Lecture Notes in Computer Science 3320

Commenced Publication in 1973
Founding and Former Series Editors:
Gerhard Goos, Juris Hartmanis, and Jan van Leeuwen

Editorial Board

David Hutchison
  Lancaster University, UK
Takeo Kanade
  Carnegie Mellon University, Pittsburgh, PA, USA
Josef Kittler
  University of Surrey, Guildford, UK
Jon M. Kleinberg
  Cornell University, Ithaca, NY, USA
Friedemann Mattern
  ETH Zurich, Switzerland
John C. Mitchell
  Stanford University, CA, USA
Moni Naor
  Weizmann Institute of Science, Rehovot, Israel
Oscar Nierstrasz
  University of Bern, Switzerland
C. Pandu Rangan
  Indian Institute of Technology, Madras, India
Bernhard Steffen
  University of Dortmund, Germany
Madhu Sudan
  Massachusetts Institute of Technology, MA, USA
Demetri Terzopoulos
  New York University, NY, USA
Doug Tygar
  University of California, Berkeley, CA, USA
Moshe Y. Vardi
  Rice University, Houston, TX, USA
Gerhard Weikum
  Max-Planck Institute of Computer Science, Saarbruecken, Germany

Kim-Meow Liew   Hong Shen
Simon See   Wentong Cai   Pingzhi Fan
Susumu Horiguchi (Eds.)

Parallel and Distributed Computing: Applications and Technologies

5th International Conference, PDCAT 2004
Singapore, December 8-10, 2004
Proceedings

 Springer

Volume Editors

Kim-Meow Liew
Nanyang Technological University
E-mail: mkmliew@ntu.edu.sg

Hong Shen
Japan Advanced Institute of Science and Technology
E-mail: shen@jaist.ac.jp

Simon See
Nanyang Technological University
E-mail: simon.see@ntu.edu.sg

Wentong Cai
Nanyang Technological University
E-mail: aswtcai@ntu.edu.sg

Pingzhi Fan
Southwest Jiaotong University
E-mail: p.fan@ieee.org

Susumu Horiguchi
Tohoku University
E-mail: susumu@ecei.tohoku.ac.jp

Library of Congress Control Number: 2004116523

CR Subject Classification (1998): F, D, C, H, I

ISSN 0302-9743
ISBN 3-540-24013-6 Springer Berlin Heidelberg New York

This work is subject to copyright. All rights are reserved, whether the whole or part of the material is concerned, specifically the rights of translation, reprinting, re-use of illustrations, recitation, broadcasting, reproduction on microfilms or in any other way, and storage in data banks. Duplication of this publication or parts thereof is permitted only under the provisions of the German Copyright Law of September 9, 1965, in its current version, and permission for use must always be obtained from Springer. Violations are liable to prosecution under the German Copyright Law.

Springer is a part of Springer Science+Business Media

springeronline.com

© Springer-Verlag Berlin Heidelberg 2004
Printed in Germany

Typesetting: Camera-ready by author, data conversion by Scientific Publishing Services, Chennai, India
Printed on acid-free paper   SPIN: 11356615   06/3142   5 4 3 2 1 0

Preface

The 2004 International Conference on Parallel and Distributed Computing, Applications and Technologies (PDCAT 2004) was the fifth annual conference, and was held at the Marina Mandarin Hotel, Singapore on December 8–10, 2004. Since the inaugural PDCAT held in Hong Kong in 2000, the conference has become a major forum for scientists, engineers, and practitioners throughout the world to present the latest research, results, ideas, developments, techniques, and applications in all areas of parallel and distributed computing.

The technical program was comprehensive and featured keynote speeches, technical paper presentations, and exhibitions showcased by industry vendors. The technical program committee was overwhelmed with submissions of papers for presentation, from countries worldwide. We received 242 papers and after reviewing them, based on stringent selection criteria, we accepted 173 papers. The papers in the proceedings focus on parallel and distributed computing viewed from the three perspectives of networking and architectures, software systems and technologies, and algorithms and applications. We acknowledge the great contribution from all of our local and international committee members and paper reviewers who devoted their time in the review process and provided valuable feedback for the authors.

PDCAT 2004 could never have been successful without the support and assistance of several institutions and many people. We sincerely appreciate the support from the National Grid Office and IEEE, Singapore for technical co-sponsorship. The financial sponsorships from the industrial sponsors, Hewlett-Packard Singapore; IBM Singapore; Sun Microsystems; SANDZ Solutions; Silicon Graphics, and Advanced Digital Information Corporation, are gratefully acknowledged.

December 2004

Kim-Meow Liew
Hong Shen
Simon See
Wentong Cai
Pingzhi Fan
Susumu Horiguchi

Organizing Committee

PDCAT 2004 was organized by the Nanyang Centre for Supercomputing and Visualisation, Nanyang Technological University, Singapore and the Asia Pacific Science and Technology Center, Nanyang Technological University, Singapore.

Conference Chairs
Kim-Meow Liew (Nanyang Technological University, Singapore)
Hong Shen (Japan Advanced Institute of Science and Technology, Japan)

Program Chair
Simon See (Sun Microsystems Inc. and Nanyang Technological University, Singapore)

Program Vice-Chairs
Wentong Cai (Nanyang Technological University, Singapore)
Pingzhi Fan (Southwest Jiaotong University, China)
Susumu Horiguchi (Tohoku University, Japan)

Conference Manager
Maddie Wong (Nanyang Technological University, Singapore)

Conference Secretariat
Shirley Soh (Nanyang Technological University, Singapore)

Conference Management System Provider
Joseph Lim (E-Link IT Enterprise, Singapore)

Local (Singapore) Program Committee Members
Sourav Saha Bhowmick (Nanyang Technological University)
Yiyu Cai (Nanyang Technological University)
Robert Gay (Nanyang Technological University)
Francis Lee (Nanyang Technological University)
Teng-Yong Ng (Nanyang Technological University)
Liang Peng (Nanyang Technological University)
Jie Song (Nanyang Technological University)
Yong-Meng Teo (National University of Singapore)
Stefan Turner (Nanyang Technological University)
Lipo Wang (Nanyang Technological University)

International Program Committee Members
Hamid R. Arabnia (University of Georgia, USA)
Richard P. Brent (Oxford University, UK)
David John Evans (Nottingham Trent University, UK)
Shi-Jinn Horng (National Taiwan University of Science and Technology, Taiwan)
Frank Hsu (Fordham University, USA)

Zhiyi Huang (University of Otago, New Zealand)
Oscar Ibarra (UC Santa Barbara, USA)
Hai Jin (Huazhong University of Science and Technology, China)
Joe Kazuki (Nara Women's University, Japan)
Francis Lau (University of Hong Kong, Hong Kong)
Minglu Li (Shanghai Jiao Tong University, China)
Yamin Li (Hosei University, Japan)
Weifa Liang (Australian National University, Australia)
Yen-Chun Lin (National Taiwan University of Science and Technology, Taiwan)
Koji Nakano (Hiroshima University, Japan)
Stephan Olariu (Old Dominion University, USA)
Yi Pan (Georgia State University, USA)
Marcin Paprzycki (Oklahoma State University, USA)
Shietung Peng (Hosei University, Japan)
Frode Eika Sandnes (Oslo University College, Norway)
Stanislav G. Sedukhin (University of Aizu, Japan)
David Taniar (Monash University, Australia)
Cho-li Wang (University of Hong Kong, Hong Kong, China)
Yuke Wang (University of Texas at Dallas, USA)
Nong Xiao (National University of Defense Technology, China)
Zhiwei Xu (Chinese Academy of Sciences, China)
Hyunsoo Yoon (Korea Advanced Institute of Science and Technology, Korea)
Huaxin Zeng (Southwest Jiaotong University, China)
Bing Bing Zhou (University of Sydney, Australia)
Albert Y. Zomaya (University of Sydney, Australia)

Technical Sponsors

IEEE Singapore Section, Singapore
National Grid Office (NGO), Singapore

Industry Sponsors

Diamond
Hewlett-Packard Singapore Pte. Ltd.

Platinum
Sun Microsystems Pte. Ltd.
IBM Singapore Pte. Ltd.

Gold
SANDZ Solutions (Singapore) Pte. Ltd.
Silicon Graphics Pte. Ltd.
ADIC South Asia

Table of Contents

Algorithms and Applications

Biological/Molecular Computing

Implementing a Bioinformatics Workflow in a Parallel and Distributed Environment
Ching-Lian Chua, Francis Tang, Yun-Ping Lim, Liang-Yoong Ho, Arun Krishnan 1

Parallel Computing Platform for the Agent-Based Modeling of Multicellular Biological Systems
Toh Da-Jun, Francis Tang, Travis Lee, Deepak Sarda, Arun Krishnan, Andrew Goryachev 5

Data Reduction in Human Vision System
Kwang-Baek Kim, Jae-Hyun Nam, Am-Suk Oh 9

Database Applications and Data Mining

Mediator-Based Architecture for Integrated Access to Biological Databases
Teh Chee Peng, Wahidah Husain, Rosni Abdullah, Rosalina Abdul Salam, Nur'Aini Abdul Rashid 13

Application of Active Database Abstraction in B2B E-Commerce
DongWoo Lee, SeongHoon Lee, ChongSun Hwang 17

An Algorithm for Mining Lower Closed Itemsets
Tian-rui Li, Ming Qing, Jun Ma, Yang Xu 21

An Update Propagation Method Based on the Tree of Replicas in Partially Replicated Databases
Misook Bae, Buhyun Hwang 25

A Parallel Electro-Optical Computer Architecture for Artificial Intelligence
Jong Whoa Na 30

Data Mining Techniques in Materialised Project and Selection View
Ying Wah Teh, Abu Bakar Zaitun 34

Parallel Text Categorization for Multi-dimensional Data
  Verayuth Lertnattee, Thanaruk Theeramunkong 38

Agent Based Distributed Data Mining
  Sung Wook Baik, Jerzy Bala, Ju Sang Cho 42

Distributed Data and Knowledge Based Systems

A Resistant P2P-Based Cooperative Storage System
  Qing-Song Wei, Qing-Feng Du 46

Distributed High-Performance Web Crawler Based on Peer-to-Peer Network
  Liu Fei, Ma Fan-Yuan, Ye Yun-Ming, Li Ming-Lu, Yu Jia-Di 50

A Peer-to-Peer Hypertext Categorization Using Directed Acyclic Graph Support Vector Machines
  Liu Fei, Zhang Wen-Ju, Yu Shui, Ma Fan-Yuan, Li Ming-Lu 54

Architecture of Agent-Based Healthcare Intelligent Assistant on Grid Environment
  Shailendra Singh, Bukhary Ikhwan Ismail, Fazilah Haron, Chan Huah Yong 58

Design of Replication Manager in Main Memory DBMS ALTIBASE^{TM}
  Kwang-Chul Jung, Kyu-Woong Lee, Hae-Young Bae 62

A Distributed Ontology Framework for the Grid
  Andrew Flahive, Wenny Rahayu, David Taniar, Bernady Apduhan ... 68

One Backward Inference Algorithm in Bayesian Networks
  Jianguo Ding, Jun Zhang, Yingcai Bai, Hansheng Chen 72

Dynamic Semantic Consistency Checking of Multiple Collaborative Ontologies in Knowledge Management System
  Dong Li, Linpeng Huang, Mingliu Li 76

High-Performance Scientific Computing

The Practice of I/O Optimizations for Out-of-Core Computation
  Jianqi Tang, Binxing Fang, Mingzeng Hu, Hongli Zhang 81

A Grid Service Based Portal for Virtual Learning Campus
  Elizabeth Sherly, Bindya George, Deepa L, Resmy S Kumar 86

Implementation of Application Collaboration Protocol
  Tomoya Sakaguchi, Hitoshi Sakagami, Manabu Nii,
  Yutaka Takahashi 90

A Componentized Approach to Grid Enabling Seismic Wave Modeling
Application
  Dheeraj Bhardwaj, Jeremy Cohen, Steve McGough,
  Steven Newhouse 94

Image Processing and Computer Graphics

Design of Algorithm for the 3D Object Representation Based on the
Web3D Using X3D
  Yun-Bae Lee, Sung-Tae Lee, Gun-Tak Oh, Young-Kook Kim,
  Young-Ho Kim 98

Motion Vector Recovery by Surrounding Region Matching Based on
Gradient Difference
  Dong-Wook Kim, Eung-Kwan Kang, Jin-Tae Kim, Yong-In Yoon,
  Jong-Soo Choi... 106

Computer Generated Holographic Image Processing for Information
Security
  Kyu B Doh, Kyeongwha Kim, Ting-C Poon 111

A Nonparametric Skin Color Model for Face Detection from Color
Images
  Kyongpil Min, Junchul Chun, Goorack Prak...................... 116

An Efficient Prediction Search Pattern for Half Pixel Motion Estimation
  Mi Gyoung Jung... 121

Analysis of Functional MRI Image Using Independent Component
Analysis
  Minfen Shen, Weiling Xu, Jinxia Huang, Patch Beadle 127

Prediction-Based Simplified Half Pixel Motion Estimation
  HyoSun Yoon, GueeSang Lee, HyeSuk Kim, Miyoung Kim 131

A New CWT-IHS Fusion Based on Edge-Intensity-Factor
  Jin Wu, Yang Liu, Jian Liu, Jinwen Tian 136

Image Segmentation Based on Fuzzy 3-Partition Entropy Approach
and Genetic Algorithm
  Jin Wu, Juan Li, Jian Liu, Jinwen Tian 140

Network Routing and Communication Algorithms

An Optimal Broadcasting Algorithm for de Bruijn Network dBG(d,k)
  Ngoc Chi Nguyen, Sungyoung Lee 144

Container Problem in Bi-rotator Graphs
  Keiichi Kaneko, Yasuto Suzuki, Yukihiro Hasegawa 149

WNChord: A Weighted Nodes Based Peer-to-Peer Routing Algorithm
  Liang Zhang, Shudong Chen, Fanyuan Ma, Minglu Li 155

A Congestion Control Algorithm for Multimedia Traffic
  Sharmin Parveen, Md Rajibul Alam Joarder, Afreen Azhari, Hasan Sarwar, Shahida Rafique 160

Improved Limited Path Heuristic Algorithm for Multi-constrained QoS Routing
  Wendong Xiao, Boon Hee Soong, Choi Look Law, Yong Liang Guan 164

Neural Networks

Weightless Neural Network Array for Protein Classification
  Martin Chew Wooi Keat, Rosni Abdullah, Rosalina Abdul Salam, Aishah Abdul Latif 168

Vector Quantization Using Enhanced SOM Algorithm
  Jae-Hyun Cho, Hyun-Jung Park, Kwang-Baek Kim 172

An Enhanced Fuzzy Neural Network
  Kwang-Baek Kim, Young-Hoon Joo, Jae-Hyun Cho 176

A Novel Anti-spam Email Approach Based on LVQ
  Zhan Chuan, Lu Xianliang, Xing Qian 180

An Application of Hybrid Least Squares Support Vector Machine to Environmental Process Modeling
  Byung Joo Kim, Il Kon Kim 184

Recurrent Neural Network for Robot Path Planning
  Ni Bin, Chen Xiong, Zhang Liming, Xiao Wendong 188

Normalized RBF Neural Network for Tracking Transient Signal in the Noise
  Minfen Shen, Yuzheng Zhang, Zhancheng Li, Patch Beadle 192

Parallel/Distributed Algorithms

An Efficient Algorithm for Fault Tolerant Routing Based on Adaptive
Binomial-Tree Technique in Hypercubes
Yamin Li, Shietung Peng, Wanming Chu 196

Genetic Local Search Based on Genetic Recombination: A Case for
Traveling Salesman Problem
*Peng Gang, Ichiro Iimura, Hidenobu Tsurusawa,
Shigeru Nakayama* 202

Study on Data Allocation Model in Distributed Storage
Qing-song Wei, Qing-feng Du 213

O(1) Time Algorithm on BSR for Constructing a Binary Search Tree
with Best Frequencies
*Limin Xiang, Kazuo Ushijima, Kai Cheng, Jianjun Zhao,
Cunwei Lu* 218

Agent Based Distributed Parallel Tunneling Algorithms
Wen Yuanqiao, Yu Shengsheng, Zhou Jingli, Huang Liwen 226

The Effect of Varying Computational Granularity and Tree Imbalance
on the Performance of Parallel Tree-Based Application
Fazilah Haron, John R Davy 230

Distributed Channel Routing Using Genetic Algorithm
Chuleui Hong, Wonil Kim, Yeongjoon Kim 234

Distributed Simulated Annealing for Composite Stock Cutting Problem
Wonil Kim, Chul-Eui Hong, Yeong-Joon Kim 238

Constant Time Algorithms for the 3-D All Nearest Neighbor Problem
on the LARPBS
Yuh-Rau Wang, Shi-Jinn Horng 243

Parallel K-Means Clustering Algorithm on DNA Dataset
*Fazilah Othman, Rosni Abdullah, Nur'Aini Abdul Rashid, Rosalina
Abdul Salam* 248

Performances of Parallel Clustering Algorithm for Categorical and
Mixed Data
Nguyen Thi Minh Hai, Horiguchi Susumu 252

Task Distribution Methods for the Reconstruction of MR Images
Hyo Jong Lee, Jessica Turner, First Birn 257

A Fault-Tolerant h-Out of-k Mutual Exclusion Algorithm Using
Cohorts Coteries for Distributed Systems
  Jehn-Ruey Jiang 267

Phylogenetic Analysis Using Maxmimum Likelihood Methods in
Homogenous Parallel Environments
  M. Till, B.-B. Zhou, A. Zomaya, L.S. Jermiin 274

Real-Time Transcoding of MPEG Videos in a Distributed Environment
  Yunyoung Nam, Eenjun Hwang 280

A Communication-Induced Checkpointing and Asynchronous Recovery
Algorithm for Multithreaded Distributed Systems
  Tongchit Tantikul, D. Manivannan 284

A Parallel Routing Algorithm on 2-Circulant Networks Employing the
Hamiltonian Circuit Latin Square
  Youngjoo Cho, Dongkil Tak, Ilyong Chung 293

Parallel Algorithms for the Process of the Biorthogonal Wavelet
Transform
  Hyung Jun Kim 297

The Subgroup Method for Collective I/O
  Hwangho Cha, Taeyoung Hong, Jeongwoo Hong 301

Utilizing Dynamic Data Value Localities in Internal Variables
  Shoichi Hirasawa, Kei Hiraki 305

A Service-Oriented Accounting Architecture on the Grid
  Jiadi Yu, Minglu Li, Ying Li, Feng Hong, Yujun Du 310

A Genetic Algorithm for Robot Navigation
  Calaiselvy, Foo Tsu Yong, Lee Wei Ping 314

Resource Allocation and Management

A Categorized-Registry Model for Grid Resource Publication and
Discovery Using Software Agents
  Lei Cao, Minglu Li, Henry Rong, Joshua Huang 318

An Adaptive Load Balancing Approach in Distributed Computing
Using Genetic Theory
   SeongHoon Lee, DongWoo Lee, Wankwon Lee, HyunJoon Cho 322

Global Stability of Optimization Based Flow Control with Time-Varying
Delays
   Yuedong Xu, Liang Wang, Zhihong Guan, Hua O. Wang 326

OITASSF: An Omnipotent Integration Technology for Application
System Security Functions
   Tang Ye, Zhang Shen-Sheng, Li Lei, Zhang Jing-Yi 332

How to Provide Continuous Services by Mobile Servers in
Communication Networks
   Satoshi Fujita, Yue Liang 337

A Framework for Price-Based Resource Allocation on the Grid
   Jiadi Yu, Minglu Li, Ying Li, Feng Hong, Ming Gao 341

RT-Grid: A QoS Oriented Service Grid Framework
   Hai Jin, Hanhua Chen, Minghu Zhang, Deqing Zou 345

Storage-Aware Harmonic Broadcasting Protocol for Video-on-Demand
   Chao Peng, Hong Shen 349

Task Mapping and Job Scheduling

Stochastic DFS for Multiprocessor Scheduling of Cyclic Taskgraphs
   Frode Eika Sandnes, Oliver Sinnen 354

A Novel Rollback Algorithm in Parallel and Distributed System
Simulation
   Xuehui Wang, Lei Zhang, Kedi Huang 363

Agent-Mediated Genetic Super-Scheduling in Grid Environments
   Gang Chen, Zhonghua Yang, Simon See, Jie Song 367

Investigating Super Scheduling Algorithms for Grid Computing: A
Simulation Approach
   Jie Song, Zhonghua Yang, Simon See 372

A New Motion Planning Approach Based on Artificial Potential Field
in Unknown Environment
   Zhiye Li, Xiong Chen, Wendong Xiao 376

Networking and Architectures

Computer Networks

Physical Frame Timeslot Switching (PFTS) in the Single User-Plane Architecture Network (SUPANET)
  Dengyuan Xu, Huaxin Zeng, Ji Li 383

Fast Address Configuration for WLAN
  Soohong Park, Pyungsoo Kim, Minho Lee, Youngkeun Kim 396

NIC-NET: A Host-Independent Network Solution for High-End Network Servers
  Keun Soo Yim, Hojung Cha, Kern Koh 401

Analysis of TCP/IP Protocol Stack for a Hybrid TCP/IP Offload Engine
  Soo-Cheol Oh, Hankook Jang, Sang-Hwa Chung 406

Techniques in Mapping Router-Level Internet Topology from Multiple Vantage Points
  Yu Jiang, Binxing Fang, Mingzeng Hu 410

Lossy Link Identification for Multicast Network
  Hui Tian, Hong Shen 416

Heterogeneous and Multimedia Systems

Scalable MPEG-4 Storage Framework with Low Bit-Rate Meta-information
  Doo-Hyun Kim, Soo-Hong Kim 420

Interconnection Networks

Micro-communication Element System
  Peng Zheng, Zeng Jiazhi, Zhang Ming, Zhao Jidong 424

Single User-Plane Architecture Network (SUPANET) and Its QoS Provisioning Mechanisms in Signaling and Management (S&M) Planes
  Jun Dou, Huaxin Zeng, Haiying Wang 429

A Commodity Cluster Using IEEE 1394 Network for Parallel Applications
  Yong Yu, Yu-Fai Fung 441

Design and Implementation of an Improved Zero-Copy File Transfer Mechanism
  Sejin Park, Sang-Hwa Chung, Bong-Sik Choi, Sang-Moon Kim 446

An M-VIA-Based Channel Bonding Mechanism on Gigabit Ethernet
  Soo-Cheol Oh, Sang-Hwa Chung 451

Optical Networks

Soft-Computing-Based Virtual Topology Design Methods in IP/DWDM Optical Internet
  Wang Xingwei, Chen Minghua, Huang Min, Xiao Wendong 455

An Analytic Model of Burst Queue at an Edge Optical Burst Switching Node
  SuKyoung Lee 459

Cost-Effective Deflection Routing Algorithm in Optical Burst Switching Networks
  SuKyoung Lee, LaeYoung Kim, JooSeok Song 464

Parallel/Distributed Architectures

On Concurrent Multi-port Test System for Routers and Its Support Tools
  Bo Song, Huaxin Zeng, Liquan Yue 469

A Temporal Consensus Model
  Hengming Zou 484

Automatically Generalized Ontology System for Peer-to-Peer Networks
  Boon-Hee Kim, Young-Chan Kim 493

Locabus: A Kernel to Kernel Communication Channel for Cluster Computing
  Paul Werstein, Mark Pethick, Zhiyi Huang 497

View-Oriented Parallel Programming and View-Based Consistency
  Z.Y. Huang, M. Purvis, P. Werstein 505

A Distributed Architecture of the Indirect IP Lookup Scheme for High-Speed Routers
  Jaehyung Park, MinYoung Chung, Jinsoo Kim, Yonggwan Won 519

A Locking Protocol for Distributed File Systems
Jaechun No, Hyo Kim, Sung Soon Park 527

Tuning Genetic Algorithms for Real Time Systems Using a Grid
Antonio Martí Campoy, Francisco Rodríguez, Angel Perles Ivar 531

An In-Order SMT Architecture with Static Resource Partitioning for Consumer Applications
Byung In Moon, Hongil Yoon, Ilgun Yun, Sungho Kang 539

ShanghaiGrid - Towards Building Shared Information Platform Based on Grid
Ying Li, Minglu Li, Jiadi Yu 545

A Cost-Optimized Detection System Location Scheme for DDoS Attack
Dong Su Nam, Sangjin Jeong, Woonyon Kim, Sang-Hun Lee, Do-Hoon Lee, Eung Ki Park 549

Dynamically Selecting Distribution Strategies for Web Documents According to Access Pattern
Keqiu Li, Hong Shen 554

An Information Sharing Structure of Broadcasting
Jianguo Ma, Ling Xing, Youping Li 558

Design and Evaluation of a Novel Real-Shared Cache Module for High Performance Parallel Processor Chip
Zhe Liu, JeoungChill Shim, Hiroyuki Kurino, Mitsumasa Koyanagi .. 564

Reliability and Fault-Tolerance

Using Computing Checkpoints Implement Consistent Low-Cost Non-blocking Coordinated Checkpointing
Chaoguang Men, Xiaozong Yang 570

The K-Fault-Tolerant Checkpointing Scheme for the Reliable Mobile Agent System
Taesoon Park, Jaehwan Youn 577

Analysis of Mobile Agents' Fault-Tolerant Behavior
Wenyu Qu, Hong Shen 582

Security

Secure Group Communication with Low Communication Complexity
  Heeyoul Kim, Jaewon Lee, H. Yoon, J.W. Cho 586

Multi-proxy Signature and Proxy Multi-signature Schemes from Bilinear Pairings
  Xiangxue Li, Kefei Chen, Shiqun Li 591

Probability Principle of a Reliable Approach to Detect Signs of DDOS Flood Attacks
  Ming Li, Jingao Liu, Dongyang Long 596

A Novel Distributed Intrusion Detection Architecture Based on Overlay Multicasting
  I-Hsuan Huang, Cheng-Zen Yang 600

Secure Group Communication in Grid Computing
  Chen Lin, Huang Xiaoqin, Li Minglu, You Jinyuan 604

Tamper Resistant Software by Integrity-Based Encryption
  Jaewon Lee, Heeyoul Kim, Hyunsoo Yoon 608

Towards an Analysis of Source-Rewriting Anonymous Systems in a Lossy Environment
  Jin-Qiao Shi, Bin-Xing Fang, Bin Li 613

Group Key Agreement Protocol Based on GH-KEP
  Mingxing He, Pingzhi Fan, Firoz Kaderali 619

The Packet Marking and the Filtering Protocol to Counter Against the DDoS Attacks
  Jeenhong Park, Jin-Hwan Choi, Dae-Wha Seo 624

A Lightweight Mutual Authentication Based on Proxy Certificate Trust List
  Li Xin, Ogawa Mizuhito 628

Proposal of a New Message Protocol for IEEE 802.11
  Seung-Jung Shin, Dae-Hyun Ryu 633

Attack Resiliency of Network Topologies
  Heejo Lee, Jong Kim 638

Matching Connection Pairs
  Hyung Woo Kang, Soon Jwa Hong, Dong Hoon Lee 642

Adaptation Enhanced Mechanism for Web Survivability
*Eungki Park, Dae-Sik Choi, Jung-Taek Seo, Choonsik Park,
DongKyu Kim* 650

Patch Management System for Multi-platform Environment
*Jung-Taek Seo, Dae-Sik Choi, Eung-Ki Park, Tae-Shik Shon,
Jongsub Moon* 654

A Generalized Proxy Signature Scheme Based on the RSA Cryptosystem
Qingshui Xue, Zhenfu Cao, Haifeng Qian 662

Novel Impostors Detection in Keystroke Dynamics by Support Vector Machine
Yingpeng Sang, Hong Shen, Pingzhi Fan 666

Wireless Networks and Mobile Computing

New Fast Handover Mechanism for Mobile IPv6 in IEEE 802.11 Wireless Networks
Pyung Soo Kim, Young Sam Lee, Soo Hong Park 670

One Hop-DAD Based Address Autoconfiguration in MANET6
Zhao Yunlong, Shi Rui, Yang Xiaozong 674

A Distributed Topology Control Algorithm for Heterogeneous Ad Hoc Networks
Lei Zhang, Xuehui Wang, Wenhua Dou 681

UbiqStor: A Remote Storage Service for Mobile Devices
MinHwan Ok, Daegeun Kim, Myong-soon Park 685

A Fan-Shaped Flexible Resource Reservation Mechanism in Mobile Wireless Internet
Wang Xingwei, Yuan Changqing, Song Bo, Huang Min 689

Security Analysis of Multi-path Routing Scheme in Ad Hoc Networks
JongMin Jeong, JoongSoo Ma 694

MSMA: A MLD-Based Mobile Multicast for Handling Source Mobility in All-IP Networks
Byoung Seob Park, Young Wook Keum 698

MQRP: A Multi-path QoS Routing Protocol in Ad Hoc Mobile Network
Peng Gegang, Liu Yan, Mao Dilin, Yang Jianghu, Gao Chuanshan ... 702

ESSHP: An Enhanced Semi-soft Handoff Protocol Based on Explicit
Node Decision in Cellular Networks
  Jae-Won Kim, Wonjun Lee, Jihoon Myung, Inkyu Lee 706

ISSRP: A Secure Routing Protocol Using Identity-Based Signcryption
Scheme in Ad-Hoc Networks
  Bok-Nyong Park, Jihoon Myung, Wonjun Lee 711

Mobility Support Algorithm Based on Wireless 802.11b LAN for Fast
Handover
  Jang Sang-Dong, Kim Wu Woan 715

A Synchronized Hello Exchange Mechanism to Enhance IEEE 802.11
PSM in Mobile Ad Hoc Network
  Sangcheol Hong, Yeonkwon Jeong, Joongsoo Ma 719

Software Systems and Technologies

Component-Based and OO Technology

Component Retrieval Using a Synaptic Connectivity Matrix
  Young Wook Keum, Byoung Seob Park 724

A Rule Filtering Component Based on Recommendation Agent System
for Classifying Email Document
  Ok-Ran Jeong, Dong-Sub Cho 729

Globally Synchronized Multimedia Streaming Architecture Based on
Time-Triggered and Message-Triggered Object Model
  Eun Hwan Jo, Doo-Hyun Kim, Hansol Park, Moon Hae Kim 736

Formal Methods and Programming Languages

A Universal Machine File Format for MPI Jobs
  Francis Tang, Ho Liang Yoong, Chua Ching Lian, Arun Krishnan ... 740

SVO Logic Based Formalisms of GSI Protocols
  Hui Liu, Minglu Li 744

A High-Level Policy Description Language for the Network ACL
  *Jangha Kim, Kanghee Lee, Sangwook Kim, Jungtaek Seo,
  Eunyoung Lee, Miri Joo* 748

Target Code Generation Using the Code Expansion Technique for Java Bytecode
Kwang-Man Ko, Soon-Gohn Kim 752

Internet Computing

A 4-Layer Robust Mobile Web Front-End Design Model
Toshihiko Yamakami 756

Study on Replication in Unstructured P2P System
Meng-Shu Hou, Xian-Liang Lu, Xu Zhou, Chuan Zhan 763

Random Walk Spread and Search in Unstructured P2P
Zhaoqing Jia, Ruonan Rao, Minglu Li, Jinyuan You 768

ODWIS as a Prototype of Knowledge Service Layer in Semantic Grid
Bo Chen, Mingtian Zhou 772

An Adaptive Proximity Route Selection Scheme in DHT-Based Peer to Peer Systems
Jiyoung Song, Sungyong Park, Jihoon Yang 778

Modeling and Simulation

Distributed Security Agent Modeling in the Policy-Based Networking
Hee Suk Seo, Tae Ho Cho 782

The Analysis of Hardware Supported Cache Lock Mechanism Without Retry
Wonil Kim, Chuleui Hong, Yeongjoon Kim 787

Modeling of Non-Gaussian AR Model with Transient Coefficients Using Wavelet Basis
Lisha Sun, Minfen Shen, Weiling Xu, Patch Beadle 791

Model for Generating Non-gaussian Noise Sequences Having Specified Probability Distribution and Spectrum
Lisha Sun, Minfen Shen, Weiling Xu, Zhancheng Li, Patch Beadle ... 795

Self-Directed Learning Evaluation Using Fuzzy Grade Sheets
Sung-Kwan Je, Chang-Suk Kim, Eui-Young Cha 799

Operating Systems

State Machine Based Operating System Architecture for Wireless Sensor Networks
  Tae-Hyung Kim, Seongsoo Hong 803

QoS-Aware Admission Control for Video-on-Demand Services
  Ilhoon Shin, Y.H. Shin, Kern Koh 807

Context Aware Thread Aggregation in Linux
  Takuya Kondoh, Shigeru Kusakabe 811

Parallelizing Compilers

Compiler-Assisted Software DSM on WAN Cluster
  Junpei Niwa 815

Performance Evaluation and Measurements

Performance Analysis of Batch Rekey Algorithm for Secure Group Communications
  Jun Zhang, Fanyuan Ma, Yingcai Bai, Minglu Li 829

Workload Dispatch Planning for Real-Time Fingerprint Authentication on a Sensor-Client-Server Model
  Yongwha Chung, Daesung Moon, Taehae Kim, Jin-Won Park 833

Explaining BitTorrent Traffic Self-Similarity
  Gang Liu, Mingzeng Hu, Bingxing Fang, Hongli Zhang 839

Scheduler Oriented Grid Performance Evaluation
  Liang Peng, Simon See 844

Tools and Environments for Software Development

Integrated Service Component Development Tool on Web Services
  Woon-Yong Kim, R. Young-Chul Kim 848

On Construction of a Large Computing Farm Using Multiple Linux PC Clusters
  Chao-Tung Yang, Chun-Sheng Liao, Kuan-Ching Li 856

On Construction of a Large File System Using PVFS for Grid
  *Chao-Tung Yang, Chieh-Tung Pan, Kuan-Ching Li,
  Wen-Kui Chang* 860

A Grid-Enabled Workflow PSE for Computational Applications
  Yoonhee Kim 864

GAD Kit - A Toolkit for "Gridifying" Applications
  *Quoc-Thuan Ho, Yew-Soon Ong, Wentong Cai, Hee-Khiang Ng,
  Bu-Sung Lee* 868

GridCrypt: High Performance Symmetric Key Cryptography Using Enterprise Grids
  *Agus Setiawan, David Adiutama, Julius Liman, Akshay Luther,
  Rajkumar Buyya* 872

Web Technologies

Planning Based Service Composition System
  Zhang Jianhong, Zhang Shensheng, Cao Jian 878

A Sparse Timestamp Model for Managing Changes in XML Documents
  Geunduk Park, Woochang Shin, Kapsoo Kim, Chisu Wu 882

Author Index 887

Implementing a Bioinformatics Workflow in a Parallel and Distributed Environment

Ching-Lian Chua, Francis Tang, Yun-Ping Lim, Liang-Yoong Ho, and Arun Krishnan

Bioinformatics Institute, 30 Biopolis St, #07-01 Matrix, Singapore 138671
{chuacl, francis, yunping, lyho, arun}@bii.a-star.edu.sg

Abstract. This paper illustrates a bioinformatics workflow and its execution in a parallel and distributed environment. Our paper is organized into two main parts. The first part describes a bioinformatics study of a genome wide analysis based on full length human transcripts (cDNA information) to determine gene expression in various tissues. The second part is the execution of the workflow in a parallel and distributed environment. We show the embarrassingly parallel structure of the workflow, its implementation in a distributed cluster environment and the efficiency that can be achieved by automation of the workflow through a parallel scripting language.

Keywords: Bioinformatics, Parallel Computing, Workflow.

1 Bioinformatics Workflow: Tissue Specific Gene Expression Analysis

The human genome encodes approximately 30,000 to 40,000 genes [1]. The availability of human transcripts from large scale sequencing projects has allowed a comprehensive evaluation of the human transcriptome. The first step to our genome-wide study focuses on high throughput extraction of exon[1] information from a genome, which is made up of exons and introns[2]. Secondly, full length complementary DNA (cDNA) is mapped to the exons. Finally, further analysis is applied to determine the human genes expressed in different tissues and the occurrences of tissue specific genes.

For our purpose, we downloaded National Centre for Biotechnology Information (NCBI)'s Human Genome Build 34 genbank files and 16,385 full length cDNAs from Mammalian Gene Collection [2]. Information such as exon sequences, position and length were extracted from the genbank files and stored in a flat file. The exon sequences were aligned against the cDNA database using BLASTN. Results from the BLAST process were summarized to list the genes whose sequences have high identity and good coverage.

---

[1] Exon - sequences found in the gene that are also represented in the mRNA product.
[2] Introns - sequences present in the gene that are not represented in the mRNA product.

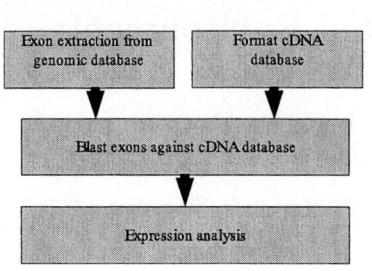

Fig. 1. Steps of the Genomic Analysis Pipeline

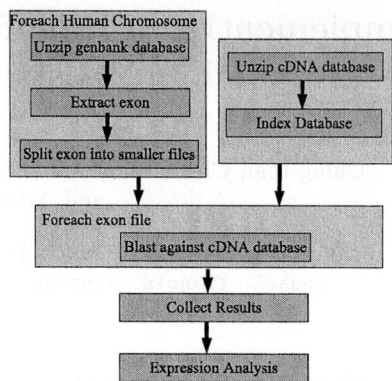

Fig. 2. Parallelised Genomic Analysis Pipeline

In order to expedite the analysis process, we identified elements of the workflow that could benefit from execution in a distributed environment and parallelise them to achieve better efficiency. The rest of the paper illustrate this parallelisation process.

2 Parallelisation of Workflow

The analysis pipeline is shown in Fig. 1. Exons are extracted from the whole set of chromosomes and blasted against the cDNA database, the results are piped into the expression analysis stage. Both the exon extraction and BLAST processes are time consuming and could benefit from parallelisation. In the following sections, we outline the steps that were taken to parallelise the workflow and its implementation on a cluster. It is important to note here that parallelisation *does not* require modifications to the application source codes but rather uses existing sequential applications in a parallel environment.

2.1 Parallelisation Steps Outlined

Parallelising the pipeline entails breaking up each stage of the pipeline into smaller components. Since the exon extraction in the first stage is independent between chromosomes, it is a simple procedure to run them in parallel. The formatting of the cDNA database can also be done concurrently at this stage.

In the second stage, the mapping of the exons to the cDNA can be processed in parallel because exon information outputs from stage one can be blasted independently. Since a BLAST run can take a long time (typically in days) depending on the number of input query sequences and size of databases, we split the exon sequences from each chromosome into 5 separate files and blasted these smaller queries against the cDNA database. Hence we were able to maximise the use of the processors available on the cluster by distributing the work load across many nodes.

This compared to the original pipeline, the modified workflow has 25 parallel processes (including formatting of the cDNA database) in the first stage and 120 processes in the second stage. The parallelised workflow with the additional components marking intermediate steps is shown in Fig. 2.

2.2 Automated Submission Through Workflow Engine

The workflow was constructed using a parallel scripting language, Grid Execution Language (GEL) [3]. It supports constructs such as parallel execution, iterations, if-else and loops. Given that its workflow engine has interface to LSF, SGE, PBS as well as Globus, the task of coordinating the workflow is simplified to just a few instruction lines in GEL.

```
noop :=          { exec = "noop.sh";
                   dir = "bin";
                   ipdir = "data"}
gunzip(gzfile) := { exec = "gunzip";
                    software_req = ":PATH=/bin";
                    args = "-f", $gzfile }
exonx(gzfile) := { exec = "exonx.sh";
                   dir = "bin";
                   args = $gzfile }
formatdb(fasta) := { exec = "formatdb";
                     dir = "bin";
                     args = "-p", "F","-i", $fasta }
dice(gzfile) :=  { exec = "DICE.sh";
                   dir = "bin";
                   args = $gzfile, "-num", 5 }
blast(query, db) :={ exec = "BLAST.sh";
                     dir = "bin";
                     args = $query, $db;
                     cmdir = "results" }
```

```
noop ; #to load the genbank files
( pforeach f of "*.gbk.gz" do
    gunzip($f) ;
    exonx($f) ;
    dice($f)
  endpforeach
| ( gunzip("hs_mgc_mrna.fasta.gz") ;
    formatdb("hs_mgc_mrna.fasta")
  )
);
pforeach g of "*_dice*.fna" do
    blast($g, "hs_mgc_mrna.fasta")
endpforeach
```

Fig. 3. Script for Workflow: The first part consist of declarative statements and the second part, the workflow construct in GEL. Note the symmetry in GEL's expression and the workflow chart in Fig. 2

3 Performance of Bioinformatics Workflow

The workflow was executed in a cluster consisting of 128 1.4GHz Intel PIII CPUs which was more than adequate to handle the 120 blast processes. While the task of mapping the cDNA using a single query consisting of the full human transcript took 54883s using the original pipeline, the same task was completed in under 6000s using the modified workflow. Clearly, the problem was too large for a single CPU and it had benefited from parallelisation. The timing diagram for the workflow is shown in Fig. 4.

4 Conclusion and Further Work

This paper shows how a bioinformatics workflow or a part of it could benefit from parallelisation. This was done through splitting up query sequences and

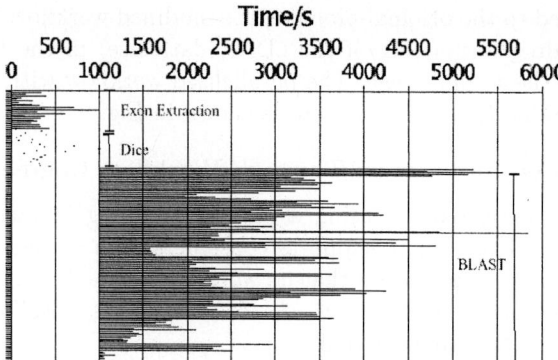

Fig. 4. Timing Diagram for Workflow: Shows the start and stop times of the exon extraction, files splitting and BLAST processes. Notice that majority of the time is taken up by BLAST (maximum 5000s), though one exon extraction process took almost 1000s. File splits are negligible operations in the workflow in this case

executing the smaller queries in a cluster. We demonstrated the use of a parallel scripting language in aid of parallelising workflow. Since it is a scripting language, the workflow is also editable and extensible through the changing of input database, extraction information and additional analysis program.

However, we recognise that improvements can still be made to the workflow, such as load balancing in BLAST. The BLAST processes could have been improved if the exon sequences from the first stage were distributed more evenly. The last stage of the workflow, namely expression analysis, was not shown, since the results from the BLAST output could be used for numerous types of analysis such as multi-alignment and structure prediction. Some of these analyses could also be parallelised while some like multi-alignment, could only be accomplished through specialised application, like MPI. Depending on the type of follow-up analysis, the same parallelisation procedures we applied to stages one and two could be implemented. In addition a comparison of the performance of GEL versus other scripting paradigms needs to be carried out.

References

1. Lander, E.S., Linton, L.M., Birren, B., Nusbaum, C., Zody, M.C.: Initial sequencing and analysis of the human genome. Nature **409** (2001) 860-921
2. Strausberg, R.L., Feingold, E.A., Klausner, R.D., Collins, F.S.: The Mammalian Gene Collection. Science **286** (1999) 455-457
3. Chua, C.L., Tang, F., Issac, P., Krishnan A.: GEL: Grid Execution Language. Journal of Parallel and Distributed Computing (2004) To be submitted.

Parallel Computing Platform for the Agent-Based Modeling of Multicellular Biological Systems

Toh Da-Jun, Francis Tang, Travis Lee, Deepak Sarda, Arun Krishnan, and Andrew Goryachev*

Bioinformatics Institute, Matrix L7, 30 Biopolis St, Singapore

Abstract. Agent-based simulation of large multicellular biological systems has become a viable option owing to affordable parallel computers, such as Beowulf-style clusters. We describe a scalable modular software platform that (i) provides for an easy integration of different solvers computing internal dynamics of the cells, and (ii) dynamically adapts to the changing loads on the cluster nodes using a load balancing algorithm. Simulations of systems of about 100,000 bacterial cells have been shown to be feasible using the platform.

1 Introduction

The overwhelming complexity of biological systems challenges our attempts to understand their function. The staggering variety of the "parts" that constitute biological systems and the highly nonlinear laws that define their interaction leave computational simulation as, perhaps, the only practical approach to the "understanding" of living matter. Steady improvements in computing hardware and recent advances in computational cell biology have given researchers powerful tools for simulation of intracellular metabolic, genetic and signal transduction networks [4]. Considerably less attention, however, has been given to the development of computational tools suitable for the biologically realistic simulation of systems comprised of many (100–100,000) interacting biological cells.

The necessity to model large ensembles of interacting cells commonly arises in the studies of disease pathology, cancer progression, embryonic development, wound healing and many other highly important processes involving creation and reorganization of biological tissue. A number of approaches based on the continuous representation of tissue with partial differential equations has been proposed in the literature [3]. They, however, do not explicitly address the discrete, cellular organization of the tissue and cannot be easily generalized to satisfy the needs of various applications.

In this work we present a computational platform capable of multipurpose simulation of large ensembles of interacting biological cells whose number varies

---

* Author to whom correspondence should be addressed.

due to the processes of cell division and cell death. The natural parallelism of biological systems is captured by implementing the cells as largely independent agents whose intracellular dynamics is computed in a parallel way on a cluster-based hardware. We demonstrate that large multi-cellular ensembles of practical importance can be simulated in a reasonable time on contemporary cluster hardware.

2 Platform Design

The platform is designed for the Beowulf-style clusters, since they provide the scalability and computing power required for the simulation of thousands of interacting cells at affordable cost. We employ agent-based simulation paradigm with three types of agents: Cell, Medium and Master. We allocate one processor each for the Medium and the Master, while the cells are allocated to the remaining processors.

A Cell encapsulates a number of variables describing the environment of a typical biological cell, such as age, cell cycle phase, and concentrations of various chemical species. It also performs autonomous calculations of the intracellular dynamics of the metabolic, genetic and signal transduction networks. This function is performed by a dedicated third-party software, such as CellWare [2]. This core engine can be readily replaced to address the specific goals of the particular simulation problem. Based on their environment and the internal state variables, cells autonomously select predefined developmental programs, such as cell division or death. Cells do not communicate directly with each other, but only through interaction with the common Medium.

The Medium models the extracellular environment where the cells are allowed to move and with which they are chemically connected through the exchange of a subset of intracellular molecules. These chemicals are allowed to freely diffuse in the Medium and be "sensed" by other cells, thus enabling the cell-cell communication. Finally, the Master acts as the administrator that manages the system clock and schedules cooperation of the Medium and the Cells. It also maintains the dynamic cell collection by satisfying the requests of individual cells for division and termination, as well as migrates cells from node to node to balance their computational load.

2.1 Load Balancing and Scheduling

Since each cell independently proliferates or dies, some processors may end up with more cells than others (see Fig. 1, left). Also, since the underlying cluster is typically a shared resource, its load may depend on other users' jobs. We created a load balancing module that monitors in real time the node performance and determines where the new cells should be created as well as proposes cell migrations should changes in the node performance be detected (Fig. 1, right).

The load balancing is achieved through a list scheduling algorithm which uses the expected run-times of cells derived from the run-times observed in the previous time steps. To reduce the amount of statistics, similar cells are grouped

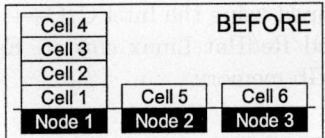 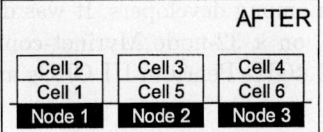

Fig. 1. Load Balancing. The load balancing algorithm dynamically redistributes the work

together. Assuming heterogeneity in the performance of processors, allows us (i) to model interference from other users' jobs, and (ii) to incorporate a cost penalty for migrations. In the case of heterogeneous processors we used a modified list scheduling algorithm based on that proposed by Davis and Jaffe [1]. The algorithm is known to give a solution at most $2.5\sqrt{m}$ times worse than the optimal for m processors.

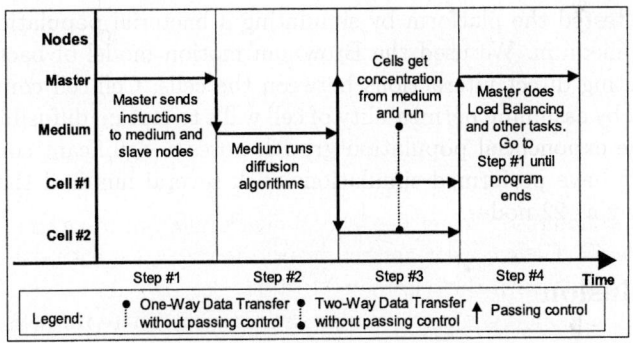

Fig. 2. Scheduling. For each time step, the Master instructs the Medium to run the diffusion algorithm. Then it instructs each cell to request the latest extracellular chemical concentrations from the Medium and run the intracellular simulation. Each cell may decide to divide, die or otherwise change its behavior, passing this decision to the Master. The Master creates, destructs and relocates the cells according to the load balancing method

In biological systems, the communication between the cells and the medium is continuous. By analogy with the Forward-Euler Method, we simulate this process by alternating the parallel intracellular dynamics of cells with the Medium communication step. Reduction of the time step length increases accuracy at the expense of the performance. The Master provides the necessary time step coordination (see Fig. 2).

2.2 Implementation and Results

The platform was implemented using a layered reference software architecture (see Fig. 3), which allows for easy upgrading of program functions, and task allocation among developers. It was developed using the Intel C/C++ compiler and MPI, on a 32-node Myrinet-connected RedHat Linux cluster. Each node had two 1.4GHz Pentium III CPUs and 2Gb memory.

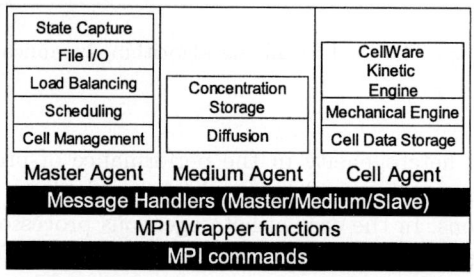

Fig. 3. Layered Reference Architecture

We have tested the platform by simulating a bacterial population in a two-dimensional medium. We used the Brownian motion model of bacterial movement, neglecting direct interactions between the cells. Cell-cell communication was modeled by assuming permeability of cell walls to certain diffusible molecules. Although the exponential population growth poses a significant computational challenge, we have performed simulations with several hundred thousand cells using as many as 22 nodes.

3 Conclusion

In this paper we have introduced a highly flexible parallel computational platform suitable for the multipurpose agent-based simulation of large multicellular ensembles of biological cells. On the example of a loosely chemically connected bacterial culture we demonstrated the feasibility of biologically realistic simulations involving hundreds of thousands of bacterial cells. We thus validated the potential of our platform to address complex biological problems and will further improve its simulation realism and computational efficiency in the future work.

References

1. E. David and J. M. Jaffe. Algorithms for scheduling tasks on unrelated processors. *J. ACM*, 28:721–736, 1981.
2. P. Dhar, Tan C. M., S. Somani, Li Y., K. Sakharkar, A. Krishnan, A. B. M. Ridwan, M. Chitre, and Zhu H. Grid Cellware: The first Grid-enabled tool for modeling and simulating cellular processes. *Bioinformatics*, 2004.
3. J. D. Murray. *Mathematical biology II: Spatial models and biomedical applications*. Springer-Verlag, 2003.
4. B. Slepchenko et al. Computational cell biology: Spatiotemporal simulation of cellular events. *Ann. Rev. Biophys. Biomol. Struct.*, 31:423–441, 2002.

Data Reduction in Human Vision System

Kwang-Baek Kim[1], Jae-Hyun Nam[2], and Am-Suk Oh[3]

[1] Dept. of Computer Engineering, Silla University, Korea
[2] Division of Computer & Information Engineering, Silla University, Korea
[3] Dept. of Multimedia Engineering, TongMyong University of Information, Korea
{gbkim, jhnam}@silla.ac.kr, asoh@tmic.tit.ac.kr

Abstract. For the effective realization of the artificial visual systems, it needs the research for the mechanism of the human visual system. In the research for retinal mechanism, we purpose the analysis of the signal transfer processing in the retina and making the retina model. A model for the characteristics of ganglion cells in the retina is proposed after considering the structure of the retina that compressed the information. The results of this study show that the recognition rate of the mechanism, processes input information, was not much different from of the machine vision model.

1 Introduction

The technologies for vision play a core role when interfacing information channels between human and machine. That is, in order to make a machine do what we want, human-like natural vision abilities are obviously necessary. However, the current visual systems are used in very restricted ways due to the insufficiency in performance of algorithms and hardware [1][2]. It is important for human to detect changes of an environment, take a judgment, interpret a situation, and do an appropriate action to adapt to changes of an environment. A research of machine vision is to play the purpose of imitating function of a human visual system, and providing it to a machine. Algorithm and applications related to machine vision are developing gradually. But the machine vision technology used in real world is still applied restricted fields. And its information processing is developing into a different form with that of human visual system because of the limited application range [2].

A human visual information processing composed with a lot of step. The primary information processing begins in the human retina. The human retina not only includes a process changing light energy into electricity chemical energy but also transmits visual information, is processed information, to visual path [1-3].

In this paper, we investigate the data compression property of retina through physiological evidence. We are going to implement a model about the visual information compression using wavelet transform that actual human gets up in a process an image. We will review information processing procedures of the retina and construct a model based on the mechanism in Chapter 2, and present the results of the experiment and conclusions.

2 Proposed Algorithms

The research of human visual system has been preceded until 1960's by neurophysiology and psychophysics. It got a lot of achievements by an appearance of cognitive science in 1970's. Knowledge about visual information processing of a human visual system has been found with a medical science, engineering recently. And study to maximize performance of a current developed computer vision through modeling about this visual information processing is proceeded in the entire world. Also, there is active study to creature artificial vision for the blind [2].

Since ganglion cell is composed with only about 1,000,000 in one eye, a lot of visual information is compressed for transferring from 125,000,000 receptors to ganglion cell. Actually it is turned into a neural signal by an operation of the retina, but the sampling image is transmitted to primary visual cortex of a brain through optic nerve of the retina. To processing of human visual information, is compressed for transferring, are very similar to wavelet transform. Information of low-band has very much delicate information to express original image in wavelet transform and much information of original image exists. As for theses, a mapping process of parvo-cellular of ganglion cell (P-cell) and the mechanism are very alike in receptor of the retina. Also, information of high-band of wavelet transform has edge information of original image compared to low-band which has a little information. These mechanisms are very similar to a mapping process of magno-cellular of ganglion cell (M-cell). Therefore, P-cell of ganglion cell deals with main information of an image like low-band, and M-cell is dealing with edge information of an image like the high-band. In this paper, we used wavelet transform in a compression process of this visual information and composed the model. We implemented the information processing model in figure 1.

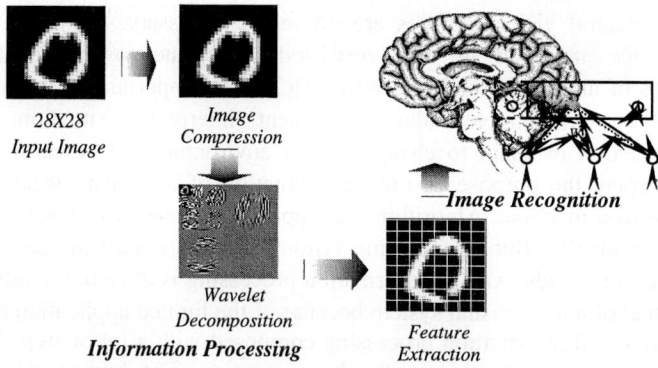

Fig. 1. Proposed Information Processing Model

To recognize the image, we did not give an answer about an input pattern having been given and adopted ART2 and the SOFM which were the unsupervised learning algorithm in which learning was possible. Especially, ART2 and SOFM the algorithm are similar to a biology recognition system. Specially, as for the SOFM, the practice speed is quite fast with neural network model proposed by Kohonen, and adaptability is excellent in a real-time with learning process and various changes about an input pattern. SOFM is the model in which application is possible on a binary input pattern and analog input pattern. And it is the same, and a connection weight change of SOFM reacts to a cluster generation having an average of all input patterns [3][4].

3 Experimental Results

In this study, a proposed image model, which is based on the human vision system, is implemented by using Visual C++ 6.0 in the environment of Pentium 2GHz, 512MB memory, and Window XP. We used the database of the AT&T Corp., which it was used in a lot of paper on face recognition at this paper and tested. It is contains a set of face images taken between April 1992 and April 1994 at the lab. The database was used in the context of a face recognition project carried out in collaboration with the Speech, Vision and Robotics Group of the Cambridge University Engineering Department. There are ten different images of each of 40 distinct subjects. For some subjects, the images were taken at different times, varying the lighting, facial expressions and facial details. All the images were taken against a dark homogeneous background with the subjects in an upright, frontal position. The size of each image is 92x112 pixels, with 256 grey levels in Fig. 2.

Fig. 2. The face database of the AT&T Corp

In the experiment of this study, we implemented the model that the primary information processing begins in the human retina and different compression rates were used over time by taking into consideration of human reflection functions.

Table 1. Experiments of face recognition

Bpp	Recognition rate	Storage (byte)
0.75	92.26%	479
0.50	91.66%	957
0.25	90.66%	1,436
0.125	90.47%	1,914
0.0625	88.09%	2,393

The image was compressed with Daubechies (9,7) filter that is often used for the loss compression. For an experiment on the recognition process, the most commonly used neural network algorithms, ART2 and SOM, were used to suggest a recognition model. The results of the experiment are presented in Table 1. As it is shown in Table 1, recognition rates gradually decreases with compression rates, whereas the efficiency of storage space gets better. Therefore, compressed data of the proposed model showed similar performance in the visual information processing. Human's memory tends to degenerate with time. Human's recollection ability also fades with time, which makes their recognition less accurate. Meantime, due to the limited capacity of human brain, humans tend to compress old memories to recollect. Thus, this dissertation took the recollection ability into account, and conducted different experiments according to the compression ratio.

4 Conclusion

The proposed model did a change from photoreceptor to ganglion cell based on human visual information processing. Machine vision technology is developing into a different form with that of human visual system because of the limited application range. Human visual information processing system goes through the process in which a great deal of information is compressed by ganglion cell in the retina, but does not feel a particular problem on an actual recognition process. The results modeling did a compression process of a human visual information processing. And also general recognition model and performance difference were able to know null.

In simulation results, there is not significant recognition result between conventional computer vision and proposed model. Future study, if it were modeling from ganglion cell to primary visual cortex, It could be applied to image recognition, object tracking, artificial vision.

References

1. Brain Science Research Center.: Research on Artificial Audiovisual System based on the Brain Information Processing. Research Paper by The Korea Advanced Institute of Science and Technology, Department of Science Technology (2001)
2. Shah, S., and Levine, M. D.: Information Processing in Primate Retinal Cone Pathways: A Model. TR-CIM-93-18. McGill University, Centre for Intelligent Machines (1993)
3. Diamantaras, K. I., and Kung, S.Y.: Principal Component Neural Networks. Theory and Applications. NY: Wiley (1996)
4. Zurada, J. M.: Introduction to Artificial Neural Systems. Boston: PWS Publishing Company (1992)
5. Burrus, C. S., Gopinath R. A., and Guo H.: Introduction to Wavelets and Wavelet Transforms. Prentice hall (1998)
6. Shapiro, J. M.: Embedded Image coding using zerotrees of wavelet coefficients. IEEE Trans. on Signal Processing, Vol. 41. No. 12 (1993) 3445-3462
7. Gonzalez, R. C., and Woods, R. E.: Digital image processing. Second edition. Prentice Hall (2001)

Mediator-Based Architecture for Integrated Access to Biological Databases

Teh Chee Peng, Wahidah Husain, Rosni Abdullah,
Rosalina Abdul Salam, and Nur'Aini Abdul Rashid

School of Computer Sciences, 11800 Universiti Sains Malaysia, Penang, Malaysia
cp.teh@plexus.com,
{wahidah, rosni, rosalina,nuraini}@cs.usm.my

Abstract. The amount of biological information accessible via the internet is growing at a tremendous rate. The biologists often encounter problems in accessing huge amount of widely spread data due to disparate formats, remotely dispersed and varying implementation on different platforms and data models. Besides that, the custom browsing and querying mechanism implemented in different data sources requires the users to uniquely query each individual database. Instead of having different custom interfaces to these public bioinformatics databases, an intuitive common integrated data access method is proposed to provide uniform transparent access to disparate biological databases. The proposed mediator-based architecture consists of three conceptual layers namely Query Formulation, Query Transformation and Query Execution.

1 Introduction

With the advancement of the microbiology technologies such as genome sequencing, microarray gene expression and mass spectroscopy, various public-accessible bioinformatics database has been developed. Simple retrieval of data from individual biological databases by multiple sequential steps is no longer practical for modern biological research. A specific biological research may require data analysis against multiple data sources and the results are fed into various application programs such as functional domain, protein structural prediction, and motive identification for various biological research purposes. The objective of this work is to create an integrated tool that access to multiple biological databases. This is implemented by applying a mediation framework that implements a transparent access to the heterogeneous data sources [1]. One main requirement of integration is that, the owner of the data maintains autonomy of each data source.

2 Proposed Design Architecture Framework

In the mediator-based architecture, the strongest feature is that it does not store any data and does not require a copy of database to reside in the local storage [2]. The queries are executed remotely in the respective data source and the results returned to end user. In this work, an integrated access to bioinformatics databases is devised based on a mediator-based architecture. The integration structure consists of three major components:

(i) GUI-based Query Formulation
(ii) Query Transformation
(iii) Query Execution

As illustrated in Fig.1, the three major components listed are mapped into a mediator-based architecture where the system first gets a general declarative query from the user. The declarative query is formulated by navigating the visual components provided in the GUI interface. The system then collects the information from the GUI and formulates the query to be fed into the next process to construct a source-dependent query. The process of query transformation is encapsulated in the mediator layer in mediator-based architecture. Query transformation is required to construct a meaningful query based on the declarative query from the GUI layer. The meaningful query is referred to as fully parameterized query that contains dependent information on data source to generate a detailed execution plan. The objectives of the query execution layer are to facilitate the physical execution of query against the data source and handling the communication with the remote database. Its responsibilities include getting the data and responses from different database sources.

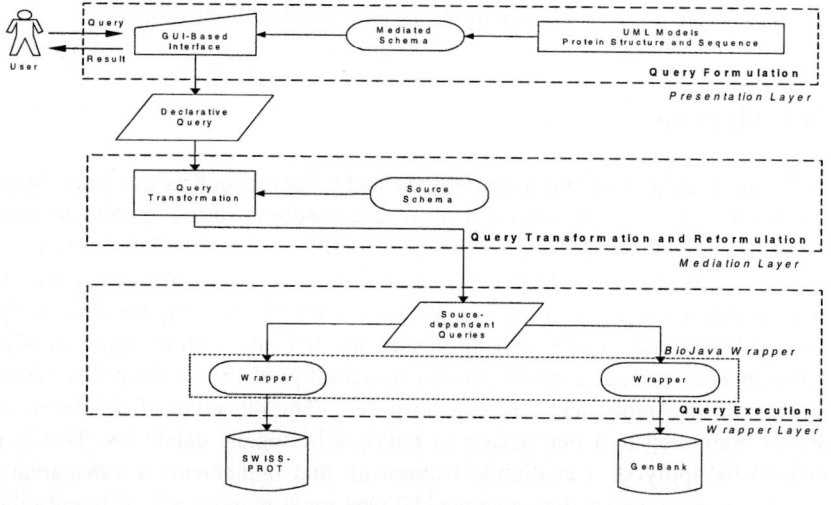

Fig. 1. Mediator-based Architecture

3 Implementation and Results

In the implementation of the mediator-based architecture in accessing Swiss-Prot and GenBank, Java's J2EE framework is adopted. The prototype is implemented as Java servlets that are executed in J2EE web application server. The servlets are used to generate GUI forms from the global schema and also to perform mediation on the queries submitted by the user. The global schema and local schemas for each individual databank are stored in a relational data model (MySQL). Each data source is implemented as a single relation in the global schema and the wrapper provides an interface that can accept queries on the data source relation; process the queries against the actual data source and return the required result. The web data sources integrated into the prototype are Swiss-Prot [3], a protein sequence bank and Gen-Bank, a popular nucleotide sequence database. The query form consists of the source dependent fields that are relevant to the desired database. However, the user does not need to specify the field name for the searched field in the individual database as the fields in the query form are rewritten in terms of source fields during the query execution in the wrapper [4]. In order to analyze the performance of the tool, a search for organism field containing "human coronavirus" in Swiss-Prot is performed in each integration method to compare the query response time. Fig. 2(a) shows the response time of mediator against other integration approaches.

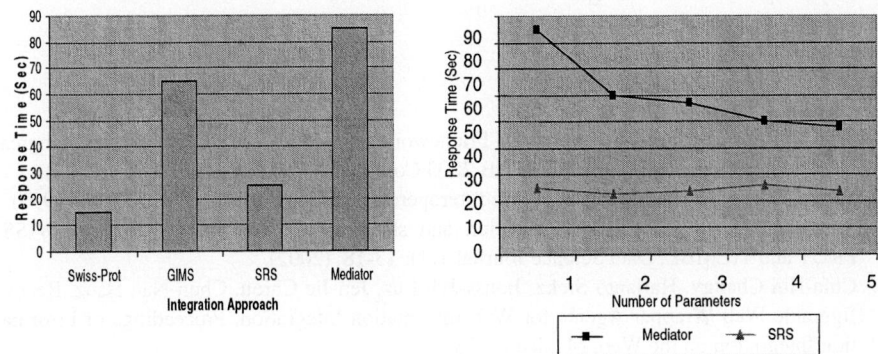

Fig. 2. Response Time for Querying Organism "Human Coronavirus" from Swiss-Prot for various integration methods; Comparison of Response Time for mediator and SRS for searching with various no of parameters

The results shown that GIM [5] and SRS have faster response time compared to mediator-based approach. The response time is slower in the mediator-based because of the delay from query translation, the process of parsing and filtering the results in the wrapper components and the network propagation time for submitting the query and getting back the result. However, as observed in Fig. 2(b), the mediator-based approach shows that the response time for querying Swiss-Prot with the less number of parameter consumes more execution time than a complicated query that has more parameters. This is because less result is returned by the data source with the specification of more search criteria. As for SRS, the response time required to generate the result does not depend on the number of parameters.

Although the mediator-based approach is slower in terms of query response time, the result generated by the mediator-based approach has high accuracy rate and the return results are also consistently up-to-date compared to other methods. This is because the mediator is querying the data sources directly and the updates of the data source are done autonomously by the owner of the data source.

4 Conclusion

In conclusion, the contribution of this work is to demonstrate the web-based bioinformatics application that utilizes different stand-alone bioinformatics database, implemented using mediator-based integration approach. This work contributes to the effort of integrating various types of biological databases and further improvement in query execution plan by engaging query optimization and dynamic execution plan generator. As for improving the response time of the mediator approach, the future work is to parallelize the result parsing in the wrapper module. The parallelism of parser could bring tremendous improvement response time especially in the situation where the query result is large.

References

1. The Mediagrid Project, A Mediation Framework for a Transparent Access to Biological Data Sources, Proceedings of the ECCB 2003 Conference Poster Session, Paris (2003).
2. Peter D. Karp. A Strategy for Database Interoperation, J Comput Biol 2(4): 573-86 (1995).
3. Magrane M., Apweiler R. Organisation and standardisation of information in SWISS-PROT and TrEMBL, Data Science Journal 1(1): 13-18. (2002).
4. Chia-Hui Changy, Harianto Siekz, Jianss-Jyh Luz, Jen-Jie Chiou, Chun-Nan Hsuz. Reconfigurable Web Wrapper Agents for Web Information Integration, Proceedings of Information Integration on the Web, Mexico (2003).
5. Mike Cornell, Norman W. Paton, Shengli Wu, Carole A. Goble, Crispin J. Miller, Paul Kirby. GIMS – A Data Warehouse for Storage and Analysis of Genome Sequence and Functional Data, 2nd IEEE International Symposium on Bioinformatics and Bioengineering, Maryland. (2001).

Application of Active Database Abstraction in B2B E-Commerce

DongWoo Lee[1], SeongHoon Lee[2], and ChongSun Hwang[3]

[1] Dept. of Computer Science, Woosong University,
17-2 Jayang-dong Dong-ku Daejeon, Republic of Korea
dwlee@woosong.ac.kr
[2] Div. of Information and Communcation Engineering, Cheonan University,
115 Anseo-dong Cheonan, Choongnam, Republic of Korea
shlee@cheonan.ac.kr
[3] Dept. of Computer Science, Korea University,
1-5 Ga Anam-dong SeongBuk, Seoul, Republic of Korea
hwang@disys.korea.ac.kr

Abstract. Close collaboration among businesses is required in B2B E-Commerce. Furthermore, emergency requests or urgent information among businesses should be processed in an immediate mode. In this paper active database abstraction based timely collaboration among businesses and an active functionality component to support it in B2B E-Commerce are proposed. The proposed active functionality component uses HTTP protocol to be applied through firewalls. It is implemented using basic trigger facilities of a commercial DBMS for practical purpose.

1 Introduction

B2B E-Commerce systems need to be coordinated and integrated for collaboration inter organizations to achieve their common business goals. Especially emergency requests or critical information among businesses should be processed in an immediate mode. Most current systems, however, due to the firewalls for systems' security and autonomy, can not handle these requirements appropriately, but handle them in a batch processing mode or an *ad hoc* manner[1].

In this work collaboration among businesses in B2B E-Commerce is analyzed and the need for timely collaboration is derived and classified in terms of inter organizational contracts. To meet the need an active functionality component(AFC) based on active database abstraction is proposed to provide B2B E-Commerce systems with flexible coordination and immediate processing in WWW environment. Since high level ECA rule programming is supported by the AFC, the collaboration among businesses and event-based immediate processing can be implemented independently to application logic. Thus, system administrators and programmers can easily program and maintain timely collaboration among businesses in B2B E-Commerce.

2 Timely Collaboration Among Businesses

Timely collaboration among businesses, i.e., immediate service request - immediate cooperation, can be seen as exceptions out of business' normal collaborations. That is, emergency requests or critical information among businesses should be transmitted to partners promptly and processed by the partners in an immediate mode. They are not frequent, but once they occur, they require special treatment and affect customers' or businesses' profits largely.

Timely collaboration procedure among businesses in B2B E-Commerce can be drawn like in Fig. 1. In order to collaborate in an immediate mode, the situation for timely collaboration should be detected, notified or transmitted to each other, evaluated and recognized, and processed promptly. It shows that timely collaboration among businesses is suitable application to ECA rule mechanism [3]. That is, the timely collaboration can be represented in ECA rules, such as occurrence of the situation for timely collaboration as event, collaboration constraints as condition, and the processing of the service as action. Then, an AFC which processes ECA rules detects automatically the occurrence of the event and notify the occurrence to partner's system. The AFC of the partner evaluates the condition and if the condition is satisfied then it executes the action promptly for collaboration. That is, the collaboration among businesses can be processed in an immediate mode without interference of applications or users.

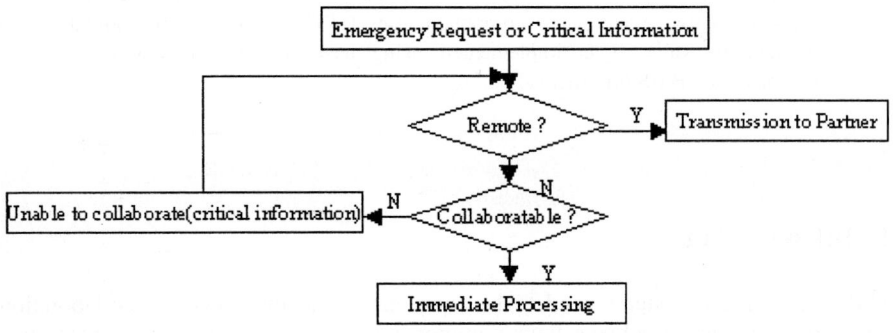

Fig. 1. Timely Collaboration Procedure in B2B E-Commerce

Thus, the timely collaboration among businesses in B2B E-Commerce can be supported by the two main elements: ECA rule programming facility and the Active Functionality Component(AFC).

3 ECA Rule Programming for Timely Collaboration

In this work new ECA rule language is not developed instead an existent ECA rule language is extended at the minimum to express timely collaboration. We adopt ECAA(Event Condition Action Alternative Action) rule pattern which is one of ECA rule patterns[3].

Example of ECA Rule Programs: Consider that a shopping mall becomes short of an item suddenly and requests a partner supplier to provide it. Then the supplier should provide the item quickly within a contracted time period. If, however, the item is out of stock in the supplier's warehouse, it should be notified to the shopping mall promptly so that the shopping mall can try to find alternate supplier to fill the item.

This example shows that a shopping mall and a supplier should collaborate in an immediate mode. It can be implemented by the following two rules;

Rule Find-Alternate-Service /* rule on a Shopping Mall */
    Event unable-special-supply(string supplier, string item-1, integer n);
    Condition true;
    Action Begin find-alternate-service(string item-1, integer n)
      End

Rule Special-Service /* rule on a Supplier */
    Event request-special-supply(string requester, string item-1, integer n);
    Condition no. of item-1 > n;
    Action Begin special-order-processing(string requester, string item-2) End
    Alternative Action Begin raise-event('notify-unable-special-supply') End

4 Active Functionality Component

Timely collaboration written in ECA rules is processed by an AFC. The architecture of an AFC consists of five modules, Communication-Manager, Event-Manager, Rule-Manager, Event-Rule-Interface, and Action/Application. The overall architecture is shown in Fig. 2.

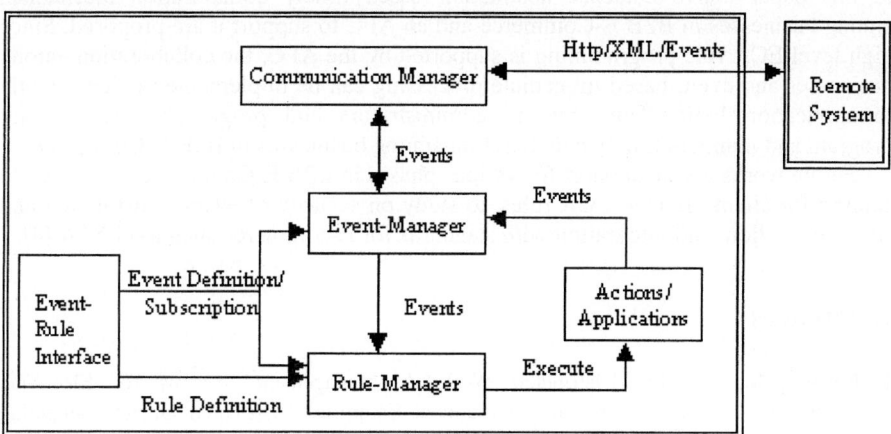

Fig. 2. Overall Architecture of Active Functionality Component

Communication-Manager: It is implemented in Java servlet of Web server and contains two roles. First it receives XML message through Web server, extracts events, and transfers them to local Event-Manager. Second it receives event from local Event-Manager, transforms into XML format, and using HTTP post command transmits to the Communication-Manager of partner's AFC.

Event-Manager: It manages schema definition of events and their subscription, identifies whether subscription of an event is local or remote, and transfers to corresponding Rule-Manager which subscribes the event.

Rule-Manager: The Rule-Manager evaluates and executes ECA rules. It is implemented with basic trigger facilities of an underlined DBMS and contains Event-Instance-Table and Rule-Table.

Event-Rule-Interface: The Event-Rule-Interface is an interface for system administrators or programmers to define events and rules as well as to manage them, *i.e.*, search, delete, and update.

Actions/Applications: The actions/applications are treatments of requested collaboration. They may generate events too.

Prototype Implementation and Application: To validate the timely collaboration mechanism and applicability of the AFC, a prototype has been implemented and applied to a typical B2B scenario. During design and implementation of the prototype, we considered practicability, interoperability with database, and platform independence. Therefore Java was chosen as an implementation language. Commercial DBMS Oracle 9i, Apache Tomcat Web server, Xerces2 Java parser were chosen.

5 Conclusion

In this paper active database abstraction based timely collaboration mechanism among businesses in B2B E-Commerce and an AFC to support it are proposed. Since high level ECA rule programming is supported by the AFC, the collaboration among businesses and event-based immediate processing can be implemented independently to application logic. Thus, system administrators and programmers can easily program and maintain timely collaboration among businesses in B2B E-Commerce.

Future works are: to support for various phases in B2B E-Commerce life cycle, to support for client oriented ECA rules, to study on security of event transmission and action execution, and integration with standards for E-commerce such as ebXML[4].

References

1. Kanaya, N., et. al.: "Distributed Workflow Management Systems for Electronic Commerce", proceedings of 4th International Enterprise Distributed Object Computing Conference(EDOC'00), IEEE 2000.
2. Skonnard, A.: "SOAP: The Simple Object Access Protocol", Microsoft Internet Developer, January 2000.
3. Paton, N. W., and Diaz, O.: "Active Database Systems", Computing Surveys, ACM, 1999.
4. Hofreiter, B., Huemer, C., and Klas, W.: "ebXML: Status, Research Issues, and Obstacles", Proceedings of 12th Int'l Workshop on Research in Data Engineering: Engineering e-Commerce/e-Business Systems (RIDE'02), 2002.

An Algorithm for Mining Lower Closed Itemsets[1]

Tian-rui Li, Ming Qing, Jun Ma, and Yang Xu

Department of mathematics, School of Science,
Southwest Jiaotong University, Chengdu, 610031, China
{trli, xuyang}@swjtu.edu.cn

Abstract. The generalized association rule base(GARB) presented by Li(2003) can efficiently solve the problem of quantity of rule in the process of acquiring rule by traditional association rule mining algorithms. Therefore, how to deduce all rules contained in the rule of GARB becomes an urgent issue in order to support more effective decision-making. In this paper, the notation of lower closed itemset of an itemset was proposed and some properties of it are proved. Then, it is concluded that the above problem can be solved if all the lower closed itemsets of frequent closed itemset(FCI) are obtained. Finally, an algorithm for mining all lower closed itemsets of an itemset was given and its validity is proved.

Introduction

Association rule mining is one of the most important research areas in data mining, to which many researchers have paid their attention[1-8]. Yet there still exist a big problem in process of acquiring rule by traditional mining algorithms, namely, the over-abundant acquired rules, which cause people hard to understand and eventually make use of this knowledge. Presently there are many methods focus on resolving this problem. Some researchers, for example, proposed the methods for reducing the amount of rules by deleting or combining derived rules such as reducing over-abundant rules by structured rule and summarizing related rule by clustering[2], the method of GSE-pattern to organize, generalize, and represent the mined rule[3]. Other researchers presented the methods of mining association rule based on constraints[4], which can reduce amount of rules by applying some special constraints provided by users to the mining process. Moreover, there are many other methods, such as mining multiple-level association rules[5], mining association rules with multiple minimum supports[6], mining φ-association rule[7] and the like.

Although the aforementioned methods can reduce the amount of rules derived to some extent, the number of mined rules is still too big. Then, in [8], the generalized association rule base(GARB) was presented which can solve this problem efficiently because we can deduce all association rules of the database from it and keep

---

[1] This work was supported by the National Natural Science Foundation of China (NSFC) and Basic Science Foundation of Southwest Jiaotong University.

information in the course of deducing, i.e., the support and confidence of rule in the deductive course do not change. Also there is no redundant rule in the base, which means no rule can be obtained by adding or deleting item of antecedent (or consequent) to another rule in this base on the basis of keeping information. Therefore, how to deduce all rules contained in the rule of GARB becomes an urgent issue that should be solved as soon as possible in order to support more effective decision-making. In this paper, the notation of lower closed itemset of an itemset was proposed firstly, then an algorithm for mining all lower closed itemsets of an itemset was given, which can be used to solve this problem.

Preliminaries

Definition 1[1]. *Let $I=\{i_1,i_2,...,i_m\}$ be a set of m different items. An association rule is an implication of the form $X \Rightarrow Y$, where $\emptyset \neq X \subset I$, $\emptyset \neq Y \subset I$, and $X \cap Y = \emptyset$.*

Definition 2[1]. *Let X be an itemset. If s percents of the transactions containing X in the transaction database, then the support of X, denoted as supp(X), is s.*

Definition 3[8]. *An itemset X is closed if there exists no itemset Y such that Y is a proper superset of X and every transaction containing X also contains Y.*

Definition 4[8]. *A closed rule is an implication expression of the form $X \Rightarrow Y$, where $\emptyset \neq X \subset I$, $Y = \emptyset$, and X is a closed itemset.*

Definition 5[8]. *Association rule and closed rule are all called generalized association rule.*

Definition 6. [8] *An upper closed set of an itemset X, denoted as X^- (called as upper closed itemset), is the smallest closed itemset containing it.*

Definition 7. *An lower closed set of an itemset X, denoted as X_- (called as lower closed itemset), is the largest closed itemset contained in it, which means that there exists no closed itemset Y, a proper subset of X, containing X_-.*

Example 1. Suppose a transaction database is shown as Table 1. {B} is one of the lower closed itemsets of itemset {B, C, E}.

Table 1. Transaction database

ID	Items
1	A C D
2	B C E
3	A B C E
4	B F
5	A C

From Definition 7, it is obviously that the following propositions hold.

Proposition 1. *Let X be an itemset, then* $X_- \subset X$.

Proposition 2. *Let Y be a lower closed itemset, then supp(X)<supp(Y).*

Proposition 3. *The lower closed itemset of an itemset X, if it exists, may not be unique.*

Example 2. The itemsets {A, C} and {B, C, E} in Talbe1 are the lower closed itemset of {A, B, C, E}, therefore, the Proposition 3 holds.

Definition 8[8]. *The rule set* $\{r | r : X \Rightarrow Y$ *is a generalized association rule,* X, $X \cup Y$ *closed itemset} are called as generalized association rule base of the database.*

Then, from the above definition of lower closed itemset and propositions, if we can obtain all the lower closed itemsets of frequent closed itemset(FCI) $X \cup Y$, all the rules will be deduced from the rule $X \Rightarrow Y$ in GARB of the database. Therefore, now the problem is development of algorithm for mining all lower closed itemsets of FCI.

An Algorithm for Mining All Lower Closed Itemsets of FCI

In the following, the concrete algorithm for mining all lower closed itemsets of FCI was given.

Algorithm 1. (Mining all lower closed itemsets of a FCI)

Input. 1. Given a FCI A and suppose its cardinal number l is greater than 1.

2. The set of all FCIs in transaction database D.

Output. All lower closed itemsets of FCI A.

Method.
1. Number FCI according to cardinal number in increasing order and lexicographic order.
2. Let FCI_1={FCIs which cardinal number is less than l} $\cup \{\phi\}$ (The cardinal number of empty set is set to 0).
3. All lower closed itemsets of FCI A, denoted as LCS(A), are obtained from calling the process GenLowerClosedSet(FCI_1, A, ϕ).

Following is the algorithm of subroutine GenLowerClosedSet(F_1, A, F_2).

Parameters:
F_1: FCIs which cardinal number is less than l;
F_2: The candidate lower closed itemset of A.
Method:
①If F_1 is an empty set, then return F_2, end;
②else
Get the last element B from F_1, and delete it from F_1;
If B is an subset of A and B is not subset of any element in F_2, then
Add B in F_2;
Recursively call GenLowerClosedSet(F_1, A, F_2).

Proposition 4. *From the above algorithm, we can obtain all the lower closed itemset of FCI A.*

Proof. It is obviously a breath-first search from top to bottom according to the cardinal number of FCI in decreasing order, therefore, the conclusion holds.

By Proposition 4, the above algorithm is valid. Following is an example to illustrate the process of the algorithm.

Example 3. Itemset {A, B, C, E} is a FCI in transaction database shown in Table 1. Here $FCI_1 = \{\phi, \{B\}, \{C\}, \{A, C\}, \{B, F\}, \{A, C, D\}, \{B, C, E\}\}$, then according to GenLowerClosedSet(FCI_1, A, ϕ), it is easily to obtain the set of all lower closed itemsets of {A, B, C, E}, namely, {{B, C, E}, {A, C}}.

Conclusions

In this paper, the concept of lower closed itemset of an itemset was proposed firstly. Then, some properties of it were obtained. Based on these properties, it is concluded that if all lower closed itemsets of FCI were obtained, all rules contained in the rule of GARB can be deduced, which is very important for effective decision-making. Finally, the algorithm for mining all lower closed itemsets of FCI is presented and its validity is proved.

References

1. Agrawal R., Scrikant R.: Fast algorithm for mining association rules. In: Proceeding of VLDB'94. Santiago, Chile, (1994) 487-499
2. Toivonen H., Klemettinen M., RonKainen P., Hatonen K., Mannila H.: Pruning and grouping discovered association rules. In: Workshop Notes of the ECML'95. Heraklion, Greece, (1995) 47-52
3. Liu B., Hu M., Hsu W.: Multi-level organization and summarization of the discovered rules, In: Proceedings of KDD'00. Boston, USA, (2000) 208-217
4. Ng R., Lakshmanan L., Han J. W., Pang A.: Exploratory mining and pruning optimizations of constrained associations rules. In: Proceedings of SIGMOD'98. Seattle, Washington, (1998) 13-24
5. Han J. W., Fu Y.: Mining multiple-level association rules in large databases. IEEE Trans. on knowledge and data engineering. 11(1999) 798-804
6. Liu B., Hsu W., Ma Y.: Mining Association Rules with Multiple Minimum Supports. In: Proceedings of KDD'99. New York, (1999) 337-341
7. Li T. R., Ma J., Xu Y.: An improving mining algorithm aiming at a kind of specific function of degree of interest. In: Proceedings of ICMLC'02. Beijing, China, (2002) 1214-1218
8. Li T. R., Niu Y. Q., Ma J., Xu Y.: Generalized association rule base mining and its algorithm. In: Proceedings of PDCAT'03. Chengdu, China, (2003) 919-922

An Update Propagation Method Based on the Tree of Replicas in Partially Replicated Databases

Misook Bae and Buhyun Hwang

Dept. of Computer Science, Chonnam National University,
300 Yongbong Dong, Kwangju, Republic of Korea
{msbae, bhhwang}@chonnam.chonnam.ac.kr

Abstract. In the single master lazy updates propagation methods that guarantee weakly consistency, they may increase the read availability, but have more chances for update conflicts. We propose an effective update propagation method to resolve this non-serializable execution. The proposed method is based on the balanced tree of replicas in the partially replicated databases and uses the timestamp and the information of the RCTL(the most Recent Committed update-Transaction List) in the status database. We made an experiment of our algorithm through the simulation, and proved that it has good performance due to reducing the abort ratio and response time of transactions.

1 Introduction and Motivation

Data replication is essential to enhance performance and to provide fault tolerance in distributed systems. [1,2,3,4,5] mentioned that replication consistency can be violated in the lazy master replication database system. The updates propagation methods can increase the workload due to executing the works likewise in all sites that have the replicated data and generate the high abort rate of transactions when the consistency is enforced [3,6]. The weakly consistency scheme allows that a write operation updates the most recent replica, but a read operation can response more stale replica. That is, a read only transaction is allowed to read data in a site even on the way of propagating updates of a committed transaction. In the case that timestamp of update transaction is less than timestamp of read transaction, the execution in the lazy propagation violates TSO(TimeStamp Ordering) rule in a site when update transaction arrives after read transaction has been committed. It makes it impossible to abort update transaction because update transaction already has been committed. We resolve this non-serializability problem and this paper assumes that the updates occur rarely and uses a single master lazy propagation technique in which a master copy is updated first.

2 Transaction in Partially Replicated Databases

2.1 System Model

We show a proposed algorithm called UPM-RT (Update Propagation Method using Replicas Tree). UPM-RT is based on the system architecture like in Fig.1.

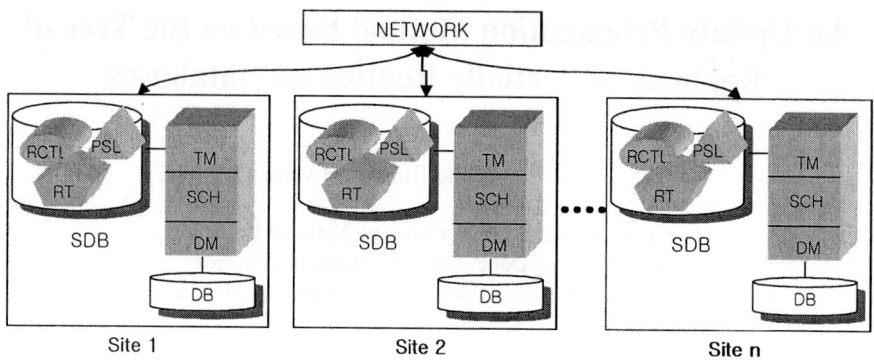

Fig. 1. Architecture of System Model

The architecture is composed of a set of sites connected through a network. Each site consists of a Transaction Manager (TM) and a SCHeduler (SCH). The data are replicated partially. Each status database (SDB) maintains the locations of primary sites (PSL) that execute the write operations and the list of transactions (RCTL). When the update transaction is committed in the primary site, RCTL is used to inform this update information to its all replica sites before its propagation-transaction arrives at each replica site. RCTL includes the information about the data items that are primary copies, and the identifier and the timestamp of transactions that have been committed most recently in the primary site. The primary site of each data item maintains replica trees(RT). RT is a tree that consists of sites that have replicas of each data. The primary site of each data is the one being accessed most frequently for the data and becomes the root of RT. The access frequency of a root is higher than that of its subtrees. The sites that have similar access frequency are in the same level in the tree. Each SCH having a primary copy propagates the updates efficiently along the branches of RT. The structure of sites needs to be reconfigured to propagate the updates efficiently using a RT, too [3]. Since the updates are propagated along the path of tree, to minimize propagation time, the tree needs to be balanced.

2.2 UPM-RT Algorithm

2.2.1 Commit of Transaction and Propagation of Updates

A coordinator of a transaction uses 2PC protocol to commit it. When committing the transaction, if a site that has executed its operations is not a primary site, the site having executed read operations informs its commit decision to its primary site. This produces a serializable history satisfying TSO rule. If there is a transaction that includes write operations, after the transaction has been committed, a trigger to propagate its updates has to be provided.

To resolve non-serializability, the transaction that includes read operations must validate its serializability before it commits its execution. To check serializability, our algorithm uses RCTL information. It is used to check the conflict of a transaction and a propagation transaction. Though PT_i did not arrive at a site, the TM can check the serializability of them by comparing $ts(T_j(x))$ with $ts(RCTL(x))$. The $ts(T_j(x))$ means the timestamp of T_j, which reads x, and $ts(RCTL(x))$ means the timestamp of a transaction in RCTL for x.

When an update transaction commits, the coordinator of it submits its write operations to the corresponding primary sites. After completing write operations of the committed transaction at all its primary sites, its propagation transaction is created for each update and is propagated along the its RT. If the coordinator site does not correspond to primary site, it should inform the primary site of the result of decision. The primary site received the commit decision updates its own RCTL information and propagates its update results to its children in the tree after it executes write operations. The timestamp of the committed transaction is assigned to the write operation to be propagated. When the read-only transaction commits, for all data x not in the primary site, it informs the primary site of x of the fact that it has committed. UPM-RT algorithm is described as follows.

```
begin
  When a transaction T is submitted to a site S_i;
  if (T is a propagation transaction PT)
       propagate the updates along the its RT;
  if (T is a Transaction) {
      TM assigns unique timestamp to T;
      distribute operations to execute in each site;
      schedule operations in the scheduling queue
              according to TSO rule;
      if (the execution of last operation in T finished)
          perform UPM-2PC; }
end.
                /* UPM-2PC */
/* COordinator */
CO sends a vote request to all PAs;
if (a participant polls RCTL information)
       a CO responses RCTL information;
CO collects voting results;
if (all PAs voted to YES) CO sends Commit to all PAs
else CO sends Abort to all PAs;

/* PArticipants */
if (the operation executed in the PAs == w(x))
       vote YES/NO to CO whether executed or not ;
if (the operation executed in the PAs == r(x))  {
       poll RCTL information to the primary site of x;
       if (ts(T) < ts (RCTL(x))   vote NO to CO;
       else if (w_ts(x) == ts(RCTL(x)) vote YES to CO;
             else {  wait until PT arrives;
                     execute PT as soon as PT arrives;
                     vote YES to CO;}}
```

3 Performance Evaluation

To evaluate performance of the proposed algorithm, we performed simulation experiment using CSIM(C SIMulator) simulator. We use transaction abort ratio and response time as performance measures. The proposed algorithm(UPM-RT) has been compared with existing methods(LHD) while varying three parameters: the number of nodes(sites), replicas ratio, and read operation ratio. The unit of response time is milliseconds. First, we simulated two algorithms while varying replicas rate; 20, 40, 70, and 100%. The replicas ratio means the rate of the number of replicas nodes to that of total nodes. Next, we experimented them while varying the number of nodes;7, 10, and 15. Third, the performance comparison has been done while varying rate of read operations: 10, 30, 50, 70, and 90%. The results of simulation are shown as in Table 1, Table 2, and Table 3. And they show that UPM-RT has better performance than LHD since transaction abort ratio and response time are reduced.

Table 1. Abort Ratio and Response Time for Replicas Ratio (Write-Operation Ratio 0.1)

Parameter Replica Ratio(%)	Abort-Ratio		Response-Time	
	LHD	UPM-RT	LHD	UPM-RT
20	0.6394	0.1960	9006.975	5603.457
40	0.6543	0.3323	7362.981	6019.116
70	0.6523	0.5106	6067.049	5564.540
100	0.5842	0.5957	5633.558	5648.176

Table 2. Abort Ratio and Response Time for the Number of Nodes

Parameter #nodes	Abort-Ratio		Response-Time	
	LHD	UPM-RT	LHD	UPM-RT
7	0.6173	0.3395	2672.837	2750.300
10	0.6546	0.2163	8946.453	5469.222
15	0.6204	0.0853	17555.79	10308.53

Table 3. Abort Ratio and Response Time for Read Operation Ratio

Parameter Read-Operation Ratio(%)	Abort-Ratio		Response-Time	
	LHD	UPM-RT	LHD	UPM-RT
10	0.2676	0.0786	7177.567	6183.731
30	0.5710	0.1810	8929.520	5763.626
50	0.6709	0.2360	9261.173	5435.796
70	0.6627	0.2230	9265.797	5434.207
90	0.4768	0.1283	6769.854	5490.742

4 Conclusion

Recently, there is a tendency that databases are to be scalable and to be partially replicated according to the degree of importance and necessity of data. For preserving consistency in the partially replicated databases, the replication management needs an efficient update propagation method that guarantees serializable execution. This paper proposed the updates propagation method UPM-RT based on the replicas tree of each data. It can be applied to the ubiquitous environment that needs partially replicated databases. The proposed method guarantees the serializable execution of transactions by using timestamp and SDB. It reduces the updates propagation delay since it uses a tree of replicas that needs only to be updated. Through the simulation experiment, we compared UPM-RT with a representative method LHD while varying the number of sites, replicas ratio, and read operation ratio. We found out performance improvement of our method compared to LHD since our method can reduce the transaction abort ratio and response time.

Acknowledgement

This work was supported by Korea Science and Engineering Foundation (KOSEF #R05-2003-000-10532-0).

References

[1] Jim, G., Pat, H., Patrick, O., Dennis, S.: The Danger of Replication and a Solution. In Procs. of ACM SIGMOD International Conf. on Management of Data, Montreal Canada (1996) 173-182
[2] Todd, A., Yuri, B., Henry, F.K. , Avishai, W.: Replication, consistency and practicality: Are these mutually exclusive?. In Procs. of the ACM SIGMOD International Conf. on Management of Data, Seattle WA (1998) 484-495
[3] Xiangning, L., Abdelsalam, H. and Weimin, D.: Multiview Access Protocols for Large Scale Replication. ACM Transaction on Database Systems Vol.23 No.2. (1998) 158-198
[4] Yuri, B., Henry, F..K.: Replication and Consistency: Being lazy helps sometimes. In Procs. of the ACM SIGACT-SIGMOD-SIGART Symposium on Principles of Database Systems, Tucson Arizona (1997) 173-184
[5] Esther, P., Eric, S.: Update Propagation Strategies to Improve Freshness in Lazy Master Replicated Databases. VLDB Journal (2000) 305-318
[6] Marta, P.M., Ricardo, J.P, B.Kemme, G.Alonso: Scalable Replication in Database Clusters. In Proc. of Distributed Computing Conf. DISC'00 volume LNCS1914, Toledo Spain (2000) 315-329

A Parallel Electro-Optical Computer Architecture for Artificial Intelligence

Jong Whoa Na

Computer Engineering Dept., Hansei University,
Kun Po Si, Kyung Gi Do, South Korea
jwna@hansei.ac.kr

Abstract. The users of the supercomputer are changing from the scientific community to the business community. However, the database and knowledge base applications are executed on the computer based on the Neumann architecture designed for the numerical processing. We propose a novel parallel computer architecture that uses optical devices to exploit the inherent parallelism of optics for the parallel processing of the rule-based systems. The proposed system uses two-dimensional spaces as basic computational entities and is therefore able to perform concurrent comparison operations of the expert system.

1 Introduction

Traditionally, the buyers of the state-of-the-art supercomputers have been from the scientific and military domain. However, this trend is changing. The ever-increasing business data of the multinational company such as Citibank and the business processes now require the performance of the supercomputer [1]. These business processes typically make use of database. What are emerging now are the facilities to make an intelligent decision by using enormous amount of data. Rule-based Database System (RBMS) is an implementation for the intelligent database [2]. The engine of the rule-based system (RBS) is a resolution engine that requires the pattern matching operation. Since the size of the data is enormous, the pattern matching operation is the bottleneck of the RBS [3]. As the size of the knowledge base becomes too enormous as in the case of the CYC, we must analyze the performance and efficiency of the underlying hardware [4].

In this paper, we propose a high performance Optoelectronic Integrated Circuit (OEIC)-based Expert System (OES) tailored for the high performance RBS implementations. Specifically, the architecture is designed for the hardware for CYC that uses the resolution principle as inference engine. We tried to exploit the natural parallelism available in the resolution operation by using the optical components [5]. The OES uses OEIC for parallel inference engine while electronics for the rest of the system. To take advantage of the OEIC properties, we represent facts and rules in two-dimensional space so that the proposed inference engine performs the three-dimensional processing. The inference engine is logically transformed into an optical interconnection network that can carry out inference optically and hence in a highly parallel passion.

2 Organization of the OEIC Expert System (OES)

The major objective of the OEIC-based Expert System (OES) is the exploitation of maximum parallelism in expert systems. It can be achieved by using two-dimensional representation of knowledge and three-dimensional knowledge processing. In order to evaluate rules in parallel, the host must maintain consistency. To maintain consistency, the host must compare a fact element with a group of related rules and facts. Thus, the size of the group can be important in that the comparison time depends on the number of data in the group. One of the major characteristics of the rule-based programming environment is modularity and hierarchy [6]. These stem from the fact that the structure of human knowledge can be modeled in a modular and hierarchical structure such as a tree, where each node represents a module which is composed of a small number of rules and facts. In this tree, the newly evaluated facts must be compared to a mutually exclusive group. Thus, the fact is compared with a specific group, which is small. Note that this checking operation is performed at compile time. Therefore, the checking time for a given fact for the group should not cause any excessive overhead at run time. In CYC, each module is termed as microtheory such that the inference is performed within each microtheory.

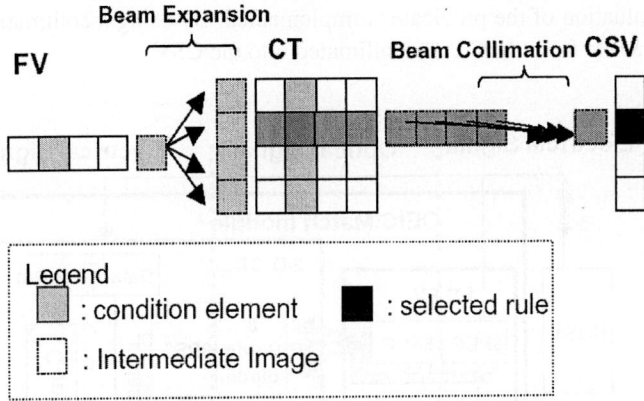

Fig. 1. Knowledge representation and operation principles in OES: FV, CT, and CSV represents fact vector, condition table, and conflict set vector respectively

2.1 Knowledge Representation in the OES

In general, to run any high level programming language on a computer, the source code must be translated into an object code. RBSs require the rules to be in human readable form as well as the object code, which is optimized for the hardware. Thus, RBSs keep their own version of the object knowledge base. For OES, we have developed a translation algorithm that translates the knowledge base into the data format suitable for the execution in the OES. OES uses a 2-D array called Condition Table

(CT) and an 1-D array called Fact Vector (FV) and one 1-D array called conflict set vector (CSV), as shown in Fig. 1.

A rule consists of a condition part and an action part. In Fig. 1, each row of the condition table (CT) represents a rule and each pixel of the row represents a condition element of a rule. The condition part of a rule consists of conjunction of the condition element. In OES, the *Object-Attribute-Value* tuple of a predicate is evaluated as follows: Each entry of the input fact vector (FV) represents the *Value* of a fact that is to be compared with the *Object* of the condition variable. The *Value*, which was an optical signal, is converted into electrical signal using photodiodes. Then the *Value* and the *Object* are processed according to the *Attribute* in of the tuple is specified by the predicate. In this way, we can exploit the data-level parallelism.

The evaluation results of each condition elements of a row are converted back into an optical signal via a LASER or LED. This is to take advantage of optical interconnect over electrical interconnect. These signals from a row of the CT are collected into a pixel representing the evaluation result of a rule. The one-dimensional conflict set vector (CSV) represents the result of the evaluation of the rules of a microtheory.

Fig. 2 illustrates the block diagram of the proposed OES. Here, the *beam expansion* implies sending the source of light representing a fact to multiple destinations representing the condition part of the rule. In the figure, the light representing the value of a fact is spread (in parallel) into the four condition slots of a rule. Thus, parallel evaluation of the predicate is implemented. By using a collimating optics, the outputs of a rule from the CT are collimated into the CSV.

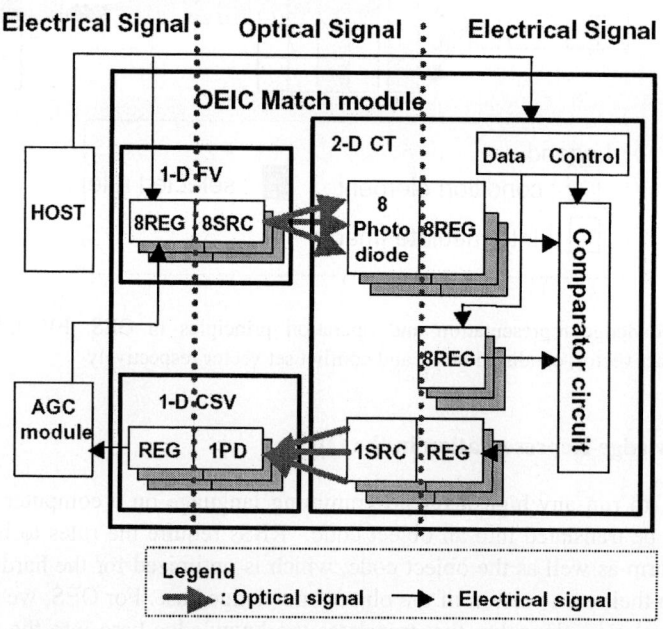

Fig. 2. Logical block diagram of the OEIC-based Expert System

The electronic AGC module receives the one-dimensional CSV from the match module to perform a conflict resolution. The action parts of the triggered rules out of the selected rules are executed and the corresponding variable of the FT are modified. If the fired rule satisfies the goal condition, the AGC stops inference cycle. Otherwise, the OM initiates another inference cycle.

3 Conclusion

The size of knowledge base of the CYC is very large and still growing [7]. The growing size of the database of the multi-national companies now requires the performance of the supercomputers. Conventional electronic parallel machines contain fast processors, but have limited communication bandwidth, which is critical in parallel processing [8]. Optical interconnect can be an alternative owing to the advantage of optical interconnects such as high speed, EMI immunity, and massively parallel structure. By using optical interconnect instead of electrical interconnect, OES can evaluate as many input data as possible to the condition elements of the rule. Since the current technology permits $10^3 \times 10^3$ optical data plane, assuming 10 bits are used to represent the *Value* of a predicate, we may be able to represent 10^5 facts at one cycle. We have explored the OEIC-based Expert System (OES) architecture. The architecture exploits the natural parallelism of RBS by using optics and the advantage of optical interconnects.

Acknowledgement

This work was supported by 2004 Hansei University Research Grant.

References

1. P. Stenstrom. Trends in shard memory multiprocessing, Computer, pp.44-50, Dec. 1997.
2. Barbara von Halle, Building a Business Rules System: Part 1, DM Review, Jan. 2004.
3. P. Harmon and D. King, Expert System: Artificial Intelligence in Business. New York: John Wiley and Sons, 1985.
4. http://www.cyc.com/cyc/technology/whatiscyc_dir/howdoescycreason
5. A. Guha and M. W. Derstine, Designing Massively Parallel Optical Computers: a Case Sturdy, Applied Optics, vol. 29, pp. 2187-2200, 1990.
6. G. E. Blelloch, CIS: a massively concurrent rule-based system, in AAAI-86, Phil., pp. 735-741, Aug. 1986.
7. http://www.cyc.com/cyc/technology/whatiscyc_dir/whatsincyc
8. B. W. Wah and G. J. Li, Design issues of multiprocessors for artificial intelligence, in Parallel Processing for Supercomputers, ch. 4, pp. 107--159, New York: McGraw-Hill, 1989.

Data Mining Techniques in Materialised Project and Selection View

Ying Wah Teh and Abu Bakar Zaitun

Faculty of Computer Science and Information Technology, University of Malaya,
50603, Kuala Lumpur, Malaysia
tehyw@um.edu.my

Abstract. This paper investigates factors such as the use of both attributes and tuples specified in the criteria of a structured query language query and their influence on the response time of a query in a data warehouse environment. To handle queries by using redundant data structures such as materialised views has already been will established by the pioneers in the data warehouse industry. With the availability of very large data storage today, redundant data structures are no longer a big issue. However, an intelligent way of managing materialised views that can lead to fast access of data is the central issue dealt with in this paper.

1 Introduction

One of the techniques employed in a data warehouse to improve the response time of a query is the creation of a set of materialised views and indexes [1]. The materialised view and index selection are two problems often studied independently in data warehouses. Studying the problem of views and index separately causes an inefficient distribution of resources (space, computation time, maintenance time, etc.) between materialised views and indexes [2].

The right materialised views can significantly improve performance, particularly for decision-support applications [1]. Both indexes and materialised views are physical structures that can significantly accelerate performance. An effective physical database design tool must therefore take into account the interaction between indexes and materialised views by considering them together to optimise the physical design for the workload on the system [1].

2 Literature Review

2.1 Microsoft SQL 2000's Tuning Wizard

Agrawal, Chaudhuri and Narasayya [1] contended that an effective physical design database tool must take into account the interaction between indexes and materialised views by considering them together to optimise the physical design for the workload on the system. In 2000, they established that, in order to pick a physical design consisting of indexes and materialised views, it is vital to explore over the combined space of indexes and materialised views. The tuning wizard has been implemented in Microsoft SQL Server 2000. The strength of the tuning wizard is that it helps the data warehouse administrators to select optimal indexes and materialised views automatically. Its weakness is that it is a black box to the data warehouse administrators as automatic tools do everything without the involvement of a data warehouse administrator. The tuning wizard uses a workload to recommend the indexes and materialised views. The workload is the logging capability of database systems to capture a trace of queries and updates faced by the system. In a data warehouse, most of the queries are read-only statements (select) rather than update statements (Insert, Delete and Update). Microsoft SQL 2000's tuning wizard and AutoAdmin face the same problem. If the tuning wizard is allowed to build the index or materialised view, it might not be suitable for a data warehouse.

2.2 Current Research in Query Processing Techniques

Current research in query processing techniques comprises either the automatic or non-automatic selection of query processing techniques (Table 1). Both approaches, however, are not suitable for a data warehouse. There are too many parameters to select in data warehouse performance tuning. Microsoft's AutoAdmin and Microsoft SQL 2000's tuning wizard use the optimiser estimated cost for all the SQL statement (Insert, Delete, Update and Select).

Table 1. Current Research in Query Processing Techniques

Non-automatic or automatic selection of indexes and/or materialised views	Comments	Actions
Data warehouse performance tuning	There are too many parameters to be selected. It is not suitable for inexperienced data warehouse administrators	Microsoft's AutoAdmin
Microsoft's AutoAdmin (index selection tool)	It uses the optimiser's estimated cost for all the SQL statements. It might not be suitable for a data warehouse (read-only statements)	To incorporate the materialised view selection (Microsoft SQL 2000' tuning wizard) as well and modify the estimated cost for selection statements only.
Microsoft SQL 2000's tuning wizard (index and materialised view)	It uses the optimiser's estimated cost for all the SQL statements. It might not be suitable for a data warehouse (read-only statements)	To modify the estimated cost for selection statements only.

Microsoft SQL 2000's tuning wizard is not an open-source software, thus, it is impossible to change the existing codes. Therefore, data mining techniques are proposed as intelligent ways to handle the query processing techniques in this research.

Most researchers apply data mining at the application level of data warehouse [4], [5], [6]. From their work [7], [8], it is known that it is important to start optimisation from the base relation to reduce large, immediate results.

An association-rule is one of data mining techniques. An association-rule involves certain association relationships among a set of objects in a database. In this context, sets of association-rules are found at various levels of abstraction from the relevant set(s) of data in a database. The weakness of the association-rule algorithms is that they use the transaction log which relies only on the frequently accessed items. Redundant data structures are built based on multiple criteria (number of bytes, the frequently accessed attributes and multiple-attribute access) rather than only frequently accessed items/attributes. Therefore, the association rule might not be suitable for selection based on multiple criteria to form redundant data structures.

3 Data Mining Techniques in MPSV

Table 2 shows a training data set with four data attributes and two classes.

Table 2. shows a training data set with four data attributes and two classes

Attribute Names	Len(x)	F (x)	Data Distribution	Class
a_5	21	1	Null	Do not MPSV
:	:	:	:	:
YJoin	2	3	30	MPSV

```
1. create a node N;
// this node is a leaf node
2. if all instances of the same class, C is positive, then create MPSV node and
   halt.
   // Class, C is positive which can be any of the conditions:
   //    a) the size of an attribute <= 8 bytes
   //    b) data distribution <=20%
   //    c) frequently accessed attributes >.mean.of frequent access F(x)
3. if all instance of the same class, C is negative, then create do not MPSV node and
   halt.
   // Class, C is negative which can be any of one the conditions:
   //    a) data distribution > 50%
   //    b) frequently accessed attributes <= mean of frequent access F(x)
// this node is a decision node
4. Select a feature, F with values v1, v2, ... vn and create a decision node.
// the first selecting feature of F is the size of an attribute
// the second selection feature of data distribution
// the third selection feature of F is Frequently Accessed Attributes
// if the size of an attribute, the values will be {<=8 bytes, between 9 and 16 bytes,
//                                                  > 16 bytes}
// if >1 attribute access at a time, the values will be {>20%, <=20%}
// if Frequently Accessed Attributes {<=Mean of Frequent Access, >Mean of Frequent
//                                    Access}
5. Partition the training instances in C into subsets C1, C2, ..., Cn according to the values
   of v1, v2, ..., vn.
// the first selection feature of F (the size of an attribute) will be partitioned
//    the training instances in C into subsets {Frequently Access Attributes, Data
//    Distribution, MPSV} according to the values of {> 16 bytes,
//    between 9 and 16 bytes, <=8 Bytes} respectively.
// the second selection feature of F (Data Distribution) will be partitioned
//    the training instances in C into subsets {Do not MPSV, MPSV} according
//    to the values of {>20%, <=20%} respectively.
// the third selection feature of F (Frequently Accessed Attributes) will be partitioned
//    the training instances in C into subsets {Do not MPSV, MPSV} according
//    to the values of {{<=Mean of Frequent Access, >Mean of Frequent Access }
//    respectively.
6. Apply the algorithm recursively to each of the sets Ci.
```

Fig. 1. Generate the Decision Tree Algorithm for MPSV

The Hunt's method for generating an Materialised Project and Selection View (MPSV) can be elaborated further as shown in Fig. 1.

4 Conclusions

The table below shows performance TPC-H [3] sample queries.

Query Name	Before the Decision Tree Model	After the Decision Tree Model
Query 1	1:17 min	47 sec
Query 2	17:09 min	1:08 min
:	:	:
Query 19	1:39 min	4 sec

The results of this work are expected to encourage wider use of data mining techniques in the MPSV. The current tools do not allow data warehouse administrators to optimise the performance of their data warehouse. The training data set has a significant impact on the model that had been built. The selected attributes indexed, only represent the behaviour of the training data set of a particular relation for a certain time.

References

1. S. Agrawal, S. Chaudhuri, and V. Narasayya : Automated Selection of Materialized Views and Indexes for SQL Databases. In: Proceedings of the 26th International Conference on Very Large Databases, San Francisco, Morgan Kaufmann (2000)
2. L. Bellatreche, K. Karlapalem, and M. Mohania: Some Issues in Design of Data Warehouse Systems , in, Dr. Shirley A. Becker (Eds.), Developing Quality Complex Database Systems: Practices, Techniques, and Technologies, Western Hemisphere, Ideas Group Publishing, (2001) 125-172
3. Transaction Processing Performance Council, *TPC-H*. Available from World Wide Web: http://www.tpc.org/tpch/default.asp Last modified: February 24, 2003.
4. Ferguson et al. : An application of data mining for product design. IEE Colloquium on Knowledge Discovery and Data Mining. (1998) 5/1 -5/5
5. Ogilvie et al. : Use of data mining techniques in the performance monitoring and optimisation of a thermal power plant. IEE Colloquium on Knowledge Discovery and Data Mining. (1998) 7/1 -7/4
6. Steele et al. Knowledge discovery in medical databases: what factors influence a successful bone marrow transplant for Hodgkin's disease. IEE Colloquium on Knowledge Discovery and Data Mining. (1998) 3/1 -3/8
7. V. Harinarayan, A. ,Rajaraman and J. Ullman, Implementing Data Cubes Efficiently. New York: ACM Press. (1996)
8. K. A. Ross, and Z. Li: Fast Joins Using Join Indices. The VLDB Journal. 8(1). (1999) 1- 24
9. Claussen et al. : Exploiting early sorting and early partitioning for decision support query processing. The VLDB Journal, 9(3), (2000) 190-213

Parallel Text Categorization for Multi-dimensional Data

Verayuth Lertnattee[1] and Thanaruk Theeramunkong[2]

[1] Faculty of Pharmacy, Silpakorn University,
Nakorn Pathom, 73000, Thailand
verayuths@hotmail.com, verayuth@email.pharm.su.ac.th
[2] Sirindhorn International Institutue of Technology,
Thammasat University, Pathum Thani 12000
thanaruk@siit.tu.ac.th

Abstract. In this paper, we propose a multi-dimensional category model (MDCM) for classifying multi-dimensional text collection. We can parallel and distribute the process of text classification in separately on each dimension. With this model, performance of classifiers improves in both accuracy and time complexity. For classification accuracy, some benefits can be obtained. Classifiers learn from larger training documents with a small number of classes on each dimension. We can select the best classifier for each dimension and combine the results from them. For time complexity, the learning and classifying phases can be in parallel and distributed manner. The efficiency of MDCM is investigated on drug information data set which assigns topics in monographs in the first dimension and primary therapeutic classes in the second dimension. The experimental results show that parallel text classification on MDCM performs better than flat model in both accuracy and time complexity.

Keywords: text classification, multi-dimensional data, parallel algorithm.

1 Introduction

With the fast growth of online text information, there has been extreme need to organize relevant information in text documents. Automatic text categorization (also known as text classification) becomes a significant tool to utilize text documents efficiently and effectively. In the past, a variety of classification models were developed in different schemes, such as probabilistic models [1], linear models [2], support vector machine (SVM) [3] and so on. For high accuracy, the text classifiers need sufficient labeled documents to learn accurately. An alternative way is that the classifiers utilize a large pool of unlabeled documents. However, the computational time for learning from unlabeled documents is very high. Some techniques for clustering and classifying documents in parallel were proposed in [4, 5]. Most researches focus on parallelizing of learning algorithms.

This paper, we propose a new category model for classifying a special type of text collection so-called multi-dimensional text collection. With this type of collection, each text document is belong to multiple predefined sets of categories, where each set corresponds to a dimension. To classify documents in multi-dimensional collection, a simple flat category model (for short, FCM) can be applied [2, 4]. Classification based on this model causes to the problems of classification accuracy and computational time. The task based on these fine-grained classes is much more difficult than those for single-dimensional data sets due to the following two reasons. Firstly, more classes may confuse a classifier since some classes will look similar to the others and may utilize more time for comparison to class prototypes. Secondly, fewer training documents per class may cause the constructed class prototypes not good enough to be a representative of all documents in the class. To cope with these problems, a new category model, called *multi-dimensional category model* (for short, MDCM), is introduced. With this model, text classifiers can classify a document on each dimension by the ways of parallelizing and distributing. The performance of classifiers should improve in both accuracy and computational time.

2 Parallel Text Categorization on Multi-dimensional Category Model

With some disadvantages of FCM as describing in previous section, MDCM is introduced in this work. The proposed model is an extension of a FCM, where documents are not classified into a single set of categories, instead they are classified into multiple sets. Each set of categories can be viewed as a dimension in the sense that documents may be classified into different kinds of categories.

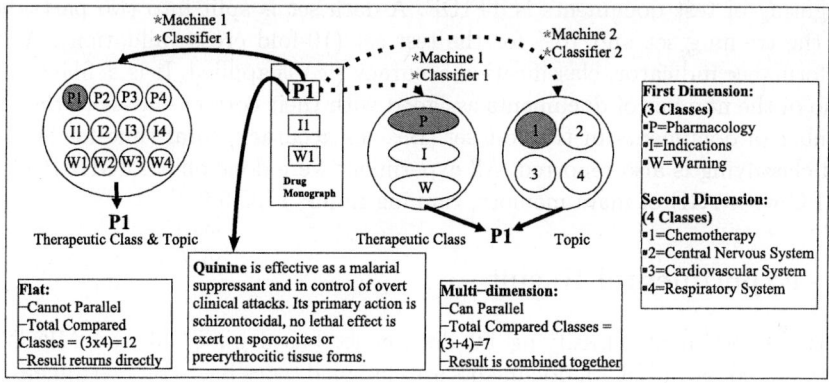

Fig. 1. Two category models for classifying a drug monograph

In Figure 1, a drug monograph is composed of three topics in the first dimension and four therapeutic classes in the second dimension. For example, a quinine monograph is composed of three parts: P1, I1 and W1 with each part representing each topic in the monograph. P1 means pharmacology of a chemotherapy drug such as quinine. This figure shows the detail of P1 and the representations for classifying P1 based on two category models: FCM and MDCM. With MDCM, several advantages can be obtained as follows. Performance of classifiers improves in both accuracy and time complexity. For classification accuracy, three benefits can be obtained as follows. (1) Classifiers learn from larger training documents than flat model. (2) The number of classes on each dimension in MDCM (3 classes in the first dimension and 4 classes in the second dimension) is usually less than in FCM (12 classes). (3) We can select the best classifier for each dimension. The results of each dimension are combined to be the suggested class for a test document. For time complexity, the learning and classifying phases can be in parallel and distributed manner. Therefore, the total time is the longest time among learning and classifying on each dimension.

3 Data Sets and Experimental Settings

To evaluate MDCM, a collection called drug information (DI) is used. DI is a collection of web documents that have been collected from *www.rxlist.com*. It is composed of 4,480 web pages providing information about widely used drugs in seven topics (the 1st dimension): *adverse drug reaction, clinical pharmacology, description, indications, overdose, patient information,* and *warning*. Moreover we manually grouped the drugs according to major pharmacological actions, resulting in five classes (the 2nd dimension): *chemotherapy, neuro-muscular system, cardiovascular & hematopoeitic, hormone* and *respiratory system*. It is organized into 35 classes (7×5). Centroid-based classifiers of bigram models are used with three different term weightings i.e., TFIDF, TFICF and IDFICF. Term weighting of test documents is TFIDF. A data set is split into two parts: 90% for the training set and 10% for the test set (10-fold cross validation). As the performance indicator, classification accuracy (%) is applied. It is defined as the ratio of the number of documents assigned with their correct classes to the total number of documents in the test set. Besides accuracy, total time for learning and classifying is also reported. All experiment were done on a 2.4GHz Pentium IV PC with 1GB of main memory, running Linux TLE 5.0.

4 Experimental Result

In this experiment, classifying DI documents based on FCM and MDCM is investigated. For MDCM, documents are classified twice based on two dimensions independently. The results of the first and second dimensions are combined to be the suggested class for a test document. The performance of classifiers based on FCM and MDCM is shown in Table 1.

In the tables, D_1 and D_2 mean the accuracy of the first and second dimensions, respectively. The two-dimensional accuracy of FCM and MDCM are denoted by F and M, respectively. From the results, classification accuracy based on MDCM outperforms FCM. The TFICF gains the highest accuracy. High accuracy may be obtained from the combination of the good classifier in each

Table 1. Performance of Classifiers based on FCM and MDCM (%)

Methods	Accuracy (%)				Time (sec)	
	D_1	D_2	F	M	F	M
TFIDF	96.07	78.28	69.29	**75.11**	11.67	**9.33**
TFICF	97.48	85.84	70.51	**83.59**	11.78	**9.44**
IDFICF	91.36	84.62	74.42	**78.21**	11.67	**9.33**
D_1 (TFIDF)+D_2(IDFICF)	81.07				9.33	

dimension. When we combine the result of D_1 (from TFIDF) and D_2 (from IDFICF), accuracy is also high. The computational time (include disk I/O) in parallel in MDCM is usually less than FCM. The conclusion is that MDCM gains high accuracy and less computational time than FCM.

5 Conclusion and Future Work

In this paper, we proposed a MDCM for classifying multi-dimensional text collection. By this model, documents were classified in separately on each dimension. A parallel text classification algorithm was applied in a MDCM. Performance of classifiers improves in both accuracy and time complexity. Classification on each dimension gave us some benefits. Classifiers learn from larger training documents with a small number of classes. We can select the best classifier for each dimension and combine the results from them. The learning and classifying phases can be in parallel and distributed manner. For our future work, it is also interesting to find out the way to generalize the multi-dimensional categories to deal with hierarchical text collection.

Acknowledgement. This work has been supported by National Electronics and Computer Technology Center (NECTEC), project number NT-B-22-I5-38-47-04.

References

1. Nigam, K., McCallum, A., Thrun, S., Mitchell, T.: Text classification from labeled and unlabeled documents using EM. Machine Learning **39** (2000) 103–134
2. Lertnattee, V., Theeramunkong, T.: Effect of term distributions on centroid-based text categorization. Information Science **158** (2004) 89–115
3. Joachims, T.: Learning to Classify Text using Support Vector Machines. Kluwer Academic Publishers, Dordrecht, NL (2002)
4. Kruengkrai, C., Jaruskulchai, C.: A parallel learning algorithm for text classification. In: Proceedings of the Eighth ACM SIGKDD International Conference on Knowledge Discovery and Data Mining, ACM Press, New York, US (2002) 201–206
5. Ruoccom, A., Frieder, O.: Clustering and classification of large document bases in a parallel environment. Journal of the American Society for Information Science **48** (1997) 932–943

Agent Based Distributed Data Mining

Sung Wook Baik[1], Jerzy Bala[2], and Ju Sang Cho[1]

[1] College of Electronics and Information Engineering,
Sejong University,
Seoul 143-747, Korea
{sbaik, jscho}@sejong.ac.kr
[2] Datamat Systems Research, Inc.
1600 International Drive, McLean, VA 22102, USA
jbala@dsri.com

Abstract. This paper presents an agent-based distributed data mining approach dealing with heterogeneous databases located at different sites. It introduces a modified decision tree algorithm on an agent based framework, which produces an accurate global model without transferring data between agents. The novel approach is evaluated over a test bed of texture feature data of 184 aerial photograph images. The experimental results show that the distributed version with more agents outperforms the version with fewer agents when the rule generation from the large database is not complicated.

1 Introduction

Recently, massive amounts of data in digital form are rapidly collected and stored for a variety of purposes with an advance in storage technologies. These data are naturally located at geographically distributed sites, and some of them are relevant to each other. In such a distributed environment, a basic approach for data mining is to move all of the data to a central data repository and then to analyze them with a single data mining system. However, even though it guarantees accurate results of data analysis, the approach requires overly expensive computation and communication costs and has a critical security problem in revealing private information data. An alternative approach is a high level learning with in-place strategies in which all the data can be locally analyzed, and local results at their local sites are combined at the central site to obtain the final result (global data model). This approach is less expensive but may produce ambiguous and incorrect global results. To make up for such a weakness, many researchers have spent great efforts looking for more advanced approaches of combining local models built at different sites. Most of these approaches are agent-based high level learning such as meta-learning [1], knowledge probing [2], and mixture of expert [3], Bayesian model averaging [4], and stacked generalization [5]. However, these approaches still only have ability to estimate a global data model through the aggregation of the local results, rather than generating an exactly correct global model. In particular, they have the critical weakness of not dealing with heterogeneous databases located at different sites.

2 System Architecture and Distributed Learning Algorithm

This paper presents an agent based distributed data mining approach, in which the modified decision tree algorithm on an agent based framework can deal with heterogeneous data sets in the distributed environment and produce accurate global results. The data mining based the algorithm takes full advantage of all the available data through a mechanism for integrating data from a wide variety of data sources and is able to handle data characterized by geographic (or logical) distribution, complexity and multi feature representations, and vertical partitioning/distribution of feature sets.

Fig. 1 shows the architecture of an agent based system, which consists of a web server, a mediator, and agents. The web server supports users with a web based interface through which they can access databases located at different sites and manipulate data mining facilities. The mediator coordinates the communication between several agents with security concerns such as authentication. Each agent is located at each heterogeneous data site to achieve coordinated learning through the cooperation of local learning and communication with the other agents. The mining engine and the communication interface within the agent are implemented in C and Java, respectively.

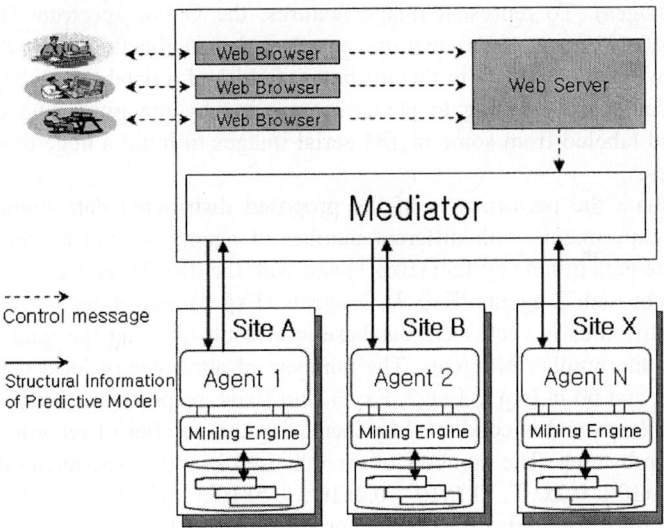

Fig. 1. System architecture of an agent based distributed data mining

The distributed learning algorithm of a decision tree in an agent-mediator communication mechanism is as follows:

1. [Mediator] Start the local data mining processes associated with local agents.
2. [Agent] Find the attribute and its associated value that can best split the data into the various training classes during local mining.
3. [Agent] Send the best local attribute and its associated value to the mediator.

4. [Mediator] Select the best attribute from the best local attributes of all the agents.
5. [Mediator] Notify each agent of its role for the next action (splitting or waiting).
6. [Agent] Split the data, according to the best global attribute and its associated split value, in the formation of two separate clusters of data in the selected agent.
7. [Agent] Distribute the structural information in each cluster and the best attribute to the other agents through the mediator.
8. [Agent] Construct the partial decision trees according to the structural information in other agents.
9. [Agent] Generate decision rules at each agent and notify the mediator for termination if there is no more splitting. Otherwise, go to step 2.
10. [Mediator&Agent] Terminate.

3 Experimentation

Experimental data are provided by the UC Berkeley Library Web [6]. They are 184 aerial photographs (scale of the originals: 1:30,000) of the San Francisco Bay area, California. Each photograph image has the size of approximately 1300 X 1500 pixels with 256 grey-level. Experiments have been conducted to generate a data pattern for two distinguished classes (i.e., downtown areas (class A) and forest areas (class B) on aerial images). To represent image features, the Gabor spectrum filtering [7] generates 240 features (40 orientations and 6 scales in the frequency domain) on each pixel, which correspond to the attributes (fields) of a database. A huge amount of feature data corresponding to pixels categorized by the given two classes are collected and labeled from some of 184 aerial images to build a huge database with 240 attributes.

We evaluate the performance of the proposed distributed data mining method under four experiments with different number of agents -- with a non-distributed version of the data mining system (Exp 1) and with the distributed version of the data mining system with 2 agents (Exp 2), 3 agents (Exp 3), and 4 agents (Exp 4). The number of attributes in each local database is a result dividing the total number of attributes by the number of agents. The numbers of attributes of local databases are 240, 120, 80, and 60 in Exp 1, Exp 2, Exp 3, and Exp4, respectively. Each experiment consists of 8 steps and is conducted by increasing the number of records in its local database, step by step. The numbers of records used in each experiment are 0.3×10^5, 0.6×10^5, 0.1×10^6, 0.2×10^6, 0.3×10^6, 0.4×10^6, 0.5×10^6, and 0.6×10^6 over 8 steps, respectively. Fig. 2 presents the estimated processing time for decision rule generation at every step in the four experiments. Each step corresponds to an index on an X axis. The decision rule sets generated in all experiments are exactly same since the proposed algorithm for distributed data mining uses all the available data located at different sites, without moving them to each other. These decision rules are revealed simply because geographical data easily discriminated on aerial images are used in the experiments. In conclusion, the experimental results show that the distributed version with more agents outperforms the version with fewer agents when the rule generation from large amount of database is not complicate with low communication overhead between agents and the mediator.

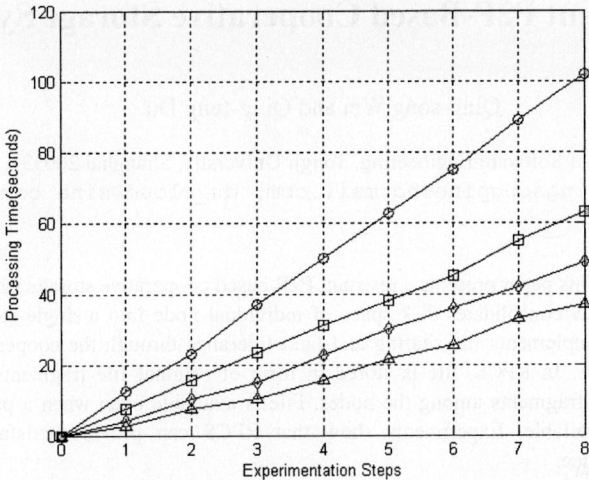

Fig. 2. The processing time for the decision rule extraction (The circle, square, diamond, and triangle indicate a non-distributed version, 2 agents, 3 agents, and 4 agents in the distributed version, respectively)

References

1. S. Stolfo, A. L. Prodromidis, S. Tselepis and W. Lee, JAM: Java Agents for Meta-Learning over Distributed Databases, Proceedings of the International Conference on Knowledge Discovery and Data Mining, pp. 74-81, 1997
2. Y. Guo and J. Sutiwaraphun, Knowledge probing in distributed data mining, In Advances in Distributed and Parallel Knowledge Discovery, 1999
3. L. Xu and M. I. Jordan, Em learning on a generalized finite mixture model for combining multiple classifiers, In Proceedings of World Congress on Neural Networks, 1993
4. A. E. Raftery, D. Madigan and J. A. Hoeting, Bayesian model averaging for linear regression models, Journal of the American Statistical Association, Vol. 92, pp. 179-191, 1996
5. D. Wolpert, Stacked generalization, Neural Networks, Vol. 5, pp. 241-259, 1992
6. http://sunsite.berkeley.edu/AerialPhotos/vbzj.html#index
7. M. Farrokhnia and A. Jain, A multi-channel filtering approach to texture segmentation, Proceedings of IEEE Computer Vision and Pattern Recognition Conference, pp. 346-370, 1990

A Resistant P2P-Based Cooperative Storage System

Qing-song Wei and Qing-feng Du

School of Software Engineering, Tongji University, Shanghai 200331, China
qingsongpine@hotmail.com, du_cloud@sina.com

Abstract. This paper presents a resistant P2P-based cooperative storage system: RPCS. RPCS consolidates disk space of individual node into a single storage spool and implements file-sharing and fault-tolerance through the cooperation of the nodes. In RPCS, file is stored in form of original file fragments and verification fragments among the nodes. File is available even when a part of nodes unavailable. Experiments show that RPCS can provide satisfactory storage service.

1 Introduction

At present, data availability becomes more and more important in our life, which requires storage system providing high reliability. Distributed storage technology can meet this expectation in lost cost.

This paper presents a resistant P2P-based cooperative storage system called RPCS. By using the disk space of distributed nodes, RPCS constructs a public storage spool. In RPCS, file is stored across nodes in form of Original Fragments and Verification Fragments to acquire fault-tolerance. Through parallel transfer mechanism, RPCS provides high-performance file read and write service [1][2].

The rest of this paper is as follows. Section 2 describes the design of RPCS. Section 3 is about measurement. Finally, we offer our conclusions in section 4.

2 The Design of RPCS

2.1 Global Directory Index and Its Synchronization Mechanism

In order to realize single name space, RPCS introduces Global Directory Index (GDI) to maintain global file information. GDI preserves how a file is stripped and where the fragments are stored. GDI is analogous to the Unix inode. Whereas inode aggregates disk blocks of a volume to a file, GDI aggregates original fragments and check fragments from distributed nodes to a file [3] shown as Figure 1.

In RPCS, each peer holds a copy of GDI. In order to maintain consistency of GDI, every node takes part in GDI synchronization. RPCS utilizes Event Driven Synchronization Mechanism (EDSM) to synchronize GDI. EDSM means when the events of reading/writing or timer expiration occur, EDSM drives node to inform all other nodes of the system to update GDI with synchronization messages. If there is no event occurring in a certain period of time, timer will activate the EDSM.

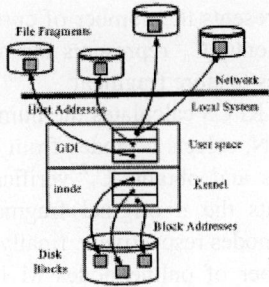

Fig. 1. GDI in comparison to UNIX inode

There are two kinds of EDSM: SYN-ANS and SYN-NOANS. SYN-ANS requests both receiver and sender to update local GDI synchronously, which is used by sender to force every node to synchronize its GDI. SYN-NOANS only need receiver to update its GDI, and the sender need not update its GDI synchronously. It is used to inform other nodes to synchronize its GDI when a node succeeds in writing.

2.2 Active Nodes List and Its Synchronization Mechanism

In RPCS, each node maintains an Active Nodes List (ANL) which keeps a list of active nodes in the system. ANL is the key of file reading and writing. When a user writes a file, the system queries the ANL firstly, selects available node array according to the network condition and free disk space of active nodes, then decides how to strip the file. When a user reads a file, the system gets the list of available nodes according to GDI and ANL and reads the file fragments from the selected nodes.

It is necessary to synchronize ANL: when a node joins, online nodes should add it to its local ANL; when a node exits normally or abnormally, online nodes must be aware of this event and update their own ANL. There are two kinds of synchronization mechanism of ANL: ANL-ONLINE and ANL-OFFLINE.

ANL-ONLINE needs sender and receivers to update their local ANL synchronously. ANL-OFFLINE is used to inform online nodes to update local ANL when a node gets out. If a node quits abnormally, the periodic ANL synchronization messages will ensure that the crashed node will be deleted from the ANL.

2.3 File Writing

RPCS utilizes Redundant Verification Segmenting Algorithm (RVSA) to acquire fault-tolerance. The important principle of RVSA is that when one writes a file, it stores not only the original file fragments but also the redundant XOR verification fragments. By doing so, one can use the XOR verification fragments to recover the file even when some of the original file fragments are not available. RVSA can be expressed by the following formula (1):

$$\begin{cases} N = n + C_n^2 & \{n \mid n \geq 2, n \in Z\} \\ N_n \leq M \leq N_{n+1} & (M \geq 3) \end{cases} \quad (1)$$

In the formula (1), M represents the number of current active nodes; n represents the number of original fragments; C_n^2 represents the number of check fragments; N represents the number of nodes to store fragment.

When a user writes a file, RPCS calculates the number n through M, then obtains the number of storing nodes N, selects N nodes from the M active nodes, strips the file into n original fragments and obtains C_n^2 verification fragments through their mutual XOR calculation, puts the n original fragments and the C_n^2 verification fragments into the N selected nodes respectively, finally updates GDI.

For example, if the number of online nodes M is 7, according to RVSA, the system obtains n=3 and N=6 firstly, selects 6 storing nodes, divides the file into 3 fragments, calculates their mutual XOR verification, stores these 6 fragments in the 6 selected nodes, and finally updates GDI as shown in Figure 2.

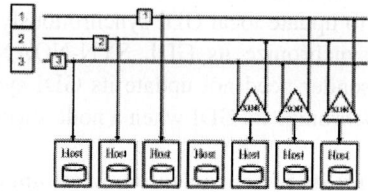

Fig. 2. File writing procedure (7 active nodes, 6 nodes are selected to store file)

2.4 File Reading

When reading a file, it needs to get enough corresponding fragments from the nodes and congregate them into the integrated file [4]. In order to reduce the overhead of calculation and speed up the reading, RPCS reads verification fragments only when the file can not be reconstructed from original fragments.

Considering the worst case, when the number of online nodes is C_n^2+1 at least and n-1 offline nodes at most, the file is still available, so the lowest available rate X of file can be calculated as formula (2).

$$X = \frac{C_n^2 + 1}{n + C_n^2} = 1 - 2\frac{1 - 1/n}{n + 1} \qquad n = 2,3,4,... \qquad (2)$$

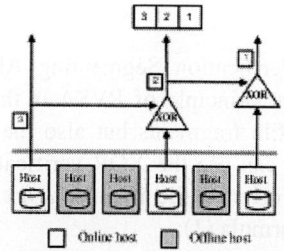

Fig. 3. File reading procedure (File is stored in 6 nodes, but 3 nodes online)

When storing nodes number is N and online nodes number is M, if M>=X*N, file can be read totally. Figure 3 shows the process of reading a file from the 3 online nodes, which is stored in the 6 nodes.

3 Experiments

We tests the performance of RPCS under different node number, reading and writing a 32M file 100 times and getting average latency shown in figure 4.

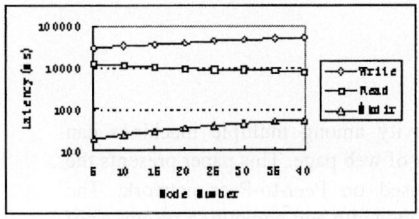
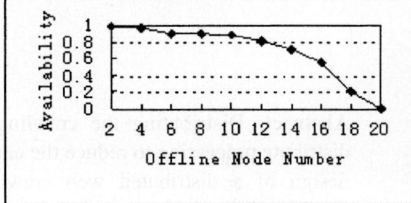

Fig. 4. RPCS performance test   **Fig. 5.** RPCS fault-tolerance test

From the figure 4, we can see that global synchronization overload increases slowly as joint nodes manifold, which means that RPCS has good scalability.

This paper tests the fault-tolerance performance of RPCS under different offline nodes. The test result is plotted in figure 5.

From the figure 5, we can see that when the number of offline nodes is less than 14, RPCS keeps high availability, when the number of offline nodes is more than 14, file availability becomes low rapidly. RPCS can obtain good fault-tolerance.

4 Conclusion

This paper presents a novel resistant P2P-based cooperative storage system called RPCS. It realizes distributed file-sharing and fault-tolerance without adding any hardware. Experiments show that RPCS achieves satisfactory performance.

References

1. James S.Plank, A tutorial for Fault-Tolerate in RAID-like systems,Technical Report UT-CS-96-332 Department of Computer Science University of Tennessee July 19,1996,10–22.
2. Sumeet Sobti, NitinGarg,Chi Zhang, et al. PersonalRAID: Mobile Storage for distributed and disconnected computers, Proceedings of the FAST 2002 Conference, USA, 2002,5–8.
3. Scott Atchley, Stephen Soltesz, James S, et al. Fault-Tolerance in the Network Storage Stack, Proceedings of the FAST 2002 Conference, California, USA , January 28-30,2002,3–5.
4. G.Gibson, Cost-effective high-bandwidth storage architecture, Proceedings of ACM ASPLOS, October 1998, 4–5.

Distributed High-Performance Web Crawler Based on Peer-to-Peer Network

Liu Fei, Ma Fan-Yuan, Ye Yun-Ming, Li Ming-Lu, and Yu Jia-Di

Department of Computer Science and Engineering,
Shanghai Jiaotong University, Shanghai,
P. R. China 200030
{liufei001, my-fy, ymm, li-ml, yujiad}@sjtu.edu.cn

Abstract. Distributing the crawling activity among multiple machines can distribute processing to reduce the analysis of web page. This paper presents the design of a distributed web crawler based on Peer-to-Peer network. The distributed crawler harnesses the excess bandwidth and computing resources of nodes in system to crawl the web. Each crawler is deployed in a computing node of P2P to analyze web page and generate indices. Control node is another node to being in charge of distributing URLs to balance the load of the crawler. Control nodes are organized as P2P network. The crawler nodes managed by the same control node is a group. According to the ID of crawler and average load of the group, crawler can decide whether transmits the URL to control node or hold itself. We present an implementation of the distributed crawler based on Igloo and simulate the environment to evaluate the balancing load on the crawlers and crawl speed.

1 Introduction

The architecture of the current crawler [1] [2] is based on a single architecture design. Centralized solutions are known to have problems like link congestion, being single point of failure, and expensive administration. To address the shortcomings of centralized search engines, there have been several proposals [3] to build decentralized search engines over peer-to-peer networks. Peer to Peer system are massively distributed computing systems with each node communicating directly with one another to distribute tasks or exchange information or accomplish task. In our system each crawler is deployed in a computing node to analyze web page and generate indices. Control node is another node to being in charge of distributing URLs to balance the load of the crawler. Control nodes are organized as P2P network---CAN [4]. The crawler nodes managed by the same control node is a group. According to the ID of crawler and average load of the group, crawler can decide whether transmits the URL to control node or hold itself. We present an implementation of the distributed crawler based on Igloo and simulate the environment to evaluate the balancing load on the crawlers and crawl speed.

2 The Structure of Single Crawler

We have implement Igloo that has three versions. This paper uses crawler in Igloo version 1.2 as single crawler to construct our system. First we introduce the architecture of single crawler (Fig. 1).

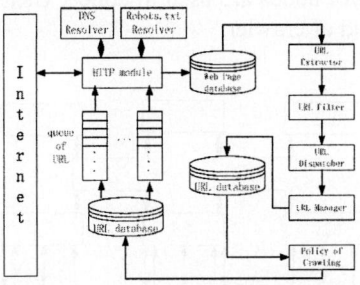

Fig. 1. The structure of single crawler

Each crawler can get IP of host with URL by DNS. Then it downloads the web page through HTTP module if Robot allows access to the URL. URL extractor extracts the URL from the downloaded web page and URL filter check whether the URL accord with the restrictions. Then the crawler uses hash function to compute the hash ID of URL. The crawler inserts the URL into its URL database. Policy of crawling is used to sort the rank of pages to make higher important resource to be crawled more prior. We adopt the PageRank [5] method to evaluate the importance of web page. HTTP module consists of several download threads and each thread has a queue of URL.

3 Control Node Overlay Network

P2P overlay network is scalable and robust so it fits to organize these control node. We organize these control nodes in CAN. Our design centers around a virtual 4-dimensional Cartesian coordinate space. This coordinate space is completely logical and bears no relation to any physical coordinate system. At any point in time, the entire coordinate space is dynamically partitioned among all the control nodes in the system such that every control node owns it individual, distinct zone within the overall space. We assume that IP of node is the identifier of control node in it. We can regard IP as a point in a virtual 4-dimensional Cartesian coordinate space which is defined as $S_a=\{(0,0,0,0),(255,255,255,255)\}$.

4 The Architecture of Our System

The ID of crawler is pair *(IP, number)* where *IP* is the IP of the node crawler being in and *number* is a random number that is not used by active crawlers start before the crawler starts. The *number* is one of the values of the crawler. Each crawler that joins our system must know at least one control node. Then the joining crawler *P1* sends packet containing its *(IP, number)* to the control node *R1* to ask for joining. *R1* checks the IP of *P1*. If the IP of *P1* is in the space controlled by *R1*, *R1* records *(IP, number)* of *P1*. Otherwise *R1* transfer *(IP, number)* to its neighbor which coordinate is closest to the IP of *P1*. Then the neighbor does the same work as *R1* until find a control node which controls the space containing the IP of *P1*. In this way crawlers are organized by control node. The control nodes are used to collect URLs and redistribute them to crawlers to balance the load of crawler.

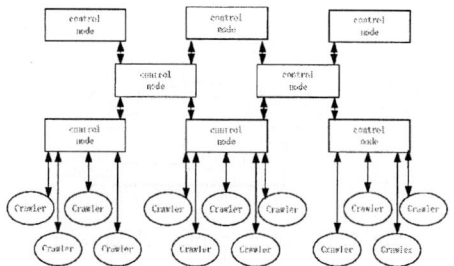

Fig. 2. The architecture of our system

Control node computes average load of its group periodiacally and send it to all crawler nodes in its group. If the load of crawler node is lighter than average load, it holds itself. Otherwise it sends the URL to control node to distribute the URL. Fig. 2 shows the architecture of our system.

5 Experimental Results

We use GT-ITM models to obtain 7 groups of nodes. One group contains 30 nodes that are used as CAN that organize information services. We implements simulation of CAN. Each of the other 6 groups of nodes contains 100 nodes and every node runs a crawler. We use seven 1.7GHz Pentium IV machine with 1GB of memory as our experiment hardware. One of these computers is used to run CAN that organizes

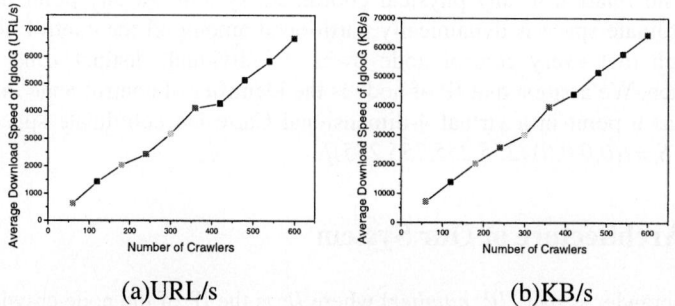

(a)URL/s (b)KB/s

Fig. 3. The average download speed of our system

information services. Each of the other 6 machines run 100 nodes to run crawlers. Fig. 3 shows the average download speed of our system scales linearly as the number of participating crawlers increase. So we know crawlers of our system are load-balanced.

6 Conclusions and Future Work

This paper presents the design of a distributed web crawler based on P2P network. This distributed web crawler is based on our previous work Igloo. The control nodes are organized with P2P network. URLs are collected by control node according to the ID of the crawler and the load of the crawler. In this way our system are load-balanced and can scale up to the entire web and has been used to fetch tens of millions of web documents.

Acknowledgements. This paper is supported by 973 project (No.2002CB312002) of China, ChinaGrid Program of MOE of China, and grand project of the Science and Technology Commission of Shanghai Municipality (No. 03dz15026, No. 03dz15027 and No. 03dz15028).

References

1. Sergey Brin, Lawrence Page, Google: The Anatomy of a Large-Scale Hypertextual Web SearchEngine" Proceedings of the 7th International World Wide Web Conference, pages 107-117, April 1998
2. Allan Heydon and Marc Najork, "Mercator: A Scalable, Extensible Web Crawler", *World Wide Web*, 2(4):219–229, 1999
3. J. Li, B. T. Loo, J. Hellerstein, F. Kaashoek, D. Karger, and R. Morrris. On the Feasibility of Peer-to-Peer Web Indexing and Search. In *IPTPS 2003*
4. S. Ratnasamy, P. Francis, M. Handley, R. Karp, and S. Shenker. A scalable -addressable network. In *ACM SIGCOMM'01*, August 2001
5. Henzinger M R. Hyperlink analysis for the Web. IEEE Internet Computing, 2001, 5(1): 45-50

A Peer-to-Peer Hypertext Categorization Using Directed Acyclic Graph Support Vector Machines

Liu Fei, Zhang Wen-Ju, Yu Shui, Ma Fan-Yuan, and Li Ming-Lu

Department of Computer Science and Engineering, Shanghai Jiaotong University,
Shanghai, P. R. China, 200030
{fliu, zwj2004, yushui, my-fy, li-ml}@cs.sjtu.edu.cn

Abstract. DAGSVM (Directed Acyclic Graph Support Vector Machines) has met with a significant success in information retrieval field, especially handling text classification tasks. This paper presents PDHCS (P2P-based Distributed Hypertext Categorization System) that classify hypertext in Peer-to-Peer networks. Distributed hypertext categorization can be easily implemented in PDHCS by combining the DAGSVM (Directed Acyclic Graph Support Vector Machines) learning architecture and Chord overlay network. Knowledge sharing among the distributed learning machines is achieved via utilizing both the special features of the DAG learning architecture and the advantages of support vector machines. The parallel structure of DAGSVM, the special features of support vector machines and decentralization of Chord overlay network lead to PDHCS being more efficient.

1 Introduction

The recent surge of interest in Knowledge Management, however, has contributed to enlarging the view on processes involving information discovery, sharing and reuse. Recent research now focuses as well on their cooperative aspects and methods for supporting these. In particular, a number of case studies have studied the cooperative nature of information search activities. The case study reported in [1][2] provides insight into the forms of cooperation that can take place during a search process. However, most researchers have studied in depth the kinds of collaboration that can occur in either the physical or digital library [2][3][4]. With the rapid change of the World Wide Web, new cooperative learning forms of the web mining play a crucial role in web information acquisition. YU Shui etc. [5] have proposed an algorithm to train classifier cooperatively based on LAN. As a typical application of web information retrieval, automatic hypertext categorization is suffering the large-scale unlabeled web page base. Since building text classifiers by hand is difficult and time consuming, it is desirable to learn classifiers from examples. The machine learning techniques have been incorporated into text categorization for many years especially the supervised learning technique. Apparently it is meaningful and necessary to extend the state-of-the-art machine learning techniques to cooperative learning environment so as to solve the problem of distributed web information retrieval.

Another motive of this extension is the local learning machines are always looking forward to knowledge share in one community. In other words, the result of local knowledge discovery should be shared and reorganized globally in the cooperative learning context.

2 Multi-class SVM and DDAG Learning Architecture

SVM was originally designed for binary classification. How to effectively extend it for multi-class classification is still an ongoing research issue. Several methods have been proposed where typically the binary SVMs are combined to construct the multi-class SVMs. There are three main methods: one-against-one, one-against-all and directed acyclic graph SVM (DAGSVM). Chih-Wei Hsu and Chih-Jen Lin have pointed out that DAGSVM is very suitable for practical use [6]. Previous experiments have proved that DAGSVM yield comparable accuracy and memory usage to the other two algorithms, but yield substantial improvements in both training and evaluation time [6][7].

In the training phase of DAGSVM, $k(k-1)/2$ binary SVMs are solved respectively (k is the category numbers). In the testing phase, it uses rooted binary directed acyclic graph which has $k(k-1)/2$ internal nodes and k leaves. Each node is a binary SVM of ith and jth classes. Given a test sample x, starting at the root node, the binary decision function is evaluated. Then it moves to either left or right depending on the output value. Therefore a decision path is passed before a leaf node is reached which indicates the final predicted class. Fig.1 shows the sketch map of decision DAG for finding the best class out of four classes [7]:

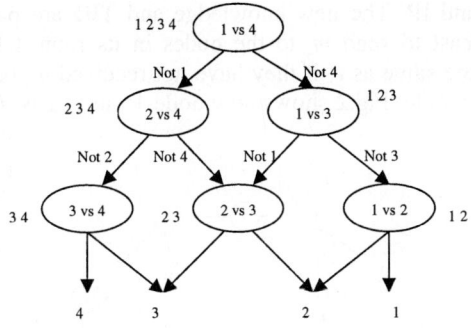

Fig. 1. The decision DAG for finding the best class out of four classes

3 Implementation of PDHCS

We denote a node of PDHCS that respond identifier i by e_i. Let $d_i^j(i \neq j)$ be the node in DAGSVM which is a binary SVM related to labeled sample of category i and labeled sample of category j. Labeled sample of category which identifier equals i is denoted by x_i. We denote launch node to be the node which start computing to renew

DAGSVM and computing node to be the node which computing the node of DAGSVM. The process of constructing PDHCS is the same as the process of constructing Chord because PDHCS is constructed through adding managed software and SVM in Chord node. After establish PDHCS system, the node of DAGSVM can be trained in PDHCS node and the knowledge can be exchanged to form a whole DAGSVM in PDHCS node.

Let PD be a PDHCS. We define the DAGSVM we want to construct as DA. We assume node $e_a(e_a \in PD)$ received samples of document DR. e_a uses SHA-1[8] to assigns each category an m-bit identifier. e_a sends $x_{il}(x_{il} \in DR)$ to PDHCS node $e_{il}(e_{il} \in PD)$ which respond to i_l. If e_{il} already has the category i_l, it merges the old labeled samples into the new labeled samples x_{il}. Then e_{il} sends x_{il} to its 20 successors. Each node in PDHCS stores information about categories in PDHCS and exchanges with each other periodically to renew the information.

Node e_{il} uses a data structure to record the computing state of DAGSVM node. When labeled samples of category which identifier equals i_l have been renewed, the computing state of DAGSVM node d_{il}^j $(j=1,2,...,m-1, d_{il}^j \in DA)$ is "unfinished". After finishing the computation of the DAGSVM node d_{il}^j, the computing state of DAGSVM node d_{il}^j $(j=1,2,...,m-1)$ is "finished". With the computing state e_{il} we can decide which DAGSVM node needs to be renewed. If the computing state of d_{il}^j is "unfinished", e_{il} sends message m_l (which contains x_{il}), computing request and timestamp to $e_j(e_j \in PD)$. e_j checks whether it has sent the same computing request. If e_j has done that, e_j and e_j will compare the two timestamps and the earlier one is accepted. For example, Node 1 requests node 2 to compute DAGSVM node d_1^2, at the same time, Node 2 requests node 1 to compute DAGSVM node d_1^2. If m_l is earlier than m_2, then node 2 will do the computing.

When computing node $e_r(e_r \in PD)$ finish computing, it produces an identifier TID with current time and IP. The new knowledge and TID are packed in message m_n. Then e_r uses multicast to send m_n to the nodes in its route table. The nodes those receive m_n will do the same as e_r if they have not received m_n before. Otherwise they ignore m_n. As an example, Fig.2 shows how node 1 multicasts m_n in a PDHCS which contains 10 nodes.

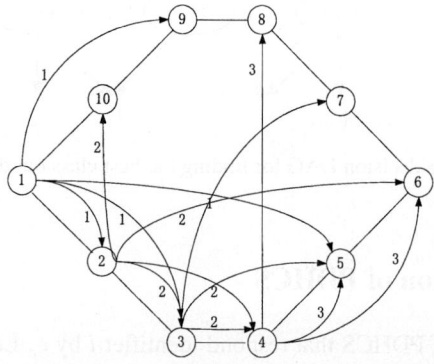

Fig. 2. The process of multicasting new knowledge

4 Conclusions and Future Work

Hypertext categorization is used for web information retrieval and web mining. Since building hypertext classifiers by hand is difficult and time consuming, it is desirable to learn classifiers from labeled categorization examples. Because training large-scale classifier is intractable, it is meaningful and necessary to build it in the distributed cooperative computing. In this paper, we have introduced a distributed hypertext classification system, which combines the DAGSVM learning architecture and P2P network. The parallel structure of DAGSVM, the special features of support vector machines and decentralization of Chord overlay network lead to PDHCS being more efficient.

Acknowledgements. This paper is supported by 973 project (No.2002CB312002) of China, ChinaGrid Program of MOE of China, and grand project of the Science and Technology Commission of Shanghai Municipality (No. 03dz15026, No. 03dz15027 and No. 03dz15028).

References

1. O'Day, V., R. Jeffries: Orienteering in an Information Landscape: How Information Seekers Get From Here to There. In: *Proc. INTERCHI '93*, 1993, pp. 438-445
2. Twidale, M. B., D. M. Nichols, G. Smith, J. Trevor: Supporting collaborative learning during information searching. *Proceedings of Computer Support for Cooperative Learning (CSCL 95)*, 1995, pp. 367-374, Bloomington, Indiana
3. Hertaum, M., and Pejtersen, A.M. The information-seeking practices of engineers: Searching for documents as well as for people. *Information Processing & Management*, 36, 2000, 761-778
4. Fidel, R. Bruce, H. Pejtersen, A. Dumias, S. Grudin, J. and Poltrock, S. Collaborative information retrieval. In: L. Höglund, ed. *The new review of information behavior research: studies of information seeking in context*. (The third international conference on information needs, seeking and use in different contexts.) London & Los Angeles: Graham Taylor
5. YU Shui PAN Leyun. DHCS: *A Case of Knowledge Share in Cooperative Computing Environment*. To appear in GCC'2003
6. Chih-Wei Hsu, Chih-Jen Lin. A comparison of methods for multicalsss support vector machines. *IEEE Transactions on Neural Networks*. March 2002, Vol. 13, No. 2, 415-425
7. J. C. Platt, N. Cristianini, and J. Shawe-Taylor. Large margin DAGs for multiclass classification. *Advances in Neural Information Processing Systems*. Cambridge, MA: MIT Press. 2000. 547-553
8. FIPS 180-1. *Secure Hash Standard*. U.S. Department of Commerce/NIST, National Technical Information Service, Springfield, VA, Apr. 1995

Architecture of Agent-Based Healthcare Intelligent Assistant on Grid Environment

Shailendra Singh[1], Bukhary Ikhwan Ismail[2], Fazilah Haron[2], and Chan Huah Yong[2]

[1] Health Informatics Research Group, School of Computer Sciences,
Universiti Sains Malaysia, Penang, Malaysia
shai_paper@hotmail.com
[2] Grid Computing Lab, School of Computer Sciences,
Universiti Sains Malaysia, Penang, Malaysia
{bukharyi, fazilah, hychan}@cs.usm.my

Abstract. In this paper we present an architecture of agent-based Healthcare Intelligent Assistant on grid environment. The Healthcare Intelligent Assistant is used by the medical practitioners to retrieve and use various existing organizational knowledge to help solve medical cases. We will use *case-based* format that captures the experiential knowledge of healthcare practitioners [1]. Using grid technologies all resources-knowledge within hospitals can be use by medical practitioner's across geographically distributed location.

1 Introduction

Healthcare practitioners use the knowledge stored in *Healthcare Knowledge Management System* to advice and diagnose their patients. Often this knowledge is bound within the hospital or organization and doctors rely only on the knowledge that is stored in his/her organization. Without facilitating knowledge sharing and proper knowledge utilizing, knowledge can not be expanded, improved or be generated. Inter-organization boundaries between hospitals may cripple knowledge creation and vital knowledge to save life cannot be used by others outside the organization. The idea behind this paper is to merge *organizational knowledge* from various hospitals and premises as one pool of knowledge resources. Using grid technology we can make this possible.

2 Related Works

Previous work that has been proposed by the authors [2] is a client-server *Agent-based Intelligent Healthcare Knowledge Assistant* framework. This framework consists of (a) *healthcare experimental knowledge web* – a portal to the experimental knowledge sources; and (b) an *agent-based healthcare assistant framework* that handles the request, matching and formatting the experimental knowledge. Query that is specified by the users is structured and formatted in the *information specification*

(IS). Based on IS, the information is passed to the agent manager and the agent manager then will activate the responsible agents for retrieving the experimental knowledge [2].

The knowledge request will be handled by an agent-based workflow framework consists of the following components. *Agent Manager:* The main agent that controls and manages all agents. It accepts the user query and forwards it to the case broker agent. *Case Broker Agent (CBA):* Central agent that is responsible of fetching and matching the knowledge from the case-based. *Presentation Agent (PA):* Prepares and formats the search results. *Web Server Agent (WSA):* Propagate the query from user to the agent manager. Figure 1 illustrates the overall architecture.

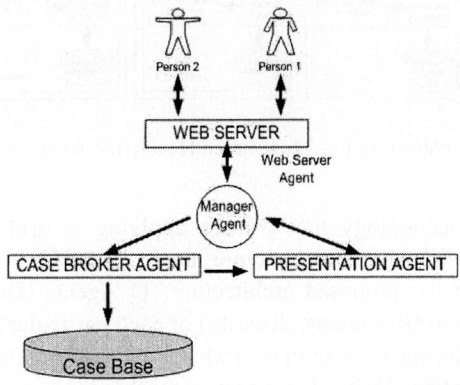

Fig. 1. The architecture of Intelligent Healthcare Knowledge Assistant framework

Existing healthcare projects or works mainly focuses on image-based processing application e.g. MammoGrid - databases of mammogram images [4] and advance simulation processing e.g. GEMSS – simulation on surgical support [3]. Both of these projects is developed using Globus technology. Our project will be focusing on designing a new framework within healthcare domain to enable knowledge sharing of patient data and past cases–experimental knowledge from distributed located hospitals. We will use standard grid technology-Globus toolkit.

3 Proposed Architecture

In reference to the existing architecture we can observe that all of the components of the system, that is the agents, are located in one single location. Looking at actual environment, data is usually widely spread across geographic location especially in the case of healthcare system. In order to cater for this distribution we have proposed to further extend the existing architecture to fit into a distributed environment. The overall proposed architecture is shown below in figure 2.

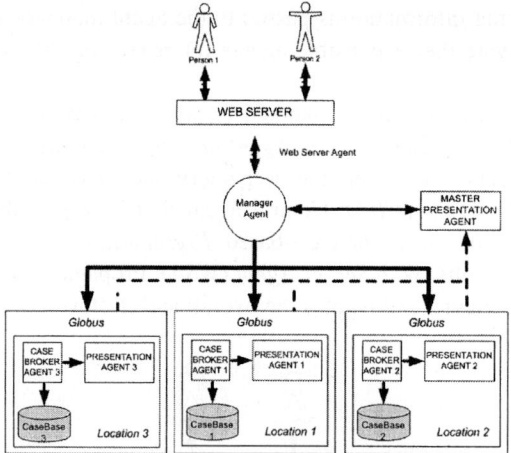

Fig. 2. Proposed Architecture for Agent-based Healthcare Assistant on Grid Environment

The distributed technology that we are applying is grid technology based on Globus Toolkit. Based on the architecture above there are mainly two components that are working in the proposed architecture: 1) Agents (Dealing with healthcare tasks). 2) Management (Resources, Security) of each particular grid nodes.

The working of the agents is similar to what we have currently except for their position i.e. physical location. Thus, once the query reaches the manager agent will query on the Monitoring and Discovery Services (MDS) of the Globus toolkit. Basically the DS will be storing the information related to the location of the particular databases herein, which is needed for query. An example of MDS working is shown in figure 3. The justification to use Globus is due to its features that it can handle well the security and resource management issues. In reality, hospitals and its data are located in a distributed environment. Hence agent-based intelligent healthcare systems match well to run on distributed environment as it caters for the realistic situation.

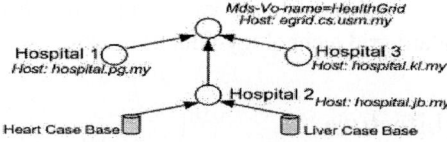

Fig. 3. Example MDS Services

In reference to figure 3 MDS will help in retrieving all the related information with regard to each database that is physically located at each hospital. Thus, upon the completion of a query process of the MDS, the manager agent will start to deploy individual case broker agents. Each of these individual agents will be having exact information of the physical location that of the particular database that it needs to query.

Upon arriving at the particular node that is the database source the agents needs to go through another Globus Service i.e. Security Services. This component mainly concerns with providing authentication and authorization services. It is used for all resource access and sharing. In our case the agent will go through authentication and authorization process before it is allowed to go further in that particular location. The central concept of authentication here is based on certificates and each agent will be given a certificate that contains vital information in identification process of a particular.

Once it passes the authentication test the agent is allowed to get into the particular location with its authorization. Following that the agents will start its query process on the particular database as designated by the manager agent earlier. The final result will be passed to the presentation agent for formatting purpose. The above stated flow is one complete flow in each grid node.

Finally the results of each of the presentation at the particular grid node will be passed to the master presentation agent. This agent acts as a mine to collect together all the distributed results based on the user query. In this agent is where the final formatting tasks will be done before the results are sent over to the user for viewing purposes.

4 Conclusion

In this paper we propose a methodology where health-care agents not only reside on a single location but can also be on a distributed environment. This further expands the capabilities and resources for the agent to retrieve information. In addition, by applying the grid technology herein the Globus toolkit we no longer need to be considering the underlying details of each node such as resource management, security etc. All of the related issued to the particular node is handled by Globus toolkits.

References

1. Zafar I.H, S S Raza Abidi, Yu-N, S.H.Zaidi.: Intelligent Agents-Based Knowledge Assistant for Enterprise – wide Healthcare Enterprise Knowledge Factory. Conference on Information Technology Research and Applications (CITRA 2002), Kuala Lumpur, Malaysia.
2. Zafar I.H, Yu-N, S.H.Zaidi, S S Raza Abidi.: Intelligent Agent-Mediated Approach for Experimental Knowledge of Healthcare Enterprise through CBR-Adaptation Techniques.
3. Siegfried Benkner, Guntram Berti, Gerhard Engelbrecht, Jochen Fingberg, Greg Kohring, Stuart E. Middleton, Rainer Schmidt.: GEMSS: Grid-infrastructure for Medical Service Provision.
4. Richard McClatchey, David Manset, Tamas Hauer, Floridal Estrella, Pablo Saiz, Dmitri Rogulin.: "The MammoGrid Project Grids Architecture", CHEP '03, San Diego March 24th 2003.

Design of Replication Manager in Main Memory DBMS ALTIBASE^{TM}

Kwang-Chul Jung[1], Kyu-Woong Lee[2], and Hae-Young Bae[3]

[1] Real-Time Tech. Lab., ALTIBASE Co., Seoul, Korea
[2] Dept. of Computer Science, Sangji Univ., Wonju, Korea
[3] School of Computer Engineering, Inha Univ., Incheon, Korea
jungkc@altibase.com, leekw@sangji.ac.kr, hybae@inha.ac.kr

Abstract. ALTIBASE^{TM} is a main memory DBMS that provides fault tolerance, high availability as well as predictable response time. ALTIBASE^{TM} supports the efficient replication mechanism in order to increase the availability. In this paper, we give an overview of architecture for replication model and our replication protocols. The performance of replicated server environment is evaluated under various circumstances.

1 Introduction

An attractive approach to providing predictable response for general DBMS is to load the whole data into main memory. It can be suggested by the increasing availability of large and relatively cheap memory. The disk-resident database system(DRDB) with a very large memory, however, is basically different from pure main memory database systems(MMDB). The key difference is that there is no need to interact with a buffer manager for fetching or flushing buffer pages. The performance of MMDB can be improved further by dispensing with buffer manager, changing the storage hierarchy into the flat structure [3,1]. The implementation techniques and traditional method of DRDB, however, cannot be adopted into MMDB directly [2]. We therefore design and implement the replication model and protocols in main memory database ALTIBASE^{TM}.

The remainder of paper is organized as follows. In section 2, we provide our system architecture and section 3 explains our replication models and protocols. In section 4, we evaluate the transaction performance of our system under our various replicated models and we give our conclusions in section 5.

2 ALTIBASE^{TM} System Architecture

Figure 1 shows our overall system architecture. ALTIBASE^{TM} system provides the various industrial standard application programming interfaces such as ODBC, JDBC, SQL CLI, and ESQL programming interface. The storage

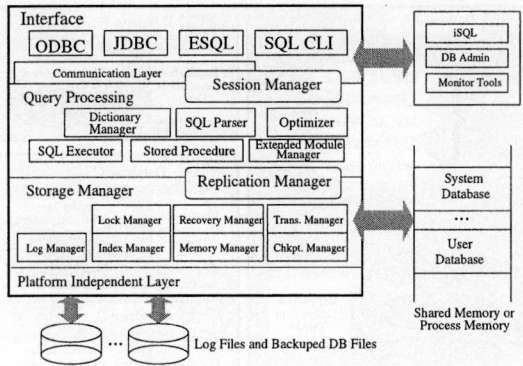

Fig. 1. System Architecture of ALTIBASE^{TM}

manager is the core part of the server process that supports main capabilities of DBMS. Its major sub-components are lock manager, recovery manager, index manager, transaction manager, memory manager, and log manager [4].

3 Database Replication of ALTIBASE^{TM}

3.1 Replication Manager and Replication Model

The replication manager was implemented with the thread architecture. The major components are *replication manager thread*, *sender thread*, and *receiver thread*. The replication manager thread has the responsibility of arbitration for replicated data between sender and receiver thread. There is one pair of the sender and receiver thread for a replicated server. Figure 2 shows an example database replication system that consists of a master node and three replicated servers.

ALTIBASE^{TM} system provides the four replication models. The replication model is categorized by the role of nodes that are participated in replicated database system. We define the three types of server and provide four replication models based on the server types. The basic replication model of ALTIBASE^{TM} is *primary-standby* model depicted, which is the typical model for fault-tolerance in the conventional distributed systems. All the database requests are handled at the primary server and their updates have to be propagated into the standby server. The standby server is only ready to immediately take over in case the primary server fails. The more flexible model for application development is the *active-active* model This replication model enable us to develop the load-balanced applications as well as the highly available applications. An active server plays as both roles of primary and standby server at a time. The primary-multi standby model is for the applications which are highly sensitive to the reliability. This model consists of one primary server and two or more standby servers. We therefore can acquire the higher availability than other models but

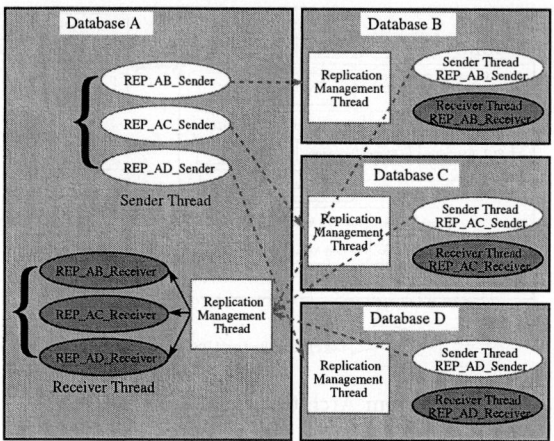

Fig. 2. Replication Thread Architecture of ALTIBASE^{TM}

pay an expensive cost for multiple replication. For the efficiency of multiple replication and supporting the reasonable response time of main memory DBMS, we adopt the *propagator* that is dedicated to broadcasting the primary server's updates to the all standby servers.

3.2 Replication Protocol and Algorithm

The basic idea of our replication management is based on the conventional log records. Only the change log, *XLOG*, is additionally maintained in order to propagate the updates to a remote server and it is plainly constructed from the general DBMS transaction log. *XLSN* is the sequence number for XLOG and it refers to the point of transaction log that is not yet reflected into the remote replicated server. The replication manager gathers the transaction log records from the XLSN to the current log record pointer and then composes the XLOG transaction from those log records. Our replication mechanism is implemented by the replication manager thread (*REP_Manager*), the sender thread(*REP_Sender*) and the receiver thread(*REP_ Receiver*). Those threads are operated cooperatively in order to reflect the update of another replicated server. Figure 3 illustrates the replication protocol and communication flow of our ALTIBASE^{TM} system. When the transaction have been committed at the primary server, the sender thread is created and then it requests a hand-shake connection for propagating the update to the remote node(Figure 3 (S1)). At the next stage, the replication manager thread creates the corresponding receiver thread as shown Figure 3 (S2). And then, the sender thread makes the update transaction based on its own change log, XLOG, of the committed transaction. The update transaction should be sent to the replication manager and receiver thread in sequence as depicted in Figure 3 (S5) and (S6). When the sender thread, however, cannot make a hand-shake connection to the

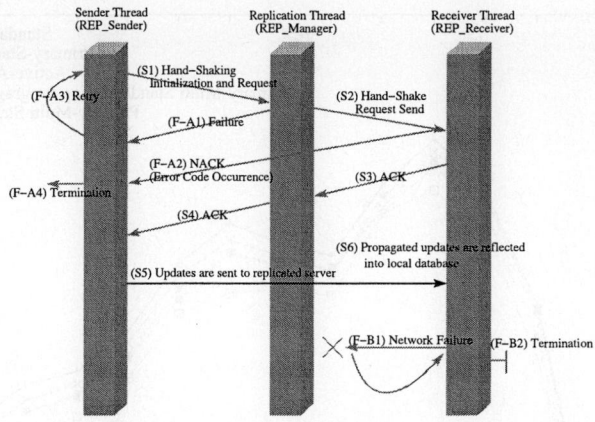

Fig. 3. Replication Protocol and Communication Flow

replication manager thread (F-A1), the connection retry occurs at the given system parameter as illustrated (F-A3). When the receiver thread cannot reply to the replication manager or sender thread, the overall replication procedure should be aborted immediately as shown in (F-B1) and (F-B2). On the other hands, when the sender thread receives the *NACK* message for the reason of logical error such as the schema conflict(F-A2) even though the connection was established completely, the sender thread should be terminated(F-A4).

4 Performance Evaluation

This section illustrates our experimental results for transaction execution of our *ALTIBASE^{TM}*. All experiments were performed on *Sun Enterprise 3500* platform with 4 CPUs and 4G bytes of memory. *Select, insert, update, and delete transaction* were evaluated under the strict condition of transaction durability and logging level. The target table consists of total 20 attributes of various data types, such as *number, real, char* and *varchar*.

Figure 4 shows the TPS values based on our various replication models. The TPS in the stand-alone server environment is compared to the TPS in the primary-standby and active-active replication model in this experiment, and it obviously outperforms the replicated environment. The performance of replicated database server, however, shows the almost same results(95%) as one of non-replicated server environment. The overhead of our replication procedure can be a ignorable factor on the overall performance. In the primary-multi standby replication model, the replication overhead of primary server may be higher than one of the basic primary-standby replication model as the number of standby server increases. Our replication system consists of one primary server, two standby servers and one propagator for this experiment. In the worst case,

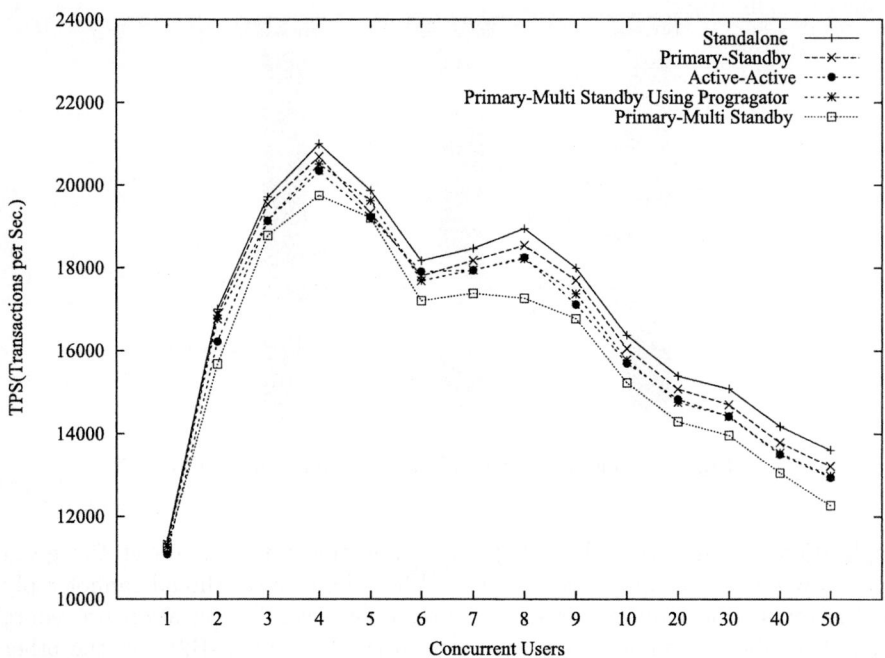

Fig. 4. Effects of Replication Models on Throughput

the TPS in the primary-multi standby model shows the 92% and 97% of TPS in the stand-alone and the basic primary-standby model, respectively. The TPS in the primary-multi standby using propagator model, however, is degraded at most as 95% of TPS in stand-alone system. Finally, we find that the overhead of replication in our $ALTIBASE^{TM}$ system can be ignorable as compared to acquiring the availability.

5 Conclusion

This paper describes replication mechanism of $ALTIBASE^{TM}$. we propose the various replication models and protocols for the reliable application development. As the comparatively higher experimental results, $ALTIBASE^{TM}$ is ensured to guarantee the better performance in time-critical applications. Currently, $ALTIBASE^{TM}$ version 3.0 is pronounced and is in the on-going project for hybrid function of disk-based facilities for large database.

References

1. Philip Bohannon and et al. Distributed multi-level recovery in main-memory databases. In *Proc. of the International Conference on Parallel and Distributed Information Systems*, pages 44–55, 1996.

2. Philip Bohannon and et al. The architecture of the dali main-memory storage manager. *Multimedia Tools and Applications*, 4(2), 1997.
3. Hector Garcia-Molina and Kenneth Salem. "main memory database systems : An overview ". *IEEE Transactions on Knowledge and Data Engineering*, 4(6), 1993.
4. K-C. Jung, K-W. Lee, and H-Y. Bae. Implementation of storage manager in main memory database system altibase^{TM}. In *Proceedings of the 10th International Conference on Real-Time and Embedded Computing Systems, Lecture Notes in Computer Science*, 2004.

A Distributed Ontology Framework for the Grid

Andrew Flahive[1], Wenny Rahayu[1], David Taniar[2], and Bernady Apduhan[3]

[1] La Trobe University, Australia
{A.Flahive, W.Rahayu}@latrobe.edu.au
[2] Monash University, Australia
David.Taniar@infotech.monash.edu.au
[3] Kyushu Sangyo University, Fukuoka, Japan
bob@is.kyusan-u.ac.jp

Abstract. Tailoring large ontologies can be a very cumbersome task. The Grid enables resource sharing to handle such tasks over a distributed environment. It makes sense then, to investigate the possibility of using resources on the Grid to tailor large Ontologies. This paper proposes a distributed ontology framework for tailoring ontologies in the Grid. The framework consists of five main categories; Ontology Processing, Ontology Location, Ontology Connection, Users' Connection and Algorithm Location.

1 Introduction

The next generation of the Internet is called the *Semantic Web*, and provides an environment that allows more intelligent knowledge management and data mining. The main focus is the increase in formal structures used on the Internet. These structures are called ontologies [1], and the success of the semantic web highly depends on the success of these ontologies.

The *Semantic Grid* is basically the same as the Semantic Web except that the former shares resources in accordance to certain architectures and standard grid infrastructures[2, 3]. Communities are starting to share large ontologies in the Grid Environment as it is an ideal medium for such a resource. But often these ontologies are too cumbersome for individuals to use it in it's entirety.

This paper explores a framework for developing ontology tailoring systems for the Grid. It aims to help the developer tune their system to make ontology tailoring more time efficient and cost effective for the intended user.

2 Background

An ontology is a shared understanding of a certain domain of information[1]. Ontologies may be very small, containing just a few concepts and relationships, or they may be ever expanding, containing many millions of concepts and relationships. The Unified Medical Language System (UMLS) [4] base ontology, has more than 800,000 concepts (nodes) and more than 9,000,000 relationships connecting the nodes. The popularity of Ontologies is largely due to what they promise: a shared and common understanding of a domain that can be communicated between people and applications.

Most user applications only require particular aspects of the ontology as they do not benefit from the plethora of semantic information that may be present. However, using the base ontology means that all the drawbacks from this extra information are encountered; complexity and redundancy rise, while efficiency falls. Smaller ontologies are much more suited to the user. Deriving Tailored Ontologies from large base ontologies, enables users to have small specific parts of the ontology for their own use. However, ontology tailoring, is computationally expensive, in part because of the size of the ontologies and also due to the complexity of the user requirements. Previous work in the area[5, 6], has addressed this problem, by proposing a distributed architecture for the extraction/optimization of a sub-ontology from a large base ontology. For the use of examples throughout this paper, we refer to the *Ontology Tailoring Program Resource* as OTPR.

The idea of Grid Computing is to share computer resources in a highly controlled area[7]. This allows the less-advantaged, remote, users, to share in the resources of the more-advantaged users. Developing a Grid Resource to tailor ontologies, will allow it to use other Grid resources to make the process even quicker.

3 Proposed Ontology Framework

Figure 1 shows an overview of the components of the proposed distributed ontology framework in the Grid environment. The OTPR is a Resource on the Grid that performs ontology tailoring based on user requirements. The users provide the base ontology (local or remote) and their specifications (algorithms) as to how they want it tailored. The OTPR processes ontology and sends the results

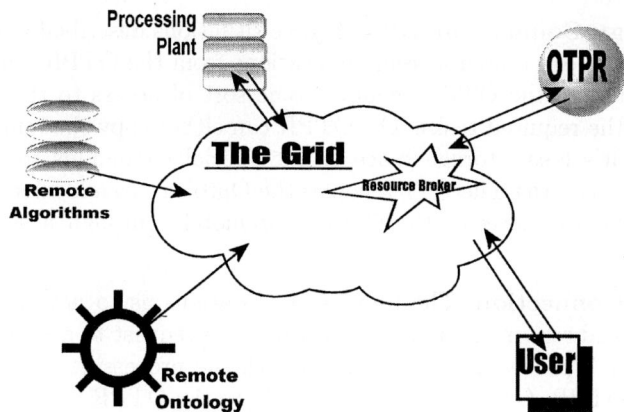

Fig. 1. Components of the Framework in the Grid Environment

back to the user. The OTPR has the ability to use other Grid Resources to help it process the ontology. For instance, a powerful Ontology Processing Resource may be employed to help out with processing the ontology.

The proposed framework is broken down into five main categories; (i) Ontology Processing, (ii) Ontology Location, (iii) Ontology Connection, (iv) User Connection and (v) Algorithm Location. These categories are shown in Fig 2.

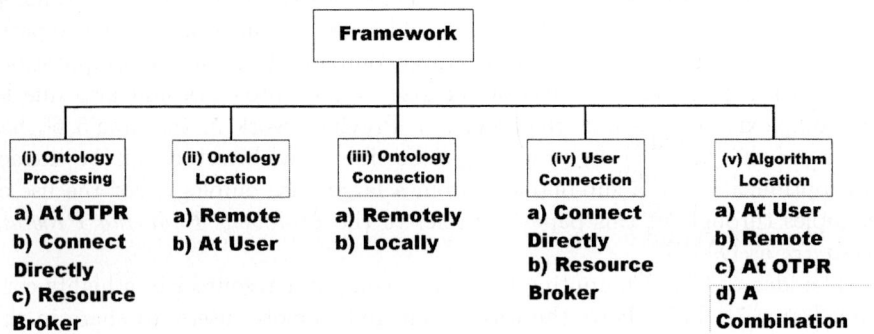

Fig. 2. The Main Framework Category's

(i) Ontology Processing. The application resource (OTPR) chooses to process the ontology itself or process the ontology at a processing plant. The three possible outcomes are: **(a)** The OTPR processes the Work itself. **(b)** The OTPR connects directly to a known Ontology Processing Plant **(c)** The OTPR connects to a Resource Broker which finds a suitable Ontology Processing Plant for it.

(ii) Ontology Location. This category comprises of two different situations based on the location of the Ontology that is required to be processed. These are: **(a)** The Ontology is located at the User site, or **(b)** The Ontology is stored at a remote site as a Grid Resource.

(iii) Ontology Connection. Both of these situations described above (section 3) have the ontology stored at remote locations from the OTPR, and therefore, in both situations, the OTPR requires some sort of access to them so that it can perform the required tasks. The OTPR can either copy the remotely stored Ontology to it's local storage space or use special commands to traverse the ontology remotely. **(a)** The OTPR copies the Ontology to a local storage space, or **(b)** The OTPR accesses the Ontology remotely through a set of request commands.

(iv) Users Connection. The user has two options as to how to employ the OTPR as a Grid resource. They are: **(a)** Submit a request to a Resource Broker to match up it's processing requirements with the processing ability, as advertised by the OTPR. Or **(b)** Connects directly to the OTPR as it's location and ability are already known.

(v) Algorithm Location. Algorithms, in this case, are used generally to describe how the ontology should be manipulated to match the users requirements. The user may have developed their own algorithms to meet their own specific needs or they may use some general algorithms created by a foreign party or by the OTPR itself. The user may either choose to: **(a)** use only the OTPR's predefined algorithms to process the ontology, **(b)** use only their own algorithms, **(c)** the OTPR accesses algorithms stored in a remote location. **(d)** use any combination of the above

4 Conclusion

This paper proposed a distributed framework for tailoring ontologies efficiently over the Grid Environment. The Framework consisted five main categories: (i) Ontology Processing, (ii) Ontology Location, (iii) Ontology Connection, (iv) User Connection and (v) Algorithm Location. It was found that these five categories combine to form many scenarios that the system developer must take into account when proposing such a project. These options reflected the most efficient method for mapping the problem into a working distributed framework for ontology tailoring.

References

1. Gruber, T.R.: Toward principles for the design of ontologies used for knowledge sharing. In: Formal Ontology in Conceptual Analysis and Knowledge Representation. Kluwer Academic Publishers, Deventer (1993)
2. Foster, I., Kesselman, C., Nick, J., Tuecke, S.: The physiology of the grid: An open grid services architecture for distributed systems integration (2002)
3. ogsi wg: Open grid services infrastructure (ogsi) version 1.0. Version 1.0 edn. Global Grid Forum (2003)
4. U.S. National Library of Medicine: UMLS Knowledge Sources. 13th edn. Unified Medical Language System. US Department of Health and Human Services, National Institutes of Health, National Library of Medicine (2002)
5. Wouters C., Dillon T., Rahayu W., Chang E. and Meersman R.: A practical approach to the derivation of materialized ontology views. In D., T., W., R., eds.: Web Information Systems. Idea Group Publishing (2004) 191–226
6. Bhatt, M., Flahive, A., Wouters, C., Rahayu, W., and Taniar, D.: A distributed approach to sub-ontology extraction. In: IEEE CS Proceedings of the 18th International Conference on Advanced Information Networking and Applications (AINA'04), Fukuoka, Japan (2004)
7. Foster, I., Kesselman, C., Nick, J., Tuecke, S.: The anatomy of the grid: Enabling scalable virtual organisations. International Journal of Supercomputing Applications (IJSA) (2001)

One Backward Inference Algorithm in Bayesian Networks

Jianguo Ding[1], Jun Zhang[1], Yingcai Bai[1], and Hansheng Chen[2]

[1] Shanghai Jiao Tong University, Shanghai 200030, P.R. China
Jianguo.Ding@sjtu.edu.cn
[2] East-china Institute of Computer Technology, Shanghai 200233, P.R. China

Abstract. When a complex information system is modelled by a Bayesian network the backward inference is normal requirement in system management. This paper proposes one inference algorithm in Bayesian networks, which can track the strongest causes and trace the strongest routes between particular effects and their causes. This proposed algorithm will become the foundation for further intelligent decision in management of information systems.

1 Introduction

With the information systems get more complex, the system maintenance and management is getting more difficult. Because the entities in the information system increase quickly, the dependency relationship between the entities and the management information tends to be incomplete and uncertain. Bayesian Networks (BNs) are effective means to model probabilistic knowledge by representing cause-and-effect relationships among key entities of a managed system. BNs can automatically generate useful predictions and decisions even in the presence of uncertain or incomplete information. BNs have been applied to problems in medical diagnosis [3, 7], map learning [4], and language understanding [5].

From the view of application, one kind of requirement is to trace particular causes from the observation of effects, particularly in error diagnosis and malfunction recovering. Another requirement is to identify the key routes between the effects and causes. In this paper the Strongest Dependence Route (SDR) algorithm for backward inference in BNs is developed. The SDR algorithm will allow user to trace the strongest dependency route from effect to causes, so that the key causal factors can be identified. It can also provide the dependency sequence of the causes from particular effects.

2 Backward Inference in Bayesian Networks

Bayesian networks use DAGs to represent probabilistic knowledge[1, 2]. In BNs, the information included in one node depends on the information of its predecessor nodes. The former denotes an effect node; the latter represents its causes. Note that an effect node can also act as a causal node of other nodes, where it then plays the role of a cause node. An important advantage of BNs is the avoidance of building huge Joint Probability Distribution (JPD) tables that include permutations of all the nodes in the network. Rather, for an effect node, only the states of its immediate predecessor need to be considered.

The most common approach towards reasoning in information system is backward inference, which traces the causes from effects. We define E as the set of effects (evidences) which we can observe, and C as the set of causes.

Consider the basic model for backward inference in BNs, which X be the set of causes of Y, $X = (x_1, x_2, \ldots, x_n)$. Then the following variables are known: $p(x_1), p(x_2), \ldots, p(x_n), p(Y|x_1, x_2, \ldots, x_n) = p(Y|X)$. Here $x_1, x_2, \ldots, x_n$ are mutually independent, so $p(X) = p(x_1, x_2, \ldots, x_n) = \prod_{i=1}^{n} p(x_i)$. By Bayes' theorem, $p(X|Y) = \frac{p(Y|X)p(X)}{p(Y)} = \frac{p(Y|X)p(X)}{\sum_x [p(Y|X)p(X)]} = \frac{p(Y|X) \prod_{i=1}^{n} p(x_i)}{\sum_X [p(Y|X) \prod_{i=1}^{n} p(x_i)]}$, which computes to $p(x_i|Y) = \sum_{X \setminus x_i} p(X|Y)$.

Hence the individual conditional probability (backward dependency) $p(x_i|Y)$ can be achieved from the JPD $p(Y|X)$, $X = (x_1, x_2, \ldots, x_n)$.

3 Strongest Dependency Route (SDR) Algorithm for Backward Inference

Definition 1. *In a BN, let C be the set of causes, E be the set of effects. For $e_i \in E$, C_i be the set of causes based on effect e_i, iff $p(c_k|e_i) = Max[p(c_j|e_i), c_j \in C_i]$, then c_k is the strongest cause for effect e_i.*

The detailed description of the SDR algorithm is described as follows:

(1) Pruning of the BNs

Generally, multiple effects (symptoms) may be observed at a moment, so $E_k = \{e_1, e_2, \ldots, e_k\}$ is defined as initial effects. In the operation of pruning, in every step only current nodes' parents are integrated and their brother nodes are omitted, because their brother nodes are independent with each other. The pruned graph is composed of the effect nodes E_k and their entire ancestor.

(2) SDR Algorithm

After the pruning operation, a simplified sub-BN is obtained. The SDR algorithm use product calculation to measure the serial strongest dependencies between effect nodes and causal nodes.

Input: $BN = (V, L, P)$; $E_k = \{e_1, e_2, \ldots, e_k\}$, $E_k \subset V$.
Output: T: a spanning tree of the BN, rooted on E_k.

Variables: $depend[v]$: the strongest dependency between v and all its descendants; $p(v|u)$: the probability can be calculated from JPD of $p(u|\pi(u))$, v is the parent of u; $\varphi(l)$: temporal variable to record the strongest dependency between nodes.

Initialize the SDR tree T as E_k;   // E_k is added as root nodes of T
Write label 1 on e_i;   //$e_i \in E_k$
While SDR tree T does not yet span the BN
    For each frontier edge l in BN
        Let u be the labelled endpoint of edge l;
        Let v be the unlabelled endpoint of edge l;   //v is one parent of u
        Set $\varphi(l) = depend[u] * p(v|u)$;
    Let l be a frontier edge for BN that has the maximum φ-value;
    Add edge l (and vertex v) to tree T;
    $depend[v] = \varphi(l)$;
    Write label $depend[v]$ on vertex v;
Return SDR tree T and its vertex labels;

The result of the SDR algorithm is a spanning tree T. Every cause node $c_j \in C$ is labeled with $depend[c_j] = p(c_j|M_k, e_i)$, $e_i \in E_k$, M_k is the transition nodes between e_i and c_j.

(3) Proof of the Correctness of SDR Algorithm
When a vertex u is added to spanning tree T, define $d[u] = weight(e_i, u) = -lg(depend[u])$. Because $0 < depend[\delta_j] \leq 1$ so $d[\delta_j] \geq 0$. Note $depend[\delta_j] \neq 0$, or else there is no dependency relationship between δ_j and its offspring.

Proof: suppose to the contrary that at some point the SDR algorithm first attempts to add a vertex u to T for which $d[u] \neq weight(e_i, u)$.

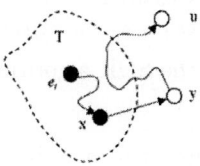

Fig. 1. Proof of SDR Algorithm

See Fig. 1. Consider the situation just prior to the insertion of u and the true strongest dependency route from e_i to u. Because $e_i \in T$, and $u \in V \setminus T$, at some point this route must first take a jump out of T. Let (x, y) be the edge taken by the path, where $x \in T$, and $y \in V \setminus T$. We have computed x, so

$$d[y] \leq d[x] + weight(x, y) \qquad (1)$$

Since x was added to T earlier, by hypothesis,

$$d[x] = weight(e_i, x) \qquad (2)$$

Since $< e_i, \ldots, x, y >$ is sub-path of a strongest dependency route, by Eq.(2),

$$weight(e_i, y) = weight(e_i, x) + weight(x, y) = d[x] + weight(x, y) \qquad (3)$$

By Eq. (1) and Eq. (3), we get $d[y] \leq weight(e_i, y)$. Hence $d[y] = weight(e_i, y)$.

Since y appears midway on the route from e_i to u, and all subsequent edges are positive, we have $weight(e_i, y) < weight(e_i, u)$, and thus $d[y] = weight(e_i, y) < weight(e_i, u) \leq d[u]$.

Thus y would have been added to T before u, in contradiction to our assumption that u is the next vertex to be added to T. So the algorithm must work. Since the calculation is correct for every effect node. It is also true that for multiple effect nodes in tracing the strongest dependency route.

(4) Analysis of the SDR Algorithm

In SDR algorithm, every link (edge) in BN is only calculated one time, so the size of the links in BN is consistent with the complexity. The number of edges in a complete DAG is $n(n-1)/2 = (n^2 - n)/2$, where n is the size of the nodes of the DAG. Normally a BN is an incomplete DAG. So the calculation time of SDR is less than $(n^2 - n)/2$. The complexity of SDR is $O(n^2)$.

Compared to other inference algorithms in BNs [2,6], the SDR algorithm belongs into the class of exact inferences and it provides an efficient method to trace the strongest dependency routes from effects to causes and to track the dependency sequences of the causes. It is useful in fault localization, and it is beneficial for performance management. Moreover it can treat multiple connected networks modelled as DAGs.

4 Conclusions and Future Work

Bayesian inference is the popular operation for a reasoning system. The SDR algorithm presents an backward efficient method to trace the causes from effects in complex information system. It is useful for information management, such as systems diagnosis and error exact location and further can be used in performance management.

References

1. J. Pearl. Probabilistic Reasoning in Intelligent Systems: Networks of Plausible Inference. Morgan Kaufmann, San Mateo, CA, 1988.
2. R. G. Cowell, A. P. Dawid, S. L. Lauritzen, D. J. Spiegelhalter. Probabilistic Networks and Expert Systems. New York: Springer-Verlag, 1999.
3. D. Nikovski. Constructing Bayesian networks for medical diagnosis from incomplete and partially correct statistics. IEEE Transactions on Knowledge and Data Engineering, Vol. 12, No. 4, pp. 509 - 516, July 2000.
4. K. Basye, T. Dean, J. S. Vitter. Coping with Uncertainty in Map Learning. Machine Learning, 29(1): 65-88, 1997.
5. E. Charniak, R. P. Goldman. A Semantics for Probabilistic Quantifier-Free First-Order Languages, with Particular Application to Story Understanding. Proceedings of IJCAI-89, pp1074-1079, Morgan-Kaufmann, 1989.
6. J. Pearl. Causality: Models, Reasoning, and Inference. Cambridge, England: Cambridge University Press. New York, NY, ISBN: 0-521-77362-8, 2000.
7. W. Wiegerinck, H.J. Kappen, E.W.M.T ter Braak, W.J.P.P ter Burg, M.J. Nijman, Y.L. O, and J.P. Neijt. Approximate inference for medical diagnosis. Pattern Recognition Letters, 20:1231-1239, 1999.

Dynamic Semantic Consistency Checking of Multiple Collaborative Ontologies in Knowledge Management System[1]

Dong Li, Linpeng Huang, and Mingliu Li

Department of Computer Science & Engineering,
Shanghai Jiao Tong University,
Shanghai 200030, P.R. China
lidong@sjtu.edu.cn, huang-lp@cs.sjtu.edu.cn

Abstract. An ontology-based knowledge management system uses an ontology to represent explicit specification of a special domain and to serve as a backbone for providing and searching for knowledge sources. But, dynamically changing domain environment implies changes in the conceptualization of the domain that are reflected on the underlying domain ontologies. Consequently, these changes have effects on the consistency and validity of the domain ontologies of the KM system. In this paper we present an approach for dynamic semantic consistency checking of multiple collaborative ontologies in KM system in the case of changes in the domain ontology. This approach is based on our research in the ontology reasoning.

1 Introduction

An ontology-based KM system consists of multiple collaborative ontologies. An ontology in a KM system is related to the business strategy and also indirectly to the business environment. Consequently in a fast changing environment it is obvious that an ontology as a domain backbone is also a matter of change. The changes have to be propagated to other dependent ontologies. Although this change propagation problem has great impact on knowledge searching process, this problem is not well addressed[1].

In this paper we present an approach that enable dynamic semantic consistency checking in the ontologies of knowledge sources in the case of changes in the domain ontology[2], From the knowledge management system point of view the proposed approach will enable us to develop a robust knowledge management solution that copes with the high-changeable business conditions.

---

[1] This work is supported by the China Ministry of Science and Technology 863 high Technology program (Grant No 2001AA113160) and 973 project (No.2002CB312002)of China, ChinaGrid Program of MOE of China, and grand project of the Science and Technology Commission of Shanghai Municipality (No. 03dz15026, No. 03dz15027 and No. 03dz15028).

2 Semantic Consistency Checking of Multiple Collaborative Ontologies

2.1 Conceptual Modeling of Composite Ontologies

In our conceptual modeling approach we present our approach on an abstract, mathematical level that defines the structure of ontology. We may support this structure with several different syntaxes.

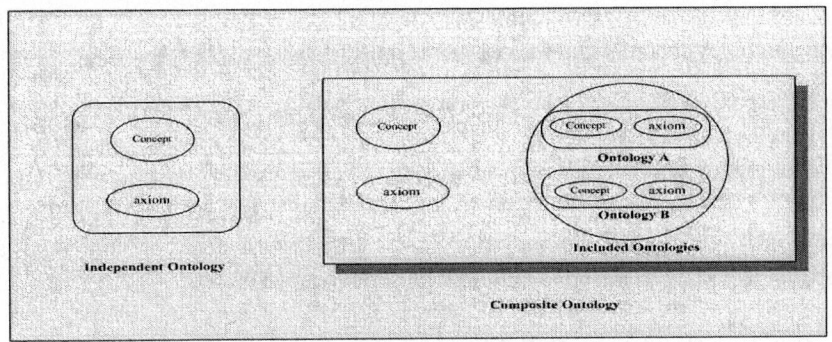

Fig. 1. Multiple Collaborative Ontologies

Definition 1(Independent Ontology Structure): An independent ontology structure is a tuple O:= (C,A) where:

- C is the set of concept of the ontology,
- A is the set of axiom of the ontology.

Definition 2 (Composite Ontology Structure): An composite ontology structure is a tuple CompO := (C,A,O_{sub}) where:

-C is the set of concept of the ontology,
-A is the set of axiom of the ontology.
-O_{sub} is the set of included independent ontology or included Composite Ontology.

An ontology represents a self-contained unit of structured information that may be reused. It may include a set of other ontologies (represented through the set O_{sub}). Different ontologies can talk about the same concept, so the sets of concept C of these ontologies don't need to be disjoint.

Definition 3 (Composite Ontology Interpretation): An ontology interpretation $\mathcal{I}$ is a model of CompO if it satisfies all concept definitions and axioms in CompO and set O_{sub}.

An ontology interpretation $\mathcal{I}$ satisfies

- a concept definition $\quad c \doteq C \quad$ iff $\quad c^T = C^T$
- an axiom $\quad\quad\quad C_1 \sqsubseteq C_2 \quad$ iff $\quad C_1^T \sqsubseteq C_2^T$

where c is a concept name, C, C_1, C_2 is complex concept of Composite Ontology or included ontologies.

Definition 4 (Composite Ontologies Modularization Constraints): If an composite ontology imports some other ontology O_i (i=0,1,2,...,n), that is, if $O_i \sqsubseteq O_{sub}$, then following ontology modularization constraints must be satisfied:

$$O_i := (C_i, A_i, O_{sub\,i})$$
$$C_i \sqsubseteq C$$
$$A_i \sqsubseteq A$$

Cyclical inclusions aren't allowed, that is, a graph whose nodes are ontologies and arcs from including to included ontology must not contain a cycle.

2.2 Ontology Consistency Definition

For Consistency of single ontologies the essential phase is the semantics of change phase, whose task is to maintain ontology consistency. Applying elementary ontology changes alone will not always leave the ontology in a consistent state. For example, deleting a concept will cause subconcepts, some properties and instances to be inconsistent.

Definition 5 (Single Ontology Consistency): A single ontology is consistent if it satisfies a set of concept and axiom in the ontology model and if all used entities is defined.

Definition 6 (Composite Ontology Consistency): A Composite ontology is consistent if the ontology itself and all its included ontologies are single ontology consistent.

Definition 7 (Multiple Collaborative Ontologies Consistency): Multiple Collaborative Ontologies is consistent if each of composite ontology or Independent Ontology of Multiple Collaborative Ontologies is single ontology consistent.

2.3 A Tableau Algorithm for Single Ontology Consistency Checking

An tableau algorithm which constructs a tableau for a concept $\mathcal{D}$ can be used as a decision procedure for the satisfiability of with respect to a role box $\mathcal{R}$. Such an algorithm have been described in detail[3].

2.4 A Consistency Checking Algorithm for Multiple Collaborative Ontologies

The algorithm for Consistency of multiple Collaborative Ontologies is presented in below. We base our algorithm implementation primarily on deductive techniques of tableau reasoning of description logics, for which it has been shown that they are crucial to achieving tractability and practicability of inferencing.

```
boolean MultriOntologyConsistencyCheckingAlgorithm(Array Ontology_Array){
   for all o in Ontology_Array
     swith (o) {
       case Type(o) is Independent Ontology
         if (not Single_Ontology_Consistency(o.getConcept(),o.getaxiom()))
           { return false; }
       case Type(o) is Composite Ontology
         if (not Composite_Ontology_Consistency(o))
           { return false; }
   }
   end for
   return true;
}
boolean Composite_Ontology_Consistency(Ontology composite_o){
   C=composite_o.getConcept(); A=composite_o.getaxiom();
   O_subArray=composite_o.getChildOntologyArray();
   if (not Single_Ontology_Consistency(C,A))
     {return false }
   if (O_subArray not is null) {
     for all o in O_subArray
       if (not Composite_Ontology_Consistency(o))
         {return false;}
     end for
   }
   return true;
}
boolean Single_Ontology_Consistency(Array_Concept C, Array_Amoin A){
   return Tableau_Algorithm_for_Single_Ontology(C,A);
}
```

3 Conclusion

This article presents present an approach for dynamic semantic consistency checking of multiple collaborative ontologies. We restricted our focus in this paper to management aspects of representing Independent, Composite ontologies. We presented a conceptual modeling approach along with its mathematical definition and formal semantics, that is suitable as a basis for a scalable implementation.

References

[1] D. Fensel, Ontologies: A Silver Bullet for Knowledge Management and Electronic Commerce.Springer, 2001.
[2] A. Maedche, B. Motik, L. Stojanovic, R. Studer, and R. Volz. Ontologies for Enterprise Knowledge Management. *To appear in: IEEE Intelligent Systems*, 2003.
[3] Jeff Z. Pan. Web Ontology Reasoning in the SHOQ(Dn) Description Logic. In Proceedings of the Methods for Modalities 2(M4M-2), Nov 2001. ILLC, Univer- sity of Amsterdam

The Practice of I/O Optimizations for Out-of-Core Computation

Jianqi Tang, Binxing Fang, Mingzeng Hu, and Hongli Zhang

Department of Computer Science and Engineering,
Harbin Institute of Technology, Harbin, 150001, China
{tjq, bxfang, mzhu, zhl}@pact518.hit.edu.cn

Abstract. Out-of-core computation needs high I/O performance as the out-of-core data stored in files has to be moved between memory and disks during the execution of an application program. In order to obtain better performance of out-of-core programs, two I/O optimizations are practiced, which are data prefetching and data reuse. This paper focuses on discussing the mechanism and implementation of each method and under which condition a method should be used. Several sets of experiments are taken to test the strategies and the results show that the I/O performance is efficiently improved by using these optimization methods.

1 Introduction

With the increasing scale of scientific computation, more and more applications involve solving problems with very large data sets, which results in out-of-core computation [1]. A typical Grand Challenge Applications could require 1Gbytes to 4Tbytes of data per run [2]. Hence in such computation, data needs to be stored on disks and during program execution only a portion of the data can be fetched into memory. This makes it necessary to move data back and forth between main memory and disks.

There are two main problems out-of-core computation is facing. One is that it is difficult to write a traditional out-of-core program which is organized around a few disk files and interspersed with many explicit I/O statements. Convenient and efficient interfaces in higher level should be provided. We developed a new programming interface using object-oriented method, which is discussed in detail in [3]. The PVFS developer team also once designed a MDBI interface to help in the development of out-of-core algorithms operating on multi-dimensional datasets [4].

Another is that out-of-core computation needs high I/O performance. Since I/O is slow, the I/O speed, and not the CPU speed, is often the bottleneck in out-of-core applications [5]. Applications that need high I/O performance must decrease the amount of I/O requests and ensure that all I/O operations access large amounts of data [6]. Most operating systems maintain a cache in main memory. However, because the cache is designed for universal codes, it is inefficient for some scientific and engineering applications.

Some I/O optimizations have been made in the level of hardware control of the processor, the interior of compilers and file systems. These methods focus on automatic optimizations which are transparent to users. But different applications have different data access patterns. It is the user who clearly knows how the data is used in the program. If flexible optimization strategies are provided for the user to adopt in various applications, the performance of out-of-core computation will be improved. In this paper, we present two main optimization methods which are implemented in a runtime library. Application programming interfaces (APIs) of optimized I/O operations are provided for users to control the data access in various out-of-core applications.

The rest of this paper is organized as follows. Section 2 and 3 respectively describe data prefetching and data reuse. The study of test results on a workstation of each method is presented in its corresponding section. All the tests are taken on a workstation with a Pentium III 450MHz processor, a 64M RAM and a 10GB disk. We used the Linux 2.4.7 kernel and GNU C/C++ 2.96. Finally, Section 4 draws the conclusions and our future work.

2 Data Prefetching

The concept of data prefetching originally appeared in accessing memory. Data is fetched into the cache from main memory in advance in order to improve the cache hit rate. The software prefetching method for single processors is first presented at Rice University [7]. Compiler-based I/O prefetching is always the hot point [8, 9]. Based on the same idea, data prefetching can also be adopted to disk access. That is to extend the cache-memory level to the memory-disk level.

The out-of-core data stored in a file is divided into a number of slabs which can fit in main memory. A typical out-of-core program execution proceeds as follows: a slab of data is fetched into memory; the computation is performed on this slab and the slab is written back to the file. This is repeated on other slabs till the end of the program. This is illustrated in Fig. 1(a) in which we assume reading, writing and computation take the same amount of time. During this process, the processor has to wait while the I/O operations are handled.

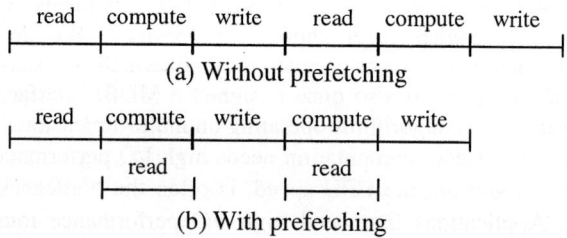

Fig. 1. Data prefetching

As shown in Figure 1(b), the execution time can be reduced by overlapping the read of next slab with the computation being performed on the current slab. This needs to allocate two user buffers and issue the non-blocking I/O request. While the computation is performed on the data in the current buffer, the next slab is fetched into another buffer. While data in the current buffer is written back to the file, the data in another buffer is copied to the current one.

If the file is divided into n slabs, the prefetching method will save n times of reading time or computation time. If the computation time is comparable to the reading time, data prefetching can result in significant improvement.

In our runtime library, multithread is used to implement the overlap between computation and I/O. The main thread performs computation and writing, and the derived thread reads the data. Users can adopt prefetching by using the API prefetch(), and prefetch_wait() to wait for the prefetching to complete.

Table 1 shows the performance of a vector inner product program. The element type is integer and the buffer is set to 1Mbytes, which means the size of each slab is 1Mbytes. There are no writing operations in this application. In all cases, prefetching improve performance considerably. The improvement ratio is around 40% in our tests.

Table 1. Performance of Inner Product between Two Vectors (time in seconds)

Element number (N)	Data space (4×N bytes)	Prefetching	No prefetching
32M	128M	15.42	25.73
64M	256M	34.28	56.81
128M	512M	70.05	105.92
192M	768M	90.63	154.38
256M	1G	148.52	249.19

3 Data Reuse

In out-of-core computation, data may be read from files many times. If a portion of the data currently fetched into memory is also needed for the computation on the next data block, that portion already in memory can be reused instead of reading it again with the next data block. This is data reuse.

For example, consider the Jacobi iteration for the Laplace equation solver. Suppose the array is distributed along rows and each block consists of s rows. Then the computation of each row requires one row from the upper and one row from the lower. As shown in Fig. 2, the buffer size for the computation on a data block should be $l+2$ rows. The lower two rows (l and $l+1$) in the current block are overlapped with the upper two rows in the next block (0 and 1). Then after the computation is performed on the current data block, the two rows at the bottom can be reused by moving them to the top location instead of reading them again with the next data block from the disk. The reuse thus eliminates the reading of two rows in this example. Because moving data in memory is quite faster than I/O, the performance of the program can be improved.

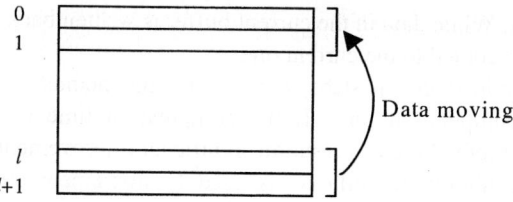

Fig. 2. Data reuse

The call datareuse() in our library is used to perform data reuse. Table 2 shows the performance improvement obtained by using data reuse for the Jacobi iteration. The buffer size is 16 rows. The array size is various from 1K×1K to 6K×6K. The results show that reuse provides good performance improvement even in the Jacobi iteration only two rows can be reused. The amount of reused data depends on the intersection of the two consecutive data block needed for computation.

Table 2. Performance of Data Reuse (time in seconds)

Array Size	With Reuse	Without Reuse
1K×1K	0.35	0.37
2K×2K	4.51	5.97
3K×3K	20.96	21.37
4K×4K	39.10	43.34
5K×5K	62.85	68.96
6K×6K	88.13	97.82

Another set of results shown in Table 3 explains the relationship between the amount of reused data and the improvement. A 40960×2048 integer matrix (320Mbytes) is read into memory block by block. Each block contains 128 rows (1Mbytes). No computation is performed on the data set. The results indicate that the more the amount of reused data is, the better the improvement is. With the increased number of reused rows, more data needs to be fetched into memory during the program execution if no reuse is performed. At the same time, if reuse is adopted, the amount of fetched data does not change and only more data needs to be moved within memory, which results in little time increase.

Table 3. Performance of Different Amount of Reused Data (time in seconds)

Number of Reused Rows	With Reuse	Without Reuse	Improvement Ratio
2	16.69	17.07	2%
8	17.92	18.47	3%
16	20.78	21.82	5%
32	22.61	25.38	11%
64	28.17	35.91	22%

4 Conclusions

The I/O performance plays a significant role in out-of-core computation. Research on I/O optimizations and high-level interface helps to solve the large-scale problems efficiently. This paper discussed two strategies to improve the I/O performance. Data prefetching hides part of the I/O latency. Data reuse reduces the amount of data fetched from disks and moves the reused data within memory instead. Both of these optimizations are implemented and provided in a runtime library. The test results have shown that the performance of out-of-core computation can be efficiently improved if the proper optimization method is performed according to the data access pattern.

In the future, there is still a lot of work to do to expand the functionality of our library. The individual method should be joined with others to obtain better performance improvement. Additional study is needed to characterize and identify the different data access patterns.

References

1. J. Ramanujam M. Kandemir, A. Choudhary and R. Bordawekar. Compilation techniques for out-of-core parallel computations. Parallel Computing, 1998, 23(3-4): 597—628
2. J. Rosario, A. Choudlhary. High performance I/O for parallel computers: problems and prospects. IEEE Computer. March 1994. 59-68
3. Jianqi Tang, Binxing Fang, Mingzeng Hu, Hongli Zhang. An Object-Oriented Method for Out-of-Core Parallel Computations on Cluster of Workstations. PDCAT'2003. Proceedings of the Fourth International Conference on Parallel and Distributed Computing, Applications and Technologies, IEEE Press, Aug.27-29, 2003, Chengdu, China, Page(s): 507 –510
4. M. M. Cettei, W. B. Ligon III, and R. B. Ross, Support for Parallel Out of Core Applications on Beowulf Workstations, Proceedings of the 1998 IEEE Aerospace Conference, pages 355-365, March, 1998.
5. Huseyin Simitci and Daniel Reed. A comparison of logical and physical parallel I/O patterns. The International Journal of High Performance Computing Applications, 1998, 12(3):364—380
6. Rajeev Thakur and William Gropp, "Parallel I/O", Sourcebook of Parallel Computing, Morgan Kaufmann Publishers, Ch. 11, pp. 331-355, 2002
7. D. Callahan, K. Kennedy, A. Porterfield. Software prefetching. In Proceedings of the 4th International Conference on Architectural Support for Programming Languages and Operation Systems, Santa Clara, CA , USA, 1991. 40- 52
8. Lian Reiqi, Zhang Zhaoqing, Qiao Ruliang. A data prefetching method used in ILP compilers and its optimization. Journal of Computers, 2000, 23(6): 576-584 (in Chinese)
9. Angela Demke Brown , Todd C. Mowry , Orran Krieger. Compiler-based I/O prefetching for out-of-core applications. ACM Transactions on Computer Systems (TOCS), 2001, 19(2): 111-170

A Grid Service Based Portal for Virtual Learning Campus

Elizabeth Sherly[1], Bindya George[2], Deepa L[2], and Resmy S Kumar[2]

[1] Indian Institute of Information Technology and Management- Kerala
Park Centre, Technopark, Trivandrum 695 581, India
sherly@iiitmk.ac.in
[2] Dept of Computer Science, University of Kerala, Trivandrum, India
{bindyageorge, deepus_ld, resmysk}@yahoo.co.in

Abstract. Grid computing makes it possible to dynamically share and coordinate dispersed, heterogeneous computing resources. In this paper we developed a grid based video and digital library portal for a Virtual Learning Campus (VLC) for easy access and deployment of various services. Our grid implementation combined with grid and factory services over GT 3.2 is capable of handling various services for seamless information processing and provides a collaborative problem-solving environment under a distributed environment.

1 Introduction

The development of the next generation collaborative problem solving environments is being influenced by rapid advances in Internet, distributed computing, and finally grid computing. Though Globus [1] provides a better framework to handle various services for seamless information processing, the successful launch of different environments under one umbrella remains a significant barrier. Grid and web services are now quickly gaining attention of grid developers and users for the easy access and deployment of services.

The Globus Toolkit provides services for the remote execution of a job, but does not attempt to provide a standard hosting environment that will guarantee the job execution correctly. This task is left to the user. The Open Grid Services Architecture (OGSA) enables grid and web services to work together and describe the structure and behavior of various services. In a web service model, the job execution and lifetime becomes the responsibility of the service provider [3]. Both web services and grid services focus on supporting applications or processes running across multiple loosely coupled systems. This enables services to dynamically locate, manage, and assure quality performance from participating systems.

Virtual Learning Campus (VLC) [5] is an advanced web portal being developed at IIITM-K. It has interfaces to various services for an easy access to different computational servers, streaming servers, digital library, course management system and collaboration servers distributed in a heterogeneous environment. In VLC, a large collection of rich course materials of learning resources are distributed in multiple servers across the region in a web based learning environment. The courses are enriched with streamed video lectures and a digital libraries supported by video and digital library servers.

The grid-based portal provides:
1. Simple and secure access to Grid applications and resources.
2. Persistent references to files, metadata, event message histories, and experiment logs.
3. Secure sharing of applications and data within group.
4. Access to group collaboration desktop applications.
5. Share course materials, video lectures and digital libraries.
6. Collaborative problem solving and data analysis environments.

We have developed a grid-based portal for managing high volumes of data and video/digital libraries in a distributed environment for the Virtual Learning Campus. We have used grid web services and Application Factory Services to launch and couple together components to build the distributed application.

1.1 OGSA and Grid Services

Web services provide a standard means of interoperating different software applications, running on a variety of platforms and/or frameworks. OGSA standardizes practically all the services one finds in a grid application (job management services, resource management services, security services, etc.) by specifying a set of standard interfaces to these services [3]. Through OGSA, the system manages many transient services including fundamental semantics, life-cycle management, and discovery, framework for fault resilience, security, and transaction management. Because of the transient, dynamic creation and destruction of services, the development of interfaces to the states of distributed activities, data analysis, and sharing of streaming video lectures become easier. OGSA also supports delegated authentication credentials using heterogeneous communications protocols [2].

2   File Services and Video Services

Two services established are File Services and Video Services in which different services are discovered, managed, named and used. Each service instances are created by factories; naming and bindings are done by unique name and services are managed by service data.

GridServicePortType is used for the creation of various services, which defines the fundamental behavior of a service with introspection, discovery and soft state life management [2]. FilePortType and VideoPortType are created using GWSDL in gwsdl namespace (gwsdl: portType). The declaration of services and functions are made accessible to client applications through the use of GridServiceHandle (GSH) and GridServiceReference (GSR). GSH points to a grid service and is identified by a URI. The GSR contains the necessary identified information to access the service instance. The steps involved in the

Grid Service creation after the establishment of connection with server and client are given below:

1. The client application calls the client stub. The client stub then turns this 'local invocation' into a proper SOAP request and sent it to the server.
2. After the receipt of the request, the server stub will convert the SOAP request into a format that the service implementation can understand.
3. The server stub sends the request to service implementation.
4. The service implementation sends the work result back to server stub.
5. The server stub converts the result into SOAP response and sent it back to the client.
6. The client stub converts the SOAP response into client application.

2.1 Portal Services

The various services have been monitored from the portal, which includes administrative services, logging services, information management services, lifetime management, load balancing, resource management and reliable file transfers.

Information Management: The service data provides a mechanism for service request to easily access the state of the service instance. Each instance of files and video services has a lifecycle. This refers to the time between an instance creation and destruction. An interface `ServiceLifeCycleMonitor` is implemented in the class `lifecyclemonitor` to know the instance lifecycle. Information Services are also available from the index service, which caches and host the service data. The details of the client, login particulars, the course materials and video lectures selected are monitored from the portal. Service details such as Service name, Grid Service Handle, service access time, and service termination time are stored as service data. A notification client is also running in parallel, which allows notification of service data and lifetime related events to subscribe to a particular service data element in a service.

Resource Management: Resource Management is done using GRAM architecture using Managed Job Factory Services [2]. From the client side, index service is created, client calls `createserviceoperator` from the factory. The factory creates the Managed Job Service and then returns to the locator. The client then returns the managed job services status.

GridFTP: GridFTP performs a third party transfer between two GridFTP Servers. This allows parallel file transfers, automatic restarting of interrupted transfers from the last checkpoint, and transfer portions of file starting at a particular offset. The implementation of the GridFTP protocol takes the form of two APIs and corresponding libraries: `globus_ftp_control` and `globus_ftp_client`. This utility is developed using java CoG Kit 1.1 API. The visualization of directory structure and attributes of files in a remote machine running GridFTP server using Net Beans IDE 3.51 [4] is shown in Fig 1. This is used to transfer the files of courses materials from any remote location to the servers.

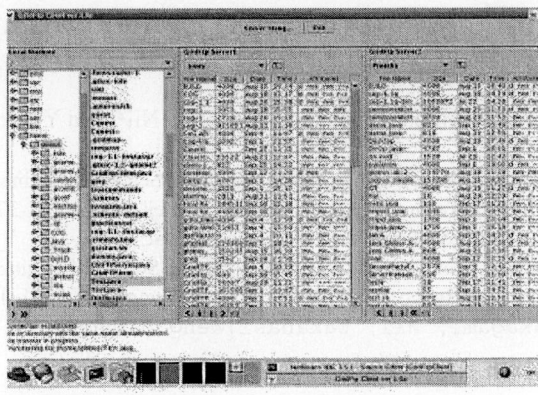

Fig. 1. Visualization of directory structure in GridFTP

The hosting of the services is done in JAVA environment in GWSDL file. The factory services and stub classes are generated from GWSDL, established in Linux environment using GT3.2. The deployment is done with WSDD (Web Service Deployment Descriptor) that makes the system a Grid Service enabled Web Server.

3 Conclusion

A video/digital library portal is developed using Grid Services. We have shown that OGSA along with Web Services and Factory Services provides an easy way to create and access any resources distributed in a heterogeneous environment. It also monitors the various services of information management, logging particulars, resource management, networking and load balancing.

References

1. Globus toolkit 3 tutorial. http://www.casa-sotomayor.net/gt3-tutorial/.
2. Foster, S. T. I. Open grid service infrastructure, white paper on ogsi. Tech. rep., Global Grid Forum. http://www.ggf.org/ogsi-wg.
3. GANNON, D., and ANANDAKRISHNAN, R. Grid web services and application factories. In *Proceedings of the International Conference on Parallel and Distributed Techniques and Application* (2002).
4. SHERLY, E. Data grid test bed for education grid. In *HiPC Workshops 2003: New Frontiers in High-Performance Computing*. Elite Publishing House Pvt. Ltd, New Delhi, India, 2003, pp. 355–364.
5. SRIVATHSAN, K. R. Virtual learning campus- india mission. Tech. rep., Indian Institute of Information Technology and Management, Technopark, Kariavottam, Trivandrum 695 581, Kerala India, 2004.

Implementation of Application Collaboration Protocol

Tomoya Sakaguchi[1], Hitoshi Sakagami[2], Manabu Nii[2], and Yutaka Takahashi[2]

[1] Division of Computer Engineering, Graduate School of Engineering,
Himeji Institute of Technology, 2167 Shosha, Himeji, Hyogo 671-2201, Japan
`tomoya@comp.eng.himeji-tech.ac.jp`
[2] Division of Computer Engineering, Graduate School of Engineering,
University of Hyogo, 2167 Shosha, Himeji, Hyogo 671-2201, Japan
`{sakagami, nii, takahasi}@eng.u-hyogo.ac.jp`

Abstract. When one application needs results calculated by another application simulating different phenomena to simulate some phenomena, users must write communication codes to exchange data between two applications. Because users require to program codes as simple as possible in general, writing communication codes should be more easier. It is, however, complicated for users to implement these codes using the existing method. In this paper, we have proposed the Distributed Computing Collaboration Protocol as a simple user interface for communication between application programs.

1 Introduction

Computer technology has continuously developed and recently enabled such a computation that could not be performed by a single computer. For example, Grid computing realizes execution of large-scale computing and huge data access by multiple computers. The cancer and anthrax research has proceeded with Grid computing in grid.org project [1]. The Globus Alliance [2] is also researching and developing to create fundamental technologies behind Grid computing. Furthermore, BOINC [3], which is a software platform for distributed computing projects like SETI@home [4] and distributed.net [5], simplifies conversion from an application to a public computing project. As mentioned above, the research in the field of distributed computing has been investigated more aggressively in various projects.

We are trying to perform simulations that need to smoothly coordinate multiple programs, which communicate each other to integrate simulations. Execution of each program is typically managed by NQS (Networking Queuing System), which is a job management system that assigns the queued task to idle CPU by turns, and we cannot define when and where these application programs are performed. Meanwhile, in order to communicate between two programs, both programs have to be simultaneously executed, and the sender program needs to know IP address of the receiver program. Thus communication between them is not necessarily possible due to NQS. In order to exchange data among programs, we therefore require a specific interface that has two features; sender and receiver programs do not have to be executed at the same time, and they can be performed at any machines. We can adopt the existing technologies to solve this problem, but these technologies are not suitable for this special kind of integrated simulations because programming with them is complicated and annoying.

In this paper, we propose the Distributed Computing Collaboration Protocol (DCCP) as a system that has the method of non-direct communication between programs, which is a high-level protocol that uses TCP/IP and builds up a unique communication system for only exchanging data. Especially collaboration of loosely coupled large-scale simulation codes is the main object for DCCP. We also discuss details of its implementation.

2 Details of DCCP

DCCP has two daemon processes, which are Arbitrator and Communicator, be resident in the DCCP network to realize the feature as is described above. Communicator receives data that is sent from codes or transferred from other Communicators, deposits the data in its storage, and sends the data to codes that request the data. In other words, Communicator actually performs data transmission instead of codes themselves. Arbitrator administrates multiple Communicators and codes. Concretely speaking, it instructs Communicators to transfer data to other Communicators, and controls communications between codes. In the network with DCCP, one Arbitrator and multiple Communicators can exist. Figure 1 shows the configuration that consists of site A where *Codes x* and *y*, *Communicator i*, and *Arbitrator* are running and site B where *Code z* and *Communicator j* are resident. Control and data communications are also shown in Fig.1. Control communications are used for management of Communicators and codes, and data communications mean transmission of data that are necessary for collaboration operations. Communicators use storage to temporarily store data for future usage.

Two daemons enable data exchange between codes by our protocol, DCCP. When *code z* needs data calculated by *code x*, the data is transferred through the process shown in Fig.2; There are only two cases of launch timing of these codes, (a) is the case where *code z* is already launched when *code x* sends data, (b) is the case where *code z* is not yet launched when *code x* sends data. We express the flow of basic processes in DCCP system using this instance.

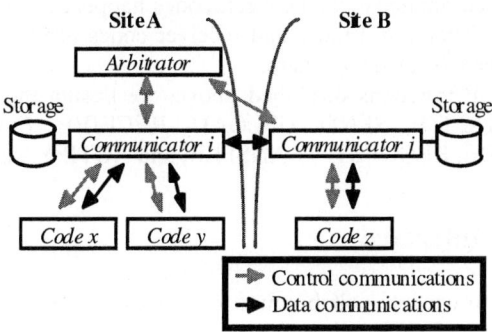

Fig. 1. Typical DCCP configuration

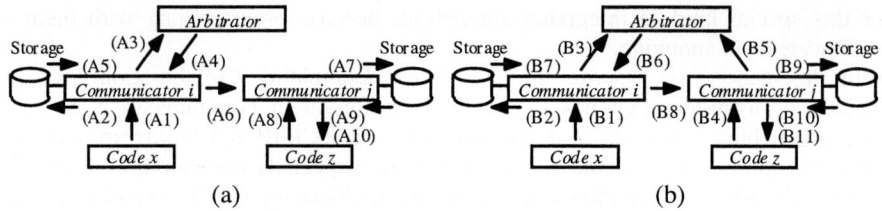

Fig. 2. Diagram of data transfer. (a) In the case where *code z* is already launched when *code x* sends data, (b) In the case where *code z* is not yet launched when *code x* sends data

Code x sends data to *Communicator i* and asks *Communicator i* to transfer the data to *code z* (A1) (B1). At this moment, the data is not actually transferred to *code z*, but the send process of *code x* is completed, and proceeds next calculation or finishes execution. *Communicator i* stores the data into its storage (A2) (B2) and inquires of *Arbitrator* to which Communicator the data will be sent to finally transfer the data to *code z* (A3) (B3).

Assume that *code z* is managed by *Communicator j*, the data should be sent to *Communicator j*. *Arbitrator* replies information of *Communicator j* to *Communicator i* (A4). Then *Communicator i* loads the data from its storage that was sent from *code x* and stored before (A5), and sends it to *Communicator j* (A6). And then *Communicator j* stores the data into its storage (A7) and waits for a request for the data. When *Communicator j* receives the data request from *code z* (A8), *Communicator j* loads (A9) and sends the data to *code z* (A10).

If *Communicator j* does not manage *code z* yet, *Arbitrator* replies *Communicator i* the fact that *Arbitrator* has no information for transferring the data to *code z*, and *Communicator i* waits for notice about *Communicator j* from *Arbitrator*. When *Communicator j* receives a demand for data from *code z* (B4), *Communicator j* requests *Arbitrator* to instruct all related Communicators to transfer the demanded data to *Communicator j* (B5). Therefore *Arbitrator* instructs information of *Communicator j* to *Communicator i* (B6), and *Communicator i* loads (B7) and sends the data to *Communicator j* by the same method as is mentioned above (B8). Then, *Communicator j* stores the data into its storage (B9) and loads (B10) and sends the data to *code z* (B11).

Thus, no direct communications between codes happen, and Communicator keeps data in its storage. Therefore sender and receiver codes need not be simultaneously launched and can be executed anywhere.

To realize DCCP functions described above, we design the interactive protocol commands, INITIALIZE, SEND, UPLOAD, RECEIVE, FINALIZE, INVOKE, INFORM, INQUIRE, REQUEST, TRANSFER, and NOTIFY, such as POP3 [6].

3 FORTRAN Interface

When users want to execute collaboration processes with DCCP, they have only to call five FORTRAN DCCP subroutines. The name and function of each DCCP subroutines are listed in Table 1. Before DCCP_SEND, DCCP_UPLOAD, and DCCP_RECEIVE are called, DCCP_INITIALIZE must be called. DCCP_FINALIZE must be called at the end of collaboration processes with DCCP.

Table 1. DCCP subroutines

Subroutine name	Function
DCCP_INITIALIZE	Request initialization of code.
DCCP_SEND	Send data to another code.
DCCP_UPLOAD	Upload data for multiple retrieve.
DCCP_RECEIVE	Receive data from another code.
DCCP_FINALIZE	Request finalization of code.

4 Conclusions

In this paper, we have proposed and implemented the Distributed Collaboration Computing Protocol that enables collaboration of application. This protocol uses Arbitrator and Communicator daemons, and these daemons transfer data from the sender application to the receiver application instead of codes themselves. These processes allow users to implement data transmission between applications easily. Users can use DCCP by calling five FORTRAN subroutines.

In addition, in order to enable DCCP communications beyond a firewall, we have introduced Transponder daemon, which relays communications between Arbitrator and Communicator and between Communicators, as a forwarder and demonstrated various configuration with DCCP [7]. At present, this protocol is actually applied to IFE (Inertial Fusion Energy) simulation in FI^3 project [8].

References

1. http://www.grid.org/
2. Foster, I., Kesselman, C., Tuecke, S.: The Anatomy of the Grid: Enabling Scalable Virtual Organizations. The Globus Alliance, (2001) http://www.globus.org/.
3. Anderson, D.: Public Computing: Reconnecting People to Science, Berkeley Open Infrastructure for Network Computing (BOINC), (2004) http://boinc.berkeley.edu/.
4. http://setiathome.ssl.berkeley.edu/
5. http://www.distributed.net/
6. Myers, J.: Post Office Protocol - Version 3. IETF, RFC 1939, (1996) http://www.ietf.org/rfc/rfc1939.txt.
7. Sakaguchi, T., Sakagami, H., Nii, M., Takahashi, Y.: Implementation of Application Collaboration Protocol. Technical Report, Himeji Inst. of Tech., Vol. 56 (2003) 27-42 (In Japanese)
8. Sakagami, H., Mima, K.: Interconnection between Hydro and PIC codes for Fast Ignition Simulations. Laser and Particle Beams, Vol. **22** (2004) 41-44

A Componentized Approach to Grid Enabling Seismic Wave Modeling Application

Dheeraj Bhardwaj[1], Jeremy Cohen[2], Steve McGough[2], and Steven Newhouse[2]

[1] Department of Computer Science & Engg., Indian Institute of Technology Delhi, India
dheerajb@cse.iitd.ac.in
[2] London e-Science Centre, Imperial College London, London, UK

Abstract. Seismic modeling is an integral part of the seismic data processing for oil and gas exploration, as it provides us the seismic response for a given earth model. Grid enabled seismic wave modeling can facilitate users in the area of geophysics to calculate synthetic seismograms using federated HPC resources and complex solution algorithms without knowing their complexities. The present paper is about componentization of the wave equation based seismic modeling algorithm and its implement using Imperial College e-Science Infrastructure (ICENI) Grid Middleware.

1 Introduction

Oil and gas companies are constantly challenged to assess promising locations for exploration and to improve production processes. The cost and availability of computational power has always been a limiting factor in the application of advanced seismic processing methods to refine subsurface images. Today, seismic data processing is as much based on complex algorithms, computation, data analysis, and collaboration. Though the computer power, data storage, and communication continue to improve exponentially, computational resources are failing to keep up with what geophysicists demand of them. The "Computational Grid" offers a potential means of surmounting these obstacles to progress [1], however they also present many challenges to their effective exploitation by non-trivial applications. Grid based programming requires a high-level programming model that performs in a resource/platform independent fashion.

ICENI uses a component-programming model to describe Grid applications. This is clearly beneficial because it promotes code reuse and reduces the task of Grid application development to that of application composition [7]. Each component in an application represents an abstract or running software resource service that can communicate to other components in the application through the ICENI middleware.

2 Wave Equation Based Seismic Modeling

The basic problem in the theoretical seismology is to determine the wave response of a given model to the excitation of an impulse source by solving the wave equations under some simplifications. In the scalar approximation, the acoustic wave equation may be solved to evaluate the waveform. The acoustic wave equation in a 3D heterogeneous medium given by

$$\frac{1}{K}\frac{\partial^2 p}{\partial t^2} = \frac{\partial}{\partial x}\left[\frac{1}{\rho}\frac{\partial p}{\partial x}\right] + \frac{\partial}{\partial y}\left[\frac{1}{\rho}\frac{\partial p}{\partial y}\right] + \frac{\partial}{\partial z}\left[\frac{1}{\rho}\frac{\partial p}{\partial z}\right] \quad (1)$$

where, p is the negative pressure wavefield, ρ is the density and K is the incompressibility. But instead of solving this second order hyperbolic wave equation, numerically one can use an equivalent first order system [5], which can be derived from equations of motion. If u, v and w are the components of the velocity vector in the x-, y- and z-directions respectively, then

$$\rho\frac{\partial u}{\partial t} = \frac{\partial p}{\partial x}, \quad \rho\frac{\partial v}{\partial t} = \frac{\partial p}{\partial y}, \quad \rho\frac{\partial w}{\partial t} = \frac{\partial p}{\partial z} \quad (2)$$

Using equations (1), and (2), we can also write a first order system of hyperbolic equations

$$\frac{\partial \mathbf{P}}{\partial t} = \mathbf{A}\frac{\partial \mathbf{P}}{\partial x} + \mathbf{B}\frac{\partial \mathbf{P}}{\partial y} + \mathbf{C}\frac{\partial \mathbf{P}}{\partial z} \quad (3)$$

where

$$\mathbf{P} = \begin{bmatrix} p \\ u \\ v \\ w \end{bmatrix}, \quad \mathbf{A} = \begin{bmatrix} 0 & \lambda & 0 & 0 \\ \rho^{-1} & 0 & 0 & 0 \\ 0 & 0 & 0 & 0 \\ 0 & 0 & 0 & 0 \end{bmatrix}, \quad \mathbf{B} = \begin{bmatrix} 0 & 0 & \lambda & 0 \\ 0 & 0 & 0 & 0 \\ \rho^{-1} & 0 & 0 & 0 \\ 0 & 0 & 0 & 0 \end{bmatrix}, \quad \mathbf{C} = \begin{bmatrix} 0 & 0 & 0 & \lambda \\ 0 & 0 & 0 & 0 \\ 0 & 0 & 0 & 0 \\ \rho^{-1} & 0 & 0 & 0 \end{bmatrix}$$

In contrast to equation (3), equation (1) requires the calculations of derivatives with respect to physical parameters. Equations (1) and (3) are usually solved by explicit finite-difference methods. The selection of the method depends on the formulation of the wave equation whether equation (1) or (3), convergence criterion, number of computations, accuracy etc. This requires a good understanding of finite difference methods for partial differential equations.

3 The ICENI Middleware

ICENI [3], [4] is an end-to-end Grid middleware system developed at London e-Science Centre. ICENI is based on an implementation independent API that interfaces to a service oriented architecture (SOA). As such, computational resources and software capabilities are exposed as services that can be discovered by the user.

ICENI is rich in metadata which is preserved at all levels within the system. This includes: metadata about how each component in a particular application works, as provided by the component developer; performance characteristics, stored from previous runs of the component within the ICENI environment; and metadata (both static and dynamic) provided by the Grid resources which are available for use by components in an application. Together these aspects enable a user to construct an application from components, to submit this workflow specification to a scheduling system capable of exploiting the application meta-data to optimize the placement of the components to reduce overall execution time.

4 Componentization Approach for Seismic Modeling

Seismic Modeling can be divided into the following four basic modules and each module will have independent components, which can be selected by the user to compose an application to execute in a Grid environment.

1. Input Data Files and Problem Parameters. This allows the user to provide input velocity, density files and their related parameters such as the size of the domain, records length, source, receiver locations etc.

2. Mathematical Model and Algorithms. This allows the user to select mathematical models such as parabolic/hyperbolic form of the wave equation. Based on the form of the partial differential equation, the user will have a choice for selecting the solution method e.g. finite difference or finite element. After selecting a solution method, the user can have a choice for selection of specific solution scheme [5].

3. Parallel System Parameter Selection. Although the intricacies of the running system will be hidden from the user, if some user wants to define the parallel system and partitioning of the domain etc, parallel system parameter selection can allow the user to select various partition algorithms [6]. The Grid middleware should be responsible for hiding the complexity of Grid usage and through performance modeling can indicate the best parallel parameters for the particular problem size on that computational resource.

4. Results and Visualization. This allows the user to define how he wants to receive and visualize the data e.g. data storage location, format and visualization tools.

We have developed various binary components for each of the above four basic modules above where the user has a choice to select according to the needs for data available for the processing. For example, in the case of a salt dome model, a user will prefer to select a hyperbolic formulation of the wave equation and will have a choice to select the finite difference scheme as McCormick for better resolution.

5 Seismic Modeling as an ICENI Application

In order to develop various components of the seismic modeling application, we have used the ICENI binary *ComponentBuilder* that allows us to expose native code as a component within a Grid environment. Further, this permits us to specify the ports of the components according to the meaning, behavior and implementation in a graphical way. Once the components have been developed, we use the ICENI Netbeans based client to browse and monitor available services in ICENI. This client also provides an intuitive way for application to be composed, whereby components can be dragged-and-dropped onto a composition pane, before being connected together to visually describe the workflow of the application. The composed application can then be submitted and launched through ICENI in order to schedule and execute the component.

Most of the components used in the Seismic Modeling application were developed independently from ICENI and work as separate binary applications. The binary applications can be accessed through the use of the ICENI *Binary Component* – a way of wrapping up an existing application to use within the ICENI framework.

Every Binary Component is associated with the binary executable that the component represents, a JDML file that describes how the application is to be executed and the arguments that it may take. The Binary Component is capable of taking input and output data from other components in ICENI. This allows a set of arguments to be passed to the binary executable (through the *stdin* ports), and/or the output of the application to be passed back to ICENI.

6 Conclusion

We have shown that the wave equation based seismic modeling application has been implemented successfully within the ICENI Grid environment. Since ICENI is an integrated Grid environment for component applications, we have componentized the seismic modeling application into various independent binary modules. Finally, they have been wrapped up by using the ICENI binary ComponentBuilder to make them available as services to compose the seismic modeling application and execute within a Grid environment.

References

1. Foster, I., Kesselman, C., eds. 2004, The Grid 2: Blueprint for New Computing Infrastructure, Morgan Kaufmann.
2. Oz Yilmaz, Seismic Data Processing Vol. 1 & 2, 2000, SEG Publication
3. Furmento, N., Lee, W., Mayer, A., Newhouse, S., and Darlington, J., ICENI: An Open Grid Service Architecture Implemented with Jini. In SuperComputing2002. (2002) USA
4. Furmento, N., Mayer, A., Newhouse, S., Field, T., and Darlington, J., ICENI: Optimization of Component Applications within a Grid Environment. J. Par. Compt, 28(12) (2002) 1753-1772
5. Phadke, S., and Bhardwaj. D., Parallel Implementation of Seismic Modeling Algorithms on PARAM Openframe, Neural, Parallel and Scientic Computations. Vol. 6 (4) (1998) 469-478
6. Chakraborty, S., Yerneni, S., Phadke, S. and Bhardwaj, D. 2003, Parallelization Strategies for Seismic modelling algorithms, Journal of Indian Geophysical Union, vol. 7, no.1, 11-14.
7. Mayer, A., McGough, Gulamali, M., Young, L., Stanton, S., Newhouse, S., and Darlington, J., Meaning and behaviour in Grid oriented components, in M. Parashar, editor, Grid Computing – GRID 2002: Third international workshop, proc., LNCS, 2536 (2002) 100-111

Design of Algorithm for the 3D Object Representation Based on the Web3D Using X3D

Yun-Bae Lee, Sung-Tae Lee, Gun-Tak Oh,
Young-Kook Kim, and Young-Ho Kim

Dept. of Computer Science, Graduate School,
Chosun University, 375 Seosuk-Dong, Dong-ku,
Gwangju, 501-759, Korea
yblee@mina.chosun.ac.kr

Abstract. The data volume of Web3D representation based on polygon meshes is so large that transferring practical data fast is a difficult problem. This paper proposes 3D object structure, a new framework for a compact 3D representation with high quality surface shape. By utilizing a free form surface technique, qualified surfaces are transferred with limited amount of data size and rendered. 3D graphic structure can be regarded as both polygon meshes and free form surfaces. Therefore, it can be easily integrated to existing Web3D data formats, for example VRML & XML. The 3D object's structure also enables modeling free form surface shapes intuitively with polygon modeling like operations. In this paper, we propose and verify an algorithm on representation of 3D objects using X3D.

1 Introduction

More attention is being drawn to the 3D animation field in order to model objects highly similar to the real ones due to the increase of 3D games or virtual reality on the Internet. We can categorise virtual reality techniques on the Internet into two groups: they are panorama based on images and Web3D based on 3D polygon. Panorama is a method of viewing from the center after mapping photographs either in a cylinder shape or a sphere. It produces high quality and the procedure is simple since it uses photographs. However Web3D uses photographs and 3D polygons so implementation procedure is more complicated. Therefore there is a need to develop a new technique to represent real world objects as 3D, as 3D games and virtual reality grows in Web3D.

VRML(Virtual Reality Modeling Language), which is the 3D version of HTML, is a standard for representing 3D on the web.

It is envisaged that X3D and XML will be common exchange formats for integrated 3D graphics and multimedia. Recently a new technique to replace VRML was announced in North Carolina. Also Web3D consortium announced that X3D was finalized as the next generation standard. X3D will be replacing VRML and supporting 3D graphics in various applications and devices. Experts comment that it is likely to have X3D as a standard due to its flexibility and extensibility [3].

In this paper, we propose and verity an algorithm on representation of 3D objects using X3D.

2 Representation of Objects Based on Web3D

2.1 Gregory Patch

If we expand the NURBS formula into 3D curved surface, control point will expand to both the u, v directions and know vector will have both directions as well. We can draw a point of 3D curved surface by multiplying blending function from the knot vector. Figure 1 shows 3D Gregory patch based on Bezier curve. Figure 2 shows the curved surface produced by u, v two directional curves.

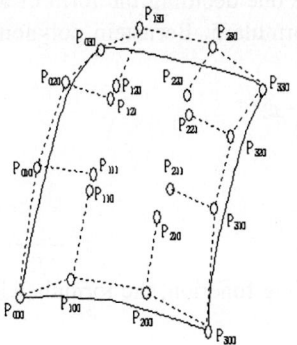
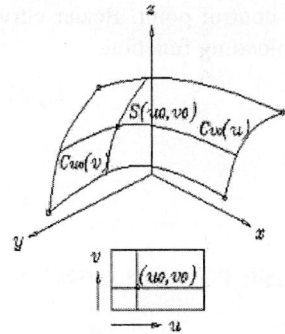

Fig. 1. 3Dimension Gregory

Fig. 2. Curved surface produced by u,v two directional curves

Formula 1 shows the formula of NURBS curved surface.

$$S(u,v) = \frac{\sum_{i=0}^{n}\sum_{j=0}^{m} N_{i,p}(u) N_{j,q}(v) w_{i,j} P_{i,j}}{\sum_{i=0}^{n}\sum_{j=0}^{m} N_{i,p}(u) N_{j,q}(v) w_{i,j}}$$

--------- formula 1

If we compare this to a curved formula, we can notice that the use of two directions of u and v is the only difference in blending function. If we simplify formula 1, it will be as formula 2, it is same as the curved formula. It is achieved by multiplying control point to weighting factor. Figure 1 of 3D Gregory patch is processed to 3D polygon by formula 2, 3, and 4.

$$S(u,v) = \sum_{i=0}^{3}\sum_{j=0}^{3} B_i^3(u) B_j^3(v) Q_{ij}(u,v)$$
$$(0 \leq u \leq 1, 0 \leq v \leq 1)$$

--------- formula 2

$$Q_{ij}(u,v) - P_{ij0}$$

---------formula 3

$$Q_{11}(u,v) = \frac{uP_{110} + vP_{111}}{u+v},$$

$$Q_{12}(u,v) = \frac{uP_{120} + (1-v)P_{121}}{u+(1-v)},$$

$$Q_{21}(u,v) = \frac{(1-u)P_{210} + vP_{211}}{(1-u)+v},$$

$$Q_{22}(u,v) = \frac{(1-u)P_{220} + (1-v)P_{221}}{(1-u)+(1-v)}$$

$$(0 \leq u \leq 1, 0 \leq v \leq 1)$$

-------- formula 4

2.2 Control of Bezier Curve

Bezier curve defines a curve using angular points of polygons that are containing the approximate curve planned. Combining the polygon's points and blending function will produce a curve. Blending function is the one deciding the form of a curve with effects of control point. Bezier curve uses formula 5, Bernstein polynomial expression as a blending function.

$$B_{i,n}(u) = {}_nC_i \, u^i (1-u)^{n-i}$$

$$_nC_i = \frac{n!}{i!(n-i)!}$$

-------- formula 5

If we apply polygon's vertexes to the blending function, the formula will be as formula 6.

$$P(u) = \sum_{i=0}^{n} {}_nC_i \, u^i (1-u)^{n-i} P_i$$

-------- formula 6

If the number of the control point is (n+1), we can know that the curve formula is a n-dimension formula because u^n member become the highest member. Therefore, the Bezier covered line is determined the dimension of the curve formula by the number of the control point. Figure 3(a) and (b) are the processed 3-dimension objects by the Bezier curved line.

 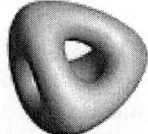

Fig. 3. (a) 3-dimension objects   (b) Objects by the Bezier curved line

3 Web3D

3.1 A Need of Web3D

X3D is extensible and is extended with VRML. The name, X3D was chosen to represent the integrity with XML. Figure 4 is the structure of X3D. There are some reasons to use X3D. First, it has backward compatibility with VRML97 so that content done in VRML97 is viewable. Second, it is integrated with XML so that VRML97 can be expressed when X3D is used with XML. Third, the extensible light core is possible by componentization. Fourth, it is extensible to add new nodes and executing code by component. XML was adapted as a solution for possible problems on the web. The reasons for using XML are re-hostability, page integration, and integration with the next generation web.

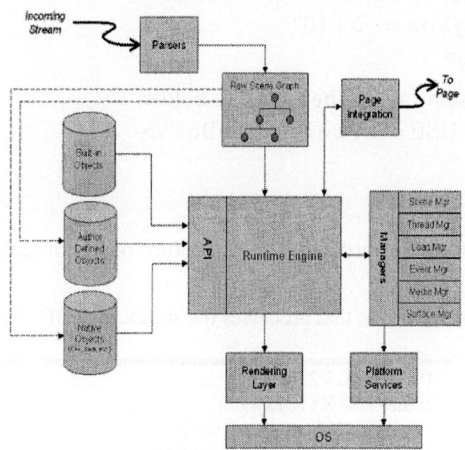

Fig. 4. Structure of X3D

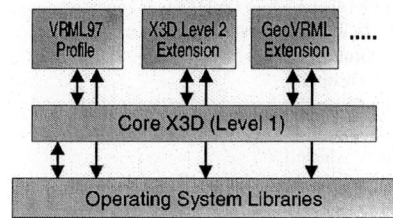

Fig. 5. Operating system and relation of VRML and X3D and it represents

Figure 5 displays operating system and relation of VRML and X3D and it represents perfect backward compatibility by putting a profile of VRML97 on top of Core X3D. X3D level2 Extension shows extensibility with XML. GeoX3D Extension is an example from a working group of Web3D consortium. Operating System Libraries are the system libraries that will be shared for core and extensible elements. VRML97 uses symbols to express 3Ds and binary format and XML will be another symbols respectively. Here is a simple example.

VRML97 : DEF MyView viewpoint

  {position 0 0 10}
  XML : <viewpoint DEF='MyView' position='0 0 10'>

The next example shows how XML syntax is used to define PROTO.
<Proto type ="myBox">
    <Field id = "mySize" type = "vec">
    <Box size = "mySize">
</Proto>

Then other documents may be used like below.
<ProtoUse type = "myBox"
    DEF = "aTwoThreeTenBox">
    mySize = "2 3 10"
</ProtoUse>

Then you can use a tag on the web like below.
<ProtoUse USE ="aTwoThreeTenBox"/>

3.2 VRML97

Table 1 is an algorithm that processes the structure of 3D objects to VRML.

Table 1. An algorithm that processes the structure of 3D objects to VRML

```
1:  #VRML V2..0 utf8
2:  PROTO XVL_EDGE [
3:    field SFFloat  round_val 0
4:    field SFVec3f  round_str 0 0 0
5:    field SFVec3f  round_end 0 0 0
6:  ]
7:  { Text { string [ " weight of adge " ] } }
8:  PROTO XVL_STATUS [
9:    field SFString status of shape" ] } }
10: Group{
11:   children [
12:     Group {
13:       children [
14:         shape {
15:           geometry IndexedFaceSet {
16:           }}]},
17: Switch {
18:   choice [
19:     XVL_STATUS {
20:       status "XVL_GREGORY"
21:     }
22:     XVL_EDGE {
23:       round_val 0.5
24:       round_str 0 0 0
25:       round_end 0 0 0
26:     }
27:     IndexedLineSet {
28:       coordIndex [ 24 103 ]
29:     }
30:   ]
31:   whichChoice -1
32: }]
33: }
```

3.3 X3D (VRML2002)

3D graphics will be presented in VRML according to the section 3.2. Nodes are based on abstract node so that each node can fit with the relevant functions. Object hierarchy structure will show interrelationship and origin of nodes. For example GeometryNode, LightNodes, SensorNode, and BindableNode are the ones that are repeated in X3D DTD after defining in VRML97. The definition of Tetrahedron came from GeometryNode, and it may be anywhere of a graph with Box, Sphere, or any other geometry node. 3D graphics in VRML are implemented in forms of dynamic X3D in XML. Table 2 is DTD of object structure of X3D.

Table 2. DTD of object structure of X3D

```
1:  <!ENTITY % XvlShellTypes "CS_POLYLN I
2:  CS_BEZIER I SS_POLYGON I SS_LATTICE I
3:  SS_GREGORY " >
4:  <!ELEMENT XvlShell (XYZ, UV, Faces*, Edges*,
5:  Vertices*0>
6:  <!ATTLIST XvlShell
7:    Type (%XvlShellTypes;) #REQUIRED
8:    DEF ID     \#IMPLLED
9:    USE  IDREF \#IMPLLED
10: >
11: <!ELEMENT Faces (Materiaal?, Texture?, Face+)>
12: <!ELEMENT Edges (Material?, Edge+) >
13: <!ELEMENT Vertices (Material?, Texture?
14:           %XvlG1T1FaceChild;) >
15: <!ATTLIST Face
16:   ix %MFInt32; #REQUIRED
17:   tx %MFInt32; #IMPLIED
18: >
19: <!ELEMENT Edge (Material?
20:           %XvlG1T1EdgeChild; ) >
21: <!ATTLIST Edge
22:   ix   %MFInt32; #REQUIRED
23:   vec  %MFInt32; #IMPLIED
24:   VRnd %SFFloat; #IMPLIED
25: >
26: <!ELEMENT Vertex (Material?) >
27: <C
28:   ix   %MFInt32; #REQUIRED
29:   VRnd %SFFloat; #IMPLIED
30: >
31: <!ELEMENT Texture (EMPTY) >
32: <!ELEMENT Texture
33:   url    CDATA  \#IMPLLED
34:   repeaatS %SFBool; "true"
35:   repeaatT %SFBool; "true"
36:   url    IDREF  \#IMPLLED
37:   url    ID     \#IMPLLED
38:   url    IDREF  \#IMPLLED
39: >
40: <!ELEMENT XYZ  \#PCDATA>
41: <!ELEMENT UV   \#PCDATA>
```

4 Application

Figure 6 demonstrates objects processed with Web3D based on the object presentation algorithm. A is base mech, b, c, d are done with division number 1, 2, and 8 respectively. When the algorithm was applied to the original image, we achieved high quality images.

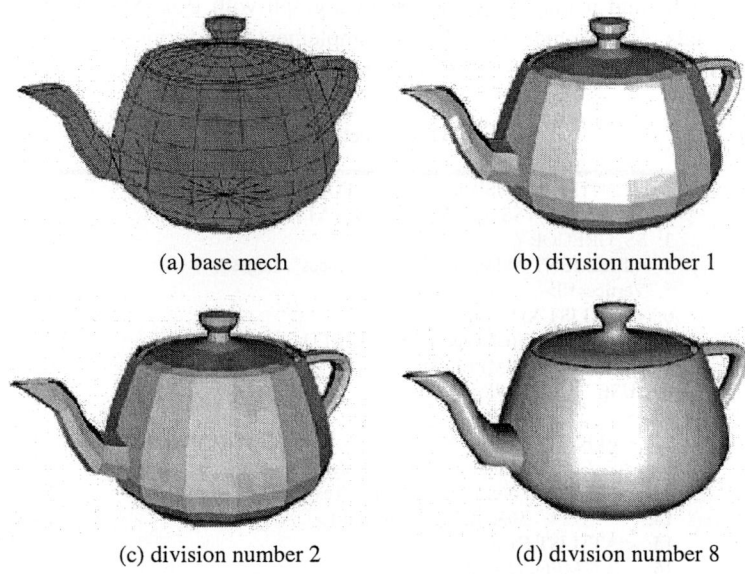

(a) base mech (b) division number 1

(c) division number 2 (d) division number 8

Fig. 6. Demonstrates objects processed with Web3D based on the object presentation

5 Conclusion and Future Study

This paper proposes use of components of 3D graphics with X3D in combination of VRML and XML. The benefits of the proposal are as follows.

First, it provides easiness in X3D execution, better maintainability, and reduced complexity of tools to developers through a set of small core functions. Second, any other functions can be added due to extensibility. Thus new functions or extended functions based on existing one are possible. Third, it is possible to execute results of VRML Working Group on a core browser because of its extensible structure with reusable Web3D Working Group. For example, H-Anim, EAL, Living Worlds or GeoVRML will be elements. Fourth, its reduced amount in coding is a very crucial factor in terms of possibility of a small browser. It is more important when it is on a set top box.

X3D is compatible with VRML97 and is envisaged that it will be integrated with XML. With further developed technology, X3D should be applied in various fields not only the Internet but also broadcast in adoption with audio/video streaming.

Acknowledgement. This study was supported by research funds from Chosun University, 2001 in Korea.

References

1. VRML97, International Standard: ISO/IEC 14772-1, December, 1997. http://www.vrml.org/Specifications/VRML97/index.html.
2. Tim Bary, et. al. XML 1.0 Specification.
3. W. Ihlenfeldt. Visualizing Chemical Data in the Internet Data Driven and Interactive Graphic. Computers and Graphics, 22(6):703-714, 1999.
4. International Standard ISO/IEC Virtual Reality Modeling Language, 1997.
5. Jon Bosak, Tim Bary, XML and the Second-Generation Web. Scientific American, May 1999
6. Danicl Lipkin. Integrating XML and VRML : A Technical Discussion.
7. World Wide Web Consortium: Extensible Markup Language(XML) http://www.w3.org/XML/(2000).

Motion Vector Recovery by Surrounding Region Matching Based on Gradient Difference

Dong-Wook Kim[1], Eung-Kwan Kang[2], Jin-Tae Kim[3],
Yong-In Yoon[4], and Jong-Soo Choi[4]

[1] Dept. Telecommunication Eng., Jeonju Univ., Chunbuk 560-759, Korea
[2] Dept. Multimedia Eng., Jeonju Univ., Chunbuk 560-759, Korea
{dwkim, kwan}@jj.ac.kr
[3] Dept. Computer & Information Sci., Hanseo Univ., Chungnam 356-756, Korea
jtkim@hanseo.ac.kr
[4] Dept. Image Eng., Graduate School of Advanced Imaging Science,
Multimedia, and Film, Chung-Ang University,
Seoul 156-756, Korea
{yoonyi, jschoi}@imagelab.cau.ac.kr

Abstract. The error concealment is a very useful technique for real-time communication systems, such as video conferencing. In this paper, we propose an error concealment technique designated to minimize discontinuities between block boundaries in consideration of the fact that the human visual system is sensitive to discontinuities. Error concealment for each loss block is performed by surrounding region matching of the loss block based on gradient difference. By computer simulation, the performance improvement for the proposed technique is shown to be superior than 1.32 dB in terms of the PSNR, in comparison with the conventional techniques.

1 Introduction

Due to the congestion in the transmission of video over the Internet or other networks, packets may be lost. In order to cope with transmission errors, several techniques have been proposed. When loss occurs while video signal is transmitted, retransmission way of a lost packet is used widely. However, in the bi-directional real-time communication systems such as video conferencing, the retransmission method can cause large delays. Therefore, in the case of the real-time bi-directional communication of image or voice, error concealment methods at the receiver end offer a better result than methods based on retransmission [1-3].

In video coding based on motion compensated prediction, the motion vector information is a very important factor. If the motion vectors of a frame are lost or received with errors, the frame is corrupted. In this paper, a new method of recovering lost motion vector is proposed.

2   Proposed Method for Motion Vector Recovery

The simplest recovery method for lost vectors involves the replacement of the lost blocks with the corresponding blocks from the previous frame. This temporal extrapolation works quite well in still parts of the picture but fails in areas containing moving objects. In general, the efficiency of this method decreases as the speed of the moving object increases.

In previous works, the overlapped motion compensation techniques and the side match criterion were proposed to take advantage of spatial pixel correlation. The side match criterion finds the best-matched motion-compensated block using one of the motion vectors of the surrounding blocks with the minimum gray-level transition across the four boundaries and replaces the lost blocks with pixel blocks of the previous frame shifted by the obtained motion vector [3-4]. The picture quality so obtained is greatly improved but the performance deteriorates when the neighboring blocks have different motion vectors, such as in the case of blocks belonging to the edges of moving objects. Moreover, this method still requires the delivery of the motion vectors of the neighboring blocks. However, if the motion vectors of the neighboring blocks include errors or are lost, the recovered blocks subjectively appear large blocking effects. In order to solve these problems, a surrounding region matching technique is proposed in this paper.

Let's the macro block with a size of M×N at location (i,j) in the frame k be denoted by $B_k(i,j)$ as shown Fig. 1. In this paper, we refer to the oblique region of Fig. 1 as the surrounding region of $B_k(i,j)$. When the block $B_k(i,j)$ is lost, in order to find the best match for it from among the blocks contained in the previous frame, a motion estimation method using the surrounding region $S_k(i,j)$ is introduced in this paper. In other words, in this method, the reference region for motion estimation is the surrounding region $S_k(i,j)$.

In motion compensated video coding, motion vectors are mostly obtained by means of a block matching algorithm (BMA). As the evaluation function in the BMA, the sum of the absolute differences is widely used. However, BMA based on the absolute sum is liable to induce several types of error. As an example, let us consider the case of two pairs of one-dimensional signals whose grey-value distributions are represented by Fig. 2 (a) and (b), respectively. Let us examine the differences between signal (a) and signal (b) of Fig. 2 using the sum of the absolute difference. In both cases, the average values of the absolute differences between the two signals are 20 within the range given in Fig. 2. Namely, the absolute differences between the two signals have the same average value both in the case of Fig. 2 (a) and (b). However, as regards the similarity between the two signals, the two signals in Fig. 2(a) are more similar than those in Fig. 2(b). That is, the two signals in Fig. 2(a) have almost the same pattern.

In this paper, we propose a new evaluation function called the Surrounding Region Matching Criterion (SRMC) for the purpose of region matching based on gradient differences, in order to minimize the discontinuity between the block boundaries. Its role is to calculate the gradient difference between adjacent pixels.

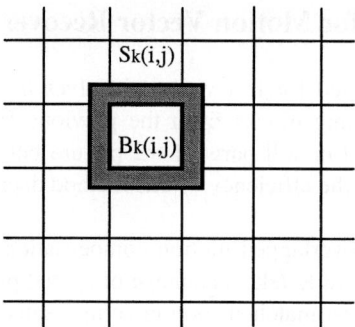

Fig. 1. Surrounding region of a block

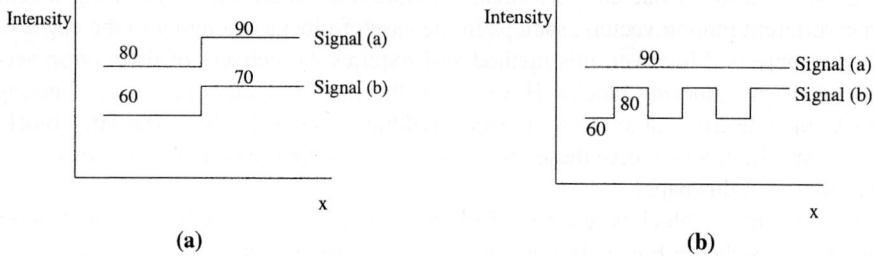

Fig. 2. Signal patterns

The new evaluation function is defined as follows:
$$SRMC(i,j) = a_1 MSE(i,j) + a_2 DOG(i,j) \tag{1}$$
where, $MSE(i,j)$ and $DOG(i,j)$ are
$$MSE(i,j) = \frac{1}{R}\sum_{p,q \in R} I_k(p,q) - I_{k-1}(p+i,q+j) \tag{2}$$

$$DOG(i,j) = \frac{1}{R}\sum_{p,q \in R}(\frac{\partial I_k(p,q)}{\partial x} - \frac{\partial I_{k-1}(p+i,q+j)}{\partial x})^2 +$$
$$\frac{1}{R}\sum_{p,q \in R}(\frac{\partial I_k(p,q)}{\partial y} - \frac{\partial I_{k-1}(p+i,q+j)}{\partial y})^2 \tag{3}$$

Where, I_k is the current frame and I_{k-1} is the previous frame. In Equation (1), a_1 and a_2 have constant values. In Equation (2), R is the area size of the surrounding region. In order to minimize the influence of noise, simplified forms of the differential factors, $\frac{\partial I}{\partial x}$ and $\frac{\partial I}{\partial y}$, defined in Equation (3) are used. These simplified forms are described in Equation (4) as follows:

$$\text{if } \frac{\partial I}{\partial x} > 0, \frac{\partial I}{\partial x} = 1$$

$$\text{else if } \frac{\partial I}{\partial x} < 0, \quad \frac{\partial I}{\partial x} = -1 \tag{4}$$

$$\text{else} \quad \frac{\partial I}{\partial x} = 0$$

Using the SRMC, motion estimation is performed for each reference region corresponding to lost block, and the vector so obtained is regarded as the recovered vector.

3 Proposed Method for Motion Vector Recovery

In order to demonstrate its performance, simulations were performed for the proposed algorithm using several image sequences. Methods used for comparison in experiment are as follows.

- Method-1: Replaces the lost block with the corresponding block to the same coordinates of previous frame.
- Method-2: Side match criterion method [3]
- Method-3: The conventional method [4]

The format of the images is 720×480, and the size of the search range is ±20. The macro block size used for motion estimation is the 16×16. We assume a block loss rate of 7.5%. In this case, losses occur in about 100 macro blocks among 1350 macro blocks for one frame, and this is set up so that in each case five successive blocks are lost. Also, the constants a_1 and a_2 of the Equation (1) have values of 1 and 2, respectively.

The image qualities obtained using the various techniques are summarized in Table 1. In Table 1, no-loss refers to the case where no blocks are lost. For the 'Football' sequence, the performance improvements for the proposed algorithm range from 0.98 dB to 1.32 dB on the average in comparison with the method 2 and the method 3, respectively. For the 'Mobile' sequence, the proposed algorithm provides performance improvements of 0.49 dB and 1.30 dB on the average in comparison with the method 2 and the method 3, respectively.

Table 1. Simulation results (average qualities, dB)

Image	Football	Mobile
No-loss	36.38	37.55
Method-1	27.68	28.98
Method-2	32.25	34.97
Method-3	32.59	35.78
Proposed Method	33.57	36.27

Fig. 3 is shows the simulation results of the proposed algorithm. Compared with the 'Mobile' sequence, the 'Football' sequence involves a great deal of movement. From the simulation results, it can be seen that when the movement of the object is large, the proposed technique is more effective.

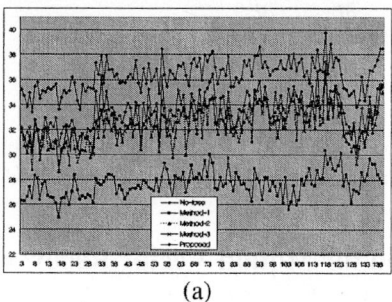

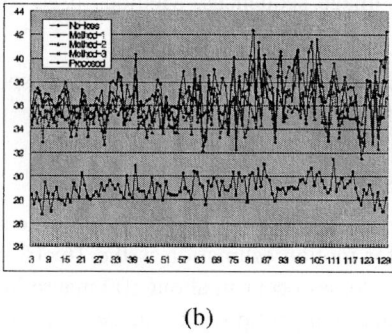

Fig. 3. Results of computer simulation (a) 'Football' sequence (b) 'Mobile' sequence

4 Conclusion

In this paper, we proposed an error concealment technique designed to minimize the discontinuity between block boundaries. The proposed algorithm is more effective in case of images that include fast moving objects. In the simulation result, the performance improvement of the proposed technique in comparison with the conventional technique was found to be 1.32 dB on the average.

References

1. Y. Wang and Q. F. Zhu, Error control and concealment for video communication: A review, *Proceedings of the IEEE*, vol. 86, no. 5, May 1998.
2. W-J. Chu and J-J. Leou, Detection and concealment of transmission errors in H.261 images, *IEEE Trans. Cir. and Sys. for Video Technology*, vol. 8, no. 1, pp. 248–258, Feb. 1998.
3. P. Salama, N. B. Shroff, and E. J. Delp, Error Concealment in Encoded Video, *IEEE Journal on Selected Areas in Communications*, vol. 18, no. 6, pp. 1129–1141, Jun. 2000
4. M-J. Chen, L-G. Chen, and R-M. Weng, Error concealment of lost motion vectors with overlapped motion compensation, *IEEE Trans. Cir. and Sys. for Video Technology*, vol. 7, no. 3, pp. 560–563, Jun. 1997.

Computer Generated Holographic Image Processing for Information Security

Kyu B. Doh[1], Kyeongwha Kim[1], and Ting-C Poon[2]

[1] Department of Telecommunication Engineering, Hankuk Aviation University,
200-1 Hwajeon-dong, Goyang-city 412-791, Korea
kdoh@hangkong.ac.kr

[2] Bradley Department of Electrical and Computer Engineering,
Virginia Polytechnic Institute and State University, Blacksburg, Virginia 24061,USA

Abstract. We propose a method for information security technique using computer generated holographic image processing. Using encryption key factors, computer generated holographic image and Fourier plane phase mask, an image or document to be secured is encrypted by digital holographic image encoding processor. The proposed image encryption technique can also be used for wireless application in real-time. For the use of real-time wireless application, the encrypted information is required to be stored as electrical signal. For reconstruction of the encrypted image in secure site, the encrypted image is, together with a decryption key, processed and sent to a decryption processor unit. If the encryption key and decryption key are matched, the decryption unit will decrypt the image. We present computer simulation of the idea.

1 Introduction

Due to the resent progress in the development of optical component and systems and their increased technical performance, optical cryptography suggests that it has significant potential for security application. The application of optical security technique to information encryption and decryption are a topic of growing interest. Several studies have been published on the digital holographic processing techniques for information security [1-7]. One of the reasons of using holographic encryption is that holographic encryption as opposed to electronic or digital encryption can provide many degrees of freedom for securing information. Another reason is that the encrypted information is difficult to reproduce with the usual reproduction device. When large volumes of information are to be encrypted, such as a 3-D object, the use of holographic encryption methods is probably the most logical choice. We aim in the present paper to propose a computer generated holographic image processor for information security. The method is based on two-pupil synthesis processor [8]. Advantages of the method include that method is easily extendible to encrypt 3-D image. In section 2 we discuss how to perform encryption and decryption with digital holographic method for information security and also provide computer simulation results to demonstrate the validity of the idea. We then give concluding remarks.

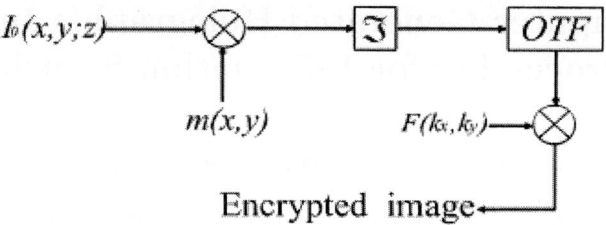

Fig. 1. Computer generated holographic image processor unit for encryption

2 Encryption and Decryption

We shall describe the computer generated holographic image processor for information security in the encryption stage as well as in the decryption stage. The holographic system is based on the two-pupil synthesis processor [8], which has been used extensively for various fields of electro-optic applications [9-13]. We now focus on describing the digital holographic encryption and decryption operation with the results of the processor. The computer generated holographic image processor unit for encryption is shown in Fig. 1. Let $I_0(x, y; z)$ denote the image to be encrypted and $F(k_x, k_y)$ denote the Fourier random phase mask. The input random phase mask, $m(x, y)$, is bonded with the image. To perform encryption on input $I_0(x, y; z)$, we use the Optical Transfer Function (OTF) of the two-pupil synthesis optical processor to apply the proposed encryption technique. The image to be encrypted is coded by a time-dependent Fresnel plate (TDFP). TDFP is created by the superposition of a plane wave with Fourier plane random phase key and a spherical wave of different temporal frequency. As we see that the choice of a Fourier plane random phase mask is a good encryption key. For this choice of the mask, according to [8], we have expression:

$$OTF(k_x, k_y) = \exp\left[j\frac{z}{2k_0}(k_x^2 + k_y^2)\right] \quad (1)$$

It can be shown that the spectrum of $i(x, y; z)$ is related to the spectrum of $I_0(x, y)$ through the following expression:

$$\begin{aligned}\Im\{i(x,y;z)\} &= \Im\{I_0(x,y;z)m(x,y)\}OTF(k_x,k_y;z)F(k_x,k_y)\\ &= [\Im\{I_0(x,y;z)\} \otimes \Im\{m(x,y)\}]OTF(k_x,k_y;z)F(k_x,k_y) \quad (2)\end{aligned}$$

where $\otimes$ denotes 2-D convolution, and (2) then becomes:

$$\begin{aligned}i(x,y;z) &= \Im^{-1}[\Im\{I_0(x,y;z)m(x,y)\}OTF(k_x,k_y;z)F(k_x,k_y)]\\ &= \Im^{-1}[[\Im\{I_0(x,y;z)\} \otimes \Im\{m(x,y)\}]OTF(k_x,k_y;z)F(k_x,k_y)] \quad (3)\end{aligned}$$

$i(x, y; z)$ is the encrypted image and can be stored by the digital computer. We can interpret equation (3) as the random phase masked image being encrypted by Fourier plane random phase mask and then the encrypted information is being recorded as a digital hologram. Figure 2 shows the original information of document to be encrypted with the simulated dimension of about $2cm$ by $2cm$. Figure 3 shows the encrypted information of the document performed according to (3). The following parameters are chosen that the wavelength of

Fig. 2. Original input image   **Fig. 3.** Encrypted information of image

light used is $0.6\mu m$, the document to be encrypted $I_0(x,y)$, has simulated depth information of $30cm$ away from the reference. Figure 4 shows the real part of the phase key. After the object has been encrypted, we need to decrypt it. For decryption, since the system is hybrid in nature, it is flexible and either optical decryption or digital decryption could be employed with the system. We let $F_d(k_x, k_y)$ denote as a decryption key. The information is now stored in the digital computer to be used to decrypt the information coming from the encryption site via transmission. To decrypt the image from (3), we provide the use of a digital decryption unit that is basically reversal processing of the digital holographic encryption unit shown in figure 1. We see that the output of the unit, $I_d(x,y)$ as follows:

$$\begin{aligned}I_d(x,y) &= \Im^{-1}\big[[\Im\{I_0(x,y;z)\} \otimes \Im\{m(x,y)\}]\\ &\quad \times OTF(k_x,k_y;z)OTF^*(k_x,k_y;z)F(k_x,k_y)F_d(k_x,k_y)\}\big]\\ &= \Im^{-1}[\Im\{I_0(x,y;z)m(x,y)\}]\\ &= I_0(x,y)m(x,y)\end{aligned} \quad (4)$$

Provided that $F(k_x, k_y) \cdot F_d(k_x, k_y) = 1$, and the digital holographic reconstruction is in focus. Condition allows us choose the functional form of the encryption key, $F(k_x, k_y)$, and the decryption key, $F_d(k_x, k_y)$, in each stages. It is apparent that the choice of phase keys would work. Figure 5 shows the decrypted information of image processed without decryption key. Since the decrypted information also has a holographic information as well, the depth information, z, play a role as an additional security key as shown in Figure 6. Figure 7 shows the intensity of decrypted information of image.

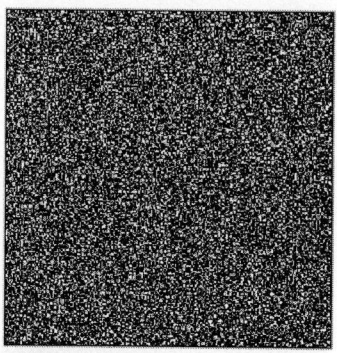 

Fig. 4. Real part of the phase key

Fig. 5. Decrypted information of image without phase key

3 Concluding Remarks

In summary, we have discussed computer generated holographic image processor and its application to information security technique. We propose coding method for information security using digital holographic cryptography. In pro-

Fig. 6. Decrypted information of image with wrong depth information

Fig. 7. Decrypted information of image

posed method, the image to be encrypted is coded by a time-dependent Fresnel plate (TDFP). TDFP is created by the superposition of a plane wave with Fourier plane random phase key and a spherical wave of different temporal frequency. The reason of using digital holographic encryption is that holographic encryption as opposed to electronic or digital encryption can provide many degrees of freedom for securing information. Another reason is that the encrypted information is difficult to reproduce with the usual reproduction device. Advantages of the method include that the method is easily extendible to encrypt 3-D information. Another advantage include that the system have a capability of producing the encrypted image in real-time for hardware implementation applications. It is important to point out that the encryption key and the decryption key are of the same functional form and they are actually the same key. The proposed system enables us to store, transmit, and decrypt the encrypted data digitally. The result demonstrates that the technique can be used to encode optical information in a complex, digital holographic pattern that cannot be viewed using conventional amplitude techniques.

The authors express their gratitude for financial support by Regional Research Center of Korea Science and Engineering Foundation ($R12-2001-051-00007-0$).

References

1. Tajahuerce, E., Javidi, B.: Encrypting three-dimensional information with digital holography, Appl. Opt. 39, 6595-6601 (2000)
2. Yoshikawa, N., Itoh, M., Yatagai, T.: Binary computer generated holograms for security applications from a synthetice double-exposure method by electron-beam lithography, Opt. Lett. 23, 1483-1485 (1998)
3. Schnarys, U., Juptner, W.P.O.: Direct recording of holograms by a CCD target and numerical reconstruction, Appl. Opt. 33, 179-181 (1994)
4. Cuche, E., Bevilacqua, F., Depeursinge, C.: Digital holography for quantitative phase-contrast images, Opt. Lett. 24, 291-293 (1999)
5. Javidi, B., Nomura, T.: Securing information by means of digital holography, Opt. Lett. 25, 28-30 (2000)
6. Nomura, T., Javidi, B.: Optical encryption system with a binary key code, App. Opt. 39, 4783-4787 (2000)
7. Javidi, B., Nomura, T.: Securing information by means of digital holography, Opt. Lett. 25, 28-30 (2000)
8. Poon, T.C.: Scanning holography and two-dimensional image processing by acouto-optic two-pupil synthesis, J. Opt. Soc. Am. A 2, 521-527 (1985)
9. Doh, K., Poon, T.C., Indebetouw, G.: Twin-image noise in optical scanning holography, Opt. Eng. Vol. 35, no. 6, 1550-1555 (1996)
10. Doh, K., Poon, T.C., Wu, M., Shinoda, K., Suzuki, Y.: Twin-imgae elimination in optical scanning holography, Optics and Laser Technology, vol. 28, no2, 135-141 (1996)
11. Poon, T.C., Qi, Ying: Novel real-time joint-transform correlation by use of acousto-optic heterodyning, App. Opt. 42, 4663-4669 (2003)
12. Kim, T., Poon, T.C., Indebetouw, G.: Depth detection and image recovery in remote sensing by optical scanning holography, Opt. Eng. 41(6), 1331-1338 (2002)
13. Schilling, B.W., Templeton, G.C.: Three-dimensional remote sensing by optical scanning holography, App. Opt. 40, 5474-5481 (2001)

A Nonparametric Skin Color Model for Face Detection from Color Images[1]

Kyongpil Min[1], Junchul Chun[1], and Goorack Prak[2]

[1] Department of Computer Science, Kyonggi University, Yui-Dong Suwon, Korea
{cabbi, jcchun}@kyonggi.ac.kr
http://giplab.kyonggi.ac.kr
[2] Department of Computer Science, Kongju National University, Kongju, Korea
ecgrpark@kongju.ac.kr

Abstract. This paper presents a novel approach to extract face and facial feature points from color image automatically based on a nonparametric skin color model. Most of introduced skin color models for face detection have lack of robustness for varying lighting conditions and need extra work to reduce such problem. To resolve the limitation of current skin color model, we utilize the Hue-Tint chrominance model and represent the skin chrominance distribution as a linear equation. Thus, the facial color distribution is simply described as a combination of the maximum and minimum values of Hue and Tint components. The decision rule to detect skin region is simplified by measuring the distance between the skin chrominance distribution function and measured input chrominance. In order to extract facial feature points defined by MPEG-4, the minimal facial feature positions detected by the skin color model are subsequently adjusted by using edge information from the detected facial region along with the proportions of the face. The experiments show that the proposed method guarantees fast and exact processing for face and facial feature point generation and is robust to various lighting conditions and input images.

1 Introduction

Human face information has been widely used in security system, criminal identifications, teleconference, 3D avatar, human computer interface and so on. The analysis of facial information has been one of the challenging problems in computer vision field. Especially, the facial region and feature detection is considered a critical work for developing various face recognition and face modeling systems. However, due to variations in illumination, background, and facial expression, the face detection and recognition have complex problems.

Many of the works to detect facial region can be broadly classified as feature-based methods and image-based methods [1]. The feature-based methods make explicit use of face knowledge and follow the classical detection methodology in which low-level

---

[1] This work as supported by grant No. (R01-2002-000-00010-0) from Basic Research Program of Korea Science and Engineering (KOSEF).

features are derived prior to knowledge-based analysis. Skin color segmentation can be performed using appropriate skin color thresholds where skin color is modeled through histograms. Skin color model, which are very efficient for detecting face from color images, have some difficulties in robust detection of skin colors in the presence of complex background and light variations [2]. Active contour models depict the actual physical and hence higher-level appearance of features. Once released within a close proximity to a feature, an active shape model will interact with local image features and gradually deform to take the shape of the feature [3]. Meanwhile, most of the image-based approaches apply a window scanning technique for detecting faces[4,5].

In this paper we propose a novel face detection method that is based on Hue-Tint chrominance. The proposed method shows efficiency for detecting face and facial feature points guided by MPEG-4 and is robust to various lighting conditions and input images. The facial feature points are subsequently used to create a realistic 3D face model.

2 A Nonparametric Skin Color Model

Color information is efficient for identifying skin region. In computer vision, since every color spaces have different properties, color space selection is a very important factor for face detection. We need to consider some criteria for selecting an efficient skin color models: how it separates color information with chrominance and luminance data, a chrominance data can describe complex shaped distributions in a given space, and the amount of overlap between the skin and non-skin distributions in that space.

RGB is one of the most widely used color spaces for image processing. But, because it consists of combination chrominance with luminance data, we must transform from RGB into 2D chrominance space to get robustness to changes in illumination conditions. To date, various color models have been proposed for face detection, but many researches do not provide strict justification of their color models. In order to select proper color components for face detection, we plot 2D distribution of the two chrominance data that have often been used for skin detection. In order to plot distribution, we use skin sample images of 14 Asian that consist of dark and light images. Generally, since YCbCr, HSV, and TSL, have been proposed to achieve better color constancy, we select Cb, Cr components of YCbCr, H(hue), S(saturation) components of HSV, and T(tint), s components (we use small letter s in distinction from S component of HSV) of TSL[6].

Figure 1 shows 15 different chrominance spaces. Because skin sample data has 14 different face regions, the most of chrominance space have broad distribution. But, H-T chrominance distribution is denser and easier to be represented by modeling method than other chrominance distribution. And we calculate amount of the intersection between the normalized skin and non-skin histogram to evaluate the degree of overlap between the skin and non-skin distribution. Table 1 illustrates the value of intersection for each chrominance space.

Table 1. Comparison of amount of the intersection between skin and non-skin region

Color space	Intersection ratio	Color space	Intersection ratio
Cb-Cr	0.1311	Cr-H	0.1331
Cb-H	0.1311	Cr-S	0.1182
Cb-S	0.1218	Cr-T	0.1214
Cb-T	0.1218	Cr-s	0.1318
Cb-s	0.1318	H-S	0.1218
H-s	0.1282	S-s	0.1318
H-T	0.1182	T-s	0.1182
S-T	0.1311		

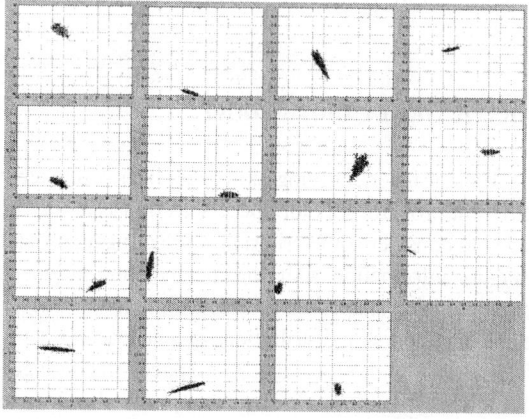

Fig. 1. Histograms in 15 different chrominance spaces of skin sample images. From top to bottom and left to right: Cb-Cr, Cb-H, Cb-S, Cb-T, Cb-s, Cr-H, Cr-S, Cr-T, Cr-s, H-S, H-s, H-T, S-T, S-s and T-s spaces

Once the combination of two chrominance components suitable for skin representation is selected, the function that models skin color distribution should be established. This function has to classify the color distribution into skin field and non-skin field and measures distance of input color value to skin field. In parametric skin modeling method it is common that the skin chrominance distribution is modeled by an elliptical Gaussian joint probability density function. But, because the boundary is defined by training data, in case of skin detection from different training image, a wrong result come out often. Therefore, nonparametric skin modeling methods can be used to evaluate skin color distribution from the training data without deriving an explicit model of the skin color. These methods are fast and independent to the shape of skin distribution.

The chrominance components we select here are Hue and Tint for skin detection. The shape of H-T distribution always looks like a straight line although distribution scatters longer than combinations of other components. We set up two points using the maximum and minimum values of H and T components. The skin chrominance distribution is modeled by a straight line function defined as

$$f(h) = \frac{T_{min} - T_{max}}{H_{max} - H_{min}}(h - H_{min}) + T_{max} \quad , H_{min} \leq h \leq H_{max} \qquad (1)$$

where h denote the H chrominance value of a pixel with coordinates (i, j), the Tmin, Hmin are minimum values of T and H components, the Tmax, Hmax represent the maximum values of T and H components. To detect skin region, a decision rule is used

$$d(x, y) = |f(x) - c(x, y)| \qquad (2)$$

where $c(x, y)$ represents the measured values of the chrominance (H(i, j), T(i, j)) of a pixel with coordinates (i, j) in an image. If equation (4) is less than threshold λ_s, then we call it a face candidate pixel. Threshold value is obtained by comparison of every pixel over the skin samples with $f(c)$.

For facial feature analysis, we divide human face in the middle horizontally and can get two areas that include eyes and mouth respectively. We inspect intensity variation to extract facial features in each area. In face candidate region, intensity of eyes, mouth and eyebrows have lower brightness than other region. The positions of eyes and mouth are determined by searching for minima in the topographic relief. We compute the mean value of every row and then search for minima in x-direction at the minima in the resulting y-relief. In Figure 2, the eyes positions can be acquired if significant minima in x-direction are detected. We can get the mouth position using the same method.

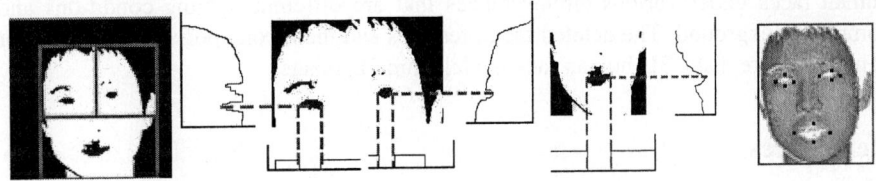

Fig. 2. Face, eyes and mouth position extraction

3 Experimental Results

To evaluate the efficiency of proposed color model to detect facial region, we have applied the model to various color images that are exposed to varing light conditions. For the comparion of the skin color detection results, we both apply the proposed model and decision technique and currently used elliptical Gaussian joint probability density function for other color spaces. Figure 3 shows the skin region detected by proposed method.

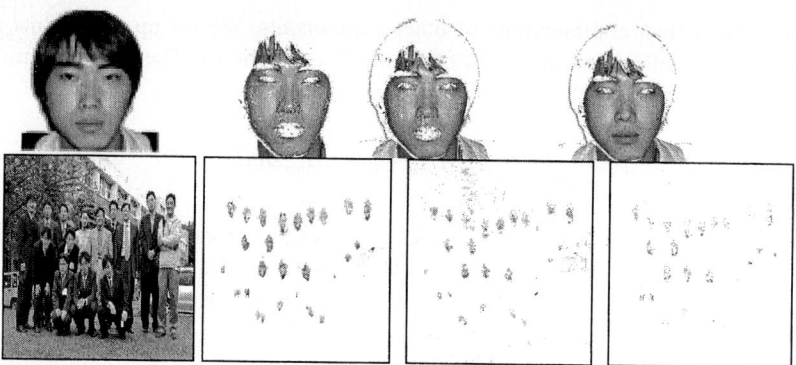

Fig. 3. Skin region detection results. From left to right: Original image, results by H-T, Cb-Cr, T-s chrominance spaces

From the results of all of those cases, we can prove the proposed skin color model efficiently detects skin color region rather than previously introduced skin color models. We apply our facial feature detection technique to 3D face modeling process.

4 Concluding Remark

In this paper, we have introduced a unique method to detect face and facial feature points based on Hue-Tint color model. The proposed method projects color image on Tint-Hue chrominance space and detects skin region by using nonparametric skin model that is defined straight line equation. Based on the evaluation of experimental results, we can prove that the proposed skin color model is suitable to characterize human faces under various circumstances that are different lighting conditions and complex background. The deteted facial features and their exact poistions are used for generating a realistic 3D human face model from 2D images.

References

1. E. Hjelmas, Boon Kee Low, Face detection: A Survey, Computer Vision and Image Understanding, (2001) 236-274
2. D. Maio and Maltoni, "Real-time face location on gray-scale static images," Pattern Recognition, vol. 33, no. 9, (2000) 1525-1539
3. Y. Zhu, S. Schwartz, and M. Orchard, Fast face detection using subspace discriminant wavelet features, in IEEE Conference on Computer Vision and Pattern Recognition, (2000)
4. B. Moghaddam and A. Pentland, Probabilistic visual learning for object representation, IEEE Trans. Pattern Anal. Mach. Intell. 19(1), (1997)
5. E. Viennet and F. Fogelman Soulie, Connectionist methods for human face processing, in Face Recognition: From Theory to Application. Springer-Verlag, Berlin/New York, (1998)
6. Jean-christophe Terrillon, Shigeru Akamatsu, Comparative performance of different chrominance spaces for color segmentation and detection of human faces in complex scene images. In Proceedings of the 12th Conference on Vision Interface, (1999) 180-18

An Efficient Prediction Search Pattern for Half Pixel Motion Estimation

Mi Gyoung Jung

Department of Computer Science, Chonnam National University,
300 Youngbong-dong, Buk-gu, Kwangju 500-757, Korea
mgjung@chonnam.ac.kr

Abstract. Motion Estimation (ME) consists of two steps, the integer pixel motion estimation and the half pixel motion estimation. Many fast integer pixel motion estimation algorithms have been developed to reduce the complexity. However, the half pixel motion estimation requires huge computational complexity. In this paper, We propose an efficient prediction search pattern for half pixel ME. The proposed search pattern reduces the computational overhead by limiting the number of interpolations of the candidate half pixel points based on the cross center-biased distribution property of Motion Vectors (MV) and the correlations between integer pixel MVs and half pixel MVs. Experiments show that the speedup improvement of the proposed algorithm over a full half pixel search (FHPS), horizontal and vertical directions as references (HVDR), chen's half pixel search algorithm (CHPS-1) and a parabolic prediction-based fast half-pixel search (PPHPS) can be up to 1.2 ~ 3.3 times on average and the image quality improvement can be better up to 0.01(dB)~ 0.25(dB).

1 Introduction

ME and motion compensation techniques are important parts of most video encoding, since it could significantly affect the compression ratio and the output quality. A typical motion vector search procedure can be divided in two steps, the integer pixel motion vector estimation and the half pixel motion vector estimation. For the first step, the integer pixel ME, integer pixel points within a search area are examined to find the integer pixel MV. Many low complexity motion estimation algorithms such as Diamond Search (DS) [1, 2], New Three Step Search (NTSS) [3], HEXagon-Based Search (HEXBS) [4], Motion Vector Field Adaptive Search Technique (MVFAST) [5] and Predictive Motion Vector Field Adaptive Search Technique (PMVFAST) [6] have been proposed to reduce the computational complexity. Most recent fast methods for integer ME can find an integer MV by examining less then 10 search points. For the second step, the half pixel ME, FHPS that is a typical method, interpolates integer pixels for half pixels and examines 9 half pixels including integer MV point to determine a half pixel MV. FHPS requires huge computational complexity. Hence, it becomes more meaningful to reduce the computational complexity of half pixel motion estimation. Some fast half pixel motion vector search algorithms have been proposed as follows. In HDVR, which is one of the fast half pixel ME algorithmes, 4 neighboring half pixel points in horizontal and vertical directions around the integer pixel motion vector are examined, and the two best matching points are found for both directions. Then, a diagonal point between the two best matching points is additionally examined [7]. Therefore, 5 search points are to be examined instead of 8 points in HDVR. CHPS-1 [8] only searches 4 horizontal and vertical directions around the integer pixel motion vector. In PPHPS, an sum of absolute differences (SAD) curve around an integer pixel motion vector is modeled as a paraboloid [8]. By using the SAD values of neighboring integer pixel points, the parameters of paraboloid equation are estimated and the SAD values of half pixel points are predicted using the paraboloid equation. Then, the best matching point having the smallest SAD value among candidate points is predicted. Finally, the real SAD values of the predicted point and its two neighboring points are examined to find the final motion vector. Therefore, PPHPS needs to examine 3 search points.

In this paper, we propose an efficient prediction search pattern for half pixel ME based on the property of MVs and the correlations between integer pixel MVs and half pixel MVs. As a result, we reduce the total number of search points used to find the half pixel MV of the current block and improve the motion estimation accuracy.

This paper is organized as follows. Section 2 describes the proposed algorithm. Section 3 reports the simulation results and conclusions are given in Section 4.

2 The Proposed Algorithm

The integer pxel positions and the half pixel positions are shown in Fig. 1(a). In Fig. 1(a), the final integer pixel MV at the integer pixel ME step is C and 8 neighbors of integer pixels with a radius of 1 pixels for C are H_1, H_2, V_1, V_2, D_1, D_2, D_3 and D_4. Also 8 neighbors of half pixels with a radius of 0.5 pixels for C are h_1, h_2, v_1, v_2, d_1, d_2, d_3 and d_4. If the centred integer pixel point (C) is selected as a minimum distance block at the integer pixel search step, then this point and 8 neighbouring interpolated half pixel candidates will be selected at the half pixel search step. The formulas for the half pixel interpolations are shown in Fig. 1(b).

Most of the real-world image sequences have cross center-biased motion vector distributions. Table 1 documents the motion vector distribution probabilities within certain distances from the search window center by exploiting the FS algorithm to three commonly used test image sequences, "Akiyo", "Carphone" and "Table", based on SAD matching criterion. As indicated in Table 1, many motion vectors are located in the center, horizontal and vertical direction rather than in the diagonal direction. We propose an efficient prediction search pattern to estimate the half pixel MV. The proposed method reduces the computational overhead by limiting the number of interpolations of the candidate half pixel points. and based on the property of MVs in Table 1 and the correlations between

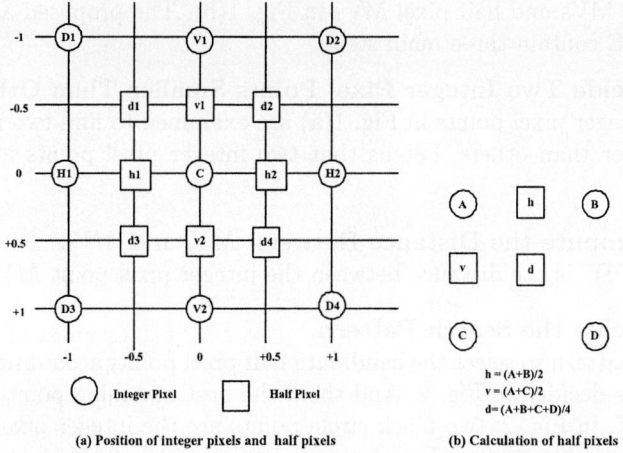

Fig. 1. The position and calculation of half pixel

Table 1. The motion vector distribution probabilities

	Akiyo	Carphone	Table
the zero radius	97.00%	73.73%	59.42%
the one radius	2.34%	15.70%	17.70%
the two radius	0.44%	4.88%	6.51%
the three radius	0.13%	1.72%	3.37%
cross	97.08%	72.52%	65.38%
diagonal	2.92%	27.48%	34.62%

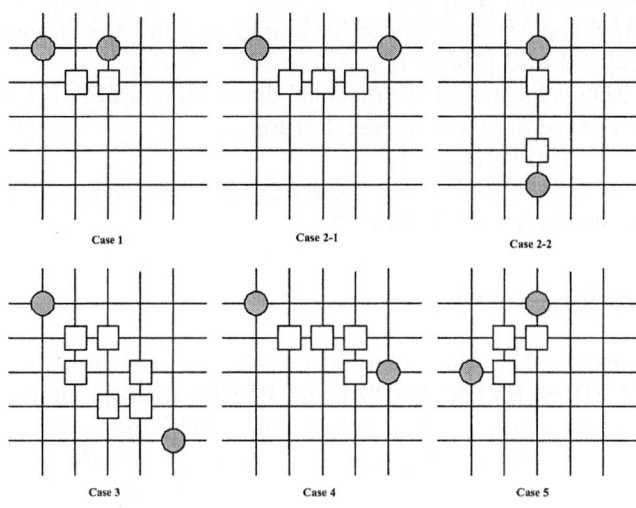

Fig. 2. The search pattern according to the case of distance

integer pixel MVs and half pixel MVs in Fig. 1(b). The proposed algorithm for half pixel ME contain three main steps.

Step 1. Decide Two Integer Pixel Points Smaller Than Others.
SAD of 8 integer pixel points in Fig. 1(a) are examined to find two integer pixel points smaller than others. Let us that two integer pixel points are MV_i and MV_j.

Step 2. Compute the Distance Between MV_i and MV_j.
Let us that "D" is the distance between the integer pixel point MV_i and MV_j

Step 3. Decide the Search Pattern.
The search pattern to select the candidate half pixel points according to the type of distance is decided in Fig. 2. And then, the best matching point is chosen as the final MV. In Fig. 2, two black circle points are the integer pixel point MV_i and MV_j and white rectangle points are the candidate half pixel points. The search pattern is categorized in five cases according to the type of distance.

Case 1: ($|Dx| = 0$ and $|Dy| = 1$) or ($|Dx| = 1$ and $|Dy| = 0$)
In this case, MV_i and MV_j are the adjacent points in case 1 of Fig. 2. For example, if D_1 and V_1 in Fig. 1(a) are two integer pixel points smaller than others, the candidate half pixel points are d_1 and v_1, i.e., The candidate half pixel points correspond to the integer pixel points.
Case 2: ($|Dx| = 2$ and $|Dy| = 0$) or ($|Dx| = 0$ and $|Dy| = 2$)
Case 2 divide into case 2-1 and case 2-2. In case 2-1, MV_i and MV_j are located in the axis of "X" or the axis of "Y" and the distance with 2 in case 2-1 of Fig. 2. This search pattern needs to examine 3 search points. In case 2-2, MV_i and MV_j are located in the horizontal or vertical direction and the distance with 2 in case 2-2 of Fig. 2.
Case 3: ($|Dx| = 2$ and $|Dy| = 2$)
In this case, MV_i and MV_j are located in the diagonal direction in case 3 of Fig. 2.
Case 4: ($|Dx| = 2$ and $|Dy| = 1$)
In this case, MV_i is located in the diagonal direction and MV_j is located in the horizontal or vertical direction in case 4 of Fig. 2.
Case 5: ($|Dx| = 1$ and $|Dy| = 1$)
In this case, MV_i is located in the horizontal direction and MV_j is located in the vertical direction in case 5 of Fig. 2.

3   Simulation Result

In this section, we show the experiment results for the proposed algorithm. We compared FHPS, HVDR, CHPS-1 and PPHPS with the proposed method in both image quality and search speed. Nine QCIF test sequences are used for the experiment: Akiyo, Carphone, Claire, Foreman, Mother and Daughter, Salesman, Table, Stefan and Suzie. The mean square error (MSE) distortion function is used as the block distortion measure (BDM). The quality of the predicted image is measured by the peak signal to noise ratio (PSNR), which is defined by

$$MSE = \left(\frac{1}{MN}\right) \sum_{m=1}^{M} \sum_{n=1}^{N} [x(m,n) - \hat{x}(m,n)]^2 \qquad (1)$$

$$PSNR = 10 \, log_{10} \frac{255^2}{MSE} \qquad (2)$$

In Eq. (1), $x(m,n)$ denotes the original image and $\hat{x}(m,n)$ denotes the reconstructed image. From Table 2 and 3, we can see that the proposed method is better than FHPS, HVDR, CHPS-1 and PPHPS in terms of the computational complexity (as measured by the average number of search points per motion vector) and is better than CHPS-1 and PPHPS in terms of PSNR of the predicted image. In terms of PSNR, the proposed method is about $0.01 \sim 0.08$ (dB) better than HVDR and about 0.01(dB)$\sim$ 0.2(dB) compare with CHPS-1 and PPHPS

Table 2. Average PSNR of the test image sequence

Integer-pel ME method	Full Search				
Half-pel Method	FHSM	HVDR	CHPS-1	PPHPS	Proposed
Akiyo	35.374	35.227	35.319	35.046	35.295
Carphone	32.213	32.161	32.181	32.172	32.225
Claire	35.694	35.619	35.655	35.466	35.629
Foreman	31.020	30.940	30.952	30.880	30.962
M&D	32.482	32.398	32.420	32.317	32.444
Salesman	33.706	33.611	33.662	33.514	33.699
Table	32.909	32.843	32.863	32.716	32.878
Stefan	28.095	28.054	28.063	27.934	28.069
Suzie	34.276	34.209	34.262	34.140	34.281
Average	32.863	32.785	32.820	32.687	32.831

Table 3. Average number of search points per half pixel motion vector estimation

Integer-pel ME method	Full Search				
Half-pel Method	FHSM	HVDR	CHPS-1	PPHPS	Proposed
Akiyo	8	5	4	3	2.31
Carphone	8	5	4	3	2.49
Claire	8	5	4	3	2.27
Foreman	8	5	4	3	3.10
M&D	8	5	4	3	2.51
Salesman	8	5	4	3	2.28
Table	8	5	4	3	2.40
Stefan	8	5	4	3	2.29
Suzie	8	5	4	3	2.47
Average	8	5	4	3	2.46

in Table 2. In terms of the average number of search points per MV, experiments in Table 3 show that the speedup improvement of the proposed algorithm over FHPS, HVDR, CHPS-1 and PPHPS can be up to 1.2 ∼ 3.3 times on average. As a result, we can estimate MV fast and accurately.

4 Conclusion

In this paper, we propose an efficient prediction search pattern for the half pixel ME. The proposed method reduces the computational overhead by limiting the number of interpolations of the candidate half pixel points. and makes an accurate estimate of the half pixel MV based on the cross center-biased distribution property of MVs and the correlations between integer pixel MVs and half pixel MVs. As a result, we reduce the total number of search points used to find the half pixel MV of the current block and improve the ME accuracy.

References

1. Tham, J.Y., Ranganath, S., Kassim, A.A.: A Novel Unrestricted Center-Biased Diamond Search Algorithm for Block Motion Estimation. IEEE Transactions on Circuits and Systems for Video Technology. **8(4)** (1998) 369–375
2. Shan, Z., Kai-kuang, M.: A New Diamond Search Algorithm for Fast block Matching Motion Estimation.IEEE Transactions on Image Processing. **9(2)** (2000) 287–290
3. Renxiang, L., Bing, Z., Liou, M.L.: A New Three Step Search Algorithm for Block Motion Estimation. IEEE Transactions on Circuits and Systems for Video Technology. **4(4)** (1994) 438–442
4. Zhu, C., Lin, X., Chau, L.P.: Hexagon based Search Pattern for Fast Block Motion Estimation. IEEE Transactions on Circuits and Systems for Video Technology. **12(5)** (2002) 349–355
5. Ma, K.K., Hosur, P.I.: Report on Performance of Fast Motion using Motion Vector Field Adaptive Search Technique. ISO/IEC/JTC1/SC29/WG11.**M5453** (1999)
6. Tourapis, A.M., Au, O.C., Liou, M.L.: Optimization Model Version 1.0, ISO/IEC JTC1/SC29/WG11 **M5866** (2000).
7. K.H., Lee, J.H., Choi, B.K., Lee and D.G., Kim: Fast Two-step Half-Pixel Accuracy Motion Vector Prediction. Electronics Letters, **36**, (2000) 625–627
8. C., Du and Y., He: A Comparative Study of Motion Estimation for Low Bit Rate Video Coding. VCIP2000, **4067(3)**, (2000) 1239–1249

Analysis of Functional MRI Image Using Independent Component Analysis

Minfen Shen[1], Weiling Xu[1], Jinxia Huang[1], and Patch Beadle[2]

[1] Key Lab. of Guangdong, Shantou University, Guangdong 515063, China
mfshen@stu.edu.cn
[2] School of System Engineering, Portsmouth University, Portsmouth, U.K.

Abstract. To understand how the brain functions work and assist the diagnosis of the brain diseases, functional magnetic resonance imaging (fMRI) has been widely used. This paper proposes an effective scheme to deal with the issue of identifying the functional signals and suppress the background noise by using independent component analysis (ICA) technique. The fastICA is discussed and applied to solve the problem of blind separation of the source functional signals. Finally, an example with the real fMRI data set was carried out in terms of the proposed method. The experimental result demonstrated the effectiveness and the robustness of the ICA and the related blind source separation approach.

1 Introduction

More and more attentions are paid to analyzing the brain images from many imaging modalities for the purposes of well understanding how the brain functions work and assisting the diagnosis of the brain diseases [1,2]. One of important functional brain imaging modalities is the functional magnetic resonance imaging which provides useful functional information regarding the neural activities under certain sensory or cognitive tasks designed. Based on the changes of the local blood supply for active neurons, fMRI provides the brain imaging data from the whole brain with a very high resolution, which carries the spatio-temporal information of the brain responses activated with some kinds of external cognitive tasks.

With a point of view in signal processing, fMRI signals are inevitably contaminated with background noises such as electrophysiological signals, electrical noises of the system and other environmental artifacts [3]. To detect the functional activities, the common method widely used is the correlation approach which statistically compares the fMRI signals of each brain voxel with the input stimulation to construct the functional maps. In order to correct the multiple comparisons and spatial correlations, the statistical maps are further investigated by employing some methods like statistical parametric mapping (SPM). However, before performing the correlation, it is necessary to preprocess the fMRI signals using effective denoising technique to suppress the additive background noises. For this purpose, this paper applies independent component analysis to identify the functional signals and suppress the other background noise [4].

2 The Method Based on ICA

ICA and closely related blind source separation (BSS) have received a lot of interests in statistical signal processing and other applications [5,6]. There are many motivating reasons to use ICA for studying the fMRI data set. First, ICA can effectively resist the strong background noises based on the fact that ICA only requires the condition of the source signals being statistically independent. Moreover, ICA does not need the precise knowledge of the system's parameters as the estimation is just based on the higher-order statistics of the given signals. As a result, some robustness against the methods using erroneous parameter estimation can be obtained in terms of ICA technique. Finally, ICA enables to suppress Gaussian noise and separate mutually independent non-Gaussian signal.

The principle of ICA is briefly described for brain imaging problems. We assume the received signal can be defined as

$$f(t) = \mathbf{A}s(t) + n(t) \tag{1}$$

where $f(t)$ denotes a vector of the observed signals with zero-mean value. $s(t)$ represents n source signals from the pure observed brain signal with no more than one Gaussian process. $n(t)$ indicates the background noise added in the received signals. The matrix $\mathbf{A}$ is defined as a full column rank. In fact, the matrix $\mathbf{A}$ means a linear mixing of the source signals involved in the collected signal $f(t)$. The aim is to identify the source signals from the observed signals and the unknown mixing matrix. As we know, if the joint probability density function of a series of processes can be represented as the product of the marginal density function, these processes are regarded to be statistically independent with each other. If the background noise is independent of the source signals, the task of estimating the source signals consist of identifying the demixing matrix $\mathbf{W}$ by no means of information regarding the mixing matrix. Thus we can estimate the source signal via the following relation:

$$\hat{s}(t) = \mathbf{W}f(t) \tag{2}$$

ICA enables to obtain the result that the demixing matrix converges to a fixed value which has the same value as the pseudo-inverse of the mixing matrix such that

$$\mathbf{W} = (\mathbf{A}^T \mathbf{A})^{-1} \mathbf{A}^T \tag{3}$$

With the higher-order statistics or second-order statistics of the source signals, ICA became one of effective procedure for BBS of the observed noisy signal [6]. For the problem of fMRI signal processing, the main task is focused on canceling the additive noise and detecting the location of the brain functional activities. Based on the discussion above, ICA can be used to perform the separation of the source signals which reflect the brain functional activities. The fastICA algorithm is used in this contribution for the purpose of source separation [7,8]. Therefore, the background noises can be effectively suppressed and the source signals are significantly detected, which enables to construct the corresponding functional maps.

3 Results and Discussion

The real fMRI data consist of the source component and the noise components, which can be expressed with a noisy ICA model as in (1). To show the ability of ICA technique, an example was carried out in this section. Fig.1 shows the BSS results of the fMRI signal with an activated voxel by using the fastICA algorithm. Fig.1 (a) demonstrated two observed signals before performing the BSS while Fig.1 (b) provided the significant result of the signals after separating the observed signals. This procedure was carried out for each voxel of the brain area. To perform the multiple comparisons and spatial correlations [9], the automatic threshold was proposed to detect the functional areas of the brain. Each activation area detected was projected to the locating image mapping with interpolation technique. Fig.2 demonstrates the corresponding results of the functional activation area with pseudocolors under four different thresholds changing from 0.3 to 0.6. The red color indicates the highest degree of the functional activation induced from the external stimulation. The result shows the success of the robustness by using ICA technique in detecting the functional activation areas.

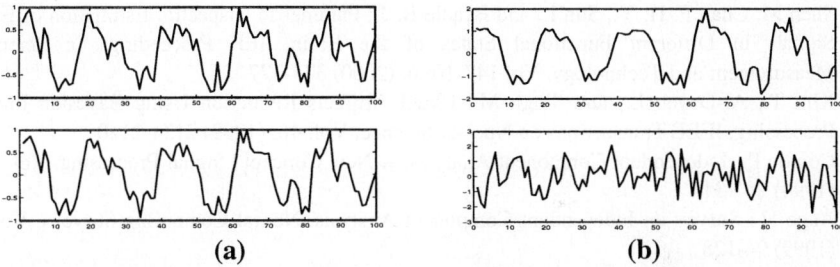

Fig. 1. Two observed signals before performing the BSS (a) and the result after separating the observed signals using ICA (b)

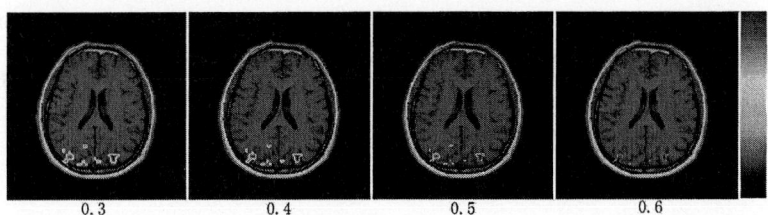

Fig. 2. The experiment result of functional activation areas detected with different thresholds

4 Conclusions

In this paper, we considered the problem of separating sources from the observe signals by means of ICA approach. The algorithm of fastICA with real valued data was proposed to identify the demixing matrix and the source signals. We focused on the application of ICA method to the detection of the brain functional activation areas. The problems of both background noise suppression and the functional activities allocation were also discussed. Real fMRI data were analyzed to prove that the proposed method can effectively improve the detection ability. The robustness of detecting the functional activation areas was also demonstrated.

Acknowledgements

The research was supported by the Natural Science Foundation of China (60271023), the Natural Science Foundation of Guangdong (021264 and 32025) and the Key Grant of the Education Ministry of China (02110).

References

1. Enzhong L. and Xuchu W.: Asymmetry of Brain Function Activity: fMRI Study Under Language and Music Stimulation. Chinese Medical Journal, Vol. 2. Chinese Medical Association Publishing House, Beijing (2000) 154-158
2. Shen M, Chan F. H. Y., Sun L, and Beadle B. J.: Parametric Bispectral Estimation of EEG Signals in Different Functional States of the Brain, IEE Proceedings in Science, Measurement and Technology. Vol.147. No.6. (2000) 374-377
3. Kim T., Al-Dayeh L., and Singh M.: FMRI Artifacts Reduction Using Bayesian Image Processing, IEEE Transactions on Nuclear Science, Vol. 46. (1999) 2134-2140
4. Comon P.: Independent Component Analysis, A New Concept? Signal Processing. Vol. 36. (1994) 287-314
5. Aapo H.: Survey on Independent Component Analysis. Neural Computing Surveys, Vol.2. (1999) 94-128
6. Cardoso J. F.: Blind Signal Separation: Statistical Principles. Proceedings of the IEEE, Vol.9. No.10. (1998) 2009-2026
7. Bingham E. and Hyvarinen X.: A Fast-Point Algorithm for Independent Component Analysis of Complex Valued Signals, International Journal of Neural System. Vol.10. No.1. (2000) 1-8
8. Hyvarinen A. and Oja. E.: A Fast-Point Algorithm for Independent Component Analysis, Neural Computation. Vol.9. (1997) 1483-1492
9. Friston K.J., Jezzard P. and Turner R.: Analysis of Functional MRI Time-Series. Human Brain Mapping, Vol. 1. (1994) 153-171

Prediction-Based Simplified Half Pixel Motion Estimation

HyoSun Yoon[1], GueeSang Lee[1,*], HyeSuk Kim[1], and Miyoung Kim[2]

[1] Department of Computer Science, Chonnam National University,
300 Youngbong-dong, Buk-gu, Kwangju 500-757, Korea
estheryoon@hotmail.com, gslee@chonnam.ac.kr, iamtina@korea.com
[2] Department of Computer Information Technology, Namdo Provincial College,
262 Hanggyo-Ri, Damgyang-Gun, Chonnam-Provice 517-802, Korea
kimmee@namdo.ac.kr

Abstract. A prediction-based simplified half pixel motion estimation algorithm is proposed to improve the search speed in half pixel motion estimation. It predicts the possible sub area and checks only three half pixel points in its possible sub area rather than eight half pixel points which are used in full half pixel search method (FHPS). Experimental results show that the proposed algorithm has a significant speedup up to 62% over FHPS and preserves the image quality

1 Introduction

Motion estimation (ME) and motion compensation techniques are an important part of video encoding systems, since it could significantly affect the compression ratio and the output quality. But, ME is very computational intensive part.

Generally, ME is made of two parts, integer pixel motion estimation and half pixel motion estimation. For the first part, integer pixel motion estimation, many search algorithms such as Diamond Search (DS) [1, 2], Three Step Search (TSS) [3], New Three Step Search (NTSS) [4], Four Step Search (FSS) [5], Two Step Search (2SS) [6], Two-dimensional logarithmic search algorithm [7], HEXagon-Based Search (HEXBS) [8], Motion Vector Field Adaptive Search Technique (MVFAST) [9] and Predictive MVFAST (PMVFAST) [10] have been proposed to reduce the computational complexity. Some algorithms among these algorithms can find an integer pixel Motion Vector (MV) by examining less than 10 search points. For the second part, half pixel motion estimation, Full Half Pixel Search (FHPS) examines eight half pixel points around the integer motion vector. This method takes nearly half of the total computations in the ME that uses fast algorithms for integer pixel motion estimation. Therefore, it becomes more important to reduce the computational complexity of half pixel motion estimation. For these reasons, Horizontal and Vertical Direction as Reference (HVDR) [11], the Parabolic Prediction-based, Fast Half Pixel Search algorithm

---
* Corresponding author.

(PPHPS) [12]and Chen's Fast Half Pixel Search algorithm (CHPS)[13] have been proposed. Since these algorithms do not have any information on the motion of the current block, they always perform half pixel motion estimation to find a half pixel motion vector.

In this paper, we propose a new half pixel motion estimation algorithm that can provide much fast search speed and less image degradation. It predicts the possible sub area and examines three half pixel points in the possible sub area for the half pixel motion vector.

This paper is organized as follows. Section 2 describes the previous works. The proposed method is described in Section 3. Section 4 reports the simulation results and conclusions are given in Section 5.

2 The Previous Works

In Motion Estimation, half pixel motion estimation is used to reduce the prediction error between the original image and the predicted image. FHPS that is a typical method, examined eight half pixel points around the integer motion vector 'C' illustrated in Fig. 1. The point with the minimum cost function value among these points is the half pixel motion vector. To reduce the computational complexity of FHPS, some fast algorithms have been proposed.

In HVDR, 4 neighboring half pixel points in vertical direction and horizontal direction around 'C' illustrated in Fig. 1 are examined to decide the best matching point in each direction. Then, a diagonal point between these two best matching points is also examined. The point having the minimum cost function value among these 5 points and 'C' is decided as a half pixel motion vector.

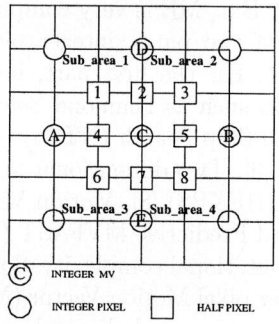

Fig. 1. The position and of half and integer pixels

CHPS examines 4 horizontal and vertical half pixel points '2','4','5','7' shown Fig. 1. The point having the minimum cost function value among these 4 points and the point 'C' is decided as a half pixel motion vector.

PPHPS predicts the possible optimal half pixel point by using the cost function values of 5 integer pixel points 'A','B','C','D','E' shown Fig. 1. The cost function values of the predicted possible optimal half pixel point and its nearest points are calculated to find the best matching point. The point of the minimum cost function value is decided as a final half pixel MV between this best matching point and the point 'C'.

CHPS can not consider the diagonal direction motion in half pixel motion estimation, it reusts in the degradation of image quality. HVDR checks more half pixel points than other fast half pixel motion estimation methods. PPHPS uses complex equations to predict the half pixel motion, it cause a little computational complexity.

3 The Proposd Method

We propose a prediction-based simplified half pixel motion estimation algorithm to provide much faster search speed and less image degradation. It predicts the possible sub area by using the cost function values of four integer pixel points and examines three half pixel points in its possible sub area to decide the half pixel motion vector. Following is a more detailed explanation.

At first, the proposed algorithm decides the best horizontal matching point between 2 horizontal integer pixel points 'A','B' and the best vertical matching point between 2 vertical integer pixel points 'C','D' depicted in Fig. 1. Then, the possible sub area is selected according to the best horizontal and vertical matching points. Three half pixel points in its possible sub area are examined. Finally, the point having the minimum cost function among these three half pixel points and the point 'C' is decided as the half pixel motion vector. For example, we assume that points 'A','D' are the best horizontal and vertical matching points respectively. The Sub_area_1 in Fig. 1 is selected as the possible sub area. The half pixel points '1','2','4' in Sub_area_1 are examined. The point having the minimum cost function among these three half pixel points and the point 'C' is decided as the half pixel motion vector.

4 Simulation Result

In this section, we show experimental results for the proposed method. The proposed method has been evaluated in the H.263 encoder. Nine QCIF test sequences are used for the experiment. The mean square error (MSE) distortion function is used as the block distortion measure (BDM).

For integer pixel motion estimation, Full Search algorithm is adopted. For half pixel motion estimation, the proposed algorithm is compared with four other half pixel motion estimation algorithms: FHPS, HVDR, CHPS and PPHPS. Table 1 and Table 2 show that the proposed algorithm achieves up to 60% speedup on the number of search points (NSP) per half pixel motion vector with a similar image quality over FHPS. The proposed algorithm can improve the search speed up to 40% over HVDR and up to 25% over CHPS while maintaining better image quality. The NSP of the proposed algorithm is equal to that of PPHPS, but the image quality of the proposed is better than that of PPHPS. Also, PPHPS uses complex equations to predict the half pixel motion, it cause a little computational complexity. Experimental results show that the proposed algorithm can get a similar PSNR of FHPS with the speedup on NSP. Thus, the proposed algorithm is a good alternative for FHPS in half pixel motion estimation.

Table 1. Average PSNR for half pixel motion estimation algorithms

Integer-pel ME method	Full search				
Half-pel ME method	FHPS	HVDR	CHPS	PPHPS	Proposed
Akiyo	34.5	34.41	34.46	34.43	34.5
Claire	35.05	35.02	35.03	35.05	35.05
Foreman	29.54	29.52	29.50	29.51	29.51
M&D	31.54	31.50	31.54	31.52	31.54
News	30.59	30.49	30.54	30.57	30.57
Salesman	32.7	32.64	32.67	32.70	32.70
Silent	31.81	31.80	31.76	31.79	31.80
Stefan	23.89	23.85	23.86	23.87	23.87
Suzie	32.19	32.17	32.15	32.19	32.19

Table 2. The Number of Search points per half pixle MV

FHPS	HVDR	CHPS	PPHPS	Proposed
8	5	4	3	3

5 Conclusion

A prediction-based simplified half pixel motion estimation algorithm is proposed to provide much faster search speed and less image degradation. Experimental results show that the proposed algorithm improves the search speed significantly without the degradation of image quality. The proposed algorithm outperforms other half pixel motion estimation algorithm in the search speed and the image quality.

References

1. Tham, J.Y., Ranganath, S., Kassim, A.A.: A Novel Unrestricted Center-Biased Diamond Search Algorithm for Block Motion Estimation. IEEE Transactions on Circuits and Systems for Video Technology. **8(4)** (1998) 369–375
2. Shan, Z., Kai-kuang, M.: A New Diamond Search Algorithm for Fast block Matching Motion Estimation. IEEE Transactions on Image Processing. **9(2)** (2000) 287–290
3. Koga, T., Iinuma, K., Hirano, Y., Iijim, Y., Ishiguro, T.: Motion compensated interframe coding for video conference. In Proc. NTC81. (1981) C9.6.1–9.6.5

4. Renxiang, L., Bing, Z., Liou, M.L.: A New Three Step Search Algorithm for Block Motion Estimation. IEEE Transactions on Circuits and Systems for Video Technology. **4(4)** (1994) 438–442
5. Lai-Man, P., Wing-Chung, M.: A Novel Four-Step Search Algorithm for Fast Block Motion Estimation. IEEE Transactions on Circuits and Systems for Video Technology. **6(3)** (1996) 313–317
6. Yuk-Ying, C., Neil, W.B.: Fast search block-matching motion estimation algorithm using FPGA. Visual Communication and Image Processing 2000. Proc. SPIE. **4067** (2000) 913–922
7. Jain, J., Jain, A.: Dispalcement measurement and its application in interframe image coding. IEEE Transactions on Communications. **COM-29** (1981) 1799–1808
8. Zhu, C., Lin, X., Chau, L.P.: Hexagon based Search Pattern for Fast Block Motion Estimation. IEEE Transactions on Circuits and Systems for Video Technology. **12(5)** (2002) 349–355
9. Ma, K.K., Hosur, P.I.: Report on Performance of Fast Motion using Motion Vector Field Adaptive Search Technique. ISO/IEC/JTC1/SC29/WG11.**M5453** (1999)
10. Tourapis, A.M., Liou, M.L.: Fast Block Matching Motion Estimation using Predictive Motion Vector Field Adaptive Search Technique. ISO/IEC/JTC1/SC29/WG11.**M5866** (2000)
11. Lee, K.H.,Choi, J.H.,Lee, B.K., Kim. D.G.: Fast two step half pixel accuracy motion vector prediction. Electronics Letters **36(7)**(2000) 625–627
12. Cheng, D., Yun, H., Junli, Z.: A Prabolic Prediction-Based, Fast Half Pixel Serch Algorithm for Very Low Bit-Rate Moving Picture Coding. IEEE Transactions on Circuits and Systems for Video Technology. **13(6)** (2003) 514–518
13. Cheng, D., Yun, H.: A Comparative Study of Motion Estimation for Low Bit Rate Video Coding. SPIE **4067(3)**(2000) 1239–1249

A New CWT-IHS Fusion Based on Edge-Intensity-Factor

Jin Wu[1], Yang Liu[2], Jian Liu[1], and Jinwen Tian[1]

[1] Huazhong University of Science and Technology, Image Information
and Intelligence Control Laboratory of the Ministry of Education,
430074 Wuhan, P. R. China
hust_wu@163.com
[2] Wuhan University of Science and Technology,
College of Information Science and Engineering,
430081 Wuhan, P. R. China
liuyang_2001@etang.com

Abstract. For the fusion of a high-resolution panchromatic image (PAN) and a low-resolution multispectral image (TM), this paper presents a new fusion algorithm based on the new characteristic wavelet transform (CWT), intensity-hue-saturation transform (IHS) and the edge-intensity-factor (EIF). First, the decomposed PAN details can be fused into the decomposed intensity component of the TM image by CWT fusion algorithm. Then, the new intensity component can be reconstructed using the new inverse CWT based on EIF. Finally, the fused image is reconstructed by means of an inverse IHS transform using the fused new intensity component, the hue and saturation components from the original TM image. Experiment results demonstrate that the proposed algorithm can achieve better combining performance in preserving the spatial characteristics and the spectral information.

1 Introduction

In order to provide increased interpretation capabilities and more reliable results from data with different characteristics, image fusion combines two or more source images from the same scene into a composite image with extend information content. What we discuss is how to fuse panchromatic image (PAN) with multispectral image (TM) in pixel level. Many image fusion algorithms have been developed, such as Intensity-Hue-Saturation transform (IHS) [1], Principal Component Analysis (PCA)[2], High Pass Filter transform (HPF)[3] and Wavelet Transform (WT)[4], etc. Because of the superior qualities of wavelet transform in both time and frequency domains, it has become the mainstream fusion technology. Furthermore, IHS transform can be used to visually improve multispectral color composites. However, the traditional fusion algorithms based on IHS or WT usually cause some color distortion, characteristic degradation or suffer from ringing. Consequently, we propose a new image fusion algorithm based on CWT, IHS and the edge-intensity-factor (EIF).

2 A New Fusion Algorithm Based on CWT and IHS Transforms

To combine the characteristics from the TM and PAN images, we adopt the CWT detail coefficients fusion rule in [5]. First, the input images f_{HR} and f_{MSI} are decomposed continuously into two parts until the desired coarser resolution 2^{-J} ($J > 0$): approximate coefficients $S_{2^{-J}} f_{HR}(x,y)$ and $S_{2^{-J}} f_{MSI}(x,y)$, and detail coefficients $W_{2^{-j}}^{k} f_{HR}(x,y)$ and $W_{2^{-j}}^{k} f_{MSI}(x,y)$. Where, $k = 1, 2, 3$, representing horizontal, vertical or diagonal direction; $j = 1, 2, \cdots, J$, representing different scale; and (x, y) presents the coordinate of pixel. Suppose $D_{2^{-j}}^{k} f_{HR}(x,y)$ and $D_{2^{-j}}^{k} f_{MSI}(x,y)$ are the local variances in 3×3 windows of $W_{2^{-j}}^{k} f_{HR}(x,y)$ and $W_{2^{-j}}^{k} f_{MSI}(x,y)$, we choose the detail coefficients at each scale as follows:

$$W_{2^{-j}}^{k}(x,y) = \begin{cases} W_{2^{-j}}^{k} f_{HR}(x,y), & D_{2^{-j}}^{k} f_{HR} > D_{2^{-j}}^{k} f_{MSI} \\ W_{2^{-j}}^{k} f_{MSI}(x,y), & others \end{cases} \quad (1)$$

In order to preserve more spectral information from the TM as well as avoid suffering from ringing and characteristic degradation, we abandon the approximate coefficients fusion rule in [5], but fuse $S_{2^{-J}} f_{HR}(x,y)$ into $S_{2^{-J}} f_{MSI}(x,y)$ using the following new fusion algorithm.

Let $S_{2^{-J}} f_{MSG}(x,y)$ be the gray value of the subimage $S_{2^{-J}} f_{MSI}$, we can reconstruct the new intensity component I_{new} as follows [6]:

$$I_{new} = (\gamma_{xy} \cdot S_{2^{-J}} f_{MSI}, (W_{2^{-j}}^{1})_{1 \le j \le J}, (W_{2^{-j}}^{2})_{1 \le j \le J}, (W_{2^{-j}}^{3})_{1 \le j \le J}) \quad (2)$$

Where γ_{xy} is the edge intensity factor and defined as:

$$\gamma_{xy} = \begin{cases} \dfrac{S_{2^{-J}} f_{HR}(x,y)}{S_{2^{-J}} f_{MSG}(x,y)}, & S_{2^{-J}} f_{MSG}(x,y) \ne 0 \\ 0, & S_{2^{-J}} f_{MSG}(x,y) = 0 \end{cases} \quad (3)$$

Finally, perform the inverse IHS transform to the new intensity component I_{new} together with the hue and saturation components, to obtain the fused RGB image.

3 Experiments and Fusion Results Analysis

To test the correctness and effectiveness of the proposed algorithm, we choose the same sized PAN and TM of a mandrill image to be fused using different fusion algorithms ($J=1$). The original and different fusion images are shown in Fig.1, from which we can see that the CWT algorithm can enhance the spatial detail information better than WT. However, the traditional CWT-IHS algorithm can preserve the spectral information well but suffers from serious ringing. Though the traditional EIF-CWT-IHS algorithm can improve the spatial resolution, it does lose some spectral information. Comparatively, the proposed algorithm can simultaneously combine and preserve the spectral and spatial information very well.

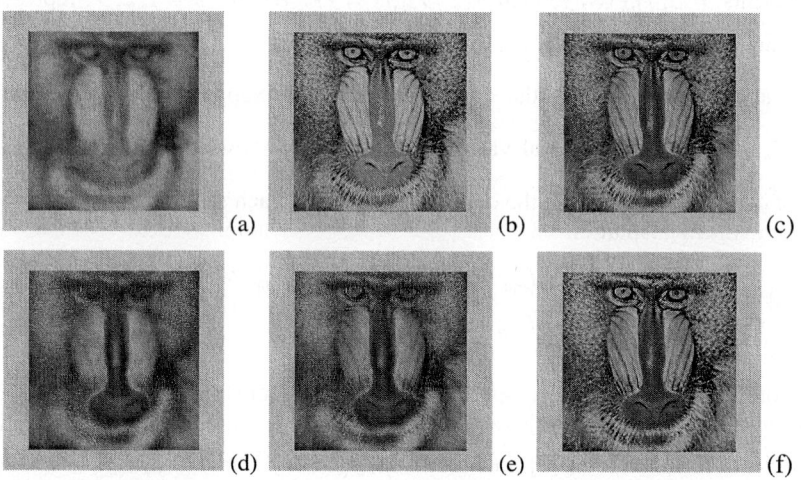

Fig. 1. Original mandrill images and the fusion results of different methods (256×256 pixels). (a), (b) The original TM, PAN images. (c) Fused image using the proposed algorithm. (d) The WT-IHS model. (e) The traditional CWT-IHS model. (f) The traditional EIF-CWT-IHS model

The statistical parameters, such as standard variance σ, entropy H, definition G, distortion degree D, deviation index D_{index}, and the correlation coefficient C [7], are chosen to quantitatively analyze the different fusion results. The statistical results are shown in Table 1. From Table 1, we can find that: (1) The σ, H, G of the proposed algorithm are higher than that of the traditional CWT-IHS and WT-IHS algorithm, which demonstrates the proposed algorithm is superior in expressing spatial details. The D and D_{index} of the proposed algorithm are a little higher and the C is a little lower than that of the latter, which means the proposed algorithm preserves the spectral information equivalent to the latter. (2) The σ, H, G of the proposed algorithm are a little lower than that of the traditional EIF-CWT-IHS algorithm, which means the proposed algorithm is a little inferior in expressing spatial details. But the C of the proposed new algorithm is much higher than that of the latter, which shows the proposed algorithm can preserve the spectral information much better. In balance, we find that the proposed fusion algorithm can achieve better performance in combining and preserving spectral-spatial information.

Table 1. Characteristic statistics of different images

Different images	σ	H	G	D	D_{index}	C
TM	29.5717	4.7693	1.9652			
PAN	39.2179	5.0042	17.1328			
Proposed Algorithm	36.1403	4.9585	15.6039	23.7977	0.1941	0.7417
WT-IHS algorithm	30.8085	4.8083	12.9527	23.5575	0.1868	0.7847
CWT-IHS (k_1=0.3)	31.7531	4.8282	13.1512	21.7999	0.1727	0.7565
EIF-CWT-IHS	38.7118	5.0292	17.3403	25.4537	0.2097	0.6745

4 Conclusion

In this paper, a new edge-intensity-factor based CWT-IHS fusion algorithm is presented, and we compare it with other fusion algorithms by fusing a high-resolution PAN and a low-resolution TM mandrill image. The visual and statistical analyses of the different fusion results all demonstrate that the proposed fusion algorithm can possess better spatial and spectral qualities simultaneously than the other algorithms.

For convenience, we choose the scale J=1 here. However, the fusion effect of wavelet based fusion algorithm is related to the scale of decomposition. With the increase of the decomposition scale, the spatial resolution of the fused image will increase, but the spectral information will decrease. So, in practice, we can appropriately choose the decomposition scale J=3 (or 4) to get a better fusion result.

References

1. Carper, W. J., T. M. Lillesand, R. W. Kiefer: The Use of Intensity-hue-saturation Transformations for Merging SPOT Panchromatic and Multi-spectral Image Data. Photogrammetric Engineering & Remote Sensing, Vol.56, No.4 (1990) 459-467
2. Chavez, P. S. Jr., A. Y. Kwarteng: Extracting Spectral Contrast in Landsat Thematic Mapper Image Data Using Selective Principal Component Analysis. Photogrammetric Engineering & Remote Sensing, Vol.55, No.3 (1989) 339-348
3. Chavez, P. S. Jr., S. C. sides, J. A. Anderson: Comparison of Three Different Methods to Merge Multiresolution and Multispectral Data: Landsat TM and SPOT panchromatic. Photogrammetric Engineering & Remote Sensing, Vol.57, No.3 (1990) 295-303
4. Hui Li, B.S. Manjunath, Sanjit K. Mitra: Multisensor Image Fusion Using the Wavelet Ttransform. ICIP'94, vol. 1 (1994) 51-55
5. Li Jun, Lin Zongjian: Data Fusion for Remote Sensing Imagery Based on Feature. China Journal of Image and Graphics, Vol. 2 (1997) 103-107
6. Li Ming, Wu Shunjun: A New Image Fusion Algorithm Based on Wavelet Transform. ICCIMA' 03, (2003) 154-159
7. Li Bicheng, Wei Jun, Peng Tianqiang: Objective Analysis and Evaluation of Remote Sensing Image Fsion Effect. COMPUTER ENGINEERING & SCIENCE, vol. 26, no. 1 (2004) 42-46

Image Segmentation Based on Fuzzy 3-Partition Entropy Approach and Genetic Algorithm

Jin Wu[1], Juan Li[1], Jian Liu[2], and Jinwen Tian[2]

[1] Wuhan University of Science and Technology,
College of Information Science & Engineering,
430081 Wuhan, P. R. China
hust_wu@163.com

[2] Huazhong University of Science and Technology,
Image Information & Intelligence Control Laboratory of the Ministry of Education,
430074 Wuhan, P. R. China
jwtian@mail.hust.edu.cn

Abstract. In this paper, a three-level thresholding method for image segmentation is presented, based on the concept of fuzzy c-partition and the maximum fuzzy entropy principle. A new fuzzy exponential entropy is defined through probability analysis. We also define simplified membership functions for the three parts respectively, while the fuzzy regions can be determined by maximizing fuzzy entropy. A genetic algorithm is implemented to search the optimal combination of the fuzzy parameters, which finally decide the thresholds. Experiments show that the proposed method can select the thresholds automatically and effectively, and the resulting image can preserve the main features of the components of the original image very well.

1 Introduction

Image segmentation is an important topic for image processing, pattern recognition and computer vision. To segment complex images, a multilevel thresholding method is required. Some techniques have been reported [1,2].

Fuzzy set theory has been successfully applied to many image processing and pattern recognition tasks, and especially image thresholding. In this paper, we will use maximum entropy principle and fuzzy 3-partition method to select the threshold values associated with the maximum entropy of the fuzzy 3-partition. Since the exhaustive search for all parameter combinations is too expensive, a genetic algorithm is employed to reduce the computation time.

2 Fuzzy 3-Partition Entropy Approach and Genetic Algorithm

Based on the definition of a fuzzy event [3], we can view an image as a fuzzy event modeled by a probability space. We assume that the image has 256 gray levels ranging from 0 to 255. The three-level thresholding classifies the pixels of the image into three parts, namely, dark, gray and bright part. Consider the three fuzzy sets dark, gray and bright, whose membership functions are defined as:

$$\mu_{dark}(x) = \begin{cases} 1, & x \leq a_1 \\ (x-c_1)/(a_1-c_1), & a_1 < x < c_1 \\ 0, & x \geq c_1 \end{cases} \quad (1\text{-a})$$

$$\mu_{gray}(x) = \begin{cases} 0, & x \leq a_1 \\ (x-a_1)/(c_1-a_1), & a_1 \leq x \leq c_1 \\ 1, & c_1 \leq x \leq a_2 \\ (x-c_2)/(a_2-c_2), & a_2 \leq x \leq c_2 \\ 0, & x \geq c_2 \end{cases} \quad (1\text{-b})$$

$$\mu_{bright}(x) = \begin{cases} 0, & x \leq a_2 \\ (x-a_2)/(c_2-a_2), & a_2 < x < c_2 \\ 1, & x \geq c_2 \end{cases} \quad (1\text{-c})$$

where x is the independent variable, a_1, c_1, a_2, c_2 are parameters, and $0 \leq a_1 < c_1 < a_2 < c_2 \leq 255$.

The probabilities of the occurrence of fuzzy sets dark, gray and bright can be calculated by

$$P_I = \sum_{k=0}^{255} \mu_I(k) P(k), \quad I \in \{dark, gray, bright\}. \quad (2)$$

The fuzzy entropy of each fuzzy set can be calculated by

$$H_I = P_I e^{1-P_I}, \quad I \in \{dark, gray, bright\}. \quad (3)$$

Then the total fuzzy entropy is

$$H = H_{dark} + H_{gray} + H_{bright}. \quad (4)$$

From entropy theory, when the three parts satisfy $P_{dark} = P_{gray} = P_{bright} = 1/3$, the total fuzzy entropy is the largest. It means that the number of the pixels in those parts should be nearly equivalent, which leads to the hopeless loss of some main features. So the new fuzzy exponential entropy, defined through probability analysis [4], is introduced as

$$H_I = \sum_{k=0}^{255} \frac{P(k) \times \mu_I(k)}{P_I} e^{1 - \frac{P(k) \times \mu_I(k)}{P_I}}, \quad I \in \{dark, gray, bright\}. \quad (5)$$

We can find an optimal combination of (a_1, c_1, a_2, c_2) so that the total fuzzy entropy H has the maximum value. Then, the two thresholds of this fuzzy

3-partition are the midpoints of the a,c pairs. That is, $b_1 = (a_1 + c_1)/2$, and $b_2 = (a_2 + c_2)/2$.

Genetic algorithm [5] is implemented to search the optimal combination of the fuzzy parameters. The detailed genetic algorithm is described below:

Step 1: Encode the randomly generated parameters (a_1, c_1, a_2, c_2) into an alphabet string.

Step 2: Choose the fuzzy entropy function in Eqs. 4 and 5 as the fitness function, and the major parameters of GA are set as MaxGen (maximal generation number) = 40; PoPs (population size) = 100; PC (probability of crossover) = 0.5; Pm (probability of mutation) = 0.01.

Step 3: Parents are selected according to their fitness by means of roulette-wheel selection.

Step 4: Exchange elements from mating of two parent chromosomes to create two new child chromosomes.

Step 5: From time to time, change one character of some string at random.

Step 6: If the MaxGen is met, stop. The desired optimum is represented by the current string of maximum fitness. Otherwise, repeat the sequence of steps starting at *step 3*. Finally, GA can find the solution (a_1, c_1, a_2, c_2) with the maximum fuzzy entropy.

3 Experimental Results

We have done experiments on many gray level images. Two typical images, showed in Fig. 1 and 2, are used to demonstrate the performances of fuzzy c-means clustering method and the proposed method.

(a)

(b)

(c)

Fig. 1. Thresholding results of the "ship" image. (a) Original image, (b) Thresholdingimage of fuzzy c-means clustering method, and (c) our approach, $(a_1, c_1, a_2, c_2) = (106, 119, 128, 211)$, $(b_1, b_2) = (113, 170)$

In Fig. 1(b), most part of the ship merges with the sky. Nevertheless, the main features of the image, such as the ship, ocean, sky and cloud, are well preserved in Fig. 1(c).

(a) (b) (c)

Fig. 2. Thresholding results of the "linkmen" image. (a) Original image, (b) Thresholding image of fuzzy c-means clustering method, and (c) our approach, $(a_1, c_1, a_2, c_2) = (14, 146, 163, 171)$, $(b_1, b_2) = (80, 167)$

In Fig. 2(b), the hole and tree disappear, and the linkmen are blurry. However, the main features of the original image, such as the linkmen, hole and tree, are well preserved in Fig. 2(c).

The experiment results of Fig. 1 and 2 show that the proposed method can segment image more effectively and properly than fuzzy c-means clustering method, retain the main features of the original image.

Computation time of the exhaustive search and the genetic algorithm is 7.5 hours and 30 seconds separately, which demonstrate that the proposed genetic algorithm is much faster than the exhaustive search.

4 Conclusions

Thresholding is an important topic for image processing. Selecting thresholds is a critical issue for many applications. In this paper, we present a three-level thresholding method for image segmentation based on the concept of fuzzy c-partition and the maximum fuzzy entropy principle. Fuzzy exponential entropy through probability analysis is used. Since the exhaustive search for all parameter combinations is too expensive, we adopt a genetic algorithm. The experimental results show that the proposed method gives good performances, can segment the image more effectively and faster.

References

1. S.S.Reddi, S.F.Rudin, and H.R.Keshavan.: An optimal multiple threshold scheme for image segmentation. IEEE Trans. Syst., Man, Cybern, Vol. SMC-14, No. 4 (1984) 661–665.
2. N.Papamarkos and B.Gatos.: A new approach for multilevel threshold selection. CVGIP: Graphical Models Image Process, Vol. 56, No. 6 (1994) 494–506.
3. L.A.Zadeh.: Probability measures of fuzzy events. J. Math. Anal. And Appl, Vol. 23 (1968) 421–427.
4. Wen-Bing Tao, Jin-Wen Tian, and Jian Liu.: Image segmentation by three-level thresholding based on maximum fuzzy entropy and genetic algorithm. Pattern Recognition Letters, Vol. 24 (2003) 3069–3078.
5. D.E. Goldberg.: Genetic algorithms in searching, optimization, and machine learning. Addison-Wesley, Reading, Massachusetts (1989).

An Optimal Broadcasting Algorithm for de Bruijn Network dBG(d,k)

Ngoc Chi Nguyen and Sungyoung Lee

Computer Engineering Department, Kyung Hee Univerity,
1, Seocheon, Giheung, Yongin, Gyeonggi 449-701 Korea
{ncngoc, sylee}@oslab.khu.ac.kr

Abstract. Recent works have classified de Bruijn graph (dBG) based broadcasting algorithms into local broadcasting and arc-disjoint spanning trees based broadcasting. However, those algorithms can only work in binary dBG. In this paper, we investigate broadcasting in bidirectional dBG for a degree greater than or equal to two. A distributed broadcast algorithm for one-to-all broadcasting in the all port communication is proposed for dBG(d,k)[1].

1 Introduction

Broadcasting is one of the fundamental communication problems of interconnection networks. Some typical broadcasting applications are synchronizing different processors in a distributed computing network, and reconfiguring multiprocessor architecture. Recently, broadcasting problems on dBG have been investigated as local broadcasting[3] and arc-disjoint spanning trees based broadcasting[4][5].

However, the above can only work in a dBG(2,k) networks. Considering this limitation we intend to investigate broadcasting in bidirectional de Bruijn graph with a degree greater than or equal to two. A distributed broadcast algorithm is proposed for dBG(d,k). Our study shows that the maximum time steps to finish broadcast procedure is k regardless of the broadcast originator, time complexity at each node is 0(3d/2), and no overhead happens in the broadcast message.

This paper is organized as follows: background is discussed in section 2, section 3 explains the algorithm and the paper is concluded in section 4.

2 Background

The dBG graph denoted as dBG(d,k)[1] has $N=d^k$ nodes with diameter k and degree 2d. If we represent a node by $d_0 d_1 ... d_{k-2} d_{k-1}$, where $d_j \in 0, 1, ..., (d-1)$, $0 \leq j \leq (k-1)$, then its neighbor are represented by $d_1 ... d_{k-2} d_{k-1} p$(L neighbors, by shifting left or L path) and $p d_0 d_1 ... d_{k-2}$(R neighbors, by shifting right or R path), where $p = 0, 1, ..., (d-1)$. Shift string of a node A is a binary string (0 for left shift and 1 for right shift) which represents path from originator to A.

---

[1] This research was partially supported by ITRC project of Sunmoon University.

For simplest broadcasting mechanism, the originator initiates the process by making a "call" to other neighboring vertices in the graph informing them of the message. Subsequently, the informed vertices call their neighboring vertices and the process continues until all vertices in the graph are informed. Basically, this mechanism is like flooding phenomenon. Note that the interval during which a call takes place will be referred to as a time step or simply step. In flooding broadcasting (FB), level of a node A is the number of steps by which a message from originator reaches A (or shortest path length between A and originator).

3 Broadcasting Algorithm in dBG(d,k)

By applying FB, we can easily obtain k as the maximum number of steps to finish broadcasting. However, message overhead is very high in FB. Thus, how to reduce message overhead (or letting each informed vertices call its uninformed neighbors only) in FB states the motivation for our algorithm. We assume that each packet sent to the other node must contain originator address, sender's level, a shift string of receiver and all calls take the same amount of time.

There are two cases of message overhead when an informed node A wants to inform node X. Case 1, node X has been informed already. Thus, X must have lower or equal level to A. Case 2, uninformed node X can be informed by nodes B,C,D, which have the same level as A, at the same time. For case 1, we need to compare the shortest-path length between X and A to originator. And X is informed by A if X level is higher than A's level and case 2 not happen. For case 2, we have to define some conditions, based on these conditions only A or B or C or... inform X. The following theorems are proposed for calculating path length.

Theorem 1: *given p is shortest-path length between node a and b, the minimum length of matched strings between a and b is k-p (dBG(d,k)).*

Proof: as shown in [1], there are 3 types for determining shortest path (R,L; RL,LR; R_1LR_2, L_1RL_2). The minimum matched string[2] can be obtained in type R,L among them. And length for this minimum matched string is k-p.

Theorem 2: *path length between node s and d is $min(2s_j + s_i + d_i, 2s_i + s_j + d_j)$, where s_i and d_i are the left indices, and s_j and d_j are the right indices of matched string in s and d respectively.*

Proof: path length $2s_j + s_i + d_i, 2s_i + s_j + d_j$ are for case $R_{s_j}L_{s_j+s_i}R_{d_i}$ and $L_{s_i}R_{s_i+s_j}L_{d_j}$ respectively . These cases are the general cases for 3 types presented in [1](ex. if $s_i, s_j, d_i, d_j \neq 0$ then they become type R_1LR_2 and L_1RL_2).

To solve the above two cases of message overhead, a Boolean valued function SPL is proposed. SPL has inputs: originator S, current node P, neighboring node X, current level n (level of P), shift string Q ($q_0q_1q_2...q_{z-1}$, length z≤k) (from S to X through P). Fig. 1a shows SPL algorithm. Step 1,2,3 solve message overhead of case 1. Step 1 is a result of theorem 1. Step 4,5,6 solve case 2 message overhead.

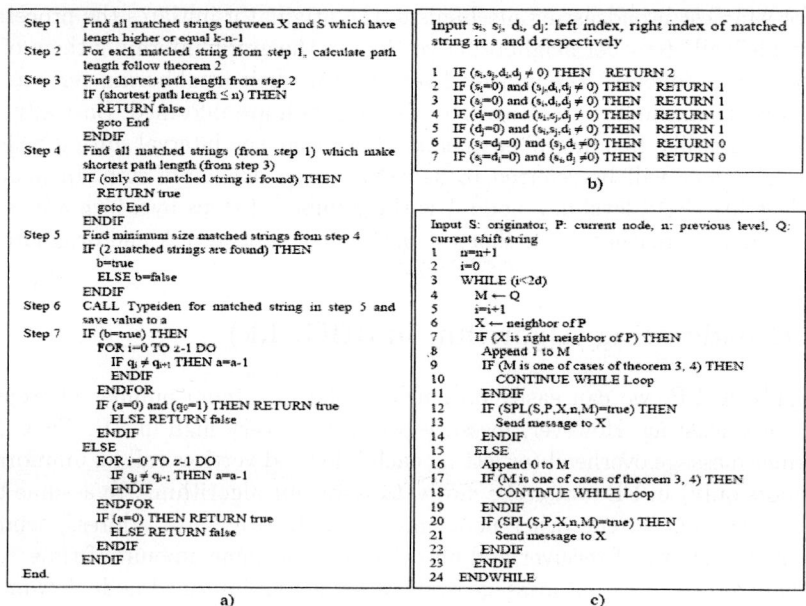

Fig. 1. a)SPL function algorithm; b)Typeiden function algorithm; c)Broadcasting algorithm for dBG(d,k)

In case 2, we have several shortest paths from S to X. One shortest path must be chosen based on the following conditions:

• The shortest path corresponds with the shortest matched string of S and X (step 5).

• In the case, there exist 2 shortest path from the first condition. Then, shortest path which begin with shifting right is chosen. (step 6)

Step 7 compares shift string Q to the condition gotten from step 5 and 6 to determine whether X should be informed or not.

Example 1: in dBG(3,10), given input S: 0012111001, P: 0111012110, n=7, X: 1110121100, Q=01111100. By applying SPL, we have

Step 1: find all matched strings[2] which have length higher or equal 10-7-1=2. These strings are 11, 111, 1110, 01, 012, 0121, 01211, 110, 1100.
Step 2: path lengths for strings in step 1 are 12, 10, 8, 14, 12, 10, 8, 13, 11.
Step 3: shortest path length is 8.
Step 4: matched string, which make shortest path length 8, are 1110, 01211.
Step 5: minimum size string from step 4 is 1110, b=false.
Step 6:Typeiden(input $s_i = 0, s_j = 6, d_i = 4, d_j = 2$)→returned value: 1,a=1.
Step 7: there are 2 places in Q in which two adjacent bits are different → a=-1 $\neq$0. Consequently, X is an uninformed node (step 3,8>n), but it isn't informed by P (message overhead case 2) due to our priority given in step 5 and 6.

If we apply SPL for all 2d neighbors of one node, then it cost 0(2d) for running our algorithm. The following theorems reduce from 0(2d) to 0(1.5d). Following are some notations used, where T is the previous shifting string.

R↔T: total number of right shift in T > total number of left shift in T
L↔T: total number of left shift in T > total number of right shift in T

Theorem 3: *by shifting RLR/LRL, results are duplicate with shifting R/L.*

Proof: given a node $a_0a_1...a_{n-1}$. By shifting RLR in dBG(d,k), we have $a_0a_1...a_{n-1} \to \alpha a_0 a_1...a_{n-2} \to a_0 a_1...a_{n-2}\beta \to \gamma a_0 a_1...a_{n-2}$, $0 \le \alpha, \beta, \gamma < d$.
Substitute α for $\gamma \to \gamma a_0 a_1...a_{n-2} \equiv \alpha a_0 a_1...a_{n-2}$.
By proving similarly for case LRL, theorem 3 is proved.

Theorem 4: *if R↔T/L↔T, results provided by next shift LR/RL are duplicate.*

Proof: assume the beginning node is $a_0a_1...a_{n-1}$. For case R↔T, we have the following cases:

- $T = R_u L_v R_w, T = L_u R_v R w, T = L_u R_v L$. By shifting LR, we have shift string $R_1 L_1 R_2 L_2$ or $L_1 R_1 L_2 R_2$, which are not existed for shortest path (as shown in Lemma 1 of [1]).
- $T = R_u L_v$ (u>v). By shifting R u times and L v times respectively, we have $a_0 a_1...a_{n-1} \to \beta_{u-1}...\beta_1 \beta_0 a_0 a_1...a_{n-u-1} \to \beta_{u-v-1}...\beta_1 \beta_0 a_0 a_1...a_{n-u-1} \delta_0 \delta_1...\delta_{v-1}$ where $0 \le \beta_i, \delta_j < d$, $0 \le i < u$, $0 \le j < v$. By shifting LR we have, $\beta_{u-v-1}...\beta_0 a_0...a_{n-u-1}\delta_0...\delta v - 1 \to \beta_{u-v-2}...\beta_0 a_0...a_{n-u-1}\delta_0...\delta v \to \gamma \beta_{u-v-2}...\beta_0 a_0...a_{n-u-1}\delta_0...\delta v - 1$ (K)
Substitute $\gamma (0 \le \gamma < d)$ for $\beta_{u-v-1} \to$ K is duplicate.
- $R=R_u$. Shift string $R_u LR$ makes duplicate as shown in theorem 3.

By proving similarly to case L↔T, we prove theorem 4.
As a result, broadcasting algorithm is proposed as shown in fig. 1c.

Theorem 5: *in the worst case, time complexity for our broadcasting algorithm is 0(1.5d).*

Proof: probability for theorem 3 happening is 25%, and for theorem 4 is less than 25%. Therefore, the probability for CONTINUE command (line 10, 18 fig. 1c) happening is 25%. So, theorem 5 is proved.

4 Conclusion

We have presented a distributed broadcasting algorithm for dBG(d,k), which requires k steps to finish broadcasting process, time complexity at each node is 0(3d/2) and no message overhead during broadcasting. Therefore, the algorithm can be considered feasible for broadcasting in the real interconnection network which is built based on de Bruijn graph dBG(d,k).

References

1. Zhen Liu, Ting-Yi Sung, "Routing and Transmitting Problem in de Bruijn Networks" IEEE Trans. on Comp., Vol. 45, Issue 9, Sept. 1996, pp 1056 - 1062.
2. Alfred V. Aho, Margaret J. Corasick, "Efficient String Matching: An Aid to Bibliographic Search", Comm. of the ACM, Vol. 18 Issue 6, June 1975.
3. A.H.Esfahanian, G. Zimmerman, "A Distributed Broadcast Algorithm for Binary De Bruijn networks", IEEE Conf. on Comp. and Comm., March 1988.
4. E.Ganesan, D.K.Pradhan, "Optimal Broadcasting in Binary de Bruijn Networks and Hyper-deBruijn Networks", IEEE Symposium on Parallel Processing, April 1993.
5. S.R.Ohring, D.H.Hondel, "Optimal Fault-Tolerant Communication Algorithms on Product Networks using Spanning Trees", IEEE Symp. on Parallel Processing, 1994.

Container Problem in Bi-rotator Graphs

Keiichi Kaneko, Yasuto Suzuki, and Yukihiro Hasegawa

Tokyo University of Agriculture and Technology, Koganei-shi, Tokyo 184-8588, Japan
k1kaneko@cc.tuat.ac.jp

Abstract. In this paper, we give an algorithm for the container problem in bi-rotator graphs. The solution achieves some fault tolerance such as file distribution based information dispersal technique. The algorithm is of polynomial order of n for an n-bi-rotator graph. It is based on recursion and divided into two cases according to the position of the destination node. Performance of the algorithm is also evaluated by computer experiments.

1 Introduction

A bi-rotator graph[7] is obtained by making each edge of a rotator graph[1] bi-directional. The average diameter is improved by this modification. A bi-rotator graph is pancycilc and Hamilton-connected while a rotator graph does not have these properties. One of unsolved issue concerning this topology is the container problem: for a pair of nodes s and d in a k-connected graph $G = (V, E)$, to find k paths between s and d that are node disjoint except for s and d. The container problem[2, 4, 8] is one of important issues in designing parallel and distributed computing systems as well as the node-to-set disjoint paths problem[3, 5, 6]. In this paper, the terms 'disjoint' and 'internally disjoint' are used to express 'node disjoint' and 'node disjoint except for source and destination' if their uses do not cause any ambiguity.

In this paper, we give an algorithm of order of n instead of $n!$. We estimate the theoretical performance of the algorithm. We also evaluate its average performance by computer experiment.

2 Preliminaries

2.1 Definitions

Definition 1. For an arbitrary permutation $\boldsymbol{u} = (u_1, u_2, \cdots, u_n)$ of n symbols of $1, 2, \cdots, n$ and an integer i ($2 \leq i \leq n$), we define positive and negative rotation operations $R_i^+(\boldsymbol{u})$ and $R_i^-(\boldsymbol{u})$ as follows:

$$R_i^+(\boldsymbol{u}) = (u_2, u_3, \cdots, u_i, u_1, u_{i+1}, u_{i+2}, \cdots, u_n),$$
$$R_i^-(\boldsymbol{u}) = (u_i, u_1, u_2, \cdots, u_{i-1}, u_{i+1}, u_{i+2}, \cdots, u_n).$$

Note that R_2^+ and R_2^- represent a same rotation operation. Therefore there are $2n - 3$ operations.

Definition 2. An n-bi-rotator graph, BR_n, has $n!$ nodes. Each node has a unique address that is a permutation of n symbols of $1, 2, \cdots, n$. The node whose address is $\boldsymbol{u} = (u_1, u_2, \cdots, u_n)$ is adjacent to the nodes whose addresses are elements of the set $\{R_i^+(\boldsymbol{u}), R_i^-(\boldsymbol{u}) \mid 2 \leq i \leq n\}$.

Figure 1 shows examples of 2- to 4- bi-rotator graphs. Note that in this figure an address $(u_1, u_2, \cdots, u_n)$ is denoted by $u_1 u_2 \cdots u_n$.

Definition 3. In an n-bi-rotator graph, a sub graph induced by nodes that have a common symbol k at the right-most positions of their addresses forms an $(n-1)$-bi-rotator graph. This sub bi-rotator graph is denoted by $BR_{n-1}k$ by indexing the common symbol k.

2.2 Algorithm A

In Figure 2, we give an auxiliary algorithm for BR_n that establishes a path between an arbitrary pair of nodes $\boldsymbol{s}$ and $\boldsymbol{d}$ in polynomial time of n.

We assume that $\boldsymbol{s} = (s_1, s_2, \cdots, s_n)$ and $\boldsymbol{d} = (d_1, d_2, \cdots, d_n)$, and introduce an order relation defined by $d_1 \prec d_2 \prec \cdots \prec d_n$. We also assume that a relation $j \succ i$ holds if and only if $i \prec j$ holds.

It is known that a path generated by Algorithm A from $\boldsymbol{s}$ to $\boldsymbol{d}$ and a path generated by the same algorithm from $\boldsymbol{d}$ to $\boldsymbol{s}$ are internally disjoint[7].

2.3 Algorithm B

For any four nodes $\boldsymbol{x}_1, \boldsymbol{x}_2, \boldsymbol{y}_1, \boldsymbol{y}_2$ in BR_n ($n \geq 3$) where $\boldsymbol{x}_1 \neq \boldsymbol{x}_2$, $\boldsymbol{y}_1 \neq \boldsymbol{y}_2$, we give an algorithm that obtains two disjoint paths each of which has one terminal in $X = \{\boldsymbol{x}_1, \boldsymbol{x}_2\}$ and the other in $Y = \{\boldsymbol{y}_1, \boldsymbol{y}_2\}$ in polynomial time of n.

Step 1. If $X = Y$, then paths are already constructed. Otherwise, if $X \cap Y \neq \emptyset$, let $\tilde{\boldsymbol{x}} = X \cap Y$, $\boldsymbol{x} = X - \{\tilde{\boldsymbol{x}}\}$ and $\boldsymbol{y} = Y - \{\tilde{\boldsymbol{x}}\}$, and obtain two internally disjoint paths between $\boldsymbol{x}$ and $\boldsymbol{y}$ by using Algorithm A to select one of them that does not include $\tilde{\boldsymbol{x}}$ and terminate.

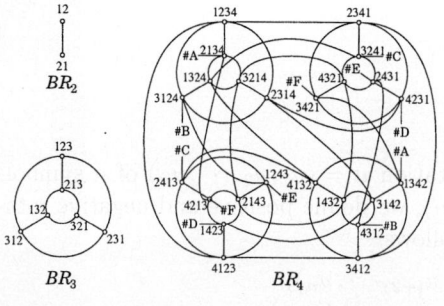

Fig. 1. Examples of 2- to 4- bi-rotator graphs

```
procedure A(s, d)
begin
    P := [s];
    Find k such that
        s_k ≻ s_{k+1} ≺ s_{k+2} ≺ ⋯ ≺ s_n;
    for i := 1 to k do begin
        Find the smallest h such that
            s_1 ≺ s_{h+1} ≺ s_{h+2} ≺ ⋯ ≺ s_n;
        s := R_h^+(s);
        P := P ++ [s]
    end
end;
```

Fig. 2. Algorithm A

Step 2. Construct two internally disjoint paths P_1 and P_2 between x_1 and y_1. If both of x_2 and y_2 are on $P_1 \cup P_2$, then there are two disjoint paths between x_1 and y_1, and x_2 and y_2, or two disjoint sub paths between x_1 and y_2, and x_2 and y_1, and select them to terminate.

Step 3. Construct internally disjoint two paths Q_1 and Q_2 between x_2 and y_2. If both of x_1 and y_1 are on $Q_1 \cup Q_2$, we can obtain two disjoint paths and terminate in the similar way in Step 2.

Step 4. If at least one of Q_1 and Q_2 is disjoint to at least one of P_1 and P_2, then we can obtain two disjoint paths and terminate.

Step 5. Let Q be one of the paths Q_1 and Q_2 that does not include neither x_1 nor y_1. In addition, let u and v be the nodes on $Q \cap (P_1 \cup P_2)$ that are nearest to x_2 and y_2, respectively. If u and v are both on either P_1 or P_2, here we assume that it is P_1, then the path P_2 from x_1 to y_1, the sub path of Q from x_2 to u, the sub path of P_1 from u to v, and the sub path of Q from v to y_2 are disjoint each other. On the other hand, if u and v are on different paths of P_1 and P_2, say u is on P_1 and v is on P_2, then the sub path of P_2 from x_1 to v, the sub path of Q from v to y_2, the sub path of Q from x_2 to u, and the sub path of P_1 from u to y_1 are disjoint each other.

2.4 Algorithm C

Finally, for $x_1, y_1, y_2 \in BR_{n-1}h$ and $x_2, x_3, y_3 \in BR_{n-1}k$ where $y_1 \neq y_2$, $x_2 \neq x_3$, $h \neq k$ and $n \geq 4$, we give an algorithm that generates three disjoint paths inside $BR_{n-1}h \cup BR_{n-1}k$ each of which has one terminal node in $X = \{x_1, x_2, x_3\}$ and the other in $Y = \{y_1, y_2, y_3\}$ in polynomial time of n.

Step 1. In $BR_{n-1}h$, select a node x_0 that is different from x_1, is not adjacent to y_3, and has an address of $(\cdots, k, h)$ or $(k, \cdots, h)$.

Step 2. For x_0, x_1, y_1, and y_2, apply Algorithm B to obtain two disjoint paths.

Step 3. Let y_0 be the neighbor node of x_0 in $BR_{n-1}k$. For x_2, x_3, y_3, and y_0, apply Algorithm B to obtain two disjoint paths.

Step 4. Select an edge (x_0, y_0) and terminate.

3 Algorithm

For a BR_3, the problem is trivial. Hence we assume that $n \geq 4$. Let the source node be $s = (s_1, s_2, \cdots, s_n)$, and the destination node be $d = (d_1, d_2, \cdots, d_n)$. Then we consider the following two cases. Theoretically our algorithm can be proved to be $O(n^4)$ for an n-bi-rotator graph and the maximum length of paths obtained to be $4n - 5$.

3.1 Case 1 ($s_n = d_n$)

Step 1. In $BR_{n-1}s_n$, apply the algorithm recursively to obtain $2n - 5$ internally disjoint paths between s and d.

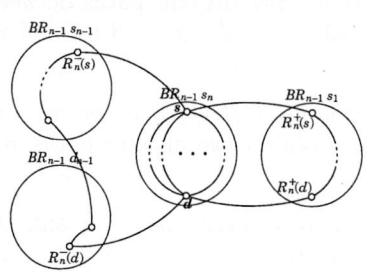
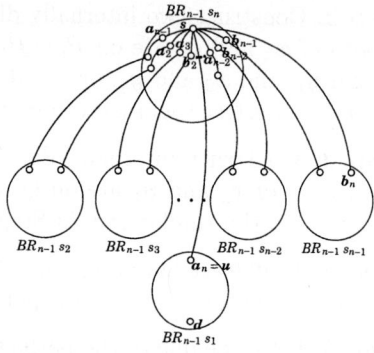

Fig. 3. Construction of outside paths ($s_1 = d_1, s_{n-1} \neq d_{n-1}$)

Fig. 4. Construction of disjoint paths from the source node to sub graphs ($d_n = s_1$)

Step 2. Select edges $(s, R_n^+(s))$, $(s, R_n^-(s))$, $(d, R_n^+(d))$, and $(d, R_n^-(d))$.

Step 3. For $R_n^+(s)$, $R_n^-(s)$, $R_n^+(d)$, and $R_n^-(d)$, if either $s_1 = d_1$ or $s_{n-1} = d_{n-1}$ holds, try to establish paths between $R_n^+(s)$ and $R_n^+(d)$, and between $R_n^-(s)$ and $R_n^-(d)$. Otherwise, try to establish paths between $R_n^+(s)$ and $R_n^-(d)$, and between $R_n^-(s)$ and $R_n^+(d)$. If the pair of nodes belong to a same sub graph, apply the auxiliary algorithm A inside the sub graph to obtain a path. Otherwise, select a path between the pair of nodes so that the path does not include any node outside of the sub graphs to which those nodes belong. See Figure 3.

3.2 Case 2 ($s_n \neq d_n$)

Step 1. First, name each of neighbor nodes of s as follows:
$$a_i = R_i^+(s) \quad (2 \leq i \leq n), \quad b_i = R_i^-(s) \quad (3 \leq i \leq n).$$

Next, construct paths from s to sub graphs $BR_{n-1}s_1, BR_{n-1}s_2, \cdots, BR_{n-1}s_{n-1}$ that are disjoint except for s as follows. Let u be the other terminal node of the path from s to $BR_{n-1}d_n$.

If $d_n = s_1$: $a_2 \to R_n^+(a_2)(\in BR_{n-1}s_2)$; $a_3 \to R_2^-(a_3) \to R_n^+(R_2^-(a_3))(\in BR_{n-1}s_3)$; $\cdots$; $a_{n-2} \to R_{n-3}^-(a_{n-2}) \to R_n^+(R_{n-3}^-(a_{n-2}))(\in BR_{n-1}s_{n-2})$; $a_{n-1} \to R_n^+(a_{n-1})(\in BR_{n-1}s_2)$; $a_n(\in BR_{n-1}s_1)$; $b_3 \to R_n^+(b_3)(\in BR_{n-1}s_3)$; $b_4 \to R_n^+(b_4)(\in BR_{n-1}s_4)$; $\cdots$; $b_{n-1} \to R_n^+(b_{n-1})(\in BR_{n-1}s_{n-1})$; $b_n(\in BR_{n-1}s_{n-1})$. See Figure 4.

If $d_n = s_{n-1}$: $a_2 \to R_n^+(a_2)(\in BR_{n-1}s_2)$; $a_3 \to R_2^-(a_3) \to R_n^+(R_2^-(a_3))(\in BR_{n-1}s_3)$; $\cdots$; $a_{n-2} \to R_{n-3}^-(a_{n-2}) \to R_n^+(R_{n-3}^-(a_{n-2}))(\in BR_{n-1}s_{n-2})$; $a_{n-1} \to R_n^+(a_{n-1})(\in BR_{n-1}s_2)$; $a_n(\in BR_{n-1}s_1)$; $b_3 \to R_n^+(b_3)(\in BR_{n-1}s_3)$; $b_4 \to R_n^+(b_4)(\in BR_{n-1}s_4)$; $\cdots$; $b_{n-2} \to R_n^+(b_{n-2})(\in BR_{n-1}s_{n-2})$; $b_{n-1} \to R_2^-(b_{n-1}) \to R_n^+(R_2^-(b_{n-1}))(\in BR_{n-1}s_1)$; $b_n(\in BR_{n-1}s_{n-1})$.

If $d_n = s_j$ ($j \neq 1, n-1$): $a_2 \to R_n^+(a_2)(\in BR_{n-1}s_2)$; $a_3 \to R_2^-(a_3) \to R_n^+(R_2^-(a_3))(\in BR_{n-1}s_3)$; $\cdots$; $a_{j-1} \to R_{j-2}^-(a_{j-1}) \to R_n^+(R_{j-2}^-(a_{j-1}))(\in$

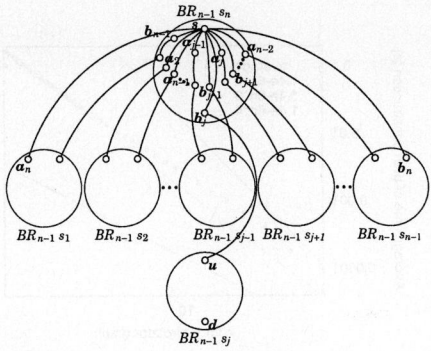
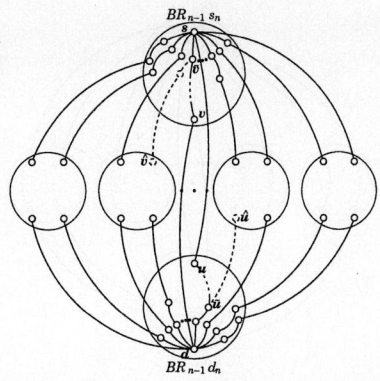

Fig. 5. Construction of disjoint paths from the source node to sub graphs ($d_n = s_j, j \neq 1, n-1$)

Fig. 6. Construction of paths between s and d

$BR_{n-1}s_{j-1}$); $a_j \to R_{j+1}^-(a_j) \to R_n^+(R_{j+1}^-(a_j))(\in BR_{n-1}s_{j+1})$; $\cdots$; $a_{n-2} \to R_{n-1}^-(a_{n-2}) \to R_n^+(R_{n-1}^-(a_{n-2}))(\in BR_{n-1}s_{n-1})$; $a_{n-1} \to R_n^+(a_{n-1})(\in BR_{n-1}s_2)$; $a_n(\in BR_{n-1}s_1)$; $b_3 \to R_n^+(b_3)(\in BR_{n-1}s_3)$; $b_4 \to R_n^+(b_4)(\in BR_{n-1}s_4)$; $\cdots$; $b_{n-2} \to R_n^+(b_{n-2})(\in BR_{n-1}s_{n-2})$; $b_{n-1} \to R_2^-(b_{n-1}) \to R_n^+(R_2^-(b_{n-1}))(\in BR_{n-1}s_1)$; $b_n(\in BR_{n-1}s_{n-1})$. See Figure 5.

Step 2. As similar to Step 1, construct paths from the destination node d to sub graphs $BR_{n-1}d_1, BR_{n-1}d_2, \cdots, BR_{n-1}d_{n-1}$ that are disjoint except for d. If $u = d$, then refrain from constructing a path from d to $BR_{n-1}s_n$. If $u \neq d$, then let v be the other terminal node of the path from d to $BR_{n-1}s_n$.

Step 3. If a path between s and d is not established yet, construct paths from u to d, and from v to d, and let $\tilde{u}$ and $\tilde{v}$ be the first nodes on the previously constructed paths that are encountered by these paths. Let $\hat{u}$ and $\hat{v}$ be the terminal nodes of these paths other than s and d, and discard sub paths from $\tilde{u}$ to $\hat{u}$ and from $\tilde{v}$ to $\hat{v}$. See Figure 6.

Step 4. In each sub graph other than $BR_{n-1}s_n$ and $BR_{n-1}d_n$, if even number of paths constructed in Steps 1 and 2 have reached to the sub graph, apply Algorithm A or B to connect terminal nodes appropriately. If there are two sub graphs both of which have three terminal nodes of paths, for these sub graphs, apply Algorithm C to connect these terminal nodes appropriately. See Figure 7.

3.3 Computer Experiment

To evaluate the performance of our algorithm, for each n between 3 and 50 we selected 10,000 random combinations of the source and destination nodes to apply our algorithm and measured the average execution time.

Figures 8 shows the result of the average execution time. From the figure, we can conclude that for an n-bi-rotator graph, our algorithm generates $2n-3$ internally disjoint paths in the average execution time $O(n^{3.0})$.

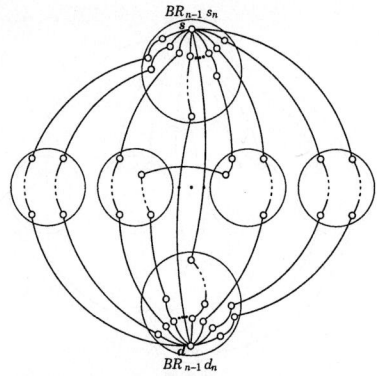

Fig. 7. Construction of paths in sub bi-rotator graphs

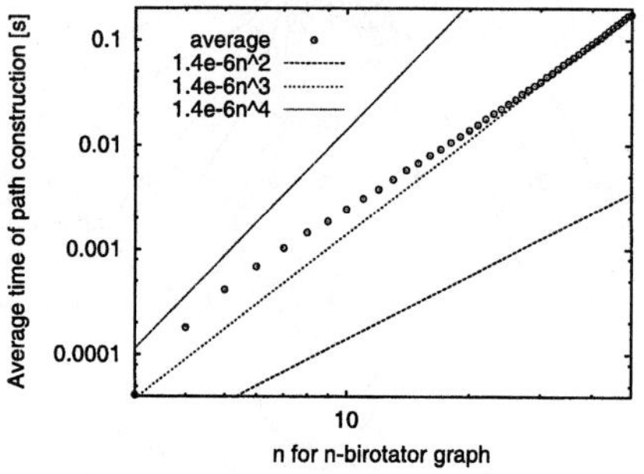

Fig. 8. Average execution time of our algorithm

4 Conclusion and Future Work

In this paper, we have proposed an algorithm that solves the container problem in an n-bi-rotator graph. Theoretical values for its time complexity and the maximum length of paths obtained by the algorithm are $O(n^4)$ and $4n - 5$, respectively. Computer experiment showed that the disjoint paths are obtained in $O(n^{3.0})$ time and the maximum length of them is $2n + 2$. The future work includes improvement of the algorithm so that the shorter paths are obtained in shorter time.

References

1. Corbett, P. F.: Rotator graphs: an efficient topology for point-to-point multiprocessor networks. IEEE Trans. Parallel and Distributed Systems, 3(5), 622–626, 1992.
2. M. Dietzfelbinger et al., Three disjoint path paradigms in star networks. Proc. IEEE SPDP, 400–406, 1991.
3. Gu, Q.-P., Peng, S.: Node-to-set disjoint paths problem in star graphs. IPL, 62(4), 201–207, 1997.
4. Hamada, Y., Bao, F., Mei, A., Igarashi, Y.: Nonadaptive fault-tolerant file transmission in rotator graphs. IEICE Trans. Fundamentals, E79-A(4), 477–482, 1996.
5. Kaneko, K., Suzuki, Y.: An algorithm for node-to-set disjoint paths problem in rotator graphs. IEICE Trans. Inf. & Syst., E84-D(9), 1155–1163, 2001.
6. Kaneko, K., Suzuki, Y.: Node-to-set disjoint paths problem in pancake graphs. IEICE Trans. Inf. & Syst., E86-D(9), 1628–1633, 2003.
7. Lin, H.-R., Hsu, C.-C.: Topological properties of bi-rotator graphs. IEICE Trans. Inf. & Syst., E86-D(10), 2172–2178, 2003.
8. Suzuki, Y., Kaneko, K.: An algorithm for node-disjoint paths in pancake graphs. IEICE Trans. Inf. & Syst., E86-D(3), 610–615, 2003.

WNChord: A Weighted Nodes Based Peer-to-Peer Routing Algorithm[1]

Liang Zhang, Shudong Chen, Fanyuan Ma, and Minglu Li

Department of Computer Science & Engineering, Shanghai Jiao Tong University,
Shanghai, 200030 China
zhangliang@cs.sjtu.edu.cn

Abstract. Considering the existing difference in load rates, computing performance and delivery latency between peers in Chord protocol, we present a weighted nodes based P2P routing algorithm(WNChord), in which each node could be treated respectively to make highly capable nodes take more tasks. Specifically speaking, the routing algorithm in peers is reformulated and is parameterized using a quantity C, which may control latency's expected value such that P2P network's total latency to become much lower by choosing proper C.

1 Introduction

In existing P2P routing algorithms (such as Chord, Tapestry, Pastry, CAN), routing is based solely on nodeID, which are chosen randomly (e.g. hashing of IP address, file name, etc). A path on the overlay network consists of a series of application-level, not IP-level, hops between the source and destination nodes. The efficiency measure used in existing routing algorithm was the number of application-level hops taken on the path. And each node is treated equivalently in most of P2P routing algorithm including traditional Chord, that is, it is assumed that all nodes have the same capacity to process messages and the same load rate. Considering that the heterogeneity observed in current P2P populations [1] is quite extreme, we propose a reformulation of the Chord such that each node could be treated respectively to make highly capable nodes take more tasks, i.e. each node is weighted, which we call the WNChord.

2 Chord Algorithm's Limitation

Chord [2] uses a one-dimensional circular key space as its ID space. As an example, consider the Chord ring in Figure 1. Suppose node 1 wants to locate the identifier 7. Since 7 belongs to the circular interval [5,0], it belongs to 1.finger[3].interval; node 1 therefore checks the third entry in its finger table, which is 5. Node 1 will ask node 5

---

[1] This paper is supported by 973 project (No.2002CB312002)of China, ChinaGrid Program of MOE of China, and grand project of the Science and Technology Commission of Shanghai Municipality (No. 03dz15026, No. 03dz15027 and No. 03dz15028).

to return the location of identifier 7. In turn, node 5 will infer from its finger table that 7's location is the node 0, and return node 0 to node 1. This is the process of Chord routing. However, as we see in the Figure 1, there exists another path which goes though node 3 from node 1 to 0. If the geographic information of node 0, 1, 3, and 5 is like the Figure 2, then we may see obviously that the latter path is better than the former one.

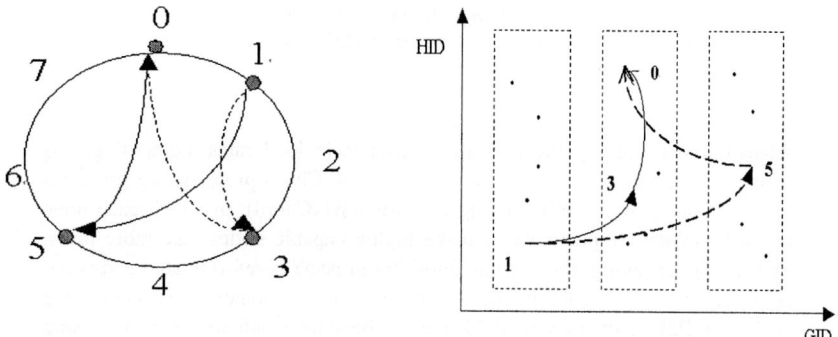

Fig. 1. An example of Chord network   **Fig. 2.** Geographic information

3 WNChord Routing Algorithm

We take into consider the load rate of each peer and its computing performance.[3] in WN-Chord. A network of P2P can be modeled by a vertex-weighted graph G=(V, E, α), where $\alpha : V \rightarrow [0,1]$ is the normalized performance of a peer: Let t_{v_0} be the time needed by a peer v_0 to execute a sequential process, and t_v the time needed on peer v, thus t_{v_0}/t_v is the performance of v with respect to v_0. At the same time considering load's effect on peers, through actual simulation we assume $\alpha_v = e^{-\beta} t_{v_0}/t_v$ is the actual performance ratio of v to v_0, where β is load rate of the peer. In order to have $\alpha \in [0,1]$ one takes the fastest peer for v_0. Here we use the parameter α to reflect the difference between peers, which is reflected in the item "finger[k].alpha" of the routing table.

Besides, the efficiency measure in Chord was the number of application-level hops taken on the path. However, the true efficiency measure is the end-to-end latency of the path. Because the nodes could be geographically dispersed, some of these application-level hops could involve transcontinental links, and others merely trips across a LAN; routing algorithms that ignore the latencies of individual hops are likely to result in high latency path. Thus the parameter latency should be introduced.

Considering the two aspects, the key location pseudocode of WNChord are shown in Figure 3. Parameter C in the *probability_locate* procedure in figure 3 reflects the tradeoff among peer's performance, next overlay hop's span distance and next overlay hop's latency. Adjusting C may affect the probability of next peer selected so as to lower latency's expected value of p2p network.

```
//ask node n to find id's successor
  n.find_successor(id)
      n'=find_predecessor(id);
      return n'.successor;
//ask node n to find id's predecessor
  n.find.predecessor(id)
      n'=n;
      while (id∉ (n',n'.successor])
          n'=n'. probability_locate (id);
      return n';
//return finger preceding id with random probability
  n.probability_locate(id)
      for i=m downto 1
      // parameter C reflects the tradeoff among peer's
      //performance , next overlay hop's span distance
      and next overlay hop's latency
      if( $e^{-C*\alpha*\log(finger[i].\text{span\_distance})/finger[i].\text{lantancy}} < rand[0,1]$ )
          return finger[i].node;
      return n;
```

Fig. 3. The pseudocode to find the successor node of an identifier id

In WNChord, a node determines which finger point should be used with a computed probability in term of the α and the delay. As an example above, consider the WNChord ring in Figure 4. We may get the path of $1 \rightarrow 3 \rightarrow 0$, other than $1 \rightarrow 5 \rightarrow 0$.

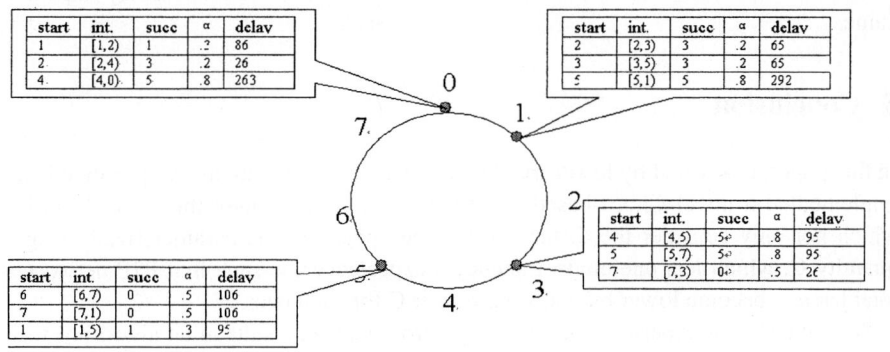

Fig. 4. Finger tables for a net with nodes 0,1,3, and 5

4 Experimental Results

In this section, we present some preliminary performance measurements of WNChord, compared to traditional Chord. We have implemented Chord and WNChord using Visual C++ on a 1.0 GHz Pentium IV processor under Windows 2000 with 512 megabytes of RAM..We use the Georgia Tech Internetwork Topological Models (GT-ITM) [4] to generate the network topologies used in our simulations. We use the "transit-stub" model to obtain topologies that more closely resemble the Internet hierarchy than pure random graph.

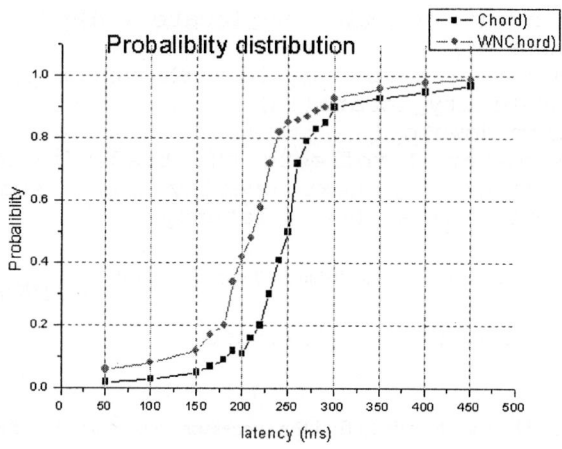

Fig. 5. Latency Probability distribution

According to the simulation, the latency probability distribution curves of the WNChord and Chord algorithms of 20000 peers are shown in Figure 5 (where $C=8$ for all peers in WNChord, ID space size is 2exp(20)), which shows that compared to the traditional Chord algorithm, WNChord has lower latency expected value.

5 Conclusion

In this paper, motivated by lower true latency in actual applications, we presented and implemented a novel Chord-based Weighed nodes routing algorithm --WNChord – which not only consider the difference between peers, but is parameterized using a quantity C, which lets one control latency's expected value such that P2P network's total latency become lower by choosing proper C for each peer.

We have shown experimentally that this reformulation results in an algorithm with lower latency for the whole P2P network. , which is very useful in actual applications. The results obtained in the example show the potential of the method.

References

1. SAROIU, S., GUMMADI, K., AND GRIBBLE, S. A measurement study of peer-to-peer file sharing systems. In *Proceedings of Multimedia Conferencing and Networking* (2002).
2. STOICA, I., MORRIS, R., KARGER, D., KAASHOEK, M. F.,AND BALAKRISHNAN, H. Chord: A scalable peer-to-peer lookup service for internet applications. In *Proceedings of the ACM SIGCOMM '01 Conference* (San Diego, California, August 2001).
3. Ohaha, Smart decentralized peer-to-peer sharing.http://www.ohaha.com/design.html.
4. Zegura, E. w., Calvert. k., and Bhattacharjee, S. How to model an Internetwork. InProceedings of IEEE INFOCOM (1996).

A Congestion Control Algorithm for Multimedia Traffic

Sharmin Parveen[1], Md. Rajibul Alam Joarder[2], Afreen Azhari[3],
Hasan Sarwar[1], and Dr. Shahida Rafique[1]

[1] Dept. of Applied Physics and Electronics, University of Dhaka, Bangladesh
[2] Dept. of Computer Science, Bangladesh National University, Dhaka
[3] Dept. of Electrical and Electronics Engineering,
Bangladesh University of Engineering & Technology (BUET)
mdhasan70@hotmail.com

Abstract. In this paper a new approach has been proposed to eliminate congestion that occurs in Internet, mostly caused by multimedia traffic. The new algorithm, Priority Queue Algorithm for multimedia traffic (PQAM) has been developed and simulated. Analysis has been performed on TEXT, AUDIO and VIDEO data packets. It has been found by simulation that PQAM gives better service in terms of less delay in comparison to Adaptive Virtual Queue Algorithm, Virtual Queue Algorithm, and DECbit Algorithm.

1 Introduction

Internet is being increasingly used for multimedia traffic. Audio, Video, animated image, telephone comprise this data traffic. To date, a number of congestion control algorithms have been evolved to handle this large amount of Non-TCP traffic. There already exist a good number of congestion control algorithms for end-to-end congestion control, namely, Drop Tail Algorithm, DECbit Algorithm, Random Early Detection Algorithm, Variations of RED Algorithm, Proportional Integral Controller Algorithm, Fair Queuing Algorithms, Random Exponential Marking Algorithm, Core Stateless Fair Queuing Algorithm, Virtual Queue Algorithm, Adaptive Virtual Queue Algorithm. In this paper, a new Congestion control Algorithm has been proposed and compared with the Adaptive Virtual Queue Algorithm (AVQ), RED, REM, PI, and VQ schemes.

2 Concept Overview

The fundamental idea of this algorithm is to give support to more users who are placing requests in the internet and thereby reducing congestion. Information consists of text, video, and audio data. It can easily be conceived that textual data is able to convey enough information to fulfill a user's request for information. For a more clear understanding of the query, a user may then ask for audio and visual demonstration. Again, a simple statement in text format can be accomodated within a very short sized packet. On the other hand, it can also be understood that, at any time interval, all users in a group may not request multimedia information simultaneously. Rather most of the users are satisfied with text formatted information most of the times. From the above analysis, it is evident that if same amount of time is allotted to provide service for text packets and video packets seperately, it will eventually ensure giving service to more number of users who are asking for text formatted information, that is, number of users being serviced at an interval can be maximized and congestion minimized.

In this approach, the order of service time for 3 different packets has been kept different. Where, $t_{st.text} < t_{st.audio} < t_{st.video}$
Here,

$t_{st.text}$ = Service time for a packet Text data
$t_{st.audio}$ = Service time for a packet Audio data
$t_{st.video}$ = service time for a packet Video data.

3 Algorithm

The proposed Priority Queue Algorithm for Multimedia Traffic (PQAM) consists of two modules. The packet arrival algorithm places incoming Text, Audio, and Video packets in Text, Audio and Video queue respectively. The server management algorithm serves each queue for a fixed amount of time.

3.1 Packet Arrival Algorithm:

1. Start Service for each Q.
2. A packet comes in.
3. if packet. type = "AUDIO" $Q_A \leftarrow$ Packet.
4. if packet. type = "VIDEO" $Q_V \leftarrow$ Packet.
5. if packet. type = "TEXT" $Q_T \leftarrow$ Packet.

3.2 Server Management Algorithm

1. For each Queue give service for a fixed amount of time t.

4 The Simulation Model

In the simulation model, packets are being generated according to an exponential distribution – having probability density function given by

$$qS(t) = \begin{cases} \lambda e^{-\lambda t} & t \geq 0 \\ 0 & t < 0 \end{cases} \quad (1)$$

In the simulation model, packets are being generated according to an exponential distribution – having probability density function given by

$$St(t) = \int \lambda e^{-\lambda} \quad (2)$$

5 Result and Discussion

The Proposed algorithm has been simulated and result has been shown graphically in the following figure.

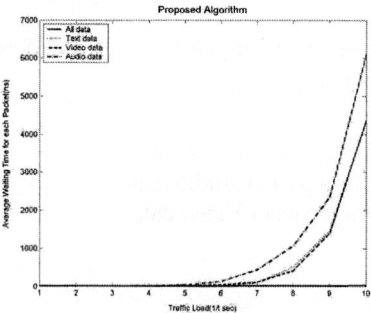

Fig. 1

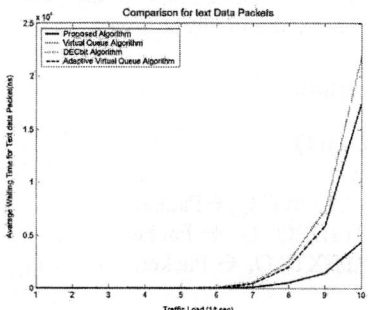

Fig. 2

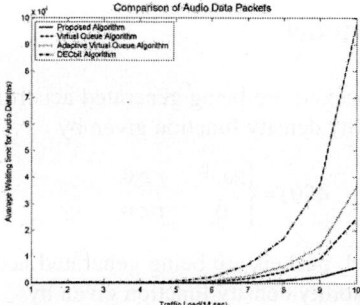

Fig. 3

Load has been considered as the inverse of mean inter-arrival time, i.e, traffic load = 1/t. In fig 1, the graph shows that for the proposed algorithm, the average waiting time increases as the traffic load increases, which is natural, but the waiting time for text packet in comparison with other packet is far less. Fig 2, 3, 4 shows the average waiting time of PQAM algorithm is less compared to DECbit algorithm, Virtual queue algorithm and adaptive virtual queue algorithm for text, audio and video data.

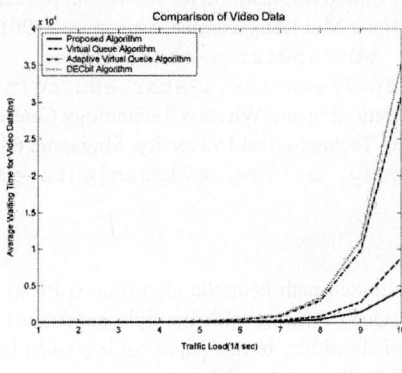

Fig. 4

In every graph, the load has been depicted on the X axis while the Y axis shows the waiting time.

6 Conclusion

It is concluded that PQAM can give better Quality of Service (QoS) by satisfying more user requests than that are supported by other algorithms.

References

1. F. Anjum and L. Tassiulas. Balanced-RED: An Algorithm to Achieve Fairness in the Internet. Proceedings of IEEE INFOCOM'99 Mar 1999.
2. B. Braden, D. Clark, et al. Recommendations on Queue Management and Congestion Avoidance in the Internet. Network Working Group, RFC2309, Apr 1998

Improved Limited Path Heuristic Algorithm for Multi-constrained QoS Routing

Wendong Xiao[1], Boon Hee Soong[2], Choi Look Law[2], and Yong Liang Guan[2]

[1] New Initiatives, Institute for Infocomm Research,
21 Heng Mui Keng Terrace, Singapore 119613
wdxiao@i2r.a-star.edu.sg
http://www.i2r.a-star.edu.sg/ni
[2] Positioning and Wireless Technology Centre,
Nanyang Technological University, Singapore 639798
{ebhsoong, ecllaw, eylguan}@ntu.edu.sg

Abstract. Recently limited path heuristic algorithm (LPHA) was proposed for Quality of Service (QoS) Routing with multiple constraints based on the extended Bellman-Ford algorithm. In this paper, an improved limited path heuristic algorithm (ILPHA) is introduced by means of two novel strategies, i.e., combining checking to deal with the path loss problem, and path selection to choose high-quality paths. Two path selection heuristics are recommended respectively based on the dominating area and maximal weight. Simulation results show that ILPHA can improve the performance of LPHA significantly. The comparison between the two path selection heuristics is also given.

1 Introduction

Quality of Service (QoS) routing is a natural requirement of real-time multimedia communications with the aim to find a feasible path that satisfies QoS constraints (usually in terms of bandwidth, delay, or delay-jitter etc.) and optimize the utilization of network resources. It is well-known that QoS routing with multiple path constraints is NP-complete, therefore many heuristics or approximation algorithms have been proposed [1]. In [2], by extension of the Bellman-Ford shortest path algorithm, Yuan proposes the limited path heuristic algorithm (LPHA) by maintaining a limited number of non-dominated paths, say X non-dominated paths[2], [3], at each node. Analytical and simulation studies indicate that LPHA is time/space efficient and relatively insensitive to the number of constraints. However, LPHA has the following drawbacks which affect its performance:

First, in LPHA, when the path table of a node is full, a new generated non-dominated path is inserted in the table only when it can dominate some existing paths in the table. Otherwise, it is discarded regardless of its quality. This simple discarding scheme can easily lose some new high-quality paths.

Second, the quality of the derived path table is affected by the checking sequence of the new generated paths, and the original sequentially checking scheme in LPHA may lose some useful paths. For example, for a network with two types of weights, suppose $X=3$, path p_1, p_2 and p_3 are 3 paths already in the path table of a node with weights (1, 6), (3, 5), and (4, 3), and path p_4 and p_5 are 2 new generated paths to this node with weights (2, 2) and (5, 1). If we check p_5 before p_4, the derived path table only includes p_1 and p_4. However, if we check p_4 before p_5, the derived path table will includes p_1, p_4 and p_5. Easy to see, the second checking sequence is better because it is more informative.

This paper presents an improved LPHA (ILPHA) with the aim to solve the above problems.

2 ILPHA

Two strategies are introduced in ILPHA, i.e., combining checking to overcome the path loss problem of LPHA and path selection heuristic to reduce the possibility to lose potential high quality paths. They are described as follows:

1) Combining Checking. Easy to see, after a relaxation operation [2] which relaxes all paths of a node, say nide i, to a second node, say node j, via a link, node j has at most $2X$ non-dominated paths (including X non-dominated paths in the original path table of node j and those new generated ones from node i). In this strategy, the path table of node j can temporarily contain all the candidate non-dominated paths. Therefore, it does not matter which checking sequence is used for the new generated paths as all of them will result in the same temporary path table in node j.

2) Path Selection Heuristics. If after combining checking, the temporary path table of node j still contains more than X non-dominated paths, some paths must be discarded in order to keep the number of paths bounded by X. Path selection heuristic is introduced for this purpose. Actually, several heuristics can be used here. In this paper, we recommend the following 2 heuristics:

- Maximal dominating area selection heuristic (Hereafter denoted as DomArea heuristic): the first X paths with maximal normalized dominating areas (each weight of a feasible path is normalized to [0,1] after divided by its corresponding constraint) are maintained, and the others are discarded.
- Minimal maximal-weight selection heuristic (Hereafter denoted as MaxXY heuristic): the first X paths with the minimal maximal-weights are maintained, and the others are discarded.

The mathematical formula for dominating area and maximal-weight of a path can be found in our previous paper [3] where they are used in path selection in the limited path Dijkstra's algorithm (LPDA) for QoS routing. The geographic explanations of DomArea and MaxXY heuristics in the 2-dimensional space are shown in Fig. 1, where $X=2$ and w_i, c_i ($i=1,2$) are the i-th weight and its corresponding constraint of the path. In both cases, p_2 is discarded because it is with the smallest dominating area and maximal-weight respectively. Easy to know, each non-dominated path dominates all the paths that lie in its dominating area where the path can be relaxed to by a later relaxation operation. DomArea heuristic is based on the knowledge that usually the bigger the domination area of a path is, the more likely that a derived path after the relaxation operation is feasible.

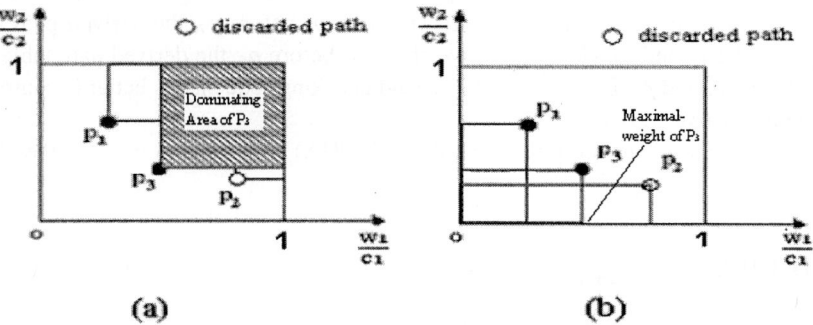

Fig. 1. DomArea heuristic (a) and MaxXY heuristic (b)

3 Experiments

The performance of ILPHA against LPHA is evaluated by experiments on the ANSNET network with 32 nodes and 52 links [3] and the grid networks. We consider 2-constrained path problem. The performance metric of a given heuristic is the competitive ratio (CR) which is defined as

$$CR = \frac{number\ of\ requests\ satisfied\ by\ the\ heuristic}{number\ of\ requests\ satisfied\ by\ the\ exhaustive\ heuristic}$$

In each routing request, for the ANSNET network, the source node s and destination node d are randomly generated. For a grid network, s and d are always selected as the two corner nodes that are farthest apart. For each routing request of both networks, the link weights are randomly generated, and the two constraints are set to the weights of the shortest path (calculated by conventional Dijkstra's algorithm) between s and d with regard to the equally weighted linear aggregate weight function. In this way, CR can be simplified to the following equation

$$CR = \frac{number\ of\ requests\ satisfied\ by\ the\ heuristic}{number\ of\ requests}$$

which is a good indication of the efficiency of a given heuristic.

The averaged CR result for the ANSNET network is shown in Fig. 2 based on 2000 generated routing requests. When X increases, the CRs of LPHA and ILPHAs increases steadily. When X is greater than or equal to 4, the CR of any algorithm is equal to 1.0, which means any of them can achieve the same performance as the exact algorithm. ILPHA with any heuristic significantly outperforms LPHA and the DomArea heuristic is slightly better than the MaxXY heuristic.

The averaged CR results for grid networks with size 10*10 and 20*20 are shown in Fig. 3 (a) and (b) respectively both based on 1000 generated routing requests.

Again ILPHA with any heuristic significantly outperforms LPHA, in addition, DomArea heuristic significantly outperforms the MaxXY heuristic. This remainders us that the dominating area based heuristic is more suitable for QoS route search.

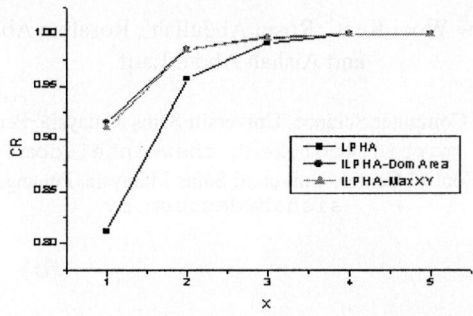

Fig. 2. CR against k with different heuristics (ANSNET network)

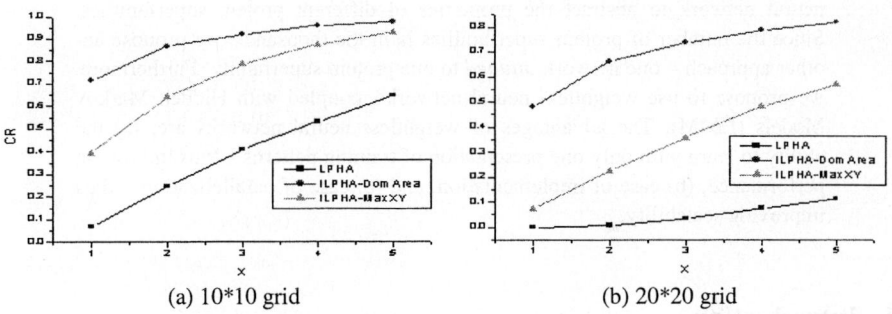

Fig. 3. CR against k with different heuristics (grid networks)

4 Conclusions

In this paper, ILPHA is introduced based on combining checking and path selection heuristics. DomArea and MaxXY path selection heuristics are also proposed. It is demonstrated that ILPHA significantly improves the performance of LPHA, and the DomArea heuristic outperforms the MaxXY heuristic.

References

1. Kuipers, F.A., Korkmaz, T., Krunz, M., Mieghem, P.V.: An Overview of Constraint-Based Path Selection Algorithms for QoS Routing. IEEE Commun. Mag. 40:12 (2002) 50–55
2. Yuan,X.: Heuristic Algorithms for Multiconstrained Quality-of-Service Routing. IEEE/ACM Trans. Netw. 10 (2002) 244–256
3. Xiao, W., Luo, Y., Soong, B.H., Xu, A., Law, C.L., Ling, K.V.: An Efficient Heuristic Algorithm for Multi-constrained Path Problems, IEEE VTC2002-Fall (2002) 1317–1321

Weightless Neural Network Array for Protein Classification

Martin Chew Wooi Keat[1], Rosni Abdullah[2], Rosalina Abdul Salam[3], and Aishah Abdul Latif[4]

[1,2,3] Faculty of Computer Science, Universiti Sains Malaysia, Penang, Malaysia
martin.wooi.keat.chew@intel.com
[4] Doping Control Center, Universiti Sains Malaysia, Penang, Malaysia
aishah@dcc.usm.my

Abstract. Proteins are classified into superfamilies based on structural or functional similarities. Neural networks have been used before to abstract the properties of protein superfamilies. One approach is to use a single conventional neural network to abstract the properties of different protein superfamilies. Since the number of protein superfamilies is in the thousands, we propose another approach – one network *attuned* to one protein superfamily. Furthermore, we propose to use weightless neural networks, coupled with Hidden Markov Models (HMM). The advantages of weightless neural networks are: (a) the ability to learn with only one presentation of training patterns – thus improving performance, (b) ease of implementation, and (c) ease of parallelization – thus improving scalability.

1 Introduction

This concept paper relates to the field of protein classification, for the purpose of functional determination, in order to assist the process of drug target discovery. Given an unlabeled protein sequence S and a known superfamily F, we wish to determine whether or not S belongs to F. We refer to F as the target class and the set of sequences not in F as the non-target class. In general, a superfamily is a group of proteins that share similarities in structure and/or function [1]. If the unlabeled sequence S is detected to belong to F, then one can infer the function of S. Neural networks have been used to classify proteins before [2]. However, our proposed approach will use an array of weightless neural networks. Weightless neural networks have been used for image recognition before [5]. We modified the concept of a weightless neural network to suit the purpose of protein classification. A particular weightless network is attuned to a particular protein superfamily. An unknown protein sequence submitted to the network array is deemed to belong to the protein superfamily represented by the network with the most positive output (i.e. the *resonant* network). We may also be able to deduce the degree of relationship of the sequence to other protein superfamilies by comparing the outputs of the other networks, relative to the resonant network.

2 System Description

The first step is to determine a particular transformation/encoding function, for the purpose of deriving from protein sequences, an array of real values to serve as inputs into the weightless network. The intention of the transformation function is to bring to surface (i.e. make explicit) the implicit feature(s) of protein sequences, for the purpose of abstraction. The transformation function plays a major role in the accuracy of the system. A particular protein superfamily is paired to the particular transformation function most suited to its properties. Each protein superfamily will be abstracted by its own weightless network. For the purpose of this paper, we will use a simple transformation function called 2-gram encoding for every protein family. The frequency of unique character *pairs* in a protein sequence is counted. Since there are 23 different amino acids, 2-gram encoding will give rise to 23x23 possible pairings. Therefore, the neural network will have 23x23 input units. Each input unit represents a particular *feature* of the protein. Different encoding techniques will give rise to different input features. For example, 3-gram encoding will give rise to 23x23x23 features. Each feature can be represented by an address. Since we have 23x23 possible pairings for 2-gram encoding, we need at least 23x23 addresses. The first feature will be mapped to address 000000000, the second feature to 000000001, etc. The content of each address will be initialized to zero. As each training sequence is presented to the weightless network, the value for a particular feature is accumulated in the address mapped to that feature.

Encoding systems such as 2-gram highlights global similarities at the expense of local similarities (i.e. local similarities such as motifs are lost during the transformation process). In order to factor in local similarities, a Hidden Markov Model (HMM) is used to abstract the motif indicative of a particular protein superfamily. HMMs have been used before, either singularly or in conjunction with conventional neural networks [3], [4]. Different superfamilies would most probably have different indicator motifs. There could also be more than one motif for a particular superfamily. First, the cluster of motifs has to be abstracted into a HMM. When a particular substring – window-scanned from a protein sequence - is submitted to the HMM, the model is able to return a probability value, indicating the consensus of the given substring, with respect to the cluster of motifs the model represents. Once these steps are done, the system is ready to be used in a predictive mode. Only addresses with final contents over a pre-determined threshold (we call this threshold the "weightless threshold") will be selected, the rest being ignored. Given an unknown protein sequence, the 2-gram encoding method is applied to extract an array of values (i.e. an integer count for each 2-gram pair). These values will serve as inputs (I) to a particular weightless network. To calculate the final output (R) of the weightless network, a mapping is done between cells of the input array and the selected addresses of the weightless network. Only cells with a count of more than 1 will be selected for the mapping, the rest being ignored. For each matching input cell and weightless address, a point will be scored. The final output (R) is the percentage of matches with respect to the number of active addresses.

3 Experimental Results

For experimental data, we relied on the Superfamily 1.65 website (http://supfam.mrc-lmb.cam.ac.uk/SUPERFAMILY/cgi-bin/align.cgi). We pulled data for three protein families (acid proteases, cytochrome b5, and cytochrome c) from the SCOP 1.63 Protein DataBase. Table 1 below shows the settings of our experiment, and Table 2 shows the results we obtained. (sample F1-1 refers to sample #1 from family F1, sample F3-3 refers to sample #3 from family F3).

Table 1. Weightless network settings

Network	Sequences	Average seq. length	Weightless threshold	Active addresses
Acid proteases	118	183	120	44
Cytochrome b5	28	81	40	7
Cytochrome c	129	120	95	14

Table 2. Results

Sample	Acid proteases (F1)	Cytochrome b5 (F2)	Cytochrome c (F3)	Correct
Sample F1-1	**65%**	0%	2%	Yes
Sample F2-2	**65%**	0%	4%	Yes
Sample F3-3	**65%**	2%	2%	Yes
Sample F2-1	28%	**57%**	28%	Yes
Sample F2-2	28%	**57%**	0%	Yes
Sample F2-3	28%	**100%**	14%	Yes
Sample F3-1	**21%**	**21%**	**21%**	No
Sample F3-2	**21%**	14%	**21%**	No
Sample F3-3	21%	21%	**50%**	Yes

We chose three random samples from each family (for a total of 9 samples), and we fed each sample into every network. Every sample scored the highest in its correct network, with the exception being sample F3-1 and sample F3-3. In other words, family 1 (acid proteases) and family 2 (cytochrome b5) was well abstracted, but not family 3 (cytochrome c). We attribute this to the loss of local similarities when the families when 2-gram encoding was applied. As we mentioned before, HMMs (each unique to a particular family) are necessary for further differentiation. In the case of the two samples of exception (sample F3-1 and sample F3-3), the HMM trained on local similarities of family 3 (cytochrome c) should return a high probability value for sample F3-1 and sample F3-3, and a low probability value for samples from other families. This will help to boost the score of sample F3-1 and sample F3-3, and push down the score of samples from the other families. The quality of the prediction will then be further improved. One drawback of this system is that the training data sets for each protein family must have sufficient members, and each member must be of sufficient length. This is necessary in order to enable the network to fully abstract the properties of the protein family. The training data sets should be filtered to exclude sequences which are too short. Another drawback is that each weightless threshold must be individually adjusted to provide the optimum results.

4 Potential Contributions to the Field of Bioinformatics

Currently, neural networks require numerous iterations over the training data set to reach convergence. Furthermore, an increase in the number of input units (e.g. from 2-gram encoding to 3-gram) could lead to an increase in training time as well. We intend to explore the use of weightless neural networks to help overcome this problem. The ease with which weightless neural networks may be implemented will help make parallelization easier. Our system requires one weightless network for one protein family. If there are a thousand protein families, we will have a thousand weightless networks. Parallelization will enable different protein families to be abstracted, and repeatedly reabstracted (in the event of a new encoding formula) in parallel. Finally, when an unknown sequence is submitted to the array of weightless networks, the outputs from the array will help us decide, not only from which protein family the unknown sequence may be from, but also, its degree of relationship to other families. Even if the array has several high outputs, this could help us narrow down the possibilities of which family an unknown sequence belongs to, by helping us to focus on a few most likely candidate families.

References

1. Pandit, Shashi B., et. al. : SUPFAM − A Database of Potential Protein Superfamily Relationships. Indian Institute of Science, Bangalore (2001).
2. Wang, J., Ma, Q., Shasha, D., Wu, C. : Application of Neural Networks to Biological Data Mining : A Case Study in Protein Sequence Classification. Department of Computer Science, New Jersey Institute of Technology (2001).
3. Krogh, A : An Introduction to Hidden Markov Models for Biological Sequence. Technical University of Denmark (1998).
4. Ohler, U., Stemmer, G., Niemann, H. : A Hybrid Markov Chain - Neural Network System for the Exact Prediction of Eukaryotic Transcription Start Sites. University Erlangen, Nuremberg, Germany. (2000).
5. Burattini, E., DeGregorio, M., Tamburrini, G. : Generating and Classifying Recall Images by Neurosymbolic Computation. Cybernectics Institute, Italy (1998).

Vector Quantization Using Enhanced SOM Algorithm

Jae-Hyun Cho[1], Hyun-Jung Park[2], and Kwang-Baek Kim[3]

[1] Dept. of Computer Information, Catholic University of Pusan, Korea
[2] Dept. of Architectural Engineering, Silla University, Korea
[3] Dept. of Computer Engineering, Silla University, Korea
jhcho@cup.ac.kr, {phj, gbkim}@silla.ac.kr

Abstract. The vector quantization for color image requires the analysis of image pixels for determinating the codebook previously not known, and the self-organizing map (SOM) algorithm, which is the self-learning model of neural network, is widely used for the vector quantization(VQ). However, the vector quantization using SOM shows the underutilization that only some code vectors generated are heavily used. This defect is incurred because it is difficult to estimate correctly the center of data with no prior information of the distribution of data. In this paper, we propose an enhanced self-organizing vector quantization method for color images. The results demonstrated that compression ratio by the proposed method was improved to a greater degree compared to the conventional SOM algorithm.

1 Introduction

In the compression methods introduced until now, the image compression by Vector Quantization (VQ) is most popular and shows a good data compression ratio. Self-organizing map (SOM) is widely applied in the vector quantization, which is the self-learning method among neural network algorithms [1][2]. SOM classifies the input vector by clustering features with similarity to the given vector and stores the information of an input vector in the winner node which corresponds to the representative class selected for the input vector. Given an input pattern, SOM adjusts the corresponding saved pattern to get the likelihood with the input pattern by reflecting the difference of the input pattern and the stored pattern to the saved. In the case which many input patterns are applicable at one class, the stored pattern is adaptively adjusted including all information of features of input patterns. The process adaptively adjusting the weight of the saved pattern in SOM algorithm is the same as the process generating dynamically a code vector in the codebook for the given input vector in the vector quantization. Therefore, the vector quantization using SOM algorithm generates the codebook dynamically for color images [3]. But, with no information of the distribution of learning vectors, the vector quantization using SOM algorithm selects randomly the initial code vectors and progresses the adaptive learning [4]. In this paper, we propose an enhanced self-organizing vector quantization for color images.

2   Vector Quantization Using Enhanced SOM Algorithm

In this paper, we improved the SOM algorithm by employing three methods for the efficient generation of codebook. In the proposed method, the codebook is generated by presenting the entire image only two times. In the first step, the initial codebook is generated to reflect the distribution of the given training vectors. The second step uses the initial codebook and regenerates the codebook by moving to the center within the decision region. To generate the precise codebook, it needs to select the winner node correctly and we have to consider the real distortion of the code vector and the input vector. For this management, the measure of the frequency to be selected as winner node and the distortion for the selection of the winner node in the competitive learning algorithm are needed. Generally the SOM algorithm uses the following equation for the weight adaptation.

$$w_{ij}(t+1) = w_{ij}(t) + \alpha(x_i - w_{ij}(t)) \tag{1}$$

α is the learning factor between 0 and 1 and is set between 0.25 and 0.75 in general. $(x_i - w_{ij}(t))$ is an error value and represents the difference between the input vector and the representative code vector. This means weights are adapted as much as the difference and it prefers to adapt the weight in proportion to the size of the difference. Therefore, we use the normalized value for the output error of the winner node that is converted to the value between 0 and 1 as a learning factor. The larger the output error, the more amount for the weight adaptation. So, the weight is adapted in proportion to the size of the output error.

Based on the above method, we use the following equation in the weight adaptation.

$$w_{ij}(t+1) = w_{ij}(t) + \alpha(x_i - w_{ij}(t))$$

$$\alpha = f(e_j) + \frac{1}{f_j} \tag{2}$$

where $f(e_j)$ is the normalization function that converts the value of e_j to the value between 0 and 1, e_j is the output error of the jth neuron, and f_j is the frequency for the jth neuron as the winner. The above method considers only the present weight change and does not consider the previous weight change. So in the weight adaptation, we consider the previous weight change as well as the present one's. This concept corresponds to the momentum parameter of BP. We will also call this concept as a momentum factor. Based on the momentum factor, the equation for the weight adaptation is as follows:

$$w_{ij}(t+1) = w_{ij}(t) + \delta_{ij}(t+1) \tag{3}$$

$$\delta_{ij}(t+1) = \alpha(x_i - w_{ij}(t)) + \alpha \delta_{ij}(t) \tag{4}$$

3 Simulation

Simulation was performed on a personal computer using C++ builder to evaluate the proposed method. Digitized color images of the (R, G, B) domain and a resolution of 128 x 128 were used for the simulation. Fig.1 shows various images used for simulation.

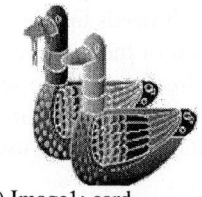 

(a) Image1: card   (b) Image2: Album cover over record

Fig. 1. Original images used for simulation

In conventional SOM, only winning neurons and their neighbors participate in learning, for a given vector. Hence, a neighborhood parameter was used in the Kohonen net. The initial values of the gain factor and the neighborhood size were given and they were decreased as the input vector cycles continued. The error tolerance limit was fixed at a very low level of $Escrit = 0.0001$ and the error tolerance for all the individual vectors was accumulated. The enhanced self-organizing vector quantization for color images proposed in this paper, can decrease the number of times the entire image data is read. Table1 show the size of the codebook file for the conventional SOM and the enhanced self-organizing vector quantization for color images.

Table 2, which shows the MSE values of images created by using the conventional SOM and the enhanced SOM and from Fig. 2 through 3.

Table 1. Size of codebook by VQ (byte)

Images / Algorithms	SOM	Enhanced SOM
Image1	32208	31968
Image3	22656	21456

Table 2. Comparison of MSE (Mean Square Error) for compressed images

Images / Algorithms	SOM	Enhanced SOM
Image1	13.1	11.2
Image2	9.2	8.4

Fig.2 and Fig.3 show respectively recovered images for original images of Fig.1. This contribution proposed an improved SOM algorithm. It improves compression and replay rate of image by the codebook dynamic allocation than the conventional SOM algorithm.

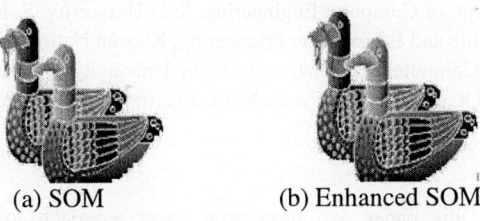

(a) SOM (b) Enhanced SOM

Fig. 2. The recovered image for Image1

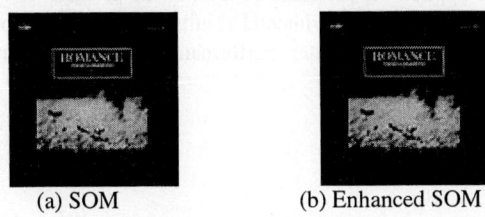

(a) SOM (b) Enhanced SOM

Fig. 3. The recovered image for Image2

4 Conclusion

The proposed method in this paper can be summarized method as follows: Using the enhanced SOM algorithm, the output error concept is introduced into the weight adaptation and the momentum factor is added. The simulation results show that the enhanced SOM algorithm for color image compression produces a major improvement in both subjective and objective quality of the decompressed images.

Generally, the procreation of the codebook is difficult work in vector quantization of color image. Therefore, we propose a new method that uses enhanced SOM learning algorithm to increase the compression and replay ratio.

References

1. Kohonen, T.: Improved versions of learning vector quantization. Proceedings of IJCNN. Vol. 1. (1990) 545-550
2. Kim, K. B., and Cha, E. Y.: A Fuzzy Self-Organizing Vector Quantization For Image. Proceedings of IIZUKA. Vol. 2. (1996) 757-760
3. Jo, L., and Kaimal, M. R.: Image Compression using Self-Organizing Neural Networks. Proceedings of National Seminar on Artificial Neural Networks and Cognitive System. (1998) 143-147
4. Madeiro, F., Vilar, R. M., Fechine, J. M., and Aguiar Neto, B. G.: A Slef-Organizing Algorithm for Vector Quantizer Design Applied to Signal Processing. International Journal of Neural Systems. Vol. 9. No. 3. (1999) 219-226

An Enhanced Fuzzy Neural Network

Kwang Baek Kim[1], Young-Hoon Joo[2], and Jae-Hyun Cho[3]

[1] Dept. of Computer Engineering, Silla University, S. Korea
[2] School of Electronic and Information Engneering, Kunsan National University, S. Korea
[3] Dept. of Computer Information, Catholic University of Pusan, S. Korea
gbkim@silla.ac.kr, yhjoo@kunsan.ac.kr, jhcho@cup.ac.kr

Abstract. In this paper, we propose a novel approach for evolving the architecture of a multi-layer neural network. Our method uses combined ART1 algorithm and Max-Min neural network to self-generate nodes in the hidden layer. We have applied the proposed method to the problem of recognizing ID number in identity cards. Experimental results with a real database show that the proposed method has better performance than a conventional neural network.

1 Introduction

Error backpropagation algorithm is a typical learning algorithm of multilayer neural networks which were proposed to solve the nonlinear problem that single percepron can not solve. In error backpropagation algorithm, the learning speed is determined by setting parameter up according to input patterns, and the paralysis and local minima problem are generated from setting the number of nodes of hidden layer [1][2]. If the hidden layer has too many nodes, the redundant nodes, which have no effect on discriminative performance, result in longer learning time. If the hidden layer does not have sufficient nodes, the possibility of placing the connection weights in local minima may be increased [3][4]. It is easy to find the number of nodes in a simple linear separation problem or in an Exclusive OR problem. But it is difficult to find the number of nodes in complex problem such as pattern recognition. Therefore, the approximated solution, which is computed by iterative calculation through heuristic methods, is generally used as the number of nodes in the hidden layer. In this paper, we proposed an enhanced fuzzy neural network, which is composed of ART1 and fuzzy neural network [5], for the solving problem of setting the number of nodes of the hidden layer in error backpropagation algorithm, which would make the learning speed of error backpropagation slow.

2 Enhanced Fuzzy Neural Network

BP learning method used widely in multilayer neural networks has a possibility of getting trapped in local minima due to inadequate weights and insufficient number of hidden nodes. Therefore, we propose an enhanced fuzzy neural network using self-organization that self-generates hidden nodes using the compound ART1 algorithm and Max-Min neural network. The proposed network is presented with a large number of patterns and each hidden layer neuron represents the cluster center. The prototype pattern for each cluster is represented by the weights from the hidden neuron to the input neuron. Vigilance criterion is used to achieve unsupervised learning which determines the actual number of clusters.

In the proposed architecture, the connection structure between input layer and hidden layer is similar to structure of the modified ART1. The output layer of the modified ART1 is used as the hidden layer in the proposed structure. A node of hidden layer represents each class. The nodes in hidden layer are fully connected to nodes in input and output layers. In the case of backward propagation by comparing target value with actual output value, we adapt a winner-take-all method to modify weighting factor of only the synapse that is connected to the neuron representing the winner class. The adaptation of weight of synapses between output layer and hidden layer is accomplished by Max-Min neural network. The creation for organizing the clustering layer nodes is based on the number of determining classes based on input patterns. Based on ART1, we assume the number of maximum initial nodes of the hidden layer as the number of classes. Starting with one node, we allocate related classes to the initially suggested pattern from the input layer of the node. Next input patterns choose a winner from the nodes in the present state. If all the existing nodes fail to choose a winner, one node is added and allocated to the class for the presented pattern. In this way, patterns are sequentially presented and the nodes for the class are created dynamically. If the stored pattern of the winner node is similar to the input pattern, it becomes the winner. Otherwise, classification is repeated until we get a winner. If an existing node is found to be a winner node, all the weights linking that node to the input layer are updated to reflect the accommodation of that input pattern into the representative class.

The proposed algorithm uses a winner-take-all method instead of the conventional error backpropagation learning to change weights. When we classify the connection between the input layer and the clustering layer, and the connection between the clustering layer and the target layer, the winner node chosen from the clustering layer becomes the representative class of input pattern. Therefore, we should adjust the weights connected to the winner node from the clustering layer to the input layer. To reflect target value for the input pattern to the actual output value by the representative class, we change only the connection weights related to the target layer node and its representative class.

3 Experiments and Performance Analysis

To analyze proposed method's performance, we simulated the algorithm using Intel Pentium-1GHz PC and Visual C++ 6.0. HP Scanjet 4200C scanner obtains the BMP files (600x400) of student ID card, and we compared the proposed algorithm with conventional backpropagation algorithm using 10 ID codes extracted from student ID cards.

The region of ID code was extracted by two procedures. First the region containing the ID numbers was extracted from the ID card image. Then the individual numbers were extracted from that field. The individual ID code was extracted as follows: The presented scheme sets up an average brightness as a threshold, based on the brightest

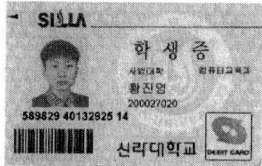

Fig. 1. Sample of test image

pixel and the least bright one for the source image of the ID card. After converting to a binary image, a horizontal histogram was applied and the ID code was extracted from the image. Then the noise was removed from the ID code region using mode smoothing with a 3x3 mask. After removing noise from the ID-code region, the individual ID code was extracted using a vertical histogram [6]. Table 1 shows the number of the success convergence by applying 50 number patterns to the error backpropagation and proposed method. In the error backpropagation algorithm, the initial learning rate is 0.3 and the momentum is 0.5. In the proposed algorithm, the vigilance parameter is 0.9. In the criterion of success convergence, the number of epoch is limited to 20,000 and TSS is 0.04.

Table 1. Comparison of Learning Convergence between BP and the Proposed Method

	# of trials	# of success	# of the nodes of hidden layer	# of epoch (average)
BP	10	4	12	10952
Enhanced Fuzzy Neural Network	10	10	15	571

As shown Table 1, the number of success convergence of the proposed method is larger and the average number of epoch of that is smaller than the error backpropagation algorithm. Table 2 presents the result of training through vigilance variable's change (0.8~0.9) in the proposed method. We set a momentum with 0.95 in Table 2.

Table 2. Epoch Number & Produced Node Number through Vigilance Parameter's Change

	Vigilance parameter	# of epoch	# of the nodes of hidden layer
Proposed Method	0.8	558	14
	0.85	571	15
	0.9	571	15

We could confirm the fact that the proposed method changed the number of hidden node according to vigilance variable's value, but did not affect training time.

Through experimental results, we found that the proposed method spent less time for training compared with the conventional training method, and had good convergence ability. This is based on the fact that winner-take-all method is adapted to the connection weight adaptation, so that a stored pattern for some pattern gets updated. Moreover, the proposed method reduced the possibility of local minima due to the inadequate weights and the insufficient number of hidden nodes. The reason is that adjustment of weights by the winner-take-all method decreases the amount of computation, and adjusting only the related weights decreases the competitive stages as a premature saturation. Therefore, there is less possibility of the paralysis and local minima in the proposed method.

4 Conclusion

This paper proposed an enhanced fuzzy multi-layer perceptron learning algorithm using self-organization that self-generates hidden nodes by the compound Max-Min neural network and modified ART1. From the input layer to hidden layer, a modified ART1 was used to produce nodes. Moreover, winner-take-all method was adapted to the connection weight adaptation, so that a stored pattern gets updated. To analyze proposed method's performance, we tested student ID-card images. Through experiments, we found that the proposed method was quite robust with respect to minor change in the momentum parameter. Moreover, it had good convergence ability, and took less training time than conventional backpropagation algorithm.

References

1. Hecht-Nielse, R.: Theory of Backpropagation Neural Networks. Proceedings of IJCNN. Vol. 1. (1998) 593-605
2. Hirose, Y., Yamashita, K., Hijihya, S.: Backpropagation Algorithm Which Varies the Number of Hidden Units. Neural Networks. Vol. 4. (1991) 61-66
3. Kim, K. B., Kang, M. H., and Cha, E. Y.: Fuzzy Competitive Backpropagation using Nervous System. Proceedings of WCSS. (1997) 188-193
4. Kim, K. B., Kim, Y. J.: Recognition of English Calling Cards by Using Enhanced Fuzzy Radial Basis Function Neural Networks. IEICE Trans. Fundamentals. E87-A(6) (2004) 1355-1362
5. Saito, T., Mukaidono, M.: A Learning algorithm for Max-Min Network and its Application to Solve Relation Equations. Proceedings of IFSA. (1991) 184-187
6. Kim, T. K., Yun, H. G., Lho, Y. W., and Kim, K. B.: An Educational Matters Administration System on The Web by Using Image Recognition. Proceedings of Korea Intelligent Information Systems. (2002) 203-209

A Novel Anti-spam Email Approach Based on LVQ

Zhan Chuan, Lu Xianliang, and Xing Qian

College of Computer Science and Engineering, UESTC of China, Chengdu 610054
{zhanchuan, xlu}@uestc.edu.cn, nancyhouse@etang.com

Abstract. Along with wide application of e-mail nowadays, a great deal of spam e-mails flood into email inboxes and bring catastrophe to people's study and life. This paper presents a novel anti-spam e-mail filter based-LVQ network in terms of spam e-mails which are mainly made up of several kinds commercial or political spam emails at present. Experiments have proved that the filter based on LVQ outperforms Bayes-based and BP-based approaches in total performances apparently.

1 Introduction

Along with wide application of the Internet, e-mail has been used widely with its characteristics of high-speed, convenient, low cost and become an efficient and popular communication medium nowadays. However, many of spam e-mails flood into email inboxes and bring catastrophes into people's study and life. Spam e-mails are annoying to most users, as they waste users time, money as well as network bandwidth. Sometimes, they even are harmful, e.g. pornographic content. Without appropriate counter-measures, the situation will continue worsening and spam emails will eventually undermine the usability of email.

In terms of content-based anti-spam email filtering, emails are usually regarded as particular texts. Sahami[1] et al. used Bayes theory to filter spam emails. James clark et al.[2] designed a 3 layers BP neural network, which had rather good effect of identifying spam emails. Duhong Chen et al.[3] compared four algorithms, Bayes, decision tree, neural networks, Boosting, and found that neural network algorithm had better performance.

This paper uses a LVQ neural network, which combines several subclasses into a single class and forms complex class boundaries, to design an anti-spam model and identify spam emails which are mainly composed of commercial and political emails. Experiments have proved that the LVQ-based anti-spam email filter has better performance than Bayes-based and BP neural network-based approaches.

2 Data Preprocessing

Email may be regarded as a vector space which is composed of a group of orthogonal key words. let the dimension of vector space be n, email d represents by $V(d) = (x_1, x_2, \cdots, x_n)$, with weight of each feature key word in email d. We use TFIDF [4] approach to calculate feature weight.

We adopt feature based on word in our experiments in order to focus on our algorithm performance and simplify our test. A mail contains many different words. A large part of words contribute little to the classification, what's more, some words may play a negative role in classifying process. Hence, it is necessary to select some words as features. We select features by MI (Mutual Information) [5] method. For multi-class, we compute MI of the word corresponding to every class respectively and then select the maximum. We will choose feature words whose MI is bigger than a threshold so as to decrease the dimensionality of vector space.

3 Anti-spam Email LVQ Model

3.1 Spam Email Category

Spam emails vary significantly in content. Related statistic [6] shows that spam emails are mainly composed of shopping online, promoting IT products, get-rich, adult products, vacation, political information, business information, pornography violence as well as other in content, shown in figure 1. Therefore, category of spam emails is rather wide. Clustering centers of different subclasses of spam emails are different so that

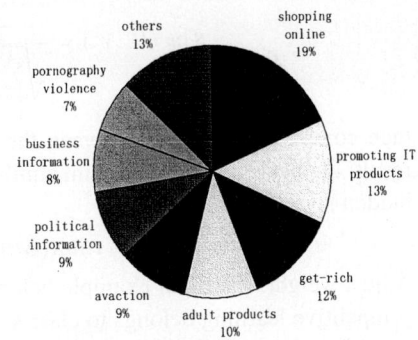

Fig. 1. category of spam email

feature words of the whole spam emails are sparse in content. Hence, it is difficult to distinguish spam emails from legitimate emails. If we divide spam emails into several subclasses according to content, feature words of every subclass is closer and more related so as to identify them easily. Therefore, in our approach, we firstly identify whether an email belongs to one of subclasses of spam emails. If so, due to legitimate emails being usually rather different from above subclasses of spam email in content, the email will be regarded as a spam email.

3.2 Learning Vector Quantization Neural Network Model

LVQ network [7] is a hybrid network, which form classification through supervise and unsupervised learning. The model is divided into two layers. The first layer is competitive layer, in which each neuron represents a subclass, and the second is output layer, in which each neuron represents a class. A class may be composed of several subclasses. The second layer combines several subclasses into a class through W^2 matrix. So LVQ network may create complex boundaries through combining several subclasses into a class. Therefore, LVQ is suited to classify spam emails which have several subclasses.

In input layer of our anti-spam email LVQ network model, we choose 100 feature words as input nodes. According to previous experiments, when the number of feature is set 100, the filter has a better performance. If the number continues to increase, the performance improves slightly, but calculation increases sharply. We choose 10 neurons in hidden layer with competitive function. In output layer, two neurons (legitimate and spam) and linear function are set.

3.3 Anti-spam Email LVQ Algorithm

- Initialize weight vectors W={ $w_1, w_2, \cdots, w_n$ }, and learning rate $a \in [0, 1]$
- Select an example from training email corpus, and calculate distance between weight vectors and it respectively. We take the place of Euclidean distance in formula with Cosine distance, which represents similarity of two texts. cosine distance is defined as follows:

$$Sim(U,V) = \frac{\sum_{k=1}^{n} w_{uk} \Box w_{vk}}{\sqrt{\sum_{k=1}^{n} w_{uk}^2} \sqrt{\sum_{k=1}^{n} w_{vk}^2}} \quad (1)$$

then compare similarities between the example and each weight vector, in the result, the neuron with maximum similarity, wins and outputs 1, other neuron of hidden layer output 0

$$a^1 = \max(Sim(x, x^i)) \quad (2)$$

- Adjust weight, if a input example belongs to class r, the neuron c which wins in competitive learning belongs to class s, we will adjust weight in accordance with formula (6)

$$\begin{cases} w_c(t+1) = w_c(t) + u(t)[x(t) - w_c(t)]; & r = s \\ w_c(t+1) = w_c(t) - u(t)[x(t) - w_c(t)]; & r \neq s \\ w_i(t+1) = w_i(t); & i \neq c \end{cases} \quad (3)$$

- Modify learning rate $u(t)$, decrease $u(t)$ when iteration increasing
- Check stopping condition, whether is iterative times enough.

4 Experiments and Result

This project makes use of email corpus from http://www. Spamassassin. org/ publiccorpus, which is open available source. We select 1000 pieces e-mails randomly from the corpus, including 580 spam e-mails, 420 legitimate e-mails. The corpus consists of all English emails whose attachments, html tags and email headers except the subject line have been stripped off.

In the experiments, we compare performances of LVQ-based approach, Bayes-based as well as BP neural network-based, shown in Table 1.

In table 1, we list the performances of three algorithms, both algorithms based on neural network, which have slight improvement in SP whereas improve SR apparently, are superior to Bayes-based approach. In two neural networks, LVQ-based is better than BP-based in both SP and SR. In the terms of F1, Naïve Bayes, ANN-BP, ANN-LVQ increase in sequence.

Table 1. Comparison of performance of three algorithms

	SP(%)	SR(%)	F1(%)
Naïve Bayes	97.63	86.48	91.72
ANN−BP	98.42	91.26	94.70
ANN−LVQ	98.97	93.58	96.20

5 Conclusion

This paper further classifies spam email into several subclasses according to spam email content, selects corresponding feature words of each subclass of spam emails, then combines the subclasses into complex classes by LVQ neural network so as to identify spam emails more accurately.

Both neural network-based algorithms are usually better than approach based on Bayes. Because neural networks take account of relationship between each feature words on the whole, and yet Bayse-based algorithm simply thinks that feature words are independent.

LVQ-based method outperforms method based on BP, because we classify spam emails into several subclasses in content so that the feature words of each subclass of spam email is more related and closer as well as characteristics of each subclass of spam emails are easier to identify.

References

1. Sahami, M, S. Dumais, et al. A Bayesian Approach to Filtering Junk E-Mail. Learing for Text Categorization –Papers from the AAAI Workshop, Madison Wisconsin. 1998.
2. James Clark, Irna Koprinska, Josiah Poon, A neural network based approach to automated e-mail classification , Proceedings of the IEEE/WIC international conference on web intelligence.
3. Duhong chen, Tongjie et al. Spam Email Filter Using Naive Bayesian, Decision Tree, Neural Network and AdaBoost, http://www.cs.iastate.edu/~tongjie/spamfilter/paper.pdf
4. Salton G. Introduction to modern information retrieval . New York McGraw-Hill Book company. 1983.
5. Kenneth Ward Church and Tatrick Hanks. Workd association norms, mutual information and lexicography. In proceedings of ACL27, Wancouver , Canada, 1989.
6. China anti-spam market research report in 2004, IResearch Inc. 2004
7. Martin T.Hagan, Howard B.Demuth, Nark H. Beale, Neural network design, China Machine Press, 2002,8

An Application of Hybrid Least Squares Support Vector Machine to Environmental Process Modeling[1]

Byung Joo Kim[1] and Il Kon Kim[2]

[1] Youngsan University School of Network and Information Engineering, Korea
bjkim@ysu.ac.kr,
[2] Kyungpook National University Department of Computer Science, Korea
ikkim@knu.ac.kr,

Abstract. In this paper we propose a hybrid model which includes both first principles differential equations and a least squares support vector machine (LS-SVM). It is used to forecast and control an environmental process. This inclusion of the first principles knowledge in this hybrid model is shown to improve substantially the stability of the model predictions in spite of the unmeasurability of some of the key parameters. Proposed hybrid model is compared with both a hybrid neural network(HNN) as well as hybrid neural network with extended kalman filter(HNN-EKF). From experimental results, proposed hybrid model shown to be far superior when used for extrapolation compared to HNN and HNN-EKF.

Keywords: Hybrid LS-SVM, Neural Network.

1 Introduction

The control of process, in which important parameters cannot be measured directly, or of which measurement is expensive or very incorrect, is a complex problem. In these cases the solution is of the type of inference control [1] which uses an machine learning method to model the unmeasurable parameters, for use in conjunction with the known part of the model. In recent years, there has been a spate of research[2] showing the utility of these hybrid model in a variety of applications with particular attention to fed-batch bioreactors[3]. The aim of this paper is to propose a hybrid model being able to perform on-line estimation of directly unmeasurable process variables. Main attention is paid to hybrid models that is combination of first principles(FP) models with least squares support vector machine(LS-SVM). We review the dynamics of microbial growth in the next section. In Section 3, we introduce a hybrid LS-SVM model which uses a LS-SVM to estimate the growth rate within the governing equations for the kinetics of process. In Section 4, we compare the performance of this model with various other strategies. Finally we investigate experimental results.

---

[1] This study was supported by a grant of the Korea Health 21 R&D Project, Ministry of Health & Welfare, Republic of Korea (02-PJ1-PG6-HI03-0004).

2 Dynamics of Microbial Growth

Bioreactors operated in a fed-batch manner and are quite difficult to model, since their operation involves microbial growth under constantly changing conditions. Nevertheless, knowledge of process parameters(such as growth rate) under a wide range of operating conditions is very important in efficiently designing optimal reactor operation policies. A fed-batch bioreactor can be described by the following equations

$$\frac{dB}{dt} = \mu(t)B(t) - \frac{Q(t)}{V(t)}B(t) \quad (1)$$

$$\frac{dS}{dt} = -\mu(t)B(t) + \frac{Q(t)}{V(t)}[S_i(t) - S(t)] \quad (2)$$

$$\frac{dV}{dt} = Q(t) \quad (3)$$

where $B(t)$ is the biomass concentration at time t, $S(t)$ is the substrate concentration, $Q(t)$ is the volumetric flow into the system, $V(t)$ is the volume, and $\mu(t)$ is the specific growth rate. It is the parameter that complicates the process, as it is a time-varying function of the biochemical variables of the system. In the literature, many models have been developed for this unmeasurable growth rate of which the most widely used are the Monod and Haldane function of the amount of substrate in the system

$$\mu(t) = \frac{\mu^* S(t)}{K_m + S(t) + \frac{S(t)^2}{K_i}} \quad (4)$$

The hybrid LS-SVM described below accomplishes the estimation of unknown growth rate, but with the added feature that is can provide reasonable extrapolation by directly estimating the growth rate.

3 Hybrid Least Square Support Vector Machine

In the last decade, neural network have been successfully used as *black-box* models of dynamic systems and, more specifically, as process variable estimators in bioreactor modeling applications. However, identification of batch processes is much more difficult, since a wide range of operating regimes is involved and less data may be available. Furthermore neural network has weak points such as the existence of local minima and how to choose the number of hidden units. Major breakthroughs are obtained at this point with new class of neural networks called support vector machines(SVM)[5]. SVM solutions are characterized by convex optimization problems what is so called quadratic programming(QP). Solving QP needs complex computation and difficulty in implementation. To solve this problem Suykens developed least squares support vector machine(LS-SVM)[6]. In this paper, we focus on function estimation using LS-SVM. The central idea of this paper is to integrate the available approximate model with a LS-SVM which approximates the unknown kinetics, in order to form a combined model structure which can be characterized as a hybrid LS-SVM process model. LS-SVM component receives as inputs the process variables and provides an estimate of the current parameter values, in this case growth rate. LS-SVM's output serves as an input to the first principles component, which produces as output the values of the process variables at the end of each sampling time. The combination of these two building blocks yields a complete hybrid LS-SVM model of the bioreaction system.

4 Experiment

We evaluate this hybrid LS-SVM(HLS-SVM) modeling scheme by comparing its prediction accuracy with hybrid neural network(HNN) proposed by Ungar[4] and hybrid neural network with extended Kalman filter(HNN-EKF). In order to test the behavior of the HLS-SVM, we simulated data via the known first principles differential equations (1)-(3) under a realistic condition. The specific growth rate was generated using the Haldane model (equation (4)) with the parameter values listed in[4], namely $\mu^* = 5, K_m = 10, K_i = 0.1$. The inlet concentration $S_i = 3.5$ and the flowrate, Q, was held constant at 0.1. Future state variables were then generated using the differential equations with random noise. We take the same initial values B_0, S_0, V_0 to generate the training, validation, test data set used in [4]. For the HNN, number of input, hidden and output node is 2,3 and 1 and weight update is done by backpropagation method to estimate the growth rate. The weights that produced the smallest SSE(Sum of Square Error) for the validation data were selected for making the predictions for the test set. In case of HNN-EKF, initial value of weight is set to 1. Covariance and error matrix in process state set to identity matrix. Variance of error in measurement state is 0.01. Weight update is done by EKF method. In HLS-SVM, we take the RBF kernel and kernel parameter $\sigma = 1.96$ and $\lambda = 0.479$ are obtained by cross-validation method. Figure 1 shows estimated and true $\mu(t)$ for training data

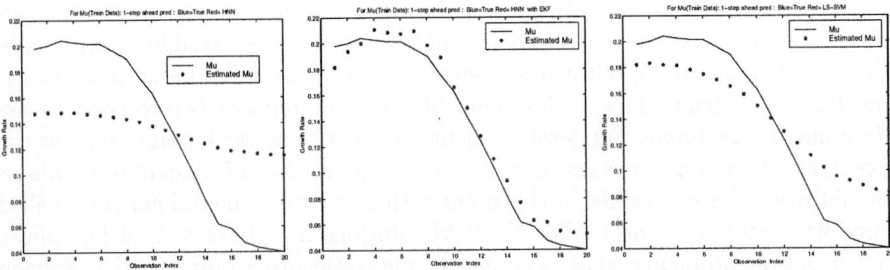

Fig. 1. From left to right estimated growth rate by HNN, HNN-EKF, HLS-SVM

by three methods. Asterisk(*) in each graph is estimated value of $\mu(t)$. As we can see HNN model can't estimate $\mu(t)$ well, whereas HNN-EKF and HLS-SVM model estimate well. From table 1 experimental results shows that in estimating B and S, HLS-SVM is about 100 times outperform than HNN because LS-SVM overcomes the overfitting problem and guarantees the global minima. Comparing HLS-SVM to HNN-EKF the former is about 3 times outperform than the later. Generalization ability of HNN-EKF is decreased because overfitting occurs more or less during learning process.

Table 1. Comparision of sum of square error(SSE) on B and S by HNN, HNN-EKF and HLS-SVM method

Method	Train		Validation		Test	
	B	S	B	S	B	S
HNN	0.22	0.22	19.57	19.52	23.5280	23.30
HNN-EKF	0.00310	0.02375	0.01846	0.01584	0.67861	0.67558
HLS-SVM	0.1206	0.03356	0.03759	0.03433	0.18469	0.19361

5 Summary and Conclusion

In this paper we propose a new hybrid model comprised of a LS-SVM, together with first principles differential equations for the forecasting and simulation an environmental process. When sufficiently large training sets of data are available, traditional black-box model gives an accurate model of the process. However limited data are available, the hybrid model gives significantly better accuracy, particularly on extrapolation. The hybrid model, once learned, can be used for process control and optimization. The concept of combining LS-SVM with first principle knowledge is a powerful one, and goes well beyond the example presented in this paper.

References

1. B. Joseph, and C. Brosilou, "Inferential Control of Processes, Part I Steady State Analysis and Design," AICHE J., Vol. 24, No. 3, 1978.
2. E.J. Molga, and K.R. Westerterp, "Neural network based model of the kinetics of catalytic hydrogenation reactions," Stud. Surf. Sci. Catal. 109,379-388, 1997.
3. B. Saxen and H. Saxen, "A neural network based model of bioreaction kinetics," Canadian Journal of Chemical Engineering 74(1), 124-131, 1996.
4. C. Dimitris, Psichogios and H. Ungar, "A Hybrid Neural Network-First Principles Approach to Process Modeling," AICHE Journal 38(10),14991511, 1992.
5. S. Gunn, Support Vector Machines for Classification and Regression, ISIS Technical Report, U. of Southampton, 1998.
6. J.A.K. Suykens, "Nonlinear Modeling and Support Vector Machines," Accessible at http://www.kdiss.or.kr/kdiss/

Recurrent Neural Network for Robot Path Planning

Ni Bin[1], Chen Xiong[1], Zhang Liming[1], and Xiao Wendong[2]

[1] Department of Electronic Engineering, Fudan University,
200433, Shanghai, PRC
{032021018, chenxiong}@fudan.edu.cn
[2] Institute for Infocomm Research, 21 Heng Mui Keng Terrance,
119613, Singapore
wxiao@i2r.a-star.edu.sg

Abstract. A novel model of organized neural network is shown to be very effective for path planning and obstacle avoidance in an unknown map which is represented by topologically ordered neurons. With the limited information of neighbor position and distance of the target position, robot will autonomously provide a proper path with free-collision and no redundant exploring in the process of exploring. The computer simulation will illustrate the performance.

1 Introduction

Dynamic path planning of robots or manipulators in an unknown or nonstationary environment is a fundamentally important issue in robotics.

Many neural network models were proposed to generate real-time path through learning. Glasius et al. [5] proposed a Hopfield-type neural network model for real-time trajectory generation with obstacle avoidance in a nonstationary environment. But it suffers from slow dynamics on the contrary. Yang and Meng [1] proposed a neural network approach to dynamic collision-free trajectory generation of a point mobile robot in nonstationary environment. But this method also needs all the information of the entire map and can not be used in an unknown map efficiently.

In this paper, we will provide a novel recurrent neural network model called "distance-orientation" model, which only has the local lateral connections among the neuron and the weight of distance from the target. The neuron model can represent the whole map and each neuron corresponds to a certain subset of the map. The distance of robot and target can be transferred to energy function to lead the robot to the right way. When the robot detected the existence of obstacles, no matter polygons and circles, the value of the corresponding neuron will be set low. Based on it, we can ignore the effect of variant shapes of obstacles and also can avoid the "too close" and "too far" problem.

The computational complexity of the model linearly depends on the number of connection of the each neuron. Therefore the model allows the high speed of calculation and fast convergence.

In this paper, all the contents are organized as follows:

In Section 2, the novel model is proposed. In Section 3, the simulations are shown to illusotrate the performance of the networks. In Section 4, a conclusion is addressed.

2 Model

In this section, we will introduce the dynamic model of "distance-orientation" model, which includes not only the short range information but the long range information. Here the short range information means the local connection with the neighbor neurons, which can be realized by the sonar or vision sensor installed on the robot. As to the long range information, it can be the position information of the target or the distance between the target and the robot.

We assume the model consists of a large collection of identical neurons which are arranged in a 2-dimensional cubic lattice. And the lattice represents a topologically ordered map and each neuron corresponds to a certain subset of the map. By properly defining the value of target and obstacles, we can guarantee that the target and obstacles stay at the peak and the valley of the activity landscape of the neural network. In the case of a continuous-time evolution the states of neurons are updated by

$$\frac{dx_i}{dt} = -Ax_i + (B - x_i) \cdot \sum_{j=1}^{n} w_{ij} x_j + \min\left[C / \|x_i - \text{target}\|, D\right] \quad (1)$$

where x_i is neural activity. A, B, C and D are positive constants. n means the number of all the neurons representing the whole map. Function $\min(x,y)$ is to find the smaller element between x and y. Function $\|x_i - \text{target}\|$ represents the Euclidean distance between x_i and *target*.

w_{ij} is the connection weight from the neighbor jth neurons to the ith neuron. w_{ij} can be defined as

$$w_{ij} = f(\|q_i - q_j\|) \quad (2)$$

The connection weight function $f(x)$ can be a monotonically decreasing function, e.g., a function defined as

$$f(x) = \begin{cases} \mu / x & \text{if } 0 < x < r_0 \\ 0 & \text{if } x \geq r_0 \end{cases} \quad (3)$$

where μ and r_0 are positive constants. w_{ij} is symmetric $w_{ij} = w_{ji}$ and does not depend on the moving of the robot. (3) make sure that the neuron has lateral connection to the ith neuron which is defined as its neighboring neurons and no weight affects the neuron itself. Therefore, the recurrent neural network model can be written as

$$\frac{dx_i}{dt} = -Ax_i + (B - x_i) \cdot \sum_{j=1}^{k} w_{ij} x_j + \min\left[C / \|x_i - \text{target}\|, D\right] \quad (4)$$

where $j \neq i$. Here in the map, robot, target and obstacle are symbolized as neurons with different activities. Make sure the target has the highest value and obstacle has the lowest value. The neuron of robot only can update its value between the highest and lowest value through the neighboring connection.

In "distance-orientation" model, we use the information of the distance between robot and target to guide the robot to find the next neuron nearest to the target in its neighbors meanwhile avoiding colliding with the obstacles. So the proposal algorithm (5) makes the target as the energy peak and obstacle as the gap in the whole map. And the peak globally influences the choice of next position of the robot, while the obstacles have only local effect.

For a given present robot position q_o in the map, the next position q_n will be got from the $q_i (i = 1,2,...,k)$, through choosing the max energy value. Here k is the number of the neighboring position of the q_0. After the robot reaches the next position, then the q_n will be the new present position.

Lyapunov method [4][2] can prove the stability of the moving robot in this model. And the robot will also find an acceptable path in the map if there is a path exists.

3 Simulation

In this section we illustrate the analytical results of the proposed model outlined above: an autonomous point-robot trying to find the target in an unknown environment.

In our demonstration we used a two-dimensional lattice with N=900 neurons ordered in a 30×30 neural map.

Here in Figure 1(a), we use the original model of non-distance orientation to compare with the new model in the same map.

As to the "distance orientation" model in Figure 1(b), by choosing $r_0 = 2$ each neuron on the lattice is connected with excitatory connections to its 24 neighbors. The connection weight function can be shown in (4). As to the closer 8 neighbors, the weight of connection is μ, and the other farther neurons get the weight of $\mu/2$. Here the value μ can be settled as 1. The other model parameters are chosen as A = B = 1, C = 10 and D = 1.

The obstacles are shown by Solid Square and the generated trajectory is shown by Solid Circles. The diamond point means the start point, and the asterisk point represents the end point.

Through the comparison shown in Figure 1 in an unknown environment, we can find that the efficiency of distance-orientation model is better than that of original model in evidence. In "distance-orientation" model shown by (b), the robot can avoid searching path aimlessly like in (a). No redundant path to explore, the robot in (b) will find the closest way with free-collision leading to the target. And (b) also can solve another problem in (a) that the robot has no ability to choose the better way when meeting the cross road. Based on its excellent efficiency the method also can save a lot of time in searching the way.

Another advantage in the comparison of Figour1 is that the robot in "distance-orientation" model will not suffer from either the "too close" or the "too far" problems, that is too near or to far from the obstacles. The robot will autonomously avoid choosing the way clinging to the obstacles and can make sure that there is enough space for the robot to pass the map.

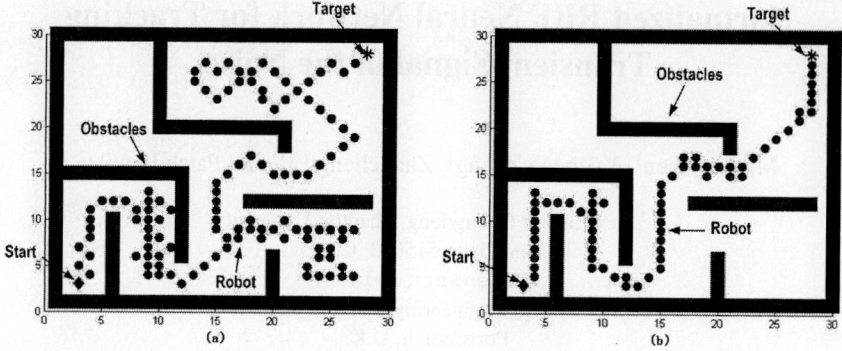

Fig. 1. Trajectory generation of a mobile robot to avoid a set of obstacles. (a) "Nondistance-orientation" model. (b) "Distance-orientation" model

4 Conclusion

In this paper we presented a recurrent neural network model, "distance-orientation model", for path-planning in an unknown environment. All the neurons in the model only have the neighbor connections and the distance information of the target. Based on the efficient neuron updating algorithm, this novel model can search the real-time path with free-collision in an unknown environment. Further more it can also avoid the "too close" and "too far" problem.

References

1. Simon X. Y and Max M, "Neural Network Approaches to Dynamic Collision-Free Trajectory Generation", *IEEE Trans. on Syst., Man, and Cybern*, Vol.31, No.3, 2001.
2. Sanqing Hu and Jun Wang, "Global Stability of a Class of Continuous-Time Recurrent Neural Networks", *IEEE Trans. on Circuits and Systems-I: Fundamental Theory and Applications*, Vol.49, No.9, 2002.
3. M. A. Cohen and S. Grossberg. "Absolute stability of global pattern formation and parallel memory storage by competitive neural networks", *IEEE Trans. on Systems, Man, and Cybernetics*, 1983.
4. S. Grossberg. "Nonlinear neural networks: principles, mechanisms, and architectures", *Neural Networks*, 1988
5. R. Glasius et al., "Neural network dynamics for path planning and obstacle avoidance", *Neural Networks*, vol.8, no.1, pp.125-133, 1995.
6. C. J. Ong and E. G. Gillert, "Robot path planning with penetration growth distance" *J.Robot.Syst.* vol.15, no.2, pp.57-74, 1998.

Normalized RBF Neural Network for Tracking Transient Signal in the Noise

Minfen Shen[1], Yuzheng Zhang[1], Zhancheng Li[1], and Patch Beadle[2]

[1] Key Lab. of Guangdong, Shantou University,
Guangdong 515063, China
mfshen@stu.edu.cn
[2] School of System Engineering, Portsmouth University,
Portsmouth, U.K.

Abstract. A novel approach is proposed to solve the problem of detecting the signal in the noise using a modified RBF neural network (RBFNN). The RBFNN is normalized to obtain optimal behavior of noise suppression even at low SNR. The performance of the proposed scheme is also evaluated with both MSE and the tracking ability. Several experimental results provide the convergent evidence to show that the method can significantly enhance the SNR and successfully track the variation of the signal such as evoket potential.

1 Introduction

There is an increasing interest in detecting and extracting the desired signal which contaminated with the background noise since the measurement of the signal is inevitably corrupted by noise of many other kinds of background activities. As a result, majority of signals should be treated as a typical non-stationary and nonlinear process [1,2,3]. Usually, various methods for solving this problem make use of ensemble averaging (EA) technique and other algorithms. However, EA method can not provide an optimal estimate of transient responses from the measured raw signal due to a number of reasons. Many adaptive filters were adopted to overcome the EA limitation, but they need a meaningful reference signal [4,5]. To take the nonlinear nature of the signal interested into consideration, RBF neural network were widely used as the filter to obtain more meaningful signals [6,7]. Unfortunately, these methods are not valid in tracking the change of the responses and working in low signal-to-noise ratio (SNR). In order to well track the variations of the desired signal, this paper proposes a novel method using modified RBFNN technique for extracting signal in noise. Normalized RBFNN is developed in terms of dividing each radial function in RBF network by the sum of all radial functions. The main task is to design a real-time estimator with which the unwanted contribution of the on-going background noise can be filtered out from the observations as much as possible. As an application, we focus on detecting the fast evoket potentials (EPs) and tracking EPs' variations across trials on time. The presented procedure is proved to provide an optional template with high SNR from the collected data.

2 Proposed Approach

General RBF neural network has been widely used in various areas. The RBFNN consist of an input of source nodes, a single hidden layer of nonlinear processing units, and an output payer of linear weights [8]. This special structure makes RBFNN a very powerful tool for solving both linear and nonlinear problems. The units in the kernel layer provide an array of nonlinear radial basis function which are usually selected as Gaussian functions. In the output layer, the value of a unit is obtained through a linear combination of the nonlinear outputs from the kernel layer. Local basis functions have advantageous because of the increased interpretability of the network, the ability of producing locally accurate confidence limits and improving computational efficiency. The normalization of the basis functions in such a network is motivated and expected to achieve a partition of unity across the input space. It results in the basis functions covering the whole input space to the same degree, i.e. the basis functions sum to unity at every point. By partition of unity, it means that at each point in the input space the sum of the normalized basis functions equals unity. Partitioning of unity is an important property for basis function networks in many applications such as noisy data interpolation and regression. This structure results in the less sensitive to the poor center selection and the cases when the network is used within a local model structure. In addition, since the basis function activations are bounded between 0 and 1, they can be interpreted as probability values. The effect of the normalization also improves the interpolation properties and makes the network less sensitive to the selection of some parameters.

3 Experimental Results

Both simulated data and real signals are carried out in this section to evaluate the performance of real-time signal detection in the following three aspects: (a) comparing the performance with relative mean square error (MSE), (b) evaluating the ability of tracking signal variation, and (c) testing the signal detection ability at different SNR conditions. Both RBFNN and the nonlinear ANC with RBFNN prefilter (ANC-RBFNN) are computed and compared with the proposed NRBFNN method.

First, to evaluate the behaviors, 50 epochs of 500 samples with input SNR at –20 dB and –40 dB were generated, respectively. The ANC-RBFNN, RBFNN and NRBFNN were performed. The performance of the estimation was also evaluated by calculating the MSE which was shown in Fig.1. Based on the MSE behaviors, NRBFNN is found having the best behavior as compared with other two models. In addition, the ability of tracking signal's variation was investigated. 1000 trials input signals was generated. The first 500 trials remain waveform I, and other 500 trials adopt a different waveform II. There existed a jump at the 500th trial. Fig.2 illustrated the error curves comparison in abrupt changing simulation. Finally, we compared the performance with different SNR from -40 dB to 0 dB. Fig.3 showed the corresponding results. It can be seen that the presented NRBFNN significantly eliminates the background noise. As an application, the visual EPs (VEP) during visual attention processing was studied. We aim at the problem of obtaining the real-time VEPs' measurement and tracking VEPs' variations across the trials. Our particular interest focuses on determining the temporal relationship of variance between trials and measuring response synchronously to each stimulus. Fig. 4 showed the real-time VEP responses detected using NRBFNN technique. It shows that NRBFNN can significantly improve the behavior of VEPs detection, even at very low SNR conditions. By employing the NRBFNN, the changes of whole real-time VEP for each trial can be clearly captured, which significantly helps our understanding of many practical problems in biomedical engineering. The NRBFNN is also more applicable to the real-time detection of signals in noise than other existing methods. The main reason for that is because the local interpolation properties of NRBFNN is greatly improved, which makes the neural network less sensitive to the choice of other parameters. The proposed scheme significantly improved the ability with respect to the responding speed and output SNR.

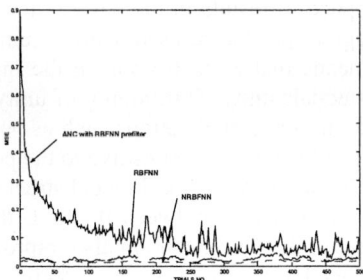

Fig. 1. Comparison of the MSE

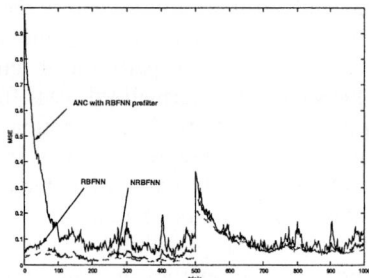

Fig. 2. Comparison of the errors

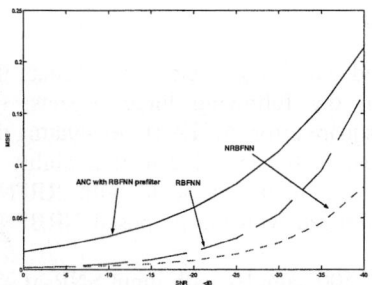

Fig. 3. Comparison of MSE versus SNR

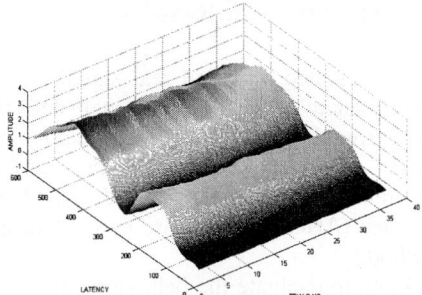

Fig. 4. Each VEP detected via NRBFNN

Based on the experimental results, we can find that the proposed NRBFNN enables to obtain preferable results for real-time signal detection. The modified RBF neural network can effectively eliminate the redundant hidden nodes of the network and obtain a reasonable network structure which can be used for the real-time detection of signal in noise. Furthermore, the performances of real-time detection were evaluated and compared with both RBFNN and the ANC-RBFNN in terms of the MSE, the ability of tracking signal variation, and the behaviors of signal detection at different SNR. All results have shown the robustness and the applicability of the presented NRBFNN model.

4 Conclusions

We have presented a novel method for signal detection in noise, utilizing the modified RBF neural network. A normalized RBFNN was developed as a new filter for dealing with the problem of extracting the time-varying responses in the noise. We also focus on the application to the detection of the real VEP responses from trail to trial. It has been shown that the NRBFNN approach enables improving the VEP analysis and facilitates tracking the amplitude peaks and the latency shift of the single VEP component. Both simulation and real VEP data analysis have proved that the presented approach is more applicable to the real-time detection of signal in background noise even under the condition of low SNR.

Acknowledgements

The research was supported by the Natural Science Foundation of China (60271023), the NSF of Guangdong (021264 and 32025) and the Key Grant of the Education Ministry of China (02110).

References

1. Husar P. and Henning G..: Bispectrum Analysis of Visually Evoked Potentials, IEEE Engineering in Medicine and Biology. January/February. (1997) 57-63
2. Boashash B. and Powers E. J.: Higher-Order Statistical Signal Processing. Wiley Halsted Press. (1996)
3. Shen M., Sun L., and Chan F. H. Y.: Method for Extracting Time-Varying Rhythms of Electroencephalography via Wavelet Packet Analysis. IEE Proceedings in Science, Measurement and Technology, Vol.148, No.1, January (2001) 23-27
4. Widrow B. and et. al.: Adaptive Noise Canceling: Principles and Applications, Proceeding of IEEE. Vol. 63. (1975) 1692-1711
5. Zhang Z.: Nonlinear ANC Based on RBF Neural Networks. Journal of Shanghai Jiaotong University. Vol.32. (1998) 63-65
6. Hartman E. J., Keeler J. D. and Kowalski J. M.: Layered Neural Networks with Gaussian Hidden Units as Universal Approximation. Neural Computation, Vol. 2. MIT Press, Cambridge (1989) 210-215
7. Platt J. C.: A Resource Allocating Network for Function Interpolation, Neural Computation. Vol. 3. (1991) 213-225
8. Shorten R. and Murray-Smith R.: On Normalizing Basis Function Networks, Proceedings of 4th Irish Neural Networks Conference. Dublin, Sept. (1994)

An Efficient Algorithm for Fault Tolerant Routing Based on Adaptive Binomial-Tree Technique in Hypercubes

Yamin Li[1], Shietung Peng[1], and Wanming Chu[2]

[1] Department of Computer Science, Hosei University, Tokyo 184-8584 Japan
[2] Department of Computer Hardware, University of Aizu, Fukushima 965-8580 Japan

Abstract. We propose an efficient fault-tolerant routing algorithm for hypercube networks with a very large number of faulty nodes. The algorithm is distributed and local-information-based in the sense that each node in the network knows only its neighbors' status and no global information of the network is required by the algorithm. For any two given nonfaulty nodes in a hypercube network that may contain a large fraction of faulty nodes, the algorithm can find a fault-free path of nearly optimal length with very high probability. The algorithm uses the adaptive binomial-tree to select a suitable dimension to route a node. We perform empirical analysis of our algorithm through simulations under a uniform node failure distribution and a clustered node failure distribution. The experimental results show that the algorithm successfully finds a fault-free path of nearly optimal length with the probability larger than 90 percent in a hypercube network that may contain up to 50 percent faulty nodes.

1 Introduction

Hypercube networks are among the most popular network models studied by researchers and adopted in many implementations of parallel computer systems, such as Intel iPSC, the nCUBE, the Connection Machine CM-2, and the SGI's Origin 2000 (1996) [1] and Origin 3000 (2000).

Much effort has been devoted to introduce more realistic definitions to measure the networks' ability to tolerate faults, and to develop routing algorithms under a large number of faults. For example, Najjar et al [2] demonstrated that for the 10-cube, 33 percent of nodes can fail and the network can still remain connected with a probability of 99 percent. Gu and Peng [3] proposed an efficient global routing algorithm for a k-safe n-cube with up to $2^k(n-k)-1$ faulty nodes. Chen et al [4] also proposed a distributed routing algorithm for hypercube with up to 37.5% faulty nodes based on local subcube-connectivity.

In this paper, based on the divide-and-conquer and adaptive binomial-tree techniques, we propose an efficient fault-tolerant routing algorithm. For hypercube network that may contain a large fraction of faulty nodes, our algorithm finds a fault-free path for any two given nonfaulty nodes with very high probability. The algorithm uses the adaptive binomial-tree to select a suitable dimension to route a node. We perform empirical analysis of our algorithm through simulations under a variety of probability distributions of node failures. The experimental results show that the algorithm successfully finds a fault-free path of nearly optimal length with the probability larger than 90 percent in a hypercube network that may contain up to 50 percent faulty nodes.

2 Fault-Tolerant Routing Algorithm

The proposed algorithm uses the following strategy: Find a fault-free k-binomial-tree $T_k(s)$ in H_{n-1}^0 starting from $k = 0$. If all the paths $(s \to u : u^{(j)})$ and $(s \to u : v : v^{(j)})$ are faulty, where $s \to u$ is a path in $T_k(s)$ and $v \in N(T_k(s)) \cap H_{n-1}^0$, then the algorithm repeats the same process using $(k+1)$-binomial-tree $T_{k+1}(s)$. The algorithm terminates when either a fault-free path $s \to s' \in H_{n-1}^1$ is found or the fault-free $(k+1)$-binomial-tree cannot be built.

Intuitively, the basic routing algorithm can be described below. In the first run, if $s^{(j)}$ is nonfaulty then we are done, where j is the dimension on which we are routing; otherwise, we build a $k = 0$ binomial-tree $T_0(s) = \{s\}$ and try to find a fault-free path $s \to s'$ of length 2, $(s : s^{(i)} : s^{(i,j)})$, where $s^{(i)} \in H_{n-1}^0$ and $i \neq j$.

If we fail to find a fault-free path in the first run then let $k = k + 1$ and try to build a fault-free k-binomial-tree $T_k(s)$. If there exists a node $u \in T_k(s)$ such that $u^{(j)}$ is nonfaulty then we are done. Otherwise, for each node $u \in T_k(s)$, we try to find a node $u^{(i)}, i \neq j$, such that $u^{(i)}$ and $u^{(i,j)}$ are nonfaulty. If such u exists then we are done and $s' = u^{(i,j)}$. The algorithm terminates if the fault-free path $s \to s'$ is found or the algorithm fails to build $T_k(s)$.

To extend $T_{k-1}(s)$ to $T_k(s)$, we use a dimension set D to keep the dimensions that are not yet routed. Initially, $D(u) = \{1, \ldots, n\}$. Once a dimension j is

---

Algorithm Hypercube_Routing(n, s, t)
Input: n-cube, nonfaulty nodes $s = s_1 s_2 \ldots s_n$ and $t = t_1 t_2 \ldots t_n$
Output: a fault-free path $P = (s \to t)$ or report *failure*
begin
$\quad P = \emptyset; D = \{1, \ldots, n\}; w = s;$
$\quad$ for $i = 1$ to n do
$\qquad$ if (there is a dimension $j \in D$ such that $w_j \neq t_j$)
$\qquad\quad D = D - \{j\};$
$\qquad\quad$ if ($w' = w_1 \ldots w_{j-1} \overline{w_j} w_{j+1} \ldots w_n$ is nonfaulty) $P = P : w; w = w';$
$\qquad\quad$ else routed = false; $k = 0;$
$\qquad\qquad$ while (routed = false) AND ($k < n - i$) do
$\qquad\qquad\quad (w', T, \text{fail}) = \text{Binomial\_Tree}(n, w, t, j, k, D);$
$\qquad\qquad\quad$ if ($w' \neq -1$) $P = P : T; w = w';$ routed = true;
$\qquad\qquad\quad$ else if (fail = true) return *failure*;
$\qquad\qquad\qquad$ else $k = k + 1;$
$\quad$ **return** P; $\qquad\qquad\qquad\qquad\qquad$ /* finish, path constructed */
end

Procedure Binomial_Tree(n, w, t, j, k, D)
begin
    $w' = -1$; $T = \emptyset$; fail = false;
    if ($k = 0$)
        $B = \{w\}$;
        reorder(w, t, D);
        if (there is an $i \in D$: $u = w_1 \ldots w_{i-1}\overline{w_i}w_{i+1}\ldots w_n$ is nonfaulty)
            if ($v = u_1 \ldots u_{j-1}\overline{u_j}u_{j+1}\ldots u_n$ is nonfaulty)
                $T = u$; $w' = v$;
                return (w', T, fail);
        return (w', T, fail);
    $N = \emptyset$;
    for (each node $s \in B$) **do**   /* 1. construct k-binomial-tree */
        reorder(s, t, D);
        if (there is an $i \in D$: $u = s_1 \ldots s_{i-1}\overline{s_i}s_{i+1}\ldots s_n \notin (B \cup N)$ is nonfaulty)
            if ($v = u_1 \ldots u_{j-1}\overline{u_j}u_{j+1}\ldots u_n$ is nonfaulty)
                $T = w \to u$; $w' = v$;
                return (w', T, fail);
            $N = N \cup u$;
        else fail = true;
    for (each node $s \in N$) **do**   /* 2. search k-binomial-tree */
        reorder(s, t, D);
        if (there is an $i \in D$: $u = s_1 \ldots s_{i-1}\overline{s_i}s_{i+1}\ldots s_n$ is nonfaulty)
            if ($v = u_1 \ldots u_{j-1}\overline{u_j}u_{j+1}\ldots u_n$ is nonfaulty)
                $T = w \to u$; $w' = v$;
                return (w', T, fail);
    $B = B \cup N$;   /* constructing $(k+1)$-binomial-tree */
    return (w', T, fail);   /* $w' = -1$; $T = \emptyset$; fail = true or false */
end

routed, j is deleted from D. When we check the neighbors of a node in the binomial-tree to find a nonfaulty node to extend the binomial-tree, we want those nodes whose jth bit have the same value as the destination node t to be searched first. Therefore, we re-order D before it is used for selecting neighbors or finding new nodes. We call this *adaptive binomial-tree routing*.

The construction of $T_k(s)$ is as follows: We apply a tree traversal on $T_{k-1}(s)$. While $u \in T_{k-1}(s)$ is visited, we try to find a nonfaulty node $v \in \{u^{(i)} | i \in D(u)\}$. If such v exists then we include edge $(u : v)$ and node v in $T_k(s)$. Otherwise, the extension fails and the algorithm terminates unsuccessfully.

The running time of the routing algorithm is analyzed as follows: For every k, each iteration for finding $s \to s'$ takes $O(|T_k(s)| \times n)$ time. In the worst case, the time for finding a fault-free path $s \to s'$ or reporting a failure will take $\sum_{k=0}^{max} O(|T_k(s)| \times n) = O(n)$, where max is the largest k we try for finding $s \to s'$. In all practical cases as we will show in the next section, we have $max \leq 4$. Then, the running time of the algorithm that performs binomial-tree routing $O(n)$ is $O(n^2)$, independent of the size of F.

3 Theoretical Analysis and Simulations

In this section, we first give a theoretical analysis on the successful routing rate of our algorithm under the uniform distribution of node failures. Then we show the simulation results of our algorithm under the uniform and clustered distributions of node failures.

The causes for the failure of the binomial-tree routing are twofolds: failure in finding a nonfaulty k-binomial-tree or failure in finding a fault-free path ($s \rightarrow s'$) using the found binomial-tree. For simplicity, we assume that k is fixed. Let p_f be the node failure probability. We calculate the successful routing rate p_s for the given values of n, p_f, and k. The formula for the approximate p_s is given in the following theorem.

Theorem 1. *Suppose that every node in the n-cube has an equal and independent failure probability p_f. For a given k, the probability of successful routing of the algorithm $p_s \approx \prod_{i=1}^{n/2}(1 - p_f(1 - (1 - p_f)^2)^{n-i})$ if $k = 0$; otherwise, $p_s \approx \prod_{i=1}^{n/2}(1 - p_f^{2^k}(1 - (1 - p_f)^2)^{2^k(n-i-k)})(1 - p_f^{n-i+1})^{2^{k-1}}$.*

We have performed extensive experiments to study the performance of our routing algorithm based on the uniform distribution and the clustered distribution of node failures. We have done simulation for the n-cube with $n = 10, 15, 16$ and 20. For each n, we simulated the node failure probability $p_f = 10\% \sim 70\%$ with 10% increment. For each pair (n, p_f), we randomly picked up 10,000 pairs of nonfaulty nodes in H_n, and simulated our routing algorithm.

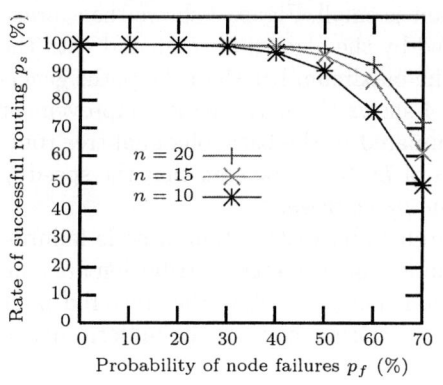

Fig. 1. Successful routing rate

Fig. 2. Ratio of p_s for $max = 1, 2,$ and 3 over $max = 0$ when $n = 16$

From Figure 1, we can see that, when the node failure probability is not very large (i.e., $p_f \leq 20\%$), the successful routing p_s is nearly 100% ($\approx 99.9\%$), and the path_plus is nearly optimal (≈ 1.04 of the node distance). When the p_f is 30% or more, the p_s starts to drop slowly, and when the p_f is 60% or more, the p_s

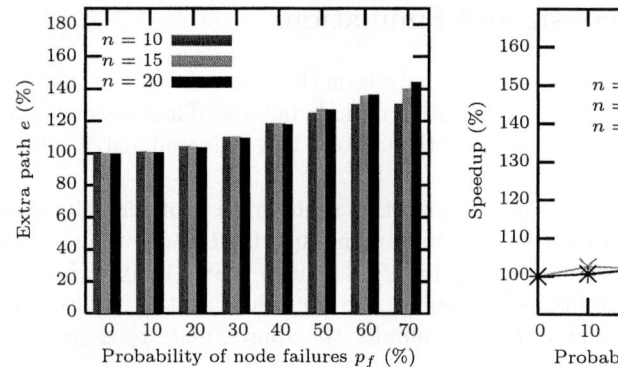
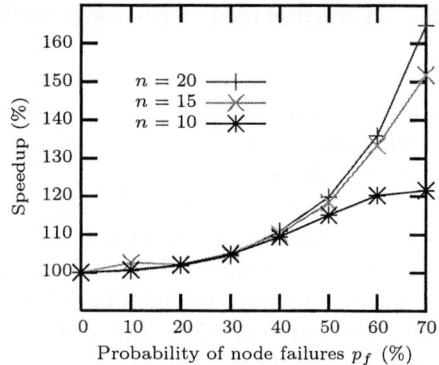

Fig. 3. Ratio of the max. length to $d(s,t)$ **Fig. 4.** Speedup of adaptive routing

drops faster. However, the p_s still maintains at about 50% for $n = 10$, and 70% for $n = 20$. For $n = 10$ and $p_f = 30\%$, Chen's algorithm finds a fault-free path at the probability of 92% [4]. In contrast, our algorithm finds a fault-free path at the probability of 99.28% with $k = 2$, much higher than Chen's algorithm.

Figure 2 indicates the improvement on p_s over the increment on max (the upper bound of the binomial-tree to be checked) for $n = 16$. We let the values of max vary from 0 to 3. From the resulting data, we see the improvement is significant for max as p_f increases. For example, when $p_f = 70$, the p_s of $max = 3$ is 5 times of that of $max = 0$. However, for $max > 3$, the improvement on performance is very little and can be ignored. We conclude that setting $max = 2$ or $max = 3$ should be enough for all practical cases. Therefore, the running time of the algorithm is efficient since the constant is small. Figure 3 shows the average ratio of the lengths of the paths generated by the algorithm compared with the distance $d(s,t)$ for $n = 16$. In all cases, the maximum length of the paths generated is bounded by $1.5 \times d(s,t)$. Figure 4 shows the performance improvement of the adaptive binomial-tree routing compared to the basic binomial-tree routing that does not reorder the dimensions of D. It can be seen that the speedup increases as the size of hypercube and the p_f increase.

We have also simulated on another probability distribution of node failures. The results show that the performance under the clustered distribution are similar to that under the uniform distribution. For $p_f > 20\%$, the clustered node failure distributions get a little bit better performance than the uniform distribution.

References

1. SGI: Origin2000 Rackmount Owner's Guide, 007-3456-003. http://techpubs.sgi.com/ (1997)
2. Najjar, W., Gaudiot, J.L.: Network resilience: A measure of network fault tolerance. IEEE Transactions on Computers **39** (1990) 174–181

3. Gu, Q.P., Peng, S.: Unicast in hypercubes with large number of faulty nodes. IEEE Transactions on Parallel and Distributed Systems **10** (1999) 964–975
4. Chen, J., Wang, G., Chen, S.: Locally subcube-connected hypercube networks: Theoretical analysis and experimental results. IEEE Transactions on Computers **51** (2002) 530–540

Genetic Local Search Based on Genetic Recombination: A Case for Traveling Salesman Problem

Peng Gang[1], Ichiro Iimura[2], Hidenobu Tsurusawa[3], and Shigeru Nakayama[4]

[1] Department of Computer and Control Engineering,
Oita National College of Technology,
1666 Maki, Oita City, 870-0152, Japan

[2] Department of Administration, Faculty of Administration,
Prefectural University of Kumamoto,
3-1-100 Tsukide, Kumamoto, 862-8502, Japan
iiimura@pu-kumamoto.ac.jp

[3] Department of Computer and Control Engineering,
Oita National College of Technology,
1666 Maki, Oita City, 870-0152, Japan
{peng, tsurusawa}@oita-ct.ac.jp

[4] Department of Information and Computer Science,
Faculty of Engineering, Kagoshima University,
1-21-40 Korimoto, Kagoshima, 890-0065, Japan
shignaka@ics.kagoshima-u.ac.jp

Abstract. Genetic Algorithms (GAs) have been applied in many different fields and optimization problem domains. It is well known that it is hard to solve the complex problems with a Simple Genetic Algorithm (SGA). Many previous studies have shown that the hybrid of local search and GAs is an effective approach for finding near optimum solutions to the traveling salesman problem (TSP). In this paper, an approach based on the Genetic Recombination is proposed and applied to the TSP. The algorithm is composed of two SGAs which only consist of the basic genetic operators such as selection, crossover and mutation. One of the SGAs is named as the Global Genetic Algorithm (GGA) and carried out in the main tours which are designed for searching the global optimal solutions. Another one is named as the Local Genetic Algorithm (LGA) and carried out in the sub tours which are designed for searching the local optimal solutions. The LGA is combined to the GGA as an operator. The local optimal solutions are recombined to the main tours for improving the search quality. To investigate the features of the proposed algorithm, it was applied to a small double circles TSP and some interesting results were presented in our experiments.

1 Introduction

The TSP is one of the well-studied combinatorial optimization problems [6], [18]. Many researchers from various fields have devoted to developing new algorithms for solving it. In the TSP, each distance between two cities is given for a set of n cities. The goal is to find the shortest tour. There are currently three general classes of heuristics for the TSP: classical tour construction heuristics such as the Nearest Neighbor method, the Greedy algorithm and local search algorithms based on re-arranging segments of the tour [15]. Many progressive results have been presented in the previous studies during the recent years even though there are still improvable spaces with the search algorithms which have been applied to the TSP, such as ant colonies [12], local search [5], neural networks [10], simulated annealing [17], and tabu search[2], genetic algorithms [9]. It has been proved that the hybrid of different algorithms is more effective than a single algorithm. For example, the local search has been successful for improving GAs in the search processes [1], [16], [19]. Most of the works on solving the TSP focused on the efficiency on how to solving the larger TSP instances. Some of the works aimed at expanding the theories of search algorithms, especially in the GAs domain.

In this paper, our attempt is to make a discussion on the GAs based on Genetic Recombination. The algorithm is composed of two SGAs which only consist of the basic genetic operators. One is the GGA which was applied to the main tours for searching the global optimal solutions. Another is the LGA which was applied to the sub tours for searching the local optimal solutions. The SGA was developed by John Holland and his original algorithm is approximately the same as shown in the Fig.1 [8]. In the early studies, the SGA played an important role in the development of GAs and attracted the researchers' attentions widely. Goldberg made a detailed discussion on how the SGA works with some simple optimal mathematical functions and other problems in his book [4]. Reeves discussed the differences and similarities between the SGA and the neighborhood search [3]. Computer scientist Michael D. Vose provided an introduction to what is known about the theory of the SGA. He also made available algorithms for the computation of mathematical objects related to the SGA [13]. All the studies have shown that the SGA is still valuable in heuristic search algorithm.

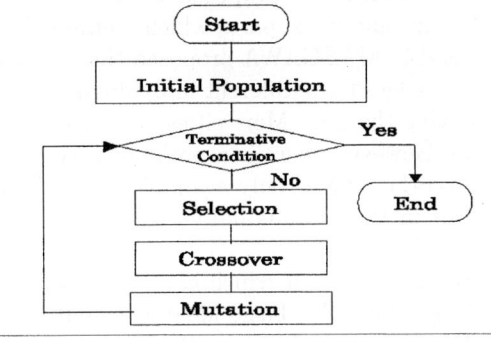

Fig. 1. Simple GA

The paper is organized as follows. Section 2 gives a general description of the local search to the TSP. Section 3 presents the detailed operations of the proposed algorithm. Section 4 gives the analyses on the experimental results. Section 5 is the summary for this paper.

2 Local Search Algorithms in GAs

Every successful strategy to produce near-optimal solutions necessarily relies upon the local search algorithm. All these algorithms differ with respect to their neighborhood structures. Any such structure specifies a set of neighboring solutions that are in some sense close to that solution. The associated local improvement operator replaces a current solution by a neighboring solution of better value if possible. The local search algorithm is repeated several times, retaining the best local optimum found. Our works focus on the local search algorithms. In the hybrid of the Local Search and the GAs, the design of the local operator is very important. There are many local search heuristics which have been combined to the GAs for the TSP. For example, the well-known 2-Opt heuristic has been used to optimize the TSP tours in connection with the GAs [18]. The 2-Opt removes two edges in a tour, and then one of the resultant segments is reversed and the two segments are reconnected. If 2-Opt results in an improved tour, the change is preserved. Otherwise, the tour is returned to the original form. The 2-Opt used a pair of edges which was formed from 4 cities in the tour. It is a powerful local search operator in the GAs. Compared with the 2-Opt, K-Opt (k=3,4...) uses more edges to rearrange the tours.

Moreover, some crossover methods also emphasis on the local operations. The crossover methods usually recombine two individuals to reproduce the new individuals. But most of them seldom utilize the shorter edges while they are applied to the tour. Some crossover methods aimed at the phenotype of the edges in the tour. They use more cities or a set of cities according to the visiting order in the tour. For example, YAMAMURA proposed the sub tour exchange crossover (SXX) which mutually exchanges the parts which contain the same continuous cities in two individuals [14]. MAEGAWA proposed the edge exchange crossover (EXX) which utilizes the edges from different individuals [11]. Both of the methods are powerful for solving the TSP. More cities are used when they are applied to re-arrange the tours. However, there is a problem with few variations of the child individuals because the SXX is only available when the parts which composed of the same cities in two various individuals are found. The EXX puts emphasis on combining edges.

Our approach is to use a sub tour which contains a set of continuous cities according to the visiting order. The basic idea is to find a better sub tour to replace the original one. This operation acts like the Genetic Recombination in the Genetic Engineering field. Genetic Recombination is the process by which the combination of genes in an organism's offspring is different from the combination of genes in that organism. This definition is commonly used in classical genetics, evolutionary biology, and population genetics. Commonly, one gene or a set of a few foreign genes is taken out of the DNA of one organism and inserted into the DNA of another organism by an artificial manipulation of genes. The manipulation disrupts the ordinary command code sequence in the DNA. This disruption may make the individual better if it is applied judiciously. As we knew, there are many good phenotypes of plants that have been created in biological field with the Genetic Recombination. The technical problem is how to find the better GENES to replace the original ones. In the TSP, it is the technique related to the local search. To find the better cities in the tour, we chose a set of continuous cities from the main tour to form a sub tour, and then applied the LGA to the sub tour to find better solutions to feed into the main tour. This operation acts as the cultivation for finding the better GENES biologically. The detailed operations are described in the following section.

3 New Algorithm

The new algorithm is shown in Figure 2. The parts a and b in the figure are separately a SGA before the part b is implemented to the part a. The part b is the LGA in the algorithm. The two parts form the new algorithm–GGA. Part b performs as a local search operator in the GGA. The GGA is applied to the main tour for searching the global optimal solutions. To obtain the global optimal solutions in the process of the TSP, the GGA may just need to improve the order of a set of cities in the best tour with evolution of the process, especially in the latter stages of the process. We chose a set of continuous cities to create the sub tour in the experiment. The LGA was applied to the sub tour for finding the local optimal solution to replace the original part chosen from the main tour.

There are two methods for initializing the sub tour: 1. Keep the original part from the main tour as an individual in the population of the LGA, and then randomly initialize the sub tour except for the start and end cities to the population size of the LGA. 2. Only reproduce the original part from the main tour to the population size of the LGA. It means the population is composed of same individuals as the original part. The same operation in the both initialization methods 1 and 2 is that the original parts from the main tours are preserved in the population of the LGA. If the solution of the LGA is shorter than the original part, the main tour will be improved when it is recombined. If no solution is found shorter than the original part in the LGA, the original part will be recombined back to the main tour. Both of the initialization methods are available for a small sub tour in the LGA. But, the first method is not suggested for a big sub tour as it takes long time to initialize.

In the LGA, the sub tour is an open tour. The length of the tour is calculated from the start city to the end city, not including the distance between the end city and the start city. Another important point is that all individuals in the population of the LGA have the same start and end cities during the processing. This operation is for avoiding that the main tour becomes longer at the connection points after the sub tour was recombined back into it.

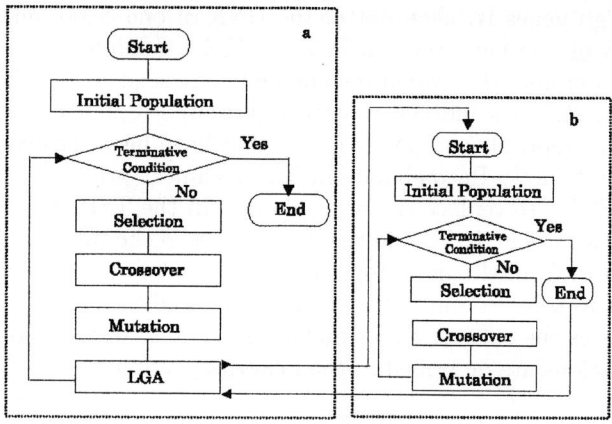

Fig. 2. New Algorithm

Because both the GGA and the LGA are complete genetic algorithms, all genetic operators for solving the TSP are probably applicable to them. In our experiments, only three genetic operators were implemented: Crossover, Mutation and Selection. The crossover is one point crossover method with two random individuals. The mutation is randomly carried out to the individuals by changing the order of two cities chosen randomly in one tour. The selection is carried out to replace the four longest individuals with the two shortest ones in the population. In the LGA, the mutation and crossover keep the diversity of the population, so the mutation rate is set higher than in the GGA. The terminative conditions are set to the total number of generations in the GGA and the LGA.

Obviously, it is computationally expensive running a big LGA in every generation of the GGA. But, it is believed that the LGA could be set as an island for improving the elite individuals of the main population in distributed or parallel processing. (This will be discussed in our future works). A small LGA is effective as an operator in the GGA. This has been confirmed in our experiments.

Local Operations: The tour which consists of n cities is expressed as $c=\{c_0,..., c_i,c_{i+1},..., c_{n-1}\}$. The distance $d(c_i,c_{i+1})$ is given for the pair of cities c_i and c_{i+1}. All cities are coded using path representation.

1. Randomly chosen one main tour $c=\{c_0, ..., c_i, ..., c_j, ..., c_{n-1}\}$ from Population of the GGA.
2. Randomly chosen one sub tour which contains N_s continuous cities in the main tour c. The sub tour $c_s=\{c_i, ..., c_j\}$. The start city is c_i and the end city is c_j. j-i$\geq$4. This is the first individual of the LGA. The length of the first individual was set as d_0.
3. Reproduced the first individual to the population size of the LGA. The start city c_i and the end city c_j were kept unchanged. The population of the LGA was created with P_s same individuals.

Table 1. Parameters in the GGA and the LGA

	GGA(Main Tour)	LGA(Sub Tour)
Population size:	100	80
Cities	24	4~ 24
Generations	1000	0,10,20,30,40,50,60,70,80,90,100
Crossover Rate	75%	75%
Mutation Rate	2%	2.5%
Selection	2 shortest individuals replace the 4 longest ones	2 shortest individuals replace the 4 longest ones

4. Run the LGA in every generation of the GGA. The start and end cities of all individuals of the LGA were kept unchanged during the processing.
5. The best individual in the population of the LGA was obtained when the LGA stopped. Its length was set as d_1.
6. The best individual was recombined back to the main tour to replace the original part.

Here we set the Ratio $R=d_0/d_1$. The range of R is $R \geq 1$. The R is discussed in the next section. The population size P_s of the LGA ranges from 4 to n. The minimum size of the sub tour is set to 4 cities due to the start and end cities are fixed in the sub tour during the processing. The maximum size is set to n because it is the largest improvable parts in the main tour. The LGA performs as the reversion operator in the GGA when the sub tour only contains 4 cities, the start and end cities were fixed.

4 Results and Discussions

The main tour which contains n cities $c = \{c_0, ..., c_i, c_{i+1}, ..., c_{n-1}\}$ is given and the distance between two cities c_i and c_{i+1} is $d(c_i, c_{i+1})$. A sub tour which contains m cities from main tour is $c_s = \{c_0, ..., c_k, c_{k+1}, ..., c_{m-1}\}$ and the distance between two cities c_k and c_{k+1} is $d(c_k, c_{k+1})$. Total distances of the main tour and the sub tour are D_{mt} and D_{st} respectively:

$$D_{mt} = \sum_{i=0}^{n-1} d(c_i, c_{i+1}) \tag{1}$$

When $i = n-1$, $c_{i+1} = c_0$.

$$D_{st} = \sum_{k=0}^{m-2} d(c_k, c_{k+1}) \tag{2}$$

The D_{mt} and D_{st} are defined as the Fitness of the individuals. The shorter the distance is, the higher the Fitness is.

The parameters are shown in the table 1. Our source code is written in the Java and run on a PC (CPU Pentium III 1.0GHz, 256 MB memory) with Windows 2000 Operating System.

The TSP instance of the double concentric circle which contains only 24 cities was used in the experiments(Fig.3.). The ratio of the inner radius(Ri) and the outer radius(Ro) is r=Ri/Ro. If r <0.58879, the optimal tour is C type (Fig.3.a.). If $r \geq 0.58879$, the optimal tour is O type(Fig.3.b.).

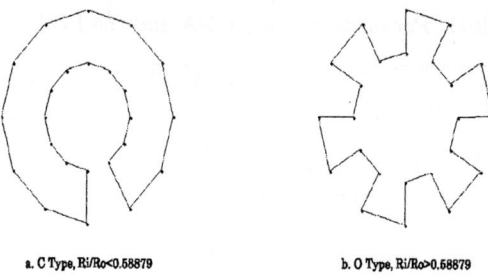

a. C Type, Ri/Ro<0.58879   b. O Type, Ri/Ro>0.58879

Fig. 3. TSP instances

4.1 Distributions of Optimal Solutions

Fig.4. shows the numbers of the optimal solutions which were obtained in 20 runs. A peak appeared around the half city numbers of main tour. The Fitness is shown in Fig.5. The process stopped at the 1000th generation. The process converged faster with the increase of city numbers in the sub tour at the beginning. This happened because there are much more improvable spaces in a big sub tour in the LGA. The stable convergences appeared when the city numbers of the sub tour range around the half that of the main tour. The result is not satisfied when the LGA performs as the reversion operator in the experiments.

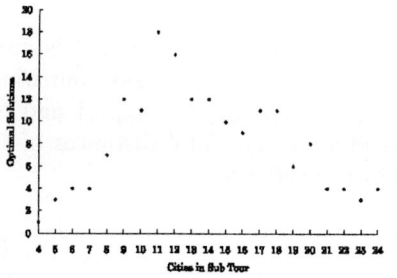
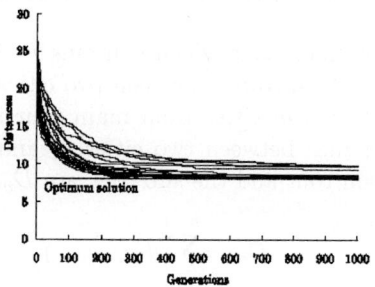

Fig. 4. Distribution of optimal solutions   **Fig. 5.** Fitness

4.2 Computation Time

The GAs usually take a long time to run to reach a good result. Consequently it increases the computation time greatly by combining the LGA to the GGA. The computation time was examined by increasing the city numbers and the generations in the LGA respectively. The results are shown in Fig.6. and Fig.7. The computation time linearly became longer with the increase of the city numbers and the generations in the LGA. Less city numbers and generations in the LGA took shorter time but it might not be sufficient for finding a better sub tour to improve the main tour.

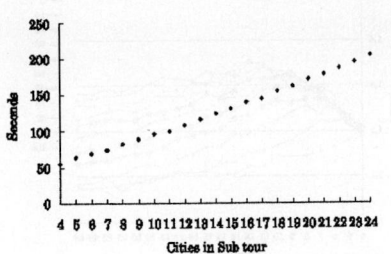
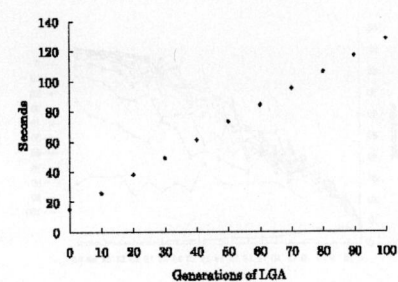

Fig. 6. Computation time with cities increase

Fig. 7. Computation time with generations increase

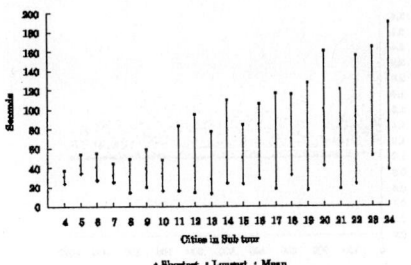
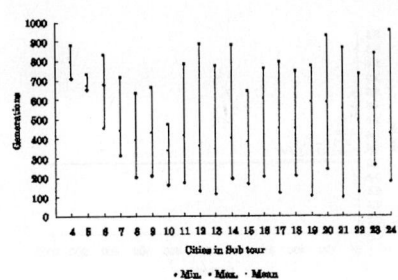

Fig. 8. Time of the optimal solution

Fig. 9. Generation of optimal solutions

4.3 Time and Generations for Obtaining the Optimal Solutions

Fig.8. shows the computational time for obtaining the optimal solutions. There are 3 points on every vertical line . The low, upper and central points show the shortest, longest and mean time for obtaining the optimal solutions respectively in 20 runs. The time became longer for finding the optimal solution while the city numbers of the sub tour increased. In Fig.9., the three points on every vertical line show the earliest, latest and mean generations for reaching the optimal solutions respectively in 20 runs. The earliest generations appeared when the city numbers in the sub tour ranged around the half city numbers of the main tour. Some optimal solutions appeared early when the sub tours contained more cities. But, it took much longer computation time when the city numbers increased in the sub tour as mentioned in 3.1 and 3.2.

4.4 Recombination Rates and Ratios

Fig.10. is the figure of the recombination rates. We suppose the number of the individuals which were recombined with the LGA is N_r and the number of the individuals which were searched by the LGA is N_s. The Recombination Rate $= N_r/N_s \times$ 100. The Recombination Rates increased with the increase of the generations and the city numbers in the sub tours. More generations are advantageous for finding a better sub tour to carry out the recombination, but

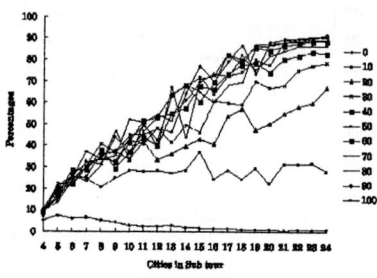
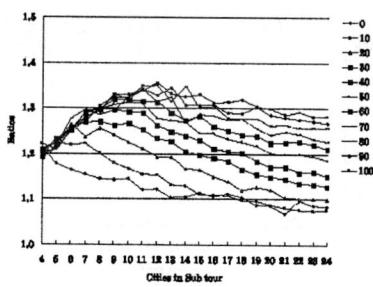

Fig. 10. Rates, Generations and population sizes

Fig. 11. Ratios, Generations and population sizes

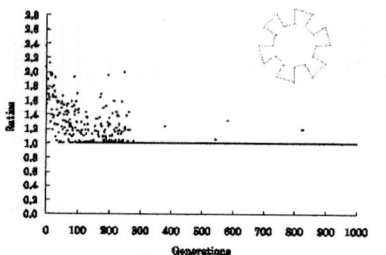
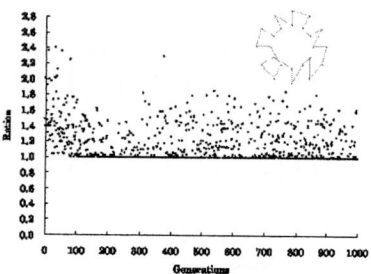

Fig. 12. Generation of Optimal Solution: 252nd

Fig. 13. Generation of Local Solution: 151st

it takes longer time to run the LGA. Same trend appeared with the changes of the city numbers because there are more improvable spaces in the bigger sub tour. The part chosen from the main tour is easier to improve. Fig.11. is the Ratio figure. The Ratio $R=d_0/d_1$ and $R \geq 1$. The peaks of the ratios appeared when the city numbers in the sub tour ranged from 8 to 13. The higher Ratio means a sub tour was found to be shorter in the LGA than the original part from the main tour. The result is correlative with the distribution of the optimal solutions in Fig.4.

4.5 Dynamics of the LGA

Fig.12. and Fig.13. show the dynamics of the LGA. Fig.12. presents the Ratio distributions of a single GGA in which the optimal solution was obtained at the 252nd generation. Because the original part from the GGA was preserved in the LGA and the Ratio $R=d_0/d_1$, the value of the $R \geq 1$. It indicates that the LGA created a shorter sub tour and recombined it to the GGA when $R > 1$. The LGA worked efficiently and more Ratios are bigger than 1 before the optimal solution was obtained at the 252nd generation. When the population converged to the optimal solution, the LGA could not create a better sub tour than the original part from the main tour and the Ratios became 1. Fig.13. shows the Ratio distributions of another GGA in which the premature convergence occurred at the 151st generation. There are many points distributed over 1 after the premature convergence occurred. It indicates that the LGA still worked efficiently even though the GGA reached the premature convergence.

5 Summary

A local search genetic algorithm based on the genetic recombination was discussed in this paper. The LGA acted as a local search operator in the GGA. A good result was presented when the city numbers of the sub tour were set around the half city numbers of the main tour. But, we think it would be reasonable running a small LGA for a big TSP instance, because half city numbers of a big TSP still forms a new big TSP instance. It may be more effective in distributed and parallel processing running the LGA as an island to improve the main tour. This will be discussed in our future works.

References

1. A. Homaifar, S. Guan, and G. E. Liepins, A New Approach to the Traveling Salesman Problem by Genetic Algorithms, in Proceedings of the 5th International Conference on Genetic Algorithms, pp. 460–466, Morgan Kaufmann, (1993).
2. C.N. Fiechter, A Parallel Tabu Search Algorithm for Large Traveling Salesman Problems, Discrete Applied Mathematics and Combinatorial Operations Research and Computer Science, vol. 51, pp. 243–267, (1994).
3. C.R.Reeves. Genetic algorithms and neighborhood search. in Evolutionary Computing, AISB Workshop, Pages 115-130. Leeds, U.K. (1994).
4. David E. Goldberg, Genetic Algorithms in Search, Optimization, and Machine Learnin, Appendix D, Addison-Wesley, Boston, MA, (1989).
5. D. S. Johnson and L. A. McGeoch, The Traveling Salesman Problem: A Case Study in Local Optimization, in Local Search in Combinatorial Optimization, (E. H. L. Aarts and J. K. Lenstra, eds.), Wiley and Sons, New York, (1996).
6. E. L. Lawler, J. K. Lenstra, A. H. G. Rinnooy Kan, and D. B. Shmoys, The Traveling Salesman Problem: A Guided Tour of Combinatorial Optimization. New York: Wiley and Sons, (1985).
7. G. Reinelt, The Traveling Salesman: Computational Solutions for TSP Applications. Vol. 840 of Lecture Notes in Computer Science, Springer Verlag, Berlin, Germany, (1994).
8. Holland, J.H. Adaptation in Natural and Artificial Systems, Univ. of Michigan Press (1975)
9. J.Grefenstette, R. Gopal, B. Rosimaita, and D. V. Gucht, Genetic Algorithms for the Traveling Salesman Problem, in Proceedings of an International Conference on Genetic Algorithms and their Applications, pp. 160–168, (1985).
10. J.Y. Potvin, The Traveling Salesman Problem: A Neural Network Perspective,ORSA Journal on Computing, vol. 5, pp. 328–348, (1993).

11. Keiji Maekawa,Hisashi Tamaki,Hajime Kita and Yoshikazu Nishikawa:A method for the traveling salesman problem based on the genetic algorithm,Transactions of the Society of Instrument and Control Engineers,Vol.31,No.5,pp.598-605,May (1995)(In Japanese).
12. L. M. Gambardella and M. Dorigo, Ant Q: A Reinforcement Learning Approach to the Traveling Salesman Problem, in Proc. 12th International Conference on Machine Learning, pp. 252–260, Morgan Kaufmann, (1995).
13. Michael D. Vose The Simple Genetic Algorithm: foundations and theory,MIT Press, (1999).
14. M.Yamamura, T.Ono, S.Kobayashi, Character-Preserving Genetic Algorithms for Traveling Salesman Problem Journal of The Japanese Society for Artificial Intelligence Vol.7, No.6, pp. 1049-1059,(1992) (In Japanese).
15. P.C. Kanellakis and C.H. Papadimitriou. Local search for asymmetric traveling salesman problem (1980).
16. R. M. Brady, Optimization Strategies Gleaned from Biological Evolution, Nature, vol. 317, pp. 804–806, *Operations Research*, 28(5):1066-1099, (1985).
17. S. Kirkpatrick, C. D. Gelatt, and M. P. Vecchi, Optimization by Simulated Annealing, Science, vol. 220, pp. 671–680,(1983).
18. S.Lin, and B. Kernighan, An Efficient Heuristic Procedure for the Traveling Salesman Problem. Operations Research., 21:498-516, (1973).
19. T. G. Bui and B. R. Moon, A New Genetic Approach for the Traveling Salesman Problem, in Proceedings of the First IEEE Conference on Evolutionary Computation, pp. 7–12, (1994).

Study on Data Allocation Model in Distributed Storage

Qing-song Wei and Qing-feng Du

School of Software Engineering, Tongji University, Shanghai 200331, China
qingsongpine@hotmail.com, du_cloud@sina.com

Abstract. According to the basic requirement of distributed storage, this paper defines several technical parameters to describe data allocation policy and presents a data allocation model by analyzing the performance of various data allocation policies. In this model, the data allocation policy is described in polyhedron view. The model can suggest an optimal data allocation policy to acquire satisfactory storage service at the less costs.

1 Introduction

Distributed storage technology is a key method to ensure data reliability, which strips data to segments and stores them across distant nodes to overcome localization of the local backup technology [1][2]. Choosing an optimized policy considering reliability, performance and costs is the key of the distributed data storage [3].

This paper presents a data allocation model in distributed storage. The model defines several parameters to describe data allocation policy according to the basic requirement of distributed storage, and establishes an estimation and decision mechanism by analyzing the performance of various data allocation policies. In this model, the data allocation policy is described in a polyhedron view. The model can suggest an optimal policy to acquire satisfactory storage service at the less costs.

The rest of this paper is as follows. Section 2 builds distributed data storage model. Section 3 presents factual analysis. Finally, we conclude in section 4.

2 Distributed Data Storage Model

We define several parameters to describe distributed storage policy [4][5]:

Backup Reliability: means file recovery probability from the rest live nodes while some nodes unavailable, marked as R.

Node Dependency: is the ratio of the minimal recovery node average number to the total node number, marked as D.

File Partition: describes how many parts a file is stripped to, marked as P.

Space Redundant: refer to an average replica number, marked as S.

2.1 One-Dimensional Model

Firstly, we study a simple case. A file is stripped to m parts marked as $\{D_1, D_2, \ldots, D_m\}$. Each segment is stored in one node and every node only stores one segment. So m nodes are needed. It is a one-to-one mapping shown as Figure 1. Accordingly, we call this case One-Dimensional Storage Model and its performance calculating method One-Dimensional Arithmetic.

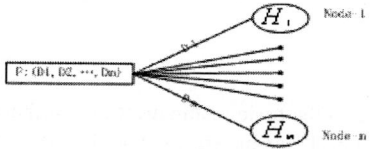

Fig. 1. One-Dimensional Storage Model

Suppose p_i be the probability of a node to be down. To recover a file, all m nodes must be available. So the Backup Reliability is:

$$R = P(H_1 * H_2 * \ldots * H_m)$$

The m nodes are insular mutually, so:

$$R = P(H_1) * P(H_2) * \ldots * P(H_m) = \prod_{i=1}^{m}(1-p_i)$$

According to definition, The File Partition is: $P = m$
The Node Dependency is: $D = m/m = 1$
The Space Redundant is: $S = 1$

2.2 Two-Dimensional Model

Similarly, a file is stripped to m parts marked as $\{D_1, D_2, \ldots, D_m\}$. Each segment D_i is stored in the N_i ($N_i>1$) nodes and every node only stores one segment. It is a one-to-more mapping shown as Figure 2. Several nodes storing same segment construct a polygon, so, we call this case Two-Dimensional Storage Model and its performance calculating method as Two-Dimension Arithmetic.

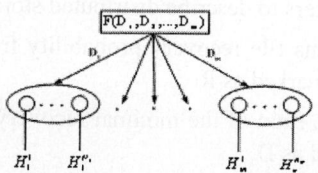

Fig. 2. Two-Dimensional Storage Model

The node j storing D_i is marked as H_i^j. Suppose p_i^j is the probability of H_i^j to be down. To recover D_i, among the nodes storing D_i, one node must be available at least. The node is insular mutually, the available possibility of D_i is:

$$P_i = P(1 - \overline{H}_i^1 * \overline{H}_i^2 * ... * \overline{H}_i^{Ni}) = P(1 - \prod_{j=1}^{Ni} P_i^j)$$

So, the Backup Reliability is: $R = \prod_{i=1}^{m} P_i$

According to definition, the File Partition is: $P = m$

The Node Dependency is: $D = m \Big/ \sum_{i=1}^{m} N_i$

The Space Redundant is: $S = \sum_{i=1}^{m} N_i \Big/ m$

2.3 Multi-dimensional Model

A file is stripped to m parts marked as $\{D_1, D_2, ..., D_m\}$. Each segment D_i is stored in the N_i ($N_i > 1$) nodes and every node stores one more segments. It is a more-to-more mapping shown as Figure 3. We call this case Multidimensional Model and its performance calculating method as Multidimensional Arithmetic.

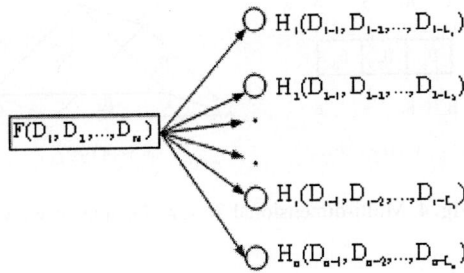

Fig. 3. Multi-Dimensional Storage Model

We present the following definition:

Un-Recovery Package: is the remote backup host set not to recover a file. That is to say, when these nodes are unavailable, it is not possible to recover the file from the other nodes.

Un-Recovery Package Operation: If a node is deleted from the Un-Recovery Package, the rest hosts set is still a Un-Recovery Package, we call this operation a Un-Recovery Package Operation.

Un-Recovery Closed Package: is a Un-Recovery Package which can not be performed Un-Recovery Package Operation any more.

Due to the definition of the Un-Recovery Closed Package, all the un-recovery cases are the union of the elements of the Un-Recovery Closed Package U, so un-recovery possibility is: $\overline{R} = P(U_1 \bigcup U_2 \bigcup ... \bigcup U_z)$.

Then, The Backup Reliability is: $R = 1 - \overline{R}$

According to definition, the File Partition is: $P = m$

The Node Dependency is: $D = ((\sum_{j=1}^{k} X_j)/k)/n$

The Space Redundant is: $S = (\sum_{i=1}^{m} N_i)/m$

3 Practical Analyses

A file is stripped into 3 parts marked as $\{D_1, D_2, D_3\}$, in which D_1 is stored in the nodes set $\{A, B, B_1, A_1\}$, D_2 is stored in the nodes set $\{B_1, B_2, A_2, A_1\}$ and D_3 is stored in the nodes set $\{B_2, B, A, A_2\}$. The Figure 4 is the geometry express of this data allocation, in which the Figure 4-A is its two-dimensional surface view and the figure 4-B is its three-dimensional solid view. In the Figure 4-B, the point represents node and surface represents segment.

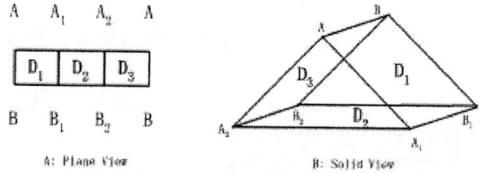

Fig. 4. Multi-dimensional Storage Geometry View

According to the above geometry view, we study the tetrahedron and hexahedron storage models. Table 1 lists their performance. From this method, we can get a perfect data allocation policy according to practical environment.

Table 1. Data Allocation Policies Performance Comparison

	Tetrahedron(4 nodes)			Hexahedron(8 nodes)		
	One-Dim.	Two-Dim.	Multi-Dim.	One-Dim.	Two-Dim.	Multi-Dim.
Backup Reliability	$(1-p)^3$	$1-2p^2+p^3$	$1-4p^2+3p^3$	$(1-p)^7$	$1-2p^4+p^7$	$(1-p)^7$	$1-6p^4+12p^6-8p^7+p^7$
Node Dependency	1	1/2	1/2	1	1/4	1/2	1/3
File Partition	4	2	4	8	2	4	6
Space Redundant	1	2	3	1	4	2	3

4 Conclusions

This paper presents an efficient method for finding optimized data allocation policy in distributed data storage, considering reliability, performance and costs. With this method, a perfect policy can be found according to practical environment.

References

1. Cabrera, L.-F, and Long, D.D.E.(1991). Swift: Using distributed disk striping to provide high I/O data rate. Computing System, 4(4):405–436.
2. Scott Atchley, Stephen Soltesz and James S. Plank, et al., Fault-Tolerance in the Network Storage Stack, Proceedings of the FAST 2002 Conference, California, USA, 2002,3–5.
3. Darrell D. E. Long, Bruce R. Montague, and Luis-Felipe Cabrera. Swift/RAID: a distributed RAID system. Computing Systems, 7(3):333–359. Usenix, Summer 1994.
4. Cao, P., Lim, S. B., Venkataraman, S., and Wilkes, J. The TickerTAIP parallel RAID architecture. ACM Transactions on Computer Systems 12(3). (August 1994) 236–269.
5. Brinkmann A,Salzwedel K,Scheideler C. Efficient Distributed Data Placement Strategies for Storage Area Networks. Proc.12 ACM SPAA, 2000.

O(1) Time Algorithm on BSR for Constructing a Binary Search Tree with Best Frequencies

Limin Xiang[1], Kazuo Ushijiam[1], Kai Cheng[1], Jianjun Zhao[2], and Cunwei Lu[2]

[1]Department of Social Information Systems, Kyushu Sangyo University,
2-3-1 Matsukadai, Higashi-ku, Fukuoka 813-8503, Japan
{xiang, ushijima, chengk}@is.kyusn-u.ac.jp
http://www.is.kyusan-u.ac.jp/
[2]Department of Computer Science and Engineering, Fukuoka Institute of Technology,
3-10-1 Wajiro-Higashi, Higashi-ku, Fukuoka 811-0295, Japan
{zhao, lu}@fit.ac.jp

Abstract. Constructing a binary search tree of n nodes with best frequencies needs $\Omega(n \log n)$ time on RAM, and $\Omega(\log n)$ time on n-processor EREW, CREW, or CRCW PRAM. In this paper, we propose an $O(1)$ time algorithm on n-processor BSR PRAM for the problem, which is the first constant time solution to the problem on any model of computation.

1 Introduction

The binary search tree is one of the most frequently used structures in computer science. Suppose that we have n keys of data and we know the relative frequency that each key is searched. We want to store them as nodes on a binary search tree so that the most commonly searched keys are the easiest to retrieve. This means that the most commonly searched keys will have the shortest paths from the root. Such a binary search tree is called the Binary Search Tree with Best Frequencies (BSTBF for short) in this paper. In other words, the root of any subtree in a BSTBF is with the maximum one of the frequencies in the subtree.

It is known that constructing a binary search tree with n nodes needs $\Omega(n \log n)$ time on RAM (Random Access Machine) [1], therefore, to construct a BSTBF with n nodes needs at least $\Omega(n \log n)$ time on RAM, and constructing the same tree will need $\Omega(\log n)$ time on n-processor EREW (Exclusive Read Exclusive Write), CREW (Concurrent Read Exclusive Write) or CRCW (Concurrent Read Concurrent Write) PRAM (Parallel Random Access Machine), since the time lower bound on n-processor EREW, CREW or CRCW PRAM is $\Omega(T(n)/n)$ for the problem that needs $T(n)$ time on RAM [2].

In this paper, we will propose an $O(1)$ time algorithm on BSR (Broadcasting with Selective Reduction) PRAM for constructing a BSTBF, which is the first constant time solution to the problem on any model of computation.

The remainder of this paper is organized as follows. Section 2 describes the BSR PRAM model. Some properties of the BSTBF are included in Section 3. Section 4 gives our $O(1)$ time algorithm on BSR PRAM for constructing a BSTBF. Section 5 illustrates an example. Finally, Section 6 concludes the paper.

2 BSR PRAM Model

Of many different computing models for parallel algorithms, the PRAM is the most popular one. There are four forms of memory access allowed by the PRAM most commonly used, namely, exclusive read (ER), exclusive write (EW), concurrent read (CR), and concurrent write (CW). The relation between processors and memory locations is of *one-to-one* correspondence for ER or EW, and of *many-to-one* (*one-to-many*) correspondence for CR or CW. CR or CW includes ER or EW as a special case. Therefore, for some problems, solutions on CREW PRAM are faster than those on EREW PRAM, and those on CRCW PRAM are the fastest. Besides ER, EW, CR, and CW, another form of memory access is allowed by the BSR (Broadcasting with Selective Reduction) PRAM model [3,4], namely, the BROADCAST Instruction (BI), for which the relation between processors and memory locations is of *many-to-many* correspondence. Thus, for some problems, solutions may be found on BSR that are faster than those possible on CRCW.

A BI is denoted by

$$u_j := \Re_{1 \leq i \leq n} d_i \mid t_i \ \sigma \ l_j$$

where,

- n : number of processors;
- d_i : datum broadcast by processor i, $1 \leq i \leq n$;
- t_i : tag broadcast by processor i, $1 \leq i \leq n$;
- l_j : limit value used by processor j;
- σ : selection operation, taken from the following set $\{<, \leq, =, \geq, >, \neq\}$;
- $\Re$: binary associative reduction operation, taken from $\{\Sigma, \Pi, \wedge, \vee, \oplus, \cap, \cup\}$ denoting sum, product, AND, OR, Exclusive OR, maximum, and minimum, respectively;
- u_j : result stored by processor j;

The above BI means that: *for $1 \leq i \leq n$, if $t_i \sigma l_j$ is TRUE, d_i is "accepted" by u_j. The set of all data accepted by u_j is reduced to a single value by the operation $\Re$, and stored in u_j. If no data are accepted by u_j, then u_j is not affected by this BI. If only one datum is accepted, then u_j is assigned the value of the datum.*

When the range of i in the above BI is understood, the instruction can be abbreviated as

$$u_j := \Re \; d_i \, | \, t_i \; \sigma \; l_j$$

Instead of the single selection $t_i \; \sigma \; l_j$, the multiple selection $\wedge_{1 \leq h \leq k} t_i^{(h)} \sigma^{(h)} l_j^{(h)}$ was also allowed by BSR in [3], and the general selection

$$\wp(t_i^{(1)} \sigma^{(1)} l_j^{(1)}, t_2^{(2)} \sigma^{(2)} l_j^{(2)}, \ldots, t_i^{(k)} \sigma^{(k)} l_j^{(k)})$$

was allowed by BSR in [5], in order to obtain time optimal solutions for more applications.

The time of memory access in EREW, CREW, or CRCW is typically assumed as $O(1)$ for simplicity when, in fact, $\Omega(\log n)$ circuit stages are needed for each processor of n processors to be able to access a same memory location. Therefore, in BSR, if the number of circuit stages is $O(\log n)$ between n processors and memory locations, then the time of memory access is assumed to be $O(1)$ for the same reason. Since the implementations of BSR, BSR with multiple criteria and BSR with general selection in [3-5] are all with $O(\log n)$ circuit stages between n processors and memory locations, a BI of BSR is of $O(1)$ time. Algorithms on BSR for Many applications can be found in [2-15].

3 Some Properties of BSTBF

To obtain a correct algorithm, some properties of BSTBF with n nodes are discussed in this section.

Definition 1.
(1) *Let* $K_n = \{k(1), k(2), \ldots, k(n)\}$ *be a set of n keys, where for $1 \leq i \leq n$, $k(i)$ is from an ordered set, and $k(i) \neq k(j)$ if $i \neq j$.*
(2) *Let* $F_n = \{f(1), f(2), \ldots, f(n)\}$ *be the frequency set for K_n, where for $1 \leq i \leq n$, $f(i)$, the frequency for $k(i)$, is a nonnegative integer. Furthermore, for ease of presentation, let $f(i) \neq f(j)$ if $i \neq j$.*
(3) *A binary search tree with n keys K_n and the frequency set F_n is denoted by* $T(K_n, F_n)$.

Thus, the BSTBF can be recursively defined as follows.

Definition 2.
(1) *An empty tree is a BSTBF,*
(2) *binary search tree $T(K_n, F_n)$ is a BSTBF, where*
   (i) *node $k(r)$ is the root of $T(K_n, F_n)$, and $f(r) = \max F_n$,*
   (ii) *$T(K_L, F_L)$ and $T(K_R, F_R)$ are the left and right subtrees of node $k(r)$, respectively, and*
   (iii) *both $T(K_L, F_L)$ and $T(K_R, F_R)$ are BSTBF's.*
(3) *a BSTBF with n keys K_n and the frequency set F_n is denoted by* $T(K_n, F_n)$.

Example 3.
$K_{10}=\{D,B,I,A,C,G,J,E,H,F\}$,
$F_{10}=\{80,65,75,10,40,45,25,15,30,5\}$ and the BSTBF T(K_{10},F_{10}) is shown as in Figure 1.

The *inorder transversal* is denoted by $IK_n=(k(I_1),k(I_2),\ldots,k(I_n))$ of K_n on T(K_n,F_n), and the subsequence $(k(I_i),k(I_{i+1}),\ldots,k(I_j))$ of IK_n is denoted by $IK_n(i,j)$. We have $k(I_1)<k(I_2)<\ldots<k(I_n)$ by the definitions of the binary search tree and the inorder transversal.

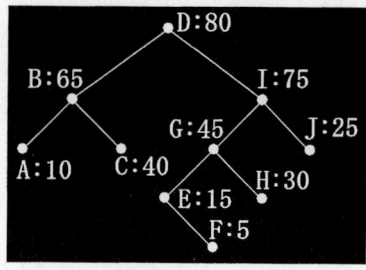

Fig. 1. T(K_{10},F_{10})

Corresponding to IK_n, the frequency sequence is denoted by $IF_n=(f(I_1), f(I_2),\ldots,f(I_n))$, namely, key $k(I_i)$ is with frequency $f(I_i)$ for i in $\{1,2,\ldots,n\}$.

For T(K_{10},F_{10}) in Figure 1, for example, IK_{10}=(A,B,C,D,E,F,G,H,I,J) and IF_{10}=(10,65,40,80,15,5,45,30,75,25).

Corollary 4.

T(IK_m, IF_m) *is a subtree of* T(IK_n, IF_n) *if and only if there are i and j so that*
(1) $IK_m = IK_n(i, j)$ and $IF_m = IF_n(i, j)$,
(2) $f(I_{i-1}) > f(I_k)$ for $i \le k \le j$, if $1 < i$, and
(3) $f(I_k) < f(I_{j+1})$ for $i \le k \le j$, if $j < n$.

Proof.

$\Rightarrow$: *Since the inorder transversal of* IK_m *in* T(IK_m, IF_m) *is the same as that in* T(IK_n, IF_n), *(1) holds. (2) and (3) hold by the definitions of the BSTBF and the inorder transversal.*

$\Leftarrow$: *By condition (1),* IK_m *and* IF_m *are the subsequences of* IK_n *and* IF_n, *respectively. By conditions (2) and (3),* T(IK_m, IF_m) *is a subtree of* T(IK_n, IF_n).

Example 5.
The left subtree of node I in Figure 1, rooted by G, is with IK_4=(E,F,G,H)=IK_{10}(5,8) *and* IF_4=(15,5,45,30)=IF_{10}(5,8), *and* $f(I_4)=80 > f(I_7)=45 < f(I_9)=75$.

From Definition 2 and Corollary 4, a recursive algorithm can be obtained easily for constructing a BSTBF from its IK_n and IF_n, which is left to the reader.

Theorem 6.
For $IK_n = (k(I_1),k(I_2),\ldots,k(I_n))$ *and* $IF_n = (f(I_1),f(I_2),\ldots,f(I_n))$, *let* $k(I_r)$ *be the root of* T(K_n, F_n),
$a = \max\{\{0\} \cup \{i \mid (1 \le i < j) \wedge (f(I_i) > f(I_j))\}\}$
$b = \min\{\{n+1\} \cup \{i \mid (j < i \le n) \wedge (f(I_i) > f(I_j))\}\}$, *and*

$$c = \begin{cases} f(I_a) & ,(a>0) \wedge (b=n+1) \\ f(I_b) & ,(a=0) \wedge (b<n+1) \\ \min\{f(I_a), f(I_b)\}, (a>0) \wedge (b<n+1) \end{cases}$$

for $1 \le j \le n$, in $T(K_n, F_n)$,

(1) if $j \ne r$ and $f(I_p) = c$, node $k(I_p)$ is the parent of node $k(I_j)$,

(2) if $b < n+1$ and $f(I_p) = c = f(I_b)$, then node $k(I_j)$ is the left son of node $k(I_p)$, and

(3) if $a > 0$ and $f(I_p) = c = f(I_a)$, then node $k(I_j)$ is the right son of node $k(I_p)$.

Proof.
When $a > 0$ and $b < n+1$, $k(I_a)$ is the nearest to $k(I_j)$ on the left side in IK_n with the frequency bigger than $f(I_j)$, and $k(I_b)$ is the nearest to $k(I_j)$ on the right side in IK_n with the frequency bigger than $f(I_j)$. Thus, $f(I_j)$ is the biggest in $IF_n(a+1, b-1)$. When $a = 0$ and/or $b = n+1$, $f(I_j)$ is also the biggest in $IF_n(a+1, b-1)$. Therefore, node $k(I_j)$ is the root of tree $T(IK_n(a+1, b-1), IF_n(a+1, b-1))$. By Corollary 4, the tree is a subtree of $T(K_n, F_n)$. Since $j \ne r$, the parent exists of node $k(I_j)$ in $T(K_n, F_n)$. From the definitions of the BSTBF and the inoder transversal, when $a = 0$ or $(b<n+1) \wedge (f(I_b) < f(I_a))$, tree $T(IK_n(a+1,b-1), IF_n(a+1,b-1))$ is the left subtree of node $k(I_b)$, i.e., node $k(I_j)$ is the left son of node $k(I_p)$ when $b < n+1$ and $f(I_p) = c = f(I_b)$, and when $b = n+1$ or $(a>0) \wedge (f(I_a) < f(I_b))$, tree $T(IK_n(a+1,b-1), IF_n(a+1,b-1))$ is the right subtree of node $k(I_a)$, i.e., node $k(I_j)$ is the right son of node $k(I_p)$ when $a > 0$ and $f(I_p) = c = f(I_a)$.

This completes the proof.

With Theorem 6, we can give our $O(1)$ time algorithm on BSR for constructing a BSTBF in the next section.

4 The Algorithm

Before giving the solution on BSR for constructing a BSTBF, we make clear the *Input* and *Output* of the algorithm as follows.

Input: $K[1..n]$, $F[1..n]$: the key sequence, and the frequency sequence.
Output: $P[1..n]$, $L[1..n]$, $R[1..n]$: if $P[i] \ne 0$, node $K[P[i]]$ is the parent of node $K[i]$, or else node $K[i]$ is the root of the BSTBF; if $L[i] = 0$ ($R[i] = 0$), node $K[i]$ has not the left (right) son, or else, node $K[i]$ has the left (right) son $K[L[i]]$ ($K[R[i]]$).

Thus, the algorithm is given below in detail.

Algorithm cBSTBF
```
{----------------------------------------------------------}
begin
   for j := 1 to n dopar
   {-- to sort K[1..n] ----------------------------------}
      s[j] := 0;
      s[j] := ∑ 1 | K[i] ≤ K[j];
      t[s[j]] := j;
      IK[s[j]] := K[j];
      IF[s[j]] := F[j];
   {-- to calculate a and b --------------------------}
      a[j] := 0;
      a[j] := ∩i | (i < j) ∧ (IF[i] > IF[j]);
      b[j] := n + 1;
      b[j] := ∪i | (i > j) ∧ (IF[i] > IF[j]);
   {-- to calculate indexes for P[1..n],L[1..n],R[1..n] --}
      h[j] := 0; d[j] := 0; e[j] := 0;
      if a[j] = 0 then
      begin
         if b[j] ≤ n then
         begin h[j] := b[j];
               d[b[j]] := j;
         end;
      end else if b[j] = n + 1 then
      begin
         h[j] := a[j];
         e[a[j]] := j;
      end else if IF[a[j]] > IF[b[j]] then
      begin
         h[j] := b[j];
         d[b[j]] := j;
      end else
      begin
         h[j] := a[j];
         e[a[j]] := j;
      end;
   {-- to calculate P[1..n],L[1..n],R[1..n] ------------}
      if h[j] = 0 then P[t[j]] := 0 else
         P[t[j]] := t[h[j]];
      if d[j] = 0 then L[t[j]] := 0 else
         L[t[j]] := t[d[j]];
      if e[j] = 0 then R[t[j]] := 0 else
         R[t[j]] := t[e[j]] ;
   pardo;
end.
{----------------------------------------------------------}
```

From Theorem 6, it is known that the algorithm above can construct the BSTBF from the key and frequency sequences correctly. Since each instruction in the algorithm above is in $O(1)$ time on BSR, the algorithm is a constant time solution on BSR.

5 An Example

Recall the example in Section 3, where, $K_{10}=\{D,B,I,A,C,G,J,E,H,F\}$, and $F_{10}=\{80,65,75,10,40,45,25,15,30,5\}$. We will still use them as the input of Algorithm cBSTBF to construct $T(K_{10}, F_{10})$ in the following.

Algorithm cBSTBF consists of four steps, namely

- *Step 1*: sorting $K[1..n]$ to obtain $IK[1..n]$ and $IF[1..n]$,
- *Step 2*: calculating middle variables $a[1..n]$ and $b[1..n]$,
- *Step 3*: calculating indexes for $P[1..n]$, $L[1..n]$, and $R[1..n]$, and
- *Step 4*: calculating $P[1..n]$, $L[1..n]$, and $R[1..n]$.

Table 1 shows the data for using Algorithm cBSTBF to construct $T(K_{10},F_{10})$ on a 10-processor BSR, where values of variables $K, F, s, t, IK, IF, a, b, h, d, e, P, R$, and L are corresponding to those in the algorithm after each step.

Let X-axis be from left to right, Y-axis be from up to down, and node $K[i]$ of $T(K_{10},F_{10})$ be placed at the coordinate decided by the rule in [11] for $1 \le i \le 10$, using the values of $R[1..10]$ and $L[1..10]$ in Table 1, we can draw a *planar upward straight-line grid tree drawing* [11] for $T(K_{10},F_{10})$, as shown in Figure 2.

From Figure 2, Theorem 6 in Section 3 and Algorithm cBSTBF in Section 4 can be understood easier, and it is also verified by the example that Algorithm cBSTBF can construct the BSTBF from its key and frequency sequences correctly.

Table 1. Data for constructing $T(K_{10}, F_{10})$

Index	1	2	3	4	5	6	7	8	9	10
K	D	B	I	A	C	G	J	E	H	F
F	80	65	75	10	40	45	25	15	30	5
s	4	2	9	1	3	7	10	5	8	6
t	4	2	5	1	8	10	6	9	3	7
IK	A	B	C	D	E	F	G	H	I	J
IF	10	65	40	80	15	5	45	30	75	25
a	0	0	2	0	4	5	4	7	4	9
b	2	4	4	11	7	7	9	9	11	11
h	2	4	2	0	7	5	9	7	4	9
d	0	1	0	2	0	0	5	0	7	0
e	0	3	0	9	6	0	8	0	10	0
P	0	1	1	2	2	3	3	6	6	8
L	2	4	6	0	0	8	0	0	0	0
R	3	5	7	0	0	9	0	10	0	0

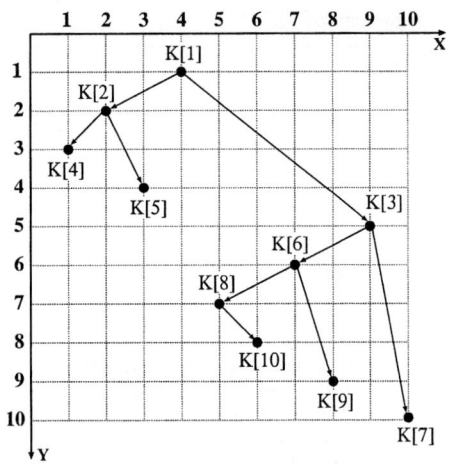

Fig. 2. $T(K_{10}, F_{10})$

6 Conclusions

Some sequences for binary trees, such as tree traversals [6], the *i-p* or *p-i* sequence [11], the bit-sting [14], and the i-sequence [15] are different from K_n and F_n (IK_n and IF_n). Therefore, methods in [6,11,14,15] for constructing binary trees from those sequences can not be used to construct the BSTBF from its key and frequency sequences.

The binary search tree is one of the most frequently used structures in computer science. In this paper, we discussed some properties of BSTBF, and based on the properties, we proposed an $O(1)$ time parallel algorithm *cBSTBF* on BSR to construct the BSTBF from its key and frequency sequences. Constructing a BSTBF with n nodes needs $\Omega(n \log n)$ time on RAM, and $\Omega(\log n)$ time on n-processor EREW, CREW, or CRCW PRAM. *cBSTBF* is the first constant time solution to the problem on any model of computation.

References

1. Devroye, L., Robson, J. M.: On the generation of random binary search tree. SIAM J. Comput. 24 (6) (1995) 1141–1156
2. Xiang, L., Ushijima, K.: On time bounds, the work-time scheduling principle, and optimality for BSR. IEEE Trans. on Parallel and Distributed Systems, 12 (9) (2001) 912–921
3. Akl, S. G.: Parallel Computation: Models and Methods. N.J.:Prentice Hall (1997) 475–509
4. Lindon, L. F., Akl, S. G.: An Optimal Implementation of Broadcasting with Selective Reduction. IEEE Trans. on Parallel and Distributed Systems. 4 (3) (1993) 256–269

5. Xiang, L., Ushijima, K., Akl, S. G., Stojmenovic, I.: An Efficient Implementation for the BROADCAST Instruction of BSR$^+$. IEEE Trans. on Parallel and Distributed Systems. 10 (8) (1999) 852–863
6. Stojmenovic, I.: Constant time BSR solutions to parenthesis matching, tree decoding, and tree reconstruction from its traversals. IEEE Trans. on Parallel and Distributed Systems. 7 (2) (1996) 218–224
7. Xiang, L., Ushijima, K.: Decoding and drawing an arbitrary tree from its pre-post sequence. Proc. PDCS'98, Las Vegas (1998) 182–185
8. Xiang, L., Ushijima, K.: Optimal Parallel Merging Algorithms on BSR. Proc. I-SPAN 2000, Dallas (2000) 12–17
9. Xiang, L., Ushijima, K.: O(1) Time Algorithm on BSR for Computing Convex Hull. Proc. PDCS 2002, Cambridge, USA (2002) 143–146
10. Xiang, L., Ushijima, K.: ANSV problem on BSRs. Information Processing Letters. 65 (3) (1998) 135–138
11. Xiang, L., Ushijima, K.: Decoding and drawing on BSR for a binary tree from its i-p sequence. Parallel Processing Letters. 9 (1) (1999) 103–110
12. Xiang, L., Ushijima, K.: Rearranging scattered information on BSR. Information Processing Letters. 71 (1) (1999) 43–47
13. Xiang, L., Ushijima, K.: A theorem on the relation between BSR_k and BSR$^+$. Information Processing Letters. 71 (2) (1999) 71–73
14. Xiang, L., Ushijima, K., Zhao, J.: Time Optimal n-Size Matching Parentheses and Binary Tree Decoding Algorithms on a p-Processor BSR. Parallel Processing Letters. 12 (3-4) (2002) 365–374
15. Xiang, L., Ushijima, K., Zhao, J., Zhang, T., Tang, C.: O(1) Time Algorithm on BSR for Constructing a Random Binary Search Tree. Proc. PDCAT'03, Chengdu, China (2003) 599–602

Agent Based Distributed Parallel Tunneling Algorithms[*]

Wen Yuanqiao[1,2], Yu Shengsheng[1], Zhou Jingli[1], and Huang Liwen[2]

[1] College of Computer Science & Technology, HUST, 430074 Wuhan, China
wenyuanqiao@yahoo.com.cn, {ssyu, jlzhou}@mail.hust.edu.cn
[2] Navigation College, WHUT, 430062 Wuhan, China
lwhuang@mail.whut.edu.cn

Abstract. This paper presents an efficient and scalable approach to solve global optimization problem by distributed parallel tunneling using mobile agents.To use the parallel and concurrent characteristic of the tunneling algorithms and increase the speed of the computing, we use mobile agents as a tool for parallel implementation in a distributed environment. The experimental results demonstrate the feasibility and the potential of the proposed method.

1 Introduction

Global optimization presents widely in practice and scientific experiments and is widely concerned and researched. The traditional optimal methods always get stuck in local minimum because their searching efficiency is effected by the initial points and the topology of the surface associated with the objective function. In order to improve the efficiency of the traditional algorithms, Levy et al firstly proposed the tunneling algorithm (TA) [1] for the global optimization of functions. And then, Yao et al suggested the dynamic tunneling algorithm (DTA) [2]. In 1993, Cetin et al used terminal repeller unconstrained sub-energy tunneling (TRUST) [3] for fast global optimization. For the parallelism of tunneling algorithms, it's convenient to realize them in a parallel [4] or distribution model. In this article, an agent based distributed parallel computing model of tunneling algorithm is designed.

2 Fundamentals of Tunneling Algorithms

The tunneling algorithms can be classified into two types: one is tunneling functions based tunneling algorithm and the other is dynamic system based tunneling algorithm [1,2,3,4]. The paper gives their brief descriptions.

For the global optimal problem, the tunneling functions based tunneling algorithm (FTA) [1,4] has two phases: minimization phase and tunneling phase.

Starting from an initial approximation x_0, the minimization phase has to find a local solution to the problem by using local search algorithm, such as steepest descent

---

[*] This paper was sponsored by National Natural Science Foundation of China (NO:40275015).

method, conjugate gradient method and quasi-Newton local optimization method. In tunneling phase, starting from x^*, to tunnel from one valley to another is the main task. The purpose is to find x^{tun} which satisfies the condition $T_{tun}(x^{tun}) \le 0$ by constructing tunneling functions $T_{tun}(x)$. The commonly used tunneling functions are classical tunneling functions and exponential tunneling functions [1]. Taking x^{tun} as the new x^* and repeating the above two phases until the convergent conditions are satisfied, the global optimal resolution x_G^* and the global optimization $f(x_G^*)$ can be found.

Dynamic system based tunneling algorithm (DTA) [2,3] is based on the dynamic system. It's also composed of two phases. In minimization phase, it can find the local optimal resolution x^* of $f(x)$ by integrating the dynamic system to seek its equilibrium point. In dynamic tunneling phase, a dynamic system [2,3] is constructed. For more details see [3].To repeat the two phases, it can find the global optimization at last.

3 Distributed Parallel Tunneling Algorithms Using Mobile Agents

In the system, there are 4 types of agent: control agent (CG), task agent (TG), resource agent (RG) and message agent (MG). CG starts the running of the whole system and is responsible for generating, dispatching and retracting, disposing TG. The first local minimum is found by CG. The tunneling directions of TG are partitioned and broadcasted by CG. CG manages and schedules all available computing resources knowing from RG. The MG is used by CG to send direction information, new starting points and new local minimum to all TG. If TG find a new local minimum, they will dispatch MG to CG about the new information.The execution roadmap of the distributed parallel tunneling algorithm is described as the following:

(i) Firstly, it's necessary to create a CG. Starting from initial point x_0, CG finds the local minimum x^*. Then, it creates and dispatches TG (remarked $TG_1, TG_2, \cdots, TG_i$) to available computing resources according to its scheduling information. TG_i carries the local minimum information and tunneling directions information from CG.

(ii) Once TG_i arrives its destination, it clones itself to create one to more children (remarked $TG_{i1}, TG_{i2}, \cdots, TG_{iK}$) according to its available computing resources. The children receive the staring point information and tunneling directions information from its parents and execute tunneling search tasks along different way.

(iii) TG_{im} should immediately reports the local minimum information found in its local searching phase to its parent TG_i. TG_i selects the best local minimum from the received local minimums and periodically reports it to CG. The reporting frequency is consulted by TG_i and CG.

(iv) CG checks if the new local minimum come from TG_i is the best found so far in which case it proceeds to send a MG with this information as well as new tunneling directions information to all TG_i s. TG_i sends the new local minimum to its children once it receives the information.

(v) TG_{im} restarts a new tunneling search from the new local minimum point along new direction partitioned by its parent if it received the new information from parent at its tunneling phase. However, TG_{im} continues the local search until it finds a new local minimum if the new information was received at its local minimization searching phase. The computed new local minimum will be compared with the received new information. If the former is not better than the latter, TG_{im} restarts a new tunneling search from the received new local minimum point. Otherwise, it reports the computed new local minimum to its parent TG_i.

(vi) The above steps are repeated until the convergent condition or the general stopping condition is satisfied. Finally, CG outputs the global optimization information and retracts and disposes all agents in the system.

4 Model Implementation and Experiments

The mobile agent execution environment used to implement the system is based on the Aglet Technology. The global optimization problem used to test the system is to find the optimal structure of small molecules which using the Lennard-Jones potential [4].

Here we test the system for the specially difficult case of 38 atoms [4]. The computing resources joined in experiments are S3 (origin300 workstation), PC1,PC2, PC3(personal computers with Windows or Linux System).In order to test the scalability, parallelism, efficiency and speedup of the system under different scenarios, 11 experiments have been designed. The details and their results are in Table 1.

Table 1 shows the performance of the system under different scenarios. As it can be seen from the results, with the joining of more and more computing resources, the speedup of the system increases and the system becomes more efficient, which proves that the system has good scalability. The use of multiple agents on different computing resources improves the parallelism of the system. However, for the communication costs between agents and the limits of working load, it's not advisable to clone more task agents on the same computing resource, which can be seen from the decreasing trend of the efficiency in Table 1.

Table 1. Details of experiments. In table, the speedup is a measurement of how much faster the same program with the same data by using multiple TGs than by using one TG. The efficiency is the ratio of Speedup compared with the corresponding TG numbers. NO.1 experiment is sequential tunneling algorithm, which is used as the contrasting case. NO.2~4 experiments mainly test the scalability of the system. NO.5~11 experiments test the parallelism of the multiple agents parallel computing

Experiment NO.	Joined computing resource and TGs working on them				TG Numbers	Time (unit:s)	Speedup	Efficiency
	PC1	PC2	PC3	S3				
1	0	0	1	0	1	1649		
2	0	1	1	0	2	443.6	3.72	1.86
3	1	1	1	0	3	274.2	6.07	2
4	1	1	1	1	4	137.5	11.9	3
5	2	2	2	2	8	47.7	34.5	4.32
6	2	2	2	8	14	26.1	63.4	4.51
7	2	2	2	12	18	19.7	83.88	4.66
8	2	2	4	12	20	17.1	96.42	4.82
9	2	2	6	12	22	16.3	101.15	4.6
10	2	4	6	12	24	15.9	103.7	4.3
11	2	4	6	16	28	15.5	106.4	3.8

5 Conclusion

Based on the intrinsic characteristics of the tunneling search and the parallelism of its tunneling search, an efficient distributed parallel tunneling algorithm is realized in an agent based ubiquitous computing system. For the mobility, autonomy, reactivity, communication, cooperation and coordination of agents, as well as the two-level control model controlling different agents, the system is flexible and scalable enough. The periodical querying and direct replacement fault tolerance strategy keeps the dependability of the system. The experiments of Lennard-Jones potential problem show that the system is a practical tool to solve real complex molecular conformational searching problems.

References

1. Levy A V, Montalvo A:The tunneling algorithm for the global optimization of functions,Vol.6. SIAM Journal on Scientific and Statistical Computing (1985) 15–29
2. Y. Yao:Dynamic Tunneling Algorithm for Global Optimization,Vol.19(10).IEEE Transactions on Systems, Man, and Cybernetics (1989) 1222–1230
3. Cetin, Barhen and Burdick: Terminal Repeller Unconstrained Subenergy Tunneling (TRUST) for fast Global Optimization, Vol.77.Journal of Optimization Theory and Applications (1993) 97–126,
4. Susana Gómez, Nelson del Castillo, Longina Castellanos, Julio Solano:The parallel tunneling method,Vol. 29(4). Parallel Computing (2003) 523–533

The Effect of Varying Computational Granularity and Tree Imbalance on the Performance of Parallel Tree-Based Application

Fazilah Haron[1] and John R. Davy[2]

[1] School of Computer Science, Universiti Sains Malaysia, 11800 Penang, Malaysia
fazilah@cs.usm.my
[2] School of Computer Studies, University of Leed, Leeds LS29JT, UK
davyjr@scs.leeds.ac.uk

Abstract. In this paper we discuss the effect of two tree application parameters, namely computational granularity and tree imbalance, on the overall performance of parallel tree structured application. We apply a technique called phased-based adaptive dynamic load balancing, a version of adaptive DLB in which a parallel computation moves through different load balancing phases identified on the basis of run-time workloads. A simulator was used to evaluate the benefit of this approach. Two DLB algorithms were used as test cases; the Generalized Dimension Exchange Method and Load server algorithms. The results show that applications with large grain computation would benefit most from our approach while tree imbalance does not show consistent advantage.

1 Introduction

We introduced the notion of phase-based adaptivity for parallel tree computation in [1]. The basic principles behind the techniques are to speed up the initial workload distribution, maintain a steady state when the machine is full and remove the overhead of the load balancing at the end of the computation.

The paper is organised as follows; section 2 discusses the existing work, section 3 briefly describes the experimental plans. Section 4 presents the results and the insights obtained from the experiments and section 5 concludes by discussing the future development of the work.

2 Related Works

Special mechanisms for the early stage of a parallel tree computation are described in [2]and [3], which is equivalent to our filling phase as discussed in [1]. Both systems use the Iterative Deepening A* algorithm to solve the 15-puzzle problem. In [2], newly expanded nodes are always migrated to free processors, though no indication is given of how it is known which processors are free. Since this implies a global migration space, it supports our hypothesis that global migration is useful for this stage.

In [3] the root node is broadcast to all processors which redundantly expand the first few levels of the tree, obtain the same set of sub trees $n_1, n_2, ...$ During the main phase of the computation, processor i then starts to expand its sub-tree $n_i, n_{p+i}, ..., n_{2p+i}$, ensuring that all processors expand different sub-trees for most of the computation. It is worth noting that in both the above systems there is a very large processor array (16 K-node SIMD and 1024-node MIMD, respectively) which makes the effects of the filling phase quite significant. Neither of these systems explicitly identifies an emptying stage, nor does them experiments on the idea of adaptivity extensively.

3 Results and Discussion

The computational granularity of a node, g, may vary from one application to another. Some of the tree applications may have different degree of tree imbalance, m, which produces irregular workload throughout the computation. For parameters g and m we carried out experiments to investigate how Improvement Through Adaptivity (ITA) varies with the given parameter. These experiments were carried out at three different processor sizes representing small, medium and large networks, and for both GDEM and LDSV.

3.1 Varying the Computational Grain Size

The purpose of this experiment is to investigate the performance improvement through adaptivity for a range of grain size, g. The values for g can either be 10, 100, 1000 or 10000 floating point operations.

Table 1. Grain size: The best improvement and technique for GDEM

p	ITA (%) and Technique			
	10	100	1000	10000
4	0.00 (t_2)	0.00 (t_2)	0.06(t_1,t_1,t_2)	0.12(t_1,t_1,t_2)
32	1.55 (t_2)	1.37 (t_2)	1.76(t_1,t_2)	2.83 (t_1,t_2)
128	21.43 (t_1,t_2)	19.64(t_1,t_2)	21.02(t_1)	25.52 (t_1)

Table 2. Grain size: The best improvement and technique for LDSV

p	ITA (%) and Technique			
	10	100	1000	10000
4	0.00 (t_2)	0.00 (t_2)	0.00 (t_2)	0.00 (t_2)
32	9.03 (t_1,t_2)	9.60 (t_1,t_2)	14.23 (t_1)	17.29 (t_1)
128	14.43 (t_2)	13.15 (t_2)	16.61 (t_2)	40.97 (t_1)

Tables 1 and 2 show which combination of transition gives the best ITA for all combination of g and p. The following observations can be made; (i) The techniques show benefits and is more significant for large networks (ii) No single technique is the best for a given algorithm or processor size (iii) The techniques t_1t_2 or t_1 alone yield the best results for large g. (iv) GDEM seems to favour t_1t_2 while LDSV favours t_1 and t_2 individually.

3.2 Varying the Tree Imbalance

This set of experiments use imbalance tree instead of random tree because the degree of imbalance can be parameterised in the former. Hence, the imbalance tree is not repeatable. The implications are; first is on the pattern of ITA and the second is how ITA is measured. In some cases, the pattern of ITA is not as consistent as those of g to enable a clear relationship being made. Despite that some general pattern can still be established.

Table 3. Tree Imbalance: The best improvement and technique for GDEM

p	ITA (%) and Technique			
	0.0	0.1	0.2	0.3
4	25.21 (t_1t_2)	0.13 (t_2)	0.84 (t_1, t_1t_2)	6.88 (t_1t_2)
32	1.14 (t_1t_2)	4.16 (t_1t_2)	14.51 (t_1t_2)	5.45 (t_1t_2)
128	24.48 (t_1)	25.92 (t_1t_2)	67.77 (t_1t_2)	166.97 (t_1t_2)

Table 4. Tree Imbalance: The best improvement and technique for LDSV

p	ITA (%) and Technique			
	0.0	0.1	0.2	0.3
4	1.20 (t_1)	0.44 (t_1t_2)	9.30 (t_1)	3.82 (t_1t_2)
32	2.69 (t_2)	24.60 (t_1t_2)	40.70 (t_1t_2)	64.08 (t_1t_2)
128	10.19 (t_2)	39.77 (t_1t_2)	47.76 (t_1t_2)	11.62 (t_2)

Tables 3 and 4 show which combination of transition gives the best ITA for all combination of m and p. The following observations can be made; (i) Adaptivity always bring improvement, and is more significant for large p for GDEM and medium p for LDSV. (ii) t_1t_2 usually yields the best results for GDEM. (iii) t_1t_2 sometimes yields the best results for LDSV.

The following are the insights obtained from the adaptivity experiments when computational grain size and tree imbalance are varied:

- The improvement gained through adaptivity increases with the grain size, and processor size. It usually increases with the degree of imbalance.
- The relative merits of the adaptivity techniques are as follows; t_1 is suitable for an application with high computation to communication ratio. t_2 on the other hand, is beneficial if the application has a low computation to communication ratio. As to the tree imbalance, there is no clear relationship that could be established. t_1t_2 exhibits a similar pattern of improvement to t_1 for all three parameters, indicating a greater advantage gained from t_1 compared to t_2 when both

techniques are combined (i.e. as the grain size increases, the benefit increases consistently). High tree imbalance does not show consistent advantage, but the pattern is similar to t_I.
- The benefit of parametric phase-based adaptivity is more significant for medium and large processor sizes.

4 Conclusion and Future Work

The results of the investigation can be summarised as follows; (i) The parametric phase-based adaptivity techniques have demonstrated good performance improvement for parallel tree computation. (ii) The conditions under which each transition (or the combination of both) provide the most benefit have been identified (e.g. the larger the computational granularity and the processor size the higher the benefit). The experimental results above have shown the potential performance benefit of phase-based adaptivity

References

1. Haron, F. and Davy, J. R., A "Framework for Phase-based Adaptive Dynamic Load Balancing for Parallel Tree Computation", To appear in the Proceedings of the 1st International Conference on Informatics 2004, 28th–30th July 2004.
2. Powley, C., Ferguson, C. and Korf, R. E., "Parallel Tree Search on a SIMD Machine", Proceedings of the 3rd IEEE Symposium on Parallel and Distributed Processing, 1991, pp. 249–256.
3. Reinefeld, A. and Schnecke, V., "Work-load Balancing in Highly Parallel Depth-First Search, Procceding of the IEEE Scalable High Performance Computing, 1994, pp. 773–780.

Distributed Channel Routing Using Genetic Algorithm

Chuleui Hong[1], Wonil Kim[2], and Yeongjoon Kim[1]

[1] Software School, Sangmyung University,
Seoul, Korea
{hongch, yjkim}@smu.ac.kr
[2] Dept. of Digital Contents, College of Electronics and Information Engineering,
Sejong University, Seoul, Korea
wikim@sejong.ac.kr

Abstract. Known as an NP-Complete problem, the channel routing problem is very important in the automatic layout design of VLSI circuit and printed circuit boards. In this paper, a distributed genetic algorithm for this channel routing problem is presented in MPI environments. Each node executes genetic operations to own sub-population and communicates synchronously with other nodes to form the global population. The experimental results show that the proposed algorithm maintains the convergence properties of sequential genetic algorithm.

1 Introduction

In the channel routing problem, a channel consists of two parallel horizontal rows of points which are called terminals. These terminals are placed at a regular interval and identified by the columns of the channel. A net consists of the same terminals must be interconnected through certain routing paths without being overlapped with others. A layer is an interconnected routing area of the nets to connect the terminals. The channel routing problem is routing the given nets between terminals on the minimum multilayer channel areas.

Although many different sequential and parallel algorithms have been proposed, the problem of finding globally optimal solution for the channel routing is still open [1, 2]. In this paper, we propose a distributed genetic algorithm (DGA) for the channel routing problems. The distributed and synchronous nature of the proposed algorithm effectively speeds up the processing time. This DGA is verified practical in the solution quality and computation time.

2 Data Representation for Channel Routing

Each net in a chromosome is represented by a scalar value from 1 to $m \times l$, where m is the number of tracks and l is the number of layers. Each net is assigned to only one track of layer. When the ith net is assigned to the jth track of layer k, $a_i = j+(k-1) \times m$.

The example representation of chromosome for 10-net, 3-track, 2-layer problem can be a string (2, 6, 5, 3, 2, 1, 4, 6, 4, 2). Then the first net is placed to (tack 2, layer 1), the second net is to (track 3, layer 2), and so on.

When a net is assigned to the track, conflicts may occur with the overlap in the vertical and horizontal direction to other nets. Since the objective is to find the placement of nets free of overlaps, the fitness is the reciprocal of the total overlaps of a chromosome. The fitness function, f, is $a / (\beta + TOTAL\_C)$, where $TOTAL\_C$ is the total number of overlaps, a is the square of the total number of nets and β is the small positive real number forbidding division by zero.

3 The Proposed Distributed Genetic Algorithm

Previous researches have shown that the parallel genetic algorithm with punctuated equilibrium yields the better problem solutions and speed-up compared to sequential genetic approaches [3, 4]. This scheme evolves independent sub-population in an isolated manner and exchanges individuals when a state of equilibrium throughout all the sub-population has been reached.

In our synchronous distributed genetic algorithm, first each node randomly generates the same size of sub-population. The sub-population and its fitness value are broadcast to all other nodes resulting in the global population. Next, the individuals are randomly selected as many as the size of sub-population from the global population. Each node executes the sequential genetic algorithm in parallel. Independent genetic operation are implemented and evaluated respectively to its sub-population. The duration of isolated evolution is called one epoch. The epoch length is the number of predefined generations for a node before synchronizing communication among the nodes. The epoch length is set to the sub-population size.

The pseudo code for the distributed genetic algorithm of each node is as follows.

```
1.   Establish MPI communications to all other nodes
2.   Get the routing information from input;
3.   Generates sub-population(P_sub);
4.   while (iteration is less than max_epoch
              or solution is not found) Begin
5.       Calculate fitness for P_sub;
6.       for generations = 1 until epoch_length Begin
7.          for i = 1 until n Begin    // n is the size of P_sub
8.             select individuals, selected[i], from P_sub;
                /*using roulette scheme */
9.          End;
10.         for i = 1 until n increasing by 2 Begin
11.            forms new P_sub by crossover
                  (selected[i], selected[i+1]);
12.         End;
13.         forms new P_sub by mutation;
14.      End;
15.      if solution is found Begin
16.         report solution configuration;
```

```
17.       break the loops;
18.    End;
19.    else Begin
20.       broadcast P_sub to all other nodes;
21.       select new P_sub randomly;
          /* the communication is done synchronously */
22.    End;
23. End;
```

4 Simulation and Evaluation

The experiment shows that the crossover probability is optimal at 0.6 and the mutation probability has a great effect on the solution quality. We simulated the proposed algorithm using various crossover and mutation probabilities. Table 1 shows the parameters in different number of nets.

Table 1. Parameters of Distributed Genetic Algorithm

# of nets	# of columns	# of tracks	# of Two-layers	Population Size	Probability of Crossover	Probability of Mutation
10	12	3	2	32	0.6	0.05
21	43	6	2	128	0.6	0.05
45	90	8	2	128	0.6	0.01
47	84	9	2	128	0.6	0.01
54	103	9	2	128	0.6	0.01
55	119	9	2	128	0.6	0.01
61	128	10	2	256	0.6	0.005
72	175	11	2	256	0.6	0.005

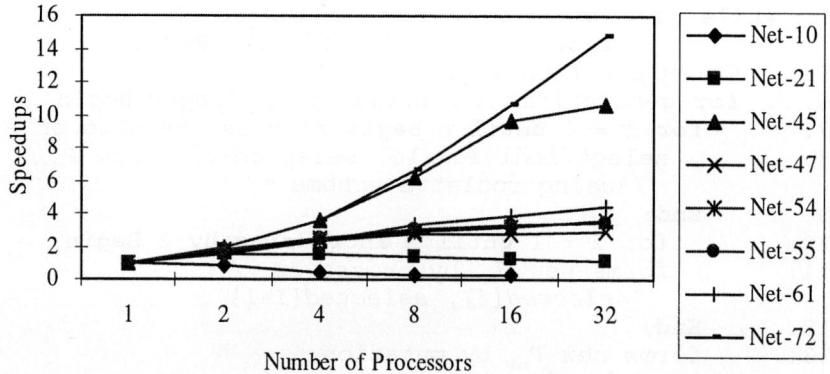

Fig. 1. Speedups of Different Nets

The parallel speedup generally increases proportional to the number of nets and the population size as in Figure 1. In some cases, as in the net-45 problem, if the problem is much complicated and the computing time is extremely long, then the speedup is lager than other problems. This shows that proposed distributed algorithm is useful as the problem size increases.

This distributed genetic algorithm was successful to find the solutions on several benchmark problems [5] as shown in Figure 2.

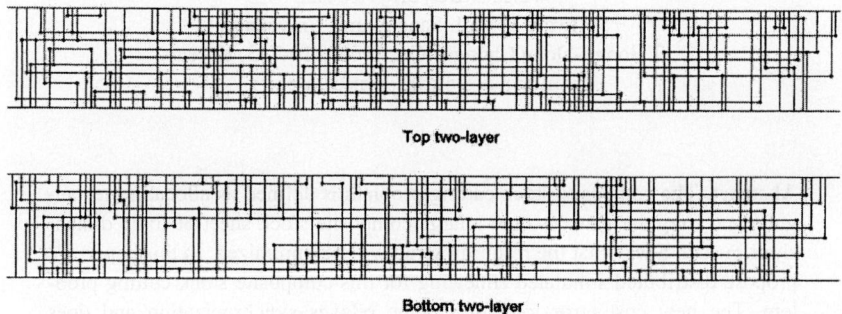

Fig. 2. The solutions of the benchmark problems

5 Conclusions

In this paper, we proposed a distributed genetic algorithm (DGA) for the channel routing problems. This new synchronous distributed algorithm was verified successful to the several benchmark routing problems. Considering the network latency in the distributed system, the results are promising. In the future, we will modify and apply this algorithm to the broad range of NP-Complete problems such as chip placement, image processing, and traveling salesman problem.

References

1. Susmita, S., Bhargab, S., Bhattacharya, B.: Manhattan-diagonal routing in channels and switchboxes. ACM Trans on DAES, Vol. 09, No. 01. (2004)
2. Ning, X.: A Neural Network Optimization Algorithm For Channel Routing. Journal Of Computer Aided Design And Computer Graphics. Vol. 14, No. 1. (2002)
3. Lienig, J., Thulasiraman, K.: A New Genetic Algorithm for the Channel Routing Problem. ACM Proc. of the 7th International Conference on VLSI Design. (1994)
4. Goni, B. M., Arslan, T. and Turton, B.: A genetic algorithm for over-the-cell and channel area optimization. Proceedings of the 2000 Congress on Evolutionary Computation (CEC-2000), Vol. 1. (2000) 586-592
5. Yoshimura, T., Kuh, E.S.: Efficient Algorithms for Channel Routing. IEEE Trans. of CAD, Vol. CAD-1, No. 1. (1982) 25-35

Distributed Simulated Annealing for Composite Stock Cutting Problem

Wonil Kim[1], Chul-Eui Hong[2], and Yeong-Joon Kim[2]

[1] Dept. of Digital Contents, College of Electronics and Information Engineering,
Sejong University, Seoul, Korea
`wikim@sejong.ac.kr`
[2] Software School, Sangmyung University,
7 Hongji-Dong Chongro-Gu, Seoul 110-743, Korea
`{hongch, yjkim}@smu.ac.kr`

Abstract. The composite stock cutting problem is defined as allocating rectangular and irregular patterns onto a large composite stock sheet of finite dimensions in such a way that the resulting scrap will be minimized. In this paper, we propose distributed simulated annealing for this composite stock cutting problem. The new cost error tolerant scheme relaxes synchronization and does move generations asynchronously in a dynamically changed stream length to keep the convergence property of the sequential annealing. This paper also proposes the efficient data structures for pattern related information.

1 Introduction

In stock cutting problem [1], rectangular and irregular patterns are allocated onto a large stock sheet of finite dimensions in such a way that the resulting scrap will be minimized. This problem is common to many applications in aerospace, shipbuilding, VLSI design, steel construction, and shoe manufacturing. Since this problem and associated theoretical problems are NP-hard [2], there is no polynomial algorithm to solve them.

In general, linear programming method involves a solution of the problem through the development of mathematical models [3]. This consists of an objective function that is to be minimized and constraint functions indicating the limitations on the variables of the objective function. Another class of heuristics often used is the tree-search method. It is difficult to determine which path to start with and whether to proceed or change to a different path once on a particular path [4]. The branch-and-bound using this method was presented in [5]. Bottom-up Left-justified (BL) algorithm represents the order of patterns to be packed as a list. This method places the pattern to the bottom as down as possible and moves it to the left. It is proven that the height of the solution of BL algorithm is less than three times of the optimal height [6]. The genetic operations have been applied to finding the optimal state that has the minimal height [7]. However, BL algorithm restricts the pattern as rectangle, which limits this method to be applied to any polygonal patterns [8].

All of these previous methods could not find the global optimum nor be applied to the various real problems. In this paper we propose a novel approach to find the global optimal for the Composite Stock Cutting problem using Distributed Simulated Annealing.

2 Data Structures for Composite Stock Cutting

In the initial step of the annealing process, a bitmap is generated for each pattern at all allowed rotations. The affinity relation is calculated for every pair of patterns in advance. Since the stock sheet is composite material, the allowable rotations are predefined to 2 (0 and 180 degree) or 4 (0, 90, 180, and 270 degree). Usually bitmap representation is used for the patterns because the overlap of two patterns can be detected easily just by examining the bitmap elements. The affinity relation between any pair of patterns displays the contribution to the packing when they are placed next.

For the bitmap of a pattern, the bounding box or Minimum Bounding Rectangle (MBR) is calculated first. The outside, boundary and inside elements of bitmap are different each other for easy calculation of affinity relation and overlap detection. The bounding box is defined as the minimal rectangle containing the pattern. Packing density increases generally as the boundaries of two patterns overlaps and the area of bounding box including two patterns is smaller. The affinity relation is defined as follows for arbitrary two patterns i and j.

$$a_{ij} = \alpha\left(a_1 + \frac{a_2}{2}\right) + \beta\rho \tag{1}$$

The variables a_1 and a_2 represent the degrees of overlap of two patterns, where α and β are weight constants. When two patterns that form the minimal bounding box fit together, the size of the final stock sheet is likely to be small. Therefore, the density ρ of the bounding box surrounding two patterns is incorporated to the affinity relation. The affinity relation for every pair of patterns is calculated on all allowed rotations in advance. The degree of overlap between two patterns is efficiently calculated by using bitmap in state transition of annealing process.

3 The Distributed Simulated Annealing Algorithm

The annealing schedule such as state transition method, objective function, cooling schedule and parallelization is devised to fit to the problem. Three types of moves are allowed in order to change the configuration of the given patterns. These three types of moves are (1) Displace a pattern to a new place, (2) Exchange the locations of two patterns and (3) Rotate a pattern to the allowed angles.

The cost function consists of the affinity relation between two patterns, $a_{i,j}$, the distance from the origin of a particular pattern, d_{io}, and the overlap penalty, $o_{i,j}$. The $d_{i,j}$ is the distance between pattern i and j, and α, β, and γ are the weights of the three term in the cost function.

$$C = -\alpha \sum_{\forall i} \sum_{\forall j} \frac{a_{ij}}{d_{ij}} + \beta \sum_{\forall i} d_{i0} + \gamma \sum_{\forall i} \sum_{\forall j} o_{ij} \qquad (2)$$

In implementing the simulated annealing, the following parameters must be specified for cooling schedule ; Initial temperature(T_o), Final temperature(T_f), Length of the Markov chain(L_k) at a certain temperature T_k and Decrement strategy of the temperature($T_{k+1} = \alpha \cdot T_k$). The cooling schedule must balance the quality of the final result with the computation time required. T_o is set such that the acceptance rate is more than 90% for L_k. T_f is set to the temperature where the value of the cost function is not changed for 5×L_k. L_k is set to the problem size, and the limit of transition is 4×L_k. A fixed decrement ratio, α, is set to 0.95 to 0.98. This strategy decreases the temperature proportional to the logarithm of the temperature.

Since simulated annealing is defined as Markov process which needs information of previous state, it is hard to parallelize the annealing. In distributed environments, the state information must be broadcast and updated for every state transition to keep the global state up to date. This is a bottleneck for performance. In order to reduce this expensive synchronization, the state information is sent to other processors independently after every processor makes state transitions several times. This is called as an *asynchronous*. Calculating the cost change under inconsistent states may result in a *cost error*. The Bound on the cost error is a function of global update frequency, or stream length s. The stream length is defined as the number of continuous moves before the global update. The cost error has been verified to have the exponential distribution [9] and can be derived with a stream length, s. ΔC_e is the estimated cost change, α is the acceptance rate of state transition, |<E>| is the average cost error in an accepted transition, and T is the temperature.

$$E = \left(\Delta C_e \pm s \cdot \alpha \cdot |\langle E \rangle|\right) \cdot \Pr[\Delta C_e > 0] \cdot \left| e^{-\frac{C_e}{T}} \cdot \left(e^{\pm \frac{s \cdot \alpha \cdot |\langle E \rangle|}{T}} - 1 \right) \right| \qquad (3)$$

Since hill climbing power decreases in proposition to cost error, Markov chain length must be increased to compensate the reduced hill climbing power. Therefore, $s \times u$ stream length is required to obtain the same hill climbing power of sequential annealing. $d_r(s)$ is the hill climbing power in stream length s without cost error and u is increment of a stream length.

$$e^{\frac{d_r(s)}{T}} \leq \frac{1}{s} \cdot \frac{1}{u} \qquad (4)$$

Among the three terms of the cost function defined in Equation (2), only the affinity relation term needs the global state. Therefore, a spatial decomposition, in which near patterns are clustered into the same processor, is desirable. The stock sheet is nearly equally divided in the x-direction. Each processor governs a space and handles patterns whose reference coordinates belong to their own space.

One processor (master) picks a pattern and sends the information of the selected pattern and the candidate displacement location to the neighboring processor (slave). If the two neighbor processors do inter-processor move operations simultaneously, then the neighbor processors become the master processors at the same time, and wait response from each other forever. In this case, a slave processor reject master's request to prevent deadlock. Each processor calculates its own affinity relation part of the cost function and the overlap penalty. Then the slave processor sums the costs from the master and makes the move decision. If the move is accepted, each processor changes its information.

4 Experimental Results

The proposed algorithm was implemented on 16-node MPI environments. For the first experiment, 16 different sets of patterns were implemented. The number of patterns varied to 160. A cooling schedule was set such that the initial temperature was about 200,000, the temperature decrement ratio was 0.98 to 0.99, and the Markov chain length was 5,000 to 20,000. The weight of the cluster term is balanced with that of the affinity relation term. Then we achieved the packed configurations. We varied the number of processors, to measure the speedup of running time comparing with a sequential implementation (Fig 1). According to the cost function defined in Equation (2), parallel processing does not degrade the solution quality while it reduces computing time.

For the second experiment, the stream lengths are varied to see cost error behavior. This experiment was done 5 times using 128 regular patterns and 16 nodes. The cost of the proposed adaptive stream length method is almost same as that of the average of the static stream length method while the computing time of the adaptive is about 1,000 seconds shorter than that of static method (Table 1). Therefore the proposed adaptive method reduces computing time while keeping the solution quality comparing with the traditional static method and the sequential one.

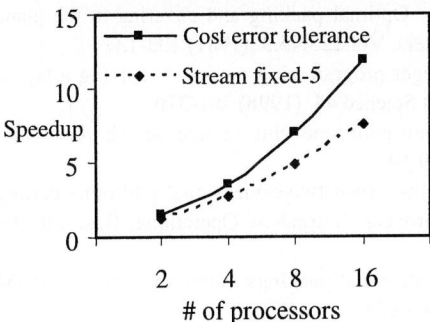

Table 1. Final cost comparison

	Time(msec)	Cost
Static	8.736e+06	788,896
Adaptive	7.207e+06	786,792
Sequential	9.345e+07	783,421

Fig. 1. Speedup of Distributed Annealing

The sample results are also shown in Figure 2. Experiments on sample nests show that the packing densities of the distributed annealing process range from 76% to 91%. Those are almost same as the packing densities of the sequential annealing with comparable speedup.

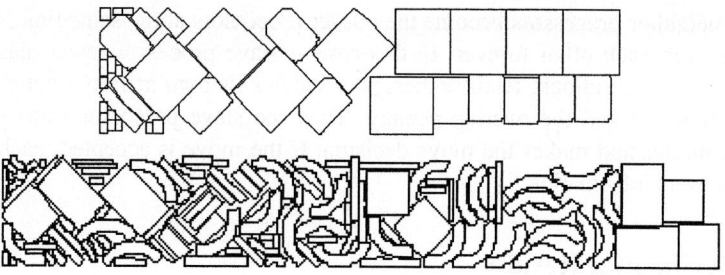

Fig. 2. Examples of composite stock cutting

5 Conclusions

In this paper, the cost error tolerant scheme is applied to the composite stock cutting problem in MPI distributed environments. The applied adaptive error control method changes the stream length dynamically keeping the convergence property as much as the sequential annealing process has. Therefore, the proposed method does not need many experiments to find the optimal stream length as in the traditional methods. The experiments show that this asynchronous distributed algorithm results in the same packing densities as the sequential algorithm with considerable speedup.

References

1. Lutfiyya, H., McMillin, B., Poshyanonda, P., Dagli, C.: Composite stock cutting through simulated annealing. Mathl. Comput. Modeling, Vol.16, No.1. (1992) 57-74
2. Fowler, R.J., Paterson, M.S., Tanimoto, S.L.: Optimal packing and covering in the plane are NP-complete. Information Processing Letters, Vol.12, No.3. (1981) 133-137
3. Degraeve, Z., Vandebroek, M.: A mixed integer programming model for solving a layout problem in the fashion industry. Management Science 44. (1998) 301-310
4. Beasley, J.E.: An exact two-dimensional non-guillotine cutting tree search procedure. Operations Research, Vol.33, No.1., (1985) 49-64
5. Morabito, R., Arenales, M.N.: Staged and constrained two-dimensional guillotine cutting problems: An AND/OR-graph approach. European Journal of Operational Research 94. (1996) 548-560
6. Baker, B.S., Coffman, E.G., Rivest, R.L.: Orthogonal packings in two dimensions. SIAM Journal on Computing, Vol.9, No.4. (1980) 846-855
7. Bean, J.C.: A multiple-choice genetic algorithm for a nonlinear cutting stock problem. Computing in Science and Engineering, Vol.2, No.2. (2000) 80-83
8. Jakobs, S.: On genetic algorithms for the packing polygons. European Journal of Operational Research88 (1996) 165-18
9. Hong, C., McMillin, B.: Relaxing synchronization in distributed simulated annealing. IEEE Trans. on Parallel and Distributed Systems, Vol. 16, No. 2. (1995) 189-195

Constant Time Algorithms for the 3-D All Nearest Neighbor Problem on the LARPBS[*]

Yuh-Rau Wang[1] and Shi-Jinn Horng[2]

[1] Department of Computer Science and Information Engineering,
St. John's & St. Mary's Institute of Technology, Taipei, Taiwan
yrwang@mail.sjsmit.edu.tw
[2] Department of Computer Science and Information Engineering,
National Taiwan University of Science and Technology, Taipei, Taiwan
horng@mouse.ee.ntust.edu.tw

Abstract. Two $O(1)$ time algorithms for solving the 3-D all nearest neighbor (3D_ANN) problem of n points using an LARPBS of size $\frac{1}{2}n^{\frac{7}{4}+\epsilon}$ and $\frac{1}{2}n^{\frac{3}{2}+\epsilon}$ respectively are proposed. To the best of our knowledge, all results derived above are the best $O(1)$ time 3D_ANN algorithms known.

1 Introduction

Given a set $\mathcal{V}$ of n points, to find a nearest neighbor (NN) from $\mathcal{V}$ for each point $v_i \in \mathcal{V}$ is defined as the all nearest neighbor (ANN) problem. The ANN problem has been applied in pattern recognition, geography, mathematical ecology, and solid-state physics. If $\mathcal{V}$ is in the k-dimensional (k-D) Euclidean space (E^k), then it is defined as the kD_ANN problem. The 2D_ANN problem has been introduced by several researchers; however, up to now, very few parallel algorithms are introduced for solving the 3D_ANN problem. Lai and Sheng [1] proposed an $O(1)$ time algorithm for the kD_ANN problem on an $n \times n$ reconfigurable mesh, which is the best previously published algorithms known. Here we present two $O(1)$ algorithms for solving the 3D_ANN problem on the LARPBS.

2 Some Fundamental Lemmas

In this paper, we base on the linear array with a reconfigurable pipelined bus system (LARPBS) [3] to devise our algorithms. First, we introduce some fundamental lemmas as follows. Here we skip the proofs in this version. Lemma 1 summarizes some primitive operations of the LARPBS model. Lemmas 2 and 4 are derived based on Lemma 1. Then, based on Lemma 2 and the column sort algorithm [2], we derive Lemma 3. Based on [5] and Lemma 4, we derive Lemma 5. In [1], Lai and Sheng proved that there are at most 48 points (i.e., $3 \times 2^{3+1}$) for

---

[*] The work was partly supported by National Science Council under the contract numbers NSC-93-2213-E-129-011 and NSC-91-2213-E-011-115.

each 3-D corner such that $d(p, c_i) < D'(p)$; more precisely, Lemma 6 shows that there are at most 3 points for each 3-D corner such that $d(p, c_i) < D'(p)$.

Lemma 1. [3] One-to-one communication, broadcasting, multicasting, multiple multicasting, binary prefix sum, binary summation, and compression can be done in $O(1)$ bus cycles on an LARPBS.

Lemma 2. [4] N items can be sorted in $O(1)$ time using an LARPBS of N^2 processors.

Lemma 3. The task of sorting an N-item sequence can be performed in $O(1)$ time on an LARPBS of $N^{1+(\frac{2}{3})^\kappa}$ processors, where κ stands for the times the column sort algorithm to be invoked. This can be proven by induction.

Lemma 4. [3] The minimum value of N data items can be computed in $O(1)$ time on an LARPBS of size $\frac{1}{2}N^2$.

Lemma 5. The minimum of an N-item sequence can be found in $O(1)$ time on an LARPBS of size $\frac{1}{2}N^{1+\epsilon}$, where $0 < \epsilon = \frac{1}{2^{c+1}-1} \ll 1$, $c \geq 1$.

Lemma 6. Given an arbitrary set S of points in E^3, and arbitrary numbers $x_1 < x_2$, $y_1 < y_2$, and $z_1 < z_2$, let $R = \{(x,y,z) | x_1 \leq x \leq x_2$ and $y_1 \leq y \leq y_2$ and $z_1 \leq z \leq z_2\}$ be a rectangular cube, let p be any point of $R \cap S$, let $d(p,q)$ be the Euclidean distance between points p and q, let $D(p) = \min\{d(p,q) | q \neq p,$ and $q \in S\}$ (i.e., the distance from point p to its global NN), and let $D'(p) = \min\{d(p,q) | q \neq p, x_1 \leq X_q \leq x_2$ or $y_1 \leq Y_q \leq y_2$ or $z_1 \leq Z_q \leq z_2, q \in S\}$ (i.e., the distance from point p to its local NN in $[x_1, x_2] \cup [y_1, y_2] \cup [z_1, z_2]$). Then, the following statements are true. a) If p is any point of $R \cap S$ and for all the 8 corners $c_i, 0 \leq i \leq 7$, of R, $D'(p) < d(p, c_i)$ holds, then $D'(p)$ turns out to be $D(p)$. b) If p is any point of $R \cap S$ such that $D(p) < D'(p)$, then there exists a corner c_i of R, such that $d(p, c_i) < D'(p)$. c) There are at most 3 points $p \in R \cap S$ such that $d(p, c_i) < D'(p)$ for each corner $c_i, 0 \leq i \leq 7$, of R.

3 The First $O(1)$ Time Algorithm

By invoking Lemma 3 ($\kappa = 1$), Lemma 5, and Lemma 6 (only once), we devise the first $O(1)$ time 3D_ANN algorithm which not only uses fewer processors but also executes faster compared with previously published best algorithm [1].

Algorithm 3D_ANN_1
  Input: A set $\mathcal{V} = \{v_i | 0 \leq i < n\}$ of n points in E^3.
  Output: For each point v_i, finding its (global) NN $\mathcal{N}_{v_i}$ in the giving set $\mathcal{V}$.

Step 1: Sort $\mathcal{V}$ by ascending h^{th}-coordinate, where $1 \leq h \leq 3$. Based on Lemma 3 ($\kappa = 1$), it takes $O(1)$ time using $n^{\frac{5}{3}}$ processors to sort the n points in each coordinate. The sorted sequence is denoted as $S^h = \{s_i^h | 0 \leq i < n\}$. Divide S^1, S^2 and S^3 into $n^{\frac{1}{4}}$ slabs S_α^1, S_β^2 and S_γ^3, respectively, each of $n^{\frac{3}{4}}$ points. Now, E^3 is divided into $(n^{\frac{1}{4}})^3 = n^{\frac{3}{4}}$ rectangular cubes $R(\alpha, \beta, \gamma)$.

Step 2: Based on Lemma 5, the local NNs, denoted as $\mathcal{N}_\alpha(s_i^1)$, and associated distances, denoted as $min_\alpha(s_i^1)$, of $\forall s_i^1 \in S^1$ (i.e., $n^{\frac{1}{4}}$ slabs S_α^1, each of $n^{\frac{3}{4}}$ points) in ascending X-coordinate can be found within their own slabs S_α^1 in $O(1)$ time using $n^{\frac{1}{4}} \times n^{\frac{3}{4}} \times \frac{1}{2} n^{\frac{3}{4} \times (1+\epsilon)} = \frac{1}{2} n^{\frac{7}{4} + \frac{1}{2}\epsilon}$ processors. The $\mathcal{N}_\beta(s_i^2)$ and $min_\beta(s_i^2)$ in ascending Y-coordinate, and the $\mathcal{N}_\gamma(s_i^3)$ and $min_\gamma(s_i^3)$ in ascending Z-coordinate are computed similarly and sequentially. Via some routing procedures, each v_i holds $min_\alpha^1(v_i)$, $min_\beta^2(v_i)$, and $min_\gamma^3(v_i)$ which are the distances from point v_i to its NNs in S_α^1, S_β^2, and S_γ^3, respectively. We then find $min_{\alpha,\beta,\gamma}(v_i) = \min\{min_\alpha^1(v_i), min_\beta^2(v_i), min_\gamma^3(v_i)\}$. Therefore, the point $\mathcal{N}_{\alpha,\beta,\gamma}(v_i)$ which associates with $min_{\alpha,\beta,\gamma}(v_i)$ is found also.

Step 3: For each point $v_i \in R(\alpha,\beta,\gamma) \cap \mathcal{V}$, we compute the distances from each point v_i to each of the 8 corners of $R(\alpha,\beta,\gamma)$. We check if any of them is smaller than $min_{\alpha,\beta,\gamma}(v_i)$. If the answer is affirmative, we mark v_i. Based on Lemma 6.(a), for each unmarked point v_i, the $min_{\alpha,\beta,\gamma}(v_i)$ turns out to be the distance from point v_i to its global NN $\mathcal{N}_{v_i}$ and we denote it as $min(v_i)$. Based on Lemma 6.(c), there are at most $24n^{\frac{3}{4}}$ marked points in E^3 and it takes at most $n^{\frac{3}{4}} \times \frac{1}{2} n^{1+\epsilon} = \frac{1}{2} n^{\frac{7}{4}+\epsilon}$ processors for all the marked points v_i to find their global NNs $\mathcal{N}_{v_i}$ in $O(1)$ time. This concludes Theorem 1.

Theorem 1. The 3D_ANN problem of n points can be solved in $O(1)$ time on an LARPBS of size $\frac{1}{2} n^{\frac{7}{4}+\epsilon}$.

4 The Second $O(1)$ Time Algorithm

We then present the second algorithm, which recursively invokes Lemma 6 three times, for solving the 3D_ANN problem of n points in $O(1)$ time on an LARPBS of size $\frac{1}{2} n^{\frac{1}{2}+\epsilon}$. The result is far better than that derived in [1]. First, we introduce Lemma 7 upon which the second algorithm is based.

Lemma 7. The ANN problem of $n^{\frac{3+i}{6}}$ points in E^3 can be performed in $O(1)$ time on an LARPBS of $\frac{1}{2} n^{\frac{6+i}{6} + \frac{3+i}{6}\epsilon}$ processors, where $1 \leq i \leq 3$.

Proof: 1) For $i = 1$: a) It takes $(n^{\frac{2}{3}})^{\frac{13}{9}} = n^{\frac{26}{27}}$ processors to sort $n^{\frac{2}{3}}$ points in ascending X-coordinate by invoking Lemma 3. b) The sorted sequence can be divided into $n^{\frac{1}{6}}$ slabs, each of $n^{\frac{1}{2}}$ points. Based on Lemma 5, the ANN problem of $n^{\frac{1}{2}}$ points can be solved in $O(1)$ time using $n^{\frac{1}{2}} \times \frac{1}{2} n^{\frac{1}{2} \times (1+\epsilon)} = \frac{1}{2} n^{1+\frac{1}{2}\epsilon}$ processors. So totally it takes $\frac{1}{2} n^{\frac{7}{6}+\frac{1}{2}\epsilon}$ processors for all of the $n^{\frac{1}{6}}$ slabs each of $n^{\frac{1}{2}}$ points to be processed in parallel. The Y- and Z-coordinates are processed similarly and sequentially. c) Since the sorted sequence of $n^{\frac{2}{3}}$ points can be divided into $n^{\frac{1}{6}}$ slabs in each coordinate, so the slab of $n^{\frac{2}{3}}$ points is divided into $(n^{\frac{1}{6}})^3 = n^{\frac{1}{2}}$ rectangular cubes. As described in Lemma 6, there are at most $24n^{\frac{1}{2}}$ marked points for each rectangular cube. The marked points can be partitioned into at most 24 groups, each of $n^{\frac{1}{2}}$ points. Each group is processed sequentially. Then, we assign $\frac{1}{2}n^{\frac{2}{3}\times(1+\epsilon)}$ processors for each of the marked points to find its NN within these $n^{\frac{2}{3}}$ points. Totally, it takes at most $\frac{1}{2}n^{\frac{7}{6}+\frac{2}{3}\times\epsilon}$ processors for all the marked points v_i to find their NNs and associated distances $min(v_i)$ within these $n^{\frac{2}{3}}$ points in $O(1)$ time. From a), b)and c), the number of processors needed is $\max(n^{\frac{26}{27}}, \frac{1}{2}n^{\frac{7}{6}+\frac{1}{2}\epsilon}, \frac{1}{2}n^{\frac{7}{6}+\frac{2}{3}\times\epsilon}) = \frac{1}{2}n^{\frac{7}{6}+\frac{2}{3}\times\epsilon}$. So, it is true when $i=1$.

2) Based on the method and result of 1), for $i=2$, the number of processors needed is $\max(n^{\frac{65}{54}}, \frac{1}{2}n^{\frac{4}{3}+\frac{2}{3}\times\epsilon}, \frac{1}{2}n^{\frac{4}{3}+\frac{5}{6}\times\epsilon}) = \frac{1}{2}n^{\frac{4}{3}+\frac{5}{6}\times\epsilon}$. So, it is true when $i=2$.

3) Also, based on the result of 2), for $i=3$, the number of processors needed is $\max(n^{\frac{13}{9}}, \frac{1}{2}n^{\frac{3}{2}+\frac{5}{6}\times\epsilon}, \frac{1}{2}n^{\frac{3}{2}+\epsilon}) = \frac{1}{2}n^{\frac{3}{2}+\epsilon}$. This proves this lemma.

Algorithm 3D_ANN_2
Input: A set $\mathcal{V} = \{v_i|\ 0 \leq i < n\}$ of n points in E^3.
Output: For each point v_i, finding its (global) NN $\mathcal{N}_{v_i}$ in the giving set $\mathcal{V}$.

Step 1: Sort $\mathcal{V}$ by ascending h^{th}-coordinate, where $1 \leq h \leq 3$. As described in Lemma 3 ($\kappa = 2$), it takes $O(1)$ time on an LARPBS of $n^{\frac{13}{9}}$ processors to sort the n points in each coordinate. The sorted sequence is denoted as S^h. Divide S^h of n points into $m = n^{\frac{1}{6}}$ slabs, each of $n' = \frac{n}{m}$ points. Then recursively sort and divide each of the new slabs of n' points into m slabs in all the 3 coordinates until each slab contains $n^{\frac{1}{2}}$ points.

Step 2: Based on Lemma 5, the local 3D_ANN problems of $n^{\frac{1}{2}}$ slabs each of $n^{\frac{1}{2}}$ points can be solved in $O(1)$ time using $n^{\frac{1}{2}} \times n^{\frac{1}{2}} \times \frac{1}{2}n^{\frac{1}{2}\times(1+\epsilon)} = \frac{1}{2}n^{\frac{3}{2}+\frac{1}{2}\epsilon}$ processors for all the n points to find their respective local NNs within their own slabs. Each S^h is processed similarly and sequentially.

Step 3: In general, since S^h can be divided into $n^{\frac{3-i}{6}}$ slabs, each containing $n^{\frac{3+i}{6}}$ points, and based on Lemma 7, the 3D_ANN problem of $n^{\frac{3+i}{6}}$ points can be performed in $O(1)$ time on an LARPBS of $\frac{1}{2}n^{\frac{6+i}{6}+\frac{3+i}{6}\epsilon}$ processors, so, from $i=1$ to 3, it will always take $n^{\frac{3-i}{6}} \times \frac{1}{2}n^{\frac{6+i}{6}+\frac{3+i}{6}\epsilon} = \frac{1}{2}n^{\frac{3}{2}+\frac{3+i}{6}\epsilon}$ processors for all the $n^{\frac{3-i}{6}}$ slabs to be processed in parallel.

Theorem 2. The 3D_ANN problem of n points can be solved in $O(1)$ time on an LARPBS of size $\frac{1}{2}n^{\frac{3}{2}+\epsilon}$.

References

1. Lai, T.H., Sheng, M.J.:Constructing Euclidean Minimum Spanning Trees and All Nearest Neighbors on Reconfigurable Meshes. IEEE Trans. Parallel and Distributed Systems., Vol. 7, No. 8, (1996) 806-817.
2. Leighton, T.: Tight bounds on the complexity of parallel sorting. IEEE Trans. Computers. Vol. 34, No. 4, (1985) 344-354.
3. Pan, Y.,Li, K.: Linear Array with a Reconfigurable Pipelined Bus System - Concepts and Applications. Journal of Information Sciences. (1998) 237-258.

4. Pan, Y., Li, K., Zheng, S.-Q.: Fast Nearest Neighbor Algorithms on a Linear Array with a Reconfigurable Pipelined Bus System. Parallel Algorithms and Applications. Vol. 13, (1998) 1-25.
5. Wang, Y.R., Horng, S.J.: An O(1) Time Parallel Algorithm for the 3-D Euclidean Distance Transform on the CRCW PRAM Model. IEEE Trans. on Parallel and Distributed Systems. Vol. 14, No. 10, (2003) 973-982.

Parallel K-Means Clustering Algorithm on DNA Dataset

Fazilah Othman, Rosni Abdullah, Nur'Aini Abdul Rashid, and Rosalina Abdul Salam

School of Computer Science, Universiti Sains Malaysia, 11800, Penang, Malaysia
{fazot, rosni, nuraini, rosalina}@cs.usm.my

Abstract. Clustering is a division of data into groups of similar objects. K-means has been used in many clustering work because of the ease of the algorithm. Our main effort is to parallelize the k-means clustering algorithm. The parallel version is implemented based on the inherent parallelism during the Distance Calculation and Centroid Update phases. The parallel K-means algorithm is designed in such a way that each **P** participating node is responsible for handling **n/P** data points. We run the program on a Linux Cluster with a maximum of eight nodes using message-passing programming model. We examined the performance based on the percentage of correct answers and its *speed-up* performance. The outcome shows that our parallel K-means program performs relatively well on large datasets.

1 Introduction

The objective of this work is to partition data into groups of similar items. Given a set of meaningless data and sets of representatives, our work will group the data according to the nearest representative. This work is useful in helping scientists explore new data and lead them to new discovery in relationships between data. It is widely employed in different disciplines which involve grouping massive data such as computational biology, botany, medicine, astronomy, marketing and image processing. A survey [1][2][3] on clustering algorithm reported that K-means is a popular, effective and practically feasible method widely applied by scientists. However, the rapid growth of data makes the processing time increase due to large computation time. [2] has implemented the K-means algorithm on DNA data using positional weight matrices (PWM) training The decreasing prices of personal computers make parallel implementation a practical approach. In this paper, we propose a parallel implementation of **K**-means clustering algorithm on a cluster of personal computers. This is to provide a practical and economically feasible solution.

2 K-Means Clustering Algorithm

K-means algorithm works conveniently with numerical values and offers clear geometric representations. The basic K-means algorithm requires time proportionate to number of patterns and number of cluster per iteration. This is computationally expensive especially for large datasets [4]. To address these problems, parallelization has become a popular alternative which exploits the inherent data parallelism within sequential K-means algorithm. Efforts in parallelizing the K-means algorithm has been done by [1][5][6][7][8] in areas such as image processing, medicine, astronomy marketing and biology. As our contribution we propose a parallel K-means clustering algorithm for DNA dataset running on a cluster of personal computers.

3 Parallel K-Means Clustering Algorithm

The sequential algorithm spends much of it's time calculating new centroid and calculating the distances between **n** data points and **k** centroids. We can cut down the execution time by parallelizing these two operations. Our parallel **K-means** algorithm is parallelized based on the inherent data-parallelism especially in the *Distance Calculation* and *Centroid Update* operations. The *Distance Calculation* operation can be executed asynchronously and in parallel for each data point (x_i for $1 \leq i \leq n$).

We designed the parallel program in such a way that each participating **P** processor is responsible for handling **n/P** data points. The basic idea is to divide the **n** data points into **P** parts which are the approximate size for the portion of data which will be processed by the **P** independent nodes.

However, each of the **P** nodes must update and store the mean and **k** latest centroid in the local cache. The master node will accumulate new assigned data points from each worker node and broadcast new global mean to all. The **k** centroids allow each node to perform distance calculation operation in parallel while the global mean permit each node to decide on the convergence condition independently.

The *Centroid Update* is performed in parallel. It is operated before the new iteration of K-means begins. New centroids will be recomputed based on the newly assigned data points in k centroids. Each node that performs *Centroid Update* need to communicate simultaneously since the computation requires the global mean accumulated by the master node. The parallel K-means algorithm design is shown in Figure 1.

4 Implementation and Result

We run the program on Aurora Linux Cluster with a maximum of 8 nodes using message passing programming model. Each node has CPU speed of 1396 MHz, swap memory of 500 Mb and total memory of 1 GB for clients and swap memory of 520 Mb and total memory of 2.0 GB for the server. We tested on three datasets which have been statistically analyzed and published by P.Chaudhuri and S.Das[9] to benchmark our cluster result. The three datasets are ribosomal RNA for twenty four organisms, vertebrate mitochondrial DNA sequences and complete genomes of roundworm. Next we are interested in studying the impact of parallelizing the sequential K-means algorithm in terms of performance. Thereby we assume our cluster result is acceptable. Figure 2(a) shows the result of executing parallel K-means algorithm on ribosomal RNA sequences of 24 organisms and Figure 2(b) shows the result of executing parallel K-means algorithm on the artificial dataset of 15.7 MB, which consist of 16 sequences, each of length 1 million base pair. We examined the performance based on the percentage of correct answers and highlight the speed-up. The outcome shows that our parallel K-means algorithm performs relatively well on large dataset.

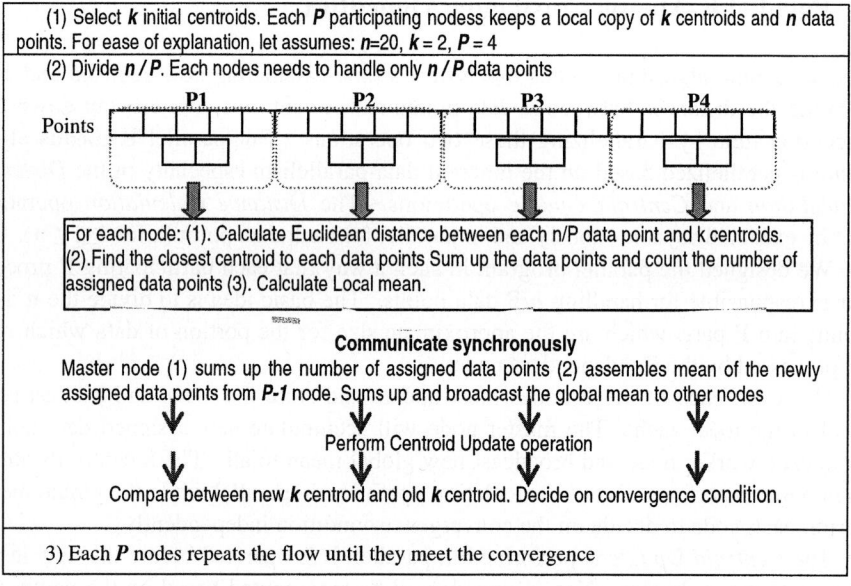

Fig. 1. The diagram of Parallel K-means Algorithm

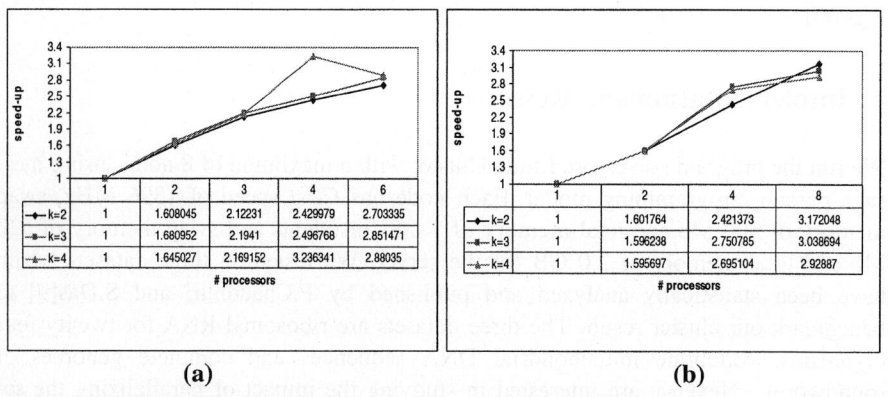

Fig. 2. (a) Speed-up performance for parallel K-means using ribosomal RNA sequences of 24 organisms; (b) Speed-up performance for parallel K-means using artificial dataset

5 Conclusion and Future Work

The experiments carried out showed that the parallel K-means algorithm starts making progress on a large dataset. In order to improve the accuracy of the cluster results, we observed that attention should be given to the data training phase. In our program, we applied the PWM method where we calculated the frequency of nucleotides A, T, C and G for each position in the sequences. However, the DNA sequence is very rich with gene information and the arrangement within the nucleotides gives crucial information. It is very interesting to employ other method called the distribution of DNA words that focus on the word frequency-based approach as reported in [9]. We hope to port our work to a high performance cluster of Sun machine. The SUN Cluster is a new facility provided by the Parallel and Distributed Computing Centre, School of Computer Science, USM. With 2 GB memory space on the server machine alone and a total hard disk external storage of 70 GB on the clusters machines, it is hoped that it will produce more encouraging results.

References

1. Inderjit S. Dillon and Dharmendra S. Modha, "A Data-Clustering on Distributed Memory Multiprocessors" in ACM SIGKDD Workshop on Large-Scale Parallel KDD System (KDD 99), August 1999.
2. Xiufeng Wan, Susan M. Bridges, John Boyle and Alan Boyle, "Interactive Clustering for Exploration of Genomic Data", Xiufeng Wan, Susan M. Bridges, John Boyle and Alan Boyle, Mississippi State University, Mississippi State, MS USA,2002
3. K.Alsabti, S.Ranka and V.Singh. An Efficient K-Means Clustering Algorithm. http://www.cise.ufl.edu/~ranka/, 1997
4. K.Murakami and T.Takagi, "Clustering and Detectionof 5' Splices Sitesof mRNA by K Wight Matrices Model",Pac Symp BioComputing,1999, pp 171-181.
5. Kantabutra S. and Couch A.L, "Parallel K-means Clustering Algorithm on NOWs",NECTEC Technical Journal,vol 1, no.6 (February 2002),pp 243-248.
6. Killian Stoffel and Abdelkader Belkoniene, "Parallel K/H-means Clustering for Large Data Sets",Proceedings of the European Conference on Parallel Processing EuroPar'99, 1999.
7. Kantabutra S., Naramittakapong, C. and Kornpitak, P, "Pipeline K-means Algorithm on NOWs," Proceeding of the Third International Symposium on Communication and Information Technology (ISCIT2003),Hatyai,Songkla,Thailand,2003.
8. Forman,G and Zhang , B., "Linear Speed-Up for a parallel Non-Approximate Recasting of Center-Based Clustering Algorithm,including K-Means,K-Harmonic Means and EM," ACM SIGKDD Workshop on Distributed and Parallel Knowledge Discovery (KDD2000), Boston, MA, 2000.
9. Probal Chaudari and Sandip Dass,"Statistical Analysis of Large DNA sequences using distribution of DNA words", CURREBT SCIENCE, vol. 80, no. 9(10 may 2001) pp 1161 – 1166.

Performances of Parallel Clustering Algorithm for Categorical and Mixed Data

Nguyen Thi Minh Hai and Horiguchi Susumu*

Japan Advanced Institute of Science and Technology, 1-1,
Asahidai, 923-1292, Japan
*Graduate School of Inf. Science, Tohoku University, Aobayama 09,
Sendai, 980-8573, Japan
{hai-ntm, hori}@jaist.ac.jp

Abstract. Clustering is a fundamental and important technique in image processing, pattern recorgnition, data compression, etc. However, most recent clustering algorithms cannot deal with large, complex databases and do not always achieve high clustering results. This paper proposes a parallel clustering algorithm for categorical and mixed data which can overcome the above problems. Our contributions are: (1) improving the k-sets algorithm [3] to achieve highly accurate clustering results; and (2) applying parallel techniques to the improved approach to achieve a parallel algorithm. Experiments on a CRAY T3E show that the proposed algorithm can achieve higher accuracy than previous attempts and can reduce processing time; thus, it is practical for use with very large and complex databases.

Keywords: clustering, categorical data, mixed data, very large databases, parallel algorithm.

1 Introduction

Clustering is used to group a set of unlabeled data objects into smaller groups of similar objects, called clusters, in order to simplify data management and extract useful knowledge. In clustering tasks, categorical data and mixed data are the most common data types. However, the various algorithms that deal with these kinds of data, such as [1] and [2], are still unstable due to the non-uniqueness of the *modes* which they use instead of *means* to deal with non-numerical data. Unlike other methods, the k-sets algorithm [3] uses *connected components* instead of *means/modes*, and achieves more stable and better results than previous algorithms tested on the same databases. However, k-sets can not deal with outliers or with very large databases. To process large databases, Sanpawat Kantabutra et al. [4] and K. Stoffel et al. [5] proposed parallel clustering algorithms based on the k-means clustering algorithm. Unfortunately, their parallel algorithms, like most others can deal only with numeric databases.

These reasons encouraged us to develop a parallel clustering algorithm for categorical and mixed data. The rest of the paper is organized as follows. Section 2 introduces the improvement of the k-sets algorithm to deal with outliers in order to achieve more accurate results, then introduces parallelization based on the improved approach to create an effective and efficient parallel algorithm, the Parallel Clustering Algorithm for Categorical and Mixed Data (PCACMD). Section 3 describes the performance of PCACMD in a parallel computer; its accuracy is also compared with that of the previous algorithms using the same datasets. Conclusions are drawn in Section 4, which also addresses future work.

2 Parallel Clustering Algorithm for Categorical and Mixed Data

2.1 Improving the k-Sets Clustering Algorithm

In k-sets, two objects o_i, o_j of the dataset S are *neighbors* if $Sim(o_i, o_j) \geq \theta$,

where: $\quad Sim(o_i, o_j) = \sum\limits_{p=1}^{m} \delta^p(o_i^p, o_j^p) / m$, m is number of attributes , (1)

in that, $\quad \delta^p(o_i^p, o_j^p) = \begin{cases} 1, \text{if } o_i^p = o_j^p \text{ and } p^{th} \text{ attribute is categorical} \\ 1, \text{if } \left| o_i^p - o_j^p \right| < \mu \text{ and } p^{th} \text{ attribute is numeric} \\ 0, \text{otherwise.} \end{cases}$ (2)

θ, μ are threshold parameters defined by the user; and o_i^p, o_j^p are p^{th} value of o_i, o_j, respectively. The *neighbor* relation is symmetric. A *connected component* (*CC*) is a set which consists and only consists of all objects that are neighbors to each other. First, k-sets separates $\mathbb{S}$ into l *connected components* (CCs). Second, the *k*-largest CCs are chosen to be *k cores* of *k* clusters. Last, each o_i in the remaining *l-k* CCs is assigned to the cluster containing a certain core CS_{hi}, if there exists $o_{hi} \in CS_{hi}$ such that $Sim(o_i, o_{hi}) \geq Sim(o_i, o_j)$, $\forall o_j \in k \text{ cores}$. Note that if o_{hi} is an outlier, then the o_i may be assigned to an incorrect cluster. To overcome this drawback, we propose the following approach: a cluster containing core CS_{hi} is determined as the cluster of the object o_i if $Sim(o_i, CS_{hi}) \geq Sim(o_i, CS_j)$, $\forall CS_j \in$ set of k cores. $Sim(o_i, CS_{hi})$ is defined as:

$$Sim(o_i, CS_{hi}) = \sum_{o_j \in CS_{hi}} \frac{Sim(o_i, o_j)}{|CS_{hi}|}, \quad CS_{hi} \in k\text{-largest } connected\ components. \quad (3)$$

With our approach, incorrect assignments caused by outliers can be avoided. Consequently, this approach should give us more accurate results in certain databases.

2.2 Design of Parallel Algorithm

To get high quality clustering results, it is necessary to execute the algorithm with numerous trials of the input parameters, say, θ, μ, k. These processes are very time-consuming. Hence, we considered applying multi-parallel techniques to these trials.

The basic idea of our multi-parallelization is to equally divide the total running times among P processors. Each processor will execute the same clustering task with the same trials for k but different trials for θ and the same or different trials for μ (depending on P, the number of possible values of θ and the number of possible value of μ). For each pair of values of θ, μ, and P, it is necessary to determine the needed processors, which will be used in the case, to avoid wasting time by sending the whole data set $\mathbb{S}$ to un-used processors. This approach balances total processing time among all the processors because tasks of two processors are different by at most only one loop.

Input: $\mathbb{S} = \{o_1, o_2, ..., o_n\}$, k, θ, $[\mu]$.
i. The number of needed-processors is determined.
ii. Data is read by one processor and is broadcasted to all other needed-processors.
iii. On each needed-processor do
    For each value of θ (value of θ is different on each processor)
    For each value of μ (value of μ is different on each processor)
    For each value of k do
    Step 1: Build connected components
        Step 2: Find k *cores* by choosing k largest connected components.
        Step 3: Find cluster for remaining objects by choosing the closest core.
iv. Choose the best result from all processors.
Output: k clusters

Fig. 1. Scheme of the PCACMD

3 Performance Evaluation:

The performance of PCACMD was estimated on a Cray T3E 1200E with: the soybean disease dataset (47 objects, each contains 35 categorical attributes [6]), the credit approval dataset (666 objects, each contains 6 numeric and 9 categorical attributes [6]), three subsets of the Connect-4 opening database (500, 1000 and 10000 objects, each object contains 42 categorical attributes), and a subset of the KDD Cup 1999 database (10000 objects; each contains 34 numeric and 7 categorical attributes [7]).

3.1 Accuracy

Accuracy is calculated in the same way as in the papers whose results are compared with the results here. Table 1 shows the accuracy of the clustering algorithms on some of the datasets. The columns from second to fifth are the accuracy of the algorithms on the soybean disease, the credit approval, and two subsets from the Connect-4 datasets, respectively. In all four cases, PCACMD achieves the higher accuracies than K-sets. Consequently, PCACMD also achieves higher accuracies than other algorithms on the soybean and credit databases [3]. In summary, PCACMD can find clusters that are more similar to the original clusters than can the previous algorithms.

Table 1. Results

Databases Algorithms	Soybean	Credit	Connect-4-500 objects	Connect-4-1000 objects
PCACMD	1.00	0.8378	0.73	0.815
K-sets [3]	1.00	0.8288	0.718	0.805

3.2 Speed-Up

Figure 2 shows the average speed-up of PCACMD from five experiments with two sub-datasets. With our parallel approach, the maximum number of processors that can be used with the mixed data (KDD database) is larger than that for the database which contains only categorical attributes (Connect-4), when the number of possible processors is larger than $\theta * \mu$. Consequently, in Figure 2, speed-up is better in case of the KDD database when the number of processors is large.

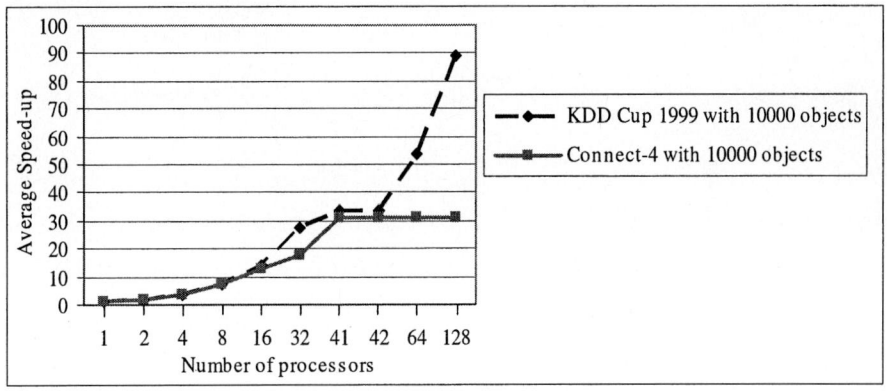

Fig. 2. Speed-up of the PCACMD

4 Conclusion

In this paper, we have implemented the PCACMD algorithm by parallelizing our improvement of the k-sets clustering algorithm [3]. This approach enabled our algorithm to achieve more accurate results than previous methods. The parallel approach significantly reduces processing time for PCACMD; it can run 90 times faster than a serial algorithm on 128 processors with the subset of KDD Cup 1999 database. It is especially efficient and effective when applied to large datasets of mixed data. In the future, new parallel techniques and new similarity measures will be invented in order to obtain a more effective and efficient clustering algorithm.

Acknowledgement

This research was supported in part by the international research project, JAIST.

References

1. Z. Huang. Clustering Large Data Sets with Mixed Numeric and Categorical Values, In Proceedings of The First Pacific-Asia Conference on Knowledge Discovery and Data Mining, World Scientific, (1997) 21–34
2. Z. Huang, Michael K. Ng. A fuzzy k-modes algorithm for clustering categorical data. IEEE Trans. Fuzzy Systems 7 (4), (1999) 446–452
3. S. Q. Le, T. B. Ho. A k-sets Clustering algorithm for categorical and mixed data. In Proc. of the 6th SANKEN Int. Symposium, (2003) 124–128
4. S. Kantabutra, A. L. Couch. Parallel K-means Clustering Algorithm on NOWs. NECTEC Technical journal, Vol.1, No. 6, (2000) 243–248
5. K. Stoffel, A. Belkoniene. Parallel K-Means Clustering for Large Databases. Proc. of the Euro-Par '99, LNCS 1685, (1999) 1451–1454
6. C.L. Blake, C.J. Merz. UCI Repository of machine Learning databases. [http://www.ics.uci.edu/~mlearn/ MLRepository.html], (1998).
7. Hettich, S., Bay, S. D. The UCI KDD Achieve [http://kdd.ics.uci.edu], (1999).

Task Distribution Methods for the Reconstruction of MR Images

Hyo Jong Lee[1], Jessica Turner[2], and First Birn[3]

[1]Chonbuk National University, Jeonju, Korea
[2]University of California, Irvine
[3]Functional Imaging Research of Schizophrenia Test bed BIRN
www.nbirn.net

Abstract. The raw data of MRI consists of series of complex numbers that represent phases and amplitudes of signals. The reconstruction procedure of the MRI requires lengthy computational time and sequence of images due to the heavy discrete Fourier transformation. Four different parallel algorithms, the Round-Robin distribution, demand distribution, minimal load distribution, and variable distribution methods were developed to handle the lengthy reconstruction process for the clustered network and analyzed. The performance of four methods were found to be similar in the current investigation.

1 Introduction

Distributed computing and cluster computing are recognized as efficient ways for high performance computing. Cluster computing has become popular among scientists and engineers from various scientific and technological areas, such as physics, chemistry, bioengineering, and fluid dynamics. The primary reason of attraction is the good ratio of performance to cost. The rapidly advancing technology of semiconductor devices today allows even lower cost computer processors with better performance than ever before. Additionally, the development of fast communication switching equipment has also added to the increasing popularity of cluster computing.

Efficient task allocation for distributed computing has been an important goal to increase the system performance in a dynamic environment. Tandiary et al's [14] investigation of possible batch processing for unused system cycles from the clustered workstations is a good example of attempts to maximize utilization of idle processors. Additionally, Kanoda and Knightly [9], have identified two key factors, load balance of system resources and minimization of communication between processors, in a similar investigation.

The maximum utilization can be approached by improving the allocation method of tasks for distributed or clustered systems. In order to achieve a high resource utilizing rate, dynamic distribution of tasks should be considered. In the current investigation four different allocation methods, the round robin distribution (RR), the demand distribution (DD), the minimal load distribution (MIN), and the variable distribution (VAR), were developed and compared within a clustered network. These methods were applied to the real problem of the reconstruction of magnetic resonance images (MRI) in order to quantify the differences in their performance.

The purpose of the current investigation is two-fold: to develop a parallel reconstruction algorithm for MRIs, and to analyze and compare the performance of four dynamic task distribution methods within clustered workstations. As such, the following sections of this article will provide detailed descriptions of: (a) the basic concepts to be considered in identifying existing flaws in the use of a heterogeneous network for MR image analyses (Section 2); (b) limitations of existing sequential reconstruction methods and the four proposed alternative parallel distribution methods (Section 3); (c) the experimental performance of each of the implemented algorithms for the reconstruction of MR images (Section 4); and (d) investigational outcomes and conclusions (Section 5).

2 Magnetic Resonance Images

Magnetic resonance imaging (MRI) has been recognized as an inevitably important diagnostic tool in the field of medical science for more than two decades. Schizophrenia, Alzheimer's disease and other various mental disorders are examples of those whose understanding depend on the neuro-imaging techniques [5, 6]. However, the reconstruction procedures of MR images, particularly functional MR, are not trivial due to the complicated nature of MRI [1]. Furthermore, the process is computationally intensive and takes a large space of memory due to the heavy discrete Fourier transformation and lengthy sequence of computation. Other medical imaging techniques, such as computerized tomography (CT) [3, 8], positron emission tomography (PET) [4, 7], and single photon emission tomography (SPECT) [2, 13] are implemented in parallel algorithms and their efficiencies are reported. Although it is demanded at many places, the functional MRI has not been parallelized except for Lee's research [11].

Reconstruction of 3-D volume images from raw data requires exhaustive computation of discrete Fourier transformation with complex numbers. The processing time is closely related to the performance of systems due to lengthy processing. For example, Sun Ultra SPARC 5 generally takes about 80 seconds to reconstruct a single volume, while a fast Sun server IIe only takes about 30 seconds. If a single scan contains 200 volumes, and a study for one subject needs ten scans, 2000 volumes must be reconstructed before any analysis can proceed. To reconstruct all volumes would take almost two days with a slower processor. However, computation of each volume is completely independent; thus, the data lends itself naturally to the use of a parallel reconstruction method.

3 Reconstruction of MR Images

There are several different kinds of reconstruction methods available [1, 12]. A heuristic reconstruction algorithm has also been developed [10]. The methods depend on the specific MRI hardware system, acquisition protocol (software), and analysis purpose. However, a general reconstruction method has common procedures. This section will describe the general reconstruction method, followed by a description of the four proposed parallel reconstruction methods.

3.1 Parallel Reconstruction Method

In order to examine the effect of distribution method, four different algorithms have been implemented. Details of algorithms are described in the following sections.

Round-Robin Distribution. This method distributes the same size of tasks to each processor in Round-Robin (RR) fashion. The minimum granularity of distributed tasks is the same as the number of total slices in the raw data to be reconstructed. If the raw data file has v volumes and each volume consists of s slices, the total number of slices f is defined as $f = s \times v$. If the chosen granularity is g, each processor may get a maximum T number of tasks, where $T = \lceil f/gp \rceil$. The first processor from the processor pool always gets the first set of tasks. The second processor gets the second set, and so on. It is possible that one more set of tasks may be distributed to the first processor. The Round-Robin distribution method is described in Figure 1.

```
01 Procedure RoundRobin
02     Input rawdata
03     Output resultImg
04 if( node==master ) { /* distribute task consecutively*/
05     for( p=0; p<noFrame*noSlice; p++) {
06         task.start = p % noSlice
07         task.end = (task.start + grain-1) % noSlice
07         des = ctr++ % nProc
08         send( task, des )
09     }
10     /* send done signal to every node */
11     for( p=0; p<nProc; p++ )
12         send( DONE, p )
13 }
14 else { /* slave processor */
15     while (true) {
16         recv( task, MASTER )
17         if ( k==DONE )   /* check if we hit the end */
18             break
19         for( j=task.start; j<task.end; j++ ) {
20             getSlice( j, image ) /* get j-th slice */
21             combineImage( resultImg, image )
22             writeImg( resultImg )
23         }
24     }
25 }
```

Fig. 1. Pseudocode of Round-Robin distribution

Communication protocol in the Round-Robin distribution is one-way from a master to clients. The master specifies task information with starting and ending indices and sends it to clients in Round-Robin fashion at for block at line 05. The while block at line 15 in the pseudocode is actual reconstruction code. A client has already received slice indices from the master node. The `getSlice()` moves the file pointer to the correct slice location and constructs each slice sequentially. Once each slice is reconstructed by `getSlice()`, the result is placed into a correct position by `combineImage()` and written into a shared file system by `writeImg()`. This process is repeated until every client receives the DONE signal.

Demand Distribution. Demand distribution (DD) is a kind of dynamic task distribution method, while the RR adapts a static method. A main goal of dynamic task distribution is to minimize processor idle time. Therefore a dynamic distribution method is a natural choice for working with dynamic systems. The DD algorithm is summarized in Figure 2.

```
01 Procedure DemandDistribution
02     Input rawdata
03     Output resultImg
04 if( node==master ) { /* dedicated master */
05     for( p=0; p<nProc; p++ ) {
06         send( task, p )
07     maxSlice = noFrame * noSlice
08     for( s=nProc*grain; s<=maxSlice; s=s+grain ) {
09         recv( task, ANY_SOURCE );
10         task.start = s % noSlice
11         task.end = (task.start+grain-1) % noSlice
12         adjust task.end if necessary
13         send( task, des );
14     }
15     for( p=0; p<nProc; p++ )   /* all done */
16         send( DONE, p )
17 }
18 else { /* slave processor */
19     while (moreData) {
20         recv( task, MASTER )
21         if ( k==DONE )
22             break
23         for( j=task.start; j<task.slice; j++ ) {
24             getSlice( j, image )  /* get j-th slice */
25             combineImage( resultImg, image )
26             writeImg( resultImg )
27         }
28         send( myId, MASTER)
29     }
30 }
```

Fig. 2. Pseudocode of demand distribution

In the DD method, a dedicated master process is required. The dedicated master process is similar to the one in the RR method. However, it only distributes tasks to each requesting processor without any computation for actual reconstruction. Initially every slave processor will get at least one task by the first **if** block at line 06 in Figure 2. Then, the master waits for requests from the slave that completes the distributed task earliest at line 09. As soon as the master gets the request, it sends a new task to the specific slave processor at line 13. The master repeats the same procedure until all frames are distributed.

After all frames are distributed, the master distributes a DONE signal to each slave processor.

The slave processor in the DD method is also very similar to those in the RR. However, the DD slave processor sends its own processor identification number to the master to indicate it is available for a new task, instead of receiving a fixed number of frames once. A slave processor reconstructs frames while the received frame number is not the DONE signal in the fixed method. While a client in RR does not send any message to a master, a client in DD should send another request as soon as it completed the allocated task. The master is waiting for slaves' requests and allocates new frames only to the requesting processors, but not to a client that does not request. Thus, this allocation method keeps every slave processor running as much as possible.

Minimal Load Distribution. The DD method does adaptively distribute tasks to clients so that it tries to maximize processor utilization. However, the master does not send tasks until a client requests it. There are two factors that make client delays longer. If multiple clients request tasks, one client must wait until the master completes the distribution to other clients first, which will cause a delay for the one client. Another delay time may occur even in the case that a single client requests a new task because the client requests a new task only after it completes the current task. The minimal load distribution (MIN) aims to remove the extra delays by predistributing the optimal size of tasks. The optimal size of tasks, G_{opt} can be defined as following:

$$G_{opt} = G_0 * (L_{max} - L_c)/L_{max} + \gamma \qquad (1)$$

where G_0, L_{max}, L_c and γ are the maximum granularity, estimated maximum load of clients, the current load of a clients, and a minimum granularity, respectively. The algorithm for MIN is described in Figure 3.

The master distributes tasks of specified granularity G_0 to each client initially. Then, it waits for the response from the client that completes the assigned task first. The message structure task contains the load of the client as well as the starting and ending slice number and volume numbers in this method. Then, the master computes the optimal size of tasks based on the client's load and distributes the optimal number of slices. The master processor may fetch the system loads of clients by making remote procedure calls. The optimal load computed at line 13 is an indirect inverse linear interpolation to the system load. If the load is close to zero, the optimal granularity will be close to the maximum granularity G_0 and vice versa. Thus, γ is the minimum granularity for the slow clients. The pseudocode for the client of MIN in Figure 3 is similar to that of DD in Figure 2.

Variable Distribution. One problem with the RR distribution is the last distribution of tasks. Thus, one or more clients processors get extra set of tasks. The variable distribution (VAR) method minimizes the difference of the last distribution by controlling the distributional size of tasks. The difference of execution

```
01 Procedure MinimumLoadDistribution
02      Input rawdata
03      Output resultImg
04 if( node==master ) { /* distribute task consecutively*/
05      for( p=0; p<nProc; p++ ) {
06          task.start = task.start + Go*p
07          task.end = task.end + Go*p
08          send( task, p )
09      }
10      maxSlice = noFrame * noSlice
11      for( s = nProc* Go; s<= maxSlice;  ) {
12          recv( task, ANY_SOURCE );
13          Gopt = Go *(Lmax - task.load) / Lmax +
14          task.start = s % noSlice
15          task.end = (task.start+ Gopt) % noSlice
16          adjust task.end if necessary
17          send( task, des)
18          s = s + Gopt
18      }
19      for( p=0; p<nProc; p++ )
20          send( DONE, p )
21 }
22 else { /* slave processor */
23      while (true) {
24          recv( task, MASTER )
25          if ( k==DONE )  /* check if we hit the end */
26              break
27          task.load = checkLoad();
28          send( task, MASTER )
29          for( j=task.start; j<task.end; j++ ) {
30              getSlice( j, image ) /* get j-th slice */
31              combineImage( resultImg, image )
32              writeImg( resultImg )
33          }
34      }
35 }
```

Fig. 3. Pseudocode of minimal load distribution

time between processors with even and odd numbers of tasks assigned will be minimized by using variable granularities. Thus, the ideal way to distribute tasks is to distribute large sizes of tasks at the beginning and smaller sizes of tasks closer to the end of processing.

Let's define α a threshold that begins reduced distribution. Then, if α of total tasks are distributed with a maximum granularity G_m and the rest of tasks are distributed linearly reduced corresponding to the remaining tasks the granularity can be calculated as follows:

$$G = G_m, \quad if \ processed \ task < \alpha$$
$$G = G_m * (T_{all} - \alpha - T_{done})/(T_{all} - \alpha), \quad otherwise \quad (2)$$

where G_m, T_{all}, and T_{done} are a maximum granularity, total tasks, and number of tasks that were completed, respectively.

The initial distribution method of the VAR is the same as the one of RR until the size of performed tasks reaches the specified size α. Then, the master processor distributes smaller and smaller sizes of tasks according to the Equation (2). The pseudocode of VAR algorithm is given in Figure 4.

The granularity *grain* is fixed until the size of the processed tasks is smaller than a given threshold α. The tasks are distributed consecutively following the

```
01 Procedure VariableDistribution
02     Input rawdata
03     Output resultImg
04  if( node==master ) { /* distribute task consecutively*/
05     for( s=0; s<noFrame*noSlice; ) {
06         if (processed <  )
07   grain = Gm
08         else
09             grain = Gm*(totalTask- -doneTask) /
10                     (totalTask -  )
11         task.start = s % noSlice
12         task.end = (task.start + Gm) % noSlice
13         des = ctr++ % nProc
14         send( task, des )
15         processed = processed + grain
16         doneTask = doneTask + grain
17         s = s + grain
18     }
19     for( p=0; p<nProc; p++ )
20         send( DONE, p )
21  }
22  else { /* slave processor */
23      while (true) {
24          recv( task, MASTER )
25          if ( k==DONE )  /* check if we hit the end */
26              break
27          for( j=task.start; j<task.end; j++ ) {
28              getSlice( j, image ) /* get j-th slice */
29              combineImage( resultImg, image )
30              writeImg( resultImg )
31          }
32      }
33  }
```

Fig. 4. Pseudocode of variable distribution

RR fashion. However, if the processed tasks are larger than the threshold, a new grain is computed based on the percentage of the remaining tasks out of total tasks, such as described at line 09 and 10 in Figure 4. The VAR method can be modified for other methods, such as DD or MIN, but it follows the simple RR method in the current investigation.

4 Experiments

Each method has been implemented with MPICH 1.2.5 and tested on the clustered network of four AMD Opteron 240s with 64K L1 cache and 1Mb L2 cache memory. Figure 5 shows the execution times of the parallel reconstruction algorithm deploying the four different distribution methods described in the previous section, for different numbers of processors.

First of all, execution times of the four methods show similar patterns. While the experiments were progressing, no one used the clustered system so that system condition of every processor is almost identical. Each execution time represents the average of ten runs of the same data file. Table 1 shows the mean execution times for different numbers of processors plotted in Figure 5. Average execution time in Figure 5 are summarized in Table 1.

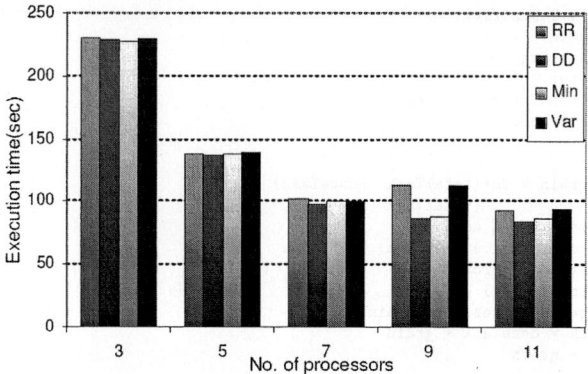

Fig. 5. Execution time of algorithms

Table 1. Execution time of four distribution methods in seconds

Number of Processors	RR	DD	MIN	VAR
1	681.99	682.91	684.15	679.59
3	230.11	228.47	227.65	229.72
5	138.53	137.12	138.48	139.54
7	101.79	98.34	100.58	100.52
9	112.72	86.20	87.88	113.47
11	93.07	84.77	86.32	93.92

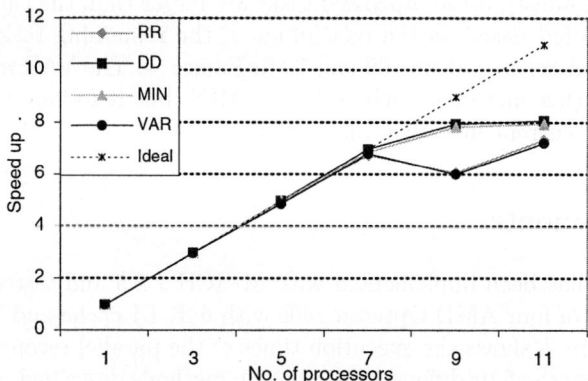

Fig. 6. Speed up of each algorithm

Execution times of the four methods for a single processor were not found to be significantly different. The RR and the VAR were slightly faster compared to the DD and the MIN methods. The speed-up of the four methods was calculated using an execution time of each method. The results of speed-up are plotted in Figure 6.

The speed-ups of the four methods were found to be very similar up to seven processors. However, the speed-up of the RR and the VAR decreased significantly when the number of processors was nine or greater. This is due to the uneven numbers of task distribution. The DD and the MIN methods are capable of handling uneven numbers of tasks. However, the RR and the VAR methods distribute tasks strictly in Round-Robin fashion, of which the last processors might be busy while the other processors are idle.

5 Conclusion

Four different task distribution methods, the Round-Robin distribution, the demand distribution, the minimal load distribution and the variable distribution methods were developed and implemented with MPICH. Each method has its own characteristics along with respective advantages and disadvantages.

The performance of the four parallel algorithms show improved performance with linear speed-up up to the number of physical processors. The algorithms mimic the processor farming model by distributing tasks to available slave processors. The performance of dynamic distribution algorithms demonstrates the behavior of good linear speed-up compared to the static method. It is expected that the speed-up will continually increase linearly, if the size of the clustered network is increased.

The utilizing rate of processors in the demand distribution and the minimal load distribution methods was found to be higher than static distribution methods for most circumstance. The performance of the parallel reconstruction algorithm has been improved significantly by distributed I/O of each client processor.

Acknowledgments

This research was supported by the Functional Imaging Research in Schizophrenia Testbed Biomedical Informatics Research Network (BIRN, www.nbirn.net), which is funded by the National Center for Research Resources at the National Institutes of Health (NIH). (5 MOI RR 000827)

References

1. M. H. Bounocore and D. C. Zhu. Image-based ghost correction for interleaved epi. *Magnetic Resonance in Medicine*, 45:96–108, 2001.
2. R. R. Brechner and M. Singh. Iterative reconstruction of electronically collimated spect images. *IEEE Trans. On Nuclear Science*, 37(3):1328–1332, 1990.
3. C. M. Chen, S. Y. Lee, and Z. H. Cho. A parallel implementation of 3-d ct image reconstruction on hypercube multiprocessor. *IEEE Trans. On Nuclear Science*, 37(3):1333–1346, 1990.

4. C. M. Chen, S. Y. Lee, and Z. H. Cho. Parallelisation of em algorithm for 3-d pet image reconstruction. *IEEE Trans. On Medical Imaging*, 10(4):513–522, 1991.
5. V. A. Diwadkar, M. D. DeBellis, J. A. Sweeney, J. W. Pettegrew, and M. S. Keshavan. Abnormalities in mri-measured signal intensity in the corpus callosum in schizophrenia. *Schizophrenia Research*, 67(2-3):277–282, 2004.
6. P. M. Doraiswamy. Magnetic resonance markers in alzheimer's disease clinical trials. *Molecular Imaging and Bilogy*, 6(2), 2004.
7. D.W.Shattuck, J.Rapela, E. Asma, A. Chatzioannou, J. Qi, and R. M Leahy. Internet2-based 3d pet image reconstruction using a pc cluser. *Physics in Medicine and Biology*, 47:2785–2795, 2002.
8. C. A. Johnson and A. Sofer. A data-parallel algorithm for tomographic image reconstruction. In *Proceedings of the 7th symposium on the Frontier of Massive Parallel Computation*, volume 67, pages 1–10, 1999.
9. V. Kanodia and E. W. Knightly. Ensuring latency targets in multiclass web servers. *IEEE Transactions on Parallel and Distributed Systems*, 14(1):84–93, January 2003.
10. Hyo Jong Lee. A heuristic method for the reconstruction of functional magnetic resonance images. In *Proceedings of International Conference on Imaging Science, System, and Technology*, 2004.
11. Hyo Jong Lee, Jessica Turner, and Steven Potkin. Scalable parallel reconstruction algorithm for magnetic resonance images. In *Proceedings of Parallel and Distributed Processing Techniques and Applications*, 2004.
12. K. J. Lee, D. C. Barber, M. N. Paley, I. D. Wilkinson, N. G. Papadakis, and P. D. Griffiths. Image-based epi ghost artifact reduction using iterative phase correction. In *Conference for Medical Image Understanding and Analysis*, 2001.
13. F. Munz, T. Stephan, U. Maier, T. Ludwig, A. Bode, S. Ziegler, S. Nekolla, P. Bartenstein, and M. Schwaiger. Now based parallel reconstruction of functional images. In *Proceedings of International Parallel and Distributed Processing Symposium*, 1998.
14. F. Tandiary, S. C. Kothari, A. Dixit, and E. W. Anderson. Batrun: utilizing idle workstations for large scale computing. *IEEE Parallel & Distributed Technology: Systems & Applications*, 4(2), 1996.

A Fault-Tolerant h-Out of-k Mutual Exclusion Algorithm Using Cohorts Coteries for Distributed Systems

Jehn-Ruey Jiang

Department of Computer Science and Information Engineering
National Central University, Jhongli 320, Taiwan
jrjiang@csie.ncu.edu.tw

Abstract. In this paper, we propose a distributed algorithm for solving the h-out of-k mutual exclusion problem with the aid of a specific k-coterie — cohorts coterie. The proposed algorithm is resilient to node and/or link failures, and has constant message cost in the best case. Furthermore, it is a candidate to achieve the highest availability among all the algorithms using k-coteries. We analyze the algorithm and compare it with other related ones.

1 Introduction

A distributed system consists of interconnected, autonomous nodes which communicate with each other by passing messages. A node in the system may need to enter the *critical section* (*CS*) occasionally to access a shared resource, such as a shared file or a shared table, etc. The problem of controlling the nodes so that the shared resource is accessed by at most one node at a time, is called the *mutual exclusion* problem. If there are k, $k≥1$, identical copies of shared resources, such as a k-user software license, then there can be at most k nodes accessing the resources at a time. This raises the k-*mutual exclusion* problem. On some occasions, a node may require to access h ($1≤h≤k$) copies out of the k shared resources at a time; for example, a node may need h disks from a pool of k disks to proceed efficiently. How to control the nodes to acquire the desired number of resources with the total number of resources accessed concurrently not exceeding k is called the *h-out of k-mutual exclusion* problem or the *h-out of-k resource allocation* problem [10].

There are at least four distributed h-out of-k mutual exclusion algorithms proposed in the literature. Raynal proposed the first algorithm in [10] and then three algorithms using k-arbiters, (h, k)-arbiters, and k-coteries are proposed in [2], [9], and [5], respectively. Among the four algorithms, only Jiang's algorithm using k-coteries is fault-tolerant. It can tolerate node and/or network link failures even when the failures lead to network partitioning. Furthermore, it is shown in [5] to have lower message cost than others. The basic idea of Jiang's algorithm is simple: a node should collect enough permissions from some set of nodes to enter CS. However, there raise some problems when a node fails to collect enough permissions repeatedly.

In this paper, we proposed another h-out of-k mutual exclusion algorithm using a specific k-coterie — *cohorts coterie* to eliminate the problems of Jiang's algorithm. A cohorts coterie [4] is a k-coterie [3], which is a collection of sets (called *quorums*) satisfying the *intersection*, the *non-intersection* and the *minimality* properties. As we will show, the proposed algorithm has constant message cost in the best case and is a candidate to achieve the highest *availability*, the probability that a node can gather enough permissions to enter CS in an error-prone environment, among all the algorithms using k-coteries.

The rest of this paper is organized as follows. In Section 2, we introduce some related work. In Section 3, we propose the h-out of-k mutual exclusion algorithm using cohorts coteries. In Section 4, we analyze the proposed algorithm and compare it with related ones. And finally, we give some concluding remarks in Section 5.

2 Related Work

In [10], Raynal proposed the first distributed h-out of-k mutual exclusion algorithm. Raynal's algorithm is extended from Ricart and Agrawala's algorithm [11]. It demands a node u to send request messages to all other nodes and wait for replies to estimate the number of unoccupied resources. A node v replies that there are k unoccupied resources if it is neither using nor requesting shared resources, or if it has lower priority than the requester (in terms of logical clock [7] order). On the other hand, node v replies that there are $k-h$ unoccupied resources if v is using h resources or if v is requesting h resources with higher priority. For such a case, node v should later reply again that there are h resources released after it leaves CS. From all the replies, if node u finds that the estimated number of unoccupied resources is larger than the number of requested resources, it can enter CS. Raynal's algorithm has message complexity between $2(n-1)$ and $3(n-1)$, where n is the number of nodes. It is not fault-tolerant since a node cannot gather replies from all other nodes if there is any failing node.

In [1], Baldoni proposed the concept of *arbiter sets* to solve the h-out of-k mutual exclusion problem. Every node is associated with an arbiter set (request set), and any k arbiter sets should have at least one common member. A node should send request messages with parameter h ($h\leq k$) to all members of its arbiter set to gather permissions to access h resources. Every node keeps the number of unoccupied resources, which is initially k and is decreased by h after granting a request for accessing h resources. The total number of resources concurrently being accessed is guaranteed to be no more than k because the common member of any $k+1$ arbiter sets can serve as the arbiter, which grants its permission only when the number of unoccupied resources is no less than the number of requested resources. The algorithm using arbiter sets has the message complexity $O(q)$, where q is the size of arbiter sets. Baldoni proved that arbiter sets have the size lower bound of $O(n^{k/k+1})$ if all arbiter sets have the same size and every node appears in the same number of arbiter sets.

The concept of the arbiter set was further formalized as the k-arbiter by Baldoni et al. in [2]. A k-*arbiter* is a collection of minimal arbiter sets (called *quorums*) where any $k+1$ quorums have at least one common member. Two k-arbiters were proposed in [2]: $(k+1)$-cube and uniform k-arbiters, with quorum sizes $(k+1)\cdot n^{k/(k+1)}$ and

$\lfloor k \cdot n/(k+1) \rfloor + 1$, repectively. In [9], Manabe and Tajima further generalized k-arbiters with (h,k)-arbiters and proposed $(k+1)$-cube and uniform (h,k)-arbiters with quorum size $(k+2-h) \cdot n^{(k+1-h)/(k+1)}$ and $\lfloor k \cdot n/(k+h) \rfloor + 1$, respectively.

The h-out of-k mutual exclusion algorithms [1, 2, 9] using arbiter sets are not fault-tolerant in the sense that a node just selects a quorum and waits for all the members of the quorum to reply. If any member of the selected quorum fails, a node may fail to gather permissions to enter CS. In [5], Jiang proposed a fault-tolerant distributed h-out of-k mutual exclusion algorithm using k-coterie. A k-coterie [3] is a collection of sets (called *quorums*) satisfying the following properties:

1. *Intersection Property*: There are at most k pairwise disjoint quorums.
2. *Non-intersection Property*: For any h ($< k$) pairwise disjoint quorums $Q_1,...,Q_h$, there exists a quorum Q_{h+1} such that $Q_1,...,Q_{h+1}$ are pairwise disjoint.
3. *Minimality Property*: Any quorum is not a super set of another quorum.

In Jiang's algorithm, a node u requesting to access h resources should randomly select h pairwise disjoint quorums and send request messages to the members of the h quorums. On receiving a request message, a node v grants its permission by replying a grant message. Node u can enter CS after it gathers permissions from members of h pairwise disjoint quorums. The correctness of h-out of-k mutual exclusion is guaranteed since every node grants its permission to only one at a time and there are at most k pairwise disjoint quorums. Jiang's algorithm is fault-tolerant in the sense that a node can reselect h pairwise disjoint quorums for sending incremental request messages when the node does not gather enough permissions after a timeout period. However, Jiang's algorithm has the following problems: First, it does not explicitly specify how to efficiently select and reselect h pairwise disjoint quorums. Second, it is difficult to determine the timeout value.

3 The Proposed Algorithm

In this section, we propose an h-out of-k mutual exclusion algorithm using a specific k-coterie — cohorts coterie [4]. The proposed algorithm does not use timeout mechanism and does not require a node to reselect h pairwise disjoint quorums. As we will show, the proposed algorithm has constant message complexity in the best case and is a candidate to achieve the highest availability among those using k-coteries.

Before presenting the proposed algorithm, we first introduce the cohorts k-coterie [6], which is constructed with the aid of *cohorts structures*. A *cohorts structure* $Coh(k, m) \equiv (C_1,...,C_m)$, $m \geq k$, is a list of sets, where each set C_i is called a *cohort*. The cohorts structure $Coh(k, m)$ should observe the following three properties:

P1. $|C_1| = k$.
P2. $\forall i: 1 < i \leq m : |C_i| > 2k-2$, for $k>1$ ($|C_i|>1$, for $k=1$).
P3. $\forall i, j: 1 \leq i, j \leq m, i \neq j: C_i \cap C_j = \emptyset$.

To sum up, a cohorts structure *Coh(k, m)* has *m* pairwise disjoint cohorts with the first cohort having *k* members and the other cohorts having more than $2k-2$ members (or more than one member when $k=1$). For example, ({1, 2}, {3, 4, 5}, {6, 7, 8, 9, 10}) is *Coh(2,3)* since it has three pairwise disjoint cohorts with the first cohort and the other cohorts having 2 (=k) and more than 2 (=$2k-2$) members, respectively.

A set *Q* is said to be a *quorum under Coh(k, m)* if some cohort C_i in *Coh(k, m)* is *Q*'s *primary cohort*, and each cohort $C_j, j > i$, is *Q*'s *supporting cohort*, where a cohort *C* is *Q*'s primary cohort if $|Q \cap C|=|C|-(k-1)$ (i.e., *Q* contains exactly all except $k-1$ members of *C*), and a cohort *C* is *Q*'s supporting cohort if $|Q \cap C|=1$ (i.e., *Q* contains exactly one member of *C*).

The family of all quorums under *Coh(k, m)* is called a *cohorts coterie*, which has been shown to be a *k*-coterie in [4]. For example, the following sets are quorums under $Coh(2, 2) \equiv (\{1, 2\}, \{3, 4, 5\})$: $Q_1=\{3, 4\}$, $Q_2=\{3, 5\}$, $Q_3=\{4, 5\}$, $Q_4=\{1, 3\}$, $Q_5=\{1, 4\}$, $Q_6=\{1, 5\}$, $Q_7=\{2, 3\}$, $Q_8=\{2, 4\}$ and $Q_9=\{2, 5\}$. Quorums $Q_1,...,Q_3$ take {3, 4, 5} as their primary cohort and no supporting cohort is needed, and quorums $Q_4,...,Q_9$ take {1, 2} as their primary cohort and {3, 4, 5} as their supporting cohort. It is easy to check that these nine sets constitute a 2-coterie.

In [6], the cohorts coterie is shown to be *nondominated (ND)*. Let C and D be two distinct *k*-coteries. C is said to *dominate* D if and only if every quorum in D is a super set of some quorum in C (i.e., $\forall Q, \exists Q': Q \in D, Q' \in C: Q' \subseteq Q$). Obviously, the dominating one (C) has more chances than the dominated one (D) to have *available quorums* in an error-prone environment, where a quorum is said to be *available* if all of its members (nodes) are *up*. Since an available quorum implies an available entry to CS, we should always concentrate on ND *k*-coteries that no other *k*-coterie can dominate. The algorithm using ND *k*-coteries, for example the proposed algorithm, is a candidate to achieve the highest availability.

The core of the proposed algorithm is a permission gathering procedure, which is named *Get_Quorum* shown in Figure 1. For a distributed system with *n* nodes organized as a *cohorts structure Coh(k, m)* $\equiv (C_1,...,C_m)$, a node requesting *h* out of *k* resources should invoke *Get_Quorum(h, k, $(C_1,...,C_m)$)*. The node can access *h* resources after *Get_Quorum* returns.

The function *Probe(C_i, g)* evoked in *Get_Quorum* performs the task of probing all the nodes in set C_i for their permissions. It returns a set of nodes of C_i that reply grant messages for the following three cases. (It will not return if none of the cases stands.)

Case 1: If $i>1$ and there are more than $|C_i|-(k-1)+(g-1)$ nodes replying grant messages, the returning set will be a set of $|C_i|-(k-1)+(g-1)$ replying nodes.
Case 2: If $i>1$ and there are more than *g* but less than $|C_i|-(k-1)+(g-1)$ nodes replying grant messages, the returning set will be a set of *g* replying nodes. (Note that $|C_i|-(k-1)+(g-1)>g$ because $|C_i| > 2k-2$ for $k>1$, or $|C_i| > 1$ for $k=1$.)
Case 3: If $i=1$ and there are more than *g* nodes replying grant messages, the returning set will be a set of *g* replying nodes. (Note that because $|C_1|=k$, only one node can make C_1 the primary cohort of a quorum. Thus, *g* replying nodes can make C_1 be the primary cohorts of *g* quorums.).

```
Function Get_Quorum( h, k: Integer; (C_1,...,C_m): Cohorts Structure):Set;
  Var R, S: Set;
  Var g: Integer;
  g = h;   //g: Storing the number of primary cohorts needed
  R = ∅;   //R: The set of replying nodes that will be returned
  For (i =m,...,2 ) Do
    S=Probe(C_i, g);
    If |S| = |C_i|–(k–1)+(g–1)
    Then {R=R∪S; g=g–1; If g=0 Then Return R;}
    /*C_i can be the primary cohort of one quorum,
      and be the supporting cohorts of g–1 quorums       */
    Else If |S|=g Then R=R∪S;
    /*C_i can only be the supporting cohorts of g quorums */
  EndFor
  S=Probe(C_1, g);
  Return R∪S;   //C_1 is the primary cohort of g quorums
End Get_Quorum
```

Fig. 1. The permission gathering procedure – *Get_Quorum*

The procedure *Get_Quorum* uses no timeout mechanism and can return a set of nodes of h pairwise disjoint quorums efficiently. It is clear that no two nodes can simultaneously gather permissions from h_1 and h_2 pairwise disjoint quorums by invoking *Get_Quorum* if $h_1+h_2>k$. Thus, the proposed algorithm guarantees the safety property of h-out of-k mutual exclusion that there are no more than k resources being accessed concurrently. To ensure the liveness (i.e., deadlock and starvation-free) property, we could rely on the well known conflict resolution mechanism of Meakawa's algorithm [8]. However, we omit the details for simplicity.

4 Analysis and Comparison

The reader can check that if a node calls the function *Get_Quorum* when there is no failing node and no request conflict, then *Get_Quorum* will return a set of the union of h pairwise disjoint quorums which take $C_m,...,C_{m-h-1}$ respectively as their primary cohorts, with C_m being the supporting cohorts of $h-1$ quorums,..., and C_{m-h} being the supporting cohort of one quorum. For such a case, the node has to send request message to $c \cdot h$ nodes if we assume all cohorts (including $C_m,...,C_{m-h-1}$) are of the same size c, $c > 2k-2$. However, if there are failures and/or request conflicts, then some of the h quorums may take $C_{m-h-2},...,C_1$ as their primary cohorts. In an extreme case, some quorums may take C_1 as their primary cohorts. In such a case, the node has to send request messages to all the n system nodes.

Like other quorum-based algorithms [1, 2, 5, 9], the proposed algorithm is a Meakawa-type algorithm [8], which relies Lamport's logical clock concept [7] and five types of messages, namely *request, grant, release, inquire* and *relinquish* messages, to avoid deadlock and starvation. In the best case, a node u needs $3c \cdot h$ messages to access h, $h \leq k$, resources. The best case occurs when u sends request messages to all members of $C_m, ..., C_{m-h-1}$, receives grant messages from all members of $C_m, ..., C_{m-h-1}$, and at last sends release message to all members of $C_m, ..., C_{m-h-1}$ on leaving CS. In the worst case, the message complexity is $6n$. It occurs when u sends request messages to each node u, u sends inquire message to some node w, w sends relinquish message to u, u sends grant message to v, v sends release message to u (after v leaves CS), and at last u sends grant message to w. The worst case message complexity can be reduced by the following mechanism. We can set a probability p for a node to decide whether or not to further probe nodes in cohorts $C_{m-h-2}, ..., C_1$ after it has probed nodes in $C_m, ..., C_{m-h-1}$. The probability p makes the worst case message complexity to be $6f \cdot n$, where f is a constant between 0 and 1. With p, we can trade fault-tolerance for message-efficiency. The reader can check that larger p will lead to higher message complexity and higher degree of fault-tolerance.

As shown in [10], Raynal's algorithm has message complexity between $2(n-1)$ and $3(n-1)$. The message complexities of the algorithms using k-arbiters and (h,k)-arbiters have been analyzed in [5]. Both the algorithms have the message complexity $3q$ in the best case and $(3h+3)q$ in the worst case, where q is the quorum size of the k-arbiter or the (h,k)-arbiter. As shown in [5], Jiang's algorithm has message complexity $3h \cdot q$ in the best case and $6e \cdot n$ in the worst case, where q is the quorum size of the k-coterie and $0 < e \leq 1$. Table 1 shows the comparison of Raynal's algorithm [10], the algorithms using k-arbiters [2] and (h,k)-arbiters [9], Jiang's algorithm [5], and the proposed algorithm.

Table 1. The comparison of various distributed h-out of-k mutual exclusion algorithms

Algorithm	Message complexity	Quorum reselection	Timeout mechanism	Fault-Tolerance
Raynal's algorithm [10]	between $2(n-1)$ and $3(n-1)$	no	no	no
The algorithm using k-arbiters [2]	between $3q$ to $(3h+3)q$, where $q=(k+1) \cdot n^{k/(k+1)}$ for the $(k+1)$-cube arbiter and $q = \lfloor k \cdot n/(k+1) \rfloor + 1$ for the uniform k-arbiter	no	no	no
The algorithm using (h,k)-arbiters [9]	between $3q$ to $(3h+3)q$, where $q=(k+2-h) \cdot n^{(k+1-h)/(k+1)}$ for the $(k+1)$-cube (h,k)-arbiter and $q = \lfloor k \cdot n/(k+h) \rfloor + 1$ for the uniform (h,k)-arbiter	no	no	no
Jiang's algorithm [5]	between $3h \cdot q$ and $6e \cdot n$, where q is the quorum size of the k-coterie used, and $0 < e \leq 1$	yes	yes	yes
The proposed algorithm	between $3c \cdot h$ and $6f \cdot n$, where $c > 2k-2$ and $0 < f \leq 1$	no	no	yes (maybe of the highest availability)

*n stands for the number of nodes, and h stands for the number of requested resources.

5 Conclusion

In this paper, we have proposed a distributed h-out of-k mutual exclusion algorithm using a specific k-coterie — cohorts coterie. The proposed algorithm becomes a k-mutual exclusion algorithm for $k>h=1$, and becomes a mutual exclusion algorithm for $k=h=1$. It is resilient to node and/or link failures and has constant message cost in the best case. Furthermore, it is a candidate to achieve the highest availability among all the algorithms using k-coteries since the cohorts coterie is ND. We have compared the proposed algorithm with Raynal's algorithm [10], the algorithms using k-arbiters [2] and (h,k)-arbiters [9], and Jiang's algorithm [5] to show its superiority.

References

1. Baldoni, R.: An $O(N^{M/(M+1)})$ Distributed Algorithm for the k-out of-M Resources Allocation Problem. 14th IEEE International Conference on Distributed Computing Systems, (1994) 81-88
2. Baldoni, R., Manabe, Y., Raynal M., Aoyagy, S.: k-Arbiter: A Safe and General Scheme for h-out of-k Mutual Exclusion. Theoretical Computer Science, 193 (1998) 97-112
3. Huang, S.-T., Jiang, J.-R., Kuo, Y.-C.: k-Coteries for Fault-Tolerant k Entries to a Critical Section. 13th IEEE International Conference on Distributed Computing Systems, (1993) 74-81
4. Jiang, J.-R., Huang, S.-T., Kuo, Y.-C.: Cohorts Structures for Fault-Tolerant k Entries to a Critical Section. IEEE Trans. on Computers, 48 (1997) 222-228
5. Jiang, J.-R.: Distributed h-out of-k Mutual Exclusion Using k-Coteries. 3rd International Conference on Parallel and Distributed Computing, Application and Technologies (PDCAT'02), (2002) 218-226
6. Jiang, J.-R.: On the Nondomination of Cohorts Coteries. IEEE Trans. on Computers, 53 (2004) 922-923
7. Lamport, L.: Time, Clocks, and the Ordering of Events in a Distributed System. Communications of ACM, 21 (1978) 558-565
8. Meakawa, M.: A $\sqrt{N}$ Algorithm for Mutual Exclusion in Decentralized Systems. ACM Trans. Comp. Sys., 3 (1985) 145-159
9. Manabe, Y., Tajima, N.: $(h\text{-}k)$-Arbiter for h-out of-k Mutual Exclusion Problem. Theoretical Computer Science, 310 (2004) 379-392
10. Raynal, M.: A Distributed Solution for the k-out of-m Resources Allocation Problem. Lecture Notes in Computer Sciences, Vol. 497. Springer Verlag (1991) 599-609
11. Ricart, G., Agrawala, A. K.: An Optimal Algorithm for Mutual Exclusion in Computer Networks. Communications of ACM, 24 (1981) 9-17

Phylogenetic Analysis Using Maximum Likelihood Methods in Homogeneous Parallel Environments

M. Till[1], B.B. Zhou[1], A. Zomaya, and L. S. Jermiin[2]

[1] School of Information Technologies,
Madsen Building, F09,
[2] School of Biological Sciences,
Heydon-Laurence Building A08
University of Sydney,
Sydney 2006, NSW Australia

Abstract. This paper describes a parallel application for phylogenetic analysis of DNA sequences. The program extends the phylogenetics program Trexml to increase the speed of this rather exhaustive tree searching program. The program uses the Advanced Stepwise Addition Algorithm (ASA) and provides two main advantages over existing applications. The size of the tree space can be chosen in such a way that we can fully utilize super computing resources. We also adopt a Single Program multiple Data (SPMD) approach in our program and use deterministic means to evaluate which processors are involved in communication. This approach alleviates the communication costs incurred in a master/slave system. Results from running the program on the AC3 Barossa supercomputer indicate that our approach scales well.

Keywords: parallel, super computing, phylogenetics, ASA, SPMD.

1 Introduction

Phylogenetics involves the study of a series of biological entities. Phylogenetic analysis examines a group of such entities and infers the evolutionary relationship between these entities. This field is growing in relevance to a variety of life science areas such as forensics, medical diagnosis and drug discovery. The Maximum-likelihood (ML) method evaluates a phylogenetic tree in terms of the probability of that tree being the correct model for the data that is given [4]. Consistency and low variance make this method a powerful approach of evaluating phylogenetic uncertainty [6]. As a result, ML methods are used in a variety of applications. The ML method involves the definition of tree topology followed by branch length optimization [6].

Given n taxa there are $\prod_{i=3}^{n}(2i-5)$ [7] possible topologies - as n increases the number of possible topologies increases exponentially. Most ML applications have therefore introduced other means to reduce this computational complexity. The Simple Stepwise Addition algorithm (SSA) [3] is one such method of reducing the search space considerably. In the SSA a starting tree with three leaves is constructed. The next taxa is added to this tree (4 possible configurations) and the best tree is kept. This process is repeated until all n taxa have been added. Using the SSA only $2i-5$ for possible trees for $i > 3$ are examined for each i leaved tree. Whilst this is a considerable reduction in computational complexity, it ignores all but the best tree in each round. It is often found that the best tree has a similar ML value to other near optimal trees.

Another drawback of the SSA is that it is found to be slow on classical sequential computing systems [2][3][4]. Modern super computing systems are assembled from hundreds and sometimes thousands of processors. Classical master / slave systems are common amongst parallel solutions to this problem [1][5][8][9][10] - however the master will be come a communication bottleneck as we add more processors. Our solution implements a more thorough method of searching the tree space - the Advanced Stepwise Addition algorithm (ASA) [11].

2 Advanced Stepwise Addition Algorithm

The ASA algorithm is an exhaustive two step algorithm. The first stage searches exhaustively for the best k trees that have a taxa. We choose a small value for a so that this search is not too time consuming. The second stage involves adding successive taxa one at a time in separate rounds. There are $n-a$ of these rounds and $k(2(a+1)-5) = k(2a-3)$ trees are generated for each tree with $a+1$ leaves. Only the top k trees are considered for the next round of the algorithm. It is noteworthy that when $a = 3$ and $k = 1$, the ASA functions in the same way as the SSA. By varying the values of a where $a <= n$

1. Choose a set, A, of a taxa
2. Generate all binary trees on A
3. Save the set, K, of k best trees
4. FOR the remaining $n - a$ taxa
   (a) FOR each tree in K
   (b) Add next taxon to all edges
   (c) Save the set, K, of k best trees [12]

Fig. 1. Advanced Stepwise Addition Algorithm

and k we can vary the size of the search space for trees with n taxa. By choosing large values of a and k we increase the search space considerably in the hope that we can obtain better results. The problem of increased computational complexity can be solved by running the application on a large scale parallel supercomputer.

3 Parallel Implementation

Several modifications were made to the original program in order to achieve parallelism. We used the MPI library for inter-processor communication. Primitive functions were composed to send a tree structure between processors and to recreate trees from input buffers. These functions are common amongst applications of this nature [8][10]. The nexttree() method was re-factored to produce the next pth tree starting from a particular processor's id number. Insertion-Sort was used whenever an ordered list of ML and processor-id pairs needed to be established. We have added timing and throughput metrics to the application to assist with the benchmarks presented in this paper.

We have adopted a SPMD paradigm in implementing a parallel ASA algorithm. Our algorithm treats all processors equally by assigning each processor (when possible) an equal amount of work. This approach makes sense when you consider that many large scale supercomputers are homogeneous. Communication is deterministic and only occurs at the end of each round of computation, thereby minimizing communication. The implementation of the ASA in Figure 1 uses a subset of a' (for $a' \leq a$). The number

1. Choose a subset, A', of a' taxa from set A
2. Generate all possible trees on A' on all processors
3. Distribute the generated trees evenly among the processors
4. On each processor generate all possible trees by adding the remaining $a - a'$ taxa
5. Save a set, K, of k best trees across the processors
6. evenly distribute k best trees among the processors
7. FOR the remaining $n - a$ taxa
   (a) Each time add one taxon
   (b) Save k best trees across the processors
   (c) Balance the workload amongst the processors [12]

Fig. 2. A parallel implementation of the ASA algorithm

of trees with a' taxa must be greater or equal to the number of processors. The number of trees with $a' - 1$ taxa must be less than the number of processors. Every processor will generate $t_0 = \prod_{i=3}^{a'}(2i - 5)$ trees and keep a different subset of size t_0/p. Each processor then has a different set of original trees to extend. The next section discusses how we can locate the best k trees in the most efficient manner possible.

3.1 Tree Cutting

One way of obtaining the best k trees across all the processors would be to carry out global sorting and listing the first k entries. This is rather time consuming for large values of k and p - we only need to find the first k trees. Figure 3 shows the parallel tree cutting procedure we have developed. Each processor keeps the trees in an ordered list with at most k elements. The tree cutting algorithm works in much the same way as a binary search works - however the median value is stored on each processor. The communications involved in the tree cutting phase where implemented using MPI_Allreduce for sharing global maximums and minimums. As described in Figure 3, the process involves determining a median value on each processor and calculating the number of trees below this value. The number of global trees with ML values below this median value is then determined. The global maximum and minimum is then re-adjusted, with the process repeating itself until the number of global trees is equal to k. It is simple to show that in the average case that this algorithm uses $\log kp$ messages - far less than a worst case of kp for global sorting.

1. On each processor
   (a) Sort the trees in a non-increasing order according their likelihood values
   (b) save the first k trees
2. Calculate global largest and smallest likelihood values
3. On each processor,
   (a) Calculate the median value according to the largest and smallest values
   (b) Partition the trees into two parts, the first part containing all the trees with their likelihood values greater than the median and the second part containing the remaining trees
4. Count the total number of trees in the first parts, say j
5. On each processor, if $j = k$, the job is done
6. Otherwise, go back to Step 3 (a) to find k best trees in the first parts if $j > k$, or (4) to find $(k - j)$ best trees in the second parts if $j < k$. [12]

Fig. 3. The tree- cutting procedure for finding k best trees

1. Each processor calculates k/p and v, the variance
2. The variances are placed in a global array
3. Whilst any process has a variance greater than zero -
   (a) Sort the variances in any order.
   (b) Take the processors with the least and the most variance
   (c) Calculate and send the required load; recalculate variances

Fig. 4. The Work balancing routine to distribute k best trees evenly across p processors

3.2 Workload Balancing

After the best k trees have been identified these trees will typically be unevenly distributed over p processors. Because we are treating each processor the same, we must ensure that at the beginning of each round each processor has the same amount of trees to extend. Our work balancing routine uses the MPI function MPI_Allgather to share globally the size of the subset of best trees each processor has. By using a deterministic method for calculating which trees are sent between processors, this information only needs to be calculated once.

The balancing takes place in a series of rounds whereby each processor determines which processors requires more trees and which ones require more trees. The processor with the most trees than sends as many trees as possible to the processor with the least number of trees. This process is repeated until all processors have roughly k/p trees. In the best case this stage is not necessary. (When all processors have k/p best trees to start with.) In the worst cast this stage will take p stages. (When one process contains all of the best k trees.) In the average case $\log p$ stages are used to balance the workload.

4 Results

Our experiment was run on the AC3 Barossa supercomputer which has a total of 152 nodes - each node contains dual 3.0Ghz processors and 2Gb of RAM. The following parameters were used for our experiment -

- Number of processors - 1 ,2, 4 , 8 , 16 , 32
- Number of Initial leaves - 6
- Number of final leaves - 15 to 55 (steps of 5)
- Number of best trees kept - 100,500,1000,5000

The input data with 56 species was obtained from the fastdnaml test suite 13. Each taxa has 820 sites. Each test was run on two occasions and the average result is used. We fix the value of a in this instance to fix the size of the tree space we are searching.

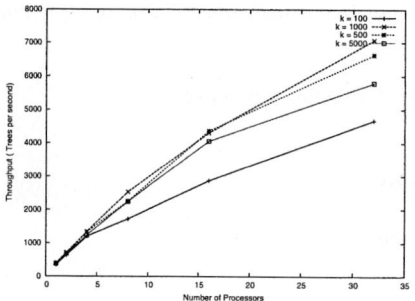

Fig. 5. Throughput vs number of processors for different values of k. These results are for trees that have 25 taxa or leaves

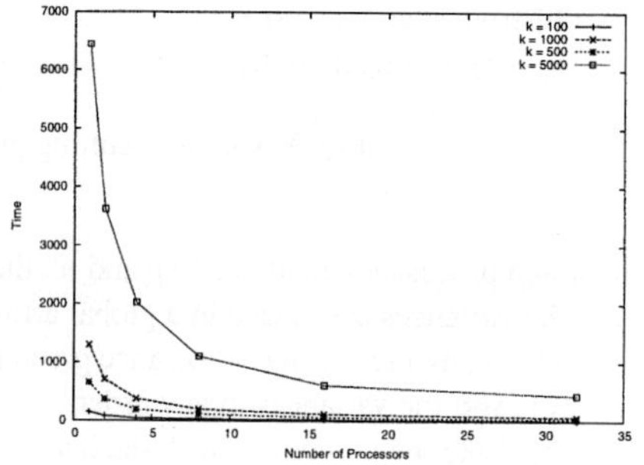

Fig. 6. Wall clock execution time vs number of processors for different values of k. These results are for trees that have 25 taxa or leaves

5 Discussions and Future Work

The results show that we have achieve good improvements over a large number of processors. The best improvements observed occur over the first 8 processors. This is expected considering the low amount of communication and waiting that occurs. When k is 1000 or less and $p >= 16$ execution time is less than 20 seconds. The largest value of k used for the experimentation indicates that the scalability is still heavily dependent on k. Future work be done to explore ways of improving the scalability when the number of processors and the value of k is quite large. Buffered communication is being considered to minimize the amount of network traffic. Furthermore an implementation that combines the ASA with large scale Grid networks is also being considered.

References

1. C. Ceron, J. Dopazo, E. L. Zapata, J. M. Carazo and O. Trelles, Parallel implementation of DNAml program on message-passing architectures, Parallel Computing, 24, 1998, pp.701-716.
2. A. W. F. Edwards, S. Cavalli, Phenetic and phylogenetic classification, Systematics Association Publication No 6, 1963, pp. 67-76.
3. J. Felsenstein, Evolutionary trees from DNA sequences: A maximum likelihood approach, j. Mol. Evol., 17, 1981, pp. 368-376.

4. D. M. Hillis, C. Moritz and B L. Mable, Molecular Systematics, 2nd ed. Sinauer Associates, Inc., 1996.
5. G. J. Olsen, H. Matsuda, R. Hagstrom and R. Overbeek, fastDNAml: A tool for construction of phylogenetic trees of DNA sequences using maximum likelihood, Comput. Appl. Biosci., 10, 1994, pp. 41-48.
6. D. Penny, M. D. Hendy and M. A. Steel, Progress with methods for construction evolutionary trees, Trends Ecol. Evol., 7, pp. 73-79, 1992
7. F. J. Rohlf, Numbering binary trees with labelled terminal vertices, Bul. Math. Biol., 45(10), 1983, pp. 33-40.
8. A. P. Stamatakis, T. Ludwig, H. Meier and M. J. Wolf, Accelerating parallel maximum likelihood-based phylogenetic tree computations using subtree equality vectors, Proceedings of SC2002, November 2002.
9. C.A. Stewart, D. Hart, D. K. Berry, G. J. Olsen, E. A. Wernert and W. Fischer, Parallel Implementation and performance of fastDNAml . A program for maximum likelihood phylogenetic inference, SC2001, November 2001.
10. Tree-PUZZLE home page, http://www.tree-puzzle.de/, last accessed August 2003.
11. J. M. J. Wolf, S. Easteal, M. Kahn, B. D. McKay and L. S. Jermiin, TrExML: a maximum-likelihood approach for extensive tree-space exploration, Bioinformatics, 16(4), 2000, pp. 383-394.
12. B. B. Zhou, M. Till, A. Zomaya and L. S. Jermiin, Parallel Implementation of Maximum Likelihood Methods for Phylogenetic Analysis, IPDPS 2004
13. Fastdnaml home page, http://ftp.cse.sc.edu/bioinformatics/fastDNAml/fastDNAml_1.2.2p/testdata/test56.phy, last accessed September 2004

Real-Time Transcoding of MPEG Videos in a Distributed Environment*

Yunyoung Nam[1] and Eenjun Hwang[2]

[1] Graduate School of Information and Communication, Ajou University, Suwon, Korea
yynam@korea.com
[2] Department of Electronics and Computer Engineering, Korea University, Seoul, Korea
ehwang04@korea.ac.kr

Abstract. As the market of mobile devices for video streaming is growing rapidly, it is necessary to convert a high bit rate MPEG stream into a low bit rate MPEG stream. However, it takes long time to transcode MPEG to another steaming media format due to the huge amount of computation in a traditional single computing environment. Furthermore, real-time MPEG transcoding also demands high computational power. Fortunately, the algorithms compliant to the MPEG standard can be parallelized. In this paper, we propose several scheduling algorithms for real-time transcoding of MPEG video that can be used in heterogeneous distributed computing environments. In the experiment, we will compare their performance through an experimental evaluation.

1 Introduction

MPEG-4[1] is used in wireless video communications due to its high compression efficiency and strong error resilience. Most mobile devices are designed to support MPEG-4 compatible video decoding. However, video content available from the Internet is usually encoded in other formats for different purposes. For example, in HDTV, the video contents stored in the video server are usually encoded in MPEG-2 format with high visual quality and spatial resolution, resulting in bit rates from 4 Mb/s up to 15Mb/s. In order to enable wireless access to the video stored in video server, video transcoding techniques can be employed to conduct both video coding format and bit rate conversions.

The video transcoding is a process of converting a previously compressed video bit stream into another bit stream with a lower bit rate, a different display format, or a different coding method, etc. The transcoding task is very expensive to encode the original video to each target format, because the transcoding process contains both decoding and encoding process steps.

Real-time processing is required for many applications such as HDTV and digital library. However, traditional sequential algorithms take a lot of time in transcoding video due to the huge amount of computation. Particularly, the discrete cosine trans-

---

* This research was supported by University IT Research Center Project.

form (DCT), the motion estimation (ME), and motion compensation (MC) are computationally intensive. In this paper, we propose two scheduling algorithms for parallel transcoding of MPEG video in a heterogeneous distributed environment, which all reduced the trascoding time a lot and the demand met on time.

2 Parallel Video Transcoding Model

The system architecture takes a classic master-slave model. The master is responsible for preparing transcoding units and communicating with slaves for parallel processing. The slaves communicate with the master for acquiring a transcoding unit and return the result. The master reads a video sequence from the disk into the memory. The video is scanned for splitting into transcoding units. In the meantime, video information such as frame size, number of GOP, average bit-rate is extracted. The transcoding units are placed into the input queue. The slave reads a transcoding unit from the input queue and performs the segmentation using a transcoding algorithm. The transcoding results by the slaves are placed into the output queue. However, the order of transcoding units in the output queue could be different from that in the input queue due to the different performance of slaves. Therefore, transcoding units in the output queue should be rearranged for the correct ordering. It may happen that some slaves do not respond to the master request, nor return the results. To handle such cases, we incorporated the time-out mechanism.

3 Scheduling Algorithms

We proposed two scheduling algorithms for transcoding. They are Size-Adaptive Round Robin, and Dynamic Size-Adaptive Round Robin scheduling algorithms.

3.1 Round Robin (RR)

The RR is one of the simplest, fairest and most widely used scheduling algorithms. However, if one slave takes more time than others, and if no slaves send results, it will cause to take more time than optimal time. In order to solve this problem, RR must be improved. We will describe improved RR in next section.

3.2 Size-Adaptive Round Robin Using Sampling (SARR)

Due to slaves' various response time and network bandwidth, the RR suffers from performance down fall. To improve this situation, performance and network bandwidth should be considered. This is the main motivation of SARR.

The master distributes a small sample video stream of equal size to all the slaves. When the master received the results from the slaves, it can estimate the performance and network bandwidth of the slaves. Using this estimation, the master splits the video stream into different size of transcoding unit and distributes them to slaves.

The SARR is more efficient than the RR. However, both master and slave may be idle due to lack of data. At the master, idle time may be avoided by using load-balancing technique. At the slaves, they are idle while other slaves preempt or communicate with the master. This idle time can sometimes be avoided by structuring a program so that the slaves perform other computation while waiting for the master.

3.3 Dynamic Size-Adaptive Round Robin (DSARR)

In the previous algorithm, the first problem is due to the fact that the master itself waits for the parsed results from the slaves. The second problem arises main from the fact that the slave itself waits for the master to receive the transcoding data. In order to solve these problems, a non-blocking strategy must be considered.

For the master, sufficient number of slaves could solve the first problem of idle time at the master. Unfortunately, an excessive number of processors are useless and waste of resources, because it causes a large number of slaves to stay idle. The sampling makes an initial estimate on the slaves' computational workload and network bandwidth at first; it adjusts each job size. When the master stays idle, the scheduler increases the number of slaves or the master execute a transcoding task. When a lot of slaves stay idle, the scheduler decreases the number of slaves in low performance order. As a result, it adjusts the number of slaves accordingly. This can reduce idle time and minimize redundant or wasted effort in the slave.

4 Experiments

For the experiments, we used 1 master machine and 10 slave machines connected via Ethernet performed. We used MPEG-2 video sequence and converted MPEG-2 into MPEG-4 without resizing of resolution.

In figure 1(a), the speedup is nearly linear to the number of machines and the SARR achieves very good speedup. When the number of machines was eleven, the speedup of the RR was 7.0 and the SARR yielded a 7.6 times better speedup than sequential transcoding. In addition, the SARR scheduling works much more efficiently as shown in figure 1(b). However, the speedup will not improve beyond the optimal number of machines. This is mainly because excessive machines cause too much communication and idle time.

Figure 2 shows the number of slaves involved according to time with the DSARR. If some of the machines have low performance and network bandwidth, it will take long time to complete video transcoding. Therefore, the master would look for more volunteer machines in order to achieve in the transcoding and reduce the number of slow machines. On the other hand, if some of the machines have high performance and network bandwidth, the master would maintain the fast machines and discard the slow machines.

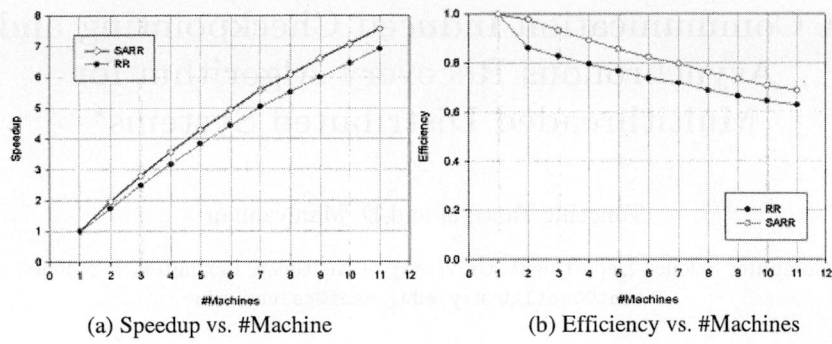

(a) Speedup vs. #Machine   (b) Efficiency vs. #Machines

Fig. 1. Speedup and Efficiency versus #machine

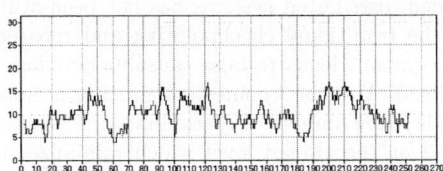

Fig. 2. #Machines versus Time (available slave machines are 20)

5 Conclusion

In this paper, we proposed two scheduling for real-time transcoding of MPEG video in heterogeneous distributed environment. Conclusively, if the number of machines is unchanging, the SARR performed better than the RR. On the other hand, if the number of machines is changing in unreliable and variable distributed environment, the DSARR is suitable.

References

1. The MPEG home page, http://mpeg.telecomitalialab.com/
2. Sun, X.H., Rover, D.T.: Scalability of parallel algorithm-machine combinations, Parallel and Distributed Systems, IEEE Transactions, Vol. 5(6). (1994) 599-613
3. Shen, K., Rowe, L. A. and Delp, E. J.: A Parallel Implementation of an MPEG1 Encoder: Faster than Real-Time!, the SPIE Conference on Digital Video Compression (1995)
4. Foster, I.: Designing and Building Parallel Programs, Addison-Wesley (1995)
5. Bilas, A., Fritts, J. and Singh, J. P.: Real time parallel MPEG-2 decoding in software. 11th International Parallel Processing Symposium (1997)
6. Shanableh T., Ghanbari, M.: Transcoding Architectures for DCT-Domain Heterogeneous Video Transcoding. Proc. IEEE Int. Conf. Image Processing (2001) 433-436
7. Lin, C.-W., Lee, Y.-R.: Fast Algorithms for DCT Domain Video Transcoding. Proc. IEEE Int. Conf. Image Processing (2001) 421-424
8. Hwang, H.-C. and Kim, D.-G.: An Efficient Requantization for Transcoding of MPEG Video. ITC-CSCC, vol 2, (2002) 1223-1226

A Communication-Induced Checkpointing and Asynchronous Recovery Algorithm for Multithreaded Distributed Systems*

Tongchit Tantikul and D. Manivannan

Computer Science Department, University of Kentucky, Lexington, KY 40506
ttant0@netlab.uky.edu, mani@cs.uky.edu

Abstract. Checkpointing and recovery in traditional distributed systems is relatively well established. However, checkpointing and recovery in multithreaded distributed systems has not been studied in the literature. Using the traditional checkpointing and recovery algorithms in multithreaded systems leads to false causality problem and high checkpointing overhead. The checkpointing algorithm is implemented at the process level to reduce number of checkpoints and the recovery algorithm is implemented at the thread level which minimizes the false causality problem. The algorithm also takes advantage of the communication-induced checkpointing method to reduce the message overhead.

Keywords: Distributed checkpointing, Communication-induced checkpointing, Fault-tolerance, Multithreaded distributed system, Asynchronous recovery.

1 Introduction

Checkpointing is the activity of saving the state of computation to stable storage. When a process fails, the recovery algorithm uses checkpoints to restore the system to a consistent global checkpoint. Applying the traditional checkpointing methods for multithreaded systems without modification has some problems. First, when we apply the traditional checkpointings to multithreaded computations by replacing the checkpointing unit from processes to threads, each individual thread is treated as a process. It increases the number of checkpoints to be proportional to the number of threads. Larger number of checkpoints require larger stable storage and slows down the normal computation. Second, when we apply checkpointings of non-threaded distributed systems directly in multithreaded systems, processes take checkpoints which contain states of all their threads. When a failure occurs, the processes and all their threads roll back to the checkpoints taken at the process level. This approach leads to the problem of false causality between threads within a process. The false causality problem occurs when some threads that do not depend on the failed processes

---

* This work was in part supported by a CAREER grant #CCR-9983584 and grant # IIS-0414791 from the US National Science Foundation.

are forced to roll back unnecessarily. Thus, traditional algorithms are unsuitable for multithreaded systems. To overcome these issues, a balanced approach has been proposed by Damani et. al. [1]. The balanced approach takes checkpoints at the process level and rollback is done at the thread level. Taking checkpoints at process level reduces the number of checkpoints. When a failure occurs, each individual thread can be rolled back independently. Threads whose state depend on the failed process directly or indirectly need to roll back, whereas threads whose state do not depend on the failed process need not rollback. It eliminates false causality problem. In coordinated checkpointing, all processes are coordinated to determine when to take checkpoints so that a globally consistent set of checkpoints is always maintained in the system [2, 3]. This approach incurs extra message overhead during checkpointing and could suspend the processes until the checkpointing is finished[2]. Processes can take checkpoints independently in uncoordinated approach [4]. Some checkpoints might become useless because they cannot be combined with other checkpoints to create a consistent global checkpoint and can create a domino effect during recovery. A communication-induced checkpointing algorithm overcomes the drawbacks of coordinated and uncoordinated checkpointing. A process can take checkpoints independently. But it also forces processes to take additional checkpoints to make all checkpoints useful [5]. So the number of useless checkpoints is minimized or eliminated. We present a communication-induced checkpointing and recovery algorithm that is suitable for multithreaded systems. The balanced approach of the checkpointing algorithm takes checkpoints at the process level, thus minimizing checkpointing overhead. The recovery algorithm minimizes the false causality problem by rolling back only selected threads when a failure occurs and the recovery method is fully asynchronous. A failed process rolls back to its latest checkpoint and continues the computation as normal without waiting for the threads of different processes to finish their rollbacks.

2   System Model

A distributed computation consists of N processes running concurrently [5]. Each process has a number of threads and a number of shared objects. Processes communicate with each other by message passing. Message passing is the way that threads of different processes communicate. Threads of the same process communicate through shared objects. Processes do not share a global memory or a global physical clock. We assume that messages are not lost, altered, or spuriously introduced. Processes are fail-stop. All failures are detected immediately and result in halting failed process and initiating recovery action [6]. When a thread fails, the process and other peer threads also fail because they share the same address space. A process local checkpoint contains the local state of the process and all its threads. During rollback, the thread state can be extracted from the checkpoint. Each thread can roll back individually and has no effect to other threads or shared objects whose state does not depend on the rolled back state. The states of threads on different processes depend on one another due to interprocess communication. The states of threads of the same process depend on one another due to shared objects. The dependency between threads due to shared objects happens when one thread sends a message to the shared object by method invocation and then another thread retrieves the return value of the method from it. Each share object is modeled as a special thread and we handle the shared object accesses as a type of message passing.

Consistent Global Checkpoint

Definition 1. *A set* $S = \{\ C_0, C_1, ..., C_{N-1}\}$ *of* N *checkpoints, one for each process, is said to be a* **consistent global checkpoint** *if* $C_p \not\xrightarrow{hb} C_q$ *for all* p, q, $0 \leq p, q \leq N - 1$. *Here,* $\xrightarrow{hb}$ *denotes the Lamport's happened before relation* [7].

3 A Communication-Induced Checkpointing and Asynchronous Recovery Algorithm

3.1 A Communication-Induced Checkpointing Algorithm

The checkpointing algorithm consists of two parts, process level checkpointing and thread triggered checkpointing. Each process independently takes checkpoints called *basic checkpoints* at every some time interval and can also be forced to take a checkpoint called *forced checkpoint*. When threads receive some messages, they trigger their processes to take a force checkpoint when the message reception is likely to make checkpoints useless. All checkpoints are part of a consistent global checkpoint.

Checkpointing Algorithm at Process P_i
Data Structures at Process P_i
$pIndex_i := 0;$ //The sequence number of the latest checkpoint C at P_i.
$next_i := 1;$ //The sequence number to be assigned to the next basic checkpoint.
When it is time for Process P_i to increment $next_i$
$next_i := next_i + 1;$ //$next_i$ is incremented periodically.
When it is time for Process P_i to take a basic checkpoint
If $next_i > pIndex_i$ then Checkpoint($next_i$);
Checkpoint(*index*)   //Checkpoint function of Process P_i.
If a checkpoint with sequence number $\geq index$ does not exist **then**
   Take checkpoint C and assign sequence number (*index*) to it;
   $pIndex_i := index;$

Checkpointing Algorithm at Thread T_{ix}

Data Structure at Thread T_{ix}
$tIndex_{ix} := 0;$ //Sequence number of P_i current checkpoint when T_{ix} received M.

When Thread T_{ix} sends a message M to Thread T_{jy} of different process ($i \neq j$)
$M.index := pIndex_i$; //Append the current checkpoint sequence number to M.
$Send(M)$;
When Thread T_{ix} sends a message M to Thread T_{iy} of the same process
$Send(M)$;
When Thread T_{ix} receives a message M from Thread T_{jy} of different process ($i \neq j$)
If $M.index > pIndex_i$ **then**   //If checkpoint number received is $>$ the current one.
    Checkpoint($M.index$);   //then take a new checkpoint at process level.
    $tIndex_{ix} := pIndex_i$;   //Update $tIndex_{ix}$ to P_i new sequence number.
else if $M.index <= pIndex_i$ **then**
    If $tIndex_{ix} < pIndex_i$ **then** $tIndex_{ix} := pIndex_i$;
Process the message;
When Thread T_{ix} receives a message M from Thread T_{iy} of the same process
If $tIndex_{ix} < pIndex_i$ **then** $tIndex_{ix} := pIndex_i$;
Process the message;

An Explanation of Checkpointing Algorithm

When P_i starts, it takes the first checkpoint with sequence number 0, sets $pIndex_i$ to 0. $pIndex_i$ represents the sequence number of the latest checkpoint of P_i and can be accessed globally by all its threads. Then it sets $next_i$ to 1. $next_i$ is a sequence number to be assigned to the next checkpoint of P_i. Processes take basic checkpoints periodically. The time interval for taking basic checkpoints by each process is chosen at the convenience of each process. P_i increments $next_i$ periodically. $next_i$ helps to keep the sequence number of the latest checkpoints of all the processes close to each other. When it is time to take a basic checkpoint, it skips taking the checkpoint if $next_i \leq pIndex_i$ because P_i took a forced checkpoint with sequence number $\geq next_i$ as a result of the reception of a message from a process that has already taken a checkpoint with sequence number $\geq next_i$. This can reduce the total number of checkpoints. Each checkpoint contains the state of P_i and all its threads. T_{ix} of P_i initializes $tIndex_{ix}$ to 0. $tIndex_{ix}$ is the index number that represents the checkpoint interval of P_i from which T_{ix} has received a message so far. $tIndex_{ix}$ is updated to the latest checkpoint sequence number of P_i, when T_{ix} receives M from a thread of the same or different process. So if the sender of M fails and has undone the sending of M by rolling back beyond the send event of M, T_{ix} can determine from the value of $tIndex_{ix}$ whether it depends on the state of the failed process or not. If it does, then it rolls back. When T_{ix} of P_i sends M to another thread of a different process, it piggybacks $pIndex_i$ with M to help the receiver to decide whether or not to take a forced checkpoint. If the sequence number appended to M is $>$ current checkpoint sequence number of the receiver, then it forces the process to take checkpoint before processing M. But when it sends M to another thread of the same process, it does not attach $pIndex_i$ to M, because $pIndex_i$ is a global variable of P_i and can be accessed by all its threads. When T_{ix} of P_i receives M from another thread of a different process and if $M.index > pIndex_i$, it notifies

P_i to take a forced checkpoint with sequence number equal to $M.index$ and sets $tIndex_{ix}$ to the new checkpoint sequence number of P_i. When T_{ix} receives M from another thread of the same processes, it compares $tIndex_{ix}$ and $pIndex_i$. If $tIndex_{ix} < pIndex_i$, it updates $tIndex_{ix}$ to $pIndex_i$.

3.2 An Asynchronous Recovery Algorithm

We assume that if T_{ix} fails, then P_i also fails because of sharing address space and when a process fails, no other process fails, until the system is restored to a consistent global checkpoint. When T_{ix} fails, P_i rolls back to its latest checkpoint with sequence number n, and P_i sends rollback requests to all other processes about its failure. Then P_i can resume its normal computation immediately and does not need to wait for other processes to finish their rollbacks. Upon receiving the rollback request, P_j ($j \neq i$) notifies its threads about the failure. Each thread determines based on the message receptions whether to roll back or not.

Recovery Algorithm at Process P_i

Additional Data Structures at Process P_i
$pInc_i := 0$;   //The current rollback incarnation number known to P_i.
$recIndex_i := 0$;   //The latest recovery line number known to P_i.
When a thread of Process P_i fails
$pInc_i := pInc_i + 1$;   //Increment the incarnation number.
$recIndex_i := pIndex_i$;   //Update recovery line number to current sequence number.
Restore the latest checkpoint C_{pIndex_i};
set $tIndex$ of all its threads to $pIndex_i$;
send $rollback(pInc_i, recIndex_i)$ to all other processes;
continue as normal;
When Process P_j receives $rollback(pInc_i, recIndex_i)$ from Process P_i
If $pInc_i > pInc_j$ **then**
   $recIndex_j := recIndex_i$;
   $pInc_j := pInc_i$;
   If $pIndex_j < recIndex_j$ **then**
      Checkpoint($recIndex_j$);   //Take a new checkpoint to form the recovery line.
   else send $T\_RollbackRequest$ to all its threads;
else Ignore the rollback message;

Recovery Algorithm at Thread T_{ix}

When Thread T_{jy} receives $T\_RollbackRequest$ from process P_j
If $tIndex_{jy} \geq recIndex_j$ **then**
   Find the earliest checkpoint C with sequence number $>= recIndex_j$;
   Thread T_{jy} rolls back to checkpoint C;
   Update $tIndex_{jy}$ to the sequence number of checkpoint C;
continue as normal;

An Explanation of Recovery Algorithm

In addition to the data structures in the checkpointing algorithm, P_i has two more variables $pInc_i$ and $recIndex_i$, which are kept in the stable storage. When one of P_i's threads fails, P_i increments the incarnation number $pInc_i$ and sets the recovery line number $recIndex_i$ to its $pIndex_i$. Then it restores the latest checkpoint and updates $tIndex$ of all its threads to $pIndex_i$. After that it sends the rollback request with $pInc_i$ and $recIndex_i$ to all other processes. When P_j receives a rollback request $rollback(pInc_i, recIndex_i)$ from P_i, first it compares its own incarnation number $pInc_j$ with incarnation number of P_i ($pInc_i$). If $pInc_i > pInc_j$, it means that P_i has started the recovery with incarnation number $pInc_i$ and P_j has not known about this recovery yet. So P_j starts its rollback procedure by updating $pInc_j$ to $pInc_i$ and $recIndex_j$ to $recIndex_i$ and P_j sends roll back requests $T\_RollbackRequest$ to all its threads. If $pInc_i \leq pInc_j$, then P_j ignores the rollback request message because P_j already knew about the failure of this incarnation. When T_{jy} receives $T\_RollbackRequest$ from P_j, it compares $tIndex_{jy}$ with $recIndex_j$. If $tIndex_{jy} \geq recIndex_j$ meaning that T_{jy} depends on the failed process directly or indirectly, then T_{jy} rolls back to the earliest checkpoint C whose sequence number is $\geq recIndex_j$ and sets its $tIndex_{jy}$ to the sequence number of checkpoint C. Otherwise, T_{jy} does not roll back.

In Fig. 1, P_0, P_1 and P_2 take basic checkpoints every t time units. T_{02} sends M_1 to T_{10} and piggies back $pIndex_0=1$ with M_1. When T_{10} receives M_1, it checks if it needs to take a forced checkpoint or directly process M_1. $M_1.index = 1$ which is equal to $pIndex_1=1$, so P_1 does not take a forced checkpoint. T_{10} updates $tIndex_{10}$ to 1 and processes M_1. When T_{11} receives M_2, P_1 took a checkpoint with sequence number 1 and $pIndex_1 = 1$. So T_{11} updates its $tIndex_{11}$ to 1. M_6 forces T_{20} to notify P_2 to take a forced checkpoint with sequence number 2 before processing M_6 because $M_6.index = 2$ and $pIndex_2(=1) < 2$ while receiving M_6. T_{20} updates its $tIndex_{20}$ to 2. Similarly, M_7 and M_8 also make T_{10} to notify P_1 to take forced checkpoints with sequence number 3 and 4 respectively. Suppose T_{00}

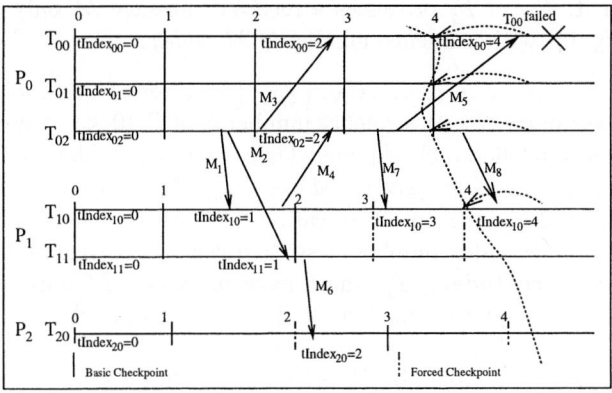

Fig. 1. Checkpointing and Recovery Algorithm

fails at X points in Fig. 1. Then, P_0 starts the recovery process and increments $pInc_0$ to 1, sets $recIndex_0$ to 4, restores it latest checkpoint with sequence number 4, sets $tIndex$ of its threads to 4, and sends $rollback(1,4)$ to P_1 and P_2. When P_1 receives $rollback(1,4)$, it sets its $pInc_1$ to 1 and $recIndex_1$ to 4. Then it sends $T\_RollbackRequest$ to T_{10} and T_{11}. T_{10} rolls back to the latest checkpoint C with sequence number 4 because T_{10} has received M_8 from T_{02}. T_{11} does not roll back because it does not depend on P_0. When P_2 receives $rollback(1,4)$ from P_0, P_2's latest checkpoint has sequence number 3 which is less than the recovery line number ($= 4$) which means that P_2 does not depend on P_0, so it does not roll back and instead takes a forced checkpoint to form the consistent global checkpoint.

Correctness of the Recovery Algorithm

Our recovery algorithm rolls back a failed thread and other threads that depend on its current state directly or indirectly to a consistent global checkpoint. After rollback, all threads restore the system to a consistent global checkpoint.

Theorem 1. *Suppose T_{ix} fails, then P_i rolls back to its latest checkpoint and sends $rollback(pInc_i, recIndex_i)$ to all other processes. Then the checkpoints to which threads of all other processes roll back form a consistent global checkpoint.*

Observation 1. If T_{jx} of P_j rolls back to checkpoint C with sequence number q, as a result of the reception of $rollback(pInc_i, recIndex_i)$ message sent by P_i ($i \neq j$), then there exists a checkpoint C of P_j that has sequence number $q \geq recIndex_i$ and all checkpoints taken by P_j prior to checkpoint C with sequence number q have sequence numbers less than $recIndex_i$.

Observation 2. For any M sent by T_{jx} of P_j, ($send(M) \xrightarrow{hb} C$ with sequence number q) $\Leftrightarrow$ ($M.Index < q$).

Observation 3. For any M received by T_{jx} of P_j, ($receive(M) \xrightarrow{hb} C$ with sequence number q) $\Rightarrow$ ($M.Index < q$). The converse is not necessarily true.

Observation 4. T_{jx} of P_j processes a received message M only after P_j had taken a checkpoint with sequence number $\geq M.Index$.

Proof. Define $S = \{C_{0,q_0}, C_{1,q_1}, ..., C_{N-1,q_{N-1}}\}$ as a set of checkpoints and C_{i,q_i} denotes the checkpoint C with sequence number q_i of P_i ($0 \leq i \leq N-1$). Suppose S is not a consistent global checkpoint. Thus, there exist M sent by T_{ix} to T_{jy} with $send(M) \notin C_{i,q_i}$, but $receive(M) \in C_{j,q_j}$. By construction timestamp, $C_{i,q_i} \leq M.index < C_{j,q_j}$ (from Observation 2,3). All the checkpoints taken by P_i prior to C_{i,q_i} have index numbers less than $recIndex_i$ (from Observation 1). Since $M.index \geq recIndex_i$, T_{jx} must have processed M only after P_j took a checkpoint with sequence number $\geq M.Index$ (from Observation 4). And $receive(M) \in C_{j,q_j}$, M must have been received by T_{jy} before C_{j,q_j} was taken. Hence there exists C_{j,q'_j} taken by P_j prior to C_{j,q_j} has a sequence number $q'_j \geq recIndex_i$. So this is contradict to our assumption. Hence, the theorem.

Table 1. Comparison with related work

	Required Message Ordering	Asynchronous	Maximum Rollbacks per Failure	Special Messages	Message Overhead	Space Overhead	False Causality
MS [5] Process-centric	None	Yes	1	No	$O(1)$	$O(N)$	Yes
MS [5] Thread-centric	None	Yes	1	No	$O(1)$	$O(NM)$	No
DG [1]	None	Yes	1	No	$O(N)$	$O(N)$	No
KND [8]	None	No	1	Yes	$O(N)$	$O(NM+J)$	No
Our algorithm	None	Yes	1	No	$O(1)$	$O(N)$	No

N is the number of processes in the system. M is the average number of threads in a process. J is the average number of objects.

4 Comparison with Existing Work

Table 1 gives the comparison of our algorithm with existing checkpointing and recovery algorithms. The *process-centric* approach applies the traditional checkpointing algorithm to multithreaded systems in the process level [1]. Applying Manivannan and Singhal algorithm (MS) [5] directly in multithreaded system creates the false causality problem. The approach that applies the traditional distributed algorithm at the thread level is called *thread-centric* approach [1]. Applying MS algorithm [5] by a thread-centric approach increases the number of checkpoints and space overhead. Damani and Garg (DG) [1] present a balanced approach. Their algorithm extends the optimistic message logging algorithm and is based on the notion of *fault tolerant vector clock*. The message size overhead is $O(N)$; since they piggyback the vector clock with the application messages. Kasbekar, Narayanan and Das (KND)[8] proposed a selective checkpointing and rollback method. The algorithm is synchronous, requires special messages to coordinate the checkpointing and the computation is blocked during checkpointing. The space overhead is $O(NM+J)$. Our algorithm is the first communication-induced method for multithreaded systems. The recovery algorithm is asynchronous and does not require messages to be ordered. It does not use vector clocks for tracking dependency between checkpoints and results in very low message overhead. The overhead to piggyback extra information with the application messages is $O(1)$. It performs the rollback at the thread level and does not suffer from the false causality problem. The space overhead is $O(N)$.

5 Conclusion

Traditional checkpointing algorithms are not suitable to multithreaded systems because they create the false causality problem between threads of a process and increasing number of checkpoints. Our algorithm is designed based on advantages of communication-induced checkpointing that has very low space overhead and message overhead. The checkpointing is handled at the process level which can reduce the number of checkpoints. The recovery reduces the false causality problem and a failed process rolls back to the latest checkpoint and other threads that depend on the failed process roll back to the consistent global checkpoint.

References

1. Damani, O.P., Tarafdar, A., Garg, V.K.: Optimistic recovery in multi-threaded distributed systems. In: Symposium on Reliable Distributed Systems. (1999) 234–243
2. Koo, R., Toueg, S.: "Checkpointing and Roll-back Recovery for Distributed Systems". IEEE Transactions on Software Engineering **SE-13** (1987) 23–31
3. Li, K., Naughton, J.F., Plank, J.S.: "Checkpointing Multicomputer Applications". In: Proceedings of 10th Symposium on Reliable Distributed Systems. (1991) 2–11
4. Bhargava, B., Lian, S.R.: "Independent Checkpointing and Concurrent Rollback for Recovery in Distributed Systems–An Optimistic Approach.". In: Proceedings of 7th IEEE Symposium on Reliable Distributed Systems. (1988) 3–12
5. Manivannan, D., Singhal, M.: "A Low-overhead Recovery Technique using Quasi-synchronous Checkpointing". In: Proceedings of the 16th IEEE International Conference on Distributed Computing Systems, Hong Kong (1996) 100–107
6. Strom, R.E., Yemini, S.: "Optimistic Recovery in Distributed Systems". ACM Transactions on Computer Systems **3** (1985) 204–226
7. Lamport, L.: "Time, clocks and ordering of events in distributed systems". Communications of the ACM **21** (1978) 558–565
8. Kasbekar, M., Das, C.: Selective checkpointing and rollbacks in multithreaded distributed systems. In: The 21st International Conference on Distributed Computing Systems. (2001) 39–46

A Parallel Routing Algorithm on 2-Circulant Networks Employing the Hamiltonian Circuit Latin Square

Youngjoo Cho, Dongkil Tak, and Ilyong Chung

Department of Computer Science, Chosun University, Kwangju, Korea
iyc@chosun.ac.kr

Abstract. In this paper, we investigate the routing of a message on circulant networks, that is a key to the performance of this network. We would like to transmit 2k packets from a source node to a destination node simultaneously along paths on G(n; $\pm s_1, \pm s_2, ..., \pm s_k$), where the ith packet will traverse along the ith path ($1 \leq i \leq 2k$). In oder for all packets to arrive at the destination node quickly and securely, the ith path must be node-disjoint from all other paths. For construction of these paths, employing the Hamiltonian Circuit Latin Square(HCLS) we present $O(n^2)$ parallel routing algorithm on circulant networks.

1 Introduction

Double-loop[1] and 2-circulant networks(2-CN)[2] are widely used in the design and implementation of local area networks and parallel processing architectures. These networks are defined as follows. Let n, s_1, s_2 be positive integers such that $0 < s_1 < s_2 < n/2$. A double-loop network is a directed graph G(n; s_1, s_2), where n nodes labeled with integers modulo n, and 2 links per vertex such that each node i is adjacent to the 2 other nodes i+s_1, i+s_2. In the undirected case, which is known as a 2-circulant network and is denoted by G(n; $\pm s_1, \pm s_2$). It is well known that G(n; s_1, s_2) and G(n; $\pm s_1, \pm s_2$) are connected iff gcd(n, s_1, s_2) =1. The routing of message is thus a key to the performance of such networks. There are routing algorithms using well-known methods, such as the Shortest Path Algorithm(the Forward Algorithm)[3], the Backward Algorithm[4], the Spanning Tree Algorithm[8]. These algorithms provide for only sequential transmission, from the source node to the desired node in a short time. We now look for algorithms that are capable of handling, multiple data items simultaneously transmitted from the staring(source) node to the destination node. There are a few algorithms on the n-dimensional hypercube network[5]-[6] that allow us to locate n disjoint paths such as the Hamiltonian path Algorithm [9], the Rotation Algorithm using Tree Structure[7], the Disjoint Path Algorithm[7], and the Routing Algorithms[9]. In this paper, we propose the algebraic approach to the

---

* Corresponding Author: Ilyong Chung(iyc@chosun.ac.kr). This study was partially supported by research funds from Chosun University, 2004.

routing of message on the G(n; $\pm s_1, \pm s_2$). As described above, four packets are simultaneously transmitted from the starting(source) node to the destination node. In this case, the ith packet is sent along the ith path from the starting node to the destination node. In order for all packets to arrive at the destination node quickly and securely, the ith path must be node-disjoint from all other paths.

2 Design of the Hamiltonian Circuit Latin Square to the Parallel Routing Algorithm on 2-Circulant Networks

Let A and B be any two nodes on G(n; $\pm s_1, \pm s_2$). The paper's objective is to find algorithms that will facilitate the transmission of data from node A to B in that network. In order for the data to traverse from node A to node B, it must cross, successively, intermediate nodes along a path.

Definition 1: The routing function R for $\pm s_i$ is as follows:

$$R(A) = A \pm s_i \pmod{n}, \text{ where A is node address}$$

Node A is physically connected to 2k neighboring nodes and these paths are node-disjoint. Data is transmitted from source node along the ith path, which is physically connected to. The path above is selected by the routing function described in Definition 1. To do this, the relative address of starting node and destination node can be obtained below.

Definition 2: The relative address r of nodes A and B on G(n; $\pm s_1, \pm s_2$) is computed as the value of difference between A and B.

$$r = B\text{-}A$$

Let two addresses of node A and node B be 1 and 3. What is the relative address of two nodes? The value of the relative address is 2.

Definition 3: Let T(A,S) be the logical transmission path of data starting from node A to the destination node B, where S is a multiset and a sequence of operations, via which data can reach at the destination node. T(A,S) is determined by the order of the elements in the set S. between A and B.

The ith packet is transmitted along the ith path, the first intermediate node of which is obtained from applying the ith operation at a starting node and the last intermediate node transmits the packet to a destination node by applying the ith operation. In some cases, the two operations can be the same.

Definition 4: Let O^s be a set of operations occurring at a starting node when four packets are transmitted simultaneously and Let O^d be a set of operations occurring at a destination node when four packets arrive. These sets are defined as follows:

$O^s = \{s_1, -s_1, s_2, -s_2\}$
$O^d = \{p_1, p_2, p_3, p_4\}$
$O^s = O^d$

We now apply the HCLS(Hamiltonian Circuit Latin Square) to find a set of m shortest and node-disjoint paths.

Definition 5: The HCLS M^1 is constructed as follows: Given distinct m points $a_0, a_2, \ldots, a_{m-2}, a_{m-1}$, a Hamiltonian circuit $a_i \to a_j \to \ldots \to a_k \to a_i$ is randomly selected. On the circuit each row of M can be obtained from the Hamiltonian path, starting at any position $a_k (0 \le k \le m-1)$, under the condition that no two rows begin at the same position. If a Hamiltonian path is $a_i \to a_j \to \ldots \to a_k$, then the row obtained from it is $[a_i, a_j, \ldots, a_k]$.

From the definition of the HCLS given in Definition 5, the MHCM(Modified Hamiltonian Circuit Matrix) is constructed below.

Definition 6: Given the HCLS $M^1 = [a_{i,j}]$, the MHCM M^2 is constructed as follows: $M^2 = [A_{i,j}]$, $A_{i,j} = \{a_{i,0}, a_{i,1}, \ldots, a_{i,j-1}, a_{i,j}\}$, $0 \le i,j \le m-1$.

We now propose a parallel routing algorithm that generates a set of m minimum-distance and node-disjoint paths for the network.

CN_Routing_Algorithm

    A ← an address of a starting node A
    B ← an address of a destination node B
    O^s ← a set of operations occurring at a starting node A
    O^d ← a set of operations requisite for reaching to a destination node B
begin

(1) Compute the relative address R of nodes A and B; R = B-A
(2) Using the relative address R, a sequence S of operations to arrive at node B in a short time are produced
(3) In order to design a set of shortest and node-disjoint paths, find a set S_1 of distinct elements in S. A set of $|S_1|$ shortest and node-disjoint paths are generated. Each path of length is $|S|$,
    (3-1) Using the set S_1, (n×n) HCLS is constructed, where n = $|S_1|$.
    (3-2) Operations in the ith row of the HCLS are performed for traversal of the ith packet and the remaining operations in S should be executed at the point except the first and the last points.
    (3-3) $O^s \leftarrow O^s - S_1$ and $O^d \leftarrow O^d - S_1$.
(4) Construct two node-disjoint paths, each path has length $|S|+2$.
    (4-1) If $O^s = \phi$, the process is finished.
    (4-2) If a set of $\{s_i, -s_i\}$ is found in O^s, then these operations are performed at the first and the last steps of two paths newly designed, and operations in S at the middle steps of them, otherwise go to (5).
    (4-3) $O^s \leftarrow O^s - \{s_i, -s_i\}$, $O^d \leftarrow O^d - \{s_i, -s_i\}$ and go to (4-1).

(5) Generate the remaining paths.
   (5-1) If $O^s = \phi$, the process is finished.
   (5-2) Produce a sequence S_2 of minimum number of operations by reducing the size of $SU\{-s_i,-s_i\}$, $s_i \in O^s$.
   (5-3) Operation g_i is performed at the first and the last steps at traversal and operations of S_2 are executed at the middle steps.
   (5-4) $O^s \leftarrow O^s$ - $\{s_i\}$, $O^d \leftarrow O^d$ - $\{s_i\}$ and go to (5-1).

end.

3 Conclusion

In this paper, we present the algorithm that generates a set of 2k shortest and node-disjoint paths on G(n; $\pm s_1, \pm s_2, ..., \pm s_k$), employing the Hamiltonian Circuit Latin Square(HCLS). Even n and k are fixed values, the algorithm can be easily extended on arbitrary circulant networks. Important steps for determining time complexity requisite for the algorithm are two things. One is to design the HCLS, which needs O(n). The other is to execute Step (5) of $CN\_Routing\_$Algorithm, which requires $O(n^2)$. Therefore, we can create $O(n^2)$ parallel routing algorithm for constructing 2k shortest and node-disjoint paths.

References

1. Bermond, J., Comellas, F., Hsu, D., "Distributed Loop Computer Networks: A Survey," J. Parallel and Distributed Computing, Academic Press, no. 24, pp.2-10, 1995.
2. Park, J., "Cycle Embedding of Faulty Recursive Circulants," J. of Korea Info. Sci. Soc., vol.31, no. 2, pp. 86-94, 2004.
3. Basse, S., Computer Algorithms : Introduction to Design and Analysis, Addition-Wesley, Reading, MA, 1978.
4. Stallings, W., Data and Computer Communications. Macmillan Publishing Company, New York, 1985.
5. Bae, M. and Bose, B., "Edge Disjoint Hamiltonian Cycles in k-ary n-cubes and Hypercubes," IEEE Trans. Comput., vol. 52, no. 10, pp. 1259-1270, 2003.
6. Thottethodi, M., Lebeck, A., and Mukherjee, S., "Exploiting Global Knowledge to Achieve Self-Tuned Congetion Control for k-ary n-cube Networks," IEEE Trans. Parallel and Distributed Systems, vol 15, no. 3, pp. 257-272, 2004.
7. Johnson, S.L. and Ho, C-T., "Optimum Broadcasting and Personalized Communication in Hypercube," IEEE Trans. Comput., vol. 38, no. 9, pp. 1249-1268, Seep. 1989.
8. Rabin, M.O., "Efficient Dispersal of Information for Security, Load Balancing, and Fault Tolerance," J. ACM, vol. 36, no. 2, pp. 335-348, Apr. 1989.

Parallel Algorithms for the Process of the Biorthogonal Wavelet Transform

HyungJun Kim

Graduate School of Information Security, Korea University,
1 5-ga Anam-dong Sungbuk-ku, Seoul 136-701, Korea
hyungjun@korea.ac.kr

Abstract. We present parallel algorithms for the process of the biorthogonal wavelet transform(BWT). We have constructed processing elements (PEs) for the decomposition and reconstruction of the BWT to minimize computational operations. They can be performed using only integer shift and superposition operations; therefore, they may be applied to the implementation of image compression standards based on BWT, such as JPEG2000.

Keywords: Wavelet transform, Parallel algorithm, JPEG2000.

1 Introduction

The performance of image compression using BWTs is superior to orthogonal wavelet transforms[1]. However, wavelet transforms have many taps and require floating point multiplication operations; thus, the derived compression systems often require long processing time. Although the lifting scheme provides insight into the construction of the wavelet transform, it is comprised of three steps: Split, Predict, and Update[2]. For image compression and real-time motion video display, it is critical that all phases of computation be performed as efficiently as possible to maximize image quality and frame rate. To do this, a common technique is to avoid multiplication and division operations wherever possible or to implement them as simple shift operations. The wavelet coefficients chosen for the proposed algorithms of decomposition and reconstruction processes are intentionally defined in this manner.

2 The Chosen Biorthogonal Wavelet Transform

In biorthogonal filter banks, one choice is

$$G_0(z) = \frac{1}{2\sqrt{2}}(z + 2 + z^{-1}), \quad H_0(z) = \frac{1}{4\sqrt{2}}(-z^2 + 2z + 6 + 2z^{-1} - z^{-2}). \quad (1)$$

The chosen filter set is the same as one of LeGall's factorized product filters[3] and is also adopted by the JPEG2000 still-image compression standard[4]. We

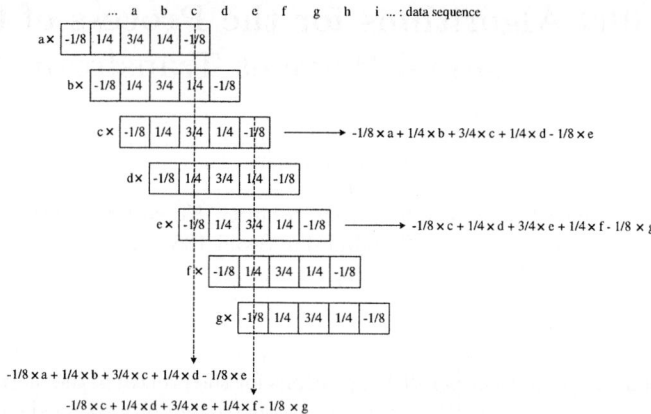

Fig. 1. An example of convolution and shift/superposition operations using a 5-tap lowpass filter for the decomposition process

avoid the factor $1/\sqrt{2}$ in the expressions by multiplying $1/\sqrt{2}$ in the analysis filters and $\sqrt{2}$ in the synthesis filters in order to create filter banks with dyadic rational valued coefficients for integer arithmetic operations. For discrete data, the wavelet transform gives the decomposition as follows

$$s_{m,k} = \sum_n h_0(n-2k)s_{m-1,n}, \quad d_{m,k} = \sum_n h_1(n-2k)s_{m-1,n} \quad (2)$$

where h_0 and h_1 are the lowpass and highpass decomposition filters, respectively. The original data can be recursively reconstructed from

$$s_{m-1,n} = \sum_k g_0(n-2k)s_{m,k} + \sum_k g_1(n-2k)d_{m,k} \quad (3)$$

where g_0 and g_1 are the lowpass and highpass reconstruction filters, respectively.

3 Algorithms for the Decomposition and Reconstruction

We use an example of shift and superposition operations using a 5-tap lowpass filter for the decomposition process. First, consider a data sequence given by $\{..,a,b,c,d,e,f,..\}$ and a 5-tap lowpass filter, h_0. At each step the signal values are multiplied by the filter coefficients and the results are summed to produce the filtered output values as illustrated by the horizontal arrows in Fig. 1. At the next clock cycle, the result of the convolution should be skipped because of the 2 : 1 decimation characteristic of a wavelet transform. The same procedure can be repeated until the final data point is reached.

Alternatively, the computation may be proceeded efficiently by shift and superposition operations as follows. One data point(a for example), which is located at the index zero of the filter mask, can be fetched and then scaled. It

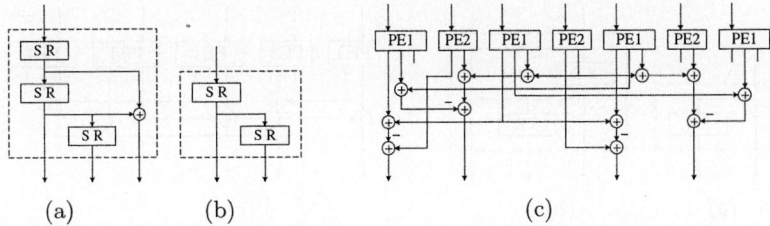

Fig. 2. (a) Even indexed filter(PE1), (b) Odd indexed filter(PE2), and (c) Parallel architecture for the 1-D decomposition process of the BWT

looks like the index zero value spreads out toward both ends of the filter and is weighted respectively by the filter coefficients. After five clock cycles, one specific column of all five intermediate data sets may be superimposed to obtain a value, shown by the first vertical arrow at the position of the input data point c, which is the same as what one would achieve from the regular convolution computation as explained previously. The same process may be repeated until one covers all the input data points in the sequence.

We split the filter into two parts, one for the even indexed coefficients and the other for the odd indexed coefficients. This splitting procedure is motivated by the inherent 2 : 1 decimation characteristic of a wavelet transform. For convenience, we refer to them as "even indexed" and "odd indexed" filters, respectively. The even indexed inputs are used only for the even indexed weights and the odd indexed inputs are used only for the odd indexed weights. Therefore, one may eliminate the redundant shift operations and accomplish efficient computation in the decomposition process of the BWT.

We constructed two PEs for the decomposition process of the BWT as shown in Fig. 2, where SR denotes a 1-bit shift-right register and $\oplus$ represents a 2-to-1 adder. Note that PEs for the even and the odd indexed filters are used for lowpass and highpass decomposition processes simultaneously. Parallel architecture for the decomposition process of the BWT is shown in Fig. 2. It can compute the odd indexed and the even indexed outputs for both lowpass and highpass processes simultaneously, at the rate of *two* data points per clock cycle T.

For the reconstruction process, consider again a data sequence given by $\{..,a,b,c,d,e,f,..\}$ and a 5-tap highpass filter, g_1. Because of the interpolation characteristic of a wavelet transform, a new data sequence $\{..,a,0,b,0,c,0,d,0,e,0,f,0,..\}$ is generated for convolution with the 5-tap filter. The lowpass and highpass data sequences are then combined for one level reconstruction.

Alternatively, the computation may be performed simply by shift and superposition operations as follows. One can fetch one data point(a for example), which is located at the index zero of the filter, and then scale it. At the next clock cycle, we do not need to calculate the intermediate data set since the input is zero. After four clock cycles, one superimposes the two intermediate data sets, except the two zero sets, which is the same result one would obtain using the regular convolution computation as explained previously.

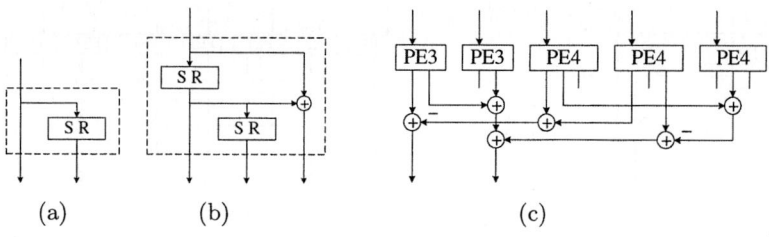

Fig. 3. (a) Lowpass filter(PE3), (b) Highpass filter(PE4), and (c) Parallel architecture for the 1-D reconstruction process of the BWT

Whereas in the regular convolution computation, even if many data points are zeroes, one must perform the convolution operation which is obviously a waste of time. In the shift and superposition operation case, if the index zero data value is zero, one may skip the whole shift and superposition operation. This method processes only the nonzero-valued pixels to minimize data access operations in performing the inverse transform. We constructed two PEs, each with lowpass and highpass filters for the reconstruction of the BWT as shown in Fig. 3. The proposed parallel architecture can compute both lowpass and highpass simultaneously. The reconstruction at one level is completed when lowpass and highpass reconstructed data sequences are superimposed.

4 Conclusions

In this paper we present parallel algorithms for the efficient computation of decomposition and reconstruction processes of BWT. Compared to the conventional wavelet transform method, the proposed parallel algorithms reduce the number of multiplications through bit-shift and addition operations by almost 30%. The proposed algorithms may be applied to the implementation of image compression standards based on BWT, such as JPEG2000.

References

1. Villasenor, J. D., Belzer, B., Liao, J.: Wavelet filter evaluation for image compression. IEEE Trans. Image Processing, **4** (1995) 1053–1060
2. Claypoole, R., Davis, G., Sweldens, W., Baraniuk., R.: Nonlinear wavelet transforms for image coding via lifting. IEEE Trans. Image Processing, **12** (2003) 1449–1459
3. LeGall, D., Tabatabai, A.: Sub-band coding of digital images using symmetric short kernel filters and arithmetic coding techniques. in IEEE Proc. Int. Conf. ASSP (1988) 761–764
4. Skodras, A., Christopoulos, C., Ebrahimi, T.: The JPEG 2000 still image compression standard. IEEE Signal Processing Magazine, **Sep.** (2001) 36–58

The Subgroup Method for Collective I/O

Kwangho Cha, Taeyoung Hong, and Jeongwoo Hong

Supercomputing Center, Korea Institute of Science and Technology Information,
52 Eoeun, Yu-seong, Daejon, 305-806 Korea
{khocha, tyhong, jwhong}@kisti.re.kr

Abstract. Because many scientific applications require large data processing, the importance of parallel I/O has been increasingly recognized. For collective I/O, one of the considerable features of parallel I/O, we suggest the subgroup method. It is the way of using collective I/O of MPI effectively in terms of application programs. From the experimental results, we could conclude that the subgroup method for collective I/O is more efficient than plain collective I/O.

1 Introduction

Because many scientific applications such as 'parallel out-of-core' require large data processing, parallel I/O of not only cluster systems but also parallel systems has received many attentions. The research about parallel I/O can be classified into the studies about parallel file system and parallel programming environment. This paper discusses collective I/O in terms of parallel programming environment such as MPI and suggests an effective way of using collective I/O which is named the subgroup method.

Collective I/O is a technique that handles discontiguous small requests from each computational nodes[1]. MPI I/O, one of the part of the MPI2, also defines collective I/O and MPI implementations such as MPICH[2] and LAM/MPI[3] provide this feature. This paper suggests a way of using collective I/O in terms of application programs, the subgroup method for collective I/O. The main concept of the subgroup method is that after splitting the entire processes group into several subgroups, only master nodes of each subgroup participate collective I/O. We tested subgroup method on the PVFS [4, 5] and the test result showed improved performance.

This paper is organized as follow. Section 2 introduces collective I/O as a related work. Section 3 describes the concept of the subgroup method. The test result of the subgroup method is described in section 4. Finally, we draw the conclusion in section 5.

2 Collective I/O

The studies about many parallel applications reported that data from each processes are stored noncontiguously in memory or file system and each process want to write or read their own data.[1, 6]. Collective I/O handles these requests efficiently by regarding separate and discontiguous I/O requests as a contiguous one. There are several implementations of collective I/O such as 2 phase I/O and disk direct I/O[6, 7].

MPI I/O defines some types of file operations such as collective, non-collective, blocking, non-blocking, and so on[8, 9]. Collective I/O of MPI I/O means all processes in the same communicator perform I/O operation in the same time. Before calling a collective I/O function, the filetype should be defined. The filetype indicates which portions of file can be accessed by the process and primitive and derived datatype are used to define the filetype. ROMIO[10] is the well known MPI I/O implementations and supports various kinds of file systems such as NFS and PVFS.

3 The Subgroup Method for Collective I/O

When collective I/O is performed, it is required that all processes exchange the information about I/O operations before executing collective write or collective read[6, 7]. In other words, collective I/O is based on collective communications among all processes in the group.

The subgroup method is a way of reducing the communication costs by decreasing the number of processes which exchange the I/O information. Like figure 1, the default communicator is divided into subgroups and only master processes of each subgroup participate collective I/O. They also collect or dispense data of their subgroup which should be written or read. In other words, in case of collective write, master processes gather data from their subgroup member and perform I/O function. For collective read, master processes scatter data to member nodes of their subgroup after I/O operation. Figure 2 shows the pseudo-code of the subgroup method. The primitive MPI function for manipulating communicators is used for generating subgroups and collective communications are used for gathering and distributing data within subgroup.

4 Performance Evaluation

To verify the performance of the subgroup method, we used 16 nodes cluster system with PVFS like table 1. To compare with the performance of non-collective

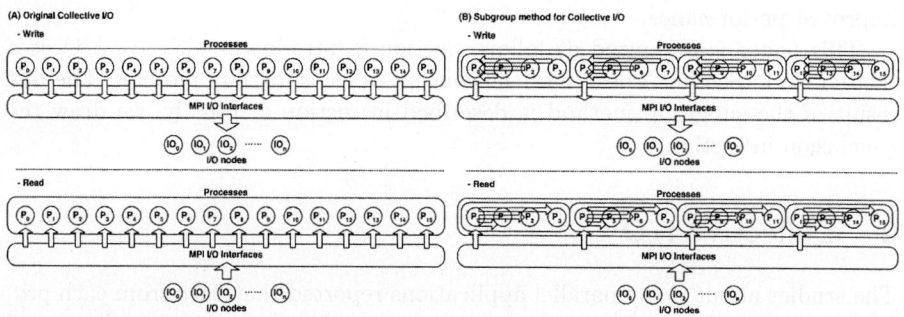

Fig. 1. The concept of original collective I/O and the subgroup method

```
/* Generate new communicator for subgroups */
MPI_Comm_split(MPI_COMM_WORLD, COLOR, KEY, &NEW_COMM);
MPI_Comm_rank(NEW_COMM, &new_rank);

/* Generate new communicator for the master processes */
if(master_process) set io_color;
MPI_Comm_split(MPI_COMM_WORLD, io_color, SUB_KEY, &IO_COMM);
    ..........
if (root_process) {
/* File Open & Generate filetype */
}
----------------------------------------------------------------
/****** READ *******/               | /****** WRITE ******/
if (master_process) {                | MPI_Gather(..., NEW_COMM);
/* Perform collective read operation */ | if (master_process) {
    MPI_File_set_view(....);         | /* Perform collective write operation */
    MPI_File_read_all(....);         |     MPI_File_set_view(....);
}                                    |     MPI_File_write_all(....);
MPI_Scatter(..., NEW_COMM);          | }
----------------------------------------------------------------
if (root_process) MPI_File_close();
```

Fig. 2. The pseudo-code of the subgroup method

Table 1. The configuration of testbed

CPU	AMD Opteron 240	Network	Gigabit Ethernet
CPU/Node	2	OS	Linux 2.4.21
The Number of Nodes	16	File System	PVFS 1.6.0
Memory	1 GB	MPI Library	LAM/MPI 7.0.6

I/O, we also tested two kinds of it which use different communications for gathering or distributing data. The first one is based on point to point communication such as MPI_Send and MPI_Recv and the other is based on collective communication such as MPI_Gather and MPI_Scatter.

Figure 3 shows the result of our experiments. The performances of non-collective I/O are better then those of collective I/O, but as the number of processes and the data size for each I/O operation are increased, it showed performance degradation. Furthermore we observed that in some case the test program with non-collective I/O was stopped abnormally while those with collective I/O performed well. From the result, we could conclude that the subgroup method give improved and reliable performance as the number of process is increased.

5 Conclusion

We have studied efficient collective I/O of MPI and this paper explains the subgroup method for collective I/O. By comparing the performances of collective I/O on a cluster system, we can conclude that the subgroup method for collective I/O is more efficient than plain collective I/O and more reliable than non-collective I/O.

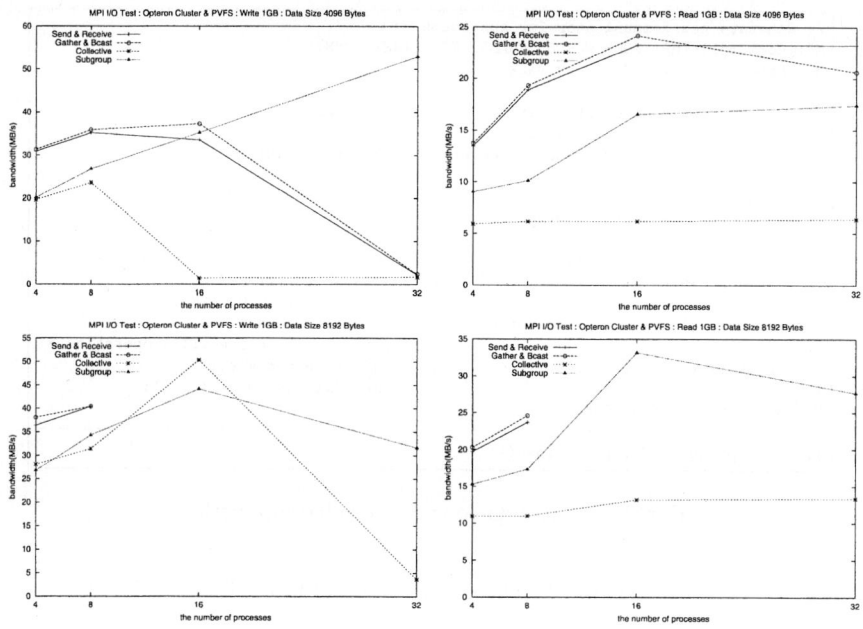

Fig. 3. The experimental results

References

1. John M. May, "Parallel I/O for High Performance Computing," *Morgan Kaufmann*, 2000.
2. MPICH-A Portable Implementation of MPI, http://www-unix.mcs.anl.gov/mpi/mpich
3. LAM/MPI Parallel Computing, http://www.lam-mpi.org
4. Avery Ching, Alok Choudhary, Wei-keng Liao, Rob Ross, and William Gropp, "Noncontiguous I/O through PVFS," *Proc. IEEE International Conference on Cluster Computing*, pp 405~414, 2002.
5. Philip H. Carns, Walter B. Ligon, III, Robert B. Ross, and Rajeev Thakur, "PVFS: A Parallel File System for Linux Clusters," *Proc. 4th Annual Linux Showcase and Conference*, pp 317~327, 2000.
6. David Kotz, "Disk-directed I/O for MIMD multiprocessors," *ACM Transactions on Computer Systems*, Vol. 15, No. 1, pp 41~74, Feb. 1997.
7. Rajesh Bordawekar, "Implementation of collective I/O in the Intel Paragon parallel file system: initial experiences," *Proc. 11th international conference on Supercomputing*, pp 20~27, 1997.
8. William Gropp, Ewing Lusk, and Rajeev Thakur, "Using MPI-2: Advanced Features of the Message Passing Interface," *The MIT Press*, 1999.
9. Hakan Taki and Gil Utard, "MPI-IO on a parallel file system for cluster of workstations," *Proc. 1st IEEE Computer Society International Workshop on Cluster Computing*, pp 150~157, 1999.
10. ROMIO: A High-Performance, Portable MPI-IO Implementation, http://www-unix.mcs.anl.gov/romio

Utilizing Dynamic Data Value Localities in Internal Variables

Shoichi Hirasawa and Kei Hiraki

Graduate School of Information Science and Technology, The University of Tokyo
{hirasawa, hiraki}@is.s.u-tokyo.ac.jp

Abstract. An effective approach to accelerate applications is to execute them in parallel. There are value localities in values of program variables. Data value reuse is able to enhance performance in applications by canceling same calculations. We propose the use of data value reuse and speculative parallelism with software to execute existing sequential applications in parallel. This study profiles value localities that exist in method arguments of benchmark programs, and evaluates performance improvements by applying data value reuse and speculative parallelism.

Keywords: Value locality, data value reuse, automatic parallel execution.

1 Introduction

A large part of enormous development of computer performance has come from the benefit of various forms of localities. When a program is running, there are value localities [2] in input values and output values of routines in the program. Some studies have explored speculative execution by predicting data values, and data value reuse [4] through the reuse of execution results. This paper proposes a novel speculative reuse method to exploit dynamic data value localities in applications by profiling. The method improves their performance through the use of value localities. We demonstrate the possibility of profiling to find high value localities in program methods. Using the value localities of such methods, we can obtain better performance from benchmark programs. We apply the method to benchmark programs and evaluate their respective performances. Section 2 describes speculative reuse. Section 3 evaluates our proposition. Section 4 shows related works and concludes.

2 Speculative Reuse

Data value reuse [4] is a method to improve performance using data value localities. It records input and output values of computation blocks. When the same computation block starts and it uses the same input values, we cancel the calculation and save execution time for it. Consider execution block A and execution block B as shown in Figure 1. If execution block A has the very same calculation, and the result is recorded (Hit) in a reuse table, we can cancel the calculation and begin executing block B with the recorded value. If the result of the same calculation does not exist in the reuse table (Miss), we must actually begin executing it. The following routine of data value reuse branches depending upon whether the data value reuse constitutes a Hit or a Miss. We can speculatively execute each branch by predicting the branch target.

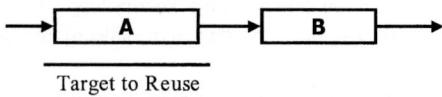

Fig. 1. Reuse the input and output values. Branches for hits and misses

2.1 Parallelization by Predicting Both Hit and Miss

Routines of data value reuse and actual calculation can be executed in parallel by predicting the branch of the data value reuse as a miss. In such a case, a rollback process is not needed because there are no data dependencies among them. Also, we can parallelize the routines of data value reuse and the following routine by predicting the branch of data value reuse as a hit, as shown in Figure 2. There is a data dependence because execution block B uses the result of the data value reuse. We have to execute the execution block B again with the correct input values if the speculative execution fails.

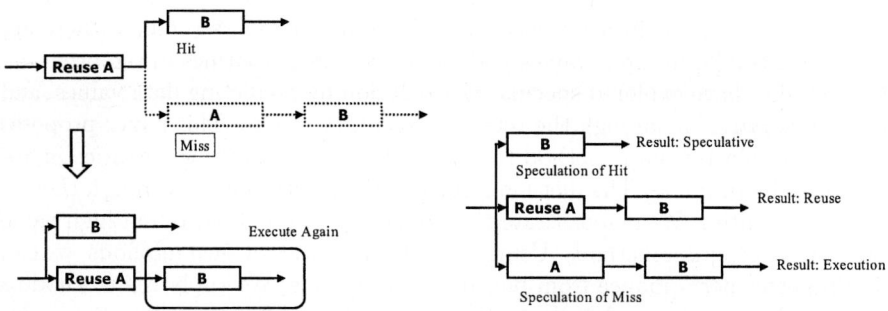

Fig. 2. Parallelized routines of reuse and the following execution block B

Fig. 3. Speculative reuse; speculatively execute both a hit and a miss of the reuse

We can execute both sides of the branch target and start both routines corresponding to the branch result as shown in Figure 3. We call this execution scheme "speculative reuse" because we speculatively execute the following routines of the data value reuse. If the reuse is eventually successful, we use the recorded result; if it fails, we must wait until the target routine ends and then use its result. These execution processes can be performed automatically using a

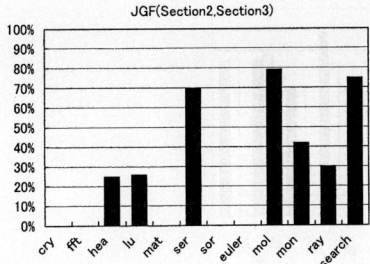 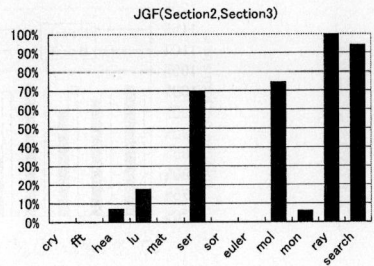

Fig. 4. Each bar shows the percentage of method arguments which have a high rate of values occurred more than once(over 90%)

Fig. 5. The percentages of method arguments which have over 90% values occurred more than once weighted by the total time of executions

speculative reuse library, which is introduced in the next section. We can achieve performance enhancement in applications without special hardwares by utilizing their high value localities.

3 Evaluation

We evaluated data value localities by profiling programs in Sections 2 and 3 of the Java Grande Forum Benchmark Suite (JGF). We developed a profiler with the Java Virtual Machine Profiler Interface (JVMPI) and the Java Virtual Machine Debug Interface (JVMDI). It record all argument values of all methods of each of the benchmark programs. We calculated the frequency of values that occurred more than once. The evaluation environment is Solaris 9, Sun Fire V880 (Ultra Sparc III 900 MHz*8 40 GB), and Sun JDK 1.4.2_03 (client VM).

Rate results of calculations for each program are presented in Figure 4. The method arguments which indicate the locality of over 90% occupy more than 60% of the entire method arguments in three applications: ser, mol, and search. In addition, We evaluated the rates of weighted localities according to how long a method requires to execute. We can elucidate value localities with this evaluation. Figure 5 shows the result. Our results showed that mol, ray and search have more than 70% of the weighted arguments show value localities of over 90%. Such percentages indicate that these applications are suitable for utilizing value localities.

By profiling, we choose one function that have the highest locality from each application, that is considered suitable for speculative reuse. We then rewrite it into two functions: one that has side effects and another that does not have side effects. We evaluate the speculative reuse performances by calling the method that does not have side effects with a software library which provides automatic creation of reuse table and threads for parallel execution. Rollback is not necessary and there is no illegal memory access because of this division and all stores are to local variables.

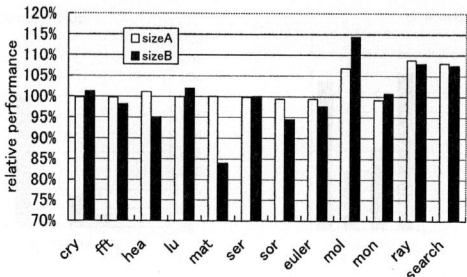

Fig. 6. Relative performances of speculative reuse applied to benchmark programs in the Java Grande Forum Benchmark Suite

We executed each program in two problem sizes. Figure 6 shows results of the original programs and the modified programs. Performance improvements are achieved in the modified programs using the speculative reuse function call. Also, we can find there is a relation between the results of profiled value localities and the performance enhancements.

4 Related Works and Conclusion

Steffan et al.[1] attempted to remove data dependencies between loop iterations and to execute them speculatively. Our proposal differs in the length of the target procedure. We execute more complex, time consuming procedures such as functions that appear in program sources. Oplinger et al.[3] evaluated speculative execution with simple prediction methods such as last value or stride value predictions. We can obtain information that is more accurate and speculatively execute functions more efficiently with accurate information because we reuse all execution data of the target function.

We have proposed a speculative reuse method with profiling for utilizing data value localities and executing sequential programs in parallel, thereby generating speculative parallelism. We profiled value localities in method arguments, and found that time weighted arguments that show over 90% value locality occupy more than 70% in three benchmark programs. The speculative reuse method reuse functions that take a long time to compute and hide overheads of reuse miss. Experimental results show that this method avoids the overhead associated with reuse. It obtained a maximum 14% performance enhancement without hardware support. Using data value localities, we can enhance parallelism and improve performance in programs without special hardware.

References

1. J G.Steffan and T C.Mowry. The potential for using thread-level data speculation to facilitate automatic parallelization. In *the Fourth International Symposium on High-Performance Computer Architecture*, February 1998.

2. Mikko H. Lipasti, Christopher B. Wilkerson, and John P. Shen. Value locality and load value prediction. In *Proceedings of the 7th International Conference on Architectural Support for Programming Languages and Operating Systems (ASPLOS-VII)*, pages 138–147, October 1996.
3. J Oplinger, D Heine, and M S. Lam. In search of speculative thread-level parallelism. In *Proceedings of the 1999 International Conference on Parallel Architectures and Compilation Techniques*, October 1999.
4. Stephen E. Richardson. Caching function results: Faster arithmetic by avoiding unnecessary computation. Technical report, Sun Microsystems Laboratories SMLI TR-92-1, September 1992.

A Service-Oriented Accounting Architecture on the Grid[1]

Jiadi Yu[1,2], Minglu Li[1], Ying Li[1], Feng Hong[1], and Yujun Du[2]

[1] Department of Computer Science and Engineering, Shanghai Jiao Tong University,
Shanghai 200030, P.R. China
{jdyu, li-ml, liying, hongfeng}@cs.sjtu.edu.cn
[2] Department of Photoelectricity Engineering, Xi'an Institute of Technology,
Xi'an, Shaanxi 710032, P.R. China
{ycardee, duyujun}@mail.xait.edu.cn

Abstract. The Computational Grid is a promising computing platform for solving the problem of large-scale resource allocation. In order to build large-scale of the grid computing systems, some obvious problems of grid computing, such as: security, resource scheduling and management, authentication and authorization, have attracted more attention and research. Charging and accounting is an important part of grid computing, and will lead to develop the grid computing systems. The aim of this paper is to propose a service-oriented accounting architecture that involves many services interaction on the grid. In this paper, we describe firstly architecture of charging and accounting and its support system. Then, we give briefly an introduction to pricing schemes and accounting policies.

1 Introduction

Grid computing has been widely accepted as a promising paradigm for large-scale distributed systems in recent years [1,2], and the main goal of it is sharing large-scale resources and accomplishing collaborative tasks [2] in science, engineering, and commerce. Grid infrastructures need support various services: security, uniform access, resource management, scheduling, application composition, computational economy, and accounting [3]. Charging and accounting is an important part of grid computing system. It needs to be decentralized, flexible, and record unambiguously resource usage of user.

Charging and accounting for grid has been taken into account for some grid projects and researchers. Various methods of "accounting" are being investigated such as "Virtual Users" at the Polish National Cluster [4], Template Accounts [5], DGAS [6] and GridBank [3]. A number of economic models for grid resource allocation have been proposed as potential frameworks such as GRACE [7].

---

[1] This paper is supported by 973 project (No.2002CB312002) of China, ChinaGrid Program of MOE of China, and grand project of the Science and Technology Commission of Shanghai Municipality (No. 03dz15026, No. 03dz15027 and No. 03dz15028).

The paper is organized as follows. In Section 2, we present the grid computing system and interaction of various services in accounting architecture. Then, we give briefly an introduction to pricing schemes and accounting policies in Section 3. Finally, we give the conclusion of this paper and the future work in Section 4.

2 Accounting Architecture

In a Grid Environment, an accounting procedure is based upon a grid computational economy model, which leads to a state of nearly stable equilibrium that can meet the needs of both resource `producers' and `consumers' [6].

2.1 Various Services Interaction

Figure 1 shows services interaction of work scheme involved in the accounting process, with the support module.

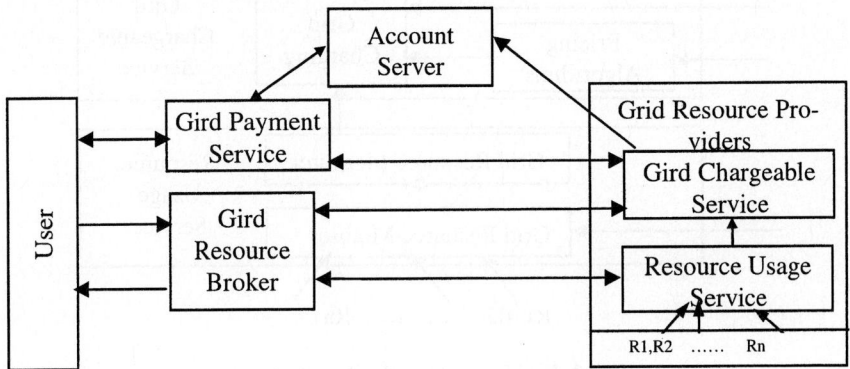

Fig. 1. Services Interaction

In Grid environment, the user submits their applications to the GRB (Grid Resource Broker). GRB is a mediator between the user and grid resources by using middleware services [7]. GRB selects suitable grid resources to user according to job criteria, and then user submits jobs to Grid Resource Provider. Grid Resource Provider executes the user job, and, at the some time, Grid Resource Provider's RUS (Resource Usage Service) measures the resources consumed while the user job is executed. Grid Resource Provider's GCS (Gird Chargeable Service) calculates total cost, and record resource usage in account server. Then GCS ask GPS (Gird Payment Service) to pay charge of resources usage. The user will pay resources usage charge by using payment strategies of GPS. In the end, the GRB returns the results to the user.

2.2 Grid Server Provider

Figure 2 show servers of Grid Server Provider Architecture and their interactions. Pricing Algorithms interacts with Grid Resource Broker to consult acceptable price of services for both grid resource provider and consumer. If they come to an acceptable price, Pricing Algorithms informs Grid Charging about negotiatory price. Then job is submitted. Grid Resource Monitor will extract resource usage information, and collect of raw date. Grid Resource Measurer measures grid resources usage, and generates a usage statistics of the grid resources after job finished. This usage statistics will be sent to Resource Usage Record (RUR) [8,9] to record. In Gird Charging, the total service cost will be calculated based on the price mutually agreed from Pricing Algorithms and the data from RUR. Finally, Gird Charging sent the total service cost to Account Server.

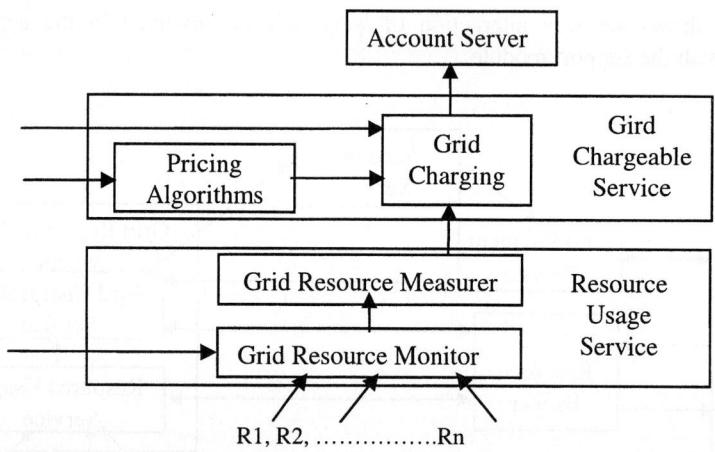

Fig. 2. Grid Server Provider Architecture

3 Pricing Schemes and Accounting Policies

Pricing schemes should base on the supply and demand for resources and the QoS requirements. In computational grid, the pricing depends on the resource supply and demand. GBR was requested to mediate resources price by grid resource producers and consumers. GBR sets firstly a price for a resource and then queries both producers and consumers whether or not accept that price. If producers and consumers agree to this price, job of user was submitted to producer. If unsatisfied, GRB will set a new price over again depending on pricing schemes supplied by Pricing Algorithms.

Once the accounting will be implemented, it will be necessary to define the rules of the system. An accounting system should be simple enough to be understood by all resource providers and consumers. In the accounting system, the user pays the charge of resource usage to resource provider. In addition, in order to complete a job, a user will need to ask resource provider for a loan, so account database should store some information about the debit and credit of the user.

Another accounting policy concern is how to charge for resource usage in some particular situations. We propose the following system policies: 1. If user job is cancelled during execution because of user action, resource provider will charge for resources already used; 2. If user job is suspended because of resource provider action, resource provider don't charge to the user; 3. If the resource usage expectations is underrated, resource provider provide a loan to user so as to complete whole job; 4. If the resource usage expectations is overrated, the job is executed.

4 Conclusions and Further Work

We have shown that a service-oriented accounting architecture on the Grid, which is a complex model that involves many services interaction, and enable to engage in grid computational economy. Then, we briefly give an introduction to pricing schemes and accounting policies.

Other work that will need to be considered and need further investigation include: Which elements should be considered for charging and accounting; The problem of the cost estimation should be considered; Moreover, the interaction of this system with related economic model needs to be investigated in further.

References

1. Foster, I., Kesselman, C.(eds.).: The Grid: Blueprint for a New Computing Infrastructure. Morgan Kaufmann (1999)
2. Foster, I., Kesselman, C., Tuecke S.: The Anatomy of the Grid: Enabling Scalable Virtual Organizations. International Journal of High Performance Computing Application, 15(3) (2001)
3. Alexander, B., Rajkumar, B.: GridBank: A Grid Accounting Services Architecture (GASA) for distributed systems sharing and integration. In 17th Annual International Parallel and Distributed Processing Symposium (IPDPS 2003) Workshop on Internet Computing and E-Commerce (2003)
4. M. Kupczyk, N. Meyer, and P. Wolniewicz.: Simplifying Administration and Management Processes in the Polish National Cluster. http://www.nas.nasa.gov/~thigpen/accountswg/Documents/VUS.pdf
5. T. J. Hacker and B. D. Athey.: Account Allocations on the Grid. http://www.nas.nasa.gov/~thigpen/accounts - wg/Documents/accountemplates.pdf
6. C.Anglano, S.Barale, L.Gaido, A.Guarise, S.Lusso, A.Werbrouck.: An accounting system for the DataGrid project -Preliminary proposal. draft in discussion at Global Grid Forum 3, Frascati, Italy, (October 2001). http://server11.infn.it/workload-grid/docs/DataGrid-01-TED-0115-3_0.pdf
7. Buyya, R.: Economic-based Distributed Resource Management and Scheduling for Grid Computing. PhD Thesis, Monash University, Melbourne, Australia, April 12, 2002. http://www.buyya.com/thesis/
8. Global Grid Forum.: Gird Economic Services Architecture (GESA). http://www.gridforum.org/3_SRM/gesa.htm
9. Global Grid Forum.: RUR - Resource Usage Record Working Group. http://www.gridforum.org/3_SRM/ur.htm

A Genetic Algorithm for Robot Navigation

Calaiselvy, Foo Tsu Yong, and Lee Wei Ping

Temasek Engineering School, Temasek Polytechnic,
Singapore 529757
calaiselvi@yahoo.com

Abstract. The sensory capabilities of the human brain makes it possible for even blind people to maneuver through unfamiliar terrain with the help of guiding devices. However, the abilities of modern robots are not so sophisticated. Given a terrain with obstacles, determining an optimally short robot navigation path poses a major search problem. In this paper, a genetic search method is developed to solve the robot navigation problem. The search node or path is represented by a string of integers, each integer representing a cell in the terrain. Simulation results comparing the proposed genetic algorithm and a sequential navigation algorithm are presented.

Keywords: Robot Navigation, Parallel search, Stochastic search, Genetic algorithms.

1 Introduction

The robot navigation problem of finding an optimal path encompassing the entire navigation terrain, poses a major search problem. Even under simplified assumptions, this problem presents a multitude of possible solutions.

In contrast to human sensory abilities, the robots have fewer sensors. In addition, the problem becomes more intensified when some of the sensor capabilities are lost due to damage or malfunctioning developed in real-time. Several approaches have been developed by researchers to handle sensor failure. This includes evolutionary learning [1], case-based reasoning[2] and Bayesian networks[3]. This paper attempts to describe how genetic search using simulations of robots and obstacles can be effective in solving robot navigation problems. These studies could be extended to solve sensor failure handling and obstacle avoidance as well. Genetic algorithms are known to be robust stochastic searching algorithms for various optimization problems [4]-[7]. Genetic algorithms use the principles of natural selection and natural genetics. They involve manipulating fixed-length strings that represent solutions to the problem at hand.

This paper starts with the introduction of the problem and genetic algorithms(GA). This is followed by the modeling for GA implementation and the complete algorithm, while section 3 presents the results of the simulation. The paper ends with a conclusion.

2 Modeling of the Problem for Genetic Algorithm

This section presents the representation of the navigation problem in a form suitable for genetic search.

The most important concern in *string representation* is that of uniqueness and completeness, with a one-to-one correspondence between the search nodes in a search space and the strings of the population. In other words, each string corresponds to a valid search node. For the navigation problem at hand, some simplifying assumptions were made. The navigation terrain was assumed to be a square area, logically divided into a 8x8 matrix of cells, sequentially numbered from 1 to 64. A simple integer string representation of the solutions was chosen. The merit of genetic search lies in the fact that it is a random, yet structured search, with parallel evaluation of nodes in the search space. This requires the generation of an *initial population*, which is done randomly. The population size was determined experimentally, as this parameter depends largely on the problem being solved.

The objective of the robot navigation problem is to optimize the navigation time, or the length of the navigation path. The fitness function determines how well the genetic search is able to progress towards the optimal solution as it is used to evaluate the search nodes and also control the genetic operators. For the robot navigation problem, the length of the navigation path is determined based on the distance traversed by the robot and defined as :

$$L(SN) = \Sigma \, d_{ij} \qquad (1)$$

where SN represents the search node and d_{ij} represents the distance traversed between cells i and j. Since the objective is to minimize the length of the path, the fitness function will be one that minimizes the length. This is done as follows:

$$Fitness = L_{max} - L(SN) \qquad (2)$$

where L_{max} is the maximum distance traversed so far. Thus the fitness value of the optimal solution will be the largest with the smallest distance traveled.

Three *genetic operators*, namely, selection, crossover and mutation were chosen to drive the genetic search. A *roulette wheel selection* that mimics a roulette wheel was chosen. Each search node in the solution space is allotted slots proportional to its fitness value in order to improve chances of selection for better strings. As for crossover, a simple single-point crossover was chosen. Mutation was implemented by swapping the integers at two mutation spots within the string. The algorithm used for the simulation of the genetic search is given below:

Algorithm *GaforRobotNavigation*

1. Initialize parameters.
2. Generate an *initial population* of 30 strings (of 64 integers each) randomly.
3. Repeat the steps 3 to 8 until convergence.
4. Evaluate each of the strings in the population to determine the *fitness value*.
5. Apply *roulette wheel selection* to form the next generation of strings.
6. Perform *crossover* on the strings with a probability *crossoverprob*.
7. Perform *mutation* on the strings with a probability *crossovermut*.
8. To prevent loss of best solution, replace the worst string in this resulting generation with the best from the previous generation.

3 Simulation Results

The genetic algorithm was implemented and compared with non-genetic algorithm results. The following parameters were used for the simulations: Population Size (30), Maximum generations (1000), Crossover Probability (0.7) Mutation Probability (0.04). Figure 1 compares the performance of the genetic algorithm for various generations. The algorithm converged to a solution with relatively high fitness during a generation between 500 and 1000, in all cases.

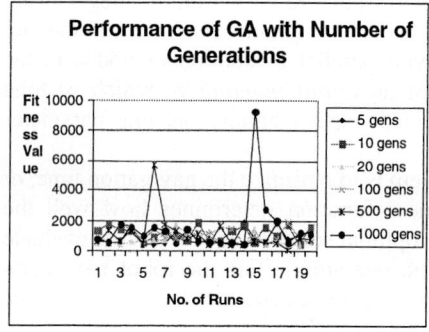
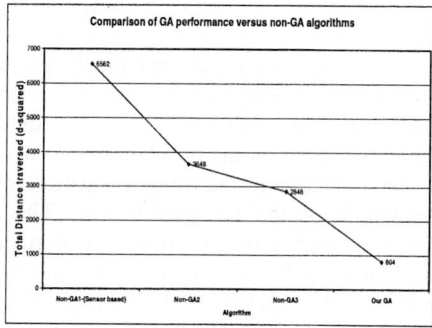

Fig. 1. Performance at different generations

Fig. 2. Comparison of performance – GA and non-genetic algorithm

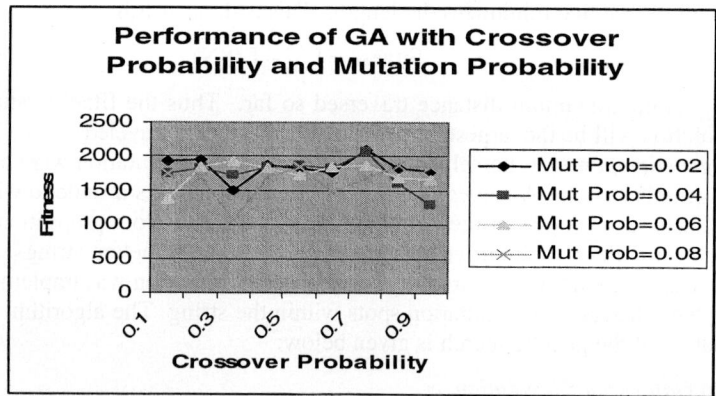

Fig. 3. Performance at various probabilities for Crossover and mutation

Figure 2 attempts to compare the distances traversed by the robot while encompassing the entire terrain, using both the genetic algorithm and non-genetic algorithm based on sensor heuristics. Figure 3 depicts the initial experimentation carried out to determine the crossover and mutation probabilities for the simulations.

4 Conclusion

In this paper, an inherently parallel search method using genetic algorithms is proposed for the problem of robot navigation. This could be used for typical applications such as collection, clearing of the terrain and so forth. Results are compared with non-genetic algorithmic results.

References

1. Schultz, A., Grefenstette, J.: Continuous and Embedded Learning in Autonomous Vehicles: Adapting to Sensor Failures. Vol.4024. Proceedings of SPIE, (2000) 55–62
2. Fox, S., Leake, D..: Modeling Case-based Planning for Repairing Reasoning Failures. Proceedings of the 1995 AAAI Spring Symposium on Representing Mental States and Mechanisms. AAAI(1995)
3. Forbes, J., Huang, T., Kanazawa, K., Russell, S.: The BATmobile: Towards a Bayesian Automated Taxi. Proceedings of the International Joint Conference on Artificial Intelligence (1995)
4. Proc. 1st International Conference on Genetic Algorithms and Their Applications. Carnegie-Mellon University, Pittsburgh, PA, July 24–26, (1985)
5. Proc. 2nd International Conference on Genetic Algorithms and Their Applications. MIT, Cambridge, MA, July 28–31, (1987)
6. Proc. 3rd International Conference on Genetic Algorithms. George Mason University, Washington, DC, June 4–71, (1989)
7. Goldberg, D.E.: Genetic Algorithms in Search, Optimization and Machine Learning. Reading, MA: Addison-Wesley, (1989)

A Categorized-Registry Model for Grid Resource Publication and Discovery Using Software Agents

Lei Cao[1], Minglu Li[1], Henry Rong[2], and Joshua Huang[2]

[1] Department of Computer Science and Engineering,
Shanghai Jiao Tong University, Shanghai 20030, China
{clcao, mlli}@sjtu.edu.cn

[2] E-Business Technology Institute, The University of Hong Kong, Hong Kong, China
{hrong, jhuang}@eti.hku.hk

Abstract. This paper presents a categorized-registry model for Grid Resource Publication and Discovery(GRPD) using software agents. We use Common Resource Model(CRM) specification to describe manageable resources as Open Grid Services Architecture(OGSA) services. We also adopt two-level registry mechanism to register corresponding resources of a Virtual Organization(VO) in order to obtain high GRPD efficiency. The "Index" node of a VO hosts the general registry. Other specific categorized registries are distributed in the VO. A large-scale Grid system may contain many VOs. "Index" nodes from various VOs connect to each other in Peer-to-Peer(P2P) mode instead of hierarchical mode. Software agent is a powerful high-level tool for modeling a complex software system. It is adopted to implement GRPD efficiently.

Keywords: Grid, GRPD, OGSA, VO, Two-level Registry, P2P, Agent.

1 Introduction

Grid technology has emerged to enable large-scale flexible resources sharing among dynamic VOs. Resource discovery in a Grid is a challenging task because of the following Grid features[1, 2]: heterogeneous, dynamic, autonomic and numerous. These characteristics create significant difficulties for traditional centralized and hierarchical resource discovery services.

In this paper, we present a categorized-registry model for GRPD using software agents. We use CRM specification to describe manageable resources as OGSA services. A large-scale Grid system may contain many VOs. Each VO has its own "Index" node that hosts the general registry. Other specific registries are distributed in the VO. All heterogeneous resources in the VO will register themselves with those specific registries in soft-state way via the general registry. This is a two-level registry mechanism by which GRPD functions can

---

[1] This paper is supported by 973 project(No.2002CB312002) of China, ChinaGrid Program of MOE of China, and grand project of the Science and Technology Commission of Shanghai Municipality(No. 03dz15026, No. 03dz15027 and No. 03dz15028).

be efficiently implemented via software agents. "Index" nodes from various VOs connect to each other in P2P mode instead of hierarchical mode.

The rest of this paper is as follows. We discuss related work in Section 2. Section 3 presents our categorized-registry model. We conclude in Section 4 with lessons learned and future research plans.

2 Related Work

Condor-G[3] agent uses the Matchmaker to make brokering decisions about where to execute user jobs. Obviously, the Matchmaker becomes the system bottleneck especially when the system's scale becomes larger.

Index Services of Open Grid Services Infrastructure(OGSI) in Globus[4] may be hierarchically included in a higher-level Index Server. It is not easy to devise scalable Grid resource discovery based on centralized or hierarchical mechanism when a large number of Grid hosts, resources, and users have to be managed[5].

Legion[6, 7] uses a Resource Management Infrastructure(RMI) in which the information collection is very similar to the Information Services in Globus. Objects are used as the main system abstraction throughout. But we can use agents as a high level abstraction.

Nimrod-G[8] uses the Globus middleware services to discover dynamic resources and dispatch jobs over computational Grids. Nimrod-G has the same shortcomings as Globus by using Globus Monitoring and Discovery Service(MDS).

In the Agent-based hierarchy model[9], the agents are responsible for GRPD. They are deployed hierarchically. In the environment where resources need to be distributed frequently, the overhead will be greatly increased and the nodes that locate in higher levels may become the bottleneck.

3 Categorized-Registry Model for GRPD

3.1 Resource Description

Grid resources have some forms of state(runtime,configuration, etc) on which management can be performed. In CRM specification[10], they are known as manageable resources. The CRM uses the OGSA grid service model for stateful resources. The CRM defines a single new port type, BaseManageableResource, which must also be implemented by manageable resource services. It extends the GridService port type. Two important Service Data Elements(SDEs) of BaseManageableResource will be used in our mechanism: serviceGroupType and searchProperty. In our mechanism we extend CRM's base resource types whose manageability port types have been given in Web Services Definition Language(WSDL) files.

3.2 Model Architecture

In a VO, all manageable resources are represented with various port types according to their types. We adopt multiple registries to accommodate coarse-grained

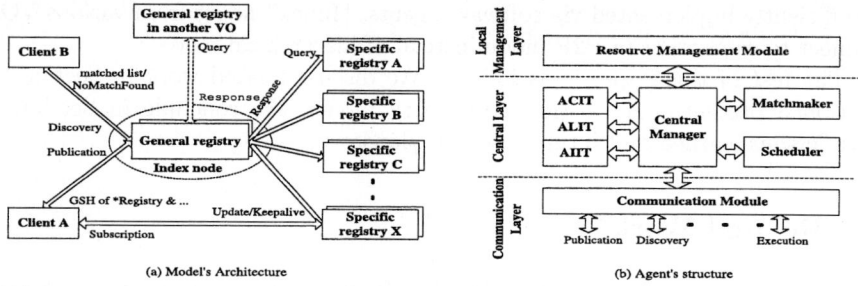

Fig. 1. Model's architecture and Agent's structure

classified resource services(See Figure 1(a)). But we also use a general registry to accommodate those registries' metadata, i.e. their GSHs. This is a two-level registry mechanism. The mechanism strengthens both the efficiency of resource discovery and the scalability of the Grid system. When a client submits a query for specific resources, the query will be submitted to the general registry at first. After being verified with the requested resource type, the query will be delivered to corresponding specific registry. We can benefit much from doing so: (1)decreasing the centralized registry's workload; (2)strengthening the system's adaptability; (3)improving the system's scalability.

We use software agents on behalf of these manageable resources to implement GRPD functions.

3.3 Super-Index Network

Use of P2P protocols is expected to improve the efficiency and scalability of large-scale Grid systems. The Grid system may contain many VOs. Every VO has its own Index node to host the general registry we mentioned above. We connect those Index nodes from different VOs into a "Super-Index network" in P2P manner. Certainly, the Index node will contain the neighbor set of other VOs' Index nodes. Because the Index node is prone to be a single point of failure and a potential bottleneck of its VO, we take some measures to avoid it: (1)Only host the general registry in the Index node to decrease the workload of the Index node; (2)Use these nodes having the largest capabilities within each VO as the Index node; (3)Introduce redundancy into the design of the Index node to provide more reliability to the VO and less workload on the Index node. However, doing so will add additional cost, so it's important to balance reliability and cost. In our model we have used two nodes sharing workload of the Index node to ensure good reliability(See Figure 1(a)). The similar measures are taken for those nodes that host specific registries.

3.4 The Structure of Agent

An agent in our model is viewed as the representative of all manageable resource services within the node at a meta-level of resource management. Each agent is able to cooperate with other agents and thereby provides resource publication and discovery for the scheduling of applications that need to utilize grid resources. An agent can be considered as both the service provider and the service requester. Those agents deployed within the VO's nodes are homogenous and have hierarchy structure. There are three layers(See Figure 1(b)). The communication layer contains a communication module that acts as an interface to the external environment. The central layer is responsible for the core GRPD functions. It has four components: Agent Information Tables(AITs), Matchmaker, Scheduler and Central Manager. The local management layer is used to perform functions such as application management, resource allocation and resource monitoring. In other means, it's the direct interface to local resources.

4 Conclusion and Future Work

This paper has described a categorized-registry model for GRPD. We have focused on the grouping of manageable resources to build some specific registries in the VO. Doing so increases both the efficiency of resource discovery and the scalability of the Grid system. Using P2P techniques we construct a Super-Index network among VOs of the Grid system. We also utilize software agent technology to complete GRPD efficiently. In the near future, we plan to do a practical performance evaluation to show that our categorized-registry model can be efficiently used in the Grid environment.

References

1. A. Iamnitchi, I.F.: On fully decentralized resource discovery in grid environments. In: Proceedings of International Workshop on Grid Computing. (2001)
2. Y. GONG, e.a.: Vega infrastructure for resource discovery in grids. Computer Science and Technology **18** (2003) 10
3. J. Frey, e.a.: Condor-g:a computation management agent for multi-institutional grids. In: Proceedings of the 10th IEEE International Symposium on High Performance Distributed Computing. (2001)
4. S. Tuecke, e.a.: Open grid services infrastructure (ogsi) version 1.0. In: Specification of GGF by OGSI-WG. (2003)
5. C. Mastroianni, D. Talia, O.V.: P2p protocols for membership management and resource discovery in grids. In: http://biblio.cs.icar.cnr.it. (2004)
6. S.J. CChapin, e.a.: The legion resource management system. In: Proceedings of Job Scheduling Strategies for Parallel Processing. (1999)
7. A. Natrajan, M.A. Humphrey, A.G.: Grid Resource Management In Legion. Kluwer Academic Publishers, Virginia (2004)
8. R. Buyya, D. Abramson, J.G.: Nimrod/g: An architecture for a resource management and scheduling system in a global computational grid. In: Proceedings of the 4th International Conference on High-Performance Computing in the Asia-Pacific Region. (2000)
9. J. Cao, e.a.: Arms: An agent-based resource management system for grid computing. Scientific Programming **10** (2002) 14
10. E. Stokes, N.B.: Common resource model(crm). In: Specification of GGF by CMM-WG. (2003)

An Adaptive Load Balancing Approach in Distributed Computing Using Genetic Theory

SeongHoon Lee[1], DongWoo Lee[2], WanKwon Lee[3], and HyunJoon Cho[3]

[1] Division of Information and Communication Engineering,
Cheonan University, 115, Anseo-dong, Cheonan,
Choongnam, Republic of Korea
shlee@cheonan.ac.kr
[2] Department of Computer Engineering,
WooSong University, 17-2, Jayang-dong, Dong-ku,
Daejeon, Republic of Korea
dwlee@woosong.ac.kr
[3] School of Information Technology & Engineering,
Jeonju University, 1200, 3rd Street Hyoja-Dong Wansan-Koo JeonJu,
Chonbuk, Republic of Korea
{wklee, chohj}@jj.ac.kr

Abstract. In sender-initiated load balancing algorithms, the sender continues to send unnecessary request messages for load transfer until a receiver is found while the system load is heavy. Meanwhile, in the receiver-initiated load balancing algorithms, the receiver continues to send an unnecessary request message for load acquisition until a sender is found while the system load is low. These unnecessary request messages result in inefficient communications, low CPU utilization, and low system throughput in distributed systems. To solve these problems, we propose a genetic based approach for improved sender-initiated and receiver-initiated load balancing in distributed systems.

1 Introduction

Load balancing for our approach is a sender-initiated and receiver-initiated algorithm. Under sender-initiated algorithms, when the distributed systems become to heavy system load, it is difficult to find a suitable receiver because most processors have additional tasks to send.

Similarly, under receiver-initiated algorithms, when the distributed systems become to light system load, it is difficult to find a suitable sender because most processors have small tasks[2,3]. So, many request and reject messages are repeatedly sent back and forth, and a lot of time is consumed before execution. Therefore, much of the task processing time is consumed, and causes low system throughput, low CPU utilization.

To solve these problems in sender-initiated and receiver-initiated algorithm, we use a new genetic algorithm and expand to a new adaptive load balancing algorithm.

2 GA-Based Adaptive Load Balancing Approach

We employ the CPU queue length as a suitable load index because this measure is known as a most suitable index [1]. This measure means a number of tasks in CPU queue residing in a processor.

We use a 3-level scheme to represent a load state on its own CPU queue length of a processor. The transfer policy is triggered when a task arrives. A node identifies as a sender if a new task originating at the node makes the CPU queue length exceed T_{up}. A node identifies itself as a suitable receiver for a task acquisition if the node's CPU queue length will not cause to exceed T_{low}.

Each processor in distributed systems has its own population which genetic operators are applied to. There are many encoding methods; Binary encoding, Character and real-valued encoding, Tree encoding [2]. We use binary encoding method in this paper. So, a string in population can be defined as a binary-coded vector $< v_o, v_1, ..., v_{n-1} >$ which indicates a set of processors to which the request messages are sent off. If the request message is transferred to the processor $P_i (0 \leq i \leq$ n-1, where n is the total number of processors), then v_i=1, otherwise v_i=0. Each string has its own fitness value.

In the sender-based load balancing approach using genetic algorithm, processors received the request message from the sender send accept message or reject message depending on its own CPU queue length. In the case of more than two accept messages returned, one is selected at random. Each string included in a population is evaluated by the fitness function using following formula 1:

$$F_i = 1/((\alpha \times TMP) + (\beta \times TMT) + (\gamma \times TTP)) \tag{1}$$

Here, α, β, γ mean the weights for parameters such as TMP, TMT, TTP. TMP(Total Message Processing time) is the summation of the processing times for request messages to be transferred. TMT(Total Message Transfer time) means the summation of each message transfer times from the sender to processors corresponding to bits set '1' in selected string. The objective of this parameter is to select a string with the shortest distance eventually. TTP(Total Task Processing time) is the summation of the times needed to perform a task at each processor corresponding to bits set '1' in selected string. The algorithm of the proposed sender-based load balancing is as shown in Fig. 1.

Initialization module is executed in each processor. A population of strings is randomly generated without duplication. Check_load module is used to observe its own processor's load by checking the CPU queue length, whenever a task is arrived in a processor. If the observed load is heavy, the load balancing algorithm performs the above modules. Individual_evaluation module calculates the fitness value of strings in the population. Genetic_operation module such as Local improvement, Reproduction, New_ProposedCrossover is executed on the population in such a way as above. Genetic_operation selects a string from the population at the probability proportional to its fitness, and then sends off the request messages according to the contents of the selected string.

```
Procedure Genetic_algorithm Approach (for sender)
   Initialization()
   While (Check_load())
      If ( Load_i > T_up )
         Individual_evaluation();
         Genetic_operation();
         Message_evaluation();
      Process a task in local processor;
Procedure Genetic_operation()
   Local_improvement_operation();
   Reproduction();
   New_ProposedCrossover();

Procedure Genetic_algorithm Approach (for receiver)
   Initialization()
   While (Check_load())
      If ( Load_i ≤ T_low )
         Individual_evaluation();
         Genetic_operation();
         Message_evaluation();
      Process a task in local processor;
```

Fig. 1. GA-based load balancing algorithm

On the other hand, GA-based receiver-initiated load balancing is shown by Fig. 1. Each string included in a population is evaluated by the fitness function using the formula 2.

$$F_i = 1/((\alpha \times TMP) + (\beta \times TMT)) + (\gamma \times TTP) \qquad (2)$$

Lastly the algorithm for adaptive load balancing is shown in Fig. 2.

3 Experiments

Our experiments have the following assumptions. First, each task size and task type are the same. Second, the number of parts(p) in a string is five. In genetic algorithm, crossover probability(P_c) is 0.7, mutation probability(P_m) is 0.05. The values of these parameters P_c, P_m were known as the most suitable values in various applications [3, 4, 2, 5]. The number of processors is 30, and the number of strings is 50.

Our experiments for sender-initiated load balancing approach have the following assumptions. The load rating over the systems is about 60 percent. The weight for *TMP* is 0.025. The weight for *TMT* is 0.01. The weight for *TTP* is 0.02. The experiment is to observe the change of response time when the number of tasks to be performed is 3000(see Fig. 3).

If (load of distributed system $< T_{low}$)
　If (a specific processor = sender)
　　Use a conventional sender-initiated load balancing algorithm
　Else
　　Use a proposed a GA-based receiver-initiated load balancing algorithm
　If (a specific processor = receiver)
　　Use a conventional receiver-initiated load balancing algorithm
　Else
　　Use a proposed a GA-based sender-initiated load balancing algorithm

Fig. 2. An Adaptive Load balancing Algorithm

Our experiment for receiver-initiated load balancing approach has the following assumption. The load rating over the systems is about 20 percent. The experiment is to observe the change of response time when the number of tasks to be performed is 2000(see Fig. 4).

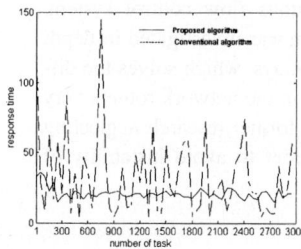

Fig. 3. Result of Sender Approach

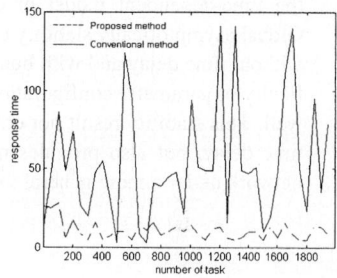

Fig. 4. Result of Receiver Approach

References

1. T. Kunz. "the influence of different workload descriptions on a heuristic load balancing scheme". *IEEE Trans on Software Engineering*, 17(7), July 1991.
2. Melanie Mitchell. *An Introduction to Genetic Algorithms*. MIT Press, 1996.
3. J.Grefenstette. "optimization of control parameters for genetic algorithms". *IEEE Trans on SMC*, SMC-16(1), January 1986.
4. J A. Miller, W D. Potter, R V. Gondham, and C N. Lapena. "an evaluation of local improvement operators for genetic algorithms". *IEEE Trans on SMC*, 23(5), Sept 1993.
5. M.Srinivas and L.M.Patnait. "adaptive probabilities of crossover and mutation in genetic algorithms". *IEEE Trans on SMC*, 24(4), April 1994.

Global Stability of Optimization Based Flow Control with Time-Varying Delays

Yuedong Xu[1], Liang Wang[2], Zhihong Guan[2], and Hua O. Wang[2]

[1] School of Computer Software Engineering,
South China University of Technology, GuangZhou, GD, 510641, P. R. China
xuyaodong2000@yahoo.com.cn
[2] Department of Control Science & Engineering,
Huazhong University of Science & Technology, Wuhan, HB, 430074, P.R. China

Abstract. Flow control and congestion control are becoming increasingly important nowadays due to explosive expansion and rapid growth of traffic in the Internet. They are inherently very complex nonlinear dynamic problems. Improper configuration of parameters can easily lead to the instability of network flow control system. An appropriate Lyapunov function is introduced aiming at the time-dependent model of deterministic continuous flow control system. Global asymptotically stability of flow control system was investigated in-depth without time delay and with bounded time varying delays, which solves the difficulty of parameter configuration of flow controller in the network routers very well. This stability result not only is consistent with former research neglecting time delay, but also provides novel criterions in order to avoid instability of network under a more general topology.

1 Introduction

Flow control schemes refer to a series of distributed and asynchronous algorithms to share network resources among competing network users. The goal of flow control strategy is to allocate network resource fairly and reasonably, and to provide good quality of service (QoS) in a stable and scalable manner [1]. We expect that flow control strategy can achieve high network efficiency, and respond to the changes of network condition rapidly. Flow control strategy adjusts the sending rate according to the network capacity, which can prevent congestion collapse effectively. It plays an important role in guaranteeing network performance such as fairness, high utility, low queuing delay and packet drop rate as well as stability.

[2][3][4][5] investigate the flow control strategies of some major protocols and link algorithms. Essentially, these algorithms are introduced to solve a strict concave optimization problem, i.e. maximizing the network utility within the constraints of network capacity. Steven. H. Low proposed duality model of TCP networks flows [4][11]. This duality model combines the utility function and link algorithm together, which is regarded as a distributed method to solve optimal rate allocation problem with proper evaluation functions. It also proves the global convergence of optimiza-

tion problems that are solved by both synchronous and asynchronous gradient projection methods. [5] proposed random exponential marking (REM) link algorithm, which decouple the congestion indication and performance objectives. REM algorithm cannot only stabilize buffer queue, but also can approximate global optimization. [7][8][9] did a lot of work over stability analysis of flow control system aiming at constant time delays. [6] also devised a masterly Lyapunov function to prove the global stability of duality model neglecting time delays.

However, time delays exist in the real Internet, which are composed of two primary parts: transmission delays and queuing delays. Time delay varies according to the changes of network conditions and cannot be regarded as a constant. Aiming at the uncertainty of time-delay in the current packet-scheduled networks, we conclude a novel global asymptotically stability based on optimization theory. We adopt the similar mathematical model as [6]. Compared with previous works, our stability condition not only takes bounded time-varying delay into consideration, but also is a global asymptotically stability result. Although [13] investigate the local stability of discrete REM algorithm with time-varying delays, our work consider the continuous time-dependent flow control model. Moreover, our result is very easy to calculate, without solving Linear Matrix Inequality (LMI).

2 Problem Formulation

Consider a network that consists of a set of unidirectional links $L = \{1, 2, \cdots\cdots L\}$. The network is shared by a set of heterogeneous sources $S = \{1, 2, \cdots\cdots S\}$, whose sending rate can be expressed as x_s. The network bandwidth of each link is denoted as C_l. Source s is characterized by four parameters $(L(s), U_s(x_s), m_s, M_s)$ [4], where $U_s(x_s)$ is a strictly increasing concave function of sending rate x_s, and m_s, M_s are the upper and the lower boundary of sending rate respectively. The goal of optimization flow control strategy is to decide the sending rate in order to maximize the aggregate source utility. Define $I_s = [m_s, M_s]$, then the objective of flow control system can be represented as follows: [4]

$$\text{Objective:} \quad Max_{x_i \in I_i} \sum_s U_s(x_s)$$

$$\text{Constraint:} \quad \sum_s x_s \leq c_l, \ l = 1, 2 \cdots\cdots L \tag{1}$$

The duality model of this optimization problem is investigated in-depth in [4]. Denote Lagrangian function:

$$L(x, p) = \sum_s U_s(x_s) - \sum_l p_l (\sum_{s \in S} x_s - c_l)$$
$$= \sum_s (U_s(x_s) - x_s \sum_l p_l) + \sum_l p_l c_l \tag{2}$$

Duality Model: $D(p) = \max_{x_s \in I_s} L(x, p) = \max_{x_s \in I_s}(U_s(x_s) - p^s x_s) + \sum_l p_l c_l$ (3)

where p_l is the price in the link l and p^s is the total price of source s in the links. $p^s = \sum p_l$. When the possible coupling problems in the each link are ignored, the complexity of flow control system will decrease considerably. The multi-source multi-links topology is very similar to multi-source single link case, thus we assume link set $L = \{1\}$.

Suppose the utility function $U_s(\cdot)$ is twice differentiable, and is a strictly concave on the interval $I_s = [m_s, M_s]$. Then $U_s^{'-1}(\cdot)$ is the inverse of $U_s'(\cdot)$, which exists over the range $[M_s', m_s']$ [4]. In both versions of TCP like Reno and Vegas, source i can be modeled to adjust the transmission rate in a smoothed version:

$$x_s(t) = [U_s']^{-1}(p(t - d_i(t)))$$

And the transmission rate x_s is achieved when $x_s = U_s^{'-1}(p^*)$. Denote $f_s(\cdot) = [U_s'(\cdot)]^{-1}$, because $U_s(\cdot)$ of different TCP versions are the strictly increasing and concave function of x_s based on previous assumption, f_s is a strictly monotone decreasing function of the link price p, which is a bit similar to the analysis in [6]. According to continuous model for the price and backlog dynamics, link algorithm can be expressed as follows:

$$\dot{b}(t) = \begin{cases} y(t) - c & \text{if } b(t) > 0 \\ [y(t) - c]^+ & \text{if } b(t) = 0 \end{cases} \quad (4)$$

$$\dot{p}(t) = \begin{cases} \gamma[\alpha(b(t) - b^*) + y(t) - c] & \text{if } p(t) > 0 \\ \gamma[\alpha(b(t) - b^*) + y(t) - c]^+ & \text{if } p(t) = 0 \end{cases} \quad (5)$$

$$y(t) = \sum_{s \in S} x_s(t - d_s(t)) = \sum_{s=1}^{S} [U_s'(p(t - d_s(t)))]^{-1} = \sum_{s=1}^{S} f_s(p(t - d_s(t))) \quad (6)$$

Here, $b(t)$ is instantaneous buffer queue size in the router, $y(t)$ represents the total input rate in the network bottleneck. $d_i(t)$ denotes time varying delay in the network. γ and α are small positive constant.

3 Global Asymptotic Stability

When this flow control system reaches equilibrium point, $y^* = c$ and $p^* > 0, b^* > 0$. Let $\delta p(t) = p(t) - p^*$ and linearize $y(t), b(t)$ and $p(t)$.

$$y(t) = \sum_{s=1}^{S} f_s(p(t-d_s(t)))$$

$$= \sum_{s=1}^{S} f_s(p^*) + \sum_{s=1}^{S} f_s'(p^*)(p(t-d_s(t)) - p^*)$$

$$= c + \sum_{s=1}^{S} f_s'(p^*)(p(t-d_s(t)) - p^*) \tag{7}$$

$$\delta \dot{y}(t) = \sum_{s=1}^{S} f_s'(p^*) \delta p(t-d_s(t)) = \delta \dot{b}(t), \tag{8}$$

$$\delta \dot{p}(t) = \gamma \alpha \delta b(t) + \gamma \delta y(t) \tag{9}$$

where $\delta y(t) = y(t) - c$, $\delta b(t) = b(t) - b^*$, $\delta p(t) = p(t) - p^*$, $p^* = \gamma \alpha b^*$.

The dynamic model of optimization based flow control system near equilibrium state is:

$$\dot{X}(t) = A_0 X(t) + \sum_{i=1}^{S} A_i X(t - d_i(t)) \qquad t \geq 0 \tag{10}$$

where $X(t) = [\delta p(t) \quad \delta b(t)]^T$, $A_0 = \begin{bmatrix} 0 & \gamma \alpha \\ 0 & 0 \end{bmatrix}$, $A_i = \begin{bmatrix} \gamma f_i'(p^*) & 0 \\ f_i'(p^*) & 0 \end{bmatrix}$.

Theorem 1: Suppose $d_i(t) = 0, \{i = 1, 2, \cdots\cdots S\}$, for $f_i(p^s)$ is strictly monotone decreasing function of p, the unique equilibrium point (b^*, p^*) is global asymptotically stable.

Generally, time delay in the network consists of two main parts: transmission delay and queuing delay in the bottleneck. Furthermore, time-delay in the network is not constant, but full of uncertainty. Thus Theorem 1 cannot guarantee that the unique equilibrium point of network flow control system is global asymptotically stable in the presence of time-varying delays. The continuous model of optimization based flow control system is as follows and we assume the initial state is θ:

$$\begin{cases} \dot{X}(t) = A_0 X(t) + \sum_{i=1}^{S} A_i X(t - d_i(t)) & t > 0 \\ X(t) = \theta & t \leq 0 \end{cases} \tag{11}$$

Theorem 2[10]: If there exist a non-singular matrix T and a set $s \subseteq \{1, 2, \cdots\cdots S\}$ that satisfy:

i) $A = A_0 + \sum_{i \in L} A_i$ is a Hurwitz matrix.

ii) $\dfrac{1}{\lambda_{max}(\mathbf{P})} > H\sum_{i=1}^{S}\sum_{j=0}^{S}\|\mathbf{TA_i A_j T^{-1}}\|$, where H is the upper boundary of time-delay, $\|\bullet\|$ is Induced Euclidean norm. $\lambda_{max}(\mathbf{P})$ is the maximum eigenvalue of matrix $\mathbf{P}$. Here $\mathbf{P}$ is the unique solution of *Lyapunov* function:

$$(\mathbf{TAT^{-1}})^T \mathbf{P} + \mathbf{P}(\mathbf{TAT^{-1}}) = -2\mathbf{I}$$

then the unique solution (p^*, b^*) of flow control system (7) is global asymptotically stable.

Lemma 1: Because $f_s(p^s)$ is a strict decreasing function of $p^s > 0$, i.e. $f_s'(p) < 0, \forall p > 0$, the real parts of eigenvalues of $A = A_0 + \sum_{i \in L} A_i$ are always negative. Thus A is always Hurwitz. If we assume $T = I$, the global asymptotically stable condition can be simplified as:

$$\dfrac{1}{\lambda_{max}(\mathbf{P})} > H \cdot \sum_{i=1}^{S}\sum_{j=0}^{S}\|\mathbf{A_i A_j}\| \tag{12}$$

P is the unique solution of *Lyapunov* function: $\mathbf{A^T P + PA} = -2\mathbf{I}$.

Remark 1: If the time delay is neglected in the optimization based flow control system, i.e. $H = 0$, Matrix is still Hurwitz. Matrix $\mathbf{P}$ will absolutely exist and $\lambda_{max}(\mathbf{P}) > 0$, which satisfy the global asymptotically stable condition of Theorem 2.

Remark 2: If all the time delays in the networks are identical to a constant d, them system (10) can be simplified as follow:

$$\mathbf{X}(t) = \mathbf{A_0 X}(t) + \mathbf{A_1 X}(t-d) \tag{13}$$

then $\mathbf{P}$ is positive definite matrix and satisfies the unique solution of *Lyapunov* function. Generally, $\gamma \ll 1$, system (10) is global asymptotically stable if $\mathbf{P}$ satisfies:

$$\dfrac{1}{\lambda_{max}(\mathbf{P})} > d \cdot (N\gamma \alpha f' + N^2 \gamma (f')^2) \tag{14}$$

Remark 3: If there are N non-responsive flows coexisting with many TCP flows, it can be regarded as bounded stochastic process with expectation a, i.e. $\{e_i^{(N)}(t)+a\}_{i=1}^{N}$, and $e_i^{(N)}(t)$ satisfies $\lim\limits_{N\to\infty}\sup\limits_{t\in[0,NT]} \dfrac{1}{N}\sum_{i=1}^{N}e_i^{(N)}(t) = 0$ [8]. Approximately, $y(t)$ can be changed in to $y(t)+a$ in system model (10). Our global asymptotically stability condition is also effective.

4 Conclusion

With the rapid development of Internet in both scale and heterogeneous services, congestion control is becoming increasingly important in guaranteeing the stability and robustness of Internet. Improper configuration of parameters in the network router can easily lead to instability of flow control system. This article investigates the duality model and its link algorithm aiming at continuous flow model with time-varying delays. A novel Lyapunov function is introduced and the global asymptotically stability condition is concluded. Our stability result not only coincides with previous research work when the time delays are neglected, but also is effective in the presence of unresponsive flows.

References

1. S.H. Low, "Network Flow Control". Technical Report, 2002. Available at: http://netlab.caltech.edu.
2. F.P. Kelly, et. al. "Mathematical Modeling of the Internet". Fourth International Congress on Industrial and Applied Mathematics, Edinburgh, Scotland, July 1999.
3. F.P. Kelly, A. Maulloo, D. Tan. "Rate Control for Communication Networks: shadow prices, proportional fairness and Stability." Journal of Operation Research, Soc. 49 (3) (1998) 237-252.
4. S.H. Low, D.E. Lapsley. "Optimization Flow Control- I: Basic Algorithm and Convergence." IEEE/ACM Trans. On Networking, Volume 7 (6), (1999) 861-874.
5. S. Athuraliya, S.H. Low, V.H. Li, Q. Yin. "REM: Active Queue Management." IEEE Networks Volume 15 (3) (2001) 48-53.
6. F. Paganini. "A Global Stability Result in Network Flow Control." Systems & Control Letters 46 (2002) 165-172.
7. R. Johari, D.K.H. Tan. "End-to-End Congestion Control for the Internet: Delays and Stability." IEEE/ACM Transactions on Networking, (December 2001), Volume: 9 Issue: 6.
8. S. Deb, S. Shakkottai, R. Srikant. "Stability and Convergence of TCP-Like Congestion Controllers in a Many-Flow Regime." Proceedings of IEEE INFOCOM, 2003.
9. X.F. Wang, G.R. Chen, K.T. Kob. "A Stability Theorem for Internet Congestion Control." Systems & Control Letters. Vol.45, (2002) 81-85.
10. Y.J. Sun, J.G. Hsieh, and H.C. Yang. "On the Stability of Uncertain Systems with Multiple Time-Varying Delays." IEEE Trans. on Automatic Control, Vol. 42, No. 1, 1997.
11. S. Athuraliya, S.H. Low. "Optimization Flow Control-- II: Implementation." Available at: http://netlab.caltech.edu/
12. B. Xu, Y. Liu. "An Improved Razumikhin-Type Theorem and Its Applications." IEEE Trans. on Automatic Control. vol. 39, pp. 839-841, 1994.
13. C. N. Long, J. Wu, X. P. Guan. "Local stability of REM algorithm with time-varying delays." IEEE Communications Letters, Volume: 7, Issue: 3, 2003. Pages: 142-144.

OITASSF: An Omnipotent Integration Technology for Application System Security Functions

Tang Ye, Zhang Shen-Sheng, Li Lei, and Zhang Jing-Yi

CIT Lab, Computer Science Department, Shanghai Jiaotong University, Shanghai 200030
{tangye, sszhang, lilei, zhangjy}@cs.sjtu.edu.cn

Abstract. The inconvenience and security risks arose from multi-system security functions are firstly analyzed as well as the limitation of Single Sign On. All kinds of methods to implement the integration of application system security functions are studied. Based on them the omnipotent integration technology for application system security functions (OITASSF) is brought forward. It employs intelligent agent combined with smart card to implement the interaction with application system security function instead of person. The technology has the characteristics of wide applicability, high agility, strong stability and good scalability. At last its simple implementation example is illustrated.

1 Introduction

There come more and more application systems employed to support all kinds of business logics in enterprises. They contain many security functions to control system data security. They have different security policies, security roles definitions, user authentication mechanisms and privilege assignment schemas. They are independent each other with different security borders. User must login the application systems with his accounts assigned by system administrators before he uses them. Some of application systems providing data encryption function need user to enter his keys when encrypting or decrypting data. Currently most of security functions rely on password based security mechanism, so user must remember a large amount of passwords and keys, which brings user a lot of troubles. If user writes them on paper, it will be very dangerous without safe keeping of the import paper. If user sets all passwords and keys to the same string, there will be very large potential risk. The data of all application systems will be menaced even only one password or key is attacked.

The problem of multiple passwords can be solved by Single Sign-On. [1] However the control security region of current Single Sign-On product is limit and some require changing the origin security mechanism of application systems. In addition, Single Sign-On can not solve the problem of passwords and keys storing and using safely. In this paper, an omnipotent integration technology for application system security functions (OITASSF) is brought forward, which makes use of smart card to save all kinds of passwords and keys. It employs intelligent agents to interact with application systems and perform security activities, overcomes the shortage of Single Sign-On, and realizes rapid integration of security functions of application systems.

2 Integration Methods for Application System Security Functions

There are three integration methods of application system security functions and their different advantages and disadvantages as listed in Table 1. [2] We implement OITASSF in security function interface presentation tier.

Table 1. Advantages and disadvantages of application system security function integrations

	Integration Methods	Advantage	Disadvantage
The integration in security function data access tier	Directly deals with security data entities and their attributes	Directly and rapidly	Difficult to integrate the cipher text data; data coupling increases
The integration in security function logic middle tier	Use security function application programming interface (API)	High reliability, easy transformation and mapping of security functions	Many systems have no defined API, and the coverage functions of API are limited
The integration in security function interface presentation tier	Employ user interface as access interface, utilize message mechanism and simulation	No special requirement for application systems and independent from the origin developers; high adaptability	Need special user interface analysis tools; additional system resources; any change for security function user interface of origin application system requires modifying integration codes

3 Omnipotent Integration Technology for Application System Security Functions

3.1 Omnipotent Integration Technology Framework for Application System Security Functions

Omnipotent integration technology framework for application system security functions includes three layers: hardware layer, agent layer and application layer, as shown in Fig. 1. Hardware layer contains smart card. Application layer covers all kinds of application systems such as OA system, financial system and mail system. Agent layer is the core of omnipotent integration technology framework. It connects hardware layer and application layer, monitors the operations of application system

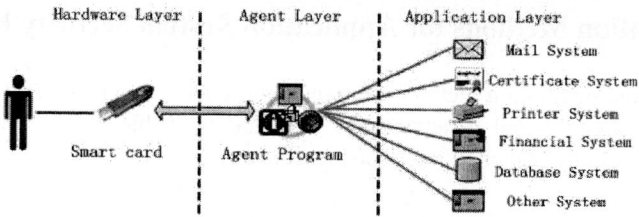

Fig. 1. Omnipotent integration technology framework

security functions in application layer and invokes smart card to provide security services.

3.2 Hardware Layer

Smart card is main supporting device in hardware layer. It both has high security ability and usability. [3] In OITASSF, authentication function and data storage function of smart card is mainly employed. The data stored in smart card include user identification information, password, X.509 certificate and keys etc. Fig. 2 shows the internal information structure of smart card.

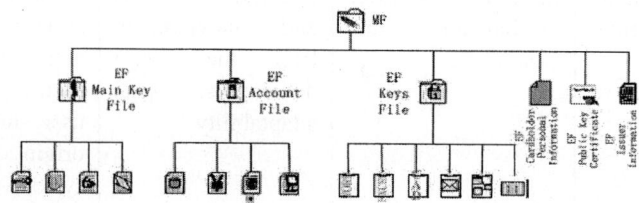

Fig. 2. Smart card internal information structure

3.3 Agent Layer

Agent layer contains intelligent agent program, which automatically monitors user operation of security functions and interacts with them instead of user. The main modules of agent are shown as Fig. 3. The core of agent program is event manager, which is comprised of message capturer module and message processing module. The main algorithm steps of agent program are listed as following:

    1) Message capturer module obtains the messages which operation system sends to integrated application system, including mouse messages and keyboard messages;
    2) The captured messages are sent to message processing module;
    3) Message processing module judges whether user is operating the integrated security functions, and invokes smart card security module;

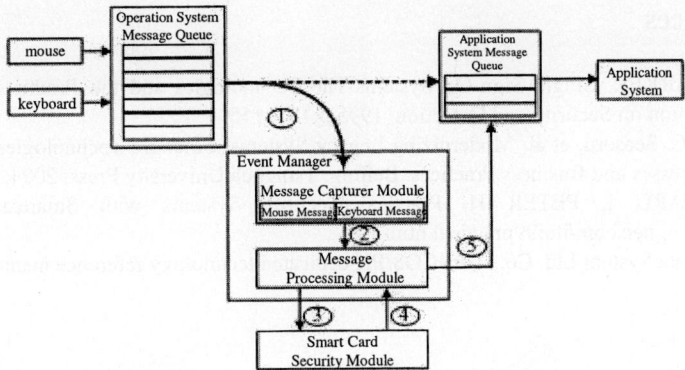

Fig. 3. The main algorithm steps of agent program

4) Smart card security module authenticates user, and gives the authentication output information to message processing module;

5) If authentication is passed, message processing module accesses data in smart card on demand of application system security functions and sends them to application system security interface.

4 The Implementation of Omnipotent Integration Technology

In order to validate OITASSF, we implement a Secure One Card system with Time-COS/PK for 32KB series smart card [4]. The system integrates user identification functions of some application systems such as Foxmail system, HiQ Workflow System. It also integrates document encryption functions of some application system such as MS Word, Excel, Access and Adobe Acrobat. As long as the feature codes for application system security function interfaces are added in agent program or removed from it, security functions can be integrated dynamically.

5 Conclusions

OITASSF utilizes smart card and intelligent agents to integrate application system security functions in interface presentation tier. User can access a lot of security functions just using single smart card. The technology can provide user large convenience and high security simultaneously.

Acknowledgements

This work is supported by Shanghai Commission of Science and Technology (Key Project, Grant No.03DZ1932) and the Zhejiang Commission of Science and Technology (Key Project, Grant No.2003C11009).

References

1. T A PARKER. Single Sign-On Systems-The Technologies and the Products, European Convention on Security and Detection, 1995.5:151~155
2. Robert C. Seasord, et al. Modernizing Legacy Systems: Software Technologies, Engineering Processes and Business Practices. Beijing: Tsinghua University Press. 2004.1
3. NAOMARU I, PETER H, Practical Security Systems with Smartcards, http://citeseer.nj.nec.com/itoi99practical.html
4. Watchdata System Ltd. Co., TimeCOS/PK dedicated technology reference manual, 2001.5

How to Provide Continuous Services by Mobile Servers in Communication Networks*

Satoshi Fujita and Yue Liang

Department of Information Engineering,
Graduate School of Engineering, Hiroshima University
{fujita, ladia}@se.hiroshima-u.ac.jp

Abstract. In this paper, we propose a new framework to provide continuous services by "mobile servers" in interconnection networks. In particular, we prove that for the classes of ring networks with n vertices, $\lceil (n+1)/3 \rceil$ mobile servers are necessary and sufficient to realize mutual transfers among configurations dominating the network, where transfer between two dominating configurations is realized by moving the role of dominating vertex from a vertex to an adjacent vertex.

1 Introduction

In this paper, we propose a new framework to provide continuous services by "mobile servers" in interconnection networks. We model servers as a subset of host nodes, and assume that a node can receive the service if at least one adjacent node is a server (i.e., we assume that the service could not be routed via the interconnection network). In other words, to provide the same service to all the users, the set of servers must be a **dominating set** [3] for the given network. Under such an abstract model, we will consider the following theoretical problem: *Given two dominating configurations A and B, can we transfer configuration A to B by keeping continuous services to the users?* The main results obtained in this paper could be summarized as follows: *For the classes of ring networks with n vertices, $\lceil (n+1)/3 \rceil$ mobile servers are necessary and sufficient to realize mutual transfers among dominating configurations.*

Readers should note that, to the authors' best knowledge, this is the first paper to investigate the mutual transferability among dominating configurations by mobile servers, although the relation between domination and server assignment has been pointed out in the literature [1–3].

2 Preliminaries

Let $G = (V(G), E(G))$ be an undirected graph with vertex set $V(G)$ and edge set $E(G)$. A dominating set for G is a subset U of $V(G)$ such that for any $u \in V(G)$, either $u \in U$ or there exists a vertex $v \in U$ such that $\{u, v\} \in E(G)$.

---

* This research was partially supported by the Grant-in-Aid for Scientific Research (C), 13680417, and Priority Areas (B)(2) 16092219.

In this paper, by technical reasons, we assume that dominating set is a multiset; i.e., it can contain each vertex in $V(G)$ several times. Let $\mathcal{D}(G)$ denote the set of all dominating (multi)sets for G. A dominating set is said to be minimal if the removal of any vertex from that violates the condition of domination (by definition, any minimal dominating set cannot be a multiset). The **domination number** $\gamma(G)$ of G is the size of a minimum dominating set for G, and the **upper domination number** $\Gamma(G)$ of G is the size of a minimal dominating set for G with a maximum cardinality [3].

For any $S_1, S_2 \in \mathcal{D}(G)$, we say that S_1 is *single-step transferable* to S_2, denoted as $S_1 \to S_2$, if there are two vertices u and v in $V(G)$ such that $S_1 - \{u\} = S_2 - \{v\}$ and $\{u, v\} \in E(G)$. Note that a single-step transfer from S_1 to S_2 is realized by moving the "role of dominating vertex" from $u \in S_1$ to its neighbor $v \in S_2$, where each vertex can own more than one roles, since each dominating set is assumed to be a multiset. A transitive closure of the relation of single-step transferability naturally defines the notion of transferability, that will be denoted as $S_1 \stackrel{*}{\to} S_2$, in what follows. Note that every subset of vertices appearing in the transfer from S_1 to S_2 must be a dominating set for G. A set $\mathcal{D}' \subseteq \mathcal{D}(G)$ is said to be **mutually transferable** if for any $S_1, S_2 \in \mathcal{D}'$, it holds $S_1 \stackrel{*}{\to} S_2$, where the sequence of single-step transfers from S_1 to S_2 can contain a subset not in $\mathcal{D}'$, although all subsets in it must be an element in $\mathcal{D}(G)$.

3 Main Theorems

In this paper, we show that for a particular class of graphs consisting of n vertices, $\lceil (n+1)/3 \rceil$ dominating vertices are necessary and sufficient to guarantee the mutual transferability among dominating configurations. The first theorem gives a tight bound for the class of trees (the proof of this theorem is omitted from this extended abstract).

Theorem 1 (Trees). *For any tree T with n vertices, the set of dominating sets for T consisting of $\lceil (n-1)/2 \rceil$ vertices is mutually transferable, and there is a tree with n vertices such that the set of dominating sets for G with cardinality at least $\lceil (n-1)/2 \rceil - 1$ is not mutually transferable.*

As for the other class of graphs, we have proved the following two theorems, which consequently imply the tightness of $\gamma(G) + 1$ for rings with n vertices.

Theorem 2 (Lower Bound). *For any $r \geq 2$ and $n \geq 1$, there is a Hamiltonian r-regular graph G with more than n vertices such that the set of dominating sets for G with cardinality at least $\lceil (n+1)/3 \rceil - 1$ is not mutually transferable.*

Theorem 3 (Rings). *For ring R_n with n vertices, the set of dominating sets for R_n consisting of $\lceil (n+1)/3 \rceil$ vertices is mutually transferable.*

4 Sketch of Proofs

4.1 Theorem 2

The given claim immediately holds for $r = 2$ since in ring networks consisting of $3m$ vertices, two dominating sets with $\lceil (3m+1)/3 \rceil - 1 = m$ vertices are not mutually transferable.

For $r = 3$, we may consider the following graph $G_1 = (V(G_1), E(G_1))$ consisting of 24 vertices, where

$$V(G_1) \stackrel{\text{def}}{=} \{1, 2, \ldots, 24\}, \text{ and}$$

$$E(G_1) \stackrel{\text{def}}{=} \{(i, i+1) \mid 1 \leq i \leq 11, 13 \leq i \leq 23\} \cup \{(12, 1), (24, 13)\}$$
$$\cup \{(i, i+12) \mid 1 \leq i \leq 12\}.$$

Note that G_1 is Hamiltonian, cubic, and $\gamma(G_1) = 6$ (e.g., $\{1, 5, 9, 15, 19, 23\}$ is a minimum dominating set for G_1). Let $S = \{1, 2, 7, 8, 16, 17, 22, 23\}$. Then, $S \in \mathcal{D}(G_1)$, and *any* dominating vertex in S cannot move the role of dominating vertex to its neighbor since each vertex in S "personally" dominates two vertices. Thus, in order to realize a transfer to other dominating sets, nine vertices are necessary. The above construction can be extended to larger cubic graphs consisting of $24x$ vertices for all $x \geq 1$, and in addition, it can be further extended to larger r's. Hence the theorem follows.

4.2 Theorem 3

A ring network consisting of n vertices is formally defined as R_n, where $V(R_n) \stackrel{\text{def}}{=} \{0, 1, \ldots, n-1\}$ and $E(R_n) \stackrel{\text{def}}{=} \{(i, i+1) \mid 0 \leq i \leq n-2\} \cup \{(n-1, 0)\}$. In what follows, we denote $i \pmod{n}$ by i, for brevity, and represent a dominating set by a binary sequence of length n; e.g., sequence 010101 represents a dominating set $\{1, 3, 5\}$ for R_6. We may assume $n \geq 4$ since the given claim obviously holds for $n \leq 3$. In the following proof, we examine the following three cases separately, where Case 2 will be reduced to Case 1, and Case 3 will be reduced to Case 2.

Case 1: When $n = 3m + 2$ for some integer $m \geq 1$.
Case 2: When $n = 3m + 1$ for some integer $m \geq 1$.
Case 3: When $n = 3m$ for some integer $m \geq 1$.

Case 1: In R_n, any vertex can dominate at most three vertices including itself. Since $n = 3m + 2$ and $k = \lceil (n+1)/3 \rceil = m + 1$, in any dominating set with k vertices, two vertices dominate five vertices, and the remaining $k - 2$ vertices dominate $3(k-2) = 3(m-1)$ vertices. Thus, any dominating set in this case can be characterized by the vertex commonly dominated by two vertices. Let S_i denote the dominating set containing vertices $i - 1$ and $i + 1$; i.e., i is the vertex dominated by two vertices. By moving the role of dominating vertex from $i + 1$ to $i + 2$, we realize a single-step transfer from S_i to S_{i+3}, and by repeatedly applying the same operation, we can reach dominating set S_{i+3x} for any $x \geq 1$. Since n is not divided by 3, there exists an integer satisfying $j \equiv i + 3x \pmod{n}$ for any $0 \leq j \leq n - 1$. Hence, the claim follows.

$$0110 \to 0101 \to 0011$$

(a) Right rotation for $n = 4$.

$$0101010 \to 0101001 \to 0100101 \to 0010101$$

(b) Right rotation for $n = 7$.

Fig. 1. Mutual transitions for $n = 4$ and $n = 7$

Case 2: When $n = 3m+1$ and $k = m+1$, we have to examine the following three subcases separately: 1) two vertices dominate four vertices and the remaining $k - 2$ ($= m - 1$) vertices dominate $3m - 3$ vertices; 2) three vertices dominate seven vertices and the remaining $k - 3$ vertices dominate $3m - 6$ vertices; and 3) four vertices dominate ten vertices and the remaining $k - 2$ vertices dominate $3m - 9$ vertices. When $n \geq 7$, any dominating set in the first subcase can be transferred to that in the second subcase (i.e., by changing subsequence 0110 010 to 0101010), and when $n \geq 10$, any dominating set in the second subcase can be transferred to that in the third subcase (i.e., by changing subsequence 0101010 010 to 01010 01010). In addition, mutual transfers for $n = 4$ and 7 can be easily verified by hand (see Figure 1). Thus, in the following, we merely consider dominating sets in the third subcase.

Any dominating set in the third subcase contains two copies of 01010 in it (the remaining part can be divided into $k - 2$ copies of 010). Let us consider a contraction of subsequence 101 to a "super vertex" of label 1, and mark it to distinguish it from the other label 1 vertices. Since this contraction reduces a dominating set with $m + 1$ vertices on R_n to a dominating set with m vertices on $R_{3(m-1)+2}$, we can apply the same argument to Case 1 to complete the proof for this case, provided that the following two operations are available on the original ring R_n:

– an exchange of super vertex of label 1 with a neighbor of label 0, and
– an exchange of super vertex of label 1 with a neighbor of label 1.

In fact, the first operation is realized in two steps as:

$$0101010010 \to 0101001010 \to 0100101010$$

and the second operation is realized in one step as: $0101010010 \to 0101001010$. A reduction from Case 3 to Case 2 can be conducted in a similar manner.

References

1. E. J. Cockayne and S. T. Hedetniemi. Towards a theory of domination in graphs. *Networks*, 7:247–261, 1977.
2. S. Fujita, M. Yamashita, T. Kameda. A Study on r-Configurations – A Resource Assignment Problem on Graphs. *SIAM J. Discrete Math.* 13(2): 227-254 (2000).
3. T. W. Haynes, S. T. Hedetniemi, P. J. Slater, *Fundamentals of Domination in Graphs*, Marcel Dekker, Inc., 1998.

A Framework for Price-Based Resource Allocation on the Grid[1]

Jiadi Yu[1,2], Minglu Li[1], Ying Li[1], Feng Hong[1], and Ming Gao[2]

[1] Department of Computer Science and Engineering, Shanghai Jiao Tong University,
Shanghai 200030, P.R. China
{jdyu, li-ml, liying, hongfeng}@cs.sjtu.edu.cn
[2] Department of Photoelectricity Engineering, Xi'an Institute of Technology,
Xi'an, Shaanxi 710032, P.R. China
{ycardee, gaoming}@mail.xait.edu.cn

Abstract. Grid computing is the key technology of next generation Internet. A promising way of solving the problem of resource allocation in a grid environment is a procedure based upon resource pricing. In Grid Computing Environment, it is very important how to allocate resources for achieving the goal of high effective utilization of resources. This paper targets the problem of resource allocation on the grid. In this paper, we propose a framework for price-based resource allocation and resources pricing algorithm to achieve maximized utilization of grid resources.

1 Introduction

Grid computing has been widely accepted as a promising paradigm for large-scale distributed systems in recent years [1,2], and The purpose of the computational grid is to provide dependable, consistent, pervasive, and inexpensive access to computational resources for the computing community in the form of a computing utility [1]. Resource management and scheduling is a complex undertaking due to large-scale heterogeneity present in resources, management policies, users, and applications requirements in these environments [6].

Grid resources may be distributed at widespread geographic location, and are administrated and owned by different organizations. In Grid Computing Environment, the mechanism built on economic is very suitable for solving the problem of resource management and scheduling. Therefore pricing has been extensively used to arbitrate resource allocation.

There are a lot of research works on manage resources for grid computing based on economics principles, which include [3,4,5,6]. Above frameworks for allocation resources can be improved, and the aim of this paper is to propose a strategy of resource management and scheduling in Grid Computing Environment.

---

[1] This paper is supported by 973 project (No.2002CB312002) of China, ChinaGrid Program of MOE of China, and grand project of the Science and Technology Commission of Shanghai Municipality (No. 03dz15026, No. 03dz15027 and No. 03dz15028).

In this paper, we propose a framework for price-based resource allocation and resources pricing algorithm, which can improve effectively the efficiency of resources utilization and maximize profit of grid resource providers. The paper is organized as follows. In Section 2, we propose a framework for price-based resource allocation. Then, we present an algorithm that computes the price and allocates resource in Section 3. Finally, we give the conclusion of this paper and the future work in Section 4.

2 System Framework

Figure 1 shows System Framework. In our resource scheduling system, the whole grid system as a global grid is organized as resource domains.

- **The Grid Resource Agents (GR-Agents)** is used to manage local resource domains, and represent the interests of the grid resource providers of the computational grid, which hope the grid resource to get maximal profit by selling local resource.
- **The Grid User Agents (GU-Agents)** is used to manage a job submitted by user, and represent the interests of grid user, which hope user to consume minimum cost to achieve goals.
- **Grid Resource Broker (GRB)** [6] is a mediator between the user and grid resources by using middleware services. It is responsible for discovers resources, negotiates for service costs, performs resource selection. It has information about the locations of current resource providers in the grid and their prices.

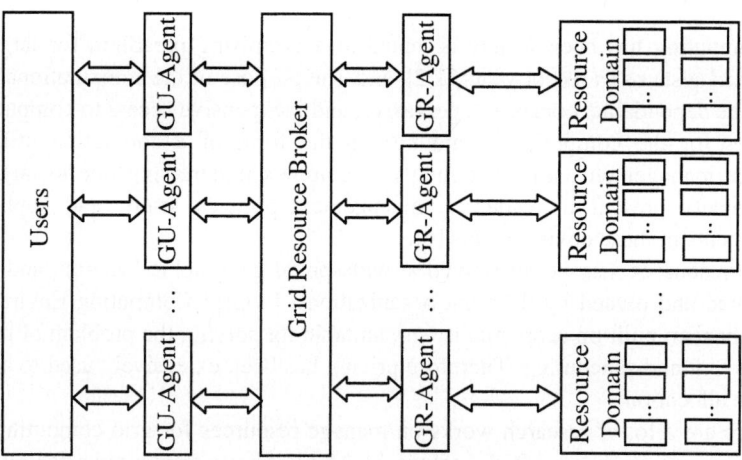

Fig. 1. System Framework

In the grid, each GR-Agent publishes resources of their resources domain to GRB. When a user prepares to submit job, a new GU-Agent is created. GU-Agent analyzes and recognizes submitted job, and then get resource information that can meet the requirement submitted job. GU-Agent orders GRB to find resources in grid resource domains according to resource information so as to meet the necessary capacity to GU-Agent.

GU-Agent queries GR-Agent price information of resource. If GU-Agent refuses the given price to make a purchase, new price may be set. When a GU-Agent purchases a portion of the resource, the price that GU-Agent pays is unable to be changed until user job is completed.

Interactions and negotiations between GU-Agents and GR-Agents are by the means of GRB, and multi GU-Agents and GR-Agents can interact and negotiate simultaneously. GRB will mediate bargaining by using price-based resource allocation algorithm. In this algorithm initial prices have been set, and GU-Agents and GR-Agents may negotiate this price by using GRB until they came to an acceptable price.

3 Resource Allocation

The whole grid system is made up of n Grid Domains. Each Grid Domain consists of k resources units, and is managed by a GR-Agent$_i$. We define a $\xi = (\xi_{i,j})_{n \times k}$ as system processing power matrix, where $\xi_{i,j}$ specifies processing power of the ith Grid Domain for the jth type of resource, and define resources prices that is stored in a vector $P_t = \{P_t^1, P_t^2, \ldots, P_t^k\}$ with the range of prices being L to H, $P_t^k \in (L, H)$, for each member of the vector i = 1,.., k and each time period t, where L is floor prices of resources, and H is the initial upper limit on prices asked. Each Grid Domain will produce a dualistic table $\Gamma_i (\xi, P_t)$ (the i index Grid Domains, i$\in$ (1,n)). GR-Agent$_i$ holds this table and publishes it to GRB in order to resources allocation. GRB initializes Γ (Γ_1, Γ_2, ... , Γ_n) according to the information submitted by all existing GR-Agents. All information of resources provided are stored in Γ. Γ should be updated by GR-Agents if the change happens within current Grid Domains. Otherwise, GR-Agents needn't update Γ.

A user submits a job to GU-Agent. GU-Agent analyzes and recognizes submitted job, and then get resources information Θ (θ, ζ, P) that can meet the requirement submitted job, where θ denotes type of requirement resource; ζ denotes processing power of requirement resource; P denotes prices expected by user.

According to information of resources provided Γ and requirement resources Θ, GRB finds resources which can meet the requirement. If resources provided do not satisfy requirement resources (for example, any θ cannot be found in Γ, or $\zeta_\theta > \xi_\theta$ exists), GR-Agents will update Γ. If appropriate resources still cannot be satisfied after some times, GRB suspends this job, and the job cannot be implemented. Then GRB sends this message to GU-Agent, and GU-Agent will cancel this job and notify the user. If appropriate resources can be found, GRB can get a quadruple table E (θ, $GR_{i,j}$, P_t, P), where θ, Pt ,P are defined above; $GR_{i,j}$ denotes the ith Grid Domain for the jth type of resource.

Resource provider attempts to get maximal profit, and simultaneously user hope the price paid should as low as possible without failing to obtain the resource. We propose two pricing functions for GU-Agent and GR-Agent. GU-Agent pricing function is $P(t) = P + \varepsilon \Delta t$, and GR-Agent pricing function is $P(t) = P_0 - \varepsilon \Delta t$, where t is the time parameter, P and P_0 denotes base price that are set respectively by GU-Agent and GR-Agent (P, $P_0 \in$ (L, H), where L, H are defined above). With time elapsing, GU-Agent and GR-Agent respectively increase or decrease the price by a small amount ε after each negotiation.

These two functions automatically make in agents, and then GR-Agent and GU-Agent negotiate resource price in GRB. If negotiation is successful, resource price is set and stored in a price vector $P = \{P_1, P_2, \ldots, P_\theta\}$; otherwise two functions must make again in GR-Agent and GU-Agent respectively until price exceed the scope of (L, H).

4 Conclusions and Further Work

In Grid Computing Environment, it is an effective approach to use economic models to schedule and manage resources. In this paper, we have shown a framework for price-based resource allocation and then present a strategy of allocating resources and resources pricing algorithm, which can improve effectively the efficiency of resources utilization and maximize profit of grid resource providers.

Other works that will need to be considered and need further investigation include: Security of the system must be further increased; Scalability needs to be addressed; Fault tolerance should be studied.

References

1. Foster, I., Kesselman, C.(eds.).: The Grid: Blueprint for a New Computing Infrastructure. Morgan Kaufmann (1999)
2. Foster, I., Kesselman, C., Tuecke S.: The Anatomy of the Grid: Enabling Scalable Virtual Organizations. International Journal of High Performance Computing Application, 15(3), (2001)
3. R. Wolski, J. Plank, J. Brevik, and T. Bryan,: Analyzing Market-based Resource Allocation Strategies for the ComputationalGrid. International Journal of High Performance Computing Applications, Sage Publications, Vol 15(3), (2001)
4. Subramoniam, K., Maheswaran, M., Toulouse, M.: Towards a Micro-Economic Model for Resource Allocation in Grid Computing System. Proceedings of the 2002 IEEE Canadian Conference on Electrical & Computer Engineering (2002)
5. B. N. Chun and D. E. Culler.: Market-based proportional resource sharing for clusters. Millenium Project Research Report, Sep. 1999.
6. Buyya, R., Abramson, D., Giddy, J.: A Case for Economy Grid Architecture for Service Oriented Grid Computing. Proceedings of International Parallel and Distributed Processing Symposium: Heterogeneous Computing Workshop (HCW 2001), San Francisco, USA.

RT-Grid: A QoS Oriented Service Grid Framework*

Hai Jin, Hanhua Chen, Minghu Zhang, and Deqing Zou

Cluster and Grid Computing Lab,
Huazhong University of Science and Technology, Wuhan, 430074, China
hjin@hust.edu.cn

Abstract. Effective and efficient *Quality of Service* (QoS) management is critical for a service grid to meet the requirements of both grid users and service providers. We incorporate QoS management into *Open Grid Services Architecture* (OGSA) and provide a high-level middleware to build complex applications with QoS guarantees. We introduce a scalable framework of information service in which capabilities of services are described and advertised as metadata of grid services. Based on that, a QoS policy based dynamic service scheduling strategy is proposed. The experiment result on the prototype proves the availability of our framework.

1 Introduction

OGSA presents a vision of an integrated approach to support both e-science and e-business [1]. The most striking technical contributions of OGSA to the Globus are in the area of extensibility and manageability. As implementation of OGSA, *Open Grid Service Infrastructure* (OGSI) [2], such as Globus Toolkit 3.0, and *Web Service Resource Framework* (WSRF) [3], such as Globus Tookit 3.9, provide the basic functionalities without QoS management.

In a highly competitive service grid environment, quality of service is one of the substantial aspects for differentiating between similar service providers. It is important for the grid platform to support dynamic service allocation in accordance with QoS policy. We provide a platform for service designers from specific organizations of business domains to publish the business semantics document described with standard interface description languages and QoS metadata schema. Different service providers implement the service semantics, deploy their services and register their service implementations with different *QoS metadata*. The semantic information and QoS metadata are managed and advertised by information service, and they are used for service selection and scheduling.

2 QoS-Based Service Grid Framework

Service-oriented view simplifies service virtualization through encapsulation of diverse implementations behind a common interface that standardizes the business function.

---

* This paper is supported by National Science Foundation under grant 60273076 and 90412010, ChinaGrid project from Ministry of Education, and the National 973 Key Basic Research Program under grant No.2003CB317003.

Our grid environment provides a set of *virtual service* (VS) to users.

$$Grid = \{VS\}$$

We develop a tool for service designer to define and advertise a *VS* by defining service interfaces as gwsdl porttypes (defined in OGSI specification). We call an implementation of *VS* a *physical service* (PS). Each *VS* is a set of redundant *PS*s.

$$VS = \{PS\}$$

All the *PS*s of the same *VS* have the uniform *operation* (O) set and are invoked in the same manner, while even the diverse implementations of the same operation by different *PS*s may have different *QoS Costs* (C).

$$PS = \{<O, C>\}$$

Here, the 2-tuple $<O, C>$ defines an operation with a QoS cost expression which may include the resource description and other capacity metadata for this operation.

We designed a XML-schema (in Fig.1) for operation cost. The schema is used as metadata schema of a service. Using the schema service providers can define the cost of any operation in the service separately. Based on the service QoS metadata schema, different policies can be designed for service scheduling.

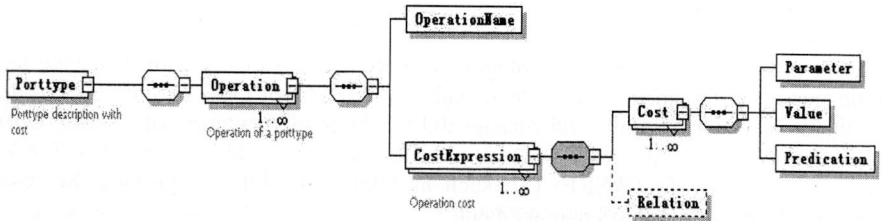

Fig. 1. XML Schema for the Service QoS MetaData

A user's request to the grid in the policy is described as following:

$$Request = VS_{request} <o_i, c_{request}>$$

A domain server is responsible for autonomous intra-domain administration and inter-domain interaction. It consists of a *Domain Service Broker* (DSB), a DIS and a *QoS Manager* (QoSM). The architecture of a domain server is shown in Fig.2.

When there comes a request, DSB looks up the DIS or GIS, selects the proper service and negotiates an SLA according to the QoS metadata of the service and the requirements of the incoming request $VS_{request} <o_i, c_{request}>$. A proxy instance is created to dispatch and monitor the coming communication. The QoSM is responsible for the QoS of network and SLAs management. The SLAs status is monitored and maintained by QoSM during the life cycle of the grid service instance. It also allows reasoning about the status of SLAs related to an application context across multiple administrative domains by contacting and querying QoSM in other domain servers.

Our grid information service architecture aims at supporting service discovery. The architecture of the GIS is like distributed *Universal Description, Discovery and Integration* (UDDI). It is a distributed system with peer-to-peer [4][5] structure. DISs and GISs are organized in hierarchical scheme. DIS updates the service information to specify group information server dynamically. When a grid customer wants to access a service, it first looks up local DIS containing the service information, and continues to search the GIS upon failure.

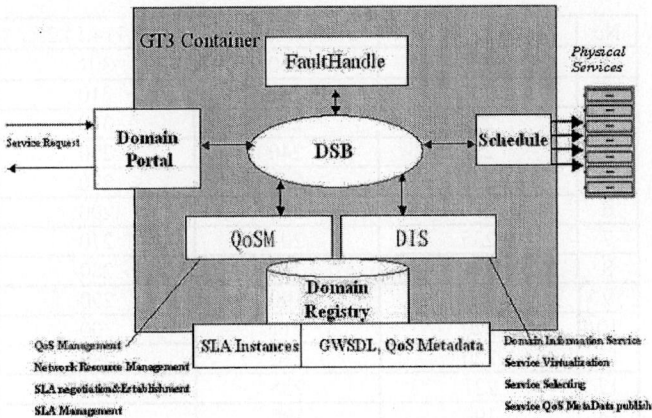

Fig. 2. Domain Server Architecture

3 Experiment Results

Our service grid prototype uses a virtual calculator service as an example, with implementations from three different domains of the Cluster and Grid Computing Lab of Huazhong University of Science and Technology. Services deployed on heterogeneous sites provide different response capacity and network cost. On site 211.69.206.128 an IBM x235 server runs, 211.69.206.199 an HP rx2600 server, and 202.114.14.252 a PC server equipped with an Intel Xeon 1GHz CPU and 512MB memory. We have three groups of experiments. In each group, 20 random recodes of requests, which have the same time constrain, are selected. The deadlines specified in the three groups are 240 ms, 260 ms, and 450ms, respectively. According to the metadata of the services all the requests are allocated to a site. Response time of each access is shown in Table.1.

The marked data shows the cases that the real-time constrains are not met. The preliminary results demonstrate that the strategies have a good role on our service grid prototype. We also implement a fault-tolerant strategy. If a fault occurs during the access, the request can be re-scheduled to another service with higher response capacity.

4 Conclusions and Future Works

We extend the service abstraction in OGSA for QoS management and provide a high-level middleware to build complex application with QoS management. QoS-based service virtualization framework is proposed. In next steps, we will enhance the QoS policy based service-scheduling model to make it support more algorithms, analyze the cost of grid middleware and try to improve the performance.

Table 1. Experiment Result: Resoponse Time

No	211.69.206.128	211.69.206.199	202.114.14.252
1	220	260	301
2	200	250	310
3	220	251	310
4	221	240	280
5	230	541	270
6	230	260	290
7	235	201	270
8	211	210	280
9	411	190	290
10	220	211	300
11	220	230	280
12	221	255	250
13	190	190	251
14	235	201	270
15	200	210	280
16	220	200	260
17	210	210	270
18	220	180	340
19	211	190	270
20	221	200	260

References

[1] I. Foster, C. Kesselman, J. M. Nick, and S. Tuecke, "The Physiology of the Grid An Open Grid Services Architecture for Distributed Systems Integration", *DRAFT document of Globus Project of the University of Chicago*, February 17, 2002.
[2] S. Tuecke, K. Czajkowski, I. Foster, J. Frey, S. Graham, C. Kesselman, D. Snelling, and P. Vanderbilt, *Open Grid Services Infrastructure*, February 17, 2003.
[3] K. Czajkowski, D. F. Ferguson, I. Foster, J. Frey, S. Graham, I. Sedukhin, D. Snelling, S. Tuecke, and W. Vambenepe, "The WS-Resource Framework", *http://www.globus.org/wsrf/*
[4] M. Ripeanu, "Peer-to-Peer architecture case study: Gnutella network", *Proceedings of International Conference on Peer-to-peer Computing*, 2001.
[5] I. Stoica, R. Morris, D. Karger, M. Kaashoek, and H. Balakrishnan, "Chord: A scalable peer-to-peer lookup service for internet applications", *ACM SIGCOMM*, 2001.

Storage-Aware Harmonic Broadcasting Protocol for Video-on-Demand

Chao Peng and Hong Shen

Graduate School of Information Science,
Japan Advanced Institute of Science and Technology,
1-1 Tatsunokuchi, Ishikawa, 923-1292, Japan
p-chao@jaist.ac.jp

Abstract. Video-on-demand (VOD) is a service that allows users to view any video program from a server at the time of their choice. The Harmonic Broadcasting Protocol has been proved to be bandwidth-optimal, but it is not efficient for the local storage. In this paper, we present a new effective broadcasting scheme, which can intelligently adjust its solution according to available bandwidth and local storage in order to achieve an ideal waiting time.

Keywords: video-on-demand, broadcasting protocols, scheduling.

1 Introduction

Usually a video-on-demand system is implemented by a client-server architecture supported by certain transport networks such as CATV, telecom, or satellite networks. Clients use web browsers or have set-top-boxes (STB) on their television sets. In a pure VOD system, each user is assigned a dedicated video channel so that they can watch the video they chose without delay and many VCR-like functions may be provided.

The bandwidth and storage cost for pure VOD is tremendous, many alternatives have been proposed to reduce it by sacrificing some VCR functions. Broadcasting is one of such techniques and is mostly appropriate for popular or hot videos that are likely to be simultaneously watched by many viewers.

In this paper, we present the *Storage-aware Harmonic Broadcasting Protocol*, which can intelligently adjust its solution to achieve an ideal waiting time according to available bandwidth and local storage.

2 The VOD Model and SHB Protocol

In a VOD model, we use L(seconds) to denote the length of a video program. B(Mb/s) denotes the available bandwidth of the server. c(Mb/s) denotes the consumption rate. S(Mb) denotes the size of a video program, $S = L \cdot c$. D(seconds) denotes the endurable maximum delay. M(Mb) denotes the minimum local storage size. R(Mb/s) denotes the minimum user I/O rate.

The mission is to find a scheduling of the video contents. We use b(Mb/s) to denote the bandwidth used in a scheme. d(seconds) denotes the max delay in a broadcast scheme. m(Mb) denotes the max local storage needed in a scheme. r(Mb/s) denotes the max I/O rate needed in a scheme. The solution must satisfy: $(b \leq B) \wedge (d \leq D) \wedge (m \leq M) \wedge (r \leq R)$.

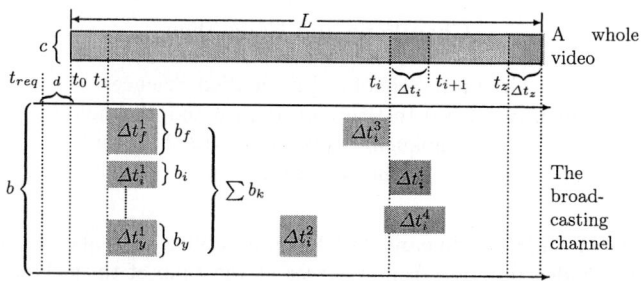

Fig. 1. A general framework for VOD scheduling

The *Harmonic Broadcasting Protocol*(HB) was proposed by Juhn and Tseng in [2]. HB equally divides a video into n segments $[S = S_1 \uplus S_2 \uplus \cdots \uplus S_n]$, and each segment S_i will be divided into i equal-size subsegments $[S_i = S_i^1 \uplus S_i^2 \uplus \cdots \uplus S_i^i]$. Then HB allocates a single channel with bandwidth $b_i = c/i$ for each segment S_i. Thus the maximum delay is the length of the first segment $d = L_1 = L/n$ and the bandwidth is $b = H_n \cdot c$(H_n is the Harmonic Number).

HB has been proved by Engebretsen and Sudan to be the Bandwidth-Optimal protocol in [4]. But in [3] it was observed that the user in HB may not get all data it needs to consume on time. The authors of [3] also proposed the *Cautious Harmonic Broadcasting Protocol*(CHB) and the *Quasi-Harmonic Broadcasting Protocol*(QHB). CHB and QHB are based on the same idea of HB, the new point is that they changed the arrangement of subsegments so that the average waiting time can be reduced by a factor near 2. However, HB is still the best for the same Maximum Waiting Time.

HB needs around 37% of the whole video size for its local storage. Unfortunately sometimes in real applications we will encounter the problem of local storage shortage. Because the STBs of some earlier VOD users usually have less local storage than those of the later users. While the consumption rate of hot videos are tend to be higher and higher. Yet before those earlier users update their hardware, the VOD service supplier still have to satisfy their demand.

Thus we propose the *Storage-aware Harmonic Broadcasting Protocol* (SHB). It equally divides a video into n segments, then arranges the first i segments according to HB and assign the same bandwidth as b_i for remain segments. In this case, the bandwidth will be $H_i + (n - i + 1)/i$ and the size of the content deposited in the local storage will be:

$$\begin{cases} f_1(t) = t \sum_{k=t}^{i} \frac{1}{k} + \frac{t \cdot (t-1)}{2} \cdot \frac{1}{i} & \text{Case1: } t \leq i, \\ f_2(t) = \frac{i \cdot (i+1)}{2} \cdot \frac{1}{i} = \frac{i+1}{2} & \text{Case2: } i < t \leq n - i, \\ f_3(t) = \frac{(2i - n + t)(n - t + 1)}{2 \cdot i} & \text{Case3: } n - i \leq t \leq n. \end{cases}$$

We can prove that $f_1(t)$ is an increasing function. Since

$$f_1(t) - f_1(t-1) = t\sum_{k=t}^{i} \frac{1}{k} + \frac{t\cdot(t-1)}{2}\cdot\frac{1}{i} - ((t-1)\sum_{k=t-1}^{i}\frac{1}{k} + \frac{(t-1)\cdot(t-2)}{2}\cdot\frac{1}{i})$$
$$= (2i\sum_{k=t-1}^{i}\frac{1}{k} - \frac{2i(t-1)}{t-1} + t^2 - t - t^2 + 3t - 2)/(2i)$$
$$= (2i\sum_{k=t-1}^{i}\frac{1}{k} + 2t - 2i - 2)/(2i)$$
$$\geq (2i\frac{i-t+2}{i} + 2t - 2i - 2)/(2i) = 1/i > 0.$$

Observe that $f_1(i) = (i+1)/2$ and $f_3(t) < (i+1)/2$, we conclude that $f_2(t) = (i+1)/2$ is the dominant case. So we only need to find the largest n and a certain i such that $H_i + (n-i+1)/i \leq B$ and $S \cdot (i+1)/(2 \cdot n) \leq M$.

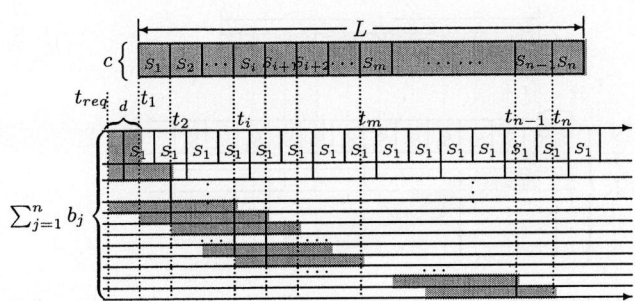

Fig. 2. The Bandwidth and Storage Situation of Storage-aware HB

For the theoretical optimal, suppose the current storage bottleneck is M. If the consumption rate is c and we divide the whole video into n segments, the length of the i-th segment is L_i, then $S_i = L_i \cdot c$ and $S = L \cdot c = \sum_{i=1}^{n} L_i \cdot c = \sum_{i=1}^{n} S_i$. The time when we should start consume S_i is $t_i = \sum_{k=1}^{i-1} L_k + \frac{S_1}{b_1} = \sum_{k=1}^{i-1} S_k + \frac{S_1}{b_1}$. If we assign bandwidth b_i to S_i, to minimize the usage of storage, we should download it from $t_i - S_i/b_i$. So the download period of S_i is $P_i = [t_i - S_i/b_i, t_i]$. W.l.o.g., let $c = 1$ and define $I(i,j) = \begin{cases} 1 & i \leq j, \\ 0 & i > j. \end{cases}$

We can write the problem we need to solve as a linear program. The goal is to find $2n$ real numbers $S_1, S_2, ..., S_n$ and $b_1, b_2, ..., b_n$ that:

minimize $\qquad \sum_{i=1}^{n} b_i$

subject to $\qquad \sum_{i=1}^{n} S_i = S, \quad \frac{S_i}{b_i} \leq \sum_{k=1}^{i-1}\frac{S_i}{b_i} + \frac{S_1}{b_1},$
$\qquad\qquad t_i = \sum_{k=1}^{i-1} L_k + \frac{S_1}{b_1} = \sum_{k=1}^{i-1} S_k + \frac{S_1}{b_1},$
$\qquad\qquad \forall t, \sum_{i=1}^{n} I(t_i - \frac{S_i}{b_i}, t) \cdot I(t, t_i) \cdot b_i \cdot (t - (t_i - \frac{S_i}{b_i})) \leq M.$

3 Performance Analysis and Comparison

Suppose there is a STB whose storage size is $2Gbytes$, which can satisfy the requirement of HB for any video whose size is less than $5.4Mbytes$. Such as a video of $c \leq 5Mbps$ and $L \leq 7200sec$. What if there is a hot video with $c = 10Mbps$ and $L = 7200sec$? Now that $L*c = 7200*10/8 = 9000Mbytes$ and $m = 7200*10*37\%/8 = 3330Mbytes > 2Gbytes$, we cannot use HB.

By SHB, we can divide the whole video into 10 segments, then arrange the first 3 segments by HB, and the following segments will be allocated a bandwidth same as that of the 3rd segment. We can check from Figure3 that at any time the content remain in the local storage will be no more than 2 segments. So the local storage is only 20% of the whole video size, which equals $1800Mbytes$ for the above case.

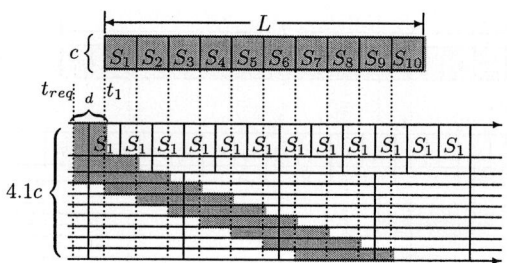

Fig. 3. An example Storage-aware HB when $n = 10$ and $i = 3$

The bandwidth used in this solution is around $b = 4.17c$, which can be further optimized. We can set $n = 9, i = 3$ and get $b = 3.83c$, while $m = 9*(3+1)/(2*9) = 2Gbytes$. Yet the delay $d = 7200/9 = 800s$ is too large, we can enlarge n and reduce d. By set $n = 63, i = 27$, we get $m = 2Gbytes, d \simeq 1.9min, b = 5.22c$, which is bearable. If we want to use HB with the same delay, then the bandwidth we need is $4.73c$ and $m = 9*0.37 = 3.33Gbytes$. So the tradeoff here is: we get a storage decrease of $1.33Gbytes$ by increasing $0.49c = 4.9Mbps$ more bandwidth. The method we used in SHB can also be applied to CHB and QHB to allay the local storage shortage problem.

4 Conclusion

In this paper we present the SHB, which can adapt the original HB to the available resources. It can be used for some cases when HB is not applicable due to the local storage shortage, the implement is quite simple and very flexible.

References

1. Chao Peng and Hong Shen. A Storage-aware Scheduling Scheme for VOD. *3rd International Conference on Grid and Cooperative Computing*, PRC, Oct. 2004.
2. L. Juhn and L. Tseng. Harmonic broadcasting for video-on-demand service. *IEEE Transactions on Broadcasting*, 43(3): 268-271, Sept. 1997.

3. J.-F. Paris, S. Carter and D. D. E. Long. Efficient broadcasting protocols for video on demand. Proc. 6th *International Symposium on Modeling, Analysis and Simulation of Computer and Telecommunication Systems (MASCOTS '98)*, Montral, Canada, pages 127-132, July 1998.
4. L. Engebretsen and M. Sudan. Harmonic broadcasting is optimal. *Proc. 6th Proceedings of the thirteenth annual ACM-SIAM symposium on Discrete algorithms*, San Francisco, California, Pages: 431 - 432, Jan. 2002.

Stochastic DFS for Multiprocessor Scheduling of Cyclic Taskgraphs

Frode Eika Sandnes[1] and Oliver Sinnen[2]

[1] Oslo University College, P.O. Box 4, St. Olav's plass, N-0130 Oslo, Norway
[2] Dept. of Electrical and Computer Engineering, University of Auckland, Private Bag 92019, Auckland, New Zealand

Abstract. DFS has previously been shown to be a simple and efficient strategy for removing cycles in graphs allowing the resulting DAGs to be scheduled using one of the many well-established DAG multiprocessor scheduling algorithms. In this paper, we investigate the inefficiencies of schedules acquired using DFS cycle removal. Further, an improved randomised DFS cycle removal algorithm is proposed that produces significantly improved results with acceptable computational overheads.

1 Introduction

Cyclic computations occur in a wide range of fields, for example digital signal processing (mobile phones and consumer entertainment electronics) [1] and feedback control (industrial robots, automobiles, airplanes and missiles) [2]. The characteristics of these systems are that the same computations are repeated continuously, where an internal state (the state vector) and the inputs (connected to some sort of sensor) are changing, resulting in different outputs (connected to some sort of actuators).

Some of the digital signal processing algorithms (such as Kalman filtering [3]) and controllers can be computationally expensive and accompanied by hard real-time constraints. Consequently, multiple processing elements must be used when single processing elements are unable to provide the necessary computational power needed to meet the hard real-time deadlines. For this purpose many researchers have resorted to multiprocessor scheduling techniques for acquiring implementations on processor networks [2,1,4].

Often such implementations need to reside in embedded systems, where resources are scarce such as limited physical space for the hardware and limited battery capacity. Recent work in multiprocessor scheduling exploits the laws of physics combined with parallel computing techniques to reduce power consumption. Power consumption increases approximately quadratically with processor clock speed. In power aware computing systems, power is saved by using multiple low-speed processors instead of one single powerful high-speed processor [5–7].

This paper addresses the scheduling of such cyclic computations, whether it is for traditional high performance computers or mobile supercomputers.

2 Scheduling Cyclic Graphs

In traditional multiprocessor scheduling the computations are usually represented as a directed acyclic graph (DAG), where the vertices represent computations and the edges represent data dependencies between these computations. Each vertex is usually referred to as a task. The problem of scheduling is to map these tasks onto a network of processors such that the precedence constraints are not violated and the schedule length, also known as the makespan, is minimised. In general, this problem is known to be NP-hard, and a large number of studies have addressed this problem. Furthermore, nearly an equal number of powerful scheduling strategies have been proposed [8, 9, 4].

In its basic form, a DAG represents a once-only computation where one starts with the entry tasks and finishes once the exit tasks are all completed. Cyclic problems are more complex. A large class of cyclic computations can be represented using cyclic graphs. A number of strategies have been proposed for scheduling cyclic computations. One avenue of research exploits retiming and is particularly used within the field of VLSI [10]. Another, strategy is graph unfolding, where a cyclic graph is transformed into a DAG where multiple iterations are represented [11]. Since multiple iterations are represented the scheduling algorithms usually produce acceptable results since most of the data dependencies between the tasks are exploited during scheduling. The drawback of the unfolding technique is that the number of iterations needs to be known at compile time (at least for complete unfolding) and that the final schedule becomes proportional to the unfolding factor. If the unfolding factor is large the resulting schedule also becomes large. This is therefore an unsuitable strategy in situations where a large problem is mapped onto a system with severe resource constraints. Also, by unfolding a cyclic graph its regular structure of computation, i.e. cyclic execution, is not exploited.

Another strategy is to simply transform the cyclic graph into a DAG (without unfolding). In order to do so some edges must be removed and all cycles must be broken. The edges must be removed in such a way that the resulting makespan after scheduling is minimised. Simultaneously, the algorithm must ensure that none of the data dependencies in the cyclic graph are violated.

In one approach [12] the cyclic graphs were unfolded into a DAG comprising of two cycles, and a genetic algorithm was used to determine the scheduling frontier that resulted in the shortest makespan (i.e. the set of tasks from the first and the second cycle). This approach produced reasonable results but the algorithm is relatively complex and the removal of cycles is intertwined with the scheduling step.

In a more recent attempt [13], the cyclic graphs were transformed into DAGs by the means of depth first search (DFS) [14]. The algorithm works as follows: Each vertex in the graph is in turn used as a start node. Then the DFS algorithm is applied to the graph with the given start node to produce a graph without cycles. The advantage of this strategy is that the DFS algorithm is simple and well known, the number of iterations need not be known at compile time, the resulting schedules do not require extraneous amounts of space and best of all

— it can be used in conjunction with most of the existing scheduling algorithms from the literature. However, as the authors pointed out, the drawbacks of the proposed DFS algorithm is that some performance in the resulting schedules might be lost due to ambiguities arising at some steps of the DFS algorithm. In particular, when the DFS algorithm is traversing a graph it ends up in a situation where it could traverse a number of vertices. The basic DFS does not specify which of these vertices should be visited, and one might be selected arbitrarily. The theme of this paper is to explore the effects of these arbitrary choices and propose an improved version of the DFS-based strategy.

3 Exploring Cycle-Removal with DFS

An experiment was carried out to explore the effects of the arbitrary choices in the DFS algorithm on the critical path and consequently the makespan of the resulting schedule. 100 random graphs for each of the densities 0.05 to 0.60 in steps of 0.05 were generated. The density of a graph indicates the probability of there being an edge between two vertices in the graph. I.e. a graph with a low density has fewer edges than a graph with a high density. These graphs were obtained by setting the values of the adjacency matrix for the graph to 0 or 1 with the given probability. Each graph was processed 100 times using the DFS algorithm and each time an ambiguous situation occurred it was resolved pseudo randomly. Each graph was also scaled into three versions, one with a communication-to-computation ratio (CCR) of 1:10 (low communication costs), 1:1 (medium communication costs) and 10:1 (high communication costs). Each of the resulting graphs where scheduled using the critical-path/most immediate successor first (CP-MISF) heuristic [4] onto a simulated fully connected eight-processor distributed memory machine.

Table 1 lists the average percentage difference between the smallest and the largest critical path and makespan obtained for each graph through the stochastic process. Clearly, the critical path for the three different communication-to-computation ratios are identical as the communication weight does not affect the critical path of the graph.

Clearly, the percentage difference between the largest and the smallest critical path is larger for more sparse graphs with a lower density and decreases gradually as the graphs become more dense with increasing graph densities. I.e. the average percentage difference is as much as 22.7 % for sparse graphs (with density 0.05) and as little as 2 % for graph with a high density (typically 0.5-0.6). Consequently, the impact of the ambiguities in the DFS algorithm is more influential in sparse graphs than for dense graphs — and real-world computations often comprise of sparse graphs.

Obviously, similar patterns can be seen for the makespans acquired when scheduling the taskgraphs. For graphs with a low communication-to-computation ratio the percentage difference between the maximum and the minimum schedule is closely matching those of the critical path. Further, for the graph with medium communication-to-computation ratio the percentage difference is about half of

Table 1. Average percentage difference between the largest and the smallest critical path (cp) and makespan

	CCR=10		CCR=1		CCR=0.1	
density	cp %	makespan %	cp %	makespan %	cp %	makespan %
0.05	22.7 %	0.0 %	22.7 %	15.2 %	22.7 %	22.0 %
0.10	16.8 %	0.0 %	16.8 %	11.1 %	16.8 %	16.2 %
0.15	9.1 %	0.0 %	9.1 %	5.0 %	9.1 %	8.7 %
0.20	7.0 %	0.0 %	7.0 %	4.0 %	7.0 %	6.7 %
0.25	5.0 %	0.0 %	5.0 %	2.0 %	5.0 %	4.7 %
0.30	4.0 %	0.0 %	4.0 %	2.0 %	4.0 %	3.8 %
0.35	4.0 %	0.0 %	4.0 %	2.0 %	4.0 %	3.8 %
0.40	5.0 %	0.0 %	5.0 %	2.0 %	5.0 %	4.7 %
0.45	3.0 %	0.0 %	3.0 %	1.0 %	3.0 %	2.8 %
0.50	3.0 %	0.0 %	3.0 %	1.0 %	3.0 %	2.7 %
0.55	2.0 %	0.0 %	2.0 %	0.0 %	2.0 %	1.8 %
0.60	2.0 %	0.0 %	2.0 %	1.0 %	2.0 %	1.9 %

what can be observed for the difference in critical path. For graphs with a high communication-to-computation ratio there is no observable difference between the minimum and the maximum makespan. We can conclude from these observations that the impact of the ambiguities in the DFS algorithm are less important when the communication to computation delay is large and that the importance of the sequence in which vertices are processed play a more important role for graphs with medium or small communication-to-computation delays.

The variances of the datasets also show a similar pattern. I.e. the variance is larger for low densities and smaller for larger densities.

At each step of the DFS we also recorded the size of the list of the ambiguous choices. I.e. how many vertices to choose between when making a choice at each step of the DFS algorithm. The results of this is shown in Table 2.

Table 2. Average number of ambiguous choices at each step of the DFS algorithm

density	% amb.
0.05	5.16
0.10	9.04
0.15	15.16
0.20	19.99
0.25	25.19
0.30	29.91
0.35	34.68
0.40	38.89
0.45	44.38
0.50	48.80
0.55	53.67
0.60	59.45

Graphs with a low density have a lower average number of ambiguous tasks, while graphs with a large density have a large average number of ambiguous tasks. When taking into consideration that the effect of the ambiguous tasks is larger in sparse graphs than dense graphs one can conclude that it is actually not the number of ambiguous cases that determines the degree of effect but rather the structure of the graph. These results also shows that the DFS in its basic form is under-specified in terms of how to remove cycles from a graph in the context of multiprocessor scheduling.

Clearly, these experiments indicate that the sequence in which nodes are processed in the DFS algorithm plays an important role. This observation is the basis for the proposed improved version of the DFS cycle removal algorithm, which we have chosen to term Random-DFS.

4 Random-DFS Cycle Removal

The proposed improved Random-DFS algorithm works as follows: At the highest level the Random-DFS algorithm is repeated s times, where s denotes the sampling size. A high value of s indicates a higher probability of finding a close to optimal solution. However, a high value of s also indicates a high computation load. At each iteration the critical path of the resulting graph is assessed and the graph yielding the smallest critical path is the result. The algorithm can be outlined as follows:

```
Random-DFS(input graph G,           // cyclic graph
           input node s,            // start node
           output graph DAG)        // acyclic graph
  begin
    repeat s times
    begin
      graph D;
      Random-decyclify(G, D);
      if D.criticalPath() < DAG.criticalPath() then
      begin
        DAG = D;
      end
    end
  end
```

The Random-decyclify algorithm can be outlined as follows

```
Random-decyclify(input  graph G,      // cyclic graph
                 output graph DAG)    // acyclic graph
  table colour;    // each vertex is assigned a colour
  begin
    DAG := G;
    for each vertex v in G do // Colour all
```

```
        colour[v] := WHITE;      // vertices white.
    done
    Random-DFS-Visit(random start node);  // Start

                              // Remove all edges
                              // crossing the
    for each edge e in G do   // iteration frontier.
      if colour[source(e)] = WHITE and
         colour[destination(e)] = BLACK then
         DAG := DAG - e;      // remove edge e
      endif
    done

                              // Check for
                              // uncovered vertices.
    for each vertex v chosen randomly from G do
      if colour[v] = WHITE then
        Random-DFS-Visit(v)
      endif
    done
end
```

Random-decyclify first colours all the vertices white then it makes a call to Random-DFS-visit, which recursively traverses the graph. Then, all the edges crossing the iteration frontier are removed and finally the unvisited nodes are visited in a random order. Random-DFS-visit can be outlined as follows:

```
Random-DFS-Visit(input node u)
  begin
    colour[u] := GREY;
    for each vertex v chosen randomly from adj(G, u) do
      if colour[v] = WHITE then     // Recursive
        Random-DFS-Visit(v)         // call
      else if colour[v] = GREY then
        DAG := DAG - edge(u,v)      // Remove
      endif                         // back edges.
    done
    colour[u] := BLACK
  end
```

Random-DFS-visit is very similar to a standard DFS-visit. The main difference is that new vertices to visit are chosen randomly instead of in a fixed order, instead of for example ordered on vertex index. Basically, for each task to visit, if its colour is white another recursive call is made and if the colour is grey an back edge is detected and this back edge is removed.

The time complexity of the DFS algorithm has been shown to be $O(E+V)$ where E is the number of edges and V is the number of vertices in the graph.

Table 3. Improvements of makespan and critical-path using Random-DFS over DFS

density	CCR=10	CCR=1	CCR=0.1	cp
0,05	0,0 %	11,0 %	12,3 %	12,5 %
0,1	0,0 %	9,6 %	10,3 %	10,3 %
0,15	0,0 %	1,1 %	4,2 %	4,4 %
0,2	0,0 %	0,0 %	1,0 %	1,1 %
0,25	0,0 %	1,0 %	2,9 %	3,2 %
0,3	0,0 %	4,0 %	4,1 %	4,1 %
0,35	0,0 %	-1,0 %	1,8 %	2,1 %
0,4	0,0 %	1,0 %	2,8 %	4,0 %
0,45	0,0 %	2,0 %	2,9 %	3,0 %
0,5	0,0 %	1,0 %	3,7 %	3,0 %
0,55	0,0 %	0,0 %	3,6 %	4,0 %
0,6	0,0 %	1,0 %	1,9 %	2,0 %

The complete time complexity of the random DFS cycle removal algorithm is therefore $O(s(E + V))$, since the basic DFS algorithm is applied s times. The randomisation within Random-decyclify does not increase the complexity.

5 Assessing Random-DFS

To evaluate the random DFS cycle removal algorithm random graphs with densities from 0.05 to 0.60 in steps of 0.05 were generated and cycles where removed using the original DFS cycle removal algorithm and the proposed Random-DFS cycle removal algorithm. Each graph comprised of 100 tasks, and each graph was scaled to match high medium and low communication-to-computation ratios, namely 10:1, 1:1 and 1:10 respectively. The resulting graphs where then scheduled using the CP-MISF scheduling heuristic [4] and the target hardware was a virtual eight processor fully connected distributed memory machine. In this experiment s (the sampling size) was set to 10,000.

Table 3 shows the results of the experiment. The first column lists the densities of the respective graphs. The second column lists the difference in percentage between the original DFS based cycle removal algorithm and the proposed Random-DFS algorithm for a system with a communication-to-computation ratio of 10:1. Similar differences for communication-to-computation ratios of 1:1 and 1:10 can be seen in columns three and four.

The table shows that for systems with a large communication-to-computation ratio the difference between the two strategies are diminishingly small. However, for systems with medium to low communication-to-communication ratios there is a noticeable improvement of Random-DFS over DFS. Clearly, the improvement is larger for lower density graphs, where the difference between the two strategies accounts for more than 10 %, namely 11 % for the system with a communication-to-computation ratio of 1 and 12.3 % for a system with a communication-to-computation ratio of 0.1. But there is a noticeable improvement also for dense graphs as it is in the region of 1 to 2 % for graphs with a density of 0.6.

It is also clear from the data that the improvement in schedules for the systems with a low communication-to-computation ratio closely matches those of the improvements in the critical path.

6 Conclusions

In this paper the inefficiencies of the static DFS cycle removal algorithm for scheduling cyclic task graphs were investigated. The results indicate that the ambiguous situations that occur at each steps of the DFS algorithm can have a significant effect on the critical path of the resulting DAG – and consequently, it can greatly affect the makespan of the schedule resulting from the DAG. The effect is more influential in systems with a medium to low communication-to-computation delay. An improved stochastic cycle removal procedure was introduced that results in significantly shorter makespans than the ones obtained using a static DFS. The computational overheads introduced are acceptable, and the quality of the result can be adjusted as a function of computational investment.

The strategy proposed in this paper is based on random sampling of the problem space. In the future, it is highly likely that the computational effort to reach high quality solutions can be reduced by introducing more efficient stochastic search algorithms such as simulated annealing, genetic algorithms or tabu search.

References

1. Wang, D.J., Hu, Y.H.: Fully static multiprocessor array realizability criteria for real-time recurrent dsp applications. IEEE transactions on signal processing **42** (1994) pp1288–1292
2. Luh, J.Y.S., Lin, C.S.: Scheduling of Parallel Computation for a Computer-Controlled Mechanical Manipulator. IEEE Transactions on Systems, Man and Cybernetics, vol SMC-12, no 2, pp214-234 (1982)
3. Bozic, S.M.: Digital and Kalman Filtering. Edward Arnold (1979)
4. Kasahara, H., Narita, S.: Practical Multiprocessor Scheduling Algorithms for Efficient Parallel Processing. IEEE Transactions on Computers, vol C-33, no 11, pp1023-1029 (1984)
5. Aydin, H., Melhem, R., Mosse, D., Mejia-Alvarez, P.: Power-aware scheduling for periodic real-time tasks. IEEE Transactions on Computers **53** (2004) 584–600
6. Liu, J.F., Chou, P.H., Bagherzadeh, N.: Power-aware task motion for enhancing dynamic range of embedded systems with renewable energy sources. Lecture Notes in Computer Science **2325** (2003) 84–98
7. Zhu, D.K., Melhem, R., Childers, B.R.: Scheduling with dynamic voltage/speed adjustment using slack reclamation in multiprocessor real-time systems. IEEE Transactions on Parallel and Distributed Systems **14** (2003) 686–700

8. Malloy, B.A., Lloyd, E.E., Soffa, M.L.: Scheduling DAG's for Asynchronous Multiprocessor Execution. IEEE Transactions on Parallel and Distributed Systems, vol 5, no 5, pp498-508 (1994)
9. Kwok, Y.K., Ahmad, I.: Dynamic Critical Path Scheduling: An Effective Technique for Allocating Task Graphs to Multiprocessors. IEEE transactions on Parallel and Distributed Processing, vol. 7, no 5, pp506-521 (1996)
10. Parhi, K.K., Messerschmitt, D.G.: Static Rate-Optimal Scheduling of Iterative Data-Flow Programs via Optimum Unfolding. IEEE Transactions on Computing, vol 40, no 2, pp178-195 (1991)
11. Yang, T., Fu, C.: Heuristic Algorithms for Scheduling Iterative Task Computations on Distributed Memory Machines. IEEE Transactions on Parallel and Distributed Systems, vol. 8m no. 6 (1997)
12. Sandnes, F.E., Megson, G.M.: Improved static multiprocessor scheduling using cyclic task graphs: A genetic approach. PARALLEL COMPUTING: Fundamentals, Applications and New Directions, North-Holland **12** (1998) 703–710
13. Sandnes, F.E., Sinnen, O.: A new scheduling algorithm for cyclic graphs. International Journal of High Performance Computing and Networking **1** (2004)
14. Cormen, T.H., Leiserson, C.E., Rivest, R.L.: Introduction to algorithms. MIT Press, pp. 477-483 (1990)

A Novel Rollback Algorithm in Parallel and Distributed System Simulation

Xuehui Wang[1], Lei Zhang[2], and Kedi Huang[1]

[1] School of Mechatronics Engineering and Automation
[2] Department of Computer Science,
National University of Defense Technology,
Chang-sha, Hunan province, P.R. China, PN 410073
{yzmailbox2003, zlmailx2000}@163.com

Abstract. Simulation is a powerful tool for the analysis of new system designs, retrofits to existing systems and proposed changes to operating rules. In this paper we limit our discussion to parallel and distributed simulation (PDS). In order to simulate large-scale complex systems with better consistency, further more as fast as possible, the universally adoptive approach of PDS is that make the execution of simulation programs on multiprocessor and distributed computing platforms. Time management algorithm is one of the key techniques in the parallel and distributed system simulation, which broadly fall into conservative and optimistic synchronization. A survey of both the two algorithms is presented focusing on fundamental principles and mechanisms. The remainder of this paper is focused on one of the novel rollback algorithm; we call it as smart rollback algorithm. And then, we provide and describe the novel rollback algorithm in optimistic time management in detail, including scheduler's priority queue, rollback manager, cancellation strategies, and roll forward operation. Among this paper, central issues concern the synchronization of computations on different processors. Finally, we discuss how to get the relatively minimal rollback, and how to realize the dynamic allocation and reclamation.

1 Introduction

Much of the work concerning the execution of analytic simulations on multiprocessor computers is concerned with synchronization. The synchronization algorithm ensures that before-and-after relationships in the system being simulated are correctly reproduced in the simulation program. Synchronization in time management is a well-studied area of research in the parallel and distributed system simulation field. There is no clear consensus concerning whether optimistic or conservative synchronization performs better.

In this paper, we first give an overview of synchronization algorithms. Then, we discuss and set forth a novel rollback algorithm, termed as smart rollback. Later we provide an emphatic study to describe the novel rollback algorithm in optimistic time management in detail.

2 Synchronization Algorithms

The goal of the synchronization mechanism is to make all LP processed events accord with the local causality constraint (LCC) or else doubtless results in *causality violations*.

A parallel simulation consists of a number of *Logical Processes* (LP) that communicate by exchanging time-stamp messages or events, typically each one running on a separate processor. The simulation progress is ensured by the processor scheduling new events to be executed in the future, and executing these events in the time-stamp order. A process can schedule an event for itself, locally thus (self-initiation), or remotely, for another process. In the latter case, a message is sent via the network to the remote process. Each process maintains a separate time clock, called the *Local Virtual Time* [1]. Synchronization algorithms can be classified as being either conservative or optimistic. In brief, conservative algorithms take precautions to avoid the possibility of processing events out of time stamp order, i.e., the execution mechanism avoids synchronization errors. For another, optimistic algorithms use a detection and recovery approach. Events are allowed to be processed out of time stamp order, however, a rollback mechanism is provided to recover from such errors.

3 Smart Rollback Algorithm

In order to avoid an explosion of cascading anti-messages and get relatively high-powered parallel and distributed simulation, we provide a novel rollback algorithm, termed as smart rollback algorithm. Simulation object manage both their set of unprocessed pending events and their processed but uncommitted events. Each event has a Rollback Manager that stores Specialized State Altering Items (SSAI) items that are created as capable-rollback operations are performed while processing the event. SSAI items undo the operation that generated them when rollbacks occur.

3.1 Schedule Priority Queue

Each node in our simulation drive provides a scheduler that coordinates event processing for its local simulation objects. The scheduler maintains each simulation object in a priority queue using each simulation object's next unprocessed event time as its priority. Priority queues have two primary operations: *insert* and *remove*. The insert operation inserts an item with a priority value (e.g., a time tag). The remove operation removes the item with the highest priority (e.g., the smallest time tag). The same priority queue data structure can be used to manage simulation object in the scheduler or events in a simulation object. The scheduler first removes the simulation object with the earliest unprocessed event time. It then processes the simulation object's next event. Afterwards, the scheduler inserts the now processed event into the simulation object's optimistically processed event list. Finally, the scheduler reinserts the simulation object back into its priority queue using the simulation object's next unprocessed event time as its priority. If the simulation object has no more pending events, then it does not need to be inserted in the scheduler's priority queue. It is possible for another simulation object to later schedule an event for a simulation object that has no pending events. When this happens, the scheduler will insert the simulation object back into its priority queue to coordinate its event processing.

3.2 Rollback Manager

To accomplish this, each simulation object maintains its set of pending events in its own priority queue. In addition, each simulation object also manages its optimistically processed but uncommitted events in a doubly linked list.[2] The optimistically processed list of events is cleaned up when Global Virtual Time (GVT) is determined. Events with time tags less than GVT are committed and then removed from the list of optimistically processed events.

Event objects contain a Rollback Manager, which stores SSAI that are created when capable-rollback operations are performed. The SSAI base class defines two virtual functions: Rollback() and Cleanup(). These functions are used to implement support for rollbacks. Each state-saving operation generates an instance of a derived SSAI class to uniquely implement those two virtual functions for the operation. The specialized SSAI classes are inserted into the event's SSAI Monitor as they are created. The event's SSAI Monitor then provides a stack of specialized SSAI items. These SSAI items are responsible for undoing the operations that caused their creation in case rollbacks occur. The Rollback() virtual function is invoked on each SSAI in reverse order to restore the simulation object back to its original state before the event was processed.

3.3 Cancellation Strategies

When a rollback occurs, some output messages may need to be cancelled. There are two categories of cancellation strategy—aggressive and lazy. [3]

Aggressive Cancellation: When the aggressive cancellation strategy is used, antimessages are sent immediately when a rollback occurs. Such messages often lead to *secondary rollbacks* in other LPs. The assumption is that the cancelled messages may be causing erroneous computation in other LPs.

Lazy Cancellation: When the lazy cancellation strategy is used, antimessages are not sent when a rollback occurs. Instead, antimessages are placed into a queue of pending antimessages. When the LP resumes execution, it will generate output messages. In the event that an output message is the same as a message that would have been cancelled during the rollback, then the pending antimessage and the new output message will annihilate.

The assumption is that after a rollback, an LP is likely to produce the same output messages. In this case, the lazy cancellation strategy will reduce the unnecessary secondary rollbacks that would occur with aggressive cancellation.[4]

3.4 Minimal Rollback

Rolling back an event requires an advanced technique that is capable of undoing changes made to state variables while also retracting any events that were scheduled.

When a node of parallel simulation receives a straggler message, it does not rollback all of the locally processed events that have a greater time value. Instead, it only rolls back the necessary events that were processed by the target simulation object. More parallelism is achieved through limiting rollbacks in this manner. [5]This approach results in fewer rollbacks and better overall parallel performance. However, it does mean that events must be associated with one and only one, simulation object. Accessing and/or modifying the state variables of another simulation object in an event are forbidden.

4 Conclusion

Parallel and distributed simulation technologies address issues concerning the execution of simulation programs on multiprocessor and distributed computing platforms. [6] Time management algorithm is one of the key techniques in the parallel and distributed system simulation. Much of the work concerning the execution of analytic simulations on multiprocessor computers is concerned with synchronization. The synchronization algorithm ensures that the cause and effect relationship in the system being simulated are correctly reproduced in the simulation program.

In our paper, we provide and describe this smart rollback algorithm in detail. Such as scheduler's priority queue, rollback manager, cancellation strategies, and minimal rollback all are discussed.

References

1. D.R. Jefferson, Virtual Time. ACM Trans. *Programming Languages and Systems*, 1995.
2. Steinman, J.S., SPEEDES: A Multiple-Synchronization Environment for Parallel Discrete Event Simulation. *International Journal on Computer Simulation*, 1992: p. 251-286.
3. Bruno R. Preiss, Ian D. MacIntyre, Wayne M. Loucks, On the Trade-off between Time and Space in Optimistic Parallel Discrete-Event Simulation, *Simulation Councils, Inc.* 1992
4. Kamil Iskra, Parallel Discrete Event Simulation Issues with Wide Area Distribution, *ASCI course a9*, March 7, 2003
5. J. Steinman, Incremental State Saving in SPEEDES Using C++. *Proceedings of the 1993 Winter Simulation Conference*, 1993.
6. R. M. Fujimoto. Parallel Discrete Event Simulation. *Communications of the ACM*, 33(10):30–53, 1990.

Agent-Mediated Genetic Super-Scheduling in Grid Environments*

Gang Chen[1], Zhonghua Yang[1], Simon See[2], and Jie Song[2]

[1] Information Communication Institute of Singapore, School of Electrical and Electronics Engineering, Nanyang Technological University, Singapore 639798
[2] Asia Pacific Science and Technology Center, Sun Microsystems Inc.

Abstract. Super-scheduling in a dynamic grid environment is a very challenging issue that remains to be solved before a grid can be deployed and effectively utilized. In this paper we investigate a paradigm based on genetic algorithms (GA) to efficiently solve the scheduling problem. This GA paradigm is architecturally combined with the multiagent system (MAS) paradigm to form a flexible super-scheduling system. A three-layered scheduling architecture is presented and the corresponding realization of a multiagent-based system is described. The experiment shows that the better scheduling results are obtained for the adopted metrics of flow time and job stretch.

Keywords: Genetic Algorithms, Agent, Grid Computing, Scheduling.

1 Introduction

Grid computing is an emerging technology to facilitate the global resource sharing and accelerate scientific computing. However, to provide an effective grid computing environment, scheduling is one of the major challenges [2]. By their very nature of grid environments, scheduling typically takes place at multiple levels, involving many players and possibly several different layers of schedulers. There are a number of papers on job scheduling in a simulated grid environments, but many of current wellknown works are focusing on local or community scheduling within a domain.

In this paper, we present a three-layered distributed scheduling system to investigate super-scheduling in a multiple domain grid setting. We rely on a paradigm, based on genetic algorithms (GA), to efficiently solve the scheduling problem. This GA paradigm is architecturally combined with the multiagent system (MAS) paradigm to form a flexible super-scheduling system. A three-layered scheduling architecture is presented and the corresponding realization of a multiagent-based system is described. Multiple agents operate at domain-scheduler layer and division-scheduler layer. They execute a GA-based scheduling algorithm and collectively achieve the robust scheduling.

---

* The authors acknowledge the contribution of Yueqin Jiang to the earlier version of this paper.

The rest of this paper is organized as follows. Section 2 illustrates the system model. The GA based scheduling algorithms are presented in Section 3. Results and conclusions are given in Sections 4 and 5, respectively.

2 The System Model

As depicted in Figure 1, our scheduling system is vertically structured into three layers, namely, *domain level*, *division level*, and *machine level*. The domain level considers job scheduling both within and across domains. A scheduler, termed *Domain Scheduler* (DoS), runs in every domain and schedules jobs both within its own domain and across domains. A domain is decomposed into a group of *divisions*. Each division involves multiple computing machines and includes a *Division Scheduler* (DiS) to schedule jobs among these machines. DiSs of a same domain do not interact directly with each other: they are coordinated by the DoS of that domain. The machines are presented at the machine level. Each machine has its own scheduler named *Machine Scheduler* (MaS) and consists one or multiple processing elements (*PEs*). A specific job queue is utilized by the machine scheduler to maintain the jobs waiting to be performed.

Jobs come to the system over times. The release times and lengths of jobs are not known *a priori*. We assume that a user can submit jobs to any machine available in the Grid at his convenience. Our layered scheduling model paves the way for a direct application of multi-agent technologies. We illustrate graphically our agent-based scheduling architecture as in Figure 2. The machine level is presented at the bottom of Figure 2. Each *machine agent* (MaA) represents a logical resource in the form of a computing machine. It controls the execution of each job allocated to it. The job scheduling among these MaAs are controlled by division agents (DiA), who function as the division schedulers at the division level. Multiple DiAs aggregate together to form a domain, the job scheduling among which is further managed by a domain agent (DoA). Domain agents work as domain schedulers and are required to schedule jobs across domains. At all levels, the decision of job re-allocations is considered as an optimization problem,

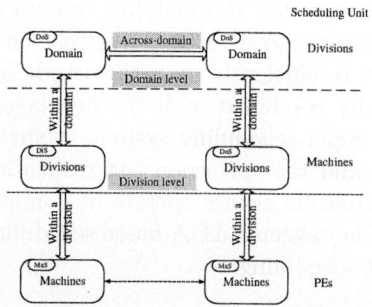

Fig. 1. The system model

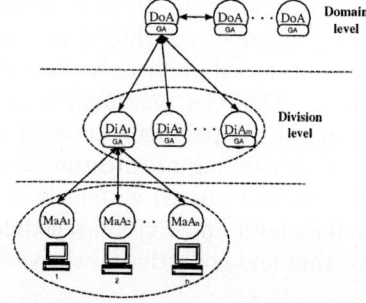

Fig. 2. The agent-based scheduling system

the solution of which is obtained through genetic algorithms. The details of these algorithms will be presented in the next section.

3 Genetic Scheduling Algorithm

In our system, scheduler agents at the domain and division levels use genetic algorithms to do job scheduling. Two key metrics, *average flow time* and *average stretch*, are adopted to measure the effectiveness of our genetic scheduling algorithm. The details of the two metrics can be found in [1]. We assume that the readers have the basic knowledge of genetic algorithms. In the remaining part of this Section, we describe in more detail the specific implementation of GA for DiS and DoS.

The GA designed for DiS conducts on a population of 100 chromosomes for a given set of jobs with the number of π. It runs for 1000 iterations before termination. Each chromosome is a π dimensional vector, where position j $(0 \leq j \leq \pi)$ represents job j, and the entry in position j is the machine to which the job has been scheduled. The initial population is generated uniformly at random. Each chromosome is characterized by a fitness value, which is the inverse of the average flow time calculated by following the schedule expressed in that chromosome. A larger fitness value indicates a better solution. After each generation of population, all chromosomes in the new population are evaluated and selected based on a roulette wheel scheme, where better chromosomes have a higher probability of being selected. Each selected chromosome is considered for crossover with a rate of 50%. Single-point crossover is performed when mating two chromosomes. The position for crossover is chosen uniformly.

After crossover, each selected chromosome is considered for mutation with a rate of 50%. Mutation selects a job within a chromosome to be mutated, and then reassigned that job to a new machine at random.

For scheduling at the domain level, each chromosome represents the mapping of jobs to divisions. The fitness value is the inverse of the approximate average response time. When performing cross-domain scheduling, the j-th entry of a π-dimensional chromosome denotes the domain to which job j is assigned. Parameters for evaluating such a chromosome include: the current simulation clock, job length, and release time of jobs. Crossover and mutation operations for this two cases are similar to those of DiS, and are used by DoS.

4 Experiment Results

This section provides the experiment results of the proposed scheduling architecture. A simulated grid environment is setup with 3 domains, containing totally 8 divisions and 36 machines. As a result, 36 MaAs, 8 DiAs and 3 DoAs are created. Not all machines receive jobs from users. For those machines that receive jobs, each of them will receive two jobs per four seconds. In total, 2000 jobs are to be processed. Job length follows Erlang distribution with an average processing time of 125 seconds. The simulation is based on the GridSim toolkit. Besides GA, another well-known scheduling heuristic MinMin is adopted to do job allocation, which aims to provide comparable results.

The experiment results are summarized in Figure 3 for both GA and MinMin. Four cases are considered. The first row of Figure 3 shows the results when jobs are only circulated within a division. In the second case (Row 2 of Figure 3), the working load is shared among divisions. In the third case, DoAs interact with each other to allocate jobs across domains. While in the fourth case, a centralized approach is adopted, where a DiA coordinates all the 36 MaAs that form a single division. In all these cases, GAs outperforms MinMin in terms of both flow time and stretch.

	Average Stretch		Average Flow Time (s)	
	GA	MinMin	GA	MinMin
DiA	3.09	3.14	379	381
DoA	2.06	2.21	266	275
DoA Co	1.94	2.24	247	262
Central	1.76	1.96	232	236

Fig. 3. The experiment results

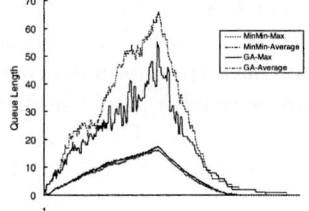

Fig. 4. Maximum and average queue length of GA and MinMin

Besides the results discussed above, Figure 4 depicts the fluctuation of queue length of machines. Only the maximum and average queue length are provided. It shows that when GA is used, the curves of queue length are all below those of MinMin. This evidenced that GA can balance the load more uniformly among domains and divisions than the common scheduling heuristics as MinMin.

5 Conclusions

In this paper, we proposed a three-layered grid scheduling system and applied genetic algorithms to do job scheduling. Scheduling instances at different levels as well as resources are modeled by agents, which facilitate the interaction among scheduling instances. The scheduling process is done by the coordination of agents. With agent interaction and coordination, better scheduling results are achieved. The results show that GA outperforms MinMin in terms of average flow time and average stretch. As agents have been recognized as a powerful high-level abstraction for modeling complex system, we believe that the combination of agent with genetic algorithm brings a promising view for further research on grid scheduling.

References

[1] Swarup Acharya and S. Muthukrishnan. Scheduling On-demand Broadcasts: New Metrics and Algorithms. In *Proceedings of the 4th annual ACM/IEEE international conference on Mobile computing and networking*, 1998.

[2] Ian Foster and Carl Kesselman (Eds.). *The Grid: Blueprint for a New Computing Infrastructure*. Morgan Kaufmann Publishers, Inc., 1999.

Investigating Super Scheduling Algorithms for Grid Computing: A Simulation Approach*

Jie Song[1], Zhonghua Yang[2], and Simon See[1]

[1] Asia Pacific Science and Technology Center, Sun Microsystems Inc.,
[2] Information Communication Institute of Singapore,
School of Electrical and Electronics Engineering,
Nanyang Technological University, Singapore 639798

Abstract. Super scheduling is notoriously difficult and challenging in grid computing due to the very dynamic and unpredictable nature. In this paper, we adopt a hierarchical scheduling architecture, within which, both online and batch mode super scheduling policies are developed. Two new online scheduling algorithms are presented and compared with the algorithms in the literature. The extensive simulation study of these algorithms is conducted. The results show that when simultaneously considering both the loads of sites and data location, the average response time and average stretch can be considerably smaller than those when using policies that only consider loads or data location alone.

1 Introduction

The grid computing environment provides us with the ability to dynamically link together resources as an ensemble to support the execution of large- scale, resource- and data- intensive, and distributed applications across independently administered domains. By definition of the Grid, the availability of resources changes dynamically, unpredictably, and subject to local control. Furthermore, not all resources will be dedicated to grid use. Clearly, efficiently scheduling jobs and resources is one of such challenges to support grid applications in such a dynamic environment.

The problem of grid scheduling can be investigated by taking *experimental* or *simulation* approach. The advantages of performing actual experiment by scheduling real applications on real resources are that it is easier and straightforward to compare the efficacy of multiple algorithms. However, the experimental study of scheduling algorithms tends to be unproductive, for example, real applications of interests might be long-lived and thus it is not feasible to perform a sufficient number of experiments for obtaining meaningful results. Furthermore, it is difficult to explore a variety of resource configurations. Typically a grid environment is highly dynamic, variations in resource availability make it difficult to obtains repeatable results As a result of all these difficulties with the experimental approach, simulation is the most viable approach to effectively

---

* The authors acknowledge the contribution of Yueqin Jiang to the early version of this paper.

investigate grid scheduling algorithms. The simulation approach is configurable, repeatable, and generally fast, and is the approach we take in this work.

In this paper, we present five online super-scheduling algorithms for the hierarchical grid scheduling architecture. The simulation results show that they are more efficient than the first three policies in terms of average response time and average stretch.

2 The System Model

We adapt Ranganathan and Ian Foster's architecture for our simulation study of super scheduling algorithms [1], including two major components for each site: a Super Scheduler (SS) and a Local Scheduler (LS) (Figure 2). A user submits jobs to a SS at his convenience. It is the SS that decides where to assign the jobs and where to get required data. The state transition of a job and its scheduling architecture is shown in Figure 1 and 2.

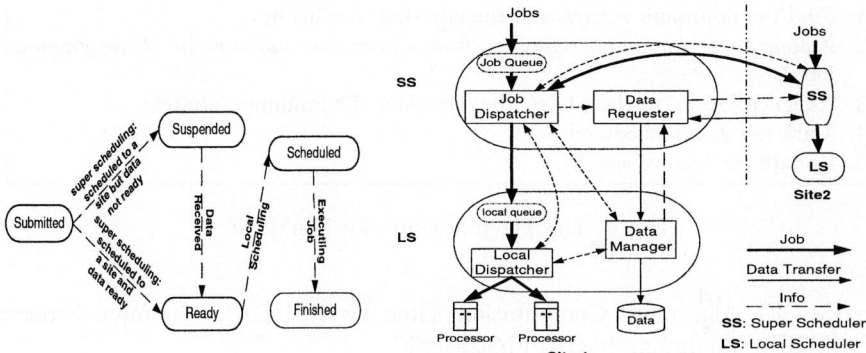

Fig. 1. The state transition of a job

Fig. 2. The Grid scheduling architecture

3 Algorithms for Super Scheduling

3.1 Online Mode Algorithms

Five online super scheduling heuristics are investigated: *DataGreedy* (DG), *DataGreedywithDataReplication* (DG-DR), *LoadGreedy* (LG), *Hybrid-C*, and *Hybrid-S*. The first two are adopted from [1]. The third one is similar to the LeastLoaded policy of [1], but the *load* is defined the sum of the computation time of all the waiting jobs, and the super scheduler makes scheduling decision based on the average load of sites, not total load. These three algorithms are adopted in this paper for comparison with our two newly proposed policies: Hybrid-C and Hybrid-S (Figure 3).

3.2 Batch Mode Algorithms

In the batch mode, all jobs in the job queue are collected into a *job set* (batch) for policy-based scheduling (Figure 4) which includes Minimum Computation Time

// The procedure for Hybrid-C	//The procedure for Hybrid-S
1. Find the site S_1 with least average load L_1 and **with** the required dataset; 2. Find the site S_2 with least average load L_2, but **without** the required dataset; 3. Calculate the approximate completion time C_1 if J_k is executed at S_1; 4. Calculate the approximate completion time C_2 if J_k is executed at S_2; 5. Return the less one of C_1 and C_2, and the corresponding site.	1. Find the site S_1 with least average load L_1 and **with** the required dataset; 2. Find the site S_2 with least average load L_2, but **without** the required dataset; 3. Calculate the approximate stretch s_1 if J_k is executed at S_1; 4. Calculate the approximate stretch s_2 if J_k is executed at S_2; 5. return the less one of s_1 and s_2, and the corresponding site.

Fig. 3. The The procedures for Hybrid-C and Hybrid-S

For all jobs in JobQueue
1. Find the minimum *stretch* and the site that obtains it;
2. Among those minimum stretches, find a *minimum* one and its corresponding job J_k;
3. Assigned job J_k to the site S_j that provides the minimum *stretch*;
4. Mark job J_k as scheduled;
5. Update the load of site S_j.

Fig. 4. The The procedures for MinMin-S

First(MiCF), Maximum Computation Time First(MaCF), Minimum Stretch First(MiSF), Maximum Stretch First(MaSF).

4 Simulation Evaluation

The simulation eveluation is based on a grid model of 5 sites, and each site has different number of processor elements: 8, 5, 5, 3, and 2, respectively. SimGrid is selected as our simulation toolkit. These processor elements have the same processing power (i.e. CPU speed). The bandwidth between sites is 5MBytes/s and constant. The model assumes that the super scheduler and local scheduler are executed on a specially designed processor dedicated to scheduling and data transfer. Communication delays for transferring jobs are neglected. Each job requires a dataset to process. The computation duration of each job is proportional to the size of the corresponding dataset in Gbytes. The sizes of datasets are distributed uniformly between 0.5 Gbytes and 2 Gbytes. The ratio of computation duration to dataset size is denoted as R. There are 20 users and 100 datasets distributed evenly among the 5 sites. Totally, there are 600 jobs, and each user has 30 jobs and submit their jobs in a Poisson process with an inter-arrival time of 90 seconds.

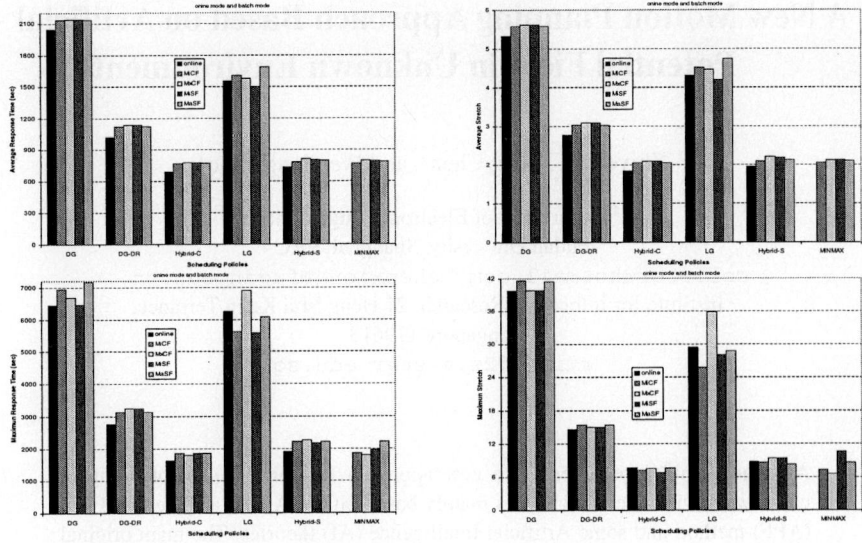

Fig. 5. Simulation results

Figure 5 show (from left to right) the average response time, average stretch, maximum response time and maximum stretch of both online and batch mode algorithms. The results of online mode are presented in the first column of the first five column groups in each figure. The bandwidth is 5MBytes/sec, and R is 300. From these figures, Hybrid-C and Hybrid-S perform much better than the other three online algorithms, in terms of average response time, average stretch, maximum response time and maximum stretch. It is also observed that the five online policies are all slightly better than their corresponding batch-mode algorithms.

The simulation also shows that the available bandwidth is as high as 100MByte / sec, the performance of LG approaches Hybrid-C and Hybrid-S, since at this time, the time consumed by data transfer is insignificant.

5 Conclusion

The super-scheduling in grid environments is notoriously challenging. In this paper, taking a simulation approach, many super-scheduling algorithms for a variety of scenarios are investigated, and their scheduling efficacy are comparatively studied. The results show that it is essential to consider data location and site load when scheduling if the bandwidth is limited.

Reference

1. Kavitha Ranganathan and Ian Foster. Simulation Studies of Computation and Data Scheduling Algorithms for Data Grids. *Journal of Grid Computing*, 1:53–62, 2003.

A New Motion Planning Approach Based on Artificial Potential Field in Unknown Environment

Zhiye Li[1], Xiong Chen[1], and Wendong Xiao[2]

[1] Department of Electronic Engineering,
Fudan University, Shanghai, PRC
celletor@hotmail.com, chenxiong@fudan.edu.cn,
[2] Institute for Infocomm Research, 21 Heng Mui Keng Terrance,
Singapore 119613
wxiao@i2r.a-star.edu.sg

Abstract. This paper presents a new approach for robots' path planning in unknown environments, which is mainly based on the Artificial Potential Field (APF) method and some Artificial Intelligence (AI) theories. The main original point of the new algorithm lies in that it puts two intelligent ideas *inertial mind* and *resistive mind*, into robots' minds. Therefore during the robots' real-time path planning in unknown environments, in addition to the repulsive force by obstacles and the attractive force by goal, there are two more forces which can influence the behavior of robots. In the new algorithm presented in this paper, robots are directed by the composite force in the environments and the local minima problems are solved efficiently. Several simulations are presented to demonstrate the effectiveness of the new approach.

1 Introduction

With detail information of the environment, robots are able to perform target finding and path planning without sensors. In this paper, we could discuss how robot performs in unknown environment. Former researchers have done much work in this area such as the Bug algorithm, the Hierarchical Generalized Voronoi Graph (HGVG), and APF([1,2,3,4]) algorithms, etc. Among these methods, each has its own flaws of which the local minima problem is the most common one.

The new approach presented in this paper mainly deals with the issue of motion planning for sensor-based car-like mobile robots. The idea is inspired by APF method and the measures used for path planning and collision avoidance by humans. The APF method looks on the whole environment as a potential field in which the goal is the lowest potential point, whereas the potential of obstacles is much higher. As a result, the robot is forced to move by both the attraction from the goal and the expulsion from the barriers just as a positive electron does in the electrical potential field. When the environment is initially unknown, the robots have to use the sensors to obtain the information of surroundings by inchmeal, so the potential field is built gradually. However, because they lack complete knowledge of the circumstances, the robots are likely to fall into the local minima problem. Our point is that we put some human behaviors into the APF algorithm to guide the robot to plan its path as humans do, and the local minima will be solved excellently by the method. We call the two minds used in this paper "inertial mind" and "resistive mind" which become two sorts of forces in potential field.

2 Method Proposed

In this section, we will discuss the new algorithm. The robot we use in the research is a car-like robot equipped with many sonar sensors around. The robot is given the task to move from a beginning configuration in the 2-dimension environment map to the destination with the lack of the knowledge of the environment. In order to simplify the planning problem, we treat the mobile robot as a represented point in the rest of this paper.

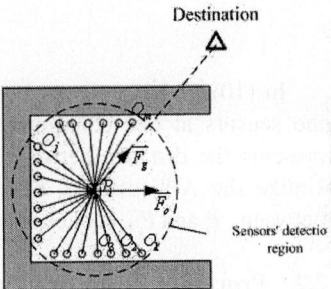

Fig. 1. The illustration of a point robot in the environment

2.1 Definitions and Assumptions

The environment of the robot is in the 2-dimensional space called configuration space, C. When the robot is working in C, because of the potential field it actually receives four sorts of forces: the repulsive force F_o by obstacles detected by sensors; the attraction F_g from the goal; the inertial force F_{in} and the resistive force F_r from the robot's own *mind*. The last two kinds of forces are a bit different from the two former ones because they are not forces caused by potential but mind. We will state them clearly in part B of this section. So the composite force F of all forces received at one time drives the robot to move:

$$\overline{F} = \overline{F}_g + \overline{F}_o + \overline{F}_{in} + \overline{F}_r \qquad (7)$$

We define d as the length of robot's each step and R as the farthest detection distance of sensors ($d<R/10$). Let P_0 be the beginning configuration in C, and let P_n (or P_g) represent the goal point, thus the path figure G built by the robot is described as:

$$G = \{(P_0, P_1), (P_1, P_2), \cdots, (P_{n-1}, P_n)\} \qquad (8)$$

In (8) n is the number of steps of the robot. So the length of the whole path L could be approximately expressed as follow:

$$L = nd \qquad (9)$$

We assume that the sensors on the robot are accurate enough to obtain precise distance data between the surface of barriers they detected and themselves. In the research the car-like robot is equipped with tens of such sensors all around, so that robot can "*see*" almost everything within the scope of detection, as shown in figure 1. Those sensors get the information of distance between the obstacles they detected within the detection region and themselves, and with these knowledge from sensors, the robot can know how far the obstacles in its surroundings are from it. Now we define two of the four forces:

$$\overrightarrow{F_g} = \frac{k_1(1/r)\overrightarrow{P_iP_g}}{\left|\overrightarrow{P_iP_g}\right|}$$

$$\overrightarrow{F_o} = \overrightarrow{F_{o1}} + \overrightarrow{F_{o2}} + \cdots + \overrightarrow{F_{om}} \qquad (10)$$

$$\overrightarrow{F_{oi}} = k_2 \frac{\overrightarrow{O_jP_i}}{\left|\overrightarrow{O_jP_i}\right|^2}$$

In (10) k_1, k_2 are constants and m is the number of obstacle points detected by the sensors at one configuration which is also clearly shown in figure 1. And r presents the distance between the current configuration of the robot and the goal. Unlike the APF method, here the attraction force is not decided by the distance between P_i and P_g but keeps the same value.

2.2 Process of Real-Time Planning

We now take into account the two *mind* forces mentioned above. Figure 2 and 3 show human's usual behaviors on path planning and obstacles avoiding. In figure 2 the man wants to get to the destination, but at P_i he finds there is a wall in the way, then he has to go round the obstacle. While trying to avoid the wall and to reach the goal, he thinks," Go ahead according to the plan unless there is an obstacle in front." That is human's inertial thought and now we give this simple thinking to the robot, and turn

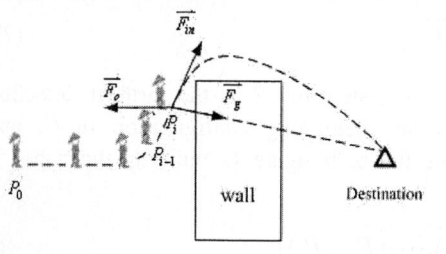
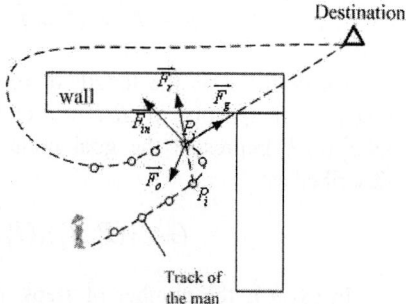

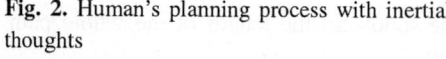

Fig. 2. Human's planning process with inertial thoughts

Fig. 3. Human behaviors to avoid obstacles

the thought into a sort of power received by the mobile robot, so the robot is effected by inertial force any time it travels. The inertial force is defined at any configuration P_i as follows:

$$F_{in} = \frac{(k_3/d)\overrightarrow{P_{i-1}P_i}}{|P_{i-1}P_i|} \qquad (11)$$

With inertial force the robot can remove many local minima problems in motion planning. For example, if a car-like robot wants to arrive at the goal in figure 2, it will be trapped into local minima around P_i with the traditional APF planning method, but it will easily find the successful way when added the inertial thought. We provide more proofs in next section.

Besides inertial mind, another thinking called resistive mind is also common in human's thought. Seen in figure 3, the man wants to find a way to the goal, but he is blocked off by the wall on the right and the upper one of the figure. When he arrives at P_j, the sensors (the eyes) find a part of his own path around P_i just now. At this time, a usual idea is that "I don't want to walk toward the region around P_i because it is the place I have passed by." We call this *resistive* mind with which the man finds the exit on the top-left. To the robot, it becomes a kind of power which affects its behavior. We define the power when the robot is at P_j as follow:

$$\overrightarrow{F_r} = \overrightarrow{F_{r1}} + \overrightarrow{F_{r2}} + \cdots \overrightarrow{F_{rl}}$$
$$\overrightarrow{F_{ri}} = k_4 \frac{\overrightarrow{P_j P_{ri}}}{|P_j P_{ri}|^2} \qquad (12)$$

where l is the number of configurations in the path detected by sensors, k_4 is a constant, and $\{P_{r1}, P_{r2}, \cdots, P_{rl}\}$ represents those detected points.

The problems we consider above are not particular ones but very common. In fact both resistive thinking and inertial mind are very basic thoughts of humans.

2.3 Algorithm

Here we express the composite force in a complete way:

$$\overrightarrow{F(i)} = \frac{k_1(1/r)\overrightarrow{P_i P_g}}{|P_i P_g|} + k_2 \sum_{j=1}^{m} \frac{\overrightarrow{O_j P_i}}{|O_j P_i|^2} + \frac{(k_3/d)\overrightarrow{P_{i-1}P_i}}{|P_{i-1}P_i|} + k_4 \sum_{j=1}^{l} \frac{\overrightarrow{P_i P_{rj}}}{|P_i P_{rj}|^2} \qquad (13)$$

Because $|P_{i-1}P_i| = d$, and P_{i-1} is also a configuration already passed by the robot and close to P_i, to simplify the algorithm, we let $k_3 = k_4$, so (7) is simplified as:

$$\overrightarrow{F(i)} = \frac{k_1(1/r)\overrightarrow{P_i P_g}}{|P_i P_g|} + k_2 \sum_{j=1}^{m} \frac{\overrightarrow{O_j P_i}}{|O_j P_i|^2} + k_3 \sum_{j=1}^{l+1} \frac{\overrightarrow{P_i P_{rj}}}{|P_i P_{rj}|^2} \qquad (14)$$

We only need the direction of $\overrightarrow{F(i)}$, but not its numerical value, which could be described as:

$$\overrightarrow{P_i P_{i+1}} = d \frac{\overrightarrow{F(i)}}{|F(i)|} \qquad (15)$$

Therefore we can normalize the three parameters with $k_1 = 1$.
The following is the pseudo-code of the algorithm:

---

1. $G \leftarrow \phi, k_1 \leftarrow 1$
2. $k_2, k_3 \leftarrow$ constants
3. $i \leftarrow 1$
4. **Loop**
5. $\overline{F(i)} \leftarrow$ the composite force at 6. P_i calculated by (13)
6. $P_{i+1} \leftarrow$ the new configuration got by 8(15).
7.   If $P_{i+1} = P_g$ **is true**
8.   the robot arrives at the destination, **break**
9. **end**

---

3 Experimental Evaluation

To illustrate our approach more explicitly and to show the robustness of the new algorithm, we present several simulations in this section. We select some very different environment maps (4 maps in figure 4) as real physical environments of the robot. The experiments are done on a PC with Pentium IV 2.4G CPU and the algorithm was executed in Matlab.

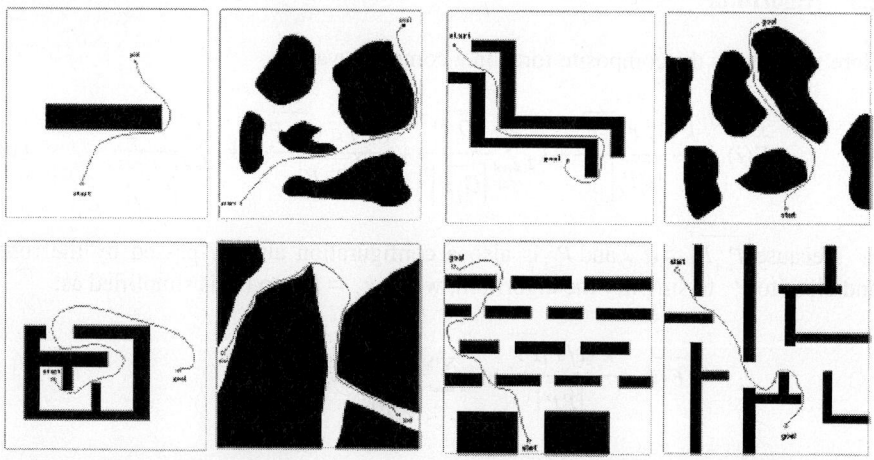

Fig. 4. The paths computed by our approach   **Fig. 5.** Four more examples which illustrate the robustness of the new algorithm

The results of the experiments shown in figure 4 display the effectiveness of the new approach that the robot can not only find a path in fairly complex unknown environments but also produce routes which are very like the paths human pass in the same circumstances. Furthermore, local minima problems are not troubles for the robot any more. Figure 5 presents more examples.

Now let us make some numerical contrasts among the three motion planning approaches: traditional APF, lazy-DRM and our approach (we call it intelligent APF, I-APF). Table I notes the numerical value of paths produced respectively by the three algorithms in sense 4 of figure 5's environment. The map size is 500x500, and the maximum detection distance of sensors is 30. The data indicates that our new approach leads to more direct compared with other two counterparts. We can also achieve similar results when the algorithms are implemented in other class of 2-dimensional environments.

Table 1. Performance data of three approaches for sense 4 of Fig. 5

Approach	Length of the path	Sensors' detection	Notation
APF	1435.2	30	
Lazy-DRM	935.54	30	500 nodes
I-APF	618.26	30	

4 Conclusions and Future Work

This paper proposes a new idea of path planning in unknown environments: to add some elementary human thought processes into the planning algorithm of robot, which makes the robot have some intelligence. The new motion planning approach in this paper develops the traditional APF method and considers two basic human thought processes in the course of planning. With the new algorithm, many problems met when we use classical APF to guide the robot in unknown environments are effectively eliminated. It is proven by the simulations that the paths of the robot built by the new algorithm are much better than those directed by the traditional motion planning methods. The favorable features are smoothness, freedom from local minima, similarities with human's paths in motion and avoiding obstacles. The approach can be applied in many sorts of static environments, including complex ones.

Despite its advantages, there are still some limitations in the algorithm. For example, if the ratio of the parameters k_1, k_2, k_3 at the beginning of the algorithm is not appropriate, the path the robot passed through will not be efficient enough. So we should study more on this problem in future work to build a scope or data base of *best ratios*. Furthermore, besides the two kinds of thinking we used in this paper, there are still some other thoughts which could be also turned into some certain forces to affect the robots' behaviors.

References

[1] J-O. Kim, P. K. Khosla, *Real-Time Obastacle Avoidance Using Harmonic Potential Functions,* IEEE Transaction on Robotics and Automation, Vol. 8, No.3, June 1996.
[2] O. Khatib, *Real time obstacle avoidance for manipulators and mobile robots,* Int. J. Robotics Res., 5(1), 90-99,1986.
[3] R. Spence, S. Hutchinson, *An Integrated Architecture for Robot Motion Planning and Control in the Presence of Obstacles With Unknown Trajectories,* IEEE Transaction on Systems, Man, And Cybernetics, Vol. 25, No. 1, January 1995.
[4] N. V. Dounskaia, *Artificial Potential Method for Control of Constrained Robot Motion,* IEEE Transaction on Systems, Man, And Cybernetics, Vol. 25, No. 3, June 1998.

Physical Frame Timeslot Switching (PFTS) in the Single User-Plane Architecture Network (SUPANET)*

Dengyuan Xu, Huaxin Zeng, and Ji Li

School of Computer and Communications Engineering,
Southwest Jiaotong University, Chengdu, 610031, China
xudave@tom.com, xudave@sina.com.cn

Abstract: In the background of future trend to merge existing separated three types of network (i.e. cable TV network, telephone switched network, and computer network), this paper presents a framework of the Single User Plane Architecture NETwork (SUPANET), with an emphasis on the switching techniques in User data transfer plane (U-plane). A novel concept called Physical Frame Timeslot Switching (PFTS) is introduced, and key issues relevant to support of QoS provisioning in PFTS are discussed in some detail, together with mechanisms in the Signaling and Management planes.

1 Introduction

The progress in fiber communication, especially that of DWDM (Dense Wavelength Division Multiplexing), has raised the transmission rate in a single wavelength up to 80 Gbps and in a single fiber towards tens of Tbps. This can effectively provide a sound communication means for a merged network to replace separated cable TV, telephone and computer communication networks. The success in Internet has surely drawn attention to Internet techniques; nevertheless, analysis has shown that existing Internet architecture is not quite suitable for such converged network [1].

Such a merging trend demands high efficiency in user data transfer and a better QoS mechanism than that of the "best effort" service in Internet. Such mechanism must be able to ensure different QoS requirements of real-time video, audio, and traditional computer network traffic. The activity of Multi-Protocol Label Switching (MPLS) is migrating from the orthodox 3-layer data transfer platform to an enhanced 2-layer structure so as to raise the data transfer efficiency and a label is used to identify traffic with the same FEC (Forward Equivalence Class) [2]. However, for lack of mechanisms in existing physical layer technology over a lambda channel with a data rate of tens of Gbps, a label shared by multiple data streams of the same class over data link protocols cannot effectively satisfy these QoS requirements [3]. This

---

* This paper is sponsored in part by NSFC (NO. 60372065) and by Ph.D student Creative Foundation of Southwest Jiaotong University.

implies that the crux of the problem lies in the physical layer to provide a better mechanism in QoS provisioning.

Faced with high data rates in a single lambda, people have been trying to develop various techniques to handle the downwards-multiplexing problem in a lambda channel. Optical Burst Switching (OBS) is trying to multiplex a lambda channel with fixed or variable length of data blocks (Bursts) by setting up the data forward lambda hop or path in advance via the burst head through another lambda [4,5]. References [6,7] have analyzed deficiency of OBS in channel utility and QoS provisioning, let alone its problems of lacking data buffering and processing capabilities in optical domain in foreseeable future.

Other people are in favor of the SDH-centric approach, with which SDH multiplexing techniques have been adopted on top of the DWDM [8]. The merit of this approach is that SDH is matured and has reached the data rate of 40 Gbps [9], nevertheless, SDH itself is complicated and has to be involved with non-trivial segmentation and re-assembly processing when interfacing with computer frames or packets.

Consequently, one could ask whether there are alternative approaches in handling downwards multiplexing with an easiness of interfacing with network data streams and in providing adequate mechanisms to support different QoS requirements in future merged networks. Should this goal be reached, the 2-layer user data transfer platform, as in MPLS networks, can be further reduced to a single physical layer. All these considerations have led to the research work, sponsored by NSFC (Natural Science Foundation of China), on the single physical User-Plane Architecture Network (SUPANET) [1] and its core switching technique – Physical Frame Timeslot Switching (PFTS) [7].

This paper is organized into 5 parts. In addition to introduction in section 1, section 2 is a brief introduce to the SUPANET, section 3 discusses the requirement for the user data transfer platform, basics of PFTS, and QoS provisioning mechanism in User plane (U-plane). Section 4 is a brief introduction to QoS provisioning mechanisms in Signaling and Management planes (S&M planes) in SUPANET. Finally, section 5 provides a forward view concerning the SUPANET and PFTS, based on the preliminary experience gained in this project.

2 The SUPANET

2.1 Incentive Behind SUPANET

The success of Internet has made IP based techniques dominating the network world for more than 20 years. "IP over Everything" and "Everything over IP" are becoming catchwords today both in network application and in system interconnection. However, one should be aware that the TCP (or UDP)/IP based protocol stack and the Internet architecture were evolved from late 1970s, when communication facilities were typically characterized by low line speed (e.g. a few to tens of Kbps) and high error rate (e.g. 10^{-6} or 10^{-5}). At that time, the focus in protocol and network architecture design is on reliable text-oriented data transfer; therefore, network architectures such as OSI/RM (Open System Interconnection/Reference Model) and Internet developed during that time had surely borne such "time-stamps", which were typically characterized by in-band signaling and 3-layer subnetwork.

However, the orthodox 3-layer subnetwork adopting in-band signaling model has shortcomings of inefficiency in user data transportation caused by multi-layer handling, and has to face difficulty in ensuring the QoS required by applications for its dependency on multiple layers. Even with out-band signaling approach as with InteServ and DiffServ, such disadvantages can still remain unless the layers in U-plane can be reduced and services offered by lower layers can be improved.

A diverted direction in network architecture development is to adopt the out-band signaling approach, which has resulted 2-layer U-plane architectures such as in B-ISDN [10] and in MPLS [11]. These architectures are more efficient in user data transfer, and will behave particularly well when SDH is used in physical layer. However, ATM cell in B-ISDN is too short (53 bytes) hence needs lots of adaptation between the cell and modern IP packets (max. 65536 bytes) or Ethernet frames (max. 1530 bytes), let alone its low efficiency in carrying user data (90%: 48 bytes payload against the 53-byte cell length). Moreover, the protocol stacks used for signaling and management in B-ISDN are too far complex and less familiar to Internet community compared with those in Internet.

MPLS inherits the 2-layer user plane architecture of B-ISDN while remaining the Internet protocol stacks in signaling and management planes intact. However, MPLS also has some shortcomings:

A. The QoS provided by MPLS, to some extent, depends on existing data link services, over which exercise of QoS control may be difficult in some cases such as connectionless MAC sublayer.
B. The extra label switching sublayer decreases the efficiency of user data transfer with extra overhead.
C. Application of MPLS to DWDM environment may not be so efficient since there is a lack of granular mechanism within a lambda. Application of MPLS over DWDM as suggested by GMPLS [12] will have to use the gigantic label (lambda) unless there is a good downwards-multiplexing mechanism within a lambda.

Analysis to existing network architectures has convinced us that:

A. Existing network architectures have not fledged for future merged networks.
B. The key for next generation network architecture lies in whether the physical layer can provide a granular transfer and switching mechanism with enough support for higher layers with regard to QoS provisioning.
C. Should be so, the user data transfer platform can be reduced to a single physical layer.

2.2 Design Criteria for SUPANET

Bearing the facts in mind, that Internet has been successful worldwide and out-band signaling can simplify the user data transfer platform, we have decided that the design criteria in the new architecture should include:

A. To improve the data transfer efficiency, the user transfer platform should be simplified as much as possible, better still as a single physical layer integrated into DWDM layered structure considering DWDM is the most prosperous high-speed optical communication technique.
B. The user transfer platform should have the power of supporting granular data transfer and switching, as well as QoS provisioning. Granularity in transmission

and switching is the essence of transportation and routing of different rates of user data, while the mechanism in support of QoS can ensure that different traffic can be delivered with required QoS features.
C. The data link can be abolished, should its main functions such as framing be combined into the physical layer functions.
D. The length of the physical frame for carrying user data should be compatible with the most popular data link frame or IP packet so as to reduce the adaptation necessity to upper layer frame or packet.
E. Last but not the least, the new architecture should utilize techniques evolved in Internet at full extent so as to interoperate with Internet for the time being and be easy to be migrated from existing Internet to a new architecture in the future, to protect the investment on Internet and make a smooth migration.

To meet the design criteria listed above, we have decided that

A. Out-band signaling approach should be adopted to simplify the user data transfer platform (or User-Plane, U-Plane for short).
B. To introduce a new switching technique called the Physical Frame Timeslot Switching (PFTS) on top of a lambda channel, the timeslot for PFTS is exactly the time duration to transfer a maximum length of the most popular Ethernet MAC frame (1530 bytes) at a given data rate of a lambda. The reason for selecting MAC frame is that the Ethernet is supported by all the computers and is also widely used in LAN, MAN, and WAN especially after the publication of 10 G bps Ethernet standards [13]. As the physical frame resembles the Ethernet MAC frame, the need for data link layer will disappear at the user data transfer platform and might potentially be abolished in S&M planes to further simplify the existing 5-layer architecture of Internet.
C. To ensure the QoS required by different type of streams, a Switched/Permanent Virtual Connection (SVC or PVC) service should be provided with various mechanisms at the physical layer as well as in signaling and management planes.
D. The Internet protocol stacks should remain unchanged, at least for the time being, to keep interoperability with present Internet. There is a need for an enhancement in the S&M planes to guarantee the required QoS together with the mechanism provided in the U-Plane.

2.3 The Architectural Framework of the SUPANET

Figure 1 is an improved architecture based on reference [1].

In figure 1, the user system is an implementation of SUPANET protocol stacks in the U-Plane and the S&M Planes, which will interacts with a SUPANET Router/Switch through the UNI_S (User-Network Interface in S&M planes) or UNI_U (User-Network Interface in User plane) respectively. It could be implemented in a computer (client/server) or be implemented as part of a router to interconnect to the SUPANET. The NNI_U (Network-Network Interface in User plane) and NNI_S, on the other hand, are defined for interactions between SUPANET routers/switches in U-plane and S&M planes respectively.

The operation between two SUPANET user systems and the SUPANET router/switch will start with use of QoS Negotiation Protocol (QoSNP) on top of UDP to establish a Switched Virtual Connection (SVC) in S&M planes. An SVC is completed when a lambda path between two SUPANET user systems can be found and all the routers along the path are capable of satisfying QoS requirements of two users, and consequently relevant resources are reserved. A PVC (Permanent Virtual Connection) service can also be provided via pre-registration manually or through On-line Registration Protocol (ORP) in M-plane.

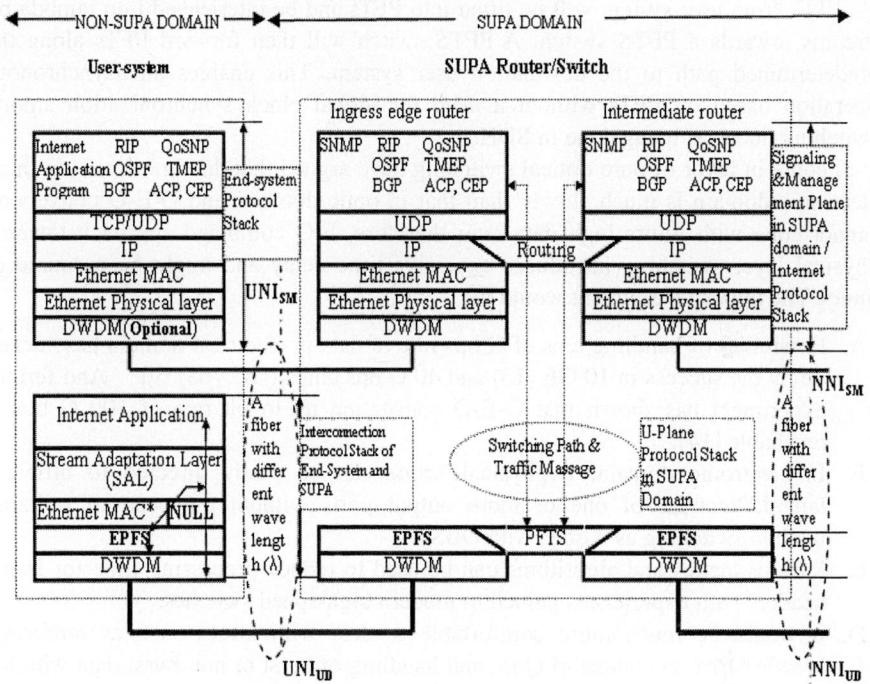

Fig. 1. Protocol stacks in SUPANET

The user data will be loaded into the physical frames called EPFs (Ethernet-like Physical Frames) and be transferred and switched in the U-plane after the SVC is completed, and the concatenated VC Identifiers (VCIs) assigned during QoSNP will be used as the path identifier at the physical-layer U-plane.

Ending of an SVC will be completed by use of the Connection Ending Protocol (CEP), either in an elegant way through bilateral agreement or in an abrupt manual. QoS provisioning for user data delivery will be ensured by the mechanisms in U-plane and those in S&M planes, which will be discussed in the following sections.

3 Physical Frame Timeslot Switching (PFTS)

3.1 Concept of PFTS

To meet the design criteria in section 2.2, the most popular Ethernet MAC frame has been adopted as the basic data unit called the Ethernet-like Physical Frame (EPF); consequently, framing function traditionally in the data link layer is merged into physical layer. A novel concept PFT (Physical layer Frame Timeslot) is defined as the transmission time for an EPF with the maximum Ethernet MAC frame length (1530 bytes including preambles, IEEE 802.3/2002) [6,7] and acts as the basis for frame-based asynchronous operation. In other words, EPFs are transmitted, switched, and synchronized on per PFT basis by detecting frame boundaries.

EPFs from user system will be fitted into PFTs and be interleaved into lambda bit streams towards a PFTS switch. A PFTS switch will then forward PFTs along the predetermined path to the destination user system. This enables an asynchronous operation based on PFTs without a need for global clock synchronization among switching nodes as being done in SDH.

People in favor of pure optical switching have argued that data transmission in an electronic domain is much slower than that in optic domain, and O-E-O conversion cannot cope with future high data rate; therefore, E/O combined approach towards physical layer switching introduces excessive time delay and might be a source of jitters. The opposite argument would be:

A. Feasibility of handling tens of G bps rate of data in electrical domain has backed up by the success in 10 GE [13] and 40 G bps chips (OC-768) [9]. And further experiment has shown that O-E-O conversion up to bit rate of 100 G bps is reachable [14].
B. In electronic domain, a physical frame can be easily directed to different lambda/lambdas of one or more output ports without the need of utilizing lambda switching as it does with OBS.
C. Various tactics and algorithms can be used to reduce processing time for frame headers with experiences gained in modern high-speed switches.
D. It would be much more comfortable to deal with issues such as buffering, broadcasting, guarantee of QoS, and handling of burst or non-burst data within a switch in an electronic domain (even with the star topology) compared with the predicament encountered with OBS.
E. Last but not the least, switching in an O/E combined domain will be much easier to interact and coordinate with signaling and management planes of a network adopting out-band signaling just as it is done with MPLS.

3.2 Format of EPF/PFT

The EPF is the basic unit for transmission and switching, and will be fitted into a PFT in a lambda over DWDM. The format of the EPF resembles an Ethernet MAC frame except that the destination address field in the MAC frame is replaced by a 4-byte switching field and be used by PFT switches. It should be stressed that the MAC addresses within the PFTS domain is no longer meaningful and can be kept at edge devices between the PFTS domain and non-PFTS domain for use in Ethernet domain. As an EPF per second represents a data rate of 12 Kbps (that means transmitting one EPF frame per second, which payload is 1500 byte long), PFTS provides a granular transmission capability; the user data transfer efficiency is up to 98%(1500 byte payload against 1530-byte EPF frame length)), which is higher than that in ATM (90.1%); the channel utility is better than that of OBS without counting the possible burst losses caused by lack of lambda resource and buffers. A detailed discussion and comparison can be found in reference [7].

Figure 2 illustrates the up-to-date format of switching field in an EPF frame.

The D-bit (Discard bit) in figure 2 is set in less significant frames if lost in case of congestion with the agreement between users and the service provider during QoS negotiation. The Burst bit (B-bit in short), on the other hand, is provided to denote that there is another EPF right after the current one in a burst belonging to the same virtual connection. This enables a burst to be output as a consecutive EPF stream through the same lambda.

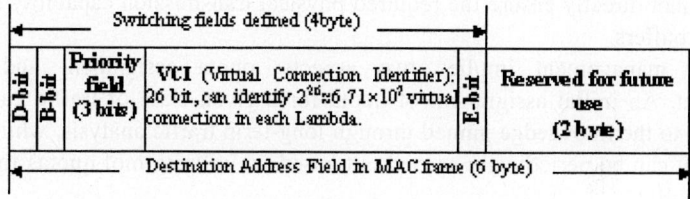

Fig. 2. Format of EPF/PFT Switching fileds

The 3-bit priority field is similar to that defined by IEEE 802.1p, and can be implemented as multi-priority queues. This field will be assigned by edge routers, according to QoS negotiation result and network control policies.

The 26-bit VCI (Virtual Connection Id) is used to identify a single user data stream or multi-user data streams multiplexed at the layer above the physical layer within a fiber and can hold up to 6.71×10^7 virtual connections. A VCI will be associated with a transmission capability represented by a number PFTs reserved, transmission priority assigned, and a contract of set of QoS parameters for that VC during QoS negotiation. It should be emphasized that a VCI only has local significance on a fiber between two PFTS switches. In other words, a complete user data path within PFTS domain is formed of concatenated local VCs.

Finally, the E-bit in PFTS switching fields is an indication of the End of data transfer in the forward direction, and the resources reserved for that VC will be returned to the switch when the frame with E-bit set has been forwarded to the next switch.

Note that in an EPF, the two bytes in the destination address field and the 6 bytes of the source address field of the MAC frame are not used for physical layer switching, and are reserved for future use, such as handling security issues of a VC at the two edge routers of PFTS domain.

3.3 Switching Mechanism Supporting QoS in PFTS

As analyzed in section 2, QoS provisioning cannot be ensured unless the physical layer is able to provide a mechanism in support of QoS; therefore, it is the major concern in PFTS. Mechanisms in PFTS with respect to QoS provisioning include:

A. PFT Reservation and Quota Management

Assignment of enough PFTs for a time-critical stream is the first resort of resource reservation to guarantee the required throughput. It is done during connection establishment and QoS negotiation in the S-plane under the condition that PFTs Quota left for that class of traffic for a given output fiber is adequate to support the throughput. Quota is defined as the maximum number of EPT/PFT for a given class of traffic in output channel (lambda/fiber). Each time a number of PFTs being reserved, the same numbers of PFTs will be deducted from the quota for that class of traffic. Since reservation of PFTs is directly associated with transmission capability, it would be much more effective and directly controllable than reservation in RSVP, which cannot directly ensure the required physical transmission capability apart from reserving buffers.

Quota management implies two aspects: quota assignment and dynamic adjustment. An initial assignment of quota for a given class of traffic can be done according to the knowledge gained through long-term traffic analysis, while dynamic adjustment can be periodically carried out based on utilization of quotas for different types of traffic.

B. Multiple Queues and Priorities

In a PFTS switch, there might be tens/hundreds I/O ports, each of which may have tens/hundreds of lambdas, and there are 8 priorities in traffic handling. Therefore, 8 FIFO queues have been designed for different priorities in each lambda, and 4 types of burst Queue have also be added for high-priority grades of traffic to cope with the bursting events. To maintain the sequence order of traffic in a VC, non-burst data prior to the first frame of a burst has to be output before start to handling the burst. Indeed, the management of the multiple queues in PFTS is not a trivial problem, and needs further thorough investigation.

C. Routing Strategy

Routing in a PFTS switch can be classified into two types: output port (fiber) selection and lambda selection within a fiber. The former is done according to inter relationship among routers and through exchange of routing information by utilization of Internet routing information protocols in S&M planes, such as RIP, OSPF, and BGP. However, route selection with traditional routing protocols, was aiming for selection of a physical line without considering distribution of traffic in individual lambdas in the DWDM environment. However, for PFTS over DWDM, traffic within a lambda must be put into account when trying to set up a VC for a given data stream. This has brought to the necessity of lambda selection within a fiber.

For a given VC, use of multiple lambdas or a dedicated lambda to output the traffic is disputable. Multi-lambda approach is more flexible and good for dynamic distribution of traffic load among lambdas; nevertheless, it is difficult to maintain the sequence order of frames when multiple queues of different lambdas with the same priority are involved. The dedicated lambda approach, on the other hand, is less flexible but comparatively to manage and maintain the sequence of consecutive frames in a VC. Another drawback of this approach is that it needs re-allocation of VCs in case of lambda failure. In our system, we have adopted the second approach.

D. Congestion Control

Congestion Control is jointly done in User plane and S&M planes in PFTS. The state of congestion in PFTS node is provided by U-plane and congestion information exchange is done by TMEP (Traffic Monitor and information Exchange Protocol) in Management plane. The congestion state in PFTS is decided by WJCW (Wavelength Jam Control Word), which takes the format as shown in figure 3:

Port Id (8 bits)	Wavelength Id (8 bits)	Congestion flags (2 bits)

Fig. 3. Format of Wavelenght Jam Control Word (WJCW)

The 8-bit Port Id and Wavelength Id in figure 3 are designed to identify up to 256 ports each of which with 256 lambdas. These fields will be used in exchanging of the congestion information to identify a lambda. Congestion flags are used to indicate whether an output lambda is in "no congestion" (00), "congestion pre-warning" (01), "congestion" (10), or "heavy congestion" (11) state. In "no congestion" state, CIR (Committed Information Rate), CBR (Committed Burst Rate) and EBR (Extended Burst Rate) agreed in negotiation should be supported in a PFTS node. In the "congestion pre-warning" state, EBR may not be ensured, consequently, EPFs with D-bit set may be discarded when data rate exceeding CBR. In the "congestion" state, EPFs with D-bit set might be discarded when data rate exceeding the CBR. In the worst state of "heavy congestion", EPFs might be discarded first with those of D-bit set.

Handling of congestion at edge routers can involve a feed-back action in the S&M planes by use of Admission Control Protocol (ACP).

E. Minimizing Variation in Transit Delay and Anti-jitters

Long transit delay will not cause problems even in transmission of time-critical streams, as long as it remains comparatively stable within tolerable limit. The most disturbing problem in transmission of time critical traffic is the variation of transit delay, which may produce jitters within a data stream. Mechanisms in anti-jitters applicable to PFTS include:

a) Making switching time stable in individual switches so as to keep variation of accumulated transit delay along a PFTS path within the tolerable range. This should be better accomplished in PFTS switch design.

b) Trying to keep time-relationship between user data as it is injected into the PFTS domain. Support of priority in switching enables data streams with higher priorities to be served first and this will help in satisfy time-critical requirements.

c) Trying to maintain the integrity of a burst – this is done in PFTS by setting the "B" bit (the first bit of the switching field) to "1". A PFTS switch will treat these multiple EPFs as an integral unit by directing them into the same lambda in consecutive PFTs. It is expected that the "B" bit will be only applied to traffic with high priorities.

F. QoS Monitoring

In order to further ensure that promised QoS is ensured, QoS monitoring in U-plane is carried out at individual output port to provide queuing information for dynamic quota adjustment, service request admission, traffic shaping, and congestion alert. QoS monitoring information is exchanged between PFTS switches in S&M planes by the way of TMEP (Traffic Monitoring information Exchange Protocol).

G. Traffic Engineering

Traffic Engineering is a process that enhances overall network utilization by attempt to create a uniform or differentiated distribution of network traffic. When network resources are insufficient or inadequate to accommodate offered load, congestion may occur. This should be handled by traditional congestion control strategies such as rate limiting, window flow control, queue management, schedule-based control, etc.

When traffic streams are inefficiently mapped onto available resources, it might cause some subsets of network resources to become over-utilized while others remain underutilized. Generally speaking, adopting load-balancing policies can ease congestion caused by inefficient resource allocation.

H. Admission Control

Admission control in PFTS involves VC acceptance control and input data rate shaping according the transmission resource available, congestion condition at edge router, and QoS commitment during negotiation. Three parameters have been used in U-plane to control the input data rate for individual VC, i.e. CIR (Committed Information Rate, CBR (Committed Burst Rate), and EBR (Extended Burst Rate).

I. Data Loss Issues

The self-similar nature observed by network community indicates that there is always bursts appeared in the volume-time spectrum disregarding the length of sampling time [15]. This phenomenon can cause instant congestions when multi-bursts from multiple input ports are directed to a single output port. Better design in switching algorithms can reduce data losses to some extent, but can never be avoided completely. The D-bit is provided in PFTS switches as the last resort to discard those frames less important within the limit agreed during QoS negotiation.

J. Fault Tolerance

Quality of service can be deteriorated in case of lambda failure, fiber fault (being disconnected or broken), or in the worst case the central component failure. In general practice, influence of central component failure can somehow be reduced to minimal by having double switching engines.

The impact of fiber failure may either be replaced by a back-up fiber or by dynamically re-routing with deteriorated performance. In the latter case, reduction of quotas is necessary. Lambda failure will incur a reduction of total throughput of an output fiber, hence it is appropriate to reduce the total PFT quota of an output port (if there are free PFTs) to restrict further reservation and try to maintain the QoS of existing connections according to traffic priorities.

4 QoS Provisioning Mechanisms in S&M Planes

QoS requirements cannot be satisfied by U-plane alone in the SUPANET, it needs joint activities between U-plane and S&M planes. A set of protocols has been defined in the S&M planes to enhance the QoS provisioning in SUPANET.

A. QoS Negotiation Protocol

QoS Negotiation Protocol (QoSNP) is the first mechanism designed in S&M planes to establish a profile for service provisioning. Many QoS parameter are negotiated between the end-system and PFTS nodes in the S&M plane before setting up a VC in the U-plane. ITU has defined a framework for QoS parameters [16], which are complete but not necessarily operable for PFTS. Important QoS parameters negotiated at present include: data rate (CIR, CBR, and EBR), jitter (average, maximum), data discarding rate in percentage (average, maximum), VC disconnection approach (negotiated, abrupt). More QoS parameters might need to be negotiated in the future with more experience gained with PFTS, such as security parameters, reliability parameters etc.

QoSNP is an application protocol, which involves all the relevant application entities in S&M plane entities in user system and in PFTS nodes, therefore, it has to utilize a transport protocol as being done with the routing protocols (RIP, OSPF, BGP). Considering that UDP is the transport protocol implemented in all Internet routers, QoSNP is implemented on top of UDP. QoS negotiation result determines whether or not a VC can be established, hence it has to be agreed between two end-systems. However, since it involves consent of all the nodes in both directions along the negotiation path, a forward-and-return process has to be carried out through hop-by-hop negotiation.

B. Traffic Monitoring Information Exchange Protocol

Traffic Monitoring information Exchange Protocol (TMEP) is another application protocol in S&M planes of the SUPANET, which performs the traffic information between neighbor nodes so as to provide information for congestion control and traffic pattern analysis. One issue similar to routing information exchange is to prevent information exchange loop, various strategies in defining neighbor relationship can be applied. By the same token as in QoSNP, TMEP is implemented on top of UDP. How far the traffic monitoring information should be propagated for global analysis and for congestion and admission control is left for further study.

The information exchanged by TMEP is obtained from the U-plane, and the Wavelength Jam Control Word (WJCW) as specified in last section, is one of the information to be exchanged.

C. Admission Control Protocol

Admission Control Protocol (ACP) is also an application protocol in S&M planes, which involves exchange of congestion information on the UNI between user system and its access node. At present, only congestion information local to the user system is used in admission control, and how to utilize the global congestion information is left for further study when we have more experiences with SUPANET.

D. Connection Ending Protocol

Connection establishment and ending are typical functions in signaling plane and usually defined in one protocol. They are separated in SUPANET for two reasons:

a) Connection establishment in SUPANET involves a lot of QoS negotiation activities therefore has been merged into the QoSNP.
b) Ending a VC in future merged network is more complicated than that in current Internet, since QoS provisioning for different types of traffic may have different requirements.

The Connection Ending Protocol (CEP) is an application protocol in S-plane, which handles two types of protocol ending process: negotiated (single way/two way) ending, and abrupt ending. Although the ending process is carried out in S-plane, but most likely it will be piggybacked in the last EPF with the E-bit set in the data stream.

5 A Forward View of SUPANET

The work presented in this paper is based on our recent experience gained in functional development of SUPANET, quantifiable experiment and analysis are needed when hardware platform under development is completed in order to make it more convincing. However, our preliminary experience has shown that SUPANET is a promising candidate for next generation network in view that it is definitely more efficient than that of the MPLS relying on existing two-layer protocol stratum and it is better in QoS provisioning than OBS for its lacking of mechanisms in this respect.

For the time being, the Signaling and Management functions and protocol stacks are collectively referred to as S&M planes, further refinement to separate the two planes and to define two protocol stacks has been planned. Apart from Internet SNMP and the REgistration Protocol (REP) under development, management issues need more consideration in the context of SUPA.

Finally, multicast issues are not discussed in this paper, which are very important for future merged service such as cable TV service, video or audio conferencing, VPN etc.

References

1. Zeng Hua-xin, et al: On the architecture for Next Generation Internet, Computer Applications (Chinese), 6 (2004) 1-5
2. draft-awduche-mpls-te-optical-01.txt - Multi-Protocol Lambda Switching: Combining MPLS Traffic Engineering Control with Optical Crossconnects, IETF, May 2002.
3. RFC 3471 - Generalized Multi-Protocol Label Switching (GMPLS) Signaling Functional Description, IETF, Jan. 2003.
4. C.Qiao and M.Yoo: Optical burst switching (OBS)-a new paradigm for an Optical Internet, Journal of High Speed Network, 8(1999) 69-84.
5. C. Guillemot, et al: Transparent Optical Packet Switching- The European ACTS KEOPS Project Approach, Journal of lightwave technology, 11 (1998) 2117-2134
6. Huaxin Zeng, et al.: On Physical Frame Time-slot Switching over DWDM, in Proceedings of PACAT03, IEEE press, 8 (2003) 535-540
7. Huaxin Zeng et.al: Promotion of Physical Frame Timeslot Switching (PFTS) over DWDM, to be published in: IEC Annual Report of Communications, Vol. 57 (2004).
8. ITU Recommendation G. 707 – Network node interface for the Synchronous Digital Hierarchy (SDH), 1996.

9. ITU: G.691 - Optical interfaces for single channel STM-64, STM-256 and other SDH systems with optical amplifiers, October 2000
10. ITU, I.120 – Integrated Services Digital Networks (ISDN).
11. RFC 3035 - MPLS using LDP and ATM VC Switching, Jan 2001
12. RFC 3471 - Generalized Multi-Protocol Label Switching (GMPLS) Signaling Functional Description, IETF, Jan. 2003.
13. IEEE 802.3ae - Local and metropolitan area networks—Specific requirements, Part 3: Carrier Sense Multiple Access with Collision Detection (CSMA/CD) Access Method and Physical Layer Specifications, Amendment: Media Access Control (MAC) Parameters, Physical Layers, and Management Parameters for 10 Gb/s Operation, June 13, 2002.
14. Roman Sobolewski: Ultrafast optoelectronic interface for digital super conducting electronics, Superconductor Science and technology, 11 (2001) 994-1000.
15. An Ge, et al: On Optical Burst Switching and Self-Similar Traffic, IEEE Communication Letters, 3 (2000).
16. ITU X.641 I ISO/IEC 13236- QoS Framework (1997).

Fast Address Configuration for WLAN

Soohong Park, Pyungsoo Kim, Minho Lee, and Youngkeun Kim

Mobile Platform Laboratory, Digital Media R&D Center, Samsung Electronics,
416 Maetan-3Dong, Yeongtong-Gu, Suwon, Gyeonggi-Do, Korea
{soohong.park, kimps, minho03.lee, ykksam}@samsung.com

Abstract. In this paper, we discuss the current mechanism for IP address configuration in the wireless networks especially 802.11 WLAN and describes its unreasonable time delay and proposes a new mechanism of address configuration which obtains an IP address more quickly. The proposed mechanism provides a reduced message exchange for address configuration in the WLAN over the current 4-way message exchange using DHCP. Performance evaluation and comparison have shown that the proposed mechanism is faster in terms of delay than the existing mechanism including reduced packet loss and stable message exchange when in motion.

1 Introduction

As WLAN becomes widely available, users can access Internet in everywhere. In this environment, data packets would be carried over IP technology, with Mobile IPv4 [1] providing handovers to allow a mobile node to communicate with other nodes after moving to a new network as soon as a new address is configured called care-of address. In addition, fast IP address configuration is strongly needed to support seamless IP connection when in motion.

Dynamic Host Configuration Protocol (DHCP) [2] is generally used for address configuration in WLAN. However the existing mechanism occurs unnecessary time-delay when configuring IP address because of DHCP 4-message exchange. Moreover, in some environments, such as those in which high mobility occurs and the network attachment point changes frequently, the existing mechanism is not beneficial to rapidly configure the mobile node and it is therefore difficult for the node to maintain its connection without packet loss because of the protections offered by the current 4-message exchange.

This paper proposes a new mechanism for address configuration scheme in WLAN. Through this mechanism, mobile node can configure its IP address by 2-message exchange rather than 4-message exchange. Particularly, current Access Point (AP) of WLAN can be used for DHCP Server to allocate unique IP address in its coverage. It is significantly efficient to reduce time delay for configuring addresses when the DHCP Server is far from the mobile node. Thus, we implemented the new mechanism into AP. The evaluation criteria are delay and packet loss. The results are encouraging and show the proposed mechanism is faster in terms of delay than the existing mechanism.

2 Comparison of New Mechanism with Existing Mechanism

As shown in Fig. 1., mobile node has to obtain its unique address through DHCP server with 4-message exchange (DHCPDISCOVER, DHCPOFFER, DHCPREQUEST and DHCPACK) when attaching to a new network. While the new mechanism reduce 2 message as DHCPOFFER and DHCPREQUEST for address configuration with a new option described in Section 2.1. Note that network administrators must only enable the use of Rapid Reply on a DHCP server if one of the following conditions is met: (1) the server is the only server for the subnet. (2) addresses are plentiful for the client population. When multiple servers are present, they may each commit a binding for all clients and therefore each server must have sufficient addresses available. A server may allow configuration for a different (likely shorter) initial lease time for addresses assigned when Rapid Reply is used to expedite reclaiming addresses not used by clients.

2.1 Rapid Reply Option

The Rapid Reply option is used to signal the use of the two messages exchange for address assignment. The code for the Rapid Reply option is to be defined by IANA (temporary code was assigned to this paper) and length is 1 octet. A client must include this option in a DHCPDISCOVER message if the client is prepared to perform the DHCPDISCOVER-DHCPACK message exchange described on the right side of Fig. 1. A server must include this option in a DHCPACK message sent in a response to a DHCPDISCVER message when completing the DHCPDISCOVER-DHCPACK message exchange.

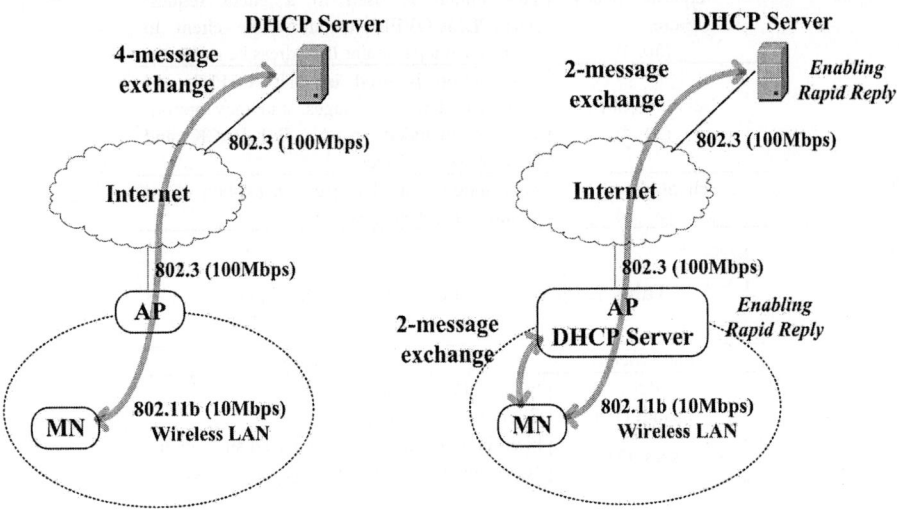

Fig. 1. Comparison of network architecture and DHCP message exchange

2.2 Operations Overview

A client that supports the Rapid Reply option must include it in DHCPDISCOVER messages that it sends. The client must not include it in any other messages. A client that sent a DHCPDISCOVER with Rapid Reply option processes responses as described in [3] because it is modeled on DHCPv6 Rapid Commit option. However, if the client receives a DHCPACK message with a Rapid Reply option, it should process the DHCPACK immediately (without waiting for additional DHCPOFFER or DHCPACK messages) and use the address and configuration information contained therein. A server that supports the Rapid Reply option may respond to a DHCPDISCOVER message that included the Rapid Reply option with a DHCPACK that includes the Rapid Reply option and fully committed address and configuration information. A server must not include the Rapid Reply option in any other messages. The Rapid Reply option must not appear in a Parameter Request List option [4]. All other DHCP operations are as documented in [4]. This paper does not mention how layer 2 operations happen when attaching a new AP.

2.3 Detailed Flow

The following is a detailed procedure that includes handling of the Rapid Reply option and both option and field description are shown in Table 1 and Table 2.

Table 1. Option description in DHCP Messages

Option (code, length)	Description
requested IP address (50, 4)	This option is used in a client request (DHCPDISCOVER) to allow the client to request that a particular IP address be assigned.
server identifier (54, 4)	This option is used in DHCPOFFER and DHCPREQUEST messages, and may optionally be included in the DHCPACK and DHCPNAK messages.
client identifier (61, n)	This option is used to pass an explicit client identifier to a DHCP server.

Table 2. Field description in DHCP Messages

Field (octet)	Description
yiaddr (4)	'your' (client) IP address
chaddr (16)	Client hardware address
secs. (2)	Field in by client, seconds elapsed since client began address acquisition or renewal process.

1. The client broadcasts a DHCPDISCOVER message on its local physical subnet and must include the Rapid Reply option if it supports this option. The DHCPDISCOVER message may include options that suggest values for the network

address and lease duration. BOOTP relay agents [4] may pass the message on to DHCP servers not on the same physical subnet.

2. Each server may respond with either a DHCPOFFER message or a DHCPACK message with Rapid Reply option (the latter only if the DHCPDISCOVER contained a Rapid Reply option and the server's configuration policies allow use of Rapid Reply) that includes an available network address in the 'yiaddr' field (and other configuration parameters in DHCP options [4]). Servers sending a DHCPOFFER need not reserve the offered network address, although the protocol will work more efficiently if the server avoids allocating the offered network address to another client. Servers sending the DHCPACK message commit the binding for the client to persistent storage before sending the DHCPACK. The combination of 'client identifier' or 'chaddr' and assigned network address constitute a unique identifier for the client's lease and are used by both the client and server to identify a lease referred to in any DHCP messages. The server transmits the DHCPOFFER or DHCPACK message to the client, using the BOOTP relay agent if necessary. When allocating a new address, servers should check that the offered network address is not already in use.

3. The client receives one or more DHCPOFFER or DHCPACK (if Rapid Reply option sent in DHCPDISCOVER) messages from one or more servers. If a DHCPACK (with Rapid Reply option) is received, the client immediately configures its network address if the offered configuration parameters are acceptable. Otherwise, the client broadcasts a DHCPREQUEST message that must include the 'server identifier' option to indicate which server it has selected, and that may include other options specifying desired configuration values. The 'requested IP address' option must be set to the value of 'yiaddr' in the DHCPOFFER message from the server. This DHCPREQUEST message is broadcast and relayed through DHCP/BOOTP relay agents. To help ensure that any BOOTP relay agents forward the DHCPREQUEST message to the same set of DHCP servers that received the original DHCPDISCOVER message, the DHCPREQUEST message must use the same value in the DHCP message header's 'secs' field and be sent to the same IP broadcast address as the original DHCPDISCOVER message. The client times out and retransmits the DHCPDISCOVER message if the client receives no DHCPOFFER messages.

4. The client may choose to relinquish its lease on a network address by sending a DHCPRELEASE message to the server. The client identifies the lease to be released with its 'client identifier', or 'chaddr' and network address in the DHCPRELEASE message. If the client used a 'client identifier' when it obtained the lease, it must use the same 'client identifier' in the DHCPRELEASE message.

3 Performance Evaluation and Comparison

In this section, we present our implementation and distinct performance against the existing mechanism especially reduced delay time and packet loss. We have conducted experiments for three situations depicted in Fig 1. We use the Linux Kernel 2.4.22 operating system for all implementation as DHCP server and mobile node and encode the Rapid Reply option in the Internet Systems Consortium DHCP source code so that Rapid Reply option is included in AP. We measured the date 50 times and the results are shown in Table 3.

Table 3. Comparson of mean value and standard deviation

	Item	Mean Value	Standard Deviation
Time Delay (Second)	Existing (4-message)	0.051269	0.002349
	New (2-message)	0.001541	0.001213
	AP (2-message)	0.000423	0.000422
Packet Loss (Packet)	Existing (4-message)	417.04	53.10322
	New (2-message)	366.02	32.55092
	AP (2-message)	082.32	11.42390

We can thus conclude that the use of AP and DHCP Server enabling Rapid Reply is efficient to configure IP addresses quickly.

4 Conclusion

In this paper, a new mechanism has been proposed for fast and stable address configuration in the WLAN such as those in which high mobility occurs and the network attachment point changes frequently. In particular, a Rapid Reply option has been newly defined in this paper to support the new mechanism and implemented in AP. It is possible to more quickly configure a mobile node's network address because the protections offered by the normal and longer 4-message exchange may not be needed. Also, performance evaluation and comparison have showed that the proposed mechanism is faster in terms of delay that existing mechanism including reduced packet loss. Especially when the mobile node is far from the DHCP server, the result might be remarkable. Through the new mechanism, a mobile node can maintain its connection when moving to a new network seamlessly because a new address, known care-of address in Mobile IP, is able to be configured quickly in a new network.

References

1. Perkins C.: Mobile networking through Mobile IP, Internet Computing, IEEE, Volume: 2 Issue: 1, p, 58-69, January (1998)
2. Droms R.: Automated configuration of TCP/IP with DHCP, Internet Computing, IEEE, Volume: 3 Issue: 4, p. 45-53, July (1999)
3. Droms R.: Dynamic Host Configuration Protocol for IPv6 (DHCPv6), IETF RFC 3315, December (2003)
4. Alexander A. and Droms R.: DHCP Options and BOOTP Vendor Extensions, IETF RFC 2132, March (1997)

NIC-NET: A Host-Independent Network Solution for High-End Network Servers

Keun Soo Yim[1], Hojung Cha[2], and Kern Koh[1]

[1] School of Computer Science and Engineering, Seoul National University, Korea
[2] Department of Computer Science, Yonsei University, Korea

Abstract. This paper discusses a host-independent network system where a network interface card is utilized in an efficient way. By eliminating protocol stack processing overheads from host system, the proposed system improves the communication speed by 11-36% under heavy network and CPU loads.

Keywords: High-end network server, protocol stack, network interface card.

1 Motivation

In a client and server computing model, the network server systems typically suffer from both heavy communication and computational loads, while they should provide high accessibilities to the clients. Recently, as communication channels become increasingly speedy, the communication bottleneck has been shifted from the limited channel bandwidth of network fabrics to the end-host software path traversed by messages. In order to improve the server performance, computer architects take the advantage from parallel and distributed computing technologies. However, as these systems typically provide an improved computing power, these systems still suffer from the lack of available communication bandwidth.

As the protocol stack resides in kernel in UNIX-like operating systems, they involve mainly three communication bottlenecks. In particular, applications have to use a system call interface, which requires two context-switching and one memory copying operation between user and kernel areas. Next, as these systems use the interrupt mechanism for handling network events, their performance can be significantly degraded at higher packet arrival rate [1]. Moreover, the host CPU has to process the heavy protocol stack, such as TCP/IP, while it takes up a relatively long time.

2 Related Work

There are several techniques that improve the end-host communication system performance by optimizing the network protocol stack, e.g. the user-level protocol architecture [2], and the related network hardware, e.g. the virtual interface architecture (VIA) [3]. The user-level architectures eliminate the kernel from its critical communication path by locating the network protocol stack in the user-level libraries. Because of this, these systems eliminate the system call overhead between the user and kernel address spaces. Although some variants use lightweight protocol stacks instead of TCP/IP, in these systems the host system has to execute the protocol stack, which typically takes up several milliseconds. Moreover, the host system suffers from handling network interrupt operations beneath higher packet arrival conditions. These defects are eliminated in NIC-NET as the network-related portion is offloaded.

In VIA, the two performance defeats of user-level protocol architectures are also addressed in the similar way as NIC-NET does. However, VIA is developed to provide the short communication latency for small packets between interconnected high-performance computers. To achieve this, VIA only uses specialized lightweight protocols and high-speed communication media, such as Myrinet. Because of this feature, VIA is not directly appreciable for the high-end network servers that use the TCP/IP protocol, while NIC-NET is suitable for the network servers as it supports the TCP/IP protocol. In EMP [4], TCP/IP protocol is offloaded to an Ethernet card to address the defeats of user-level system. In order to further improve the performance of EMP, we present novel communication interfaces between the host and NIC and evaluate the performance under various design spaces and runtime conditions.

3 Host-Independent Network System (NIC-NET)

In order to overcome these technical hurdles, in this paper we present a host-independent network system, namely NIC-NET, where a network interface card (NIC) is utilized in an efficient manner. The following features are the main benefits obtained with NIC-NET. First, as the network-related portion is offloaded from the kernel to the NIC, the host can fully utilize its computing power for other useful purposes. Note that the protocol stack processing time for a packet between the physical layer and the socket interface takes about 1-2 ms depending on the CPU computing power. Second, it eliminates the aforementioned system call overheads, since the host communicates with the NIC through its user-level libraries. In order to further reduce the communication costs, we provide novel communication interfaces between the user-level libraries of the host and the socket interface of NIC. Third, it also reduces the network interrupt operation count because the host handles interrupts in terms of a segment (a unit used in TCP) instead of a packet. Typically, the packet count is twice to four times than the segment count mainly due to packet fragmentation and control packets (such as ACK, SYN, and FIN). Fourth, it has a potential of reducing the kernel size due to its offloaded protocol architecture and also has high flexibility, which means that NIC-NET could be easily implemented with current operating systems by modifying its libraries and network device drivers.

In NIC-NET, the host system interacts with the NIC for various socket operations. Since each socket operation has different objectives and working mechanisms, the communication interfaces should be adapted to the each socket operation to maximize the performance benefits. We design three key communication methods that are employed depending on the type of socket operations as shown in Figure 1.

First, the asynchronous mode method is designed for asynchronous operations, i.e. *sendto*, *write*, *select*, *bind*, *listen*, and *create*. Second, the synchronous mode method aims to achieve synchronous operations such as *recvfrom*, *read*, *connect*, *accept*, and *close*. Although these two methods are sufficient in that they cover the entire generic socket interfaces, we provide the urgent mode method for high-performance network servers in order to avoid the risk of NIC memory overflow due to the heavy network traffic without having to be equipped with a larger memory size. Also it can be used to quickly deliver the urgent messages to the host without delaying them in the NIC.

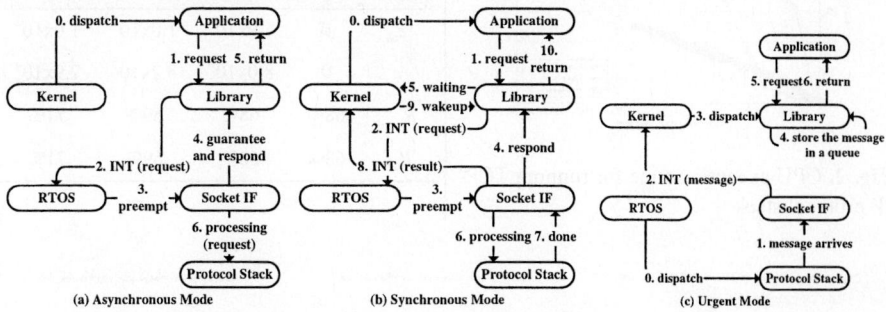

Fig. 1. Communication methods between the host and the NIC

4 Performance Evaluation

We used a modeling and simulation method so as to evaluate the performance under various design spaces and runtime conditions. As the existing network simulators such as *ns2* are based on kernel-resided protocol architecture, we specifically modeled the kernel-resided, user-level, and the proposed systems, measured the execution time of TCP/IP stack on a real machine, and finally developed a custom-simulator.

First, as shown in Figure 2, we measure the host CPU execution time for network system when a server application responds to sixty requests from a client through TCP. The straight lines without symbols denote the host reads the incoming messages from the NIC by using its interrupt handler routine. As the message count and size are much smaller than the packet count and size, NIC-NET reduces the interrupt service time significantly. This figure also shows that NIC-NET significantly reduces the protocol processing time marked by symbols due to its offloaded protocol architecture. The CPU overhead reduction rate of NIC-NET in comparison with the kernel-resided (R_{kernel}) and user-level (R_{user}) systems is about 68-71% as a function of average packet error rate as summarized in Table 1.

As NIC-NET significantly reduces the CPU overhead for the network system, it has a high potential of improving the performance of high-end network computers, which suffer from heavy network traffics and computational loads. Figure 3 illustrates the message roundtrip time consumed when a client count varies from 1 to 9 and each client generates a request in every 10ms. Figure 3(a) shows that the kernel-resided system processes the client requests in a stairway fashion because it stores incoming packets in a queue placed in the link layer to shorten the interrupt service time, and then it handles them using its kernel thread. A major observation in Figure3(b) is that

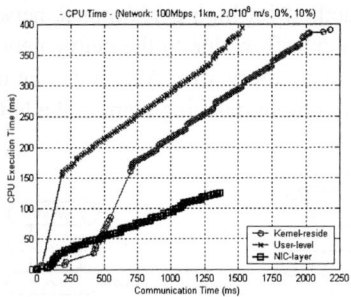

Fig. 2. CPU execution time for running TCP/IP protocol stack

Table 1. Reduction rate of CPU time for the network system as a function of packet error rate (e) in NIC-NET

Type	Ideal	Wired	Wireless	
e_{bit}	0	1.0×10^{-7}	1.0×10^{-6}	1.0×10^{-5}
e	0	8.0×10^{-4}	8.2×10^{-3}	7.9×10^{-2}
R_{kernel}	68%	68%	69%	71%
R_{user}	68%	68%	69%	71%

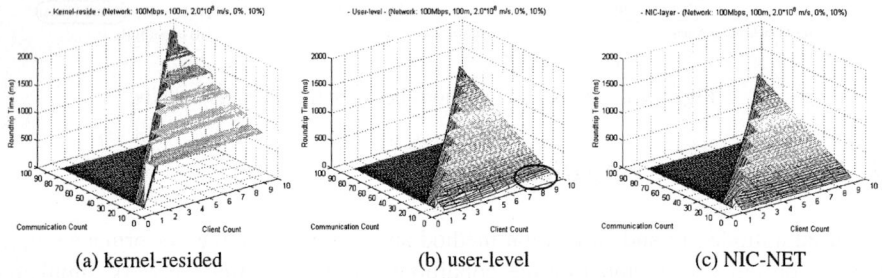

(a) kernel-resided   (b) user-level   (c) NIC-NET

Fig. 3. Message roundtrip time Versus network traffic

the user-level system does not response under the heavy traffic conditions directed by a circle because the host only reads arrived packets from the NIC during such duration. In contrast to the user-level system, NIC-NET responses under heavy traffic conditions, as shown in Figure 3(c), because the host runs the server application while the IC receives and processes the incoming packets. The message roundtrip time reduction rates of NIC-NET as compared with the kernel-resided and user-level systems are 32-83% and 11-36%, respectively. We also monitored the message roundtrip time by controlling the scheduling rate of the server application to reflect heavy computational load conditions. The results have quite similar characteristics of the former experiment.

As the performance of NIC-NET depends on the processor clock in the NIC, we evaluated the performance of NIC-NET with various CPU clocks and the NIC processor clocks under heavy network traffic conditions. If the CPU clock is 1GHz (baseline model is Intel Celeron) and the NIC processor clock is varying between 50MHz and 1GHz, we observed that the message roundtrip time becomes increased when the NIC processor clock is smaller than or equal to 200MHz, and this feature is not related in anyway to the host CPU clock. Therefore, the NIC processor clock of 200MHz is most suitable for achieving the best cost-benefit ratio in NIC-NET.

5 Conclusion

We have presented an efficient NIC-driven network system that uses a TCP/IP protocol stack and an Ethernet interface for high-end network server computers. The evaluation results have shown that the proposed NIC-NET significantly improves the communication speed under the conditions that the network and CPU are heavily loaded. For future work, we plan to extend NIC-NET using remote DMA operations.

References

1. J. Mogul and K. K. Ramakrishnan, "Eliminating Receive Livelock in an Interrupt-driven Kernel," *Proc. USENIX Annual Technical Conference*, 1996.
2. T. von Eicken, A. Basu, *et al.*, "U-Net: A User-Level Network Interface for Parallel and Distributed Computing," *Proc. ACM Symposium on OSs Principles*, pp. 40-53, 1995.
3. D. Dunning, G. Regnier, *et al.*, "The Virtual Interface Architecture," *IEEE Micro*, Vol. 18, No. 2, pp. 66-76, 1998.
4. P. Shivam, P. Wyckoff, and D. Panda, "EMP: Zero-copy OS-bypass NIC-driven Gigabit Ethernet Message Passing," *Proc. ACM Conference on Supercomputing*, No. 57, 2001.

Analysis of TCP/IP Protocol Stack for a Hybrid TCP/IP Offload Engine*

Soo-Cheol Oh, Hankook Jang, and Sang-Hwa Chung

School of Electrical and Computer Engineering,
Pusan National University, Pusan, 609-735, Korea
{osc, hkjang, shchung}@pusan.ac.kr

Abstract. TCP/IP, the most popular communication protocol, is processed on a host CPU in traditional computer systems and this imposes heavy loads on the host CPU. Recently TCP/IP Offload Engine (TOE) technology, which processes TCP/IP on a network adapter instead of the host CPU, has become an important alternative approach to this problem. In this paper, we analyze TCP/IP components that impose high loads on the host CPU by measuring processing times for each function in a TCP/IP protocol stack. Based on these analyses, we propose a hybrid TOE architecture, in which functions imposing high loads on the host CPU are implemented using hardware, and other functions are implemented using software.

1 Introduction

Ethernet technology has been widely used in many areas, and has already achieved a bandwidth of one Gigabit per second. Recently, 10-Gigabit Ethernet was standardized. TCP/IP, the most popular communication protocol for Ethernet, is processed on a host CPU in all computer systems, and this imposes heavy loads on the host CPU, thus degrading the performance of computer systems for users. Moreover, the loads on the host CPU increase as the physical bandwidth of networks increases. To solve this problem, TCP/IP Offload Engines (TOEs), in which TCP/IP is processed on a network adapter instead of in the host CPU, have been introduced. TOEs can reduce many of the loads imposed on the host CPU and help the CPU concentrate on executing computation jobs other than communication, thus improving the performance of the computer system.

There are two approaches in developing TOE. In the first approach, used in Intel's PRO/1000T IP Storage Adapter [1], which is based on Gigabit Ethernet, a processor embedded in the network adapter processes TCP/IP using software. This approach has the advantage that it is easier to implement than

---

* This research was supported by the Program for the Training of Graduate Students in Regional Innovation which was conducted by the Ministry of Commerce, Industry and Energy of the Korean Government.

a hardware-based approach. In Intel's Storage Adapter, the TCP/IP protocol is processed by an Intel 80200 StrongARM processor installed on the adapter. According to experiments performed at Colorado University [2], the unidirectional bandwidth of this adapter does not exceed 30 MB/s, which is about half the bandwidth of 70 MB/s achieved by general Gigabit Ethernet adapters. This shows that software-based TOE has a disadvantage in network performance. The other approach is to develop a specialized ASIC processing TCP/IP. Alacritech's SLIC [3], QLogic's ISP4010 [4] and Adaptec's NAC-7211 [5] are examples of hardware-based TOE products. The bandwidth of Alacritech's SLIC is over 800 Mbps, which approaches the peak bandwidth of Gigabit Ethernet. This shows that the hardware-based approach guarantees network performance. However, it takes much time to implement a hardware-based TOE. Moreover, in the near future, demand for TOEs to support IPv6 will increase, and it will be difficult for hardware-based TOEs supporting IPv4 to migrate to IPv6 quickly.

In this paper, we analyze the TCP/IP factors imposing high loads on a host CPU by measuring the times spent processing each function in the TCP/IP protocol stack. Based on these analyses, we propose a hybrid TOE architecture that combines the hardware and software approaches to guarantee both network performance and fast implementation.

2 Analysis of TCP/IP Protocol Stack

When TCP/IP was implemented in early UNIX systems such as BSD UNIX, data in a packet was repeatedly copied at every layer in the TCP/IP protocol stack. This redundant data copying degraded network performance. Linux adopts a socket buffer structure to remove unnecessary data copies between layers of the TCP/IP protocol stack. When sending a data packet, a socket buffer consisting of a header region and a data region is created. A pointer to the socket buffer is then passed through each layer of the protocol stack instead of copying the whole socket buffer, and each layer fills its associated header region of the socket buffer with the required values. When receiving a packet, each layer processes its associated header and passes a pointer to a socket buffer to the upper layers.

We chose Linux as a basic operating system for this study because Linux has higher network performance than other operating systems. In this section, we measure processing times for each function in the TCP/IP protocol stack and analyze the primary factors that generate heavy loads on a host CPU. For our experiments, two nodes were connected using Intel PRO/1000MT Gigabit Ethernet server adapters without a switch. Each node had a 1.8 GHz Intel Xeon CPU and 512 MB of main memory. The operating system was based on Linux kernel 2.4.7-10, and the device driver for the network adapter was version e1000-5.2.20 provided by Intel. The TCP packet size was varied from 1.4 KB to 1 MB, and the time unit is the number of CPU clock cycles.

Table 1 shows the processing times for the TCP functions that consume the most time in sending data. *tcp_alloc_skb()*, *skb_add_data()* and *wait_for_tcp_memory()* take up about 70 - 90 % of the total send time. *tcp_alloc_pskb()* creates a

Table 1. Times spent in processing functions in sending data

(time unit : 1000 CPU clocks)

	1.4 KB		14 KB		144 KB		1 MB	
tcp_alloc_skb()	9	(52 %)	105	(57 %)	957	(16 %)	7,291	(16 %)
skb_add_data()	3	(18 %)	46	(25 %)	413	(7 %)	2,525	(5 %)
wait_for_tcp_memory()	0	(0 %)	0	(0 %)	4,092	(69 %)	31,298	(67 %)
Total send time	17	(100 %)	185	(100 %)	5,918	(100 %)	46,511	(100 %)

Table 2. Times spent on processing functions in receiving data

(time unit : 1000 CPU clocks)

	1.4 KB		14 KB		144 KB		1 MB	
tcp_v4_rcv()	11	(19 %)	12	(5 %)	111	(6 %)	720	(4 %)
ACK functions (tcp_send_ack())	13	(22 %)	54	(21 %)	99	(5 %)	294	(2 %)
tcpt_copy_to_iovec()	17	(29 %)	72	(28 %)	767	(39 %)	7,413	(45 %)
__kfree_skb()	5	(8 %)	51	(19 %)	720	(36 %)	5,710	(35 %)
Total receive time	59	(100 %)	263	(100 %)	1,974	(100 %)	16,308	(100 %)

socket buffer, and *skb_add_data()* copies data in user space to a socket buffer in kernel space. *wait_for_tcp_memory()* makes the send process sleep until enough free send buffer space is available. The relative processing times of these three functions change as the data size increases. When the data size is relatively small, such as 1.4 KB to 14 KB, the time spent in processing *tcp_alloc_pskb()* is over 50 % of the total send time and *skb_add_data()* occupies 18 - 25 % of the total send time. When the data size is 140 KB to 1 MB, *wait_for_tcp_memory()* spends about 70 % of the total sending time. When a user process requests to create a socket buffer to send data, free memory space must be allocated to this socket buffer. If enough free memory space is not available in main memory, *wait_for_tcp_memory()* changes the state of this process to 'sleep' for multitasking. This process is awoken and resumes its job when enough free memory space is available. The scheduling process of the Linux operating systems consumes much time and this makes processing time for *wait_for_tcp_memory()* near to 70 % of the total sending time.

Table 2 shows the processing times for the TCP functions that consume the most time in receiving data. *tcp_v4_rcv()*, *tcp_copy_to_iovec()*, *__kfree_skb()* and acknowledgement (ACK) processing functions including *tcp_send_ack()* consume 73 - 86 % of the total receive time. *tcp_v4_rcv()* processes TCP headers. *tcp_copy_to_iovec()* copies data from a socket buffer to the corresponding INET socket, which is located on upper layer of the TCP layer. ACK processing functions including *tcp_send_ack()* generate an ACK packet and send it to the corresponding node. *__kfree_skb()* frees a socket buffer after data is copied to an INET socket. The relative processing times of these functions change as the data size increases. When the data size is relatively small such as 1.4KB to 14KB, the time spent in processing ACK functions and *tcp_copy_to_iovec()* is about 50 % of the total receive time. When the data size is 140KB - 1MB, *tcp_copy_to_iovec()* and *__kfree_skb()* spend 39 - 45 % and 35 - 36 % of the total receive time, respectively.

In summary, the three functions listed in Table 1 and the four functions listed in Table 2 use 70 - 92 % of the total TCP processing time. These seven functions must be optimized for implementing a TOE.

3 Hybrid TOE Architecture

Based on the experimental results of Sections 2, we propose a hybrid TOE architecture. The key idea of the hybrid TOE is that the time-consuming functions are implemented using hardware and other functions are implemented using software. The hybrid TOE consists of one ASIC-based hardware module and two embedded processor cores. The functions except *wait_for_tcp_memory()* listed Table 1 and Table 2 are implemented in the hardware module. The task scheduling load generated by *wait_for_tcp_memory()* can be avoid by preventing the task switches between send and receive processes. The task switches between two processes can be removed by handling send and receive processes on separate embedded processors. An advantage of the hybrid TOE is that it guarantees network performance, because the functions requiring the most processing are implemented using hardware. Another advantage is fast implementation because most functions of TCP/IP, which do not consume much time, are implemented by software.

4 Conclusions and Future Works

We analyzed primary factors of loads imposed on a host CPU by measuring the times spent in processing each function in the Linux TCP/IP protocol stack, and it is shown that three functions used in sending data and four functions used in receiving data spend 70 - 90 % of the total processing time. Based on the results of these analyses, we proposed the hybrid TOE architecture that combines the hardware and software approaches to guarantee both network performance and fast implementation. In future work, we will implement the hybrid TOE proposed in this paper and will develop a network adapter with the hybrid TOE module.

References

1. Intel PRO/1000T IP Storage Adapter, Data Sheet, Intel, 2003.
2. S. Aiken, D. Grunwald, A. R. Pleszkun, and J. Willeke: A Performance Analysis of the iSCSI Protocol, *Proceedings of the 20th IEEE/MSS'03*, 2003.
3. SLIC Technology Overview, http://www.alacritech.com/html/tech_review.html, Alacritech, Inc.
4. iSCSI Controller, http://download.qlogic.com/datasheet/16291/isp4010.pdf, qlogic Corp., 2003.
5. Adaptec TOE NAC 7711, Data Sheet, adaptec, Inc., 2003.

Techniques in Mapping Router-Level Internet Topology from Multiple Vantage Points

Yu Jiang, Binxing Fang, and Mingzeng Hu

School of Computer Science and Technology, Harbin Institute of Technology,
150001 Harbin, P. R. China
{jiangyu, bxfang, mzhu}@hit.edu.cn
http://pact518.hit.edu.cn/

Abstract. Accompanying the Internet rapid expansion and the great changes in Internet underlying topology, research communities have paid ever-increasing attention to the challenging task of measuring Internet topology. This paper discusses the limitation of using public traceroute servers for router level topology measurement. In our distributed three-level architecture for mapping individual ISP topologies by a third party, an on-demand probing at each hop and centralized DNS query are employed to reduce network overload and improve probe efficiency. The effects of these two techniques are exhibited in this paper.

1 Introduction

Mapping each national or continental ISP topology individually becomes an alternative method to router level Internet topology measurement. Like a world atlas, each national or continental ISP topology is a portion of Internet, and the combination of them will reflect the topology of the whole Internet.

Previous studies have shown that Internet topological data should be collected simultaneously from multiple vantage points during the same period of time in order to make the measured graph more complete [1-5]. To this end, we have presented a three-level architecture - *DRIMA* (*D*istributed *R*outer-level *I*nternet *M*apping *A*rchitecture) - to measure ISPs (Internet Service Provider) topologies [6]. Our goal is to map ISPs topologies from multiple vantage points in a cooperative way by a third party.

In this paper, after presenting an analysis of the necessity to design *DRIMA*, we discuss the effect of two techniques that are in favor of improving probe performance in router level topology measurement, which include an on-demand probing at each hop and centralized DNS (Domain Name Server) query. In this regard, this paper is a supplement to [6] and other details related to *DRIMA* are referred to [6].

2 Consideration in Designing *DRIMA*

We develop our probe engine instead of using public traceroute servers (PTrSs) for the reason that an independent and easy deployed probe engine is capable of meeting the requirement of on-demand deployment and is flexible in adding other functions in order to get a relatively complete topology graph and easy maintenance. Also, there are some limitations of using PTrSs to measure router level Internet topology.

2.1 Limitations of Using PTrSs

First, the distribution of PTrSs is uneven. It is not the case that each ISP hosts PTrSs (e.g., in the mainland of China there is only one national ISP hosting two PTrSs that are merely supporting single probe source). Meanwhile, there are few PTrSs (5.8%) supporting multiple probe sources in the world [2]. Therefore, for most ISPs we can only conduct topology measurement from a single source within the target ISP. However, the measured topology from a single source is far from being complete [1][7].

Second, an ISP is usually connected to Internet eXchange Points (IXP) at limited points. Thus, using other ISP's PTrSs to map the target ISP topology is equivalent to probing from the limited points adjacent to IXPs, even for the case that the target ISP has more than one links with an IXP. This scenario is illustrated in Fig. 1. In this figure, solid lines represent links that can be discovered and dashed lines represent links that cannot be discovered. An additional $PTrS_4$ is of no use. In fact, there may exist this kind of limitation in the traceroute-like measurement whose measurement scope traverses a national ISP with no active source in the very ISP.

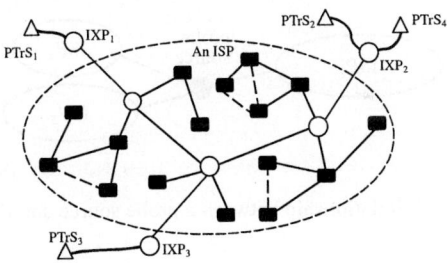

Fig. 1. No way to further improve measurement completeness with additional PTrSs

Third, generally we are unable to control the running way of PTrSs. This involves the following five aspects. (1) Using PTrSs might produce a great deal of DNS queries for reversal domain name resolution. Interfaces addresses presented in different probed paths are not unique, and a traceroute server would send a DNS query for each hop in each path. The more passive destinations, the more repeated queries. (2) In order to avoid PTrS being used as a source of DDoS attack, in general only after obtaining the cooperation and trust with the administrator of PTrSs can we gain limited control on the running way of PTrSs and perform an automated probe; otherwise, we can only manually conduct the probe. However, it is not an easy work to win the cooperation and trust from the administrators of PTrSs. (3) Even having obtained the limited control on PTrSs, we might only send UDP or ICMP packets for topological data collection. However, out of security consideration, ICMP echo request/reply packets and UDP port probing packets are prone to be blocked. For instance, in order to block Worm.Blaster, ICMP echo request/reply packets are blocked unconditionally. Meantime, UDP packets are prone to be routed by policy routing. If we ourselves develop the probe engine, when UDP and ICMP packets do not meet our needs, we might employ TCP packets for path collection. At present, all of these three probe ways are implemented in our probe engine that employs traceroute-like method, and different ways are scheduled according to the actual situation. (4) Even having obtained the limited control on PTrSs, we might not be able to control the number of packets sent at each hop (refer to section 3.1). (5) Even having obtained the limited control on PTrSs, we might not be able to terminate a probe process when there are three timeout hops in a probe path [7][1], and we can only let it go until Time-To-Live reaches the threshold (e.g. 30 hops). This would affect probe performance.

Therefore, we develop our probe engine and measurement system for topology measurement. Our goal is *to map each of national ISP topology in a cooperative way by a third-party, and the same measurement system is employed in mapping different ISP topologies*. Each probe source is connected to the Points of Presence (PoP) of relevant ISPs via a router, as depicted in Fig. 2, and thus it is equivalent to conducting the measurement within the target ISP by a third party from multiple vantage points.

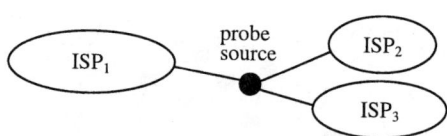

Fig. 2. Relationship between a probe source and ISPs

2.2 Strength of the Three-Level Deployment Framework

Previous efforts for mapping router level Internet topologies, including *Rocketfuel* [2] and *skitter* [3], employ a two-level deployment framework, i.e. multiple probing level and centralized processing level. When there are dozens or hundreds of vantage points, a two-level deployment framework would result in exerting much pressure on the centralized processing for a large amount of raw data from multiple sources, since the normalization of millions of hops and the parsing for processing are resource- and time-consuming procedures. Fox example, suppose the average number of hops in a probe path is h, the total number of passive destinations is d, and the number of probe sources (vantage points) is s, then the total number of records would be $h \times d \times s$. If h=15, d=20000, and s=10, the total number of records would be 30 millions. Instead, our three-level deployment framework can reduce much pressure on the centralized *post-processing* with the help of *pre-processing* at the middle level. *Post-processing* is not responsible for the normalization of raw paths and the parsing for processing (refer to the Fig. 2 in [6]). What it processes is the logical sub-graphs with merely thousands of items constructed by pre-processing. Each of the logical sub-graphs represents the *summary view* from multiple vantage points that are under the control of the same module at the middle level. This is in favor of system scalability and efficiency.

3 The Effects of Two Techniques

In this section, we present that the on-demand probing at each hop and centralized DNS query are efficient in improving probe performance.

3.1 On-Demand Probing at Each Hop

Topology measurement from multiple vantage points should not produce much overload in the network. In general, one response is enough for each hop in the course of probing paths. Similar to the idea in [8], at each hop we send another packet only in the situation that the response for the preceding probe packet is timeout, and at most three packets are sent. The proportion of packets needed at each hop for each probe source is shown in Fig.3. We can see that at each hop the case that only one packet is needed is at least 89.08%, and the case that at most two packets are needed is at least 99.79%. It suggests that due to the effect of congestion and route change, if one sole packet is sent at each hop, the completeness of link discovery might be decreased (see Fig. 3 (b)). On the other hand, compared with the way of sending default three packets at each hop in using PTrSs, the way of on-demand probing at each hop will decrease the overload and improve the probe efficiency.

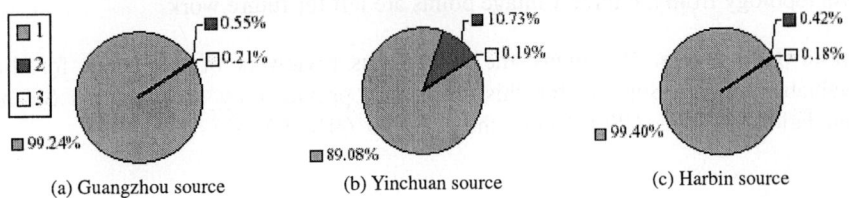

(a) Guangzhou source   (b) Yinchuan source   (c) Harbin source

Fig. 3. The proportion of packets needed at each hop

3.2 Centralized DNS Query

In our architecture, instead of querying DNS servers for reversal domain name resolution at each hop during path probe from multiple vantage points, we do DNS queries only for all distinct IP addresses that are selected from the union graph after all probe processes terminate. Thus, we do DNS query for each IP address at most once in one measurement cycle. In this way, the total number of DNS queries in mapping an ISP topology will neither be determined by the number of probe sources nor by the number of passive destinations. It will only be determined by the number of distinct router interfaces within the target ISP's network, and the unnecessary DNS queries are reduced dramatically. In our experiments of 17.8 thousand destinations from each of the three vantage points, there are about 529 thousands valid hops in total. However, we need only 2866 (0.54%) DNS queries. The relevant results are shown in Table 1.

Table 1. Numbers of valid hops and actual queries

Probe Source	# of valid IP addresses	# of distinct IP addresses	Queries(%)
Guangzhou	166740	2261	1.36%
Yinchuan	175157	2242	1.28%
Harbin	187644	1961	1.05%
Total	529541	2866	0.54%

4 Conclusion Remarks

In this paper we have discussed the limitation of using public traceroute servers as probe sources in router level Internet topology measurement. The strength of our three-level deployment framework is also discussed. The effects of on-demand probing at each hop and centralized DNS query are also exhibited. Though the centralized DNS query is simple, it reduces the number of DNS queries significantly by delaying the query till all the probing is done. In a cooperative way, we are able to transport our traceroute-like probe engine to every probe source at the stage of deployment and schedule it on-demand at the stage of measurement by an integrated configuration interface presented in [6]. Analyses of the topology properties of the measured router level topology from the three vantage points are left for future work.

Acknowledgements. We thank the anonymous reviewers of the paper for their invaluable efforts. Support for this work was provided by the National Science Foundation of China (NSFC) under the grant No. 60203021.

References

1. Jiang, Y., Hu, M. Z., Fang, B. X., Zhang, H. L.: An Internet router level topology automatically discovering system. J. China Institute of Communications, Dec. 2002, 23 (12) 54-62
2. Spring, N., Mahajan, R., Wetherall, D.: Measuring ISP Topologies with Rocketfuel. ACM SIGCOMM Computer Comm. Review, Oct. 2002, 31(4) 133-145
3. Huffaker, B., Plummer, D., Moore, D., claffy, k: Topology discovery by active probing. In: Proc. of SAINT'02w, IEEE press, New York, (2002) 90-96
4. Subramanian, L., Agarwal, S., Rexford, J., Katz, R. H.: Characterizing the Internet hierarchy from multiple vantage points. In: Proc. of INFOCOM 2002, IEEE Press,NY,(2002) 618-627
5. Barford, P., Bestavros, A., Byers, J., Crovella, M.: On the Marginal Utility of Network Topology Measurements. In: Proc. of IMW2001, ACM press, New York, (2001) 5-17

6. Jiang, Y., Fang, B. X., Hu, M. Z., Zhang, H. L., Yun, X. C.: A Distributed Architecture for Internet Router Level Topology Discovering Systems. In: Proc. of PDCAT 2003, IEEE press, New York, 47-51
7. Govindan, R., Tangmunarunkit, H.: Heuristics for Internet map discovery. In: Proc. of IEEE INFOCOM 2000, IEEE Press, New York, (2000), 1371-1380
8. Pansiot, J., Grad, D.: On Routes and Multicast Trees in the Internet. ACM SIGCOMM Computer Communication Review, Jan. 1998, 28 (1) 41-50

Lossy Link Identification for Multicast Network

Hui Tian and Hong Shen

Graduate School of Information Science
Japan Advanced Institute of Science and Technology

Abstract. Use of multicast traffic as measurement probes has been shown effective to infer network-internal characteristics. In a network the links that have a packet loss rate greater than a given threshold are called lossy links. Lossy links adversely affect network performance and collectively cause break-down of network service in many cases. We propose a new approach to identify the lossy links from multicast end-to-end measurements. It is based on hamming distance of sequences on receipt/loss of probe packets maintained at each pair of sibling nodes. With prior knowledge of multicast network topology, all lossy links can be effectively identified by our approach.

Keywords: Multicast network, lossy link, identification.

1 Introduction

How to measure network performance accurately plays an important role in the successful design, control and management of networks. Generally, it is evaluated by such measurements as packet loss rates and link delays. Lossy links in a network are those links whose packet loss rates exceed a predefined threshold. Identifying lossy links can benefit many network management tasks such as locating link failures and service break-down. How to effectively identify lossy links is therefore an interesting problem of great significance to network administration.

In this paper, we propose a new approach to identify the lossy link in a network based on multicast end-to-end measurements. It differs from the previous work which paid much attention to identify the network-internal characteristics such as [1, 2, 4, 5]. Inferring detailed network-internal characteristics is quite difficult and costly, and making such an effort is not always worthwhile. In our problem context, we are only interested in those ill-performing links in the network and we want to identify and recover them quickly without invoking a complex process of network-internal characteristics inference. To accomplish this task, we apply hamming distance to compare the sequences on receipt/loss of probe packets maintained at different nodes.

The paper is organized as follows. In Section 2 the mathematical model of multicast network is given. Section 3 describes the identification approach and simulation is given. Section 4 concludes the paper.

2 The Network Model

We begin the section with description of mathematical model for the real multicast network as presented in [3]. In this model, the physical multicast tree is represented by a tree comprising the nodes and communication links connecting them.

Let $T = (V, L)$ denote a multicast tree with node set V and link set L. The root node 0 is the source of probe packets, and $R \subset V$ denotes the set of leaf nodes representing the receivers. A link is said to be internal if neither of its endpoints is the root or a leaf node. Each non-leaf node k has a set of children node $d(k) = \{d_i(k) \mid 1 \leq i \leq n_k\}$, and each non-root node k has a parent $p(k)$. The link $(p(k), k) \in L$ is denoted by link k. Let $a(U)$ denote the nearest common ancestor of a node set $U \subset V$. Nodes in U are said to be siblings if they have the same parent, i.e., if $f(k) = a(U), \forall k \in U$. Assume the progress of each probing packet down the tree is described by an independent copy of a stochastic process $X = (X_k)_{k \in V}$ as follows. $X_0 = 1$, $X_k = 1$ if the probing packet reaches node $k \in V$ and 0 otherwise. If $X_k = 0$, $X_j = 0, \forall j \in d(k)$. Otherwise, $P[X_j = 1 | X_k = 1] = p_j$ and $P[X_j = 0 | X_k = 1] = 1 - p_j = \alpha_j$. Define $p_0 = 1$. We use a boolean variable $X_k^{(i)}$ to denote the loss measurement of node k for ith probe packet. For n probe packets, the 0-1 sequence maintained on the node k is denoted by $\{X_k^{(i)}\}, 1 \leq i \leq n, k \in V$.

3 Lossy Links Identification

The problem of lossy link identification can be stated as follows: given the topology of a multicast network and a packet loss threshold, we want to identify all links in the multicast network whose packet loss rates are greater than the threshold. In the multicast tree, the root is the source and leaves are the receivers. Internal nodes and their connections are also given in the topology. We focus on identifying the lossy links by use of measurements made with access to the source and receiver. Binary multicast tree is mainly considered for simplicity. Extension to general tree case can easily deduced from our approach.

3.1 Lossy Links Identification for Binary Trees

When a probe packet is sent from the root of the multicast tree, several copies are generated at each router encountered. Thus, each receiver will receive one copy of the probe packet in case of transmitting without loss in the path. $X_k^{(i)}$ is set to 1 if node k receives the ith probe packet or its copy, otherwise set to 0. The same holds for those internal routers. Thus with n probe packets, each node in the network will maintain a "0-1" sequence. The sequences of receivers can be observed directly. The sequences of those internal nodes can be deduced by the following equation.

$$X_k^{(i)} = \vee_{l \in R(k)} X_l^{(i)}. \tag{1}$$

Thus, each node obtains a "0-1" sequence $\{X_k^{(i)}\}$, $0 < i < n$, $k \in V$. These sequences imply correlations among all the nodes. As the paths from the root to receivers vary, the sequences maintained by all nodes are, more or less, different from one another, which is shown by different correlation between any pair sequences. Because for a 2-component sequence, hamming distance is the simplest and most efficient method to identify the similarity and dissimilarity among different sequences. We propose the use of hamming distance of each pair sequences for lossy links identification.

The hamming distance between two nodes, denoted by $H_d(\cdot,\cdot)$, is defined to be the number of components whose corresponding values are different. $\oplus$ is the exclusive-OR operator and $0 < i < n$, $s_1, s_2 \in V$.

$$H_d(s_1, s_2) = \sum_{i=1}^{n} X_{s_1}^{(i)} \oplus X_{s_2}^{(i)}, \qquad (2)$$

Because only the hamming distances of all siblings pairs are of interest, we assume s_1 and s_2 are siblings. Suppose the total No. of probe packets is n. s is parent node of s_1 and s_2. Assume the No. of probe packets reaching s to be n_s^1. The hamming distance between the sequences at both nodes are determined only by their separative link condition. If a link has great loss, or even fails, it can be identified directly by comparison of the hamming distance and a threshold $\epsilon \cdot n_s^1$. For those nodes who haven't siblings we determine if the No. of lost packets on the single-branch path is great by comparing the No. of "0" in the sequence of the node with that in the sequence of its nearest multi-children ancestor. If the ratio of them exceeds loss rate threshold α_h, there is at least one lossy link on the path. In this case, we consider the link nearest to the multi-children ancestor to the lossy link.

Let $n_{s_1}^1$ denote the No. of probe packets transmitted trough link s_1 successfully, and $n_{s_1}^0$ denote the No. of lost probe packets on link s_1. $n_{s_1 s_2}^0$ is denoted the No. of probe packets lost on both links s_1 and s_2 at the same time. We assume α_{s_1} is the loss rate of link s_1. The loss rate of the common links from the root to the siblings' parent node is supposed to be α_s. Then,

$$H_d(s_1, s_2) = n_{s_1}^0 + n_{s_2}^0 - 2n_{s_1 s_2}^0 = n_s^1 \cdot (\alpha_{s_1} + \alpha_{s_2} - 2\alpha_{s_1}\alpha_{s_2}). \qquad (3)$$

The main steps of identification algorithm is given as follows.

1. *Input*: The network $T = (V, L)$, the set of receivers R, the number of probe packets n, and the sequences observed at all receivers $(X_r^{(i)})_{r \in R}^{i=1,\cdots,n}$;
2. Give the threshold α_h, ϵ, initialize the lossy link set to be identified L';
3. Calculate each node's sequence according to $X_k^{(i)} = \vee_{l \in R(k)} X_l^{(i)}$;
4. If a node has no siblings, compare the number of "0" in the sequence with that of its nearest multi-children ancestor. Otherwise, compare the hamming distance of each pair of siblings with the threshold; if $H_d(s_1, s_2) > \epsilon \cdot n_s$, the link connecting the node whose number of "0", saying s_1, is more than that of its siblings is identified as one of the lossy links. Add link s_1 to L'.
5. *Output*: The identified lossy link set L'.

3.2 Simulation on Identification Algorithm

We define AR as accuracy rate which is the ratio of the number of correctly identified lossy links to the number of real lossy links. With different given loss rate α_h, we evaluate the AR as ϵ varies in the simulation.

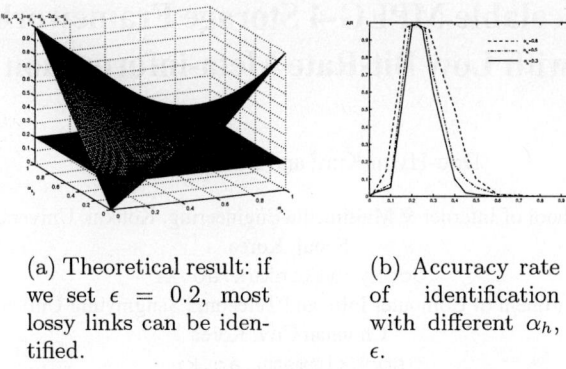

(a) Theoretical result: if we set $\epsilon = 0.2$, most lossy links can be identified.

(b) Accuracy rate of identification with different α_h, ϵ.

Fig. 1. Simulation Result

Figure1(a) shows the theoretical choice of ϵ based on Equation (3). In practice, it is shown that if ϵ is set around 0.2, the accuracy rate is near to 1. In this case, our approach can identify those interested lossy links accurately.

4 Conclusion

A new and simple approach to identify the lossy link in the multicast network has been proposed in this paper. It is based on comparison of hamming distance between the sequences on receipt/loss of probe packets maintained at siblings. The simulation has shown that the accuracies of lossy links identification for different values of ϵ and loss rate threshold α_h are quite satisfactory.

References

[1] R. Caceres, N. G. Duffield, J. Horowitz, and D. Towsley. Multicast-based inference of network-internal loss characteristics. *IEEE Trans. Information Theory*, 1999.
[2] R. Careres, N. G. Duffield, H. Horowitz, D. Towsley, and T. Bu. Multicastbased inference of network internal loss characteristics: Accuracy of packet loss estimation. In *Proc. Of Infocom'99. New York, NY*, 1999.
[3] N. G. Duffield, J. Horowitz, F. Lo Presti, and D. Towsley. Multicast topology inference from measured end-to-end loss. *IEEE Trans. Information Theory*, 2002.
[4] F. Lo Presti, N. G. Duffield, J. Horowitz, and D. Towsley. Multicast-based inference of network-internal delay distributions. *IEEE/ACM Transactions on Networking*, Vol. 10, No. 6, Dec. 2002.
[5] Hui Tian and Hong Shen. Multicast-based inference of network internal loss performance. In *Proceedings of ISPAN'04*, May. 2004.

Scalable MPEG-4 Storage Framework with Low Bit-Rate Meta-information

Doo-Hyun Kim[1] and Soo-Hong Kim[2]

[1] School of Internet & Multimedia Engineering, Konkuk University,
Seoul, Korea
doohyun@konkuk.ac.kr
[2] Department of Computer Info. and Telecom., Sangmyung University,
Chonnan City, Korea
soohkim@smu.ac.kr

Abstract. In this paper, we have shown a many-fold layered encoding mechanism that can provide fine-grained scalable storage, hence, improve the degree of QoS adaptability. Our scheme provides both the temporal scalability and fidelity scalability, simultaneously, by segmenting the stored MPEG-4 data in the DCT coefficient domain as well as the temporal domain with low bit-rate meta-information.

Keywords: MPEG-4, layered storage, temporal scaling, fidelity scaling.

1 Introduction

A QoS adaptive multimedia streaming architecture is composed of three sub-systems: decomposer, streaming server, and streaming client. The decomposer, mainly focused on in this paper, is composed of two modules, MPEG DeMuxer and Media Decomposer. MPEG DeMuxer separates an original MPEG file into a video stream and an audio stream. Media Decomposer splits the MPEG-4 video stream into multiple layers by applying temporal slicing and fidelity slicing, and simultaneously generates meta-information data containing the layering information. And then each of the layers and the audio data is stored into a repository. Therefore, these modules are performed in off-line.

Most of works conducted for improving adaptability with layered encoding scheme are confined to selecting layers from only one base layer and only one or two enhancement layers [1, 2]. Thus, it seems not to be fine-grained enough to reflect the QoS dynamicity. For instance, the base layer may still be large to transfer over current Internet in a timely manner in case of network congestion. Meanwhile, Scalable layered MPEG-2 Video Multicast method [3] tries to divide the DCT coefficient into several layers. The base layer contains the DC coefficient, AC coefficients with lower frequency, and header information for decoding. This method is similar to our approach in the point that total bit-stream size is not increased compared with original MPEG stream and that it can adapt flexibly for the dynamic QoS variation without overloading the server. However, this method was applied to only MPEG-2 and did not reveal the structure for preparing proper layered storage. In this paper, we propose a mechanism for building a fine-grained layered MPEG-4 storage providing both of the temporal scalability and fidelity scalability.

2 Scaling Framework

Temporal Scaling Framework. The temporal scaling is referred to reduce the resolution of the video stream in the time domain by decreasing the number of video frames transmitted within a time interval. The temporal scaling extracts the pictures from the MPEG-4 video stream according to the picture types, I-, P-, and B-VOP, and consequently, results in three intermediate representations of an I-substream, a P-substream, and a B-substream. I-substream can be decoded by itself at the MPEG-4 decoder. In this case, the frame rate is reduced since all of P-pictures and B-pictures are dropped. But, the P- and B-substreams are not self-contained. Thus, in order to decode the P-substream, it should be merged with the I-substream at first. Similarly, B-substream should be merged with both the I-substream and the P-substream. One problem occurring when a frame is skipped is an effect on the presentation time of other frames. To prevent changing of presentation time, the inserting a dummy frame in the place of dropped frame may be considered. Because the client cannot find the order of original stream using the received bit-stream with the some dropped frame, the insertion point of dummy frame cannot be estimated. Therefore additional information has to be transmitted to the clients for merging and decoding.

Fidelity Scaling Framework. The fidelity scaling degrades picture quality by reducing the number of DCT coefficients applied to the compression of a picture. 2-D(8x8) DCT coefficients of a block are converted to 1-D sequence by using either zig-zag scanning or alternate scanning rules. So, the sixty-four 1-D ordered DCT coefficients are decomposed into proper number of DCT groups. The DC term must be included in the first group. Fidelity scaling can be applied to inter-pictures(I-substream) as well as intra-pictures (P-substream and B-substream). As one block is divided into several

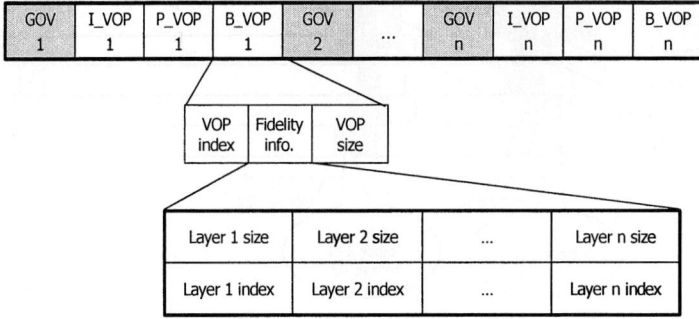

Fig. 1. Structure of Meta Data

layers, the searching method for the end of block is required for each layer. While MPEG-2 generates the Huffman code for run and level, MPEG-4 generates the Huffman code for run, level and last. Run value represents the number of occurrence of zero before the coefficient and level value represent the ac coefficient. Using these characteristics of MPEG-4, we set the last field value as '1' for the end of each layer.

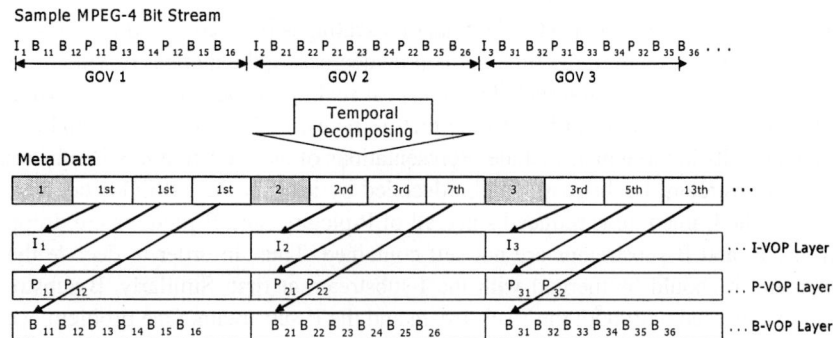

Fig. 2. Example Meta data with only temporal scaling information

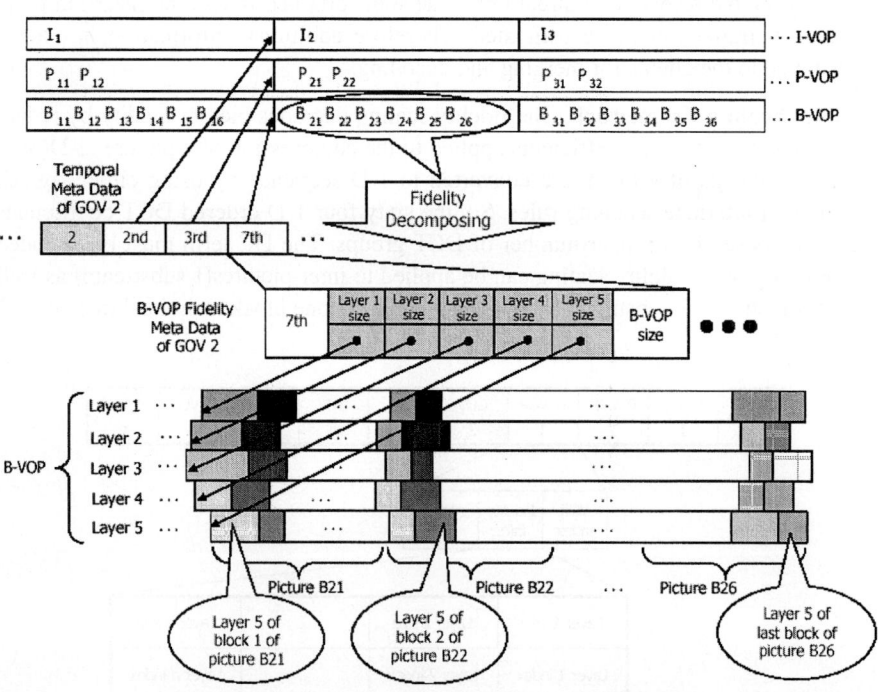

Fig. 3. Example meta data with fidelity scaling information

3 Meta Information Processing

The stored layer files stored in a repository are selected according to the adaptation level and reconstructed as an MPEG-4 bit-stream. The meta-information that is needed to reconstruct the MPEG-4 bit-stream is stored in separate file as shown in Fig. 1. The Meta data is generated by a scalable media splitter at off-line, and stored into the server's storage together with corresponding MPEG-4 data. The amount of the meta-information depends on the number of VOPs in MPEG-4 data, but it is revealed that it does not exceed 1% of the given MPEG data, hence, does not affect the overall transmission cost significantly. Fig. 2 and Fig. 3 explain the mechanisms to build meta-information for temporal scaling and fidelity scaling, respectively. The Table 1 reveals the adaptability of the layered files and meta-information by illustrating fidelity scaled images of the I-VOP in the first GOV of "suzie.mpg" reconstructed from one to four layer files and the corresponding meta-information.

Table 1. I-VOP in the first GOV of "suzie.mpg"

4 Layers	3 Layers	2 Layers	1 Layer

4 Conclusions

In this paper, we have shown a many-fold layered encoding mechanism that can provides both the temporal scalability and fidelity scalability of MPEG-4, simultaneously. It is experimentally revealed that the newly generated meta-information does not exceed 1% of the given MPEG data, hence, does not affect the overall transmission cost significantly. This ratio is expected to be similarly small for other MPEG-4 sources as long as the meta-information is generated per GOV. Because the mechanism focuses on fine-grained scalable MPEG-4 storage, it is expected to contribute on improving QoS adaptability by combining previous researches focusing on dynamic bit-rate predicting and controlling mechanism reflecting network QoS dynamicity.

References

[1] D. Wu, Y.T. Hou, and Y.Q. Zhang, "Transporting Real-Time Video over the Internet: Challenges and Approaches", *Proceedings of the IEEE*, Vol. 88, No. 12, 2000.
[2] R. Rejaie and M. Handley, "Quality Adaptation for Congestion Controlled Video Playback over the Internet," *ACM SIGCOMM'99*, 1999, pp.189-200.
[3] F. Ruijin, L. B. Sung, and A. Gupta, "Scalable Layered MPEG-2 Video Multicast Architecture," *IEEE Tr. on Consumer Electronics*, Vol. 47, No. 1, pp. 55-62, 2001.

Micro-communication Element System

Peng Zheng, Zeng Jiazhi, Zhang Ming, and Zhao Jidong

School of Computer Science and Engineering,
UESTC, Chengdu, 610054, China
peppeng@hotamil.com, {jzzeng, jdzhao}@uestc.edu.cn,
davidzm@sina.com.cn

Abstract. Based on the research on Service Unit based Network Architecture (SUNA), this paper presents a Micro-Communication Element System (MCES) which is a new interconnecting network system and is easy for applications and users from TCP/IP environment to be converted into. MCES is constructed of organized micro-communication elements, and the entire network system consists of many micro-communication systems. Beside interal flexibility, MCES is compact and easy to be implemented.

1 Introduction

Since 1990s, research on high-performance network architecture has been conducted internationally. For instance, D. Clark, D. Tennenhouse et al proposed ALF (Application Level Frame) in 1990 [1] and Active Network Technique in 1996 [2]. Later, A. Lazar proposed a programmable network model [3]. These researches on optimizing network performance are based on layered architectures. So it is difficult for them to solve the problems that are inherent in layer-based networks.

The Modular Communication System (MCS) [4][5][6][7], introduced by Stefan Boecking, is an object-oriented network architecture designed to satisfy diversified requirements of performance and Qos. In 2002, Braden and his fellows proposed a non-layered paradigm, called RBA (role-based architecture) [8], which can communicate between network layers and accommodate additional services in existing network.

Function redundancy impairs the practicability of usage in the broadband network, as revealed in a number of studies [9][10][11]. To resolve existing defects in layer-based architecture, another non-layered network architecture, service unit based network architecture (SUNA) was introduced in 2003 [12], and its Micro-Communication Element System (MCES) is proposed in this paper.

2 Service Unit Based Network Architecture (SUNA)

Service unit based network architecture is a modularized structure where modules are SUs (service units). A SU is a minimal entity (hardware or software) that provides services without any exposure of its inner details. Another feature distinguishing a SU from a layer is that the SU merely provide services while the other one not only offers services but also requests services. The services from SUs are implemented by service data units (SDUs), which are also titled packages. SU can be the sender (source), receiver (destination), forwarder or transformer.

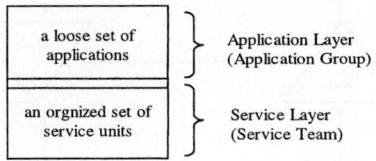

Fig. 1. Node model of SUNA

In the new network architecture, end-to-end addresses are employed instead of layer addresses. End-to-end addresses are expected to be an ordered pair made up of node address and port number.

End-to-End Address = (Node Address, Port Number)

The node model of SUNA can be divided into two parts, as is shown in Fig. 1: an application group and a service group. An application group could only receive services, while service group accommodate applications with services.

3 Micro-communication Element System Architecture

A SU and network media constitute active communication channels. Since SUs are relatively small, a single node may contain many SUs. We therefore call them "Micro-Communication Elements". Furthermore, a service team, which is made up of relevant nodes, organizes these micro-communication elements into a micro-communication system. A number of micro-communication systems then consolidate to form a network system. That is exactly why we call the first network system in SUNA as MCES (Micro Communication Element System).

3.1 A Reference Model for MCES Architecture

A reference model for MCES architecture is shown in Fig. 2. Here, squares and triangles stand for SUs. As is mentioned in this [12], there are five general types of SUs in a network and there are several distinct SUs in each general type to perform different functions. They are denoted by i and j as suffixes respectively.

Connectionless and connection-oriented SUs are of the first SU type. We could also confirm the SUs for segmentation, ICMP, IGMP and RTCP belong to the second type. Similarly, passive services fall into category three, routing-like SUs pertain to the fourth type, and SUs for encryption, NIC and so on should be of the fifth type.

The sequence of SUs of the 5th type in the same node could be either the same or not the same. One host could thereupon communicate with distinct nodes simultaneously in different ways such as encrypted or common communication. In addition, the SU sequence structure could be decided during initiating period or after the negotiation between other nodes.

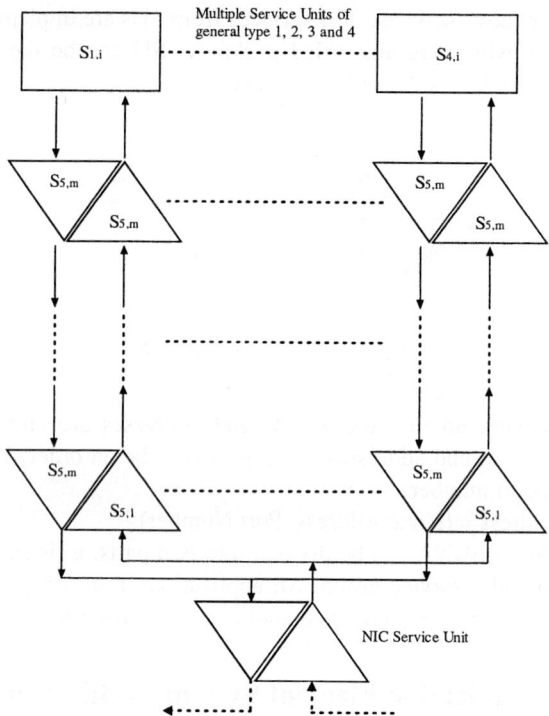

Fig. 2. A reference model for MCES architecture

Moreover, user-defined SUs are also available to extend network functions. For instance, users could define their own routing SUs to implement voluntary network function in a custom way.

3.2 The Package Format of MCES Architecture

As is shown in Fig. 3, a package is composed of headers and bodies (data plus check) in which the data can be transmitted on behalf of applications.

The basic header is indispensable, and is public to every SU in a service team. A bit map is employed in a header to denote the existence of each special field. Every special field includes several columns. For example, the special field for connection is divided into four columns: serial number, confirm number, window size and emergency pointer. Furthermore, every special field could be shared by multiple SUs. Returning to the previous example, special fields for connections are shared by SUs of connection establishing, data sending, data receiving, connection releasing and so on.

Protocols, such as OSPF, RIP, EGP, and BGP, make use of data fields instead of headers. There should be different type flags to identify the existence of these different protocols. Routing and forwarding SUs merely forward packages to the 5th SUs in corresponding ports. All these SUs may change data, headers, or the entire packages. For example, compression and decompression SUs only alter the data, while NIC SUs transform whole packages.

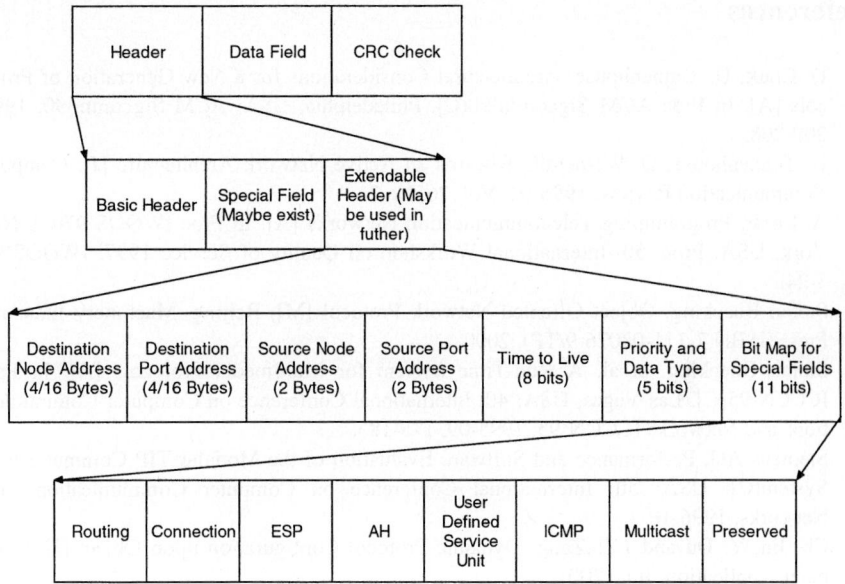

Fig. 3. Package Format of MCES

4 Transition to the SUNA

The original network adapter can be still employed after minor changes. As mentioned before, the interfaces of most system calls would remain to guarantee the tremendous amount of TCP/IP applications and software based on TCP or UDP are used as usual. Besides, additional SUs could be incorporated to extend system calls so that the real time transmission of voice and video can be supported directly. In SUNA, without frame processing, hardware structure, package forwarding rate and price of routers would be close to current layer 2 switches. With a package converter, our low-cost network can communicate with Internet.

5 Conclusion

The MCES adopts many successful experiences and productions of TCP/IP, including state transition diagram which make it possible to adopt the modeling result immediately. With the avoidance of redundant functions and service transfer overheads, performance of MCES would be improved. And it is easy for MCES reference model to be implemented using modular or object-oriented programming methods. Consequently, MCES can be improved continually to suit broadband network for the next generation applications.

References

1. D. Clark, D. Tennenhouse. Architectural Considerations for a New Generation of Protocols [A]. In Proc ACM Sigcomm'90[C]. Philadelphia, USA: ACM Sigcomm'90, 1990. 200-208.
2. D. Tennenhouse, D. Wetherall. Towards an Active Network Architecture [J]. Computer Communication Review, 1996-04, Vol. 26, No.2.
3. A. Lazar. Programming Telecommunication Networks [A]. In Proc IWQOS'97[C]. New York, USA: Proc. 5th International Workshop on Quality of Service 1997, IWQOS'97, 3-24.
4. Stefan Boecking, Object Oriented Network Protocol [M], Beijing, Machinery Industrial Press (ISBN 7-111-08076-9/TP), 2000.
5. Stefan Boecking, et al. A Run-Time System for Multimedia Protocols [A]. In Proc ICCCN'95[C]. Las Vegas, USA: 4th International Conference on Computer Communications and Networks ICCCN'95, 1995-09, 178-185.
6. Siemens AG. Performance and Software Evaluation of the Modular TIP Communication System[C]. USA: 5th International Conference on Computer Communications and Networks, 1996-10.
7. Ch. Jin, Y. Du and J.Zh.Zeng, Dynamic Protocol Configuration upon Object [J], Computer Application, June 2001.
8. B. Braden, T. Faber, M. Handley. From Protocol Stack to Protocol Heap - Role-Based Architecture[R]. First Workshop on Hot Topics in Networking, 2002-10.
9. J. Kay, J. Pasqucde. Profiling and Reducing Processing Overheads in TCP/IP [J]. IEEE/ACM Trans.Net, 1996-12, Vol.4, No.6: 817-828.
10. R. Stewart, C. Metz. SCTP: New Transport Protocol for TCP/IP [J]. IEEE Internet Computing, 2001-11 to 2001-12, Vol.5, No.6: 64 –69.
11. R. Engel, D. Kandlur, A. Mehra, D. Saha. Exploring the Performance Impact of QoS Support in TCP/IP Protocol Stacks[C]. Proceedings of IEEE INFOCOM98, 1998-03, 883-892.
12. Zeng Jiazhi, et al, Service Unit based Network Architecture[C], International Conference on Parallel and Distributed Computing, Applications and Technologies (PDCAT), 2003

Single User-Plane Architecture Network (SUPANET) and Its QoS Provisioning Mechanisms in Signaling and Management (S&M) Planes

Jun Dou, Huaxin Zeng, and Haiying Wang

School of Computer and Communication Engineering,
Southwest Jiaotong University, Chengdu, Sichuan, China 610031
doujun@126.com

Abstract. It is becoming tangible to merge three types of separated network (i.e. cable TV network, telephone switched network, and computer networks) into an integrated one, when the data rate on a single fiber with DWDM approaches Tbps. However, existing network architectures evolved from late 1970s' have not yet fledged for this event with respect to efficient high-speed data switching and QoS provisioning. This paper discusses the Single User Plane Architecture Network (SUPANET) in the perspective of QoS provisioning, with an emphasis on mechanisms in Signaling and Management planes (S&M plane). Mechanisms both in S&M plane and in the data transfer platform consisting of a single physical layer make the SUPANET highly efficient in application data transfer and ready for providing the QoS required by different applications.

1 Introduction

In recent years, there is a common point that existing Internet technologies need to be improved. However, in the activities of Next Generation Internet (NGI) [1] and Next Generation Network (NGN) [2], no radical architecture-change to Internet has been attempted except that Multi-Protocol Label Switching (MPLS) [3], which has reduced the orthodox 3-layer user data transfer platform to an enhanced 2-layer architecture.

In the last few years, trying to re-examine the deficiencies and redundancies of the Internet architecture, some of the research groups are strongly against the traditional layered network architecture and promote the layer-less architectures, such as Service Element Based Architecture (SEBA) [4], and Role-Based Architecture (RBA) [5], which are all trying to solve the problems by introduction of concepts (objects or roles) of software realm. Nevertheless, neither of them has treated the network as a whole, which involves hardware too. Important issues pertinent to providing a guaranteed QoS in future high-speed, converged network have not been discussed either.

The SC-Netcom-lab (Sichuan Network Communication key Laboratory) of Southwest Jiaotong University has been working on the next generation network architecture from a different angle and has led to the research work on a Single User-Plane Architecture (SUPA) [6] and a novel technique called the Physical Frame

Timeslot Switching (PFTS) [7]. The work is based on the analysis that: DWDM in optics provides a huge communication capability for merging existing separated networks into a converged one; The worldwide success of Internet has directed such converging activities to utilization of Internet techniques; The efficiency of the 3-layer Internet for data transfer is low and mechanisms in QoS provisioning in Internet are inadequate; Finally, there is no satisfactory mechanism on top of DWDM to provide granular downward multiplexing and to support the QoS promised by upper layers.

This paper discusses the SUPA Network (SUPANET) in the perspective of QoS provisioning, with an emphasis on those in Signaling and Management plane (S&M plane). Mechanisms both in S&M plane and in the data transfer platform (U-plane) consisting of a single physical layer make the SUPANET highly efficient in application data delivery and suitable for providing the QoS required by different applications.

The rest of the paper is organized as follows. Section 2 is an explanation of incentives behind the development of SUPANET, while section 3 presents the framework of the SUPANET. Section 4 gives a brief description of the PFTS techniques and its mechanism in QoS provisioning. Finally, in section 5, control protocols pertinent to QoS provision in S&M plane are discussed in detail.

2 Incentives Behind the SUPANET

2.1 Inadequacy in the Internet Architecture

Internet is inadequate in architecture and has been traditionally viewed as an in-band signaling network providing "best effort" service. Techniques such as Integrated Service (IntiServ) [8], Differentiated Service (DiffServ) and MPLS [9] have been recommended by IETF to improve such service. MPLS has also been recognized by IETF and ITU as the future technique over DWDM [10], but for the difficulties in exercising QoS over the 3-layer or 2-layer data transfer platform and for lack of mechanisms to support QoS at the physical layer, these techniques are not so satisfactory. This implies that the crux of the problem lies in the physical layer to provide a better mechanism in QoS provisioning.

2.2 Problems in Switching Techniques Over DWDM

International standardization works relevant to DWDM on ASON [11] and ASTN [12] in ITU have been focused on the automatic switching optical network and the transport network up to the lambda switching and no effort has been made with regard to downward multiplexing within a lambda. Faced with high data rates in a single lambda, people have been trying to develop various techniques to handle the downward multiplexing problem in a lambda channel.

Optical Burst Switching (OBS) is trying to multiplex a lambda channel with fixed or variable length of data blocks (Bursts) by pre-setting up a forwarding lambda-hop or a path via the burst head through another lambda [13]. Reference [7] has analyzed the deficiency of OBS in channel utility and the inadequacy in QoS provisioning, let alone the problems of lacking data buffering and processing capabilities in optical domain in foreseeable future.

Other people are in favor of the SDH-centric approach, with which SDH multiplexing techniques have been adopted on top of the DWDM [14]. The merit of this approach is that SDH is matured and has reached the data rate of 40 Gbps [15], nevertheless, SDH itself is complicated and has to be involved with global clock synchronization and non-trivial segmentation and re-assembly processing between 251-byte payload in SDH and computer frames or packets.

2.3 PFTS, SUPA, and SUPANET

In order to solve the downward multiplexing problem, the SC-Netcom-lab has been working on an alternative approach over DWDM since 2000. The design criteria for new techniques include:

A. High efficient in application data transfer and switching;
B. Easy to interface with existing data link layer with little segmentation and re-assembly effort;
C. To provide a satisfactory mechanism in support of different QoS requirements.

Should this goal be able to reach, the problem faced with MPLS can be solved. Furthermore, the necessity of data link layer may disappear if framing function can be incorporated into the physical layer. All these considerations have led to a novel technique called the PFTS and a new network architecture called the Single physical User-Plane Architecture (SUPA). The two techniques have formed the basis of the network called the SUPANET discussed in this paper.

3 The Framework of SUPANET

3.1 Design Criteria for SUPANET

Bearing the facts in mind, that Internet has been successful worldwide and out-band signaling can simplify the user data transfer platform, we have decided that the design criteria in the new architecture should include:

A. To improve the data transfer efficiency, the user transfer platform should be simplified as much as possible, better still as a single physical layer.
B. The user transfer platform should be able to support granular data transfer and switching, as well as QoS provisioning. Granularity in transmission and switching is the essence of transportation and routing of different rates of user data, while the mechanism in support of QoS can ensure that different traffic can be delivered with required QoS.
C. The data link can be abolished, should its main function such as framing be combined into the physical layer functions.
D. The length of the physical frame for carrying application data should be compatible with the most popular data link frame or IP packet so as to simplify adaptation between data units at the physical layer and frames of upper layers.

E. Last but not the least, the new architecture should be easy to interact with Internet and to migrate from existing Internet to a new architecture in the future.

To meet the design criteria listed above, we have decided that

A. Out-band signaling approach should be adopted to simplify the user data transfer platform (or User-Plane, U-Plane for short).
B. The new switching technique - Physical Frame Timeslot Switching (PFTS) should be easy implemented on top of a lambda channel and integrated with DWDM sublayers. Therefore, the timeslot for PFTS is set to equal to the time to transfer a maximum length of the Ethernet MAC frame (1530 bytes) for a given data rate of a lambda. The reason for selecting MAC frame is that the Ethernet is supported by all the computers and is also widely used in LAN, MAN, and WAN especially after the publication of 10 G bps Ethernet standards [16]. As the physical frame resembles the Ethernet MAC frame, the need for data link layer will disappear at the user data transfer platform and might potentially be abolished in S&M plane to further simplify the existing 5-layer architecture of Internet.
C. To ensure the QoS required by different type of streams, a Switched/Permanent Virtual Connection (SVC or PVC) service should be provided with embedded QoS mechanisms in PFTS at the physical layer.
D. The Internet protocol stacks should remain unchanged, at least for the time being, in order to interoperate with Internet, but in order to perform QoS negotiation, traffic information exchange, and admission control, new control protocols should be added in S&M plane to enhance the existing Internet protocol stacks.

3.2 The Framework of the SUPANET

Figure 1 is an improved architecture based on reference. In figure 1, the user system is an implementation of SUPANET protocol stacks, which will interacts with a SUPANET Router/Switch through the UNI_S (User-Network Interface in S&M plane) or UNI_U (User-Network Interface in User plane) respectively. A user system can either be an implementation in a computer (client/server) or part of implementation in a router interfacing to the SUPANET. The NNI_U (Network-Network Interface in User plane) and NNI_S, on the other hand, are defined for interactions between SUPANET routers/switches in U-plane and S&M plane respectively.

The operation between two SUPANET user systems and the SUPANET router/switch will start with use of QoS Negotiation Protocol (QoSNP) on top of UDP to establish a Switched Virtual Connection (SVC) in S&M plane. An SVC is completed when a lambda path between two SUPANET user systems can be found and all the routers along the path are capable of satisfying QoS requirements of two users. During negotiation, relevant resources are reserved. A PVC (Permanent Virtual Connection) service can also be obtained via pre-registration manually or through on-line REgistration Protocol (REP) in M-plane.

The user data will be loaded into the physical frames called (EPFs – Ethernet-like Frames) and be transferred and switched in the U-plane after the SVC is completed. Concatenated VC Identifiers (VCIs) assigned during QoS negotiation will be used as the path identifier at the single physical-layer U-plane.

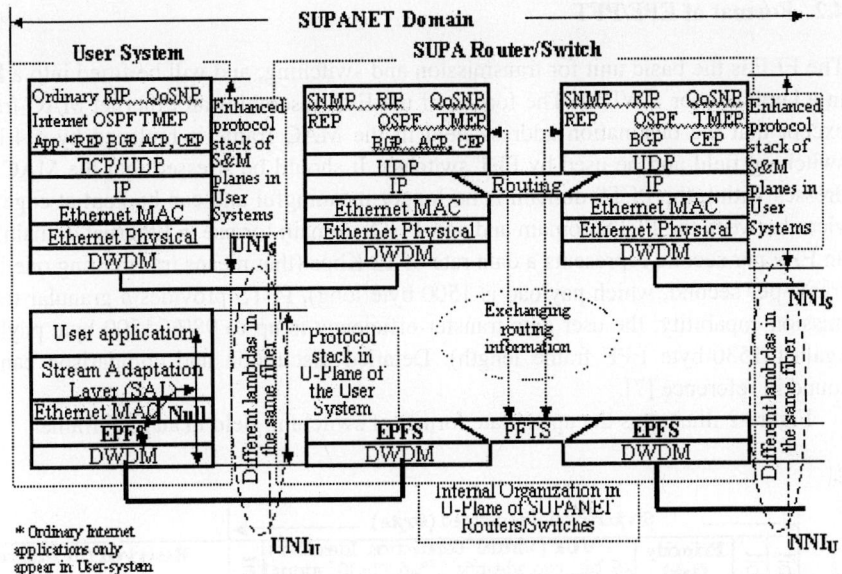

Fig. 1. Protocol stacks in SUPANET

Ending of an SVC will be completed by use of the Connection Ending Protocol (CEP), either in an elegant way through bilateral agreement or in an abrupt manner. QoS provisioning for user data delivery will be ensured by the mechanisms in U-plane and those in S&M plane, which will be discussed in the following sections.

4 PFTS and Its Embedded QoS Mechanisms

4.1 Concept of PFTS

To meet the design criteria in section 2.3, the most popular Ethernet MAC frame has been adopted as the basic data unit called the Ethernet-like Physical Frame (EPF); consequently, framing function traditionally in the data link layer is merged into physical layer. A novel concept PFT (Physical layer Frame Timeslot) is defined as the transmission time for an EPF with the maximum Ethernet MAC frame length (1530 bytes including preambles, IEEE 802.3/2002) and acts as the basis for frame-based asynchronous operation. In other words, EPFs are transmitted, switched, and synchronized on per PFT basis by detecting frame boundaries.

EPFs from user system will be fitted into PFTs and be interleaved into lambda bit streams towards a PFTS switch. A PFTS switch will then forward PFTs along the predetermined path to the destination user system. This enables an asynchronous operation based on PFTs without a need for global clock synchronization among switching nodes as being done in SDH.

4.2 Format of EPF/PFT

The EPF is the basic unit for transmission and switching, and will be fitted into a PFT in a lambda over DWDM. The format of the EPF resembles an Ethernet MAC frame except that the destination address field in the MAC frame is replaced by a 4-byte switching field and be used by PFT switches. It should be stressed that the MAC addresses within the PFTS domain is no longer meaningful and can be kept at edge devices between the PFTS domain and non-PFTS domain for use in Ethernet domain. As an EPF per second represents a data rate of 12 Kbps (that means transmitting one EPF frame per second, which payload is 1500 byte long), PFTS provides a granular transmission capability; the user data transfer efficiency is up to 98%(1500 byte payload against 1530-byte EPF frame length). Detailed discussion and comparison can be found in reference [7].

Figure 2 illustrates the up-to-date format of switching field in an EPF frame.

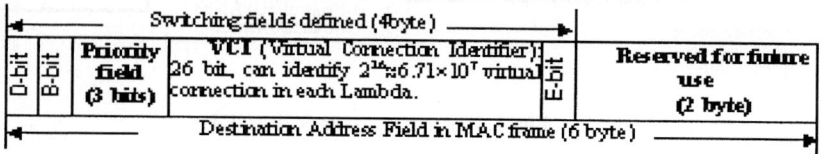

Fig. 2. Format of EPF/PFT Switching

4.3 QoS Mechanisms Embedded in PFTS

As analyzed in section 2, QoS cannot be ensured unless the physical layer is able to provide a mechanism to support QoS provisioning, which is the major concern in design of PFTS switches. Indeed, there are a few mechanisms embedded in PFTS to ensure the switching efficiency and to support the QoS activities in S&M plane.

A. PFT Reservation and Quota Management

Reservation of enough PFTs for a time-critical stream is the first resort of resource reservation to guarantee the required throughput if Quota left for that class of traffic for a given output fiber is enough. The quota is defined as the maximum number of EPT/PFT for a given class of traffic in an output lambda. Since reservation of PFTs is directly associated with transmission capability, it would be much more effective and directly controllable than reservation buffers in Internet with RSVP. Quotas can be dynamically adjustment based on utilization of quotas for different types of traffic.

B. Multiple Queues and Priorities

8 FIFO queues have been designed in a PFTS switch for individual output traffic with different priorities for each lambda, and 4 types of burst Queue have also be added for bursts with high-priorities (i.e. EPFs with B-bit (see figure 2) set).

C. Routing Strategy

Routing in a PFTS switch differs from that in Internet in that a route is associated with QoS. In other words, a route selected in PFTS domain will ensure that the QoS required by a pair of user system will be satisfied.

D. WJCW (Wavelength Jam Control Word)

The WJCW (Wavelength Jam Control Word) as shown in figure 3, is used to signal the congestion state for a given lambda, to selectively discard EPFs with D-bit set, and to be distributed by TMEP in S&M plane for congestion control. Figure 3 shows the format of WJCW.

Port Id (8 bits)	Wavelength Id (8 bits)	Congestionflags (2 bits)

Fig. 3. Format of Wavelength Jam Control Word (WJCW)

E. Mechanisms of Minimizing Variation in Transit Delay and Anti-jitters

Long transit delay will not cause problems even for time-critical streams as long as it remains comparatively stable within tolerable limit. The most disturbing problem in transmission of time critical traffic is the variation of transit delay, which may produce jitters within a data stream. Hardware based design and switching algorithms are carefully selected to reduce variation in PFT switches design.

F. QoS Monitoring

QoS monitoring in U-plane is carried out on the basis of individual lambda to provide queuing information for dynamic quota adjustment, service request admission, traffic shaping, and congestion alert.

G. Traffic Engineering and Admission Control

Traffic Engineering and Admission Control are mechanisms used in congest prevention and lyses. Selectively discarding EPFs with D-bit set is used as the last resort in congestion condition; while information distributed by TMEP in S&M plane will be used in global traffic analysis, traffic shaping, and admission control.

5 QoS Provisioning Mechanisms in S&M Plane

5.1 Generic Format of PDUs of QoS Protocols in S&M Plane of SUPANET

The QoS related protocols in S&M plane of the SUPANET, such as QoSNP, TMEP, ACP, CEP, and REP, have many similarities, therefore, it is better to define a generic format for all these application protocols. Figure 4 illustrates this format and the relationship to IP and UDP Headers:

The Source or Destination field in figure 4 will be the IP address of a host (Client/Server), which supports PFTS within the PFTS domain or does not support PFTS outside of the PFTS domain. In the second case, QoS activities will end at "user systems" (refer to description of the "user system" in figure 1) of the PFTS domain, since QoS protocols are local to PFTS domain. In other words, an edge router half in PFTS domain and half in non-PFTS domain will handle the issues across the PFTS domain. The half implementation in the edge router interfacing with PFTS domain will on behalf of the end-system outside of PFTS domain handle the QoS protocols, and mapping of QoS requirements onto the QoS mechanisms. The relevant parameters are left for further study.

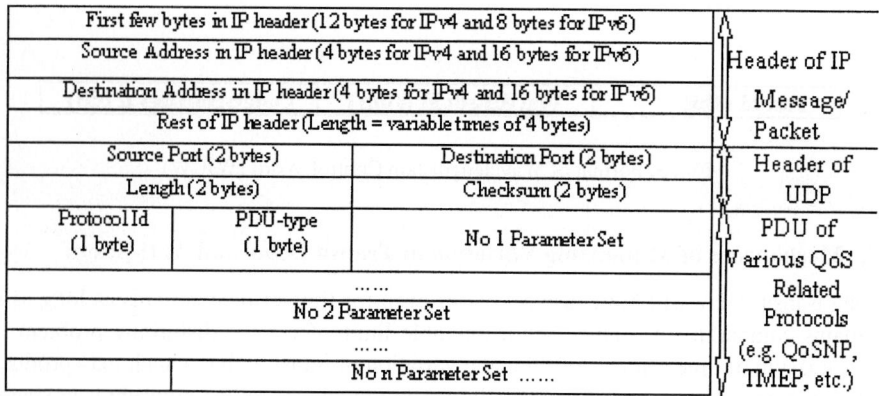

Fig. 4. Generic Format of PDUs of QoS related protocols in S&M plane

To follow the regulation in Internet, the "protocol" field in IPv4 message has to be set in "17" (decimal) to indicate that UDP is used in the Transport layer, while for IPv6, nothing is needed since there is no "protocol" field. Source or Destination Port are application dependent in Internet, therefore, at present a special port number (400) is defined to identify the transport port for QoS protocols. As in figure 4, there is a field called protocol Id, which is used to distinguish different QoS protocols, where "1" stands for QoSNP, "2" for TMEP, "3" for ACP, "4" for CEP, and "5" for REP. This two-byte field provides plenty of space for future expanding.

1 byte	1 byte	1 byte	1 byte
Offset to Next (in byes)	Parameter Set Id	Parameter Length (bytes)	......
		......	

Fig. 5. Generic Format for Parameter Set

The PDU-type field in figure 4 is prepared for different control purposes for each protocol. Finally, a mechanism for describing the relationship between adjacent parameter sets with variable length is defined as in figure 5, which always start with a one-byte field - Offset to Next parameter set to indicate the bytes from the first byte of current parameter set to that of the next set and followed by one-byte Parameter Set Id and one-byte Parameter Length.

With the format shown in figure 5, a group of parameters may be defined as a parameter set with an Identifier when their parameter lengths are the same, this could simplify the representation of information exchanged. Alternatively, a single parameter can be defined as a parameter set if it has to be singled out for convenience and in this case, the parameter length field will be used to check the end of this parameter set. It should be noted that for the last parameter set in a QoS related PDU, the Offset to Next field eventually points to the byte right after the current parameter set. The length field in UDP header will count all the bytes including the padding if the total number of bytes in a QoS PDU is not the integral times of 4 (required by Internet).

Parameters or parameter set will be defined in individual protocols including its parameter Set Id, parameter length, and their exact formats.

5.2 QoS Negotiation Protocol

The purpose of QoS Negotiation Protocol (QoSNP) in S&M plane is to negotiate the possibility of setting up an end-to-end virtual path between two user systems in PFTS domain, to satisfy the QoS requirements of two end users and to be supported by all the PFTS switches along path. Therefore, it is an application layer protocol in S&M plane relying on an end-to-end protocol. Considering that UDP is the transport protocol implemented in all Internet routers, QoSNP is implemented on top of UDP and takes the format as illustrated in figures 4 and 5.

A. Operation of QoSNP

Negotiation process involves commitment to the traffic in single direction or in both directions from all the routers along the negotiated path; hence a forward-and-return process has to be carried out through hop-by-hop negotiation. Two types of negotiation modes have been defined to cater for different requirements, i.e. FRN (Forward-and-Return single direction Negotiation) and TSN (Two-direction Simultaneous Negotiation). TSN should be adopted if both directions require a guaranteed QoS and the negotiation initiator knows the QoS requirements in both directions. Otherwise, FRN is chosen if it knows the QoS requirement in one direction only. It has been envisaged that in an unbalanced situation, where traffic in one direction is very little, it could be more efficient in utilization of a VC that multiple streams share a VC between a pair of edge routers. This requires a multiplexing mechanism within a VC and it is left for further study in the future.

Before negotiation, the initiator will prescribe type groups of QoS parameters (favorable and acceptable) and specify an Id for the VC between the user system and the first router in PFTS domain. The first router in PFTS domain will assign a priority level to this VC according to the strategy decided by administration. As negotiation in progressing, QoS negotiation entities of a PFTS router will try to find a best output port (a fiber) available in the router, by looking up the IP routing table; and to find a suitable lambda in that port, according to the Quota available for supporting the VC. An Id will be assigned to identify the output VC between current node and the next in forwarding direction; and an association between the input VC Id and the output VC

Id will be established in switching tables of the current node. The next node will be notified when the negotiation process is pushed forward to the next one. In FRN mode, the reverse negotiation will be carried out after the remote partner has provided the required QoS parameters. In other word, negotiation has to be done in two directions separately; and only when negotiations in both directions are successful, can a pair of single direction VC be set up, otherwise the negotiation fails.

In TSN mode, on the other hand, a network works node handles the negotiation at the same time; therefore, a backward output VC Id has to be assigned before forwarding the QoSNP-PDU to the next node. In this case, a constraint has to be imposed on selection of the backward output port that it has to be one directly connected to the previous node. Without this constraint, the new backward routing might involve another round of negotiation and make the process too complicated. In other words, only the QoS can be satisfied in both directions, can a node in PFTS propagate the negotiation process to the next node; otherwise, a reject PDU is returned to the previous node and resources reserved for that VC will be returned to the node. This rejection process will be pushed back until reaching the initiator. A successful negotiation will be completed until the remote user system agrees to accept the connection and to be satisfied with the QoS committed by all the nodes along the path by sending back the QoS negotiation successful message.

B. QoS Parameters in QoSNP

ITU has defined a complete set of QoS parameters [17]. In the context of PFTS, only a sub-set of these QoS parameters has been defined in QoSNP in consideration of importance, measurability, and controllability. For example, transit delay has been defined in the QoS framework of ITU, but it is not so important for time critical streams as long as the transit delay is comparatively stable. On the other hand, significant jitters are more influential to videos or audios, which can cause unpleasant senses or feelings to people. At present, parameters adopted in negotiation include:

a) Data rate in Kbps - CIR (Committed Information Rate), CBR (Committed Burst Rate), and EBR (Extended Burst Rate), which will be used in control of EPF switching and in congestion control in the U-plane on per VC basis.

b) Maximum jitter (in ms) – an end-to-end parameter decided by addition of that of individual PFTS switches along the path between a pair of user systems.

c) Maximum data discarding rate (in percentage) – this parameter is used in deciding how many EPF with the Discard bit (D-bit) set can be dropped without causing significant bad effect in different congestion conditions.

d) VC disconnection approach (negotiated/abrupt, single way/bi-directions) – this parameter is negotiated between two user systems to agree on whether any user can disconnect a single way VC when it has no data to send and on whether a pair of VC should be disconnected simultaneously by either side of the communication partner.

More QoS parameters may be needed in the future when more experience gained with PFTS. A few parameters are currently under consideration such as security parameters and reliability parameters.

Detailed coding of QoS parameters and state transitions in QoSNP are not discussed in this paper considering that they are complex and difficult to explain in a short paper.

5.3 Traffic Monitoring Information Exchange Protocol

Traffic Monitoring information Exchange Protocol (TMEP) is another application protocol in S&M plane of the SUPANET, which performs the traffic information between neighbor nodes for congestion control and traffic pattern analysis. One issue similar to routing information exchange is to prevent information exchange loop, some strategies used by RIP and OSPF in establishment of neighboring relationship are adopted in TMEP. By the same token as in QoSNP, TMEP is implemented on top of UDP and utilizes the generic format for QoS protocols in figure 4 and the generic format of parameter in figure 5.

One of important parameters exchange by TMEP is the Wavelength Jam Control Word (WJCW) as in figure 3 generated by PFTS switches in the U-plane.

Congest control is a global issue in a network, it can be caused by instant traffic converged into an output port instantly, therefore distribution of traffic monitoring information can be very useful to prevent from congestion and to ease congestion condition when congestion takes place. However, how far traffic monitoring information should be propagated for global analysis, for congestion, and admission control is not yet explored at present and is left for further study.

5.4 Admission Control Protocol

Admission Control Protocol (ACP) is part of congestion control mechanism in PFTS domain. At present, the WJCW (Wavelength Jamming Control Word) as in figure 3 within an edge PFTS node is used in admission control in U-plane. The incentive behind the ACP is further to feed back the congestion information to data source and to force it to refrain from sending at EBR in case of light-congestion, or to constrain its sending within CBR or CIR in congestion or heavy congestion so as to reduce the data to be dropped within the PFTS domain and to ease the congestion.

As discussed in section 5.3, algorithms for distribution the congestion information and how to utilize the global congestion information are not considered at present. Consequently, how to use the global congestion information in ACP is left for further study when we have more experiences with SUPANET.

6 Epilogue

The work presented in this paper is very limited; some issues such as adaptation between EPFs and application streams, and management mechanisms are not discussed. Although there are a lot works have to be done, our preliminary experience has shown that SUPANET could a promising candidate for next generation network in view that it is definitely more efficient than that of the MPLS relying on existing two-layer protocol stratum.

The work presented in this paper has been sponsored by NSFC (Natural Science Foundation of China, ratification No: 60372065), and the authors wish to acknowledge the financial support from NSFC. Authors also wish to express our thanks to our colleagues in SC-Netcom-Lab for their useful discussions.

References

1. President's Information Technology (IT) Advisory Committee Review of the Next Generation Internet Program and Related Issues, April 28, 1999.
2. "Focus on the Future of Networking" - Proceedings of 17th Annual Conference on Next Generation Networks, Nov. 3-7, Boston, 2003
3. Daft-awduche-mpls-te-optical-01.txt - Multi-Protocol Lambda Switching: Combining MPLS Traffic Engineering Control with Optical Crossconnects, IETF, May 2002.
4. Zeng jiazhi et al., "Service Unit based Network Architecture," in: Proceedings of PACAT03, IEEE press, PP. 12-16, Aug (2003).
5. Robert Braden, et al., From Protocol Stack to Protocol Heap – Role-Based Architecture, http://www.isi.edu
6. Huaxin Zeng, et al., "On Three-Dimension Ethernet MAN (3D-EMAN) Architecture," in: Proceedings of PACAT03, IEEE press, PP. 535-540, Aug (2003).
7. Huaxin Zeng, et al., "On Physical Frame Time-slot Switching over DWDM," in: Proceedings of PACAT03, IEEE press, PP. 286-291, Aug (2003).
8. RFC 1633 - Integrated Services in the Internet Architecture: an Overview, June 1994.
9. RFC 3035 - "MPLS using LDP and ATM VC Switching", Jan 2001
10. RFC 3471 - Generalized Multi-Protocol Label Switching (GMPLS) Signaling Functional Description, IETF, Jan. 2003.
11. ITU: G.8080/Y.1304 - Architecture for the automatically switched optical network (ASON), November 2001.
12. ITU Recommendation G.872 - Architecture of optical transport networks, November 2001.
13. C.Qiao and M.Yoo, "Optical burst switching (OBS)-a new paradigm for an Optical Internet, " Journal of High Speed Network, vol. 8, pp.69-84 (1999).
14. ITU Recommendation G. 707 – Network node interface for the Synchronous Digital Hierarchy (SDH), 1996.
15. ITU: G.691 - Optical interfaces for single channel STM-64, STM-256 and other SDH systems with optical amplifiers, October 2000.
16. IEEE 802.3ae - Local and metropolitan area networks-Specific requirements, Part 3: Carrier Sense Multiple Access with Collision Detection (CSMA/CD) Access Method and Physical Layer Specifications, Amendment: Media Access Control (MAC) Parameters, Physical Layers, and Management Parameters for 10 Gb/s Operation, June 13, 2002.
17. ITU X.641 I ISO/IEC 13236:1997- QoS Framework

A Commodity Cluster Using IEEE 1394 Network for Parallel Applications

Yong Yu and Yu-Fai Fung

Department of Electrical Engineering, The Hong Kong Polytechnic University,
Hong Kong
yongyu.ee@polyu.edu.hk, eeyffung@inet.polyu.edu.hk

Abstract. IEEE 1394 is now a widely used interface for connecting PC peripherals. Since it provides high data transmission rate at low price, The IEEE 1394 bus can also be a cost-effective solution for linking a Network Of Computers (NOWs), or Cluster. In this paper, we tested the performance of IEEE 1394 on the Linux system, and discussed the implementation of a new communication library for using the IEEE 1394 network as NOWs interconnection.

1 Introduction

Network Of Workstations (NOWs), is a popular approach to construct a parallel computing platform, it is a more cost-effective way for setting up a parallel computing platform than dedicated parallel computers. The effectiveness of the NOWs system is highly depended on the communication mechanism between the workstations. Currently, the most commonly used networking technology for a NOWs is the Fast Ethernet, which gives a 100Mbps transfer rate. Economical as it is, the Fast Ethernet NOWs performance is not very good. Other high-end technologies such as the Gigabit Ethernet, and the Myrinet [1], can sustain higher bandwidth to Gigabits per second but they are rather expensive. The IEEE 1394 bus [2], which has a transfer rate of 400Mbps but costs much less than the Gigabit Ethernet is a suitable candidate for interconnection of NOWs.

The 1394 bus attracted many attentions when it emerged, several ip-over-1394 drivers exist, but research on networking workstations using the 1394 bus for Linux workstations is still very limited. In this paper, we will discuss how the IEEE 1394 can be used in cluster computing and the implementation of a new communication library for using the IEEE 1394 device in cluster computing.

2 Possible IEEE 1394 Clusters

Although the IEEE 1394 bandwidth is shared on the whole bus, it is especially suitable for some specific parallel application, take the railway simulation system as in [3] for example.

Fig. 1 depicts the cluster structure of the railway simulation system. Since this system employs 3D animations to display the simulated railway system in real time. Between the central simulator and the graphical workstations that run the virtual reality display, there are strong data communications. Such data communications are in constant time interval and almost in a steady throughput.

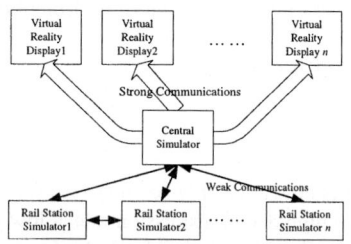

Fig. 1. A Cluster for Railway Simulation System

The performance of such a system on an Ethernet cluster is not good. Since IEEE 1394 is designed to carry multimedia data, with the Isochronous mode of the IEEE 1394 bus, the guaranteed constant delivery time of the Isochronous mode makes the 3D animation display steady, and the broadcasting nature, if can be utilized properly, can enable the system to accommodate much more virtual reality displays.

Urban traffic simulation is another popular parallel application that runs on a cluster. On such cluster, there is strong data communications between one node and all its neighbors, while few data communications between the node and other nodes. This makes a point-to-point network topology a quite ideal solution for such system.

Fig. 2 shows a cluster of 4 * 4 nodes, each node has a direct link to all its neighbors, and 48 cards are needed in this structure. The cost of the interconnection for such cluster is USD1440, which is much cheaper than using Gigabit Ethernet.

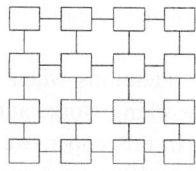

Fig. 2. A cluster of 4 * 4 nodes

3 A Communication Library on IEEE 1394 for Clustering

The Asynchronous mode of the IEEE 1394 offers a guaranteed delivery of the network data, but its throughput is not as good as that of the Isochronous mode. While on the other hand, the Isochronous mode offers higher throughput but no guarantee of the success data delivery. To fully utilize the IEEE 1394 bandwidth, we implement a communication library over the linux1394 driver, an acknowledgement mechanism over the Isochronous mode was developed so that the success of data delivery can be guaranteed while at the same time higher throughput can be achieved, and a packet multiplexing mechanism over the Isochronous mode is also introduced so that the Isochronous mode can be used to carry data between random nodes.

3.1 Implementing Acknowledgement Over the Isochronous Mode

We use the Asynchronous mode to implement the Acknowledgement. When two nodes are communicating, data packet is sent out via the Isochronous transfer, on a channel number that is previously negotiated. The receiver receives the data packet at the same channel number, with each success delivery of the packet, an acknowledgement to that packet, with the SN number that is obtained from the SN field, will be sent through the Asynchronous mode to the sender, which is obtained from the *Src* field. Since an acknowledgement is normally a small packet, this should incur little interference to the Isochronous transfer.

We conduct a simple test of the Isochronous mode throughput with the acknowledgement mechanism using our library. We send sustained Isochronous data flow from one node to the other, the data packet size is set to be 1024, 2048, 2072, 4096 respectively, the result is shown in Fig. 3.

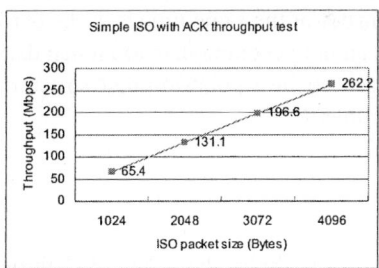

Fig. 3. The throughput of Isochronous mode with acknowledgement mechanism

3.2 Packet Multiplexing for Isochronous Mode

With the acknowledgement mechanism on the Isochronous transfer, our library can offer better throughput with guaranteed data delivery. But there is a drawback of the Isochronous transfer, when there are several Isochronous transfers in the IEEE 1394 bus at the same time, the sum of the packet size of all the transfers can not exceed 4096 bytes. If one wants to accommodate 8 Isochronous transfers on the bus at the same time, each transfer's packet size can only be 512 bytes. Such packet size is too small for most cases, and that will cause too much protocol overhead when transferring random size upper layer data. So we introduce a multiplexing mechanism in our communication library, with the benefit of the broadcasting nature of the Isochronous mode.

The throughput of such multiplexing mechanism is tested on a IEEE 1394 network with 4 nodes. We tested the throughput with fixed packet size, from 1 sender to 2 receivers, packet size is 2048, and 1 sender to 3 receivers, packet size is two 1024 and one 2048, and 2 senders each sending data to 2 receivers, packet size of each is 1024 respectively. Fig. 4 depicts the results.

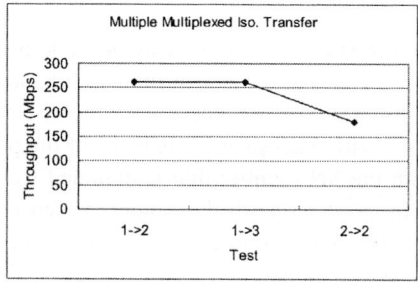

Fig. 4. The multiplexing throughput of the Isochronous mode with fixed packet size

In Figure 4, we can see that with the fixed packet size, maximum throughput can be around 260Mbps, that is almost the same as using bare Isochronous mode, but when data flows that transfer at the same time is 4, the performance drops, this shows that such a mechanism can not accommodate too much data transfers, but considering the IEEE 1394 is being used in a point-to-point structure as shown in Figure 2, it should not be a major problem.

4 Conclusion

With our new communication library the IEEE 1394 throughput can be improved to 260Mbps with guaranteed data delivery, which is much better than the throughput of Fast Ethernet. The IEEE 1394 device can fulfill the requirement of cluster computing for the applications we described using our communication library, and we can expect the performance of such clusters to be much better than a Fast Ethernet cluster. The IEEE 1394 is still under fast evolutions, the 800Mbps interface cards are now available, and higher speed interface card up to 3.2Gbps will be available in the near future [4], This makes the IEEE 1394 bus is a promising option for cluster computing.

References

1. Nanette J. Boden, Danny Cohen, Robert E. Felderman, Alan E. Kulawik, Charles L. Seitz, Jakov N. Seizovic, and Wen-King Su: Myrinet - A Gigabit Per Second Local Area Network, IEEE MICRO, Feb (1995)

2. IEEE Std. 1394-1995, IEEE Standard for a High Performance Serial Bus, The Institute of Electrical and Electronics Engineers, (1996)
3. Yang Zhaoxia, Jiang Xi, Yu Yong, Tan Ligang, Du Peng, Miao Jianrui: mulation system of technological process at marshalling station,Proceedings of the Conference on Traffic and Transportation Studies, ICTTS, (2000), p 17-21.
4. IEEE Std 1394b-2002, 1394b IEEE Standard for a High-Performance Serial Bus---Amendment 2, The Institute of Electrical and Electronics Engineers, (2002)

Design and Implementation of an Improved Zero-Copy File Transfer Mechanism

Sejin Park, Sang-Hwa Chung, Bong-Sik Choi, and Sang-Moon Kim

Department of Computer Engineering, Pusan National University, Pusan, Korea
{sejnpark, shchung, guyver3, listman}@pusan.ac.kr

Abstract. This paper[1] presents the design and implementation of an improved zero-copy file transfer mechanism that improves the efficiency of file transfers for Linux-based PC cluster systems. This mechanism, based on the Virtual Interface Architecture (VIA), presents a file transfer primitive that does not require the file system to be modified. This allows the NIC to transfer data from the kernel buffer to the remote node directly, without copying to a user buffer or page flipping. In addition, we apply the RDMA write technique to this mechanism to minimize the CPU utilization of the receive node. To do this, we have developed a hardware-based VIA network adapter for use as a NIC. We demonstrate the performance of the improved zero-copy file transfer mechanism experimentally, and compare results with those from existing file transfer mechanisms.

Keywords: Zero-Copy, File Transfer, Gigabit Ethernet, VIA, PC Cluster.

1 Introduction

As high-performance network like Gigabit Ethernet have shown, the performance of network devices has improved through reducing data copying between the kernel and the user buffer, decreasing context switching time, and minimizing the communication protocol overhead. User-level communication, such as the VIA [3] and InfiniBand [4], and zero-copy file transfer algorithms, such as *sendfile* [1] [2] and the Direct Access File System (DAFS) [5], have been developed. The DAFS, based on the VIA, is a user-level file system that uses RDMA and can be applied to various other applications [6]. However, *sendfile* is not efficient for high-performance cluster systems because it is based on TCP/IP. The DAFS is a standard for network-attached storage, and so the file system must be modified to use it. Meanwhile, there is no special mechanism or library for file transfers on the VIA, so three methods are used to transfer files on VIA-based cluster systems.

---

[1] This research was supported by the Program for the Training of Graduate Students in Regional Innovation which was conducted by the Ministry of Commerce, Industry and Energy of the Korean Government and IDEC at Pusan National University.

The file can be read to a user buffer and sent using the VIA, or transferred using sockets, or through using the DAFS. However, it is convenient and efficient to construct cluster systems that support zero-copy file transfer primitives without the need to modify the file system.

2 File Transfer Methods Based on TCP/IP and the VIA

Fig. 1 shows the various file transfer mechanisms that use TCP/IP and the VIA on Linux cluster systems. In the case of TCP/IP, there are three mechanisms: (1) $read->send$ (A->B), (2) $mmap->send$ (C), and (3) $sendfile$ (D). As shown in the figure, the number of data copies and context switches is reduced in $sendfile$, and $sendfile$ can achieve zero-copy file transfers. The general file transfer mechanism of the VIA is $read->VipPostSend$, and one copy occurs. For the DAFS, file data is transferred without data copying by using the remote memory addressing capability of DAT (Direct Access Transport). This mechanism is somewhat complicated, so we omit the details in this paper.

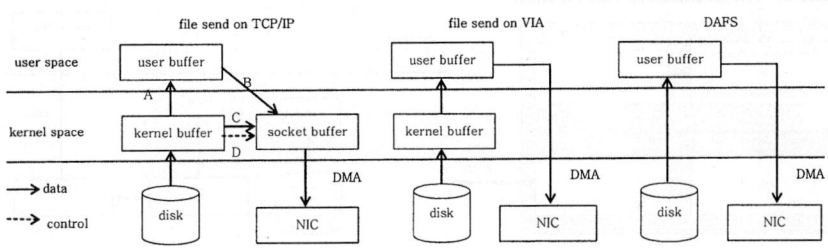

Fig. 1. File transfer mechanisms for TCP/IP and the VIA

3 Implementation of an Improved Zero-Copy File Transfer

Fig. 2 (left) shows a block diagram of the hardware-based VIA network adapter that we have developed. The network adapter is a 32-bit/33MHz PCI plug-in card using an FPGA for the VIA Protocol Engine and the Gigabit Ethernet chip set to construct a high performance system area network. The network adapter performs virtual-to-physical address translation, doorbell, RDMA writes, and send/receive completion operations in hardware without kernel intervention. In particular, the Address Translation Table is stored in the local memory of the network adapter, and the VIA Protocol Engine efficiently controls the address translation process by directly accessing the Address Translation Table. This network adapter has a minimum latency of 12.2 μs, and a maximum bandwidth of 96.3 MB/s.

Fig. 2 (right) shows the suggested zero-copy file transfer mechanism presented in this paper. This mechanism is identical to the send/receive and RDMA write operations on the VIA, except that the kernel buffer is transferred under DMA control from the NIC instead of the user buffer, and therefore the sender does not use the VI descriptor. This mechanism behaves as follows. First, two nodes establish a communication channel using VI, and the receiver allocates the user buffer. The sender then calls our suggested primitive, *VipSendFile*, and the NIC driver receives the physical address of the kernel buffer and provides information about the transaction *(e.g. the physical address, VI handle, and size)* to the NIC directly. The NIC then sends the data from the kernel buffer to the receiver without a VI descriptor, and the receiver must be able to handle this data. The VIA Protocol Engine of our hardware-based VIA network adapter can transmit file data without copying or using a VI descriptor, so it consequently minimizes the CPU overhead. In the receiver, the NIC copies data directly to the user buffer, as it does with the VIA protocol. Our NIC copies data faster, because of its address translation table. In addition, by using RDMA writes, the CPU utilization in the receiver is reduced further.

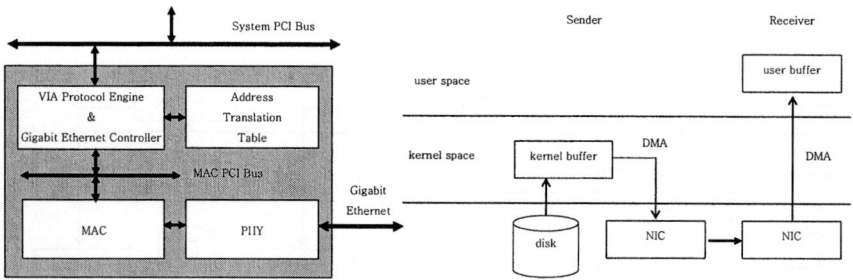

Fig. 2. Hardware-based VIA network adapter(left) and zero-copy file transfer mechanism(right)

4 Experimental Results

The performance of the improved file transfer mechanism was evaluated using two 800 MHz Pentium III PCs, each with a 32-bit/33MHz PCI bus. The PCs were running with Linux kernel 2.4. For comparison purposes, the performances of other TCP/IP-based mechanisms were measured using AceNIC's Gigabit Ethernet card. We have focused our experiments on the sender's behavior, and so *VipSendFile* is identical in the sender, both with and without the RDMA write operation. Additionally, as the initial disk accesses took longer than the time for transmission, data copying, and other overheads, we have excluded them and measured through iteration.

Fig. 3(a) shows the elapsed time for the sender to transfer the file, and Fig. 3(b) shows the ping-pong bandwidth between two nodes for five file transfer mechanisms. Three results are based on TCP/IP, while the other two are based on the VIA using our hardware-based VIA network adapter. From Fig. 3(a),

VipSendFile was 1.2-1.9 times faster than *sendfile* or *read−> VipPostSend*, showing that zero-copying, less context switching, and minimal protocol overheads are important factors in file transfer mechanisms. Fig. 3(b) shows the overall performance, including network speed and receiver's overhead. *VipSendFile* has lower overheads for both sender and receiver. In addition, while experimental results are not presented in this paper, the receiver's CPU is not used for RDMA write operations because there is no explicit VipPostRecv function call, and a VI descriptor is not necessary.

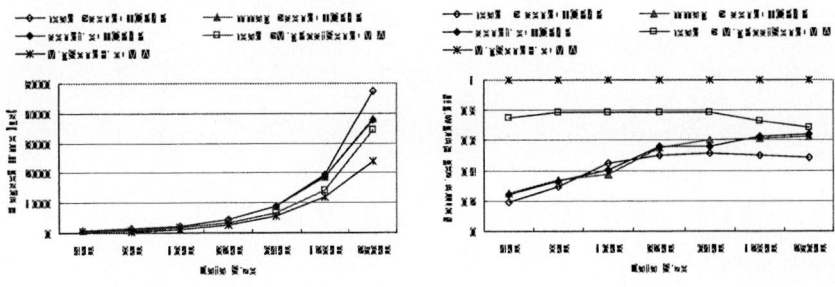

(a) Time taken in the sender   (b) Bandwidth between two nodes

Fig. 3. Performance comparisons of file transfer

5 Conclusions

This paper has presented an improved zero-copy file transfer mechanism for a hardware-based VIA network adapter that does not require file system modifications. As shown in the experiment results, performance is improved compared with existing mechanisms because of the zero-copy mechanism, less context switching, and a lower communication protocol overhead. This system also supports file transfers using RDMA writes, minimizing the CPU utilization of the receiver.

References

1. D. Stancevic: "Zero Copy I: User-Mode Perspective", *Linux Journal*, Volume 2003, Issue 105, January 2003
2. J. Tranter: "Exploring The Sendfile System Call", *Linux Gazette, Issue91*, June 2003
3. Virtual Interface Architecture Specification. http://www.viarch.org/
4. $InfiniBand^{TM}$ Architecture, http://www.infinibandta.org/

5. DAFS Collaborative. Direct Access File System Protocol, Version 1.0, September 2001. http:// www.dafscollaborative.org
6. A. Feforova, M. Seltzer, K. Magoutis, S. Addetia: "Application performance on the Direct Access File System", *ACM SIGSOFT Sofrware Engineering Notes, Proc. Of the 4th international workshop on Software and Performance, vol 29*, January 2004

An M-VIA-Based Channel Bonding Mechanism on Gigabit Ethernet*

Soo-Cheol Oh and Sang-Hwa Chung

School of Electrical and Computer Engineering,
Pusan National University, Pusan, 609-735, Korea
{osc, shchung}@pusan.ac.kr

Abstract. This paper proposes an M-VIA-based channel bonding mechanism on Gigabit Ethernet to improve network bandwidths of cluster systems. M-VIA is a software implementation of a user-level communication protocol that replaces the time-consuming TCP/IP protocol in cluster systems. Channel bonding techniques manage multiple network cards as a virtual single network card and expand network bandwidth by sending data concurrently through the multiple network cards and their associated networks. According to experiments with two Gigabit Ethernet adapters, the M-VIA-based channel bonding mechanism on Gigabit Ethernet showed a bandwidth improvement of 29 % over an M-VIA on a single channel.

1 Introduction

It is extremely important to improve network performance in constructing high-performance cluster systems. Because TCP/IP, a representative communication protocol for Gigabit Ethernet, has many software overheads, user software cannot fully utilize the available physical bandwidth [1] and this limits the performance improvement of the cluster system. TCP/IP's many overheads include kernel intervention, multiple data copies and context switching from user level to kernel level. To solve this problem, user-level communication protocols [2] that remove the overheads of TCP/IP have been developed and VIA (Virtual Interface Architecture) [3] is representative. In VIA, the context switching overhead is removed by performing the communications tasks at the user level instead of the kernel level, and data is copied less frequently by simplifying protocol layers. M-VIA [4], developed by Lawrence Berkeley Laboratory, is a software implementation of VIA.

Another strategy that improves network performance is channel bonding, in which data are sent concurrently through multiple network cards installed in one computer node. An advantage of channel bonding is that network performance can be improved without using expensive higher performance network cards.

---

* This work was supported by grant No.(R05-2003-000-10726-0) from the Korea Science and Engineering Foundation.

Ethernet channel bonding [5] from the Beowulf cluster and MuniSocket (Multiple NIC Interface Socket) [6] from the University of Nebraska-Lincoln are examples of previous research on channel bonding. These studies are based on TCP/IP and no channel bonding mechanism based on M-VIA has been developed.

This paper proposes an M-VIA-based channel bonding mechanism on Gigabit Ethernet to improve network bandwidth. A new channel bonding layer is inserted into the protocol stack of M-VIA and manages multiple network cards as a virtual single network card.

2 M-VIA Based Channel Bonding Mechanism

Figure 1-(a) shows the protocol stack of M-VIA. The VI Provider Library, the uppermost layer, is the Application Programming Interface (API) of M-VIA. To send data to a remote node, a connection between the two nodes is established by the M-VIA Kernel Agent. This agent, a hardware-independent layer, provides the necessary kernel services, which include connection management and memory registration, to establish connections between nodes. After establishing the connection, data is transferred to a Gigabit Ethernet adapter through two device drivers. via_ering, developed for M-VIA, handles common features for Ethernet-based network cards and partitions the data according to the Maximum Transfer Unit (MTU) size of the network card, which is 1514 bytes for Ethernet devices. via_e1000, provided by the network card manufacturer, includes functions to handle a specific adapter, and new functions for M-VIA implementation are added to this device driver. The partitioned data is sent to remote nodes by the adapters.

A channel bonding layer for M-VIA is located between the via_ering and via_e1000 layers, as shown in Fig. 1-(b). The channel bonding layer manages the multiple Gigabit Ethernet adapters as a virtual single adapter. An important issue in sending each block of partitioned data is to determine which network card is used. For this study, we chose the round robin algorithm, which is adopted for TCP/IP channel bonding in Linux. The round robin algorithm guarantees fair distribution of packets in most cases and generates little overhead because of its simplicity. The selected Gigabit Ethernet adapter and via_1000 layer form a packet from the partitioned data and send it to the remote node.

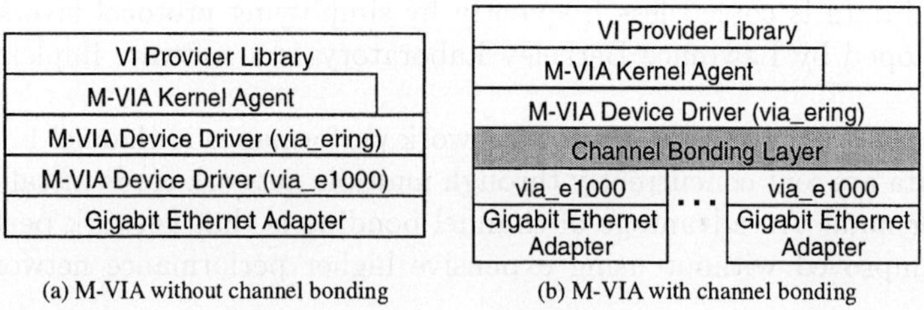

Fig. 1. Protocol stack of M-VIA

When the packet arrives at the remote node, it is transferred to the channel bonding layer. The channel bonding layer transfers packets received from the multiple Gigabit Ethernet adapters to via_ering as if these packets were received from one adapter. A problem for the channel bonding layer is that packets sent earlier from the send-node can arrive later at the receive-node because the packets are sent by different adapters. M-VIA without channel bonding checks a sequence number in each packet and discards packets without consecutive sequence numbers. The channel bonding layer for TCP/IP stores such packets in a buffer or discards them. This increases the time spent in processing the packet and degrades the performance of the Gigabit Ethernet adapter. To solve this problem, our implementation utilizes an offset field in the M-VIA packet header. The offset field indicates the location where the received packet data should be stored in the receive buffer. M-VIA with the channel bonding layer stores the received packet directly at this offset location in the receive buffer instead of buffering or discarding. This mechanism does not generate additional processing overhead because it utilizes the offset field, which is already included in the M-VIA header and replaces the process of checking the sequence number process with the process of checking the offset.

3 Experiments

We performed experiments on a PC cluster system with two nodes. Each node had a 1.4 GHZ Pentium III processor, 512 MB of main memory and a 64 MHz/64 bit PCI bus. The operating system was based on Linux kernel 2.4.7. Two Intel 1000/Pro Gigabit Ethernet cards were installed on each node, and two 3Com SuperStack3 4900 Gigabit Ethernet switches were used to form two distinct networks connecting the two computers.

Figure 2 shows the bandwidths of M-VIA and TCP/IP with channel bonding. For TCP/IP, the channel bonding layer implemented in Linux was used. The bandwidth of the M-VIA version with bonding is 1.14 Gbps, which is higher than the 0.88 Gbps obtained with the single-M-VIA version, so the M-VIA version with bonding is 29 % superior to the single-M-VIA version. However, the bandwidth of the bonding TCP/IP version is lower than that of the single TCP/IP version. As explained in section 2, packets sent earlier from the send-node can arrive later at the receive-node when multiple networks are used. The channel bonding layer of TCP/IP handles these packets using buffering or rejection, and this degrades the performance of the TCP/IP version with bonding. However, our channel bonding layer for M-VIA adopted the algorithm utilizing the offset field of M-VIA header, which does not generate additional processing overhead, and this leads to the performance improvement.

In this experiment, only a single thread was used to generate network traffic but this does not generate sufficient network traffic to fully utilize two Gigabit Ethernet adapters. We plan to perform experiments with multiple threads and we expect the bandwidth improvement of M-VIA with bonding will be better than the 29 % of Fig. 2.

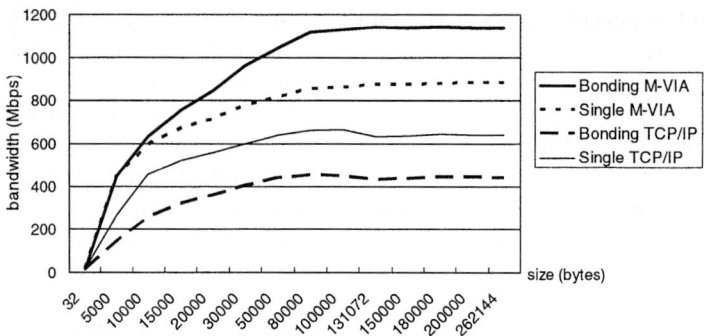

Fig. 2. Bandwidths of M-VIA and TCP/IP with channel bonding

4 Conclusions

This paper proposes an M-VIA-based channel bonding mechanism on Gigabit Ethernet to improve the network bandwidth of cluster systems. M-VIA is a software implementation that replaces the time-consuming TCP/IP protocol in cluster systems. The channel bonding layer is inserted into the M-VIA protocol stack and manages multiple Gigabit Ethernet adapters as a virtual single adapter. The channel bonding layer adopts the round-robin algorithm to distribute packets to multiple adapters. This layer also utilizes the offset field of the M-VIA header to collect the packets delivered through the multiple Gigabit Ethernet networks and this mechanism did not generate any additional processing overhead. According to the experiments, the M-VIA-based channel bonding mechanism on Gigabit Ethernet showed a bandwidth improvement of 29 % over an M-VIA on a single channel.

References

1. J. Kay and J. Pasquale: Profiling and Reducing Processing Overheads in TCP/IP, *IEEE/ACM Transactions on Networking*, Vol. 4, No. 6, pp. 817-828, Dec. 1996.
2. R. A.F. Bhoedjang, T. Ruhl, and H. E. Bal: User-Level Network Interface Protocols, *IEEE Computer*, Vol. 31, No. 11, pp. 53-60, Nov. 1998.
3. D. Dunning et al.: The Virtual Interface Architecture, *IEEE Micro*, Vol. 18, No. 2, pp. 66-76, 1998.
4. P. Bozeman and B. Saphir: A Modular High Performance implementation of the Virtual Interface Architecture, *Proc. Of the 2nd Extreme Linux Workshop*, June 1999
5. http://www.beowulf.org/intro.html
6. N. Mohamed, J. Al-Jaroodi, H. Jiang, and D. Swanson: A Middleware-Level Parallel Transfer Technique over Multiple Network Interfaces, in *Proceeding IPDPS 2003, Workshop on Advances in Parallel and Distributed Computational Models*, Nice France, April 2003.

Soft-Computing-Based Virtual Topology Design Methods in IP/DWDM Optical Internet[*]

Xingwei Wang[1], Minghua Chen[1], Min Huang[2], and Wendong Xiao[3]

[1] Computing Center, Northeastern University, Shenyang, 110004, China
wangxw@mail.neu.edu.cn
[2] College of Information Science and Engineering, Northeastern University, Shenyang, 110004, China
[3] New Initiatives, Institute for Infocomm Research, 21 Heng Mui Keng Terrance, Singapore 119613

Abstract. Virtual topology design is considered to be one of the key problems in the IP/DWDM optical Internet. Due to its NP-hard nature, with the objective of minimizing the sum of traffic-weighted hop count, two soft-computing-based methods to design the virtual topology are presented, adopting genetic algorithm and simulated annealing algorithm respectively. A simulation environment is developed and performance evaluations have also been done.

1 Introduction

IP/DWDM optical Internet is considered to be one of the most potential candidates for NGI (Next Generation Internet) backbone [1]. Its performance can be improved substantially by determining an optimal virtual topology for it. In this paper, oriented to mesh networks, two soft-computing-based virtual topology design methods are proposed, with the objectives of minimizing the sum of traffic-weighted hop count. Due to its NP-hard nature, GA (Genetic Algorithm) and SAA (Simulated Annealing Algorithm) are adopted respectively [2]. Simulation results have shown that the proposed methods are feasible and effective.

2 Problem Formulations

The physical topology of IP/DWDM optical Internet can be modeled as a graph $G(V,E)$, where V is the set of nodes representing optical routers or switchers and E is the set of edges representing optical fibers. Graph $G(V,E)$ contains $|V|$ nodes and $|E|$ edges. $[\lambda_{sd}]_{|V|\times|V|}$ is a matrix, describing the amount of traffic flowing from one node to another. Here, s represents the source node and d represents the destination one, $\lambda_{ss} = 0$.

---

[*] This work was supported by the NSFC under Grant No.60473089, No.60003006 and No.70101006; the National 863 Plan under Grant No.2001AA121064; the NSF of Liaoning under Grant No.20032018 and No.20032019; Modern Distance Education Engineering Project of MoE.

Given G and $[\lambda_{sd}]_{|V|\times|V|}$, generate a corresponding virtual topology G_v, and route the traffic over it. The objective function is defined as follows:

$$F = \min\left(\frac{\sum_{sd} \lambda_{sd} H_{sd}}{\sum_{sd} \lambda_{sd}}\right) \quad (1)$$

Here, H_{sd} is the count of hops, which lightpath (s,d) has traversed.

3 Soft-Computing-Based Virtual Topology Design Methods

3.1 GA-Based Virtual Topology Design Method

Numerical coding is adopted to denote the solution, which is called chromosome here. The initial population is generated randomly and the population size is set to P (a preset value). Three kinds of crossover schemes are chosen randomly to do the crossover operation, i.e., parallel, exchanging and odd-even. Fitness function is defined as follows:

$$F_t = MAX - \left(\frac{\sum_{sd} \lambda_{sd} H_{sd}}{\sum_{sd} \lambda_{sd}}\right) \quad (2)$$

Here, MAX is a large enough positive number to ensure that all possible values of F_t are positive. Each chromosome corresponds to a virtual topology. Once the virtual topology is constructed, assign the wavelengths to it and route the traffic over it adopting the following wavelength assignment algorithm and the traffic routing algorithm [2], and then compute the value of F_t.

3.1.1 Wavelength Assignment Algorithm
Determine the physical links that make up an optical channel and the wavelength that the optical channel will occupy. The wavelength continuity constraint only has to be satisfied between two wavelength converters. When passing through the same physical link, different optical channels need use different wavelengths, otherwise wavelength assignment conflict will happen[3]. Hence, the following measures are taken: number all wavelengths available on the physical links at first; every time, try to find out the wavelength with the smallest number, which has not yet been assigned; whenever such a wavelength is not available, release the whole lightpath.

3.1.2 Traffic Routing Algorithm
The proposed algorithm tries to find the shortest paths for the traffic node pairs by greedy algorithm over the constructed virtual topology [2]. It also tries to route traffic as much as possible to the path with hops as less as possible without exceeding the optical channel capacity [2].

To speed up the population evolution, select the $P \times (1 - p_c)$ best chromosomes from the P father chromosomes and reserve them directly as son chromosomes, and then have crossover operation on the remaining $P \times p_c$ chromosomes in the father population to generate the new son population. Here, p_c is the crossover probability. Father chromosomes in the crossover operation are selected from the father population according to the roulette wheel.

To ensure the solution quality, a safety valve is established reserving the elitist (the chromosome with the largest fitness value), which need not take part in the selection and crossover operation. Only when the best chromosome of the current population is better than the reserved elitist, does the former replace the latter. If the elitist remains unchanged after the preset maximum evolution times of generations, the algorithm ends.

3.2 SAA-Based Virtual Topology Design Method

This method is different from that GA-based one mainly on the fitness function definition and the annealing mechanism. Its fitness function is defined as follows:

$$F_t = \frac{\sum_{sd} \lambda_{sd} H_{sd}}{\sum_{sd} \lambda_{sd}} \tag{3}$$

A suitable initial temperature is the one that can bring the higher average initial state accepted probability. Generate two solutions randomly, and then compute their fitness values, denoted by F_1 and F_2 respectively. If these two values are equal, generate a new solution, till they are unequal. Set the initial temperature as follows: $t_{ini} = -|F_2 - F_1| \times \log(e) / \log(\beta)$, where β is a constant between 0 and 1. Use exponential cooling scheme to control the temperature.

4 Performance Evaluations and Conclusions

Simulation researches and performance evaluations have been done over some actual network topologies [2]. For GA-based virtual topology design method, set the virtual degree [2] to 6 and the wavelength number to 6; when the PS (Population Size) is set to 20, the effect of the CP (Crossover Possibility) on the AHC (Average Hop Count) is shown in Fig.1-(a) and its effect on the AEOC (Amount of the Established Optical Channels) is shown in Fig.1-(b), whereas the effect of the MP (Mutation Probability) on the AHC is shown in Fig.1-(c) and its effect on the AEOC is shown in Fig.1-(d); the effect of the PS on the AHC is shown in Fig.1-(e) and its effect on the AEOC is shown in Fig.1-(f). For SAA-based virtual topology design method, with the MTTD (Maximum Temperature Declined Times) increased, the produced solutions are getting better and better; however, the MTTD cannot be increased without limitation, otherwise the running time of the algorithm will become unbearable; at the same time, after the MTTD has become large enough, its effect on algorithm performance changes little.

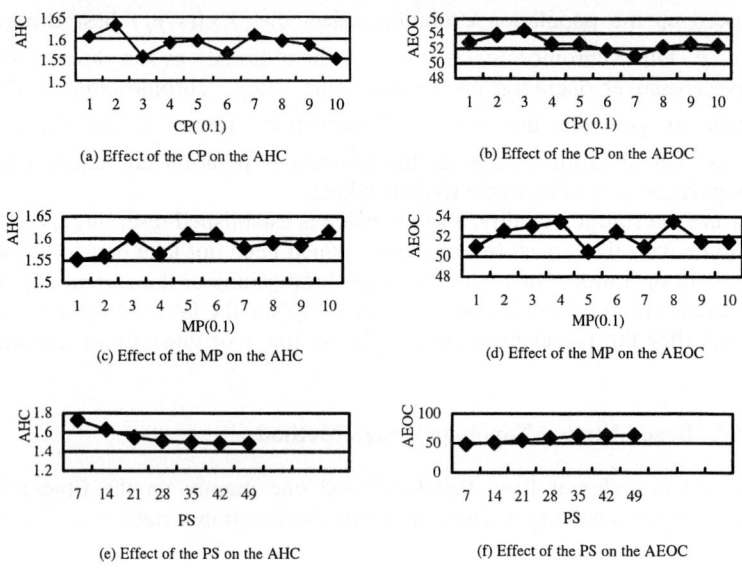

Fig. 1. Simulation results

In conclusion, the proposed methods are both feasible and effective, and can help to improve the performance of IP/DWDM optical Internet.

References

1. Mário M. F., Joel J. R., Rui M. C.: The Role of Network Topologies in the Optical Core of IP-over-WDM Networks with Static Wavelength Routing. Telecommunication Systems, Vol. 24, No. 2. (2003) 111-122
2. Chen M.H., Research and Simulated Implementation of Virtual Topology Design Algorithms in IP/DWDM Optical Internet. Sy: Northeastern University, (2003) (in Chinese)
3. Wang X.W., Cheng H., Li J., Huang M.: A Multicast Routing Algorithm in IP/ DWDM Optical Internet. Journal of Northeastern University (Natural Science), Vol. 24, No. 12. (2003) 1165-11681 (in Chinese)

An Analytic Model of Burst Queue at an Edge Optical Burst Switching Node[*]

SuKyoung Lee

Sejong University, Seoul, Korea
sklee@sejong.ac.kr

Abstract. In Optical Burst Switching (OBS) networks, most of processing and buffering are concentrated at the edge. Thus, we propose an analytic model of burst queue at an edge in terms of IP packets with the aim to obtain the average number of packets in burst queue the size of which influences the cost of constructing OBS networks.

1 Introduction

In order to realize such IP-over-WDM paradigms, optical burst switching has attracted more attention as a quite suitable network architectures for future Optical Internet backbones. One of the key problems in the application of burst switching in an optical domain is the aggregation of several IP packets in a single optical burst. In particular, once IP packets are aggregated into much larger bursts, they should wait in the burst queue [1] till the enough wavelength is reserved, before transmission through the network. Thus, in this paper, we focus on developing an analytical model of burst queue with burst assembler in terms of IP packets. We investigate the expected number of packets in burst queue following the burst assembler at an edge OBS node because most of processing and buffering are concentrated at the edge in an OBS network. This investigation is meaningful in the aspect that the size of burst queue would be decided on the basis of the expected number of packets in the burst queue with the tolerable delay limit of each traffic class.

2 Burst Queue Modeling at an OBS Edge Node

A number of user traffic flows are connected to an edge OBS node. Each incoming packet for a given burst needs to be stored in a burst assembler until the last packet of the burst arrives. As soon as the last packet arrives, all packets of the burst are transferred to the burst queue. The arrival process to a burst queue can be modelled as a superposition of N independent effective On/Off processes, each coming from N user traffic flows. If we assume that both On and Off periods are

---

[*] This work was supported in part by Korea Science and Engineering Foundation (KOSEF) through OIRC project.

geometrically distributed with the same parameters α and β which denote the transition rates from Off to On and On to Off states, respectively, an Interrupted Bernoulli Process (IBP) can be used to model each burst assembler. Within the On state, at each time instant, there is a packet arrival with probability γ from each active user and generated packets during an On period form a single burst. Supposing the event that the burst assembler is not empty, the conditional probability, Π_i that the burst assembler contains i packets is given by

$$\Pi_i = \frac{\beta}{\beta + \gamma(1-\beta)} \left(1 - \frac{\beta}{\beta + \gamma(1-\beta)}\right)^{i-1}, \quad \text{for } i \geq 1 \tag{1}$$

and for the number of packets in burst assembler, N_{ba}, $E[N_{ba}] = \frac{\beta + (1-\beta)r}{\beta}$. The data bursts in a burst queue are assumed to be drained virtually in terms of packet. Thus, the burst queue is investigated using a discrete-time system where one time slot is equivalent to the duration a packet is transmitted on a wavelength.

In OBS networks, it is known that a burst in burst queue is transmitted to an output port after waiting sometime called offset. Thus, if t_c denotes an offset time for the bursts belonging to a service class c and L is the mean burst length, the one packet service time becomes t_c/L. Under the assumption that the packets are not bound to arrive back-to-back, inter-arrival times of successive packets are independent identically distributed [2]. In terms of activity cycle, let β^{-1} and α^{-1} be the active period and the idle period, respectively. Then overall one cycle T becomes $\alpha^{-1} + \beta^{-1}$. The probability of such a traffic source being in the On state, p_{on} is given by $\frac{\beta^{-1}}{T}$. Then we get the probability that a single source transits from On state to Off state in a time slot as followings

$$p_t = P[\text{Transition\_to\_Off}|\text{Being\_in\_On}] = p_{on}\beta. \tag{2}$$

The probability that i out of N active sources transit from On state to Off state in a time slot, Γ_i, can be expressed as $\Gamma_i = b(i; N, p_t)$ where $b(i; n, p)$ represents the binomial distribution with all n sources.

Let x be the probability distribution of burst queue. We define x_i as the steady-state probability that the burst queue contains i packets under a total of N On/Off sources. Let $\mathbf{x}_i$ denote the probability vector with N components, $x_{i,n} (1 \leq n \leq N)$ which is the probability that the burst queue contains i packets and n sources are at On state. We can describe the aggregate arrival process by a discrete-time batch Markovian arrival process (D-BMAP). However, it brings about the computational complexity in getting $\mathbf{x}_i$ [3].

In advance of computing the approximation of $\mathbf{x}_i$, the traffic density can be defined as $\rho = \frac{E[N_{ba}]N}{T}$. Taking $N \to \infty$, $\lambda\rho \ll 1$, we obtain

$$\Gamma_i \approx \frac{(\lambda\rho)^i}{i!} e^{-\lambda\rho} \approx \begin{cases} e^{-\lambda\rho} \approx 1 - \lambda\rho, & i = 0 \\ \lambda\rho e^{-\lambda\rho} \approx \lambda\rho, & i = 1 \\ 0, & \text{otherwise} \end{cases} \tag{3}$$

where λ denote $1/E[N_{ba}]$. Due to Eq. 3, β_i that i packets arrive to form a burst transiting from an On state to an Off state is expressed as

$$\beta_i = \begin{cases} \Gamma_0 = 1 - \lambda\rho, & i = 0 \\ \Gamma_1 \Pi_i = \lambda^2 \rho (1-\lambda)^{i-1}, & i \geq 1 \end{cases} \quad (4)$$

According to the state transition diagram of the burst queue working on the basis of one time slot in [4], a system of difference equations may be derived for the approximation of x_i, $\tilde{x}_i$ as follows:

$$\tilde{x}_0(1-\beta_0) = \tilde{x}_1\beta_0, \qquad \tilde{x}_1(1-\beta_1) = \tilde{x}_2\beta_0 + \tilde{x}_0\beta_1 \quad (5)$$

$$\tilde{x}_i(1-\beta_1) = \tilde{x}_{i+1}\beta_0 + \tilde{x}_0\beta_i + \sum_{n=1}^{i-1} \tilde{x}_i\beta_{i-n+1}, \quad \text{for } i \geq 2$$

Then,

$$(1-\beta_1)\sum_{n=2}^{\infty} \tilde{x}_n z^n = \frac{\beta_0}{z}\sum_{n=2}^{\infty} \tilde{x}_{n+1} z^{n+1} + \tilde{x}_0 \sum_{n=2}^{\infty} \beta_n z^n + \sum_{n=2}^{\infty}\sum_{i=1}^{n-1} \tilde{x}_i \beta_{n-i+1} z^n \quad (6)$$

and z-transform of $\tilde{x}_i$, $X(z)$ and $\tilde{x}_n$ are derived as follows:

$$X(z) = (1-\rho)\left(1 - \frac{\lambda \rho z}{z(1-\lambda) - (1-\lambda\rho)}\right) \quad (7)$$

$$\tilde{x}_n = \frac{1}{n!}\frac{d^n X(z)}{dz^n}\bigg|_{z=0} = \frac{\lambda\rho(1-\rho)(1-\lambda)^{n-1}}{(1-\lambda\rho)^n}. \quad (8)$$

Finally, the expected number of packets in the burst queue under N users is derived as

$$E[n] = \sum_{n=0}^{\infty} n\tilde{x}_n = \frac{\rho(1-\lambda\rho)}{\lambda(1-\rho)} \quad (9)$$

From Eq. 9, the mean waiting time in burst queue becomes $\bar{T}_{bq} = \frac{E[n]}{\lambda} = \frac{\rho(1-\lambda\rho)}{\lambda^2(1-\rho)}$. Even if each burst is at the head of the burst queue, it could not be transmitted into a network since it should wait for an offset time during which the control packet reserves the wavelength. Therefore, to reduce the delay which each burst experiences at an edge, the control packet generator can transmit the control packet when the remaining waiting time of the burst in the burst queue becomes equal to the offset time. As can be seen in a simple flow of Fig. 1(a), the mean waiting time can be reflected in determining the time when the control packet will be sent, to reduce the overall waiting time at the edge, resulting in better end-to-end delay performance.

3 Performance Evaluation

In order to capture the burstiness of data at the edge nodes, the traffic from a user to the edge node is generated by Pareto burst arrivals with 10 and 50

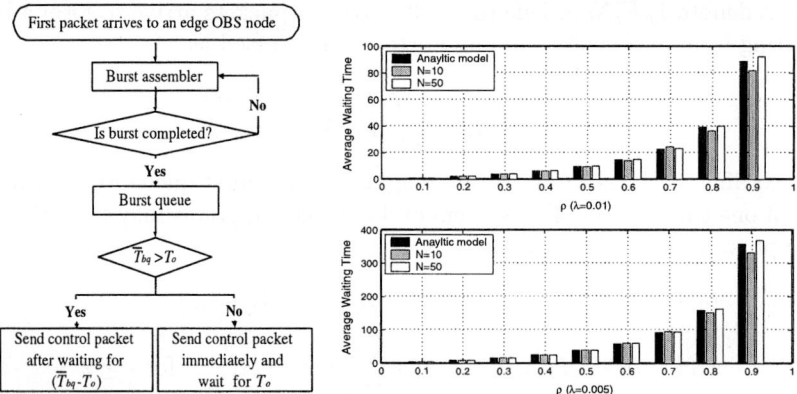

Fig. 1. (a) The desired actions to reduce the waiting time in burst queue (b) Average waiting time at an edge OBS node when $\lambda = 0.01$ and 0.005

independent traffic sources with On/Off periods which are assumed to be exponentially distributed. The length of the burst is fixed to the average burst length in the Poisson case, i.e., 100 fixed-sized packets. The Hurst parameter is 0.525.

Fig. 1(b) plots the average waiting time in burst queue with burst assembly times versus the traffic density for different number of sources and the analytical model. We observe that the error increases as the ρ increases, that is, the traffic density increases. There may be some concern that the analytical model may not work very well if there are just a few sources. But this concern falls off in Fig. 1(b) for $N=10$ and $N=50$. From the simulation results (due to the lack of space, other results for different traffic arrivals are not included), we could see that the analytical result tracks the simulation result more closely as the traffic arrivals increase, because $\lambda\rho \ll 1$ is assumed in our analytical model.

4 Conclusion

It is possible that the processing at an edge would be a bottleneck to real-time multimedia applications. Therefore, in this paper, we investigated the burst queue with burst assembler at an edge OBS node. From this analytic model, Internet Service Providers may expect how tolerable delay limit could be provided for different service classes in an OBS network. As a future research, we are extending the simple mechanism in Fig. 1(a) to support different QoS.

References

1. Chaskar, H.M., Verma, S., Ravikanth, R.: Robust Transport of IP Traffic over WDM Using Optical Burst Switching. Optical Networks Mag. Vol.3, No.4 (Jul./Aug. 2001) 47-60.

2. XU, L., Perros, H.G., Rouskas, G.N.: A Queueing Network Model of an Edge Optical Burst Switching Node, IEEE INFOCOM, San Francisco CA USA, (2003).
3. Widjaja, I., Neuts, M.F., Li, J-M.: Conditional Overflow Probability and Profile Curve for ATM Congestion Detection. IEEE INFOCOM, San Francisco CA USA, (1996).
4. Lee, S.: Packet-based Burst Queue Modeling at an Edge in OBS Networks. Submitted.

Cost-Effective Deflection Routing Algorithm in Optical Burst Switching Networks[*]

SuKyoung Lee[1], LaeYoung Kim[2], and JooSeok Song[2]

[1] Graduate School of Information & Communication,
Sejong University, Seoul, Korea
sklee@sejong.ac.kr

[2] Dept. of Computer Science, Yonsei University, Seoul, Korea

Abstract. In this paper, we propose a cost-effective deflection routing algorithm with wavelength conversion in order to provide more guarantee of resource for contending bursts on alternate path. The proposed scheme dynamically decides alternate path with optimal cost in terms of blocking and wavelength conversion performance.

1 Introduction

In an OBS network, contention is a major concern and contention resolution is necessary. Thus, several contention resolution schemes have been proposed such as optical buffering using Fiber Delay Lines (FDLs), wavelength conversion, and deflection routing. Recently, various deflection routing schemes have emerged [1],[2]. However, they can not guarantee that control packet will reserve all the wavelengths successfully to the destination on alternate path, especially when traffic load is high in a network [3]. In this paper, to reduce the blocking rate on alternate path, we propose a cost-effective deflection routing with wavelength conversion scheme that attempts to seek the least congested alternate path unlike traditional deflection routing. Further, the proposed deflection routing scheme also aims to reduce wavelength conversion cost as well as burst blocking rate.

2 Cost-Effective Deflection Routing

We now provide a formulation of the deflection routing policy. Consider a physical network represented by a graph $G(N, L)$ where N and L are the set of nodes and the set of links connecting the nodes, respectively. Let W denote the maximum number of wavelengths per link. Given the set of established primary lightpaths, $\mathbf{P}$ for the ongoing bursts, $P_p \in \mathbf{P}$, make an assumption that an alternate path, P is established for the contending burst. Here we introduce three

---

[*] This work was supported in part by Korea Science and Engineering Foundation (KOSEF) through OIRC project.

network costs C_c, C_t, and C_b denoting wavelength conversion cost, transmission cost and the blocking cost for P and the relevant indicators are:

- C_i^{kl} : the wavelength conversion cost from wavelength k to l at node i
- C_{ij}^t : the transmission cost on link (i,j)
- C_{ij}^b : the blocking cost due to contention from node i to node j $(i \neq j)$
- $x_{ij,p}^k$: a binary variable telling whether wavelength k is already reserved on link (i,j) over P_p
- x_{ij}^k : a binary variable telling whether the contending burst uses wavelength k on link (i,j) over P
- $y_{i,p}^{kl}, y_i^{kl}$: binary variables telling whether wavelength k needs to be converted to l at node i on P_p and P, respectively
- x_{ij} : a binary variable denoting whether alternate route includes a link (i,j) (i.e. $\sum_{k=1}^{W} x_{ij}^k > 0$) or not

In this formulation, an objective function is designed to establish an alternate path, P for the contending burst from the congested node to the destination such that the above three network costs are minimized, and is stated as

$$\text{Minimize} \quad \sum_{i=1}^{|N|}(C_c + C_t + C_b) \tag{1}$$

where $C_c = \sum_{l=1}^{W} \sum_{k=1}^{W} C_i^{kl} y_i^{kl}$, $C_t = \sum_{j=1}^{|N|} \sum_{k=1}^{W} C_{ij}^t x_{ij,p}^k$ $(i \neq j)$ and $C_b = \sum_{j=1}^{|N|} C_{ij}^b x_{ij}$. The set of constraint conditions is are defined as follows:

$$\sum_{l=1}^{W} \sum_{k=1}^{W} y_i^{kl} = \sum_{k=1}^{W} \sum_{j=1}^{|N|} x_{ij}^k \tag{2}$$

$$\sum_{k=1}^{W}(y_i^{kl} + y_{i,p}^{kl}) \leq 1, \quad \sum_{l=1}^{W}(y_i^{kl} + y_{i,p}^{kl}) \leq 1, \quad \forall P_p \in \mathbf{P} \tag{3}$$

$$\sum_{j=1}^{|N|} \sum_{k=1}^{W}(x_{ij,p}^k + x_{ij}^k) \leq W, \quad \forall P_p \in \mathbf{P} \tag{4}$$

At a node, Eq. 2 ensures wavelength conversion while Eq. 3 requires that a specific wavelength only appears at most once in both the incoming and outgoing links. Eq. 4 ensures, in a link, that the number of wavelengths occupied by both primary and deflected paths should not be larger than that provided by a link.

In this paper, the "hub-node" concept proposed in [2] is adopted due to lower complexity and here the "hub-node" is called deflection router which has an out degree sufficiently higher than other nodes in a network. Thus, every node in a network does not need to be equipped with our proposed deflection routing module and FDL for delaying the contending burst. When contention occurs, the proposed deflection routing module in deflection router determines an alternate path on the basis of its predefined deflection routing policy with network status information (e.g. link status, transmission cost and wavelength conversion cost in this paper). The detailed operation of exchange and distribution of information about network status can be found in [4]. To decrease the complexity and support our deflection routing algorithm on-demand, a heuristic algorithm is proposed as follows.

Procedure Heuristic DR()
  $\mathbf{P}_{\text{DRT}}$ = FindAlternatePath(N, L); \\ Initialization of DRT
  ComputeCost($\mathbf{P}_{\text{DRT}}$, C_{ij}^b); \\ Computation of blocking cost of alternate paths
  While (contention) \\ On-demand when there is contention
    $Burst$=GetBurstAttribute(ControlPacket); \\ e.g. burst length, traffic class
    P_s=SelectLeastCongestedAlternatePath($\mathbf{P}_{\text{DRT}}$);
    If ($Burst$ is loss-sensitive)
       Then P=AssignVirtualWavelenghs(P_s, $Burst$, C_i^{kl}, C_{ij}^t);
       If (No Available Wavelengths)
          Then Drop the burst & Notify the source that the burst is dropped;
          Go back to while loop;
       EndIf
    EndIf
  EndWhile

The FindAlternatePath searches all possible alternate paths to each destination limiting the distance in a network and initializes Deflection Routing Table (DRT) (i.e. $\mathbf{P}_{\text{DRT}}$) which is maintained in each deflection router, with the found alternate paths. The ComputeCost computes the blocking cost of the alternate paths in the DRT. The blocking cost is collected periodically. When a contention occurs, the deflection router delays the contending burst using FDL if needed. The proposed algorithm allows some contending bursts belonging to loss-sensitive traffic flows to be transmitted on an alternate path with wavelength assigned virtually. On the other hand, other contending bursts belonging to delay-sensitive traffic flows are routed via traditional Shortest Path Deflection Routing (SPDR). As soon as the procedure determines an alternate path, the deflection router sends the data burst.

3 Performance Evaluation

We compare the heuristic deflection routing algorithm to SPDR and full Wavelength Conversion (WC) schemes. All the simulation results are obtained on a 14-node NSFNET network with 26 links. Each link is composed of the same number of wavelengths, W (16 and 32) on which the transmission rate is 1Gbps. For the proposed scheme and SPDR scheme, three nodes that have the highest out degree in the simulation network are operated as deflection router while performing full wavelength conversion for WC scheme. For the proposed scheme, four nodes that have the secondary highest out degree, are configured with full wavelength conversion capability. Five pairs of source and destination nodes are randomly chosen. It is assumed that burst arrivals follow the Poisson process and

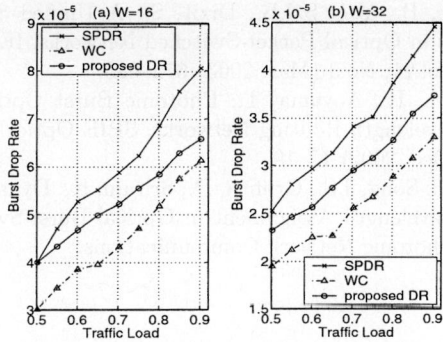

Fig. 1. Burst blocking rate versus offered load

their lengths are exponentially distributed with an average length of 1Mbyte. As shown in Figs. 1(a) and (b), for the two cases of W=16 and 32, the burst blocking rate of the proposed scheme is much lower than the SPDR at most loads. This is because the proposed scheme transmits the contending burst over the alternate path with minimum blocking rate and provides the information of available wavelengths as well as output port to the contending burst. As expected, the proposed scheme has higher loss than the WC. Under current technology, however, adding wavelength conversion capabilities to optical switches will definitely increase its complexity and cost. The wavelength conversion cost of the proposed scheme is improved by about 60% up to 70% over the WC. Thus, it can be known that WC enhances the burst blocking performance at the expense of wavelength conversion cost, while the proposed scheme keeps the wavelength conversion cost significantly low maintaining moderate burst blocking rate which is much better than what SPDR achieves.

4   Conclusion

In this paper we proposed a cost-effective deflection routing algorithm for OBS networks. The proposed algorithm aimed to reduce the burst blocking rate by finding least-congested alternate routes and assigning proper wavelengths virtually. The simulation results demonstrated that the proposed scheme achieves better burst blocking performance than SPDR scheme while it can keep wavelength conversion cost lower maintaining moderate burst loss compared with WC scheme without deflection routing.

References

1. Yao, S., Yoo, S.J.B., Mukherjee, B., Dixit, S.: All-Optical Packet-Switched Networks: A Study of Contention Resolution Schemes in an Irregular Mesh Network with Variable-Sized. SPIE OPTICOMM 2000, Vol.4233 (Oct. 2000) 235–246.

2. Yao, S., Mukherjee, B., Yoo, S.J.B., Dixit, S.: A Unified Study of Contention-Resolution Schemes in Optical Packet-Switched Networks. IEEE Journal of Lightwave Technology. Vol.21, No.3 (Mar. 2003) 672–683.
3. Wang, X., Morikawa, H., Aoyama, T.: Photonic Burst Optical Deflection Routing Protocol for Wavelength Routing Networks. SPIE Optical Networks Magazine, Vol.3, No.6 (Nov./Dec. 2002) 12–19.
4. Lee, S.K., Kim, L.Y., Song, J.S., Griffith, D., Sriram, K.: Dynamic Deflection Routing with Virtual Wavelength Assignment in Optical Burst-Switched Networks. To appear in Kluwer Photonic Network Communications.

On Concurrent Multi-port Test System for Routers and Its Support Tools

Bo Song, Huaxin Zeng, and Liquan Yue

School of Computer and Communication Engineering,
Southwest Jiaotong University, Chengdu, 610031, China
sb_000@263.net, yanwuxin@126.com

Abstract. Having analyzed the inadequateness of existing test technique and requirements of concurrent testing for routers, this paper presents a framework of distributed Concurrent Multi-Port Router Test System under development at Sichuan Network Communication Key Laboratory. Based on the system, its core components - Concurrent Multi-Port Test Manager (CMPTM) and Two-Port Tester (TPT) including their architectures, functional components, message format for communication between CMPTM and TPT-s are discussed in some detail. Moreover, its test case support tools are also discussed in detail and based on shortages of TTCN3 in describing multi-port test, the paper introduces a new test definition language - the Concurrent Multi-Port Test Definition Language (CMPT-TDL).

1 Introduction

With the advent of IPv6, testing for IPv6 routers had redrawn attentions of the network community. During transition from IPv4 to IPv6, equipments and products based the two different IP protocols need interconnect and interoperability. As relay system supporting IP protocols of the two versions, router plays an important role in interconnection between network systems. Therefore, research of test technology and development of test system for IP routers has a very important significance.

At present, test activities for router's protocols can be classified into three classes according to their test purposes: conformance testing, interoperability testing and performance testing [1]. Conformance testing and interoperability testing belong to functional test. Conformance testing aims at checking if protocols under test are in accordance with the RFC document. The aim of interoperability testing is assured of interconnection and interoperability between products from different vendors. The purpose of performance testing is to test the characteristic parameters of protocol implementations, such as packet transfer delay and throughout, so as to evaluate the efficiency of protocol implementations. However, so far the test methods for router are still restricted to the Loop-back Test Method (LTM) and the Transverse Test Method (TTM) [1] defined in ISO 9646. LTM excises testing by sending test data to a router and being looped back to the tester by the router, and had been the most popular test method until early 1980's for its convenience in application. For its testing capability is restricted to the implementation related to a single port and the routing function, the TTM is introduced in 1984 [2], which enable a pair of testers to test and observe the router through a pair of ports. TTM is more powerful than LTM and more appropriate for thorough test.

TTM and LTM can only test one or a pair of ports for router. Modern routers or switch routers could have tens of ports with two sets of protocol-stack implementation inside: the 3-layer user data transfer plane and the 5-layer signaling and management plane [3]. Therefore, existing testing techniques such as LTM or TTM, designed for testing routers on per port or a pair of ports basis, are unable to cope with the complexity and concurrency in multiple-port interactions.

There are some activities involving parallel multi-port testing, such as those in Interoperability Laboratory (IL) [4] of US and Institute of Computing Technology of Chinese Academy of Sciences (ICT); nevertheless they did not attempt to handle the concurrent issues among multi-ports. The IL's test experiments are carried out in the moonv6 collaboration project between US and Europe. However, it don't adopt the standard test definition language –TTCN (at present, it has been developed to the 3rd version -TTCN3) to describe test data, therefore, its test suites are lack of universality and difficult to apply to other test systems. Moreover, it cannot perform performance testing because of the far distance. As for the ICT, although the project IPv6CTS can realize multi-port test, it don't take into account concurrent problem for router testing and its test configuration is not flexible. In generally, although research on multi-port test has been carried out in some organizations, while in industry testing of IP routers is mainly restricted to testing one port or a pair of ports of a router only.

This has stimulated the activity of research on techniques of Concurrent Multi-Port-Testing Test System (CMPT-TS) presented in this paper. The attribute "concurrent" here is intended to emphasize that parallel tests are taking place at the same time and in a controlled (or synchronized) manner, which differs from existing parallel testing (sometimes also being referred to as concurrent testing though)[5]. In order to handle concurrency in network traffic on multiple ports, there is a strong need for CMPT (Concurrent Multi-Port Testing) as well as for a concurrent test definition language.

This paper first examines the inadequacy of existing test techniques, the necessity and requirement of concurrency testing for routers in section 2. Section 3 presents a framework of the CMPT-TS under development at Sichuan Network Communication Key Laboratory (SC-NetComLab), its functional components are explained in some detail. Section 4 deals with issues of test definition language and its support tools. The inadequacy of TTCN-3 in multi-computer based CMPT-TS is examined, our enhancement to TTCN-3 and the Concurrent Multi-Port Test Definition Language (CMPT-TDL), are analyzed and explained. Finally, section 5 provides a forward view of concurrent multi-port testing based on the experience gained in development of the CMPT-TS.

2 Necessities and Requirement of Concurrent Multi-port-testing

IP routers have been traditionally viewed as a network device with a 3-layer architecture adopting the in-band signaling technique. However, this point of view cannot explain why management protocol (SNMP) and the routing information exchange protocols such as RIP, OSPF, and BGP in a router are actually implemented on top of a transport protocol – UDP/TCP.

This contradiction can be avoided by adopting out-band signaling concept. In other words, a router is actually composed of two sets of protocol stack, one for user data transfer (up to network layer, usually being referred to as User Plane, or U-Plane for short), and the other for singling and management (up to the application layer, usually being referred to as Signaling & Management plane, or S&M plane for short) [3].

With this perception, a router transfers and routes IP packets at the network layer by utilizing routing tables, pre-defined or dynamically reconstructed by exchanging routing information in the S&M plane. In other words, SNMP and other routing information exchange protocols are application protocols in the S&M plane; hence their functions are different from those of the Network Relay System/Intermediate System as defined in ISO/RM. As a result, testing of routers involves not only the layer 3 function in U-plane, but also the layer 5 functions in S&M plane. Furthermore, functions in different planes are interrelated, e.g., routing functions in U-plane can be affected by the exchange of routing information in S&M plane; therefore, there is a need to test routing function jointly with routing information exchange activities.

With existing loop-back or transverse test methods, testing of routers can only be carried out on per port/a pair of ports basis. Even if S&M plane functions are deliberately used in controlling the routing tables in advance, the real operation environment cannot be simulated with LTM or TTM for a router with two more ports. It should be pointed out that simultaneously testing and observing on all the ports is even more important in measuring and evaluating the performance of a router than that in conformance testing.

Observation results from long-time monitoring of different networks have shown that network traffic has the "similar nature " [6], i.e. the spectrum of data volume of traffic vis-à-vis the time always has the same pattern disregarding the sampling time duration (hundreds of seconds/ milliseconds/ microseconds). The most prominent feature in these spectrums is that there are always high spectrum lines (representing data bursts) along the comparatively flat outline of the spectrum. This implies output congestion might arise whenever multiple bursts from different input-ports are instantly directed to a single output-port. Bearing in mind that routing table updating duration is with RIP is 30 seconds and with OSPF is even longer, there is no way to avoid this happening when routing table is temporarily unchangeable.

The behavior of a router in such condition cannot be tested by LTM and TTM; nevertheless, with the concurrent testing approach, all possible situations can be simulated by way of injecting test data into multi-ports in a controllable manner. This could be also very useful in robustness test and tolerance test.

As discussed above, for complete router testing, multi-port concurrent testing is more versatile; and is the very reason to have spurred the activity of development of CMPT-TS at SC-NetComLab.

3 A Framework of CMPT-TS

3.1 The Main Architecture of the CMPT-TS

The CMPT-TS is a test center-oriented system (Notes: hardware design of portable tester and its internal complicated concurrent arithmetic are not discussed in this paper.), which is designed for conformance testing and performance measurement for single router, and for interoperability testing and arbitration between routers. With the CMPT-TS, a router with multi-ports can be tested on all ports simultaneously in a controllable manner and thus its real operation environment can be simulated. With the system architecture shown in figure 1, the Two-Port Tester can be turned into an independent portable tester.

As shown in figure 1, the CMPT-TS are composed of two parts: CMPT system on the left and Test case support tools on the right. The main function of CMPT system is to deal with testing issues by utilizing executable test suites pre-compiled from test definition languages. Test case support tools include CMPT-TDL (Concurrent Multi-Port Test Definition Language), Test and Test Control Notation version 3 (TTCN-3), and relevant compilers. The CMPT-TDL is used in define concurrent test suite, and the CMPT-TDL compiler separates the concurrent control functions for CMPTM (Concurrent Multi-Port Test Manager) from tests for TPT-s. The TTCN-3 compiler further converts test suites in TTCN-3 into C programs, which will be further converted into machine executable codes by C compiler.

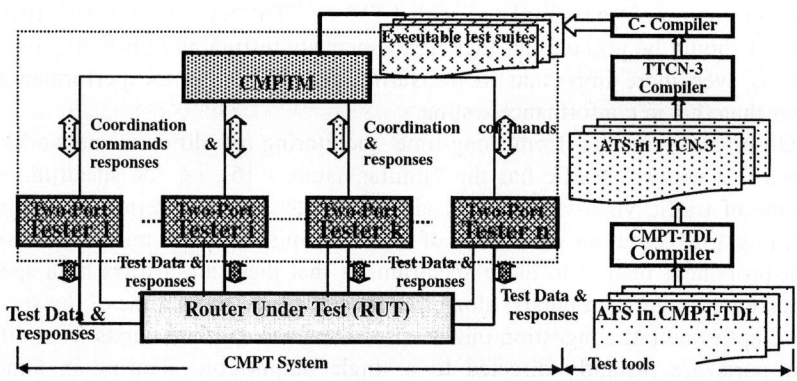

Fig. 1. The CMPT-TS composed of CMPT System & Test Case Support Tools

The main function of CMPTM in figure 1 is to handle multiple parallel testing in a controllable manner. The functionality of the CMPTM spans from test configuration of Two-Port Testers (TPT), assignment of executable test suite/groups/cases to individual TPT-s, initiation of a test session, graphic display of test progression, synchronization and coordination of concurrency in parallel tests, dynamic parallel test thread selection, parallel test information logging, ending a test session, and production of test reports.

As shown in figure 1, a TPT adopts either LTM or TTM as defined in ISO 9646 to test single port or a pair of ports. Which test method should be chosen and how a router should be tested, are decided by test requirement for a given router, the test system configuration, and test control data thus selected (test suite, test groups, and test cases). Adopting LTM or TTM, a TPT may act as an elementary test executor in a CMPT-TS, or as an independent tester in single port or two ports testing. Figure 3 further decomposes the functional diagrams of a TPT.

3.2 Concurrent Multi-port Test Manager (CMPTM)

As depicted in fig.2, CMPTM is control center of the whole CMPT-TS, which is in charge of initiating system, selecting test cases/groups to execute, assigning test tasks to Two-Port Tester (TPT) to execute, coordinating and synchronization TPT-s to assure of finishing test tasks successfully, receiving responses from every TPT, summing up middle test effects, and based on middle results collected from every TPT and log information getting a final test verdict and test report.

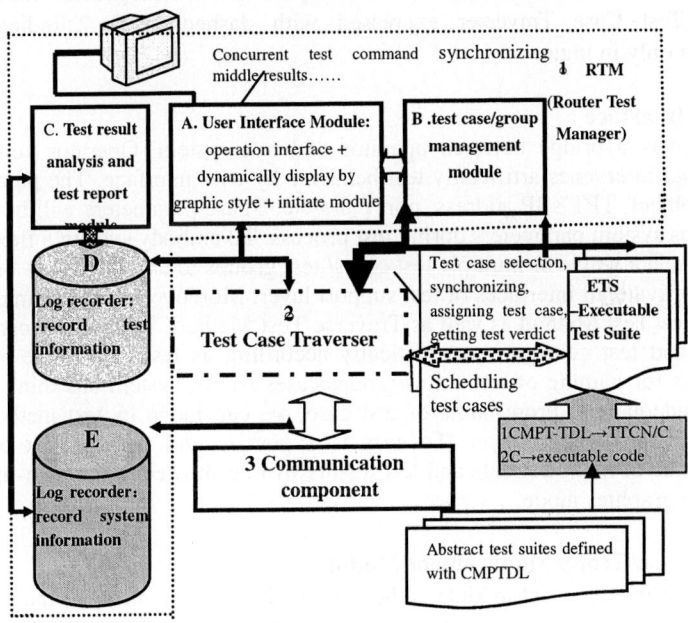

Fig. 2. Architecture of CMPTM and It's Support Tools

CMPTM is composed of router test manager (RTM), test case traverser, communication component. CMPTM is the entry of the whole test behavior as well as the end of test. Executable test suites compiled from abstract test suites written with Concurrent Multi-Port Definition Language (CMPT-TDL) are a series of commands to test, which are put into a database. When test is beginning, CMPTM will read commands from the database to execute by pointer. With the command's outspread,

CMPTM will call some TPT-s to execute corresponding operation. In here, there are two methods to make TPT execute these operations. One is TPT downloads concrete test commands from CMPTM to execute; the other is that these concrete test operations are beforehand saved in TPT to wait for being called. The former is more intuitive and easier, but in the distributed environment the velocity is too slow. Especially in performance testing, the velocity will affect test results directly. The later makes program in TPT bigger but can assure of test velocity to some extent, therefore, it makes test more accurate. Based the reason, the later is adopted in our CMPT-TS. Different from in CMPTM, these executable test cases in TPT is directly compiled from TTCN3, and perform concrete test operations under the management of CMPTM.

Test Case Traverser is a program to begin from a single test case entry and send PDU-s to SUT(system under test) along embranchment of test tree, and turn to next embranchment based on SUT's response. It executes test case assigned by RTM ,and after finishing the test case executes next test case by the order arranged beforehand or selected dynamically by RTM. To simplify communication interface between modules of test system, test case traverser is compiled into ETS together with abstract test suites. Test Case Traverser expressed with dashed in fig.2 indicates its independence only in logic.

3.2.1 User Interface

User interface is a bridge between operator and test system. Operator configures parameters and intervenes artificially test behavior by user interface. The parameters include test object, TPT's IP address, port pairs etc. These parameters will be passed to test cases as system parameters during test process. To embody system's flexibility, operator can select single or multiple test cases/ test groups to execute at one time and system will activate all interfaces of test support layer. Moreover, this system can test with Loop-back Test Method as well as Traverse Test Method. Test system can select test method and test configure automatically according as test case name selected artificially. As for naming of test suites/groups/cases /steps, system has think of this requirement adequately. From name of test case, we can judge its test method, test protocol layer and support layer. To easy to supervise and manage test process, alteration course of main test data and test results will be showed in the man-machine interface with graphics mode.

3.2.2 Test Case/Group Management Module

Test case/group management module is the main body of test control. At the phase of initiation of system, it expresses time-sequence relation between test cases/groups by means of list in the light of selection of operator. Afterward, test cases are performed in sequence of the list. And then this module passes over some test cases to execute based on last test verdict and principle of dynamic selection. One of main rules of dynamic selection makes use of the relation "not A is not B" between test cases. It means that when the verdict of test case A is fail, the verdict of test case B is sure to fail. Therefore, dynamic selection for test case can advance test efficiency largely.

3.2.3 Log Recorder and Test Report Module

C~E in fig.2 are respectively test result analysis and report module, two log recorders. The former can collect middle test verdicts from TPT-s and after analysis give a final verdict, finally form a test report displayed in man-machine interface. In some situations, system cannot give a confirmative verdict, namely the verdict is "inconclusive". At this time, test final verdict needs be analyzed artificially in the light of test report and logs. Accordingly, a supplement verdict is gotten or a new test case is designed to confirm the final test verdict. It should be pointed out that log recorder D is used to record test information which results from running test case, but log recorder E to record test system information which results from test system itself, such as network breaks.

3.2.4 Communication Component

This component is in charge of exchanging messages with every TPT which takes part in testing. All commands and data sent to TPT-s are passed by the communication component. As a management component in charge of sending control command and receiving response from TPT-s, different from TPT, CMPTM has no test support layer, which only need send and receive messages in a definite format. The message format has two classes: control message format and data message format. Table 1 shows their detail formats.

Table 1. Message Format

Message Type (1bit)	Request & Response (1bit)	Control type (6bit)	Data

Message Type		Request & Response	Control Type	Data	Memo.
0	Data Message	0: Request message	000000	Data	
		1: Response message			
1	Control message	0 : Request message	000001	Data information	HELLO message
			000010	Data information	SYN message
		1: Response message	000011	Data information	START message
			000100	Data information	STOP message
			others		reserve

As showed in table 1, the front is the general message format, and the back is the detail explanation. As for data message, the field Message Type is 0, but for control message, it is 1. The second field indicates the orientation of message, and if it is request message, the value is 0, whereas it's 1. As to data message, the field Control Type is 0 and the next field is data to transport. Data message format is simpler than control message format. In fact, control message has many different control types such as synchronization, initiation, starting, stop etc. Every control type has different value in field Control Type, and maybe is also different in field Data. Table 1 lists only partial control types and it is possible to be extended with the farther research.

3.3 The Two-Port Tester (TPT)

As depicted in figure 3, the TPT Manager is the test commander of a TPT under the control of CMPTM or the test operator. It controls test progression through the following functions: tester configuration, test case selection, giving order to the Test Case Traverser, starting or ending a test session, graphic display on the visual monitor, and so on. A Test Case Traverser is the single test case executor; it traverses through a single executable test case, calls up the E/D to encode/decode the PDU of the protocol under test, loading the encoded PDU into the PDU of the top layer in Test Support layers and de-loading in reverse direction (represented by the bold-line arrow).

Note that E/D is represented by a dotted box to indicate that an E/D has been included in the Executable Test Suite (ETS) before being compiled. Therefore, the two vertical dotted-arrows only imply conceptual data flows.

The two logging files in figure 3 differ from one another. The log file on the top in figure 3 loges the PDU events and data from the interface between TPTM and the test case traverser for post-analysis and TPT test report generation; selected events will also be passed TPTM or TPT monitor for display. The log file at the bottom in figure3 loges PDU events underneath the layer to be tested to provide an extra post analysis means.

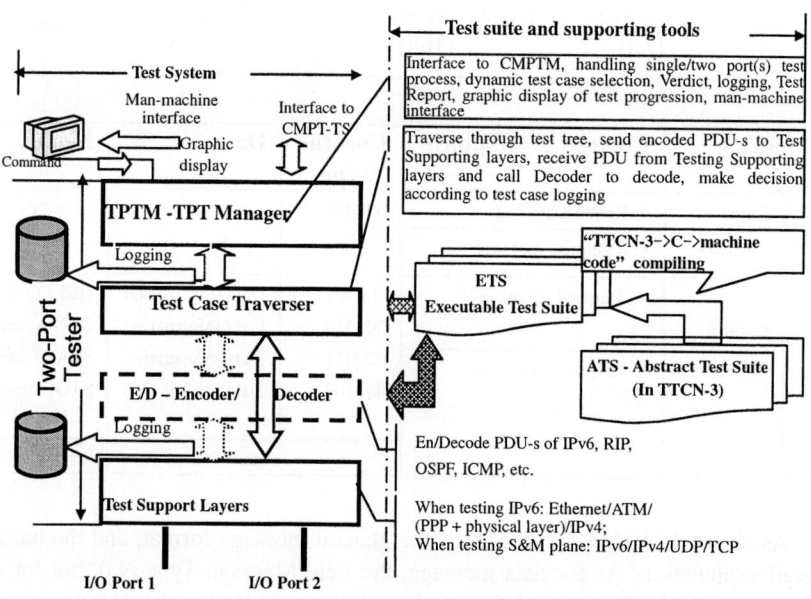

Fig. 3. Functional Components of Two-Port Tester

The Support layers in figure 3 represent different protocol stratum from the layer underneath the layer to be tested down to physical interface corresponding to those in the router under test. For example, they are Ethernet implementation when testing the IPv6 routing functions over Ethernet; while for encapsulated test of IPv6 as in 6-bone project, the highest layer in Support layers will be an IPv4 implementation. When come to testing of routing protocols, Support layers would be an implementation of the protocol stratum from physical layer up to UDP/TCP. In other words, the TPT should be designed as flexible as possible to adapt to different layer focused on and different support protocol stratum corresponding to those in the router under test.

3.4 Decision-Making Issues for CMPT-TS

Having decomposed the functionalities of the CMPT-TS into two parts as shown in figure 1, a systematic refinement is needed in system development. Figure 3 can be thought of as the result of the first-step refinement to TPT, in which four modules have been defined. Detailed function specification for individual modules needs to be done before programming.

There are many decision-making issues involved in development of CMPT-TS:

A. *What Kinds of Testing Capability Should be Included in CMPT-TS*
In design of the CMPT-TS, we have decided that the flowing test capability should be included in our system:

- Straightforward testing and encapsulated testing – As existing IPv6 routers can be realized either as an IPv6 implementation on top of the data link layer, or on top of existing IPv4 implementation. Therefore, the CMPT-TS should be able to test IPv6 straightforward on data link layer, as well as being encapsulated in IPv4 (as is done in 6-bone [7]).
- Considering that existing test activities on routers, by and large, focus on conformance testing with LTM and TTM, the new system should be able to cover performance testing as well with an emphasis on concurrent multi-port testing. The merits of such extension can be twofold: first, it enables testing interrelationship among routing functions in U-plane and routing information exchange and routing table up-dating; second, it enables measuring the performance of routers in real operation environment in terms of average data rate, transit delay, jitter, and worst case data rate, robustness, data discarding rate etc.
- Interoperability test and arbitration – with the concurrent multi-port testing capability, it should be natural to cover the interoperability test and arbitration test. This would be especially useful in test and diagnosis of behaviors of routers from different manufacturers in interconnection. This can be done by assigning of some TPT-s as active testers to issue test data while others as passive testers to observe the traffic between adjacent routers.

B. *Compiling or Interpreting*
There are two approaches with regard to produce final executable test cases: compiling and interpreting. Essentially, this is a decision of making trade-offs

between on-line processing time and storage space. For following reasons, we have taken the first approach:

- On-line processing speed is important in CMPT-TS for testing the performance of high-speed routers. The interpretation approach relies on case-by-case on-line interpretation and therefore it has to repeatedly go through the interpretation process every time to run a test case (even for the same one). Furthermore, it is also not a favorable feature for future development of portable tester. Last but not the least, the TTCN compiler developed at Chengdu Institute of Computer Applications [8] has provided us with useful experiences.
- With this approach, test suite defined in CMPT-TDL can be discomposed into two parts: one for concurrency control executable for CMPTM and the other for TPT-s to be converted into TTCN-3 format. This helps to compare test cases derived from CMPTM with test cases directly specified with TTCN-3 (possible defined by others) and provides a means to utilize existing test cases in TTCN.

C. Single Computer System or Multi-computer System

For three reasons, we have finally decided to build CMPT-TS with multiple microcomputers: one PC server for TMPTM plus PC stations for TPT-s.

- A single computer capable of supporting more than ten ports with different lower layers, especially the data link and physical layer, most likely requires a mini-computer. Therefore, the performance/price ratio of the system would be low compared with low-cost microcomputers.
- Another factor effecting our decision is the feasibility of making the TPT into a standalone portable tester in the future. The success of the OSI Transport protocol test system [9] in PCs has further strengthened our belief.

With this approach, test suites defined in TTCN-3 can still be used in TPT-s possibly with necessary modifications, which could save a lot of human power in test definition. Consequently, specification of a new test definition language – CMPT-TDL needs only to focus on test concurrency and coordination and leave ramification of single-thread test definition to TTNC-3.

4 Test Support Tools

4.1 Inadequacy of Existing TTCN and TTCN-3

TTCN (Trees and Tabular Combined Notation) has been around for many years as a standard semi-formal test definition language with two text-oriented and graphic versions [1]. However, it was designed for the four abstract test methods for end-systems, and for LTM and TTM for relay systems in the perception of only one or two testers involved in testing.

TTCN-3 is an extension to TTCN with the perception of parallel testing. It has defined a unified tester called the MTC (Main Test Component) and can be extended to multiple parallel test components called the PTC. It is supposed that this will enable to handle both the single thread test and multi-thread test in a testing system with a mechanism called "MESSAGE" to exchange information among multi-test threads. In other word, the perception of TTCN-3 is a single-machine model. More specifically, the current TTCN-3 is inadequate in following aspects:

A. It is difficult to be realized in a parallel testing system within a single machine to test a router with tens of ports, let alone the low performance/cost ratio of big machines.
B. Synchronization among parallel test threads in a computer is comparatively simple via inter-process communication. But for a multi-computer based test system, the mechanism - "MESSAGE" as defined in TTCN-3 needs to be refined in order to cope with problems of coordination, clock synchronization, message transmission delays between distributed CMPTM and TPT-s.
C. Writing parallel test cases with TTCN-3 is a big headache and error-prone since the definer has to consider both detailed test steps in a single thread and the interrelationship among multiple test threads. It would be better to decompose the definition process into two steps: one for global specification focused on parallelism and concurrency handling and the other for single-thread test details.

4.2 Extension to TTCN-3

According to the discussion in section 4.1, we have extended the TTCN-3 and focused on two aspects: addition of Macros to adapt to requirement in performance testing and new statements for synchronization and coordination.

A. *Macros for Specifying Data Required in Performance Testing*
Since TTCN is a conformance-testing oriented language, it lacks mechanism to define a large amount of data, which is vital in measuring parameters like throughput, transit delay, jitters. For this purpose, we have introduced a few global macro data, which can be predefined and included in data library.

- DATA SEQUENCE$_i$ – a mechanism for forming macro data by utilization of predefined data with a constraint on the sequence order of individual data. Its general format is: DATA SEQUENCE$_i$ [DATA$_m$, ..., DATA$_z$].
- BURST$_j$ – a mechanism for forming a large amount of data. A BURST may or may not need be synchronized at the time to be sent out among parallel test threads depending on the SYN bit, data length per packet and sending speed may also be specified. It is used for measuring quantifiable parameters, a synchronized BURST$_j$ would be most useful in testing of the response of an output port or ports when multi-port input bursts try to overwhelm to specific out ports. Its general format is: SYN BURST$_k$ [SYN, Total Length (KB), Basic Unit length (KB), Speed (KB/S)].

B. *New Mechanisms for Synchronization*
In order to adapt to the synchronization requirement between CMPTM and TPT-s, new synchronization mechanisms should be added to those in TTCN-3. Synchronization issues could be initiated by the CMPTM defined in CMPT-TDL or by a TPT specified in TTCN-3 test cases. Synchronization process involves a pair of message exchange between the CMPTM and a TPT. Initiatives from the CMPTM are

called Commands and require Response(s) from a TPT or TPT-s depending on whether a Command is a one-to-one or one-to-many command. Initiatives from a TPT are called Report or Request, and demand Instructions from the CMPTM. The mechanisms so far defined for TTCN-3 are represented as Statements in terms of programming languages, which include:

- ERROR REPORT [Condition, Error code] - whenever the Condition specified in TTCN-3 test case is met, an Error Report will be sent to CMPTM. Error codes at present can be "Timeout", "Channel Idle", "No Response", "Cannot Send", and "Request to exit". With more experiences, new error code may be needed. The ERROR REPORT is an enhancement to "OTHERWISE" in TTCN-3.
- Request for SYN [Condition, Last synchronized point] - whenever the Condition specified in TTCN-3 test case is met, a Request for SYN will be sent to CMPTM. The parameter "Last synchronized point" will be the name of previous test case completed. The response from the CMPTM could be "Sign out" to exclude a TPT in parallel testing, or "SYN confirmation" which will be broadcast to all TPT-s and indicate the name of test case to rerun.

It should be noted that new statements in TTCN-3 is not intended to replace the communication mechanism provided in TPT-s but to utilize underlying mechanisms those. Furthermore, those statements are used only whenever synchronization between the CMPTM and TPT-s must be specified in test cases explicitly.

4.3 Basics of CMPT-TDL

In this sub-section, we shall briefly describe the new features directly relevant to concurrent testing, rather than the details of the CMPT-TDL. As mentioned earlier, the necessity of the CMPT-TDL comes from complicity in specifying multi-thread test sets with TTCN-3. In other word, the functionality of CMPT-TDL is to handle the parallelism and concurrency in parallel testing without the need for specifying the details in single thread testing. Apart from statements used in ordinary programming languages, there are a few statements catered for this purpose in CMPT-TDL:

A. *Mechanisms for Management and Synchronization*
These are essentially Commands from CMPTM to TPT-s, which require responses from TPT-s.

- SYN Clock – This command will be used in CMPT-TDL to synchronize the clock whenever multiple test threads must start at the same time. The command will be broadcasted to all TPT-s and Synchronization will be done between CMPT-TS and TPT-s, therefore no parameter is needed in this statement.
- PARAMETERIZATION [TPT Id, Parameter list] – This is used to order TPT-s to parameterize the machines code test suite since they are generic and have to be adapted for the router under test and the TPT-s' configuration. The CMPTM will maintain a parameter list table for the router under test and the TPT-s' configuration. The content of the parameter list table come from three resources:

PIXIT of the router under test, system initialization of CMPTM and TPT-s, and those specified in test cases. This command requires responses from the TPT-s. This command also can be used in dynamic parameterization.

B. Macro Data

There two macro data corresponding to those added to TTCN-3: DATA SEQUENCE$_i$ and BURST$_j$, which can be used in specification and be parameterized.

4.4 Compilers, Executable Codes, and Parameterization

Test case support tools in CMPT-TS include CMPT-TDL compiler and the enhanced-TTCN-3 compiler. The CMPT-TDL compiler will first scan a concurrent test suite specified in CMPT-TDL to make syntax and semantic check as any other compiler of programming languages. One thing special about the CMPT-TDL compiler is that the final program in machine code will be distributed to the CMPTM and multiple TPT-s. Therefore, an important task for the compiler is to discompose a test suite/test group/test case into two parts. The codes for CMPTM mainly involve concurrent control and multi-thread management and synchronization, while the other will be parallel TTCN-3 test sets, each thread of test will be executed in a TPT. The TTCN-3 compiler, on the other hand, converts the test case in TTCN-3 into program code in "C", and in turn the C compiler will produce the machine codes.

It should be stressed that the program in machine code from the process mentioned above is not really executable since all test cases are defined for the same type of testing. They have to be parameterized before putting into test operation. For example, in testing routing functions of an IPv6 router, IPv6 address for each port has to be supplied to the CMPT-TS through control panel or predefined parameter tables. There are many other parameters, such as naming throughput for each port, and protocol stacks supported related to individual ports etc.

Table 2. Some Basic Elements of CMPT-TDL

Element name	Description
Arithmetic operator	+, -, *, /
Relational operator	and, or, not
Data types	NUMBER,STRING, TIME,POINTER,LIST,ARRAY,ENUMERATE
Basic Statement	Assignment-statement, select-statement, circle-statement
Macro	To easy to describe, some special macros are defined and some micros represent partial TTCN3 codes,
Function management	Every TPT's test cases are called by POINTER as a function in LIST.
Partial keywords	PACKET,INITIATE,SEND,RECEIVE,PORT, EXECUTE,ADDRESS,TPT[x],SYN,ERROR,LOG, PAIR,BURST,Vi

For the purpose of parameterization, ISO 9646 has provided a more systematic way, which requires user to provide a form called PIXIT (Protocol Implementation extra Information for Testing) to testing authorities before testing. Table.2 shows some basic elements of CMPT-TDL.

5 Epilogues

The work presented in this paper is still in its experimental stage, and there are many works have to be done before the CMPT-TS is put into full test service. The main reason is the compiler has not been finished yet. However, by translating test cases manually into C codes, and compiling them into executable test cases, authors have had some simple tests for IP routers. These tests have shown its merits over existing practices on router testing, not only in performance testing but also in conformance testing. It can advance test efficiency largely, compared with existing test systems. One test can finish former multiple tests. On other hand, test becomes simpler and more flexible. Only changing few configurations, operator can finish different tests. The use of CMPT-TDL makes test definition simpler and clearer. It breaks a new path for concurrent test definition. The authors wish that this work could be helpful for testing community in widening the scope of testing and in exploring concurrent testing techniques.

Acknowledgement

The work presented in this paper is part of the research work on a new network architecture called SUPA (Single-layer User Plane Architecture) sponsored by NSFC (Natural Science Foundation of China). In SUPA, a set of application protocols has been added to the Internet protocol stacks and been used in its Signaling and Management planes. Testing of the Internet protocols in SUPANET router involves not only those in Internet routers, but also the new functions. The authors wish to acknowledge the financial support from NSFC. Our thanks also go to our colleagues at SC-NetComLab for their efforts in this project.

References

1. ISO/IEC JTC1/SC21, "Information System Technology - Open System Interconnection – Conformance Testing Methodology and Framework" (part 1 – 7), March 14, 1994
2. Huaxin Zeng and Dave Rayner, "Gateway Testing Technique", in: "Protocol Specification, Testing, and Verification", IV edited By Y. Yemini, and etc., North-holland Publishers,1984, pp. 637 – 656
3. Huaxin Zeng, Xun Zhou, and Bo Song, "On Testing of IP Routers", in: Proceedings of PACAT03, IEEE press,,PP. 535–540, Aug (2003).
4. Interoperability Laboratory, http://www.iol.unh.edu/
5. MingWei Xu,JianPing Wu, "An Extension to Concurrent TTCN", In: Proceedings of IEEE INFOCOM98, San Francisco, U.S.A. March,1998. 447–454

6. Will E. Leland, et al., "On Self-similar Nature of Ethernet Traffic", IEEE/ACM Transactions on Networking, Vol. 2, No 1, February 1994, pp. 1–15.
7. 6-bone project, http://www.6bone.net/
8. 8 L. X. Wang, H. X. Zeng et al., "An Executable Test Case Generation Tool - the CICA TTCN Tool Kit", in: Proceedings of International Conference on Communication Technology", Sep. 1992, Beijing, China.
9. C. S. He, H. X. Zeng et al., "A Benchmark on the Design of ferry based Test Systems", in: Proceedings of 4th IFIP International Workshop on Protocol Test Systems (IWPTS), Leidschendam, Netherlands, October 1991.

A Temporal Consensus Model

Hengming Zou

Department of Computer Science and Engineering,
Shanghai Jiao Tong University,
Shanghai, China 200030
zou-hm@cs.sjtu.edu.cn

Abstract. The active (state-machine) replication protocol has been one of the commonly adopted approaches to provide fault tolerant data services. In such a scheme, service state is replicated at all participating servers and client requests are presented to *all* the servers. A strict consensus protocol executed by the servers ensures that all servers receive all the requests in the same order. The output of each request from all the servers are then compared to mask the result of faulty server(s). However, the overhead associated with running the strict consensus protocol tends to slow down the response to client requests, which makes it unsuitable for real-time applications where timing predictability is a necessity. This paper presents a weak consensus model called "temporal consensus" that reduces such overhead and enable the active scheme to meet the timing constraint of real-time applications.

Keywords: Replication, weak consensus, temporal consensus, x-kernel.

1 Introduction

Active replication is a commonly used approach by modern systems to provide fault-tolerant data services. However, due to the overhead associated with running the consensus protocol, traditional active replication model is unsuitable for real-time applications where timing dependability is a necessity.

Consider the case that a client requests the value of an object. If the value is static or the frequency of change is small such that there is enough slack between two successive updates for the replicas to reach a consensus on the value of the object, then the replicas can give the client an exact answer. Now, suppose the object's value changes frequently such that the slack between two successive updates is not enough for the system to reach an agreement. Then it is unclear what the correct behavior would be for the replicas. Since the data could go through many changes as the query is spreading among the servers, each replica may hold a different value for the object when the query is received at each replica. Traditional solutions to this problem involve either holding back the response until the servers reach a consensus or letting the servers take a vote and sending the value that the majority servers agree on to the client.

However, there are serious flaws in the above two approaches. if the frequency of change is high, then there may not be enough slack between any two successive updates for the consensus protocol to run to completion. Hence, the servers may never reach a consensus (provided that data loss is not permitted). Moreover, the time the consensus protocol takes would delay the response to clients, which could lead to violation of timing constraints imposed by the target real-time applications. The problem for the second approach is that an answer is not guaranteed in a real-time environment because the data are continuously changing and there may not exist any single value that is agreed upon by a majority of servers.

The solution to the above problem lies in the relaxation of the requirement that the value returned must be a copy of the object that is agreed upon by all correct replicas. Since many applications do tolerate some staleness of data, a value that not all correct processes agree on could still be acceptable for these applications, provided that such a value is within some limited bound of the copies on all correct processes. Hence, we relax the criteria for the traditional consensus agreement to the requirement that all correct processes agree on a limited range of values for the object. We call this kind of consensus *weak consensus*.

In a weak consensus environment, a replica can send a response to the client as long as the value is within the acceptable range, and the client can then simply pick any of the responses (if many) it receives as a correct answer. Thus, we avoids the costly consensus protocol and the voting process.

Next we present the detail of a weak consensus protocol and construct a real-time active replication service that achieves a balance between fault tolerance and timing predictability.

2 Temporal Consensus

Under weak consensus, the requirement for consensus is weakened to that all correct processes agree on some range of values for the object. Two values that are within some bounded range from each other are said to be consistent with each other. The "range" used here can be specified on a variety of domains such as value, version, and time. In this paper, we choose time as the "range" domain because we are mainly concerned with real-time applications where time is the basic element. In such case, consistency is achieved if the timestamp of the last update of the object on one replica is within some bound of the timestamps of the last update for the same object on other replicas.

Next we present our assumptions before defining the concept of *temporal consensus*.

2.1 Assumptions

For simplicity, we assume the existence of a clock synchronization mechanism. We also assume that processes can suffer crash or performance failures. (We do not assume Byzantine or arbitrary failures.) Send omissions and receive omissions are also allowed, e.g., due to transient link failures, or discard by the receiver, due to corruption or buffer overflow. Permanent link failures (resulting in network partitions) are not considered. We also assume that the environment is deterministic, i.e. the pattern and probability of a fault occurring is known or can be bounded.

Furthermore, we assume that a message is either delivered in bounded time or the message is never delivered. Thus, by taking into consideration of the probability of failure, we can schedule enough updates to ensure that messages are delivered in bounded time.

2.2 Temporal Consensus Model

We define a system to be in a *temporal consensus* state if the timestamps of the copies on all correct replicas for the same object are within some bound of some time units with each other. Let T_i^s denote the timestamp of the last update for object i at server s, δ denote the bound on the range of timestamp for the same object, then temporal consensus requires that the difference between the timestamps of the same object on different servers be bounded by the given constraint, i.e. $|T_i^s(t) - T_i^r(t)| \leq \delta, i = 1, 2, \ldots, m$, where m is the total number of objects in the system. This concept is illustrated in Figure 1.

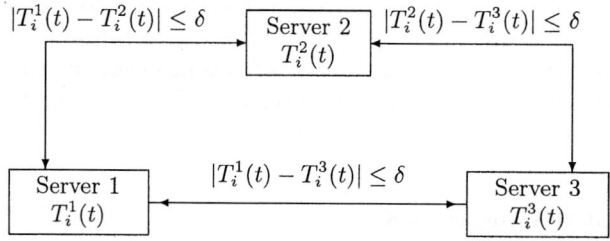

Fig. 1. System View of Temporal Consensus

Next we define two types of temporal consensus: *strict* and *sequential*. Each type of temporal consensus is useful for one class of applications.

2.3 Strict Temporal Consensus

From the perspective of a client, strict temporal consensus is achieved if any read to a data object in the server group returns a value whose timestamp is no more than δ time units earlier than the timestamp of the last write of the same data object in the system. Let $W(x,t)$ denote the operation that writes data item x with a value of timestamp t, $R(x,t)$ denote the operation that reads data item x with a returned value of timestamp t. ThenFigure 2 shows examples of legal and illegal operations under this strict temporal consensus model (x-axis represents real time line).

Below, we give an update protocol that maintains strict temporal consensus among a collection of cooperative processors. We divide update messages into

$$\frac{P_1:\ W(x,t_1)}{P_2:\qquad R(x,t_2)}$$
cond: $t_2 \geq t_1 - \delta$

$$\frac{P_1:\ W(x,t_1)}{P_2:\qquad R(x,t_2)}$$
cond: $t_2 < t_1 - \delta$

(a) Legal operation   (b) Illegal operation

Fig. 2. Strict Temporal Consensus

two categories. One is called *ordinary updates* issued by the client, the other is called *forced updates* issued by another server. Forced update must be done regardless of the status of the server's last update and acknowledgement is required. Forced update messages can also be regarded as consensus messages in some sense. If we let t_h denote the timestamp of the last update for the concerned object at a local host, let t_m denote the timestamp of the incoming message, then a protocol that achieves strict temporal consensus is as follows:

Every process p executes the following:

receive(m,t_m) occurs as follows:
  if m is an ordinary update message **then**
    if $t_m \leq t_h$ **then**
      discard the message
    else
      update object and its timestamp locally
      multicast a forced update message

  if m is a forced update message **then**
    send acknowledgement to the *sender*
    if $t_m > t_h$ **then**
      update object its timestamp locally

The above algorithm achieves strict temporal consensus if there is no fault in the system and messages are delivered in bounded time. In case of message transmission error, we can modify the multicast behavior by scheduling enough forced updates to ensure that updates arrive at destinations in bounded time.

2.4 Sequential Temporal Consensus

Not all applications require the same level of temporal consensus. For example, in modern programming practice, people writing parallel programs do not assume any order of execution between instructions of separate programs. But the order within each program is fixed. This kind of practice, in real-time applications, can in effect be supported by an even weaker consensus semantics. Sequential temporal consensus extends the basic form of temporal consensus and addresses this class of practice. It is achieved if the result of any execution is the same as if the operations of all processors were executed in some sequential order, and the operations of each individual processor appear in this sequence in the order specified by its program, and *each read returns a value whose timestamp is no more than δ time units apart from the timestamp of the value written by the latest write proceeding the read in this sequence.*

P_1:	$W(x, t_1)$
P_2:	$R(x, t_2), R(x, t_3)$
cond:	$t_2 \geq t_1 - \delta, t_3 \geq t_1 - \delta$
Legal:	$W(x, t_1), R(x, t_2), R(x, t_3)$

P_1:	$W(x, t_1)$
P_2:	$R(x, t_2), R(x, t_3)$
cond:	$t_2 < t_1 - \delta, t_3 \geq t_1 - \delta$
Legal:	$R(x, t_2), W(x, t_1), R(x, t_3)$

P_1:	$W(x, t_1)$
P_2:	$R(x, t_2), R(x, t_3)$
cond:	$t_2 < t_1 - \delta, t_3 < t_1 - \delta$
Legal:	$R(x, t_2), R(x, t_3), W(x, t_1)$

P_1:	$W(x, t_1)$
P_2:	$R(x, t_2), R(x, t_3)$
cond:	$t_2 \geq t_1 - \delta, t_3 < t_1 - \delta$
Illegal:	no possible sequential sequence

Fig. 3. Legal and illegal sequential consensus

Figure 3 depicts some legal and illegal operations under the sequential temporal consensus model. In the illegal case, the only sequence that satisfies the conditions of $t_2 \geq t_1 - \delta$ and $t_3 < t_1 - \delta$ is $R(x, t_3), W(x, t_1), R(x, t_2)$ which violates the program order of processor P_2.

An alternative but equivalent view of the sequential temporal consensus is as follows: if a read returns a value whose timestamp is no more than δ units apart from the timestamps of some writes, then all subsequent reads must return a value that is no more than δ time units earlier than those of the same writes. In other words, a later read is at least as, if not more than, temporally consistent as an earlier one. In light of this alternative view, two processors need not see the same sequence of operations as long as every pair of neighboring reads in each individual sequence is temporally consistent, i.e. their corresponding timestamps are no more than δ time units apart. For example, P_1 may see a sequence of $R_1 R_2 R_3$ while P_2 may see the sequence of $R_2 R_1 R_3$. As long as R_1 is temporally consistent with both R_2 and R_3, and R_2 is temporally consistent with R_3, then sequential temporal consensus is preserved in this instance. In fact, we have the following theorem:

Theorem 1. *If for every process p, and the sequence of neighboring reads observed by p, $R = \{R_1 R_2 \ldots R_n\}$, the condition $R_{i+1} \geq R_i - \delta$ holds for all $i \in \{1, 2, \ldots, n\}$, then sequential temporal consensus is achieved.*

In essence, sequential temporal consensus guarantees that a later read always returns a better value in the temporal sense. It is not difficult to see that sequential temporal consensus is a relaxation of the basic form of temporal consensus since it does not guarantee that any particular read returns a value that is temporally consistent with any particular write. To ensure this, explicit semaphore or synchronization mechanisms should be used. Using the same notations we introduced in strict temporal consensus, we can write a similar protocol that achieves sequential temporal consensus among a collection of cooperative processors. Due to space limit, we omit the protocol.

3 Prototype Construction

We have constructed a real-time active replication system with sequential temporal consensus within the x-kernel framework. Due to the page limit imposed by LNCS, this section is removed from the original manuscript. Interested parties please contact the author for the omitted part.

4 Prototype Performance

Our prototype evaluation considers three performability metrics: *average response time*, *average maximum inter-server temporal distance*, and *average probability of temporal consensus*. These metrics are influenced by several parameters, including client write rate (minimum time gap between two successive updates), temporal constraint, number of objects accepted, communication failure, and optimization.

4.1 System Response Time

Figure 4 depicts average system response time with (a) showing the metric as a function of the number of objects accepted in the system for a fixed temporal constraint of 100ms and (b) showing the graph as a function of the temporal constraint placed on the system for a fixed number of objects of 500. From the graphs, we see that the average client response time is fast for both graphs, ranging from 0.23 to 0.4ms, which means the system is indeed suitable for real-time applications. The fast response time was the result of the decoupling of client request processing from server updates and internal communication within the server group. The relaxation of the traditional consensus requirement to temporal consensus is also a significant contributor.

Other facts we observe from the graphs include: (1) the number of objects only has a modest impact on the response time. This is due to the fact that the admission control in the system acts as a gate keeper that prevents too many objects from being admitted. (2) temporal constraint has an inverse impact on the response time. (3) For the same number of objects or the same value of temporal constraint, the smaller the minimum time gap (the more frequent the updates are), the longer the response time. This is because more frequent updates consume more resources and hence leave less resources for processing client requests, which consequently increase the response time.

4.2 Inter-server Temporal Distance

One objective of our temporal consensus model is to bound data inconsistency between any two replicas to a given range. Figure 5 shows the *average maximum*

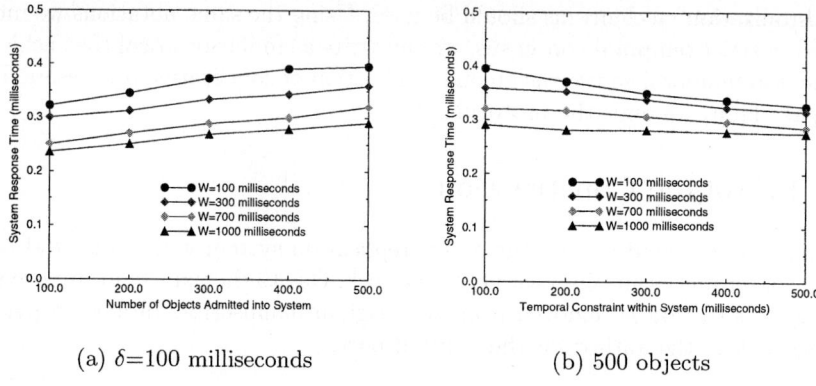

(a) δ=100 milliseconds

(b) 500 objects

Fig. 4. Average Response Time of RTA

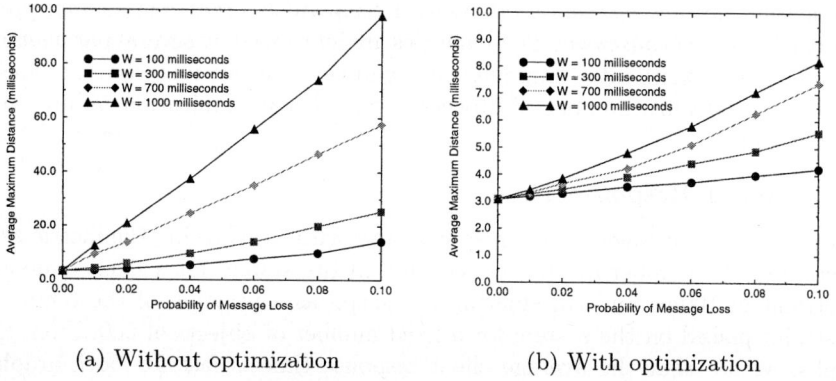

(a) Without optimization

(b) With optimization

Fig. 5. Maximum Inter-Server Temporal Distance

inter-server temporal distance as a function of the average probability of message loss between any two communicating servers. The difference between graph (a) and (b) is that optimization is introduced in (b). Both graphs plot the average maximum temporal distance for various minimum time gaps between successive updates.

From the figures, we see that the average maximum inter-server temporal distance between any two servers is roughly the one way message transmission time of 3ms when there is no message loss. However, as message loss rate goes up, the distance also increases. Graph (b) shows that optimization has a significant impact on the average maximum temporal distance.

We conclude from the graphs that the performance of the prototype is good when message loss rate is low. But as message loss rate goes up, the performance could become unacceptable to some applications if no optimization is used. The graph that uses message optimization has a better performance under severe message loss because the impact caused by message loss is compensated to some extent by the optimization since it schedules as many updates to the other servers as system resources allow.

4.3 Probability of Temporal Consensus

In this experiment, we take snapshots of system state at regular time intervals. For each snapshot, if the replicas are in temporal consensus, we count it as a consistent snapshot. We then sum up the total number of temporally consistent snapshots and divide it by the total number of snapshots to derive the probability. Figure 6 shows the average probability of temporal consensus within the system as a function of the temporal constraint. The difference between (a) and (b) is that (a) does not use optimization while (b) uses optimization to ensure better performance.

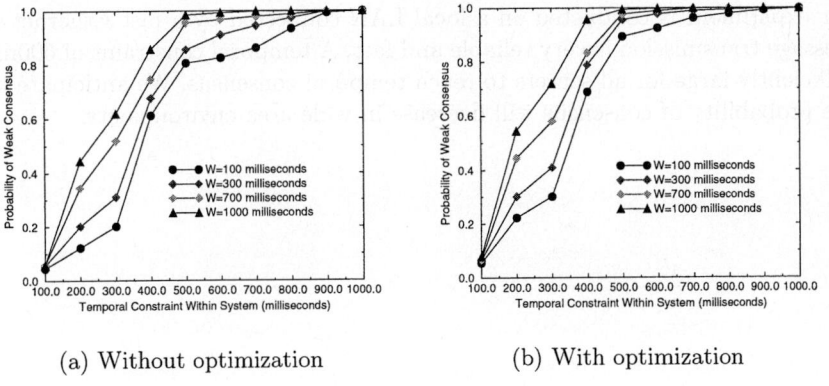

(a) Without optimization   (b) With optimization

Fig. 6. Average Probability of Temporal Consensus

From the graphs, we see that the average probability of temporal consensus is lower for smaller temporal constraint and update time gap. This is because the smaller the temporal constraint, the harder it is to achieve temporal consensus because the message delivery takes time and the temporal constraint may not allow sufficient slack for the message to be delivered. Furthermore, the more frequent the updates are (the smaller the update time gap), the more updates need to be broadcasted to the system to achieve temporal consensus which may be difficult as the available system resources are bounded.

The comparison between (a) and (b) shows that optimization significantly improves performance with respect to probability of temporal consensus in the system. Overall, the performance is improved by about 35%. A re-draw of the graphs in Figure 7 depicts more clearly the improvement.

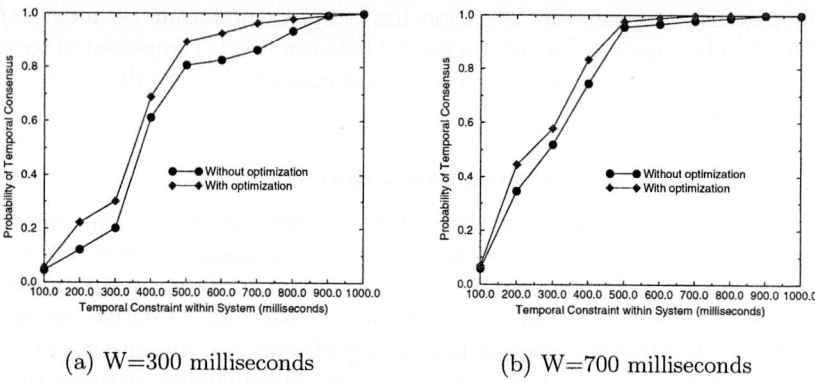

(a) W=300 milliseconds (b) W=700 milliseconds

Fig. 7. Probability of Temporal Consensus

With or without optimization, we see that the system remains in a temporal consensus state if the temporal constraint is 600ms or larger. This is because our experiment is conducted on a local LAN connected by a fast Ethernet and message transmission is very reliable and fast. A temporal constraint of 600ms is sufficiently large for all servers to reach temporal consensus. We anticipate that the probability of consensus will decrease in wide area environments.

Automatically Generalized Ontology System for Peer-to-Peer Networks

Boon-Hee Kim and Young-Chan Kim

ChungAng Univ., Bobst-Hall 5 floor, System Software Lab,
Dept. of Computer Science & Engineering,
Seoul, 221, 156-756, Republic of Korea
bhkim@sslab.cse.cau.ac.kr

Abstract. The P2P(Peer-to-Peer) system basically has search engine as its main module, and the search engine aims to ensure fastness and accuracy when searching information resources. Likewise, to ensure the best accurate search technology, the application of Semantic Web techniques is deemed to be optimal. Although experiments have been conducted gradually to apply Semantic Web technologies to P2P systems, there has been no case of automatically creating Semantic Web technologies in configuring existing or new P2P systems. In this paper, we present a structure to automatically create Semantic Web technologies (functioning to extract accurate semantic information) in P2P systems.

1 Introduction

This research gave its first priority to accuracy in all of its searched results instead of cutting search-time in searching through relevant techniques. Although many techniques have been provided to cut search-time, this research sought to address problems surrounding P2P systems that do not guarantee the accuracy of search-result objects. Also, this paper sought to research the methods of applying a module that guarantees the accurate search-result to the existing P2P systems with the least modification, and of creating P2P systems without in-depth knowledge on Semantic Web in designing the P2P system that guarantees the accurate search-result. With various P2P systems, their search resources vary[6]. Of various education and multimedia resources, search resource tends to be integrated. This paper aimed to design a structure to reflect this exclusivity.

Ontology, which clarifies the concept and relations of resources, must first be defined in order to provide search linkage chains between peers of target and actual data, namely, in order to implement Semantic Web. These ontology's are created by domain experts, but this paper sought to use ontology's within various domains already created by many experts and provide interfaces for users to reconfigure (ontology's) to fit the use of P2P systems being designed. Likewise, this paper sought to provide structures to configure users' questions into Metadata questions in P2P systems and treat them, as well as modules that are required in the process of actually matching Semantic Web resources. This research focused on the reuse of existing models as

Semantic Web application models in Index Server-based P2P system, and on the expandability and user convenience as developed Semantic Web models.

This paper is organized as follows: the next section describes the automatic generated ontology. Section 3 presents the structure of P2P system based on semantic web. Section 4 concludes the paper and discussed future works.

2 Automatic Generated Ontology

Semantic Web is created based on XML and RDF, and in implementing Semantic Web, ontology describes the meaning of terminologies contained Web texts, which is necessary for the upper level of RDF. The ontology's are expressed by many domain experts in various formats of mark-up languages[1][3][8]. And, to create ontology's fitting P2P system developers using these various formats, the ontology search step must first be accomplished. This paper follows the Metadata search format, DCME(Dublin Core Metadata Initiative)[7], for search keyword, in searching ontology. According to search keywords, ontology crawlers transfer search-result of relevant ontology, and the user chooses his desired ontology of these outputs. In case ontology is updated to boost its search efficiency, outputs should be created after entries are made in relevant DCME elements.

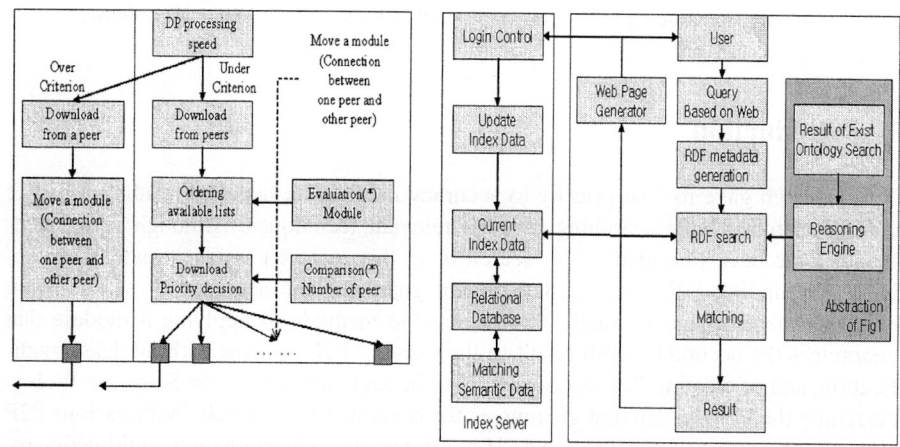

Fig. 1. Connection between Download Peer and Index Server

3 Structures of Peer-to-Peer System Based on Semantic Web

After completing the process of searching the existing ontology and making the use of the outcome, the research sought to use selected ontology and create Semantic Web-based P2P systems. The paper verified the application in Index Server-based P2P systems. Figure 1 shows the connectivity between the peer that intends to download resources and Index Server. The peer that intends to download resources must basically conduct the process of search first. The user first completes the process of logging in to Index Server, and then asks Web-based questions. Likewise, this questioning itself is the selected ontology-based RDF metadata, which is automatically created and undergoes the process of RDF search. The search step undergoes a complete search of Index Server's current RDF-based index data. Index Server, based on the login information of peers, renews existing index data for the last time, and presents index data comprised of semantic data to relevant peers. The data resulting from this process show their values by the user's web browser through the web page creator.

Download Peer is given the right to select peers from among a list of popularity order-arranged peers that own relevant resources. The popularity here is assessed by the number of downloads and accuracy of the same resources, and serves as the criteria for the Download Peer user to select relevant peers. The list, basically, features peers in the order of popularity, and also shows the current status of the network, thus enabling the Download Peer user to select peers after considering the time in downloading relevant resources and have a wider scope of choice. Likewise, certain peers tend to intensively be selected, and this should be improved through further research.

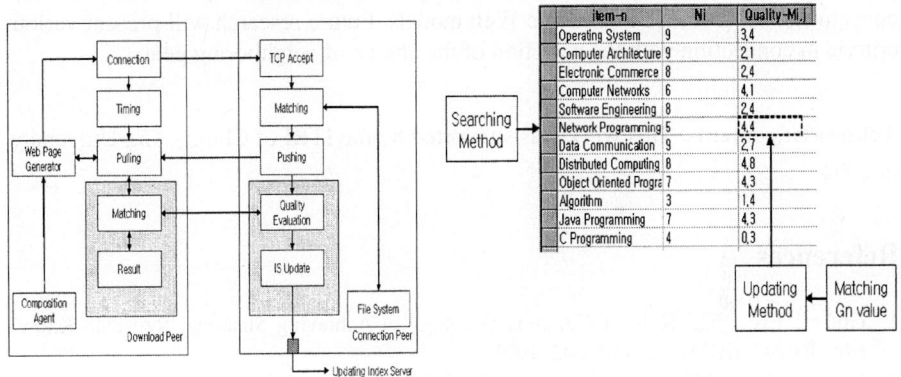

Fig. 2. Connection between Connection Peer and Download Peer

After Connection Peer(Peer of including resource), determined by Download Peer, receives Download Peer requirements, it undergoes the process of Figure 2 and provides relevant resources to Download Peer. Download Peer's demand for connection first leads to the right treatment result in the process of Connection Peer's acceptance of the connection, and the relevant file is transferred to Download Peer after searching through Connection Peer's file system and finding the file matching the required file. Likewise, the module of identifying whether the required file matches the found file and selecting the file is significant. Download Peer determines whether the downloaded file is correct or not, and the Connection Peer's popularity management module sends the evaluation of the updated file. The peer that downloaded the final result value generated through this process presents the resulting value through Web user interface by the Web page creator helped by CA.

Index Server receives renewed Connection Peer information from Connection Peer, and renews the index in realtime. Based on the renewed information sent from Connection Peer, the file undergoes the examination of its popularity, and if it exceeds a certain critical value, and is copied to neighboring peers. The selection of neighboring is limited to directly connected peers, and random selection is adopted. If the critical value is lower than a certain critical value, the outcome value is renewed through statistical addition operation, and this is informed to the relevant peer. Future research will present various criteria in connection with the selection of the choice of neighboring peers.

4 Conclusions and Future Works

This paper sought to use ontology's within various domains already created by many experts and provide interfaces for users to reconfigure (ontology's) to fit the use of P2P systems being designed. Likewise, the paper sought to provide structures to configure users' questions into Metadata questions in P2P systems and treat them, as well as modules that are required in the process of actually matching Semantic Web resources. This research focused on the reuse of existing models as Semantic Web application models in Index Server-based P2P system, and on the expandability and user convenience as developed Semantic Web models. Future research will present various criteria in connection with the selection of the choice of neighboring peers.

Acknowledgements. This work was supported by the ITRI of Chung-Ang University in 2004.

References

1. Gruber, T.R., "The Role of Common Ontology in Achieving Sharable, Reusable Knowledge Bases", KR'91, pp.601-602, 1991.
2. Brian McBrids, "Jena: Implementing the RDF Model and Syntax Specification", http://www-uk.hpl.hp.com/people/bwm/papers/20001221-paper
3. Aditya Kalyanpur, and so on, "SMORE-Semantic Markup, Ontology, and RDF Editor", http://www.mindswap.org/papers/SMORE.pdf
4. Boon-Hee Kim, Young-Chan Kim, "Ptops Index Server for Advanced Search Performance of P2P System with a Simple Discovery Server", GCC2003, 2003.
5. Ian Horrocks, "DAML+OIL: A Description logic for the Semantic Web, IEEE Bulletin of the Technical Committee on Data Engineering, vol.25, no.1, pp. 4-9, 2002
6. David Liben-Nowell, Hari Balakrishnan, and David Karger. Analysis of the evolution of peer-to-peer systems. In Proceedings of ACM Conference on Principles of Distributed Computing, 2002.
7. Dublin Core Metadata Element Set, http://www.dublincore.or.kr
8. Welty, Ferrucci, "A formal ontology for re-use of software architecture documents", Automated Software Engineering, pp. 259-262, 1999.

Locabus: A Kernel to Kernel Communication Channel for Cluster Computing

Paul Werstein, Mark Pethick, and Zhiyi Huang

Department of Computer Science,
University of Otago,
Dunedin, New Zealand
{werstein, mpethick, hzy}@cs.otago.ac.nz

Abstract. This paper proposes a kernel to kernel communication system for use in cluster computers. It is implemented directly on the Ethernet data link layer. This allows use of Ethernet's inherent broadcast capability. This system is implemented and performance tests are run. The results show significant improvement in broadcast performance.

1 Introduction

Many of the operations of cluster computers and the parallel processes running on them rely on some message passing system. The underlying network protocol for such message passing is usually TCP/IP or UDP/IP. The goal of this research is to develop a high performance, reliable, lightweight communications channel for use in cluster computers. This channel makes use of Ethernet's broadcast capability as well as providing point-to-point communications.

In the cluster environment, we can make optimizations over TCP/IP since there is no need for routing. Ethernet switches are commonplace, and we can assume a highly reliable network where packet loss is rare.

The proposed communications channel is called Locabus. It provides a reliable, connectionless, datagram-based service for broadcast traffic within a cluster computer environment. It also provides for point-to-point communications. It is implemented as a kernel module for the Linux kernel.

The rest of this paper is organized as follows. Section 2 describes related work. Section 3 give the details of the Locabus implementation. A preliminary set of performance results are given in Section 4. Finally, we give conclusions and directions for further research in Section 5.

2 Related Work

Many reliable broadcast and multicast protocols have been proposed for wide area networks. Examples of broadcast protocols include [1, 2]. Examples of multicast protocols are [3–8]. In contrast, this research concentrates on broadcast in a cluster of computers. Such an environment allows us to take advantage of the characteristics of the environment including rather reliable transmission, short delays, and lack of need for routing decisions.

Lane, Daniels, and Yuan in [9] study a cluster environment, but their studies are based on implementing multicast using the UDP interface. In this research, our approach is implemented directly on the Ethernet interface rather than using UDP/IP. This approach contrasts with [10] which implements MPI by modifying the Ethernet device driver.

Four types of protocols can be used to assure reliability of broadcast or multicast transmissions: sender-initiated, receiver-initiated, tree-based, or ring-based protocols [11]. In the sender-initiated approach, a message is broadcast and each receiver unicasts an ACK to the sender. This leads to the ACK implosion problem with a large number of nodes. In the receiver-initiated approach, receivers inform the sender when they detect an error or missing packet. Quite often a polling technique is used to determine periodically that receivers are alive and have received all messages. In a tree-based protocol, nodes are divided into groups with each group having a leader. The group leader is responsible for reliable delivery within the group and informing the sender of errors. In a ring-based protocol, receivers take turns being the token site. The token site is responsible for sending an ACK to the sender. Receivers send NAKs to the token site when they detect an error. Since the token site rotates among the receivers, the sender can determine the status of the receivers.

3 Locabus

In designing the Locabus communications system, certain assumptions are made to take advantage of the cluster environment. These assumptions include:

- The underlying network is Ethernet. This allows use of its broadcast capabilities. The network is unreliable, but the error rate is very low.
- An Ethernet switch is used so collisions are rare.
- All nodes in the cluster are on a private network with a gateway to any public network. The gateway takes care of authentication of any outside communications. Thus there is no need for authentication or encryption between nodes. There also is no need for routing.
- The underlying operating system is homogenous. In this case, Linux is used. It is not necessary that the machines be homogenous in capabilities or processor type.

To minimise administration, Locabus employs a distributed, self-discovery technique. As nodes are booted in the cluster, they periodically broadcast a discovery message for up to one minute. The existing nodes reply with a list of the nodes they know about. Thus each node learns about the presence of all other nodes.

Timestamps are used to detect reconnects. A reconnect causes other nodes to reset the information they maintain about the reconnected node. This action provides for an orderly recovery from a node which fails and recovers. A probe function is provided to deal with missing nodes.

The Locabus packet header is shown in Table 1. The *type* field specifies the type of packet. Currently implemented types include: data, ACK, NAK, connection establishment. The *proto* field specifies the protocol for the packet. The currently implemented protocols are described in Section 3.2. The *node_to* and *node_from* fields specify the source and destination for the packet. This allows for 65,535 nodes in a cluster. 0xFFFF is the address used for broadcast. Currently, the lower 16 bits of the IP address are used for these fields since they are unique in the cluster and require no additional administration.

Table 1. Locabus packet

Field	Type	Description
type	__u8	Packet type
proto	__u8	Application protocol identifier
node_to	__u16	Recipient node (0xFFFF = broadcast)
node_from	__u16	Sending node
seq_num	__u16	Packet Sequence Number
ack_num	__u16	Ack num if ack packet
len	__u16	Packet length including header
window	__u16	Current credit window of sender
csum	__u16	16 bit checksum of data + header

Seq_num is the packet sequence number. Locabus numbers packets, not bytes as in TCP/IP. *Ack_num* is an acknowledgment number if the packet is performing acknowledgment. Piggyback ACKs are used when possible. The total length of the packet including the header is specified in the *len* field. *Window* is used to implement a TCP/IP-style credit system for the number of unacknowledged packets allowed. Finally, *csum* is a 16 bit checksum of the data and header. The data follows the header. The data size can be up to 1484 bytes to maintain compatibility with the underlying Ethernet network.

The Locabus system uses a 3-way handshake to establish connections. The disconnect is done by a 2-way handshake. The kernel maintains 160 bytes of state data per connection in contrast to 360 bytes required for TCP.

3.1 Flow Control

When doing point-to-point or unicast communication, a go-back-N flow control scheme is employed. The window size is 1024 with an acknowledgment time of 0.2 seconds. Locabus uses 2 levels of cache for socket buffers. The first level is a set of per node buffers with the hardware headers precomputed. The second level is a set of general buffers.

For broadcast communication, Locabus uses a NAK based protocol with polling and random acknowledgment. This design prevents the ACK implosion problem associated with ACK based broadcast and is simpler to implement than a tree based or ring based protocol. It also reduces the workload on the receivers.

3.2 Implementation Details

Figure 1 shows the overall design of the system. The basic Locabus system is implemented as a kernel module. This is shown in the figure as the *mod_locabus* box.

Currently two protocols are implemented using Locabus. Those protocols are locamonitor, and locasock. They are shown on the figure just below the dashed line dividing kernel space from user space. The boxes for *LocaExec* and *load balancing* represent research in process. Work is ongoing on a complete implementation of MPI [12] called *LocaMPI*. Currently only the broadcast and send/receive functions are implemented.

LocaSock implements a socket interface using Locabus as the communications channel instead of TCP/IP or UDP/IP. LocaSock provides a reliable datagram service with a maximum datagram size of 64KB. Existing UDP socket code can be used simply by changing the domain from *AF_INET* to *AF_LOCABUS*. The LocaSock header is shown in Table 2.

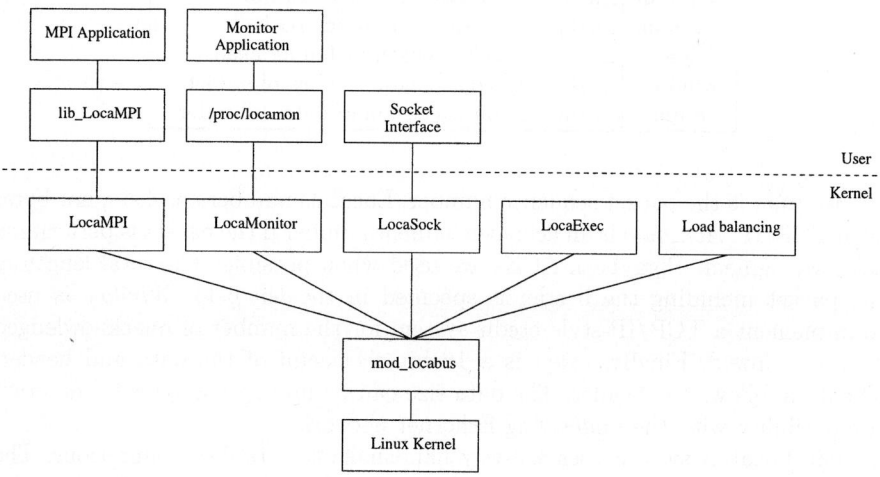

Fig. 1. Design of Locabus

Table 2. LocaSock header

Field	Type	Description
sport	_u16	Source Port
dport	_u16	Destination Port
ident	_u16	Fragmentation Identifier
frag	_u8	fragment number
nfrags	_u8	Number of fragments for packet

Sport and *dport* are the source and destination port numbers respectively. *Ident* is a fragmentation identifier and *frag* is the fragment number. *Nfrags* is a count of the total number of fragments in the packet.

LocaMonitor is a distributed cluster monitoring protocol. It also is implemented as a kernel module. Each node which runs LocaMonitor periodically broadcasts statistics such as CPU utilisation, memory usage, and disk and network statistics. These statistics are collected by all nodes which maintain the data in the */proc* filesystem. A separate display application reads the */proc* files and displays the data in an humanly readable form. The data will be used in the future for load balancing.

4 Performance Results

To determine the efficiency of the Locabus implementation, we conduct a benchmark of communication time. It compares the time to send data over the standard TCP/IP interface with the time for Locabus.

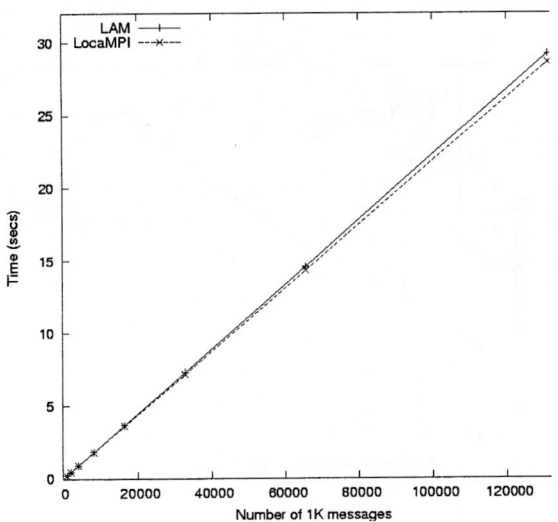

Fig. 2. Send/receive benchmark

For this test, we implement MPI_Send(), MPI_Recv(), and MPI_Bcast() using Locabus as the underlying communications system. These functions are the message sending, receiving, and broadcasting functions of MPI, respectively. We compare these functions to the same functions that exist in the LAM implementation of MPI. This removes any computational costs associated with a particular application.

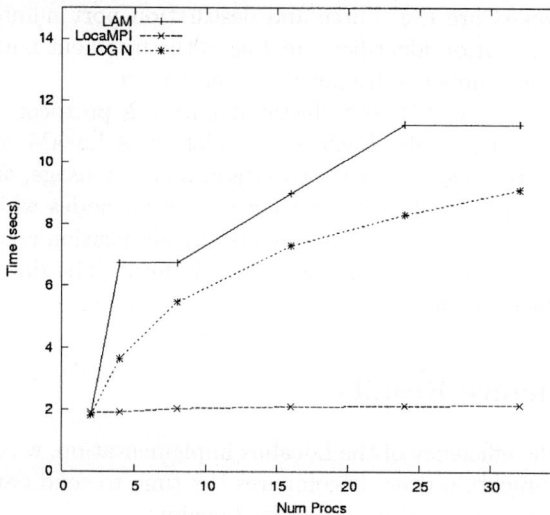

Fig. 3. Broadcast benchmark (8192 1KB messages)

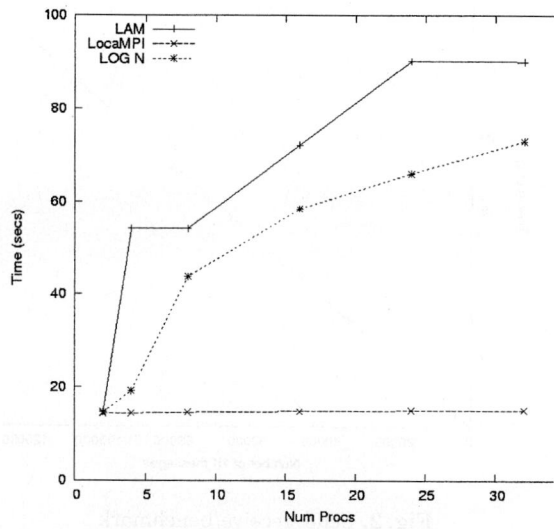

Fig. 4. Broadcast benchmark (65,536 1KB messages)

The first benchmark tests the send/receive performance. It compares the time to send/receive a varying number of 1KB messages between two nodes. The results are shown in Figure 2. As expected, Locabus exhibits only a slight performance increase owing to having not to use the IP layer software. The performance increases slightly with increasing number of messages due to the smaller overhead and smaller packet header size.

The second benchmark compares the performance of the broadcast performance for 8192 1KB messages and 65,536 1KB messages with a varying number of nodes. The results are shown in Figures 3 and 4, respectively. In this benchmark, a root node broadcasts a series of 1KB messages, and the receivers send a single acknowledgment.

In both broadcast tests, LocaMPI outperforms standard MPI. The time for LocaMPI is almost constant with a slight increase in time as the number of nodes increases. This is due to the increasing number of ACKs required. For LAM/TCP is increase is slightly worse than $O(\log_2 N)$. (The $\log_2 N$ line is shown on the figures for reference.) This result is due to the need to decompose the broadcast into a series of unicast messages.

5 Conclusions

In this paper, we present a kernel to kernel communication system implemented directly onto the Ethernet data link layer. This implementation allows the use of Ethernet's broadcast capability. The implementation is called Locabus.

Over the Locabus software, a number of protocols are built. They include a socket interface (locasock) with is similar to Berkeley sockets. Locamonitor allows each node to know the status of all other nodes. It makes extensive use of Locabus's broadcast capability. A MPI-like interface for parallel programming, called LocaMPI, is partially implemented.

Our tests compare the LocaMPI's send/receive and broadcast performance to that of standard MPI. The broadcast benchmark tests show considerable performance compared to using MPI over TCP/IP.

We are continuing to explore ways to use Locabus in a cluster environment. The LocaMPI implementation is being developed so it has most of the functions contained in the MPI standard. A set of parallel applications will be benchmarked to determine their performance when using LocaMPI. Other areas currently under investigation include load balancing and remote process submission and monitoring.

References

1. Kaashoek, M., Tanenbaum, A., Hummel, S., Bal, H.: An efficient reliable broadcast protocol. ACM SIGOPS Operating Systems Review **23** (1989) 5–19
2. Melliar-Smith, P., Moser, L., Agrawala, V.: Broadcast protocols for distributed systems. IEEE Transactions on Parallel and Distributed Systems **1** (1990) 17–25
3. Barcellos, M., Ezhilchelvan, P.: An end-to-end reliable multicast protocol using polling for scalability. In: Proceedings of the Conference on Computer Communications (IEEE INFOCOM'98), San Francisco, California, USA (1998) 1180–1187

4. Crowcraft, J., Paliwoda, K.: A mulitcast transport protocol. ACM SIGCOMM Computer Communication Review **18** (1988) 247–256
5. Floyd, S., Jacobson, V., Liu, C.G., McCanne, S., Zhang, L.: A reliable multicast framework for light-weight sessions and application level framing. IEEE/ACM Transactions on Networking **5** (1997) 784–803
6. Holbrook, H., Singhal, S., Cheriton, D.: Log-based receiver-reliable multicast for distributed interactive simulation. ACM SIGCOMM Computer Communication Review **25** (1995) 328–341
7. McKinley, P., Rao, R., Wright, R.: H-RMC: A hybrid reliable multicast protocol for the Linux kernel. In: Proceedings of the IEEE/ACM SC-99 Conference, Portland, Oregon, USA (1999)
8. Talpade, R., Ammar, M.: Single connection emulation (SCE): An architecture for providing a reliable multicast transport service. In: Proceedings of the 15th International Conference on Distributed Computing Systems (ICDCS '95), Vancouver, Canada (1995) 144–151
9. Lane, R., Daniels, S., Yuan, X.: An empirical study of reliable multicast protocols over Ethernet-connected networks. In: Proceedings of the 2001 International Conference on Parallel Processing (ICPP'01), Valencia, Spain (2001) 553–560
10. Dougan, C.: KMPI: Kernel-level message passing interface. Technical report, Finite State Machine Labs (2003) http://hq.fsmlabs.com/~cort/papers/kmpi/kmpi.pdf.
11. Levine, B., Garcia-Luna-Aceves, J.: A comparison of reliable multicast protocols. Multimedia Systems **6** (1998) 334–348
12. Gropp, W., Lusk, E., Skjellum, A.: A high-performance, portable implementation of the MPI message passing interface standard. Parallel Computing **22** (1996) 789–828

View-Oriented Parallel Programming and View-Based Consistency

Z. Y. Huang[†], M. Purvis[‡], and P. Werstein[†]

[†] Department of Computer Science,
[‡] Department of Information Science,
University of Otago,
Dunedin, New Zealand
{hzy, werstein}@cs.otago.ac.nz, mpurvis@infoscience.otago.ac.nz

Abstract. This paper proposes a novel View-Oriented Parallel Programming style for parallel programming on cluster computers. View-Oriented Parallel Programming is based on Distributed Shared Memory. It requires the programmer to divide the shared memory into views according to the nature of the parallel algorithm and its memory access pattern. The advantage of this programming style is that it can help the Distributed Shared Memory system optimise consistency maintenance. Also it allows the programmer to participate in performance optimization of a program through wise partitioning of the shared memory into views. The View-based Consistency model and its implementation, which supports View-Oriented Parallel Programming, is discussed as well in this paper. Finally some preliminary experimental results are shown to demonstrate the performance gain of View-Oriented Parallel Programming.

1 Introduction

A Distributed Shared Memory (DSM) system can provide application programmers the illusion of shared memory on top of message-passing distributed systems, which facilitates the task of parallel programming in distributed systems. Distributed Shared Memory has become an active area of research in parallel and distributed computing with the goals of making DSM systems more convenient to program and more efficient to implement [1–9].

The consistency model of a DSM system specifies ordering constraints on concurrent memory accesses by multiple processors, and hence has fundamental impact on DSM systems' programming convenience and implementation efficiency. The Sequential Consistency (SC) model [10] has been recognized as the most natural and user-friendly DSM consistency model. The SC model guarantees that *"the result of any execution is the same as if the operations of all the processors were executed in some (global) sequential order, and the operations of each individual processor appear in this sequence in the order specified by its (own) program"* [10](p690). This means that in an SC-based DSM system, memory accesses from different processors may be interleaved in any sequential order that is consistent with each processor's order of memory accesses, and the orders of memory accesses observed by different processors are the same. One way to strictly implement the SC model is to ensure all memory modifications be totally ordered and memory modifications generated and executed at one processor be propagated to and executed in that order at other processors instantaneously. This implementation is correct but it suffers from serious performance problems [11].

In practice, not all parallel applications require each processor to see all memory modifications made by other processors, let alone to see them in order. Many parallel applications regulate their accesses to shared data by synchronization, so not all valid interleavings of their memory accesses are relevant to their real executions. Therefore, it is not necessary for the DSM system to force a processor to propagate **all** its modifications to **every** other processor (with a copy of the shared data) at **every** memory modification time. Under certain conditions, the DSM system can select the *time*, the *processor*, and the *data* for propagating shared memory modifications in order to improve the performance while still appearing to be sequentially consistent [12]. For example, consider a DSM system with four processors P_1, P_2, P_3, and P_4, where P_1, P_2, and P_3 share a data object x, and P_1 and P_4 share a data object y, as shown in Fig. 1. The data object v is shared among processors at a later time not shown in this scenario.

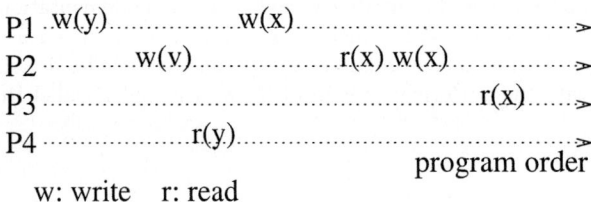

w: write   r: read

Fig. 1. A scenario of a DSM program

Suppose all memory accesses to shared data objects are serialized among competing processors by means of synchronization operations to avoid data races. Under these circumstances, the following three basic techniques can be used for optimisation of memory consistency maintenance [12].

- Time selection: Modifications on a shared data object by one processor are propagated to other processors *only at the time* when the data object is to be read by them. For example, modifications on x by P_1 may be propagated outward only at the time when either P_2 or P_3 is about to read x.
- Processor selection: Modifications on a shared data object are propagated from one processor to *only one other processor* which is the next one in sequence to read the shared data object. For example, modifications on x by P_1 may be propagated to P_2 (but not to P_3) if P_2 is the next one in sequence to read x.

– Data selection: Processors propagate to each other *only those shared data objects* that are really shared among them. For example, P_1, P_2, and P_3 may propagate to each other only data object x (not y and v), and P_1 and P_4 propagate to each other only data object y (not x).

To improve the performance of the strict SC model, a number of Relaxed Sequential Consistency (RSC) models have been proposed [9, 13–17], which perform one or more of the above three selection techniques. RSC models can be also called conditional Sequential Consistency models because they guarantee Sequential Consistency for some class of programs that satisfy the conditions imposed by the models. These models take advantage of the synchronizations in data race free (DRF) programs and relax the constraints on modification propagation and execution. That means modifications generated and executed by a processor may not be propagated to and executed at other processors immediately. Most RSC models can guarantee Sequential Consistency for DRF programs that are *properly labelled* [14] (i.e., explicit primitives, provided by the system, should be used for synchronization in the programs).

However, properly-labelled DRF programs do not facilitate data selection in consistency models. There has been some effort exploring data selection in consistency models. Examples are Entry Consistency (EC) [16], Scope Consistency (ScC) [17], and View-based Consistency (VC) [9]. Either they have to resort to extra annotations, or they cannot guarantee the SC correctness of some properly-labelled DRF programs. For example, EC requires data objects to be associated with locks and barriers and ScC requires extra scopes to be defined, while VC cannot guarantee the SC correctness of some properly-labelled DRF programs [18]. Those extra annotations are inconvenient and error-prone for programmers. To facilitate the implementation of data selection in consistency models with the SC correctness intact, we propose a novel parallel programming style for DSM, called View-Oriented Parallel Programming (VOPP). This programming style can facilitate data selection in consistency maintenance. Sequential Consistency can be guaranteed for the VOPP programs with the presence of data selection in consistency maintenance.

The rest of this paper is organised as follows. Section 2 presents the VOPP programming style and some program examples. Section 3 presents the VC model being associated with VOPP and its correctness. Section 4 discusses implementation issues of the VC model. Section 5 compares VOPP with related work. Section 6 presents and evaluates the preliminary performance results. Finally, our future work on VOPP is suggested in Section 7.

2 View-Oriented Parallel Programming (VOPP)

A *view* is a concept used to maintain consistency in distributed shared memory. A view consists of data objects that require consistency maintenance as a whole body. Views are defined implicitly by the programmer in his/her mind, but are explicitly indicated through primitives such as *acquire_view* and *release_view*. Ac-

quire_view means acquiring exclusive access to a view, while *release_view* means having finished the access.

The programmer should divide the shared memory into views according to the nature of the parallel algorithm and its memory access pattern. Views must not overlap each other. The views are decided in the programmer's mind and must be kept unchanged throughout the whole program. A view must be accessed by processors through using *acquire_view* and *release_view*, no matter if there is a data race or not in the parallel program. Before a processor accesses any objects in a view, *acquire_view* must be called; after it finishes operations on the view, *release_view* must be called. For example, suppose multiple processors share a variable A which alone is defined as a view, and every time a processor accesses the variable, it needs to increment it by one. The code in VOPP is as below.

```
acquire_view(1);
A = A + 1;
release_view(1);
```

A processor usually can only get exclusive write access to one view at a time in VOPP. However, VOPP allows a processor to get access to multiple views at the same time using nested primitives, provided there is at most one view to write (in order that the DSM system will be able to detect modifications for only one view). The primitives for acquiring read-only access to views are *acquire_Rview* and *release_Rview*. For example, suppose a processor needs to read arrays A and B, and puts their addition into C, and A, B and C are defined as different views numbered 1, 2, and 3 respectively, a VOPP program can be coded as below.

```
acquire_view(3);
acquire_Rview(2);
acquire_Rview(1);
C = A + B;
release_Rview(1);
release_Rview(2);
release_view(3);
```

To compare and contrast the normal DSM programs and VOPP programs, the following parallel sum problem is used, which is very typical in parallel programming. In this problem, every processor has its local array and needs to add it to a shared array. The shared array with size *a_size* is divided into *nprocs* views, where *nprocs* is the number of processors. Finally the master processor calculates the sum of the shared array. The normal DSM program is as below.

```
for (i = 0; i < nprocs; i++) {
  j=(i+proc_id)%nprocs*a_size/nprocs;
  k=((i+proc_id)%nprocs+1)*a_size/nprocs;
  for (;j < k;j++)
      shared_array[j] += local_array[j];
  barrier(0);
}
```

```
if(proc_id==0){
  for (i = a_size-1; i > 0; i--)
    sum += shared_array[i];
}
```

The VOPP program has the following code pattern.

```
for (i = 0; i < nprocs; i++) {
  j=(i+proc_id)%nprocs*a_size/nprocs;
  acquire_view((i + proc_id)%nprocs);
  k=((i+proc_id)%nprocs+1)*a_size/nprocs;
  for (;j < k;j++)
    shared_array[j] += local_array[j];
  release_view((i + proc_id)%nprocs);
}

barrier(0);

if(proc_id==0){
  for(j=0;j<nprocs;j++)acquire_Rview(j);
  for (i = a_size-1; i > 0; i--)
    sum += shared_array[i];
  for(j=0;j<nprocs;j++)release_Rview(j);
}
```

In the VOPP program, *acquire_view* and *release_view* primitives are added, while the normal DSM program only uses barriers. These primitives do not add much complexity to the VOPP program. On the contrary, they make the programmer feel more clear about which part of the shared array a processor needs to access. However, these primitives generate messages in DSM systems. The more primitives are used, the more messages have to be passed in DSM systems. By comparing the above two programs, it seems the VOPP program will generate more messages. But if we look more closely at the two programs, we can find the VOPP program has reduced the number of barriers since it uses view primitives to achieve exclusive access and thus does not need barriers in the first *for* loop. This advantage enables programmers to optimise VOPP programs by reducing barriers, since barriers tend to be more time-consuming than the view primitives (which will be demonstrated in our experimental results).

Read-only access to views can be explicitly declared with *acquire_Rview* and *release_Rview* in VOPP. Programmers can use them to improve the performance of VOPP programs, since multiple read-only accesses to the same view can be granted simultaneously, so that the waiting time for acquiring access to read-only views is very small. Programmers can use them to replace barriers and read/write view primitives (*acquire_view* and *release_view*) wherever possible to optimise VOPP programs.

The VOPP style allows programmers to participate in performance optimization of programs through wise partitioning of shared objects into views and wise use of view primitives. VOPP does not place an extra burden on programmers since the partitioning of shared objects is an implicit task in parallel programming and VOPP just makes the task explicit. In this way, parallel programming is less error-prone in terms of handling shared objects.

More importantly, VOPP offers a huge potential for efficient implementations of DSM systems. When a view primitive such as *acquire_view* is called, only the data objects associated with the related view need to be updated. Therefore some optimal consistency maintenance protocol can be designed based on this simplicity, and data selection can be achieved straightforwardly.

VOPP requires that a view be defined initially and not changed throughout the program. In this way, it has placed some restriction on programming and thus has brought some inconvenience to the programmer. To offer some flexibility to the programmer, we provide some primitives such as *merge_views* to merge views into a global view as done in TreadMarks' barriers and/or to redefine views at some stage of a program. The price paid for this flexibility, of course, is the DSM efficiency.

To demonstrate more about the features of VOPP, we provide the following VOPP program for a task-queue based parallel algorithm. In the algorithm every processor can access the task queue to either enqueue a new task or dequeue a task. Before a processor enqueues a new task it generates a new view for the new task with *acquire_view*(−1) which will return a system-chosen view id. The VOPP code is as below.

```
V = acquire_view(-1);
create_task(T);
release_view(V);
T.view_id = V;
acquire_view(0);
enqueue(task_queue, T);
release_view(0);
```

When a processor dequeues a new task, the VOPP code is shown below. V and T are local variables, and T is a structure with a pointer element pointing to a shared task.

```
acquire_view(0);
dequeue(task_queue, T);
release_view(0);
V = T.view_id;
acquire_view(V);
consume_task(T);
release_view(V);
```

3 View-Based Consistency

A processor will modify only one view between *acquire_view* and *release_view*, which should be guaranteed by the programmer. Therefore, we can detect modified data objects for each view in order to achieve view consistency.

Consistency maintenance in views requires updating data objects of a view when a processor calls *acquire_view*. More precisely, the following consistency condition is given for the View-based Consistency (VC) model that supports the VOPP programs. Any implementation of VC should satisfy the condition.

Definition 1. *Condition for View-Based Consistency*

- Before a processor P_i is allowed to access a view by calling *acquire_view*, all previous *write* accesses to data objects of the view must *be performed with respect to* P_i according to their causal order.

A write access to a data object is said to *be performed with respect to* processor P_i at a time point when a subsequent read access to that object by P_i returns the value set by the write access.

In VOPP, barriers are only used for synchronisation and have nothing to do with consistency maintenance for DSM.

Since a processor will modify only one view between *acquire_view* and *release_view*, which should be guaranteed by the programmer, we can detect modified data objects for each view and use them later to maintain the consistency of the view.

SC Correctness

Processors are synchronised to modify the same view, one after another, but may modify different views concurrently in any view-oriented parallel program. Based on this observation, for any parallel execution of a view-oriented parallel program, we can produce a global sequential order of the modifications on views. In this sequential order, the modifications on the same view are ordered in the same way as the synchronised order of the parallel execution, and the modifications on different views are put in program order if they are executed sequentially in the program; otherwise they are parallel and put in any order. Parallel modifications on different views can be executed in any order, which will not affect the execution result. Obviously, according to the consistency condition for VC, the parallel execution result of the program under VC is the same as the above sequential execution of the modifications. Therefore, a global sequential order has been found to match the parallel execution result under VC. According to the definition of the SC model, VC can guarantee Sequential Consistency for view-oriented parallel (VOPP) programs.

In this way, VC achieves time selection (at the time of calling *acquire_view*), processor selection (by passing an updated view to the next processor waiting to access the view), and data selection (by updating only the data objects of the view).

Any implementation of the VC model should conform with the above consistency condition. There are two important technical issues in the implementation: view detection and view consistency. View detection means identifying all the data objects (particularly modified objects) of a view. View consistency means updating all the modified data objects of a view before a processor gets (exclusive) access to the view using *acquire_view*.

Correctness and accuracy are two important issues in view detection. A correct view should include all data objects that are previously modified while the view is exclusively accessed. An accurate view should include those and only those data objects. The correctness of view detection must be satisfied in a VC implementation, while inaccuracy of view detection may only affect its performance (e.g., propagation of irrelevant modifications of data objects).

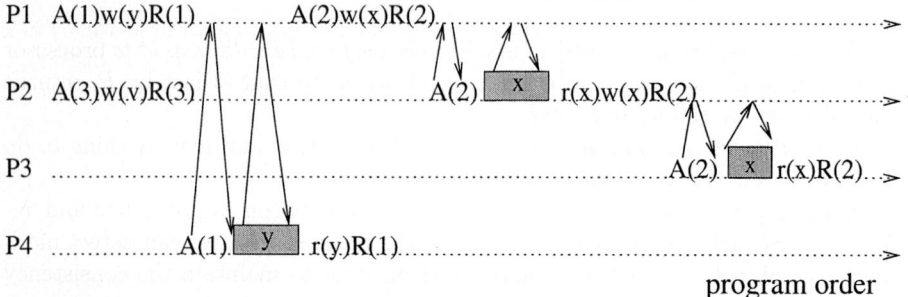

w: write   r: read   A: acquire_view   R: release_view

$\boxed{x}$: request update on x and update x at the processor

Fig. 2. View-based Consistency in action

Fig. 2 shows how the VC model works. In Fig. 2, there are two views numbered 1 and 2. View 1 includes y when P_4 enters the view, and view 2 includes x when P_2 and P_3 enter the view. When P_4 enters view 1, only the modification of y is propagated to the processor to update the view. For P_2 and P_3, only the modification on x is propagated to them to update view 2. The view acquisition and modification propagation are separate in the figure, but they can be combined in an implementation in order to improve DSM performance, i.e. the modifications can be piggy-backed on the *release_view* message.

In the following section, we will discuss our implementation of the VC model.

4   Implementation

We have implemented the VC model based on TreadMarks [7], which is a page-based DSM system. In TreadMarks, a *diff* is used to represent modifications on a page. Initially a page is write-protected. When a write-protected page is first modified by a processor, a *twin* of the page is created and stored in the system space. When the modifications on the page are needed, a comparison of the *twin* and the current version of the page is done to create a *diff*, which can then be used to update copies of the page in other processors. We use this same mechanism in our view detection. We associate all modifications (in the form of diffs) made between *acquire_view* and *release_view* with the related view.

We have also implemented the VC model based on the home-based protocol [19], in which every page has a home node (processor) and the diffs of a page are passed to its home to maintain an up-to-date copy (called home page), and thus to update a page is to fetch the home page from the home node. This home-based implementation uses pages to represent data objects, which is a coarse-grained solution to data selection.

4.1 View Detection

In consistency maintenance we only need to know which are the modified data objects and then update them. Likewise, to maintain the consistency of a view, we only need to update the modified data objects in the view. Therefore, we are not interested in the unchanged pages of a view and thus only the modified parts of pages (in the form of diffs) are recorded for the related view in our implementation of view detection.

In our implementation, view detection is achieved at run time. We use the concept of interval in TreadMarks to represent view modifications. An interval is a data structure which represents the modifications (e.g. diffs) made on a number of pages between *acquire_view* and *release_view*. We make an interval whenever a processor finishes updating a view by calling *release_view*. Note that when an interval is created, we make the diffs of related pages immediately. The diffs can be piggy-backed on the *release_view* message when another processor acquires access to the view, which is another potential optimisation for our VC implementation. When we implement VC with the home-based protocol, the diffs are passed to respective home nodes when an interval is created.

When an interval is created, it is associated with the related view whose ID number is the argument of the *release_view* causing the creation of the interval. This interval represents a modification of data objects in the view and will be used to update the view later when a processor accesses the view with *acquire_view*. Once an interval is created, the related view's version number is increased by one.

4.2 View Consistency

To achieve view consistency is to make a view up to date. When a view is to be accessed by a processor calling *acquire_view*, view consistency must be achieved for the view. Write notices are created according to the intervals associated with the related view and the current version number of the view of the calling processor. Those write notices are passed to the calling processor to invalidate the related pages. When an invalid page is accessed, a page fault will cause the processor to fetch the diffs (or to fetch the home page in the home-based consistency protocol). In this way view consistency is achieved.

View consistency is an area where we can improve the performance of the DSM system based on our VC model. In TreadMarks diffs are used to update pages, while home pages are used to update pages in the home-based protocol. In our experiments we found, when diffs are accumulating, more data and messages are passed through the network in TreadMarks than in the home-based protocol, since the cost of updating a page in the home-based protocol is constant and involves only one transmission of a page. Therefore, if we can merge accumulating diffs, transmission of diffs can be reduced.

5 Comparison with Related Work

VOPP is different from the programming style of Entry Consistency in terms of the association between data objects and views (or locks). Entry Consistency [16] requires the programmer to explicitly associate data objects with locks and barriers in programs, while VOPP only requires the programmer to implicitly associate data objects with views (in the programmer's mind). The actual association is achieved in view detection in the implementation of the VC model. VOPP is more flexible than the programming style of Entry Consistency.

VOPP is also different from the programming style of Scope Consistency in terms of the definition of view and scope. Views in VOPP are non-overlapped and constant throughout a program, while scopes in ScC can be overlapped and are merged into a global scope at barriers.

VOPP is more convenient and easier for programmers than the message-passing programming style such as MPI or PVM, since it is still based on the concept of shared memory (except the shared memory is divided into multiple non-overlapped views). Moreover, VOPP provides experienced programmers an approach to fine-tune the performance of their programs by carefully dividing the shared memory into views. Partitioning of shared memory into views becomes part of the design of a parallel algorithm in VOPP. This approach offers the potential for programmers to make VOPP programs perform as well as MPI programs.

6 Preliminary Experimental Results

In this section, we present our preliminary experimental results based on two (currently sub-optimal) versions of the VC implementation. The first VC version (called VC_d) uses diffs to update views, while the second one (called VC_h) uses the home-based protocol to achieve view consistency. Their performance is compared with that of the LRC (Lazy Release Consistency) model implemented in TreadMarks [7]. We have tested our implementations on two clusters. One cluster, called Vodca, consists of 8 PCs running Linux 2.4, which are connected by a 100 Mbps Ethernet hub. Each of the PCs has a 800 MHz processor and

128 Mbytes of memory. The other cluster, called Godzilla, consists of 32 PCs running Linux 2.4, which are connected by a N-way 100 Mbps Ethernet switch. Each of the PCs has a 350 MHz processor and 192 Mbytes of memory. The page size of the virtual memory for both clusters is 4 KB.

We chose one application, Integer Sort (IS), in the experiment because of the limited resources available for converting the applications to VOPP programs. *IS* (Integer Sort) is a benchmark application provided by TreadMarks research group. It ranks an unsorted sequence of N keys. The rank of a key in a sequence is the index value i that the key would have if the sequence of keys were sorted. All the keys are integers in the range $[0, B_{max}]$ and the method used is bucket sort. The problem size in our experiment is $(2^{25} \times 2^{15}, 40)$. The memory access pattern is very similar to the pattern of our sum example in Section 2. *IS* is an application that cannot demonstrate the performance advantage of our VC model since it does not need locks for synchronisation, but we will see how the VOPP program itself can improve its performance.

VC Versus LRC Versus VC_{vopp}

Table 1 shows the running time (in sec.) of IS on LRC and VC. VC_d is the VC implementation using diffs to update views, which is the same as the LRC implementation in TreadMarks. $VC_{d_{vopp}}$ shows the running time of an optimised VOPP program of *IS* which uses less barriers. The table shows the running time on the cluster Godzilla for 2 nodes, 4 nodes, 8 nodes and 16 nodes. The running time on one node is not displayed because it is abnormally large (around 4000 seconds) due to excessive memory usage on one node.

Table 1 shows that VC is generally more efficient than LRC, with a 21% performance gain on 16 nodes. The optimised VOPP program runs generally faster than the original one, with 8.5% performance gain on 16 nodes.

Table 1. Running time of IS on LRC and VC

	2-node	4-node	8-node	16-node
LRC	143.8	78.4	56.7	68.7
VC_d	144.6	77.5	51.5	54.3
$VC_{d_{vopp}}$	144.3	77.4	49.8	49.7

Table 2 shows the detailed statistics of IS on 16 nodes. In the table, Ba is the number of barriers called in the program, Ac is the number of lock/view acquire messages, Da is the total amount of data transmitted, Msg is the number of messages, and Rxm is the number of messages retransmitted. From the statistics we find the number of messages and the amount of data transmitted in VC are more than in LRC, which may not be the case in many other applications. Then why is the VC implementation faster than LRC? The reason is two-fold. The barriers in LRC need to maintain consistency while those ones in

VC do not. The consistency maintenance in barriers in LRC is normally time-consuming and centralised at one processor which can be a bottleneck, while consistency maintenance in VC is distributed among the processors through the view primitives.

Table 2. Statistics of IS on 16 nodes of Godzilla

	Ba	Ac	Da	Msg	Rxm
LRC	682	1	1.23G	123941	118
VC_d	682	20481	1.27G	180212	2
$VC_{d_{vopp}}$	122	20481	1.27G	163418	12

In addition, LRC has more message loss than VC according to the statistics. On 16 nodes of Godzilla, LRC has 118 retransmissions while VC only has 2 and 12 retransmissions. On 8 nodes of Vodca as shown in Table 3, the number of retransmissions in LRC is as high as 782. Nodes in Vodca are connected by a hub, so the bursty traffic at barriers causes more message loss. One message retransmission results in about 1 second waiting time. Therefore, the distribution of data traffic in VC can reduce message retransmissions and improve the performance of applications.

Table 3. Statistics of IS on 8 nodes of Vodca

	Time	Ba	Ac	Da	Msg	Rxm
LRC	324.7	362	1	285M	44288	782
VC_d	256.8	122	5121	297M	53255	410

Home-Based Versus Diff-Based Page Consistency

Table 4 shows the running time of IS on the two different VC implementations: VC_d and VC_h. The performance of VC_h is significantly better than that of VC_d when the number of nodes becomes larger. On 16 nodes of Godzilla, VC_h performs 40.9% faster than VC_d!

Table 4. Running time of IS on home-based and diff-based protocols

	2-node	4-node	8-node	16-node
VC_d	144.6	77.5	51.5	54.3
VC_h	143.6	75.5	43.5	32.1

The data (mainly diffs) transmitted in VC_d is significantly increased when the number of nodes is large. This diff accumulation problem affects the performance of diff-based implementations. The home-based implementation VC_h can resolve

Table 5. Statistics of IS on 16 nodes of Godzilla

	Time	Ba	Ac	Da	Msg	Rxm
VC_d	32.1	682	20481	1.27G	180212	2
VC_h	54.3	682	20481	0.235G	170727	0

diff accumulation by using home pages and thus reduce the amount of data transmitted, as demonstrated in Table 5. The amount of data reduced in VC_h is 81.5% compared with VC_d.

From the above results we realize that VC can be further improved if accumulated diffs can be integrated into a single diff. The single diff should integrate all previous modifications just as the home page does in home-based protocol. Also we can piggy-back those diffs associated with a view on the *release_view* messages. This improvement is one of our objectives for the near future.

7 Conclusions

We have proposed a novel VOPP programming style for DSM parallel programs on cluster computers. Our preliminary results have demonstrated the performance advantage of VOPP. We will use more applications to demonstrate its performance gain and its programming features. We will also investigate efficient implementation techniques of the associated VC model, such as an update protocol based on diff integration in order to integrate accumulated diffs for the same view. Our ultimate goal is to make shared memory parallel programs as efficient as message-passing parallel programs such as MPI programs.

References

1. Li, K., Hudak, P.: Memory coherence in shared virtual memory systems. ACM Trans. on Computer Systems **7** (1989) 321–359
2. Fleisch, B., Katz, R.H.: Mirage: A coherent distributed shared memory design. In: Proc. of the 12th ACM Symposium on Operating Systems (1989) 211–223
3. Lenoski, D. et al: The Stanford DASH multiprocessor. IEEE Computer **25** (1992) 63–79
4. Dasgupta, P. et al: The design and implementation of the Clouds distributed operating system. Computing Systems Journal **3** (1990)
5. Carter, J.B., Bennett, J.K., Zwaenepoel, W.: Implementation and performance of Munin. In: Proceedings of the 13th ACM Symposium on Operating Systems Principles (1991) 152–164
6. Bershad, B.N., Zekauskas, M.J., Sawsonm W.A.: The Midway distributed shared memory system. In: Proc. of IEEE COMPCON Conference, (1998) 528–537
7. Amza, C., Cox, A.L., Dwarkadas, S., Keleher, P., Lu, H., Rajamony, R., Yu, W., Zwaenepoel, W.: TreadMarks: Shared memory computing on networks of workstations. IEEE Computer **29** (1996) 18–28

8. Huang, Z., Lei,W.-J., Sun, C., Sattar, A.: Heuristic diff acquiring in Lazy Release Consistency model. In: Proc. of 1997 Asian Computing Science Conference (ASIAN'97) (1997) 98–109
9. Huang, Z., Sun, C., Purvis, M., Cranefield, S.: View-based Consistency and its implementation. In: Proc. of the First IEEE/ACM Symposium on Cluster Computing and the Grid (2001) 74–81
10. Lamport, L.: How to make a multiprocessor computer that correctly executes multiprocess programs. IEEE Transactions on Computers **28** (1979) 690–691
11. Tanenbaum, A.S.: Distributed Operating Systems. Prentice Hall (1995)
12. Sun, C., Huang, Z., Lei, W.-J., Sattar, A.: Towards transparent selective sequential consistency in distributed shared memory systems. In: Proc. of the 18th IEEE International Conference on Distributed Computing Systems, Amsterdam (1998) 572–581
13. Dubois, M., Scheurich, C., Briggs, F.A.: Memory access buffering in multiprocessors. In: Proc. of the 13th Annual International Symposium on Computer Architecture (1986) 434–442
14. Gharachorloo, K., Lenoski, D., Laudon, J.: Memory consistency and event ordering in scalable shared memory multiprocessors. In: Proc. of the 17th Annual International Symposium on Computer Architecture (1990) 15–26
15. Keleher, P.: Lazy Release Consistency for distributed shared memory. Ph.D. Thesis (Rice Univ) (1995)
16. Bershad, B.N., Zekauskas, M.J.: Midway: Shared memory parallel programming with Entry Consistency for distributed memory multiprocessors. CMU Technical Report (CMU-CS-91-170) Carnegie-Mellon University (1991)
17. Iftode, L., Singh, J.P., Li, K.: Scope Consistency: A bridge between Release Consistency and Entry Consistency. In: Proc. of the 8th Annual ACM Symposium on Parallel Algorithms and Architectures (1996)
18. Huang, Z., Sun, C., Cranefield, S., Purvis, M.: A View-based Consistency model based on transparent data selection in distributed shared memory. Technical Report (OUCS-2004-03) Dept of Computer Science, Univ. of Otago, (2004) (http://www.cs.otago.ac.nz/research/techreports.html)
19. Zhou, Y., Iftode, L., Li, K.: Performance evaluation of two home-based lazy release consistency protocols for shared virtual memory systems. In Proc. of the Operating Systems Design and Implementation Symposium (1996) 75–88

A Distributed Architecture of the Indirect IP Lookup Scheme for High-Speed Routers[*]

Jaehyung Park[1], Min Young Chung[2], Jinsoo Kim[3,**], and Yonggwan Won[1]

[1] Dept. of Electronics, Computer, & Information Eng., Chonnam National University,
300 Yongbong-dong, Puk-ku, Kwangju, 500-757, Korea
{hyeoung, ykwon}@chonnam.ac.kr
[2] School of Information and Communication Engineering, Sungkyunkwan University,
300, Chunchun-dong, Jangan-gu, Suwon, Kyunggi-do, 440-746, Korea
mychung@ece.skku.ac.kr
[3] Division of Computer and Applied Science, Konkuk University,
322, Danwol-dong, Chungju-si, Chungbuk, 380-701, Korea
jinsoo@kku.ac.kr

Abstract. In order that routers forward a packet to its destination, they perform IP address lookup which determines the next hop of an incoming IP packet by its destination address. Hence, IP address lookup is an important issue in designing high speed routers. For implementing a fast IP lookup scheme in high speed routers, this paper proposes a distributed architecture of the indirect IP lookup scheme which consists of several IP lookup engines. Also, we propose a simple rule for partitioning route entries among several IP lookup engines. And we evaluate the performance of the proposed scheme in terms of the memory required for storing lookup information and the number of memory accesses on constructing the forwarding table. With additional hardware support, the proposed scheme can drastically reduce the amount of required memory and the number of memory accesses for constructing the forwarding table.

1 Introduction

The increment of hosts and users and the enhancement of service quality cause the Internet traffic to be on the radical increase. Demand for the higher bandwidth requires faster packet transmission in physical media and faster packet processing in network routers [9]. Faster transmission media can be achieved by replacing their copper wires with optical fibers, and this work is on progress rapidly in the Internet backbone. However, researches on high speed routers have been going on in order to keep up with the transmission bandwidth of physical media.

A router plays an important role that performs an IP lookup in processing IP packets on the router. The router determines packets' output ports by IP

---

[*] This work was supported by Korea Research Foundation Grant(KRF-2003-003-D00255).
[**] Corresponding author.

lookup and forwards packets to them. The IP lookup is done by referencing the forwarding table, which maps packets' destination IP addresses to output ports. This IP lookup is performed by the longest prefix matching which has more computational overhead than the exact matching due to CIDR (Classless Inter Domain Routing) [5, 11].

To perform the longest prefix matching faster, IP lookup has been studied by using two general approaches. The first one is software-based schemes on trie data structure which were used as lookup methods in early routers [4, 10, 13]. However, software-based lookup schemes are not appropriate for current high speed routers. The second one is hardware-based schemes [2, 3, 6–8, 14]. To implement IP lookup scheme in hardware, there are three performance criteria; the number of memory access to lookup information in the forwarding table and the size of memory required to store information in the forwarding table should be as small as possible. Also it is required to fast update of information stored in the forwarding table.

Among these hardware-based schemes, the simplest IP lookup scheme is to construct the forwarding table for all IP addresses having 32 bits length under IPv4 environment. Then an output port can be obtained with only one memory access since the index of the forwarding table is the destination IP address within an incoming IP packet. So this scheme is called a *direct IP lookup scheme* [6]. However, this scheme is too large to be implemented because it requires $4G(=2^{32})$ entries for the forwarding table. To reduce the size of the forwarding table, an *indirect IP lookup scheme* has been proposed [2, 3, 6–8, 14]. Most of such a indirect lookup scheme, the forwarding table consists of two-level tables, which are called the primary and the secondary tables. Especially, Chung et al. [2] evaluated the performance of an indirect IP lookup scheme with two-level tables which is implemented in IQ2200 [12]. However, the lookup scheme with high performance needs to modify the already fabricated IQ2200 lookup chips.

In order to implement a fast IP lookup scheme for high speed routers, this paper proposes a distributed architecture of the indirect IP lookup scheme which is constructed from K same lookup engines having their own IP lookup chip. Also, we propose a simple rule for partitioning route entries into several IP lookup engines. In our distributed IP lookup scheme based on the indirect IP lookup, the prefix matching and the route updating are performed on only corresponding one of the K lookup engines which contains the IP address. We analyze the performance of the distributed IP lookup scheme on practical routing entries in terms of the memory required for storing lookup information and the number of memory accesses on constructing the forwarding table. The proposed indirect IP lookup scheme can be applied with the already fabricated IQ2200 lookup chips without modification, by using the prefix partitioning rule.

The paper is organized as follows. In Section 2, we propose a distributed architecture of the indirect IP lookup scheme and a prefix partitioning rule. We analyze the performance of the distributed IP lookup scheme in Section 3 and evaluate its performance by practical routing entries in Section 4. Finally we conclude in Section 5.

2 Distributed Architecture of the Indirect IP Lookup Scheme

Our distributed architecture of the IP lookup scheme consists of K lookup engines and a selector as shown in Figure 1. In each lookup engine, there are a checker and a IP lookup chip. Each IP lookup chip is implemented in the indirect IP lookup scheme and contains only specific route entries by a prefix partitioning rule. As another component of the lookup engine, the checker examines whether an inputted route entry exists in its lookup engine or not. Only if the entry does exist in its memory, the checker starts up performing operations such as lookup and update process. Otherwise, the checker does nothing but return null result. The selector returns non-null information on looked-up IP address among K lookup engines' results.

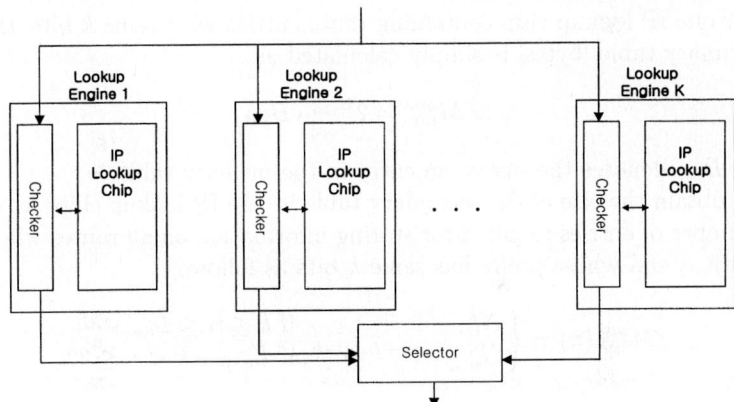

Fig. 1. Distributed architecture of the IP lookup scheme

IP address lookup for the incoming IP packet's address is processed in only one lookup engine which contains its address prefix. Lookup is proceeded in the same way of the indirect IP lookup scheme [2]. In order to perform IP prefix operations on our distributed architecture, it is necessary for an effective mechanism to partition the route entries into lookup engines. In our distributed IP lookup scheme, k bits are used as prefix partitioning mechanism, where $K = 2^k$. This mechanism partitions route entries with same k bit values at k identical bit positions, respectively. And then, the checker simply determines whether an inputted route entry exists in its own lookup chip or not, by comparing k bit positions.

By such a k-bits partitioning rule, the same k bits are useless in the IP lookup chip of the lookup engine containing such route entries. The reason is that the IP lookup chip contains only route entries with same k bit values at k identical bit positions. Therefore, the already fabricated IP lookup chip need not to be modified by the checker removing k bit positions from an inputted route entry.

3 Mathematical Analysis

In this section, we analyze the performance of the distributed IP lookup scheme designed from the indirect IP lookup chip [12]. To calculate the required memory size and the number of memory access, we define the following notations. In the notations, superscript k means that routes has same k bit values at k identical bit positions, respectively. Assume that the length of expansion bits in one IP lookup chip is L_{exp} and k identical bit positions are smaller than L_{exp}.

- N_n^k : Number of routes with prefix length n in a routing table
- $N_{n,D}^k$: Number of routes with prefix length n such that high $(L_{exp}+k)$ bits of the routes are different from those of other routes
- $N_{n,S,h}^k$: Number of routes with prefix length n such that high $(L_{exp}+k)$ bits of the routes are the same as those of other routes, where h is the largest prefix length among them.

For one IP lookup chip containing route entries with same k bits, the size of the primary table [bytes] is simply calculated as

$$M_{1st}^{one} = 2^{L_{exp}} \cdot B_{1st}, \quad (1)$$

where B_{1st} denotes the size of an entry in the primary table.

To obtain the size of the secondary table in one IP lookup chip, we calculate the number of entries required for storing information on all routes whose prefix length is n and whose prefix has same k bits as follows;

$$M_{2nd}^{one}(n) = \begin{cases} N_n^k, & \text{if } k \leq n \leq L_{exp}+k, \\ N_{n,D}^k \cdot 2^{n-L_{exp}-k}, & \text{if } L_{exp}+k < n \leq 32. \end{cases} \quad (2)$$

From Eq. 2, we obtain the size of required memory for storing information on all route entries with same k bits in the secondary table as the sum of $M_{2nd}^{one}(n)$ for all n $(1 \leq n \leq 32)$.

For one IP lookup chip containing route entries with same k bits, the lookup chips's memory size [bytes] is calculated as

$$M^{one} = 2^{L_{exp}} \cdot B_{1st} + \sum_{n=k}^{L_{exp}+k} N_n^k \cdot B_{2nd} + \sum_{n=L_{exp}+k+1}^{32} N_{n,D}^k \cdot 2^{n-L_{exp}-k} \cdot B_{2nd}, \quad (3)$$

where B_{2nd} denotes the number of bytes of an entry in the secondary table. Therefore, in our distributed architecture of the IP lookup scheme, the total size of required memory is sum of K lookup chips' required memory sizes. If any of k identical bit positions is larger than prefix length n for all route entries, the route entry should be expanded in order that a checker determines the entry's existence in its own IP lookup chip.

Information is inserted(deleted) into(from) the primary or the secondary tables whenever information on routes in a routing table is updated. The number of memory access depends on the characteristics of IP route entries, such as the prefix length, the size of expansion bits, and the relationship between prefixes of routes. To analyze the performance of the scheme under the worst condition, we consider that the primary and the secondary tables are newly constructed for a route insertion(deletion) request.

Updating a route whose prefix length is n and whose prefix has same k bits, the numbers of memory access to the primary and the secondary tables in one IP lookup chip can be obtained as

$$A_{1st}^{one}(n) = \begin{cases} N_n^k \cdot 2^{L_{exp}+k-n}, & \text{if } k \leq n < L_{exp} + k, \\ \sum_{h=n+1}^{32} N_{n,S,h}^k, & \text{if } L_{exp} + k \leq n \leq 32, \end{cases} \quad (4)$$

and

$$A_{2nd}^{one}(n) = \begin{cases} N_n^k, & \text{if } k \leq n < L_{exp} + k, \\ \sum_{h=n+1}^{32} N_{n,S,h}^k \cdot 2^{h-n}, & \text{if } n = L_{exp} + k, \\ N_{n,D}^k \cdot 2^{n-L_{exp}-k} + \sum_{h=n+1}^{32} N_{n,S,h}^k \cdot 2^{h-n}, & \text{if } L_{exp} + k < n \leq 32. \end{cases} \quad (5)$$

From Eqs 4 and 5, the total number of memory access for constructing the forwarding table in one lookup engine is calculated as

$$A^{one} = \sum_{n=1}^{32} [A_{1st}^{one}(n) + A_{2nd}^{one}(n)]. \quad (6)$$

The number of memory access for all forwarding entries is equal to that in one IP lookup engine, if all route entries are partitioned uniformly among K lookup engines. Therefore, in our distributed architecture of the IP lookup scheme, the total number of memory access for constructing the forwarding table on all route entries is equal to A^{one}.

4 Experimental Results

For evaluating the performance of the proposed scheme in terms of the required memory size and the number of table access, we use five samples of routing tables on different AS domains [1]. Assuming that L_{exp} be 18, B_{1st} be 4 bytes, and B_{2nd} be 32 bytes as same values in the already fabricated IQ2200 lookup chip.

Figure 2(a) shows prefix length distributions on five different AS domains. The ratios of prefixes whose lengths are 24 bits or less 99.89, 99.99, 99.61, 99.99, and 99.99 % for *AS 1, 234, 1668, 3277,* and *6079*, respectively. Especially, the number of routes whose prefix length is less than 8 is 0 for all AS domains. And Figure 2(b) shows the percentage of prefixes with 0 at each bit position for *AS 1, 1668,* and *6079*. Only 20% of prefixes on AS domains has 0 at 1st and 2nd bit position of prefixes. On the contrary, 80% of prefixes has 0 at 3rd bit position. From Figure 2(b), prefixes with 0 at some bit position are biased and unequally distributed. However, the percentage of prefixes with 0 whose bit position is larger than 9th bit position is nearly 50%, that is evenly distributed.

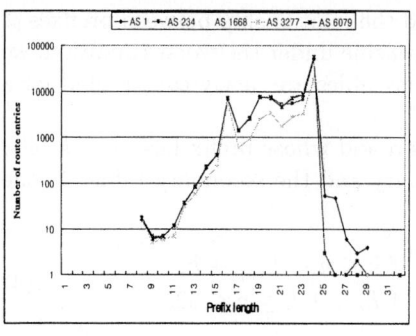 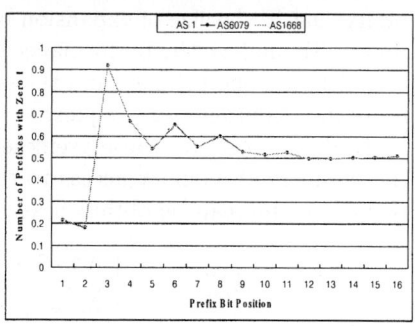

(a) Prefix Length Distribution (b) Prefix Bits Distribution

Fig. 2. Prefix length and bits distributions of five different AS domains (*AS 1* on Aug. 08, 2002, *AS 234* on Aug. 06, 2002, *AS 1668, 3277,* and *6079* on Sep. 05, 2002)

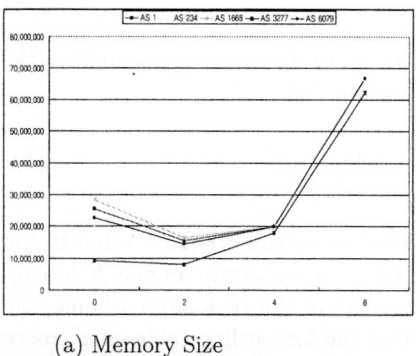 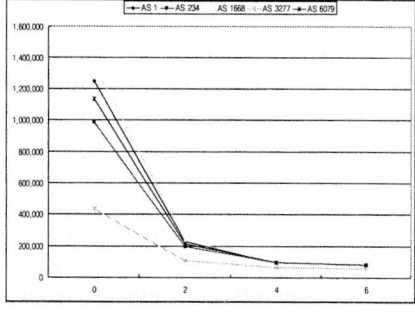

(a) Memory Size (b) Number of Memory Access

Fig. 3. Memory size and number of memory access varying the number of partitioning bits, k

As this result, the k bit positions of prefixes are chosen in larger than 9th bit position in order that so much prefixes may not be expanded. For example, the 2 bit positions are chosen 12 and 13 in case of $k = 2$.

In Figure 3(a), the required memory size is shown for storing route entries (prefixes) varying the number of k. When the number of k is fixed, the required memory size is larger as the ascending order of numbers of route entries in routing tables. As shown in Figure 3(a), the required memory size storing route entries is rather increasing in case that k is more than 4. The reason is that the number of route entries that should be expanded and stored in the secondary table is radically increasing. Especially in $k = 2$, the required memory sizes on *AS 1, 234, 1668, 3277,* and *6079* are reduced about 40, 34, 43, 13, and 36 %, respectively, compared with those in $k = 0$(the IP lookup scheme in IQ2200 Chipset). In general, we can efficiently use memory for storing routing information as the number k is set to 2.

Figure 3(b) shows the number of memory access for inserting(deleting) lookup information into(from) the forwarding table varying the number of k. The number of memory access depends on the value of $N_{n,D}^{k}$. For $k = 2$, numbers of memory access on *AS 1, 234, 1668, 3277*, and *6079* are about 225,000, 196,000, 235,000, 106,000, and 214,000, respectively. They are reduced about 82, 80, 83, 75, and 81 %, respectively, compared with those in $k = 0$(the IP lookup scheme in IQ2200 Chipset).

5 Conclusions

In order to design high speed routers, we proposed the distributed architecture of the IP lookup scheme which is constructed from several lookup engines having their own IP lookup chip. Also, we proposed a simple rule for partitioning route entries among several IP lookup engines. The performance of the distributed IP lookup scheme based on the indirect IP lookup depended on both the characteristics of IP route prefixes and the number of lookup engines. From our results, when 4 lookup engines are used, the amount of required memory are greatly minimized about 30% and the numbers of memory access are reduced about 80% or more, compared with the original IP lookup scheme in IQ2200 Chipset. The proposed indirect IP lookup scheme can be applied with the already fabricated IQ2200 lookup chips without modification, by using the prefix partitioning rule.

References

1. BGP Reports. http://bgp.potaroo.net
2. Chung, M.Y., Park, J., Ahn, B.J., Ko, N., and Kim, J.H.: Performance Analysis of an IP Lookup Algorithm for High Speed Router Systems. Lecture Note on Computer Science: Information Networking Vol. 2662 (2003) 35–45
3. Degermark, M., Brodnick, A., Carlsson, S., and Pink, S.: Small Forwarding Tables for Fast Routing Lookups. Proc. of ACM SIGCOMM (1997) 3–14
4. Doeringer, W., Karjoth, G., and Nassehi, M.: Routing on Longest Matching Prefixes. IEEE/ACM Trans. on Networking Vol. 4 No. 1 (1996) 86–97
5. Fuller, V., Li, T., Yu, J., and Varadhan, K.: Classless Inter-Domain Routing (CIDR): and Address Assignment and Aggregation Strategy. IETF RFC1519 (1993)
6. Gupta, P., Lin, S., and Mckewon, N.: Routing Lookups in Hardware at Memory Access Speeds. Proc. of IEEE INFOCOM (1998) 1240–1247
7. Huang, N.-F. and Zhao, S.-M.: A Novel IP Routing Lookup Scheme and Hardware Architecture for Multigigabit Switching Routers. IEEE JSAC Vol. 17 No. 6 (1999) 1093–1104
8. Jean, S., Chung,S.-H., Cho, J.W., and Yoon. H.: A Scalable and Small Forwarding Table for Fast IP Address Lookups. Proc. of ICCNMC (2001) 413–418
9. Keshave, S. and Rharma, R.: Issues and Trends on Router Design. IEEE Comm. Mag. Vol. 36, No. 5 (1998) 144–151
10. Nilsson, S. and Karlsson, G.: IP-Address Lookup using LC-Tries. IEEE JSAC Vol. 17 No. 6 (1999) 1083–1092

11. Ruiz-Sanchez, M. A., Biersack, E. W., and Dabbous, W.: Survey and Taxonomy of IP Address Lookup Algorithms. IEEE Network Vol. 15 No. 2 (2001) 8–23
12. Design Manual: IQ2200^{TM}, Family of Network Processors. Revision 2. Vitesse Semiconductor Corporation (2002)
13. Waldvogel, M., Varghese, G., Turner, J., and Plattner, B.: Scalable High Speed IP Routing Lookups. Proc. of ACM SIGCOMM (1997) 25–36
14. Wang, P.-C., Chan, C.-T., and Chen, Y.-C.: A Fast IP Routing Lookup Scheme. Proc. of IEEE ICC (2000) 1140–1144

A Locking Protocol for Distributed File Systems*

Jaechun No[1], Hyo Kim[2], and Sung Soon Park[3]

[1] Dept. of Computer Software,
College of Electronics and Information Engineering,
Sejong University, Seoul, Korea
[2] System Software Laboratory,
MacroImpact, Inc.,
Gangnam-gu, Seoul, Korea
[3] Dept. of Computer Science & Engineering,
College of Science and Engineering,
Anyang University, Anyang, Korea

Abstract. In this paper, we present a distributed locking protocol that enables multiple client nodes to simultaneously write their data to distinct data portions of a file, while providing the consistent view of client cached data, and conclude with an evaluation of the performance of our locking protocol on a Linux cluster.

1 Introduction

Many large-scale scientific applications are data intensive and generate huge amounts of data. As the data size generated goes beyond the local storage capacity, scientific applications have to turn to large network-oriented, high-performance distributed computing resources where distributed file systems [1, 2] take responsibility for providing coordinated accesses to remotely stored data and for providing consistent views of client cached data. A major issue in achieving high I/O bandwidth and scalability on the distributed file system is to build an efficient locking protocol. However, many of the locking protocols integrated with distributed file systems are based on a coarse-grained method [1, 3, 4] where only a single client at any given time is allowed to write its data to a file. In this paper, we present a distributed locking protocol based on multiple reader/single writer semantics for a data portion to be accessed. In this scheme, a single lock is used to synchronize concurrent accesses to a data portion of a file. But, several nodes can simultaneously run on the district data sections in order to support data concurrency. We conclude our paper by discussing the performance evaluation of our locking protocol on a Linux cluster.

---

* This work was supported in part by KOSEF award R05-2004-000-12543-0.

2 Implementation Details

2.1 Overview

Figure 1 illustrates the distributed lock interface that is integrated with distributed file systems. Applications issue I/O requests using the local file system interface, on top of VFS layer. Before performing an I/O request, each client should acquire an appropriate distributed lock from GLM (Global Lock Manager) in order to maintain data consistency for the cached data on clients and for remote, shared data on servers. The lock request is initiated by calling lock interface, snq_clm_lock.

Figure 2 represents a hierarchical overview of the locking construct. The lock modes that we provide for are SHARED for multiple read processes and EXCLUSIVE for a single write process. The lock structure consists of three levels: metalock, datalock, and childlock. The metalock, inode0 on node 0 in Figure 2, synchronizes accesses to files and the value of a metalock is an inode number of the corresponding file. Below the metalock is a datalock responsible for coordinating accesses to a data portion.

The lowest level is a childlock that is of a split datalock. Given that a datalock is granted, the datalock can be split further to maximize local lock services as long as the data section to be accessed by a requesting process does not exceed the data section of the datalock already held. In other words, in Figure 2, the datalock for the data portion 0-999 is split into three childlocks that control accesses to the data portions 0-100, 100-199, and 800-899, respectively. The childlock is locally granted and therefore the requesting process needs not communicate with GLM to obtain the childlock.

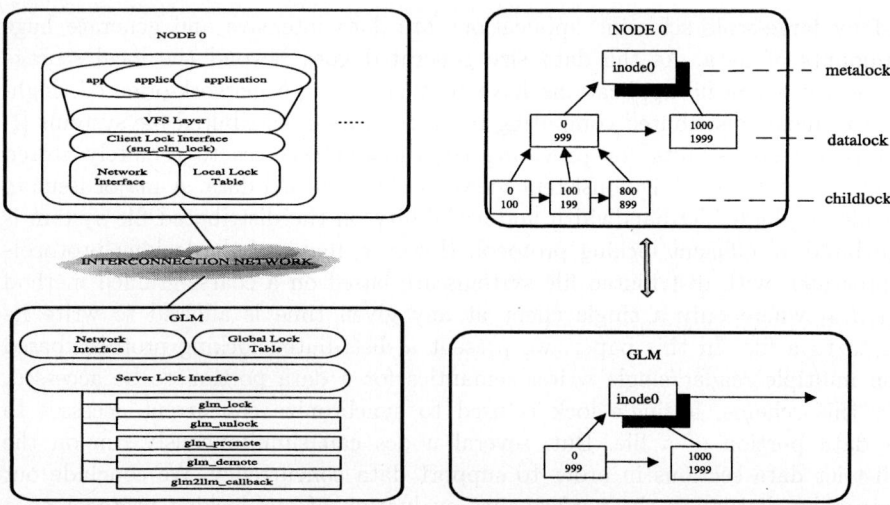

Fig. 1. A distributed lock interface **Fig. 2.** A hierarchical overview

3 Performance Evaluation

We measured the performance of the distributed locking protocol on the machines that have Pentium3 866MHz CPU, 256 MB of RAM, and 100Mbps of Fast Ethernet. The operating system installed on those machines was RedHat 9.0 with Linux kernel 2.4.20-8. Also, four machines were configured as GLMs.

Figure 3 represents the time to obtain the locks with the exclusive mode in write operations and with the shared mode in read operations, as the number of clients increases from 4 to 16. In this case, the lock requested by each client is newly created on GLM and returned to the requesting client, causing no callback message to be sent to the remote lock holder.

Figure 4 shows the time to obtain the locks with the exclusive mode and with the shared mode, while moving each client's data section to access to the one given to the neighbor at the previous step. Figure 4 illustrates that the overhead of the lock revocation is significant with the exclusive mode because only a single client is allowed to write to a data section at any given time. With the shared mode, there is no need to contact the remote lock holder since a single lock can be shared between multiple nodes.

In Figure 5, we changed the number of clients running on each node, while keeping the total number of clients as 16. With two clients running on the same node, the callback message is sent to the remote lock holder every two I/O operations to revoke a lock. With four clients, the callback message is sent to the remote lock holder every four I/O operations, resulting in the lock negotiation overhead decrement, compared to two clients on each node.

Figure 6 shows the effect of childlocks exploiting locality in the lock requests. The lock locality ratio means how often childlocks are taken. Figure 6 shows that, with the exclusive lock mode, the more childlocks are generated, the smaller time

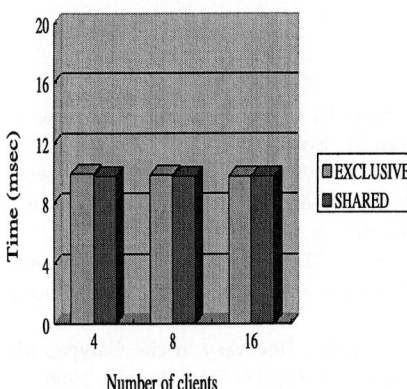

Fig. 3. Time overhead to acquire a distributed lock. Each client read or wrote 1Mbytes of data to the distinct section of the same file

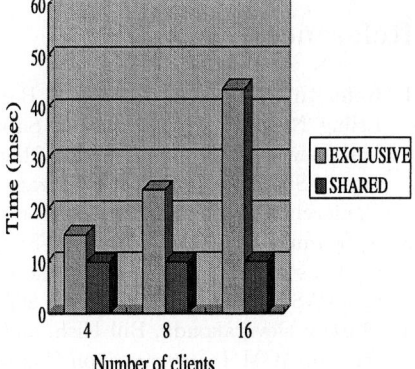

Fig. 4. Time to acquire a distributed lock. A client's data section is shifted to the one given to the neighbor at the previous step

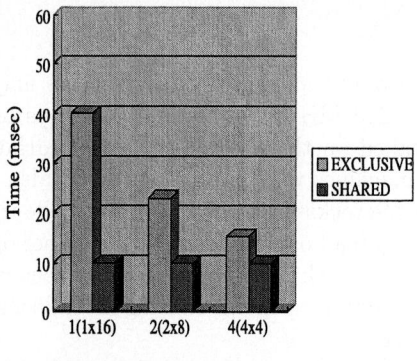
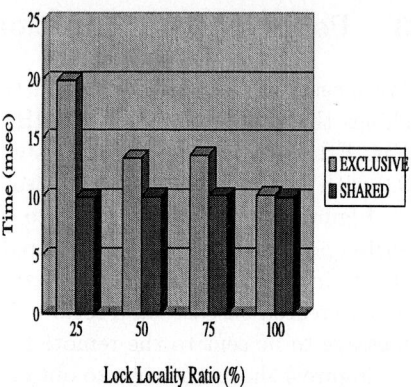

Fig. 5. Time overhead to acquire a distributed lock as a function of number of clients running on each node

Fig. 6. Time to obtain a distributed lock as a function of lock locality ratio using four clients

is taken to serve a lock request due to the drop in time to negotiate with GLM and remote lock holders.

4 Conclusion

In this paper, we presented a distributed locking protocol with which several nodes can simultaneously write to the distinct data portions of a file, while guaranteeing a consistent view of client cached data. The distributed locking protocol has also been designed to exploit locality of lock requests to minimize communication overhead with GLM and remote lock holders.

References

1. Kenneth W. Preslan, Andrew P. Barry, Jonathan E. Brassow, Grant M. Erickson, Erling Nygaard, Christopher J. Sabol, Steven R. Soltis, David C. Teigland, and Matthew T. O'Keefe. A 64-bit Shared Disk File System for Linux. In Proceedings of Sixteenth IEEE Mass Storage Systems Symposium Seventh NASA Goddard Conference on Mass Storage Systems & Technologies, March 15-18, 1999
2. F. Schmuck and R. Haskin. GPFS: A Shared-Disk File System for Large Computing Clusters. In Proceedings of the First Conference on File and Storage Technologies(FAST), pages 231–244, Jan. 2002
3. Murthy Devarakonda, Bill Kish, and Ajay Mohindra. Recovery in the Calypso file system. ACM Transactions on Computer Systems, 14(3):287–310, August 1996
4. Chandramohan A. Thekkath, Timothy Mann, and Edward K. Lee. Frangipani: A Scalable Distributed File System. In Proceedings of the Symposium on Operating Systems Principles, 1997, pages 224–237

Tuning Genetic Algorithms for Real Time Systems Using a Grid

Antonio Martí Campoy, Francisco Rodríguez, and Angel Perles Ivar

Departamento de Informática de Sistemas y Computadores,
Universidad Politécnica de Valencia, Camino de Vera s/n, Valencia 46022, Spain
{amarti, prodrig, aperles}@disca.upv.es

Abstract. The use of locking caches has been recently proposed to ease the analysis of the performance and predictability of a cache when used in a real-time system. One promising method to adequately select the cache contents is the use of a genetic algorithm. However, this method requires the tuning of analysis parameters and this step requires a huge computational cost that can be reduced only if a massively parallel computing infrastructure is used. The work presented here analyses the specific requirements of the genetic algorithm tuning and the facilities provided by commercial grid software. Although the grid eases the resource management and job execution it lacks some communication link with submitted jobs, which is solved by the use of a specialized program called the Experiment Manager. This experiment manager supplements the grid and offers a completely automated environment for algorithm tuning to the researcher.

1 Introduction

Locking cache has shown its goodness as an alternative to dynamic, conventional caches for its use in real-time systems. The use of a locking cache offers two advantages: its behavior is fully predictable, allowing the system designer to compute the response time of tasks in a simple way and it provides similar performance than conventional, non-predictable caches [1] [2]. The operation of a locking cache is simple: a sub-set of instructions, belonging to any task in the system, is loaded and locked in cache during the system start-up. Those instructions remain in cache for the whole system operation; that is, there are no cache replacements. In this way, the behavior of the cache is fully predictable and execution times can be easily estimated.

The resulting performance is highly dependent on the loaded and locked instructions. The response time of tasks, their slack time, and global system utilization varies as a function of what instructions are locked in cache. Adequate selection of these instructions is a hard problem because the number of possible solutions is huge. Equation 1 shows the number of solutions, where n is the number of main memory blocks occupied by all the tasks in the system, and m is the number of lines of the locking cache. As an example, a system of 500 main memory blocks (around 8Kbytes) and a locking cache of 250 lines (around 4Kbytes), requires the analysis of more than 10^{149} possible solutions.

$$\binom{n}{m} = \frac{n!}{m!\,(n-m)!} \qquad (1)$$

In this kind of problems, genetic algorithms [3] are a very interesting solution. In [4] a genetic algorithm is presented, that efficiently solves the problem of selecting the locking cache contents. This algorithm was developed in the C language, and its execution time in a medium performance computer is between four and twelve hours, depending on the experiment parameters. Although this time may appear too large, the cache content selection is accomplished once during system design, so the significance of this computation is relatively low.

2 The Problem

Results obtained from the genetic algorithm are, in general terms, good. But these results vary widely with several parameters, both algorithm parameters —seed, population size, number of generations, probabilities of mutation, crossover, etc— and system parameters —cache size, particular set of tasks, cache mapping function, etc—. Table 1 shows the main parameters that may affect the goodness of algorithm results with their range of possible values. Value range of parameters is established from typical values found in literature, or preliminary experimentation.

Table 1. Experimental values of parameters

Parameter	Value
Seed	Between 10 and 100 different seeds
Population size	100, 150, 200, 250
Number of generations	From 1000 to 10000 in 10 steps
Selection probability	0.05, 0.1, 0.2
Mutation probability	0.001, 0.002, 0.003
Crossover probability	0.4, 0.5, 0.6
Cache configurations	50 different cache configurations
Set of tasks	30 different sets, synthetically created

Genetic algorithm runs using different values for these parameters must be carried out to identify the optimal configuration of the genetic algorithm, providing: i) the best performance when locking cache is used, or ii) a relationship between system and algorithm parameters in order to best configure the algorithm for each particular system configuration.

The first issue in this work is the computational time needed to accomplish all the experiments. Considering an average execution time of 6 hours for the algorithm, more than 11,000 years are needed to perform them using a single computer. But the processor time is not the only temporal issue. Setting, loading, launching and processing the experiments requires a huge human researcher time. Next section presents how to minimize these temporal costs.

Another important issue is the number of replicas with different seeds. Since genetic algorithms perform a pseudo-random search, the effect of the initial seed may be significant. But the number of replicas may vary for each experiment in order to achieve the required confidence level on the results, so it is not easy to determine a-priori how many replicas are required for each configuration.

3   The Proposal

To make possible the experiments, several requirements must be accomplished:

- The number of cache configurations and set of tasks must be reduced. Grouping systems and using a factorial design of experiments [5] this becomes possible.
- Replication of experiments with different initial seeds must be dynamically determined. That is, confidence interval at desired percentage of confidence level for average result must be computed at run time and new replicas will run if needed only.
- Effect of number of generations must be obtained as partial results, setting the maximum number of generation in a dynamic way, and not as static, pre-defined value.
- A massively parallel computing infrastructure must be used, like grid computing [6]
- Automatic setup and run-time post-process of the experiment results is needed.

Using factorial design of experiments the number of required experiments is drastically reduced because not all the possible combination of parameters must be analyzed (this does not apply to the initial seed and number of generations, their effect must be computed as results are available). This reduces the time needed to perform them to around three years of a single computer. Using grid-computing techniques this time may be also reduced.

Innergrid [7] is a grid software that allows to use, in an easy way, interconnected, heterogeneous computers to distribute jobs. Innergrid architecture is based in one server and several agents. Agents run in each of the networked computers, and are inquired by the server to run the programs demanded by the grid's user. The grid's user submits the set of jobs to be executed to the server and the server polls the agents to find non-busy computers to run those jobs. Also, Innergrid takes care of questions like security, fault tolerance and system scalability making its use very simple.

Fig. 1 depicts the Innergrid architecture and operation.

Innergrid is used today by several research groups in the Technical University of Valencia as isolated grids of a dozen computers each, testing the environment

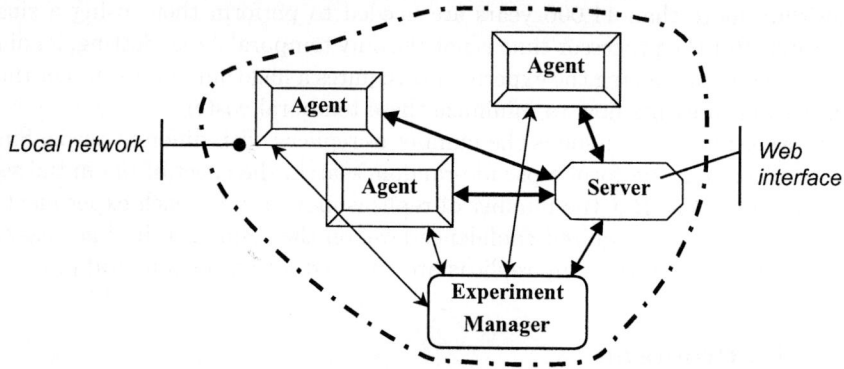

Fig. 1. Innergrid scheme with EM and relationship between elements

before around 3000 computers are interconnected in one large, high performance grid, integrating computers devoted to research and teaching purposes. Although the usefulness of Innergrid for the here presented problem is evident, there are two operational characteristics that preclude the direct use of Innergrid:

- The server offers a web-based interface to submit the jobs that must be run in the grid. This interface is very human friendly but there is no provision to ease automation of this interface by means of scripts or similar. Also, this web-based interface is the only way to retrieve results from the jobs once they finish their execution.
- There is no facility to provide a communication link with the jobs running in the agents. This way, run-time computing the confidence interval for results and dynamically determining when there are enough runs of one experiment is not possible.

4 Experiment Automation: The Experiment Manager

This section describes the work developed to automate the experiment setup and to provide a communication link with submitted jobs. This capabilities are carried out by a specialized program called the Experiment Manager (EM). This experiment manager may run in any computer that can connect to the grid server, and performs three main operations:

1. Connects with the Innergrid server and load the set of experiments into the grid. The set of experiments is read from a configuration file, created by the human researcher, where the factorial design is defined. The desired confidence interval for the results and the threshold to determine that no new generations are needed is also specified into this file. In order to connect with the Innergrid server, the EM implements a background http client without graphic interface but capable to interpret the html documents received from the server and upload the forms.

2. Communicates with genetic algorithms running in all agents, receiving partial results. During the execution of those algorithms, the EM computes the confidence interval. If the error from the confidence interval is not as small as specified in the EM configuration file it connects again with the Innergrid server and launches new replicas into the grid. Also, the improvement of the function fitness between generations is computed. If this improvement overpass the threshold, the EM connects with the server to finish the jobs.
3. When a set of experiments finish execution in the grid, the EM connects with the Innergrid server and download results, storing them in a tabular format to allow an easy and fast processing by statistical tools.

Fig. 1 shows the Innergrid architecture supplemented with the EM, and the relationships between the different elements.

The EM is required on top of the Innergrid software because the grid does not directly support the computation model used. First, the number of replicas is not fixed but dynamically determined using the confidence interval metric instead. Second, the number of generations each replica must perform before finishing execution is also determined at run time, once the EM collects its intermediate results and determines it has reached a steady-state condition.

5 Implementation and Operation Details

This section describes some important remarks in the implementation and use of the several elements involved in the described experimental process.

5.1 Genetic Algorithm

The genetic algorithm has evolved from the first version, written in the C language. In order to allow its execution in several architectures with different operating systems the algorithm was rewritten using the Java language. And inter-process communication links have been added using TCP/IP sockets. Several operating parameters —like finish condition, provided output, initial seed and system configuration— are loaded from files.

Using its communication link, a replica can provide intermediate results and accepts commands to finish early, reducing the number of generations that must be run up to completion.

5.2 Experiment Manager

Five modules form the experiment manager: Configuration parser, client, communications, analyzer, and database.

The configuration parser reads the configuration file and creates the particular files needed by the Innergrid server. The EM http client sends these files to the Innergrid server. This http client can process a reduced set of html tags, only those used by the Innergrid server. For each entry in the factorial design, a grid experiment —formed by several replicas— is created.

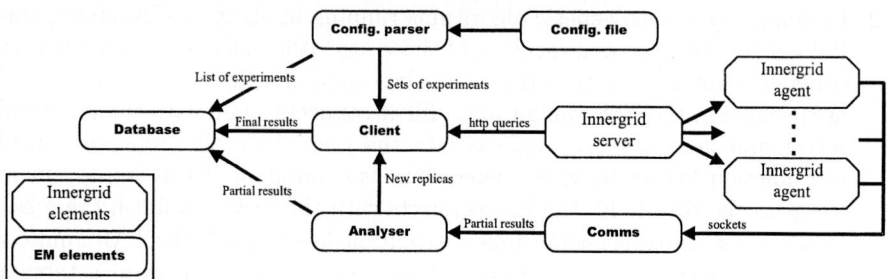

Fig. 2. EM modules and their interactions with Innergrid

The communication module accepts connections from each instance of the algorithm running in the grid and receives their results. With these results, the analyser determines if new replicas are needed or if the algorithm may finish its execution in the current generation. If new replicas are needed, the client submits them to the grid as new experiments. The amount of data the EM must manage is very large, because confidence intervals and threshold of improvement is computed for isolated subsets of experiments. The database module offers the functionality required to efficiently manage all the data.

Fig. 2 shows how the modules interact.

5.3 Experiment Framework

The only work the researcher must do to run the experiments is creating the configuration file for the EM. This file includes the factorial design that may be easily created using statistical software and other parameters like confidence interval, improvement threshold, initial number of replicas, maximum number of generations, and step of generations to produce partial results.

It is clear that parameters in the factorial design —number of systems, range of different probability values, number of cache configurations— indirectly determines the amount of time needed to accomplish the in-depth evaluation of the generic algorithm, because these parameters determine the number of experiments that must be ran. But other parameters have a direct impact on the experimental time because the directly affect the throughput of the grid:

- Initial number of replicas: naively the number of initial replications may be set to a large value [8]. This causes, for some experiments, the execution of non-necessary instances of the experiment delaying the execution of other experiments while grid resources are busy doing nothing significant. Initial number of replicas must be set to a value that allows the grid to run simultaneously different entries of the factorial design, taking advantage of the EM ability to dynamically compute and launch the replicas as they are needed.
- Step of generations: when the genetic algorithm reaches a step in the number of generations, connects with the EM and sends the results. Setting a low

value for this parameter results in an increase of network traffic. Taking into account that the grid shares the network with processes of other users, the traffic generated must be restrained.

6 Conclusions

The use of locking caches has been recently proposed to ease the analysis of real-time systems that use a cache to increase its performance. One promising method to adequately select the cache contents is the use of a genetic algorithm. However, an in-depth evaluation of the genetic algorithm is required to tune its parameters and this process needs huge computational resources, even when a factorial design of the experiments is used.

The "griddization" process is not easy when the number of execution runs or the algorithm finish condition may be not statically, a-priori defined. This is the case of experiment setups where the confidence interval for each result must be obtained with multiple executions of the same program using different seeds, for example.

The grid used to carry out the experiments offers an abstraction to the user of a large computer system where many independent programs may be submitted, performing a complex resource management policy to map jobs to lightly loaded computers from a heterogeneous network.

However, the grid does not provide an adequate abstraction to execute a large number of jobs with inter-process communication in which executing programs may submit partial solutions or intermediate results to a central repository. Submitted jobs are assumed to be independent and the results are available once the program has finished only. This lack of flexibility has led the authors to supplement the grid with specialized software, the Experiment Manager (EM), to provide the programs executing in the grid this result repository that may be accessed at any time using TCP/IP sockets.

This experiment manager complements the services offered by the grid and provides a completely automated environment for the genetic algorithm tuning process or any other situation where the grid abstraction is not enough and must be supplemented with inter-process communications. Although specifically developed to solve a genetic algorithm tuning problem, the confidence interval method to dynamically determine the number of jobs submitted to the grid is extensible to many problems with statistical analysis of their results.

The EM, coupled with the resource management provided by the grid, offers the possibility to the researcher to dynamically increase the number of submitted jobs to achieve the desired confidence interval. The EM may be also used to cancel already submitted jobs to minimize the number of replicas executed when the confidence interval has been reached increasing the grid utilization.

References

1. Martí Campoy, A., Perles, A., Busquets-Mataix, J.V.: Static Use Of Locking Caches In Multitask, Preemptive Real-Time Systems. IEEE Real-Time Embedded System Workshop, London, UK (2001)
2. Vera, X., Lisper, B., Xue, J.: Data Cache Locking for Higher Program Predictability. International Conference on Measurement and Modeling of Computer Systems (SIGMETRICS), San Diego, California, USA (2003) 272–282
3. Mitchell, M.: An Introduction to Genetic Algorithms. Mit Press (1996)
4. Martí Campoy, A., Pérez Jiménez, A., Perles Ivars, A., Busquets-Mataix, J.V.: Using Genetic Algorithms in Content Selection for Locking-Caches. IASTED International Symposia Applied Informatics. Innsbruck, Austria (2001) 271–276
5. Jain, R.: The Art of Computer Systems Performance Analysis. Techniques for Experimental Design, Measurement, Simulation, and Modeling. Wiley-Interscience, New York (1991)
6. Foster, I., Kesselman, C.: The Grid. Blueprint for a Future Computing Infrastructure. Morgan Kaufmann Publishers, USA (1999)
7. InnerGrid, by GridSystems. http://www.gridsystems.com
8. Law A. M., Kelton W. D.: Simulation Modeling and Analysis. McGraw-Hill (2000)

An In-Order SMT Architecture with Static Resource Partitioning for Consumer Applications

Byung In Moon, Hongil Yoon, Ilgu Yun, and Sungho Kang

Yonsei University, 134 Shinchon-dong, Seodaemoon-gu, Seoul 120-749, Korea
bihmoon@soc.yonsei.ac.kr, {hyoon, iyun, shkang}@yonsei.ac.kr

Abstract. This paper proposes a simplified simultaneous multithreading (SMT) architecture aiming at CPU cores of embedded SoCs for consumer applications. This architecture reduces the hardware cost and design complexity of the SMT architecture by adopting in-order execution within threads and static resource partitioning among threads. In our architecture, processor resources are divided into three types depending on their related pipeline stages and static partitioning is applied individually to each resource type. Each thread can perform its operation using the resource partition to which it belongs. Simulation results show that reasonable static partitioning reduces the hardware cost and design complexity of SMT processors while having little negative impact on or even improving performance, compared with full resource sharing.

1 Introduction

Consumer applications such as mobile phones, PDAs and home gateways are increasingly demanding high-performance processors with reasonable cost. On the other hand, to overcome the architectural performance limit of superscalar processors, many microprocessor designers are now turning their attention to multithreading, particularly SMT [1]. The SMT architecture converts thread-level parallelism (TLP) to instruction-level parallelism (ILP) through inter-thread resource sharing, increasing performance notably. However, the SMT architecture is not appropriate for embedded applications, due to its high-cost and high-complexity features. This paper seeks to reduce the cost and complexity for the purpose of applying SMT to embedded processors, and shows that this goal can be accomplished by in-order execution within threads and static resource partitioning among threads.

Most recent SMT designs [2, 3] feature full out-of-order execution within and across threads. However, SMT processors have little need to support out-of-order execution for instructions within the same thread, because TLP between multiple threads compensates for the lack of ILP of each single thread. The work by Moon et al. [4, 5] presented the SMT architecture adopting the in-order execution scheme. But it didn't give fair analysis of the impact of static resource partitioning, and had no consideration for applying SMT to low-cost embedded applications. Raasch and Reinhardt [6] presented an analysis of the impact of resource partitioning on SMT processors. However, their work uses high-cost out-of-order execution and its partitioning is limited to execution resources without consideration for fetch and decode resources. Our paper applies static resource partitioning to all the resources.

2 In-Order SMT Architecture with Static Resource Partitioning

Out-of-order execution results in high-cost features such as register renaming and complicated recovery mechanisms for branch misprediction and exception. To save hardware cost and simplify design, our SMT architecture features in-order execution within threads and is pipelined into simplified 8 stages: *select* (S), *fetch* (F), *decode* (D), *issue* (I), *read* (R), *execute* (E), *memory* (M), and *write* (W). This architecture is constructed through applying some changes to the processor architecture introduced in [4,5], and the interested reader is referred to [4,5] for more details.

By sharing hardware resources among all threads, SMT processors dramatically improve resource utilization and performance. This full resource sharing, however, increases the cost and complexity of the SMT processor. For this reason, we propose a resource partitioning scheme as a method to reduce the cost and complexity of our SMT architecture. Our partitioning scheme divides hardware resources into three types: *fetch*, *decode*, and *execute*, depending on their related pipeline stages, as shown in Table 1. Our scheme applies static partitioning individually to each type of resources. Resource partitions of each type are shared only among threads belonging to them. For example, if our SMT architecture supports four threads and divides the *fetch* type of resources into two partitions, two threads are assigned to each partition, and each two-thread set can use only their respective partitions for performing fetch operation. This static resource partitioning greatly simplifies the design of SMT processors and reduces hardware cost. To be concrete, by static partitioning of *execute* resources, the register file part is implemented as small register files with fewer ports, instead of one large register file, so the register file accesses become faster. Resource partitioning of other types also gives similar benefits, as summarized in Table 1.

3 Simulation Results

We perform our evaluations using an execution-driven, cycle-based simulator modelling in detail our SMT architecture. The simulator adopts the ARM architecture [7] as its instruction set architecture (ISA), and its base parameter values are listed in Table 2. The evaluations are separated into two parts: integer control, and data processing for consumer applications. The workload for control performance evaluation is from the four SPEC CPU2000 benchmarks: parser, twolf, vortex, and mcf. Threads of the simulator execute the four bench-

Table 1. Resources to which static partitioning is applied, and the benefits of partitioning

Resource type	Statically partitioned resources	Benefits to hardware cost and complexity
Fetch	Instruction cache ports, instruction TLB ports, and BTB ports	The thread selector is simplified. Address paths to the instruction cache, instruction TLB and BTB are simplified. Instruction paths from the instruction cache to the IFQ are simplified.
Decode	Instruction fetch queues, decode slots, and instruction issue queues	The IFQ part is divided into multiple IFQs with fewer entries. The IIQ part is divided into multiple IIQs with fewer entries. The management of the IFQ and IIQ is simplified.
Execute	Instruction issue control logic, read/write ports of the register files, read/write ports of the scoreboard arrays, functional units, data cache ports, and data TLB ports,	The register file part is implemented as small register files with fewer ports, instead of one large register file. The instruction issue control logic is simplified. Register address paths to the register file are simplified. Register data paths from and to the register files are simplified. Data forwarding logic is simplified. Data paths to and from functional units are simplified.

mark programs in different execution orders from each other. For the evaluation of data processing performance, we adopt a routing program based on LC-trie lookup algorithm [8]. This routing program uses a routing table in which the average depth of the trie is 4.3. During the simulation, each thread processes the different sets of 5000 68-byte packets, using the same routing program and table. For performance evaluations, we use instructions per cycle (IPC) and bit rates as metrics for control performance and routing performance, respectively. For routing performance, we assume a clock frequency of 500 MHz.

Table 3 shows performance results for various configurations of our SMT architecture. Applying static partitioning to *fetch* resources has little effect on processor performance. We further find that static partitioning to *decode* resources causes performance improvement. Storage resources such as the instruction fetch queue (IFQ) and instruction issue queue (IIQ) have a tendency to frequently suffer from starvation, where one or a few threads possess most of resource elements for a relatively long time, leaving insufficient elements for other threads. Performance improvement due to static partitioning of *decode* resources is because it

Table 2. Base processor parameters

Configuration parameter	Parameter value
Issue width (IW)	2, 4 or 8 instructions per cycle
Fetch width	(1 × IW) instructions per cycle
IFQ(s)	(8 × IW) entries
IIQ(s)	(8 × IW) entries
Register file(s)	(2 × IW) read ports, (1 × IW) write ports
Functional units	(1 × IW) integer ALUs, (1/2 × IW) integer multipliers, (1/2 × IW) load/store units
Latencies	1 cycle except integer multiplication (2 cycles)
BTB	Branch prediction using 2-bit saturation counters, (32 × IW) entries
Instruction and data TLBs	64 entries each
Instruction and data caches	(1/2 × IW) ports, (8 × IW)-KB size, (1 × IW)-way set associative, 32-byte line size, 1-cycle hit latency, 10-cycle miss latency, random replacement
Fetch policy	Give higher priority to threads with fewer instructions in the IFQ(s) and IIQ(s)
Issue policy	Give higher priority to instructions closer to the head(s) of the IIQ(s)

helps to eliminate or reduce the starvation, and this benefit generally outweighs the loss due to static partitioning. On the other hand, static partitioning for *execute* resources is found to cause the performance to decrease notably. This is because *execute* resources are reallocated every cycle, preventing threads from undergoing starvation for multiple cycles. Overall, our results strongly recommend that static partitioning be applied to *fetch* and *decode* resources to the full extent, and to *execute* resources moderately considering trade-offs for cost and complexity, and performance.

Table 3 shows that the 4-issue, 4-thread configuration is the most cost-effective among all the 4-issue configurations and shows similar results for the 8-issue SMT processors. Putting these results together, we have discovered the fact that in-order SMT processors are the most cost-effective when the number of threads is equal to that of instructions that can be issued in one cycle. In addition, the routing performance of the 4-issue, 4-thread in-order SMT processors (over 7 Gbps) is expected to suffice for the increasing performance demand of next-generation home network devices such as home gateways.

Table 3. Performance results for a variety of the in-order SMT processors with static resource partitioning

Issue width/ number of threads	Number of partitions (fetch/decode/execute)	Control performance (IPC)	Routing performance (Gbps)
4 instructions/ 2 threads	1/1/1	1.471	4.106
	2/1/1	1.475	4.111
	2/2/1	1.523	4.239
	2/2/2	1.428	3.980
4 instructions/ 4 threads	1/1/1	2.799	7.741
	2/1/1	2.792	7.706
	2/2/1	2.811	7.818
	2/4/1	2.826	7.997
	2/4/2	2.631	7.317
4 instructions/ 8 threads	1/1/1	2.902	7.994
	2/4/2	2.742	7.576
8 instructions/ 4 threads	1/1/1	2.833	7.854
	2/1/1	2.943	7.850
	4/1/1	2.998	7.892
	4/2/1	3.035	8.285
	4/4/1	3.310	8.789
	4/4/2	3.126	8.664
	4/4/4	2.829	8.166
8 instructions/ 8 threads	1/1/1	4.577	12.752
	2/1/1	4.621	12.668
	4/1/1	4.689	12.502
	4/2/1	4.754	12.779
	4/4/1	4.780	12.776
	4/8/1	4.897	13.011
	4/8/2	4.692	12.901
	4/8/4	4.435	12.523
8 instructions/ 16 threads	1/1/1	4.937	13.292
	4/8/2	5.101	13.533

4 Conclusion

In-order SMT architectures and the effect of static partitioning on the cost and performance of the SMT processors have not been widely studied. So we propose an in-order SMT architecture aiming at CPU cores of embedded SoCs for consumer applications. In addition, this paper applies static partitioning to three types of resources: *fetch*, *decode*, and *execute*, in order to save hardware cost and simplify design, and provides full analysis of partitioning effects.

Static partitioning to *fetch* resources causes little performance degradation. Static partitioning to *decode* resources has a tendency to improve performance. In contrast, static partitioning to *execute* resources decreases performance by a certain amount (under 8% for four partitions). We recommend that static partitioning be applied to *fetch* and *decode* resources to the full extent, and to *execute* resources reasonably. And we have found that in-order SMT processors are the most cost-effective when the number of threads is equal to that of instructions issued per cycle. Besides, 4-issue in-order superscalar processors (currently demanding reasonable cost) are expected to provide enough performance for next-generation performance-demanding consumer applications, by adopting 4-thread SMT.

Acknowledgements

The work reported in this paper was supported by the Brain Korea 21 Project in 2004. And we would like to thank Chung Bin Lim and In Pyo Hong for their support for the routing program used in this work.

References

1. Tullsen, D.M., Eggers, S.J., Levy, H.M.: Simultaneous multithreading: Maximizing on-chip parallelism. Proc. 22nd International Symposium on Computer Architecture. Santa Margherita Ligure, Italy (1995) 392–403
2. Tullsen, D.M., Eggers, S.J., Emer, J.S., Levy, H.M., Lo, J.L., Stamm, R.L.: Exploiting choice: Instruction fetch and issue on an implementable simultaneous multithreading processor. Proc. 23rd International Symposium on Computer Architecture. Philadelphia, Pennsylvania (1996) 191–202
3. Preston, R.P. et al.: Design of an 8-wide superscalar RISC microprocessor with simultaneous multithreading. Proc. 2002 IEEE International Solid-State Circuits Conference, Vol. 1. San Francisco, California (2002) 334–335
4. Moon, B.I.: Study of an in-order SMT architecture and grouping schemes. Ph.D. Thesis. Deptartment of Electrical and Electronic Engineering, Yonsei University, Seoul, Korea (2002)
5. Moon, B.I., Kim, M.G., Hong, I.P., Kim, K.C., Lee, Y.S.: Study of an in-order SMT architecture and grouping schemes. International Journal of Control, Automation, and Systems, Vol. 1, No. 3 (2003) 339–350
6. Raasch, S.E., Reinhardt, S.K.: The impact of resource partitioning on SMT processors. Proc. 12th International Conference on Parallel Architectures and Compilation Techniques. New Orleans, Louisiana (2003) 15–25
7. Jagger, D., Seal, D.: ARM Architecture Reference Manual, 2nd Edition. Addison-Wesley, Boston, Massachusetts (2000)
8. Nisson, S., Karlsson, G.: IP-address lookup using LC-tries. IEEE Journal on Selected Areas in Communications, Vol. 17, No. 6 (1999) 1083–1092

ShanghaiGrid: Towards Building Shared Information Platform Based on Grid[1]

Ying Li[1,2], Minglu Li[1], and Jiadi Yu[1]

[1] Department of Computer Science and Engineering,
Shanghai JiaoTong University,
Shanghai 200030, China
[2] Computer Science and Technology School,
Soochow University, Suzhou 215006, China
{liying, li-ml, jdyu}@cs.sjtu.edu.cn, ingli@suda.edu.cn

Abstract. Compared with Computational Grid, the Information Grid currently has no clearly definition. In terminology of the Shanghai Information Grid, to meet the requirement of Information Grid, we design a QoS-aware Information Service which can provide efficient search ability and reliable Index Service and the Information Grid Portal which acts as an access point to Information Grid.

1 Background

Shanghai is a municipality of eastern China at the mouth of the Yangtze River. Today, it has become the largest economic center and important port city in China. The primary goal of ShanghaiGrid is to develop a set of system software for the Information Grid and establish an infrastructure for the grid-based applications. By means of flexible, secure, open standards sharing and coordinating of computational resources, data information and dedicated services among virtual organizations, this project will build an Information Grid tailored for the characteristics of Shanghai and support the typical applications[1].

Information Grid currently has no clear definition. The ShanghaiGrid gives users and applications secure access to any information anywhere over any type of network [2] and integrates heterogeneous information on the web into a homogenous presentation. The terminology of the Shanghai Information Grid is a Grid environment that provides information to the end users rather than provides computational power, data access, and storage resources which are the key activities in Computational Grid. The rest of the paper introduces our research on the Information Service and Grid Portal of Information Grid.

---

[1] This paper is supported by 973 project (No.2002CB312002) of China, grand project (No.03dz15027) and key project(No.025115033) of the Science and Technology Commission of Shanghai Municipality.

2   Information Service in Information Grid

Grid Information Service plays very important role in Grid technique. It provides for locating resources based on the characteristics needed by a job (OS, CPU count, memory, etc.). The Globus Toolkit [3] provides a Monitoring and Discovery Service (MDS)[4] to support development of grid-aware applications which includes Grid Resource Information Service (GRIS), Grid Index Information Service (GIIS) and Information Provider. But for information Grid, it lacks some key features:

- QoS Support. MDS adopts a hierarchical structure to collect and aggregate service information. Systems load in high-level information servers will increase violently, and information searching efficiency could not be guaranteed [5]. Moreover, MDS can not provide a reliable index service, for subscriptions are transient in current GT3 implementation. Data loss or inconsistency can occur when the Index Service or any of the aggregated grid service instances are restarted.
- Grid-Aware Application Information Support. The information such as workflow, transaction, user information, software licenses must be addressed by Information Service.

Fig.1 shows the framework of the Information Service. We define the Information Service Domain (ISD) as a group of services which has same taxonomy, such as booking services domain, financial services domain. Every ISD has one or more Global Information Services (GIS), where all grid resources can deliver their own service data (SD). The resource also stores the information in a Local Information Service (LIS). Service Provider (SP) registers to corresponded LIS. LIS can answer the query of the local information in certain ISD. In Information Grid, a lot of queries are certain Domain-oriented, using LIS will enhance the search efficiency. Each GIS can serve as Yellow Page to provide all the Grid service's information. Client can use parallel arithmetic to find information from GISs. GIS using GIS-GIS protocol to query or duplicate service information among each GIS. There also exist LIS-GIS protocol, SP-LIS protocol and LIS query protocol in the framework to exchange service information.

To achieve the reliable indexing, we use the notification method. Notification is a frequently used software design pattern also known as Observer/Observable. The notification applied in GT3 provides a mechanism which Grid Service can send notification messages to any number of clients. Because the Index Service is also a Grid Service, we can send notification messages between Grid Service and Index Service. When the Grid Service instance starts, it calls Index Service's add subscription interface to add itself as a new subscription, when the state of the Grid Service Instance has any change, it asks Service Data Element (SDE) to notify Index Service, the Index Service can remove it from the Index. A set of MDS extension is to be developed to address grid-aware application requirements in the framework.

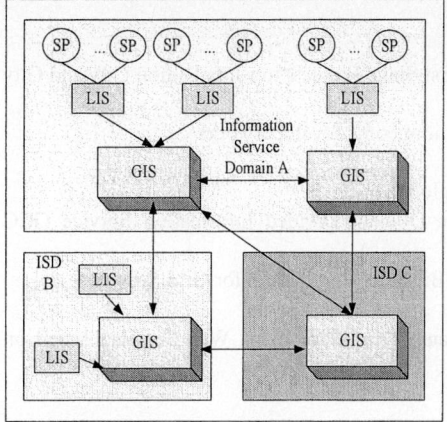 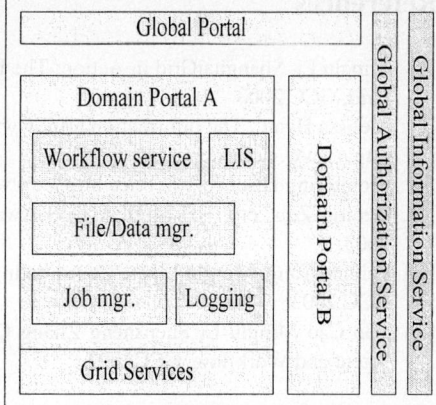

Fig. 1. The framework of Information Service   **Fig. 2.** Information Grid Portal

3 Information Grid Portals

ShanghaiGrid is a platform for varieties Grid Applications such as City Emergency system, intelligent traffic control system, public health management system. The Grid Portal acts as an access point for public user to access Grid Portal like traditional WWW Portal. Currently the existing Grid Portals are mainly Computational Grid Portal which helps to alleviate the complexity of task management through customizable and personalized graphical interfaces for the users (mainly scientists), emphasizes the need for end users to have more domain knowledge than on the specific details of grid resource management such as how to create a job, schedule and monitor its running in distributed resources, get the results and so on. In contrast, the IGP helps the end users (mainly the people without much knowledge about computer science) get the information they want such as long-term weather forecast, traffic information. The Portals in ShanghaiGrid are divided into Global Portal (GP) and Domain Portal (DP). Fig.2 shows the portal model in detail. The transaction support and workflow management are very important for information Grid which could be found in our previous study [6][7].

4 Summary

In this paper we introduce our research on the implement of Information Grid. Compared with Computational Grid, Information Grid provides information rather than computational power. So the QoS-aware Information Service and workflow supported Portal are much more important in Information Grid. Our next step is to build a set of Information Grid develop toolkit to facilitate the development of ShanghaiGrid.

References

[1] Minglu Li, ShanghaiGrid in Action: The First Stage Projects towards Digital City and City Grid, GCC 2003.
[2] Melissa Hyatt , The information grid, www.ibm.com/ developerworks/
[3] http://www.globus.com
[4] Monitoring Discovery Service http://www.globus.org/mds/
[5] Deqing Zou, etc. HH-MDS:A QoS-Aware Domain Divided Information Service GCC 2003.
[6] Feilong Tang, Minglu Li, etc.Coordinating Business Transaction for Grid Service.
[7] GCC 2003
[8] Jian Cao Minglu Li Shensheng Zhang Qianni Den, Composing Web Services based on Agent and Workflow. GCC2003.

A Cost-Optimized Detection System Location Scheme for DDoS Attack

Dong Su Nam[1], Sangjin Jeong[2], Woonyon Kim[1], Sang-Hun Lee[1], Do Hoon Lee[1], and Eung Ki Park[1]

[1] National Security Research Institute,
KT 62-1 Hwaam-dong, Yuseong-gu, Daejeon 305-348, Korea
[2] Protocol Engineering Center, ETRI,
161 Gajeong-dong, Yuseong-gu, Daejeon, 305-350, Korea
{dsnam, wnkim, melsh, dohoon, sjjeong}@etri.re.kr

Abstract. DDoS attack presents a very serious threat to the stability of the Internet. In this paper, we propose cost-optimized detection system location scheme based on the zero-one linear programming model. The performance of proposed model is evaluated based on a manually created network topology. From the evaluation results, we present that the total location cost increases exponentially according to the number of detection system, and the number of hop is reduced by adapting relative weights to the scheme.

1 Introduction

Distributed denial of service (DDoS) is a relatively simple, but very powerful technique to attack various resources (host, router, or entire network). DDoS attacks do not rely on particular network protocols or system weaknesses. Instead, they simply exploit the huge resource asymmetry between the Internet and the victim in that a sufficient number of compromised hosts are amassed to send useless packets toward a victim around the same time. The magnitude of the combined traffic is significant enough to jam, or even crash, the victim (system resource exhaustion), or its Internet connection (bandwidth exhaustion), or both, therefore effectively taking the victim off the Internet.

A taxonomy of DDoS defenses is well defined and classified by Jelena and Peter. Based on the activity level of DDoS defense mechanisms, they differentiate between preventive and reactive mechanisms [1]. Preventive mechanisms attempt either to eliminate the possibility of DDoS attacks altogether or to enable potential victims to endure the attack without denying services to legitimate clients. Reactive mechanisms strive to alleviate the impact of an attack on the victim. To attain this goal they need to detect the attack and respond to it.

An attacker installs a DDoS master program on one computer using a stolen account. The master program, at a designated time, then communicates to several dozens or even hundreds of agent programs installed on computers anywhere on the Internet. The agents, when they receive the command, initiate the attack. Using client-server technology, the master program can initiate hundreds or even thousands of agent programs within seconds. The goal of attack detection is to detect every attempted DDoS attack as early as possible and to have a low degree of false positives. In order to detect the attack, the intrusion detection system has to exchange gathered information with other systems[2][3].

In this paper, we propose a cost-optimized detection system location scheme (CDSLS) originated from File Assignment Problem (FAP) and based on the Tree based Replica Location Scheme(TRLS). The goal of CDSLS is to minimize the cost of data transfer between DSs, when they send to other DSs their information for DDoS attacks [6].

2 Related Works

An Intrusion Detection System (IDS) is a software program that performs any set of actions that attempt to compromise the integrity, confidentiality, or availability of a resource [4]. IDSs are usually classified as host-based or network-based Host-based systems base their decisions on information obtained from a single host, while network-based systems obtain data by monitoring the traffic of information in the network to which the hosts are connected [4].

Some problems in the IDS architecture are described in [5]. In the host-based model, the central analyzer is a single point of failure. If an attacker can somehow prevent it from working, the whole network is without protection. Processing all the information at a single host implies a limit on the size of the network that can be monitored. After that limit the central analyzer becomes unable to keep up with the flow of information. Distributed data collection can also cause problems with excessive data traffic in the network.

Although IDSs have a lot of problems, distributed IDSs are more powerful than host-based and centralized IDSs for DDoS attacks. In this paper, we define a detection system as DS, such as distributed Intrusion Detection Systems(IDS). If DSs share the gathered intrusion information, they can come to an agreement whether it is reliable information or not. This consensus can be more powerful for a reflector attack, an indirect attack in that intermediary nodes (routers and various servers), better known as reflectors, are innocently used as attack launchers. In the indirect attack, DSs can easily estimate and detect the hidden attacker's location because all of the geographically distributed DS has worked in cooperation.

Wolfson and Milo considered the communication complexity of maintaining the availability and proposed a new method, called the minimum spanning tree write, by which a processor in the network should multicast a write of a logical data-item to optimize the communication cost for various interconnection networks [7]. Heuristics for solving a file location problem with replication are investigated in [8], using a mixed integer programming formulation of the problem. Dowdy and Foster have studied the optimal file assignment problem and they survey a number of Mixed Integer Programming (MIP) models for the file allocation problem [9]. Kalpakis et al proved that the optimal capacitated residence set problem for trees is NP-complete [10].

3 CDSLS

Route-based distributed packet filtering uses routing information to determine if a packet arriving at a router, border router at an autonomous system (AS), given the reachability constraints imposed by routing and tree based network topology [3].

Figure 1 illustrates the impact of route-based distributed filtering on curtailing the attacker's ability to engage in spoofing. Without route-based filtering, an attacker residing at AS 1 can disguise himself with undetectable spoofed IP addresses belonging to AS 0-8, i.e., S1,9={0,1,...,8}, when attacking a server in AS 9.

With route-based filtering at AS 8, the spoofable address range shrinks to {0,1,...,5}. With distributed filtering at AS 8 and AS 3, S1,9={1,2}.

As we decide the number of DSs and its location, the cost is increased or decreased.

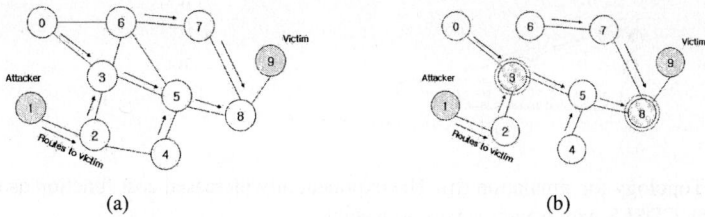

Fig. 1. (a) Route-based filtering architecture with 10 nodes. (b) Distributed filtering with filtering with filter at AS 3 and AS 8

The main goal of this paper is how to determine cost-minimized locations for DS while guaranteeing cost and deadline requirements. We present optimal cost function for locating DS by using integer-programming model. Our cost function is as followed.

$$g = \sum_{i=1}^{n} \frac{(x_i)(L)(\$_i)}{(w_i)} + \sum_{i=1}^{n-1} \sum_{j=i+1}^{n} (x_i)(x_j)(L)(\overleftrightarrow{\$}_{ij}) \quad (1)$$

We consider a tree based graph model $G = (V, E)$, a DS in node i transfer an intrusion data file to node j. The cost of storing intrusion data $\$_i$ forms a $1 \times n$ vector Γ and the cost of transferring intrusion data $\overleftrightarrow{\$}_{ij}$ forms a $n \times n$ triangular matrix Φ. The weight factor is regarded as w_i that represents a utilization ratio of the DS, when intrusion data passes through any DS. Intrusion data file size is defined as L.

Since (1) is zero-one nonlinear integer programming model, it is hard to solve this model as the original form. Therefore, zero-one linear integer programming model, g', can be solved with constraints (3),(4) and (5) by mathematical package such as CPLEX [11]. Our changed linear model is bellowed.

$$g' = \sum_{i=1}^{n} \frac{(x_i)(L)(\$_i)}{(w_i)} + \sum_{i=1}^{n-1} \sum_{j=i+1}^{n} (y_{ij})(L)(\overleftrightarrow{\$}_{ij}) \quad (2)$$

$$(x_i)(x_j) = y_{ij} \quad (3)$$

$$y_{ij} + (1-x_j)M \geq x_i \qquad (4)$$

$$y_{ij} \leq Mx_j + 0, \text{ where } M \text{ is large positive integer} \qquad (5)$$

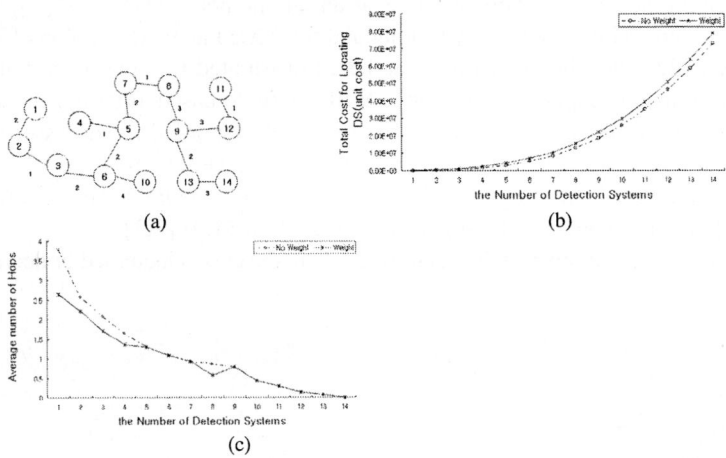

Fig. 2. (a): Topology for simulation (b): The exponentially increased cost function as the number of DS (c): CDSLS with weight versus no weight

4 Conclusion

In this paper, we have discussed the CDSLS for optimizing cost and deadline on distributed DSs. We assumed the tree based network topology that could be applicable for actual distributed networks From the File Assignment Problem, we proposed a cost function that is composed of the storage cost and communication cost. We evaluated computational analysis using Mixed Integer Programming based on the zero-one linear programming model. The DS location cost augmented exponentially as increasing the number of DS. Also we reduced the number of hops by adapting relative weights to our proposed scheme. Our results showed that how much of the cost is needed to locate and this result could be regarded as a basic economic model to decide the location.

References

1. J.Mirkovic and P.Reiher, "A Taxonomy of DDoS Attack and DDoS Defense Mechanisms", ACM, Transactions 2002.
2. Rocky K.C.Chang, "Defending against Flooding-Based Distributed Denial-of-service Attacks: A Tutorial", IEEE Communications Magazine, October 2002.
3. K.Park and H.Lee, "On the Effectiveness of Route-Based Packet Filtering for Distributed DoS Attack Prevention in Power-Law Internets, SIGCOMM, 2001
4. B.Mukherjee, T. L. Heberlein, and K. N. Levitt. "Network Intrusion Detection" IEEE Network, 8(3):26-41, May/June 1994.

5. Jai S. B, Jose O. G et al. "An architecture for intrusion detection using autonomous agents" Computer Security Applications Conference, 1998, Proceedings, 14th Annual, Dec. 1998
6. D.S Nam and C.H Youn et al "Tree-based Replica Location Scheme(TRLS) for Data Grids, IEEE ICON2004, Singapore
7. O. Wolfson and A. Milo, "The Multicast Policy and Its Relationship to Replicated Data Placement, ACM Transactions on Database Systems, vol. 16, no. 1, pp. 181-205, 1991.
8. Fisher ML, Hochbaum DS, "Database Location in Computer Networks", Journal of ACM, Vol. 27, No. 4, pp. 718–735, 1980.
9. L.W. Dowdy, D.V. Foster, "Comparative Models of the File Assignment Problem", ACM Computing Surveys, Vol. 14, No. 2, pp. 287–313, 1982.
10. K. Kalpakis, K. Dasgupta and O. Wolfson, "Optimal Placement of Replicas in Trees with Read, Write, and Storage Costs", IEEE Transactions on Parallel and Distributed Systems, 2001.
11. http://www.cplex.com

Dynamically Selecting Distribution Strategies for Web Documents According to Access Pattern

Keqiu Li and Hong Shen

Graduate School of Information Science,
Japan Advanced Institute of Science and Technology

Abstract. In this paper we present a group-based method for dynamically selecting distribution strategies for web documents according to access patterns. The documents are divided into groups according to access patterns and the documents in each group are assigned to the same distribution strategy. Our group-based model combines performance metrics with the different weights assigned to each of them. We also use trace data to simulate our method. The experimental results show that our group-based method for document distribution strategy selection can improve several performance metrics, while keeping others almost the same.

Keywords: Web caching and replication, distribution strategy.

1 Introduction

Although web caching and replication can enhance the delivery efficiency of web contents and reduce response time, they also bring some problems, such as maintaining consistency of documents, propagating content updates to replica servers and caches, and so on. In this paper, we present a group-based method for dynamically selecting distribution strategies for web documents according to access patterns. We divide the documents into groups according to access patterns and assign the same distribution strategy to the documents in each group. Further, we present a group-based model that combines performance metrics with the different weights assigned to each of them. Finally, we use both trace data to simulate our methods. The experimental results show that our group-based method for document distribution strategy selection can outperform improve several performance metrics compared to the document-based method, while keeping the others almost the same.

The rest of the paper is organized as follows. Section 2 focuses on our group-based method. The simulation experiments are described in Section 3. We conclude our paper in Section 4.

2 Selection of Document Distribution Strategy

We also considered the following document distribution strategies as those in [3], including 1. No Replication (*NoRepl*); 2. Verification (*CV*); 3. Limited verification (*CLV*); 4. Delayed verification (*CDV*); 5. $SU50$ (Server Update); 6. $SU50 + CLV$.

Now we begin to present our group-based method. First we introduce a method to group the documents into P groups according to their access patterns. The main factors that influence the access patterns are web resource and user behavior. According to [1], we group the documents according to the value of v_d, which is defined as $v_d = (c_d + f_d/u_d)s_d$, where c_d denotes the cost of fetching document d from the server, f_d denotes the access frequency of document d, u_d denotes the update frequency of document d, and s_d denotes the size of document d. We can see that when P is equal to the number of the documents, i.e., when there is only one document in each group, then our method is the same as the document-based method in [3]. Therefore, from this point of view the method proposed in [3] can be viewed as a special case of our method. For the case of $P = 1$, our method can be considered a global strategy method, since all the documents are assigned to the same strategy.

Now we present our group-based model considering the total effect of the performance metrics from a general point of view, e.g. we define the total function for each performance metric according to its characteristics. The existing method [3] defines the total function for each performance metric by summing the performance metrics of each document. We argue that this method does not always work well for some performance metrics such as total hit ratio.

Let $S = \{s_j, j = 1, 2, \cdots, |S|\}$ be the set of distribution strategies, $G = \{G_j, j = 1, 2, \cdots, |G|\}$ be the set of groups, $M = \{m_j, j = 1, 2, \cdots, |M|\}$ be the set of performance metrics such as total turnaround time, hit ratio, total consumed bandwidth, etc. A pair arrangement $(strategy, group)$ means that a strategy is assigned to the documents in a group. We denote the set of all the possible arrangements as A. We can define a function f_k for each metric m_k on a pair $a \in A$ by $R_{ka} = \sum_{j=1}^{|G|} r_{kaj} = \sum_{j=1}^{|G|} f_k(a, G_j)$, where R_{ka} is the aggregated performance result in metric m_k and r_{kaj} is the performance result in metric m_k for G_j.

Let $w = \{w_1, w_2, \cdots, w_{|M|}\}$ be the weight vector which satisfies $\sum_{k=1}^{M} w_k = 1, w_k \geq 0, k = 1, 2, \cdots, |M|$. We can get the following general model $R_a^* = \min_k w_k R_{ka}$. We refer to R_a^* as the total cost function for different weight vector w for an arrangement a.

Since there are a total of $|S|^{|G|}$ different arrangements, it is not computationally feasible to achieve the optimal arrangements by the brute-force assignment method. The following result shows that it requires at most $|G||S|$ computations to obtain an optimal strategy arrangement for the documents in each group. Therefore, we have $R_a^* = \min_{a \in A} \sum_{k}^{|M|} w_k R_{ka} = \min_{a \in A} \sum_{k=1}^{|M|} w_k (\sum_{j=1}^{|G|} r_{kaj}) = \min_{a \in A} \sum_{k=1}^{|M|} \sum_{j=1}^{|G|} w_k r_{kaj} = \min_{a \in A} \sum_{j=1}^{|G|} \sum_{k=1}^{|M|} w_k r_{kaj} \geq \min_{a \in A} \sum_{j=1}^{|G|} (\min_j \sum_{k=1}^{|M|} w_k R_{kaj})$.

From the above reasoning, we can obtain the total optimal arrangement by computing the optimal arrangement for each group. Therefore, the computation is the sum of that for obtaining the optimal arrangement for the documents in each group, whereas the computation workload for the method in [3] is about $|D||S|$, where $|D|$ is the total number of documents. Thus, our method requires less computation than the method in [3] by $(|D| - |G|)|S|$. If we suppose that there are 100 documents, and we divide the documents into 10 groups, we can see that the computation can be reduced by 90%.

In our experiments we mainly considered the following performance metrics: (1) Average Response Time per request (ART): the average time for satisfying a request. (2) Total Network Bandwidth (TNB): the total additional time it takes to transfer actual content, expressed in bytes per milli-second. (3) Hit Ratio (HR): the ratio of the requests satisfied from the caches over the total requests. (4) Byte Hit Ratio (BTR): the ratio of the number of bytes satisfied from the caches over the total number of bytes.

3 Simulation

In this section we apply trace data to simulate our results. The trace-based simulation method is similar to that introduced in [2]. In our experiments, we collected traces from two web servers created by the Vrije Universiteit Amsterdam in the Netherlands (VUA) and the National Laboratory for Applied Network Research (NLANR).

We describe our experiment for assigning the same distribution strategy to the documents in each group. The simulation results shown in Table 1 were obtained when the number of groups was 100 and 200 for VUA and NLANR, respectively. We simulated a case in which there are two performance metrics, ART and TNB.

From Figure 1, we can see that the results of our method approximate those of the existing method when we group the documents into 117 and 211 groups for VUA and NLANR, respectively. From our experiments, we conclude that there is almost no improvement in result as the number of groups increases. However,

Table 1. Performance Results for Per-Group Strategy

$w = (w_1, w_2)$	VUA		NLANR	
	TNB(GB)	ART(Sec)	NB(GB)	TT(hours)
(0.9,0.1)	95.3	8.82	162.2	5.37
(0.8,0.2)	110.2	6.95	175.7	5.68
(0.7,0.3)	126.5	6.24	196.7	5.83
(0.6,0.4)	136.5	5.86	212.5	6.04
(0.5,0.5)	150.7	5.57	256.5	6.27
(0.4,0.6)	167.4	5.33	283.5	6.62
(0.3,0.7)	178.2	5.20	314.5	6.89
(0.2,0.8)	191.7	5.11	346.8	7.05
(0.1,0.9)	205.6	5.05.1	379.4	7.24

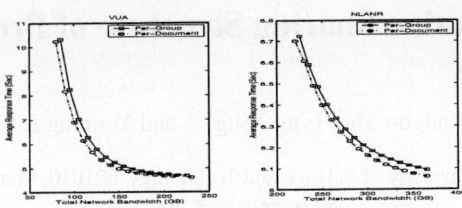

Fig. 1. Different Arrangements

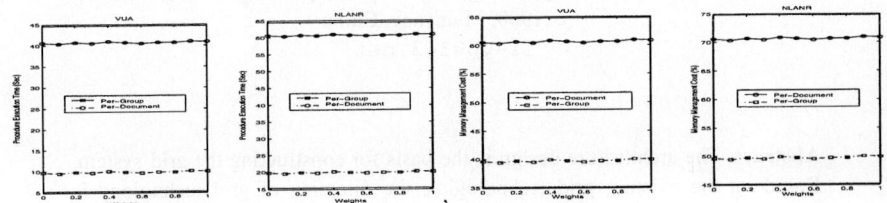

Fig. 2. Experiment Results

our method can significantly improve both the procedure execution time and the memory cost, as can be seen in Figure 2.

4 Concluding Remarks

In this paper, we presented a method for dynamically selecting web replication strategies according to the access patterns. We also used web trace data to simulate our method.

References

1. Krishnamurthy, B. and Rexford, J. (2001) *Web Protocols And Practice*. Addison-Wesley, Boston.
2. Pierre, G. and Makpangou, M. (1998) *CSaperlipopette!: a distributed web caching systems evaluation tool*. Proceedings of 1998 Middleware Conference, The Lake District, England, 15-18 September, pp. 389-405.
3. Pierre, G. and Steen, M. (2002) *Dynamically selecting optimal distribution strategies for web documents*. IEEE Transactions on Computers, 51, 637-651.

An Information Sharing Structure of Broadcasting

Jianguo Ma[1], Ling Xing[1,2], and Youping Li[3]

[1] Southwest University of Science and Technology, 621010, Mianyang, China
mjg_my@263.net
[2] University of Science and Technology of Chian, 230027, Hefei, China
xl_my@ustc.edu
[3] Institute of Electronics Engineering, China Academy of Engineering Physics,
621900, Mianyang, China
li-yp@163.net

Abstract. The architecture design is the basis for constructing the grid system. Based on the existing grid technologies, the dilemma of grid technology is analyzed. The new architecture of broadcasting grid is built in view of information sharing theory and Scale-Free Networks, and the sandglass pattern is drawn up. The results of simulation demonstrate the feasibility and validity of the architecture in DVB-C networks for distance educations. Also, the satellite channel experiments results verify its value by China Education Television Station (CETV).

Keywords: grid, broadcasting grid, information sharing, UCL.

1 Foreword

Grid technology displays a tempting view and makes people optimal about the future of computer. But what is grid? The answer is not formed in academic fields. Mr. Li Youping, an academician of Chinese Academy of Engineering, thinks that the computing capacity largely belongs to the non-generating material resource while the information resource can be largely replicated [1]. Is it possible that this property of being able to be replicated can bring about a revolutionary advance to information grid? So a new grid, different from the Internet-based grid, is generated according to the research about information sharing, which is broadcasting grid.

2 The Principle and Structure of Broadcasting Grid

2.1 Principle for Broadcasting Grid

Information sharing is different from material sharing, and the essence is not the distribution or sharing of the matrix, but the unlimited copy of the matrix. Theories have shown that the energy of only 0.693kT (k is the Boltzmann's constant) is needed to copy one bit under normal temperature T. It is a very tiny amount. Following this formula, less than 1J is needed to copy 1GB information for every body of the total 5 billion people of the earth. This, on the other hand, shows that information sharing should not have been as difficult as it is today. Internet is the excellent structure of exchanging information, but not of information sharing. The digital divide for information sharing among people will ultimately be conquered by some more effective sharing structures.

A.L. Barabasi and E. Bonabeau made a statistic research of access to nearly 100 thousand WWW sites, and found that less than one 10 thousandth controls almost the operation of the whole network, being visited far more frequently than other sites. It is a characteristic of Scale-Free Network [2]-[4]. This characteristic demonstrates at least two points theoretically. Firstly, with integrating hundreds and thousands of mainstream culture resource, broadcasting grid can satisfy most of the individual needs of users. Secondly, broadcasting-storing structure can undertake some streaming load of Internet, lessening the jam problems around the popular sites. It can also reduce the huge investments in broad bandwidth network [5].

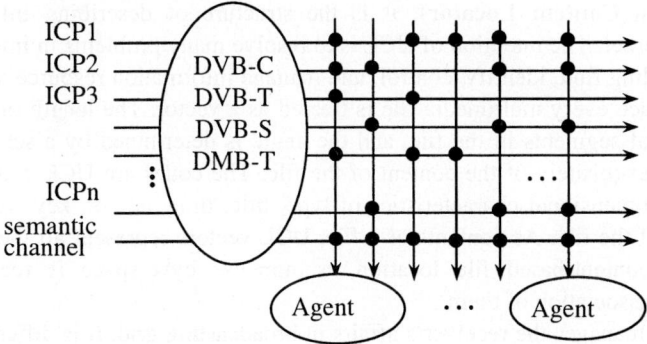

Fig. 1. Broadcasting Grid with semantic channel

2.2 Broadcasting Grid Framework [6]

Broadcasting Grid framework is shown in Fig.1. Horizontal lines represent the pervasive integration of resource, which are independent-management and uniformly-transmitted by content providers. Transmitted ways include direct broadcasting satellite, cable digital network, and wireless cell-network. Perpendicular lines are common user groups. Intelligent agents choose information content according to the needs of users.

In simple time-division, bandwidth is directly allocated to information resource, resulting in the confliction in bandwidth between different resources. By using storing technology, all users are not aware of the limited bandwidth. For example, bandwidth B=32Mbps is distributed evenly to 1,000 ICP, thus every one of them gets a sub-bandwidth of &B=32Kbps. Although &B is less than the bandwidth of dialing network, it can store information in bytes continuously due to the storing equipment at the user's end. In 24 hours, 345.6MB can be delivered to users, which is significantly greater than the total content offered by a large-scale. In this way of time accumulation, small bandwidth can transmit large files.

$$32 \text{kbps} \times 3600 \times 24 \div 8 = 345.6 \text{MB} \qquad (1)$$

3 Key Technologies of Broadcasting Grid and the Sandglass Model

3.1 Key Technologies

Parallel Broadcasting. To utilize efficiently the resource of data broadcast, and to activate the ICP, competition mechanism is introduced, namely the 'large-scale parallel broadcasting'. The principle is to divide one channel of data broadcasting (line analog bandwidth of 8M) into several independent sub-channels; thus competition mechanism of independent operation is formed.

UCL (Uniform Content Locator). It is the structure of describing information resource in Internet. The intention of UCL is to resolve many problems in information network, including find, identify, control, and manage information resource and so on [7]. In cyberspace every multimedia file is treated as a vector. The length of a vector is the number of segments in the file, and the angle is determined by a set of codes used to locate exquisitely of the content of the file. The codes are UCL codes. They describe multidimensional characteristics of type, title, time, author, key words, and classification of the file. As contents of a file, UCL vectors represent all the reader's needs. Exact content-based file location in immense cyberspace is realized by computing the association of them.

UCL agent manages the receiver's affairs in broadcasting grid. It is different from traditional agent in that UCL agent works under the indexing and mapping method of UCL in the transmitter. It can choose the download tasks, filter information, form user interest spectrums, construct of the user profiles, offer active service, and so on.

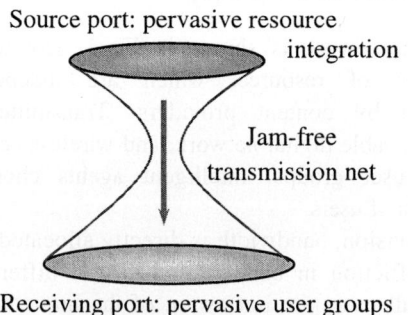

Fig. 2. Sandglass model of broadcasting grid

3.2 Sandglass Model of Broadcasting Grid

The sandglass model of broadcasting grid is shown in Fig.2. The model is composed of the pervasive integration in source ports, and the pervasive user groups, and the jam-free transmission network in receiving ports.

4 Characteristics of Broadcasting Grid

Broadcasting Grid has such characteristics:

(1) The pervasive integration of source ports: Broadcasting Grid differs greatly with WWW in the uniform information resource. Users will no longer have to face numerous isolated information islands, but real service of integration of time, space, and content. This task is performed by independent ICPs.

(2) No sharing confliction between transmission networks: Under transmission way of Internet, a message traverses many gateways and routers, which limit the transmission. Broadcasting Grid is in essence free of confliction and bottleneck because it has not so many gateways and routers.

(3) Most pervasive user groups in receiving ports: There can be limitless number of user groups, causing no such 'more cars more jams' phenomenon, which in return eases the confliction of bandwidth.

(4) Diminish semantic divide: Source port uses uniform, standard UCL codes, and users can communicate semantically with the author under the help of UCL intelligent agent.

5 Experiments

5.1 Basic Contents

Scale of Parallel-Broadcasting: 32 groups 1024 channels
Scale of Transmission Signals: 5 groups 160 channels

In an 8MHz bandwidth of analog channel, when 64-QAM modulation is used, the modulation efficiency is 6bit/band, and the maximum bit rate is (the coefficient of raised cosine is 1.15) as below:

$$\text{(Modulation efficiency)} \times \text{(bandwidth of analog channel)} \div \text{(coefficient of raised cosine)} = 6 \times 8\text{MHz} \div 1.15 = 41.7\text{Mbps} \quad (2)$$

Under the data rate of 32Mbps, the number of transmitted TS in every 100ms is:

$$\text{(Data rate)} \div \text{(TS package length in bits)} \times 0.1\text{s}$$
$$= 32\text{M} \div (188 \times 8 \times 10) = 2231 \quad (3)$$

There are at most 4 TS packages in one UCL file. If 32 programs are transmitted every time, 128 TS packages are transmitted. When the number of programs is very large, packages can be transmitted group by group.

If the time interval between two UCL messages is required to be less than 100ms, then the number of programs between the intervals of UCL packages is:

$$2231 - 128 = 2103 \qquad (4)$$

When transmission rate is low, the number of programs between the intervals is also small.

From the three formulas (2), (3), (4), data transmission rate is computed as:

$$2103 \div 2231 = 94.3\% \qquad (5)$$

The experiment shows that this method is efficient, capable of satisfying receiving requirements.

5.2 Experiment Network

Network in Fig.3 shows the experiment we did. The integration in source port is carried out in the Ethernet network. Resource is divided into three kinds: image of web sites (of www.sina.com.cn, for example), distribution of courseware (multiplexing of courseware), and on-time courses (digital video). Two stages of multiplexing, indexing of UCL, mapping of UCL, transform of data format, and QAM modulation, are also shown. The receiving port consists of data users and digital video users. UCL parsing, control of download, and agent based on UCL semantic are researched in the receiving port, too.

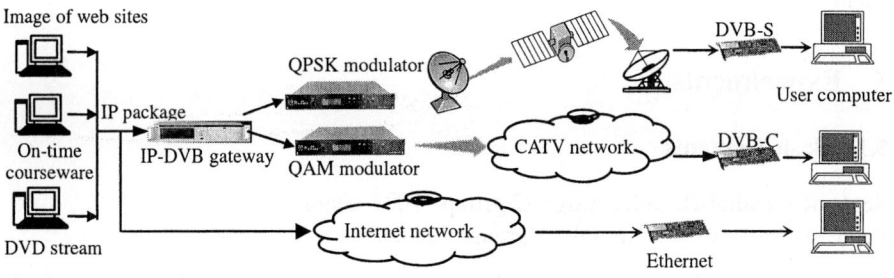

Fig. 3. Experiments Network

6 Conclusions

The research gives us these conclusions as below at least:

(1) Establishment of broadcasting grid has definite application background, and there are urgent market needs.
(2) Results of experiment show that broadcasting grid is feasible in theory according to information sharing theory and the large-scale parallel-broadcasting technology. And it is high information integration in time, space, and content.

(3) Parallel-broadcasting technology and UCL technology are compatible in general DVB-C transmission network. Displacing QAM modulator, results of this experiment can be spread to DVB-S, DVB-T, DMB-T, and so on. Also, the satellite channel experiments results verify its value by China Education Television Station (CETV).
(4) UCL technology works efficiently to dispel information rubbishes and the semantic divide; therefore it makes active service possible.

Further researches in receiving port of broadcasting grid are progressing, for example, the establishment of user interests spectrum and user profile, and the semantic agent based on UCL.

References

1. Li Youping. The second type network of information sharing [J]. Chinese Engineer Science, 2002, 4(8): 8-11
2. Ian Foster. The grid:computing without bounds [J]. Scientific American, 2003, 4:79-85
3. Ian Foster. The Grid: A New Infrastructure for 21st Century Science [J]. Physics Today, 2001, 2(55): 42-47
4. Ibert-Laszlo Barabasi and Eric Bonabcau. Scale-Free Networks [J]. Science American, 2003, (5): 50-59
5. Tim Berners-Lee. The Semantic Web [J]. Science American, 2001, (5): 21-24
6. Ma Jianguo. Information sharing technology with content indexing [D]. Doctoral dissertation. University of Electronics Science technology of China, 2004.6
7. Ma Jianguo, Liu Guihua, and Xing Ling. An agent of data broadcasting based on UCL [A]. IEEE NLP-KE 2003 [C]. IEEE press: 215-220

Design and Evaluation of a Novel Real-Shared Cache Module for High Performance Parallel Processor Chip

Zhe Liu, JeoungChill Shim, Hiroyuki Kurino, and Mitsumasa Koyanagi

Department of Bioengineering and Robotics, Tohoku University,
01 Aza-Aoba, Aramaki, Aoba-ku, Sendai 980-8579, Japan
zheliu@sd.mech.tohoku.ac.jp

Abstract. Nowadays, it is very important that integrating parallel processors on a chip offers high performance and low interactive response time on applications with fine-grained parallelism and high degree of data sharing. We propose a novel real-shared cache module with new multiport ring-bus architecture to overcome the bus bottleneck problem of the existing parallel processors chip on shared cache level. A testbench of solving a large scale of simultaneous linear equation is also designed to evaluate such architecture. The evaluation results show that it can offer immediate data sharing without conflicts or delay, and the performance of parallel processors chips with such novel real-shared cache module improves in proportion to the number of processor elements.

1 Introduction

Parallel processor system can offer outstanding computational throughput and low interactive response time. It has been taken as a popular solution for large applications with high parallelism. The progress of advanced integrated circuit (IC) processing and package technology in recent years has made it available to integrate parallel processors on one chip. It makes parallel processor chip more abstractive because of its high bandwidth and low latency. Compared with printed circuit boards (PCBs), both the on-chip bus with high bandwidth and quite close distance among different processor units improve the performance of parallel processor chips greatly.

How to implement data sharing is a very important point of designing such parallel processor chips. The snooping-based protocol [1] is the traditional basic schemes to solve the problem of cache coherence in parallel processor systems. Fig.1 shows the architecture of it. Snooping-based protocol uses a shared bus, just be the path from the processors to the main memory, to transfer coherence transactions. The snooping unit in each cache decides whether it can update or invalidate its corresponding cache entry. However, if it is used for parallel processor chips, the board-level data transfer among different caches becomes the main bottleneck of performance. Moreover, for applications with fine-grained parallelism such as large scale of linear equation calculation, the high degree of data sharing not only increases the load greatly on the shared bus in Snooping-based protocol, but also requires lower response delay. Therefore, sharing data on cache level maybe a good alternative in the designing of parallel processor chips. Therefore, we propose a "novel real-shared cache module" with the special multiport ring-bus architecture, in this paper. The new shared cache is employed to integrate a high performance parallel processor chip, because both high access bandwidth and low response delay can be achieved for the applications with fine-grained parallelism and high degree of data sharing.

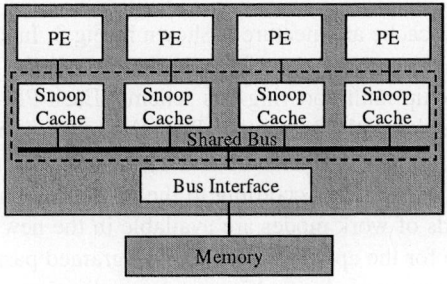

Fig. 1. Snoop cache architecture

2 Multiport Ring-Bus Architecture

In this design of the novel real-shared cache module, we utilized a special "multiport ring-bus"[2] architecture as its interface replacing the conventional common bus. Moreover, we implement the data sharing in it with an "overlaid data mode"[3]. In the new shared cache, each processor element (PE) has a private generic cache block, but not a snoop cache. All the cache blocks are also connected by an on-chip multiport ring-bus. Each PE can access the respective cache block simultaneously and independently from other PEs and the shared data from any PE can be overlaid to all cache blocks, immediately. The concept of multiport ring-bus is shown in Fig.2. The multiport ring-bus is used in the new shared cache to receive the shared data form every PE and transport them overlaying all the cache blocks for realizing the high

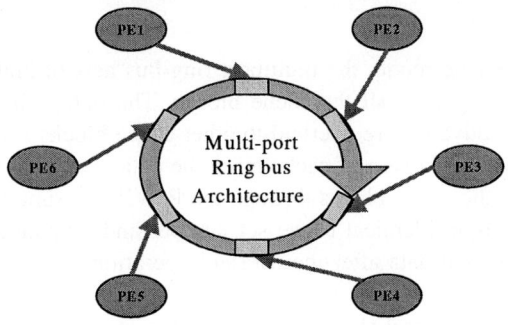

Fig. 2. Concept of multi-port ring bus

speed data sharing. The multiport ring-bus has more ports than general ring-bus structure. It can be considered as a combination of some micro buses inside of chip that more PEs can be connected to the multiport ring-bus at the junction of each two micro buses. Therefore the multiport ring-bus is advantage over the common buses.

3 Novel Real-Shared Cache Architecture

The novel real-shared cache architecture is shown in Fig.3. In contrast to snoop cache structure, each PE has a private generic cache block. All the cache blocks are also connected by an on-chip multiport ring-bus scheme. Each PE can access the respective cache block independently from other PEs. Every PE is permitted to access the multiport ring-bus, simultaneously. The Memory Interface Unit controls the activity of refill or writeback operations According to the configuration of the multiport ring-bus scheme, two kinds of work modes are available in the new shared cache module: a shared-cache mode for the applications with fine-grained parallelism and data sharing, and a multi-program mode for multi-program applications.

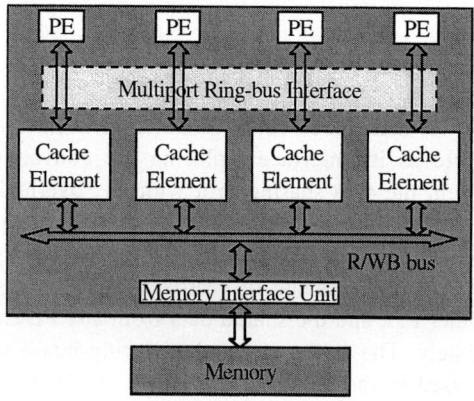

Fig. 3. Novel real-shared cache architecture

In the shared-cache mode, the multiport ring-bus acts to high speed transporting the shared data overlaying all the cache blocks. The data, which stored to a cache block by the respective PE are overlaid to other cache blocks simultaneously through the multiport ring-bus. In case of cache miss, the data read from the external memory is refilled into all the cache blocks through the R/WB bus simultaneously. Therefore, the cache line with an identical cache set number and way number in all the cache blocks has an identical data after the overlaid operation. These identical data can be simultaneously read by all PEs without conflicts, even if all PEs point to the same address. Therefore, the real-shared cache scheme in shared-cache mode is able to provide immediate data sharing. Fig.4 shows the concept of the data sharing process. Since the multiport ring-bus can be used by all PEs at any cycle and the data should be broadcasted to all other cache block, simultaneously. Therefore, there is not serious conflict when more than one PE store data. Moreover, because the frequency of store is much less than that of read in actual program executions, it is profitable to trade the performance of store operations for the immediate data sharing.

In the shared-cache mode, the multiport ring-bus is not used and all the cache blocks act as independent data caches. Moreover, each cache block also always multiplexes the data from its private PE to the data SRAM. In this mode no copy operation is performed among the cache blocks and the data in all the blocks is not all identical again. This mode is used for multi-program applications without data sharing.

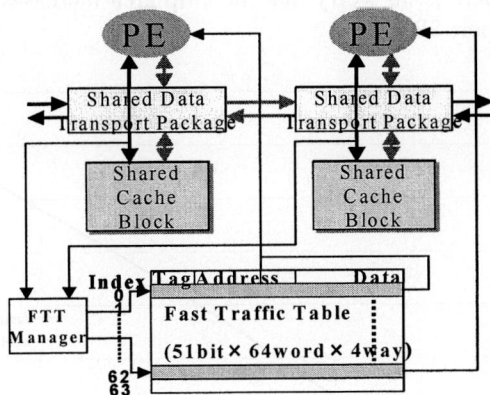

Fig. 4. Concept of data sharing process

4 Performance Evaluation

We have evaluated the performance of parallel processor chip with the novel real-shared cache module in 12 simulation modes that have 4, 6, 8 PEs respectively on chip and the cache block size is 8Kbytes, 16Kbytes, 32Kbytes and 64Kbytes respectively. Each PE is designed as a 32-bit standard RISC. The Memory Interface Unit can manage the external SDRAM memory totaling up to 256MB and the clock is set at 100MHz. All the parallel processor chips are implemented on RTL mode in VHDL and FPGA EP20K1500E (Altera APEX20KE device) is used to evaluate them.

We also solve a large scale of simultaneous linear equation on simulator as a test. Except that the master PE is also responsible for initialization and outputting the results, all the PE execute the calculation instructions in parallel. Fig.5 shows the performance evaluation of different processors chip whose cache blocks are all 64Kbytes. It is obvious that the performance improves in proportion to the number of processor elements. We also can see that the speedup ratio decreases a little as the PE number increases. It is because the latency of store conflicts increases as the PE number increases. However, since the immediate data sharing is available for all the PEs, not like the snoop cache that the read latency increases greatly with the PE number, the high performance is still possible even for large-scale parallel processor chip.

Fig.6 shows the cache miss ratio comparison of 12 simulation modes with different number of PEs and different cache block size. It shows that, for a certain PE number, the cache miss ratio decreases as the cache block size increases. The reason is because the effective utilization of cache block also decreases with the PE number. However, since generic cache is used for cache blocks in our real-shared cache, it is profitable to trade large cache block for the high performance. Moreover, there is no worry that the chip area increases unacceptably like the existing multiport SRAM.

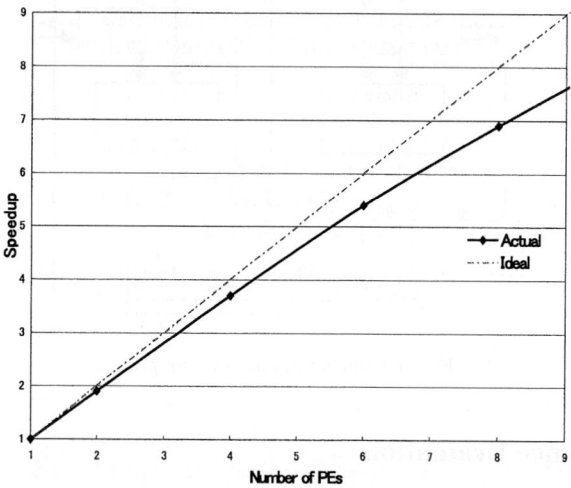

Fig. 5. Speedup of parallel processor chip performance of different number of processors

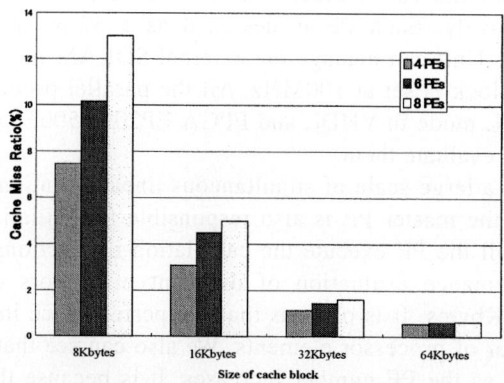

Fig. 6. Cache miss ratio of different number of PEs and different cache block size

5 Conclusion

How to implement data sharing is an important point in integrating parallel processor system on a chip. Sharing on cache level is an effective alternative not only to reduce the communication load on outside system, but also to narrow the performance gap between the parallel processor chip and external memory. We have proposed a novel real-shared cache module with higher performance than the existing snooping cache. It supports two work modes: a shared-cache mode and a multi-program mode. The evaluation shows that the performance of parallel processor chips with real-shared cache architecture improves in proportion to the number of processor elements. Moreover, the new real-shared cache has the advantage in scalability, and there is no worry that the chip area increases more than the linear proportion of the port number.

References

[1] D. E. Culler, J. P. Singh, with A. Gupta, "Snoop-based multiprocessor design", in Parallel Computer Architecture, pp.377–446, Morgan Kaufmann, California, 1998
[2] Z. Liu, J. Shim, H. Kurino, M. Koyanagi, AINA, pp241–244 (2004)
[3] S. Shimatani and M. Koyanagi, SSDM, pp.330–332 (1995)

Using Computing Checkpoints Implement Consistent Low-Cost Non-blocking Coordinated Checkpointing

Chaoguang Men[1,2] and Xiaozong Yang[1]

[1] School of Computer Science and Technology, Harbin Institute of Technology, Harbin, Heilongjiang, 150001, P.R. China
{mencg, xzyang}@Hit.edu.cn

[2] School of Computer Science and Technology, Harbin Engineering University, Harbin, Heilongjiang, 150001, P.R. China

Abstract. Two approaches are used to reduce the overhead associated with coordinated checkpointing: one is to reduce the number of synchronization messages and the number of checkpoints; the other is to make the checkpointing process non-blocking. In this paper, we introduce the concept of "computing checkpoint" to design an efficient consistent non-blocking coordinated checkpointing algorithm that combines these two approaches. Through piggybacking the information that which processes have taken new checkpoints in the broadcast committing message, the checkpoint sequence number of every process can be kept consistent in all processes, so that the unnecessary checkpoints and orphan messages can be avoided in the future running. The algorithm needn't block any process and has lower overhead than other proposed consistent coordinated checkpointing algorithms.

1 Introduction

Checkpointing has been an attractive technique for providing fault-tolerance in distributed computing system. When a fault occurs, the processes can be rolled back to previous checkpoints by reloading the checkpoints state to recover the system [1]. Two approaches are used to reduce the overhead associated with coordinated checkpointing: one is to reduce the number of synchronization messages and the number of checkpoints, but it will block processes [2-4]; the other is to make the checkpointing process non-blocking, but it will take unnecessary checkpoints [5-6]. We introduce computing checkpoint, which is taken when a process receives computing message sent by other process that takes its tentative checkpoint, to design a low-cost non-blocking consistent coordinated checkpointing algorithm that combines these two approaches, named as LNCC.

The paper is organized as follows: Section 2 introduces the system model and some definitions. Section 3 presents LNCC algorithm. Section 4 gives its correctness proofs. Section 5 compares our scheme with earlier relative consistent coordinated checkpointing schemes. Section 6 concludes the paper.

2 System Model and Definitions

The distributed computation consists of N sequential processes denoted by $P_1, P_2, \ldots, P_N$ running concurrently on fail-stop. The way for processes to communicate with each other is implemented by message passing. Each process progresses at its own speed and messages are exchanged through reliable communication channels, whose transmission delays are finite but arbitrary. Every process saves its local state to stable memory to produce its local checkpoint and each checkpoint taken by a process is assigned a unique checkpoint sequence number (CSN). The ith ($i \geq 0$) checkpoint of process P_k is assigned a sequence number i and is denoted by $C_{k,i}$. Any event $e_{k,x}$ that exists between $C_{k,i-1}$ and $C_{k,i}$ is said "$e_{k,x}$ belongs to $C_{k,i}$", denoted as $e_{k,x} \in C_{k,i}$. The ith checkpoint interval of a process denotes all the computation performed between its ith and $(i+1)^{th}$ checkpoint, including the ith checkpoint but not the $(i+1)^{th}$ checkpoint.

Definition 1. Orphan Message: A process P_i takes checkpoint $C_{i,x}$, process P_j takes checkpoint $C_{j,y}$, then P_i sends computation message M to P_j, we call M orphan message if and only if (deliver(M)$\in C_{j,y}$) $\wedge$ (send(M)$\notin C_{i,x}$).

The orphan message between processes is the reason for resulting in inconsistent [7]. A global checkpoint is a set of local checkpoints, one from each process. A global checkpoint is consistent if no message is orphan with respect to any pair of its local checkpoints [8-10].

Definition 2. Dependent Relation: A process P_i takes checkpoint $C_{i,x}$, process P_j takes checkpoint $C_{j,y}$, then P_i sends computation message M to P_j, we say that P_j at its yth checkpoint interval depends on P_i at its xth checkpoint. Simply we say P_j depends on P_i, denoted as $R_j(i)=1$. If P_j takes its new checkpoint, P_i must take checkpoint too; otherwise M becomes orphan between P_i and P_j. If P_j depends on P_k, and P_k depends on P_i, we say P_j transitively depends on P_i.

Definition 3. Computing Checkpoint: Assume that P_i has taken its $(x+1)^{th}$ tentative checkpoint and sends a computation message M to P_j. Before receiving M, P_j knows P_i in its xth checkpoint. Hence P_j must take forced checkpoint before delivering M. The checkpoint taken by P_j is called computing checkpoint. If P_j doesn't take computing checkpoint, M may become an orphan in the future.

3 The LNCC Algorithm

3.1 The Basic Idea of LNCC Algorithm

The solutions to ensure low-cost non-blocking coordinated checkpointing depend on two methods. One is to make the dependent relation not to induce unnecessary checkpoint [11]. The other is to make a receiver decide correctly whether it should take forced checkpoint before delivering a received massage to avoid orphan message and unnecessary checkpoint. We use two-phase checkpointing, these processes on which the initiator depends should take tentative checkpoint, and computing checkpoint is used to avoid orphans. When a process takes a computing checkpoint, it does not request these processes on which it depends to take checkpoint. The computing checkpoint should be transformed to a tentative checkpoint when the process that has taken the computing checkpoint receives request or discarded when the process receives committing message. Additionally, computing checkpoint can be saved in the main memory to reduce storage overhead and be saved into the stable memory only if it is transformed to tentative later. In the second phase, the initiator broadcasts committing message to all processes in the system, piggybacking the information that which processes have taken checkpoints. According to the information, each process can ensure that the *CSNs* of all processes are consistent in every process. So orphan message and unnecessary checkpoint can be avoided.

3.2 The Data Structure of LNCC Algorithm

R_i: a Boolean array. $R_i(j)$ ($i \neq j$) is initialized to 0 but $R_i(i)=1$ in each P_i.

Tem_R_i: a Boolean array. It is used to save temporary dependent relations after taking tentative checkpoint. It is initialized to 0 but $Tem\_R_i(i)=1$ in every P_i. If P_i makes tentative checkpoint permanent, $R_i:=Tem\_R_i$; If P_i discards tentative or computing checkpoint, $R_i:= R_i \cup Tem\_R_i$.

Rep_R_i: a Boolean array. It is used to save the information that which processes have taken new checkpoints. It is initialized to 0 but $Rep\_R_i(i)=1$ in every P_i.

$CSN_i[j]$: an integer array. $CSN_i[j]=X$ means process P_j takes X^{th} checkpoint that P_i expects. CSN_i is initialized to 0 in every process.

Cp_state: a Boolean variable initialized to 0, and it is set to 1 in P_i if P_i is during its checkpointing.

Com_state: a Boolean variable initialized to 0, and it is set to 1 in P_i if P_i has taken a computing checkpoint.

Weight: a non-negative variable of type real with maximum value of 1. It is used to detect the termination of the checkpointing [12].

Trigger: a tuple (*pid,inum*). *pid* indicates the checkpoint initiator that triggered this node to take its latest tentative checkpoint. *inum* indicates the *CSN* at node *pid* when it takes its local checkpoint on initiating consistent checkpointing.

3.3 The LNCC Algorithm

3.3.1 Initiating Checkpointing

Any process can initiate a checkpointing. When a process P_i initiates a checkpointing, it takes a local checkpoint, increments its $CSN_i[i]$, sets weight to 1, sends a checkpoint request to each process P_j such that $R_i[j]=1$ and resumes its computation. Each request carries the trigger of the initiator, R_i, and a portion of the *weight* of the initiator, whose *weight* is decreased by an equal amount.

3.3.2 Reception of a Checkpoint Request

When a process P_i receives a request from P_j, it first compares the $CSN_j[j]$ which is in the request message with its $CSN_i[j]$ to see if it needs to inherit the request. If $CSN_j[j] \leq CSN_i[j]$ or $Cp\_state:=1$, P_i does not need to inherit the request, it sends the appended *weight* to the initiator and then exits. Otherwise, if $Com\_state=1$, it makes computing checkpoint tentative. And then set $Com\_state:=0$; $Cp\_state:=1$; propagates the request of taking checkpoint. If there isn't a computing (or tentative) checkpoint, P_i takes a tentative checkpoint and increases $CSN_i[i]$. For each process P_k on which P_i depends, but P_j does not, P_i sends a request to P_k. P_i appends the initiator's *trigger* and a portion of the received *weight* to all those requests. At last, P_i sends a reply to the initiator with the remaining *weight* and resumes its underlying computation.

3.3.3 Sending and Receiving Computation Messages During Checkpointing

When a process P_j in checkpointing sends a computation message to a process P_i, it piggybacks his $CSN_j[j]$. When P_i receives a computation message M from P_j and P_i has not taken new checkpoint, P_i compares $CSN_j[j]$ with its local $CSN_i[j]$. If $CSN_j[j] \leq CSN_i[j]$, P_i delivers M directly. Otherwise, it implies that P_j has taken a checkpoint before sending M. P_i takes computing checkpoint and increases $CSN_i[i]$, then delivers M.

3.3.4 The Termination of the Checkpointing

When the initiator P_i receives a reply message from P_j, P_i adds the *weight* which is in the reply message to its own *weight* and set $Rep\_R_i[j]=1$. When its *weight* becomes equal to 1, it concludes that all processes involved in the checkpointing have taken their tentative checkpoints. Then, it broadcasts committing message with Rep_R_i to all processes. On receiving the committing message, if a process has taken a tentative checkpoint, it makes tentative permanent; if a process P_i has taken a computing checkpoint, it discards the computing checkpoint and decreases $CSN_i[i]$. Each process P_j updates its CSN and its R_j according to Rep_R_i piggybacked on the committing message. If a process P_j has not taken checkpoint, but a process P_k on which P_j depends has taken checkpoint, the dependent relation $R_j[k]=1$ should be cancelled to avoid unnecessary checkpoint in the future.

3.4 An Example of LNCC Algorithm

Figure 1 is an example of a distributed system with LNCC. In Fig.1, solid line means transmitting computing message and dashed line means request message. P_4 as initiator takes checkpoint $C_{4,1}$ and sends request to the processes on which it depends. After taking checkpoint $C_{3,1}$, P_3 sends $M4$ to P_2 with $CSN_3(3)=1$. Due to $CSN_2(3)=0$, $CSN_2(3)<CSN_3(3)$, P_2 takes computing checkpoint $C_{2,1}$ before delivering $M4$. Due to $CSN_1(2)=0$, $CSN_2(2)=1$, P_1 takes computing checkpoint $C_{1,1}$ before delivering $M5$. After receiving request, P_1 makes computing checkpoint $C_{1,1}$ tentative and sends request to P_2. P_2 makes computing checkpoint $C_{2,1}$ tentative. The system is consistent.

4 Correctness of the Algorithm

Theorem 1. Computing checkpoint is necessary.

Proof: Assume that P_j piggybacking $CSN_j[j]$ sends M to P_i. If $CSN_j[j]>CSN_i[j]$, it means P_j has taken a checkpoint before sending M. Assume that P_i doesn't take computing checkpoint before delivering M. Since the communication delays are finite but arbitrary, and at the same time the processes needn't be blocked, the processes' future running situations are unforeseen. Later, P_i may receive a request from another process P_k. P_i will take checkpoint, and then M becomes an orphan. If P_i takes computing checkpoint before delivering M, when P_i receives a request from P_k, the computing checkpoint can be transformed to tentative checkpoint, avoiding M becomes an orphan. After making computing checkpoint tentative, P_i propagates taking checkpoint request to the processes on which it depends but P_k does not depend. If P_i doesn't receive request message, the computing checkpoint will be discarded and the system is still consistent.□

Theorem 2. The LNCC algorithm is consistent.

Proof: Assume that there is an inconsistent after checkpointing. There is a message M sent from P_i to P_j such that P_j saves the event of delivering M and P_i doesn't save the event of sending M. P_j is an initiator or it depends on initiator because it takes a checkpoint. M is sent from P_i to P_j, so there is $R_j(i)=1$. If P_j takes checkpoint, P_i must take checkpoint. The computing checkpoint is used to avoid orphan and can not induce inconsistent (Theorem 1), so LNCC is consistent.□

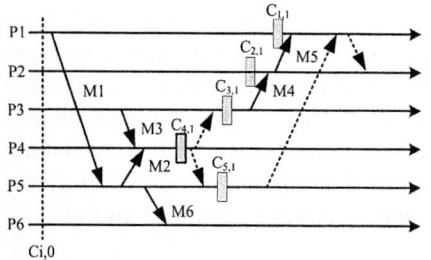 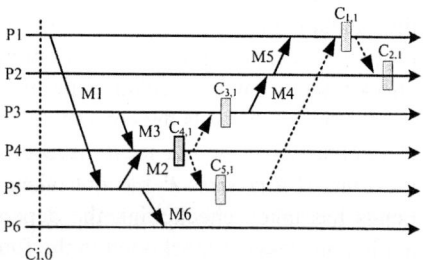

Fig. 1. An example of a distributed system with LNCC algorithm

Fig. 2. An inconsistent example of Cao-Singhal's algorithm

5 Comparisons with Existing Work

Many checkpointing schemes have been proposed for the distributed computing. In Ref.[2], only the processes on which the initiator depends take coordinated checkpoints, but Ref.[2] must block processes while checkpointing. Blocking algorithms may dramatically degrade the system performance [5]. To address this issue, non-blocking algorithms [5-6] are proposed. In non-blocking algorithms, processes need not be blocked during checkpointing by using a checkpoint sequence number to identify orphan messages. However, these algorithms require all processes in the system to take checkpoints during checkpointing, even though many of them may not be necessary.

Prakash–Singhal's algorithm [12] was the first algorithm that attempts to combine min-process with non-blocking two approaches. It only forces minimum number of processes on which initiator depends to take checkpoints and does not block the underlying computation during the checkpointing. However, this algorithm may result in an inconsistency in some situations [11]. Cao-Singhal's algorithm improves Prakash–Singhal's algorithm by using mutable checkpoint and implements a non-blocking algorithm [11]. In Cao-Singhal's algorithm, when P_i receives a computation message M from P_j, P_i should take mutable checkpoint if the following three conditions have been satisfied: (1) P_j is in checkpointing process before sending M; (2) P_i has sent a message since last checkpoint and (3) P_i has not taken a checkpoint associated with the initiator [11]. The algorithm is inconsistent in some situations.

Figure 2 is used to illustrate the inconsistency of Cao-Singhal's algorithm by the example in 3.4. In Fig.2, P_4 as initiator takes checkpoint $C_{4,1}$ and sends requests to the processes on which it depends. After taking checkpoint $C_{3,1}$, P_3 sends $M4$ to P_2. P_2 doesn't take mutable checkpoint before delivering $M4$ because it hasn't sent a message since last checkpoint (condition (2) has not been satisfied). After receiving $M5$ from P_2, P_1 receives request to take checkpoint and requests P_2 taking checkpoint. So $M4$ becomes an orphan message.

In table 1, we use four parameters to evaluate the performance of a checkpointing algorithm: the number of checkpoints during a checkpointing process, the blocking time (in the worst case), the system message overhead, whether the algorithm is distributed or not. Since Prakash–Singhal's [12] and Cao-Singhal's [11] algorithm are inconsistent, we don't compare LNCC with them.

Table 1. A comparison of system performance

algorithm	checkpoints	Blocking time	messages	distributed
Koo–Toueg[2]	N_{min}	$N_{min}*T_{disk}$	$3*N_{min}*N_{dep}*C_{uni}$	yes
Elnozahy [5]	N	0	$2*C_{broad}+N*C_{uni}$	no
LNCC	$N_{min}+N_{comp}$	0	$2*C_{uni}*N_{min}+C_{broad}$	yes

The variables are illustrated as follows. C_{uni}: cost of sending a message from one process to another process; C_{broad}: cost of broadcasting a message to all processes; T_{disk}: delay incurred in saving a checkpoint on the stable storage; T_{comp}: delay incurred in saving a computing checkpoint; N_{min}: the number of processes on which the initiator depends [2]; N: the total number of processes in the system; N_{comp}: the number of redundant computing checkpoints during a checkpointing process, a computing checkpoint is redundant if it isn't transformed into a tentative checkpoint; N_{dep}: the average number of processes on which a process depends. Note that $1 \leq N_{dep} \leq N-1$. If computing checkpoint is saved on the memory, T_{comp} is much less than T_{disk}; if computing checkpoint is saved on the stable storage, T_{comp} is equal to T_{disk}. Our experiment shows that N_{comp} is less than 4 percent of the number of tentative checkpoints. In the best situation, N_{comp} is equal to zero. Since a computing checkpoint is saved in the main memory, the delay incurred in saving a computing checkpoint is very little. The delay of saving computing checkpoint can be ignored compared with the delay of saving tentative checkpoint. The overhead of LNCC is $N_{min}*T_{disk}+ N_{comp}*T_{comp}+2*C_{uni}*N_{min}+C_{broad}$, less than other algorithms.

6 Conclusion

In this paper, we present a low-cost non-blocking checkpointing algorithm. Through using computing checkpoint and piggybacking the information that which processes have taken checkpoint in the broadcast committing message, the unnecessary checkpoints and orphan messages can be avoided in the future running. Our algorithm is the real consistent coordinated checkpointing algorithm that combines the two approaches of reducing the number of checkpoints and making the checkpointing process non-blocking. The algorithm is better than other coordinated checkpointing algorithms.

References

1. E.N.Elnozahy, L.Alvisi, Y.M.Wang and D.B.Johnson: A Survey of Rollback-Recovery Protocols in Message-Passing Systems. ACM Computing Surveys.2002, 34(3):375-408.
2. R.Koo, S.Toueg: Checkpointing and Rollback-Recovery for Distributed Systems. IEEE Transactions on Software Engineering.1987, 13(1):23-31.
3. J.L.Kim, T.Park: An Efficient Protocol for Checkpointing Recovery in Distributed Systems. IEEE Transactions on Parallel and Distributed Systems.1993, 5(8):955-960.
4. Y.Deng, E.K.Park: Checkpointing and Rollback-Recovery Algorithms in Distributed Systems. Journal of Systems Software.1994, 4:59-71.
5. E.N.Elnozahy, D.B.Johnson, W.Zwaenepoel: The Performance of Consistent Checkpointing. In: Proceedings of 11th Symposium on Reliable Distributed Systems, IEEE Press, Houston, 1992:39-47.
6. L.M.Silva, J.G.Silva: Global Checkpointing for Distributed Programs. In: Proceedings of 11th Symposium on Reliable Distributed Systems, IEEE Press, Houston, 1992:155-162.
7. J.M.Helary, R.H.B.Netzer, and M.Raynal: Consistency Issues in Distributed checkpoints. IEEE Transactions on Software Engineering.1999, 25(2):274-281.
8. J.M.Helery, A.Mostefaoui and M.Raynal: Communication-Induced Determination of Consistent Snapshots. IEEE Transactions on Parallel and Distributed Systems.1999, 10(9):865-877.
9. R.H.B.Netzer, J.Xu: Necessary and Sufficient Conditions for Consistent Global Snapshots. IEEE Transactions on Parallel and Distributed Systems.1995, 6(2):165-169.
10. J.M.Helary, A.Mostefaoui, R.H.B.Netzer and M.Raynal: Preventing Useless Checkpoints in Distributed Computations. In: Proceedings of 16th Symposium on Reliable Distributed Systems, IEEE Press, Durham, 1997:183-190.
11. Guohong Cao, M.Singhal: Checkpointing with Mutable Checkpoints. Theoretical Computer Science.2003, 290:1127-1148.
12. R.Prakash, M.Singhal: Low-Cost Checkpointing and Failure Recovery in Mobile Computing Systems. IEEE Transactions on Parallel and Distributed System.1996, 7(10):1035-1048.

The K-Fault-Tolerant Checkpointing Scheme for the Reliable Mobile Agent System

Taesoon Park and Jaehwan Youn

Department of Computer Engineering, Sejong University,
Seoul 143-747, Korea
{tspark, rivian}@sejong.ac.kr

Abstract. This paper presents a k-fault-tolerant checkpointing scheme for the reliable mobile agent system. The proposed scheme employs $2k$ observer agents which manage the checkpoints saved at the previously visiting sites. When the execution site fails, one of the observers recovers the agent from the checkpointed state so that the system can achieve a high degree of fault tolerance. To evaluate the performance, the proposed scheme and other replication schemes have been implemented on the Aglet system.

1 Introduction

As the mobile agent has drawn an attention as a new distributed computing paradigm, many mobile agent systems have been developed. However, for the agents to be used in more various application areas, agent execution should be reliable. Several fault-tolerant schemes have been proposed for the mobile agent, which are categorized into the replication scheme [3] and the checkpointing scheme [4]. The checkpointing scheme is known to require very low overhead compared to the replication scheme. However, considering the degree of fault-tolerance, the replication scheme is more plausible since in the checkpointing scheme, an agent may get blocked or lost due to the concurrent site failures.

In this paper, we present a k-fault-tolerant checkpointing scheme to improve the fault-tolerance degree of the checkpointing scheme while maintaining the low overhead of the checkpointing scheme. In the checkpointing scheme, an agent takes a checkpoint at the end of each execution stage. Our scheme utilizes these checkpoints and to manage these checkpoints and perform any recovery action, an observer agent is employed for each stage. In case of a site failure, the agent can recover from one of the previous checkpoints so that the system can achieve a high degree of reliability. We have implemented the k-fault-tolerant checkpointing scheme and other replication schemes to evaluate the performance.

2 Mobile Agent System Model

A mobile agent system consists of a number of system sites connected by a communication network. Each of the sites, to support execution and migration of agents, provides one or more *places*. A place is responsible for the migration of agents and provides the access point to the local resources. The execution of an agent in a place is called a *stage*. We denote a mobile agent with an identifier i as MA_i and the α-th stage of MA_i as $SG_{i,\alpha}$. The stage $SG_{i,\alpha}$ means the execution of a task after the α-th place migration and we also denote the agent in $SG_{i,\alpha}$ as $MA_{i,\alpha}$. For the failure types, the fail-stop model is assumed; that is, once a component fails, it stops its execution and does not perform any malicious actions.

3 K-Fault-Tolerant Checkpointing

Checkpointing is a well-known operation to save intermediate states of an agent into a stable storage so that the agent can recover from the checkpoint when a system failure occurs. One possible problem of the existing checkpointing schemes is that the agent may get blocked for a long time until the system site recovers from the failure. In the worst case, the agent may get lost if the system site cannot be recovered.

Hence, for the k-fault-tolerant checkpointing, a checkpoint is taken at the end of each stage and an observer agent is created to manage the checkpoint. When an agent is migrated to the next site, it is first replicated and the replica is transferred to the next site using the *Remote Method Invocation*. The agent in the previous site is terminated, when the migration is successfully completed. In the proposed scheme, the agent remained in the previous site is used as an observer agent instead of being terminated. The observer manages the checkpoint of the site and detects any possible failure of the next site so that the observer can recover the agent from the checkpoint in case of a system failure.

Also, to tolerate up to k concurrent site failures , $2k+1$ agents are used. Among them, one called a primary agent is responsible for the initial execution of each stage and k observer agents manage the checkpoints. With these k observer agents, the primary agent can be recovered from one of the checkpointed states even after k concurrent failures. The other k observers are also used to reach the agreement when more than one observer concurrently detect the failure of the execution site and try the recovery action. Since in such a case, only one observer agent obtaining the majority votes successfully completes the recovery action, up to k failures during the consensus process can also be tolerated with one primary and $2k$ observer agents.

These $2k$ observers are created along the agent's traveling path. Figure 1 shows an example of the observers where the value of k is one. As shown in the figure, a primary agent, $MA_{i,\alpha}$, saves its current state as a checkpoint and creates an observer, $O_{i,\alpha}$, before the migration. The notation, $O_{i,\alpha}$, denotes the observer created at the end of the stage, $SG_{i,\alpha}$.

$MA_{i,\alpha}$ also sends out the $M_{exec\_end_{i,\alpha}}$ messages to the observers before the migration. The $M_{exec\_end_{i,\alpha}}$ message informs the observers of the end of the stage $SG_{i,\alpha}$. Also, the message implicitly informs that there has been no failure for the stage $SG_{i,\alpha}$ and one more observer for $SG_{i,\alpha}$ has been created. Therefore, upon the receipt of this message, the observer with the lowest priority can safely be terminated so that only $2k$ observers can be managed. To maintain the priority of observers, each observer, $O_{i,\alpha}$, maintains a counter variable, $O\_CNT_{i,\alpha}$. The counter value is initially set to one and incremented by one whenever the observer receives the M_{exec_end} message.

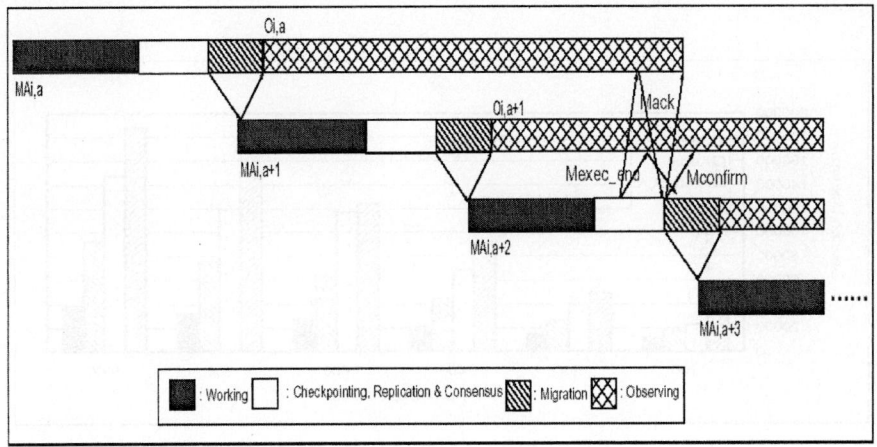

Fig. 1. K-Fault-Tolerant Checkpointing and Observer Management

The agent and the observers also perform the consensus at the end of each stage, in order to agree on the completion of the stage $SG_{i,\alpha}$ and eliminate any duplicate execution by the observer. If any observer falsely detects the failure of the agent, there can be duplicate execution of one stage by the observer. To guarantee no duplicate execution, on the receipt of the $M_{exec\_end_{i,\alpha}}$ message, each observer sends back the acknowledgment message, $M_{ack_{i,\alpha}}$ to the primary agent. When the primary agent, $MA_{i,\alpha}$, receives the $M_{ack_{i,\alpha}}$ messages from the majority of the observers, it can confirm that there is no duplicate execution for the current stage, $SG_{i,\alpha}$, and sends back the $M_{confirm_{i,\alpha}}$ messages to the observers. $MA_{i,\alpha}$ then migrates for the next stage.

To detect any failure of the primary agent, the time-out is used. Each observer sets a certain time-out value for each stage, $SG_{i,\alpha}$. If an observer receives the $M_{exec\_end_{i,\alpha}}$ message before the time-out timer expires, it resets the time-out value for the next stage, knowing that there is no failure during the current stage, $SG_{i,\alpha}$. However, if the timer expires without receiving the $M_{exec\_end_{i,\alpha}}$ message, the observer suspects the failure of the primary agent, $MA_{i,\alpha}$ and begins the consensus process. For the consensus, the scheme proposed in [3] is used, in which the observer with the highest priority can take care of the recovery.

4 Performance Study

To evaluate the performance of k-fault-tolerant checkpointing, the proposed scheme and three replication schemes discussed in [2] have been implemented on top of the Aglet [1] system. A cluster of forty Pentium IV 1 GHz PCs connected through a 100 Mbps Ethernet was used for the experiments.

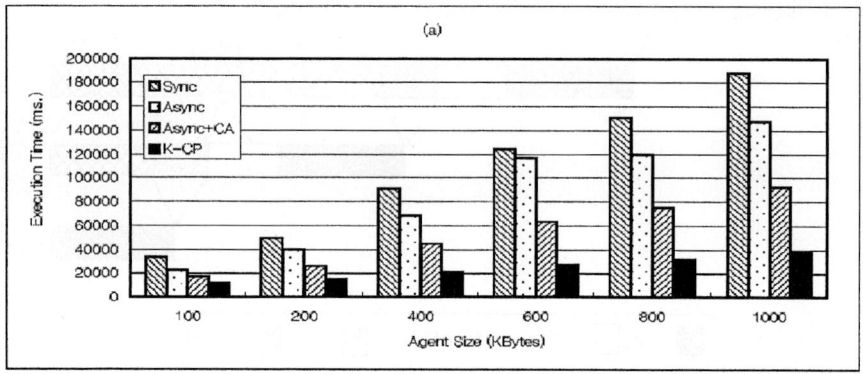

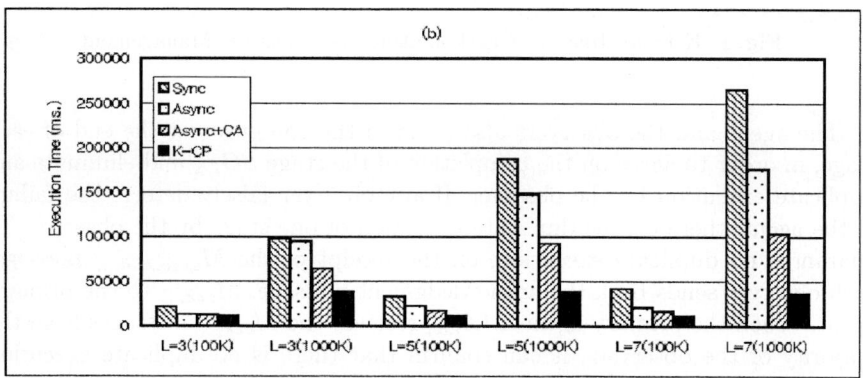

Fig. 2. Experimental Results

Figure 2.(a) first shows the performance of four fault-tolerant schemes when the size of an agent varies from 100 KBytes to 1000 KBytes. For these results, an agent worked for 1000 ms. for each stage and one primary agent and four observers (or replicas) were used for each stage. When the agent size becomes 10 times larger, the execution time of the synchronous replication scheme (denoted by Sync) and the asynchronous replication scheme (denoted by Async) become 5.65 times and 6.62 times longer, respectively. Also, the asynchronous scheme using the consensus agent (denoted by Async+CA) shows the 5.40 times longer execution time. Comparing with these performance, the k-fault-tolerant checkpointing scheme (denoted by K-CP) shows a very stable performance. When the agent size is 100 KBytes, the K-CP scheme achieves 69% reduction of the execution time compared to the Sync scheme while it achieves 79% reduction when the agent size is 1000 KBytes.

Figure 2.(b) compares the performance of four schemes when the number of the primary and the observer (or replica) agents is three, five and seven. The label, $L = X(YK)$, in the figure denotes that the number of the agents was X and the agent size was Y KBytes for that result. As it is noticed from the figure, the increase of the replica number has the same effect as the increase of the agent size. However, the increase of the observer number in the K-CP scheme does not have much effect on the increase of the execution time. The execution time increases only 2% when the value of L is seven, since in the K-CP scheme, there is no replica migration and the number of observers only affects the consensus time.

5 Conclusions

In this paper, we have proposed a k-fault-tolerant checkpointing scheme for the reliable mobile agent system and presented the performance of the proposed scheme. In the proposed scheme, to tolerate up to k failures, $2k$ observer agents are used and the consensus action is performed among the $2k + 1$ agents. The performance results confirmed that the proposed scheme achieves significant performance improvement over the other replication schemes and it also shows very stable performance.

Acknowledgments

This work was supported by grant No. R04-2002-000-20102-02004 from the Basic Research Program of the Korea Science & Engineering Foundation.

References

1. Karjoth, G., Lange, D.B., Oshima, M.: A Security Model for Aglets. IEEE Internet Computing (1997)
2. Park, T., Byun, I., Kim, H., Yeom, H.Y.: The Performance of Checkpointing and Replication Schemes for Fault Tolerant Mobile Agent Systems. Proc. of the 21st Symp. on Reliable Distributed Systems (2002) 256–261
3. Pleisch, S., Schiper, A.: FATOMAS - A Fault-Tolerant Mobile Agent System Based on the Agent-Dependent Approach. Proc. of the Int'l Conf. on Dependable Systems and Networks (2001) 215–224
4. Strasser, M., Rothermel, K.: System Mechanism for Partial Rollback of Mobile Agent Execution. Proc. of the 20th Int'l Conf. on Distributed Computing Systems (2000)

Analysis of Mobile Agents' Fault-Tolerant Behavior

Wenyu Qu and Hong Shen

Graduate School of Information Science,
Japan Advanced Institute of Science and Technology

Abstract. Mobile agent-based technology has attracted considerable interest in both academia and industry in recent years. Many agent-based execution models have been proposed and their effectiveness have been demonstrated in the literature. However, these models require a high overhead to achieve the reliable execution of mobile agents. In this paper, we propose a new mobile agent-based execution model. Extensive theoretical analysis on the population distribution of mobile agents is provided to evaluate the performance of our model. The analytical results reveal new theoretical insights into the fault-tolerant execution of mobile agents. Our model provides an efficient way to increase overall performance and a promising method in achieving mobile agent system reliability.

Keywords: Mobile agents, stochastic analysis, fault tolerance.

1 Introduction

As defined in [3], mobile agents are software entities that can migrate across the network (hence mobile) representing users in various tasks (hence agents). The kernel of this technology is to move the computation to the data rather than the data to the computation [2]. When a large amount of data are stored at remote hosts, mobile agents allow users to package their requests, dispatch it to a destination host where interactions take place locally, and return with a comparatively small result. Furthermore, mobile agents can sense their execution environment and react autonomously to changes. These merits often motivates programmers to use mobile agent technology in distributed system design. Successful examples of mobile agent systems include Aglets, Voyager, Agent Tcl, Tacoma, Knowbots, and Telescript.

As mobile agents are the medium for implementing various executions, their behaviors are paramount for the network performance. Clearly, one of the pivotal tasks ahead, if mobile agents are to have significant impact, is to explore quantitative studies on the behaviors of mobile agents, which can reveal the inherence of the mobile agent approach and ultimately guide future researches. This issue, unlike that of system design using mobile agents, has not yet been adequately addressed so far.

In this paper, we propose a fault-tolerant model for mobile agents executing in large distributed networks and analyze the population distribution of mobile agents in our model. The key idea is the use of stochastic regularities of mobile agents' behavior – all the mobile agents in the network as a whole can be stochastically characterized though a single mobile agent may act randomly. In effect, our analytical results reveal new theoretical insights into the statistical behaviors of mobile agents and provide useful tools for effectively managing mobile agents in large networks.

2 The Fault-Tolerant Execution Model

Our execution model is built on a mobile agent-based network as stated in the previous section. For a large network with a large number of nodes, suppose that agents can be generated from every node on networks, and each node on networks provide mobile agents an execution environment. Initially, there are a pile of tasks generated in the network. Then a pile of agents, whose number is equal to that of the tasks, is generated. Each task is carried by an agent. Those agents wander among nodes in the network to search for their destinations. At each node, agents have local information about the error rate of each adjoin link, but they do not have global knowledge on the state of the network. The sequence of nodes visited by the agent compose the agent's itinerary. Agents' itineraries can be either static or dynamic. A static itinerary is entirely defined at the source and does not change during the agent travelling; whereas a dynamic itinerary is subject to modifications by the agent during its execution [4].

Since mobile agents are capable of sensing the execution environment and reacting autonomously to changes [2], a dynamic itinerary is adopted in this context, i.e., an agent decides its itinerary on the fly. Let h_i denote the ith host in the itinerary and $NB(i)$ denote the set consisted by the neighbor hosts of h_i. The number of neighbor hosts in set $NB(i)$ is denoted by d_i, i.e., the connectivity degree of host h_i. Once an agent reaches a node, say h_i, it executes locally. After completed its execution, the agent selects a node from $NB(i)$ to move to. Suppose that there is an error rate for each candidate direction, mobile agents will prefer a route with a low error rate to shun failures. The selected node in $NB(i)$ is denoted by h^1_{i+1}. In case that a failure takes place on h^1_{i+1}, the agent is blocked and has to return to the previous host h_i. Then, it will reselect another neighbor host from $NB(i)$ and move to. The jth selected host in $NB(i)$ is denoted by h^j_{i+1}. An agent is supposed will not jump to the same neighbor host twice since in a general way a failure host will not recover in a very short time. This process will continue until the agent successfully enters a host and completes its execution there. The final visited host in $NB(i)$ is denoted by h_{i+1}. In case that all the d_i neighbor hosts are out of work, the agent dies. In this context, we say a host is down if it is out of work; otherwise, it is up. Furthermore, if host h_i subjects to a failure when the agent moves to a down host in $NB(i)$, the agent is also lost.

3 Population Distribution

In an agent-driven system, agents must be generated and dispatched frequently. Thus, they will hold a certain amount of resources. This section analyzes the population distribution of mobile agents, which reflects the occupation status of computational resources.

Let $p_j(t)$ be the number of agents running in the jth node at time t, the number of agents running in the ith node can be given be the following equation:

$$p_i(t) = \sum_{k=0}^{d_i} \sum_{l=1}^{p_i(t)} \delta_{ilk}(t),$$

where d_i is the connectivity degree of the ith node in the network, and δ_{ilk} indicates the situation of the lth agent running on the ith at time t, i.e.,

$$\delta_{ilk}(t) = \begin{cases} 1 & \text{if it is the } k\text{th time that the } l\text{th agent returns back to the } i\text{th node;} \\ 0 & \text{otherwise.} \end{cases}$$

It is easy to see that $\sum_{k=0}^{d_i-1} \delta_{ilk}(t) = 1$ and $\sum_{l=1}^{p_i(t)} \delta_{ilk}$ is equal to the total number of agents running on the ith node that come back at the kth time. Especially, $\delta_{il0} = 1$ implies that the lth agent never moves out from the ith node. These agents can be further subdivided into two kinds: newly generated in the ith node or came from neighboring nodes. Let $g_i(t)$ be the number of agents newly generated in the ith node at time t and $p_{ij}(t)$ be the number of agents running on the ith node which come from the jth node at time t. Then, the dynamical change of the agents in the network can be given by the following stochastic equation:

$$p_i(t) = \sum_{l=1}^{p_i(t)} \delta_{il0}(t) + \sum_{k=1}^{d_i}\sum_{l=1}^{p_i(t)} \delta_{ilk}(t) = g_i(t) + \sum_{j \in NB(i)} p_{ij}(t) + \sum_{k=1}^{d_i}\sum_{l=1}^{p_i(t)} \delta_{ilk}(t)$$
$$= A_i(t) + B_i(t) + C_i(t).$$

Suppose that $r_i(t-1)$ is the number of requests received by the jth node at time $t-1$, we have $g_i(t) = r_i(t-1)$, since an agent will be generated for each request. As the failing possibility of each neighboring node is same, all the nodes in set $NB(i)$ have the same probability to be selected. Therefore, the average number of $p_{ij}(t)$ equals $(1-p)p_j(t-r)/d_j$. Since each time an agent returns to the previous node cost $2r$ time, $\delta_{ilk}(t) = 1$ indicates that the lth agent running on the ith node at time t must come from other nodes or be generated in the ith node at time $t - 2kr$. Therefore, the average number of $\sum_{l=1}^{p_i(t)} \delta_{ilk}(t)$ equals $[A_i(t) + B_i(t)]P\{\delta_{ilk}(t) = 1\}$. Taking expectations on both sides of the above equation, we have

$$\vec{p}(t) = \vec{r}(t-1) + A\vec{p}(t-r) + \sum_{k=1}^{d_j} \vec{r}(t-2kr-1)P\{\delta_{ilk}(t) = 1\}$$
$$+ \sum_{k=1}^{d_j-1} A\vec{p}(t-2kr-1)P\{\delta_{ilk}(t) = 1\},$$

where $\vec{p}(t) = (E[p_1(t)], \cdots, E[p_n(t)])^T$, $\vec{r}(t) = (E[r_1(t)], \cdots, E[r_n(t)])^T$, and $A = (a_{ij})_{n \times n}$ is an n by n matrix with elements

$$a_{ij} = \begin{cases} (1-p)/d_j & \text{if } j \in NB(i); \\ 0 & \text{otherwise.} \end{cases}$$

Let X_i^j be a 0 or 1 valued random variable with probability $p = P(X_i^j - 1)$ for $i = 1, 2, \cdots$ and $j = 1, 2, \cdots, d_i$. The event $\{X_i^j\}$ indicates that the agent can not enter the host h_i^j in set $NB(i)$, then the parameter p measures the incidence of failure in the network. Since the event $\{\delta_{jlk}(t) = 1\}$ is equivalent to the event $\{X_j^1 = 1, X_j^0 = 0, \cdots, X_j^k = 1, X_j^0 = 0\}$, where $\{X_i^0 = 0\}$ indicates the event that the host h_i is up, the probability $P\{\delta_{jlk}(t) = 1\}$ can be evaluated as follows

$$P\{\delta_{jlk}(t) = 1\} = P\{X_j^1 = 1, X_j^0 = 0, \cdots, X_j^k = 1, X_j^0 = 0\}$$
$$= P\{X_j^1 = 1\} P\{X_j^0 = 0\} \cdots P\{X_j^k = 1\} P\{X_j^0 = 0\}$$

due to the fact that whether a machine will fail or not is an independent event to other machines in the network and $P\{x_i^k = 1\} = p$ for $k = 1, 2, \cdots, d_i$. Here $x = (1-p)p$. Thus, the dynamic change on the number of agents running in the network can be expressed as follows:

$$\vec{p}(t) = \sum_{k=0}^{d_j} x^k \vec{r}(t - 2kr - 1) + \sum_{k=0}^{d_j - 1} x^k A \vec{p}(t - 2kr - 1).$$

4 Conclusion Remarks

In this paper, we proposed a fault-tolerant execution model of mobile agents and analyzed the population distribution to characterize the behavior of mobile agents in our model. Our results show that the agents' behavior is influenced by hosts' error rate and network connectivity. Thus, the behavior of mobile agents can be effectively managed according to network characteristics.

References

1. M.J. Fischer, N.A. Lynch, and M.S. Paterson. *Impossibility of Distributed Consensus with One Faulty Process*. Journal of the ACM, 32(2), pp. 374-382, Apr. 1985.
2. D. B. Lange and M. Oshima. *Seven Good Reasons for Mobile Agents*. Communication of the ACM, 42(3), pp. 88-89, Mar. 1999.
3. D. Milojicic. *Trend Wars: Mobile Agent Applications*. IEEE Concurrency, 7(3), pp. 80-90, 1999.
4. M. Straßer and K. Rothermel. *Reliability Concepts for Mobile Agents*. Int'l Journal of Cooperative Information Systems, 7(4), pp. 355-382, Dec. 1998.

Secure Group Communication with Low Communication Complexity

Heeyoul Kim, Jaewon Lee, H. Yoon, and J.W. Cho

CS Division, Korea Advanced Institute of Science and Technology,
373-1 Guseong-dong, Yuseong-gu, Daejeon, Republic of Korea
{hykim, jaewon, hyoon, jwcho}@camars.kaist.ac.kr

Abstract. In this paper we propose a secure group communication model with low communication complexity using multiplicative one-way functions and exclusive keys. When totally n users are in the group, it reduces the complexity of multicast message required in join or leave operation from $O(\log n)$ to $O(1)$ keeping other complexities comparable. Therefore, it is very applicable to a wide area network environment or a low-bandwidth channel such as ad hoc network.

Keywords: Networking and Communications, Security, Secure Group Communication.

1 Introduction

Secure group communication enables only the users in that group securely communicate with each other [7, 3, 6]. The major demand of it is to preserve security for a dynamic group by updating group key whenever a new user joins or an existing user leaves. Because key update is very consumptive and frequently performed due to the nature of group communication, the way to update it in a scalable and secure fashion is required.

The main focus of this paper is on the communication complexity, especially the complexity of multicast message. In almost network environments, the dominant cost is rather communication cost than computational cost [1, 8]. In particular, multicasting to all group members is very costly because not only group members but also other users or routers connected by the network must forward the message.

Many models with tree-based structure in [5, 9, 13, 14] reduce communication complexity of key update to logarithmic with the increase of storage complexity. In those models, each node in the tree represents a key and each leaf node corresponds to each user. The key corresponding to a node is shared between the users in the subtree rooted at the node and each user is given all the keys on the path from the corresponding leaf node to the root. But even in those models $O(\log n)$ multicast complexity is required.

In this paper, we present a communication-efficient secure model for secure group communication. Our model has also tree-based structure, but the keys shared between group members have the opposite property. With them, our model needs only $O(1)$ multicast complexity in the key update process keeping storage complexity and computation complexity similarly to previous models.

2 Modular Squaring Function

A modular squaring function plays a significant role in our model, especially in deriving children keys from parent key. Suppose N is a Blum integer, which means it is a composite integer of the form $N = pq$ where p and q are distinct primes each congruent to 3 modulo 4. Then the modular squaring function $f: Z_N^* \rightarrow Z_N^*$ defined by $f(x) = x^2 \bmod N$ has both one-wayness property and multiplicative property.

- *One-wayness Property.* The function f has one-wayness property. The inverse function of f is

$$f^{-1}(x) = x^{((p-1)(q-1)+4)/8} \bmod N, \qquad (1)$$

but computing a square root is computationally equivalent to factoring and thus intractable if the factorization of N is not known [10].
- *Multiplicative Property.* The function f has multiplicative property from the following equation :

$$f(x)f(y) = (x^2 \bmod N)(y^2 \bmod N) = (xy)^2 \bmod N = f(xy). \qquad (2)$$

3 A Communication-Efficient Model

Main Idea. In our model, we construct a tree that n_1 is a root node and n_{2k} and n_{2k+1} are children of n_k. We define that an *exclusive key*, EK_i, of a node n_i is the key which is shared between the users not in the subtree rooted at the node n_i. If n_i is a leaf node, EK_i is shared between all users except the one corresponding to the node.

To reduce storage complexity, we use modular squaring functions previously described. Let f_L and f_R be the publicly known functions having different composite integers. Then all EK_is except EK_1 are derived from the following equation :

$$EK_{2i} = f_L(EK_i), \quad EK_{2i+1} = f_R(EK_i) \quad \text{for } i \geq 1. \qquad (3)$$

In other words, the exclusive key of a node can be computed from the key of parent node and the function f_L if it is a left child, or f_R otherwise.

If a user has all keys of sibling nodes of the nodes along the path from the root to him, he can compute all keys of leaf nodes except his own node. For example, a user in a leaf node n_9 is able to compute the keys of all leaf nodes except EK_9 if he knows EK_3, EK_5 and EK_8. On the other hand, he can not compute the keys not permitted such as EK_4 because the functions have one-wayness property. The storage complexity for the keys of each user is only $O(\log n)$.

Initialization. As other centralized models in [2,4,11], we assume there is a center that manages the group and distributes keys. Initialization is executed only once when n initial users and center establish a new group communication. The steps to be performed by the center are described as follows:

1. It generates $m_L = pq, m_R = p'q'$ where p, q, p', q' are distinct primes each congruent to 3 modulo 4 and the bit lengths of m_L and m_R are the same. Then two modular squaring functions f_L and f_R are constructed as

$$f_L(x) = x^2 \bmod m_L, \quad f_R(x) = x^2 \bmod m_R \qquad (4)$$

2. It constructs a logical key tree with the users. It then uniformly chooses a root key $EK_1 \in Z^*_{m_L}$ and computes all exclusive keys from (3). Totally, at most $2n$ times of modular squaring are computed.
3. It uniformly chooses a group key GK which will be shared between all users. The messages that will be transferred are to be encrypted with this key.
4. For each user, the center authenticates him. Then it securely sends GK and exclusive keys of sibling nodes of the nodes along the path from the root to him. Communication complexity per each user is $O(\log n)$ and storage complexity is also $O(\log n)$, which is the same as in other models.

Join Operation. When a new user joins the group, a new leaf node is to be added and key update is to be done to prevent him from guessing past messages. The steps to be performed are as follows:

1. The center authenticates him. Then it finds a node n_k that does not have two children and the index k is the smallest. In the case that n_k is a leaf node, the user in n_k is set to be in n_{2k} and then n_{2k+1} is added. Then EK_{2k+1} is sent to n_{2k}. Otherwise, a child node of n_k is added.
2. The center uniformly chooses a new group key GK', encrypts it with current key GK and multicasts it. All users can decrypt it and also participate in the next communication. The complexity of multicasting message is only $O(1)$.
3. The center securely sends a new group key and EK_is of sibling nodes of the nodes along the path from the root to him. The complexity of unicast message is $O(\log n)$.

Leave Operation. When a user leaves the group, a corresponding leaf node is to be removed and key update is to be done to prevent him from guessing future messages. Denote n_k as the leaf node. The steps to be performed are as follows:

1. The center uniformly chooses a new group key GK' and an update value $R_1 \in Z^*_{m_L}$. They are encrypted with the key EK_k and multicasted. The complexity of the message is only $O(1)$.
2. Each user except the leaving user receives the ciphertext. He computes EK_k from the keys he holds and gets GK', R_1. For each exclusive key EK_j he holds, R_j is computed from R_1 similarly to the computation of exclusive keys. Then EK_j is updated as

$$EK_j = \begin{cases} EK_j \cdot R_j \bmod m_L & \text{if } j \text{ is even} \\ EK_j \cdot R_j \bmod m_R & \text{if } j \text{ is odd} \end{cases} \qquad (5)$$

Whole key computation of each user requires $\log n$ modular multiplications and $2\log n - 1$ function computations because intermediate values can be reused.

4 Analysis of Proposed Model

Security Analysis. Basically the security of our model is based on the difficulty of finding square root modulo composite number. Based on it, our model satisfies three major security properties encountered in group communication [9, 12]. It guarantees group key secrecy that any adversary can not discover the group key because each group key is independent from others, thus indistinguishable. It also guarantees forward and backward secrecy because update values are transferred securely and only group members can get them. Moreover it guarantees subkey secrecy that any adversary who knows some exclusive keys cannot discover any other keys not permitted. He cannot guess any ancestor key of some key he holds because both functions have one-way property.

Performance Analysis. The major measurements of performance evaluation are storage complexity for the keys, communication complexity and computation complexity. Among them, the complexity of join or leave operation is more important because it is carried out very frequently. Especially in wide area network or ad hoc network, the dominant bottleneck is not the computation cost but the communication cost.

In Table 1, we compare the performance of proposed model with tree-based model in [14]. Our model reduces the complexity of multicast message to $O(1)$ in join and leave operations. Also it reduces symmetric key decryptions of a user to just one. Additionally $O(\log n)$ function computations are executed in leave operation, but modular squaring is comparable to symmetric key decryption.

Table 1. Performance comparison between tree-based model and proposed model

		Tree-based	Proposed Model
	Key storage per user	$O(\log n)$	$O(\log n)$
Join/	Complexity of multicast message	$O(\log n)$	$O(1)$
Leave	# of decryptions per user	$O(\log n)$	$O(1)$
operation	# of function computations per user	-	$O(1)$ / $O(\log n)$

5 Remark and Conclusion

In this paper, we proposed a new model which reduces the complexity of multicast message in join or leave operation to $O(1)$ compared with $O(\log n)$ in the other models. In view of it, our model is more applicable to a wide area network environment or a low-bandwidth channel such as ad hoc network. Moreover it can be easily extended to control multiple join/leave requests at the same time or merge/partition operations although detailed descriptions are omitted due to the lack of space.

Acknowledgement

This work was supported by the Korea Science and Engineering Foundation (KOSEF) through the advanced Information Technology Research Center(AITrc) and University IT Research Center Project.

References

[1] Y. Amir, Y. Kim, C. Nita-Rotaru, and G. Tsudik. On the performance of group key agreement protocols. In *Proc. 22nd IEEE International Conference on Distributed Computing Systems*, pages 463–464, 2002.
[2] J. Anzai, N. Matsuzaki, and T.Matsumoto. A quick group key distribution scheme with "entity revocation". In *Proceedings of the International Conference on the Theory and Applications of Cryptology and Information Security*, pages 333–347. Springer-Verlag, 1999.
[3] M. Burmester and Y. Desmedt. A secure and efficient conference key distribution system. In *Advances in Cryptology, Eurocrypt '94*, pages 275–286. LNCS 950, 1994.
[4] I. Chang, R. Engel, D. Kandlur, D. Pendarakis, and D. Saha. Key management for secure internet multicast using boolean function minimization techniques. In *Proceedings IEEE Infocomm'99*, volume 2, pages 689–698, 1999.
[5] G. D. Crescenzo and O. Kornievskaia. Efficient re-keying protocols for multicast encryption. In *Proceedings of the SCN 2002*, pages 119–132, 2003.
[6] J. Katz and M. Yung. Scalable protocols for authenticated group key exchange. In *Advances in Cryptology, Crypto '03*, pages 110–125. LNCS 2729, 2003.
[7] Y. Kim, A. Perrig, and G. Tsudik. Simple and fault-tolerant key agreement for dynamic collaborative groups. In *ACM Conference on Computer and Communications Security*, pages 235–244, 2000.
[8] Y. Kim, A. Perrig, and G. Tsudik. Communication-efficient group key agreement. In *Proceedings of the 16th international conference on Information security: Trusted information*, pages 229–244, 2001.
[9] Y. Kim, A. Perrig, and G. Tsudik. Tree-based group key agreement. *ACM Trans. Inf. Syst. Secur.*, 7(1):60–96, 2004.
[10] A. J. Menezes, P. C. van Oorschot, and S. A. Vanstone. *Handbook of Applied Cryptography*. CRC Press, 2001.
[11] R. Safavi-Naini and H. Wang. New constructions for multicast re-keying schemes using perfect hash families. In *Proceedings of the 7th ACM conference on Computer and communications security*, pages 228–234. ACM Press, 2000.
[12] M. Steiner, G. Tsudik, and M. Waidner. Key agreement in dynamic peer groups. *IEEE Trans. Parallel Distrib. Syst.*, 11(8):769–780, 2000.
[13] D. Wallner, E. Harder, and R. Agee. Key management for multicast: Issues and architectures. RFC 2627, 1999.
[14] C. K. Wong, M. Gouda, and S. S. Lam. Secure group communications using key graphs. In *Proceedings of the ACM SIGCOMM '98 conference on Applications, technologies, architectures, and protocols for computer communication*, pages 68–79, 1998.

Multi-proxy Signature and Proxy Multi-signature Schemes from Bilinear Pairings*

Xiangxue Li, Kefei Chen, and Shiqun Li

Department of Computer Science and Engineering, Shanghai Jiaotong University,
Shanghai 200030, China
{xxli, chen-kf, sqli}@cs.sjtu.edu.cn

Abstract. In electronic world, proxy signature is a solution of delegation of signing capabilities. Proxy signatures can combine other special signatures to obtain some new types of proxy signatures. Due to the various applications of the bilinear pairings in cryptography, many pairing-based signature schemes have been proposed. In this paper, we propose a multi-proxy signature scheme and a proxy multi-signature scheme from bilinear pairings. We also show that both of them satisfy all the security properties required by proxy signatures.

1 Introduction

In 1996, Mambo, Usuda and Okamoto first introduced the concept of proxy signatures([5]). In the proxy signature scheme, an original signer is allowed to authorize a designated person as his proxy signer. Then the proxy signer is able to sign on behalf of the original signer. Proxy signature schemes have been shown to be useful in many applications, particularly in distributed computing where delegation of rights is quite common, such as e-cash systems, mobile agents for electronic commerce, mobile communications, grid computing, global distribution networks, and distributed shared object systems. In 2000, S.Hwang first proposed the concept of multi-proxy signatures([3]). In a multi-proxy signature scheme, an original signer could authorize a proxy group as his proxy agent. Then only the cooperation of all the signers in the proxy group can generate the proxy signatures on behalf of the original signer. At the same time, a contrary concept, proxy multi-signature, was introduced by Yi et al. ([6]). In a proxy multi-signature scheme, a designated proxy signer can generate the signature on behalf of a group of original signers.

In this paper, we propose a multi-proxy signature scheme and a proxy multi-signature scheme using Boneh et al.'s short signature scheme proposed at the Asiacrypt'01 conference([1]). Both of them are based on bilinear pairings. We also show that they provide all the security properties required by proxy signatures.

---

* This work is supported by NSFC under the grants 60273049 and 90104005.

2 Preliminaries

Let G_1 be a cyclic additive group generated by P, whose order is a prime q, and G_2 be a cyclic multiplicative group of the same order q. Let a, b be elements of Z_q^*. We assume that the discrete logarithm problems (DLP) in both G_1 and G_2 are hard. A bilinear pairing is a map $e : G_1 \times G_1 \longrightarrow G_2$ with the following properties: 1) Bilinear: $e(aP, bQ) = e(P, Q)^{ab}$; 2) Non-degenerate: There exists P and $Q \in G_1$ such that $e(P, Q) \neq 1$; 3) Computable: There is an efficient algorithm to computa $e(P, Q)$ for all $P, Q \in G_1$.

Basically, a secure proxy signature scheme should satisfy the following requirements([4]): Strong unforgeability, Verifiability, Strong identifiability, Strong undeniability, and Prevention of misuse.

3 Multi-proxy Signature Scheme from Bilinear Pairings

This section proposes a pairing-based multi-proxy signature scheme. Our multi-proxy signature scheme with the clerk architecture is divided into four phases: System setup phase, Proxy key generation phase, Multi-proxy signature generation phase, and Verification phase.

System Setup Phase. The system parameters are $\{G_1, G_2, e, q, P, H_1, H_2\}$. The original signer Alice has private key s_o and corresponding public key $PK_o = s_o P$. The proxy signers $\{B_j\}$ have private keys $\{s_{bj}\}$ and corresponding public keys $\{PK_{bj} = s_{bj} P\}$. Without loss of generality, assume that there are l proxy signers in the proxy group, who will cooperate to generate proxy signatures on behalf of the original signer Alice.

Proxy Key Generation Phase. To delegate the signing capability to a group of proxy signers, the original signer Alice does the following to make the signed warrant m_w. If the following process is finished successfully, each proxy signer B_j gets a proxy key S_{P_j}.

−Alice computes $S_{o_{mw}} = s_o H_2(m_w)$, and sends $(m_w, S_{o_{mw}})$ to $\{B_j\}$.
−B_j in the proxy group accepts $S_{o_{mw}}$ as a valid key only if $e(S_{o_{mw}}, P) = e(H_2(m_w), PK_o)$. If $S_{o_{mw}}$ passes this checking, each proxy signer B_j computes his proxy key as $S_{P_j} = S_{o_{mw}} + s_{bj} H_2(m_w)$.

Multi-proxy Signature Generation Phase. To generate a multi-proxy signature on a message m that conforms to the warrant m_w, one proxy signer in the proxy group is designated as a clerk, whose task is to combine partial proxy signatures to generate the final multi-proxy signature.

−$B_j(j = 1, 2, ..., l)$ chooses $x_j \longleftarrow_R Z_q^*$, computes $r_{P_j} = e(P, P)^{x_j}$ and broadcasts his r_{P_j} to the other l-1 proxy signers.
−$B_j(j = 1, 2, ..., l)$ computes $r_P = \prod_{j=1}^{l} r_{P_j}$, $c_P = H_1(m||r_P)$, $U_{P_j} = x_j P - c_P S_{P_j}$, and sends (c_P, U_{P_j}) to the clerk as his partial proxy signature on m.

-The clerk verifies those partial proxy signatures $\{U_{P_j}\}$ by the following equations $c_P = H_1(m||(\prod_{k \neq j} r_{Pk}) \cdot e(P, U_{P_j}) e(PK_o + PK_{bj}, H_2(m_w))^{c_P})$, for $j = 1, ..., l$.

Once all partial proxy signatures are correct, the multi-proxy signature of message m can be generated as (c_P, U_P, m_w) by computing $U_P = \sum_{j=1}^{l} U_{P_j}$.

Verification Phase. After receiving the multi-proxy signature (c_P, U_P, m_w), and the message m, the verifier compute $r_P = e(U_P, P) e(H_2(m_w), \sum_{j=1}^{l}(PK_o + PK_{bj}))^{c_P}$ and accept the multi-proxy signature if and only if $c_P = H_1(m||r_P)$.

3.1 Security Concerns

On the one hand, we assume that there is explicit description of the relative rights and information of all original signers and the proxy signer in the warrant m_w, therefore, it is straightforward to show that the properties of verifiability, identifiability, undeniability, and prevention of misuse stated in Section 2 are satisfied. On the other hand, we can show that the proposed scheme also provides unforgeability.

Unforgeability. As for multi-proxy signature, there are mainly three kinds of attackers: outsiders, who do not participate the issue of the multi-proxy signature; some proxy signer, who play an active in the signing process; and the signature owner. Firstly, since we use Hess's scheme([2]), which is proven secure, to generate the multi-proxy signature, any third party who can even get Alice's signature on the warrant m_w can not forge the multi-proxy signature. On the other hand, the original signer Alice can not generate a valid multi-proxy signature since those proxy signers' private keys $\{s_{bj}\}$ are used in the multi-proxy signature generation algorithm. Secondly, even the clerk, who has more power than other proxy signers in the proxy group, cannot forge a multi-proxy signature. To see this, suppose that the clerk wants the proxy group to sign a false message m'. Of cause, he can change his own r_{Pj}, therefor r_P. Then he tries to compute c'_P and U'_P such that $r_P = e(U'_P, P) e(H_2(m_w), \sum_{j=1}^{l}(PK_o + PK_{bj}))^{c'_P}$ and $c'_P = H_1(m'||r_P)$ hold. But due to the security of the basic identity based signature scheme and the hash function H_1, it is impossible. Lastly, since the signature owner can not obtain more information than the clerk, he can not generate a valid multi-proxy signature.

4 Proxy Multi-signature Scheme from Bilinear Pairings

This section proposes a pairing-based proxy multi-signature scheme.

System Setup Phase. The system parameters are $\{G_1, G_2, e, q, P, H_1, H_2\}$. Let $A_1, ..., A_n$ be n original signers with private key s_{oi} and corresponding public key $PK_{oi} = s_{oi}P$, B be a proxy signer designated by all A_i. B has a secret key s_b and corresponding public $PK_b = s_b P$.

Proxy Generations Phase. To delegate the signing capability to B, the original signers do the following to make the signed warrant m_w.

– For $1 \leq \forall i \leq n$, A_i computes $S_{oi} = s_{oi}H_2(m_w)$ and sends m_w and S_{oi} to the proxy signer as a sub-proxy key.
– For $1 \leq \forall i \leq n$, B confirms sub-proxy key S_{oi} by an equality such that $e(P, S_{oi}) = e(PK_{oi}, H_2(m_w))$. If S_{oi} passes this equality, he accepts it as a valid sub-proxy and continues; otherwise, he requests from A_i a valid one, or he terminates this protocol.
- If B confirms all the sub-proxy keys $S_{oi}(1 \leq \forall i \leq n)$, then he computes the proxy key as $S_P = \sum_{i=1}^{n} S_{oi} + s_b H_2(m_w)$.

Proxy Multi-signature Generation Phase. When B signs a document m for $A_1, ..., A_n$, he chooses $x \xleftarrow{R} Z_q^*$ and computes $r = e(P, P)^x$, $c = H_1(m||r)$, $S = xP - cS_P$, and outputs (c, S, m_w) as the proxy multi-signature on m.

Verification Phase. After receiving the proxy multi-signature (c, S, m_w), and the message m, the verifier compute $r = e(P, S)e(PK_b + \sum_{i=1}^{n} PK_{oi}, H_2(m_w))^c$, and accepts the proxy multi-signature if and only if $c = H_1(m||r)$.

4.1 Security Concerns

It is straightforward to show that the properties of verifiability, identifiability, undeniability, and prevention of misuse are satisfied. Here we only show that the proposed scheme also provides unforgeability.

Unforgeability. Any third party, who wants to forge the proxy signature of an message m' for the proxy signer and these original signers, must have the original signers' signatures on the warrant m_w. But he can not forge those signatures, since these original signers use Boneh et al.'s pairing-based short signature scheme([1]): The scheme is proven to be secure against existential forgery under a chosen message attacks (in the random oracle) assuming the Computational Diffie-Hellman Problem is hard on the chosen elliptic curves. Since we use Hess's scheme([2]), which is secure under the hardness of CDHP and the random oracle, to generate the proxy multi-signature, even these original signers can not generate a valid proxy signature.

5 Conclusions

In electronic world, proxy signature is a solution of delegation of signing capabilities. Various type proxy signatures are important in many applications. In this paper, we proposed a multi-proxy signature scheme and a proxy multi-signature scheme from bilinear pairings. We have shown that both of them satisfied all the security properties required by proxy signatures.

References

1. D.Boneh, B.Lynn, H.Shacham. Short signatures from the weil pairing. In: *Advances in Cryptology-Asiacrypt* 2001, LNCS2248, pages 514-532. Springer-Verlag, 2003.
2. F.Hess. Efficient identity based signature schemes based on pairings. *Proceedings of SAC*2002. Lecture Notes in Computer Science. Springer-Verlag.

3. S.Huang. C.Shi. A simple multi-proxy signature scheme. *Proceedings of the 10th National Conference on Information Security*. Taiwan, ROC, 2000, pages 134-138.
4. B.Lee, H.Kim, K.Kim. Strong proxy signature and its applications. *Proceedings of SCIS*. pages 603-608, 2001.
5. M.Mambo, K.Usuda, E.Okamoto. Proxy signature: delegation of the power to sign messages. *IEICE Trans.Fundamentals*. E79-A:9, pages 1338-1353, 1996.
6. L.Yi, G.Bai, G.Xiao. Proxy multi-signature scheme: a new type of proxy signature scheme. *Electronics Letters* 36(6), 2000, pages 527-528.

Probability Principle of a Reliable Approach to Detect Signs of DDOS Flood Attacks

Ming Li[1], Jingao Liu[1], and Dongyang Long[2]

[1] School of Information Science & Technology, East China Normal University,
Shanghai 200026, PR China
ming_lihk@yahoo.com, jgliu@ee.ecnu.edu.cn
[2] Department of Computer Science, Zhongshan University, Guangzhou 510275, PR China
issldy@zsu.edu.cn

Abstract. Attentions are increasingly paid to reliable detection of intrusions as can be seen from [1, 2]. As a matter of fact, the challenge is to develop a system that detects close to 100 percent of attacks with minimal false positives. We are still far from achieving this goal [1, p. 28]. In this regard, our early work discusses a reliable approach regarding detection of signs of distributed denial-of-service (DDOS) attacks [3], where arrival time series of a protected site is specifically featured by autocorrelation function. As a supplementary to [3], this article specifically focuses on abstractly discussing probability principle involved in [3] such that the present probability principle of detection is flexible in practical applications. In addition to this, the selection of a threshold for a given detection probability is also given.

Keywords: Anomaly intrusion detection, intrusion prevention, DDOS, statistical detection, probability, reliability.

1 Introduction

For detection of intrusions with unknown patterns, a key point is reliable detection as can be seen from [1, 2]. By reliable detection, we mean that a sign of attack can be reported for a given detection probability. In our previous work [3], an approach of reliable detection of sings of distributed denial-of-service (DDOS) has been proposed, where arrival traffic time series on a monitored site is featured by autocorrelation function. We did so because autocorrelation function is a tool to model traffic time series, see e.g., [5-7]. However, from a view of traffic engineering, other traffic models may also be available, see e.g., [8-12]. Therefore, this article uses an abstract symbol to characterize a monitored series. In this way, we may purely focus on the probability principle of anomaly intrusion detection for DDOS flood attacks discussed in [3].

Basically, no matter what attack tool (old or new) is used, the basic feature of DDOS attacks is that attack packets coming from sources distributed all over the world are sent to an attacked site such that the site is overwhelmed to deny services it normally offers [13-15]. For that reason, signs of DDOS attacks can be detected by analyzing arrival data of a protected site [3]. It should be noted that techniques involved in information security has the multi-disciplinary characteristics [4]. This article, however, focuses on probability principle analysis.

Let $\{x_l\}$ be an arrival process at a protected site, where x_l is the lth sample of $\{x_l\}$ for integer l. The symbol x_l may represent whatever a feature of arrival data series monitored (e.g., autocorrelation function of arrival series within the lth interval, or distribution of connection number within the lth interval and so forth). Suppose a sign of suspicious attack is identified individually based on x_l only. Then, it may usually have large false alarm to report that the protected site is being attacked. However, assume that a sign of suspicious attack is detected based on a series of samples x_l for $l = 1, 2, \ldots M$. Then, the detection probability may be large in qualitative. From a view of reliable detection, nevertheless, it is not satisfactory only to report detection qualitatively with the term large detection probability or small probability. The key (also challenging) question in this regard is what the quantitative detection probability (or miss probability) is. In other words, what reliability is for the detection?

The rest of paper is organized as follows. Section 2 discusses probability principle of detection. Conclusions are given in Section 3.

2 Probability Analysis of Detection

Let X be a metric space of arrival data. Let $N \subseteq X$ be a space consisting of normal arrival data. Let $d(x_l, N)$ be a distance between x_l and N. Note that distance herein is a mathematics term [16]. Let $V > 0$ be a threshold of identification. Then, one may see that $x_l \in N$ if $d(x_l, N) \leq V$ while $x_l \notin N$ if $d(x_l, N) > V$. Though $d(x_l, N) > V$ implies a sign of suspicious attack according to the lth sample x_l, the identification based on an individual sample may not provide a reliable detection because one cannot know the detection probability based on $d(x_l, N) > V$ alone. To achieve a reliable detection, there is one step to go further.

Now, consider M samples of $\{x_l\}$. Then, $d(x_l, N)$ is a series of M length. Divide $d(x_l, N)$ into L non-overlapped groups. Each group has K samples. In practical terms, $K \approx 10$ may work well. Let $E[d(x_l, N)]$ be the mean of the ith group, where E is the mean operator. Denote

$$E[d(x_l, N)]_i = \xi_i \text{ for } i = 1, 2, \ldots, L. \tag{1}$$

Then, a detection sign is more reasonably given by $\xi_i > V$ than $d(x_l, N) > V$. Consequently, instead of studying the detection probability $P(x_l \notin N)$, we are interested in the probability expression $P(\xi > V)$.

Clearly, ξ_i is a sample mean series of L length. Usually,

$$\xi_i \neq \xi_j \text{ for } i \neq j. \tag{2}$$

Hence, ξ_i is a random variable. As known, ξ_i quite accurately follows the standard normal distribution for large L (e.g., $L > 10$) [17]. In what follows, large L is assumed. If no confusions arise, ξ_i is denoted by ξ for short. In this case,

$$\xi \sim \frac{1}{\sqrt{2\pi}\sigma} e^{-\frac{(\xi-\mu)^2}{2\sigma^2}}, \qquad (3)$$

where μ and σ^2 are the mean and the variance of ξ, respectively. Let

$$\Phi(t) = \int_{-\infty}^{t} \frac{1}{\sqrt{2\pi}} e^{-\frac{t^2}{2}} dt. \qquad (4)$$

Then, detection probability is given by

$$P_d = P\{V < \xi < \infty\} = 1 - \Phi[(V-\mu)/\sigma]]. \qquad (5)$$

Let P_m be the miss probability. Then, $P_d + P_m = 1$. Thus

$$P_m = \Phi[(V-\mu)/\sigma]]. \qquad (6)$$

From (5), one sees that the detection probability is a function of V and we denote it as $P_d(V)$. Practically, one often wants to find a threshold, say V_D, such that $P_d(V_D) \geq D$ for a given a detection probability D. From statistics, one may easily see that the following holds:

$$V_D \leq \mu - \sigma\Phi^{-1}(D), \text{ if } \mu - \sigma\Phi^{-1}(D) > 0. \qquad (7)$$

Equ. (7) provides an expression to select V for a given detection probability. In the case of $D = 1$ and the precision in numerical computation being 4,

$$V_D \leq \mu - 4\sigma, \text{ if } \mu - 4\sigma > 0. \qquad (8)$$

Due to the limited space of this paper, further details (e.g., a simulation case to verify the principle) are omitted.

3 Conclusions

This article has discussed a probability principle with respect to statistical detection of DDOS attacks. The expressions regarding detection probability and the criterion to select detection threshold have been given. The significance of the present detection probability is that it is suitable for any features as long as they characterize arrival data series. In addition, the distance mentioned is an abstract one. Hence, flexible in applications.

Acknowledgments

The paper is partly sponsored by SRF for ROCS, State Education Ministry, PRC, Shanghai-AM Fund under the project number 0206, and the Natural Science Foundation of China (Project No. 60273062). Anonymous referees' comments on this work are appreciated.

References

1. R. A. Kemmerer and G. Vigna, Intrusion detection: a brief history and overview, *Supplement to IEEE Computer (IEEE Security & Privacy)*, 35 (4), April 2002, 27-30.
2. J. Leach, TBSE— an engineering approach to the design of accurate and reliable security systems, *Computer & Security*, 23 (1), Feb. 2004, 22-28.
3. M. Li, An approach to reliably identifying signs of DDOS flood attacks based on LRD traffic pattern recognition, 23(7), *Computer & Security*, 2004, 549–558.
4. C. C. Wood, Why information security is now multi-disciplinary, multi-departmental, and multi-organizational in nature, *Computer Fraud & Security*, Vol. 2004, Issue 1, Jan. 2004, 16-17.
5. M. Li, et al, Modeling autocorrelation function of self-similar teletraffic in communication networks based on optimal approximation in Hilbert space, *Applied Mathematical Modelling*, 27 (3), 2003, 155-168.
6. M. Li and C.-H. Chi, A correlation based computational model for synthesizing long-range dependent data, *Journal of the Franklin Institute*, 340 (6/7), Sep.-Nov. 2003, 503-514.
7. M. Li, et al, Correlation form of timestamp increment sequences of self-similar traffic on Ethernet, *Electronics Letters*, 36 (19), Sep. 2000, 1168-1169.
8. A. Adas, Traffic models in broadband networks, *IEEE Communications Magazine*, 35 (7), 1997, 82-89.
9. H. Michiel and K. Laevens, Teletraffic engineering in a broad-band era, *Proc. of IEEE*, 85 (12), Dec. 1997, 2007-2033.
10. W. Willinger and V. Paxson, Where mathematics meets the Internet, *Notices of the American Mathematical Society*, 45 (8), 1998, 961-970.
11. J. Levy-Vehel, E. Lutton, and C. Tricot (Eds), *Fractals in Engineering*, Springer, 1997.
12. R. J. Adler, R. E. Feldman, and M. S. Taqqu, *A Practical Guide to Heavy Tails: Statistical Techniques and Applications*, Birkhauser, Boston, 1998.
13. 13 L. Garber, Denial-of-service attacks rip the Internet, *IEEE Computer*, 33 (4) April 2000, 12-17.
14. E. G. Amoroso, *Intrusion Detection: An Introduction to Internet Surveillance, Correlation, Traps, Trace Back, and Response*, Intrusion.Net Book, 1999.
15. J. Raymond, Traffic analysis: protocols, attacks, design issues and open problems. In H. Federrath, editor, *Designing Privacy Enhancing Technologies: Proceedings of International Workshop on Design Issues in Anonymity and Unobservability*, volume 2009 of *LNCS*, pages 10–29. Springer-Verlag, 2001.
16. D. H. Griffel, *Applied Functional Analysis*, Ellis Horwood, John Wiley & Sons, 1981.
17. J. S. Bendat and A. G. Piersol, *Random Data: Analysis and Measurement Procedure*, 3rd Edition, John Wiley & Sons, 2000.

A Novel Distributed Intrusion Detection Architecture Based on Overlay Multicasting

I-Hsuan Huang and Cheng-Zen Yang

Department of Computer Science and Engineering,
Yuan Ze University, Taiwan, R.O.C.
{ihhuang, czyang}@syslab.cse.yzu.edu.tw
http://syslab.cse.yzu.edu.tw/

Abstract. In this paper, we propose a novel distributed intrusion detection system called AIMS based on overlay multicasting to achieve low control message overhead. Besides, AIMS is dynamically reconfigurable by using domain overlapping cooperation. This paper presents these main techniques that are novel in intrusion detection. Preliminary experimental results on system performance are also reported.

1 Introduction

Network intrusions are serious threats to the Internet. According to the survey by the CSI and the FBI [1], the total losses in the US caused by computer crime in 2003 are $201,797,340. Therefore, developing an effective mechanism to detect such a large number of network intrusions becomes very crucial for current cyber-society.

According to our survey, distributed intrusion detection systems (DIDS) are a future trend in network intrusion detection [4, 6–8]. A DIDS collects intrusion information from distributed detection sensors and performs network-wide intrusion analyses. There are two advantages to employ a DIDS. First, the distributed detection sensors can perform intrusion detection in parallel and the detection coverage is much larger than the coverage visible from a single detection host. Second, a DIDS can synthesize the distributed detection information to find system-wide abnormal behaviors that are hard to be discovered by a single host in traditional IDS design.

However, although many research efforts have concentrated on designing a DIDS, they do not address the effectiveness of detection coverage maintenance. Since the number of maintenance control messages is proportional to the exponentially growing number of intrusions of new types, a new architecture is required to consider this issue.

In this paper, we present a novel DIDS architecture incorporated in our proposed DIDS called AIMS (Active Intrusion Monitor System) [2] based on overlay multicasting and domain overlapping. It has three distinct design features. First, with overlay multicasting, control messages are localized in a small subset of the overall detection coverage. Therefore, the number of control messages is reduced. Second, with domain overlapping, system update messages can be efficiently propagated to cooperative domains by exchanging a minimal number of messages. Third, as benefited by the previous features, AIMS is highly scalable to construct a large-scale DIDS.

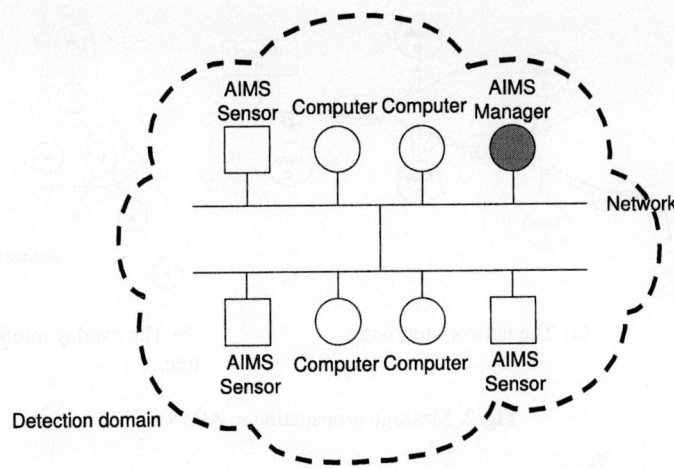

Fig. 1. The AIMS architecture

The rest of the paper is organized as follows. Section 2 describes the AIMS architecture and the communication protocol design. Section 3 describes the prototype implementation and the preliminary experimental results. Finally, Section 4 concludes the paper and discusses the future research plan.

2 Architecture Design

In AIMS, the detection coverage is controlled by a set of AIMS sensors and an AIMS domain manager. The sensors and the AIMS domain manager form the *detection domain*, as depicted in Figure 1. The AIMS domain manager maintains an overlay multicast tree for the detection domain, deploys new intrusion patterns and detection modules, and collects intrusion alarms. The AIMS sensor collects intrusion information from networks and reports alarms when it detects intrusions. The communication between the AIMS domain manager and the AIMS sensors is performed with the overlay multicast scheme that achieves low network traffic group communication without router support. There are three tasks in overlay multicast: sensor registration, overlay multicast tree maintenance, and propagation of control messages.

Figure 2 illustrates message propagation from the manager M. Suppose that the domain has six AIMS sensors A, B, C, D, E, and F. When M starts to deploy control messages to all AIMS sensors, it only sends them to C. C then forwards them to B and D according to the structure of the overlay multicast tree. Then, D chooses F instead of A as the forwarding destination because A is on the path and can intercept all messages. In our scheme, the multicasts are maintained by the intermediate sensors instead of IP routers. Message propagation is thus localized in the propagation subset.

Each detection domain can be overlapped with another domain by assigning an AIMS sensor to several AIMS domain managers. Therefore, the overlapped AIMS sensor becomes the intermediary to exchange updates and intrusion information. If an

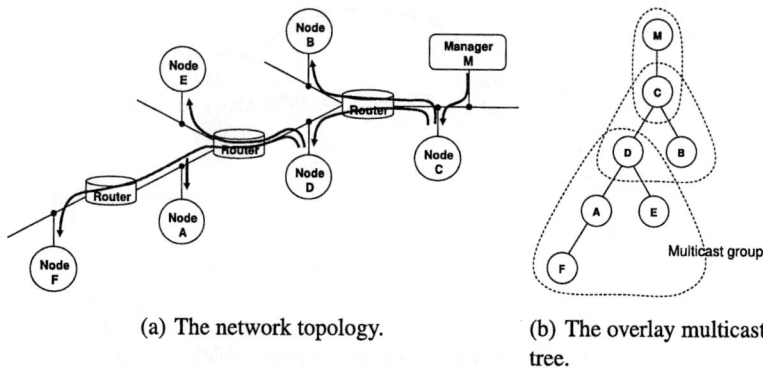

(a) The network topology. (b) The overlay multicast tree.

Fig. 2. Message propagation in AIMS

intermediary AIMS sensor gets updates from a domain, it will report to other AIMS domain managers. Accordingly, several domains can cooperate with sharing updates and intrusion information. Due to the paper limitation, more details can be found in [3].

3 Prototype Implementation and Experiments

We have implemented an AIMS prototype. The prototype contains an AIMS domain manager and two AIMS sensors. They are all implemented on Linux 2.4 in Cyclone 0.6, a high-level, type-safe dialect of C [5], for security reason. In addition, Cyclone is benefitted from that many legacy C libraries can be easily ported.

We verified the prototype by sending CodeRed signatures. The prototype successfully detected them and reported to the manager. We then measured the performance of the AIMS sensor in three different configurations. We used a packet generator to perform stress test on the AIMS sensors. Both the packet generator and the AIMS sensor were installed in an isolated 100Mbps Ethernet environment.

Figure 3(a) illustrates the experimental results. In the first configuration, the intrusion detection functionality was enabled, but the rule database in the AIMS sensor had no rule. This shows the necessary processing overhead of AIMS sensors. In the second configuration, the intrusion detection functionality was enabled with a predefined intrusion pattern, and all network packets were matched. This demonstrates the best-case performance of intrusion pattern matching. Finally, the third configuration was for measuring the worst-case performance where there were 1000 patterns but no one was matched. In all cases, the sensor could successful executed the detection work without packet loss. We also collected some network traffic traces to estimate the potential processing throughput of AIMS sensors. Figure 3(b) presents the estimated performance of an AIMS sensor. As shown in Figure 3(b), AIMS can fluently operate in a 100Mbps network environment.

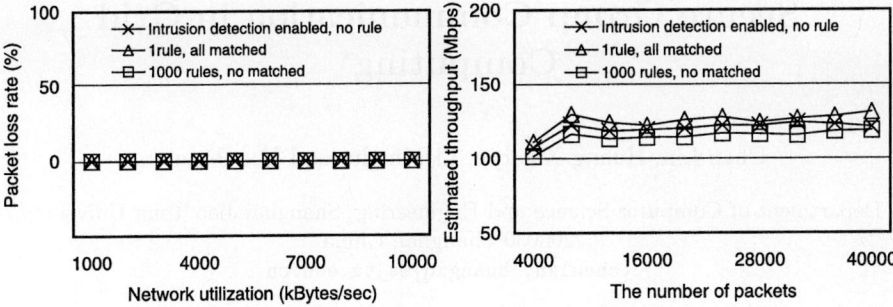

(a) The performance of the AIMS sensor prototype under fast Ethernet network.

(b) The estimated performance of the AIMS sensor prototype.

Fig. 3. The performance of the AIMS sensor prototype

4 Conclusions and Future Work

In this paper, we present a novel DIDS architecture based on overlay multicasting and domain overlapping. It has been exploited in AIMS and achieves a highly scalable DIDS. Several issues need to be further studied. First, authentication will be in depth discussed for secure message deployment. Second, we plan to enhance the AIMS architecture so it can be survival when the manager becomes the intrusion target. Third, we plan to set up a large-scale experimental environment to investigate the practical performance of AIMS.

References

1. Gordon, L. A., et al.: 2004 CSI/FBI Computer Crime and Security Survey. (2004) http://www.gocsi.com/
2. Huang, I-H., Yang, C.-Z.: Design of an Active Intrusion Monitor System. Proc. 37th IEEE ICCST'03, (Oct. 2003) 485–492
3. Huang, I-H.: Design of an Active Intrusion Monitor System. Master Thesis. Dept. of CSE. Yuan Ze Univ. (June 2004)
4. Janakiraman, R., Waldvogel, M., Zhang, Q.: Indra: A Peer-to-Peer Approach to Network Intrusion Detection and Prevention. Proc. 12th IEEE WET ICE'03 (June 2003) 226–231
5. Jim, T., et al.: Cyclone: A Safe Dialect of C. Proc. USENIX'02. (June 2002)
6. Porras, P. A., Neumann, P. G.: EMERALD: Event Monitoring Enabling Responses to Anomalous Live Disturbances. Proc. 20th NISSC'97. (Oct. 1997) 353–365
7. Snapp, S. R., et al.: A System for Distributed Intrusion Detection. Proc. 36th IEEE COMPCON Spring'91. (Feb. 1991) 170–176
8. Spafford, E. H., Zamboni, D.: Intrusion Detection using Autonomous Agents. Computer Networks. **34**, 4 (Oct. 2000) 547–570

Secure Group Communication in Grid Computing*

Chen Lin, Huang Xiaoqin, Li Minglu, and You Jinyuan

Department of Computer Science and Engineering, Shanghai Jiao Tong University,
200030 Shanghai, China
{chenlin, huangxq}@sjtu.edu.cn

Abstract. We discuss the security requirements and analyze the requirements for secure group communication in grid circumstance. When several processes generated by a user want to communicate securely, they have to share a secret key to communicate. We propose a secret key administration algorithm in dynamically circumstance. The security and efficiency of our scheme is analyzed.

1 Introduction

"Grid" refers to systems and applications that manage and access resources and services distributed across multiple control domains [1, 2]. While scalability, performance and heterogeneity are desirable goals for any distributed system, the characteristics of computational grids lead to security problems that are not addressed by existing security technologies for distributed systems [3]. The user population is large and dynamic. The resource pool is large and dynamic. A computation may acquire , start processes on , and release resources dynamically during its execution. The processes constituting a computation may communicate by using a variety of mechanisms, including unicast and multicast. While these processes form a single, fully connected logical entity, low-level communication connections may be created and destroyed dynamically during program execution. Group context management is needed to support secure communication within a dynamic group of processes belonging to the same computation [3]. In this paper, we discuss the secure group communication mechanism in grid circumstance.

2 Security Requirements

Grid systems may require any standard security functions, including authentication, access control, integrity, privacy, and nonrepudiation [3]. In order to develop security grid architecture, we should satisfy the following characteristics:

---

* This paper is supported by the National Natural Science Foundation of China under Grant No.60173033 and 973 project (No.2002CB312002)of China, ChinaGrid Program of MOE of China, and grand project of the Science and Technology Commission of Shanghai Municipality (No. 03dz15026, No. 03dz15027 and No. 03dz15028).

- Single sign-on: A user should be able to authenticate once.
- Protection of credentials: User credentials must be protected.
- Interoperability with local security solutions: Security solutions may provide interdomain access mechanisms.
- Exportability: We require that the code be (a) exportable and (b) executable in multinational testbeds.
- Uniform credentials/certification infrastructure: Interdomain access requires a common way of expressing the identity of a security principle such as an actual user or a resource.

Support for secure group communication. A computation can comprise a number of processes that will need to coordinate their activities as a group. The composition of a process group can and will change during the lifetime of a computation. Therefore, secure communication for dynamic groups is needed. So far, no current security solution supports this feature; even GSS-API has no provisions for group security contexts [3].

The computational grid security architecture is as follows: In our diagram, there are a lot of processes. These processes need to communicate securely. They have to share a common secret key.

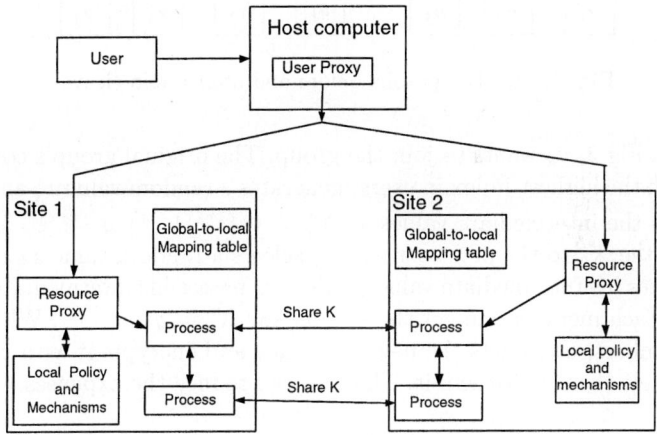

Fig. 1. A computational grid security architecture

3 Our Secure Group Communication Scheme in Grid Computing

In Grid computing circumstance, a group member often joins/leaves the group dynamically. When a user joins the group, the group key should change to a new value. Also when a user leaves a group, the original key should become invalid and the remaining member should have a new group key. So our group communication scheme should support the dynamic circumstance. Our algorithm consists of three steps as follows:

Setup: Suppose our system have three members initially (It can be extended to a lot of users easily). They want to achieve a shared key. A finite cyclic group $G = <g>$ of order a k-bite prime number p. The structure is as Figure 2.

As in [4,5], the algorithm consists of two stages: up-flow and down-flow. Player u_1 chooses at random a private value x_1 in $[1, p-1]$ and generates his intermediate value $X_1 := \{g, g^{x_1}\}$. Then u_1 delivers X_1 to the next player u_2. Player u_2 chooses at random a private value x_2 in $[1, p-1]$ and generates his intermediate value $X_2 := \{g^{x_2}, g^{x_1}, g^{x_1 x_2}\}$. Then u_2 delivers X_2 to the next player u_3. The last user u_3 receives the last up-flow. He performs the same steps as a player in the up-flow and broadcasts the set of intermediate values $X_3 := \{g^{x_2 x_3}, g^{x_1 x_3}, g^{x_1 x_2}\}$ only. Finally, each member calculates the session key $K := g^{x_1 x_2 x_3}$.

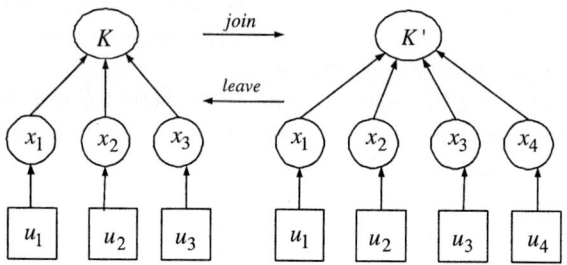

Fig. 2. Star key graphs before and after a join (leave)

Join: As in Fig 2, u_4 wants to join the group. The original group's controller u_3 (player with the highest-index in users) generates a random value x_3' and x_3^{-1}. u_3 recalculates the intermediate values as $X_3' := \{g^{x_2 x_3 x_3^{-1} x_3'}, g^{x_1 x_3 x_3^{-1} x_3'}, g^{x_1 x_2 x_3'}\}$. u_3 passes the X_3' to the new user u_4. u_4 selects a random value x_4 in $[1, p-1]$ and generates his intermediate values. Also, u_4 passes his intermediate values to u_1, u_2, u_3. Each member can get the session key $K' := g^{x_1 x_2 x_3' x_4}$. When there is a lot of members, u_{max} gets the new secret key and encrypts it with the group's old secret key, then multicasts it. Thus we can reduce the expenses.

Remove: Suppose u_2 wants to be deleted, the group controller u_3 selects randomly x_3^{-1} and x_3'. Now $X_3' := \{g^{x_2 x_3'}, g^{x_1 x_2}\}$ and sends it to all remainder users. Then u_1 can get the $K := g^{x_1 x_2 x_3'}$ and the u_3 can get the shared key $K := g^{x_1 x_2 x_3'}$.

When there exists sub-processes, for example a parent process generates three sub-processes. The three sub-processes and the parent process can get their shared secret key as above. If a user generates three separate processes in order to complete a task, he generates three processes and each process generates three sub-processes. Each sub-group generates their shared key as above: For u_1, u_2, u_3, the session key is $g^{x_1 x_2 x_3}$. For u_4, u_5, u_6, the session key is $g^{x_4 x_5 x_6}$. For u_7, u_8, u_9, the session key is $g^{x_7 x_8 x_9}$. For the whole group, the session key is $g^{x_1 x_2 x_3 x_4 x_5 x_6 x_7 x_8 x_9}$. The shared key also changes dynamically as above when a member joins/leaves the group.

4 Security and Efficiency Analysis

In our secure group communication scheme especially in the dynamic case, we use the group Diffie-Hellman key-exchange protocol. The security of the protocol is proved in [4]. Our scheme takes some measures in improving the efficiency. In the join phase, when u_{max} gets the new secret key, he can encrypts it with the group's old secret key and then multicasts it. So we can reduce the expenses. In the move phase, u_{max} recaculates his intermediate values and sends it to all remainder users. We don't take the method to repeat the process as setup phase, so we can improve the efficiency.

5 Conclusions

In this paper, we have discussed some security requirements in grid circumstance. Because secure group communication is seldom considered before, we propose an authenticated Diffie-Hellman key-exchange protocol . The protocol also considers the dynamic situation when the members join/leave the group. The situation that processes have sub-processes is also being considered.

References

1. Foster, I., Kesselman, C.: The Grid: Blueprint for a new computing infrastructure. Morgan Kaufmann. (1999) 2–48.
2. Welch, V., Siebenlist, F., Foster, I. et al.: Security for grid services. Proceedings of the 12th IEEE International Symposium on High Performance Distributed Computing(HPDC'03). (2003).
3. Foster, I., Kesselman, C., Tsudik, G.: A security architecture for computational grids. ACM Conference on Computers and Security. (1998) 83–91.
4. Chevassut, O.: Authenticated group Diffie-Hellman key-exchange: Theory and practice. PhD thesis. Louvain-la-Neuve. Belgique. October (2002).
5. Chung, K.W., Mohamed, G., Simon, S.L: Secure group communications using key graphs. Proceedings of ACM SIGCOMM'98,(1998) 68–79.

Tamper Resistant Software by Integrity-Based Encryption

Jaewon Lee, Heeyoul Kim, and Hyunsoo Yoon

Division of Computer Science, Department of EECS, KAIST, Deajeon, Korea
{jaewon, hykim, hyoon}@camars.kaist.ac.kr

Abstract. There are many situations in which it is desirable to protect a piece of software from illegitimate tampering once it gets distributed to the users. Protecting the software code means some level of assurance that the program will execute as expected even if it encounters the illegitimated modifications. We provide the method of protecting software from unauthorized modification. One important technique is an *integrity-based encryption*, by which a program, while running, checks itself to verify that it has not been modified and conceals some privacy sensitive parts of program.

Keywords: Security, Tamper Resistant Software, Software Protection.

1 Introduction

A fundamental limitation faced by designers of e-commerce and network security application is that software is easy to reverse engineer in order to determine how the software works and discover embedded secrets and intellectual properties and to make unauthorized changes for the functionality of the software. Therefore, unprotected software deployed on suspicious hosts cannot be trusted by the other hosts even the server. This situation is namely called a *malicious host problem* [1]. This problem is central in the cases that the client programs are executed in arbitrary user environment, such as DRM (Digital Right Management), e-commerce, on-line game, etc.

Our goal for tamper resistant software is to defend up to the level of dynamic modification for program, and can be summarized as following objectives: 1) (**Confidentiality**) Privacy sensitive algorithms which have been implemented into executable binary code shall be protected so that they may be concealed from competitors of program producer or analysis of adversary and 2) (**Integrity**) The dynamic modification by its user shall be detected by program itself, and it helps to cope with some proper reaction.

To fulfill these goals, we propose an *integrity-based encryption* scheme, which is composed of self-decrypting and self-integrity checking methods. The self-decryption makes a program enable itself to decrypt own parts of encrypted code. The decryption key is extracted by hashing other parts of program, so we can also preserve the integrity of those parts. Furthermore, we offer interleaving and mutual guarding mechanism to enhance the security. With our scheme, neither specialized compiler nor hardware is needed and additional implementation in source code is minimal, so it makes efficient to use in practice.

2   Related Work

Previous work to response malicious host problem can be classified into two categories as passive and active prevention. *Passive prevention* refers making software to be resistant against static analysis. Obfuscation [2, 3] is a major example and it attempts to thwart reverse engineering by making it hard to understand the behavior of a program. Also, software watermark and fingerprint [4, 5] allow tracking of misused program copies by providing an additional deterrent to tampering. However, it may be effective for the cases that decompilation of binary code produces some high level of human recognition such as Java. Also, it requires specialized compiler and may result in degradation of performance.

Secondly, *active prevention* protects the software from dynamic analysis, which uses debuggers or processor emulators [1, 6]. However, in an absolute sense, this type of prevention is impossible on the PC due to the characteristics of open architecture. Any defense against this type of attacks must, at best, merely deter a perpetrator by providing a poor return on their investment.

3   Our Approach

In our scheme, a program code is classified into three classes, i.e. algorithm private, integrity sensitive, and normal classes of code. Algorithm privacy is realized by the code encryption with guarding chain. It does not require an explicit decryption key while program running. Furthermore, decryption routines and integrity sensitive codes are protected by guarding chain, as shown in Fig. 1, to guarantee that those parts are not illegitimately modified by malicious user.

3.1   Notations and Assumptions

Program Structural Notations

$A||B$: Concatenation of program fragments A and B.
q_i : The integrity sensitive class of program.
Q_i, $1 \leq i \leq n$: The concatenation of integrity sensitive fragments, i.e.,
$Q_i = q_{i_1}||\cdots||q_{i_m}$, for example in Fig. 1, $Q_1 = q_1$, $Q_2 = q_1||q_2$, $Q_3 = q_1||q_3||q_4$.
P_i, $1 \leq i \leq n$: The algorithm private class of program in plain form.
C_i, $1 \leq i \leq n$: The algorithm private class of program in encrypted form.
D_i, $1 \leq i \leq n$: The decryption routines to decrypt C_i.

Cryptographic Notations

$\mathcal{H}(m)$: A one-way, collision-resistant hash function.
$Enc_k(m)$: Symmetric encrypt function on message m with the key k.

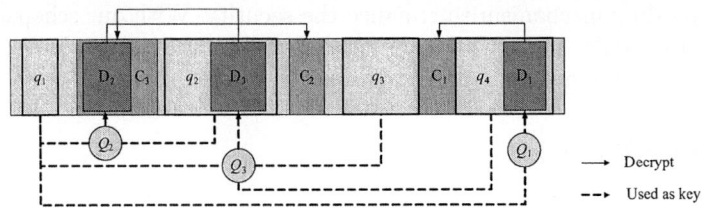

Fig. 1. Program image of mutual protecting cipher code

$Dec_k(c)$: Symmetric decrypt function on ciphertext c with the key k.
$C : A \rightarrow B$: Replace A with B by C.

Magic codes are used to denote the beginning and ending positions of each P_i and to store some meta data. But, they do not affect the program execution. $Q_1, \ldots,$ and Q_n are the integrity sensitive parts of program, whose hash values are taken as the keys for the both of encryption of P_i and decryption of C_i.

3.2 Code Encryption

To realize the algorithm privacy, we adopt a conventional symmetric encryption algorithm to encrypt privacy sensitive fragments of program, but use the hash value of other parts of program as key. The following steps are appended to the original flow of software development.

Step 1) Initialize : Complete the source code with insertion of magic codes
Step 2) Compile : Compile the source code with ordinary compiler.
Step 3) Encrypt : Encrypt the P_i into C_i using external encrypting utility.

$$\text{Utility} : P_i \rightarrow C_i, \text{ where } C_i = Enc_{\mathcal{H}(Q_i)}(P_i), \ 1 \leq i \leq n \quad (1)$$

3.3 Code Decryption and Integrity Checking

In the beginning of program execution, the encrypted segment, C_i, should be decrypted into executable code, P_i, as follows:

$$D_i : C_i \rightarrow Dec_{\mathcal{H}(Q_i)}(C_i), \ 1 \leq i \leq n \quad (2)$$

If a Q_i has been tampered into Q_i', decryption key will be $\mathcal{H}(Q_i') \neq \mathcal{H}(Q_i)$, so D_i cannot properly decrypt C_i.

4 Security Analysis

Reverse engineering is the process of analyzing a subject system 1) to identify the system's components and their interrelationships and 2) to create representations of the system in another form or at a higher level of abstraction [7]. It can be broadly classified into the static analysis and dynamic analysis, according to the attacker's aptitude for analysis.

Our goal for tamper resistant software is to defend against static analysis and dynamic analysis up to the level of dynamic substitution for the program instruction. The security of our scheme is supported by two points of view. The first is the integrity and secrecy of program and the second is the guarding chain.

4.1 Program Execution Integrity and Secrecy

Program execution integrity is guaranteed by the hashing used to generate decryption key. If the integrity sensitive code Q_i is modified into Q'_i by the perpetrator, it's hash value $\mathcal{H}(Q'_i)$ will not correspond to it's origin $\mathcal{H}(Q_i)$ which was used in encryption. After all, C_i cannot be properly decrypted, therefore program execution will be obstructed. Furthermore, through the encryption of privacy sensitive part of program, algorithm privacy can be preserved against static analysis. Also, we can deter a perpetrator against dynamic analysis by providing a fine granularity of encrypted fragment.

4.2 Guarding Chain

As shown in Fig. 1, the chain of key usage can provide sophisticated protection scheme that is more resilient against attacks. For example, if an adversary wishes to modify some codes in q_1, D_1, D_2, and D_3 cannot properly decrypt C_1, C_2, and C_3, respectively. Also, D_2 is affected by the modification of q_2 and D_3 is affected by q_3 and q_4. In another sense, the corruption of D_3 by modification of q_1, q_3, or q_4 will cause the failure of decrypting C_3. It also affects decrypting C_2. In this manner, the adversary would have a difficulty to track down the dependency.

5 Conclusion

This paper presents and discusses the techniques for protecting software from the malicious users trying to reverse engineer and modify the code on their own purpose. The integrity-based encryption scheme is proposed to guarantee the code integrity and to promise algorithm privacy with minimal effort in development of software. Furthermore, the guarding chain would make the adversary more difficult to analyze the dependency of protection mechanism. Our scheme defend against static analysis for algorithm privacy and dynamic analysis for execution integrity.

Acknowledgement

This work was supported by the Korea Science and Engineering Foundation (KOSEF) through the Advanced Information Technology Research Center(AITrc) and University IT Research Center (ITRC) Project.

References

1. Sander, T., Tschudin, C.F.: Protecting Mobile Agents Against Malicious Hosts. In: Proceedings of Mobile Agents and Security, LNCS 1419. (1998) 44–60
2. Collberg, C., Thomborson, C., Low, D.: A Taxonomy of Obfuscating Transformations. Technical Report Technical Report 161, Department of Computer Science, The University of Auckland, New Zealand (1997)
3. Ogiso, T., Sakabe, Y., Soshi, M., Miyaji, A.: Software Obfuscation on a Theoretical Basis and Its Implementation. IEICE Trans. Fundamentals **E86-A** (2003) 176–186
4. Esparza, O., Fernandez, M., Soriano, M., Muñoz, J.L., Forné, J.: Mobile Agent Watermarking and Fingerprinting: Tracing Malicious Hosts. In: Proceedings of DEXA 2003, LNCS 2736. (2003) 927–936
5. Myles, G., Collberg, C.: Software Watermarking Through Register Allocation: Implementation, Analysis, and Attacks. In: Proceedings of 6th International Conference on Information Security and Cryptology -ICISC 2003. (2003) 274 – 293
6. Aucsmith, D.: Tamper Resistant Software: An Implementation. In: Proceedings of First International Workshop on Information Hiding, LNCS 1174. (1996) 317–333
7. Chikofsky, E.J., II, J.H.C.: Reverse Engineering and Design Recovey: A Taxonomy. IEEE Software **7** (1990) 13–17

Towards an Analysis of Source-Rewriting Anonymous Systems in a Lossy Environment

Jin-Qiao Shi, Bin-Xing Fang, and Bin Li

Research Center of Computer Network and Information Security Technology,
Harbin Institute of Technology, Harbin 150001, People's Republic of China
{sjq, bxfang, libin}@pact518.hit.edu.cn

Abstract. Anonymity that protects the identity of participants is a basic requirement for many network-based applications. For practical anonymous communication systems, strong anonymity, reliability and efficiency are three critical properties, but they may degrade in a lossy environment (nodes failure or links crash). This paper takes *Crowds* system as an example and statistically analyzes the degradation of these properties in lossy environment. Theoretical deduction and numerical analysis illustrate that *Crowds* is reliable enough to tolerate nodes failure, but both efficiency and anonymity will degrade. With the theoretical analysis results in this paper, a *Crowds* system operator can adjust the parameter p_f to be tolerant of different node failure rate and node corruption rate.

1 Introduction

With the worldwide growth of open telecommunication networks and in particular the Internet, the privacy and security concerns of people using these networks have increased. Great efforts have been done in developing anonymous communication systems to protect the identity of participants. These systems can be grouped into three categories[1]: *source-rewriting*, *broadcast* and *DC-nets*[2], of which source-rewriting is the most commonly adopted mechanism. Source-rewriting anonymous systems, such as *Crowds*[3], *Onion-Routing II*[4] and *Hordes*[5], achieve anonymity via packets reshuffling, where messages are rewritten and rerouted between nodes to hide the identity of the sender.

For a practical anonymous communication system, four properties are quiet critical: *strong anonymity*, *scalability*, *reliability* and *efficiency*. Previous efforts in evaluating source-rewriting anonymous systems of these properties are most under the assumption that the number of participants in the system is a constant. But in the real world, anonymous communication systems such as *Crowds*[3] and *Tarzan*[6] are composed of volunteers and facing the threat of nodes failure and link crash. Thus these properties may degrade in a lossy environment.

This paper takes *Crowds* as an example to investigate the degradation of source-rewriting anonymous system in a lossy environment. The remainder is organized as follow. Section 2 briefly introduces *Crowds* system with assumption of failure. Section 3 details the theoretical and numerical analysis in the lossy environment. Section 4 closes the paper with our conclusions and future work.

2 *Crowds* System with Failure

The *Crowds* system was developed by Reiter and Rubin for protecting users' anonymity on the Web. A crowd is a collection of users, each of whom is running a special process called a *jondo* acting as the user's proxy. In *Crowds*, messages are routed within a set of jondos to hide the identity of the sender. Some of the jondos (called *malicious nodes*) may be corrupt and/or controlled by the adversary. Corrupted jondos may collaborate with each other to compromise the honest users' anonymity. Meanwhile, some jondos (called *unavailable nodes*) may no longer be able to forward messages because of link crash or node failure. The malicious nodes are assumed to still forward messages as normal so as not to be detected by others. A crowd member has no way of determining whether a particular jondo is malicious or not, nor can it determine whether a jondo is unavailable beforehand. The routing procedure of *Crowds* is shown as follow:

– The initiator selects a crowd member at random (possibly itself) from its own list of the crowds membership, and forwards the request to it. The selected member is called the *forwarder*.
– The forwarder flips a biased coin. With probability $1 - p_f$ it delivers the request directly to the destination. With probability p_f, it selects a crowd member at random (possibly itself) as the next forwarder in the path, and forwards the request to it. The next forwarder then repeats this step.
– When an unavailable crowd member is selected as the next forwarder, the forwarder will retry and retry till a available is selected as successive node.

3 Analysis the Degradation of *Crowds*

Strong anonymity, *scalability*, *reliability* and *efficiency* are the four critical properties of an anonymous communication system. This paper concentrates on the degradation of anonymity, reliability and efficiency of *Crowds* in a lossy environment. Scalability is not concerned in this paper as it mainly depends on the membership mechanism, network topology, message routing strategy and so on, which are not the emphasis of this paper. To quantitatively evaluating the properties, the following metrics are proposed:

Reliability: the probability of successfully routing messages from the source to the destination.

Efficiency: time expectancy for successfully routing messages from the source to the destination. The time is composed of two parts: the time for transmitting messages between nodes and that for fault-and-retry.

Strong Anonymity: $\Pr(I|H_{1+})$ for measuring anonymity degree[3] is adopted. The larger the probability is, the lower the anonymity degree is.

The analysis is based on a *Crowds* system of n numbers, of which are c unavailable nodes and z malicious nodes. To measure efficiency, $\triangle t_0$ is introduced for the time consumed for transmitting messages between two nodes while $\triangle t_1$

is the time for detecting a node failure and selecting an alternative successive node. The definitions of I, H_k, H_{k+} go from $Crowds$[3].

Theorem 1. *The message can be definitely routed to the destination with unavailable nodes number $c < n$.*

Proof. We want to prove $\Pr(E) = 1$ where E is the event of the message successfully routed to the destination. The probability for some path length l_i is

$$\Pr(E|l = l_i) = \sum_{j=0}^{\infty} P_{l_i}^j \left(\frac{n-c}{n}\right)^{l_i} p_f^{l_i-1}(1-p_f) \qquad (1)$$

where j is the retry times, $P_{l_i}^j = C_{j+l_i-1}^j \left(\frac{c}{n}\right)^j$ is the probability of j retries happened during the last l_i intermediate nodes, $C_0^j = 1$.

$$\Pr(E) = \sum_{l=0}^{\infty} \sum_{j=0}^{\infty} P_l^j \left(\frac{n-c}{n}\right)^l p_f^{l-1}(1-p_f) = \sum_{s=0}^{\infty} \sum_{t=0}^{s-1} C_s^t \left(\frac{c}{n}\right)^t \left(\frac{(n-c)p_f}{n}\right)^{s-t} \qquad (2)$$

Thus, we can prove that $\Pr(E) = 1$. □

Theorem 1 illustrates that $Crowds$ is fault-tolerant as long as there are existing available nodes. This is evident as a node can certainly find an available successive node with infinite times of retry. Below is the analysis of time efficiency, taking the transmission time $\triangle t_0$ and fault-and-retry time $\triangle t_1$ into account.

Theorem 2. *The time expectancy for successfully routing messages from source to destination against c unavailable nodes is*

$$E(T) = \frac{p_f + 2(1-p_f)}{1-p_f}\triangle t_0 + \frac{c}{(n-c)(1-p_f)}\triangle t_1 \qquad (3)$$

Proof. First, for some path length $l_i \geq 1$, the time expectancy is

$$E(T|l = l_i) = \sum_{j=0}^{\infty} P_{l_i}^j \left(\frac{n-c}{n}\right)^{l_i} p_f^{l_i-1}(1-p_f)((l_i+1)\triangle t_0 + j\triangle t_1) \qquad (4)$$

Thus,

$$E(T) = \sum_{l=1}^{\infty} \sum_{j=0}^{\infty} P_l^j \left(\frac{n-c}{n}\right)^l p_f^{l-1}(1-p_f)((l+1)\triangle t_0 + j\triangle t_1) \qquad (5)$$

Using the method in (2), we can get (3). □

Theorem 2 illustrates that the time expectancy is composed of two parts, time expected for transmission and expected for fault detection. When the unavailable node number is 0, $E(T) = \frac{p_f+2(1-p_f)}{1-p_f}\triangle t_0$ is the same as is proved in $Crowds$ [3].

Theorem 3. *The probability* $\Pr(I|H_{1+})$ *against c unavailable nodes and z malicious nodes is:*

$$\Pr(I|H_{1+}) = 1 - \frac{(n-c-z)(n-z-1)}{(n-c)(n-z)} p_f \qquad (6)$$

Proof. First, the probability of the first malicious node occupies the i_{th} position on the path is:

$$\Pr(H_i) = \sum_{j=0}^{\infty} P_i^j \left(\frac{(n-c-z)p_f}{n}\right)^{i-1} \left(\frac{z}{n}\right) \qquad (7)$$

also

$$\Pr(H_{k+}) = \sum_{i=k}^{\infty} \Pr(H_i) \qquad (8)$$

Then, with $\Pr(I|H_1) = 1$, $\Pr(I|H_{2+}) = \frac{1}{n-c}$, $I \Rightarrow H_{1+}$ and $\Pr(I) = \Pr(H_1)\Pr(I|H_{1+}) + \Pr(H_{2+})\Pr(I|H_{2+})$, we can get

$$\Pr(I|H_{1+}) = \frac{\Pr(I \wedge H_{1+})}{\Pr(H_{1+})} = \frac{\Pr(I)}{\Pr(H_{1+})} \qquad (9)$$

put $\Pr(I|H_{1+}), \Pr(I|H_{2+})$ into (9), we can get (6). □

When the unavailable node number is 0, the probability becomes $\Pr(I|H_{1+}) = 1 - \frac{(n-z-1)}{n} p_f$ which is is the same as is proved in *Crowds* [3].

Theoretical analysis above illustrates that *Crowds* is reliable enough to tolerate nodes failure. The degradation of efficiency and anonymity is analyzed by numerically calculating $E(T)$ and $\Pr(I|H_{1+})$ with total nodes number $n = 1000$, malicious nodes number $z = 100$ and node failure rate $p = \left(\frac{c}{n}\right)$. $p_f = 0.6$ is determined by the restriction of $\Pr(I|H_{1+}) \leq \frac{1}{2}$ in the ideal environment. $\Delta t_0 = 75$ seconds and $\Delta t_1 = 30$ seconds is estimated by the experimental result of *Crowds*. Figure 1 reveals that both efficiency and anonymity will degrade in the lossy environment and this degradation may compromise the system's performance. When the node failure rate is above 40%, the system can not guarantee the anonymity degree of *probable innocence*[3] while the time expectancy has increased by a factor of about 20% than the ideal value. As a result, the system operator must adjust the parameter p_f beforehand to be tolerant of different node failure rate and node corruption rate with the restriction of $p_f \geq \frac{(n-c)(n-z)}{2(n-c-z)(n-z-1)}$ derived from $\Pr(I|H_{1+}) \leq \frac{1}{2}$. This work can help guarantee the anonymity degree of *probable innocence* in the lossy environment.

4 Conclusion and Future Work

The research of anonymity protecting techniques has been an attracting topic over the recent years. Previous analysis of anonymous communication systems

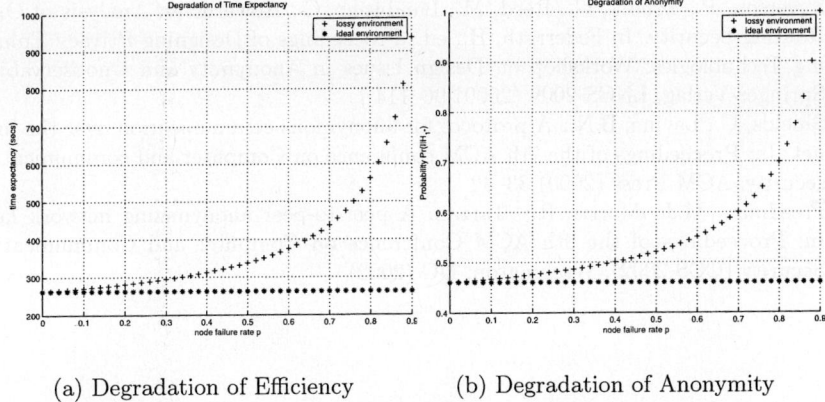

(a) Degradation of Efficiency (b) Degradation of Anonymity

Fig. 1. Numerical Analysis of Efficiency and Anonymity

are most under an ideal environment. But in practical terms, many systems are suffering from nodes failure or links crash.

This paper takes *Crowds* system as an example and statistically analyzes the degradation of reliability, efficiency and anonymity in a lossy environment. Theoretical deduction and numerical analysis illustrates that *Crowds* is reliable enough to tolerate nodes failure, but both efficiency and anonymity will degrade. With the theoretical conclusions in this paper, a *Crowds* system operator can adjust the parameter p_f to be tolerant of different node failure rate and node corruption rate.

However, this work analyze the system performance in a static view that the number of malicious nodes and unavailable nodes are the same while analyzing. But practically, these numbers are ever changing with nodes joining and leaving the system dynamically. Thus, analyzing the degradation of the properties in a dynamical view should be done in the furture. Other future work includes the analysis of systems with path length limitation or retry time limitation, this may help an anonymous systems designer for developing optimal routing strategy of secure, efficient and fault-tolerance systems.

References

1. Goel, S., Robson, M., Polte, M., Sirer, E.G.: Herbivore: A Scalable and Efficient Protocol for Anonymous Communication. Technical Report 2003-1890, Cornell University, Ithaca, NY (2003)
2. Chaum, D.: The dining cryptographers problem: Unconditional sender and recipient untraceability. Journal of Cryptology **1** (1988) 65–75
3. Reiter, M., Rubin, A.: Crowds: Anonymity for web transactions. ACM Transactions on Information and System Security **1** (1998)

4. Syverson, P., Tsudik, G., Reed, M., Landwehr, C.: Towards an Analysis of Onion Routing Security. In Federrath, H., ed.: Proceedings of Designing Privacy Enhancing Technologies: Workshop on Design Issues in Anonymity and Unobservability, Springer-Verlag, LNCS 2009 (2000) 96–114
5. Shields, C., Levine, B.N.: A protocol for anonymous communication over the internet. In: Proceedings of the 7th ACM conference on Computer and communications security, ACM Press (2000) 33–42
6. Freedman, M.J., Morris, R.: Tarzan: A peer-to-peer anonymizing network layer. In: Proceedings of the 9th ACM Conference on Computer and Communications Security (CCS 2002), Washington, DC (2002)

Group Key Agreement Protocol Based on GH-KEP

Mingxing He[1, 2, 3], Pingzhi Fan[2], and Firoz Kaderali[3]

[1] Xihua University, Chengdu 610039, P.R. China
mingxing_he@yahoo.com
[2] Southwest Jiaotong University, Chengdu 610031, P.R. China
p.fan@ieee.org
[3] University of Hagen, D-58084 Hagen, Germany
firoz.kaderali@fernuni-hagen.de

Abstract. An efficient group key agreement protocol is proposed based mainly on the 2-party GH key exchange scheme (GH-KEP) and the intractability of discrete logarithm of finite field $GF(p^t)$. It is shown that, compared with the existing DH-based protocols, the new protocol is computationally more efficient. The proposed protocol can be used to establish contributory group key for dynamical group communications such as ad-hoc networks.

1 Introduction

A classical and simple solution to the two-part key agreement problem is the Diffie-Hellman key exchange protocol (DH-KEP) [1] proposed in 1976. Since then there have been considerable amount of efforts to extend its simplicity and elegance to a group setting. Notable solutions were proposed in [2, 3, 4, 7, 11, 12]. These protocols made their contributions to message authentication, dynamical property consideration and security improvement, etc. But computation complexity in all of these protocols is high due to the modulus exponentiation operation adapted. However, how to compute efficiently the agreement group key is really an important issue especially in the case of cooperation for emergency. Therefore, the research objective in this paper is to cut down the computation complexity of group key agreement protocols without reducing their security by finding and utilizing more efficient operation components.

Recently Gong and Harn published papers [4, 5] in which a 2-part key exchange protocol (GH-KEP) has been proposed. The GH-KEP enjoys the benefit of using a shorter key to achieve high security and the GH-KEP can be resistant to power analysis attack without increasing cost of computations. By using these good properties of GH-KEP, we propose a computationally efficient group key agreement protocol.

2 GH-2 Party Key Exchange Protocol

In this section, the S-multiplication is defined and the 2-party key exchange protocol is introduced [5].

Definition of S–Multiplication. Given an irreducible polynomial $f(x)=x^3-ax^2+bx-1$ over $F=GF(q)$ with period $Q=q^2+q+1$ and set $\{s_r\}$ as the characteristic sequence generated by $f(x)$ [5]. We define pair of (s_r, s_{-r}) as S_r, $s_k S_r$ as $s_k(s_r, s_{-r})$, $S_k S_r$ as $(s_k S_r, s_k S_{-r})$, where s_k is considered as a mapping. Given k and r, we can determine $S_k S_r = (s_k(s_r, s_{-r}), s_k(s_r, s_{-r}))$, it is called as S–multiplication of S_k and S_r. The operation result of $S_k S_r$ is a pair in $F \times F$.

If we set $S = \{S_e \mid 0<e<Q, \gcd(e, Q)=1\}$, then for every S_r, S_e in S, it follows that

1) S–multiplication SeSr is well defined given e and r;
2) S–multiplication is commutative: $S_e S_r = S_r S_e = S_{re}$.
3) S–multiplication is subject to combination law: $(S_e S_r) S_k = S_{erk} = S_r(S_e S_k)$, where S_e, S_r, S_k are all in S. Therefore, notation $S_e S_r S_k = S_k S_r S_e$ make sense.
4) Computing e from $S_e = (s_e, s_{-e})$ is equivalent to solving the discrete logarithm in $GF(q^3)$. It is believed much harder than solving discrete logarithm in the $GF(q)$ for the same q.

GH- 2 Party Key Exchange Protocol (GH-KEP). User Alice chooses e, $0 < e < Q$, with gcd $(e, Q) = 1$ as her private key, computes $S_e = (s_e, s_{-e})$ and transmits S_e to Bob by public channel. Similarly, user Bob choose r, $0 < r < Q$, with gcd $(r, Q) = 1$ as his private key, computes $S_r = (s_r, s_{-r})$ and transmits S_e to Alice by public channel. Then they can compute their common key $K_{AB} = (s_{re}, s_{-re}) = S_{er} = S_e S_r = S_r S_e$.

3 Group Key Agree-ment Protocol (GKAP)

It is assumed throughout this section that the routing security of networks can be guaranteed by some efficient securing routing protocols and the neighboring nodes have already authenticated each other by an authenticated channel.

Initialization. All of initial group members $P=\{P_1, ..., P_n\}$ or participants agree a public system parameter p that is a large prime number, say 170 bits, $q = p^2$ and $f(x) = x^3 - ax^2 + bx - 1$ in $GF(q)$ such that $f(x)$ is an irreducible polynomial over $GF(q)$ with period $Q = q^2 + q + 1$. This is computational feasible for a network as once look-up-table can carry it out, then make the (p, a, b) public for dynamical group key establishment in future.

Round i ($1 \le i < n$). Upon received the message sent by P_{i-1} (except P_1), participant i, denoted by P_i, randomly choose a integer r_i such that gcd $(r_i, Q)=1$, then P_i commutates and transmit data set $\{S_{(r_1 r_2 ... r_i)/r_j} \mid j \in [1, i]\}$ and $S_{r_1 r_2 ... r_i}$ to P_{i+1}.

Round n. Participant P_n, randomly choose a integer r_n such that gcd $(r_n, Q)=1$, then P_n broadcast to $P_1, P_2, ..., P_{n-1}$: $\{S_{(r_1 r_2 ... r_n)/r_i} \mid i \in [1, n]\}$.

4 Complexity Analysis

The efficiency of the proposed protocol is compared with that of some previous ones based on DH-KEP by the following tables. In all of the comparison tables, n is the number of nodes in the protocol. A message means a single packet of information sent from one party to single recipient (no matter how long it is). In a broadcast, one party sends a message to every other participant simultaneously.

Table 1. Communication Efficiency of the Proposed Protocol

	Without broadcast	With broadcast
message	n	n
exchange	n	n
Simple rounds	n	n
Synchronous rounds	n	1
Message sent by $P_i(P_n)$	1 (1)	1 (n-1)
Message received by $P_i(P_n)$	2	2

It should be noted that given k, compute a dual pair $S_k = (s_k, s_{-k})$ in GF (p^2) by using Algorithm 1 introduced in [6] needs at most $20 \log_2 k$ multiplications in $--(p)---$ on the best case only needs $4 \log_2 k$ multiplications in $--(p)$. While by using the ordinary square and multiplication method, computing $g^k \mod p$ takes an expected $23.4 \log_2(k)$ multiplications in $GF(p)$[6]. Using the repeated squaring algorithm, $g^k \mod p$ can be computed in time $(\log_2 k)O((\log_2 p)^2)$. Note that the algorithm takes linear time in the length of k. And multiplying two elements x, y in GF(p) can be done in quadratic time in the length of p. For an n bit integer p faster multiplication algorithms work in time $O(n^{1.7})$ (rather than $O(n^2)$). Therefore, we get the following comparative table 2 and Table 3.

Table 2. Computation Complexity Comparison (DH vs. GH, one side)

Two party (n=2)	DH-agreement protocol	GH-agreement protocol
k	$0 < k < p$	$0 < k < Q = q^2 + q + 1$
Public key	$g^k \mod p$	$S_k = (s_k, s_{-k})$
Multiplications in $F(p)$	$23.4 \log_2(k)$	$20 \log_2 k$
Length of shared key	$|p|$	$2|p|$

Table 3. Computation Complexity of Group Key Agreement Protocol

Group (n-party)	DH-agreement protocol	GH-agreement protocol
Computation for P_i	(i+1) exponentiations	(i+1)S–multiplications
Computation for P_n	n exponentiations	n S–multiplications
Multiplications in $F(p)$ for P_i	$23.4(i+1)\log_2(k)$	$20(i+1)\log_2 k$
Multiplications in $F(p)$ for P_n	$23.4 n \log_2(k)$	$23.4 n \log_2(k)$

* Where $\log_2(k)$ is the average length of all k, $0 < k < p$ ($0 < k < Q = q^2 + q + 1$).

From these tables, we can see the advantage of our protocol with respect in computation efficiency. Besides, the protocol generates group key pair as long as $2|p|$ bits, which can be split into two parts for different security applications.

5 Conclusions

This paper deals with the group key generation in secure group communications by the following contributions: (1) A new group key agreement protocol based on GH-KEP is proposed. (2) The computational complexity for the new protocol are lower than that of those existing group key agreement protocols based on DH two party scheme [4, 7, 11, 12]. The complexity of adding or deleting a member to the group will be analyzed in the full version of this paper.

Acknowledgements

This work was supported by the University Doctorial Research Foundation under the grant No.20020613020, Ministry of Education, PR China, and the German Academic Exchange Service (DAAD), Germany.

References

1. W. Diffie and M. Hellman, New directions in cryptography, IEEE Transactions on Information Theory, vol.22, 644–654, 1976.
2. M. Burmester and Y. Desmedt, A secure and efficient conference key distribution system, Eurocrpto'94, Springer-Verlag, 1994.
3. W.G.Tzeng and Z.Tzeng, Round-Efficient Conference Key Agreement Protocols with Provable Security, Asiancrypt2000, LNCS 1976, Springer-Verlag, pp. 614–627, 2000.
4. M. Steiner, G. Tsudik, and M. Waidner, Diffie-Hellman key distribution extended to groups, Third ACM Conference on Computer and Communications Security, ACM Press, pp. 31-37, 1996.
5. G. Gong and L. Harn, Public-key cryptosystems based on cubic finite field extensions, IEEE Transactions on Information Theory, vol 45, no 7, pp 2601–2605, 1999.
6. G. Gong, L.Harn, and H. Wu, The GH Public-Key Cryptosystem, SAC 2001, LNCS 2259, pp. 284–300, 2001.
7. M.Steiner, G.Tsudik, and M.Waidner. Key agreement in dynamic peer groups. IEEE Transactions on Parallel and Distributed Systems, Vol.11, no.8, pp.769–780, 2000.
8. K.Giulianli, G.Gong, Generating large instances of the Gong-Hern cryptosystem, Technical Report of Waterloo university, 2002.
9. U.Maurer and S.Wolf, Diffie-Hellman, Decision Diffie-Hellman, and Discrete Logarithms, Proceedings of ISIT '98, IEEE Press, pp. 327, 1998.
10. Dirk Balfanz, D. K. Smetters, Paul Stewart and H. Chi Wong, Talking To Strangers: Authentication in Ad-Hoc Wireless Networks, Network and Distributed System Security Symposium, San Diego, California, 2002.

11. G. Ateniese, M. Steiner and G. Tsudik, New Multi-party Authentication Services and Key Agreement Protocols, IEEE Journal on Selected Areas in Communications, special issue on Secure Communication, 2000.
12. Emmanuel Bresson, Olivier Chevassut, and David Pointcheval. Provably authenticated group Diffie-Hellman key exchange – the dynamic case. Asiacrypt 2001, Springer-Verlag, pp. 290–309. 2001.

The Packet Marking and the Filtering Protocol to Counter Against the DDoS Attacks

Jeenhong Park[1], Jin-Hwan Choi[1], and Dae-Wha Seo[2]

[1] School of Electrical Engineering and Computer Science, Kyungpook National University,
1370 Sankyuk-dong Buk-gu Daegu, Republic of Korea
{grassman, kingka9594}@palgong.knu.ac.kr
[2] School of Electrical Engineering and Computer Science, Kyungpook National University,
1370 Sankyuk-dong Buk-gu Daegu, Republic of Korea
dwseo@ee.knu.ac.kr

Abstract. In this paper, we propose Node Status Feedback Protocol (NSFP) as a countermeasure for the distributed denial of service (DDoS) attacks. The aggregation-based traffic control can result in the loss of the legitimate packets under the distributed denial of service attacks. Therefore we propose the filtering method based on the deterministic packet marking to distribute the filtering points of the flow-based traffic control.

1 Introduction

The Internet is based on the TCP/IP protocol that implements the packet switching. However, the packet switching network has the problem of the network bottleneck. The DDoS attack can interfere with the legitimate service of the server by concentrating the traffic of many hosts at one point of the network. The notorious incident related to the DDoS attack was the attack to the Yahoo, eBay sites in 2000[1].

Now there are many countermeasures to the various DDoS attacks. The methods can be divided into two categories - the traceback and the defense. The traceback method is to trace the attacker's location by analyzing the information of the traceback packets. A typical method in this category is iTrace[2]. However iTrace cannot be used when the router blocks the ICMP messages for the security problem. The defense method is to reduce or block the DDoS traffic. A typical method in this category is the pushback[3]. However this method is not flow control but aggregation control, therefore can result in the loss of the legitimate traffic.

We propose a packet filtering protocol named Node Status Feedback Protocol (NSFP) based on the deterministic packet marking method. The deterministic packet marking is to mark the routing path information to every packet. The information marked in the packet can easily be exploited by the attackers. Therefore we maintain the network with the reliable security protocol NSFP. The NSFP is the protocol to distribute the filtering load throughout the network and maintain the network security. In this paper, we will define a deterministic packet marking along with a secure message protocol NSFP and describe the modules to implement the protocol.

2 The Deterministic Packet Marking and the NSFP Network

The Deterministic Packet Marking. The basic idea of the deterministic packet marking can be described as follows: Each node in the network has a unique number k and incoming packet has the field to mark a number m. All nodes have the same function f(x, y) which has the parameter x, y and returns a number. Each node marks the incoming packet with the value m' which is the result of the function f(k, m). If there are many packets with the same transmission route, the destination node will be able to receive the packets with same marking. It means that the victim node will be able to filter the massive attack traffic with the same attack route even if the source addresses of the packets are spoofed. And if the function f(x, y) has the inverse function, we will be able to find the previous node that sends the massive traffic by the packet marking value m which is the result of the inverse function $f^1(k, m')$. The function f(x, y) can be simple operations such as 'x XOR y' or 'x + y'. There are many nodes with two or more network interface and we need to distinguish the network interface with incoming attacking traffic from other interfaces. As a result, each network interface has its unique number and there may be many unique numbers per node.

The NSFP Network. It is required to define some terms to describe the network configuration. The term NSFP node means the node that implements the deterministic packet marking and NSFP. The NSFP network is defined as a set of the NSFP nodes. We assume that the NSFP nodes are secure and there's no intruder inside the NSFP network. The role of the NSFP network is to guarantee the integrity of the packet marking and distribute the filtering point to avoid the bottleneck of the network.

The edge node is located at the edge of the NSFP network and has the possibility to receive the spoofed packet from the neighbor nodes. In other words the edge node has the unreliable network interfaces that can receive the spoofed packet and the reliable ones connected to the NSFP nodes. The edge nodes initialize the marking field of the packets which are received from the unreliable network interfaces.

3 The Modules and the Protocol Definition

A NSFP node performs the packet marking and filtering of the packets that pass thorough the node. And it maintains the secure connection of the NSFP network. A NSFP node consists of three modules that are the traffic control module, the security module and the node status management module.

3.1 The Modules in the NSFP Node

The node status management module manages the filtering status and the status of the neighbor nodes. The node status consists of the current filtering list, the filtering list of neighbor NSFP node and the list of the neighbor NSFP node. The change in the status information is broadcasted to the neighbor NSFP nodes. It can update the filtering list of the traffic control module and communicate with neighbor NSFP nodes via security module. The traffic control module performs the packet filtering and marking of the packets passing through the NSFP node. The traffic control module is installed as the network filter module in the OS kernel. The security module establishes secure connection to exchange the NSFP messages.

3.2 The Node Status Feedback Protocol

Connection Establishment. The node status feedback protocol session begins from the secure connection between the NSFP nodes. The connection sequence has the following algorithms.

1. When the NSFP node A tries to establish a connection to the NSFP node B, the node A encrypts the public key e_A of the node A with the public key e_B of the node B and sends the encrypted packet to the node B.
2. The node B checks if the public key is correct and sends ACK message to node A when the connection is valid. The ACK message is encrypted with the public key e_B and includes a random symmetric encryption key K. Because there is the possibility to allow the Man-in-the-Middle attack[4], the two nodes must know about the public keys of each other.
3. The node A decrypts the encryption key K and sends ACK messages to node B. By this time, the encryption is changed to symmetric key encryption. The ACK message is encrypted with the symmetric encryption key K and the first NSFP message is also included.

Node Status Feedback Protocol. The NSFP message consists of various messages. The messages are divided into two categories - the message filtering and the status transmission. The status transmission is done periodically and the detailed description is omitted here. The NSFP filtering request message has the following algorithms.

1. The node status management module receives the filtering request from the downstream NSFP node then it performs the following operations: In case the filtering load is lower than that of the requesting node, the node status management module saves its filtering request information. Otherwise the node status management module sends NACK message to the requesting node and quit.
2. The node status management module adds the received filtering information to the traffic control module.
3. The traffic control module finds the address of the upstream NSFP node and the packet marking value. Then it reports the information to the node status management module.
4. In case that the filtering load of the current node is lower than that of the upstream NSFP node, the node status management module sends the filtering request to the upstream NSFP node.

4 The Simulation Result

We simulated the DDoS attack with the NS-2 simulator[5]. To compare with the NSFP, we chose the pushback protocol. The simulated network consists of 3 backbone routers and 6 ASP routers and 30 hosts. One of the hosts is the victim and there are 4 zombie hosts. All routers are NSFP nodes and the backbone routers are the

DDoS reflectors. The link delay is 10ms. The link bandwidth of the backbone routers is 20Mbps, that of ASP routers is 10Mbps and the hosts have 700Kbps link. All traffic is CBR. Each attack is done at 200Kbps and the legitimate traffic is sent at 500Kbps. During the 22sec of simulation the pushback showed the overall packet loss of the 28% and the loss of the legitimate traffic is 64%. In contrast, the NSFP showed the packet loss of 2% and the legitimate traffic is 1%. Because of the problem of the detection algorithm the victim did not send the filtering message immediately so the NSFP showed 2% loss.

5 Conclusion

We proposed the Node Status Feedback Protocol to distribute the filtering point and showed its possibility to counter the DDoS attacks. The Node Status Feedback Protocol operates like pushback but its performance differs under the DDoS attack. As the pushback cannot determine the DDoS attack traffic, it filters the legitimate traffic along with the DDoS attack traffic.

We also showed that the deterministic packet marking can simplify the procedure to determine the DDoS attack. The DDoS attack can be easily detected from victim host but the information about the source of the attack is unknown. However the packet marking can provide the attacking information to the victim and the attacking traffic can easily be filtered.

In this paper, the simulation is not enough to show the overall performance. The packet marking can result in the performance degradation. Later, we will examine the performance issue of the NSFP.

References

1. http://www.computerworld.com/news/2000/story/0,11280,43010,00.html
2. S.M. Bellovin: "ICMP Traceback Messages," IETF draft, 2000
3. Ratul Mahajan, S.M. Bellovin, Sally Floyd, John Ioannidis, Vern Paxson, and Scott Shenker: "Controlling High Bandwidth Aggregates in the Network", ACM SIGCOMM Computer Communications
4. http://www.fact-index.com/m/ma/man_in_the_middle_attack.html
5. http://www.isi.edu/nsnam/ns/

A Lightweight Mutual Authentication Based on Proxy Certificate Trust List

Li Xin and Mizuhito Ogawa

Japan Advanced Institute of Science and Technology,
1-1 Asahidai Tatsunokuchi Nomi Ishikawa, 923-1292 Japan
{li-xin, mizuhito}@jaist.ac.jp

Abstract. We propose Proxy Certificate Trust List (PCTL) to efficiently record delegation traces for grid computing. Our security solution based on PCTL provides functions as follows: (1) On-demand inquiries about real time delegation information of grid computing underway; (2) Lightweight mutual authentication that is beneficial for proxy nodes with limited computation power as wireless devices in mobile computing; (3) A kind of revocation mechanism for proxy certificates to improve the security and availability of grid computing.

Keywords: Grid Computing, Proxy Certificate, Mutual Authentication.

1 Introduction

Proxy certificate (PC) is used in grid computing for securing private keys, delegation and single-sign-on[1] [2]. PC is issued by either grid users or grid proxys with limited life span. However there are some open problems. First, Grid Security Infrastructure (GSI) provides weak control on agents without a revocation mechanism for PCs. For instance, a PC may become invalid while computing is still underway due to network latency, underestimate, etc. Next, proxy certificate path verification is mechanically repeated in each mutual authentication, placing a heavy burden on agents to keep and exchange a long proxy certificate chain. Last but not least, grid participants often need to know the current delegation information, but GSI provides no means to do this.

In this paper, Proxy Certificate Trust List (PCTL) is proposed to partially solve these problems by providing on-demand delegation trace inquiries, lightweight mutual authentication, and a proxy certificate revocation mechanism.

2 Core Strategy for System Based on PCTL

2.1 Certificate Register Authority (CRA)

Our system is based on the existing Certificate Authority (CA)[3]. The additional and independent module is a trusted third party named the Certificate Register Authority (CRA). The main functions of the CRA are: (1) Maintain the trust relations for PCs. (2) Respond to on-demand inquiries for detailed information about PCs and delegation traces. (3) Generate PCTL. (4) Revoke compromised or expired PCs. The data structure PNode is for recording PC information, as shown in Table 1. The information of End Entity Certificate (EEC), a standard X.509 certificate, is supplied directly from CA/LDAP servers. The IP address plus port number of the agent are contained in the PC's Relative Distinguished Name (RDN) to ensure unique names as well as active service from the CRA.

Table 1. Data Structure PNode for Proxy Certificate in CRA

Entry	Value
Index	Relative Distinguished Name + Certificate Serial Number
Delegation Depth	Permitted length of the delegation trace
Certificate Identifier_1	Hash code of proxy certificate
Certificate Identifier_2	Hash code of public key
Certificate Status	"Valid","Wait for Update","Invalid"
Validity	Life span of proxy certificate
Public Key	Public key of proxy certificate
Parent Pointer	Pointers to the issuer
Child Pointer	Pointers to all the issued grid proxys

2.2 Definition of PCTL

PCTL records trusted delegation traces for grid computing. An n-ary dual-linked tree, TrustLogicTree, is constructed based on PNode to maintain delegation relations (Figure 1). PCTL records PC information on some trusted delegation trace with short life span, issuer information, security context, etc and is signed by CRA. The format for each PCTL entry differs at various security levels. An example of PCTL with a high security level is shown in Figure 2.

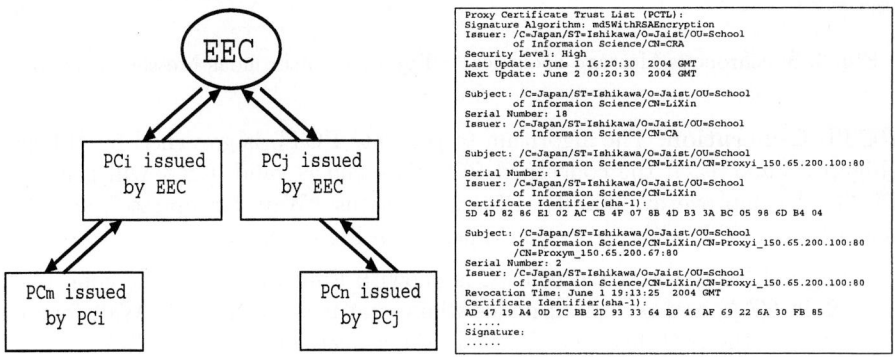

Fig. 1. N-ary dual-linked tree TrustLogic   Fig. 2. Example for PCTL in High Level

- High Level: An entry is a triplet (Index, Issuer, Certificate Identifier_1), each item of which corresponds to the definition in PNode. The hash of PC ensures the integrity of the whole certificate information.
- Middle Level: An entry is a triplet (Index, Issuer, Certificate Identifier_2). The hash of the PC's public key ensures the binding of the proxy name and its public key. Thus none can pretend to be another proxy by issuing PC with the same RDN.
- Low Level: An entry is a pair (Index, Issuer). It runs with the highest efficiency and benefits mobile computing with limited computation power.

2.3 Basic Algorithms

Register. When delegation is needed, the issuer is required to register the new PC to the CRA after signing. The CRA will find the entry for the issuer by Index and verify the PC to be issued. If verification succeeds, CRA will create a corresponding PNode for the new PC and add it into the TrustLogicTree.

PCTL Acquisition. Figure 3 shows a synchronous manner to get a PCTL when delegation and register are bounded together and the sequence order is preserved. Sequence (1)-(3) in Figure 4 shows an asynchronous manner where delegation and register are independent. It is a more lightweight handshake, but may require a timeout and retry if mutual authentication proceeds right after the delegation, that is, if an update of TrustLogicTree is later than a correlative PCTL use. Sequence (4)-(5) shows an on-demand inquiry for PCTL.

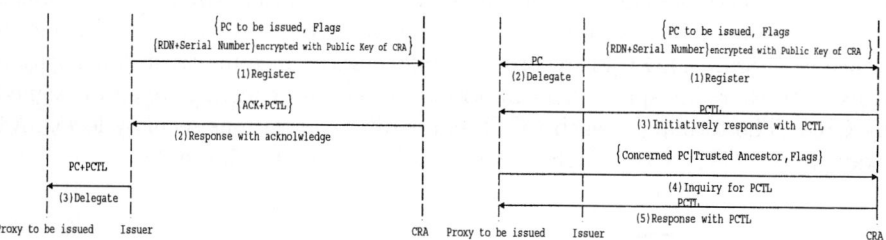

Fig. 3. Synchronous Message Sequence   **Fig. 4.** Asynchronous Message Sequence

PCTL Generation. The algorithm to generate PCTL is governed by "Flags" (Figures 3 and 4). If the concerned PC exists and is valid, CRA will generate PCTL. To improve availability, PCs with status "Wait for update" are also recorded in PCTL with revocation times, as in Figure 2.

- Flags=0 (Only the concerned PC is known): Find PNode for the concerned PC in CRA, and record all nodes whose status is "Valid" or "Wait for update" on the path between EEC and the concerned PC into PCTL.
- Flags=1 (Only the trusted ancestor of the concerned PC is known): Traverse the subtree rooted with the trusted ancestor by Depth-First-Search, and ignore the subtree rooted with PNode whose status is "Invalid". Then record all the nodes in the subtree into the PCTL.

– Flags=2 (Both the concerned PC and its trusted ancestor are known): Traverse the subtree rooted with the trusted ancestor by Depth-First-Search, then record all the nodes whose status is "Valid" or "Wait for update" on the path between the trusted ancestor and the concerned PC into PCTL.

Proxy Certificate Revocation. (1) When some private key leaks, CRA will be notified to disable all the sub-trees rooted with the attacked PC by resetting all nodes' status from "Valid" to "Invalid". (2)When some PC expires, CRA does similarly to (1). The difference is only the expired PC will be disabled by resetting the status to "Wait for update" to improve availability.

Free. Once an end entity finishes its task, CRA will release the subtree rooted with its EEC.

2.4 A Lightweight Mutual Authentication with PCTL

Let Proxy A and Proxy B be under a mutual authentication. Let PC_B be the PC of Proxy B. Let $PCTL\_B$=(Index, Issuer, CI) be the PCTL of Proxy B. Certificate verification with PCTL for Proxy A is shown briefly as follows: First, A decrypts $PCTL\_B$ with CRA's public key and check its validity. If it expired, A updates $PCTL\_B$ from CRA or asks B to provide a fresh one. After that,

– High Level: Proxy A finds the entry for B by Index in $PCTL\_B$, and then computes the hash of PC_B and compares it with CI.
– Middle Level: Proxy A finds the entry for B by Index in $PCTL\_B$, and then computes the hash of B's public key and compares it with CI.
– Low Level: If there is an entry for Proxy B in $PCTL\_B$, Proxy B can be trusted without any computation.

3 Compatibility with GSI

Figure 5 shows the relationship between CRA and the current GSI system. To support PCTL, the required modification is kept to a minimum: (1) Additional negotiation is needed for SSL/TLS protocol when PCTL is enabled. (2) A new Object Class pkiProxyLDAP is needed for LDAP Schema [4] [5] (Figure 6).

4 Conclusions and Future Work

Our solution provides a "One-Time-Verification" on behalf of grid agents. A delegation tracing method was proposed in [6] by suggesting use of a ProxyCertInfo extension field. However this method can not reflet dynamic delegation changes. With the introduction of CRA, bottle-neck and single-point failure problems need to be considered. Fault-tolerant techniques similar to those applied to CA can be used in a real implementation. Since in the current system agents might access CA for a Certificate Revocation List (CRL), the only additional overhead is the handshake with CRA in the register phrase, which doesn't take the time of computing in asynchronous manner. In our solution, certificate chain exchange

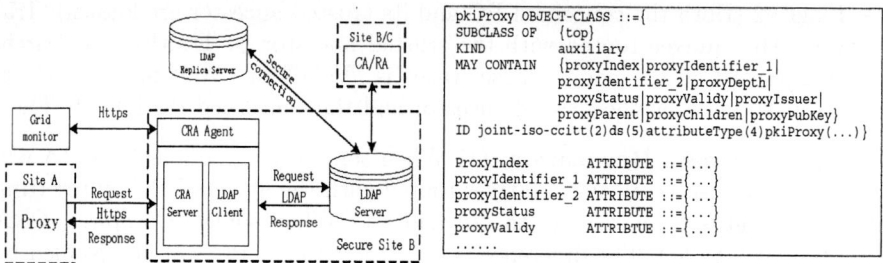

Fig. 5. CRA implementation based on PKI   **Fig. 6.** LDAP schema to support PC

can be avoided by exchanging a much smaller PCTL or by getting the PCTL itself. Certificate chain verification can also be avoided by simple hash manipulation. Assume L be the delegation depth and W the delegation width, the rough time cost of mutual authentication for the current system is $O(LW)$. So the advantages of our solution loom large when delegation is deep and frequent.

Acknowledgments

The authors thank Professor Kefei Chen (Shanghai Jiao Tong University) that work in this paper begin with his guidance, Li Qiang (Shanghai Jiao Tong Unversity) for providing an openssl platform to run examples, and Professor Yasushi Inoguchi (JAIST) for his helpful comments. This research is supported by Special Coordination Funds for Promoting Science and Technology by Ministry of Education, Culture, Sports, Science and Technology.

References

1. I. Foster, et al. The Anatomy of the Grid: Enabling Scalable Virtual Organizations. Supercomputer Applications, 15(3), 2001.
2. V. Welch, et al. Security for Grid Services. *Twelfth International Symposium on High Performance Distributed Computing (HPDC-12)*, PP.48-57, 2003.
3. Internet X.509 Public Key Infrastructure Certificate and CRL Profile. RFC 2459, 1999.
4. Internet X.509 Public Key Infrastructure LDAPv2 Schema. RFC 2587, 1999.
5. Internet X.509 Public Key Infrastructure LDAP Schema and Syntaxes for PKIs. draft-ietf-pkix-ldap-pki-schema-00.txt, 2002.
6. V. Welch, et al. X.509 Proxy Certificates for Dynamic Delegation. *3rd Annual PKI R&D Workshop*, 2004.

Proposal of a New Message Protocol for IEEE 802.11

Seung-Jung Shin and Dae-Hyun Ryu

Dept. of IT, Hansei Univerisity, Dang Jung Dong, Gun Po Si,
Kyung Gi Do, South Korea
{expersin, dhryu}@hansei.ac.kr

Abstract. The New Message Protocol is to cope with the documentation of the message transfer protocol that integrates the electronic signature, distribution and the authentication of public key in information technology. They are classified into security technology, security policy, and electronic document processing, electronic document transportation, encryption and decryption keys in its function. The measures of items for the message security protocol are produced for documentation of the implemented documents in every function for IEEE 802.11.

1 Introduction

The purpose of this study is to take a look at the actual security measures that a user must be kept in mind in today's wireless communication world. There are so many methods and forms of hacker attacks to steal commercial data that wireless measures designed for convenience can be exceedingly harmful without actually taking the proper measures.

The focus of this research is on the safety of document transfer on the Web. In an attempt to be in favor of this trend, the new message security protocol is developed than the conventional message security protocol at the IEEE 802.11. It is a new protocol that validated those main functions that are extracted from information technology. Those functions are derived and analyzed for the features of security, integrity, send negation blocking and receiver negation blocking from the information technology. Additionally, the comparison in security policy is done in terms' of message access security degree and multi degree security.

2 The Structure of Message Security Protocol

2.1 Factors of Security Protocol

Primary factors that define security in a wireless environment can be boiled down to six elements; they are shown as tightly integrated interdependent components in Figure 1.

The basic structure of message protocol is shown in the Figure 1. The major focus of this research is to augment the safety and security features on the IEEE 802.11x protocols.

Table 1. The variants of 802.11x

802.11 Variants	Description
802.11a	Created a standard for WLAN operations in the 5 GHz band with data rates of up to 54 Mbps.
802.11b	Created a standard (also known as Wi-Fi) for WLAN operations in the 2.4 GHz band with data rates of up to 11Mbps.
802.11c	Provided documentation of 802.11-specific MAC procedures to the International Organization for Standardization/(IEEE 802.1d) standard. Work has completed.
802.11d	Publishing definitions and required to enable the 802.11 standard to operate in countries that are not currently served the standard.
802.11e	Attempting to enhance the 802.11 MAC to increase the quality of service (Qos) possible. Improvements in capabilities and efficiency are planned.
802.11f	Developing recommended practices for implementing the 802.11 concepts of APs and distributed systems(DSs).
802.11g	Developing a higher-speed PHY extension to the 802.11b standard while maintaining backward compatibility with current 802.11b devices.
802.11h	Enhancing the 802.11 MAC and 802.11a PHY to provide network management and control extensions for spectrum and transmit power management in the 5 GHz band.
802.11i	Enhancing the security and authentication mechanisms of the 802.11 standard.
802.11j	Also aimed at enhancing security of 802.11b.

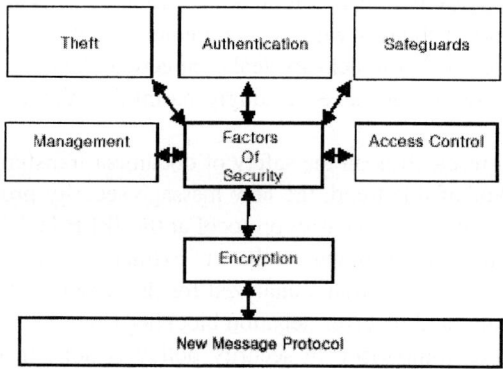

Fig. 1. The architecture and function of message protocol

2.2 The Analysis of Message Security Protocol and IEEE 802.11

The proposed message security protocol is designed to support different levels of security needs. The level of safety and security of the system employing the proposed protocol can dynamically adapt the requirement of the system. It is important in that the wireless environment is exposed to the unintentional and intentional attacks.

The message uses the header, which is made from the complicate encryption procedure. Table 1 illustrates the functions of headers of the 802.11 message protocol. The security transportation of message security protocol is designed to process within the application layer. NMP (New Message Protocol) is designed to guarantee the secure transportation depended on SSL (Secure Socket Layer) and on registration of the document the protocol is selected according to the degree and loaded in the protocol with header adding to the front side of the message.

3 The Documentation and Results

An event is evaluated for a number of items and the weight of the items is different, Information technology is a good method for integrating the evaluations. Therefore, the NMP is designed to adapt to various situations by updating the security protocols – security policy, technology, etc. First of all after the prerequisites of security protocol are decided, the relative weights are decided. In an attempt to apply fuzzy integral for the documentation of security protocol the functional parts of message security protocol is classified according to its items; and the weights of the frequency is described in the survey. In particular five items security technology, security policy, electronic document management, electronic document transfer, and encryption/decryption key are classified in detail.

Table 2. The comparison of new massage protocol (PEA means Public key Encrypted Algorithm and SEA means Secret Encryption Algorithm)

		NMP1		NMP2		NMP3		remarks
Transfer Processing time		Low speed		Medium speed		High speed		
PEA	Security function Transfer based	KCDSA	SSL	KCDSA	SSL	KCDSA	SSL	The Korean Certificate-based Algorithm
SEA	Hash value	SEED	MD5	SEED	MD5	-	MD5	The Korean Encryption Standards
Message Header		Entire		Sender/receiver information		Key Info		Class use
Document Send	Key Management	Entire	Card in access	Parts	Secret Key	Contents oriented	Secret Key	Layer4 Layer7
Counterfeit/ modulation Certification		recv_stemp;		recv_stemp;		recv_stemp;		
Sending/ receiving file		Classification						Integration management possible
Certification Service		Authentication management by sender/receiver information		Authentication management by sender/receiver information		Authentication by sender signature		

The results of message protocol of each item are summarized in table 3. We calculated those values using fuzzy integral of Eq. 1. Each subset is the calculated result of an event that combined the fuzzy measure of the function of the number of items.

$$\int_x h(x) \circ g(\cdot) = \sup_{E \subseteq X} \text{Min} \left[\min_{x \in E} h(x), g(E) \right]$$

4 Conclusion

Security evaluation and quality evaluation about NMP are developed which can be in favor of Korean wireless environments depended on the multi-degree security with the complement of message environments of message security protocol. In an attempt to efficiently process the document according to each different weight of the document, the low positions of items are applied for the documentation of NMP.

Using message protocol it proves that the results of each protocol are different according to message security protocol and IEEE 802.11b. In the future, the configuration of evaluation data must be complemented efficiently and the evaluation measure of NMP is a little low. Therefore this approach will be a good reference in designing and implementing the new security service as well as the secure and efficient security service will be designed through the uniform management and development and analysis. Hereafter, we are going to pursue various researches and developments to evaluate methods that can apply to actuality products.

Table 3. The evaluation values of table using fuzzy integral

	Factors of security	Evaluation values		
		NMP1	NMP2	NMP3
Authentication	security technology, electronic document management, electronic document transfer, encrypt·decrypt key	0.062	0.0624	0.0616
Access Control	security technology, security policy, electronic document transfer, encrypt·decrypt key	0.0663	0.0651	0.0642
Management	security technology, security policy, electronic document management, encrypt·decrypt key	0.0568	0.0579	0.0562
Encryption	security technology, security policy, electronic document management, electronic document transfer, encrypt·decrypt key	0.0637	0.0647	0.068
Safeguard	security technology, electronic document management, electronic document transfer, encrypt·decrypt key	0.05624	0.05462	0.05214
Theft	security policy, electronic document management, electronic document transfer, encrypt·decrypt key	0.0657	0.0666	0.0688

Acknowledgement

This work was supported by Hansei University, Republic of Korea.

References

1. Caption J. Detombe CD, A Comparison of Two Protocols - PEM vs MSP, 7th ACCESS, May, 1995.
2. Chin Teng Lin and George Lee, Neural Fuzzy Systems, PHIPE, International Edition, pp. 80-82, 1996.
3. Frank Ohrtman. Konrad Roeder, Wi-Fi Handbook, McGrawHill, 2003.
4. Harold Whitaker and John Halas, Timing for Animation, Focal Press, 2003.
5. Mark O'Neill, Web. Services Security, McGrawHill,2003.
6. Ministry of Information and Communication, Development of Information Security Industry, pp. 70-77, 1977.
7. Raymond Smith, WiFi Home Networking, McGrawHill, 2003.
8. Seung-jung Shin, 3rd Asia Pacific International Symposium on Information Technology Istanbul, Turkey, pp. 414-421, 2004.
9. Seung-jung Shin, FAR EAST JOURNAL OF APPLIED MATHEMATICS, 9(3), pp.157-169, 2002.
10. Stewart S.Miller, WiFi Security, McGrawHill, 2003.
11. Tom Meigs, Ultimate Game Design, McGrawHill, 2003.
12. http://www.armadillo.huntville.al.us/index.html
13. http://www.imc.org/workshop/sdn701.txt , 1994
14. http://www.imc.org.workshop/sdn701.txt , 1997.
15. http://www.redstone.army.mil/documents/c4itecharch/section3.html

Attack Resiliency of Network Topologies

Heejo Lee[1] and Jong Kim[2]

[1] Korea University, Seoul 136-701, South Korea
heejo@korea.ac.kr
[2] POSTECH, Pohang 790-784, South Korea
jkim@postech.ac.kr

Abstract. Network topology has no direct effect on the correctness of network protocols, however, it influences on the performance of networks and the survivability of the networks under attacks. In this paper, we examines the attack resiliency of network topologies and shows that the topological structure has direct impact on the robustness of a network under attacks.

1 Introduction

One research direction on Internet topology is to analyze the robustness of the Internet under network attacks [1–5]. One important nature of an attack is target-oriented and that nature can cause catastrophic failures on Internet connectivities [2, 3]. From the analysis of susceptibility to attacks as well as faults, Internet connectivities are more susceptible to malicious attacks than random failures [3], and failures on only a part of components of the Internet can break down the overall Internet infrastructure [2, 4]. On the other hand, the Internet has threads of connection with properties such as small vertex cover [1], which can be a potential "choke point" of the Internet. Thus, exploring topological characteristics of the Internet can be a springboard to enhance the robustness of the Internet infrastructure under malicious attacks.

In this paper, we analyze the resiliency of network topologies under various attacking scenarios. Given a graph G that represents a network topology, the target of an attack can be a set of "nodes", "edges" or "paths", where a path is a series of consecutive edges. Failures caused by an attack influence on the connectivity among nodes, which is represented by deleting the target elements on a graph G. The debilitating effects by attacks are measured for different types of topologies.

2 System Model

A network topology represents the connectivity structure among nodes. Fig. 1 shows three topologies with 10 nodes and 10 edges. Average distances among nodes decrease from the left graph to the right graph, while the dependencies on a single node increases.

---

* This work was supported in part by the ITRC program of the Korea Ministry of Information & Communications, the BK21 program of the Korea Ministry of Education.

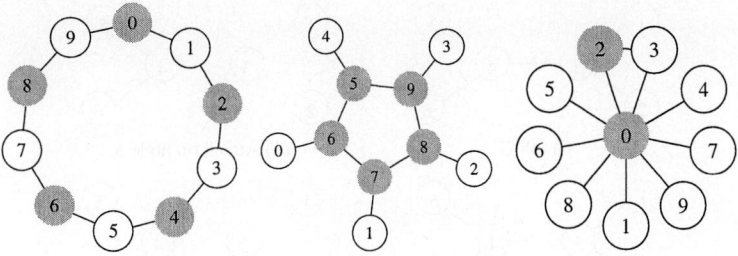

Fig. 1. Network topologies with 10 nodes and 10 edges

One node failure in the left graph does not disrupt the connectivity of other nodes, whereas the failure of the node 0 in the right graph significantly disconnects other nodes. Thus, the topology of a network gives impact on the networking performance and the robustness under attacks.

A network topology is given as an undirected graph $G = (V, E)$, where V is the set of nodes and E is the set of edges. Let T denote the target of an attack, where T is a subset of G, i.e., $T \subseteq G$. T can be a set of nodes, edges or paths. A path $\mathcal{P}[x, y]$ is a set of consecutive edges from a source x to a destination y such that $[x, y] = \{x, v_1, v_2, ..., v_{d-1}, y\}$ where $(v_i, v_{i+1}) \in E$ for all $i = 0 .. d - 1$ with $x = v_0$ and $y = v_d$. Let $\mathcal{A}$ denote an *attack* which represents an operation of deleting a subgraph T from G such that

$$\mathcal{A}(T) : G - T.$$

Deletion of a node or an edge in a graph G is a well-defined operation as described in [6]. Deletion of a path is analogous to the deletion of every edge belonging to the path. As a result of an attack $\mathcal{A}$, the failure can be measured by $\mathcal{F}(\mathcal{A}) = T \cup D$, where D is a set of nodes in $G - T$ that have no remaining edges. It implies that the failure by an attack could be larger than the target of the attack, i.e., $\mathcal{F}(\mathcal{A}) \supseteq T$.

There are three attacking types according to their targets: node attacks, edge attacks, and path attacks. Hardware faults and human errors are not considered as separate items since they can be modeled as "random" attacks. Fig. 2 shows three attack types: node attack with $T = \{3\}$, edge attack with $T = \{(3, 4)\}$ and path attack with $T = \{[1, 4]\}$.

We use α to represent the attack ratio where $0 \leq \alpha \leq 1$. For instance, $\alpha = 0$ means no attack so that $T = \{\}$, whereas $\alpha = 1$ means $T = G$. Thus, α implies the severity of an attack.

Attacks and their effects are separated by "cause" and "effect" such that an attack is a cause and the failure is its effect. The following failure metrics are used for measuring the effect of an attack. Node failure ratio is defined by $f_n = n_f/n$ where n_f is the number of failed nodes. Path failure ratio is defined by $f_p = 2 \cdot p_f/n(n-1)$ where p_f is the number of failed paths.

3 Resiliency Evaluation

To evaluate the attack resiliency, we use both AS-level Internet topologies and artificial graphs. We use AS connectivity graphs archived by NLANR from Oregon RouteView

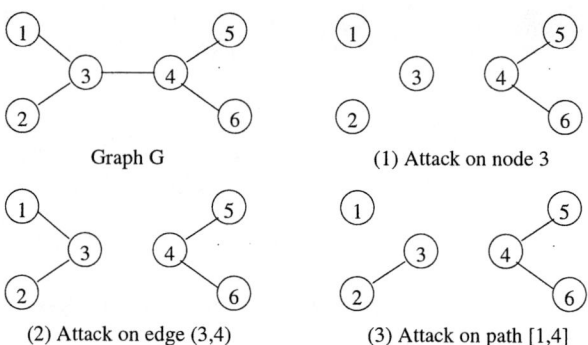

Fig. 2. Three attack types: (1) node attack, (2) edge attack, and (3) path attack

Project [7], which is the most widely used and publicly available data set for studying the Internet topologies. Random graph is generated by connecting two nodes with the linking probability corresponding to the AS connectivity at year 1997, which is $p = 0.001135$ from $p = 2e/n(n-1)$. Internet-like artificial graphs are created by using well-known topology generators such as Brite2.1 [8] and Inet3.0 [9]. Node distributions in the descending order of degree ranks are shown in Fig. 3 (Left), for the AS graphs and the artificial graphs, respectively. These figures show how far from the power-law distributions.

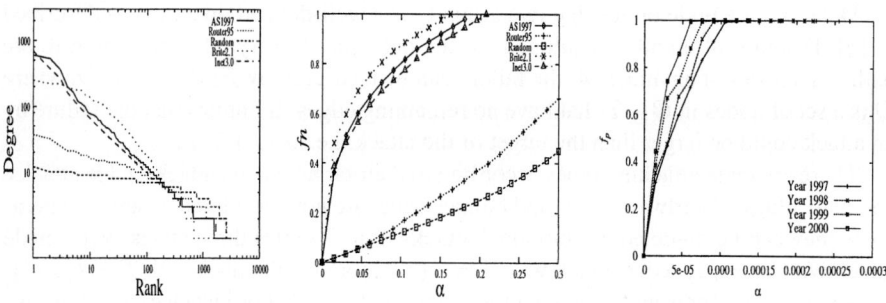

Fig. 3. (Left) Rank-degree distribution of network topologies. (Middle) Distribution of f_n on the node attack. (Right) Distribution of f_p on the path attack

The effects of network topologies are measured with both AS connectivities and router connectivities. Figure 3 (Middle) shows the distribution of f_n as a function of α on the node attack. This shows that AS1997, Brite2.1 and Inet3.0 are weaker than Random and Router95 under the node attack. This confirms that the robustness of the Internet is not better than the random topology.

The node failure ratio f_n jumps up to reach $f_n = 1.0$ at $\alpha = 0.18$, which is the ratio of vertex covering nodes in the Internet topologies [1]. This shows that an attack on vertex covering nodes significantly disconnects the network so that $\alpha = |VC|/n$ can make $f_n = 1$.

Experimental results on the Internet connectivities are shown in Figure 3 (Right). The distributions of f_p under the path attack show similar behaviors for the periods of year 1997 $\sim$ 2000. From the experiments, we can see that the Internet becomes more vulnerable as time goes on.

4 Conclusions

We have proposed several new techniques to model attacks on the Internet, as well as new failure metrics to evaluate the resiliency of the network. Path-based attacks could result in more severe damage on the connectivity of a network. From the comparison of topologies, the Internet is more vulnerable than random graphs, and even becomes worse as time goes on. The purpose of this study is to provide a foundation for finding protection mechanisms. Recent study argued that breakdown of the Internet by attacking nodes is not feasible due to the high connectivity of concentrated nodes. However, judicious placement of attacking sources and their well-targeting could render the whole network disability.

From the fact that performing different types of attacks requires different amount of resources and different degree of controls, we will study on attack costs required to mount attacks and their effectiveness. Also the goal of an attacker can be represented as partitioning a network instead of disconnecting an entire network. Network partitioning can be effective if it isolates some section of a network from desired destinations, particularly from crucial resources such as high-level name servers. Thus, evaluation of attack cost and effectiveness is the future work of this study. As well, this work will continue to find evolving strategies for making networks more resilient to attacks.

References

1. Park, K., Lee, H.: On the effectiveness of route-based packet filtering for distributed DoS attack prevention in power-law internets. ACM SIGCOMM. (2001) 15–26
2. Albert, R., Jeong, H., Barabasi, A.L.: Error and attack tolerance of complex networks. Nature (2000) 378–382
3. Park, S.T., Khrabrov, A., Pennock, D.M., Lawrence, S., Giles, C.L., Ungar, L.H.: Static and dynamic analysis of the internet's susceptibility to faults and attacks. IEEE INFOCOM. (2003)
4. Chakrabarti, A., Manimaran, G.: Internet infrastructure security: A taxonomy. IEEE Network (2002) 13–21
5. Magoni, D.: Tearing down the internet. IEEE JSAC (2003)
6. Gross, J., Yellen, J.: Graph Theory and Its Applications. CRC Press (1998)
7. Nat'l Lab. for Applied Network Research: Routing data (2001) Supported by NFS, http://moat.nlanr.net/Routing/rawdata/
8. Medina, A., Lakhina, A., Matta, I., Byers, J.: Brite: Universal topology generation from a user's perspective. BUCS-TR-2001-003, Boston University (2001)
9. Winick, J., Jamin, S.: Inet-3.0: Internet Topology Generator. CSE-TR-456-02, University of Michigan (2002)

Matching Connection Pairs

Hyung Woo Kang[1], Soon Jwa Hong[1], and Dong Hoon Lee[2]

[1] National Security Research Institute,
161Gajeong-Dong, Yuseong-Gu, Daejeon, 305-350, Korea
{kanghw, hongsj}@etri.re.kr
[2] Center for Information Security Technologies(CIST),
Korea University, Seoul, 136-704, Korea
Donghlee@korea.ac.kr

Abstract. When an intruder launches attack not from their own computer but from intermediate hosts that they previously compromised, these intermediate hosts are called stepping-stones. In this paper, we describe an algorithm to be able to detect stepping-stones in detoured attacks. Our aim is to develop an algorithm that can trace an origin system which attacks a victim system via stepping-stones. There are two kinds of traceback technologies: IP packet traceback and connection traceback. We focused on connection traceback in this paper and proposed a new intruder tracing algorithm to distinguish between an origin system of attack and stepping-stones using process structures of operating systems.

Keywords: Traceback, Stepping stone, Connection pairs, Detoured attack, Backdoor.

1 Introduction

In recent years, the network security community has made reasonably good progress in developing attack prevention and intrusion detection technologies. Although there is still a big room for improvement, these security technologies have been valuable and useful in protecting hosts against direct attacks by an intruder. However, when an intruder attacks a victim via stepping-stones, it is impossible to identify the source in real-time with current intrusion detection technologies. Therefore, an intruder tracing algorithm against detoured attacks is in need.

In this paper, we propose an intruder tracing algorithm which is effective against detoured attacks. The rest of this paper is organized as follows: In chapter 2, we define detoured attacks and notations used in this paper. In chapter 3, we review related researches [1, 3, 4, 7, 9]. A new algorithm matching connection pairs is introduced in chapter 4. Finally, in chapter 5, we draw conclusions.

2 Terminologies

First, we begin with terminologies. When a person logs into one computer, and this computer logs into other computers, we refer to this sequence of logins as a connection chain [6]. Any intermediate host on a connection chain is called a stepping-stone. Figure 1 shows the problem of identifying an origin system.

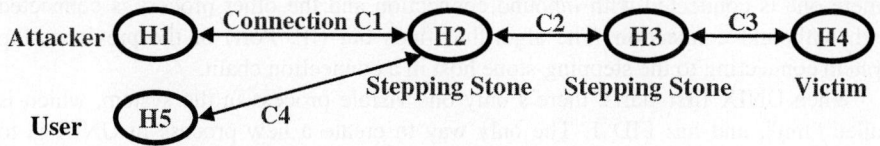

Fig. 1. Connection chains of a legal user and an attacker

There are 5 hosts named H1, H2, H3, H4 and H5, respectively. The attacker is in H1 and H4 is the victim host. H2 and H3 are called stepping-stones. H5 is a legal user. First, Host H1 connects to H2 and exploits it. Second, H2 connects to H3 and exploits it. Finally, H3 attacks the victim host H4. In this case, H2 and H3 are remotely controlled by the attacker H1, and C1, C2, and C3 are composed of a connection chain.

When an IDS detects an attack accident from H3 to H4, the problem of tracing the attacker is equivalent to the problem of finding H3's inbound connection that is C2 which matches with H3's outbound connection C3. In the same way, however, when H2 try to find inbound connection matching outbound connection C2, there are two inbound connection. One is C1 connected from H1. The other is C4 connected from H5. H2 has to find a correct inbound connection that matches with the outbound connection C2.

In this paper, we designed an algorithm which can find the correct inbound connection C1 that matches with the outbound connection C2.

3 Related Works

In this chapter, we will review existing related researches. We can classify connection traceback mechanisms into the following three types: host-based, network-based, and active network-based traceback. Host-based Traceback pursues intruders with authentication of the connection request system and analyzes logs in the system. Traceback module should be installed in every system in computer networks. Therefore, it is hard to apply this type of traceback to current Internet environments. Network-based Traceback pursues intruders by extracting the information from packets on the network. Traceback module should be installed in the location that can monitor all packets. Therefore, there is a disadvantage that monitor systems need every network segment. However, there is an advantage that it can be applied to the current Internet environment. Active network-based traceback can only be applied to Active Network environments. This is a big handicap.

4 Proposed Algorithm

The proposed algorithm can differentiate between stepping-stone hosts and the origin host in detoured attacks. If a system turns out to be a stepping-stone, there are two kinds of connections that are inbound connections and outbound connections. Then, the inbound connection is closely related with the outbound connection. In this paper, we developed an algorithm to match connection pairs using relations of two processes, where one is connected with inbound connection and the other process is connected with outbound connection. The algorithm finds out (IP, Port) of the previous stop system connecting to the stepping-stone host in a connection chain.

When UNIX first starts, there's only one visible process in the system, which is called "init", and has PID 1. The only way to create a new process in UNIX is to duplicate an existing process, so "init" is the ancestor of all subsequent processes. Similarly, all subsequent processes of windows system have a same ancestor which is explorer process.

4.1 Process Structure in the Stepping-Stone

We can classify processes patterns in a stepping-stone into following three types. We take case of UNIX system to show processes pattern in detail.

4.1.1 Interactive Connection Using Telnet, SSH (Connection Chain Type 1)

Inetd daemon serves network services in the UNIX system. When an attacker connects with stepping-stones using the telnet program, inetd daemon forks the in.telnetd process. After a log-in user enters correct id and password, in.telnetd forks a shell process to provide shell command service for the log-in user. Now, the attacker obtains a shell service and can connect with the victim using the telnet program. It is the most general connection type.

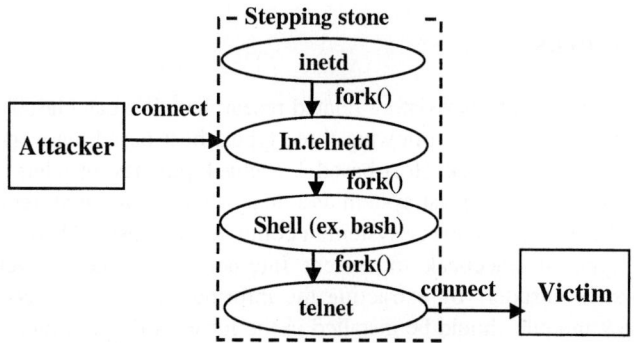

Fig. 2. Connection chain Type 1

4.1.2 Direct Connection Backdoor (Connection Chain Type 2)

In this type, an attacker installs a backdoor program, and then the backdoor process opens a network port and the process is listening to inbound connections of the attacker. When the attacker connects with the backdoor process in a stepping-stone, the backdoor acts previously arranged behaviors(e.g., DoS) to the victim.

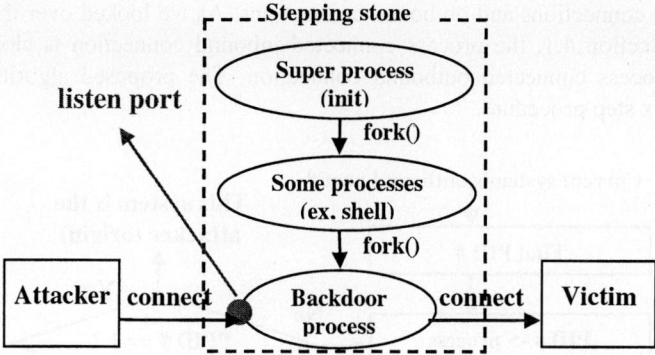

Fig. 3. Connection chain Type 2

4.1.3 Indirect Connection Backdoor (Connection Chain Type 3)

This type is very similar to Type 2, but there is a difference that a backdoor process of Type 3 does not connect with the victim directly, but the backdoor process forks a child process, and then the child backdoor process connects with the victim and attacks it. Fork of backdoor processes could happen multiple times. Most of backdoors(e.g., port redirect backdoor) belong to Type 3.

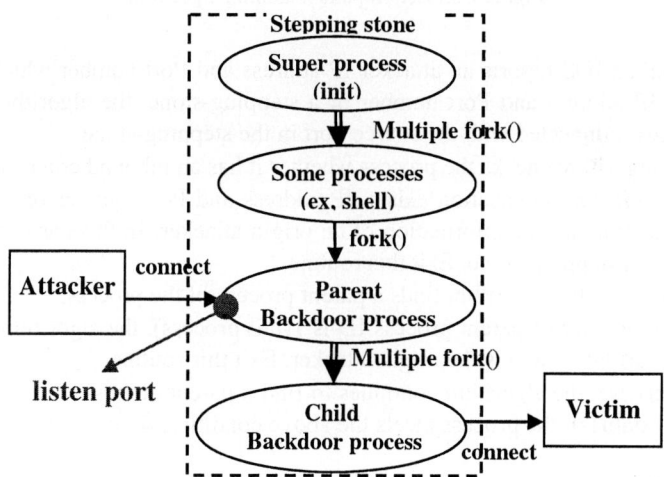

Fig. 4. Connection chain Type 3

4.2 The Algorithm Matching Connection Pairs

There are two basic ideas of this algorithm. First, init process (PID 0) is the ancestor of all subsequent processes including a malicious process created by attacker. Second, when a system turns out to be a stepping-stone, there are two kinds of connections that are inbound connections and outbound connections. As we looked over the processes pattern in Section 4.1, the process connected inbound connection is closely related with the process connected outbound connection. The proposed algorithm has the following six step procedure.

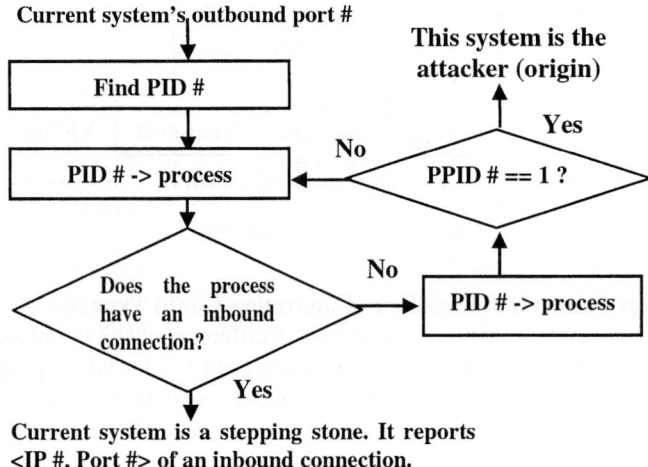

Fig. 5. Connection pairs matching algorithm

- When an IDS reports an attacker IP address and Port number which are actually IP address and Port number of a stepping-stone, the algorithm finds the process connected with the source port in the stepping-stone.
- The algorithm checks the process whether it has an inbound connection or not.
- If an inbound connection exists, IP address and Port number of the inbound connection are the information of an origin attacker. In this case, current system is a stepping-stone. Exit this routine.
- Otherwise, the algorithm finds a parent process of the process.
- If the number of parent process ID is 1(init process), the algorithm concludes that current system is the origin attacker. Exit this routine.
- Otherwise, the algorithm continues to find a parent process of current process until status of the process meets the above condition ③ or ⑤.

4.2.1 Advantages
- Proposed algorithm can detect all kinds of stepping-stones. (No False-Positive and Very-Low False-Negative)
- Proposed algorithm can matches not only interactive connection pairs (e.g., `telnet`), but also connection pairs using backdoors (e.g., `port redirect backdoor`).
- Even though a data of one side is different with a data of the other side or a data is encrypted, proposed algorithm nicely finds connection pairs in a stepping-stone unlike the thumbprint and other works [7].

- Proposed algorithm nicely finds connection pairs not only in detoured attacks using the connection oriented protocol (e.g., TCP), but also in detoured attacks using the connectionless protocol (e.g., UDP).
- Proposed algorithm doesn't need to do any job(e.g., capturing network packet) until detoured attack happens. Therefore, proposed algorithm is more efficient than existing related works [4, 7].
- If the algorithm records the data of process connected inbound connections and outbound connections as logs, the logs can be used in forensic tools for the post tracing.

4.2.2 Disadvantages

Because a traceback module should be installed in every system, it is hard to apply the proposed algorithm to current Internet environment. But, proposed algorithm (traceback module) can be applied to OS(Operating System). If OS producers (e.g., SUN) insert the traceback module into their OS and distribute it widely, the proposed algorithm can be applied to Internet environment.

4.3 Experiment

In this section, we present an implementation and results of experiments on the proposed algorithm.

4.3.1 Implementation of Our Algorithm

We implemented our proposed algorithm using `Lsof` tool and `/proc/PID/psinfo` file on solaris platform.

- System environment: Sun Sparc Solaris 2.8, Gcc 3.0 compiler
- How to get an information about matching network port and process: using Lsof tool
    - `Lsof`(List Open File) lists information about files(including network file) opened by processes for the UNIX system.
- How to get an information that process has inbound connection: using `Lsof` tool
    - `Lsof` is useful in tracking down all sorts of information. For example, it allows you to see what program is operating on an open port, which daemons have established connections, and what ports are open on your server.
- How to get a information of processes: using `/proc/PID/psinfo` file
    - There is a lot of information on process in `/proc/PID/psinfo` file. The information consists of PID (Process ID Number), PPID (Parent Process ID Number), file name, process status and so on.

4.3.2 Result of the Experiment

We made an experiment on 3 types of detoured attacks which are mentioned in Section 4.1. Table 1 shows that the proposed algorithm correctly detects stepping-stones and finds the origin attacker in all 3 types of detoured attacks. In other words, the algorithm succeeds in finding inbound connection matching malicious outbound connection.

Table 1. Results of the experiment

Detoured Attack Type	The tool used in the experiment	Existence of connections	Number of processes created by inbound connection	Results of the trace-back
Type 1	`Telnet`	Yes	2	Success
Type 1	`SSH`	Yes	3	Success
Type 1	`Rlogin`	Yes	2	Success
Type 2	`DDos agent`	No	0	Success
Type 2	`Bo2k port redirector`	Yes	0	Success
Type 3	`Port redirector`	Yes	1	Success
Type 3	`Cd00r.c(packet coded backdoor)`	Yes	1	Success
Type 3	`Httptunnel`	Yes	2	Success
Type 3	`NetCat`	Yes	1	Success

5 Conclusion

The computer communication technologies brought us many benefits including the explosive uses of the internet. However, these new technologies are facing some serious side effects, such as a computer virus or hacking problems. When an unauthorized user (attacker) accesses the computer resources and data via stepping-stones, the Intrusion Detection System (IDS) can only detect information of the last stepping-stone. Therefore IDS cannot find the information of the real attacker. This is a limitation of IDS. Due to the above reason, in this paper, we developed and proposed a connection pairs matching algorithm which can trace origin attackers. As we mentioned in Section 4.2.1, there are a lot of advantages in this algorithm in contrast to other approaches. As we mentioned in Section 4.3, this algorithm has excellent results in intruder tracing tests. Our immediate research results include the design of a connection pair matching algorithm and implementation of the algorithm. Finally natural extensions to this work will be to implement the trackback module more efficiently to various OSs.

References

1. X. Wang, D. Reeves, S. F. Wu, and J. Yuill, "Sleepy Watermark Tracing: An Active Network-Based Intrusion Response Framework", Proceedings of IFIP Conference on Security, Mar. (2001)
2. Buchholz, Thomas E. Daniels, Benjamin Kuperman, Clay Shields, "Packet Tracker Final Report," CERIAS Technical Report 2000-23, Purdue University, (2000)
3. K. Yoda and H. Etoh, "Finding a Connection Chain for Tracing Intruders," In F. Guppens, Y. Deswarte, D. Gollamann, and M. Waidner, editors, 6th European Symposium on Research in Computer Security - ESORICS 2000 LNCS -1985, Toulouse, France, Oct. (2000)
4. H.T. Jung et al. "Caller Identification System in the Internet Environment," Proceedings of the 4th Usenix Security Symposium, (1993)

5. Steven R. Snapp, James Brentano, Gihan V. Dias, "DIDS(Distributed Intrusion Detection System) – Motivation, Architecture, and An Early Prototype," Proceedings of the 14th National Computer Security Conference, (1991)
6. S. Staniford-Chen and L.T. Heberlein. "Holding Intruders Accountable on the Internet," In Proceedings of the 1995 IEEE Symposium on Security and Privacy, (1995)
7. Y. Zhang and V. Paxson, "Detecting Stepping stones," Proceedings of 9th USENIX Security Symposium, Aug. (2000)
8. D. Schnackenberg, K. Djahandari, and D. Sterene, "Infrastructure for Intrusion Detection and Response," Proceedings of DISCEX, Jan. (2000)
9. D. Schnackenberg, K. Djahandary, and D Strene, "Cooperative Intrusion Traceback and Response Architecture(CITRA)," Proceedings of the 2nd DARPA Information Survivability Conference and Exposition(DISCEXII), June (2001)
10. Dawn X. Song and Adrian Perrig, "Advanced and Authenticated Marking Schemes for IP Traceback," Proceedings of InfoCom (2001)
11. Stefan Savage, David Wetherall, Anna Karlin "Practical Network Support for IP Traceback," Proceedings of the 2000 ACM SIGCOMM Conference, Stockholm, Sweden, Aug. (2000) pp295-306.
12. Graham Glass, "UNIX for Programmers and Users : A Complete Guide", Prentice Hall (1993)

Adaptation Enhanced Mechanism for Web Survivability

Eungki Park[1], Dae-Sik Choi[1], Jung-Taek Seo[1], Choonsik Park[1], and Dongkyu Kim[2]

[1] National Security Research Institute
62-1 Hwa-am-dong, Yu-seong-gu
Daejeon, 305-718, Republic of Korea
{ekpark, dschoi, seojt, csp}@etri.re.kr
[2] School of Information & Computer Engineering
Ajou University, Suwon
Republic of Korea
dkkim@madang.ajou.ac.kr

Abstract. there are increasing needs of undisturbed web services despite of attacks. In this paper, we proposed adaptation mechanism for a web-server intrusion tolerant system. Our proposed adaptation mechanism allows the system to provide continuous web services using various techniques, such as intrusion tolerant types, replication degree, server allocation mechanism, adaptive access control method and so on.

Keywords: intrusion tolerance, survivability, web services.

1 Introduction

According to CSI/FBI reports, even though 95 percent of organizations have firewalls, 61 percent of them have IDS, 90 percent of them use access control, and 42 percent of them use digital signatures, attacks still occurred. These data indicate that both intrusion detection mechanisms and intrusion blocking mechanisms apparently have limitations, so there should be new directions toward research areas, such as intrusion tolerant systems.

In this paper, we proposed adaptation mechanism for a web-server intrusion tolerant system. Our proposed adaptation mechanism allow the system to provide continuous web services using various techniques, such as intrusion tolerant types, replication degree, server allocation mechanism, adaptive access control method and so on. The rest of this paper is organized as follows: after reviewing previous approaches in Section 2, Section 3 shows an overall structure of our Advanced Web-server Intrusion Tolerant System and Section 4 shows adaptation policies, followed by conclusions and future directions in Section 5.

2 Related Work

Feiyi Wang et. al [1–3] proposed an intrusion tolerant system called SITAR. In their approach, requests are forwarded to several web servers through acceptance monitors, and responses are monitored in acceptance monitors and ballot monitors. adaptive reconfiguration module takes care of reconfiguration and adaptation when attacks are detected. There are several problems with their approach. 1) Their modules lack detailed design and implementation descriptions, and many issues are not addressed in their paper. It is not clear how the reconfiguration module works. 2) Since a request is forwarded to several web servers simultaneously, there is performance problem for handling requests. Daesik choi et. al [4] suggests Web server Intrusion tolerant system called WITS. In their approach, WITS consists of four modules (resistance, recognition, reconstruction and adaptation) for continuous services. Detailed adaption methods are not fully discussed in their paper.

Even though there are some previous researches on intrusion tolerant systems, more research and experiments are in need, especially on adaptive policies. Therefore, after reviewing previous approaches, we designed an intrusion tolerant system and currently work on implementing a prototype.

3 Our System Overview

An intrusion tolerant server lies in front of more than one web server which includes wrapper-based web servers, and these web servers share a database. Each server can have more than one identical web service for redundancy and diversity, and more than one web server runs simultaneously. An intrusion tolerant server acts as a proxy server, and it relays requests and responses between clients and servers.

Data flow in AWITS is as follows: for requests from each client in the Internet, a new FRM (filtering and request handling module) process and a new VOM (voting module) process are created. An FRM process forwards requests to MRM (masking and recognition module) according to policies of ARM (adaptive reconstruction module). FRM executes request validation procedures (These will be explained later), and if the request passed validation tests, the request is forwarded to a web server through MRM. Then, the MRM gets results from the web server and performs result validation procedures. If the results are ok, then they are forwarded to VOM. Otherwise, the validation test results are sent to ARM and the ARM performs filtering and reconstruction. In VOM, a selected result through voting is transmitted to the client that sent the request. AMs(admin modules) reside in web servers, and collect information about web servers. Based on results of request and response validations, 'black' lists are maintained. The policies established here are used by FRM when requests are forwarded to MRM. Unknown attacks are detected through the response validation process. LHM(logging and health monitoring module) is responsible for collecting logs from modules in the system as well as checking web server status or contents of web servers. To check integrity of contents, LHM keep MD5 hash values of contents that must be protected, and AM's periodically recalculate hash values and send them to LHM , monitor Web server health and modify wrapper based web server policy.

4 Adaptation Policies

The most important and critical function of AWITS is how to adapt to new attacks. In this section, we proposed several adaptation policies.

Policy 1: Decision of an Intrusion Tolerant Type. In AWITS, intrusion tolerance types are divided into two types: *Prevent(active defense)* type and *Recover(Passive defence)* type. Let the size of blacklist be B, threshold value be T, active defense be A, and passive defense be P, then
$$if B \geq T \Rightarrow A \rightarrow P$$
How can we decide the threshold value? This value is influenced by external alert condition, administrator's judgement, etc. This policy is adaptively selected considering security strength and performance.

Policy 2: Web Server Assignment. There are two kinds of web server assigning policies: *all active* and *primary/backup*. Initially, web servers are set to the *all active* mode. As the number of attacks increases, the assigning method is changed to the *primary/backup* mode.

>**Heterogeneous Web Server.** Web server that is composed to AWITS is consisted of heterogeneous two kind of web server. Usually, web server more than 3 exists to single system.
>
>**Black List.** Blacklist means statistical data to manage AWITS's whole Adaptation. This statistical data(Blacklist) is used by judgment value of whole adaptation element. Statistical data generated in VOM are sent to ARM so that ARM updates policies of request filtering. To collect statistical data, the following validity scores are collected: Based on collected validity scores, scores per web server, URL, and client are calculated. These calculated scores are used to update policies for filtering requests, assigning MRM processes for requests, and the like.

Policy 3: Reconstruction Policy. Basically, reconstruction is executed based on collected statistical data, such as Blacklist statistics. These data are used for impact masking and determination of degrees of web server redundancy.

>**Impact Masking.** Let each request be I, A be request validation percentage, B be response validation percentage, V be Valid percentage, and threshold be T, $T_1 > T_2 > T_3$.
>
>– if $\frac{A+B}{V} \geq T_1$ then put I to blacklist, and execute response masking.
>– if $\frac{A+B}{V} \geq T_2$ then put I to blacklist, and execute request masking.
>– if $\frac{A+B}{V} \geq T_3$ then put I to blacklist, and store I for future calculation.

Using this policy, AWITS can dynamically prevent exploit codes from doing malicious action.

Degree of Web Server Redundancy. To determine degrees of web server redundancy, AWITS considers information, such as web server access statistics, performance, and admin commands. Let heterogeneous web server be $W_1, W_2, ...,$

W_n, voting winner for web server be VW, the validity score of url vs web server be VU, the validity score of client vs web server be VC, the voting result be V.

if $VW \geq T_{W_n}$ then invoke $T_{W_{n+1}}$, and redirect the request flow considering VU, VC. Because heterogeneous web servers are running concurrently, AWITS reduces $W_1, W_2, ..., W_n \rightarrow W_1$ for performance efficiency.

Let the average of all voting scores be $Q_{average}$, Wrapper-based web server be WW. if $VW \geq Q_{average}$ then invoke WW, and redirect the request flow considering response validation which is used as a criterion for privileged read/write. If VW becomes less than $Q_{average}$, ARM invokes W, redirects the request flow, and deactivates WW.

Let request/response utilization be U, utilization threshold be T, text-based web server be TW. if $U \geq T$ then invoke TW, and redirect the request flow for continuous of service. If the utilization becomes normal and situation is stable, then this flow is deactivated.

5 Conclusions and Future Directions

In this paper, we proposed adaptation mechanism for an intrusion tolerant system. Suggested mechanism executes active and passive protections against attacks, and it is designed to provide continuous web services and higher availability of data. Especially, Suggested mechanism makes use of various adaptation element such as Wrapper based web server, text-based web server. these diversity helps more adaptively reconstruction for survivability. The main advantages of this mechanim are 1) it can provide more continuous service than other IA systems, 2) it can block some unknown attacks, and 3) it can adapt against attacks.

References

1. Wang, F., Upppalli, R.: SITAR: a scalable instrusion-tolerant architecture for distributed services - a technology summary. In: Proceedings of the DARPA Information Survivability Conference & Exposition (DISCEX) 2003. (2003) 153–155
2. Wang, R., Wang, F., Byrd, G.T.: Design and implementation of acceptance monitor for building scalable intrusion tolerant system. In: Proceedings of the Tenth International Conference on Computer Communications and Networks, Scottsdale, AZ, USA (2001) 200–205
3. Wang, F., Gong, F., Sargor, C., Goseva-Popstojanova, K., Trivedi, K., Jou, F.: SITAR: A scalable intrusion-tolerant architecture for distributed services. In: Proceedings of the 2001 IEEE Workshop on Information Assurance and Security, United States Military Academy, West Point, NY (2001) 38–45
4. Choi, D.S., Im, E.G., Lee, C.W.: Intrusion-tolerant system design for web server survivability. In Chae, K., Yung, M., eds: Proceedings of the 4th International Workshop on Information Security Applications, Jeju Island, Korea, also published in *Lecture Notes in Computer Science 2908*, Springer-Verlag, Berlin (2003) 124–134

Patch Management System for Multi-platform Environment

Jung-Taek Seo[1], Dae-Sik Choi[1], Eung-Ki Park[1],
Tae-Shik Shon[2], and Jongsub Moon[2]

[1] National Security Research Institute,
62-1 Hwaam-dong, Yuseong-gu, Daejeon 305-348, Republic of Korea
{seojt, dschoi, ekpark}@etri.re.kr
[2] CIST, Korea University,
1-Ga, Anam-dong, Sungbuk-Gu, Seoul, Republic of Korea
{743zh2k, jsmoon}@kroea.ac.kr

Abstract. Patch management is one of the most important processes to fix vulnerabilities of softwares and to ensure a security of systems. Since an institute or a company has distributed hierarchical structure and the structure consists of many heterogeneous systems, it is not easy to update patches timely. In this paper, we propose a patch management framework with patch profiling mechanism and patch dependency solving mechanism. We implemented the proposed patch management framework with JAVA environments. We argue that the proposed framework can improve the patch management processes.

1 Introduction

Operating systems and application programs tend to have vulnerabilities as most of softwares do, and computer incidents increases with the advance of Internet technologies. To fix vulnerabilities and bugs of application programs and operating systems, most vendors usually provide patch programs or patches. The patch is defined as a program that makes up to fixing the weaknesses of target systems. It is important for system administrators to distribute these patches securely to every host within a domain without exception.

If the attacker knows which patches are required for the target system, he/she can easily crack the system. Thus information about the required patches for a system is a critical security information. In addition, if a worm is installed in the target system via a corrupted patches, it will cause several critical security problems in the system and its neighbor systems. Therefore a patch management is very important to ensure security in the network.

In this paper, we propose patch management framework for a distributed and heterogeneous networks. The proposed framework manages the information about the installed patches on a system using the patch profile. The proposed system automatically maintains the patch database that involves the information on currently available patches. It controls the patch dependency problems properly.

The rest of this paper are organized as follows. Section 2 addresses existing patch management solutions. The proposed patch management framework and its design are explained in section 3. This is followed by the example scenarios and experimental results in section 4. Section 5 concludes.

2 Existing Patch Management Systems and Problems

Table 1 shows the result of the analysis on existing patch management systems from the viewpoint of the various functions. According to the result of the analysis, we defines following several critical requirements that should be satisfied by the patch management system.

Table 1. The functional analysis on the patch management systems; the 'O' in the each cell means *'supported'*, while the 'X' in the each cell means *'not supported'*

	This Paper	Patch Link	BigFix	Shavlik	Gravity Storm	Safe Patch
Agent Based	O	O	O	X	X	O
Hierarchical distribution	O	X	X	X	X	X
Multiplatform	O	O	O	X	X	X
Client scanning	O	O	O	X	X	X
Secure transfer	O	O	O	X	X	O
Patch support for user application	O	O	O	O	O	O
Group	O	O	X	X	O	X
Patch file Encryption	O	O	O	O	O	O

- **Agent Based System:** there are two types of system; one is agent based system, the other is non-agent based system. It is easy to maintains the non-agent based system since it does not use the agent. However it must periodically analyze the target system through network in order to acquire the information of the target host and update the system timely. It causes many network traffic [2], [5], [6], [7], [8], and [9]. We think that it is important to collect the information of related hosts in the patch management system. Therefore the proposed framework uses the agent based system.
- **Hierarchical Distribution:** in general, one patch system manages many target systems. However, due to its limitation of computation power, the number of target systems added to it is restricted. Moreover, the size of the network is lager and larger. Hierarchically structured patch management method is able to solve this scalability problem. Until now there is no product to support hierarchical structure.
- **Multi-platform Function:** in order to manage several different platform altogether, multi-platform function should be supported by the patch management system.

- **Client Scanning:** the number of the product that supports scanning the client is getting larger since it gives a convenience to manage the client by collecting client information related to the patch management system.
- **Secure Transfer:** distributing patch data via internet has a severe dangerious point, which the malicious user can monitor the transfer channel and analyze the patch and modify it. Thus secured data transfer should be supported to solve this potential problem.

Not only operating system patch but also application patch is supported by most patch management system, and patch file encryption is also does. The group management can improve ease of management the system.

3 The Proposed Patch Management Framework

3.1 Overall Framework

To manage patches in distributed and heterogeneous networks, various and many servers and client systems are necessary. Thus an administrator manages a lot of servers. Consequently high cost and lots of time is required to collect the neccesary patch, distribute them, and test them [3]. We propose a network topology in order to reduce the cost and the time.

Fig. 1 shows the schematic view of the proposed framework. The patch management framework consists of seven components such as patch DBs, patch pri-

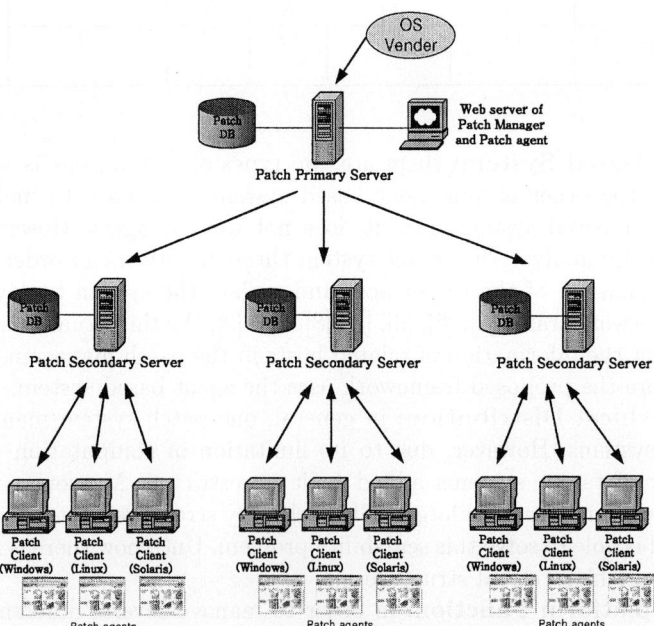

Fig. 1. The schematic view of the propsed patch management framework

mary server, patch secondary servers, patch manager, patch agents, and patch clients.

- **Patch DB:** It has various patch packages, profiles of client systems and users, and information about systems in the target domain. These profiles are used to keep tracks of clients information regarding patch updates. This is connected with patch server.
- **Patch Primary Server:** This is a system in which patch manager resides. There is only one primary server in the patch management system.
- **Patch Secondary Server:** It connects the patch client with primary patch server.
- **Patch Manager:** It manages the patch DB, fetches any required patches from the patch DB, and distributes patches to the clients. For the convenience of the adminitration, the proposed system employs the Web-based user interface.
- **Patch Agent:** It resides in each patch client. It requests required patches to the patch server, or receives patches from the patch server. The patch clients communicate with the server periodically to find new patch information.
- **Patch Client:** This is a system in which patch client resides.

To distribute the required patches, a patch primary manager transmits the new patch package and its information to patch secondary servers when a system administrator registers the new patch from vendors. The patch manager in patch secondary servers distributes the received package to patch clients in order to select adequately.

3.2 Managing Patches with the Patch Profiling

The patch profile is a set of information about the installed patches and the system. These information is important that the patch management system distributes the required patches timely and manages whole system efficiently. The profile is created by scanning the client system. It is consists of following information; the system/client name, OS type, OS version information, MAC address, IP address, the number of the installed program/patch, a list of the installed program/patch. Table 2 is an example of the patch profile.

The procedure that installs a patch file is consists of two steps; one is the distribution of the patch file, the other is the installation of the patch file. The details of the procedure as follows;

- **When a Patch is Distributed to Client Via Patch Server**
    1. First of all the server get the operating system information from the profile and select a DB table for the system. For example, when the operating system is 'Windows' and the version is 'XP', we restrict the searching target within the record included 'XP' from Windows table.
    2. Secondly, create an array with the installed patch number and list field of the profile. For example, when 'Q230652' and 'Q318245' are installed,

Table 2. Prototype of the Profile

```
system_name=comanz
user_id=turbo
OS_type=Windows
OS_version=XP
ip_addr=163.152.155.237
mac_addr=00-A0-B0-10-2C-72
patch_number=2
patch_1=Q816093
patch_2=Q282522
program_number=2
program_list_1=MS-WORD
program_list_2=MS-EXCEL
```

the client program creates an array "installed patch list = Q230652, Q318245".
3. Then, the server program create a SQL statement for getting a patch list by using the result of the first and second procedure.
4. In the end, the server queries the SQL statement, lists clients needed for receiving the new patch file and distributes it.

– **When a Patch Client Installs the Patch File**
There is no problem when the client installs the automatically downloaded patch file. However, when the client installs a patch file downloaded by a user, the installation may cause problems. For this reason, before installing the patch file, the patch client must check whether the file was already installed or not.

3.3 Patch Dependecy

When the patch or the package is installed in the LINUX(RedHat) or UNIX(Solaris), there is a possiblity that occurs the installation failure with the dependency problem. Depending on the pakage, various problems are occured, and the failure makes the system still vulnerable.

Fig. 2 shows the sequence(flow) of the method that solves the patch dependency problem. When the patch client receives the patch package, it performs the patch dependency checking procdure. If there is a dependency problem, the client requests the required files to the server in order to solve the problem. Until the required files are received and installed, the current patch intallation tasks are stored (PUSH) in the procedure stack. Moreover, there can be a mutual dependency problem among current package and existing packages in the procedure stack. In this case, the client continues related tasks by compulsion after solving any other dependency problem.

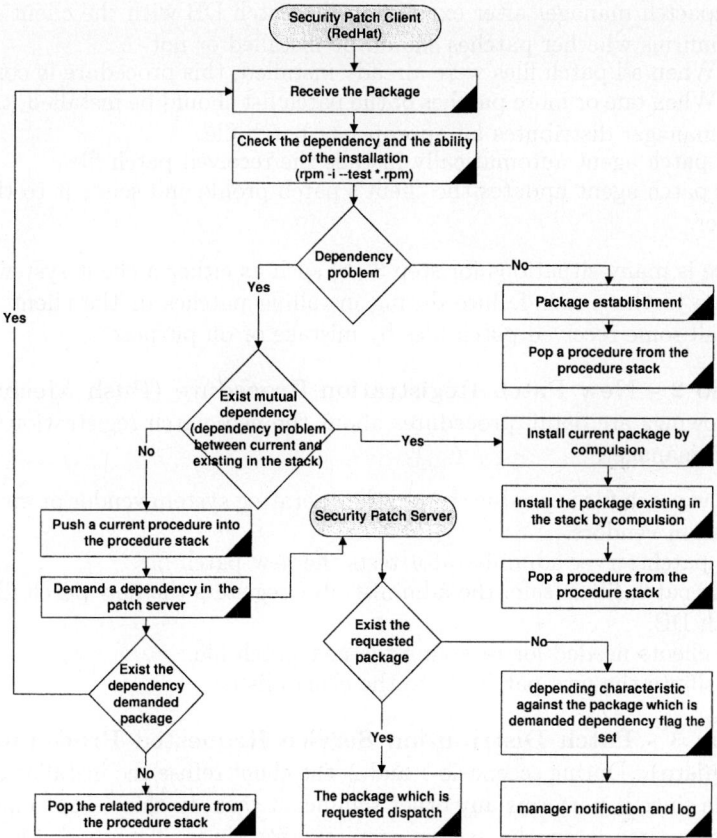

Fig. 2. The flow chart of the method that solves the patch dependency problem

4 Implementation Results

4.1 An Optimized Patch Distribution Scenario

In this paper, we propose three kind of scenarios to verify the proposed patch management system. These mechanisms are based on the push and pull distribution. In a push mechanism, a server sends patches to clients when new patches arrive at the patch DB. Patch agents receive these new patches and install them in patch client. In a pull mechanism, a client agent sends patch requests when its system environments are changed. The patch manager looks up the patch DB for new environments, and sends corresponding patches to the patch agent.

Scenario 1 - Patch Manager Initiates the Procedure (Pull Mechanism). The followings are detail procedures which are initiated by patch manager.

1. Turn on the patch client and the system completes the booting procedure.
2. The client agent is automatically executed (connected with the patch server).

3. For pactch manager after examining the patch DB with the client's profile, it confirms whether patches should be installed or not.
   (a) When all patch files were already installed, this procedure is completed.
   (b) When one or more patches of the patch list should be installed, the patch manager distributes an appropriate patch file.
4. The patch agent automatically installs the received patch file.
5. The patch agent updates the client's patch profile and sends it to the patch server.

There is many situations for step 3-(b) such as either a client system is shut down due to the power failure during installing patches or the client user did not install some received patch files by mistake or on purpose.

Scenario 2 - New Patch Registration Procedure (Push Mechanism). The followings are detail procedures about the new patch registration scenario by patch manager.

1. A new patch file is produced from the operating system vendor or application program vendors.
2. The patch server administrator tests the new patch file.
3. If the patch file is safe, the administrator registers the new patch file to the patch DB.
4. List clients needed for receiving the new patch file.
5. Distribute the new patch file to the clients listed.

Scenario 3 - Patch Distribution Service Requested Procedure (Pull Mechanism). During secenario 1 and 2, the client refuse the installation of the patch file since it performs any other significant task. In this case, to install the patch some time later, the system employs two kinds of method. One is that the client request the patching service to the server. The other is that the patch management task performs by the patch schedule.

– Request by a client agent; this mechanism supports when a client agent checks his system situation and want to install uninstalled patches.
   1. A client agent connect to patch server.
   2. The client agent confirms uninstalled patch list.
   3. The client downloads uninstalled patches and install them.
   4. Patch client Updates the client's profile and send it to the patch server.
– Scheduling; this mechanism is a general way of periodically updating patches such as virus's detection engine.
   1. Patch client is executed and start a timer for scheduling.
   2. Connected with the patch server by periods.
   3. Execute from 1st to 3rd step in scenario 1.

4.2 Implementation

The proposed systems is implemented with Java language in RedHat7.3 platform. Security patch distribution system constructed java multi-thread server and java client agent. Also, security patch manager and security patch agent is implemented with Apache web server and PHP. Security patch database based on Mysql. Finally, crypt related implementation used JCSI, JCE based on the Java Cryptography Architecture.

5 Conclusions and Future Works

In this paper, we proposed patch management framework to reduce vulnerabilities in distributed and heterogeneous networks. This framework uses hierarchical structure to distribute the patch file. This makes the system scalable and efficiently supports multi-platform based network. We also proposed patch profiling mechanism and patch dependency solution. We implemented our proposed patch management framework with Java. The implemented framework is verified by optimized patch distribution scenarios. In addition, centralized controls of the proposed framework enable timely updating of the patch. As a result, the proposed framework improves the security of the domain.

In the future, we will add more operating systems and extend patch applications. Also we have to consider more various network environment and its performance when our framework is applied to network which has many users.

References

1. CERT/Coordination-Center: CERT/CC statistics, (http://www.cert.org/stats/cert_stats)
2. Bashar,M.A.,Krishnan,G.,Kuhn,M.G.:Low-threat Security Patches and Tools. Proceedings of the International Conference on Software Maintenance.(1997) 306-313
3. Shon, T.S., Moon, J.S., Seo, J.T., Im, E.K., Lee, C.W.: Safe Patch Distribution Architecture in Intranet Environments, SAM 2003 (2003)
4. Lee, C.W., Im, E.G., Seo, J.T., Moon, J.S., Kim, D.K., Design of a secure and consolidated patch distribution architecture // Proceedings of the International Conference on Information Networking 2003 (2003)
5. PatchLink http://patchlink.com
6. BigFix Patch Manager. http://www.bigfix.com
7. Shavlik HFNetChkPro Security Patch Management. http://www.shavlik.com
8. Service Pack Manager 2000. http://www.securitybastion.com
9. LLNL SafePatch, Lawrence Livemore National Laboratory

A Generalized Proxy Signature Scheme Based on the RSA Cryptosystem[1]

Qingshui Xue[1,2], Zhenfu Cao[1], and Haifeng Qian[1]

[1] Department of Computer Science and Engineering, Shanghai Jiao Tong University, 200030, Shanghai, P.R.C.
{xue-qsh, zfcao}@cs.sjtu.edu.cn
[2] Department of Basic Theory, Shangdong P.E. Institute, 250014, Jinan, P.R.C.
{ares, xue-qsh}@sjtu.edu.cn

Abstract. In proxy signature schemes, original signers delegate proxy signers to sign messages on behalf of original signers. Based on the RSA cryptosystem, a generalized proxy signature scheme is proposed. The proposed scheme can resist all of known possible attacks such as forgery attacks. In the random oracle model, the scheme can provide security properties of strong unforgeability, verifiability, strong undeniability, strong identifiability, distinguishability and prevention of misuse of proxy signing right.

1 Introduction

In 1996, Mambo et al. [1] introduced the concept of one proxy signature scheme, which allows the original signer to delegate his/her signature power to a proxy signer. The proxy signer could stand proxy for the original signer to generate signatures. Since proxy signature schemes were introduced, many proxy signature schemes have been proposed [2-3].

In 2003, Shao proposed a proxy signature scheme using the RSA cryptosystem [2]. Based on Shao's scheme, we will propose one generalized version of proxy signature. As to the security and performance of the scheme, due to the paper limit, we will discuss them in another paper.

2 The Proposed Scheme

The following participants are involved in the scheme: the original group $G_o = \{U_{o_1}, U_{o_2}, ..., U_{o_{n_1}}\}$, the proxy group $G_p = \{U_{p_1}, U_{p_2}, ..., U_{p_{n_2}}\}$, the verifier **V**, and a trustable **CA** (Certificate Authority). We specify that any t_1 or more out of n_1

---

[1] This paper is supported by the National Science Fund for Distinguished Young Scholars under Grant No. 60225007 and the National Research Fund for the Doctoral Program of Higher Education of China under Grant No. 20020248024.

original signers ($1 \leq t_1 \leq n_1$) can delegate the signing capability to the proxy group. Similarly, any t_2 or more out of n_2 proxy signers ($1 \leq t_2 \leq n_2$) can represent G_p to sign messages on behalf of G_o.

Throughout the paper, h is a secure one-way hash function; m_w is a warrant that records the identities of the original signers in G_O and the proxy signers in G_P, the parameters (t_1, n_1), (t_2, n_2), the valid delegation period, etc; $AOSID$ is the identities of the actual original signers and $APSID = \{P_1, P_2, ..., P_{t_1}\}$ is the identities of the actual proxy signers. Each user U_i has a randomly selected private key (p_i, q_i, d_i) and public key (n_i, e_i), which is certified by the **CA**. For each user U_i, its identity is ID_i.

2.1 Proxy Share Generation Phase

Step 1 Each actual original signer U_{O_i} calculates the partial proxy signature key as follows

$$v_{ij} = h(m_w, ID_{P_j})^{-d_{o_i}} \pmod{n_{o_i}} \tag{1}$$

$$u_{ij} = \lfloor v_{ij} / n_{Pj} \rfloor \tag{2}$$

$$w_{ij} = v_{ij}{}^{e_{Pj}} \pmod{n_{P_j}} \tag{3}$$

Then U_{O_i} sends (w_{ij}, m_w, u_{ij}) to the proxy signer U_{P_j} $j = 1, 2, ..., n_2$.

Step 2 Upon receiving (w_{ij}, m_w, u_{ij}) from U_{O_i}, the proxy signer U_{P_j} recovers the partial proxy signature key by $v_{ij} = u_{ij} \times n_{Pj} + (w_{ij}{}^{d_{Pj}} \bmod n_{P_j})$, which can be verified by checking Eq. (4)

$$v_{ij}{}^{e_{o_i}} \cdot h(m_w, ID_{P_j}) = 1 \pmod{n_{o_i}} \tag{4}$$

If these equations from all of actual original signers hold, the proxy signer U_{P_j}'s proxy signing key is $(v_{1j}, v_{2j}, ..., v_{t_1 j})$.

2.2 The Proxy Signature Generation Phase

Without loss of generality, assume that $n_{P_1} < n_{P_2} < ... < n_{P_{t_2}}$.

The first proxy signer U_{P_1} at random selects $t_{11} \in [1, n_{O_1}], t_{12} \in [1, n_{O_2}], ..., t_{1t_1} \in [1, n_{O_{t_1}}]$, computes $r_{11} = t_{11}{}^{e_{o_1}} \pmod{n_{o_1}}, r_{12} = t_{12}{}^{e_{o_2}} \pmod{n_{o_2}}, ..., r_{1t_1} = t_{1t_1}{}^{e_{o_{t_1}}} \pmod{n_{o_{t_1}}}$, and sends $(r_{11}, r_{12}, ..., r_{1t_1})$ to the second proxy signer U_{P_2}.

The second proxy signer U_{P_2} randomly selects $t_{21} \in [1, n_{O_1}], t_{22} \in [1, n_{O_2}],..., t_{2t_1} \in [1, n_{O_{t_1}}]$, computes $r_{21} = r_{11} \cdot t_{21}^{e_{o_1}} \pmod{n_{O_1}}, r_{22} = r_{12} \cdot t_{22}^{e_{o_2}} \pmod{n_{O_2}},..., r_{2t_1} = r_{1t_1} t_{2t_1}^{e_{o_1}} \pmod{n_{O_{t_1}}}$, and sends $(r_{21}, r_{22},..., r_{2t_1})$ to the third proxy signer U_{P_3}.

The last proxy signer $U_{P_{t_2}}$ at random selects $t_{t_2 1} \in [1, n_{O_1}], t_{t_2 2} \in [1, n_{O_2}],..., t_{t_2 t_1} \in [1, n_{O_{t_1}}]$, computes

$$r_1 = r_{t_2 1} = r_{(t_2-1)1} \cdot t_{t_2 1}^{e_{o_1}} \pmod{n_{O_1}}, r_2 = r_{t_2 2} = r_{(t_2-1)2} \cdot t_{t_2 2}^{e_{o_2}} \pmod{n_{O_2}},..., \\ r_{t_1} = r_{t_2 t_1} = r_{(t_2-1)t_1} t_{t_2 t_1}^{e_{o_1}} \pmod{n_{O_{t_1}}}$$ (5)

and broadcasts $(r_1, r_2, ..., r_{t_1})$.

Each actual proxy signer computes $k = h(m, r_1, r_2, ..., r_{t_1})$.

The first proxy signer U_{P_1} computes
$y_{11} = t_{11} \cdot v_{11}^{k} \pmod{n_{O_1}}, y_{12} = t_{12} \cdot v_{21}^{k} \pmod{n_{O_2}},..., y_{1t_1} = t_{1t_1} \cdot v_{t_1 1}^{k} \pmod{n_{O_{t_1}}}$,
$k_1 = k^{d_{r_1}} \pmod{n_{P_1}}$ and sends $(y_{11}, y_{12},..., y_{1t_1}, k_1)$ to U_{P_2}.

The second proxy signer U_{P_2} can verify $(y_{11}, y_{12},..., y_{1t_1}, k_1)$ by checking

$$y_{11}^{e_{o_1}} \cdot h(m_w, ID_{P_1})^k = r_{11} \pmod{n_{O_1}}, y_{12}^{e_{o_2}} \cdot h(m_w, ID_{P_1})^k = r_{12} \pmod{n_{O_2}},..., \\ y_{1t_1}^{e_{o_n}} \cdot h(m_w, ID_{P_1})^k = r_{1t_1} \pmod{n_{O_{t_1}}}, k_1^{e_{r_1}} \pmod{n_{P_1}} = k$$ (6)

Then, U_{P_2} computes
$y_{21} = y_{11} \cdot t_{21} \cdot v_{12}^{k} \pmod{n_{O_1}}, y_{22} = y_{12} \cdot t_{22} \cdot v_{22}^{k} \pmod{n_{O_2}},..., y_{2t_1} = y_{1t_1} \cdot t_{2t_1} \cdot v_{t_1 2}^{k} \pmod{n_{O_{t_1}}}$,
$k_2 = k_1^{d_{r_2}} \pmod{n_{P_2}}$ and sends $(y_{21}, y_{22},..., y_{2t_1}, k_2)$ to U_{P_3}.

The third proxy signer U_{P_3} can verify $(y_{21}, y_{22},..., y_{2t_1}, k_2)$ by Eq. (7)

$$y_{21}^{e_{o_1}} \cdot (h(m_w, ID_{P_1}) \cdot h(m_w, ID_{P_2}))^k = r_{21} \pmod{n_{O_1}}, \\ y_{22}^{e_{o_2}} \cdot (h(m_w, ID_{P_1}) \cdot h(m_w, ID_{P_2}))^k = r_{22} \pmod{n_{O_2}}, \\ ...... \\ y_{2t_1}^{e_{o_n}} \cdot (h(m_w, ID_{P_1}) \cdot h(m_w, ID_{P_2}))^k = r_{2t_1} \pmod{n_{O_{t_1}}}, \\ (k_2^{e_{r_2}} \pmod{n_{P_2}})^{e_{o_1}} \pmod{n_1} = k$$ (7)

The last proxy signer $U_{P_{t_2}}$ can verify $(y_{(t_2-1)1}, y_{(t_2-1)2},..., y_{(t_2-1)t_1}, k_{t_2-1})$ by checking

$$y_{(t_2-1)1}^{e_{o_1}} \cdot (h(m_w, ID_{P_1}) \cdot h(m_w, ID_{P_2}) \cdot ... \cdot h(m_w, ID_{P(t_2-1)}))^k = r_{(t_2-1)1} \pmod{n_{O_1}}, \\ y_{(t_2-1)2}^{e_{o_2}} \cdot (h(m_w, ID_{P_1}) \cdot h(m_w, ID_{P_2}) \cdot ... \cdot h(m_w, ID_{P(t_2-1)}))^k = r_{(t_2-1)2} \pmod{n_{O_2}}, \\ ... \\ y_{(t_2-1)t_1}^{e_{o_n}} \cdot (h(m_w, ID_{P_1}) \cdot h(m_w, ID_{P_2}) \cdot ... \cdot h(m_w, ID_{P(t_2-1)}))^k = r_{(t_2-1)t_1} \pmod{n_{O_{t_1}}}, \\ ((k_{(t_2-1)}^{e_{r_2}} \mod n_{P_{(t_2-1)}})^{e_{r_{2-1}}} ... \mod n_{P_2})^{e_{r_1}} \mod(n_{P_1}) = k$$ (8)

Then, $U_{P_{t_2}}$ computes

$$y_1 = y_{t_2 1} = y_{(t_2-1)1} \cdot t_{t_2 1} \cdot v_{1t_2}^{k} \pmod{n_{O_1}}, y_2 = y_{t_2 2} = y_{(t_2-1)2} \cdot t_{t_2 2} \cdot v_{2t_1}^{k} \pmod{n_{O_2}}, \\ ..., y_{t_1} = y_{t_2 t_1} = y_{(t_2-1)t_1} \cdot t_{t_2 t_1} \cdot v_{t_1 t_2}^{k} \pmod{n_{O_{t_1}}}$$ (9)

$$k = k_{t_2} = k_{t_2-1}^{d_{n_2}} \pmod{n_{P_{t_2}}} \tag{10}$$

and sends $(m, m_w, y_1, y_2, ..., y_{t_1}, k, AOSID, APSID)$ to the verifier.

2.3 The Proxy Signature Verification Phase

Step 1. According to m_w, $AOSID$ and $APSID$, the verifier gets the public keys of the original signers and proxy signers from **CA** and knows who are the actual original signers and proxy signers.

Step 2. The verifier computes

$$k' = ((k^{e_{p_2}} \mod n_{P_{t_2}}) e^{P(t_2-1)} ... \mod n_{P_2})^{e_{p_1}} (\mod n_{P_1}) \tag{11}$$

$$\begin{aligned} r_1' &= y_1^{e_{o_1}} (h(m_w, ID_{P_1}) \cdot h(m_w, ID_{P_2}) \cdot ... \cdot h(m_w, n_{P_{t_2}}))^{k'} (\mod n_{O_1}), \\ r_2' &= y_2^{e_{o_2}} (h(m_w, ID_{P_1}) \cdot h(m_w, ID_{P_2}) \cdot ... \cdot h(m_w, n_{P_{t_2}}))^{k'} (\mod n_{O_2}) \\ &... \\ r_{t_1}' &= y_{t_1}^{e_{o_n}} (h(m_w, ID_{P_1}) \cdot h(m_w, ID_{P_2}) \cdot ... \cdot h(m_w, n_{P_{t_2}}))^{k'} (\mod n_{O_n}) \end{aligned} \tag{12}$$

Step 3. The verifier checks if the following equation holds.

$$h(m, r_1', r_2', ..., r_{t_1}') = k' \tag{13}$$

3 Conclusions

In the paper, we have proposed a generalized version of the proxy signature scheme based on the **RSA** cryptosystem. The scheme can resist all of known possible attacks such as equation attacks and provide nearly all of security properties of proxy signatures.

References

1. Mambo, M., Usuda, K., Okamoto, E.: Proxy Signature for Delegating Signing Operation. In: Proceedings of the 3.th ACM Conference on Computer and Communications Security, New Dehli, India, ACM Press, New York (1996) 48-57
2. Shao, Z.H.: Proxy Signature Schemes Based on Factoring. Information Processing Letters 85 (2003) 137–143
3. Li, J.G., Cao, Z.F., Zhang, Y.C.: Improvement of M-U-O and K-P-W Proxy Signature Schemes. Journal of Harbin Institute of Technology (New Series) (2002) 145-148

Novel Impostors Detection in Keystroke Dynamics by Support Vector Machine

Yingpeng Sang[1], Hong Shen[1], and Pingzhi Fan[2]

[1] School of Information Science, Japan Advanced Institute of Science and Technology,
1-8, Asahidai, Tatsunokuchi, Ishikawa, 923-1211, Japan
{yingpeng, shen}@jaist.ac.jp
[2] School of Computer and Communications Engineering, Southwest Jiaotong University,
Chengdu, Sichuan, 610031, China
p.fan@ieee.org

Abstract. To detect the novel impostors whose data patterns have never been learned previously in keystroke dynamics, two solutions are proposed in this paper. Unlike most other research in keystroke dynamics, this paper surveys the performance tradeoff and time consumption, which are valuable for practical implementation, of the solutions. Besides, it is our intention to attempt verifying computer users' identities based on pure numeric password which is more difficult than verification of any other kinds of passwords.

1 Introduction

Keystroke dynamics captures the keystroke timing characteristics (key-hold time and inter-key time) of keyboard users, analyzes the patterns to which the users are belonging, and verifies whether the users are the people they've claimed to be. The rate of authorized users wrongly authenticated as impostors is called false rejection rate (FRR), and the rate of impostors wrongly authenticated as authorized users is called false acceptance rate (FAR).

Statistical methods such as T-test, mean and median examination, autoregressive model, probability observation have been employed in keystroke dynamics but they didn't achieve very satisfactory authentication accuracy. There has also been some work done using neural networks such as BPNN [1]. Though neural networks can accurately classify the impostors under the circumstances that their patterns have been captured in the training set, it might be incompetent to detect novel impostors whose patterns haven't been learned previously.

In this paper we use keystroke dynamics to verify the identities of users when passwords are being pressed. To solve the problem of novel impostors detection, support vector machine (SVM) is employed because of its capability of presenting consistent algorithm status and low complexity. Specifically, two solutions are proposed. The first solution employs two-class (TC) SVM and provides the training data with an overall coverage on the possible impostors. The second one uses one-class (OC) SVM to capture the domain of the normal data patterns where probability lives.

2 Principles of Support Vector Machine

TC SVM and OC SVM differ in their training sets, quadratic programming (QP) problems, and so on. TC SVM aims to find an optimal hyperplane to maximumly separate the two classes in the training set $(\mathbf{x}_i, y_i)$ ($i=1,...,n$, $\mathbf{x} \in R^d$, $y \in \{+1,-1\}$). Solutions of its QP problem should be found with the given values of C and γ [2]. OC SVM contains only the normal data patterns $x_1,...,x_l \in \mathbf{x}$ ($l \in N$, $\mathbf{x} \in R^d$) and separates them from the origin with a maximum margin. Its QP problem should be solved with the given values of ν and γ [3].

3 Detection Method

3.1 Data Preprocessing

Using TC SVM, we can treat the impostors' data patterns as one different class from the authorized user's. Its training set can be constructed by the following way to cover data patterns of impostors as many as possible.

1. Calculate the mean vector $\mathbf{u}$ and standard deviation (SD) vector $\mathbf{s}$ of the authorized user's patterns.
2. Construct mean vectors $\mathbf{u}_i'$: $\mathbf{u}_i' = \{u_{-ki},...,u_{-1i},u_{0i},u_{1i},...,u_{ki}\}$ ($i=1,...,n$). Here, $u_{(j+1)i} - u_{ji} = d$, $u_{0i} = u_i$, $u_i \in \mathbf{u}$. d is a given value.
3. Construct SD vectors $\mathbf{s}_i'$: $\mathbf{s}_i' = \{s_{-ki},...,s_{-1i},s_{0i},s_{1i},...,s_{ki}\}$ ($i=1,...,n$). Here, $s_{-ki} = ... = s_{0i} = ... = s_{ki}$, $s_{0i} = s_i$, $s_i \in \mathbf{s}$.
4. Generate m samples according to the normal distribution for each vector $v_j = \{(u_{j1},s_{j1}),...,(u_{jn},s_{jn})\}$ ($j=-k,...,k$, $j \neq 0$).
5. Add the 2k·m samples into the training data set as the impostors' data.

It's unnecessary for OC SVM's training set to contain data patterns of impostors. OC SVM can find the domain where the authorized user's patterns probably live, and then impostors can be detected as outliers because their patterns are outside the domain.

3.2 Learning and Test

In the learning phase, the QP problems should be solved by learning the training sets. Sequential minimal optimization can be employed to find the solutions of the two QP problems [2, 3]. In the test phase, the test sets can be put into the decision functions of the two SVMs, and then FAR and FRR can be computed.

4 Experiment

Altogether 10 people were participated. Specifically, every participant acted as an authorized user and was attacked by 5 impostors who had been notified of the authorized user's passwords. The 5 impostors were also selected from the other 9 participants. As an authorized user, every participant had his own two passwords: alphabetic password (such as "fjkarebbcd") and numeric password (such as "19781105").

5 Performance Evaluation

5.1 Performance Comparison Between the Two SVMs

For vector C, v and γ, cross-validation can be employed, which takes every pair of (C_i, γ_j) or (v_i, γ_j) ($C_i \in C, v_i \in v, \gamma_j \in \gamma$) and uses the detection method to find the ranges of FAR and FRR. Based on these ranges, receiver operating characteristic (ROC) curves, which describe the tradeoff between TN (TN=1-FAR) and TP (TP=1-FRR), are shown in Fig. 1. The upper right area of each ROC curve is a valuable reference to make tradeoffs between FAR and FRR in practical implementations.

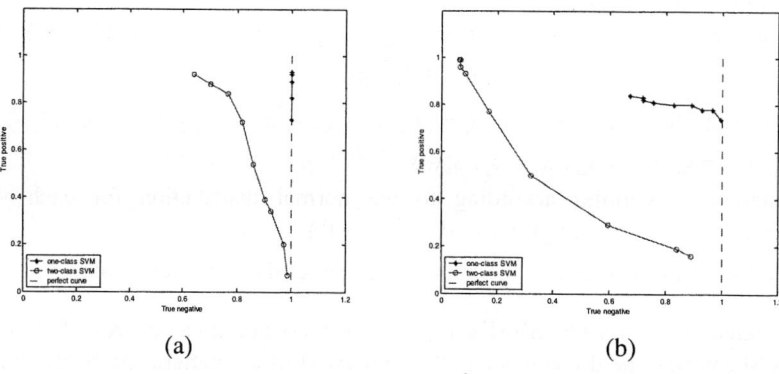

Fig. 1. ROC curves of TC SVM and OC SVM. (a) is for the alphabetic password verification, and (b) for the numeric password verification

In Fig. 1(a) and (b), ROC curves of OC SVM are closer to the perfect curve than those of TC SVM. Thus, OC SVM performs better from the view of accuracy.

5.2 Performance Comparison Between SVM and Neural Network

In table 1, comparing with Back-Propagation NN and Levenberg-Marquardt NN [4], TC and OC SVM consume much less time and achieves much better FAR.

Table 1. Performance comparions between SVM and NN

	OC SVM	TC SVM	LMNN	BPNN
Time Consumption (seconds)	0.08	0.1	8	180
Best FAR	0.02	0.1	0.7	0.74
Best FRR	0.1	0.1	0.1	0.1

6 Conclusions and Future Work

It can be concluded from this paper that TC SVM performs less efficiently than OC SVM in novel impostors detection of keystroke dynamics. Both of them consume much less time than BPNN and LMNN. The verification of numeric passwords is also applicable because a TN of 0.89 and a TP of 0.8 can be achieved simultaneously.

We have also developed an identity verification system based on keystroke dynamics. The system runs on Windows 2000 and XP, and the inside verification algorithm is OC SVM.

Some simpler methods other than cross-validation should be tried to reduce the time complexity of comprehensive survey on TP and TN.

Acknowledgements

This research is conducted as a program for the "Fostering Talent in Emergent Research Fields" in Special Coordination Funds for Promoting Science and Technology by Ministry of Education, Culture, Sports, Science and Technology, Japan. The work of Pingzhi Fan is partly supported by the University Doctorial Research Foundation under the grant No.20020613020, Ministry of Education, China.

References

1. Obaidat, M.S., Sadoun, B.: Verification of Computer Users Using Keystroke Dynamics. IEEE Trans. on Systems, Man and Cybernetics, Vol.27, No.2 (1997) 261–269.
2. Platt, J.C.: Fast training of support vector machines using sequential minimal optimization. In: Schölkopf, B., etc,: Advances in Kernel Methods-Support Vector Machine. MIT Press, (1999a) 185–208.
3. Schölkopf, B., Platt, J., Shawe-Taylor, J., Smola, A.J., Williamson, R.C.: Estimating the support of a High-Dimensional Distribution. Neural Comput, Vo.13, No. 7, (2001) 1443–1472.
4. Sang, Y., Fan, P., Hao, L.: Keystroke Characteristics Identity Authentication Based on Levenberg-Marquardt Algorithm. Computer Applications, Vol. 24, No. 7. (2004) 1–3. (in Chinese)

New Fast Handover Mechanism for Mobile IPv6 in IEEE 802.11 Wireless Networks

Pyung Soo Kim[1], Young Sam Lee[2], and Soo Hong Park[1]

[1] Mobile Platform Lab, Digital Media R&D Center,
Samsung Electronics Co., Ltd, Suwon City, 442-742, Korea
kimps@samsung.com
[2] School of Electrical Engineering, Inha University,
Inchon City, Korea

Abstract. In this paper, a new mechanism is proposed for Mobile IPv6 fast handover in IEEE 802.11 wireless networks. The proposed mechanism provides the faster acquisition of new access router's network information than the existing one, which might be advantageous for the low handover latency. In addition, the proposed mechanism might reduce amount of traffic in comparison with the existing one, which might be remarkable when there are many mobile nodes that are now connecting to current access router. Moreover, in the proposed mechanism, a mobile node can know whether it changes access router or access point, which can remove redundant traffic of the existing one.

1 Introduction

In this paper, a new Mobile IPv6 fast handover mechanism is proposed to reduce the L3 handover latency for IEEE 802.11 wireless network environment where there are several access routers (ARs) connected by access points (APs).

To implement the proposed mechanism, the beacon message used in L2 is defined newly by adding a specific subfield to the existing reserved field. Using this message, a MN can know whether it changes AR or AP. In addition, Router Table Request/Reply messages used in L3 are defined newly. Using these messages, the MN can acquire network information about all ARs in ESS, such as ARs' IP addresses, prefix lengths, and identities, which is performed once only at the booting time and isn't performed in real-time communication. It is shown that the proposed mechanism provides the faster acquisition of new access router's network information than the existing one, which might be remarkable for low L3 handover latency. In addition, the omission of above two messages might reduce amount of traffic when there are many MNs that are now connecting to the current access router. Moreover, in the proposed mechanism, the MN can know whether it changes AR or AP while the existing one cannot. Thus, when the MN changes AP, the proposed mechanism can remove redundant traffic of the existing one. Finally, an extensive experiment is performed and shows that the proposed mechanism can outperform two existing ones in [1], [2].

	ARID	IPv6 Address	Prefix Len
AR1	0x01	3ffe:2e01:2a:4::1	64
AR2	0x02	3ffe:2e01:2a:4::2	64
AR3	0x03	3ffe:2e01:2a:4::3	64

Fig. 1. Router Table shared by ARs

2 Main Works

In this section, a new Mobile IPv6 fast handover mechanism is proposed for the IEEE 802.11 wireless network with serveral access routers (ARs). As shown in [2], all ARs in this wireless network share each other's network information, such as ARs' IP addresses, prefix lengths, and identities, and thus may have information table that will be called the Router Table. Note that the access point (AP) can know its AR's identity (ARID) by a system administrator's presetting. Fig. 1 shows the Router Table for the wireless network where there are three ARs.

In order to implement the proposed mechanism, some L2/L3 messages are defined newly. Firstly, the beacon message used in L2 is defined newly. The beacon message contains information such as timestamp, beacon interval, capability information, SSID, etc [3]. In this paper, the capability information field is modified by adding the specific subfield "ARID". Since this field uses the existing reserved field, other fields are not affected. Using this beacon message, the MN can know whether it changes AR or AP, which will be explained later. Secondly, Router Table Request/Reply messages used in L3 are defined newly. These messages are made from the Internet Control Message Protocol for IPv6 (ICMPv6) in [4]. Then, using these messages, the MN performs the Router Table Request/Reply at its booting time.

When the MN is booting, it sends a Router Table Request message using all routers multicast address to current subnet in oder to acquire network information about all ARs in ESS, ARs' IP addresses, prefix lengths, and identities. In response to Router Table Request message, the current AR (CAR) on the current subnet sends a Router Table Reply message using the Router Table shown in Fig. 1. Then, the MN receives this reply message and caches the Router Table in this reply message. Note that this Router Table Reqeust/Reply is performed once only at the booting time and thus isn't performed in real-time communication. Assume that the MN communicates with the corresponding node (CN). In real-time communication, when the MN moves, the "trigger" may arrive from specific L2 events that might determine the need for handover. Since this trigger is based on the beacon message given by AP, the MN can know the ARID of its AP from the trigger. Then, the MN checks this ARID using the Router Table cached previously, in oder to determine whether the MN changes AP or AR. If the MN changes AP, it continues real-time communication via the CAR. Otherwise, the MN finds the new AR (NAR) corresponding to ARID from the Router Table, and formulates a new care-of address (NCoA) using the prefix of the NAR's address. After then, the MN associates its current CoA (CCoA) with NAR's IP address for forwarding purposes using a Fast Binding Update (FBU). Then, the CAR sends a Fast Binding Acknowledgment (FBACK) message to the MN and the NAR. The FBACK message confirms whether NCoA could be used, only after which the MN must use NCoA on the new subnet. At this time, the CAR sends a Handover Initiate (HI) message to NAR, after looking up the IP address corresponding to ARID supplied by the MN using its Router Table. This FBU/FBACK and HI/HACK allows that packets arriving at the CAR can be tunneled to the NAR. When the MN has confirmed its NCoA and then completes the Binding Update procedure with its CN, the MN continues real-time communication with the CN using NCoA as its source IP address via the NAR.

The proposed mechanism provides several advantages over the existing one in [2]. As shown in Fig. 2, the proposed mechanism can omit RtSolPr/PrRtAdv messages used in the existing one, in real-time communication. The proposed mechanism provides the faster acquisition of NAR's network information than the existing one, which might be advantageous for the low L3 handover latency. In addition, the omission of above two messages might reduce amount of traffic in comparison with the existing one, which might be remarkable when there are many mobile nodes that are now connecting to the CAR. Moreover, in the proposed mechanism, the MN can know whether it changes AR or AP, while the existing one cannot. Thus, when the MN changes AP, the proposed mechanism can remove redundant traffic of the existing one.

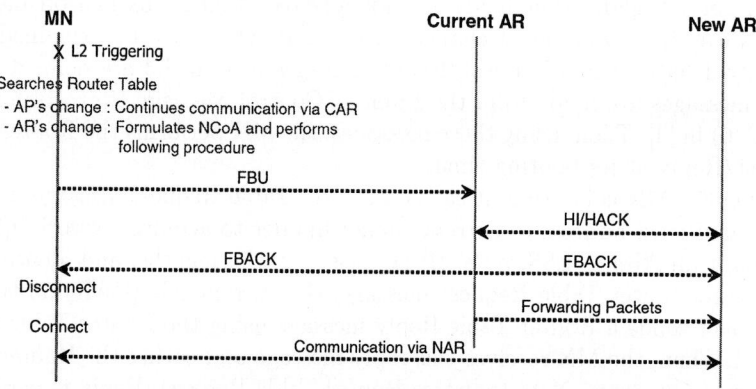

Fig. 2. Operation procedure for proposed mechanism

Finally, to evaluate the proposed mechanism, an extensive experiment will be performed for a testbed that has two ARs and a single CN communicating with the MN over IEEE 802.11b wireless network. For this testbed, a single MN ping-ponging between two ARs is experimented for the proposed mechanism, existing two mechanisms [1], [2]. The ARs are configured to send a router advertisement within 3 4 seconds as per [5]. Three mechanisms are compared by the L3 handover latency that is measured from L2 trigger to binding CoA. To make a clearer comparison, 40 handovers are performed. It can be shown in Fig. 3 that the proposed mechanism outperforms two existing ones in [1], [2].

3 Conclusions

The proposed mechanism provides several advantages over the existing one. The proposed mechanism provides the faster acquisition of NAR's network information than the existing one, which might be advantageous for the low L3 handover latency. In addition, the proposed mechanism might reduce amount of traffic in comparison with the existing one, which might be remarkable when there are many MNs that are now connecting to the CAR. Moreover, in the proposed mechanism, the MN can know whether it changes AR or AP, which can remove redundant traffic of the existing one.

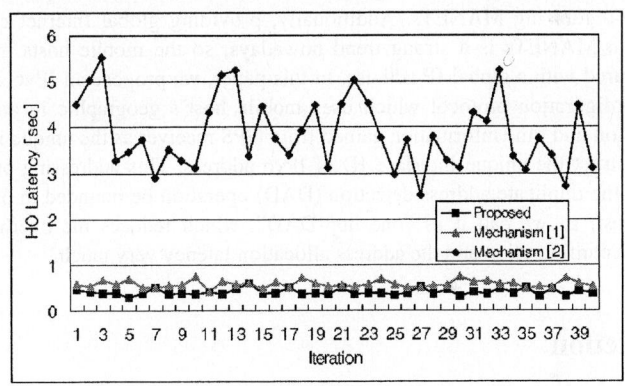

Fig. 3. Experimental results

References

1. Johnson, D. B., Perkins, C. E., Arkko, J: Mobility Support in IPv6. IETF RFC 3775 (2004)
2. Koodli, R.: Fast Handovers for Mobile IPv6. IETF Draft:draft-ietf-mipshop-fast-mipv6-02.txt (2004)
3. ISO/ICE.: Wireless LAN Medium Access Control (MAC) and Physical Layer (PHY) Specifications. ANSI/IEEE Std 802.11 (1999)
4. Conta, A., Deering, S.: Internet Control message Protocol (ICMP) for the Internet Protocol Version 6 (IPv6) Specification. IETF RFC 2463 (1998)
5. Narten, T., Nordmark. E., Simpson, W.: Neighbor Discovery for IP Version 6 (IPv6) IETF RFC 2461 (1998)

One Hop-DAD Based Address Autoconfiguration in MANET6

Zhao Yunlong, Shi Rui, and Yang Xiaozong

School of Computer Science and Technology, Harbin Institute of Technology,
Harbin, Heilongjiang 150001, P. R. China
{yl_zhao, shirui, xzyang}@hit.edu.cn

Abstract. Mobile ad hoc networks (MANETs) are autonomous and infrastructureless networks that support multi-hops wireless communications among mobile hosts. Autoconfiguration of hosts is an important open problem in self-organizing MANETs. Additionally, providing global Internet connectivity to MANETs is a strong trend nowadays, so the mobile hosts must be configured with a global IP address. In this paper, we propose an IPv6 address autoconfiguration protocol which uses mobile host's geographic location information and time information gained from GPS receiver as the unique metrics to construct the unique Interface ID of IPv6 address. This addressing protocol makes the duplicate address detection (DAD) operation be bounded in one hop broadcast, so we call it as "one hop-DAD", which reduces the overhead of address configuration and the address allocation latency very much.

1 Introduction

All Mobile ad hoc networks have so many cheerful application prospects that more and more researchers have taken interest in it. Although the route between each pair of hosts communicating with each other is an important and focus researching problem, these routing protocol researches are all based on the assumption that each host of the MANETs has been allocated a unique identifier, generally IP address beforehand. Because the MANETs aim at autonomous and autoconfiguration deployment, the unique IP address should be allocated automatically.

The research on automatic configuration of IP address for MANETs is relatively less, and the previous address autoconfiguration solutions can be divided into three categories:

1. *Independent Addressing Approach*: An unallocated address node chooses an IP address at random independently and then performs the uniqueness checking by DAD scheme. Several typical independent addressing protocols have been proposed, such as [1] and [2].
2. *Agent-Based Addressing Approach*: When a new node joins the ad hoc networks, it registers with a neighboring configured node that then acts as its address-agent. The address-agent is responsible for allocating the new node an IP address, then

processing the selected IP address's uniqueness checking. Typical researching works on this approach have been done in [3], [4] and [5].
3. *Distributed Addressing Approach*: The approach is based on the assumption that nodes taking part in the allocation hold disjoint address pools. The very first node in ad hoc networks gets an IP address and maintains the entire address pool, and then splits his address pool in half and gives one half of the address pool to the second coming node, so the new node can choose a unique IP address from his own address pool and be ready to configure others new. This approach was first proposed in [6] and extended in [7].

All the three approaches have the commonness. First, the uniqueness of selected configuration parameters to form the IP address can not be guaranteed, so that extra DAD operation must be implemented. Second, the nodes which have been configured with the same IP address may separate far away from each other, so the DAD operation, which issues some broadcasting messages to the whole ad hoc networks, should bring more extra overhead. Lastly, the DAD operation will increase the delay of address autoconfiguration.

For the sake of overcoming the aforementioned drawbacks, we propose a more efficient independent addressing scheme, which not only increases the uniqueness probability of IP address but also limits the duplicate address nodes to at most one hop DAD operation by equipping each node with an additional GPS receiver. We refer to it as one hop-DAD.

Because of the limitation of IPv4 and the inevitability of replacement with IPv6, we focus on researching the address autoconfiguration for IPv6 MANETs, which is necessary for future more and more mobile devices connecting to Internet.

The paper is organized as follows. In section 2 we describe the basic idea of the proposed addressing protocol. Section 3 gives the simple analysis of our one hop-DAD based address autoconfiguration protocol. In section 4, we implement a prototype in the OPNet simulator and give the simulation result. Finally, the conclusions are given in section 5.

2 Basic Idea

Among three kinds of address autoconfiguration methods mentioned in section 1, we prefer to the independent addressing approach for the sake of saving extra communications between the unallocated node and at least one node having been configured address which acts as addressing agent or master. On second thoughts of the independent addressing solution, it is obviously that the extra broadcast overhead initiated by DAD will be reduced to save the limited bandwidth if the picking IP address by the new node itself can be guaranteed uniqueness. So we decide to use the mobile node location information and joining time information, which can be gained by GPS receiver, as the unique part of IP address.

Before proceeding further, we would like to state three simplifying assumptions, which can be relaxed with simple changes to the proposed scheme:

1. Presently, we assume that the life-time of a mobile node will not be longer than 24 hours due to the limit of power, so the occupation time to one IP address will also be less than 24 hours.
2. Based on the matter of fact, we limit the transmitting radius of wireless transceivers between 200 meters to 10 kilometers. And the MANETs cloud will not span from the Northern Hemisphere to the Southern Hemisphere or from the Eastern Hemisphere to the Western Hemisphere.
3. Because we don't consider that a new node which first joins the MANETs will demand the global connectivity to the Internet, we assume to assign the MANETs site-local IPv6 address to the new node.

2.1 GPS Information Selection

GPS provides two levels of service, the Standard Positioning Service (SPS) and the Precise Positioning Service (PPS). The SPS is a positioning and timing service which will be available to all GPS users on a continuous, worldwide basis with no direct charge. SPS provides a predictable positioning accuracy of 100 meters (95 percent) horizontally and 156 meters (95 percent) vertically and time transfer accuracy to UTC within 340 nanoseconds (95 percent). National Marine Electronics Association (NMEA) defines a GPS receiver data format standard and has about 7 types of NMEA sentence. Among them, GGA type data contains both the position and time information which meets our demand. Table 1 presents the GGA type position and time information. There need totally 74 bits to record the GPS information.

Table 1. GPS information of NMEA data format

Data Item	Time Field			Longitude Field			Latitude Field		
	Hour	Min.	Sec.	E/W	Degree	Min.	S/N	Degree	Min.
Threshold(dec.)	24	60	60	0/1	180	60	9999	0/1	90	60	9999
Binary Digit(b.)	5	6	6	1	8	6	14	1	7	6	14
Useful Item	√	√	√	X	X	√	√	X	X	√	√

In fact, the higher 64 bits of 128 bits IPv6 address are preassigned to network prefix, which is defined as fec0:0:0:fffe::/64 for IPV6_MANET_PREFIX[1]. So the GPS information can only be added to the lower 64 bits Interface ID. Basing on the assumption 1 and 2, we can ignore the E/W、S/N and degree data items in longitude and latitude field, which are illustrated in the last row of Table 1. Eventually the selected information from GPS receiver totally occupies 57 bits.

2.2 MANETs IPv6 Address Format

According to the selection of GPS information, the format of IPv6 address can be defined like Fig.1. Where "u" is the universal/local bit which has the same meaning with EUI-64's[8] corresponding bit, and "f" is a flag bit which is set to one to indicate adopting GPS information and it is set to zero to indicate not receiving any GPS

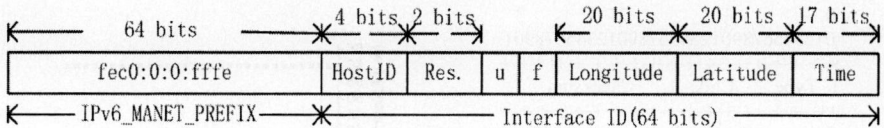

Fig. 1. MANETs IPv6 address format

information because of GPS receiver not finding enough available satellites. The left two bits of "u" are reserved for future extension. The four bits "Host ID" are randomly selected by itself. The other three sections of Interface ID are respectively consistent with the selecting GPS information.

The motivation for inserting the flag "u" is to distinguish the Internet global IPv6 address with EUI-64 based interface identifiers from MANETs IPv6 address, where the "u" bit is set to one to indicate a globally unique EUI-64 based IPv6 address and is set to zero in our MANETs IPv6 address's "u" bit.

2.3 One Hop-DAD Based Address Autoconfiguration Protocol

When a new mobile node wants to join a MANET cloud, it firstly decides if it can receive GPS information from its GPS receiver. If so, it will construct its address according to MANETs IPv6 address format, by inserting the longitude, latitude and time value to corresponding section, setting "f" bit to 1, "u" to 0 and "Res." bits with double zero and randomly selecting a number from 0 to 15 for "Host ID". Having been allocated an IPv6 address, the node starts one hop-DAD operation, which only broadcasts Address Request (AREQ) message to its direct neighbor, to detect the duplicate address. If one of its direct neighbors has allocated the same address, the neighbor will unicast an Address Reply (AREP) message back to the original node to inform it having selected a duplicate address, then it will reconfigure a new MANETs IPv6 address again by only replacing the time section's value with the current time. If it doesn't receive any AREP message for a predefined period (we set it as 20ms in our later simulation), it will rebroadcast one hop AREQ again. After a predefined repeating times (usually retry 3 times), the uniqueness of address can be guaranteed and the address can be ultimately allocated to itself.

The AREQ and AREP packets have the same format, shown in figure 2[9], the difference between them is the value of 'Type' section.

Each section of format has the same meaning with [9], except for the 'Type' section. In our protocol, the 'Type' section of AREQ and AREP is set different special values respectively, which indicate it is a one hop-AREQ or one hop-AREP message.

If the new coming node's GPS receiver can not work due to the lack of enough available satellites, it will get location information from the GPS receiver's cache and the computer operating system's (OS) time to construct the new IPv6 address, and continue the one hop-DAD operation presented in last paragraph.

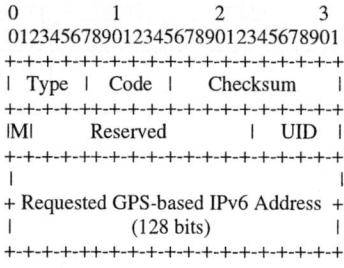

Fig. 2. AREQ & AREP packet format

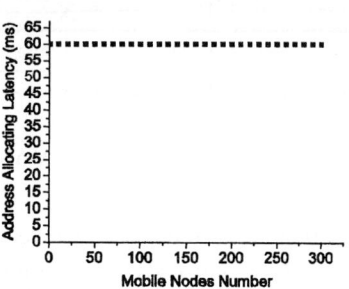

Fig. 3. Delay

3 Analysis

Considering the MANETs IPv6 address format, there are four parts to provide uniqueness: Host ID, Longitude, Latitude and Time. Because the longitude and latitude data can be computed to 0.0001 minute, we can calculate the minimum distance is approximately equal to 20 centimeter by assuming the perimeter of the equator is 40075.13 kilometers. Although one GPS receiver's positioning accuracy is about 156 meters, two nearby GPS receivers' relative difference will approach to the theoretic value 20 centimeter, much less than 156 meters, at the same moment. That can be well understood by analogy with the working theory of Difference GPS. So the probability of two or more nodes with the same position is very small, especially adding the time and random Host ID values. Even though at the same moment there are two nodes have the same longitude, latitude and Host ID value, the distance between them must be constrained no more than 200 meters, which is less than the wireless transceiver's lower bound on transmission radius of 200 meters. So the DAD process can be limited within on hop broadcast.

Considering the merger of two isolated MANETs, there would not be the duplicate address because different MANETs lie in different locations where the longitude and latitude are different at their own original time, so the GPS-based IP addresses of mobile nodes residing in different MANETs clouds must not be duplicate and no extra weak DAD operation must be implemented.

4 Performance Evaluation

To evaluate the proposed IPv6 address autoconfiguration protocol, we have implemented a prototype in the OPNet Modeler with wireless module. The protocol is evaluated using the following three metrics:

1. *Duplicate Address Probability*: The number of generating duplicate address by all mobile nodes compared with the number of mobile nodes.

2. *Address Allocating Latency*: The average delay of addressing from the boot time of one mobile node to its finishing time of IPv6 address confirmation.
3. *Protocol Overhead*: The number of addressing control packets (mainly including one hop-DAD broadcast packets and DAD reply packets) transmitted per node. Each hop-wise forwarding of a control packet is counted as one transmission.

4.1 Simulation Setup

The protocol performance is evaluated with different mobile nodes number. The scenario studied considers from one node to 300 nodes that move randomly over a square flat space (1000m x 1000m) for 40 minutes of simulated time. Each node boots up at a random generating time which is randomly distributed between zero (zero not included) and 40 minutes, and at each booting time, there are random numbers of nodes (which is also randomly distributed between zero and 5) booting up together.

All mobile nodes move according to the random waypoint mobility model[10]. Node speeds are randomly distributed between zero (zero not included) and the maximum speed 20m/s. The pause time is consistently 10 seconds.

The maximum transmission range of each mobile node is 200 meters. If the distance between two mobile nodes is larger than 200m, they can not communicate with each other directly.

4.2 Simulation Result

Figure 3 shows that the address allocating latency almost keep constant as the number of nodes increases, which means that our protocol has a good scalability and there is no duplicate address during the simulation. The protocol overhead is shown in figure 4. The overhead is also keep constant due to no duplicate addresses generation.

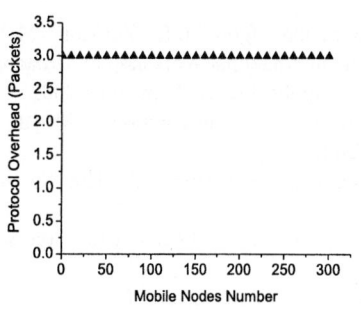
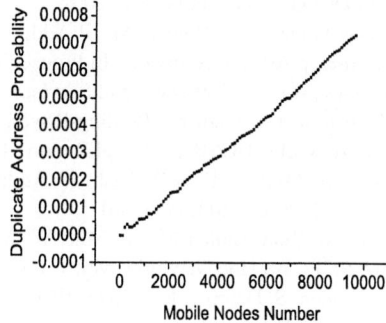

Fig. 4. Overhead   **Fig. 5.** Duplicate address probability

Finally, we calculate the duplicate address probability with the nodes number increasing. As figure 5 shows, when there are about 10000 nodes in our simulation range (1000m x 1000m), which means the nodes density is terribly high, the duplicate probability is very low to 0.00075, that indicates there are almost no duplicate address generation during our first two simulations. So the delay and overhead of our protocol are reasonably constant always.

5 Conclusion

We have presented a GPS-based IPv6 address autoconfiguration protocol for mobile nodes in MANET6, which enables MANET6 to configure their own unique IPv6 addresses of new nodes entering the network. The proposed solution can reduce the overhead of addressing protocol very much by limiting the DAD broadcasting to one hop. The one hop-DAD is realized by inserting the nodes' precise geographic position information to the IPv6's Interface ID section. The addressing method is also to tolerate network mergers, which will not produce any more overhead using our solution. The simulating result of our addressing protocol is given at last. From the simulation result, we can find that the unique metrics selected in our protocol can almost make the address exclusive, so maybe the one hop-DAD is not necessary. In our future work, we will eliminate the one hop-DAD operation and only utilize one hop Weak DAD operation to reduce the overhead more.

References

1. Jae-Hoon Jeong, Hyun-Wook Cha, Jung-Soo Park, Hyoung-Jun Kim, Ad Hoc IP Address Autoconfiguration(work in progress), Internet Engineering Task Force, May 2003
2. N. Vaidya, Weak Duplicate address detection in mobile ad hoc networks, Proceedings of the 3rd ACM International Symposium on Mobile Ad Hoc Networking and Computing (MOBIHOC'02), Lausanne, Switzerland, June 2002
3. S. Nesargi, R. Prakash, MANETconf: Configuration of Hosts in a Mobile Ad Hoc Nemtwork, In Proceedings of the IEEE Conference on Computer Communications (INFOCOM), New York, NY, 2002
4. Mesut Günes, Jörg Reibel, An IP Address Configuration Algorithm for Zeroconf. Mobile Multi Hop Ad Hoc Networks, In Proceedings of the International Workshop on Broadband Wireless Ad-Hoc Networks and Services, Sophia Antipolis, France, September 2002
5. Yuan Sun, Elizabeth M. Belding-Royer, Dynamic Address Configuration in Mobile Ad hoc Networks, UCSB Technical Report 2003-11, June 2003
6. Mansoor Mohsin, Ravi Prakash, IP Address Assignment in A Mobile Ad Hoc Network, MILCOM2002, (2002)856–861
7. Hongbo Zhou, Lionel M. Ni, Matt W. Mutka, Prophet address allocation for large scale MANETs, Ad Hoc Networks, vol. 1, (2003)423–434
8. R. Hinden, S. Deering, RFC2373: IP Version 6 Addressing Architecture, July 1998
9. Charles E. Perkins, Jari T. Malinen, Ryuji Wakikawa, Yuan Sun, IP Address Autoconfiguration for Ad Hoc Networks (work in progress), Internet Engineering Task Force, Nov 2001
10. Tracy Camp, Jeff Boleng, Vanessa Davies, A Survey of Mobility Models for Ad Hoc Network Research, Wireless Communications & Mobile Computing (WCMC): Special issue on Mobile Ad Hoc Networking: Research, Trends and Applications, 2002

A Distributed Topology Control Algorithm for Heterogeneous Ad Hoc Networks

Lei Zhang[1], Xuehui Wang[2], and Wenhua Dou[1]

[1] School of Computer,
National University of Defense Technology, Changsha 410073, China
findzhanglei@hotmail.com
[2] School of Mechatronics Engineering and Automation,
National University of Defense Technology, Changsha 410073, China
yzmailbox2003@163.com

Abstract. Topology control is an effective mechanism to save energy for ad hoc networks. In this paper, we propose an energy-saving topology control algorithm for heterogeneous ad hoc networks with non-uniform transmission ranges: Minimum-power Ingress Neighbor Sub-network (MINS), which is fully distributed, asynchronous and localized. MINS not only preserves the network connectivity, but also has low communication overhead compared with other topology control algorithms. Simulation results show the effectiveness of our proposed algorithm.

1 Introduction

Wireless ad hoc networks have been the focus of many recent research and development efforts for its applications in military, commercial, and educational environments. Since wireless nodes are usually powered by batteries, energy-saving is a prime consideration in these networks. Topology control via per-node transmission power adjustment has been shown to be effective in extending network lifetime and increasing network capacity (due to better spatial reuse of spectrum), but reducing transmission power arbitrarily on each node may result in a disconnected network. Energy-saving topology control aims at reducing the transmission power as much as possible while maintaining the network connectivity. Most of the literature in this area has focused on the topology control problem in homogeneous ad hoc networks with uniform transmission ranges, but the assumption of homogeneous nodes does not always hold in practice. In this paper, we propose an energy-saving topology control algorithm for heterogeneous ad hoc networks with non-uniform transmission ranges, which not only preserves the network connectivity, but also has low communication overhead compared with other topology control algorithms.

2 Network Model

Let V denote the node set in the network, we assume the wireless channel is symmetric and obstacle-free, each node has the ability to gather its location information via position system, such as GPS. $\forall u \in V$, suppose d_u^{max} is its maximum transmission range, we define ingress neighbor and ingress neighbor set as follows.

Definition 1. *Ingress Neighbor and Ingress Neighbor Set.* $\forall u, v \in V$, $d(u,v)$ is the distance between node u and v, if $d_u^{max} > d(u,v)$, u is an ingress neighbor of v, denoted as $u \to v$, all these ingress neighbors of node v constitute its ingress neighbor set V_{IG}^v (including node v itself).

Since the maximum transmission range of each node may be different, ingress neighbor is asymmetric, i.e., $u \to v$ does not imply $v \to u$. If u is an ingress neighbor of v, there exists a directed link (u,v) from u to v, its weight is $d(u,v)$. The network topology generated by having each node transmit with its maximum power is a directed graph, denoted as $G = (V, E)$, where $E = \{(u,v) : u \to v, u \in V, v \in V\}$.

3 The MINS Topology Control Algorithm

3.1 Topology Information Collection

Each node in the network periodically broadcasts a HELLO message using its maximum transmission power (in this paper, broadcast means 1-hop broadcast, global broadcast means broadcast in the entire network). The information contained in a HELLO message should at least include the node id, the node position and its maximum transmission range. If $u \to v$, v will receive u's HELLO message, using all the received HELLO messages node v can construct its ingress neighbor topology $G_{IG}^v = (V_{IG}^v, E_{IG}^v)$, where V_{IG}^v is the ingress neighbor set, $E_{IG}^v = \{(x,y) : x \to y, x \in V_{IG}^v, y \in V_{IG}^v\}$ is the directed edge set among all the nodes in V_{IG}^v, obviously G_{IG}^v is a subgraph of $G = (V, E)$.

3.2 Local Topology Construction

With the knowledge of ingress neighbor topology $G_{IG}^v = (V_{IG}^v, E_{IG}^v)$, node v constructs a minimum-power ingress neighbor sub-network $G_{IG}^{v'} = (V_{IG}^v, E_{IG}^{v'})$ using the following algorithm.

Step 1. Construct a subgraph $G_{IG}^{v'} = (V_{IG}^v, E_{IG}^{v'})$ without any edges and initialize the minimum transmission range d_v^{min} of each node in V_{IG}^v to 0.

$$E_{IG}^{v'} = \phi \qquad d_v^{min} = 0 \qquad V_t = V_{IG}^v - v$$

Step 2. Sort the edges in E_{IG}^v according to its weight $d(u,v)$ in a non-decreasing order, the sort result is denoted as S.

Step 3. Retrieve the first directed edge (x,y) from S.

Step 4. If $x \in V_t$ and node x is not connected to node y, add edge (x,y) to $E_{IG}^{v'}$ and update d_x^{min}:

$$\text{if } d_x^{min} < d(x,y), \text{ set } d_x^{min} = d(x,y)$$

Step 4. If node x is connected to node v, delete node x from V_t.

Step 5. If V_t is empty, terminate the algorithm, else go to step 3.

3.3 Transmission Power Adjustment

On termination of the local topology construction algorithm, node v obtains the minimum transmission range for each ingress neighbor. It will send these information to its ingress neighbors within a transmission power control (TPC) message.

Since ingress neighbor is not symmetric, node v may be unable to reach some of its ingress neighbors directly using its maximum transmission power. In this case, if v broadcasts the TPC message globally, it will result in excessive communication overhead. Instead of globally broadcasting the TPC message to all the ingress neighbors, node v only broadcasts the TPC message to those ingress neighbors that are directed connected to it in $G_{IG}^{v}{'} = (V_{IG}^{v}, E_{IG}^{v}{'})$, which is sufficient to guarantee the network connectivity (proved in Theorem 1). Extensive simulations show this method dramatically reduces the communication overhead caused by global broadcast (see Section 4).

Each node can determine the minimum power level required to reach its neighbors by the information in the TPC messages and by mesuring the receiving power of HELLO messages as in [4]. Node v then uses the power level that can reach its farthest neighbor as its transmission power. The final network topology is denoted as $G_0 = (V, E_0)$ after the transmission power adjustment.

3.4 Mobility Manipulation

To manipulate the mobility of wireless nodes, each node should broadcast HELLO message periodically, the interval between two broadcasts is determined by the mobility speed. When any node finds the ingress neighbor topology is changed, it will readjust the transmission power from scratch.

Theorem 1. *If the original topology $G = (V, E)$ is strongly connected, then $G_0 = (V, E_0)$ obtained by MINS algorithm is also strongly connected.*

Proof. Since $G = (V, E)$ is strongly connected, $\forall u, v \in V$, there exists a directed path form u to v in $G = (V, E)$, without loss of generality, we denote it as $p(u, x_1, x_2...x_{k-1}, x_k, v)$, where $x_1, x_2...x_{k-1}, x_k$ are the k intermediate nodes from u to v.

Since $x_k \to v$, by the MINS algorithm, there must exist a directed path in $G_0 = (V, E_0)$ through which node x_k can reach node v. Similarly, $x_{k-1} \to x_k$ implies x_{k-1} can reach x_k, $x_{k-2} \to x_{k-1}$ implies x_{k-2} can reach x_{k-1}, which continues until node u can reach node x_1. As a result, node u can reach node v in $G_0 = (V, E_0)$, therefore $G_0 = (V, E_0)$ is strongly connected.

4 Performance Simulation

We evaluate the performance of the MINS algorithm through simulations. Assume n nodes are uniformly distributed in a $1000m \times 1000m$ square area, we increse n from 50 to 300 and observe the average out degree, communication overhead and average transmission power of the topologies generated using maximum

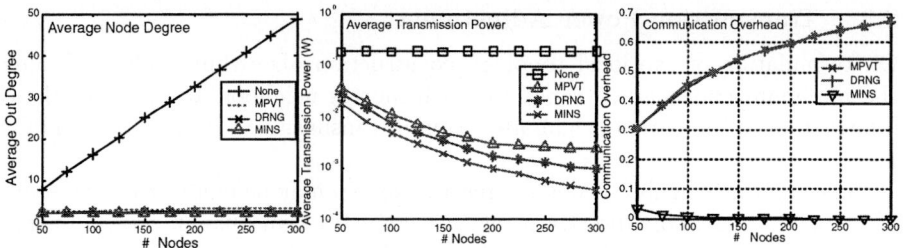

Fig. 1. Performance Comparison of MPVT, DRNG and MINS algorithm

transmission power, MPVT, DRNG and MINS algorithm. As illustrated in Fig. 1, the topology under MINS algorithm has less average out degree and lower transmission power, which implies it provides better spatial reuse and higher energy efficiency. We quantify the communication overhead as the percentage of the nodes that make global broadcast during the execution of topology control algorithms. Fig. 1 shows that in the MINS algorithm only a few nodes globally broadcast the TPC messages, and the percentage decreases rapidly with the increase of node density, while in MPVT and DRNG, plenty of nodes need global broadcast to construct the neighbor topology.

5 Conclusion

In this paper, we propose a distributed topology control algorithm (MINS) for heterogeneous ad hoc networks, which preserves the network connectivity and has less communication overhead. Performance simulation shows the effectiveness of our proposed algorithm.

References

1. Jilei Liu e Baochun Li, "Distributed Topology Control in Wireless Sensor Networks with Asymmetric Links," in Proc. GLOBECOM 2003, San Francisco, USA, Dec. 2003.
2. N. Li and J. C. Hou, "Topology Control in Heterogeneous Wireless Networks: Problems and Solutions," in Proc. IEEE INFOCOM 2004, Hong Kong, China, Mar. 2004.
3. R. Ramanathan and R. Rosales-Hain, "Topology control of multihop wireless networks using transmit power adjustment," in Proc. IEEE INFOCOM 2000, Tel Aviv, Israel, Mar. 2000, pp. 404–413.
4. N. Li, J. C. Hou, and L. Sha, "Design and analysis of an MSTbased topology control algorithm," in Proc. IEEE INFOCOM 2003, San Francisco, CA, USA, Apr. 2003.
5. L. Li, J. Y. Halpern, P. Bahl, Y.-M. Wang, and R. Wattenhofer, "Analysis of a cone-based distributed topology control algorithm for wireless multi-hop networks," in Proc. ACM Symposium on Principles of Distributed Computing, Newport, Rhode Island, United States, Aug. 2001, pp. 264–273.

UbiqStor: A Remote Storage Service for Mobile Devices

MinHwan Ok, Daegeun Kim, and Myong-soon Park

Dept. of Computer Science and Engineering, Korea University,
Seoul, 136-701, Korea
panflute@korea.ac.kr, {vicroot, myongsp}@ilab.korea.ac.kr

Abstract. In Ubiquitous computing environment the mobile devices such as PDAs necessarily connect to remote storage servers. We present an iSCSI caching system that localizes iSCSI target to overcome the shortcomings of iSCSI performance dropping sharply as the latency increases.

1 Motivation

Mobile devices such as PDAs are evolving to be incorporated into Ubiquitous computing environment. Due to lightly equipped storage, they lack enough capacity to process application of large data, thus it has been necessitated supplying vast storage capacity from remote machine. For mass storage service, SCSI has been representative protocol in its widespread application. We have built a remote storage system for mobile appliances using iSCSI protocol, which mobile devices can use the storage of a remote server through wireless link but just as their own local storage. It enables mobile appliances to overcome the limitation of storage capacity, as well as the ability to adapt various applications of wired environment in need of mass scale data.

1.1 iSCSI

The iSCSI (Internet Small Computer System Interface) is an emerging standard storage protocol that can transfer a SCSI command over IP network. Since the iSCSI protocol can make clients access the SCSI I/O devices of server host over an IP Network, client can use the storage of another host transparently without the need to pass through a server host's file system[1]. Fig. 1 illustrates iSCSI protocol linkage.

In iSCSI layer common SCSI commands and data are encapsulated in the form of iSCSI PDU (Protocol Data Unit). The iSCSI PDU is sent to the TCP layer for the IP network transport. The encapsulation and the decapsulation of SCSI I/O commands over TCP/IP enable the storage user to access a remote storage device of the remote server directly[2].

1.2 iCache

iCache is developed to improve iSCSI performance using local cache of a client system. Initiator's systems have specific cache space for iSCSI data, and iSCSI block

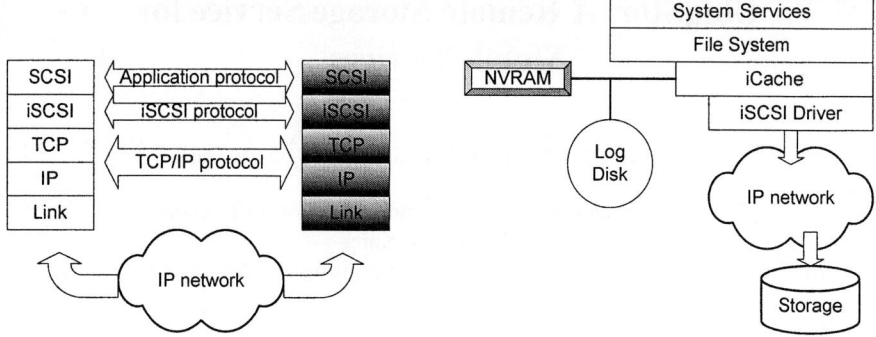

Fig. 1. Remote Storage Service with iSCSI protocol **Fig. 2.** iCache Architecture

data is cached to minimize network block I/O. Thus iSCSI does not send I/O requests through the network every time the disk I/O happens. Instead it reads cached blocks or sends blocks cached in LogDisk at once to the server for improving iSCSI performance. iCache's buffer space consists of two hierarchical caches comprising Non-Volatile RAM and LogDisk. Data is stored sequentially in NVRAM. When enough data is gathered, iCache process moves data from NVRAM to LogDisk. Blocks which are frequently accessed, are kept in NVRAM where access speed is fast. iCache stores less accessed data in the LogDisk. Caching techniques used in iCache are based on DCD technology, [3] proposed to improve Disk I/O performance. However storage subsystem like iCache is not adequate to mobile devices since it needs additional NVRAM and LogDisk to embody the local cache.

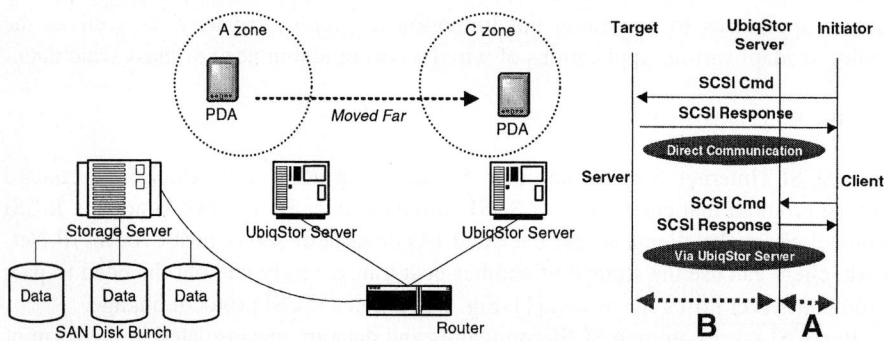

Fig. 3. iSCSI Target Localization by UbiqStor **Fig. 4.** SCSI Response Time Reduction

2 Cache Server for Ubiquitous Storage Service

We developed *UbiqStor*, an iSCSI cache server, for reduced the packet transfer delay time between a storage server and the mobile client, and higher practical utilization of the network bandwidth. UbiqStor prefetches the next block to be used by the client for iSCSI read operations and can give quick responses for iSCSI write operations. The nearest UbiqStor server from mobile client is selected by iSNS and the client connects to the UbiqStor that has an iSCSI connection with a remote storage server. By using this caching service response delay times of I/O requests shortens, instead of those of a long-distant remote storage. Fig. 3 illustrates the UbiqStor working.

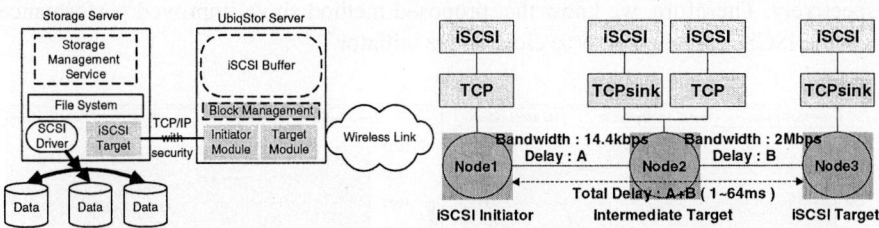

Fig. 5. iSCSI Caching System   **Fig. 6.** The Configuration of Network Simulator 2

Fig. 5 shows a modular diagram of the iSCSI caching system. The system consists of iSCSI initiator, target, and block management module. An UbiqStor server has two iSCSI connections. One is a connection between the UbiqStor server and mobile client and the other is the connection with the storage server. The *target module* has an iSCSI session with a mobile client's iSCSI initiator and the *initiator module* has one with the iSCSI target module of the storage server. Two modules perform the same role, such as general iSCSI Target/Initiator module. However, the first iSCSI connection between mobile client and UbiqStor server is used for I/O requests of the client, and the latter is used to prefetch next blocks to be used by the client from the storage server or to deliver write blocks back to the storage server. The target/initiator module of an UbiqStor server is controlled by a block management module.

3 System Simulations

In Fig. 6, the network of an iSCSI initiator, a target and the UbiqStor server is simulated using a Network Simulator 2.27. The bandwidth of the link between node1 and node2 is limited by 14400bps to simulate wireless network (CDMA 2000 1x). The change in iSCSI performance according to the distance between iSCSI initiator and target Performance is measured by the delay times from 1ms to 64ms under the supposition that delay is proportional to distance. We selected 512 bytes as data size that is SCSI block size used in PDA of MS-Windows CE-based.

Fig. 7 and 8 show the difference in iSCSI performance by data type. No intermediate is the case the UbiqStor server has not intervened. In cases where iSCSI has a short delay, and when the distance of iSCSI initiator from target is short, the transmission delay is much bigger than the difference of propagation delay by introducing UbiqStor. Therefore it has little influence on iSCSI performance. However, when the iSCSI initiator is distant from the target, the difference of propagation delay time is much longer than that of transmission delay. Fig. 8 shows that iSCSI performance difference gets greater as propagation delay between the iSCSI initiator and target gets longer. Performance differences according to data type are due to the fact that the iSCSI buffer hit rates for a read block are different. We suppose that the hit ratio of multimedia data, which is accessed sequentially, is 90 percent and 80% and 50% for text and application data, respectively. In each case of distance ratio, A:B = 5:5, A:B = 3:7, and A:B = 1:9, performance elevation of 25%, 40%, and 59% was achieved, respectively. Therefore, we know that proposed method show improved performance when the iSCSI caching server is close to the initiator.

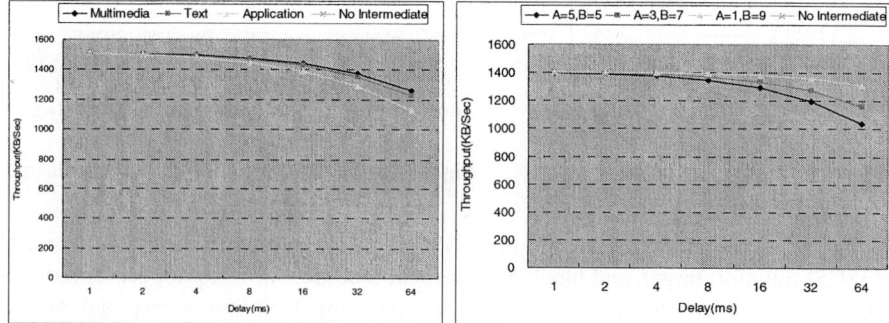

Fig. 7. Read Operations with Data Types   **Fig. 8.** Write Operations by Distance Ratios

4 Summary

In the presented system localizing the iSCSI target improved the link utilization and iSCSI performance when the target come closer to the initiator(mobile client). Through this storage subsystem the mobile devices is supplied with fluent delivery of vast storage space, which would lead to broad migration of various applications from wired environment to wireless environment that is evolving into Ubiquitous computing environment.

References

1. Y. Lu, D. H.C. Du: Performance Study of iSCSI-Based Storage Subsystems, IEEE Communication Magazine. (2003)
2. T. Clark: IP SANs: A Guide to iSCSI, iFCP, and FCIP Protocols for Storage Area Networks. Addison-Wesley (2002)
3. Y. Hu and Q. Yang: DCD-disk caching disk: A New Approach for Boosting I/O Performance. Proc. of 23rd Annual Intl. Symposium on Computer Architecture. (1996)

A Fan-Shaped Flexible Resource Reservation Mechanism in Mobile Wireless Internet[*]

Xingwei Wang[1], Changqing Yuan[1], Bo Song[1], and Min Huang[2]

[1] Computing Center, Northeastern University, Shenyang, 110004, China
wangxw@mail.neu.edu.cn
[2] College of Information Science and Engineering, Northeastern University,
Shenyang, 110004, China

Abstract. With user movement characteristics and QoS (Quality of Service) requirements being considered, a fan-shaped flexible resource reservation mechanism is presented, based on motion prediction and QoS negotiation. It also considers solutions to the frequent handover problem. Simulation results have shown that QoS guarantees can be provided to certain degree.

1 Introduction

MWI (Mobile Wireless Internet) provides ubiquitous personalized information service [1, 2]. Under MWI, when one MU (Mobile User) moves from one cell to another and handover occurs, advanced resource reservation is an effective way to ensure QoS (Quality of Service) [3]. In this paper, a fan-shaped flexible resource reservation mechanism that depends on motion prediction and QoS negotiation is presented.

2 Motion-Prediction

As shown in Fig. 1, the magnetic field intensity values p_1, p_2, p_3, p_4 within the cell for the MU at four time points t_1, t_2, t_3, t_4 are recorded in the base station. According to the cell magnetic field intensity distribution and the specific p_1, p_2, p_3, p_4 values, compute the distances s_1, s_2, s_3, s_4 between the base station and the MU at t_1, t_2, t_3, t_4. The values of MU movement velocity and acceleration $|v|$ and $|a|$ are computed as follows:

$$|v| = [(s_2 - s_1)/(t_2 - t_1) + (s_4 - s_3)/(t_4 - t_3)] \tag{1}$$

$$|v_1| = (s_2 - s_1)/(t_2 - t_1) \tag{2}$$

$$|v_2| = (s_4 - s_3)/(t_4 - t_3) \tag{3}$$

---

[*] This work was supported by the National 863 Plan under Grant No.2001AA121064; the NSFC under Grant No.60473089, No.60003006 and No.70101006; the NSF of Liaoning under Grant No.20032018 and No.20032019; Modern Distance Education Engineering Project by MoE.

$$s = [(s_3 + s_4) - (s_1 + s_2)]/2 \tag{4}$$

$$|a| = (|v_2|^2 - |v_1|^2)/2s \tag{5}$$

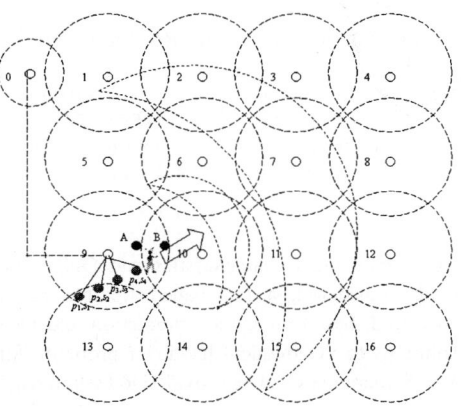

Fig. 1. Fan-shaped resource reservation

In general, except low speed movement schemes, such as moving on-foot or by bicycle, high speed ones, such as moving by car, train or airplane, often can be considered as to be on the straight-line alike track, especially within one cell; even if one MU is indeed changing his movement direction within the current cell, the movement diversion is still not considered occurred. According to [4], in the proposed mechanism, define the probability distribution function of β as follows:

$$P(\beta) = \frac{1}{\sqrt{2\pi}\sigma} e^{-\left(\frac{\beta}{\sigma}\right)^2} \tag{6}$$

$\sigma = k(|v| + |a|\Delta t)$ (k is a constant), Δt is a short time period (usually determined according to the actual situation). $|a|$ is used to tune the effect of the current $|v|$, so that the influence of future movement has also been taken into account.

3 Fan-Shaped Flexible Resource Reservation

3.1 Fan-Shaped Resource Reservation

As shown in Fig. 1, the arrow indicates the movement tendency of one MU. Assume he is communicating with someone in cell 0, cell 10 should be considered as the most probable target one for resource reservation. However, in order to prevent QoS guarantees disrupted or degraded due to his sudden diversion, the resource reservation should also be done within cell 5, 6, and 14. If he moves very rapidly, resource reservation should also be considered within cell 1, 2, 3, 7, 11 and 15. When he changes movement tendency along the vertical direction of the fan radius or along the radial direction of the fan, the fan-shaped piece angle or the radius should be adjusted respectively (enlarged or contracted accordingly).

Referring to DiffServ, suppose the user QoS class is L. The bigger L means the higher priority. According to the probability distribution of β, set a guaranteed probability threshold for the class $L=i$, i.e., $\mu_i = k_0/i$, k_0 is a constant, and then $P(\beta_i) = \mu_i$. Suppose $P^{-1}(\mu_i)$ is the reverse function of $P(\beta_i)$, then $\beta_i = P^{-1}(\mu_i)$.

The fan-shaped piece radius r, the resource reservation initiating time t_{ini} and the original resource releasing time t_{res} are computed as follows:

$$r = k_1 |v| QL \tag{7}$$

$$t_{ini} = \begin{cases} k_2 \dfrac{e^{-|v|}}{LQ} & |v| < |v_0| \\ 0 & |v| \geq |v_0| \end{cases} \tag{8}$$

$$t_{res} = k_3 \dfrac{P_f L}{Q} \tag{9}$$

In formula (7), (8) and (9), k_1, k_2 and k_3 are tuning coefficients, and Q is the network load measurement. The bigger Q means the higher network load. v_0 is a preset movement velocity threshold according to the actual situations. If t_{ini} is zero, it means to initiate the resource reservation immediately. P_f is the user coming back probability, and according to formula (6), $P_f = P(180°)$.

In fact, here is no strict boundary between neighboring cells, as shown in Fig. 1. For a high-speed MU, when he moves to point A, the probability of his moving into the neighboring cell is very high, and then resource reservation should be initiated and handover occurs at point A. However, for a low speed MU, the movement diversion probability is relatively high; therefore, only when he has moved across point B, be resource reservation initiated and handover performed. The action of releasing the original reserved resources should be postponed (if permitted), keeping them in soft reserved state for a while; if he returns to the original cell again within one certain period (refer to t_{res} definition), it is unnecessary to do resource reservation.

The proposed mechanism supports soft and hard reservation. The former is a shared style of resource reservation, other MU can use the reserved resources when the original MU is not using them, however, those temporarily borrowed resources must be returned to him immediately if needed. The latter is an exclusive style of resource reservation, only the MU who has made reservation can use the reserved resources. For example, in Fig. 1, the proposed mechanism makes hard resource reservation in the cell 10, and soft reservation in cells 5,6,14 and even in 1,2,3,7,11,15.

3.2 QoS Negotiation

In this paper, when the available network resource cannot meet with the MU QoS requirement, network and user negotiation stages are performed. In the former stage, check whether there is enough deprivable resource along the involved route in the network, and the higher priority MU can deprive the resource occupied by the lower priority one. If failed, enter into the latter stage, negotiate with the MU, and ask him whether the QoS requirement could be degraded or not. There are also two styles of deprivation at the former stage, i.e., soft and hard. For the former, before the MU handover, other low priority MU can use his reserved resources, however, once handed-over, the temporarily borrowed resources must be returned to him immediately; for the latter, the reserved resources must be allocated to the high priority MU at once. For the cells where the MU will enter with low probability, soft deprivation is carried out; however, for the cells where the MU will enter with high probability, hard deprivation is performed.

3.3 Procedure Description

The procedure of fan-shaped flexible resource reservation mechanism is as follows:

Step 1: The MU monitors magnetic field intensity of the current cell; if lower than the preset threshold, go to step 2, otherwise continue monitoring.

Step 2: The MU sends a request message to the access router of the current cell. When it has received the message, it determines the $|v|$ and $|a|$ of the MU, and computed the values of t_{ini}, t_{res}, β and r, determining the target cells.

Step 3: According to t_{ini}, the access router of the current cell sends request messages to the access routers of the target cells determined in step 2, notify them of the amount of bandwidth to be reserved and reservation style (soft or hard), etc.

Step 4: The access routers of the target cells issue resource reservation signaling packets. If the available resources in some cells cannot sustain the required QoS levels of the MU, the corresponding access routers and the MU will do QoS negotiation. If succeeded, go to step 8; otherwise go to step 5.

Step 5: If the MU chooses giving up his request, go to step 6; if he chooses waiting for a while, go to step 7.

Step 6: The access router of the current cell sends notifications to those access routers that have failed in resource reservation or have not used the reserved resources, and tell them to release the resources. The procedure ends.

Step 7: The access router of the current cell continue to send request messages to the access routers of those cells that have failed in resource reservation, try to do resource reservation again, according to the original request. If succeeded, go to step 8; otherwise go to step 6. If the times of resource reservation done are beyond the preset threshold, the procedure ends.

Step 8: Within the cell which the MU has moved into, he uses the reserved resource to continue communication, the procedure ends. For the cell which the MU does not move into, go to step 6.

4 Performance Evaluations and Conclusions

The proposed mechanism is compared with the one in [5] and fan-shaped rigid resource reservation (just support hard resource reservation and hard deprivation) on hitting rate, as shown in Fig. 2. If the MU moves very rapidly, the fan-shaped resource reservation will be done in several cells, supporting several times of handovers by one time of reservation. Table 1 is the corresponding results, and RV refers to relative velocity, RRRS1 refers to resource reservation ratio supporting one time of handover, RRRS2 refers to resource reservation ratio supporting two times of handovers, RRRS3 refers to resource reservation ratio supporting three times of handovers, SR refers to Saving Ratio, RRHR refers to resource reservation hitting rate.

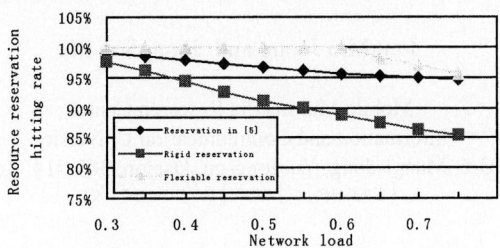

Fig. 2. Comparison of resource reservation hitting rate

Table 1. The statistics of the resource reservation

RV	RRRS1 %	RRRS2 %	RRRS3 %	SR %	RRHR%
8	85.23	14.77	0	12.87	99.9
10	60.29	29.48	10.23	33.31	99.9
12	56.87	29.27	13.86	36.30	99.9
14	49.39	34.70	15.91	39.95	99.9
16	44.80	37.28	17.92	42.24	99.7
18	41.61	40.15	18.24	43.38	99.2
20	36.80	40.78	22.42	46.13	98.3

In summary, the proposed mechanism can provide QoS guarantee to the MUs and optimize the network resource utilization to certain degree.

References

1. Jon, C.-S.W., Cheng, C.-W.: Intelligent Handover for Mobile Wireless Internet. Mobile Networks and Applications, Vol. 6, No. 1. (2001) 67-79
2. Wang, X.W., Zhang, Y.H., Liu, J.R., Li, H.T.: Research on Quality of Service Management Mechanisms in Distributed Multimedia Systems. Journal of Software, Vol. 9, No. 2. (1998) 87-90 (in Chinese)
3. Sarantis, P., Alexandros, K.: An Efficient RSVP-Mobile IP Interworking Scheme. Mobile Networks and Applications, Vol. 8, No. 3. (2003) 197-207
4. Tsai, I.F., Jan, R.H.: The Lookahead Strategy for Distance-Based Location Tracking in Wireless Cellular Networks. ACM Sigmobile Mobile Computing and Communications Review, Vol. 3, No. 4. (1999) 27-38
5. Huang, Q.B., Li, H., Gao, C.S.: An Improvement to Call Admission and Control Scheme in Next Generation Wireless Networks. Mini-Micro Systems, Vol. 24, No. 8. (2003) 1437-1440 (in Chinese)

Security Analysis of Multi-path Routing Scheme in Ad Hoc Networks

JongMin Jeong and JoongSoo Ma

Mobile Multimedia Research Center,
Information and Communication University,
103-6, Mungi-dong, Yuseong-gu, Daejon, 305-714, Korea
{minee, jsma}@icu.ac.kr

Abstract. When selecting a routing scheme for an ad hoc network, we must consider security as well as the network performance. In this paper, we numerically analyze the route availability of the multi-path routing schemes (MPRS) against malicious actions. After defining the class of multi-path routing schemes and the attack model, we compare the expectation of routes disruption of the MPRS with the single path routing scheme (SPRS). Our results show that the MPRS is twice as robust as the SPRS.

1 Introduction

Because of burdens of setting up and maintaining multiple routes, most routing protocols in ad hoc networks have avoided multi-path routing. Recently several studies on the MPRS have shown that it can be superior to the SPRS in network performance measures such as the throughput and the end-to-end delay [1], [2], [3], [4], [5]. However we must also consider the effects of the MPRS on route security because security is an important issue in ad hoc networks [6].

Our goal here is to show that the MPRS improves the route security as well as the network performance. After defining the general attack models which may be present in ad hoc networks, we evaluate the availability of routes in both the MPRS and the SPRS. Our analytical results show that the MPRS is more secure, and the MPRS should be considered as the future secure routing protocol in ad hoc network. We conduct combinatorial analysis in section 2, evaluate the security in section 3 and we conclude in section 4.

2 Numeric Analysis

2.1 System and Attack Model

For a given destination, the SPRS uses only one of the shortest paths to the destination, while the MPRS uses a shortest path and others whose path length may be equal to or longer than the shortest path. We assume each intruder attacks one node at a time but several intruders may attack the same node simultaneously. We select the expected value of path disruption as the metric for evaluating the route availability. In the SPRS, a route is disrupted if at least one of the nodes along the path is exposed by intruders. On the other hand, in the MPRS, routes are disrupted if every path has at least one exposed node. Table 1 shows the parameters for analysis of the route availability.

Table 1. Parameters and definition

p	The probability that node is disrupted by intruders $(0<p\leq 1)$
a	The number of intruders $(a = 1,2,3.....N)$
q	The number of paths in MPRS $(q =1,2,3,...N)$
n_i	The number of nodes along the i-th path in MPRS $(i = 1,2,3...q)$
r	The number of intruders attacking the same node simultaneously $(1< r \leq a)$
	The total number of nodes in route(s) $(N_t = \sum_{i=1}^{q} n_i$ in MPRS)

Definition 1: $E_q(a, N_t)$-The expectation that the route with q paths is disrupted by a intruders. In SPRS, $q=1$ and $N_t = n$. In MPRS, $q \geq 2$ and $N_t = n_1 + n_2 +,...,+n_q$.

Definition 2: $R_{q,r}(a,N_t)$-The expectation that there is at least the case that r intruders out of a intruders attack one node among N_t nodes at the same time.

From the above definitions, we can draw the following relation between $E_q(a, N_t)$ and $R_{q,r}(a, N_t)$.

$$E_q(a,n) = \frac{\sum_{i=1}^{a} R_{q,i}(a,n)}{\text{The number of possible attack types}}$$

2.2 Analysis of Route Disruption

In the SPRS, the number of path is always one $(q=1)$, and we omit q for notational simplicity. When a is one, there is only one possible attack pattern and the expectation of route disruption is $E(1,n) = R_1(1,n) = p$. As we have more intruders, there are many possible attack patterns. We found that the number of attack patterns gradually increases until r reaches $2/a$ and then decreases until r reaches $a-1$. We can express the total expectation that the route is disrupted in the SPRS as follows:

$$R_r(a,n) = \begin{cases} rp \sum_{i=0}^{r-1} \binom{n}{a-r-i+1} \frac{a!}{r!(i+1)!} & (r \leq \frac{a}{2}) \\ rp \sum_{i=0}^{a-r-1} \binom{n}{a-r-i+1} \frac{a!}{r!(i+1)!} & (\frac{a}{2} < r < a) \\ rp \binom{n}{1} & (r = a) \end{cases} \quad (1)$$

Here, the left term in the summation is the number of possible attack patterns by intruders and the right term is the permutation of these events.

In the MPRS, route disruption does not occur unless every path is disrupted. Therefore, to find the probability of the route disruption in the MPRS, we first consider the case where at least one path is not disrupted. To aid this process, we introduce the notation, $m(i,a)$.

Definition 3: $m(i,a)$ – the number of events that all a intruders attack the nodes only within the i paths out of the total q paths, $i = 1,2,3...,q-1$. If this event occurs, $q-i$ paths are absolutely secure.

With this definition, we can express the expectation of the route disruption in the MPRS as follows:

$$R_{q,r}(a,n) = \begin{cases} rp \sum_{i=0}^{r-1} (\binom{N_t}{a-r-i+1}) - \sum_{j=1}^{q-1} m(j,r)) \frac{a!}{r!(i+1)!} & (r \leq \frac{a}{2}) \\ rp \sum_{i=0}^{a-r-1} (\binom{N_t}{a-r-i+1}) - \sum_{j=1}^{q-1} m(j,r)) \frac{a!}{r!(i+1)!} & (\frac{a}{2} < r < a) \end{cases} \quad (2)$$

In the case of $r = a$, because every a nodes attack only one node at the same time, route disruption is not generated in the MPRS. The $m(i,a)$ is easily calculated with combinatorial analysis.

3 Estimation of Route Security

In this section we present the security improvement of the MPRS through numerical results for three special cases as in [6]. In case 1, every path from source (S) to destination (D) has the same path length. This implies the "best case" scenario for the MPRS, where q disjoint shortest paths exist between the given source-destination pair. In the following two cases, we assume that there are q disjoint paths of increasing path lengths, with the primary route being the shortest path. In case 2, the successive path lengths increase by one, and in case 3, they increase by two.

Fig.1-(a) shows the expectation of route disruption in the SPRS. As the number of intruder increases or the path length decreases, there is a higher probability of route disruption. In fig. 1-(b), we compare the MPRS with the SPRS. Note that the MPRS with three or four paths is twice as secure as the SPRS under the same network attack model. It also shows that the number of paths does not greatly improve the security. When the number of path in the MPRS is three or four, the improvement of network performance is the most remarkable. Therefore we consider three or four numbers of paths for security analysis. Fig 1-(c) shows the expectation of route disruption with respect to the path lengths (cases 1, 2 and 3). Note that differences in path lengths contribute very little to the overall route disruption.

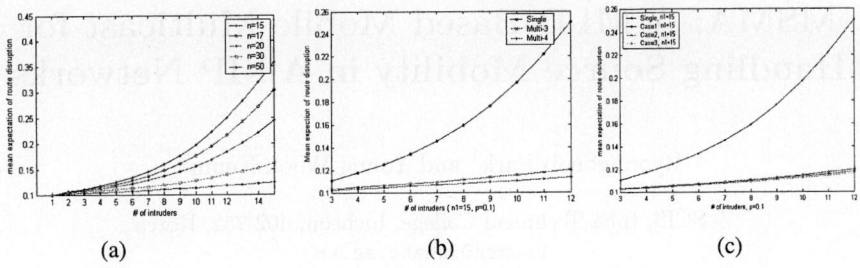

Fig. 1. Expectation of route disruption between the MPRS and SPRS

4 Conclusions

Using the technique of broadcasting of route requests, the source node can easily setup multiple paths to a destination in ad hoc networks. In this paper, we analyzed the route availability of the MPRS under a plural attack model. We showed that the MPRS is twice as secure as the SPRS. One does not require a large number of paths per route to achieve a high route availability. In the future, we will study the MPRS based security framework for further strengthening ad hoc routing security.

Acknowledgement

This research was supported by University IT Research Center Project.

References

1. Pham, P.P., Perreau, S.: Performance Analysis of Reactive shortest Path and Multi-path Routing Mechanism with Load Balance. Twenty-Second Annual Joint Conference of the IEEE Computer and Communications Societies, Vol.1, April 2003
2. 2. Marina, M.K., Das, S.R.: On-demand Multi-path Distance Vector Routing in Ad Hoc Networks. Network Protocols 2001, 9'th International Conference, Nov. 2001.
3. 3. Tsirigos, A., Hass, Z.J.: Analysis of Multi-path Routing-Part I: The Effect on the Packet Delivery Ration. IEEE Transaction on Wireless Communications, Vol.3, No. 1, January 2004
4. 4. Tsirigos, A., Hass, Z.J.: Analysis of Multi-path Routing-Part 2: Mitigation of the Effects of Frequently Changing Network Topologies. IEEE Transaction on Wireless Communications, Vol. 3, No. 2, March 2004
5. Nasipuri, A., Das, S.R.: On-Demand Multipath Routing for Mobile Ad Hoc Network. Computer Communication and Network, October 1999
6. Zhou, L., Hass, Z.J.: Securing Ad Hoc Networks, IEEE Network, Vol.13, Issue: 6, November-December 1999

MSMA: A MLD-Based Mobile Multicast for Handling Source Mobility in All-IP Networks

ByoungSeob Park[1] and Young Wook Keum[2]

[1] SCIS, Inha Technical College, Incheon, 402-752, Korea
bspark@inhatc.ac.kr
[2] School of Computer Engineering, Sungkyul University,
Anyang Gyeonggi-do, 430-742, Korea ywkeum@sungkyul.edu

Abstract. This paper explores the issues of mobile multicast scheme using Mobile-IPv6, and addresses the case when a mobile host is a source as well as a recipient of a given multicast operation. A new multicast routing protocol, called MSMA(MLD-based mobile multicast for handling Source Mobility in All-IP networks), with the MLD(Multicast Listener Discovery) and MDA(Multicast Delivery Agent) functionality to mobile hosts in Mobile-IPv6 based All-IP networks is proposed. The proposed MLD-based multicasting protocol asks its HA(Home Agent) to stop forwarding multicast for group using tunneling. Thus, the proposed protocol satisfies the maximum tolerable transfer delay and mitigates the forwarding task of HA.

1 Introduction

A multimedia application such as Internet TV and radio, videoconferencing, and network games has become extremely popular and attractive. IP multicasting requires specific mechanisms to track group membership. This dynamic membership management is done via the IGMP(Internet Group Management Protocol)[1] for IPv4 and MLD(Multicasting Listener Discovery)[2] for IPv6. Two basic mechanisms have been proposed by the IETF in Mobile-IP to support multicasting [3, 4, 5]; that is, remote subscription(RS) and bi-directional tunneling(BT). Recent proposals [6, 7, 8, 9] to provide multicasting over MIP(Mobile-IP) focus mainly on recipient mobility and little attention has been given to the case when mobile host is also the source. And, early researches on the topic "Mobile multicast" mainly focus on Mobile-IPv4 environments. Therefore, we propose a multicasting scheme with MLD functionality and cost analysis model for handling source movement to reduce HA forwarding tasks in the All-IP networks supporting Mobile-IPv6.

2 MSMA: A New MLD-Based Multicasting Protocol

2.1 MLD and MDA Operations

The proposed MLD-based mobile multicast routing employs MLD to collect multicast group membership information. The MLD [2] is used by IPv6 multicast routers to learn the existence of multicast group members on their connected links. It does so by periodically sending *queries* and having hosts sending *REPORT* about their multicast group memberships. The collected multicast group information is then provided to the multicast routing protocol. In order to reduce tunneling path, we also introduce a MDA node. The MDA is an access router to minimize the tunneling path on foreign network moving, where the MH receives multicast datagrams through a tunnel from a selected MR(Multicast Router) called MDA, located a network close to the foreign networks.

2.2 The Proposed Approaches

For the proposed MLD-based multicast protocol, we apply new types of MLD message called MLD *stop* and *MEM-ACK*. The *stop* message, when sent by an MH, notifies an HA that it should stop forwarding multicast datagram delivery. The *MEM-ACK* that sent by MDA is a response message for group membership ownership. Fig.1 demonstrates a multicast routing scenario without join operation using MDA concept. With MDA functionality, the protocol reduces network traffic by decreasing the number of duplicated datagrams and reduces multicast data delivery path length since datagrams are forwarded to the MHs by the MDA close to the foreign network. In the proposed scheme, when MH receives MLD *MEM-ACK* message from a serving MDA, multicast datagrams are delivered directly to the MH through tunneling path from MDA without join operation.

For a multicast routing scenario with source mobility handling method, it needs a tree-join operation using MLD and MDA concept for handling source movement. Until the MH that acts as a source gets a MLD *MEM-ACK* message from a new access router, it sends multicast packets to HA. However, after it receives a MLD *MEM-ACK* message from MDA, The MH starts sending multi-

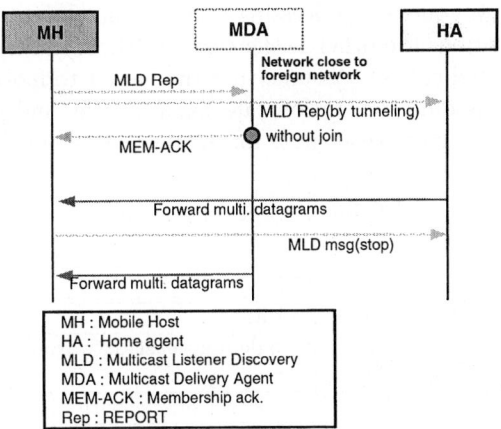

Fig. 1. Message exchange during multicast datagram delivery without join delay

cast packets through MDA, and sends MLD *stop* message to HA. The effect of MH movement that localized enhances the system performance and is serving as a source as well as a receiver for multicast group.

3 Performance Evaluation

We have analyzed a simplified cost analysis model of average cost per mobile host for our model. Then, the mobile multicast models are compared. Measures for cost analysis are processing cost and transmission cost. Fig.2 shows system cost architecture model used by mobile multicast models. It is extended from [10] with a little variation for our model. The distance between two nodes is expressed as number of hops such as H_a, H_b, H_c, H_d, and H_e. Three schemes which we com-

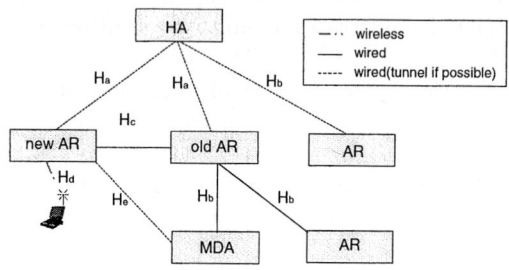

Fig. 2. The system cost model

pare are MIP-bidirectional tunneling(MIP-BT), MIP-remote subscription(MIP-RS), and the proposed model(MSMA). As the performance measure, we consider a control message cost and datagram transfer cost. The cost consists of two factors, $C_{control} + C_{data}$; one is a processing cost of control data including binding and group construction, the other is the cost to deliver multicast datagrams to a mobile in the visited subnet. Assume that the packet to mobility ratio(PMR), p is λ/μ, where, λ is data generation rate for a mobile, and μ is mobility rate between subnets. The cost parameters for analysis are defined as follows.

Table 1. Cost parameters

parameter	description
l	the datagram length ratio, l_{data}/l_{contol}
C_{tunnel}	the cost to forward single multicast data from a specific agent to MH by tunneling
m	the prob. that a MH visits a subnet with no other member
r	the average cost of processing control packets at any host
N	the mean number of the MHs per group

Then, $C_{control}$ is given by a registration cost and membership construction overhead, and C_{data} consists of the PMR and delivery cost of multicast datagrams to a MH in visited network. Consequently, the average cost, C_{total} per mobile of three multicast approaches are analyzed by the follow equation (1);

$$C_{total} = \begin{cases} (2(H_a + H_d) + 5r) + p \times [l(H_b + H_c + H_d) + 2r], & \text{for MIP-BT} \\ (2(H_a + H_d) + 5r) + m[(H_b + H_d + 2r)] + p \times [l(H_b + H_d)/N], & \text{for MIP-RS} \\ (2(H_a + H_d) + 5r) + m[2H_e + 3r] + p \times [l(H_e + H_d)/N], & \text{for MSMA} \end{cases} \quad (1)$$

where the C_{data} of a MSMA is $p \times [C_{tunnel}/N]$, and C_{tunnel} is the cost of multicast datagram delivery through tunneling from the MDA.

4 Conclusions

We propose an efficient MDL-based multicast scheme with source mobility to reduce the number of multicast tunnel and service disruption time in All-IP network environments. For this purpose, we define a new MLD extention and MDA operation, and describe the routing scenarios for two operations. The proposed MLD-based mobile multicast protocol, MSMA asks its HA to stop forwarding multicast for group. Also, we address cost analysis model to evaluate the proposed multicast scheme. As the results, the proposed protocol satisfies the maximum tolerable transfer delay and mitigates the forwarding task of Home Agent.

References

1. W. Fenner : Internet Group Management Protocol. RFC 2236, (1997)
2. S. Deering and et al. : "Multicast Listener Discovery (MLD) for IPv6", RFC 2710, Oct. (1999)
3. J. Mysore and V. Bharghavan : "A New Multicasting-based Architecture for Internet Host Mobility," Proc. ACM / IEEE MOBICOM'97, pp.161-172, Sep. (1997)
4. T.G Harrison, C.L. Williamson, W. L. Mackrell, and R.B.Bunt : "Mobile Multicast (MoM) Protocol : Multicast support for Mobile Host," Proc. ACM/IEEE MOBICOM'97, pp.151-160, Sep. (1997)
5. 3GPP2 : "Wireless IP Architecture Based on IETF Protocols," 3GPP2 P.R0001, ver1.0, Jul. (2000)
6. C.R. Lin and K.M. Wang : "Mobile Multicast Support in IP Networks," IEEE INFOCOM'2000, pp.1664-1672, (2000)
7. J. Ioannidis, D. Duchamp, and G.Q. Maguire Jr. : "IP-based Protocols for Mobile Internet-working, Proc. of ACM SIGCOMM, pp.235-245, Sep. (1991)
8. C.Bettstetter, A.Riedl, and Geler : "Interoperation of Mobile IPv6 and Protocol Independent Multicast Dense Mode," Proceedings of the ICPP'2000, (2000)
9. C.Jelger and Tomas Noel : "Multicast Mobile Hosts in IP networks : Progress and Challenges", IEEE Wireless Comm., Oct. (2002)
10. R.Jain et al. : "Mobile Internet Access and QoS Guarantees Using Mobile IP and RSVP with Location Register," Proc. IEEE ICC'98, (1998)

MQRP: A Multi-path QoS Routing Protocol in Ad Hoc Mobile Network

Peng Gegang, Liu Yan, Mao Dilin, Yang Jianghu, and Gao Chuanshan

Department of Computer Science and Engineering,
Fudan University, 220 Handan Rd, Shanghai, China
cgao@fudan.edu.cn

Abstract. In the paper, we propose a Multi-path QoS routing protocol MQRP, which constructs and adopts multiple routes of disjoint paths. The protocol can minimize route recovery process and routing control overhead by providing multiple routes. We evaluate the performance of the QoS routing protocol using extensive simulation.

1 Introduction

Due to the dynamic nature of ad hoc wireless network, ad hoc routing faces a lot of unique problems not present in wired networks[3]. Much work has been done in this area and many routing protocols for mobile ad hoc networks have been proposed [1][2][5], but all these protocols focus on best-effort traffic. In recent years QoS routing in ad hoc network has received increasingly intensive attention and some QoS routing protocols for ad hoc network have been proposed[6][7][8]. However, all these protocols are not concerned about multi-path routing. In QoS routing in wired networks, multi-path routing has been widely explored. Studies, however, have shown those proposed multi-path protocols for wired networks are not suitable for ad hoc networks. In this paper we propose a Multi-path QoS routing protocol MQRP, which constructs and adopts multiple routes of disjoint paths. The protocol can minimize route recovery process and routing control overhead by providing multiple routes.

2 QoS Parameter Calculation

Node Mobility and wireless radio properties make it more difficult than in wired networks to provide QoS in MANETs. Bandwidth calculation and reservation are the first step for further control in such an environment. Therefore, we used bandwidth as a main QoS parameter in this paper. In general, to calculate available bandwidth of a path in wireless network based on time-slots not only needs information about the available bandwidth on the links along the path, but also needs to know how to schedule the free slots. Therefore, to compute available bandwidth in MANETs is difficult and is actually NP-complete. Some heuristic algorithms have been proposed to solve the problem. In MQRP, we use the heuristic algorithm proposed in [4] to compute and reserve bandwidth.

3 MQRP Protocol

3.1 Route Establishment

When a source node needs to establish a route but does not have the route information to the destination, it broadcasts a QRP (QoS Route Probe) packet to its neighbors. When a node receives the QRP, it executes a bandwidth admission decision. In order to use hop-by-hop means to compute available bandwidth, intermediate nodes in MQRP do not use route cache to directly reply QRP. Table 1 formally shows the algorithm of dealing with a QRP at an intermediate node N in the form of pseudo-code. Upon receiving the first QRP, destination node sends a QRR (QoS Route Reply)packet to source node and records the route which the first QRP indicates. After that, the destination will wait for $ROUTE\_WAIT$ to collect other QRP control packets. The destination can receive more than one QRP in $ROUTE\_WAIT$, each of which indicates a feasible route from source node to destination node. In terms of the route information of the first route and all other candidate routes, destination node can execute a selection algorithm for disjoint routes given in table 2. Then destination sends another QRR to the source. Thus, there can be two disjoint routes between source and destination.

The intermediate nodes traveled by a QRR perform resource reservation in terms of free slots calculated in advance. If source node can receive the QRR, an

Table 1. Pseudo-code for dealing with a QRP at node N

```
If(CheckRedundantPkt(QRP.Source, QRP.QRPSN)||IncludedInNodelist
(QRP.Node_list, N))
    DropAndExit(QRP);
AvailableBandwidth = ComputeBandwidth(QRP, N);
If(AdmissionDecision(AvailableBandwidth, QRP.Bmin) == 0)
    DropAndExit(QRP);
Else
{
    QRP.TTL = QRP.TTL − 1
    If(QRP.TTL == 0)  DropAndExit(QRP);
    LogSlotInfo(QRP.Slot_list_array);
    AppendToNodelist(QRP.Node_list, N);
    If(N! = QRP.Destination)  Forward(QRP);
}
```

Table 2. Pseudo-code for selecting disjoint route

```
NodeDisjointRoute = FindNodeDisjointRoute();
If(NodeDisjointRoute == 0)
{
    LinkMaxDisjointRoute = FindMaxLinkDisjointRoute();
    If(LinkMaxDisjointRoute > 1)  SelectRoutewithMinHop();
}
ElseIf(NodeDisjointRoute > 1)  SelectRoutewithMinHop();
```

end-to-end resource reservation has been finished. When source node receives a QRR, it uses the first established route to send data packets. When the second QRR is received, the source has two routes to destination node. MQRP adopts a simple per-packet allocation to split traffic into the two routes.

3.2 Route Maintenance

When a node finds that the link to its downstream fails, it sends a $MQRP\_Route\_Error$ packet to source node. Nodes along the route from the interrupted node to source node release reserved resource for the QoS request when they receive the $MQRP\_Route\_Error$ packet, and drop all data packets of the QoS request waiting for sending in the queue. On receiving the $MQRP\_Route\_Error$ packet, the source deletes all entries which use the broken link. If only one of the two routes of the session fails, the source still can use the other valid route to send data. The source will initiate a new route establishment process only when both routes of the session are invalid.

4 Performance Evaluation

We utilized the Global Simulation Library to evaluate the performance of MQRP protocol. Our simulation environment consists of 50 mobile nodes within a 1000m*1000m area. The nodes are randomly placed in the area and each of them has a radio propagation range of 250 meters. The pause time of mobile nodes is 10 seconds. Mobility speed varies from 3m/s to 18m/s. The channel bandwidth is assumed to be 2Mbits/sec and each frame includes 16 data slots. QoS bandwidth request is 2 data slots. Constant bit rate (CBR) flows are deployed for data transmission. To validating the effectiveness of MQRP, in our simulation we implement a QoS routing protocol QDSR based on DSR. Besides providing QoS, QDSR adopts the similar mechanism with DSR and uses single route. Fig.1 shows a performance comparison of different protocols in packet delivery ratio at different levels of node mobility. Both of two protocols become more inefficient as the mobility speed increases. On the other hand, MQRP has better performance than QDSR. MQRP gets higher packet delivery ratio than QDSR and are less affected by node mobility. This is because the control packets, which more route re-establishment processes in QDSR bring about, cause more collision and contention with data packets. However, MQRP will have the other available route after one route is disturbed. MQRP can still deliver data packets without increasing control packets as long as the other route remains valid. Therefore, MQRP can get a good throughput performance. Fig.2 illustrates the end-to-end delay. MQRP has shorter delays compared to QDSR. The main cause is that in the process of more route reconstruction, QDSR brings out longer delay and during route establishment, data packets' wait time leads to larger end-to-end delays. MQRP, however, can use the remaining available route when the other route is invalid, and thus it does not need additional route acquisition latency. Fig. 3 presents routing control overhead. It can be seen from the figure that MQRP has a little more routing overhead in low speed than QDSR, which can be expected because MQRP produces more control packets while constructing multi-path route. MQRP, however, displays better performance than QDSR with the increase of mobility speed. This is due to the fact that as mobility speed increases, QDSR produces more route reconstruction than MQRP, in which source node initiates a new route establishment process only when both routes of a session are disconnected, and thus the number of reconstruction is less Compared to QDSR.

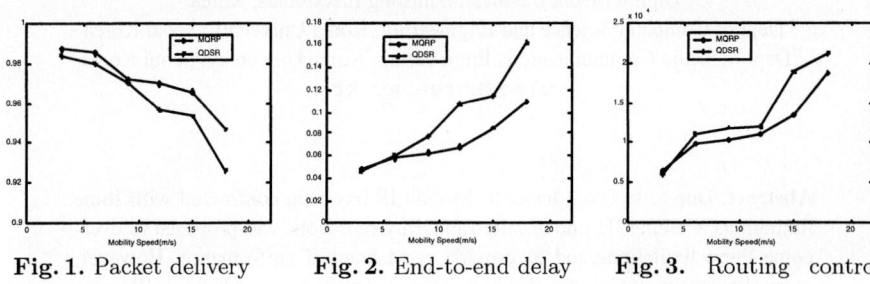

Fig. 1. Packet delivery ratio   **Fig. 2.** End-to-end delay (sec)   **Fig. 3.** Routing control overhead (packets)

5 Conclusion

In the paper, we propose a Multi-path QoS routing protocol MQRP, which constructs and adopts multiple routes of disjoint paths. The simulation results further show that the protocol accomplishes an effective multi-path QoS routing and can obtain good performance in dynamic network environment.

References

1. I. D. Chakeres and E. M. Belding-Royer. Aodv routing protocol implementation design. In *Proceedings of the International Workshop on Wireless Ad Hoc Networking (WWAN), Tokyo, Japan*, March 2004.
2. T. Fujiwara, N. Iida, and T. Watanabe. An ad-hoc routing protocol in hybrid wireless networks for emergency communications. In *Proceedings of WWAN2004 / IEEE, pp.748-754*, 2004.
3. I. Gruber, O. Knauf, and H. Li. Performance of ad hoc routing protocols in urban environments. In *In Proceedings of European Wireless 2004 (EW'2004), Barcelona, Spain, February 24 - 27*, 2004.
4. C. R. Lin and J.-S. Liu. Bandwidth routing in ad hoc wireless networks. In *IEEE Globecom*, 1998.
5. A. K. Saha and D. B. Johnson. Self-organizing hierarchical routing for scalable ad hoc networking. In *Mesh Networking Summit 2004, Salish Lodge Spa, Snoqualmie, Washington*, 2004.
6. K. N. S.Chen. Distributed quality-of-service routing in ad hoc networks. *IEEE Journal on Selected Areas in Communications, 17(8)*, pages 1488–1505, Aug. 1999.
7. R. Sivakumar, P. Sinha, and C. Bharghavan, V. a core-extraction distributed ad hoc routing algorithm. *Selected Areas in Communications, IEEE Journal on, Volume: 17 Issue: 8*, pages 1454 –1465, Aug. 1999.
8. H. Sun and H. Hughes. Adaptive qos routing based on prediction of local performance in ad hoc networks. In *Proc. of IEEE WNCN*, 2003.

ESSHP: An Enhanced Semi-soft Handoff Protocol Based on Explicit Node Decision in Cellular Networks*

Jae-Won Kim[1], Wonjun Lee[2],♦, Jihoon Myung[2], and Inkyu Lee[3]

[1] Digital Media Business, Samsung Electronics, Korea
[2] Dept of Computer Science and Engineering, Korea University, Seoul Korea
[3] Dept of Radio Communications Engineering, Korea University, Seoul Korea
wlee@korea.ac.kr

Abstract. Due to frequent handoff, Mobile IP has been confronted with some limitations. Cellular IP, one of micro-mobility protocols, was proposed to overcome these limitations and to provide good handoff performance. However, some drawbacks of Cellular IP like packet loss have been addressed. We propose an enhanced semi-soft handoff protocol based on a node's decision to cope with these drawbacks. With a bi-casting mechanism based on an explicit node decision, the proposed protocol can achieve fast and seamless handoff.

1 Introduction

Mobile IP [1] designed to support host mobility has been faced with some limitations – packet loss and high control overhead - due to frequent handoff. To cope with these limitations, micro-mobility protocols such as Cellular IP [2] and HAWAII [3] have been proposed. Especially, Cellular IP [2] has shown good performance despite of frequent handoff. Cellular IP has been designed to support seamless mobility and fast handoff. It uses the mobile routing mechanism instead of the tunneling mechanism so that it has shown better performance than hierarchical Mobile IP-based protocols [4].

However, some drawbacks of the bi-casting scheme for semi-soft handoff - packet loss and duplication - in Cellular IP have been addressed by [2][5][6]. These problems are caused by inconsistence of hop counts and amount of traffic between two paths – one between a crossover node and an old BS and the other between a crossover node and a new BS. To solve them, one approach [5] tries to calculate accurate delay time, and another approach [6] uses an indication message. These approaches still have limitations such as difficulty to measure delay and occurrence of packet duplication due to frequent changes of network conditions. Therefore, we propose an Enhanced Semi-Soft Handoff Protocol (ESSHP), which can overcome these problems.

The proposed semi-soft handoff protocol has aimed at seamless handoff without packet loss and duplication. This handoff scheme improves the semi-soft handoff

---

* This work was supported by KRF Grant (KRF-2003-041-D00509), KOSEF Grant (No. R01-2002-000-00141-0), and ETRI.
♦ Correspondent Author.

mechanism in Cellular IP, using a mobile node's decision. Thereby, the proposed protocol can ensure fast and seamless handoff without packet loss and duplication.

The rest of this paper is organized as follows: In Section 2, we present the overview and features of ESSHP. In Section 3, we compare ESSHP with Cellular IP through simulation results. Finally, in Section 4, we conclude this paper.

2 Enhanced Semi-soft Handoff Protocol (ESSHP)

The proposed semi-soft handoff protocol builds on a mobile node's decision and the fast handoff mechanism [7]. To protect packet loss and duplication, ESSHP depends on the decision of a mobile node because only a mobile node surely knows which packet it should receive. Basically, ESSHP handoff operations are based on the fast handoff mechanism, but we have modified some parts to eliminate unnecessary messages related to tunnels, to support the proposed bi-casting mechanism, and to reflect the decision of a mobile node.

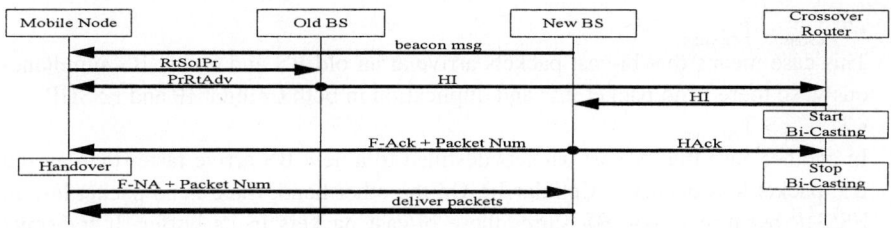

Fig. 1. Handoff Procedure of ESSHP

The handoff procedure of ESSHP is shown in Fig 1. When a mobile node starts handoff, it sends a Router Solicitation for Proxy (RtSolPr) message to inform an old BS with the information of a new BS. While the old BS replies a Proxy Router Advertisement (PtRtAdv) message to the mobile node, it sends a Handover Initiate (HI) message to the new BS via a crossover router. When the crossover router receives a HI message, it starts bi-casting. The new BS sends a Fast Acknowledgement (F-Ack) message to the mobile node to notify that it is ready to send packets. This F-Ack message includes useful information - *the first packet number* - to help the mobile node's decision. Also, it replies a Handover Acknowledgement (HAck) message to stop bi-casting. With the F-Ack message, the mobile node determines whether it attaches the new BS. If *the received packet number* which the mobile node has been received from the old BS is smaller than *the first packet number* from the new BS, it continues to receive packets from the old BS utile *the received packet number* is the same as *the first packet number - 1*. If *the received packet number* is bigger, it immediately attaches the new BS and transmits a Fast Neighbor Advertisement (F-NA) with its decision - *the next packet number* which it wants to receive. If *the next packet number* is bigger than the packets which the new BS has, the new BS waits for the packets which the mobile node requests. If *the next packet number* is smaller than the packets which the new BS contains, the new BS drops all packets prior to *the next packet number*. Thereby, ESSHP can provide seamless handoff without packet loss and duplication.

3 Performance Evaluation

We have experimented with NS-2 simulator [8] to examine the amount of packet loss and duplication and to measure TCP performance. Before showing simulation results, we describe three kinds of situations based on packet delivery time.

Table 1. Two Kinds of Packet Delivery Time

Notation	Definition
$T_{CR->OBS}$	Packet delivery time from a crossover node to an old BS
$T_{CR->NBS}$	Packet delivery time form a crossover node to a new BS

- $T_{CR->OBS} = T_{CR->NBS}$

This case means that bi-cast packets arrive at an old BS and a new BS simultaneously, so there is no packet loss and duplication in both Cellular IP and ESSHP.

- $T_{CR->OBS} > T_{CR->NBS}$

In another case that bi-cast packets destined to a new BS arrive faster than an old BS, packet loss occurs in Cellular IP. On the other hand, there is no packet loss in ESSHP because a new BS stores these bi-cast packets in its buffer. It transmits these packets when a mobile node requests.

- $T_{CR->OBS} < T_{CR->NBS}$

In the other case that bi-cast packets destined to an old BS arrive faster than a new BS, packet duplication occurs in Cellular IP. However, there is no packet duplication in ESSHP because a new BS drops all duplicated packets which a mobile node already receives from an old BS.

Fig2 (a) and (b) illustrate examples of packet loss and duplication in Cellular IP, and Fig2 (c) and (d) present examples of no packet loss and duplication in ESSHP.

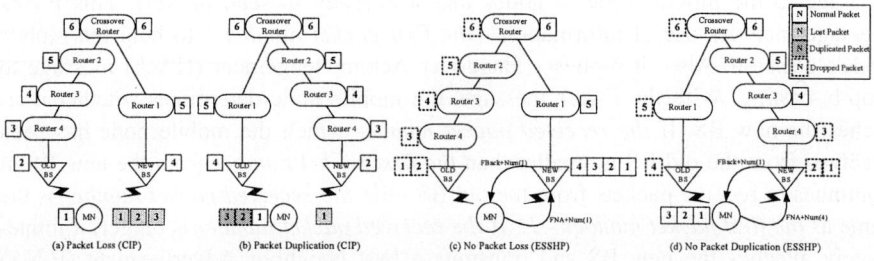

Fig. 2. Comparison of Cellular IP and ESSHP

To examine the performance of ESSHP and Cellular IP, we have implemented the proposed handoff protocol using the ns-2 simulator [8] and Cellular IP based on [9]. According to the first simulation results described in Fig 3 (a) and (b), amount of packet loss and duplication rises rapidly in Cellular IP as the gap between two distances increases. However, packet loss and duplication do not happen in ESSHP regardless of the increase of the gap. In TCP performance shown in Fig 3 (c) and (d), as the gap between two paths becomes bigger, the performance of Cellular IP becomes worse whereas that of ESSHP is not affected by the gap. In Cellular IP, the slow start mechanism is triggered by packet loss during handoff so that TCP throughput is degraded sharply. On the other hand, ESSHP shows stable TCP performance even though the gap increases. Based on the results of these experiments, it is obvious that ESSHP can provide seamless handoff without packet loss and duplication.

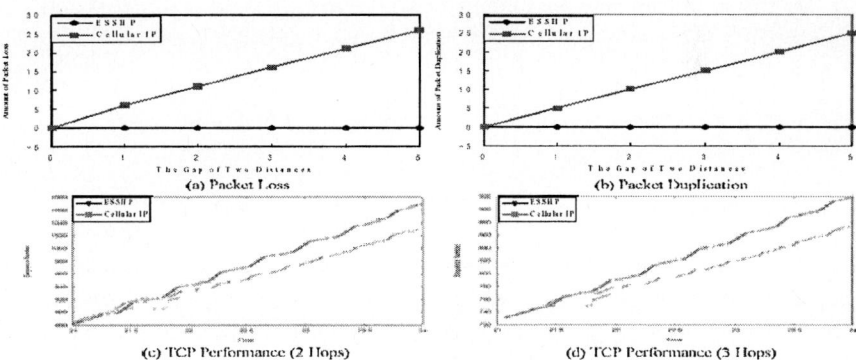

Fig. 3. Simulation Results

4 Conclusions

In this paper, we present an enhanced semi-soft handoff protocol which improves Cellular IP. To provide seamless and fast handoff, ESSHP depends on the fast handoff mechanism [7] and the decision of a mobile node which is helpful information for handoff. Especially, the decision of a mobile node assists to prevent occurrence of packet loss and duplication. With these features, we can insist that ESSHP be a suitable micro-mobility protocol in cellular network environment.

References

1. C. Perkins, "Mobile IP", IEEE Communications Magazine, May 2002.
2. A.T. Campbell, J. Gomez, S. Kim, Z. Turanyi, C-Y. Wan, and A. Valko, "Internet Micromobility", Journal of High Speed Networks, Special Issue on Multimedia in Wired and Wireless Environment, Vol. 11, No. 3-4, pp. 177-198, September 2002.

3. R. Ramjee, K. Varadhan, L. Salgarelli, S. Thuel, S.Y. Wang, and T. La Porta, "HAWAII: A Domain-based Approach for Supporting Mobility in Wide-area Wireless Networks", IEEE/ACM Transactions on Networking, Vol 10, No. 3, June 2002.
4. A.T. Campbell, J. Gomez, S. Kim, Z. Turanyi, C-Y. Wan, and A. Valko, "Comparison of IP Micro-Mobility Protocols", IEEE Wireless Communications Magazine, February 2002.
5. J. Lee, S. Kimura, and Y. Ebihara, "Advanced Semisoft Handoff Method of Cellular IP Access Networks", In Proceedings of AINA, Fukuoka, March 2004.
6. J.D. Kim, K.A. Kim, C. Kim, and J.Y. Park, "An Enhanced Handoff Mechanism for Cellular IP", In Proceedings of Third International Network Conference (INC 2002), July 2002.
7. R. Koodli, "Fast Handovers for Mobile IPv6", Internet-Draft, draft-ietf-mobileip-fast-mipv6-08, October 2003.
8. NS-2 simulator, http://www.isi.edu/nsnam/ns.
9. Micromobility home page, http://comet.ctr.columbia.edu/micromobility.

ISSRP: A Secure Routing Protocol Using Identity-Based Signcryption Scheme in Ad-Hoc Networks*

Bok-Nyong Park, Jihoon Myung, and Wonjun Lee[†]

Dept of Computer Science and Engineering,
Korea University, Seoul, Republic of Korea
wlee@korea.ac.kr

Abstract. We present a secure routing protocol based on identity-based signcryption scheme in ad-hoc networks. Because the proposed protocol uses identity-based cryptography, it can eliminate storage consumption and a certificate of public key exchange. Also, our protocol has very short ciphertexts/signatures and efficient computation time than other protocols based on RSA because it uses pairings over elliptic curves. In addition, the signcryption scheme fulfills both the functions of digital signature and encryption, and it thus can give savings in computation cost and communication overhead.

1 Introduction

The studies of secure routing in ad-hoc network have been carried out by ARAN [1], Ariadne[9], SRP [8], and so on [7]. ARAN [1] protocol consists of a preliminary certification process, a mandatory end-to-end authentication stage, and an optional second stage that provides secure shortest paths. Ariadne [9] protocol is an on-demand secure ad-hoc routing protocol based on DSR that withstands node compromise and relies on only highly efficient symmetric cryptography like hash function. SRP [8] provides correct routing information. However, such routing protocols neglect the inheritance feature of ad-hoc network such as resource-constrained in bandwidth, computational ability, energy, and so on. Also, they have high computation cost and communication overhead.

In this paper, our aim is to evaluate and optimize the effect in ad-hoc network when we apply the security schemes to be integrated with the ad hoc routing protocols. To improve the efficiency of computation, the proposed protocol, named ISSRP, uses the authentication algorithms based on the identity-based signcryption scheme [2]. The identity-based cryptography does not need to authenticate a public key [4]. The signcryption scheme can carry out both encryption and signature at one time [2]. In addition, the ISSRP can guarantee the efficiency of computation cost and communication overhead. Moreover, it can reduce the load of communication and

---

* This work was supported by Korea Research Foundation Grant (KRF-2003-041-D00509).
[†] Corresponding Author.

reply faster because it operates over elliptic curves [5]. This paper is organized as follows. Section 2 explains the secure routing protocol which uses identity-based signcryption scheme and section 3 shows the simulation and the performance analysis. Finally, Section 4 concludes the paper.

2 ISSRP

The protocol is abstracted as the exchange of two messages: route request and route reply. Our protocol is based on the following assumptions: (1) ISSRP is satisfied in the managed-open environment [1], (2) ISSRP is based on the identity-based signcryption scheme from pairings on elliptic curves [2], (3) All links between the nodes are bi-directional, and (4) We do not differentiate compromised nodes.

A sender achieves the route discovery to establish a path to a destination. The procedures of route request phase in the protocol are shown below:

Source → Intermediate: $< RREQ \parallel ID_S \parallel T \parallel Sig_S\{H(RREQ \parallel ID_S \parallel T)\} >$

Intermediate → Destination: $< RREQ \parallel ID_S \parallel ID_X \parallel T \parallel T_X \parallel Sig_S\{H(RREQ \parallel ID_S \parallel T)\} >$

A source node begins route instantiation to a destination node by broadcasting to its RREQ packet with the message for authentication. The functions of RREQ fields in this protocol are the same as those of RREQ fields of the general AODV [3]. Using ID, the source node computes public key and private key. An intermediate node X computes authentication information T for the authentication of the node which sends the message and it checks the message for the validity of T after verifying the sign. When this process is finished successfully, the intermediate node can trust the received message, and then it computes T_x using the same method. Finally, it broadcasts the message to the neighbor nodes. When the destination node receives the message, it checks the destination address. If the destination address is the same as its address, it verifies the signature, T, and T_x. If the verification is successful, it is ready to reply.

The destination node sends a RREP message to the source node. The procedures of route reply phase in the protocol are shown below:

Destination → Intermediate: $< RREP \parallel ID_D \parallel T \parallel T_D \parallel Sig_D\{H(RREP \parallel ID_D \parallel T \parallel T_D)\} >$

Intermediate → Source:
$< RREP \parallel ID_D \parallel ID_X \parallel T \parallel T_D \parallel T_X \parallel Sig_D\{H(RREP \parallel ID_D \parallel T \parallel T_D)\} >$

The destination node unicasts a RREP packet with a message for authentication back along the reverse path to the source node. RREP packet adds T_D which it generates including because the source node can trust the right reply to the message which the source sent. The computation method of T_D in the route reply follows the similar way in RREQ. Nodes that receive the RREP message forward the packet back to the predecessor from which they received the original RREQ message. When the source node receives the RREP packet with a message for authentication, it verifies that the correct hash value is returned by the destination node as well as the destination node's signature. If the verification of the digital signature and the T value is successful, the route can be established securely.

3 Performance Analysis

We have used the ns-2 simulator [6] for our evaluation. We start the simulations in order to compare the original AODV routing protocol without any security requirements and the AODV routing protocol with routing authentication extension.

3.1 Simulation Results

We simulated some simple scenarios by varying pause times in order to see the throughput in 900 second simulation time. For the 25 node experiments we used 5 and 20 traffic sources and a packet rate of 4 packets/s. We have done this study to illustrate that our scheme works for many security issues in the routing protocol, without causing any substantial degradation in the network performance.

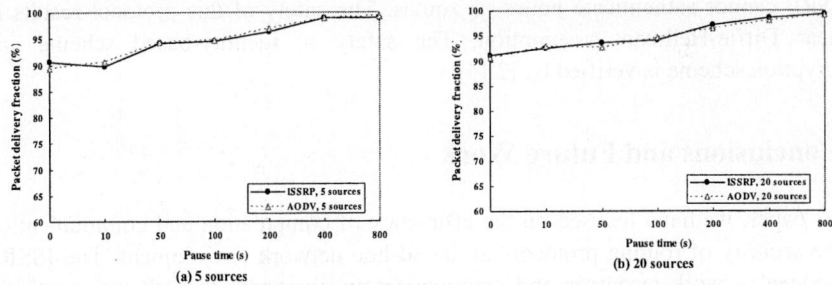

Fig. 1. Packet delivery fraction (%)

As results from Fig. 1, our ISSRP could work well in experiment because the effect of throughput of the network is small around 2-10%. The packet delivery fractions for AODV and ISSRP are very similar with 5 and 20 sources. With 20 sources, however, ISSRP has a better delivery fraction than AODV at higher pause times (Fig. 1b).

3.2 Efficiency Analysis

Protocols in ad-hoc network should be designed to satisfy the following requirements to provide the efficiency routing: low communication overhead, fast computation, and safety from widely known attacks. To satisfy these requirements, we use identity-based signcryption scheme based on pairings over elliptic curves [2][4] for checking the generation and verification of the digital signature instead of RSA algorithm. Generally, an elliptic curve whose order is a 160bit prime offers approximately the same level of security as RSA with 1024bit [5]. Thus ISSRP can use smaller parameters than with old discrete logarithm systems but with equivalent levels of security. In the Fig. 2, the graphs show that the overhead of the ISSRP in terms of routing load is very low because computation cost of the signcryption is very low than the other schemes.

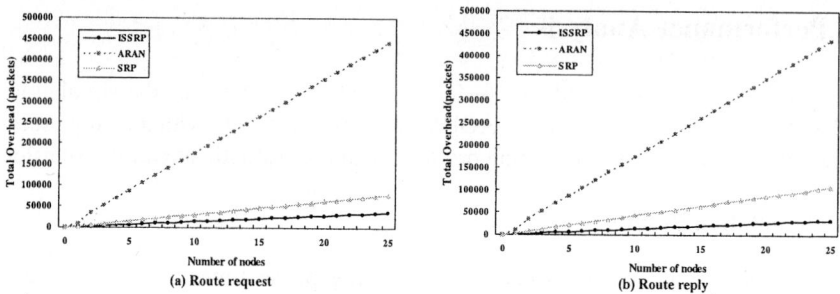

Fig. 2. Total Overhead

The proposed routing protocol can authenticate all of the nodes on routes with T generated by parameters based on identity-based signcryption scheme while ARAN and SRP cannot authenticate nodes on routes. The safety of this protocol results in Bilinear Diffie-Hellman Assumption. The safety of identity-based scheme and signcryption scheme is verified by [2][4].

4 Conclusions and Future Work

In this paper, we have focused on the efficiency of computation and communication for the security of routing protocols in the ad-hoc network environment. The ISSRP can reduce network resources and communication overheads than the conventional secure routing because of the features of identity-based signcryption and elliptic curve cryptography. We will study a secure protocol to guarantee the robustness in the wide area and not only to protect external attacks but also to detect the serious attacks from the compromised nodes and selfishness nodes.

References

1. B. Dahill, B. N. Levine, E. Royer, C. Shields, "ARAN: A secure Routing Protocol for Ad Hoc Networks," UMass Tech Report 02–21, 2002.
2. B. Libert, J-J. Quisquater, "New identity based signcryption schemes from parings," full version, available at http://eprint.iacr.org/2003/023/.
3. C. Perkins and E. Royer, "Ad-Hoc On-Demand Distance Vector Routing," in Proceedings of 2nd IEEE Workshop on Mobile Computing Systems and Applications, February 1999.
4. D. Boneh, M. Franklin, "Identity Based Encryption From the Weil Pairing," Advances in Cryptology-Crypto'01, LNCS 2193, Springer, 2001.
5. J. Lopez and R. Dahab, "Performance of Elliptic Curve Cryptosystems," Technical report IC-00-08, 2000., http://www.dcc.unicamp.br/ic-main/publications-e.html.
6. K. Fall and K. Varadhan, Eds., "ns notes and documentation," 1999; available from http://www-mahs.cs.berkeley.edu/ns/.
7. M. Ilyas, The Handbook of Ad-Hoc Wireless Networks, CRC PRESS, 2002.
8. P. Papadimitratos, Z. Haas, "Secure Routing for Mobile Ad Hoc Networks," in proceedings of CNDS 2002, San Antonio, TX, January 27–31, 2002.
9. Y. C. Hu, A. Perrig, D. B. Johnson, "Ariadne: A secure On-Demand Routing Protocol for Ad Hoc Networks," in proceedings of MOBICOM 2002.

Mobility Support Algorithm Based on Wireless 802.11b LAN for Fast Handover*

Sang-Dong Jang[1] and Wu Woan Kim[2]

[1] Division of Computer Science and Engineering, Kyungnam University,
Masan, South Korea
angong@kyungnam.ac.kr

[2] Division of Computer Science and Engineering, Kyungnam University,
Masan, South Korea
wukim@zeus.kyungnam.ac.kr

Abstract. IEEE 802.11 based wireless networks have seen rapid growth and deployment in the recent years. Critical to the 802.11 MAC operation, is the handover function which occurs when a mobile node moves its association from one access point to another. This paper presents a new approach adopting handover prediction to support seamless handover. In addition, the main idea of proposed method in this paper is to generate nCoA(new Care of Address) for fast handover by using CAM(Content associated Memory). nCoAs are constructed before entering into the new radio coverages of neighbor APs(Access point). When MN(Mobile Node) moves toward new AP, MN achieves BSSID(Basic Service Set ID) from new AP. And then MN compares it to decide nCoA that matches one of candidate Prefixes with BSSID in the MN's cache. If it matches, MN sends hit information to oAR. And then AR's cache writes this hit information to its own cache. And then the rest of FMIPv6 procedure is processed properly.

1 Introduction

The fast Internet evolution together with the enormous growth in the number of users of wireless technologies has resulted in a strong convergence trend towards the usage of IP as the common network protocol for both, fixed and mobile networks. Future *All-IP* networks will allow users to maintain service continuity while moving through different wireless systems.

Actually, the handover latency can be too long regarding real time multimedia applications. In most cases, the impact of the handover latency strongly degrades the IP stream of the mobile node. Therefore, there are many extensions to MIPv6 and new protocols proposed to improve the IP connectivity of mobile nodes. Hierarchical Mobile IPv6 [1] is the current IETF IPv6 micro-mobility proposal. Additionally, for applications that could suffer from long interruption times due to handoffs, Fast Handovers for Mobile IPv6 [2] has been designed.

---

* This work was supported by Kyungnam University Research Fund.

IEEE 802.11 based wireless local area networks (WLANs) have seen immense growth in the last few years. The predicted deployment of these networks for the next decade resembles that of the Internet during the early 90s. In public places such as campus and corporations, WLAN provides not only convenient network connectivity but also a high speed link up to 11Mbps (802.11b). In this paper, we are concerned with the IEEE 802.11b network which operates in the 2.4GHz range.

The IEEE 802.11 network MAC specification [4] allows for two operating modes namely, the ad hoc and the infrastructure mode. In the ad hoc mode, two or more wireless stations (STAs) recognize each other and establish a peer-to-peer communication without any existing infrastructure, whereas in infrastructure mode there is a fixed entity called an access point (AP) that bridges all data between the mobile stations associated to it. An AP and associated mobile stations form a Basic Service Set (BSS) communicating in the unlicensed RF spectrum.

In [5][6][7][8] tried to reduce the handover latency in IEEE 802.11 network, but it is not quite advanced method to reduce the latency.

The purpose of this paper is to reduce the time needed by these two protocols (MIPv6, FMIPv6) to move the flow of a mobile node from one access network to another. Our new approach is based on wireless IEEE 802.11b LAN. The main idea in this paper is to reduce handover latency by preparing some candidates(New CoAs and BSSIDs) in a MN's cache.

2 The Proposed Algorithmic Approach

2.1 Simulation Model

The follwing assumptions are made for simplicity.

1. The radio coverages of all APs are identical circles centered by the serving APs.
2. The Bolded line separates two regions connected to AR1 and AR2. Each AP has its own BSSID.
3. AP has a independent number if two or more AR's regions are overlapped
4. ARs have several information such as BSSIDs in some new AR's regions, new ARs prefixes, and independent number described in step. 3.
5. A independent number is a direction to indicate the new AP.

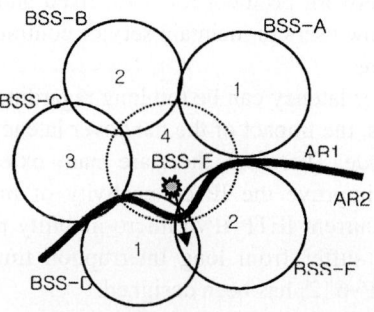

Fig. 1. Simulation Model

2.2 An Handover Algorithm in Wireless 802.11b LAN

For making new CoAs and performing its handover, the proposed approach is done by following procedures.

1. AR has its neighbor AR's prefixes, their AP's BSSID, each direction of overlapped regions and uses these information to make candidates of new CoA in advance. Table. 1 shows these information in AR1's cache.

Table 1. AR1's Information in Cache

Independent Number	BSSID	Candidate Prefix	Hit
1	BSS-D's ID	R2's Prefix	0
2	BSS-E's ID	R2's Prefix	0

2. MN predicts a place where it moves to. The place information is achieved by using predictive mobility management scheme in [7]. The predicted place is a independent number used as a direction. And then MN sends a message with a direction to oAR(current AR).
3. oAR receiving this message finds Candidate Prefixes that matches with a direction.
4. Once the oAR receives information that a MN wants to move to nARs, it constructs nCoAs based on the MN's interface ID and the nAR's subnet prefixes. It then sends a Proxy Router Advertisement (PrRtAdv) to the MN containing the proposed nCoAs and the nAR's IP addresses and link layer Addresses and BSSIDs. And then MN writes some of these information in the cache memory. At the same time, the oAR sends a Handover Initiate (HI) messages to the nARs, indicating the MN's oCoA and the proposed nCoA.

Table 2. MN's Cache Enrty

BSSID	nCoA
BSS-D's ID	R2's Prefix
BSS-E's ID	R2's Prefix

5. Upon receiving of the HI message, the correspond nAR establishes nCoA if the message is proper Neighbor Cache entry for the proposed nCoA..
6. If the nCoAs are accepted by the nARs, the nARs adds it to the Neighbor Cache for a short time period so they can defend it. The nAR then responds with a Handover Acknowledge (Hack), indicating that the proposed nCoA is valid.
7. Now, if MN moves toward some predicted neighbor AP, it compares neighbor's BSSID with its own cache's BSSID.
8. If it matches, then MN uses this nCoA that matches BSSID. After this step, the handover procedure is processed the way in[1].

3 Conclusions

Mobile IPv6 represents a key element of future *All-IP* wireless networks to allow a MN to freely roam between different wireless systems. A lot of researches have tried to reduce the handover latency in IEEE 802.11 network, but it is not quite improved to reduce the latency. The most of these results introduce unacceptable delay for real time applications.

Therefore, this paper presents a new approach adopting handover prediction method to support seamless handover. In addition, the main idea, which results in generating the fastest nCoA, with the proposed method is to generate nCoA for fast handover by using CAM. This keeps the order of *nano seconds* delay times for constructing nCoA.

However, it needs additional hardware for performing the proposed approach. Nevertheless it is not a serious problem due to the low cost hardware and the improved fabricating technologies for the necessary CAM.

The primary contribution of this paper is to provide a new approach. In the future, we plan to adopt these information in AR's cache to MPLS mechanism. Its information in MN's cache is useful to pingponging.

References

1. G.Tsirtsis, A.Yegin, C.Perkins, G.Dommety, K.El-Malki, and M.Khalil.: Fast Handovers for Mobile IPv6. IETF Internet Draft (March 2003)
2. Z. Shelby, D. Gatzounas, A. Campbell and C.-Y. Wan.: Cellular IPv6. IETF Internet Draft (November 2000)
3. Hinden, R. and S. Deering.: IP Version 6 Addressing Architecture. IETF RFC 2373 (July 1998)
4. Arunesh Mishra, Minho Shin, William Arbaugh.: An Empirical Analysis of the IEEE 802.11 MAC Layer Handoff Process. ACM SIGCOMM Computer Communication Review, Vol. 33. (April 2003)
5. Xavier Pérez-Costa, Marc Torrent-Moreno, Hannes Hartenstein.: A Performance Comparison of Mobile IPv6, Hierarchical Mobile IPv6, Fast Handovers for Mobile IPv6 and their Combination. ACM SIGMOBILE Mobile Computing and Communication Rev, Vol. 7. (Oct. 2003) 5–19
6. Arunesh Mishra, Minho Shin, William Arbaugh.: An Empirical Analysis of the IEEE 802.11 MAC Layer Handoff Process. ACM SIGMOBILE Computer Communication Rev, Vol. 33. (Apr. 2003)
7. G. Liu and G.Q. Maguire Jr., Efficient mobility management support for wireless data services. Proc. 45th IEEE Vehicular Technology Conference (VTC'95), Chicago, Illinois (July 26–28, 1995)
8. G. Liu and G.Q. Maguire Jr.: A virtual distributed system architecture for supporting global-distributed mobile computing. Technical Report, ITR 95-01 (December 1994).
9. T. Cornall, B. Pentland, and P. Khee.: Improved Handover Performance in Wireless Mobile IPv6, in Communication Systems, 2002. ICCS 2002. The 8th International Conference on, Vol. 2. (Nov. 2002) 857-861.

A Synchronized Hello Exchange Mechanism to Enhance IEEE 802.11 PSM in Mobile Ad Hoc Network[1]

Sangcheol Hong, Yeonkwon Jeong, and Joongsoo Ma

School of Engineering, Information and Communications University,
Deajeon, 305-714, Korea
{h3722, ykwjeong, jsma}@icu.ac.kr

Abstract. In this paper, we suggest a Synchronized Hello Exchange Mechanism improve IEEE 802.11 DCF-PSM in Mobile Ad-hoc Network. When IEEE 802.11 Power Saving Mode works with AODV, Power Saving Mode would be inefficient. PSM changes its state into a doze state when the node does not have any data to transmit or receive. However, in AODV, a node may determine connectivity by listening for hello packet from the neighbors. In stand-by state, because of the periodical local connectivity information exchange, nodes do not go into doze state, regardless of no data to transmit or receive. The node would dissipate the power staying in awake state. To solve this problem, we propose a Synchronized Hello Exchange Mechanism which makes distributed hello packet exchange synchronize. This proposal improves the performance of IEEE 802.11 PSM in stand-by state.

1 Introduction

MANET is a collection of wireless mobile hosts forming a temporary network without the established infrastructure or centralized control. Each node of the MANET uses a battery as a power source and designing techniques to reduce energy consumption is one of important research issues. IEEE 802.11 standard defines PSM for this purpose [2]. When each node does not have frames to receive or transmit, it stays in doze state during a BI(Beacon Interval). PSM can save energy because the electric current of doze state is less than that of wakeup state. In doze state, a node consumes very low power. On the other hand, every node should have routing path information to reach some destination nodes which want to transmit packets from a source node. AODV is one of the popular routing protocols to setup and maintain one or more routing paths in MANET environments [1].

As long as we choose IEEE 802.11 DCF-PSM for low power consumption MAC and AODV for routing protocol in a MANET, they make a critical problem in the viewpoint of the power saving due to the HELLO packet exchange. To maintain the MANET, each node must periodically exchange control information such as the HELLO packet of AODV. The period is defined by HI(HELLO Interval). The HELLO packet broadcasting requests all doze state nodes to wake up, even

---

[1] This research was supported by University IT Research Center Project.

though they do not have any application layer packets to transmit or receive. Therefore their power consumption increases exponentially while the number of participating nodes is linearly increased in a MANET.

Most of the former study about PSM centralized on only IEEE 802.11 MAC however nobody attempts to study the relationship between IEEE 802.11 DCF-PSM and HELLO packet in AODV. In this paper we will refine above problem with numerical model and propose our new SHEM(Synchronized Hello Exchange Mechanism) in Section 2. Section 3 will give the measurement results at CISCO 350 interface card and energy consumption model of IEEE 802.11 DCF-PSM and SHEM. Finally, we will make a conclusion in Section 4.

2 Observed Problem and Solution

2.1 Observed Problem

We point out that IEEE 802.11 DCF-PSM is inefficient in stand-by state when it operates with AODV. PSM mechanism saves energy by different power consumption between awake and doze state [3]. Our experiment shows that the amount of being consumed energy in the idle phase of awake state is approximately 4.7 times greater than that in the sleep phase of doze state. A HELLO packet helps IEEE 802.11 to organize efficient multi-hop ad-hoc networks by their own neighbors' local connectivity information. However, to broadcast a HELLO packet in IEEE 802.11 DCF-PSM, each node should send an ATIM frame within ATIM window to all neighbor nodes. After this broadcasting period, all nodes have to stay in awake state to send or receive HELLO packets.

To calculate the wasted amount of energy by broadcasting HELLO packet in stand-by state, we need to know what is $E[K]$, the expectation function of the number of BIs with N nodes during one HI. We use three parameters to get the $E[K]$ as follows:

- N is the number of stand-by state nodes of a MANET.
- S is the number of slots calculated by HI/BI. At the default values, S is 10 because of 1sec/100msec.[1]
- K is the number of BIs HELLO exchange will be expected to occur within one HI. Thus, the K means the number of BIs being wakeup state. By gathering the probabilistic cases of K, we can express $P(K)$, such as the formula (1).

Thus, Fig.1 shows our analysis result of $E[K]$, the expectation of K in a MANET, at increasing N. We know that each node broadcasts HELLO packets at 80% of slots when the number of nodes is 1.5 times greater than slots. For example, if N is 15 and S is 10 respectively, then each node has to wake-up within 8 slots. The number of dose node is only 3 nodes. So, the HELLO packet of AODV prevents the IEEE 802.11 DCF-PSM from sleeping and brings about high energy consumption in the stand-by state.

$$P(K) = \begin{pmatrix} sP_K \times (\frac{1}{S})^N \times \sum_{i_1=1}^{K} \times \cdots \times \sum_{i_{N-K}=1}^{i_{N-K-1}} (i_1 \times \cdots \times i_{N-K}) & ,1 \leq K < N \text{ and } 1 \leq K \leq S \\ sP_K \times (\frac{1}{S})^N & ,K = N \text{ and } 1 \leq K \leq S \end{pmatrix} \quad (1)$$

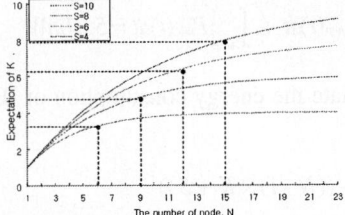

Fig. 1. $E[K]$ (expectation value of K) when N (the number of nodes) increases

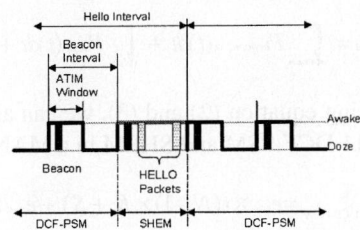

Fig. 2. Hello packet transmitting in SHEM

2.2 A Synchronized Hello Exchange Mechanism

We propose a SHEM to resolve the power consumption problem, which is due to HELLO packets in MANET. In SHEM, all nodes periodically wake up at predefined time interval and HELLO packet exchanges are only permitted during that interval.

For this purpose, we define two counters, *WakeUpCfg* and *WakeUpSts*, to maintain time synchronization among the nodes: *WakeUpCfg* counter contains the HI value of a MANET and is decided on the MANET initialization time, and *WakeUpSts* counter indicates the point when the node will wake up to exchange HELLO packet. We add these counter values on the reserved fields in capability element of beacon packet. It requires a simple modification to the current IEEE 802 standard and can be easily implemented. SHEM works as follows:

- First, the node setting up a MANET sets *WakeUpCfg* be HI and *WakeUpSts* to 0.
- When newly incoming node j makes association, *WakeUpCfg(j)* and *WakeUpSts(j)* are set into received values from beacon packet.
- In each beacon interval, node j wakes up to exchange HELLO packet if *WakeUpCfg(j)* mod *WakeUpSts(j)*=0. And set *WakeUpSts(j)*=0.
- At the end of a beacon interval, each node increases its *WakeUpSts(j)* by 1.

Fig. 2 shows the operations and the relationship between DCF-PSM and SHEM.

3 Experimental and Numerical Results

We measure circuit values of CISCO 350 interface card through experiments to get real values required to define an energy consumption model in stand-by state. We follow the process of Feeny's measurements [3]. Table 1 shows the measured currents and powers. Equation (2) and (3) give the energy consumption of an awake node($e_{s,a}$) and that of a doze node($e_{s,d}$) in stanad-by state.

$$e_{s,a} = \int_{t_{beacon}} P_{beacon,tx}(t)dt + \int_{t_{idle,aw}} P_{idle}(t)dt = 16.14mW \quad (2)$$

$$e_{s,d} = \int_{t_{beacon}} P_{beacon,rx}(t)dt + \int_{t_{sleep}} P_{sleep}(t)dt + \int_{t_{warmup}} P_{warmup}(t)dt + \int_{t_{idle,dz}} P_{idle}(t)dt = 5.67mW \quad (3)$$

Using equation (2) and (3), we can also calculate the energy consumption of IEEE 802.11 DCF-PSM and SHEM in a MANET.

$$E_{DCF-PSM} = e_{s,a} \times ((N-1) \times K + S) + e_{s,d} \times (N \times S - ((N-1) \times K + S)) \quad (4)$$

$$E_{SHEM} = e_{s,a} \times (N + S - 1) + e_{s,d} \times (N - 1) \times (S - 1) \quad (5)$$

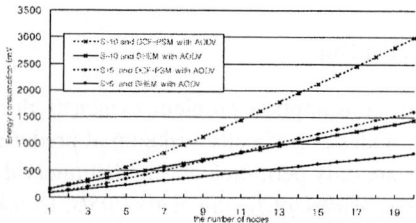

Phase	Current (mA)	Power (mW)
Sleep	35.07	168.91
Warmup	105.75	509.35
Idle	164.12	790.47
Receiving	198.17	954.51
Transmitting	270.83	1,304.48

Fig. 3. Energy consumption of SHEM and IEEE 802.11 DCF-PSM with AODV

Fig 3 shows total energy consumption of all nodes located on one hop range during one HI. In SHEM with AODV, we can see that the slope is stable. But in DCF-PSM with AODV, the slope increases gradually and the slope comes to about two times more steep than the slope of SHEM with AODV.

4 Conclusion

In this paper, we point out that 802.11 DCF-PSM is not efficient under stand-by state when it operates with AODV through the simulation. We also conduct measurement to get real values of energy consumption in the CISCO 350 interface card, and compare the energy consumption between 802.11 DCF-PSM and SHEM with AODV.

References

1. Charles E. Perkins, Elizabeth M. Belding-Royer, and Samir Das. : Ad Hoc On Demand Distance Vector (AODV) Routing, IETF RFC 3561.

2. IEEE 802.11 Standard: Part 11: Wireless LAN Medium Access Control (MAC) and Physical Layer (PHY) Specifications, 1999.
3. L. M. Feeney, M. Nilsson: Investigating the Energy Consumption of a Wireless Network Interface in an Ad Hoc Networking Environment. In Proc. of the 20th Annual Joint Conference of the IEEE Computer and Communications Societies (INFOCOM), Anchorage, AK, USA, April 2001.

Component Retrieval Using a Synaptic Connectivity Matrix

Young Wook Keum[1] and ByoungSeob Park[2]

[1] School of Computer Engieering, Sungkyul University,
Anyang Gyeonggi-do, 430-742, Korea
ywkeum@sungkyul.edu

[2] School of Computing and Information Systems, Inha Technical College,
Inchon, 402-752, Korea
bspark@inhatc.ac.kr

Abstract. Efficient retrieval of software components is an essential aspect of component-based software development. Enhancing the retrieval of such components has been the focus of significant prior research. We propose a new component retrieval method using a synaptic connectivity matrix. This new method supports queries with logical operators, which are not supported by existing facet retrieval methods. We show that the search complexity is considerably reduced with our proposed method.

1 Introduction

Component-based software development becomes more important due to the complexity and the high cost of software development. One of the essential issues is to find suitable components. Extensive research has been conducted on the component retrieval from the component repositories[1]. This paper contributes to the study of component-based software development as follows.

1. By extending a synaptic connectivity matrix, we devise a new retrieval method enabling queries with logical operators such as OR, AND and NOT, which are not supported with existing facet schemes.
2. The method uses matrix addition instead of matrix multiplication and the complexity reduces from $O(N \cdot F)$ to $O(N)$.

The rest of the paper is organized as follows. Section 2 describes the facet scheme, a widely used component retrieval method. Section 3 presents a new retrieval method and shows how we reduce complexity. Section 4 discusses related approaches. Lastly, section 5 summarizes our work and outlines future research plans.

2 Facet Scheme

Facets are groups of related terms in a subject area. This approach better structures the terms used for classifying the components. Facet schmes [2–4] use a facet list to describe a component, which is relatively easy to maintain.

3 New Method of Component Retrieval

3.1 Synaptic Connectivity Matrix

Neural network technology is popular in the knowledge representation, reasoning and rule extraction area[5]. To implement a facet scheme and enhance it for the retrieval with logical operators, we use the synaptic connectivity matrix(SCM) W, user query vector Q and retrieval output vector O in [3]. In the $N \times F$ SCM(where N is the number of the components in a component repository and F is the number of facet values), columns of the matrix represent components and rows represent facets. We define the following matrix to reflect the fact that a facet value may be contained in several components and/or a component may contain several facet values[3].

Definition 1. *Weighted synaptic connectivity matrix(WSCM) W'*

$$w'_{ij} = w_{ij} \cdot \frac{N/n_i}{\sum_{z=1}^{F} w_{zj}(N/n_z)}, \text{ where } \sum_{i=i}^{F} w'_{ij} = 1 \qquad (1)$$

In the definition, n_i is the number of components that contains facet value i.

3.2 Retrieval with Logical OR

We define the retrieval output vector of logical OR retrieval.

Definition 2. *Output vector O_{OR} of logical OR retrieval*

$$O_{OR} = Q \cdot W' \qquad (2)$$

3.3 Retrieval with Logical AND

To find a component that most closely satisfy a user query, we define the hit ratio vector and then the output vector of logical AND retrieval.

Definition 3. *Hit ratio vector H for a given query*

$$h_j(1 \leq j \leq N) = \frac{f_j}{f}, where\ f = \sum_{i=1}^{F} q_i, f_j = \sum_{i=1}^{F} q_i \cdot w_{ij} \qquad (3)$$

Definition 4. *An i−th element o_{AND_i} of output vector of logical AND retrieval*

$$o_{AND_i} = h_i \cdot o_{OR_i} \qquad (4)$$

3.4 Retrieval with Logical NOT

If we do not want a component with a facet value in the $k-th$ row of the SCM, we select a component j if $w_{kj} = 0$, or discard it if $w_{kj} = 1$. A new SCM is defined to support the NOT retrieval. Let $\overline{F}$ be a set of indexes in Q which require logical NOT retrieval.

Definition 5. *Synaptic connectivity matrix $\overline{F}W$ for NOT retrieval.*

$$\overline{F}W_{ij} = \begin{cases} 1 - w_{ij}, & \text{if } i \in \overline{F}, \\ w_{ij}, & \text{otherwise.} \end{cases} \quad (5)$$

Definition 6. *Weighted synaptic connectivity matrix $\overline{F}W'$ for NOT retrieval.*

$$\overline{F}w'_{ij} = \overline{F}w_{ij} \cdot \frac{N/n_i}{\sum_{z=1}^{F} \overline{F}w_{zj}(N/n_z)} \quad (6)$$

The complexity of computing $\overline{F}W'_{ij}$ is $O(F)$, so the complexity of computing $\overline{F}W'$ is $O(N \cdot F)$. To reduce the complexity we define the following vector.

Definition 7. *Weighted sum vector S.*

$$s_j = \sum_{i=1}^{F} w_{ij} \cdot (N/n_i), (1 \leq j \leq N) \quad (7)$$

The vector S is stored and used for the computation of $\overline{F}W$. If the weighted sum vector for the logical NOT retrieval is computed as in the following algorithm, the complexity is reduced from $O(N \cdot F)$ to $O(N)$.

Algorithm 1. Weighted Sum Vector $\overline{S}$ for Logical NOT Retrieval. An element $\overline{s}_j (1 \leq j \leq N)$ of $\overline{S}$ can be computed as follows.

$\overline{s}_j = s_j$
$for\ every\ k \in \overline{F}$
$\{\quad if\ w_{kj} = 0,\ \overline{s}_j = \overline{s}_j + N/(N - n_k)$
$\quad else \quad \overline{s}_j = \overline{s}_j - N/n_k\ \}$

We now compute an $i-th$ row of WSCM $\overline{F}w'$ for logical NOT retrieval.

Algorithm 2. Computing. $\overline{F}w'_{ij}(1 \leq j \leq N)$ **which is the i-th row of $\overline{F}W'$.**
$for\ (j = 1; j \leq N; j + +)$
$\{\quad if\ i \in \overline{F}$
$\quad\quad if\ w'_{ij} = 0$
$\quad\quad\quad \overline{F}w'_{ij} = \frac{N/(N - n_i)}{\overline{s}_j}$
$\quad\quad else$
$\quad\quad\quad \overline{F}w'_{ij} = 0$
$\quad else$
$\quad\quad \overline{F}w'_{ij} = \frac{w'_{ij} \cdot s_j}{\overline{s}_j}\ \}$

The complexity of computing the i-th row of $\overline{F}W'$ is reduced from $O(N \cdot F)$ to $O(N)$. The complexity of computing the i-th row of $\overline{F}W'$ is $O(N)$ because we have a few indexes in $\overline{F}$.

3.5 The Procedure of Computing a Retrieval Output Vector

In summary, we show how an output vector is computed for a given query.

1. A query is received.
2. Obtain two sets of indexes: Set $A(\overline{F})$ which has all the indexes that are listed as $1(\overline{1})$ in the query.
3. For any index in $\overline{F}$ which represents NOT retrieval, recompute the index-th row of the WSCM using the algorithm 1 and 2.
4. Compose new matrix TW' with only rows whose indexes appear in A or $\overline{F}$. The order of rows in the matrix does not matter any more at this stage.
5. Obtain an output vector by summing up entries in each column of TW'.
6. If this is an AND retrieval, multiply the output vector by h_i.
7. Sort and display the indexes of the output vector in the descending order.

We replace the matrix multiplication with the matrix addition in step 5. In step 6 we also use matrix addition in computing h_i with rows only in A and $\overline{F}$.

4 Related Work

The other facet methods[2–4] consider only OR retrieval. The approach in [3] uses sparse matrix multiplication but we reduce the complexity much further.

5 Conclusion and Future Works

Efficient retrieval of components in a component repository is important for component-based software development. Our new proposed retrieval method provides more powerful retrieval with logical operators such as OR, AND and NOT. In computing an output vector from a synaptic connectivity matrix and a query vector, the complexity is reduced from $O(N \cdot F)$ to $O(N)$ and matrix addition is used instead of complex matrix multiplication.

Our further research plan includes implementing a component repository applying our retrieval method thus producing performance comparison with our proposed method and other retrieval methods.

References

1. J. Guo and Luqi, "A survey of Software Reuse Repositories," Proceedings of the 7th IEEE Int. Conf. and W/S on the Eng. of Computer Based System, pp.88-96, 2000
2. R. Priesto-Diaz, "Implementing Faceted Classification for Software Reuse," CACM, Vol. 34, No. 5, pp. 89-97, May 1991.
3. Zhiyuan Wang, "Component-Based Software Engineering," Doctorial Dissertation, Department of Computer and Information Science, New Jersey Institute of Technology, Newark, New Jersey, 2000

4. Hsian-Chou Liao et al, "Using a Hierarchical Thesaurus for Classifying and Searching Software Libraries," Proc. of the COMPSAC '97, pp. 210-216, 1997
5. F.J. Kurfess, "Neural Networks and Structured Knowledge," Special Issue of Journal of Applied Intelligence, vol. 11, no. 1, pp. 135-146, 1999.

A Rule Filtering Component Based on Recommendation Agent System for Classifying Email Document

Ok-Ran Jeong and Dong-Sub Cho

Department of Computer Science and Engineering,
Ewha Womans University,
11-1 Daehyun-dong, Seodaemun-ku, Seoul 120-750, Korea
{orchung, dscho}@ewha.ac.kr

Abstract. The increased use of Internet generalizes the use of e-mail, a medium for information exchange. E-mail is used not only for individual purposes but also in a variety of purposes that users have to process significant volume. In this study, we propose a recommendation agent system the enable users for direct and optimal classification with the recommendation of the applicable category when a mail arrives as a way of efficient management of e-mail. For this purpose, three pre-processing algorithms are suggested for accurate classification, the core part of this study, and, it considers the scalability and reusability with the major filtering part is based on the rule-filtering component.

Keywords: recommendation system, e-mail, pre-processing algorithm, rule filtering component.

1 Introduction

Together with the trend of increasing use of Internet, the volume of e-document has been on the rise exponentially. On-line document, e-mail document, Internet news document, medical information document, digital library document and others that are encountered on WWW are the electronic documents. As the electronic document significantly expanded quantitatively, classifying these numerous information for each service by human is literally impossible. Accordingly, there is a growing demand on the tools that help making appropriate classification for document. In response to these demands, this study applies the existing document classification to the e-mail system to execute the automatic classification in advance in a way to propose the system to recommend the applicable category to the users in the order of priority. The document classification system in general means the system to automatically classify the text document into the category already set. There are studies on actual application [1]. by using this type of automatic classification of document, such as classification of news, routing of vast volume of e-mail to the applicable department and the like.

In this study, three pre-processing algorithms are proposed for accurate and automatic classification of e-mail for users, and by utilizing the system; the e-mail application system is designed and realized with the recommendation of most appropriate category for users. First, the preponderance of the e-mail document is considered. The e-mail document is composed of the title and the main text with the added weight on the title more than that of the main text. Second, for automatic classification, there is a need of feature extraction and learning stage. In order to improve the accuracy in this stage, the selection of learning document for feature extraction when generating the rules is very important. The rules can be made through learning by using the discretional learning document group just the way it is, but if this is intelligently reconfigured and used, more accurate rules may be formulated. Lastly, determining the accuracy of the document classification is the algorithm that presumes the formulation of rules. The role of this algorithm is to form the rules in final by using the learning document group selected by the configuration of the learning document group. There are decision tree algorithm, k-nearest neighbor algorithm, neural network algorithm, Naive Bayesian algorithm, and support vector machine [2, 3]. The document classification system using the Naive Bayesian algorithm is known to have relatively higher accuracy of the document classification than other algorithms [3]. In addition, according to this algorithm, the rule generation for the classification is very simple, and furthermore, with the speed of the document classification, structuring of the document classification system is frequently used. Therefore, The works to heighten the accuracy of the e-mail document classification based on the Naive Bayesian algorithm. The existing algorithm used the threshold, and under this study, the threshold is improved for dynamic threshold in a way of enhancing the accuracy of the document classification. In addition, by the component-based module that takes an important role when the recommendation system is visualized in a way of heightening of the scalability and reusability.

2   Existing Automatic Classification System

The Existing automatic classification system had been verified only be the experiment of standardized data that, in the event of processing the e-mail document that is not standardized and with a lot of noise, the capability is not up to the expectation. There is a high interest in classification system studies related to its characteristics, however, the practical comparative experiment analysis has been very trivial. It may not be the concrete experiment analysis related to the pre-processing module introduction to improve the classification capability, but the study related to the e-mail automatic classification of document for designing of pre-processing algorithm is summarized in two folds. It describes the method of feature extraction that can be the core parts in the Naive Bayesian algorithm and pre-processing, the foundation theory of classification by using the probability. Nave Bayesian algorithm receives the document and classify the document in the way of calculating the probability allotted to each category. In order to calculate the probability belong to a specific category. The automatic classification of document means the use of various classification techniques to divide the new document to already defined types automatically. The process is largely classified into the pre-processing stage, feature extraction stage, and document classification stage. In this study, the pre-processing stage, that is the previous step of the document classification stage and the feature extraction stage are collectively defined as the pre-processing stage.

3 E-Mail System Based Pre-processing Algorithm

3.1 Weight Assigning Method

The e-mail document, subject for the pre-processing, is consisted of the title and main body. The pre-processing machines remove the special signs, the unnecessary element in expression the information of the document. And, the title and main body are classified and generate the token and arrange it. In this stage, the tag along the 1-byte signs is removed. In the next stage, the 1-byte signs and tag are removed. For the next stage, the pre-processor loads the expressions belonged to abbreviation, slang and specific group onto the user dictionary that standardizes the expressions to maintain in serial condition. In the next stage, the pre-processor maps the e-mail document and loaded user dictionary made in vector form by removing the unnecessary sign and tag information to convert the non-standardized words shown on the e-mail document into the standardized words. Along with that, in order to heighten the insights on the words shown on the title of this e-mail document, the duplication method is used and heightens the weight value. Manager of the mail server adjusts the weight value on the title when used in the feature extraction stage.

3.2 Uncertainty Based Sampling Algorithm

Active learning algorithm selects the document with the large information volume from the entire document group, and adds into the learning document group for formulating rules. Well-drafted rule takes the largest role in raising the accuracy when classifying that the learning document group for formulating the rules is very important and the uncertainty based sampling algorithm is applied at this time. Another word, the standard to determine the document with large information volume from the active learning algorithm is in diverse, and the most representative thing is to use the uncertainty concept [4–6]. From the active learning algorithm, the algorithm that uses the foregoing concept is referred in particular as the uncertainty based sampling algorithm. According to it, the document with large volume of information is the document that the current document classification rule is difficult to classify. The document that is difficult to classify the document classification rule means the document that has little confidence when determining the category of document given by inputting the document classification rule. This type of document is located on the boundary that divides a category and a category that it would be difficult to allot in what category with any kind of certainty. When selecting these as the learning document and allot to the accurate categories, more accurate document classification rule can be developed. The uncertainty based sampling algorithm measures the uncertainty in all documents within the document group that has no labeling, and then select the document with significant uncertainty and selects it as the learning document. The uncertainty can be defined under the document classification algorithm that may forecast the category and display the assurance on this forecast in figures. From the Naive Bayes document classification algorithm, the two measure values that specify the uncertainty is typically the reliability and the mean absolute deviation (MAD). In this study, the later with more effective in accuracy was used. Looking at the uncertainty measurement by using the MAD [5], the uncertainty is measured by using how the values of $P(c|x)$ defined earlier is separated from the average of the values μ. This is defined as follows.

$$U_{MAD}(x) = \frac{1}{|c|}\sum_{i=1}^{|c|}(P(c_i|x) - \mu), \mu = \frac{1}{|c|}\sum_{i=1}^{|c|}P(c_i|x) \quad (1)$$

$U_{MAD}(x)$ means the probability that the distance of document x belongs to each category or the average distance separated from the average of the values that the uncertainty is larger as $U_{MAD}(x)$ becomes smaller, and the uncertainty is smaller as it becomes larger. As shown on the experiment of the next person, the uncertainty based sampling algorithm is applied to the Naive Bayesian document classification algorithm to greatly improve the accuracy of the e-mail recommendation system.

3.3 Dynamic Threshold

The existing threshold used in the Naive Bayesian algorithm is improved in dynamics to improve the accuracy of the filtering. Under this study, the e-mail document classification is made through the representative teaching algorithm for document classification, Bayes learning technique. C is referred to asentire category group, and C_0 is the case where classification is impossible. Let's assume that the entire group of the e-mail documents is D. Under the Naive Bayes Classification Method, the conditional on each category of c_j for document d_i is calculated under the equation(2).

$$\Re(d_i) = \{P(d_i|C_1), P(d_i|C_2), P(d_i|C_3), ..., P(d_i|C_k)\} \quad (2)$$

In most systems, the classification is made for category with the highest probability value, as in equation (3), on the subject document for classification. However, in this study, the threshold T that used the existing Bayes algorithm is converted to the dynamic threshold T' by equation (4). When dynamic threshold T' was applied for the capability assessment of this system, the improved accuracy result was displayed.

$$P_{max}(d_i) = max\{P(d_i|C_t)\}, \ t = 1, 2, ..., k \quad (3)$$

$$C_{best}(d_i) = \begin{cases} \{C_j|P(d_i|C_j)\} = P_{max}(d_i) & \text{if } P_{max}(d_i) \geq T' \\ & \text{where } T' = 1 - \frac{P_{max}(d_i)}{\sum_{j=1}^{k}P(d_i|C_j)} \\ C_0 & \text{otherwise} \end{cases} \quad (4)$$

In one category, the probability value of each e-mail document following the applicable drawing, and here, use T' to adjust the threshold to improve the classification speed and prevent the erroneous classification.

4 Component Based Application System

4.1 Implementation of Application System

In order to apply the earlier proposed pre-processing algorithm to actual e-mail system, the web-mail based e-mail system is implemented. For the use of environment, Windows 2000 Professional is used, and MS-SQL 2000 Server for DB control, MS Visual C++ 6.0 for rule formation and execution of algorithm, COM+ to make component for major functions, and ASP and ASP components are used for other functions. The overall system is designed by module and each module communicates by shared files. The details roles are explained below.

- The Web Mail Interface Module (WMI): When a new mail arrives, the system firstly monitors and learns the mail processing of a user. This module helps to extract the features and set the rules. Furthermore, it is the process to set the categories suitable for the personal needs of a user.
- The Category Rule Generation Module (CRG): It extracts the features in mail processing and generates the rules in accordance with the personal needs as applying Bayesian algorithm.
- The Mail Classification & Recommendation Module (MCR): When a new mail arrives, it classifies mails by category on the basis of defined rules and recommends the mails by category in accordance with the priority.

The user interface belongs to the WMI module is used in the user observation process, and the actual user may make the category generation and store. Through this process, the feature extraction is made and the document classification rule is formed under the CRG module. On the basis of the formulated rules, the automatic classification is made at the MCR module in advance, and recommends the applicable category to the users. Under this application system, the main functions, namely, the feature extraction, formation of learning and rule, actual classification and recommendation function are re-implemented in COM+ so that it considered the scalability and reusability to be applied in other document classification system. In addition, it may be conveniently used under the dispersion environment. Major interface and method are shown on Fig. 1.

4.2 Experiment and Result Analysis

The performance evaluation of document classification system is measured in general by the barometers of recall ratio and precision ratio. The ratio call is the ratio of appropriate records and documents classified by the classification system from the appropriate records and documents within the document classification

```
IRuleFilter
{
HRESULT SetDBOpen(BSTR bstrDBConnect,BSTR bstrDBID,BSTR bstrDBPW);
HRESULT MergeMail(BSTR bstrID,BSTR bstrRuleName,BSTR bstrMailData);
HRESULT CheckFolder(BSTR bstrID, BSTR bstrMailData,[out,retval] BSTR *pRet);
HRESULT CheckFolders(BSTR bstrID, BSTR bstrMailData,[out,retval] BSTR *pRet);
};
SetDBOpen(DBOPEN, DBID, DBPW);
MergeMail(ID, RuleName, MailData);
CheckFolder(ID, MailData);
CheckFolders(ID, MailData);
```

Fig. 1. Rule Filtering Component

system, and the precision ratio is the ratio of appropriate records and documents from the entire records and documents classified [7]. These two measure value are all very important in assessing the document classification system that there is a need for measure value that reflected both points, and measure value F_1 is used for this purpose. The following is the expression of the F_1 measure value.

$$F_1 = \frac{2 * recall * precision}{recall + precision} \quad (5)$$

The above described recall and precision F_1, measure values are to assess individually for each of the category capability. In order to assess the average capability on all categories, the macro-averaging method is used herein. For the equation (5), the recall, precision, and F_1 measure value for each category are calculated, and by using this value, the macro averaging is calculated to assess the capability of the entire system.

Table 1. F1 measure and Macro-averaging of each pre-processing algorithm

Num	Category Item	Total	F1 (BA)	F1 (DV)	F1 (SA)	F1 (DT)
1	Sale	38434	0.860	0.870	0.880	0.910
2	Autos	23712	0.920	0.910	0.900	0.920
3	Sports	17124	0.890	0.870	0.880	0.870
4	Electronics	12354	0.940	0.950	0.950	0.990
5	Politics	7971	0.840	0.840	0.830	0.850
6	Computer	573	0.930	0.950	0.940	0.970
7	Graphics	23579	0.910	0.910	0.920	0.860
8	Hardware	1578	0.830	0.830	0.840	0.850
9	Space	11694	0.850	0.870	0.860	0.940
10	Talk	62915	0.890	0.870	0.870	0.850
11	Language	14180	0.880	0.910	0.910	0.910
12	Spam	7260	0.890	0.900	0.920	0.920
	Macro-averaging		0.886	0.890	0.892	0.903

5 Conclusion

Today, numerous volume of information is exchanged through e-mail, and users would demand custom-made e-mail interface. If the mail document applies the general document classification system to enable the users to recommend the accurate categories for classification, the mail system can be managed much more conveniently. For the accurate classification for each category of the e-mail document, this study suggests 3 steps for the useful pre-processing algorithm. When managing ever-extending mail, the e-mail application system using the pre-processing algorithm that we suggested would be utilized very usefully. For the future studies, we have applied the pre-processing algorithm onto the document classification presumption algorithm. Naive Bayes, however, recently, it may be applied to the SVM algorithm that is frequently used in structuring the document classification system in recent days. In addition, the major module parts are made in components that the experiment is made by using the Reuteer-21578 document group, the standard data of the text classification for comparative analysis with the outcome of the time it is applied to the general text document.

References

1. Sebastiani, F.: Machine Learning in Automated Text Categorization, Technical Report IEI-B4-31-1999, Istituto di Elaborazione dell' Informazione, Consiglio Nazionale delle Ricerche, Pisa, IT, (1999). 313-331
2. Pedro Domingos and Michael Pazzani. Beyond Independence: Conditions for the Optimality of the Simple Bayesian Classifier. In Proceedings of the 13th International Conference on Machine Learning, (1996) 105-112
3. Jee-Haeng Lee and Sung-Bae Cho :An Automatic Classification System for Hanmail Net Questions Using Multiple Neural Networks, Proceedings of the 27th KISS Fall Conference,(2000) 232-234
4. David D. Lewis and William A.Gale: A Sequential Algorithm for Training Text Classifiers. In Proceedings of the 17th Annual International ACM-SIGIR Conference on Research and Development in Information Retrieval, (1994) 3-12
5. David D. Lewis and Jason Catlett.: Heterogeneous Uncertainty Sampling for Supervised Learning. In Proceedings of the 11th international Conference on Machine Learning, (1994) 148-156
6. M. Trensh, N. Palmer, and A. Luniewski : Type Classification of Semi-structured Documents. In Proceedings of the 21st ACM SIGMOD International Conference on Management of Data, (1995) 263-274
7. Konstan, J.A., Miller, B.N., Maltz, D., Herlocker, J.L., Gordon, L.R. and Riedel, J. : GroupLens: Applying Collaborative Filtering to Usenet News. CACM, 40(3), (1997) 77-87

Globally Synchronized Multimedia Streaming Architecture Based on Time-Triggered and Message-Triggered Object Model*

Eun Hwan Jo, Doo-Hyun Kim, Hansol Park, and Moon Hae Kim

Konkuk University, Seoul, Korea
{ehjo, doohyun, parkhs, mhkim}@konkuk.ac.kr

Abstract. In this paper, we present a new multimedia stream synchronization mechanism based on a real-time object model named Time-triggered Message-triggered Object (TMO). Especially, the global time and time-triggered features of TMO are used to achieve *inter-location synchronization* among multiple receivers. The usage of the global clock not only enhances the accuracy of the synchronization among distributed nodes, but also provides developers simple but powerful means for specifying the synchronization requirements from the design time. By showing experimental results of the one-sender two-receivers streaming application, we suggest, in this paper, that this global time based approach is also practically meaningful.

1 Introduction

Stream is a sequence of media data units with temporal constraints. Streaming, which is the processing of a stream, is embodied by a chunk of codes or an object which receives a stream, changes certain characteristics of the stream by applying filtering operations, and outputs the processed stream. In this paper, we present a real-time multimedia streaming architecture, called MMStream TMO, to facilitate the development of globally synchronized distributed multimedia applications.

Our architecture uses TMO model as a fundamental framework and utilizes TMOSM(TMO Support Middleware) as the execution engine for our experiments [1, 2]. TMO is a natural, syntactically minor, and semantically powerful extension of the conventional object(s) [1]. Particularly, TMO is a high-level real-time computing object. Member functions (i.e., methods) are executed within specified time. Timing requirements are specified in natural intuitive forms with no esoteric styles imposed. As depicted in Fig. 1, the basic TMO structure consists of four parts:

- *Spontaneous Method (SpM)*: A time-triggered (TT) method which is triggered when the real-time clock reaches specific values determined at design time and specified in *AAC*(Autonomous Activation Condition) as the time-windows for execution.
- *Service Method (SvM)*: A method similar to the conventional service method which is triggered by service request messages from clients.

---

* This research was supported by University IT Research Center Project, MIC, KOREA, 2004.

- *Object Data Store (ODS)*: A basic unit of storage which can be exclusively accessed by a certain TMO method at any given time or shared among concurrent of TMO methods (SpMs or SvMs).
- *Environment Access Capability (EAC)*: A list of entry points to remote object methods, logical communication channels, and I/O device interfaces.

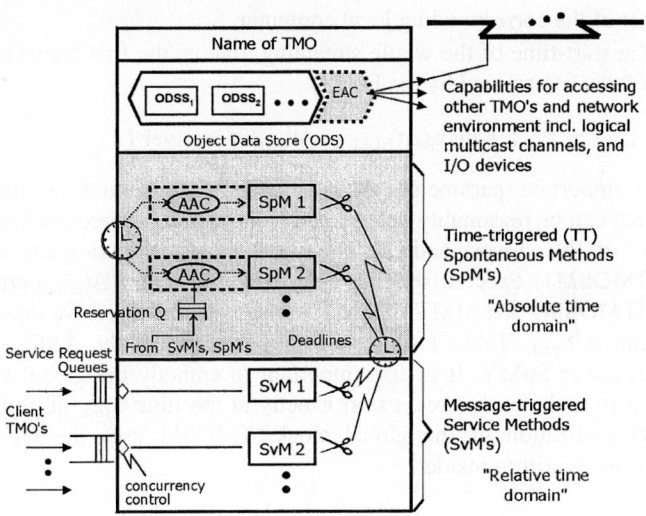

Fig. 1. Structure of TMO[1]

2 Global Synchronization Mechanism

Among the various features of the TMO programming scheme mentioned above, some of the fundamental features can enable efficient programming of complex distributed multimedia applications. TMO enables the programmer to design global time based coordination of distributed multimedia actions, and provides a sound foundation for programming and executing distributed multimedia streaming and presentation requiring global synchronization among the media units or among the nodes. Also, the clear separation and BCC between SpMs and SvMs allow the use of the SpM, the time-triggered spontaneous method, as an accurate means for periodic stream processing. Furthermore, when the TMO execution engine is supported by real-time platforms, the SpM can perform more precise inter- and intra-stream synchronizations [3].

Utilizing the global time feature of the TMO, we can simply devise a novel synchronization mechanism that provides *inter-location* synchronization among multiple receivers distributed through the network. The key of the mechanism is to make the period of processing each streamed frame be started as exactly same global time as possible at each receiver side. In order to achieve such relatively fine-grained global action, the SpM can be effectively used by carefully determining following parameters at design time and defining AAC's of each engaged SpM according to the determined parameters:

- Δt_{intra}: the period for processing each frame.
- Δt^i_{NDEL}: the maximum delay of communication caused by routing, transmission and protocol processing.
- Δt^i_{buff}: the maximum of buffering delay for de-jittering the jitters possibly caused by communication and OS. This parameter should also be the worst-case estimation that can be reasonably determined from the statistics of short-term behavior of the corresponding local computer.
- t_{synch}: the start-time of the whole streaming, that is, the first frame actually. This parameter is determined by the Eq. (1).

$$t_{synch} = t^1_{start} + \max_i(\Delta t^i_{NDEL} + \Delta t^i_{buff}) \ \forall receiver\ I \qquad (1)$$

The two important parameters, Δt^i_{NDEL} and Δt^i_{buff}, should be the worst-case estimation that can be reasonably determined from various sources such as short-term QoS statistics of the network and OS. The Fig. 2 shows a situation when the sender's SpM (MMTMOSM1) execute sending each frame at every Δt_{intra} period, and two SpM's (MMTMOSM2 and MMTMOSM3) at receiver nodes receive these frames and start rendering at t_{synch}. Table 1 illustrates specifications of the AAC's for both the sender and receiver SpM's. It is also important to embody the global clock at each node in order to make each stream start exactly at the time t_{synch} in global time. For this physical realization of the global clock, TMOSM uses the GPS and clock synchronization algorithm inside.

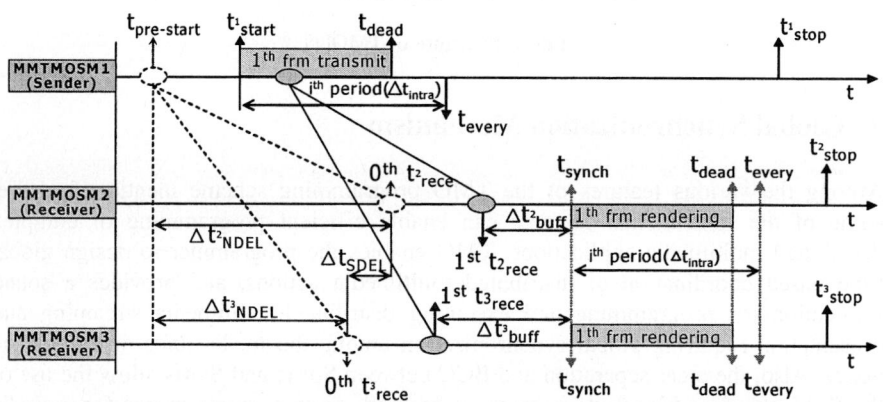

Fig. 2. Global synchronization mechanism for two-receiver streaming

Table 1. AAC Specifications for global synchronization among multiple receivers

AAC Specification for Sender SpM	AAC Specifications for Sender SpMs
for t = from t^1_{strat} **to** t^i_{stop} **every** Δt_{intra} **start-during**(t, t + OS_DELAY) **finish-by** t + t_{dead}	**for** t = from t_{synch} **to** t^i_{stop} **every** Δt_{intra} **start-during**(t, t + OS_DELAY) **finish-by** t + t_{dead}

3 Experimental Results

Fig. 3 shows our experimental results of one-sender two-receivers streaming of an audio data in a LAN environment. For our experiment, we made artificial situation where every other two packets toward one receiver is delayed by one period. Fig. 3(a) shows that the synchronization skews between the corresponding audio packets span the range of 50ms in case when we did not used our proposed TMO-based synchronization mechanism. Fig. 3(b), however, reveals that the synchronization skews are dramatically decreased to the range of 1ms and fairly steady as the two SpM's in each node play out those packets at right global time with accurate regularity. We used TMOSM/Linux [3] and PC's with 1.5 GHz Pentium IV processor, and packetized the 8 KHz PCM audio data at every 512 bytes.

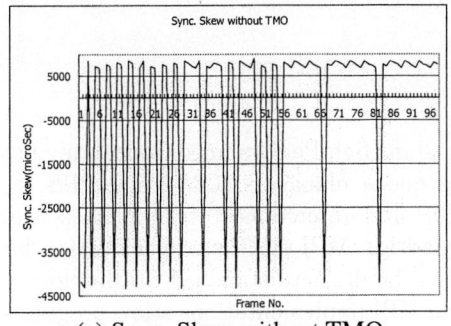 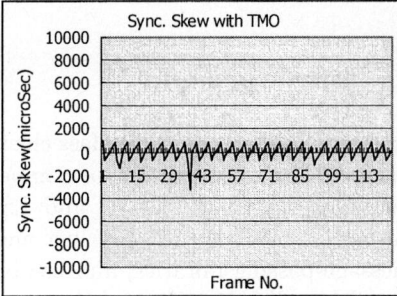

(a) Sync. Skew without TMO (b) Sync. Skew with TMO

Fig. 3. Traces of Synchronization Skew between two receivers of an audio stream

4 Conclusions

We, in this paper, presented a mechanism for inter-location synchronization using the global time and time-triggered features of TMO, and also explained the usage of the global clock for enhancing the accuracy of the synchronization among distributed nodes. The time-triggered spontaneous feature of TMO was also used to enhance the tolerance to the irregular deliveries of media units. By showing experimental results of the one-sender two-receiver streaming application, we have shown that our global time based approach is practically meaningful for such applications that the global or inter-location synchronization is mandated.

References

1. Kim, K.H., "APIs for Real-Time Distributed Object Programming," *IEEE Computer*, June 2000, pp.72-80.
2. Kim, D.H, "A TMO-based Software Architecture for Distributed Real-time Multimedia Processing," *Proc. WORDS2003*, Guadalajara, Mexico, Jan. 2003.
3. Kim, H.J., Park, S.H., Kim, J.G., and Kim, M.H., "TMO-Linux: A Linux-based Real-time Operating System Supporting Execution of TMOs", *Proc. ISORC '02*, Apr. 2002.

A Universal Machine File Format for MPI Jobs

Francis Tang, Ho Liang Yoong, Chua Ching Lian, and Arun Krishnan

Bioinformatics Institute, Matrix L7, 30 Biopolis St, Singapore
{francis, lyho, chuacl, arun}@bii.a-star.edu.sg

Abstract. Beowulf-class clusters use a diverse collection of queue management software, and interconnect technology, often causing inter-cluster operability issues. We present a Universal Machine File format to allow easy migration between these modern supercomputers.

1 Introduction

The popularity of Beowulf-class clusters [2] in High Performance Computing has resulted in a proliferation of competing queue managers (QM), e.g. PBS [6], Sun GridEngine (SGE) [1] and LSF [9], and interconnect technologies, e.g. Fast-/Gigabit-Ethernet, Myrinet and Quadrics. MPI [3, 4] is a specification for message-passing libraries, and has become the de facto standard for developing parallel applications. Interconnect-specific MPI implementations allow programs to be optimised for different interconnects.

A user can submit a job script to the QM requesting to run an MPI program across several cluster nodes. Each QM has a different convention for communicating the parallel environment (i.e. which nodes have been allocated). Similarly, each MPI implementation requires a slightly different procedure to run an MPI program, often requiring a *machine file*. It is the responsibility of the job script to run the MPI program in the parallel environment allocated by the QM.

The ad hoc approach of writing a job script for a specific QM/MPI combination used to suffice. However, their transition from exclusive to commodity status has resulted in some university departments and research institutes running several clusters. This and the rapid adoption of grid computing has escalated the need for inter-cluster operability.

One solution for MPI interoperability is to run TCP/IP over the interconnect, and then use a standard TCP/IP-based MPI implementation such as MPICHp4. However, this is inefficient since TCP/IP was designed for wide-area, internet communications. A similar but improved solution is VMI [8], a communication layer which is designed for communications within cluster interconnects. However, since VMI is still a run-time abstraction, message latency is inevitably increased. Neither of these solutions addresses interoperability between QMs.

We propose a Universal Machine File format, encapsulating a parallel environment, which allows users to mix-and-match QM-specific with MPI-specific scripts to suit the cluster. The user uses the native MPI-implementation without intermediate abstraction layers, and thus does not have to compromise performance. We have used this to support PBS, SGE and LSF, and MPICHp4 (MPI over IP), MPICHGM (MPI over Myrinet) and QsNet (MPI over Quadrics).

2 Universal Machine File

A solution based on one script for each QM/MPI combination clearly does not scale since for M QMs and N MPI-implementation, a total of MN such scripts are required. We propose an XML-based *Universal Machine File* format (UMF) as an intermediate representation of the parallel environment between the QM and MPI-implementation. For a given QM/MPI combination, we mix-and-match one of M QM-UMF scripts with one of N UMF-MPI scripts (Fig. 1), thus a total of $M + N$ scripts are required to support all MN combinations.

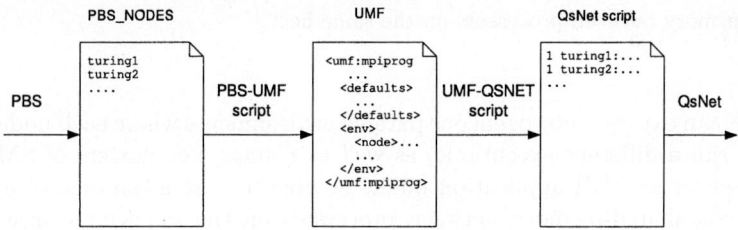

Fig. 1. Example of how UMF can be used for PBS and QsNet (Quadrics). The PBS-UMF script takes the parallel environment from PBS and generates a UMF script, an XML-based intermediate format; then the UMF-QSNET script generates a QSNET script which is run through prun. Since UMF is an XML application, new Queue Managers and MPI implementations can be supported by writing translation scripts using standard XML tools, and the scripts can be mixed-and-matched as required

```
<umf:mpiprog
   xmlns:umf="http://www.bii.a-star.edu.sg/~francis/xml"
   xmlns:xsi="http://www.w3.org/2001/XMLSchema-instance"
   xsi:schemaLocation="http://www.bii.a-star.edu.sg/~francis/xml umf.xsd">
   <defaults>
      <exec>cpi</exec>
      <numproc>4</numproc>
   </defaults>
   <env>
     <node><hostname>turing1</hostname></node>
     <node><hostname>turing2</hostname></node>
     <node><hostname>turing3</hostname></node>
     <node><hostname>turing4</hostname></node>
   </env>
</umf:mpiprog>
```

Fig. 2. A simple Universal Machine File. Here we are running program cpi across the four nodes turing1–4, using one processor per node

```
<umf:mpiprog
    xmlns:umf="http://www.bii.a-star.edu.sg/~francis/xml"
    xmlns:xsi="http://www.w3.org/2001/XMLSchema-instance"
    xsi:schemaLocation="http://www.bii.a-star.edu.sg/~francis/xml umf.xsd">
  <defaults>
     <numproc>8</numproc>
  </defaults>
  <env>
    <node>
      <count>4</count><hostname>linux1</hostname><exec>cpi-linux</exec>
    </node>
    <node>
      <count>4</count><hostname>sun1</hostname><exec>cpi-sun</exec>
    </node>
  </env>
</umf:mpiprog>
```

Fig. 3. A more advanced Universal Machine File. This is a request to run a program on a heterogeneous cluster. We request 4 processors on linux1 and 4 processors on sun1. On linux1, we run program cpi-linux, whereas on sun1, we run program cpi-sun. If supported by the MPI implementation, the parallel program would communicate via shared memory between processors on the same host

UMF can express heterogeneous parallel environments where each node might need to run a different executable, as well as *clumps*, i.e. clusters of SMP machines, where an MPI application might be able to take advantage of message passing via shared-memory between processors on the same node (see Fig. 3 for an example). We have developed a small utility library using Apache Xerces which allows programs to read and write the XML-based UMF files. Developers can use this library, or other XML-libraries directly, to support new MPI-implementations and QMs.

3 GEL: An Application

GEL [7] is a portable parallel scripting language for cluster and grid computing. Different GEL interpretors support different underlying hardware: presently the GEL interpretors support SMP machines, LSF/SGE/PBS-based clusters and Globus-based grids [5]. Since GEL scripts do not have middleware-specific references, e.g. hostnames, they can be run on different target machines without source code modifications.

The architecture of the interpretors is designed so that the majority of the code is shared between implementations. By using a simple intermediate language based on DAGs, the interpretors share a front end, the *DAG builder*, which translates GEL scripts into intermediate DAGs which are executed by the corresponding back end, the *DAG executor*. For example: the SMP DAG executor forks processes using an OS call; the PBS DAG executor submits jobs using the "qsub" command; and the Globus DAG executor uses GridFTP to stage files and GRAM to submit jobs. Thus there are interpretors to support many hardware configurations yet keeping a scalable code-base.

The atomic components of GEL scripts are jobs in the sense used by Globus, LSF, SGE and PBS. The current interpretors support only sequential jobs (i.e. not MPI jobs). UMF and various QM-UMF and UMF-MPI scripts will allow simple modifications to the GEL interpreters to support MPI jobs for different QM/MPI combinations while at the same time maintaining (1) portability of GEL scripts, and (2) a scalable interpreter code-base.

4 Conclusion

The adoption of Grid computing will put scientists in a situation where a diverse collection of clusters are at their disposal. Subtle incompatibilities between queue managers and MPI implementations add extra complexity to the problem of migration between clusters. The Universal Machine File (UMF) format is a scalable platform allowing us to improve inter-cluster operability. We intend to incorporate UMF into GEL interpreters and thus provide a portable mechanism for using MPI jobs as workflow components.

Acknowledgements

The authors would like to thank Stephen Wong for comments and suggestions for improvement.

References

1. Sun grid engine. White paper available at http://wwws.sun.com/software/gridware/sgeee53/wp-sgeee/index.html.
2. D. J. Becker, T. L. Sterling, D. F. Savarese, J. E. Dorband, U. A. Ranawak, and C. V. Packer. Beowulf: A parallel workstation for scientific computation. In *Proceedings of the International Conference on Parallel Processing*, 1995.
3. Message Passing Interface Forum. MPI: A message-passing interface standard. *International Journal of Supercomputer Applications*, 8(3/4):165–414, 1994.
4. Message Passing Interface Forum. MPI2: A message-passing interface standard. *International Journal of High Performance Computing Applications*, 12(1–2):1–299, 1998.
5. Ian Foster and Carl Kesselman. Globus: A metacomputing infrastructure toolkit. *The International Journal of Supercomputer Applications and High Performance Computing*, 11(2):115–128, Summer 1997.
6. R. Henderson and D. Tweten. Portable Batch System: External reference specification. Technical report, NASA Ames Research Center, 1996.
7. Chua Ching Lian, Francis Tang, Praveen Issac, and Arun Krishnan. GEL: Grid execution language, 2004. Submitted for publication.
8. Scott Pakin and Avneesh Pant. VMI 2.0: A dynamically reconfigurable messaging layer for availability, usability, and management. In *Proc. 8th Int. Symp. on High-Performance Computer Architecture*, 2002.
9. S. Zhou. LSF: Load sharing in large-scale heterogeneous distributed system. *Proc. Workshop on Cluster Computing*, 1992.

SVO Logic Based Formalisms of GSI Protocols*

Hui Liu and Minglu Li

Department of Computer Science and Engineering,
Shanghai Jiaotong University, 200030 Shanghai, China
{liuhui, li-ml}@cs.sjtu.edu.cn

Abstract. This paper employs SVO logic to describe the interoperability protocols of GSI. As a successor of BAN logic, SVO logic can be used to assume certain goals a protocol must hold. Because the messages exchanged in a protocol depend on the credential format and encryption mechanism, these protocols are formalized in terms of protocol goals using the credential of X.509 certificates.

1 Introduction

Grid security components are fundamental building blocks to bring the grid application into reality [1]. Because GLOBUS is one of the widely deployed and employed grid middleware, its security infrastructure, namely GSI (Grid Security Infrastructure), is almost installed throughout the grid communities worldwide.

The core of current GSI are four interoperability protocols, handling U-UP, UP-RP, RP-P and P-P interactions corporately [2]. However, there is no published proof or analysis to indicate that these protocols are reasonable and sound enough. For this reason, this paper describes some GSI protocols with SVO logic for future formal analysis.

The rest of this paper is organized as follows. Section 2 introduces some related work about SVO logic. Formalization of GSI interoperability protocols are presented in section 3 and section 4 concludes this paper.

2 Related Work

Formal analysis is a widely accepted method to check the correctness of a security protocol and uncover its potential flaws. BAN (Burrows, Abadi and Needham) logic has been a highly successful computation model for this intention. Being logic of belief, BAN can be used to analyze authentication protocols by deriving

---

* This research is supported by the National Grand Fundamental Research 973 Program of China (No.2002CB312002), China Grid Project, China Postdoctoral Science Foundation, and Grand Project of the Science and Technology Commission of Shanghai Municipality (No.03dz15027).

the beliefs that honest principals correctly executing a protocol can come to as a result of the protocol execution [3].

After an evolution intending to overcome limitations of BAN, SVO (Syverson and van Oorschot) logic becomes a notable successor that unifying different predecessors, i.e., GNY, AT and VO [4]. Therefore, it comprises almost all distinct advantages added to BAN. Detail information about SVO notation, SVO rules and SVO axioms can be found in literature [4]. SVO logic has been used to build protocol analysis tool C3PO [5].

Recent improvement includes introducing synchronization, revocation and recency into authentication logic, such as the one suggested in literature [6]. However, this logic seems too complicated for normal protocols.

3 Formalization of GSI Interoperability Protocols

GSI provides a specific security architecture comprising four interoperability protocols. These protocols support different credentials, including identity password pair, Kerberos ticket, X.509 certificate, etc. This paper prefers using PKI based mechanism to illustrate formalism of these protocols.

User Proxy Creation Protocol. The main issue in this protocol is how the proxy credential is created and given to the proxy. In addition to the notation used in literature [2], denote the user by U, the host from which the user proxy is created by UP, the X.509 certificate of I by C_I, and the key of I by k_I, the goals of this protocol are described below:

1. UP believes (U says (U has C_U ∧ C_U has $PK_\psi(U, k_U)$ ∧ U controls k_U^{-1}) ∧ $fresh(PK_\psi(U, k_U))$ ∧ U has 'access right on UP to create proxy')
2. U controls ($\lfloor$user-id, host, start-time, end-time, auth-info,...$\rfloor_{k_U^{-1}}$, C_{UP}) ∧ C_{UP} has $\lfloor$user-id, host, start-time, end-time, auth-info,...$\rfloor_{k_U^{-1}}$ ∧ U believes (UP believes (U says C_{UP} ∧ $fresh(C_{UP})$) ∧ UP has C_{UP})
3. UP controls 'user proxy process' ∧ 'user proxy process' has $F(C_{UP})$

In goal 3, the message 'user proxy process' indicates that a user proxy process is created and provided with C_{UP}. At the same time, the user proxy process must protect the integrity of C_{UP}.

Resource Allocation Protocol. This protocol is used for the allocation initiated by a user proxy. Denote the user proxy by UP, the resource proxy by RP, the key of I by k_I, and the user that create UP by U, the goals of this protocol are described below:

1. RP believes (UP says (UP has C_{UP} ∧ C_{UP} has $PK_\psi(UP, k_{UP})$ ∧ UP controls k_{UP}^{-1}) ∧ $fresh(PK_\psi(UP, k_{UP}))$) ∧ UP believes (RP says (RP has C_{RP} ∧ C_{RP} has $PK_\psi(RP, k_{RP})$ ∧ RP controls k_{RP}^{-1}) ∧ $fresh(PK_\psi(RP, k_{RP}))$)

2. $UP\ controls\ \lfloor resource\text{-}req \rfloor_{k_{UP}^{-1}} \wedge \lfloor resource\text{-}req \rfloor_{k_{UP}^{-1}}\ has\ 'allocation\ specification' \wedge UP\ believes\ (RP\ believes\ (UP\ says\ \lfloor resource\text{-}req \rfloor_{k_{UP}^{-1}} \wedge fresh(\lfloor resource\text{-}req \rfloor_{k_{UP}^{-1}})) \wedge RP\ has\ \lfloor resource\text{-}req \rfloor_{k_{UP}^{-1}})$
3. $RP\ believes\ (U\ controls\ C_{UP} \rightarrow U\ has\ 'access\ right\ on\ RP\ to\ allocate\ resources' \wedge \lfloor resource\text{-}req \rfloor_{k_{UP}^{-1}}\ has\ 'be\ honored\ by\ local\ policy')$
4. $RP\ controls\ \lfloor user\text{-}id,\ host,\ resource\text{-}name,\ldots \rfloor_{k_{RP}^{-1}}$
5. $RP\ believes\ (UP\ believes\ (RP\ says\ \lfloor user\text{-}id,\ host,\ resource\text{-}name,\ldots \rfloor_{k_{RP}^{-1}} \wedge fresh(\lfloor user\text{-}id,\ host,\ resource\text{-}name,\ldots \rfloor_{k_{RP}^{-1}})) \wedge UP\ has\ \lfloor user\text{-}id,\ host,\ resource\text{-}name,\ldots \rfloor_{k_{RP}^{-1}})$
6. $UP\ controls\ (\lfloor user\text{-}id,\ host,\ resource\text{-}name,\ldots \rfloor_{k_{UP}^{-1}}, C_P) \wedge C_P\ has\ \lfloor user\text{-}id,\ host,\ resource\text{-}name,\ldots \rfloor_{k_{UP}^{-1}}$
7. $UP\ believes\ (RP\ believes\ (UP\ says\ \{C_P\}_{k_{RP}} \wedge fresh(C_P)) \wedge RP\ has\ C_P)$
8. $RP\ controls\ 'processes\ for\ resources' \wedge 'processes\ for\ resources'\ has\ C_P$

In goal 7, we suppose that the public key k_{RP} is used to encrypt the credential of process, namely C_P, and securely pass it to the resource proxy.

Resource Allocation from a Process Protocol. This protocol is more widely used than previous one, because in more common case is that resource allocation will be initiated dynamically from different processes. Denote the process by P, and the user proxy by UP, the goals of this protocol are described below:

1. $P\ believes\ (UP\ says\ (UP\ has\ C_{UP} \wedge C_{UP}\ has\ PK_\psi(UP, k_{UP}) \wedge UP\ controls\ k_{UP}^{-1}) \wedge fresh(PK_\psi(UP, k_{UP}))) \wedge UP\ believes\ (P\ says\ (P\ has\ C_P \wedge C_P\ has\ PK_\psi(P, k_P) \wedge P\ controls\ k_P^{-1}) \wedge fresh(PK_\psi(P, k_P)))$
2. $P\ controls\ \lfloor allocation\ parameters \rfloor_{k_P^{-1}} \wedge P\ believes\ (UP\ believes\ (P\ says\ \lfloor allocation\ parameters \rfloor_{k_P^{-1}} \wedge fresh(\lfloor allocation\ parameters \rfloor_{k_P^{-1}})) \wedge UP\ has\ \lfloor allocation\ parameters \rfloor_{k_P^{-1}})$
3. $UP\ controls\ 'request\ has\ been\ honored' \wedge UP\ believes\ 'all\ goals\ of\ Resource\ Allocation\ Protocol\ have\ been\ achieved' \wedge UP\ has\ 'handle\ of\ resulting\ process'$
4. $UP\ controls\ \lfloor handle\ of\ resulting\ process \rfloor_{k_{UP}^{-1}} \wedge UP\ believes\ (P\ believes\ (UP\ says\ \lfloor handle\ of\ resulting\ process \rfloor_{k_{UP}^{-1}} \wedge fresh(\lfloor handle\ of\ resulting\ process \rfloor_{k_{UP}^{-1}})) \wedge P\ has\ \lfloor handle\ of\ resulting\ process \rfloor_{k_{UP}^{-1}})$

Mapping Register Protocol. This protocol is used to map a global subject to a corresponding local subject. Because it is not designed for authentication, formalizing it with SVO logic is of no usage for formal analysis. In fact, its essential are finding matched arguments for the requests of MAP-SUBJECT-UP and MAP-SUBJECT-P, and acknowledging these requests in time.

4 Discussion and Conclusion

A protocol can be formalized in two different levels, i.e., the level of message exchanging and the level of authentication goals. Because the message sequence exchanged in one protocol varies with the credential format and encrypts mechanism, this paper formalizes GSI protocols in terms of authentication goals, which reveal beliefs that all principals must hold at the end of a run. Since GSI protocols support different credentials, such formalisms establish a more systematic view of these protocols.

As shown in section 3, GSI protocols can be classified into four protocols according to their functionality. However, these protocols are not designed for U-UP, UP-RP, RP-P and P-P interactions respectively. Indeed, these interactions may occur in one protocol simultaneously. Therefore, only three GSI protocols are formalized with SVO logic in this paper, which are more authentication oriented. These protocols have been widely used in grid communities, thus, they are correct in normal scenarios and security contexts. However, they are described with natural languages.

Formalism of GSI protocols has some advantages: firstly, the protocols in this form are more accurate and regular than that in the form of natural language; secondly, formal analysis could be conducted to check the correctness of these protocols; thirdly, it lays a foundation for us to find protocol flaws and prevent potential attacks.

Because formal analysis is a common way to design sound security protocols, we hope the formalisms of GSI protocols in this paper would benefit the future further research on them.

References

1. Ferreira, L., Berstis, V., Armstrong, J., Kendzierski, M., Neukoetter, A., Takagi, M., Bing-Wo, R., Amir, A., Murakawa, R., Hernandez, O., Magowan, J., Bieberstein, N.: Introduction to Grid Computing with Globus. IBM Corp. (2002)
2. Foster, I., Kesselman, C., Tsudik, G., Tuecke, S.: A Security Architecture for Computational Grids. In: G, Li, Reiter, M. (eds.): Proc. of the 5th ACM Conf. on Computer and Comm. Sec. ACM Press, New York (1998) 83-92
3. Burrows, M., Abadi, M., Needham, R.: A Logic of Authentication. ACM Trans. on Computer Syst. 1 (1990) 18-36
4. Syverson, P., Cervesato, I.: The Logic of Authentication Protocols. In: Batini, C., Giunchiglia, F., Giorgini, P., Mecella, M. (eds.): Proc. of 9th Intl. Conf. on Coop. Inf. Syst. Lecture Notes in Computer Science, Vol. 2172. Springer-Verlag, Berlin Heidelberg Trento Italy (2001)
5. Dekke, A.: C3PO: A Tool for Automatic Sound Cryptographic Protocol Analysis. Proc. of 13th IEEE Computer Sec. Foundations Workshop IEEE Press, Cambridge UK (2000) 77-87
6. Stubblebine, G., Wright, N.: An Authentication Logic with Formal Semantics Supporting Synchronization, Revocation, and Recency. IEEE Trans. on Software Eng. 3 (2002) 256-285

A High-Level Policy Description Language for the Network ACL

Jangha Kim[1], Kanghee Lee[1], Sangwook Kim[1],
Jungtaek Seo[2], Eunyoung Lee[2], and Miri Joo[2]

[1] Department of Computer Science, Kyungpook National University,
1370 Sankyuk-dong Buk-gu, Daegu, 702-701, Korea
[2] National Security Research Institute,
161 Gajeong-dong Yuseong-gu, Daejeon, 305-350, Korea
{jhkim, khlee, swkim}@cs.knu.ac.kr, {seojt, eylee, mrjoo}@etri.re.kr

Abstract. Malicious codes and worms comprise the largest portion of the loss caused the security problem in the Internet. Small worms such as the "Blaster" spread quickly through the enormous network. It causes the network to lock down within an hour or so[1]. The situation worsens before it can be monitored and notified by the supervisor. Since the network is not available, it becomes hard to serve a node with an order. It is difficult for most large networks to introduce a consistent monitoring tool and reporting system. It is also more difficult to manage the configuration of network nodes with the matter of policy. We represent abstract language that supports various functions. Functions are in grouping, event, compliance and intermediate forms. This high-level language abstracts the control behavior of the network nodes that have various setting-up methodologies. We will describe the features of the language and give examples of the preliminary implementation on the test-bed.

1 Introduction

The most important process in the management of network security is the protection of the network from automated worms that spread quickly through the Internet. It is for this reason that the abstract policy language and hierarchy security management system are necessary in delivering security information such as the policies among the nodes and domains. The purpose of this study is to design and implement a high-level ACL description language for the large-scale network of the hierarchy security management system. The large-scale network consisting of many hosts and nodes is divided into sub-networks.

The rest of this paper is organized as follows: section 2 describes a specific large-scale network and explains the necessity of high-level security management; section 3 reviews the features of the proposed high-level language; section 4 and 5 explain the environment of implementation and show the results of its comparisons to the other high-level languages; and section 6 presents the conclusion and future applications.

2 The Large Network and the Abstraction of Policy

In this paper, the organization that forms itself into a logical hierarchy from highest to the lowest is called the "Domain". The generic spread process of the malicious code transfers harmful traffic from one infected domain to another. To prevent the spread of harmful traffic in the system requires collaboration between the Domains. When harmful traffic is detected, coherent policies have to report within the Domains.

In constructing hierarchal Domains in the large-scale network, each Domain is recursively constructed. The highest Domain, such as the back-born, is the highest network not only logically but also physically. The highest Domains are constructed as 'Nets'. Many researches connected to the collaboration of the highest Domains are currently in progress. To keep in line with the purpose of this paper, we will not take this matter up in detail. Figure 1 represents the Domain constitution of the large-scale network described above.

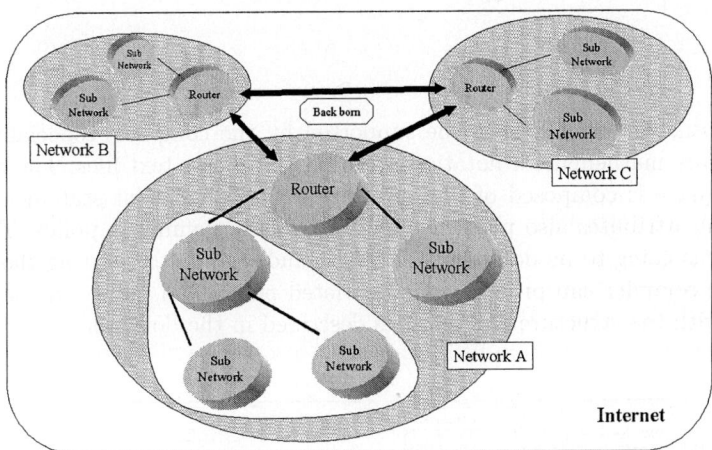

Fig. 1. The constitution of the Domain of large-scale networks

3 Triton Language

The Domain management policies must describe the high-level abstract language used to control the large-scale network in the block. It is necessary to describe the heterogeneous and configurative information of various network nodes. This approach provides the highest Domain with a methodology to manage the large-scale network. A high-level Triton offers various political functions that manage lower network nodes. This mechanism provides five perspectives of a description:

- Abstract description for the configuration of a lower node
- Mechanism of policy compliance
- Grouping
- Event for a polymorphous policy
- Semi-structured communication framework

We will illustrate with a simple example[2].

```
policy SamplePolicy triggered by EVENT_ALERT
{
    Range R1 = [ x:IP | "10.1.1.5" <= x <= "10.1.1.20" ];

    incoming {
        for ( "DomainA", "DomainB", "DomainC" ) {
            if ( src_addr in R1 && dst_port == 8080 ) {
                deny ( 3, essential );
            }
        }
    }
}
```

The other features have to be supported by the compiler, especially those that require mathematical notations in order to process text files. The description language is composed of a group of structure dependent statements. The statement attributes also play an important role in defining a policy. The system that is going to be designed will also include an editor creating the policy. A Triton compiler can process an instantiated policy and build a management system with the structure and features described in the document.

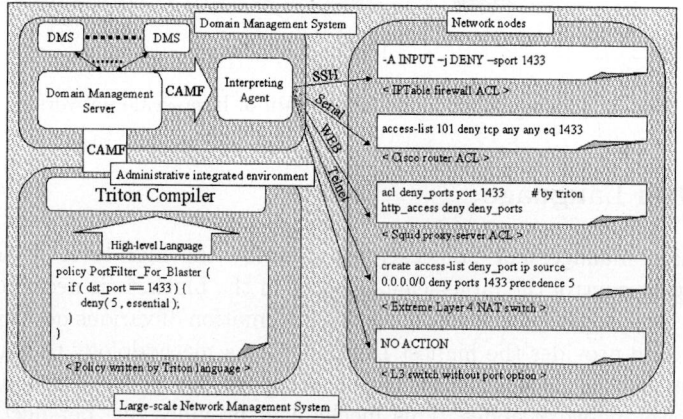

Fig. 2. An abstract language for the configuration of the lower node

4 Evaluation

This paper compares the Triton language to the other languages representing policies for the evaluation of a proposed language. There are various policies description languages used in managing network security. Most of the languages have individual properties. We looked into the policy description language, with a similar purpose, for the comparison and selection of five network policy languages[3][4].

Table 1. The comparison of police represented languages

Language	Target Architecture	Compliance	Group	Event	Reference	Represent
Policy term	Distributed	Low	Low	Low	Low	Low
PFDL	Centralized	Medium	Low	Medium	Low	Low
RPSL	Centralized	Low	Low	Low	Low	Low
PAX	Centralized	Low	Low	Low	Low	Low
SRL	Distributed	Low	Low	Low	Low	Low
NetSPoC	Centralized	Low	High	Low	Low	Medium
Triton	Distributed	High	Medium	Medium	Medium	High

5 Conclusion

The policy manager has summarized and abstracted the information on large-scale networks to set up a coherent policy. Additionally, if the Domain server accommodates a policy delivered from the other trustable Domains, the lower Domain then, is improving in security. In the lower Domain, it collects information of harmful traffic and forwards the useful information to the higher Domain. In the higher Domain, it sends useful policies to the lower Domains. In this manner, the high-level ACL description Language and related management systems perform abstracted policy descriptions and various policy services, such as compliance to policy, grouping, an event-based approach and an intermediate form. This gives a tried manager the important function of managing the security of the large-scale network.

References

1. Mohit Lad, Xiaoliang Zhao, Beichuan Zhang, Dan Massey and Lixia Zhang : "An Analysis of BGP Update Burst during Slammer Attack," IWDC, Calcutta, 2003
2. Triton BNF, http://woorisol.knu.ac.kr/lab/content/triton-bnf.txt, 2004
3. G.N.Stone, B.Lundy, and G.G.Xie : "Network Policy Languages: A Survey and a New Approach," IEEE Network, Vol.15, No.1, pp. 10-20, 2001
4. NetSPoc homepage, http://netspoc.berlios.de/, 2004

Target Code Generation Using the Code Expansion Technique for Java Bytecode

Kwang-Man Ko* and Soon-Gohn Kim**

*School of Computer, Information and Communication, Sang Ji University,
660 Woosan-dong, Wonju-si Kwangwon-do 220-702, Korea
kkman@mail.sangji.ac.kr
**Division of Computer Engineering, Information and Communication, Joongbu University,
101 Daehak-ro, Chubu-myeon, Kumsan-gun, Choongchungnam-do, 312-702, Korea
sgkim@joongbu.ac.ac.kr

Abstract. The execution speed is not an important factor for Java programming language when implementing small size application program which is executed in the web browser, but it becomes the serious limitation when it comes to implement the huge size program. To overcome these kinds of problems, the various researches are investigated for translating the Bytecode into target code which can be implemented in the specific processor using classical compiling methods. In this paper, we have designed and realized the native code generation system which directly generate Pentium code from the Bytecode to improve the execution speed of Java application programs. The native code generation system composed of the class file information analyzer, code translation information table, and native code generator. And then, the result generated by the native code generator has been verified by comparing the final outcome of *.class file executed by JDK interpreter.

1 Introduction

Java programming language supports various development environments such as Objected-Oriented paradigm as a language designed for easy and effective development of API in the Internet and distributed system. In Java language system, Bytecode which is virtual machine code is used and the interpreter in the virtual machine executes the program to make Java program independent of platform. It causes slowdown in performance. For a small sized applet program run in web browser, the slowdown of program running speed is not a significant factor. However, overall performance is degraded to a large extent compared to that of existing programming language such as C/C++. Many researches have been done to find out the ways to get around with performance slowdown problem. One method is suggested to make a processor for Bytecode and to use Java chip with the intention of direct execution of program in hardware. Another is to compile as a method unit whenever it is needed in run-time following JIT method. It is also suggested that during compile time to change Bytecode into object code that can be executed in a special purposed processor using the traditional compile method. SUN also uses the method which compile Bytecode into native code in a special purposed processor in parallel with using JVM interpreter to improve the running time of Java API.[6][7].

JIT compiler has been implemented as an attempt to develop various methods to execute Java language apart from JVM interpreter method in research labs and industry. CACAO[8] as a 64-bit JIT compiler for Alpha processor gets Bytecode input and generates native code for Alpha processor.

2 Related and Base Works

2.1 Native Code Generation System

CACAO[8] as a 64-bit JIT compiler for Alpha processor generates a native code for Alpha processor from the Bytecode. In the process of native code generation, stack based Bytecode is transformed into CACAO-implemented register based intermediate language and then the register based intermediate language into the native code for Alpha processor. NET compiler[7] as an optimized compiler generating native code from Bytecode is a native code generation system proposed by IMPACT. It also employs register based intermediate language devised to generate the native code appropriate for a specific processor from stack based Bytecode. From the class file, NET compiler makes Java IR, which is an internal language format for the native code generation.

2.2 Code Generation System

The target code generation system is the part that generates actual target code based on code generation rules and machine information, which is described on the machine description table through putting in intermediate code in a formalized method. It is composed of the code-generator generator and the code generator.

The code-generator generator gets the target machine description table through input and produce information in the form of a table, and it is reference by the code generator at the time of target machine code generation. In order to generate a table, after you should analyze syntax and semantics about target machine description table when they come in through input, and then you either directly generate table date in a file, or save it temporarily.

The code generator is the part that actually generates target code based on table information that is generated by the code-generator generator by receiving intermediate code through input, and it uses fake stack to generate code of good quality. Fake stack is a logical expansion of an actual stack that is used when an actual program is at work, and it is used to maintain and manage generated token as it carries out intermediate code included in code generation rules for the target machine description table.

3 Native Code Generator from the Java Bytecode to Pentium Code

3.1 Overview

Native code generation system which reads the Java class(*.class) and then generates the Pentium code composed of the Class file information analyzer, code translation information table, native code generator as following Fig. 1.

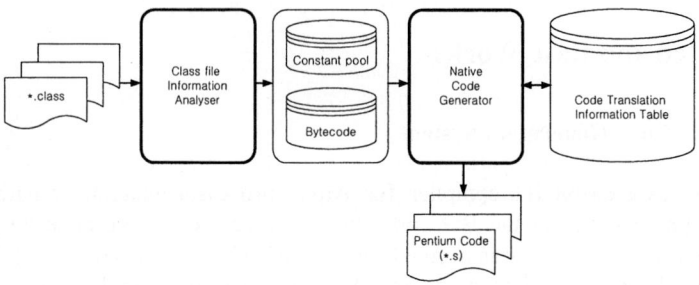

Fig. 1. Native Code Generation System Configuration

3.2 Code Translation Information Table: Java Bytecode to Pentium Code

Computation Operations: This table describes the translation information about an arithmetic/local/bit manipulation Bytecode as following Table 1.

Table 1. Integer and float arithmetic operations translation table

IADD {	IDIV {	FSUB {	FMUL {
popl %ecx	popl %ecx	fld %st(1)	fmul %st(1)
popl %eax	popl %eax	fsub %st(1)	}
addl %ecx, %eax	cltd	}	
pushl %eax	idivl %ecx		
}	pushl %eax		
	}		

Stack Management Operations: Stack manipulation or control instruction, SWAP, DUP_X1, ..., should be described because of Bytecode based on the stack machine as following Table 2.

Table 2. Stack management operations translation table

SWAP {	POP2 {	DUP_X1 {	DUP {
popl %ecx	popl %ecx	popl %eax	popl %eax
popl %eax	popl %eax	popl %ecx	pushl %eax
pushl %ecx	movl $0x00, %eax	pushl %eax	pushl %eax
pushl %eax	movl $0x00, %ecx	pushl %ecx	}
}	}	pushl %eax	
		}	

4 Conclusion

The ultimate goal of this paper is to translate the Bytecode into i386 native code. The result has been verified with the completed code translation information table about the most basic Load/Store, arithmetic or logical operation, stack management and array management commands for the native code generation of 230 Bytecode. In this paper, the native code generator is designed and implemented which generates i386 Pentium code from Bytecode to improve the performance of Java application programs. Specially, the Native Code generator plays an essential role in generating Pentium code corresponding Bytecode. It looks up the code translation information table and makes use of the 1:N macro expansion technique to each Bytecode. Code translation information table keeps the record of the practical information about native code generation and is made of command groups holding related information considering the Bytecode characteristics. Lastly, the result generated by the Native code generator has been verified by comparing the final outcome of JDK *.class file executed by JDK interpreter.

Acknowledgement. This work was supported by grant No. (R01-1999-000-00236-0) from the Basic Research Program of the Korea Science & Engineering Foundation.

Reference

1. Alfred V. Aho, Mahadevan Ganapathi, Steven W. K. Tjiang, "Code Generation Using Tree Matching and Dynamic Programming," ACM TOPLAS, Vol. 11, No. 4., pp.491-516, Oct., 1989.
2. R. G. G. Cattell, "Automatic Derivation of Code Generators from Machine Descriptions," ACM TOPLAS, Vol. 2, No. 2, pp.173-190. Apr., 1980.
3. Mahadevan Ganapathi, Charles N. Fischer, John L. Hennessy, "Retargetable Compiler Code Generation", ACM Computing Surveys, Vol. 14, No. 4, pp.573-592, Dec., 1982.
4. Susan L. Graham, "Table-Driven Code Generation", IEEE Computer, Vol.13, No.8, pp. 25-34, Aug., 1980.
5. Karen A. Lemone, Design of Compilers : Techniques of Programming Language Translation, CRC Press, 1992.
6. Hans van Staveren, "The table driven code generator from ACK 2nd. Revision," report-81, Netherlands Vrije Universiteit, 1989.
7. Wen-mei W. Hwu, "Java Bytecode to Native Code Translation: The Caffeine Prototype and Preliminary Results", The proceeding of the 29th Annual International Symposium on Microarchitecture, Dec., 1999
8. A. krall and R. Grafl, CACAO : A 64 bit Java VM Just-in-Time Compiler, Concurrency: practice and experience, 1997. http://www.complang.tuwien.ac.at/~andi.
9. Ronald Veldema, Jcc, A Native Java compiler, Vrije Universiteit Amsterdam, July, 1998.
10. Jon Meyer and Troy Downing, JAVA Virtual Machine, O'REYLLY, 1997.
11. Ken Arnold and James Gosling, The Java Programming Language, Sun Microsystems, 1996.
12. Jonathan Meyer, Jasmin Assembler, http://www.cat.nyu.edu/meyer/

A 4-Layer Robust Mobile Web Front-End Design Model

Toshihiko Yamakami

ACCESS, 2-8-16 Sarugaku-cho, Chiyoda-ku, Tokyo, 101-0064 Japan
yam@access.co.jp

Abstract. The author describes the lessons learned from the 4-year non-stop operation of the mobile Internet services to identify the robust mobile web design issues from an operational viewpoint. In order to maintain the user confidence during the unexpected situations, the author describes a 4-layer fallback design model to manage the real world mobile web operations and to give a sense of continuity to the mobile users. The author discusses issues in the open mobile Internet services in relation to the proposed front-end design model for the robust tolerant mobile web operations.

1 Introduction

Internet with information appliances is quickly emerging and penetrating into the every-day life [1]. There will be close to one billion wireless devices capable of Internet connectivity within five years, outnumbering the installed base of traditional wired compute devices. Not only these restrictions make the content management challenging, but also make the robust operation difficult due to the limited communication channel. In this paper, the author summarizes the lessons learned from the 4-year experience of mobile Internet content service operation and proposes a 4-layer level robust front end user interface design.

The mobile handsets have distinguished restrictions as follows: small display space, small memory capacity, low-power CPU, limited user interface components, and narrow bandwidth. The small display space is a restricting factor not only for the regular content, but also for the help content at the exceptions. This needs the careful design for proactive user interface to prepare for any troubles. The mobile Internet content service should cope with robust operation with its 24-hour services, scalable operation, diversity of the device environments, dynamic evolution of the networks and carrier-level evolution requirements.

Content adaptation is a hot topic in the diversity challenges in the mobile Internet [2]. In addition, the mobile Internet technical issues like session handoff were studied by researchers like [3]. These technical challenges like content adaptation were visible, however, the underlying operation challenges were often uncovered. The mobile Internet service operation includes the four design challenges: user interface design, service design, system and network design, and operation design. The user interface design includes: regular user interface design, and exception-tolerant robust user interface design. In the 24-hour nonstop services, the latter user interface design is critical in the mobile Internet services. This gives the three issues to be resolved: exception detection, graceful fallback user interface and operational control on the content at exceptions. This paper focused the latter two issues in order to sustain user confidence in the services. It highlights the front-end design in order to follow an operation-oriented service software architecture presented in [4].

2 Lessons Learned in the Long-Term Mobile Internet Service Operation

The lessons learned from the 4-year mobile Internet content service operation is split into the following categories: operation usability and flexibility, operation robustness, network integration and extensibility. The lessons include the followings:

- User interface needs the on-the-fly update from the content providers,
- Carrier systems are not stable during the mobile evolution,
- Carriers performs regular or irregular maintenance works,
- Carriers modify the fundamental features during their service evolutions,
- Network, database, and server capabilities are largely unknown at the design stage.

When there are some troubles in the subscription-based content, it is one of the highest priority issues to keep the subscribers update about the situation and to maintain the customer relation with sense of continuity in services. The flexible wording by the content provider is critical 24 hours and 365 days. It is critical that this type of flexible user interface update is provided to the original content provider over the mobile content platform. The lessons tell that the arbitrary assertion of the temporary notice from the original content provider and the mobile content platform provider should be incorporated in an integrated manner.

In March 2002, there was a large subscription authentication system failure in one of the major Japanese mobile carriers. From this lesson, we learned that the subscription-check on the top page is failure-prune. It is common that the content is customized at the top level after checking user identifiers for subscription. It was a nice design, however, the web did not work when the carrier-based subscription authentication system failed and did not return a result. This type of events should be incorporated in the system design because some of the mobile carriers stop their services weekly or monthly based for system maintenance. Sometimes, they carry out the system halts for maintenance in a region-by-region base. The lesson tells us that the free content provision without the subscription check is a good way in order to retain the user confidence on the content services. In this fallback scheme, we do not hurt the relation to the subscribed customers.

When it is a temporary problem, the damage to provide the content to the non-subscribed users for a short span of time is not significant.

In some rare occasions, the mobile carriers update the fundamental properties. For example, at the 3G-service launch, a carrier modified the user identifier to indicate the 3G users. It is sometimes convenient, but some of the users lost their content contexts like records and preferences. The lesson tells that the interface should be flexible to accommodate the end users unintentionally forced to have the new user identifier in this case.

In March 2004, the PC Internet web with one of our services had the performance deterioration problems. The web page was attached with the notice and apology for this performance deterioration. In this service, the user experienced frequent timed-out because the response time to the PC Internet was inherited to that of the mobile Internet content. In the PC case, the notice worked. With the limited display size and easy gone-away user characteristics, it is a challenge to notify the mobile users about the temporary system performance degradation. The lesson tells that the service can notify the temporary system troubles using the registered user email address. Also, the mail based system status query can work. It keeps the customer confidence that the service is well managed.

3 A 4-Layer Mobile Front-End Web Design Model

The author proposes 4-layers for front-end fallback design as follows: mail based status interface, fixed content, partial subset content, and regular content. The detailed function model is depicted in Fig. 1.

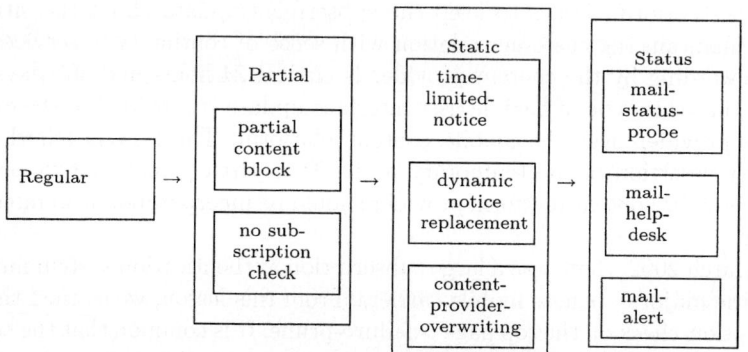

Fig. 1. A 4-layer web front-end design model

For the status query level, it is safe to anticipate these external events and prepare for them. To reduce the server load, the trade-off between the server generated dynamic pages and static pages should be carefully considered. It is desirable for improving turn around time to have the most frequently accesses pages as static ones, which avoids the server or database bottlenecks. For the fixed content level, the design should incorporate built-in operation design that enables the cooperation of the content providers and platform providers. For the robust operation, the easy operational interface for content providers to make the partial and temporal content update is valuable to add cautions, explanations and status update. It is useful to enable multiple ways to guide the end users in the various network and system conditions in the operation level. The operational access security should be designed to cope with a wide variety of the operation outsourcing.

From lessons learned, the operation design should consider the following stages in order to finalize multiple user interface fall back design: (a) one page notice, (b) static page only operation, (c) service without database operations, (d) service without mobile carrier provided functions, and (e) full operations. The proactive design from the operational viewpoint needs considerations in the following time out cases: authentication, database query, networks. The following four criteria are considered for sustained user confidence: (a) reliable fast feedback expectation, (b) fallback expectation, (c) alternative channel expectation, and (d) operation awareness. In the flexible operation level design, the operation designers should consider how to guide end users in exceptional operational conditions. Lessons told us that the mobile specific instability and low visibility needs special care in the front-end user interface design in the total integration design.

In the built-in extensible operation design, the operation design should pay attention to the future evolution that may not be captured in advance. The operational switches in the operation levels, extensible database design and built-in adaptation mechanisms can help the evolutions over a long span of time. On-the-fly web page generation should be minimized at the operation troubles, because it makes the user help desk operation more difficult.

4 Discussion

The important factor on the mobile Internet front-end design is the gap analysis in the system status and user mental models. The slim information channel is vulnerable under the open mobile environment with unexpected events. It leads to the gaps in the mental models in the fluctuations in the mobile Internet. The fast mobile Internet evolution with 24-hour 265-day non-stop services makes the network and system integration challenging. The fallback based layered model of the user interface fits this open and dynamic situation. The trust building process include the following aspects:

- Operation awareness at the troubleshooting,
- Stable first-page expectation, and
- Fallback awareness.

The trust building depends on the three different issues:

- Stable service quality,

- Trouble transparency,
- Feedback,
- Operation awareness, and
- Cause awareness.

The mobile Internet is convenient, but not a dominant information channel. The users easily come and easily go. When users cannot tolerate unexpected user experiences, they will easily switch the services. The alternatives can be telephone, TV, email, PC-web, etc. Users may prefer these alternatives, even if they are inadequate in certain respects, because they are more familiar and better controlled. The mobile communication reliability depends the contexts and network situations. Users may have some patience, but when they find their efforts to maintain the user relationship are not rewarded, they switch to other media.

Trust building is a central issue in every-day life penetrating mobile Internet with a challenge to build trust with the remote, virtual, and anonymous entities in a slim channel. When the reliability was improved in the early Internet a decade ago, the social trust building issues were highlighted in a similar manner. Hoffman et al discussed the trust building for the cyber consumers including privacy [5]. Friedman et al criticized technology-centric trust building approach [6]. Gefen argued that the single dimension trust building was not appropriate, and proposed the multi-dimensional trust building with integrity, capability and benevolence [7]. Luo et al extended this multi-dimensional trust building with different trust building processes in their health care web sites [8]. The mobile commerce trust-building process itself was discussed by Siau et al [9]. They discussed how the initial trust formation leads to the continuous trust development. From our learned lessons, the past literature under-evaluated the user mental model transitions in the unexpected experiences in the mobile Internet where end users are isolated and at loss in most exceptions. In the past literature, this aspect was enclosed in the deployment dimension, not user interface level. The reliable and robust service deployment needs further user support to survive these situations. The proposed 4-layer model enhanced the mobile web trust building factors depicted in Fig. 2. The proposed 4-layer design model reflects these 4 fallback stages of user confidence on the service operations.

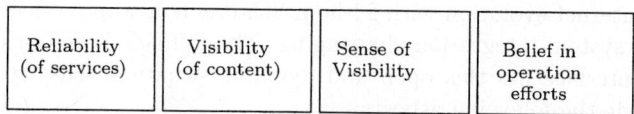

Fig. 2. A 4-stage fallback stage model

Usually, the three stages (a) visibility, (b) sense of visibility, and (c) belief in operation efforts, are not distinguished in the PC Internet. *Sense of visibility* is the user mental status that makes user confident on the content visibility even when content visibility is lost on some occasions. The belief in operation efforts is linked to the user conception of continuity of the service operations. It is because the end users have ability to verify and test the working status of the web, URL addresses and the markup language content. The user mental model of the system impacts the locus of control. The researcher dated back to 1970's studied the locus of control. It is not controllability in the user interface, but the sense of the control in the user mental model. It impacts the user preference of the systems. Lee et al noted that locus of control relates to the perception an individual has of his/her influence over events. Rickenberg [10] mentioned that results showed that the effects of monitoring and individual differences in thoughts about control worked as they do in real life, and that users felt more anxious when characters monitored their website work and this effect was strongest for users with an external control orientation. The visibility and verifiability common in the PC Internet is not available in the mobile Internet. Therefore, the micro-stage awareness and the fallback mechanisms in these stages are important for the sustained trust in the mobile Internet. As Friedman mentioned in [6], *people trust people, not technology.* The belief in the operational efforts is a key issue, and the dynamic and timely shift in the 4-layer model front-end interface provides the base for this trust building process. This paper does not cover the quantitative measures to evaluate these three factors in the mobile web trust building process. It is a further study as well as the comparisons with the proposed layered model and legacy solutions. The fault tolerant operation in the mobile web service cannot depend on the sustainable server design issues. It should be noted that the user mental model of the mobile web could not be underestimated. There are multiple reasons why the end users may make different mental cognition on the mobile web status including:

– access failure due to the local wireless conditions,
– access failure due to the temporary gateway conditions, and
– link failures.

It is important because the mobile users have difficulty to verify and pursue the exact failure reasons on a small mobile handset. When the mobile Internet experience will increase, the users will lead to the mental models similar to the PC Internet today. However, the multiple user interfaces restrictions will sustain in some of the side. The mobile web design should focus on the trust building issues and pay attention to the immature trust building process on the mobile users. The good fall back interface gives a reasonable guidance for building up the user trust in a sustainable manner.

Comparison with a server modification approach is shown in shown in Table 1. The flexible user interface approach is operation-built-in, therefore, it needs close cooperation with the content providers. From the lessons, the author concludes that the early and transient stages of the mobile Internet, it is critical to include these operational features in the front-end design. This comes from the two facts: (a) the services need to evolve during the unexplored integration issues, and (b) the user needs graceful fallback mechanisms due to a limited information channel.

Table 1. Comparison with a server modification approach

	server-modification	4 layer-approach
design	×	○
fine-tuning on operation	×	○
robustness on exceptions	×	○
code-size	×	○

5 Conclusions

From the long-term operation experience, the author describes the exception tolerant front-end design to maintain the user confidence in the mobile services in a constraint slim information channel. The author presents a 4-layer robust mobile web front-end design model to implement the graceful and visible fallback for the mobile services. The adaptive and flexible design to cope with the unexpected system troubles during 24-hour operation needs operational design and considerations for proactive design. The robust mobile web front-end 4-layer model is linked to the underlying trust building process in the mobile Internet. The operation-oriented layered approach supports the close collaboration between web operators and content providers to cope with exceptions during operation. It also facilitates the sense of service continuity in the fall back design to be aware of the underlying trust building process in a slim information channel.

References

1. Cerf, V.: Beyond the post-PC internet. CACM **44** (2001) 34–37
2. Billsus, D., Brunk, C., Evans, C., Gladish, B., Pazzani, M.: The adaptive web: Adaptive interfaces for ubiquitous web access. CACM **45** (2002) 34–38
3. Phan, T., Guy, R., Bagrodia, R.: A scalable, distributed middleware service architecture to support mobile internet applications. In: Proceedings of the first workshop on Wireless mobile internet, ACM Press (2001) 27–33
4. Yamakami, T.: Mobile content operation design: Lessons learned in the long-term experience. In: NBiS2003, IEEE Computer Press (2003)
5. Hoffman, D., Novak, T., Peralta, M.: Building consumer trust online. CACM **42** (1999) 80–85
6. Friedman, B., Khan, P., Howe, D.: Trust online. CACM **43** (2000) 34–40
7. Gefen, D.: Reflections on the dimensions of trust and trustworthiness among online consumers. ACM SIGMIS Database **33** (2002) 80–85
8. Luo, W., Najdawi, M.: Trust-building measures: a review of consumer health portals. CACM **47** (2004) 108–113
9. Siau, K., Shen, Z.: Building customer trust in mobile commerce. CACM **46** (2003) 91–94
10. Rickenberg, R., Reeves, B.: The effects of animated characters on anxiety, task performance, and evaluations of user interfaces. In: Proceedings of the SIGCHI conference on Human factors in computing systems, ACM Press (2000) 49–56

Study on Replication in Unstructured P2P System

Meng-Shu Hou, Xian-Liang Lu, Xu Zhou, and Chuan Zhan

School of Computer Science and Engineering,
University of Electronic Science and Technology of China,
Chengdu 610054, P. R. China
{mshou, xlu, xzhu, zhanchuan}@uestc.edu.cn

Abstract. To improve unstructured peer-to-peer system performance, one wants to minimize the number of peers that have to be probed before the query is answered. In this paper, we propose a replication strategy with the consideration of heterogeneous resources among peers in the unstructured P2P system. In our strategy, the system copies the replication of the popular file to high capacity peers. Experimental result shows our replication strategy reduces the network traffic greatly, and improves the popular file availability effectively.

1 Introduction

In peer-to-peer (P2P) system, a peer in network can be a client and server simultaneously, called servent. The servent of equal roles or capabilities exchange information directly with each other. P2P system were classified by [1] into three different categories - unstructured, structured, loosely structured. Each has their advantages and disadvantages. However, the unstructured P2P systems are the most commonly used in today's Internet. But unstructured P2P system which retrieves the sharing data with flooding mechanism also raises an important performance issue, such as a lot of network traffic caused by flooding query.

To improve unstructured P2P system performance, one wants to minimize the number of peers that have to be probed before the query is answered. One way to do this is to replicate the sharing data on several peers. In this paper, we propose a replication strategy in that the data mostly popularity is replicated on the peers which is high capacity.

2 Replication Strategy

2.1 Zipf Distribution

Many popularities in the real world distribution in Internet world such as web server requests, web caching and P2P are presented as the Zipf distribution. In the Zipf distribution, the number of requests for the rth most popular item is proportional to $r^{-\alpha}$, where α is a constant. For example, the popularity of data requested from a web caching (with 0.65 < α < 0.85), web server data popularity (with 0.75 < α < 0.85), and P2P query popularity (with 0.63 < α < 1.24) [2] all exhibit as Zipf distributions.

According the P2P system query following the Zipf distributions, the query converge few file. The few file is the popular file. So if we replicate the popular file on more peers which have high capacity, we could minimize the number of peers that have to be probed before the query is answered. This will reduce the network traffic greatly. What's more important: it will improve the popular file availability for it's replication on more capacity peers in the unstructured P2P system.

2.2 Server-Like Peers

In our replication strategy, a sharing data was replicated at peers who fit high-bandwidth, enough computation power, long online time, and a large amount of storage space. We called the peers with above characters as sever-like peer. A peer can be a server-like peer only if above criteria is satisfied.

The basic requirement is a high bandwidth connection. Saroiu and Gribble[2] who study on Gnutella indicate that 60% of the peers in Gnutella use broadband connections. Furthermore, 30% of the peers in Gnutella have very high bandwidth connections, at least 3 Mbps.The second criterion is that the server-like peers must have enough computation power because they need to deal with most system workloads. Our prototype implementation ignores the effects of computation power. Third, server-like peers can not join/leave system frequently; otherwise its efficiency will be greatly reduced. The capacity of peers can be weighted by how long the node has been in system. At last, server-like peers should have large amount of storage space which store the replication of the sharing data.

2.3 Replication Algorithm

When a peer join in the unstructured P2P system, the system decided a peer whether is server-like peer according with above criteria. Once a peer becomes a server-like peer, it not only processes the query message but also processes the query hit message. When server-like peer receives a query hit message, it decides whether download the replication according with its status. Figure 1 shows that the system selects peer G as target of the replication of the sharing data. Peer D is in the way of the query hit message, but peer D isn't a server-like peer. Peer C is server-like peers, but it isn't in the way of the query hit message. Peer E already has the replication. So peer D, C and E are not selected as target of the replication of the sharing data.

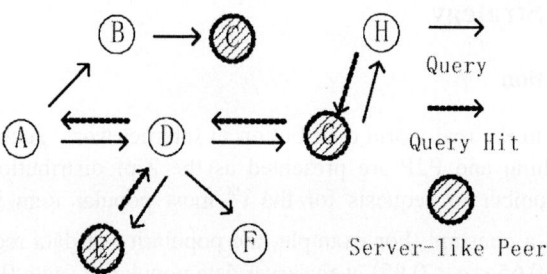

Fig. 1. Replicate the result of query

All information storage systems must deal with the problem of finite storage capacity. If the sharing storage of server-like peers was exhausted at end, it is managed as an LRU (Least Recently Used) cache in which replications are kept sorted in decreasing order by time of most recent request (or time of insert, if a replication has never been requested). When a new replication arrives (from a successful requested) which would cause the sharing storage to exceed the designated size, the least recently used replication are evicted in order until there is room. This mechanism make the popular replication was kept longer time in the system.

3 Experimental Results

To evaluate our replication strategy, we create a P2P simulation environment and vary the input parameters. For the topology of the P2P system we use BRITE[3], the topology generator for network simulation to generate. In our simulation, we assume about 30% of the peers in simulation network have very high bandwidth connections, at least 3 Mbps, 50% of the peers in simulation network are on-line above 5 hours[2]. The total number of the peers in simulation network is 10000, and the simulation network contains 5000 files which divide into 50 categories. Each of the categories has different amount. For brevity, we called the unstructured P2P system with replication strategy as RP2P, and called the unstructured P2P system without the replication strategy as GP2P.

In Figure 2 shows the network traffic generated for different requested result sizes with RP2P and GP2P respectively. The average size of query result record is 76 bytes and the average size of query message is about 82+ L(Q) bytes and the query string is L(Q) bytes[4]. In the graph, we observe that the GP2P generates more traffic than the RP2P do in the condition of requesting same results. This indicates that the RP2P can reduce the traffic greatly.

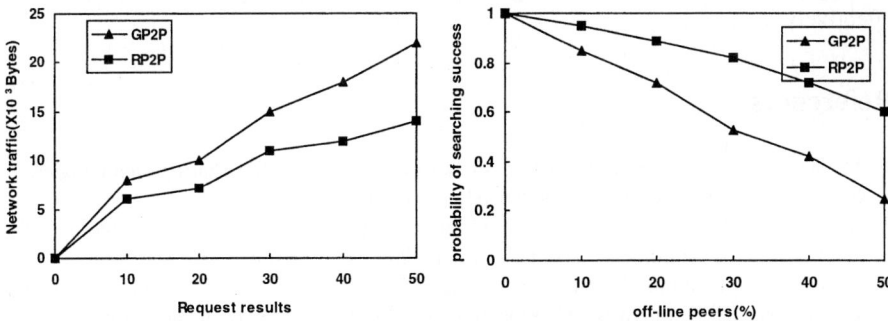

Fig. 2. Traffic vary with request results

Fig. 3. probability of searching success vary with off-line peers

In Figure 3 shows the probability of searching file success varied with off-line peers' percent with RP2P and GP2P respectively. From the graph, we observe that the

RP2P hold high probability of searching file success though the off-line peer is 50% of the total peer in stimulation network, about 60%, while the probability of searching file success only is 25%. This indicates that the RP2P can achieve more file availability than the GP2P do.

4 Related Work

Gnutella does not support proactive replication, but at least part of FastTrack-based P2P systems can be attributed to replication: FastTrack[5] designates high-bandwidth peers as search-hub (supernode, ultranode). In FastTrack a supernode replicates the index of the sharing data. In our replication strategy a server-like peer replicates the copy of the sharing data. So FastTrack caches the index of the sharing data, but our replication strategy write the replication of the sharing data into disk. Freenet allow for more proactive replications of sharing data, where the sharing data may be replicated at a peer even though the peer has not requested the sharing data. This is similar to ours strategy, but Freenet treats all peers in the system without the consideration of heterogeneous resources among peers. In [6], the author addresses the question: given fixed constraints on per-probe capacity, what is the optimal way to replicate data. In [7], this paper address the question: is it possible to place replicas of shared files in such a way that, despite constant changes to the online membership, files are highly available without requiring the continual movement of replicas.

5 Conclusions

In this paper, we propose a replication strategy with the consideration of heterogeneous resources among peers in the unstructured P2P system, and copy the popular file to the high capacity peers. Experimental result shows our replication strategy decreases network traffic greatly, and improve the popular file availability effectively.

References

1. Stephanos Androutsellis-Theotokis a survey of peer-to-peer file sharing technologies. In http:// www.eltrun.aueb.gr/whitepapers/p2p_2002.pdf 2002.
2. S. Saroiu, P. K. Gummadi, and S. D. Gribble. A measurement study of peer-to-peer file sharing systems. Multimedia Systems Journal, 2002, 8(5) 156-170.
3. A.Medina, A.Lakhina, I.Mattaf, et al. BRITE: An Approach to Universal Topology Generation. IEEE International Workshop on Modeling, Analysis, and Simulation of Computer and Telecommunication Systems, 2001, 346-353
4. B.Yang and H.Garcia-Molina. Improving search in peer-to-peer networks. Proceedings - International Conference on Distributed Computing Systems, 2002, 5-14

5. Peter Backx, Tim Wauters, Bart Dhoedt, et al. A comparison of peer-to-peer architectures. In Germany http://allserv.rug.ac.be/ ~pbackx/A% 20comparison% 20of% 20peer-to-peer%20architectures.pdf. 2002.
6. E. Cohen and S. Shenker, Replication strategies in unstructured peer-to-peer networks. Performance Evaluation Review, v 30, n 1, 2002, 258-259
7. Francisco Matias Cuenca-Acuna, Richard P. Martin, Thu D. Nguyen, Autonomous Replication for High Availability in Unstructured P2P Systems. In the 22nd IEEE International Symposium on Reliable Distributed Systems, 2003.

Random Walk Spread and Search in Unstructured P2P*

Zhaoqing Jia, Ruonan Rao, Minglu Li, and Jinyuan You

Department of Computer Science and Engineering, Shanghai Jiao Tong University,
Shanghai 200030, China
jiazhaoqing@hotmail.com

Abstract. Unstructured Peer-to-Peer applications are very popular on the Internet. An efficient technique for improving performance of search method of these systems is to replicate file location information in P2P. In this paper we present random walk spread mechanism, and random walk spread and search method. Simulation results show that it achieves high success rates at low cost.

1 Introduction

In recent years, unstructured P2P applications are very popular, such as Gnutella [1]. In general, they employ flooding scheme for searching object, and waste a lot of bandwidth [1]. Today, bandwidth consumption attributed to these applications amounts to a considerable fraction (up to 60%) of the total Internet traffic [2]. It is of great importance to reduce the total traffic of them for the user and the broad Internet community.

A search for a file in a P2P network is successful if it discovers the location of the file. The ratio of successful to total searches made is the success rate of the algorithm. The performance of an algorithm is associated with its success rate, while its cost relates to the number of messages it produces.

Many search methods have been proposed for reducing the overhead of flooding scheme. A random walks search method is proposed in Ref.[3], and total traffic is largely reduced. But its success rate is very low. Ref.[4] proposed a search algorithm which utilized high degree nodes and success rate is still low.

In this paper, we present a random walk spread mechanism and Random Walk Spread and Search (RWSS) algorithm. We perform extensive simulations and compare RWSS with the method in Ref.[4], RWSS achieves great results in the success rates, message production and average hops.

2 Random Walk in Power-Law Network

Random walk is a well-known technique, which forwards a query message to a randomly chosen neighbor at each step until the object is found. This message

---

* This paper is supported by 973 project (No.2002CB312002)of China, ChinaGrid Program of MOE of China, and grand project of the Science and Technology Commission of Shanghai Municipality (No. 03dz15026, No. 03dz15027 and No. 03dz15028).

is known as "random walker". In a power-law graph, p(k) is the probability that a randomly chosen node has degree k, and a random edge arrives at a node with probability proportional to the degree of the node, i.e., $p1(k) = kp(k)/\sum kp(k)$, where $\sum kp(k)$ is equal to average degree $<k>$. For enough high degree k_c, when $k > k_c$, there is only one node with degree=k in the graph, and its p(k)=1/N, so $p1(k) = k/(N<k>)$. Let maximum degree $m = N^{1/\tau}$[5], A random edge arrives at the highest degree node with probability $p1(m) = 1/(N^{(\tau-1)/\tau} <k>)$. So, the probability that a random walker walks through the highest degree node with steps=n is given by $q = 1 - (1 - \frac{1}{N^{(\tau-1)/\tau}<k>})^n$. Table 1 displays the probability that a random walker walks through the highest degree node in a graph with N=100000, $\tau = 2.1$, and $<k> \geq 6$. The probability is 86.6% at n=5000, and comparing with N=100000, 5000 is very low. The difference between maximum degree and degree of every other high degree node is small, thus the probabilities that a random walker walks through every other high degree node is close to the one of the highest degree node.

Table 1. Probability at Different Steps of Random Walker

Steps	1000	2000	3000	4000	5000	6000	7000	8000	9000	10000
Probability(%)	33.0	55.1	69.9	79.9	86.6	91.0	94.0	95.9	97.3	98.2

3 RWSS Algorithm

Unstructured P2P networks display a power-law distribution in their nodes degree [6]. Based on the analysis of the section 2, random walk in power-law networks naturally gravitate towards the high degree nodes. If file location information is placed on the high degree nodes, then it will be easily found through random walk. Hence, we design a replica spread method employing random walk for placing files information on the high degree nodes, and present RWSS algorithm. RWSS includes two phases: random walk spread and random walk search. To reduce delay in RWSS, a node sends b messages, and each message take its own random walk. The simulations in Ref.[3] confirm that b walkers after T steps reach roughly the same number of nodes as 1 walker after bT steps.

We have the following assumptions about our algorithm:

1. Each node has a LocalDirectory (LD) that points the shared files on this node.
2. Each node has a FileInformationDatabase (FID) that cache the location information of the remote files managed by other nodes.
3. FileInformation(*filename, loc, ttl*) is a message and used for spreading *loc* (location information) of file *filename* with *ttl* steps.

In the spread mechanism, when a node wants to share its files, it sends out b FileInformation messages to an equal number of randomly chosen neighbors.

Each of these messages follows its own path, having intermediate nodes forward it to a randomly chosen node at each step.

Spread Mechanism (Node sId spreads location information of file *filename*):

```
Spread Procedure on Source Node sId:
  add filename to LD;
  fi = New FileInfornation(filename,loc,ln(N));
  for J=1 to b {
    randomly choose a neighbor node ni of the node sId;
    forward fi to node ni;
  }
Spread Procedure on Intermediate Node ni:
  receive FileInformation(filename,loc,ttl) from node n1;
  if filename not in LD
    if filename not in FID
      add (filename,loc) to FID;
  if ttl>0 {
    randomly choose a neighbor node n2 of the node ni;
    forward FileInformation(filename,loc,ttl-1) to node n2;
  }
```

The search mechanism is similar to the spread mechanism. The only difference between them is that file information is forwarded in the spread mechanism and query message is forwarded in the search mechanism. The average path length of a random graph is proportional to $\ln(N)/\ln(<k>)$, so TTL value of query message is set at $\ln(N)$, and messages per request is $O(b\ln(N))$.

4 Simulations

In simulations, we used two power-law graphs: graph GI, which is produced by Innet-3.0 [7], and graph GP, which is produced by Pajek [8]. Graph GI has 20000 nodes with m=3159, $<k>= 5.26$ and $\tau = 2.3$. Graph GP has 20000 nodes with m=441, $<k>= 5.84$ and $\tau = 2.1$. 1000 files are used in all simulations and accessed at same probability.

4.1 Performance of RWSS

We focus on three metrics: Success Rates, Messages per Request and Average Hops. For $<k>$ of each graph is close to 6, 6 random walkers are used to spread file information. Usually, 16 to 64 walkers give good results [3]. Hence, 32 random walkers are employed for searching object. Table 2 show that RWSS achieves high success rates. Each request produces about three hundreds of messages. In contrast to flooding mechanism query cost is very low. For the degrees of the high degree nodes of the graph GI are higher than those of the graph GP, random walk can arrive at them more quickly on the graph GI. Hence, the performance on the graph GI is better than that on the graph GP.

Table 2. Simulation Results of RWSS Method and Ref.[4] Method

Graph	RWSS			Ref.[4]		
	Succ. Rates	Mess./Req.	Aver. Hops	Succ. Rates	Mess./Req.	Aver. Hops
GI	100%	228.2	1.818	80.8%	116.3	37
GP	77.73%	342.1	4.992	23.5%	373.1	122.9

4.2 Comparison with Ref [4] Method

Table 2 displays simulation results of Ref.[4] method with search steps=450 and show that success rates of RWSS are higher than those of Ref.[4] method and average hops are much lower. In Ref.[4], each node indexes all files on its neighbors, and a node chooses the highest degree neighbor node to forward the query to. The high degree nodes have not any information about the files on many low degree nodes which do not neighbor on them. The probability is that the files on the low degree nodes can not be found, so success rate is low. For the degrees of the high degree nodes of the graph GP are very low and they have few neighbor nodes, the success rate on the graph GP is very low.

5 Conclusion

This paper presents random walk spread mechanism for improving search in unstructured P2P. We proposed RWSS search method, and extensive simulations show that it achieves high performance at low cost. Comparing RWSS with Ref.[4] method, RWSS exhibits higher success rates for similar message consumption.

References

1. Gnutella website:http://gnutella.wego.com.
2. Sandvine Inc. An Industry White Paper: The Impact of File Sharing on Service Provider Networks. Dec. 2002.
3. Q. Lv, P. Cao, E. Cohen, K. Li and S. Shenker. Search and Replication in Unstructured Peer-to-Peer Networks. ICS'02. Jun. 2002. Pages:84-95.
4. L. Adamic, R. Lukose, A. Puniyani, and B. Huberman. Search In Power-Law Networks. Phys. Rev. E64(2001), 046135.
5. W. Aiello, F. Chung, and L. Lu. Random Evolution in Massive Graph. STOC'00. 2000. pp. 171-180.
6. M.A. Jovanovic. Modeling Large-sacle Peer-to-Peer Networks and a Case Study of Gnutella. Master Thesis. Apr. 2001.
7. C. Jin, Q. Chen, and S. Jamin. Inet: Inernet Topology Generator. Technical Report CSE-TR443-00, Department of EECS, University of Michigan, 2000.
8. Pajek website: http//vlado.fmf.uni-lj.si/pub/networks/pajek/.

ODWIS as a Prototype of Knowledge Service Layer in Semantic Grid

Bo Chen and Mingtian Zhou

School of Computer Science & Engineering,
University of Electronic Science & Technology of China,
Chengdu, Sichuan, China 610054
bluesbeyond@vip.sina.com, mtzhou@uestc.edu.cn

Abstract. As proposed to be an infrastructure of e-Science environment, the Semantic Grid is an evolution of Grid in that it incorporates ontologies as essential ingredients, which is logically structured into a 3-layered architecture from viewpoint of services by its advocates: Computation/Data, Information and Knowledge Service Layer. Based on a Granular Representation Calculus adapted for representing Internet information sources, the authors first presented an Ontology-Driven Web Information System (ODWIS) as a Knowledge Integration model of Web information system, to facilitate complex knowledge retrieval on the Web. The present paper discusses both functional and computational aspects of ODWIS, with open issues left for a full-fledged implementation. Intrinsic with built-in ontologies, ODWIS is a promising candidate of a prototype for Knowledge Layer implementation for Semantic Grid. Feasible approach to building a Semantic Grid can be the integration of extended ODWIS with common grid computing environments built with well-known toolkits. The authors hope such an interdisciplinary topic can be of significance to promote cross cooperation among researchers.

Keywords: Semantic Grid, Ontology-Driven Web Information System, Granular Representation Calculus.

1 Preliminaries

Coordinate resource sharing in dynamical Virtual Organizations (VO) is the core of Grid Computing. Resource representation is the first step for resources to be discovered and shared. The representation form of resources should be easy to be automatically generated and ready for further processing.

Chen et al. presented Granular Representation Calculus (GRC) in [1, 2] to represent Information Systems in the context of Rough Set Theory research, which describes systems starting from a natural language viewpoint and then synthesizes complex systems from the primitive notion of atomic information granules. Over the granular representation, an alternative approach of investigating roughness is achieved, namely the Granular Rough Theory (GRT). In [3], the fundamental role of GRC in GRT motivates Chen et al. to adapt GRC to be appropriate for representing media resources over Internet, so as to take advantages of soft computing capability of GRT. The adapted GRC is tightly bound to ontologies for full-fledged expressive power on par with Resource Description Framework (RDF).

In [4, 5], Roure et al proposed the Semantic Grid as an infrastructure of e-Science, which is appealing in that it incorporates ontologies to evolve Grid Computing to be knowledge oriented, as is the trends of Web to evolve to be the Semantic Web. From a service-oriented view, Roure et al gave a layered architecture of it, as illustrated in Fig.1, namely Data/Computation Services Layer, Information Services Layer and Knowledge Services Layer. The Knowledge Layer is concerned with the way that knowledge is acquired, used, retrieved, published and maintained to assist e-Scientists to achieve their particular goals and objectives.

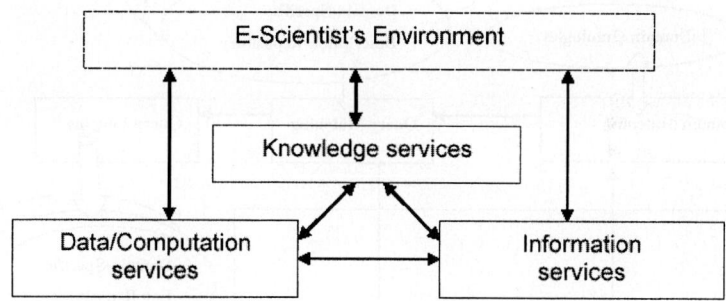

Fig. 1. Three-layered architecture viewed as services (see [4])

As rudimental efforts, an Ontology-Driven Web Information System (ODWIS) is proposed first to take account in only issues related to generic Web resources, which is a Knowledge Integration model of Web information system, built for facilitating complex knowledge retrieval on the Web. The ODWIS is then proposed to deploy in Semantic Grid as its Knowledge Service Layer, in order that Soft Computing technologies intrinsic in Granular Rough Theory can be applied to complex Knowledge processing in Semantic Grid.

2 An Embryo: Ontology-Driven Web Information System ODWIS

The ODWIS system acts as a mediator between users and information sources, collecting descriptions of sources all over the Internet, answering queries from clients and additionally providing knowledge discovering supports over descriptions or query logs, as in Fig. 2.

2.1 Functional Aspects

2.1.1 Domain Ontologies

Domain ontologies play a core role in ODWIS, which gives the global worldview for all domains of interest. A domain is referred to as a particular discourse of universe, which stands for phenomena in a specific context, for instance, bibliographical domain, medical domain, and automobile manufactory domain. For each domain, there is a domain specific ontology, which is crucial to specify what classes of entities are presented in the information source, what aspects we can inspect over the entities, what component/integral-object mereological relation may exist between granules, what attribute set can be for entities in a sub-universe, and so on. Domain-specific ontology defines a schema of Information Repository for information granules, to which the GRC can then be applied.

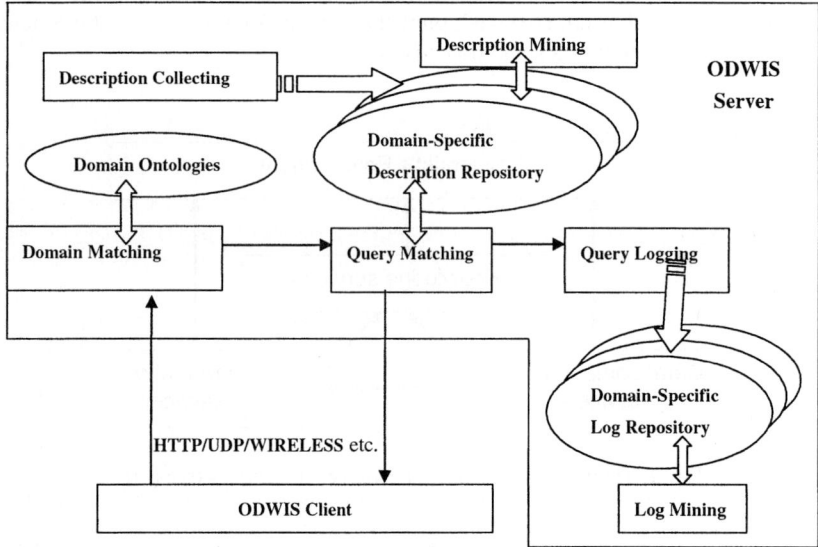

Fig. 2. An ODWIS framework on functional aspects

2.1.2 Domain-Specific Description Repositories
There are as many domain-specific Information Repositories as domains of interest, each of which conforms to the "schema" defined by the corresponding domain-specific ontology mentioned above, termed as *Domain-Specific Description Repository (DescRep)*. A DescRep contains information granules describing aspects of Web information sources, extracted from *RDF*-like annotations of these sources. For a given information granule, it must describe aspects for entities of the exact types specified in the domain-specific ontology, whereas due to the independency of granular representation, information granules in DescRep need not be complete in the sense to describe every aspects of an entity, which makes it tolerable to the incompleteness of information.

2.1.3 Description Collecting
Since ODWIS intends to act as a mediator system, it is natural for ODWIS to have facilities for collecting descriptions of widespread heterogeneous Web information sources in the *RDF*-like annotations so as to answer complex queries. A prerequisite condition for description collecting is meta-level annotation mechanism due to the Domain Ontologies is well adopted in construction of Web information sources,

which is beyond the reach of this work. There may be two styles fulfilling such functionality: *ODWIS Initiated Collecting* and *Description Registry Service Provider*. The former is closely related to agent technologies, which makes use of agents (so-called Web Crawler) that crawl on the Web to gather descriptions from annotations residing with each information source. The latter provides open description registry facilities in the same way some global name servers supply their naming services. The collected annotations are then processed to validate their conformance to the specified Domain Ontologies in ODWIS. If there are inconsistencies, a semantics oriented domain-specific ontology translation is performed or the inconsistent descriptions are discarded. The resulted annotations are then transformed into information granules and added to corresponding domain-specific DescRep.

2.1.4 Query Answering

End user initiates an ODWIS query through different kinds of communication mechanisms, such as HTTP, UDP and Wireless. From the viewpoint of the end users, the most desirable form of queries is a natural English propositional sentence. By some auxiliary utilities, such a sentence in natural language can be parsed into triple form information granules, due to their intrinsic affinities. It is of paramount significance that queries must follow the specification of domain ontologies. Such a conformance can be reinforced by predefined Web pages that provide standard domain ontology oriented query generation forms.

On the ODWIS Server side, the received queries are then matched to their corresponding domains. The matching is mainly based on the domain information encoded in the query granules. There may be occasion that no such information is encoded, which makes it hard to determine information sources in what particular domain the user are intended to retrieve. In such a situation, the domain information for some of them can be extracted by comparing the attribute collections of query granules to each domain-specific ontology for their names and value types. This issue is potentially profound and further efforts on it would be necessary. Once the domain-specific ontology is matched, the domain-specific DescRep is also determined, which is the totality of description granules of information sources in the specified domain. Then these description granules are compared with the query granules to obtain the resulted granules. From the viewpoint of the Granular Calculus, the comparison is to find out the *aspect cluster granule* with respect to the attribute and valuation collection of the query granule. The resulted granules are transformed into sentences as answers to users.

Optionally, query results cache mechanism can be incarnated into realized system for higher performance.

2.1.5 Knowledge Discovering

Knowledge Discovering components in ODWIS take advantage of the intrinsic connection of the underlying representation model. By applying the Granular Rough Theory to description granules in each domain-specific description repositories, association or decisional rules between multiple aspects of information sources can be obtained, and information sources can be classified into predefined classifications. Furthermore, clustering of information sources can also be achieved. It is often more desirable to analyze the activities of end users, which calls for the mining functionalities for historical queries. There is *Query Logging* component that log all the compound query granules into domain specific *Log Repositories* (*LogRep*). Then similar knowledge discovering mechanism applied to DescRep can be adapted into the logging context, with augmented requirements such as sequential user activities mining.

2.2 Issues for Computational Aspects

It is obvious that the GRC is by nature a representation calculus, viz. it provides a way of expressing information structures by its operations rather than really specifies underlying implementation. Since there are a great number of information granules in the system, efficient comparison and query methodology for information granules are crucial for our approach to be practical and realizable. In other word, a mapping from the symbolic operations of the GRC to computational realizable constructs is the key to a full-fledged system. So far, it has not been well investigated and left for future efforts, but there are some potential candidates to adapt to this context. Since the query of information granules is by nature an object query, a mapping of GRC to realizable data models for Object-Oriented Database Management Systems (OODBMS) can help. Two of the most promising models can be data models in ODMG [6] and Java Data Object (JDO) [7]. One may question why we develop an additional representation model other than models in ODMG and JDO themselves, for such a challenge, we could say that the standards in OODBMS are developed from a pure database point of view, but GRC are originally developed to be an alternate to tabular representation for Information Systems so as to be a fundamental representation model for an alternate theory of roughness. The distinction between their origins makes it reasonable to be such a calculus, which is not so general an object model for all the OODBMS needs but dedicated to a more specific operational context.

3 ODWIS Extension as the Knowledge Service Layer

The ultimate goal of the authors' efforts is to establish an ontology-driven grid computing environments, which incorporates interdisciplinary methodologies and technologies. ODWIS is general purpose for Web intelligent systems and no specifications of its deployment in grid context. A feasible approach to achieve the ultimate goal can be based on a common Grid computing environment implemented

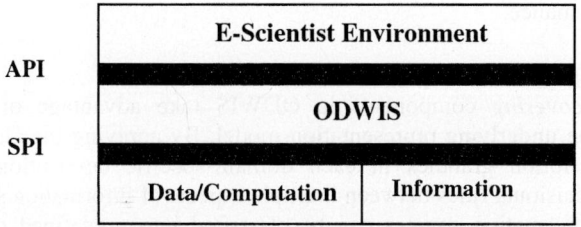

Fig. 3. ODWIS in Semantic Grid Service Layers

with Grid computing toolkits such as Globus [8], and integrate ODWIS as its knowledge service layer. ODWIS must be extended to supply both Application Programming Interface (API) and Service Provider Interface (SPI), to facilitate e-Scientist Layer implementation and underlying Data/Computation and Information Layer utilization, respectively, as illustrated in Fig.3.

4 Conclusions

Semantic Grid is the future infrastructure of e-Science, which bears the very objective to support cross-disciplinary cooperation of researchers and practitioners. By such a topic, the paper is intended to promote the cooperation of building such an interdisciplinary problem-solving environment.

References

1. Chen B, Zhou M. A Pure Mereological Approach to Roughness. In Wang G, Liu Q, Skowron A et al (Eds.): Proceedings of RSFDGrC 2003, Chongqing, China, LNCS/LNAI 2639, Springer 2003, pp.425–429.
2. Chen B, Zhou M. Adapting Granular Rough Theory to Multi-agent Context. In Wang G, Liu Q, Skowron A (Eds.): Proceedings of RSFDGrC 2003, Chongqing, China, LNCS/LNAI 2639, Springer 2003, pp. 701–705.
3. Chen B, Zhou M. Extending Granular Representation Calculus for Internet Media Resources. In Li J et al. (Eds): Proceedings of the 3rd International Conference on Active Media Technology (ICAMT'04), Chongqing, China, World-Scientific, 2004, pp.571–576.
4. Roure D, Jennings N, Shadbolt N. The Semantic Grid: A Future e-Science Infrastructure. In Berman F, Fox G, Hey A, (Eds). Grid Computing - Making the Global Infrastructure a Reality, pages pp. 437–470. John Wiley and Sons Ltd.
5. Roure D, Jennings N, Shadbolt N. "Research Agenda for the Semantic Grid: A Future e-Science Infrastructure" Technical Report of the National e-Science Center, UKeS-2002-02, 2001.
6. Catell R (Eds). The Object Database Standard: ODMG 3.0. Morgan Kaufmann, 2000.
7. Craig Russell (Eds.), JSR-000012 Java Data Objects (JDO) Specification. http://jcp.org/aboutJava/communityprocess/final/jsr012/index2.html.
8. Foster I, Kesselman K. Globus: A metacomputing infrastructure toolkit. Journal of Supercomputer Applications 11, 2 (1997), 115–128.

An Adaptive Proximity Route Selection Scheme in DHT-Based Peer to Peer Systems*

Jiyoung Song, Sungyong Park, and Jihoon Yang

Dept. of Computer Science, Sogang University,
Seoul, South Korea
{itsuki, parksy}@sogang.ac.kr, jhyang@ccs.sogang.ac.kr

Abstract. This paper presents a proximity route selection scheme which is adaptive to the underlying network conditions. The proposed scheme repeatedly estimates and updates the total lookup latency based on the information from the neighborhoods. The updated information is used to select the next peer dynamically to route the query, which results in reducing the overall lookup latency. We implemented the scheme using the Chord, one of the most popular DHT-based peer to peer systems, and compared the performance with those of original Chord and the CFS' server selection scheme. The proposed scheme shows performance improvement over other schemes.

1 Introduction

Chord [1] is one of the most popular distributed hash table (DHT) based peer to peer systems which provides scalable services for the storage and retrieval of (key, data) pairs. In Chord, a hash function such as SHA-1 assigns a key (or identifier, ID) from the circular m-bit identifier space to each node and data. Each node maintains a routing table (finger table in Chord) of other live members (neighborhoods). The size of the routing table is either constant or $O(log\ p)$, where p is the number of participating nodes. The ith entry in the routing table of node n points to a node with the smallest identifier clockwise from $n+2^{i-1}$. During the query routing process, Chord selects the next routing peer in the finger table whose identifier is the closest to the data's key to minimize the total routing hops.

However, the overlay hops along the routing path may contain heavy links and the lookup latency increases although we have minimal routing hops. In order to solve this problem, CFS [3] proposes a server selection scheme for Chord on the domain of proximity route selection (PRS) [2]. In CFS, each node predicts the entire lookup latency which is calculated by using the total number of nodes and average overlay hop delay. Among these neighborhoods, one with the minimum cost is selected as the next routing peer. The problem of this approach is that it is hard to approximate the total number of nodes and the average hop latency from the local, since the number of neighborhoods for each node is too small. The inaccurate estimation may also result in decreasing the performance.

---

* This work was supported by grant No. R01-2003-000-10627-0 from the Basic Research Program of the Korea Science & Engineering Foundation.

In this paper, we propose an adaptive proximity route selection (APRS) scheme in order to reduce the total lookup latency by modifying the Chord protocol. Unlike CFS, our scheme estimates the query delivery time using previous estimation history, where the new estimated value is calculated by combining the observed latency and the old estimated value. This scheme does not require any knowledge of total number of nodes and the average hop latency.

The rest of the paper is organized as follows. Section 2 presents the adaptive proximity route selection scheme in detail. In Section 3, we evaluate the APRS scheme and present the experimental results. Section 4 concludes the paper.

2 Adaptive Proximity Route Selection Scheme (APRS)

The APRS scheme uses recursive lookup. Each node on the routing path forwards a query for a specific key to one of its neighborhoods and updates the estimation about the expected lookup latency based on the information from their neighborhoods unless the node is the predecessor whose ID is just previous to the key on the ID space. In what follows, we provide the detailed description of our scheme.

For a given node with ID n, if a key q of query in $[n+2^i, n+2^{i+1})$, where i is an integer between 0 and $m-1$ (on the m- bit identifier space), is received, we assume that node n is in i-state. (Similar to the term Range used in [5])

For the query q, the candidates set of the next routing peer in node n is determined as follows:

$$candidate\_set_n(q) = \{\text{Node } x \mid \forall x \text{ in the routing table which satisfies its ID} \in (n, q]\} \quad (1)$$

Note that the route is restricted by the candidate set.

Each node obtains the routing policy by predicting which one of $candidate\_set_n(q)$ can reduce the total lookup latency for routing the query. To do this, APRS requires additional information for each entry in the finger table. For each entry with ID x, the form is,

$$(x, \text{cost}_i, \text{cost}_{i+1}, ..., \text{cost}_m) \text{ for all entry in the routing table} \quad (2)$$

where the integer i starts at the state of neighborhood peer ID. The value of cost_i which is denoted by $Q_n(x,i)$ means the estimated lookup latency by selecting x of candidates for i-state query at node n. This extended table is called a lookup table.

The node periodically updates this lookup table by the rule shown below.

$$Q_n^{new}(x,i) = (1-\alpha) \cdot Q_n^{old}(x,i) \\ + \alpha \cdot (\text{observed latency to } x + \min_{z \in \text{neighborhoods of } x} Q_x(z,i)) \quad (3)$$

where α [†] is a constant between 0 and 1. This update rule (3) is drawn from Q-routing algorithm [4] based on reinforcement learning on the domain of distributed packet routing algorithms.

There are two strategies to update the lookup table by receiving the information[‡] from neighborhoods. According to the original Chord protocol, each node in the

---

[†] We set alpha to 0.5 in our simulation for experimental reason.
[‡] This is the second part given in equation (3).

system runs the stabilization protocol periodically in the background for neighborhoods to refresh its entries. It is possible to add additional information corresponding to the term $Q_x(z,i)$ and measure the latency to x based on the latencies observed while performing the background process. The advantage of our scheme is that no additional control message exchange is needed. However, due to this delayed updating, the adaptability to the network can be decreased. The other alternative is to update the lookup table by requesting the response message for the forwarded query, immediately. In our simulation, the latter is adopted for the fast convergence.

The decision rule of selecting the next peer to route the query is greedy. If node n is in i-state for the query q, the greedy decision rule is as follows:

$$\pi_n(i_q) = \arg\min_{c \in candidate_n(q)} Q_n(c, i_q) \tag{4}$$

where $\pi_n(i_q)$ is the routing policy for node n during the routing process.

3 Experimental Results

We have conducted our experiment over modified SFS-simulator [6] to implement our scheme. Two different topologies, ring and transit-stub random graph with Waxman model by GT-ITM [7], are used for underlying physical connectivity between nodes and we have compared the performance of our scheme (APRS) with those of unmodified Chord and the CFS' server selection scheme.

The simulation consists of three phases. First, each node joins one-by-one. At this time, each node selects its underlying network position in the topology and ID randomly. In the second phase, each node inserts about 50 documents (in average) into the system. In the third phase, we measure the lookup latency by generating 50 requests for randomly selected documents. During the simulation, we do not consider the dynamics of nodes (e.g. node joins and leaves) in the system explicitly.

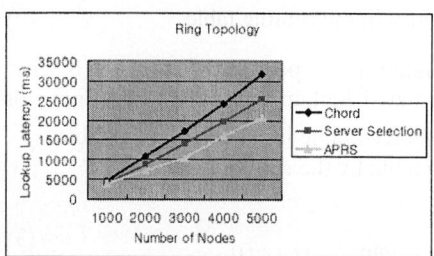 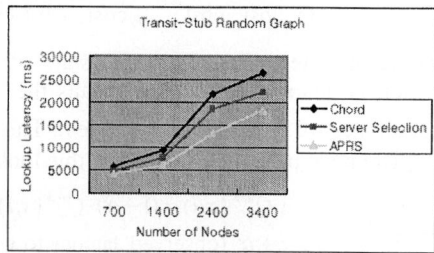

Fig. 1. Average lookup latency for Ring and Transit-Stub Random Graph

Fig. 1 shows the average lookup latency for the ring and transit-stub random graph by varying the number of nodes ranging from 1000 to 5000 and from 700 to 3400, respectively. APRS scheme shows performance improvement over the original Chord and server selection method by about 31% and 20%, respectively. Note that server selection has the advantage of knowing the number of nodes in the system.

Fig. 2 shows the time required for the latency to converge into a certain level. The 1 time unit in Fig. 3 (i.e., x-axis) means the time when one request on all nodes in the system has been resolved. As we can see from Fig. 2, after about 21 requests are reached, the average lookup latency is converged to a certain level. This means that the proposed scheme adapts to the network changes within a reasonably short period.

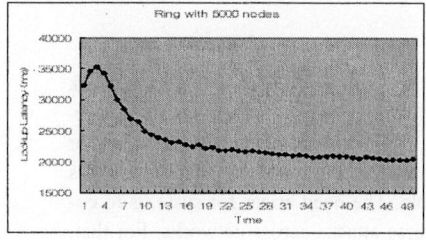 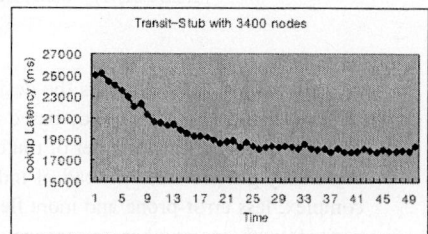

Fig. 2. Convergence time

4 Conclusion

In this paper, we have proposed an adaptive proximity route selection scheme. Nodes in Chord are able to obtain the distributed routing policy by using APRS. To show that, we have implemented and compared our scheme with the original Chord that does not aware of the network proximity and CFS' server selection through simulation. From the experiments, we showed that the performance of our proposed scheme was better about 20% and 31% than the server selection and original Chord, respectively without much network overhead and computation. We also showed that the period of adapting to network changes is also reasonably short.

References

1. Stoica, I. et. al. : Chord : A Scalable Peer-to-Peer Lookup Protocol for Internet Applications, IEEE/ACM Transactions on Networking Vol. 11 Issue 1 (2003) 17-32.
2. Gummadi, K. et. al. : The impact of DHT Routing Geometry on Resilience and Proximity, Proc. of the 2003 Conference on Applications, Technologies, Architectures, and Protocols for Computer Communications (2003) 381-394.
3. Dabek, F. et. al. : Wide-area cooperative storage with CFS, Proc. of the 18th ACM Symposium on Operating Systems Principles (2001) 202-215.
4. Boyan, J., Littman, M.: Packet routing in dynamically changing networks: A reinforcement learning approach, Proc. of Neural Information Processing Systems (1994) 982-988.
5. Zhang, H., Goel, A., Gobindan, R.: Incrementally Improving Lookup Latency in Distributed Hash Table, Proc. of the 2003 ACM SIGMETRICS International Conference on Measurement and Modeling of Computer Systems (2003) 114-125.
6. Chord Simulator, http://pdos.lcs.mit.edu/cgi-bin/cvsweb.cgi/sfsnet/simulator.
7. GT-ITM, http://www.isi.edu/nsnam/ns/ns-topogen.html.

Distributed Security Agent Modeling in the Policy-Based Networking[1]

Hee Suk Seo and Tae Ho Cho

School of Information & Communications Engineering, Modeling & Simulation Lab,
Sungkyunkwan University, Suwon, 440-746, South Korea
{histone, taecho}@ece.skku.ac.kr

Abstract. This paper presents the design and modeling of distributed network security agents based on policy-based networking (PBN) which has some merits. Configuring a high number of routers, IDS (Intrusion Detection System), or servers by generic rules instead of individual configuration appears to be less complex, less error-prone and more flexible. The need arises for systems to coordinate with one another, to manage diverse attacks across networks. For that, we have designed the policy-based framework which has distributed intrusion detection agents and diverse network components.

1 Introduction

Networks are developed to make computers more accessible to the outside world. Making computers more accessible to the outside is a mixed blessing. Network security is a problem that has gotten larger with the growth of the Internet [1]. For the simulation of the policy-based framework environment, ID agent models, network component models and Firewall models are constructed based on the DEVS (Discrete EVent system Specification) formalism [2]. Since evaluating the performance of a security system directly in real world requires heavy costs and efforts, an effective alternative solution is using the simulation model. In concrete terms, using the model we can build various simulation situations, perform iterative runs, and decide which security configuration is effective in meeting the change of network environment [3]. The paper describes the design and modeling of network security agents based on policy-based framework which has some merits. The need arises for systems to coordinate with one another, to manage diverse attacks across networks and time.

2 Agent Model

2.1 Security Agent

Intrusion detection is the process of monitoring computer networks and systems for violations of security policy [4]. Intrusion detection agent is decomposed into four sub-components: Audit, Packet Distributor, Alarm, and Detection model. Audit model

---

[1] This research was supported by University IT Research Center Project.

is specialized into Auditlog and Buffer model. Audited information is generally considered security critical and deemed suitable for storage in a protected log.

Packet Distributor model receives network packets that are generated by the network packet generator model and classifies them according to attack types. Then it filters sorted packets to reduce processing time in the following processes. Packet Allocator model in Packet Distributor model sends the received packets to each type model according to the policies. If the intrusion is detected, this situation is reported to Alarm model and policy-based system model. As intrusion detection system technology matures, alarms must evolve into more dynamic directives from sensor components and processors to other components in the system. Detection is core model in the Intrusion Detection Agent and transforms the packets that are delivered by Packet Distributor into facts to be used by expert system. Expert system inferences according to the facts thus generated. If a new attack is to be added to intrusion detection model later on, the administrator classifies the attack and adds a proper subcomponent model to Packet Distributor and its corresponding rules to Detection model. Firewall agent is decomposed into Controller and Filter model. If attack is detected by ID agent, ID agent reports this information to the firewall through the policy enforcement point of the policy-based framework. Firewall model changes the policies itself. Then attack packets are prevented from the Internet.

2.2 Policy-Based Networking Agent

Policy-based networking [5] is decomposed into five sub-components: PC, PR, PDP, PEP, and PMP model. Policy console model helps an administrator edit policy rules and configurations. PR model stores the policies. PDP model is decomposed into Supervision, Policy Transform, and Policy Distributor model. Policy Transform model is responsible for ensuring that the high-level policies specified by the network administrator and mutually consistent, correct, and feasible with the existing capacity and topology of the network. Policy Distributor model is responsible for ensuring that the low-level policies are distributed to the various devices in the network. PEP model is specialized into six sub-components: Gateway model, Router model, Switch model, IDS model, firewall model, and Authentication model. PMT model applies the policies that is defined by the network management policies and stores the information to the policy repository model. It is decomposed again into Resource Discovery, Model Interface, and Model Valid Check. Model Interface is specialized into Model Interface Administrator, Model Interface PR, Model Interface IDS, Model Interface Firewall, and Model Interface VDB. Vulnerability database (VDB) contains the network vulnerability. Valid Check model inspects the attributes that is set by the network management policies and checks if the new policy conflicts with the used it. Resource Discovery model determines the topology of the network, the users, and applications operational in the network.

3 The Coordination Among the Multi-agents by the PBN

Policy server reports the information which is defined by the policy-based framework to other network components. Firewall uses this information to prevent harmful packets from external network. Intrusion detection agent of each subnet detects the intrusion and reports the intrusion information to the policy-based framework. The policy management tool in the common policy-based framework is used by the network administrator but we have appended the a few interface modules for the more automatic control. The policy management tool in the proposed system is accessed by the administrator, vulnerability database, and intrusion detection system. Vulnerability database helps the system manager to find bugs that enable users to violate the network security policies. The policy server reports to the firewall for the prevention from damaging the network.

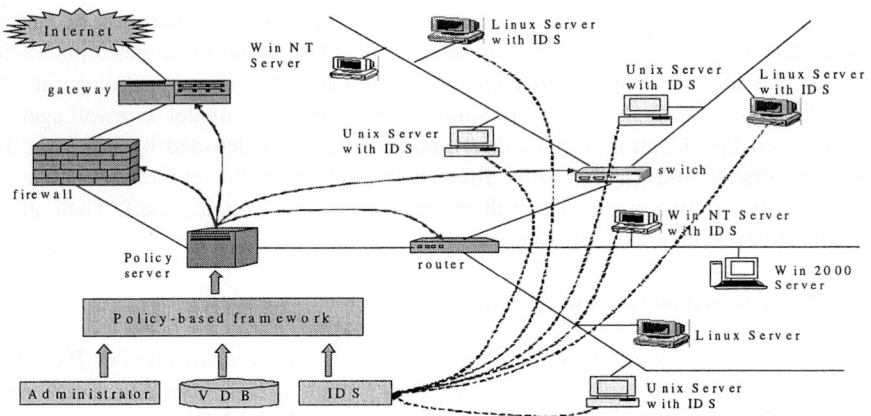

Fig. 1. Network components coordination

4 Simulation Result

We have executed simulations for two cases. One is the case for using the PBN, the other is the case for not using the PBN. Scanning attack is used for the simulation in both cases. The intrusion detection time, false positive and false negative error ratio are measured for the performance indexes in the simulation [6].

Scanning checks for any network-accessible insecurities that would allow a intruder to get onto victim machine or gather information that could aid in other hacking attempts. This research shows that the proposed system with PBN is superior. Fig. 4,5 shows the false positive error ratio of the proposed system with PBN for the scanning attack. A false positive is basically an alarm on acceptable behavior. Figure shows that the false positive error ratio is increased by strengthening of the security level. This increase in the error ratio is due to the fact that the higher the security level, the more error IDSs make in both cases. Fig. 6,7 shows the false negative error ratio of the proposed system with PBN for the scanning attack. A false negative is basically a missed alarm condition. Fig. 6,7 shows the decrease of the false positive error ratio as the security level is strengthened. For all cases, the error ratio of the proposed system is lower than that of the previous system since the intrusions are detected based on the shared information.

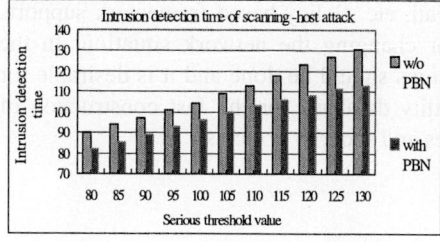

Fig. 2. Intrusion detection time of scanning attack - a case of host attack

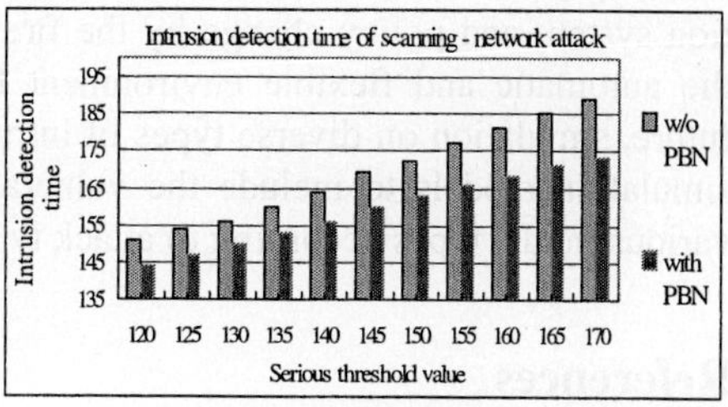

Fig. 3. Intrusion detection time of scanning attack - a case of network attack

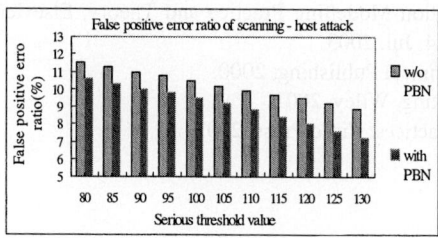
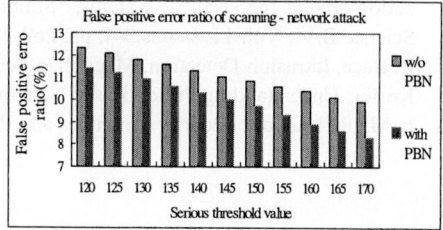

Fig. 4. FPER of scanning attack- a case of host attack

Fig. 5. FPER of scanning attack – a case of network attack

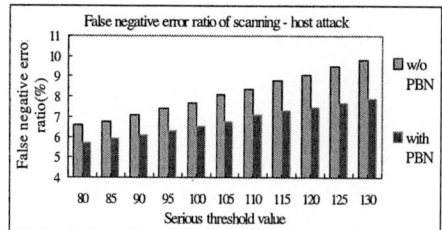
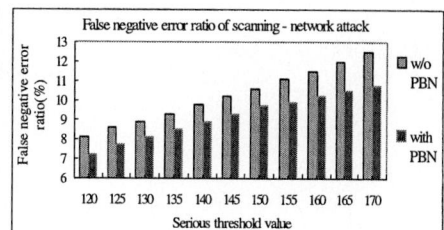

Fig. 6. FNER of scanning attack – a case of host attack

Fig. 7. FNER of scanning attack – a case of network attack

5 Conclusion and Future Work

As the usage of the network increases, intrusions occur more frequently and become more widespread and sophisticated. Policy-based network management provides a means by which the administration process can be simplified and largely automated.

The proposed system has an advantage of the management. The administrator can easily apply the policies to the network components with the policy-based framework. The security system makes a various network situations-the policies should be applied to change the network states. These situations include the response of intrusion detection system and policy change by the firewall, etc. Policy-based framework supports the automatic and flexible environment for changing the network situation. In the future, simulation on diverse types of intrusions should be done and it is desirable for simulation models to include the vulnerability database for the fast construction of various model types according to attack types and security policies.

References

1. C. M. King, C. E. Dalton, T. E. Osmanoglu, Security Architecture, RSA press, 2001.
2. B. P. Zeigler, H. Praehofer and T.G. Kim, Theory of Modeling and Simulation, Academic Press, 2000.
3. Seo, Hee Suk and Cho, Tae Ho, "An application of blackboard architecture for the coordination among the security systems," Simulation Modelling Practice and Theory, Elsevier Science B.V., Vol. 11, Issues 3-4, pp. 269-284, Jul. 2003.
4. R. Bace, Intrusion Detection, Macmillan Technical Publishing, 2000.
5. Kosiur, Understanding Policy-Based Networking, Wiley, 2001.
6. S. Malik, Network Security Principles and Practices, Cisco Press, 2003.

The Analysis of Hardware Supported Cache Lock Mechanism Without Retry

Wonil Kim[1], Chuleui Hong[2], and Yeongjoon Kim[2]

[1] Dept. of Digital Contents, College of Electronics and Information Engineering,
Sejong University, Seoul, Korea
wikim@sejong.ac.kr
[2] Software School, Sangmyung University,
Seoul, Korea
{hongch, yjkim}@smu.ac.kr

Abstract. A lock mechanism is essential for synchronization on the multiprocessor systems. This paper proposes the new locking protocol, called WPV (Waiting Processor Variable) lock mechanism. It uses the cache state lock mechanism and has only one lock-read bus traffic. This paper also derives the analytical model of WPV lock mechanism as well as conventional memory and cache queuing lock mechanisms. The simulation results on the WPV lock mechanism show that access time is reduced comparing with the memory and queuing lock mechanism as the number of processors increases.

1 Introduction

An efficient lock mechanism is required in a shared memory parallel architecture because many processors should be able to write shared data simultaneously [1]. The locking mechanism using the cache coherence protocol is an approach to reduce the bus usage dramatically [2, 3]. The newly proposed WPV (Waiting Processor Variable) lock mechanism takes advantage of the pipelined protocol [4]. The sub-phase of waiting for the locked data is held until the data is transferred directly to the next waiting processor by the cache-to-cache data transfer mechanism without retry.

The WPV lock mechanism changes the cache coherence protocol slightly and reduces the bus usage more considerably than the existing cache lock mechanism. In the WPV mechanism, which is shown in Figure 1, the cache block has both *LOCKED* and *LOCK-WAIT* states, therefore the data block can be locked directly without a separate lock bit. Because of this mechanism, lock/unlock operations can be performed without any overhead, as the reads/writes to the target data execute the lock/unlock operations simultaneously. A *LOCK-WAIT* state indicates another processor is waiting for the shared data to be unlocked.

The WPV lock mechanism does not retry locking and saves one bus usage comparing with the conventional cache lock mechanism. Each processor has its own single buffer called WPV. The ownership of the shared lock data is shifted according to the WPV's of processors which want to lock the shared data. This guarantees FIFO operation as a fairness criterion on the arbitration scheme. Therefore, WPV mechanism sets the upper bound on the waiting time of locking and guarantees the deadlock free operations. It also prevents the processor from waiting for locking forever.

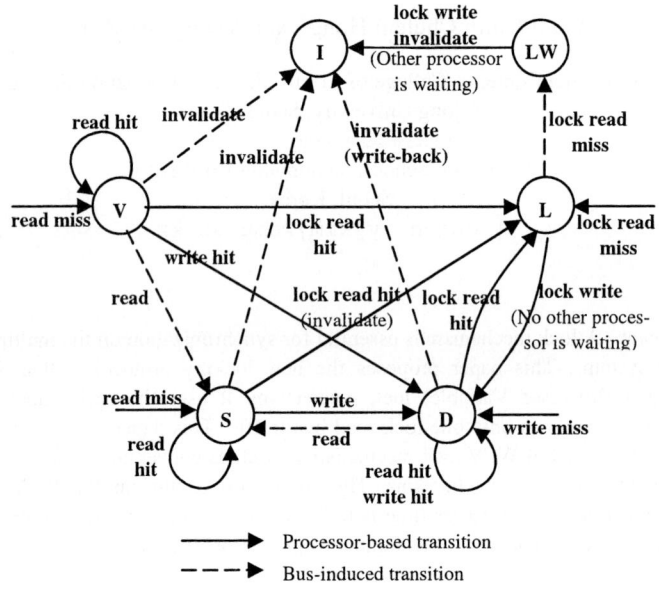

Fig. 1. WPV Cache State Diagram

2 Analytical Modeling of WPV

In this section, we analyze and compare the performances of (1) memory lock, (2) queuing lock using cache coherence protocol, and (3) the proposed WPV lock mechanism. The actual lock reference ratio, r, is derived by summing the initial and retrying lock references. Let the number of processors be N, the total lock variables be L, and the number of routings be B. Then the probability of arbitrary processor to access any lock variable is r/L, and the probability of any processor not accessing any lock variable is $(1-(r/L))^N$. Let q be the probability that at least one processor access any lock variable. If the lock variable references are independent and uniformly distributed, the probability, f, that i lock variables are referenced among L lock variables is binomially distributed. Therefore, the average number of referenced lock variables in 1 cycle is qL, and only B lock variables are referenced among those. The bandwidth BW is derived as in Eq. (1).

$$q = 1-\left(1-\frac{r}{L}\right)^N, \; f_i = \binom{L}{i} q^i (1-q)^{L-i}, \; BW = \sum_{i=1}^{B-1}(i \cdot f_i) + B\sum_{i=B}^{L} f_i \qquad (1)$$

We first analyze the memory lock mechanism. The average lock interval time, T, is defined by summing the average execution interval time, $x=(1-p)/p$ where p is initial lock reference ratio, the average delayed time by the lock variable and network contention, d_l, and the average lock operation time, l_{op}. d_n is a delayed average time by only network contention. Lock/unlock operation is assumed to be completed in 1 cycle. N_{req} is defined as the reference number in T times through network. Since the completion ratio of lock operation is $BW/2N$, the average lock interval time $T=2N/BW$. Therefore, the lock reference ratio in a memory lock mechanism, r_{mem}, is defined in Eq. (2).

$$T = x + d_l + l_{op} + d_n + 2, \quad N_{req} = d_l + d_n + 2 = r \times \frac{2N}{BW}$$

$$r_{mem} = \frac{\frac{2rN}{BW}}{x + l_{op} + \frac{2rN}{BW}} = \left(1 + \frac{BW \cdot (x + l_{op})}{2rN}\right)^{-1} \quad (2)$$

With a analytical model of memory lock mechanism, we derive the analytical model of cache queuing lock, r_{queue}, and WPV lock mechanism, r_{WPV} in Eq. (3). α represents lock variable contention probability, where $w = \alpha \cdot d_l$. Figure 2 shows time sequences of memory, cache queuing, and WPV lock mechanisms respectively.

$$r_{queue} = \left(1 + \frac{BW \cdot (x + l_{op} + w)}{r \cdot (\alpha + 2) \cdot N}\right)^{-1}, \quad r_{WPV} = \left(1 + \frac{BW \cdot (x + l_{op} + w)}{r \cdot 2 \cdot N}\right)^{-1} \quad (3)$$

<Memory Lock>

execution interval	blocked req. for lock	lock	locking operation	blocked req. for NW	unlock
x	d_l	1	l_{op}	d_n	1

<Cache Queuing Lock>

execution interval	blocked req. for NW	lock	wait	additional req.	lock	locking operation	blocked req. for NW	unlock
	d_n	1	w	α	1	l_{op}	d_n	1

<WPV Lock>

execution interval	blocked req. for NW	lock	wait	locking operation	blocked req. for NW	unlock
x	d_n	1	w	l_{op}	d_n	1

Fig. 2. The time sequences of various lock mechanisms

3 Simulation Results and Conclusions

The memory, queuing and WPV lock mechanisms are based on a single bus which has pipelined protocol. In the simulation, we assumed that the miss ratio of a cache is 3% on each processor [5]. The lock frequency and the size of the critical section is set to 1% and 10 instructions respectively.

The Figure 3 shows that average lock access time of memory lock increases sharply when the number of processors is increased over 8 as the bus utilization increases over 8 processors. The high bus contention increases the probability of the critical section execution, and the write operation for releasing the lock variable fails by bus contention. This causes an increase in the average lock access time. The utilization of processor is inversely proportional to the bus utilization because the processors will be idle due to retry or waiting for the lock variable under lock contention. This simulation shows that the lock performance does not depend on the lock frequency and the size of the critical section, but on the sharing rate.

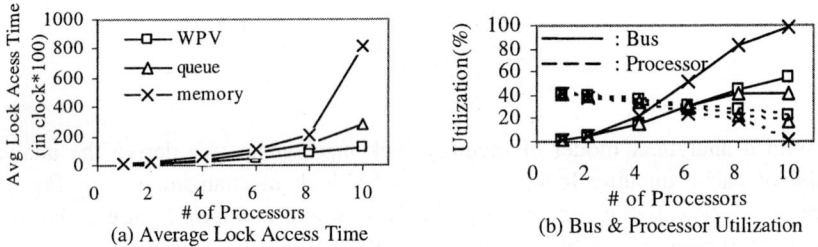

Fig. 3. Average Lock Access Time and Bus & Processor Utilization

The WPV lock mechanism is efficient in fine grain granularity lock operations. It takes advantage of the pipelined data transfer protocol. Since it does not retry locking for the contested shared data at all, locking is done with one bus command instead of two bus commands of the conventional cache queuing lock mechanism. The WPV mechanism increases the system performance dramatically because the bus is likely to be a bottleneck in multiprocessors. The simulation shows that about 50% of the access time are reduced comparing with the conventional queuing lock mechanism. Moreover, this method adopts the cache state lock to reduce the locking overhead. It also sets the upper bound on the waiting time of locking and guarantees the deadlock-free operations.

References

1. Moon, E., Thang, S., Jhon, C.: Analysis of the Relation of Synchronization Algorithm and Parallel Programs in Shared-Memory Multiprocessor Systems. Proceedings of High Performance Computing Symposium. (2000)
2. Cho, H.: Cache coherency and concurrency control in a multisystem data sharing. IEICE Transactions on Information & Systems. Vol. E82-D. No. 6. (1999) 1042–1050
3. Nikolopoulos, D., Papatheodorou, S.: Fast Synchronization on Scalable Cache Coherent Multiprocessors using Hybrid. Proceedings of the 14th International Parallel & Distributed Processing. (2000) 711–719
4. Ki, A.D., Park, B.K.: Highly pipelined bus : HiPi-Bus. Proceedings JTC-CSCC '91. (1991)
5. Yamamura, S., Hirai, A., Yamamoto, M: Speeding Up Kernel Scheduler by Reducing Cache Misses. Proceedings of the Freenix Track 2002 USENIX Annual Technical Conference. (2002) 275–285

Modeling of Non-Gaussian AR Model with Transient Coefficients Using Wavelet Basis

Lisha Sun[1], Minfen Shen[1], Weiling Xu[1], and Patch Beadle[2]

[1] Dept. of Electronic Engineering, Shantou University, Guangdong 515063, China
lssun@stu.edu.cn
[2] School of System Engineering, Portsmouth University, Portsmouth, U.K.

Abstract. This paper focuses on the modeling of non-Gaussian autoregressive (AR) model for a wide range of physical signals. A practical algorithm based on higher-order cumulants is proposed to deal with the problem of estimating the non-Gaussian AR model with transient coefficients. Wavelet basis is used to identify the transient coefficients. The performance in terms of Haar and Morlet basis is evaluated with non-stationary processes. The experimental results show the flexibility of capturing the local events by using the presented model.

1 Introduction

The issue of identifying time-varying linear systems has received more attention during the last decade since we need to deal with these problems in practice such as system analysis, data analysis and modeling [1]. Generally, most of time series are assumed that they are both stationary and Gaussian. The stationarity requires that the underlying statistics and the model parameters that characterize the process are not dependent on time. However, more and more physical signals have been proved to be non-stationary and non-Gaussian nonlinear [2,3]. To describe and capture the local characteristics of the underlying non-stationary non-Gaussian process, more explicit modeling of the processes evolution is required. But up to now, it is still difficult to effectively solve the problem of identifying the time-varying linear system driven with a non-Gaussian noise. For this purpose, based on the method of modeling the third-order stationary non-Gaussian process [4], we extend the model to the situation of non-stationarity and develop an algorithm for detecting the local non-Gaussian statistical characteristics in this contribution. The proposed scheme consists of the linear systems with time-variant parameters, which is expressed by a finite set of constant coefficients of basis functions. We construct the transient AR model with the input of the non-stationary non-Gaussian signals. The wavelet basis functions are used for describing the time-varying parameters of the AR model. Several simulations are carried out based on both Haar and Morlet wavelet basis functions for the time-varying coefficients estimation of the proposed model. The empirical results demonstrate that the proposed scheme is much suited for modeling the practical time-varying non-Gaussian processes.

2 The Proposed Model

For a non-stationary non-Gaussian series f(t), it can be generated via an AR(p) process with time-varying coefficients [5,6]

$$\sum_{i=0}^{P} a_i(t) f(t-i) = v(t) \quad (1)$$

where v(t) denotes an independent identically distributed (i.i.d.) stationary, non-Gaussian sequence with finite nonzero cumulants. The time-varying coefficients can be further described with a sum of basis functions

$$a_i(t) = \sum_{k=1}^{q} b_{i,k} \xi_{i,k}(t) \quad (2)$$

where $\xi_{i,k}(t)$ represent a number of orthonormal basis functions. Thus $a_i(t)$ are projected on the space of the basis functions. Our task become to determine the unchanged coefficients of $b_{i,k}$. We define a new expression:

$$F(t) = -\sum_{i=1}^{P} A(i).F(t-i) + V(t) \quad (3)$$

where $F(t) = [\xi_0(t)f(t), \cdots, \xi_q(t)f(t)]^T$ and $V(t) = [\xi_0(t)v(t), \cdots, \xi_q(t)v(t)]^T$. We have $A(i) = [\xi_0(t)a_i, \cdots, \xi_q(t)a_i]$ in which $\alpha_i = [b_{i0}, \cdots, b_{iq}]^T$.

With the *mth* order cumulants $C_{m,F}$ of $F(t)$, we have the recursive relation [7,8]:

$$\sum_{i=0}^{P} A(i) C_{m,F}(\tau_1, \cdots, \tau_{m-2}, \tau-i) \equiv 0 \quad (4)$$

Hence, a series of unchanged coefficients in (2) are determined. Next, we focus on selecting the wavelet basis function for model (2). Since wavelet basis function consists of enough information regarding the changes of the coefficients of the model, we use wavelet basis to identify the model coefficients and capture the time-varying characteristics of the system. In addition, proper wavelet basis must be evaluated and chosen for different kinds of time-varying non-Gaussian processes. More discussion regarding wavelet basis can be found in the references [9,10]. In this paper, two types of wavelet basis functions are considered. Haar basis is proposed to detect the abrupt change of the coefficients while Morlet basis is used to track the changes of the coefficients of the model.

3 Experimental Results

In this section, two simulations were investigated. First of all, we generated a non-Gaussian AR(2) model with time-varying coefficients of a1(k)=0.6sin(4.4(k./n)) and a2(k)=-0.7cos(3.8(k./n)). The corresponding time-varying process was shown in Fig.1 while two transient coefficients were estimated using Morlet wavelet basis and compared with the theoretical results as shown in Fig.2.

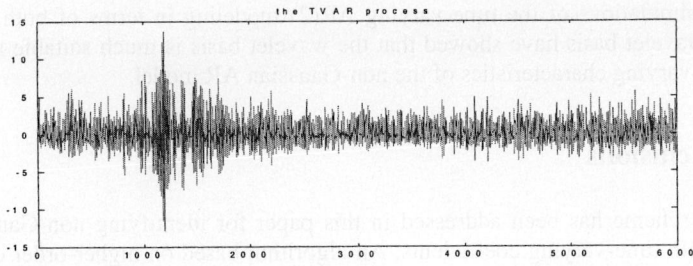

Fig. 1. The generated AR(2) time-varying non-Gaussian process

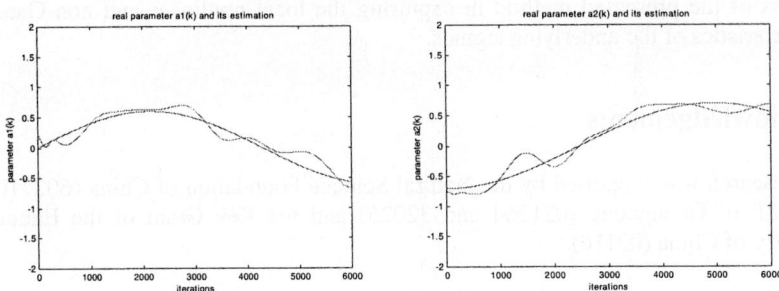

Fig. 2. Two time-varying model coefficients estimated based on Morlet wavelet basis and compared with the theoretical results (dotted lines)

The next example employed Haar basis to approximate the changes of the model coefficients described above. As sown in Fig. 3, two true time-varying coefficients were shown with the smooth solid lines while the estimated results based on Haar basis functions were demonstrated with the dotted lines of abruptly change.

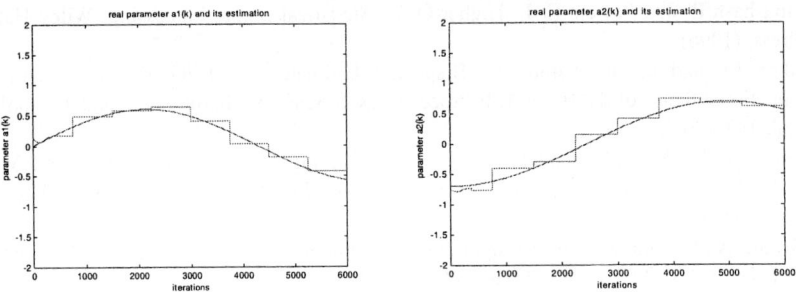

Fig. 3. The true time-varying coefficients with the smooth solid lines, compared with the estimated results based on Haar basis demonstrated with the abrupt dotted lines

The simulations of the time-varying AR(2) modeling in terms of both Haar and Morlet wavelet basis have showed that the wavelet basis is much suitable to identify the time-varying characteristics of the non-Gaussian AR model.

4 Conclusions

A novel scheme has been addressed in this paper for identifying non-Gaussian AR model with time-varying coefficients. An algorithm based on higher-order cumulants was also developed to directly estimate the transient model coefficients. We employed both Haar and Morlet wavelet as the basis functions for approximating each coefficient, which was proved to be able to track the changes of the time-varying non-Gaussian processes effectively. Two simulations were carried out to demonstrate the success of the presented method in capturing the local nonlinear and non-Gaussian characteristics of the underlying signals.

Acknowledgements

The research was supported by the Natural Science Foundation of China (60271023), the NSF of Guangdong (021264 and 32025) and the Key Grant of the Education Ministry of China (02110).

References

1. Charbonnier R. and et. al.: Results on AR Modeling of Nonstationary Signals, Signal Processing. Vol.12, No.2. (1987) 143–151
2. Shen M., Sun L., and Chan F. H. Y.: Method for Extracting Time-Varying Rhythms of Electroencephalography via Wavelet Packet Analysis. IEE Proceedings in Science, Measurement and Technology, Vol.148, No.1, January (2001) 23–27
3. Giannakis G. B. and Mendel M.: Cumulant-Based Order Determination of Non-Gaussian ARMA Models. IEEE Transaction on Acoustics, Speech, and Signal Processing. Vol. 38. No. 8. (1990) 1411–1423
4. Boashash B. and Powers E. J.: Higher-Order Statistical Signal Processing. Wiley Halsted Press. (1996)
5. Shen M. and et. al.: Parametric Bispectral Estimation of EEG Signals in Different Functional States of the Brain, IEE Proceedings in Science, Measurement and Technology. Vol. 147, (2000) 374–377
6. Tsatsanis M. K. and Giannakis G. B.: Time-Varying System Identification and Model Validation Using Wavelet, IEEE Trans. on Signal Processing. Vol. 41, No. 12. (1993) 3512–3523
7. Swami A., Giannakis G. B.: Computation of Cumulants of ARMA Processes, Proceedings of IEEE ICASSP-89. (1989) 2318–2321
8. Bakrim M., Aboutajdine D. and Najim M.: New Cumulant-Based Approaches for Non-Gaussian Time Varying AR Models. Signal Processing, Vol. 39. (1994) 107–115
9. Mallat S.: A Wavelet Tour of Signal Processing, Academic Press, 525 B Street, Suite 1900, San Dieogo, CA92101-4495. USA (1998)
10. Daubechies: Ten Lectures on Wavelets. SIAM. Ph. (1992)

Model for Generating Non-gaussian Noise Sequences Having Specified Probability Distribution and Spectrum

Lisha Sun[1], Minfen Shen[1], Weiling Xu[1], Zhancheng Li[1], and Patch Beadle[2]

[1] Dept. of Electronic Engineering, Shantou University, Guangdong 515063, China
lssun@stu.edu.cn
[2] School of System Engineering, Portsmouth University, Portsmouth, U.K.

Abstract. This paper is motivated to generate a specified correlated non-Gaussian time series, which has widely applications such as communication and radar system evaluation. The method presented provides a simple procedure for modeling the required correlated non-Gaussian random sequences with good performance. The simulation results are carried out to show the simplicity and effectiveness of the proposed method.

1 Introduction

The topic regarding the generation of desired correlated non-Gaussian time series has received a lot of interests during the last two decades in connection with the practical problems such as the communication systems evaluation, radar test and other physical measurements. For the problem of producing the non-Gaussian random series, various methods were developed to simulate the expected sequences or clutters. Usually, the practical random sequence or clutter has its joint probability density function (pdf). In addition, the random sequence may be highly correlated. Thus, both probability distribution and correlation function of the random series must be taken into account [1,2]. It is a challenge to deal with this complicated problem. However, majority of the current methods for producing such a random series were based on the consideration of just obeying the Gaussian or non-Gaussian distribution. The correlation function was always ignored or excluded for the problem. In order to overcome this limitation and simulate different types of non-Gaussian sequence having expected correlation or power spectrum density (PSD), we proposed a practical procedure to model the random sequence which has the statistical characteristics of the desired joint non-Gaussian pdf and the required correlation. The main task of this paper is to establish a proper model which can be employed to generate many different types of random sequences with not only a jointly desired non-Gaussian pdf but also a specified correlation or PSD. In other words, both statistical aspects of the pdf and the PSD can be controlled simultaneously when the model was used to generate such a specific non-Gaussian random sequence.

2 The Principle

The simulation procedure for modeling the desired correlated non-Gaussian random sequence is briefly discussed. As shown in Fig.1, the block diagram provides the proposed scheme which mainly involves the pointwise linear and nonlinear transformation of white Gaussian noise.

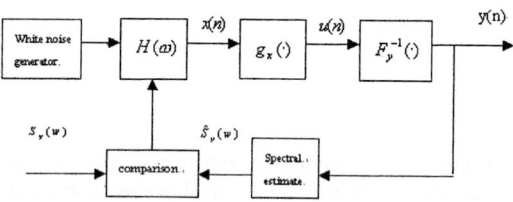

Fig. 1. The proposed procedure for generating a desired correlated non-Gaussian sequence

The output $y(n)$ denotes the required non-Gaussian sequence with probability distribution $F_y(\cdot)$ and the spectrum $S_y(f)$. Basically, this scheme consists of the linear transformation $H(z)$, the nonlinear transformation $G(\cdot)$ and the the spectral comparison. First of all, $H(z)$ is designed to transform a white Gaussian noise into a colored Gaussian sequences $x(n)$ [3]. Next, the nonlinear system $G(\cdot)$ includes the normalized Gaussian distribution function $g_x(\cdot)$ and the inverse of the distribution function of the desired sequence $y(n)$. The former is used for transforming the Gaussian sequences $x(n)$ into a sequence $u(n)$ which is uniformly distributed in the unit interval [4-5], and thus the output sequences $y(n)$ have the specified probability distribution due to the transformation of $F_y^{-1}(\cdot)$. Furthermore, the desired spectrum of the sequence $y(n)$ must be satisfied. The nonlinear transformation can be expressed as

$$G(x) = F_y^{-1}[g(x)] \tag{1}$$

If the auto-correlation function of the random sequences $y(n)$ has been specified, our task is to determine the auto-correlation function $R_x(m)$ based on the nonlinear transformation. Once $R_x(m)$ is decided, the linear system $H(z)$ can be definitely determined. Hence, the proposed procedure in Fig. 1 has been described such that when a white Gaussian noise input to the linear system, the output generate a stationary non-Gaussian sequence $y(n)$ with both specified probability distribution and correlation function. Finally, to obtain a more accurate power spectrum of the simulated sequence, a feedback procedure is proposed to compare the spectral estimate of $y(n)$ with the specified spectrum $S_y(\omega)$ and to adjust the parameters of the linear system via the error of the spectral estimation.

3 Basic Algorithm

The nonlinear function $G(x)$ is described provided the probability distribution $F_y(\cdot)$ has been definitely provided. The nonlinear function is supposed to be expanded into the Hermite polynomials [1-2]

$$G(x) = \sum_{K=0}^{\infty} b_K H_K(x) \qquad (2)$$

where $H_K(x)$ represents the K th Hermite polynomial. The coefficients of Hermite polynomial b_K is expressed as

$$b_K = (K-1)^{-1} \int_{-\infty}^{\infty} g(x) H_K(x) f(x) dx \qquad (3)$$

where $f(X)$ denotes the normalized Gaussian density function. Since $x(n)$ can be normalized into a standard Gaussian sequence, the relationship of the auto-correlation between the input and output of the nonlinear system can be described as [1]

$$R_y(m) = \sum_{K=1}^{\infty} C_K^2 R_x^K(m) \qquad (4)$$

Once the coefficients C_K is computed and $R_y(m)$ is specified, the $R_x(m)$ can be found by solving the equation (4). In general, there are several methods for finding the coefficients of the $H(z)$ [1,4,5]. However, most of these methods require a very complicated optimization procedure to achieve the design of the linear system. To overcome this limitation, AR model is proposed to provide Gaussian sequence with the required $R_x(m)$. The AR model makes the calculation of the parameters of the AR model more convenient and effective. Also the model parameters can be modified in terms of the error of the spectral estimation. Hence, after a white Gaussian noise is driven to the linear system followed by the nonlinear system, the output of the system is such a random sequence with not only a specified non-Gaussian pdf but also a desired correlation function.

4 Simulation Results

In this section, we focus on simulating s random sequence with Weibull marginal pdf which has the form

$$p(y) = aby^{b-1} \exp(-ay^b) \qquad (5)$$

The corresponding correlation is specified as the exponential function. Fig. 2 (a) and (b) show the estimated and theoretical results for both pdf and correlation function of the sequence generated. The solid lines represent the theoretical results while the bar denotes the empirical or estimated result. The simulation shows that the estimated results of the simulated non-Gaussian sequence is consistent with the theoretical results in both pdf and correlation function.

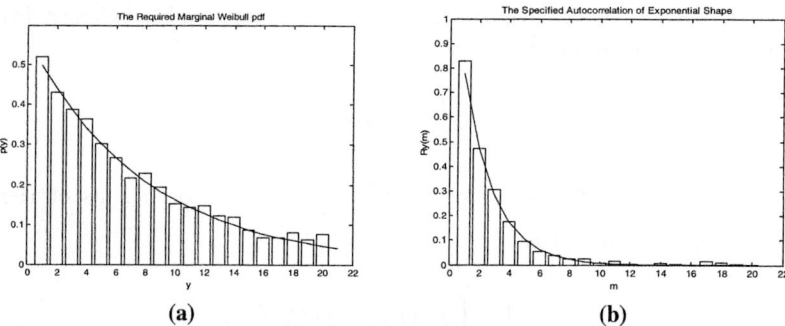

Fig. 2. The example of a random sequence with a specified Weibull probability density and an exponential auto-correlation function. (a=0.5, b=1)

5 Conclusions

This contribution considers the problem of computer generation of a desired correlated non-Gaussian sequence by means of a pointwise of linear and nonlinear transformation. Excellent agreement between theoretical and experimental results proved that the proposed approach can be effectively used in practice.

Acknowledgement

The research was supported by the Natural Science Foundation of China (60271023), the NSF of Guangdong (021264 and 32025) and the Key Grant of the Education Ministry of China (02110).

References

1. Shen J.: Approach of A Method for Generating A Random Sequence, Technique of Fire-Controlled Radar. Vol.3. (1986) 56–62
2. Li G. and Yu. B.: Modeling and Simulation of Coherent Weibull Clutter, IEE Proceedings. Part F. Communication, Radar and Signal Processing. Vol.136(1). (1989) 2–12
3. Whalen A. D.: Detection of Signals in Noise, Academic Press, Inc. (1971)
4. Haykin S.: Nonlinear Method of Spectral Analysis, Springer-Verlay. (1983)
5. Liu B. and Munson D.C.: Generation of a Random Sequence Having A Jointly Specified Marginal Distribution and Auto-Covariance, IEEE Trans. on ASSP. Vol.30. No. 6. (1982) 973–983

Self-Directed Learning Evaluation Using Fuzzy Grade Sheets

Sung-Kwan Je[1], Chang-Suk Kim[2], and Eui-Young Cha[3]

[1,3] Dept. of Computer Science, Pusan National University, Korea
[2] Dept. of Computer Education, Kongju National University, Korea
{jimmy374, eycha}@pusan.ac.kr, csk@kongju.ac.kr

Abstract. In this paper, we propose that the evaluation of the methods of self-directed learning use the triangle-type function of the fuzzy theory so that the learner can objectively evaluate their own learning ability. The proposed method classifies the result of learning into three fuzzy grades to calculate membership, and evaluate the result of an exam according to the final fuzzy grade degree as applied to the fuzzy grade sheets.

1 Introduction

The evaluation method of self-directed learning gives the initiative to each individual so they can plan how to learn, how to find the necessary information, how to search the data, and how to evaluate learning [1][2]. In existing evaluation methods, the evaluation of learning is determined by the score of an exam, which is either a multiple-choice type or single choice type question [3][4]. The method of self-directed learning using the Web (WWW) doesn't show the objective evaluations that cause some negative opinions about the evaluation. This paper proposes using the evaluation method of self-directed learning which uses the fuzzy theory where by the learner objectively evaluates his/her own learning ability. The proposed method classifies the result of learning into three fuzzy grades to calculate membership, and evaluates the result of an exam according to the final fuzzy grade degree as determined by the fuzzy grade sheets.

2 Evaluation Method of Self-Directed Learning Using Fuzzy Theory

In this paper, we propose a method of self-directed evaluation using the triangle-type membership function of the fuzzy theory.

2.1 Membership Function on the Number of Response to Learning

The membership function on the number of response to learning is organized into C_{HC}, C_{MC}, C_{LC} as Table 1.

Table 1. Parameters of the fuzzy membership function on the number of response to learning

Fuzzy Parameter	Fuzzy Value	Fuzzy Interval
C_{Hc}	Count $_{\text{High Much}}$	[8, 14]
C_{Mc}	Count $_{\text{Middle Common}}$	[4, 10]
C_{Lc}	Count $_{\text{Low Little}}$	[0, 6]

C_{LC} has a high fuzzy membership degree on the number of response to learning and has an interval [0,6]. When the number of learning is 3, membership degree is 1. In Fig. 1, the membership of C_{Lc} is computed as follows: The membership function of the number of response to learning can be shown as Fig. 1.

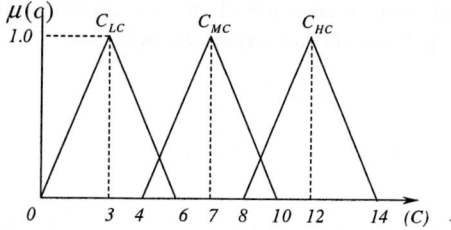

Fig. 1. Membership function on the number of response to learning

2.2 Membership Function on the Test Evaluation

The examination's problems of information process engineering are organized into four examples. To evaluate the learning ability of organized problems, the membership function is applied. The pivot is the total mean value and is computed with the number of responses to learning, which are the previous mean value, and the present mean value. The following equation (1) is shown in the above method. In this equation, I is the total number of response to learning, M is the previous mean value, K is the present mean value, and TM is the total mean value. The previous mean value (M) means the mean value of previous problem's evaluation on a test evaluation and the present mean value (K) means the mean value of the present problem evaluation. Therefore, we decided that the fuzzy grade sheets on learning ability uses the total mean value.

$$TM = (M + K)/I \qquad (1)$$

Fig. 2 is shown as the membership function on learning ability evaluation. This is organized into three fuzzy values (T_{HS}, T_{MS}, T_{LS}).

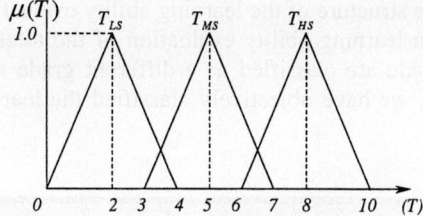

Fig. 2. Fuzzy membership function on test evaluation

2.3 Fuzzy Grade Sheets

The grade of the fuzzy scores is evaluated as follows. S (F,M) is used to represent the similarity of two fuzzy scores and is computed as an equation (2).

$$S(F, M) = (F \bullet M) / \max(F \bullet F, M \bullet M) \quad (2)$$

In this equation, F represents the standard scores $(\alpha, \beta, \gamma, \delta, \varepsilon)$ of the fuzzy grade sheets, M is a fuzzy score on the learning ability evaluation of any learner. When we define A, B that fuzzy set of universal set X, operation of A•B can be defined as equation (3). Then, it is defined as U satisfying the following conditions using the total mean value TM, the grade of fuzzy score M is shown as equation (4).

$$A \bullet B = \sum (\mu_A(x_i) \bullet \mu_B(x_i)) \quad (3)$$

$$S(U, M) = \max\{S(\alpha, M), S(\beta, M), S(\gamma, M), S(\delta, M), S(\varepsilon, M)\} \quad (4)$$

According to the fuzzy grade sheets, a grade can be produced in spite of the equal total score and we can't conclude that it is equal to the fuzzy grade of learning ability. Therefore, the proposed method classifies grades using the fuzzy grade sheets.

3 Implemental Results

This paper computes the evaluation of learning ability by using JAVA as the reading database information, which is connected by JDBC in Web.

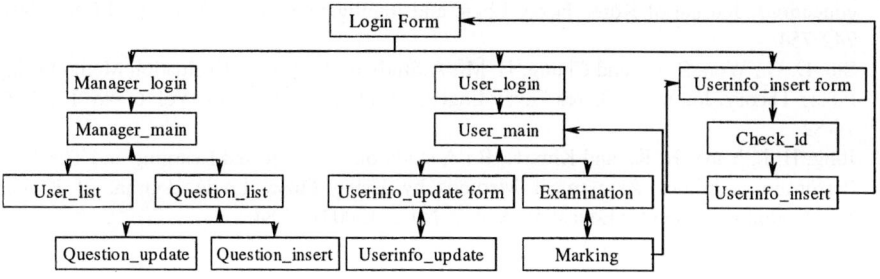

Fig. 3. Structure of learning ability's evaluation

Fig. 3 represents the structure of the learning ability evaluation. Fig. 4 represents a screen of the results on learning ability evaluation of the total learners. Because the results of the fuzzy grade are classified as a different grade among learners having same total mean value, we have objectively classified the learning ability evaluation of the test score.

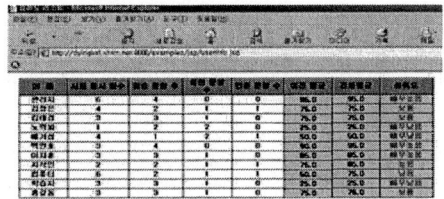

Fig. 4. Results on learning ability's evaluation of total learner

4 Conclusions

In this paper, we proposed a method of self-directed learning evaluation, which uses the triangle-type membership function and the fuzzy grade for the self-directed learning evaluation. In the proposed self-directed learning evaluation method, the total mean value is computed by the number of applied tests and previous mean value. After the computed total mean value is applied in the membership function, it is classified according to the fuzzy grade. According to the fuzzy grade sheets, in cases where there are the same total score and a different grade, we classify the fuzzy grade of the learning ability evaluation. Therefore, we have objectively evaluated the learning of the learner by eliminating the learner's subjectivity.

References

1. Kim, H. J., and Cho, S. H.: Design and Development of Web-Based Learning System Using Self-Directed Collaborative Learning Model. Journal of Korean Association of Computer Education. Vol. 5. No. 1. (2002) 67-73
2. Jang, L. H., and Kim, T. K.: Fuzzy performance assessment methods and mathematical educations. Journal of Korea Fuzzy Logic and Intelligent Systems. Vol. 11. No. 8. (2001) 742-754
3. Sin, D. G., Won, S. H., and Chung, H. M.: A Study on Education Evaluation Method using Fuzzy Theory. Journal of Korea Fuzzy Logic and Intelligent Systems. Vol. 6. No. 1. (1996) 74-82
4. Jung, H. I., Yang, H. K., and Kim, K. B.: A study on Self-Directed Learning and The Test-Performing Abilities Assessment Methods by Using Fuzzy Logic. Journal of Korean Association of Computer Education. Vol. 7. No. 2. (2004) 77-84

State Machine Based Operating System Architecture for Wireless Sensor Networks

Tae-Hyung Kim[1] and Seongsoo Hong[2]

[1] Department of Computer Science and Engineering, Hanyang University, Ansan, Kyunggi-Do, 426-791, South Korea
tkim@cse.hanyang.ac.kr
[2] School of Electrical Engineering and Computer Science, Seoul National University, Seoul 151-741, South Korea
sshong@redwood.snu.ac.kr

Abstract. A wireless sensor network is characterized as a massively distributed and deeply embedded system. Such a system requires concurrent and asynchronous event handling as a distributed system and resource-consciousness as an embedded system. State machine based software design techniques are capable of satisfying exactly these requirements. In this paper, we present how to design a compact and efficient operating system for wireless sensor nodes based on a finite state machine. We describe how this operating system can operate in an extremely resource constrained sensor node while providing the required concurrency, reactivity, and reconfigurability. We also show some important benefits implied by this architecture.

1 Introduction

Sensor networks consist of a set of sensor nodes, each equipped with one or more sensing units, a wireless communicating unit, and a local processing unit with small memory footprint [1]. In recent advancement of wireless communication and embedded system technologies, the wireless and distributed sensor networks become a prime technical enabler that can provide a way of noble linkage between the computational and the physical worlds. Since the precise delivery of real-time data on the spot is an essential basis for constructing a context-aware computing platform, the recent advancement of low-cost sensor node provides an important opportunity towards the new realm of ubiquitous computing. Positioned at the very end-terminal from the computational world side, wireless sensor nodes convey unique technical challenges and constraints that are unavoidable to system developers, which can be characterized by three aspects. First, they bear extremely limited resources including computing power, memory, and supplied electric power. Nonetheless, a sensor network can be perceived as a traditional distributed computing platform consisting of tens of thousands of autonomously cooperating nodes. Third, the computing platform does not allow recycling of the network, thus is disposable without having re-programmability.

Such characteristics of a networked sensor node call for a unique operating system architecture that can not only run on an extremely lightweight device with very low power consumption but can also support dynamic reconfigurability to cope with changing environments and applications. Such an operating system should also possess concurrent and asynchronous event handling capabilities and support distributed and data-centric programming models. In order to meet such seemingly contradictory requirements, we propose a state machine based operating system architecture, rather than following a traditional structure of an operating system and adopting it for sensor nodes like TinyOS [2]. To provide re-programmability, TinyOS employs the bytecode interpreter called Maté that runs on it. In a state machine based operating system like ours, each node is allowed to simply reload a new state machine table. Moreover, the state machine based software modeling offers a number of benefits: (1) it enables designers to easily capture a design model and automatically synthesize runtime code through widely available code generation tools; (2) it allows for controlled concurrency and reactivity that are needed to handle input events; and (3) it enables a runtime system to efficiently stop and resume a program since the states are clearly defined in a state machine. In this paper, we explore a state machine based execution model as an ideal operating system design for a networked sensor node and present the end result named SenOS.

2 State Machine Based Execution Environment

While many embedded applications should exhibit a reactive behavior, dealing with such reactivity is considered to be the most problematic. To cope with the complexity of designing such systems, Harel introduced a visual formalism referred to as statecharts [3]. Since then, a state machine has been recognized as a powerful modeling tool for reactive and control-driven embedded applications. Sensor network applications are one of those applications that can mechanize a sequence of actions, and handle discrete inputs and outputs differently according to its operating modes. Being in a state implies that a system reacts only to a predefined set of legal inputs, produces a subset of all possible outputs after performing a given function, and changes its state immediately in a mechanical way. Formally, a finite state machine is described by a finite set of inputs, outputs, states, a state transition function, an output function, and an initial state. When a finite state machine is implemented, a valid input (or event) triggers a state transition and output generation, which moves the machine from the current state to another state. A state transition takes place instantaneously and an output function associated with the state transition is invoked.

A state machine based program environment is not only suitable for modeling sensor network applications but also can be implemented in an efficient and concise way. Since sensor node functionalities are limited, although multi-functional, all those possible node functionalities are defined statically in a callback function library in advance. All we need to do as a programmer is simply to define a legal sequence of actions in tabular forms. To this end, SenOS has four system-level components: (1) an event queue that stores inputs in a FIFO order, (2) a state sequencer that accepts an input from the event queue, (3) a callback function library that defines output functions, and (4) a re-loadable state transition table that defines each valid state transition and its associated callback function. Each callback function should satisfy the "run-to-completion" semantics to maintain the instantaneous state transition semantics.

SenOS exposes another important opportunity for developers. There exist quite a few CASE tools that help designers capture state machine based system models and automatically synthesize executable code for them. UML-RT is one such tool widely used in the embedded systems industry [4]. Under our state machine based operating system, application programmers can take advantage of high-level CASE tools like UML-RT to synthesize executable code for a sensor node.

3 Implementing SenOS Architecture

The SenOS kernel architecture is comprised of three components: the Kernel consisting of a state sequencer and an event queue, a state transition table, and a callback library. The Kernel continuously checks the event queue for event arrivals; if there are one or more inputs in the queue, it takes the first one out of the queue and triggers a state transition if the input is valid. It then invokes an output function associated with the state transition. To do so, the Kernel keeps track of the state of the machine and guards the execution of a callback function with a mutex that can guarantee the run-to-completion semantics. The callback library provides a set of built-in functions for application programmers, thus determining the capability of a sensor node. The Kernel and callback library should be statically built and stored in the flash ROM of a sensor node whereas the state transition table can be reloaded or modified at runtime. The SenOS can host multiple applications by means of multiple co-existing state transition tables and provide concurrency among applications by switching state transition tables. Note that each state transition table defines an application. During preemption, the Kernel saves the present state of the current application, restores the state of the next application, and changes the current state transition table. The SenOS architecture also contains a runtime monitor that serves as a dynamic application loader. Considering the sheer number of sensor nodes, this is essential to dynamically reconfigure a new sensor network management scheme like dynamic power management. When the SenOS receives an application reload message via an interrupt from a communication adapter, the Monitor puts the Kernel into a safe state, stops the Kernel, and reloads a new state transition table. Note that the Monitor is allowed to interrupt the Kernel at any time unless it is in state transition. Since state transition is guarded by a mutex, the safety of a state machine is not compromised by such an interruption.

We have implemented our SenOS on 8-bit MCU AT89S8252 equipped with Radiometrix's BIM433 RF module that has a reliable 30m in-building range. A sensor node has four independent memory banks, each of which has 32KB flash memory as shown in Fig. 1. In our experimental implementation, we hire three sensor nodes and one sink node (PC). The SenOS is downloaded onto the sensor node that is directly connected to the host PC via a serial communication initially, and then all other nodes obtain the same OS via wireless RF communication. The SenOS was written in about 700 C lines of code, and compiled using Keil 8051 v7.0 compiler, which is compact enough to reside in a 32KB memory bank. We used four FSM tables (FSM_Serial, FSM_Network, FSM_Timer, FSM_Sensor) and defined nine output functions for wireless and serial communications, sensor and timer operations, and network man-

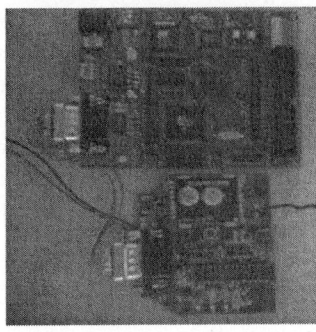

8051 Board Specifications
- ATMEL89S8252
- 8 KB Flash ROM, 2 KB EEPROM
- 32KB SRAM
- Serial Port Interface

RF Module (BIM433) Specifications
- 433.92 MHz (ETS 300-220)
- FM Transmission at -6dBm ERP
- -107dBm receive sensitivity
- Half duplex data at up to 40 kbit/s
- Reliable 30m in-building range
- Single 4.5 to 5.5 V < 15mA

Fig. 1. Sensor node module used for our implementation and its specifications

agement in our implementation. We confirmed the compactness and efficiency of a state machine based operating system by this implementation.

4 Conclusion

We have presented SenOS, a state machine based operating system for a wireless sensor node. Programmers can easily write a SenOS application via techniques on state machines and load the executable code at runtime using the Monitor as an agent. SenOS offers a number of benefits. First, its implementation is very compact and efficient since it is based on a state machine model. Second, it supports dynamic node reconfigurability in a very effective manner using replaceable state transition tables and callback libraries. Third, it can be extended to implement a sensor network management protocol, which is one of the largely untouched regions of sensor network research. Without having reconfigurability, the sensor network boils down to a hard-wired system because it is hard to reprogram that many nodes manually. These benefits render SenOS ideal for a networked sensor node. The associated tools with SenOS are underway and we further explore the applicability of reconfiguration.

References

1. Hill, J., Szewczyk, R., Woo, A., Hollar, S., Culler, D., and Pister, K.: System Architecture Directions for Networked Sensors. Proceedings of International Conference on Architecture Support for Programming Languages and Operating Systems (2000)
2. Levis, P. and Culler, D.: Maté: A tiny virtual machine for sensor networks. Proceedings of International Conference on Architecture Support for Programming Languages and Operating Systems (2002)
3. Harel, D.: Statecharts: A Visual Formalism for Complex Systems, The Science of Computer Programming, pp. 231-274 (1987)
4. IBM (former Rational Software): http://www.rational.com

QoS-Aware Admission Control for Video-on-Demand Services*

Ilhoon Shin, Y. H. Shin, and Kern Koh

School of Computer Science and Engineering, Seoul National University, Korea
{jeje, yhshin, kernkoh}@oslab.snu.ac.kr

Abstract. Admission control schemes for video-on-demand servers try to achieve the maximum admission rate. However, the quality of service (QoS) reduction caused by admitting requests has not been considered adequately. Thus, it is doubtful that servicing the maximum number of sessions can bring in the maximum revenue. We presents a QoS-aware admission control scheme that admits requests after considering both QoS reduction and resource utilization. Simulations with various traces show that the QoS-aware scheme delivers higher service revenue than a scheme that maximizes the admission rate.

1 Introduction

Video-on-demand services are emerging as a killer application in both wired and wireless network environments. The essence of video-on-demand services is the timely display of multimedia objects, and this requires that the number of concurrent sessions should be maintained at below a system's capacity. Therefore, streaming servers use an admission control module that estimates system capacity and controls requests for admission. To maximize the admission rate, existing admission control schemes try to admit as many requests as possible up to system capacity, under the assumption that if current resource utilization is below system capacity, admitting a new request will not hurt the quality of service (QoS) of the existing sessions significantly. However, this assumption does not work in disk subsystems, as shown previously [1]. That is, the occurrence of jitter can become significant as the number of concurrent sessions increases, even if the current disk bandwidth utilization is low enough to service a new request. Therefore, it is doubtful that servicing the maximum number of sessions can bring in the maximum revenue.

In this paper, we present a QoS-aware admission control scheme that maximizes the service revenue. The scheme admits a new request only when admitting the request does not hurt the QoS of existing sessions severely and it is beneficial in terms of service revenue. Performance evaluation results show that the scheme delivers more service revenue than a scheme that maximizes the admission rate.

---

* This research was supported by Brain Korea 21.

2 The QoS-Aware Admission Control Scheme

The QoS-aware admission control scheme determines whether to admit a new request by comparing the QoS reduction caused by admitting the new request with the profit resulting from servicing the new request. If the reduction in QoS exceeds the profit, the scheme rejects the new request. Only when the loss is less than the profit, it admits and services a new request. The conditions under which the QoS-aware scheme admits a new request can be abstracted as:

$$\sum (reduction\ in\ QoS) \leq the\ price\ of\ a\ new\ session \quad (1)$$

The abstraction of the QoS-aware scheme is concretized by computing the QoS reduction, which differs according to which disk-scheduling algorithm is used. Owing to the paper length limit, we implemented the QoS-aware scheme using the cycle-based disk-scheduling with a various cycle length, which is one of the most widely used for VOD servers. Cycle-based disk scheduling issues disk requests in a periodic manner, and guarantees continuous playback by reading the data required for current playback during a previous cycle. For continuous playback, the data read in a previous cycle should be sufficient for playback in the current cycle, and the previous cycle length should be long enough to read all the required blocks. The minimum cycle length that satisfies these conditions is calculated using (2). $T(s)$, s, τ_i, θ, T_{seek}, T_{lat}, and T_{full_seek} denote the cycle length, the number of concurrent sessions, playback rate of session i, disk transfer rate, aggregate seek time, aggregate rotational delay, and full seek time, respectively. A detailed explanation of the equations is given in [1].

Although the cycle length, $T(s)$ computed using (2) guarantees continuous playback when the number of concurrent sessions is s, starting a new session increases the cycle length to $T(s+1)$, which exposes existing sessions to jitter. As the data read in a previous cycle are only sufficient to feed the cycle length before it is extended, the length of jitter equals to the degree to which the cycle length is extended, i.e., $T(s+1) - T(s)$. Therefore, when the number of concurrent sessions is s, the jitter length caused by servicing a new session is calculated as (3). To compute the total reduction in QoS and the profit of servicing a new request, we need to define a price model. As it is reasonable that the price of a new session will depreciate with the occurrence of jitter and startup latency, we assume that the ideal price of a session is $M, and that it is depreciated by C_{jitter} per unit time jitter and by $C_{latency}$ per unit time startup latency. Therefore, the total loss caused by admitting a new session is calculated as (4), and the price of a new session j is calculated as (5). The lat_j denotes the startup latency of the new session. Using (4) and (5), the condition under which the QoS-aware scheme admits a new request is finally concretized as (6).

Of course, the utilization of other resources, such as memory and communication bandwidth, should also be below the maximum capacity. If the utilization of any resource exceeds its capacity, the QoS-aware scheme rejects a new request, even if (6) is satisfied.

$$T(s) = (s \cdot (T_{seek} + T_{lat}) + T_{full\_seek}) \bigg/ (1 - \frac{1}{\theta} \times \sum_{i=1}^{s} \tau_i) \quad (2)$$

$$jitter(s) = T(s+1) - T(s) \tag{3}$$

$$loss(s) = \sum jitter(s) \cdot C_{jitter} \tag{4}$$

$$price_j = M - C_{latency} \cdot lat_j \tag{5}$$

$$\sum jitter(s) \cdot C_{jitter} \leq (M - C_{latency} \cdot lat_j) \tag{6}$$

3 Performance Evaluation

We compared the QoS-aware admission control scheme with a scheme that admits requests up to 90% of the disk bandwidth capacity, in terms of the service revenue. We used three synthetic traces (Syn 1, Syn 2, and Syn 3) and one real video on demand (VOD) trace obtained from a commercial site that operates educational VOD services [2]. Syn 1 is the trace for MPEG1, Syn2 is for MPEG2, and Syn 3 is for HDTV streams. Detailed descriptions of the traces are given in Table 1. In all of the traces, the ideal prices depreciate at 10% per second of jitter and at 1% per second of startup latency, and the VOD storage device is an IBM Deskstar 120 GXP hard disk [3].

Figure 1 illustrates the results. The figure shows that the QoS-aware scheme delivered more revenue than the 90% utilization scheme overall. The improvements were conspicuous in MPEG1 and the real trace, and reached 100% and 37%, respectively. This means that servicing as many sessions as possible up to the disk bandwidth capacity was not effective, due to the considerable jitter. The QoS-aware scheme limited admission requests by considering the occurrence of jitter, and consequently delivered high revenue. By contrast, the improvements were relatively small in the MPEG2 and HDTV traces, and were 8% and 0%, respectively. This was because the disk bandwidth was easily saturated with a small number of sessions, as movies have large playback rates, so the degree of cycle extension caused by admitting a new session, i.e., the occurrence of jitter, was not significant. Note that the QoS-aware scheme still performed as well as the 90% utilization scheme in these cases, by admitting as many requests as possible up to the disk bandwidth capacity.

4 Conclusion

In this paper, we present a QoS-aware admission control scheme for VOD services. The QoS-aware scheme admits a request by considering the QoS reduction of existing sessions, as well as current resource utilization. Trace-driven simulations showed that the QoS-aware scheme performs better in terms of the service revenue than a scheme that maximizes the admission rate.

Table 1. The trace descriptions

	Syn1 (mpeg1)	Syn2 (mpeg2)	Syn3 (HDTV)	Real trace
Average playback rate	1.5Mbps	4Mbps	19.2Mbps	266Kbps
Average playback length	100 minutes	100 minutes	100 minutes	52 minutes
Average inter-arrival time	1 second	1 second	1 second	9 seconds
Ideal price	$1	$2	$4	$0.1
Simulation time	8 hours	8 hours	8 hours	39 hours

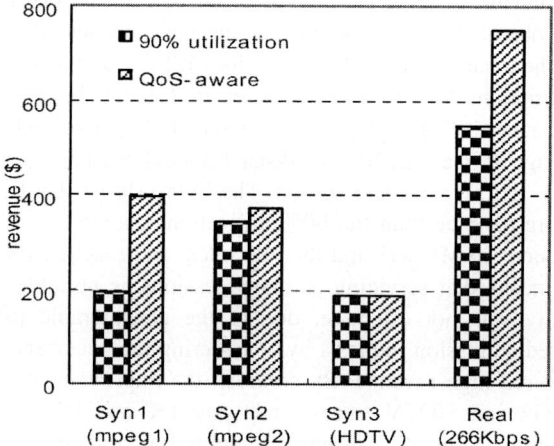

Fig. 1. The service revenue for various traces

References

1. Y. Won, K. Cho, and S. Park, "Mitigating impact of starting new session in zoned disk",. In Proceeding of ACM Multimedia, pp. 549-551, 2001.
2. KT Hitel Co. Ltd, http://edu.hanmir.com/.
3. IBM Deskstar™ 120GXP hard disk drives, http://ssddom01.hgst.com/tech/techlib.nsf/techdocs/E0B26749E1A7728C87256B290055ECA5/$file/D120GXP_ds.PDF

Context Aware Thread Aggregation in Linux

Takuya Kondoh and Shigeru Kusakabe

Grad. School of Information Science and Electrical Engineering, Kyushu University,
6-10-1, Hakozaki, Higashi-ku, Fukuoka, Japan

Abstract. Recent versions of Linux operating system employ $O(1)$ scheduler to reduce the overhead in thread scheduling. However, $O(1)$ scheduler does not take account of the affinity of threads which share the same memory address space. We propose a scheduling scheme to aggregate threads which share the same memory address space based on $O(1)$ scheduler. Our scheduler can reduce context switches and exploit locality of reference. Our performance evaluation shows our scheduler can improve throughput of a chatroom server benchmark.

1 Introduction

Although recent versions of Linux operating system employ $O(1)$ scheduler to reduce the thread scheduling overhead[1], $O(1)$ scheduler does not take account of the affinity of threads that share the same memory address space. As the gap between CPU speed and memory access speed is getting wider and wider, we need to exploit memory hierarchy to achieve high throughput. We can reduce context switches and exploit locality of reference by being aware of the context of the most recently executed thread when choosing the next thread. We develop a new scheduler which takes account of the affinity of threads and aggregates threads sharing the same memory address space. In this paper, we use $O(1)$ scheduler in Linux 2.4 as a base scheduler to implement our scheduler.[1]

2 Linux Scheduler

Linux kernel 2.4 scheduler uses a single runqueue for the entire system. The runqueue is made of doubly linked list of runnable threads. When a scheduling selection needs to be made, *schedule()* is invoked and scans all runnable threads. The scheduler can be aware of process context by comparing runnable threads and the most recently executed thread. In selecting the next thread, the scheduler gives a small priority bonus to the threads that share the same memory address sapce with the most recently executed thread. However, this runqueue scan becomes severe overhead as the number of runnable threads increase. Thus Linux kernel 2.4 scheduler lacks scalability.

In order to reduce the scheduling overhead, recent versions of Linux have $O(1)$ scheduler. The scheduling overhead of $O(1)$ scheduler is independent of the number of

---

[1] From the view point of Linux process scheduler, threads are almost the same as processes. We use "thread" and "process" interchangeably unless it matters.

runnable threads. Fig.1 shows the outline of $O(1)$ scheduler runqueue. $O(1)$ scheduler runqueue consists of two queues: an active queue and an expired queue. The active queue manages currently runnable threads that have not consumed its time quantum yet. When a thread has consumed its time quantum, it is moved to the expired queue. Once the active queue has become empty, the expired queue becomes the active queue. Each queue consists of a bitmap and an array of doubly linked list of runnable threads is associated with the bitmap. Each bit of the bitmap is a flag that indicates weather any threads exist or not in the associated list. First, $O(1)$ scheduler searches this bitmap, and finds the list of the most highest priority. Next, $O(1)$ scheduler executes the thread at the head of the list. The search overhead of $O(1)$ scheduler is a constant order and independent of the number of runnable threads. However $O(1)$ scheduler does not take account of the affinity of threads that share the same memory address space.

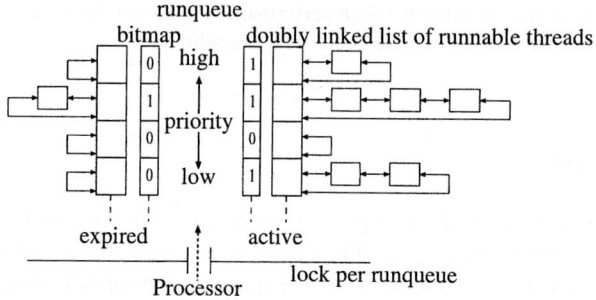

Fig. 1. Outline of $O(1)$ scheduler

3 Thread Aggregation

We improve $O(1)$ scheduler to be aware of the current thread context. Our approach tries to successively execute threads that share the same memory address space. We prioritize the threads that share the same memory address space with the most recently executed thread. Overhead of the address space switch at the time of thread switch can be omissible. Processor cache hit rate is improved by the locality of reference.

4 Implementation

In our scheduler, an auxiliary runqueue is allocated when a thread creates another thread which shares the memory address space for the first time. Thus, we have one auxiliary runqueue per group of threads that share the same address space. We also add an additional flag to a process descripter. The flag indicates weather the thread shares its address space with others or not. In creating a new thread from the parent thread, we set the flag both in the child and parent. Runnable threads with the flag set are managed by regular $O(1)$ scheduler runqueue and auxiliary runqueue. The process descripter has a pointer

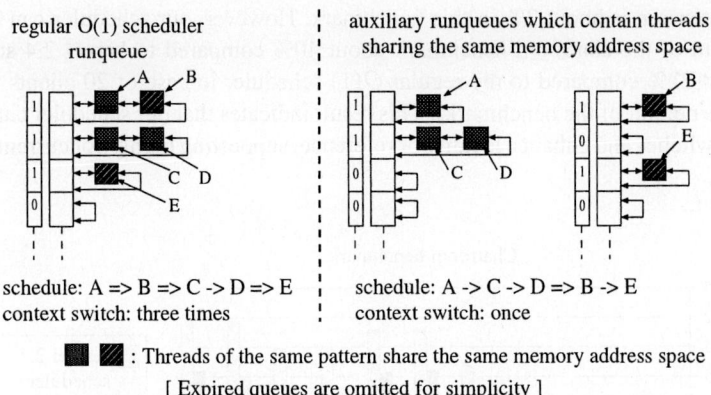

Fig. 2. Aggregating threads of the same address space

to our memory descripter, and our memory descripter has a pointer to the auxiliary runqueue. Thus our scheduler can refer to threads that share the same address space with the most recently executed thread via these pointers.

$O(1)$ scheduler simply executes threads according to the thread priority. But our scheduler executes threads in the order that reflects the thread priority and the current thread context. Our scheduler checks p_{reg}, the highest priority in regular $O(1)$ scheduler runqueue, and p_{aux}, the highest priority of the auxiliary runqueue for threads which share the same context with the most recently executed thread. Then our scheduler compares these two priorities, and if the $p_{reg} - p_{aux}$ is less than a threshold, our scheduler executes the first thread in the auxiliary runqueue. Since the threshold value corresponds to the priority bonus of Linux kernel 2.4, our scheduler tries to maintain almost the same policy of fairness of Linux kernel 2.4. In Fig.2, regular $O(1)$ scheduler executes threads A, B, C, D, and E, in that order. Our scheduler executes threads A, C, D, B, and E, in that order. Regular $O(1)$ scheduler switches the address space twice between A and B and between D and E. Our scheduler switches the address space once between D and B.

5 Evaluation

We use a chatroom benchmark[2, 3] for the performance evaluation of our scheduler. The chatroom benchmark simulates chat rooms each of which includes both a server and clients. The benchmark creates a number of threads and tcp connections, and sends and receives a number of messages. The client side of the benchmark reports the number of messages sent per second as throughput. The number of chat rooms is set to 10. Each chat room has 20 clients by default, but we change the number of clients per chat room from 5 to 55. The system configuration of our evaluation experiment is Pentium4 2.6GHz of 8 KB L1 data cache, 512 KB L2 cache, and 512 MB memory. Fig.3 shows the result of the evaluation. The horizontal axis is the number of the clients per chat room. The vertical axis shows the improvement ratio of throughput compared to that of kernel 2.4 scheduler. Higher bar indicates better throughput. The estimated overhead due to our extension is about 2% in this benchmark. However, our scheduler can improve throughput of the chatroom benchmark about 40% compared to kernel 2.4 scheduler and about 22% compared to the regular $O(1)$ scheduler in case of 20 clients per chat room (the default of the benchmark). This result indicates that our scheduler can reduce context switches and enhance locality of reference, supporting highly concurrent threads activities.

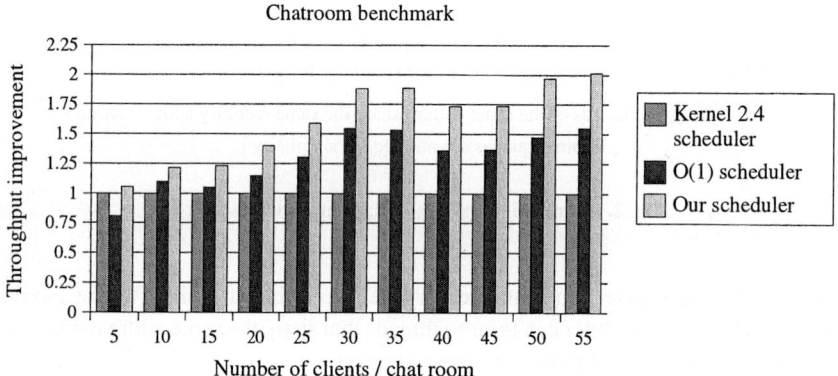

Fig. 3. Throughput improvement of chatroom benchmark

6 Concluding Remarks

We proposed the scheduling scheme to aggregate threads which share the same memory address space based on $O(1)$ scheduler. Our scheduler can reduce context switches, exploit locality of reference and support highly concurrent threads activities. Our performance evaluation showed that our scheduler can effectively improve throughput of the chatroom server benchmark.

References

1. Ingo Molnar. Ultra-scalable $O(1)$ SMP and UP Scheduler. http://www.uwsg.iu.edu/hypermail/linux/kernel/0201.0/0810.html
2. Shuji Yamamura, Akira Hirai, Mitsuru Sato, Masao Yamamoto, Akira Naruse, and Kouichi Kumon.*Speeding Up Kernel Scheduler by Reducing Cache Misses.*Proceeding of the USENIX Annual Technical Conference 2002 FREENIX Track.
3. Linux Benchmark Suite Homepage. http://lbs.sourceforge.net/

Compiler-Assisted Software DSM on a WAN Cluster

Junpei Niwa

"Information and Systems" Presto, Japan Science and Technology Agency,
Department of Astronomy, Graduate School of Science, University of Tokyo,
2-11-16 Yayoi, Bunkyo-ku, Tokyo, 113-0032, Japan
`jniwa@astron.s.u-tokyo.ac.jp`

Abstract. Recent progress in high-speed and high-bandwidth backbone networks has led to computer clusters over wide-area network (WAN), called *global computing systems*.

The shared-memory programming model makes it much easier for programmers to write parallel applications on global computing systems than the message-passing model. The question is whether or not shared-memory parallel programs can run on global computing systems efficiently.

This paper proposes techniques for optimizing software distributed shared memory (S-DSM) on global computing systems. Both the compiler optimization and the run-time optimization make the latency of remote-memory access small and provide scalable shared memory.

These techniques for optimizing S-DSM system have been implemented, and they are evaluated through the experiments under pseudo WAN environment using Comet delay.

1 Introduction

Recently, new generation applications for E-science (I will refer to them as *E-science applications*), such as the formation of a disk galaxy and the structure prediction and function analysis of biomolecules are gaining in popularity.

These E-science applications require a great deal of computational power and supercomputers are no longer suitable because of their cost-performance. Of course, considering the cost-performance, computer clusters are better, though their computational powers over local area network (LAN) are not enough.

Now, domestic high-speed backbone networks such as SuperSINET have been prepared and inter-continent high-speed backbone networks are also being prepared. Thus, it becomes feasible to construct computer clusters over wide are network (WAN). These clusters over WAN, i.e., "global computing systems" are the keys to execute these applications efficiently.

Many of these E-science applications are written under message-passing system, such as PVM and MPI. In the message-passing model, each process has its own address space and can access only the local memory of the processor executing that process. Programmers must distribute the data and explicitly specify the communication codes for accessing data in the local memories of the other processors. This makes the parallel programs difficult to develop and debug.

The shared-memory model assumes that all the memory locations can be accessed by any processor. There is no need to distribute the data, and irregular computation (such as fluid dynamics computation and N-Body simulations with treecodes) is easier to handle when all the processors have direct access to all the shared data.

The shared-memory model can thus be expected to make it much easier for programmers to write E-science applications, and to further simplify the programming. Thus, we need global computing systems that provide the shared-memory model. To execute explicitly shared-memory parallel programs efficiently on distributed-memory computers, it is required to maintain shared-address space at run-time by software. This is called the software DSM (S-DSM) [15, 13]. Thus, the question asked here is whether or not a S-DSM system can provide high performance on the global computing system.

Unfortunately, there has been little emphasis placed on the design of S-DSM in a WAN environment because many of S-DSM systems have been developed on high-speed LAN environments [15, 13, 11, 24, 25]. This paper proposes techniques for optimizing S-DSM on WAN environment. Both the compiler optimization and the run-time optimization make the latency of remote-memory access small and provide scalable shared memory. These techniques for optimizing S-DSM system have been implemented, and they are evaluated through the experiments under pseudo WAN environment using Comet Delay [1] that provides configurable delayed packet transmission with bridging (L2) between networks connectable to a Comet Network Adapter (Comet).

The rest of this paper is organized as follows. Section 2 describes problems with existing S-DSM system and Section 3 describes our proposed compiler-assisted S-DSM on WAN. Section 4 overviews the compiler optimization and Section 5 describes the runtime optimization. Section 6 describes the experimental environment. We present the results of our experiments in Section 7. We discuss related work in Section 8 and conclude in Section 9.

2 Problems with Existing S-DSM Systems

Most of existing S-DSM systems are designed on the assumption of using sequential compilers [15, 13, 11, 25], such as gcc and icc. An executable object made by a sequential compiler only issues a shared-memory access as the ordinary memory access (load/store). Thus, a coherence-management mechanism is triggered only by the trap. To utilize bandwidth, a runtime system has to buffer the remote memory access by using twin/diff mechanism [13, 5]. It is safe to say that these approaches do not provide interfaces that enable compilers/programmers to perform optimization.

3 Compiler-Assisted S-DSM

Our idea is that an optimizing compiler directly analyzes shared-memory source programs, and optimizes communication and coherence management for S-DSM execution [21, 12]. Our target is a page-based S-DSM, WAN-based distributed shared memory (WDSM). For shared-read operations, WDSM uses both virtual memory mechanism and explicit user-level coherence-management codes (we will refer to them as "read commitments"). For shared-write operations, WDSM uses two kinds of explicit user-level coherence-management codes. One is a "write detection" and the other is a "write commitment".

This enables static optimization of both shared-read and shared-write operations. Static optimizing information about them can reduce the overhead of the runtime system. Shasta[24] and DSZoom[23] are another S-DSM system assuming optimizing compiler support. Since they analyze objects generated by sequential compilers, it only performs limited local optimizations. Our compiler ("Remote Communication Optimizer": RCOP) [18, 22] analyzes a source program directly. Therefore, RCOP performs array data-flow analysis interprocedurally.

4 Compiler Optimization

4.1 Compilation Process

Figure 1 describes the overall compilation process. The input is a shared-memory program written in C extended with PARMACS [3] that provides the primitives for task creation, shared-memory allocation, and synchronization (barrier, lock, and pause). The consistency of shared memory follows lazy release consistency (LRC) model [14]. Our compiler RCOP inserts user-level coherence-management codes, i.e., read commitments, write detections and write commitments for S-DSM into a given shared-memory program. The backend sequential compiler compiles the instrumented source program and links it with a runtime library.

– Read Commitments
  To inform the runtime system that a read will happen onto a contiguous shared region, we use a pair found by the initial address and the size of the region. We call this pair a *(shared) read commitment*. In order to ensure coherence, a read commitment is inserted before the corresponding load instruction.

  If the page is invalid, cache-miss request is issued in the read commitment. Thus, we can consider a read commitment as "prefetch" because cache-miss request can be issued asynchronously earlier than the corresponding actual memory access.

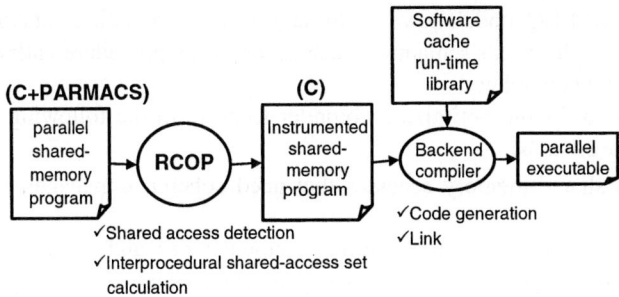

Fig. 1. Overall compilation process

The single read commitment can represent a lot of shared reads onto a large contiguous region. When there are succeeding read commitments with the same parameters, we can eliminate them but the first one.

- Write Detections

  To inform the runtime system that a write will happen onto a contiguous shared region, we use a pair found by the initial address and the size of of the region. We call this pair a *(shared) write detection*. In order to ensure coherence, a write detection is inserted before the corresponding store instruction. The write detections are optimized like read commitments.

  The write detection is required when the total shared memory allocated is larger than the physical memory of one processor. When the number of locally kept remote pages is larger than the maximum number allowed, some old cached pages must be replaced (unmapped) to make room for the new page. As for the written pages, the written contents must be sent to the page-home processors, that is to say, the corresponding write commitments must be issued before they are unmapped. Therefore, it is required to record which regions will be written before the corresponding actual stores in preparation for cache replacement.

- Write Commitments

  To inform the runtime system that a write happened onto a contiguous shared region, we use a pair found by the initial address and the size of of the region. We call this pair a *(shared) write commitment*. Besides the start address and the size, a write commitment also requires the written contents of the region. Therefore, a write commitment is inserted after the corresponding store instruction.

  When a write commitment is issued, the written memory contents are sent to the page-home processor with asynchronous communication. The size parameter of the write commitment corresponds to the length of the data transfer. The parameters recorded in the corresponding write detection are deleted in the write commitment. The single write commitment can represent a lot of shared writes onto a large contiguous region. When there are succeeding write commitments with the same parameters, we can eliminate them but the last one.

4.2 Overview of Optimizing Techniques

The coherence-management codes incur instruction overheads and communication overheads. Under the LRC model, however, these overheads are reduced at *compile-time* by exploiting the application's semantics (such as loops and procedure-calls). This is done by the optimizing compiler.

It is required for the optimizing compiler to perform the following operations to reduce these overheads:

- It detects shared-memory accesses that need coherence-management codes precisely,
- It eliminates redundant coherence-management codes, and
- It merges fine-grained coherence-management codes into a middle-grained/coarse-grained one.

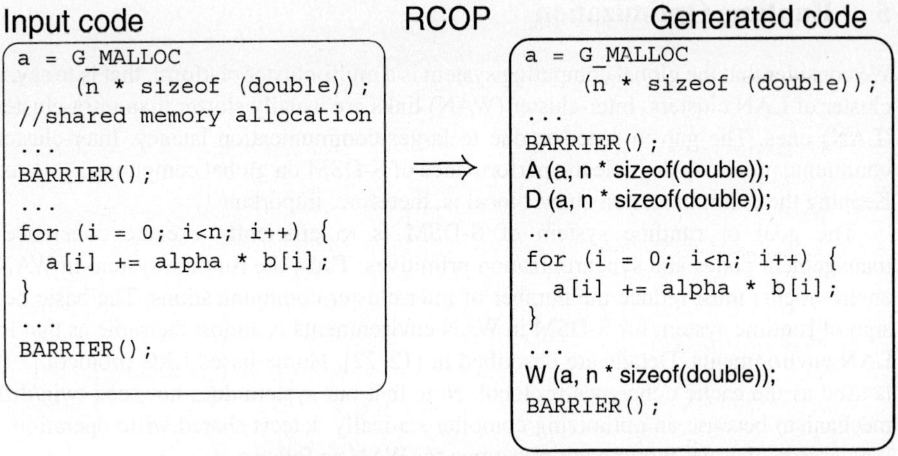

Input code	RCOP	Generated code
| ```
a = G_MALLOC
    (n * sizeof (double));
//shared memory allocation
...
BARRIER();
...
for (i = 0; i<n; i++) {
  a[i] += alpha * b[i];
}
...
BARRIER();
``` | ⟹ | ```
a = G_MALLOC
    (n * sizeof (double));
...
BARRIER();
A (a, n * sizeof(double));
D (a, n * sizeof(double));
...
for (i = 0; i<n; i++) {
  a[i] += alpha * b[i];
}
...
W (a, n * sizeof(double));
BARRIER();
``` |

R: read commitment, D: write detection, W: write commitment

Fig. 2. RCOP Optimization in WDSM

The followings are required to achieve these operations:

- *Precise points-to information*
  This is required for shared-access detection. It is also required when the coherence-management codes are moved. The reason for this is that when a statement may modify the parameters of the coherence-management routine, this routine cannot be moved across the statement. This information is obtained by *interprocedural points-to analysis* [8, 26, 27]. This analysis is context-sensitive and computes all the side-effects of the procedure-call.
- *Efficient framework for redundancy elimination*
  This is required because a control flow graph (CFG) with many cycles (i.e. loops) must be handled when eliminating redundant coherence-management codes [7, 19]. An *interval analysis* approach [4] is used to handle the hierarchical CFG, and this approach requires the interval (i.e., loop) summary to be calculated efficiently. A *shared-access set* [12, 22] is represented by systems of linear inequalities and used to help calculate the interval summary of the coherence-management codes easily and precisely. Shared-access sets are also used in the following optimization techniques.

  - Fusion
  - Coalescing
  - Redundant Index Elimination
  - Fission

  Shared-access sets across procedures are computed efficiently by using the results of points-to analysis.

Our proposed approach has been implemented fully in RCOP. Details are described in Ref. [12, 22].

5 Runtime Optimization

We consider that the global computing system is a multi-cluster platform, that is to say, a cluster of LAN clusters. Inter-cluster (WAN) links are usually slower than intra-cluster (LAN) ones. The gap in speed is due to larger communication latency. Inter-cluster communication may degrade the performance of S-DSM on global computing systems. Keeping the communication cluster-local is, therefore, important.

The goal of runtime system of S-DSM is to efficiently execute coherence-management codes and synchronization primitives. Thus, the runtime system in WAN environments must reduce the number of inter-cluster communications. The basic design of runtime system for S-DSM in WAN environments is almost the same as that in LAN environments. Details are described in [12, 22]. Home-based LRC protocol [29] is used as the cache-coherence protocol. Note that our system does not need twin/diff mechanism because an optimizing compiler statically detects shared write operations. We describe the two runtime optimizations for WAN as follows.

5.1 Cluster Cache

In the S-DSM in LAN environments, the latency of a local-memory access is much smaller than that of remote-memory access. Thus, data in the remote processor is cached in the local memory to reduce the latency of remote-memory access. We introduce the cluster cache for S-DSM in WAN environments to reduce the latency of remote-cluster memory access. Data in the remote cluster is cached in the local cluster, i.e., a processor's local memory in the local cluster to reduce the latency of inter-cluster communication. By accessing its cluster cache, a processor can share data previously requested by another processor of its cluster, thereby hiding the cost of inter-cluster communication.

We call the processor whose memory is used for cluster cache as "cluster-cache processor". We describe the scenario of how cluster caching works. Suppose that in a cluster C, a processor q caches a shared page p, i.e., q is the cluster-cache processor of

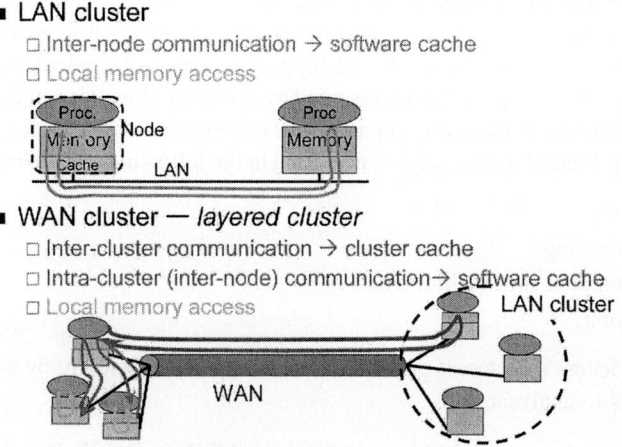

Fig. 3. Cluster Cache

p. For simplicity, we assume that the page-home processor of p (we call it as h) does not reside in a cluster C. All the processors in a cluster C send the cache-miss request of the page p to the cluster-cache processor q.

1. If the cluster-cache processor q has valid copy of the page p, q sends the page contents to the requesting processor. Thus, inter-cluster communication does not occur.
2. If the cluster-cache processor q does not have valid copy of the page p, q redirects the cache-miss requests to the home-processor h. Note that h does not reside in the cluster C. h sends the contents of the page p to q. q updates the page p in its local memory and sends the contents of the page p to the requesting processor. After that, the situation becomes the same as the case 1.

If the page-home h resides in the cluster C, we consider that the cluster-cache processor q is identical with h. Note that we do not prepare processors dedicated to execute cluster caching, as described in [2]. A cluster-cache processor not only executes cluster-cache management but also takes part in the application execution like page-home processor. In our system, users can specify not only page-home processors but also cluster-cache processors.

This scenario will work effectively for barrier-based applications. The reason is that once the cluster-cache processor q has the valid copy of the page p, the copy is never invalidated until the subsequent barrier operation is performed. However, for lock-based applications, this does not hold true. When processors except for q in the cluster C acquire an lock, it is necessary for q to perform the coherence management for the page p, and p in q may be invalidated. The cluster-cache becomes no longer the cache because the number of inter-cluster communication is not reduced. Therefore, when cache-miss requests are issued in critical sections (i.e., the intervals covered by lock and unlock operations), they are transmitted to the page-home processors directly.

5.2 Hierarchical Barrier

At a barrier operation, we can reduce the number of inter-cluster communications. There is one barrier-master processor in the system. For each local cluster, there is one cluster-master processor. The following steps are executed:

1. Each processor checks whether all the preceding page-home updates have been completed and it sends its own dirt bit table to its cluster-master processor.
2. Each cluster-master processor merges the sent dirty bit tables and sends the merged dirty bit table to the barrier-master processor.
3. The barrier-master processor merges the sent dirty bit tables and sends the merged dirty bit table to each cluster-master processor.
4. Each cluster-master processor transmits the sent dirty bit table to all the processors in its cluster.
5. Each processor invalidates its copies using the sent dirty bit table and unmaps them and it clears not only its dirty bit table but also the dirty bit tables of synchronization tags which it manages.

6 Platform

The experiment environment is as follows

- Nodes : Dell PowerEdge 1650 × 8 (1.26GHz PentiumIII with 512KB Cache, 2GB Memory and Intel 1000XT NIC)
- OS : FreeBSD 5.1-RELEASE
- Network Protocol :TCP/IP protocol
- Network : Each node is connected by Gigabit Ethernet with Extreme Summit 5i switch.
- Compiler: The sequential compiler is gcc 3.3. The optimizing compiler is RCOP.
- Runtime system : WDSM runtime library described in Sec. 5

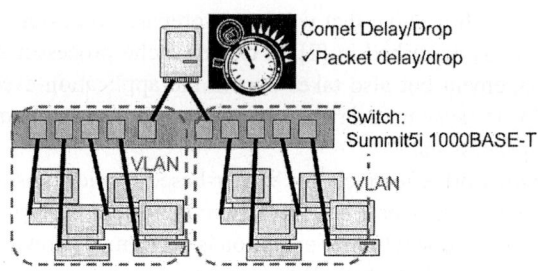

Fig. 4. Pseudo WAN Environment

We construct pseudo WAN environment in a LAN described in Figure 4.

We logically divide the machines into two clusters. Each cluster has 4 nodes. This is implemented by Virtual LAN (VLAN) mechanism in a Summit 5i switch. Messages between VLAN are transmitted via the Comet Delay (machine equipped with Comet [1]). Comet Delay provides configurable delayed packet transmission with bridging (L2) between networks connectable to a Comet Network Adapter (Comet). This tool is made to observe the effect of delay on the networks to Internet communication. In the real working WAN, communication is obstructed by the routers and other packets behaviors as well as transmission delay caused by long distance. However, for the previous step to experiment on WAN, it is important to comprehend pure delay effect without those complex parameters.

7 Experiment

The compiler optimization techniques described in Sec. 4 and the runtime optimization techniques described in Sec. 5 have been fully implemented under FreeBSD. The effects of the optimization techniques developed in this work are evaluated by running the following three benchmarks from SPLASH-2 [28], LU-Contig, a contiguous version of LU decomposition (4K×4K), Water-Spatial (32K mols) and Barnes-Spatial (256K bodies). We set transmission delay as $0 \sim 5$ (msec), found in Metro Area Network (MAN), considering the problem-sizes of applications.

7.1 LU-Contig

The LU-Contig program uses a tiled data partitioning with each tile of the matrix allocated as a contiguous region. Many shared-read and shared-write operations are performed to each tile. Their coherence-management codes are combined into one code by optimizations such as coalescing and fusions.

Table 1. 2-cluster (8-proc) execution time (secs) for LU-Contig

delay(msec)	0	1	2	3	4	5
ADSM	35.04	53.32	70.78	88.38	106.32	123.85
WDSM	32.56	42.95	55.23	68.67	75.38	**63.07**

1-cluster execution time = 64.23 (sec)

Table 1 shows both ADSM execution times and WDSM execution times on the two clusters (i.e., eight processors) for each transmission delay. The row of "ADSM" shows the results of ADSM, page-based compiler-assisted S-DSM on LAN [17, 22] and the row of "WDSM" shows the results of WDSM. We can see that WDSM is more robust over transmission delays than ADSM. In WDSM, if transmission delay is less than 3 (msec), two-cluster execution is faster than one-cluster execution. On the other hand, in ADSM, if transmission delay is less than 2 (msec), two-cluster execution is faster than one-cluster execution.

Table 2. Average time breakdowns(secs) for LU-Contig (delay=5(msec))

	Task	Msg	C-Miss	WC	Sync
ADSM	27.85	2.14	43.52	0.06	50.26
WDSM	28.13	**12.48**	**1.26**	0.06	**21.12**

Table 2 shows the results of breaking down the execution times on the two clusters when transmission delay is 5 (msec).

"Task" is the estimated time for the original computation. "Task" times in ADSM include time for page-fault traps at cache misses. "Task" times in WDSM include time for read commitments and write detections, and they also include time for page-fault traps when prefetches were not successful. "WC" is the time for executing write commitments. "C-Miss" is the waiting time for cache misses. "Msg" is the message-handling time for remote-requests. "Sync" is the time spent for synchronization operations (including waiting time). Each time is measured by using the "rdtsc" instruction. These notations are used throughout this section.

In LU-Contig, the pivot is modified by one processor and used for every processor. Thus, cluster cache works effectively. Furthermore, LU-Contig has an access pattern for which prefetch mechanism works effectively. Handling asynchronous cache-miss requests incurs "Msg" time slightly. This is because "Msg" time in WDSM includes time for mapping invalid pages when page-update messages arrive. In ADSM, this vm-mapping time is included in "C-Miss" time because cache-miss request is issued synchronously in the page-fault handler and the processor wait for the page contents to arrive in the page-fault handler. Though the read commitment (i.e., prefetch) optimization and cluster cache optimization make "Msg" time slightly increase, they make "C-Miss" time of WDSM much shorter than that of ADSM. Owing to the hierarchical barrier optimizations, WDSM "Sync" time becomes one third of ADSM "Sync" time. Note that there are no remote writes in LU-Contig. Thus, "WC" times are well reduced by compiler optimization.

7.2   Water-Spatial

The Water-Spatial program computes the forces and potentials in a system of water molecules by spatially partitioning a uniform 3-D grid of cells. Table 3 shows both

Table 3. 2-cluster (8-proc) execution time (secs) for Water-Spatial

delay(msec)	0	1	2	3	4	5
ADSM	3.77	5.60	7.34	9.10	10.88	12.64
WDSM	3.53	4.11	5.42	5.95	7.08	5.72

1-cluster execution time = 7.12 (sec)

ADSM execution times and WDSM execution times on the two clusters for each transmission delay. The difference of "ADSM" and "WDSM" becomes larger as transmission delay becomes larger. In WDSM, two-cluster execution is always faster than one-cluster execution. However, in ADSM, two-cluster execution is faster than one-cluster execution if transmission delay is less than 2 (msec).

Table 4. Average time breakdowns(secs) for Water-Spatial (delay=5(msec))

	Task	Msg	C-Miss	WC	Sync
ADSM	3.06	0.34	8.984	0.02	0.22
WDSM	3.02	1.38	1.03	0.02	0.26

Table 4 shows the results of breaking down the execution times on the two clusters when transmission delay is 5 (msec). In Water-Spatial, the history pointer prefetching technique [16] is applied. At the first iteration, all the addresses that cause the cachemisses are recorded and at the second iteration or later, the cache-miss requests for these addresses are sent not at the corresponding read commitments but at the previous barrier operations. Therefore, "Sync" time of WDSM becomes slightly large. However, prefetching makes "C-Miss" time of WDSM and "Task" time of WDSM small.

7.3   Barnes-Spatial

The Barnes-Hut algorithm solves an N-body problem by using the oct-tree. The space itself is partitioned among processors for tree-building. Each processor is responsible for loading particles in its assigned sub-space into the tree. If different sub-spaces are assigned to different processors, then two particles assigned to different processors will never have to be inserted in the same cell. Therefore locking is not required.

Table 5. 2-cluster (8-proc) execution time (secs) for Barnes-Spatial

delay(msec)	0	1	2	3	4	5
ADSM	742.33	918.03	1085.03	1251.76	1421.16	1590.50
WDSM	737.22	860.80	1009.03	1173.52	1310.38	1192.19

1-cluster execution time = 1426.52 (sec)

Table 5 shows both ADSM execution times and WDSM execution times for each transmission delay. We can see that WDSM is more robust over transmission delays than ADSM. Even in ADSM, two-cluster execution is faster than one-cluster execution when the delay is 4 (msec) or less. In WDSM, two-cluster execution is always faster than one-cluster execution. One of the reason is that the computation to communication ratio in Barnes-Spatial is much higher than the two applications described above.

In WDSM, the execution time of 5 (msec) transmission delay is faster than that of 4 (msec) transmission delay, as seen in the applications described above. The situations are not seen in the results of ADSM. We are now investigating the reasons.

Table 6. Average time breakdowns(secs) for Barnes-Spatial (delay=5(msec))

	Task	Msg	C-Miss	WC	Sync
ADSM	681.82	36.30	861.65	2.81	7.90
WDSM	703. 66	167.30	270.22	2.70	48.29

Table 6 shows the results of breaking down the execution times on the two clusters when transmission delay is 5 (msec). The prefetch optimization and the cluster-cache optimization reduce "C-Miss" time of WDSM and increase "Msg" time of WDSM. Since the history pointer prefetching technique is also applied to Barnes-Spatial, "Sync" time of WDSM slightly increases.

8 Related Work

Many researches have been done about global computing. One of the most famous one is Grid [9, 10, 20]. Grid aims to realize single system image (SSI) by middle-ware. Many researches have been done about constructing an open set of standards and protocols that enables across heterogeneous, geographically dispersed environments. Our research aims to efficiently execute parallel shared-memory programs on global computing systems.

Interweave [6] provides shared states on a hierarchical distributed environments in WAN (such as cluster of LAN clusters). In a tightly coupled LAN cluster, a page-based

S-DSM, Cashmere-2L [25] functions. Thus, twin/diff overheads still exist. InterWeave adopts version-based coherence management in WAN. In order to minimize communication and obtain high performance, user-specified coherence models are required, which imposes burdens upon programmers. Our proposed WDSM uses both compiler optimization and runtime optimization in order to minimize communication and obtain high-performance in WAN. There are no needs for user-specified coherence models. In our approach, programmers write shared-memory parallel applications without considering the WAN platforms.

Arantes et.al [2] have introduced and implemented per cluster cache for SDSM on WAN cluster. It is composed of inherent cache and extended cache. The first one is implemented by changing the way LRC protocol requests a list of casual related diffs, while the second involves an extra process which is dedicated to store remote diffs and requests. Our system uses Home-based LRC protocol and fetches the whole page at cache-miss. However, our system does not suffer from twin/diff overheads and does not require extra process for twin/diff.

9 Conclusion

This paper proposes techniques for optimizing S-DSM on global computing system. Both the compiler optimization and the run-time optimization make the latency of remote memory access small and provide scalable shared-memory. These techniques for optimizing S-DSM system have been implemented and evaluated through the experiments under pseudo WAN environment using Comet Delay.

From the experiments, we can find that our optimizing techniques are effective, although application sizes are small and WAN latency is small. It is possible to obtain high performance on S-DSM in the WAN with small transmission delay, such as campus GRID. In the real working WAN, communication is obstructed by the routers and other packets behaviors as well as transmission delay caused by long distance. Thus, we will experiment in the real WAN environment and confirm that our proposed optimizing techniques are really effective.

References

1. http://www.comet-can.jp/Applications/CometDelay/.
2. L. Arantes, P. Sens, and B. Folliot. The impact of caching in a loosely-coupled clustered software dsm system. In *Proc. of 2000 Conference on Cluster Computing*, pages 27–34, 2000.
3. J. Boyle, R. Butler, T. Disz, B. Glickfeld, E. Lusk, R. Overbeek, J. Patterson, and R. Stevens. *Portable Programs for Parallel Processors*. Holt, Rinehart and Winston, Inc., 1987.
4. M. Burke. An Interval-Based Approach to Exhaustive and Incremental Interprocedural Data-Flow Analysis. *ACM Transactions on Programming Languages and Systems*, 12(3):341–395, July 1990.
5. J. B. Carter, J. K. Bennett, and W. Zwaenepoel. Implementation and performance of Munin. In *Proc. of 13th ACM Symposium on Operating System Principles*, October 1991.

6. DeQing Chen, Sandhya Dwarkadas, Srinivasan Parthasarathy, Eduardo Pinheiro, and Michael L. Scott. Interweave: A middleware system for distributed shared state. In *Languages, Compilers, and Run-Time Systems for Scalable Computers*, pages 207–220, 2000.
7. J. Cocke. Global Common Subexpression Elimination. *Proc. of a Symposium on Compiler Optimization, SIGPLAN Notices*, 5(7):20–24, July 1970.
8. M. Emami, R. Ghiya, and L. J. Hendren. Context-Sensitive Interprocedural Points-to Analysis in the Presence of Function Pointers. In *Proc. of '94 Conf. on PLDI*, pages 242–256, June 1994.
9. I. Foster and C. Kesselman. *The Grid: Blueprint for a New Computing Infrastructure*. Morgan Kaufmann, San Fransisco, 1999.
10. Globus Project, http://www.globus.org.
11. L. Iftode, C. Dubnicki, E. W. Felten, and K. Li. Improving Release-Consistent Shared Virtual Memory using Automatic Update. In *Proc. of the 2nd HPCA*, February 1996.
12. T. Inagaki, J. Niwa, T. Matsumoto, and K. Hiraki. Supporting Software Distributed Shared Memory with a Optimizing Compiler. In *Proc. of the 1998 ICPP*, pages 225–234, August 1998.
13. P. Keleher, A. L. Cox, S. Dwarkadas, and W. Zwaenepoel. Treadmarks: Distributed Shared Memory on Standard Workstations and Operating Systems. In *Proc. of the Winter 1994 USENIX Conf.*, pages 115–131, January 1994.
14. P. Keleher, A. L. Cox, and W. Zwaenepoel. Lazy Release Consistency for Software Distributed Shared Memory. In *Proc. of the 19th ISCA*, pages 13–21, May 1992.
15. K. Li. IVY: A Shared Virtual Memory System for Parallel Computing. In *Proc. of the 1988 ICPP*, pages 94–101, August 1988.
16. Chi-Keung Luk and Todd C. Mowry. Compiler-based prefetching for recursive data structures. In *Architectural Support for Programming Languages and Operating Systems*, pages 222–233, 1996.
17. T. Matsumoto and K. Hiraki. Memory-Based Communication Facilities and Asymmetric Distributed Shared Memory. In *Proc. of the 1997 International Workshop on Innovative Architecture for Future Generation High-Performance Processors and Systems*, pages 30–39, Los Alamitos, CA, 1998. IEEE Computer Society.
18. T. Matsumoto, J. Niwa, and K. Hiraki. Compiler-Assisted Distributed Shared Memory Schemes Using Memory-Based Communication Facilities. In *Proc. of the 1998 PDPTA*, volume 2, pages 875–882, July 1998.
19. E. Morel and C. Renvoise. Global Optimization by Suppression of Partial Redundancies. *Communications of the ACM*, 22(2):96–103, February 1979.
20. Ninf Project, http://ninf.apgrid.org.
21. J. Niwa, T. Inagaki, T. Matsumoto, and K. Hiraki. Efficient Implementation of Software Release Consistency on Asymmetric Distributed Shared Memory. In *Proc. of the 1997 ISPAN*, pages 198–201, December 1997.
22. J. Niwa, T. Matsumoto, and K. Hiraki. Comparative Study of Page-based and Segment-based Software DSM through Compiler Optimization. In *Proc. of 2000 International Conference on Supercomputing*, pages 284–295, May 2000.
23. Zoran Radović and Erik Hagersten. Dszoom – low latency software-based shared memory. Technical Report 2001:03, Parallel and Scientific Computing Institute (PSCI), Sweden, April 2001.
24. D. J. Scales, K. Gharachorloo, and C. A. Thekkath. Shasta: A Low Overhead, Software-Only Approach for Supporting Fine-Grain Shared Memory. In *Proc. of ASPLOS-VII*, pages 174–185, October 1996.

25. Robert Stets, Sandhya Dwarkadas, Nikolaos Hardavellas, Galen C. Hunt, Leonidas I. Kontothanassis, Srinivasan Parthasarathy, and Michael L. Scott. Cashmere-2l: Software coherent shared memory on a clustered remote-write network. In *Symposium on Operating Systems Principles*, pages 170–183, 1997.
26. R. P. Wilson. *Efficient Context-Sensitive Pointer Analysis for C Programs*. PhD thesis, Stanford University, December 1997.
27. R. P. Wilson and M. S. Lam. Efficient Context-Sensitive Pointer Analysis for C Programs. In *Proc. of '95 Conf. on PLDI*, pages 1–12, June 1995.
28. S. C. Woo, M. Ohara, E. Torrie, J. P. Singh, and A. Gupta. The SPLASH-2 Programs: Characterization and Methodological Considerations. In *Proc. of the 22nd ISCA*, pages 24–36, June 1995.
29. Y. Zhou, L. Iftode, and K. Li. Performance Evaluation of Two Home-Based Lazy Release Consistency Protocols for Shared Virtual Memory Systems. In *Proc. of the 2nd Symp. on OSDI*, 1996.

Performance Analysis of Batch Rekey Algorithm for Secure Group Communications*

Jun Zhang, Fanyuan Ma, Yingcai Bai, and Minglu Li

Department of compute Science and Engineering, Shanghai Jiao Tong University,
Shanghai 200030, China
Alphaz@sh163.net

Abstract. The efficiency of rekeying is a main factor that influences the performance of secure group communications. Periodic batch rekeying for users join/leave is an effective way to improve the efficiency of rekeying. In this paper, we introduce queue theory into the batch rekey algorithm, and construct a model of batch rekey algorithm based on the queue theory. We then analyze the performance influence of the parameters—rekeying periods and the degree of key tree. Finally, we found 3-degree key tree is the best structure for the batch rekey algorithm, and we also analyze the reason why it is not consistent with the result before.

1 Introduction

Many emerging Internet applications, such as software and content delivery, pay per view, teleconferencing, and real-time information services, will benefit from using a secure group communications model. Thus, secure group communications (i.e., providing confidentiality, authenticity, and integrity of messages delivered between group members) will become an important Internet design issue.

In a group communications model, members of a group share a group key, which is known only to the group users and the key server. The group key is distributed by a group key management system, which changes the group key from when group membership changes (called rekeying), to get backward/forward secrecy.

Rekeying efficiency is important to group security. The key graph approach [1, 2, 3] has been proposed for scalable rekeying. Then the batch rekey algorithm for key management based on key tree introduced by [4] enhances the efficiency further. In this paper, we will study deeper in batch rekey algorithm, analyze the performance influence of the parameters—rekeying periods and the degree of key tree, until finding the best parameters.

---

* This paper is supported by 973 project (No.2002CB312002) of China, ChinaGrid Program of MOE of China, and grand project of the Science and Technology Commission of Shanghai Municipality (No. 03dz15026, No. 03dz15027 and No. 03dz15028).

2 Batch Rekey Algorithm

In rekeying system, both the server's computation and communication costs in key tree[1,2,3] are proportional to the number of encryptions to be performed. Thus, we use server cost to mean the number of encryptions the key server has to perform. If the key tree degree is d and there are N users, assuming the tree is a completely balanced tree, the server cost is $2\log_d N$ for a join and $d\log_d N - 1$ for a leave[1,2,3].

The batch rekey algorithm introduced in [4] for key management based on key tree enhances the efficiency further. In this algorithm, J join and L leave requests are collected during a period and are rekeyed in a batch.

3 Model

Batch rekey is a queue condition, we will use queue theory to analyze it. Queue system has three characters: 1. Input or arrival process: here join and leave requests are inputs; 2. Serve process: one server serves all inputs in a period; 3. Rule of queue: every input waits after arrival until the period is over, then server serves all the inputs together.

So batch rekey algorithm is an infinity queue length-infinity source, single server model. Its specialties are: 1. Clients belong to two categories: join requests and leave requests; 2. There exists a period. When the period is over, server serves all the inputs together. According to the speciality, we suppose: 1. Arrivals of the clients are totally random, which obeys Poisson distribution; 2. Server time is the cost of group key management.

4 Performance Analyze

We calculate the average cost on the assumption that key tree always keeps balanced. Let J be the join requests number and L be the leave requests number in a batch period, d be the key tree's degree, h be the key tree's height, and N be the group number. The average cost can be calculated in formula (1) [4]:

$$C_{tree}(N,d,J,L) = \begin{cases} d\sum_{l=0}^{h-1} d^l \left(1 - \dfrac{C^L_{N-N/d^l}}{C^L_N}\right) & \text{if } J=L \\[2ex] d\sum_{l=0}^{h-1} d^l \left(1 - \dfrac{C^L_{N-N/d^l}}{C^L_N}\right) - \sum_{l=0}^{h} d^l \dfrac{C^{N/d^l}_{L-J}}{C^{N/d^l}_N} & \text{if } J<L \\[2ex] \left\lceil \dfrac{dJ}{d-1} \right\rceil + 2\log_d N & \text{if } J>L, L=0 \\[2ex] d\sum_{l=0}^{h-1} d^l \left(1 - \dfrac{C^L_{N-N/d^l}}{C^L_N}\right) + \left\lceil \dfrac{d(J-L)}{d-1} \right\rceil & \text{if } J>L, L>0 \end{cases} \quad (1)$$

Based on the model in section 2, we suppose λ as the average join requests number and μ as the average leave requests number in a period. So the probability of J join requests and L leave requests in a period can be represented with formula (2).

$$P(J,L) = \frac{e^{-\lambda}\lambda^J}{J!} \cdot \frac{e^{-\mu}\mu^L}{L!} \quad (2)$$

Then the average cost for single request in a period is represented with formula (3).

$$C_{tree}(N,d) = \sum_J \sum_L C_{tree}(N,d,J,L) \cdot P(J,L)/(\lambda+\mu) \quad (3)$$

4.1 Simulation

We built a simulator for the batch rekey algorithm. The simulator first constructs a key tree and randomly picks L users to leave; it then runs the marking algorithm and calculates the server cost. We ran the simulation for 100 times and calculated the mean server cost. The results match the formula (1) well and it proves [4]'s correctness again.

4.2 Performance Comparison

After proving formula (1)'s correctness, we analyze the period based on formula (3). The period corresponds to the average join and leave requests number λ and μ in a period. Because join and leave numbers tend to be equal when a group is steady, so we suppose $\lambda=\mu$. Table 1 shows the cost when N=1024,4096, $2 \le d \le 5$, $1 \le \lambda = \mu < 10$ based on formula (3); and the last line shows the average cost of single join and single leave not using batch rekey algorithm.

Table 1. Server Cost

$\lambda=\mu$	(1024,2)	(1024,3)	(1024,4)	(1024,5)	(4096,2)	(4096,3)	(4096,4)	(4096,5)
1	11.774	11.028	11.459	11.640	14.236	12.842	13.921	14.504
2	9.4012	8.6093	8.9804	9.0392	11.512	10.061	11.091	11.563
3	8.5216	7.7173	8.0556	8.0452	10.544	9.0768	10.078	10.487
4	8.0598	7.2543	7.5724	7.5172	10.058	8.5866	9.5699	9.9379
5	7.7455	6.9427	7.2470	7.1593	9.7347	8.2652	9.2358	9.5742
6	7.4993	6.7005	6.9943	6.8810	9.4844	8.0184	8.9789	9.2941
7	7.2928	6.4984	6.7837	6.6489	9.2752	7.8135	8.7654	9.0612
8	7.1135	6.3235	6.6014	6.4480	9.0936	7.6364	8.5809	8.8597
9	6.9547	6.1689	6.4404	6.2703	8.9327	7.4799	8.4177	8.6815
indiv	19.5	15.273	14.5	14.574	23.5	18.428	17.5	17.588

We can see from table 1 that batch rekey algorithm is more efficient than single rekey, it's the same as [4]'s result. When (N,d) is fixed and period increases, as join and leaver requests in a period increase, it will further enhance the efficiency; and it also increases the waiting time of group number. We can choose large period time as possible as the requirement, so get more efficiency.

As to the choice of key tree's degree, we found $d=3$ is the optimal value. This is not only different with single rekey's result $d=4$ [2], but also different with the result $d=4$ of [4] which presents batch rekey algorithm. It is because:

1. Single rekey algorithm is different with batch rekey algorithm, so the result will not be the same.

2. [4] directly compares the result when (N,J,L), is fixed and d changes. That paper did not discover that the probability of (J,L), in a batch period is not equal. It treated them as a same value. So we should apply queue theory, compute the probabilities of every group (J,L), and then compute the average cost based on these probabilities (see formula (3)). The result is meaningful only through these processes.

In table 1, we also find that when d increases ($d \geq 3$), the server cost also increases. But when (N,d) is (1024, 5) and if the period is large, cost is less than (1024, 4)'s result. This is because that when N is small relative to d and the period, it will be in this situation. When N is large enough, this situation will not happen. For example when N=4096, there is no such a problem.

5 Conclusion

In this paper, we introduce queue theory into the batch rekey algorithm, and construct a model of batch rekey algorithm based on queue theory. We then analyze the performance influence of the parameters—rekeying periods and the degree of key tree. We conclude that when period increases, the algorithm is more efficient. Our results show 3-degree key tree is the best structure for batch rekey algorithm, at the same time we analyze the reason why it is not consistent with the result before.

References

1. M. Waldvogel, G. Caronni, D. Sun, N. Weiler, B Plattner, "The VersaKey Framework: Versatile Group Key Management", IEEE Journal on Selected Areas in Communications, Vol. 17, No. 8, August 1999.
2. D. Wallner, E. Harder, R. Agee, "Key Management for Multicast: Issues and Architectures", RFC 2627, 1999.
3. C. K. Wong, M. Gouda, S. S. Lam, "Secure Group Communications Using Key Graphs", ACM SIGCOMM'98, 1998.
4. Li XS, Yang YR, Gouda MG and Lam SS (2001), "Batch Rekeying for Secure Group Communications". Proceedings of 10th International WWW Conference, Hong Kong, China, May 2001, pp. 525-534.

Workload Dispatch Planning for Real-Time Fingerprint Authentication on a Sensor-Client-Server Model

Yongwha Chung*, Daesung Moon**, Taehae Kim*, and Jin-Won Park[†]

* Department of Computer and Information Science, Korea University, Korea
{ychungy, taegar}@korea.ac.kr
** Biometrics Technology Research Team, ETRI, Daejeon, Korea
daesung@etri.re.kr
[†] School of Electrical, Electronic & Computer Engineering, Hongik University, Korea
jinon@hongik.ac.kr

Abstract. In this paper, we analyzed the collective performance of the task assignment of the fingerprint authentication on the sensor-client-server model. We first estimated the performance of primitive operations on the sensor, the client, and the server, respectively. Then, based on these primitive performance results, the workload of each scenario of the task assignment was applied to the M/D/1 queueing model representing the sensor-client-server model, and the collective performance of each scenario was analyzed quantitatively. The modeling results showed that extracting features and matching on the server could provide both fast response time and secure authentication with small numbers of clients. As the number of clients was increased, however, a bottleneck was observed on the server. The bottleneck can be eliminated by either performing the feature extraction on the client or increasing the number of processors in the server.

Keywords: Performance Evaluation, Fingerprint Verification, Authentication Protocol.

1 Introduction

Traditionally, verified users have gained access to secure information systems, buildings, or equipment via multiple PINs, passwords or smart cards. However, these security methods have the weakness that the important information can be lost, stolen, or forgotten. In recent years, there is an increasing trend of using **biometrics**, which refers the personal biological or behavioral characteristics used for verification.

The **fingerprint** is chosen as the biometrics for verification in this paper. It is more mature in terms of the algorithm availability and feasibility[1]. At present time, the personal authentication system is mainly used at close range, such as for in-house room entry control, access to safes, and systems operation. In the future, it will be widely applied and diversified, particularly for a variety of approvals and settlements over networks, information access control, e-commerce via the Internet, and remote personal identification.

In this paper, the performance of the fingerprint authentication service is examined as the number of clients increases. To protect the fingerprint information transmitted, the sensor is assumed to have a low-end processor to execute the required cryptographic functions. In the **sensor-client-server model**[2], the sensor is connected to a specific client and the client is connected to a server through the Internet. In this model, security issues ensure that the opponents will neither be able to access the individual information/measurements nor be able to pose as other individuals by electronically interjecting stale and fraudulently obtained fingerprint measurements into the system[2-4]. To the best of our knowledge, however, there has been no previous work in evaluating performance of fingerprint authentication on the sensor-client-server model.

To derive an optimal task assignment for a given number of clients on the sensor-client-server model, we consider typical scenarios of the task assignment of the fingerprint verification and its corresponding authentication protocol to guarantee the integrity and the confidentiality of the fingerprint information transmitted. To obtain the characteristics of the workload of both the fingerprint verification and the authentication protocol, we first estimate the performance of primitive operations on the sensor, the client, and the server, respectively. Then, the workload of each scenario of the task assignment is applied to the M/D/1 queueing model representing the sensor-client-server model, and the collective performance of each scenario is analyzed quantitatively.

2 Fingerprint Verification System

A fingerprint verification system has two phases: *enrollment* and *verification*. In the off-line enrollment phase, an enrolled fingerprint image for each user is preprocessed, and the minutiae are extracted and stored in a system database. In the on-line verification phase, the input minutiae are compared to the stored template, and the result of the comparison is returned.

In general, there are three steps involved in the verification phase[1]: Image Pre-Processing, Minutiae Extraction, and Minutiae Matching. **Image Pre-Processing** refers to the refinement of the fingerprint image against the image distortion obtained from a fingerprint sensor. **Minutiae Extraction** refers to the extraction of features in the fingerprint image. After this step, some of the minutiae are detected and stored into a pattern file, which includes the position, orientation, and type(ridge ending or bifurcation) of the minutiae. Based on the minutiae, the input fingerprint is compared with the enrolled database in **Minutiae Matching** step.

Note that Image Pre-Processing and Minutiae Extraction steps require a lot of integer computations, and the computational workload of both steps occupies 96% of the total workload of the fingerprint verification[5].

3 Fingerprint Authentication Scenarios

We consider a sensor-client-server model[2] for remote user authentication using fingerprint. The sensor-client-server model for remote user authentication using fingerprint must guarantee the security/privacy as well as the real-time execution requirements. To satisfy those requirements, we first consider possible scenarios for remote user authentication using fingerprint in terms of assigning tasks of fingerprint authentication to each entity. Then, we evaluate the performance of each scenario.

First, simplifying proposed scenarios, we assume that each entity is shared the same session key when the system is installed. Also, the entity authentication is completed using proper methods such as trusted Certificate Authority(CA).

In the Scenario 1, the sensor captures a fingerprint image and sends the client the image in an encrypted form by using the shared session key. After receiving the encrypted fingerprint image $E(image)$, the client decrypts it using the same session key, extracts some features from the image, and finally sends the server the extracted features in an encrypted form by using the same key. Then, the server compares the extracted features with the stored features and returns a matching result to the client. Like other scenarios, the resource-constraint sensor can only capture a fingerprint image and encrypt it. Note that this is a typical scenario of assigning fingerprint verification tasks to the sensor-client-server model.

Unlike the Scenario 1, all tasks except the fingerprint acquisition are executed in the server in the Scenario 2. This scenario can improve the security level of a fingerprint authentication system because the server can be more secure than the client. For example, compared to the server possibly protected by security experts, the client maintained by an individual user is more vulnerable to several attacks such as Trojan horse[3]. On the other hand, the computational workload of the server increases as the number of clients increases. Note that, the sensor can be connected to the server through the client, and the client only transmits the data received from the sensor to the server.

In the Scenario 3, all tasks except the fingerprint acquisition are executed in the client. After encrypting the fingerprint features of the requested user stored in the server's database, the server only transmits it to the client. Thus, this scenario can reduce the workload of the server significantly by distributing the fingerprint authentication tasks into the clients. However, the security level of a fingerprint authentication system can be degraded because the client more vulnerable to several attacks than the server executes most of the tasks.

To evaluate the performance of each scenario, we assume the following configuration. First, the sensor, the client and the server have *StrongARM*(206 MHz) processor, *Pentium 4*(2 GHz) processor and *Xeon*(3 GHz) processor, respectively. Also, the USB interface between the sensor and the client is *USB 2.0* that is able to transfer at *400Mbps*. We assume that the transmission speed of the Internet is *10Mbps*. To guarantee both the integrity and the confidentiality of the transmitted information, *Triple-DES* is used as our symmetric encryption algorithm[6].

4 Performance Evaluation of Three Scenarios

In the fingerprint authentication scenarios described in the previous section, the response time being less than 2 *seconds* has to be satisfied for real-time execution. As we might easily expect, the clients do most of the time-consuming tasks in Scenario 1, whereas the server has the heavy workload in Scenario 2. The extreme case is Scenario 3 where the clients do almost everything. However, it is known that Scenario 3 has some security problems as explained previously.

In this section, we will evaluate three scenarios in terms of the response time versus workloads imposed on the server. In other words, we will investigate the maximum workload that the server can give less than 2 *seconds* response time, or system time in queueing theory, in each scenario. We adopt M/D/1[7] queueing results assuming that the clients request services to the server in a random fashion, but the server processes the jobs in deterministic fashion.

In an M/D/1 system, the response time is given by

$$W = \frac{1}{\mu} + \frac{\lambda}{2\mu(\mu - \lambda)} \qquad (1)$$

where W is the response time(or the systems time), μ is the service rate and λ is the arrival rate. Here, λ is the job request rate to the server by the clients, and the value of λ is assumed to increase as the number of clients increases.

In Scenario 1, fingerprint acquiring(1,000*ms*), encryption(130ms), transmitting to USB(1.4*ms*) tasks are done by the sensor, whereas decryption(1.2*ms*), feature extraction(225*ms*) and encryption(1.2*ms*) tasks are done by the client, sums to the total of 1,358.8*ms*. Transmitting the encrypted data to the server(0.8*ms*, 1KB by 10Mbps Internet transmission), decryption(1.2*ms*), matching(6.5*ms*) and returning the matching result to the client(0.8*ms*) are done by the server, sums to the total of 8.5*ms*, which plays the service time($1/\mu$). Thus, we may build the response time(W) in the M/D/1 systems using eq. (1). When we solve eq. (1) with the numbers given above, we have λ being less than 0.1168 in order to meet the total response time being less than 2 *seconds*. Here, the workload can be interpreted as the number of job requests by the clients to the server in unit time(*milisecond*).

Similar approach can be applied to Scenario 2. Fingerprint acquiring(1,000*ms*), encryption(130*ms*) and transmitting to USB(1.4*ms*) tasks are done by the sensor, sums to the total of 1,131.4*ms*. Transmitting the encrypted data to the server(56*ms*, 70KB by 10Mbps Internet transmission), decryption(1.2*ms*), feature extraction(147*ms*), matching(6.5*ms*) and returning the matching result to the client(0.8*ms*) are done by the server, sums to the total of 211.5*ms*, which plays the service time($1/\mu$). When we solve eq. (1) with the numbers given above, we have λ being less than 0.00407 in order to meet the total response time being less than 2 *seconds*.

In Scenario 3, the server is doing practically nothing except encrypting the stored template and sending the encrypted data to the clients. Fingerprint acquiring(1,000*ms*), encryption(130*ms*), transmitting to USB(1.4*ms*) tasks are done by the sensor, whereas decryption(1.2*ms*), feature extraction(225*ms*) and matching(10*ms*) tasks are done by the client, sums to the total of 1,367.6*ms*. Sending the encrypted data and the signal to the client(1*ms*) and transmission(0.8*ms*, 1KB by 10 Mbps Internet transmission) are done by the server, sums to the total of 1.8*ms*, which plays the service time($1/\mu$). When we solve eq. (1) with the numbers given above, we have λ being less than 0.5548 in order to meet the total response time being less than 2 *seconds*.

Table 1. Summary of Performance Evaluation

Scenario	1	2	3
Maximum Workload	0.1168	0.00407	0.5548
Relative Workload	28	1	136

Summarizing the results obtained in this section is depicted in Table 1. As we see in Table 1, the server should handle the lowest level of workload with Scenario 2, whereas the server can handle 136 times heavier workload with Scenario 3. In most reasonable case of Scenario 1, the server needs to handle 28 times heavier workload compared to the case of Scenario 2. Note that the bottleneck observed on the server(Scenario 2) can be eliminated by either performing the feature extraction on the client(Scenario 1,3) or increasing the number of processors in the server.

5 Conclusions

Biometrics is expected to be widely used in conjunction with other techniques such as the cryptography on the network. For large-scale, remote user authentication services, the real-time issue as well as the security/privacy issue should be managed. In this paper, the performance of the fingerprint authentication service was examined as the number of clients increased.

We first defined the sensor-client-server model, and considered typical scenarios of the task assignment of the fingerprint verification and its corresponding authentication protocol to guarantee the integrity and the confidentiality of the fingerprint information transmitted. Then, we estimated the performance of primitive operations on the sensor, the client, and the server, respectively. Based on these primitive performance results, the workload of each scenario of the task assignment was applied to the M/D/1 queueing model representing the sensor-client-server model, and the collective performance of each scenario was analyzed quantitatively.

Acknowledgement

This work was supported by Korea University Grant.

References

[1] D. Maltoni, et al., *Handbook of Fingerprint Recognition*, Springer, 2003.
[2] R. Bolle, J. Connell, and N. Ratha, "Biometric Perils and Patches", *Pattern Recognition*, Vol. 35, pp. 2727-2738, 2002.
[3] B. Schneier, "The Uses and Abuses of Biometrics", *Communications of the ACM*, Vol. 42, No, 8, pp. 136, 1999.
[4] S. Prabhakar, S. Pankanti, and A. Jain, "Biometric Recognition: Security and Privacy Concerns", *IEEE Security and Privacy*, pp. 33-42, 2003.

[5] D. Moon, et al., "Performance Analysis of the Match-on-Card System for the Fingerprint Authentication", *Proc. of International Workshop on Information Security Applications*, pp. 449-459, 2001.
[6] W. Stallings, *Cryptography and Network Security: Principles and Practice*, Prentice Hall, 2003.
[7] B. Bunday, *An Introduction to Queueing Theory*, Halsted Press, 1996.

Explaining BitTorrent Traffic Self-Similarity

Gang Liu, Mingzeng Hu, Binxing Fang, and Hongli Zhang

Department of Computer Science and Engineering, Harbin Institute of Technology,
Harbin, Heilongjiang 150001, China
{lg, mzhu, bxfang, zhl}@pact518.hit.edu.cn

Abstract. Peer-to-peer applications have become killer network applications. Understanding the nature of network traffic is critical in order to properly design and implement peer-to-peer network. Recently BitTorrent which is one of primary peer-to-peer applications has become one of most important information share tools on Internet. In this paper we examine the mechanisms that give rise to self-similar BitTorrent network traffic. We present an evidence for traffic self-similarity, and show that the self-similarity in such traffic can be explained based on the heavy-tailed distributions of BitTorrent transmission times and quiet times.

1 Introduction

Peer-to-peer applications have become killer network applications. Understanding the nature of network traffic is critical in order to properly design and implement peer-to-peer network [1]. Recently BitTorrent [6], which is one of primary peer-to-peer programs, has been one of most important information share tools on Internet. Examinations of LAN [2], WAN traffic [3] and World Wide Web traffic [4] have showed self-similarity models for network traffic. Traffic that is bursty on many or all time scales can be described statistically using the notion of self-similarity. Self-similarity is the property we associate with fractals — the object appears the same regardless of the scale at which it is viewed.

2 Background

2.1 Self-Similarity and Statistical Methods

Let $X = (X_t : t = 0, 1, 2, ...)$ be a covariance stationary (sometimes called wide-sense stationary) stochastic process. In particular, we assume that X has an autocorrelation function of the form $r(k) \sim k^{-\beta} L_1(k)$, as $k \to \infty$. Where $0 < \beta < 1$ and L_1 is slowly varying at infinity, that is, $\lim_{t \to \infty} L_1(tx)/L_1(t) = 1$ for all $x > 0$ (examples of such slowly varying functions are $L_1(t) = const$, $L_1(t) = \log(t)$). For each $m = 1, 2, 3, \cdots$, let $X^{(m)} = (X_k^{(m)} : k = 1, 2, 3, ...)$ denote a new time series obtained by averaging the original series X over non-overlapping blocks of size m. That is, for each $m = 1, 2, 3, \cdots$, $X^{(m)}$ is given by

$X_k^{(m)} = 1/m(X_{km-m+1} + \cdots + X_{km})$, $k = 1, 2, 3, \cdots$. Note that for each m, the aggregated time series $X^{(m)}$ defines a covariance stationary process; let $r^{(m)}$ denote the corresponding autocorrelation function. The process X is called (exactly second-order) self-similar [7] with self-similarity parameter $H = 1 - \beta/2$ if the corresponding aggregated processes $X^{(m)}$ have the same correlation structure as X, i.e.

$$r^{(m)}(k) = r(k), \quad for\ all\ m = 1, 2, \cdots \quad (k = 1, 2, 3, ...) \quad (1)$$

In this paper we use three methods to test for self-similarity [5]. The first method, the *variance-time plot*, relies on the slowly decaying variance of a self-similar series. The variance of $X^{(m)}$ is plotted against m on a log-log plot; a straight line with slope (β) greater than -1 is indicative of self-similarity, and the parameter H is given by $H = 1 - \beta/2$. The second method, the R/S plot, uses the fact that for a self-similar dataset, the *rescaled range* or R/S statistic grows according to a power law with exponent H as a function of the number of points included (n). Thus the plot of R/S against n on a log-log plot has slope which is an estimate of H. The third approach, the *periodogram* method, uses the slope of the power spectrum of the series as frequency approaches zero. On a log-log plot, the periodogram slope is a straight line with slope $\beta - 1 = 1 - 2H$ close to the origin.

2.2 Heavy-Tailed Distributions

The distributions we use in this paper have the property of being heavy-tailed. A distribution is heavy-tailed if

$$P[X \geq x] \sim x^{-\alpha}, \quad as\ x \to \infty, \quad 0 < \alpha < 2. \quad (2)$$

That is, regardless of the behavior of the distribution for small values of the random variable, if the asymptotic shape of the distribution is hyperbolic, it is heavy-tailed.

3 Examining and Explaining BitTorrent Traffic Self-Similarity

3.1 Data Collection

We collected traffic data at three border routers across the campus network in Harbin Institute of Technology, which consists of 92 entire Class C Internet address. The traffic data was transmitted to the three servers each of which runs Linux, and has double Intel Xeon processors, a 2G ram, a 120G SCSI hard disk, and a Gigabit fiber card. We used a tool libpcap based on Linux to capture BitTorrent traffic. Libpcap is a system-independent interface for user-level packet capture. In order to capture accurately BitTorrent Traffic, we implemented BitTorrent protocol stack upon TCP/IP protocol stack in libpcap to assemble BitTorrent session from the traffic data captured. The final data captured consists of Timestamp, internal, external IP and port information, BitTorrent command information, and BitTorrent data packet size.

Timestamps were accurate to 1 microsecond. We collected data from January 2004 through March 2004.

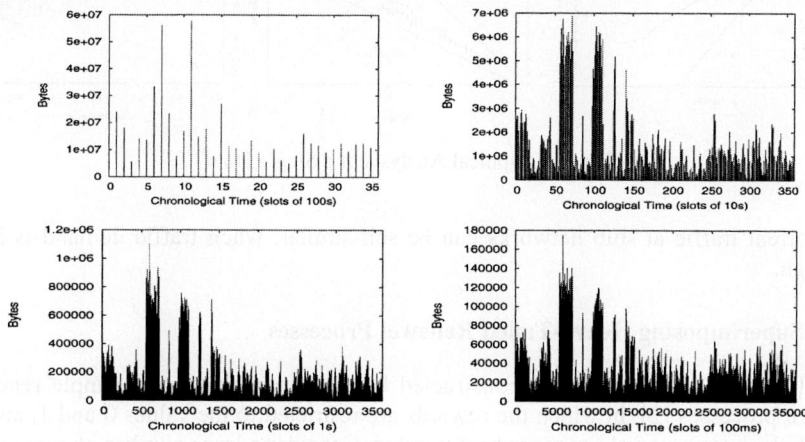

Fig. 1. Traffic Bursts over Four Orders of Magnitude; Upper Left: 100, Upper Right: 10, Lower Left: 1 second, and Lower Right: 100 Milliseconds Aggregations

3.2 Self-Similarity of BitTorrent Traffic

3.2.1 Burstiness at Varying Time Scales

One of the most important aspects of self-similar traffic is that there is no characteristic size of a traffic burst; as a result, the aggregation or superimposition of many such sources does not result in a smoother traffic pattern. One way to assess this effect is by visually inspecting time series plots of traffic demands. In Figure 1 we show four time series plots of the traffic induced by our reference traces. The plots are produced by aggregating byte traffic into discrete bins of 100 milliseconds, 1, 10, or 100 seconds. These plots show significant bursts occurring at the second-to-second level.

3.2.2 Statistical Analysis

We used the three methods for assessing self-similarity described in Section 2: the variance-time plot, the rescaled range (or R/S) plot, the periodogram plot. We concentrated on individual hours from our traffic series, so as to provide as nearly a stationary dataset as possible. To provide an example of these approaches, analysis of a single hour (4pm to 5pm, Thursday 26 Feb 2004) is shown in Figure 2. The figure shows plots for the three graphical methods: variance-time (left), rescaled range (middle), and periodogram (right). The variance-time plot is linear and shows a slope that is distinctly different from -1 (which is shown for comparison); the slope is estimated using regression as -0.36, yielding an estimate for H of 0.82. The R/S plot shows an asymptotic slope that is different from 0.5 and from 1.0 (shown for comparison); it is estimated using regression as 0.77, which is also the corresponding estimate of H. The periodogram plot shows a slope of -0.66 (the regression line is shown), yielding an estimate of H as 0.83. Thus the results in this section show that

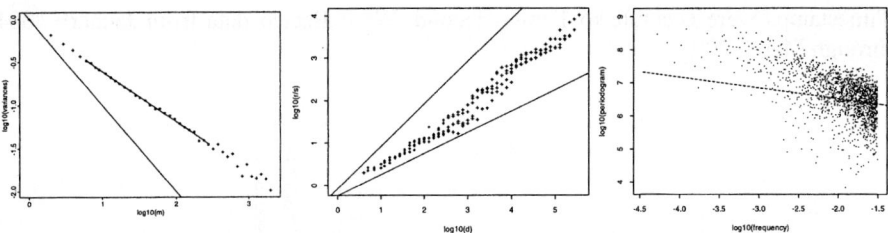

Fig. 2. Graphical Analysis of a Single Hour

BitTorrent traffic at stub networks can be self-similar, when traffic demand is high enough.

3.3 Superimposing Heavy-Tailed Renewal Processes

A self-similar process may be constructed by superimposing many simple renewal reward processes [2], in which the rewards are restricted to the values 0 and 1, and in which the inter-renewal times are heavy-tailed. Consider a large number of concurrent processes that are each either ON or OFF. At any point in time, the value of the time series is the number of processes in the ON state. If the distribution of ON and OFF times for each process is heavy-tailed, then the time series will be self-similar. Adopting this model to explain the self-similarity of BitTorrent traffic requires an explanation for the heavy-tailed distribution of ON and OFF times. In our system, ON times correspond to the transmission durations of individual BitTorrent session (connection), and OFF times correspond to the intervals between transmissions.

3.4 The Distribution of BitTorrent Transmission Times and Quiet Times

Our first observation is that BitTorrent session transmission times are in fact heavy-tailed. Figure 3 (left side) shows the LLCD plot of the durations of all 7715 sessions that occurred during the measurement period. The figure shows that for values greater than about 10, the distribution is nearly linear – indicating a hyperbolic upper tail.

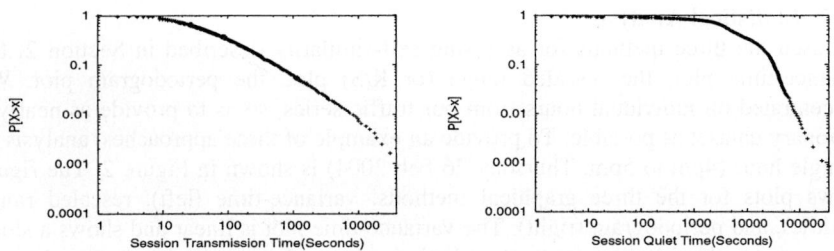

Fig. 3. The Distribution of BitTorrent Transmission Times and Quiet Times

We attributed the self-similarity of BitTorrent traffic to the superimposition of heavy-tailed ON/OFF processes, where the ON times correspond to the transmission durations of individual BitTorrent session and OFF times correspond to periods when a workstation is not receiving or sending BitTorrent data. Thus we see that the OFF times measured in our traces are heavy-tailed, shown in Figure 3 (right side).

4 Conclusions

In this paper we examine the mechanisms that give rise to self-similar BitTorrent network traffic. We present an evidence for traffic self-similarity, and show that the self-similarity in such traffic can be explained based on the heavy-tailed distributions of BitTorrent transmission times and quiet times.

References

1. Shubho Sen, Jia Wang: Analyzing Peer-to-Peer Traffic Across Large Networks, ACM/IEEE Transactions on Networking, Vol. 12, No. 2(2004)
2. W.E. Leland, M.S. Taqqu, W. Willinger, D.V. Wilson: On the self-similar nature of Ethernet traffic (extended version). IEEE/ACM Transactions on Networking, 2:1–15(1994).
3. Vern Paxson, Sally Floyd: Wide-area traffic: The failure of poisson modeling. In Proceedings of SIGCOMM '94(1994).
4. Mark E. Crovella, Azer Bestavros: Self-Similarity in World Wide Web Traffic: Evidence and Possible Causes. In IEEE/ACM Transactions on Networking Vol 5, Number 6, pages 835-846(1997).
5. Walter Willinger, Murad S. Taqqu, Robert Sherman, Daniel V Wilson: Self-similarity through high-variability: Statistical analysis of Ethernet LAN traffic at the source level. In Proceedings of SIGCOMM '95, pages 100–113, Boston, MA(1995).
6. BitTorrent, http://bittorrent.sourceforge.net.
7. Jan Beran: Statistics for Long-Memory Processes. Monographs on Statistics and Applied Probability. Chapman and Hall, New York, NY(1994).

Scheduler Oriented Grid Performance Evaluation

Liang Peng and Simon See

Asia Pacific Science and Technology Center, Sun Microsystems Inc.
Nanyang Center for Supercomputing and Visualization,
Nanyang Technological University, 50 Nanyang Avenue, Singapore 639798
{pengliang, simon}@apstc.sun.com.sg

Abstract. Grid computing is a fast developing technology as an approach to do high performance scientific and engineering computation. The research work on Grid performance evaluation and modeling, an important supporting factor, is still immature and not considered inherently grid middleware design. In this paper, we proposed a scheduler oriented grid performance evaluation approach so that it closely cooperates with grid schedulers. A typical scenario of how the the grid performance modules interact with the scheduler is also introduced and analyzed. The advantage is that the grid scheduler is able to get more performance information about remote sites and hence improve the scheduling policy for grid jobs and ensure the quality of service to some extent.

Keywords: Grid computing, Performance evaluation, Benchmarking, Grid scheduling.

1 Introduction

Grid computing is a fast developing technology as an approach to do high performance scientific computing. Most people in the community are working on the fundamental grid architecture (for example, grid schedulers, resource management tools) and development environments. Grid performance evaluation, as an important factor, is still immature. The grid middleware usually does not reveal or utilize performance information that can be used to improve the efficiency of grid management. Meanwhile, the grid performance study should also be grid scheduler oriented and not isolated from the grid software architecture.

Scheduler oriented grid performance evaluation is an approach that enables performance evaluation, monitoring, and modeling units to closely cooperate with grid schedulers. Consequently, the grid scheduler is able to achieve more performance information of remote site and hence improves the scheduling policy for grid jobs and ensures the quality of service. Meanwhile, grid performance results directly affect the overall efficiency of grid architecture by inherent consideration with grid schedulers.

The remainder of this paper is organized as follows: In section 2 we introduce grid computing and performance issues in computational grid environments; section 3 proposes the scheduler based grid performance architecture. Some related work are introduced in section 4 and finally we give a conclusion in section 5.

2 Grid Computing and Grid Performance

Grid performance should mean the performance of both the grid infrastructure and grid applications. Performance is historically related to speed in the parallel and distributed systems. However, grid performance evaluation is more about how the grid schedulers assign the available and more suitable resources to the grid jobs so that both the grid infrastructure and applications can achieve optimal performance. So in this case, grid performance is not only about speed, but also the efficiency and ability of allocating computing resources and keeping the quality of services by the schedulers. Since the computational grid environment is dynamic, the grid schedulers should also be adaptable, and this requires dynamic performance modeling, monitoring, and evaluation.

The grid performance technically includes at least following issues: grid performance evaluation, theoretical performance modeling, real-time performance monitoring and adaptation, performance tuning and optimization, etc. With a performance evaluation architecture, the user should be able to evaluate the application performance on the particular grid architecture. He may also want to do performance tuning and optimization based on the performance he observed. The job execution will be monitored and performance data will be collected and fed back to adjust performance models. All performance components should interact with grid scheduler so that the scheduler can evaluate the performance, allocate the most suitable resource according to the performance model of each resource, etc.

3 Scheduler Oriented Grid Performance Architecture

Figure 1 shows the scheduler oriented grid performance architecture. The grid user can monitor the performance with the architecture, and the data collected by monitor can also be fed to performance modeling and performance tuning module, which in turn affect the grid performance evaluation. The Grid super scheduler takes the performance evaluation results into consideration, selects the most appropriate resource, and distributes the job to the local scheduler of selected resource. A more detailed typical scenario is shown in Figure 2.

In this scenario, the user submits jobs to the computational grid via his local agent. The local agent forwards the user's resource requirements to the super scheduler, which will interact with the virtual resource index to find the most suitable resource. Here the virtual resource index may contain the performance model (this might be achieved by analyzing historical benchmarking results) and corresponding parameters (e.g. hardware/software configuration) of the computing resources. The super scheduler may take the performance model

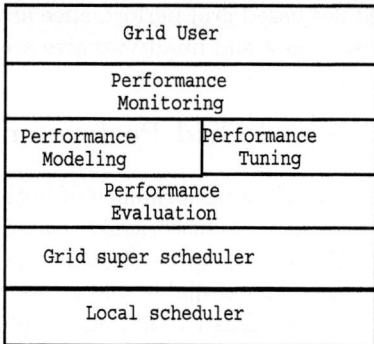

Fig. 1. The scheduler oriented grid performance architecture

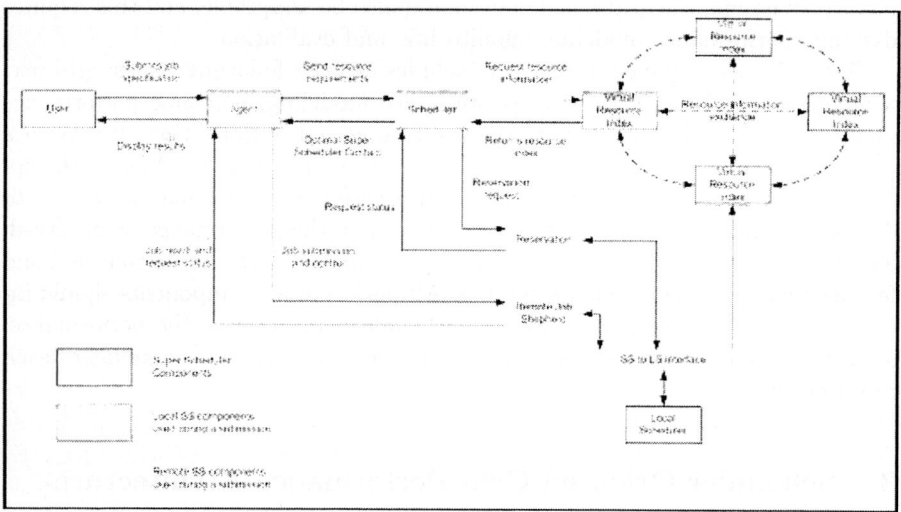

Fig. 2. A scenario of grid performance evaluation, scheduling, and monitoring

into consideration and find the most appropriate resource for the grid job. The information about the selected resource will be send back to the user's local agent, so that the local agent can submit the grid job to the remote site with the selected resource. When the job is being executed, the job monitoring module is activated as well. The job status and some performance data are collected and sent back to the agent and the scheduler, so that the user is able to watch the performance and status, while the super scheduler is able to update the existing performance model accordingly. If possible, the super schedule might also do performance tuning and optimization by migrating the job to some other computing resources if the monitored performance is not as good as expected. In this scenario, the performance issues are considered by the scheduler in almost every step of the job submission and execution. This ensures that the job scheduling policies are performance-aware and the overall grid performance is optimal.

4 Related Work

There is a grid performance working group in GGF and they proposed a grid monitoring architecture [6]. They mainly use a producer-consumer model to define the relationship between the nodes, which mainly describes the scenario of how the performance can be monitored. But it is basically a simplified specification and many important open issues (like scalability, performance, etc) are not addressed. Some initiative work has been done based on NAS Grid benchmarks [4]. They also did some work on tools and techniques for measuring and improving grid performance [3]. GridBench [2] is a tool for benchmarking grids and it is a subproject of CrossGrid [1]. GridBench provides a framework for the user to run the benchmarks on grid environments by providing functions like job submission, benchmarking results collection, archiving and publishing. The GridBench people also discuss the grid benchmark metrics, but so far still no novel metrics are proposed and measured. Performance forecasting in metacomputing environment also has been explored in FAST system [5], which heavily relies on the Wolski et al.'s Network Weather Service [7]. It also provides routine benchmarking to test the target system's performance in executing the standard routines so that a prediction can be made on these results.

5 Conclusion

In this paper we present some preliminary analysis on grid performance issues and their relationship with grid super scheduler. We show that the grid performance components/modules in the grid architecture should interact with grid scheduler and inherently embedded into the scheduler, so that the overall optimal performance of both grid application and grid infrastructure can be achieved. Our implementation work of this proposed architecture is still on going in the future we will evaluate the architecture on real computation grid environments.

References

1. CrossGrid. http://www.cs.ucy.ac.cy/crossgrid/.
2. GridBench. http://www2.cs.ucy.ac.cy/ georget/gridb/gridb.html.
3. R. Biswas, M. Frumkin, W. Smith, and R. V. der Wijngaart. Tools and Techniques for Measuring and Improving Grid Performance. In *LNCS 2571*, pages 45–54, 2002.
4. R. F. V. der Wijngaart and M. Frumkin. NAS Grid Benchmarks Version 1.0. Technical Report NAS-02-005, NASA Advanced Supercomputing Division, 2002.
5. M. Quinson. Dynamic Performance Forecasting for Network-Enabled Servers in a Metacomputing Environment. In *International Workshop on Performance Modeling, Evaluation, and Optimization of Parallel and Distributed Systems*, Apr. 2002.
6. B. Tierney, R. Aydt, D. Gunter, W. Smith, M. Swany, V. Taylor, and R. Wolski. A Grid Monitoring Architecture. Technical Report GWD-Perf-16-3, GGF Performance Working Group, 2002.
7. R. Wolski, N. T. Spring, and J. Hayes. The Network Weather Service: A Distributed Resource Performance Forecasting Service for Metacomputing. *Future Generation Copmuting systems, Metacomputing Issue*, 15(5-6):757–768, Oct. 1999.

Integrated Service Component Development Tool on Web Services

Woon-Yong Kim[1] and R. Young-Chul Kim[2]

[1] Dept of Computer Science, Kwang-Woon University,
Seoul, 139-701, Korea
wykim@kw.ac.kr
[2] Dept of Computer Information Comm., Hong-Ik University,
Jochiwon, 339-701, Korea
bob@hongik.ac.kr

Abstract. The web services based on the HTTP protocol and XML are the efficient way to integrate distributed applications on the Internet. The web services contain SOAP, WSDL and UDDI standard, and various technologies related to them are researched now. In this paper, we design and implement an efficient integrated development tool for web services components. Generally a structure of web service components is constructed by combining other components closely. For this, it may be required the efficient mechanism during design of service components. Therefore we propose an integrated model of the functions required and some composition techniques of service components. Then we develop the integrated service component development tool. This automatic tool provides UML design on the GUI and includes some procedures that are creation and registration of WSDL document for accessing the web service component efficiently and that create wrapper class composing with the other services. As a result, this tool will provide the opportunity of faster and stable component development.

1 Introduction

The web services are the interface, which describes the group of operations that access networks through the standard XML messages. One way of web service integrations, the web services easily make system integration through the web [8]. This is recognized as new substitute for the distributed computing models like CORBA, Java RMI, DCOM. The web services are consisted of open-oriented standards with SOAP, WSDL, UDDI on the XML. Various toolkits for web application development are released. These toolkits are providing with API and tools.

In this paper, we develop the integrated automatic development tool for developing the efficient web service components. Generally, the web service component has service structures either with independent-structured service or with other web service components [2]. As a result, the processes of the component design and implementation on the web service should be required the mechanisms during design of service For supporting them, our tool provides the efficiency of component design and implementation with integrating the functions required for the design and implementation of the web service component. This tool provides UML design and implementation on the GUI, and includes creation and registration of WSDL document for accessing the web service component and wrapper class to use the other services. This tool includes each step for software design, code generating, web service wrapper class creation, web services component creation and registration, and UDDI browser. In this paper, the chapter 2 describes the technologies and toolkits of web services, and the chapter 3 suggests the system structure and the component development process of the web services. The chapter 4 describes characteristics and techniques of integrated development tool on web services, and the chapter 5 is conclusion.

2 Related Researches

2.1 Web Services and Development Toolkit

It is recognized the web service as new technology, which makes system integration on the web environment based on XML, and HTTP possible. It consists of 3 open-oriented standards: the one of elements is SOAP(Simple Object Access Protocol) for the protocol of XML transmission[4], and the second one is WSDL(Web Service Description Language), the language for web service description[9], and the final one is UDDI(Universal Discovery Description Integration), the standard of storehouse for sharing information [6]. Also to solve the security problem which the web service technology does not support, BPEL4WS(Business Process Execution Language for Web Services) specs, WS-Security, WS-Coordination and WS-Transaction specs were released[7]. The architecture of web service is shown in fig. 1.

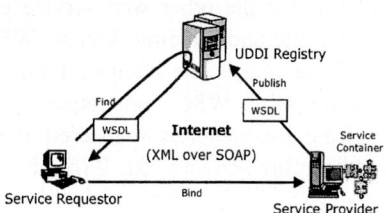

Fig. 1. Web services architecture

Various toolkits for developing web services being released. SUN releases JWSDP(Java Web Services Developer Pack)[5] version 1.3 as web service development pack. IBM starts to develop WSTK(Web Services ToolKit) as AlphaWorks project, and now releases WSTK version 1.2 including ETTK (Emerging Technologies Toolkit)[3]. Also Apache as public software group starts to develop SOAP toolkit, and now Axis version 1.2 Alpha [1]. This paper uses this toolkit for web service development. In addition, UDDI4J module in the ETTK [3] is used for making UDDI browser.

2.2 Web Services Platform

Many platforms on web services are released. Those platforms have their own arrangement methods. The representative platforms are SUN's Java Web Service Development Pack(JWSDP), Cape Clear's CapeConnect, Iona's XMLBus, Apache's Axis, Systinet's Web Applications and Service Platform(WASP), and Mind Electronic's GLUE etc[2]. This paper only uses the platform of JWSDP's environment.

3 Integrated Web Services Component Development Tool

Our tool is providing with two mechanisms by creating new component, and by using the existing web service component during design process. Also, it provides web services component development environment.

3.1 The System Structure of Tool

Our tool is provided with web services component development environment based on the structure of JAVA. Fig. 2 (left) shows structure in this integrated tool. This tool is implemented by JWSDP, which SUN supported, and its XML Parser is Apache Xerces. In addition, UDDI4J in the IBM AlphaWorks's project is used for UDDI browser.

This tool provides GUI environment based on UML 1.3. Also it provides efficiency of design through use-case, class diagram, and collaboration diagram on graphical environment. UDDI browser searches the web service component required at design step, and provides WSDL information required to composite components. The code-generation module creates skeleton code required to generate components through design information. WSC (Web Service Component) wrapper generation module creates wrapper class for the other web service components. The wrapper class provides the class for static and dynamic access. WSC generator module is in charge of WSDL creation that makes the documentation of designed web service component and service description. WSC registration is providing the registration process that new web service components are registered to web service container. The relationships of all the elements are shown in fig. 2 (right).

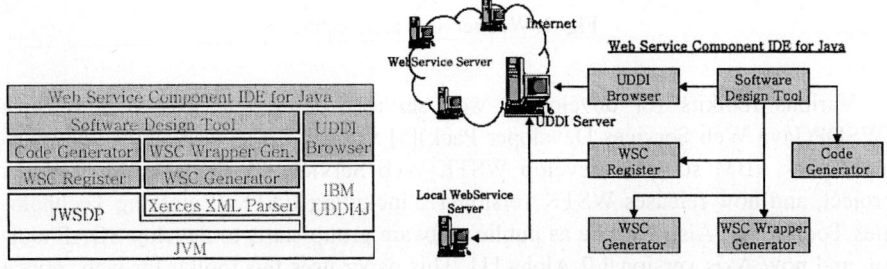

Fig. 2. Structure (left) and relationship of elements (right) in our development tool

3.2 The Web Services Component Development Process

The development process of web services component consists of the web services component design process, the code generation process, WSDL document and web service creation, and the registration process that registers web service component into the web server container. The web service component development process in our integrated tool is shown in fig. 3.

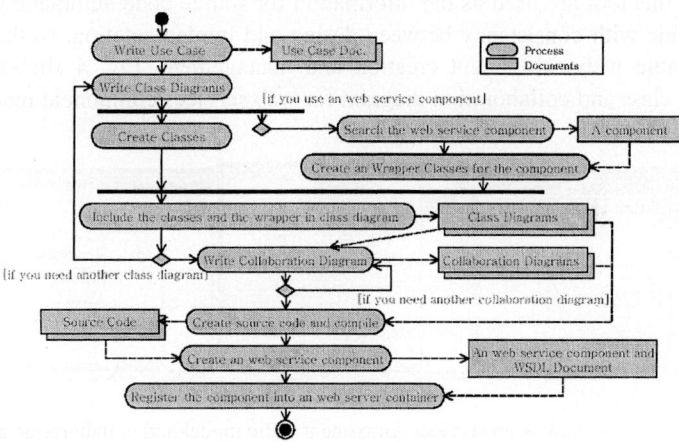

Fig. 3. Process of web services component development

Our process of web services starts from defining the web services component. The functions of component are defined by Use case doc., and class diagram is created based on this defined documentation. If the usage of other web service is necessary locally, the information of web services component will be gained by searching UDDI, and wrapper class will be created. The class diagram is composed of original class and wrapper class. Also collaboration model required for the service can be composed. The next step is generating source code. The generated source code will be the service-runnable class file after compiling and building. Through this information, WSDL required in the web services is created, and also composed as one component possible for web service. This component can be serviced through the registration on web server container. Our development tool includes the above steps. We may give a faster and stable component development chance to the developer.

4 Implementation of the Integrated Web Services Component Development Tool

Our tool environment consists of the component design, wrapper class creation, code generation, and web service component creation and registration tool. This tool provides the interface environment that manages and runs components per each project.

4.1 Web Services Component Design Tool

Our design tool provides the creation and management of Use case, class diagram and collaboration diagram based on UML 1.3. The Use case part composes the description of web service component. The class diagram part, as a core component of web services development, is in charge of designing static web services component models with original classes and classes created from the wrapper class. The collaboration diagram represents method-calling relationships on objects. These class models created by this tool are used as the information for source code automatic generation. They provide with consistency between design and implementation, so that they can provide stable web component creation and management. Fig. 4 shows Use case document, class and collaboration diagram for web services component model.

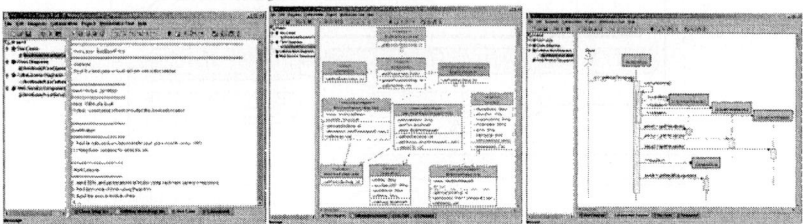

Fig. 4. Use case view, web services component static model and collaboration diagram

4.2 Web Services Wrapper Class Creation Tool

The web services component can compose of not only web services client program, but also other web services. To use the web services component when developing a program, many steps are required. WSDL document registered UDDI should be referenced, and class file should be created based on this WSDL document, and then this file applies to the program. Generally, the way to access web services is classified three mechanisms; static stub, dynamic proxy which create object on runtime, and DII(Dynamic Invocation Interface). The wrapper class creation tool provides 3 types introduced above. Fig. 5 shows the activity of wrapper class creation.

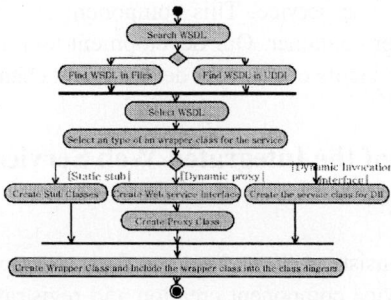

Fig. 5. Web services wrapper class creation activity

As a user use one of three different mechanisms, developers may concentrate on only service domain because of hiding functional part to access the service. The process of web services wrapper class creation is classified several parts; selection process, wrapper class creation process, and wrapper class registration. Fig. 6 shows the dialog when class creation tool is selected and UDDI Browser.

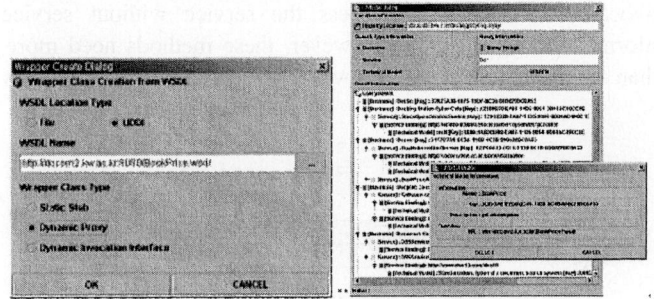

Fig. 6. Wrapper class creation view(left) and UDDI browser(right)

This dialog (left) can create the desired wrapper classes with selecting WSDL document required wrapper class creation and wrapper class type. When WDSL is acquired by UDDI, the WSDL document can be selected with UDDI browser. The UDDI browser searches on views of business, service, and t_Model. Through the chosen WSDL documentation, wrapper class can be created as one of static stub, dynamic proxy, and DII. These wrapper classes will be discussed as followed.

4.2.1 Wrapper Class Creation for Static Stub

The wrapper class for static stub is made of the structure that uses stub created before runtime. This wrapper class has structure shown as fig. 7 (left). The wrapper class for static stub is in charge of acquiring stub object and making it available.

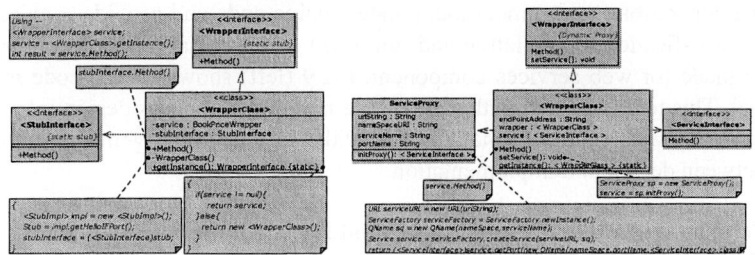

Fig. 7. Wrapper class for stub (left) and for structure based on Dynamic proxy (right)

4.2.2 Creation of Wrapper Class to Access Web Services on Dynamic Proxy

The static stub about web services depends on the implementation environment. To overcome this limit, the dynamic proxy, which creates web service object during runtime, is using for it. This creation of dynamic proxy is done through WSDL documentation. This wrapper class is in charge of management of web service information and creation of dynamic proxy. Fig. 7 (right) shows structure based on dynamic proxy.

4.2.3 Creation of Wrapper Class Based on Dynamic Calling Interface

The stub or dynamic proxy needs service interface information before running, but Dynamic Invocation Interface can access the service without service name and procedure information until runtime. However, these methods need more informative procedures than other methods. Fig. 8 shows the wrapper class that provides DII access.

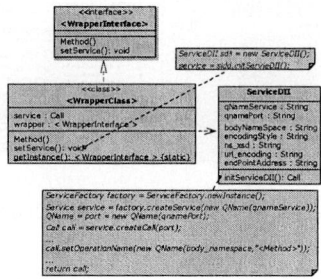

Fig. 8. Wrapper class structure for access DII

The wrapper class creation tool provides with creating the desired wrapper class automatically based on the WSDL information and class structure of desired wrapper type. In addition, it provides class information for creating component through the process of registering them to the class diagram. The web services developer can hide the functional requirements for access. So the developer can construct the stable component from the service point of view.

4.3 Code Generation Management Tool

The code generation management tool creates source code and provides environment for code modification, compilation and run based on class diagram and collaboration diagram made for web services component. Fig.9 (left) shows source code management tool. This tool is related with class diagram, and it composes design information related directly with code information. It provides efficient management with consistency between design and implementation.

4.4 Web Services Component Creation and Registration Tool

The web service component creation and registration tool creates WSDL document, and registers the component to the Tomcat on the JWSDP. The WSDL document is created as setting up several options, which are interface for service, package information, service registration location, service name, WSDL document name and WSDL style information. The created WDSL document and running classes are integrated, and registered to the web server container. This is shown in fig. 9 (right).

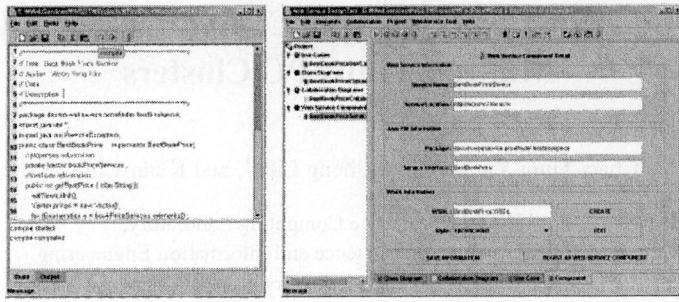

Fig. 9. Source code management (left) and component creation and registration tool (right)

5 Conclusion

Nowadays. Web service technologies have many standards like SOAP, WSDL, UDDI. They should be applied quickly for changing existing user oriented and application oriented web environment and replacing the existed distributed environment like CORBA, DCOM, Java RMI. Many specs. are modified consistently.

To solve this problem, we suggest to our integrated development tool, which may provide the efficient environment for faster and stable component development on web services. In this paper, we show to design and implement our integrated development tool for supporting efficient development on web services. Our integrated environment include as follows. Web services component design tool based on UML 1.3, Web service wrapper class creation tool, Code generation management tool, web services component creation and registration tool. As a result, we believe to develop faster and stable service component. We need consistent studies for supporting evaluated specs and additional web service functions.

References

1. Apache Web Services - Axis, "http://ws.apache.org/axis/index.html"
2. Harvey M. Deitel, Paul U. Deitel, "Java Web Services For Experienced Programmers", Prentice Hall, 2003
3. IBM AlphaWorks Emerging Technologies ToolKit, "http://alphaworks.ibm.com/tech/ettk, April 8 2003
4. Simple Object Access Protocol Spec. http://www.w3.org/TR/soap12
5. Sun Java Web Services Developer Pack (JWSDP), "http://java.sun.com/webservices/jwsdp/index.jsp"
6. UDDI Technical White Paper, http://www.uddi.org/pubs/Iru_UDDI_Technical_White_Paper.pdf
7. W3C Web Services Activity, http://www.w3.org/2002/ws
8. Web Services Architecture "http://www.w3.org/TR/2004/NOTE-ws-arch-20040211"
9. Web Services Description Languages (WSDLv2.0), http://www.w3.org/TR/wsdl20

On Construction of a Large Computing Farm Using Multiple Linux PC Clusters*

Chao-Tung Yang[1], Chun-Sheng Liao[1], and Kuan-Ching Li[2]

[1] High-Performance Computing Laboratory,
Department of Computer Science and Information Engineering,
Tunghai University,
Taichung, Taichung 407, Taiwan ROC
ctyang@mail.thu.edu.tw, g922803@student.thu.edu.tw
[2] Parallel and Distributed Processing Center,
Department of Computer Science and Information Management,
Providence University,
Shalu, Taichung 433, Taiwan ROC
kuancli@pu.edu.tw

Abstract. In addition to the traditional massively parallel computers, distributed workstation clusters now play an important role in scientific computing, due to the advent of commodity high performance processors, low-latency/high-bandwidth networks and powerful development tools. In a cluster environment, we add more and more workstations for reaching more computing performance. Unfortunately, in general case, we don't have enough space for setting up many PCs to form a large-scale PC cluster, and more questions we are concerned about, for example, network topology, electric power, and management question etc. Thus, we can use several places for setting up a number of machines on each place, and enabling networking for transparent computing on each cluster node for enable an enormous node cluster. In this paper, we use some routing policy and a kernel module named Netfilter to enable three or more clusters to be connected as a big one. In our experimental environment we use three different quantities of nodes in each PC cluster connected via a Fast-Ethernet network environment. As experiment, we performed matrix multiplication for performance analysis.

Keywords: Cluster computing, Linux PC cluster, Performance, Netfilter.

1 Introduction

Extraordinary technological improvements over the past few years in areas such as microprocessors, memory, networks, and software have made it possible to assemble groups of inexpensive personal computers and/or workstations into a cost effective system that functions in concert and possesses tremendous processing power. Cluster computing is not new, but in company with other technical capabilities, particularly in

---

* This work is supported by National Center for High-Performance Computing (NCHC), Taiwan under Grant No. NCHC-KING_010200.

the area of networking, this class of machines is becoming a high-performance platform for parallel and distributed applications [1, 2, 3, 4, 5].

Inexpensive systems such as Beowulf clusters have become increasingly popular in both commercial and academic sectors of bioinformatics community [6, 7, 8, 9]. Clusters typically consist of a master node that distributes the bioinformatics application amongst the other nodes (slave nodes).

In our laboratory, we have several Linux PC clusters. Unfortunately, the public IP addresses are not enough for setting used on all slave nodes. It means that the private IP address is used for slave nodes in a PC cluster. If we want to use a cluster with 64 CPUs or more for some experimentation like gene sequence analysis or large computing job. Currently, our setting is not suitable for allocating all computing resources. Therefore, to find a solution that can combine more Linux PC clusters for parallel computing is our main motivation in this paper.

2 System Construction

In this section, the construction procedure is described. First we need a solution that causes the slave nodes of PC clusters with private IP address that can communicate with others with public IP address. The Linux kernel version 2.4 provides a subsystem called Netfilter [1]. We use this feature for IP-Masquerade, a solution of network address translation (NAT), in the setting, we just open the capability of packet forwarding module.

You can change the "**/proc/sys/net/ipv4/ip_forward**" value to 1 to enable kernel IP forward function. Then using "**iptables**" command to change Netfilter chains. The command line is like below:

iptables -t nat -A POSTROUTING -o <eth> -s <private_net> -j MASQUERADE

under the command, the "**eth**" parameter is the mapped to your master node's public address interface and the "**private_net**" parameter is your cluster's private network address, if your private network is 192.168.1.0 and its netmask is 255.255.255.0. You should type "**192.168.1.0/24**".

Second we need a routing policy for combine our clusters to a big one. The policy is simple, if we must combine N cluster together, each master must add (N-1) route trains to satisfy each cluster communications together.

3 Experimental Results

In our experimental environment, the network topology is shown in Figure 1. There are one server node and several computing nodes in each cluster. The server node has two AMD ATHLON MP 2000+ processors and 2GB of ECC shared local memory. Each AMD ATHLON processor has 128K on-chip instruction and data caches (L1 cache), a 256K on-chip four-way second-level cache with full speed of CPU. Each computing node has dual AMD ATHLON MP 2000+ with 1GB shared-memory.

We respectively conduct the experimentation on a 32-processor Linux PC cluster and a multiple PC clusters that consists of three clusters (8 processors in amd1, 8

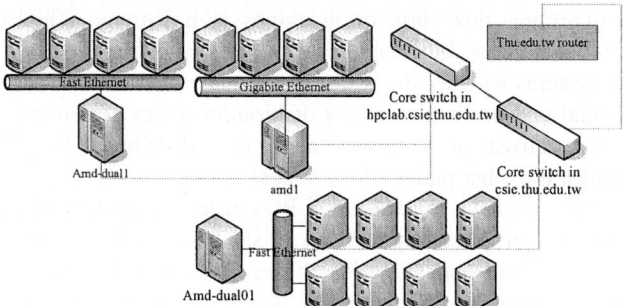

Fig. 1. Experimental environment in HPC Lab consists of three PC clusters

processors in amd-dual1, and 16 processors in amd-dual01). Figure 2 shows the execution times of matrix multiplication on single PC cluster and our multi-clusters. From the results, we can easily to find out the multi-clusters can reduce more time to perform the computation then single cluster.

Second, we conduct the experimentation by comprising performance form a Linux PC cluster and another five cases. Figure 3 shows the execution times of matrix

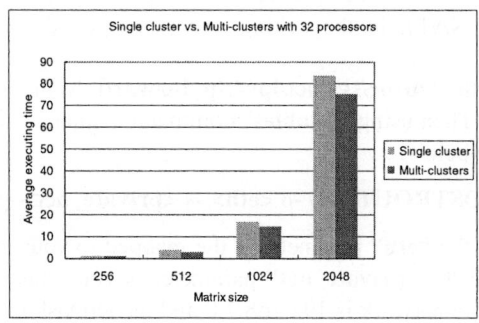

Fig. 2. Comparison of execution time by single cluster and multi-clusters with 32 processors

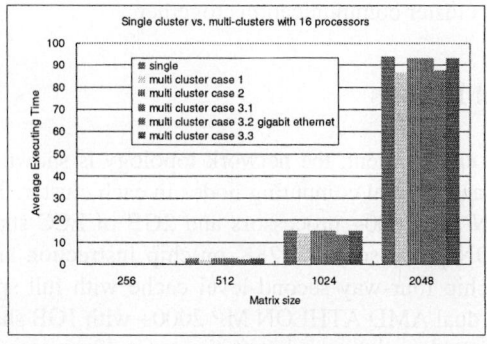

Fig. 3. Comparison of execution time by single cluster and multi-clusters with 16 processors

multiplication on single PC cluster and our multi-clusters (five cases). These five cases are summarized as in Table 1.

Table 1. The description of each case

	Machines used		
Cases	amd-dual01	amd-dual1	amd
Case 1	4	2(master)	2
Case 2	2	4(master)	2
Case 3.1	2	2(master)	4
Case 3.2	2	2	4(master)
Case 3.3	2(master)	2	4

4 Conclusion

In cluster computing environment, we commonly use many workstations for reaching more computing performance. But in general case, we don't have enough space for setting up many PCs on it, and more questions we are concerned about, for example, network topology, electric power, and management question etc. So we can use several places for setting up a number of machines on each place, and enable networking for transparent computing on each cluster node for enable an enormous nodes cluster. In this paper, we use some routing policy and a kernel module called Netfilter to enable three or more cluster to connect a big one. In experimental environment we use three different amounts of PC cluster in a Fast-Ethernet network environment.

References

[1] R. Buyya, High Performance Cluster Computing: System and Architectures, Vol. 1, Prentice Hall PTR, NJ, 1999.
[2] R. Buyya, High Performance Cluster Computing: Programming and Applications, Vol. 2, Prentice Hall PTR, NJ, 1999.
[3] T. L. Sterling, J. Salmon, D. J. Backer, and D. F. Savarese, *How to Build a Beowulf: A Guide to the Implementation and Application of PC Clusters*, 2nd Printing, MIT Press, Cambridge, Massachusetts, USA, 1999.
[4] B. Wilkinson and M. Allen, *Parallel Programming: Techniques and Applications Using Networked Workstations and Parallel Computers*, Prentice Hall PTR, NJ, 1999.
[5] Chao-Tung Yang, Chi-Chu Hung, and Chia-Cheng Soong, "Parallel Computing on Low-Cost PC-Based SMPs Clusters," *Proc. of the 2001 International Conference on Parallel and Distributed Computing, Applications, and Techniques (PDCAT 2001)*, Taipei, Taiwan, pp 149-156, July 2001.
[6] http://www.epm.ornl.gov/pvm, PVM – Parallel Virtual Machine.
[7] http://www.mpi-forum.org/, MPI Forum main page
[8] http://www-unix.mcs.anl.gov/mpi/mpich/, MPICH main page
[9] http://www.lam-mpi.org/, LAM-MPI (Message Passing Interface) main page

On Construction of a Large File System Using PVFS for Grid

Chao-Tung Yang[1], Chien-Tung Pan[1], Kuan-Ching Li[2], and Wen-Kui Chang[1]

[1] High-Performance Computing Laboratory,
Department of Computer Science and Information Engineering,
Tunghai University,
Taichung, 407 Taiwan, R.O.C.
{ctyang, wkc}@mail.thu.edu.tw
g912910@student.thu.edu.tw
[2] Parallel and Distributed Processing Center,
Department of Computer Science and Information Management,
Providence University,
Shalu, Taichung 433 Taiwan ROC
kuancli@pu.edu.tw

Abstract. Grid is the largest advance of network after Internet since the Grid System provides a specialty that can be used popularly and effectively. However, it is a challenge to the consistency and community of use on the data storages space of a Grid System. Therefore, the problem of application for the Computational Grid and Data Grid is more important. It can set up a usability, expandability, high operation capability, and large memory space in Grid with the Cluster system and parallel technique in order to solve the problem. In this paper, we provided a Grid with high operation capability and higher memories to solve the problem. As to the Grid setting, we take use of the Cluster computing to increase the operation effect for computing, and a PVFS2 with more storages effect for data. It can supply a quite correct platform for Grid user whether for large data access or huge operation.

Keywords: Cluster, Grid Computing, Data Grid, Parallel Virtual File Systems.

1 Introduction

High performance, distributed computing and computational sciences require large data sets, fast and efficient ways of getting to that data, and a security model that will protect the integrity of the stored data. In order to create enough usable space without spending large amounts of money for storage, multiple storage servers need to be used in groups.

Grid computing is a form of distributed computing that involves coordinating and sharing computing, application, data, storage, or network resources across dynamic and geographically dispersed organizations [1,2, 3, 4, 5]. Grid technologies promise to change the way organizations tackle complex computational problems. However, the vision of large scale resource sharing is not yet a reality in many areas - Grid computing is an evolving area of computing, where standards and technology are still being developed to enable this new paradigm.

Data grids are used to provide secure access to remote data resources: flat-file data, relational data, and streaming data [7, 8]. For example, two collaborators at sites A and B need to share the results of a computation performed at site A, or perhaps design data for a new part needs to be accessible by multiple team members working on a new product at different sites and in different companies.

Grid is a great progress of network after Internet because the Grid System provides a specialty that it can be used popularly and effectively. It can set up a usability, expandability, high operation capability, and large memory space in Grid with the Cluster system and parallel technique in order to solve the problem. In this paper, we provided a Grid with high operation capability and higher memories to solve the problem. As to the Grid setting, we take use of the Cluster computing to increase the operation effect for computing, and a PVFS2 with more storages effect for data. All the system use the Channel Bonding method to raise the effect of data reading, writing and transmission, so that it can provide a higher memories effect.

2 System Model

The PVFS is an effort to provide a parallel file system for PC clusters [6]. As a parallel file system, PVFS provides a global name space, striping of data across multiple I/O nodes, and multiple user interfaces.

The system is implemented at the user level, so no kernel modifications are necessary to install or run the system. All communication is performed using TCP/IP, so no additional message passing libraries are needed, and support is included for using existing binaries on PVFS files.

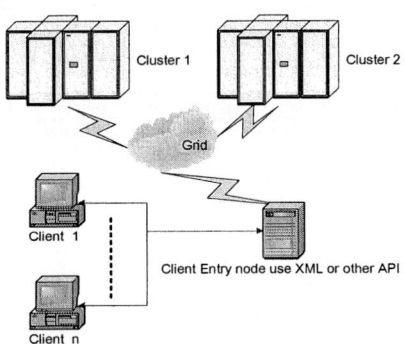

Fig. 1. Our system architecture

First, we use four dual processors PC (SMP structure) with 60GB of hard disk; divided into 10GB installation system, the rest 50GB is provided for PVFS use, total

4 PCs have 200GB capacity space. Because the setting of PVFS2 Linux OS Kernel needs a 2.6.x, we adopt Mandrakelinux-10.0-Community version, the Kernel is 2.6.3 version, MPI 6.5.9.

We set up two Cluster systems in the system, each Cluster is equipped with Linux OS Kernel 2.6.3, and set up NFS, NIS and MPI-2.0 in order to present the feature of whole set of cluster as shown in Figure 1. Therefore, in Client1 group, we can get the divided hard disk capacity of each Client 50GB, the total hard disk capacity of 4 PCs is 200GB, as to the Cluster2 group, the hard disk capacity is 150GB. Further, the Host of each group has Globus Toolkits 3 version [7] for connecting via Grid system. We use the real IP of Host IP for the two systems, which have transmitted to the simulating remote terminal IP (in fact, to link Globus PC should have a real IP) in order that the outer terminal of Client can pass through GridFTP or XML direct access the space shared by Cluster1 and Cluster2.

3 Experimental Results

Whether install PVFS2 on Cluster1 and Cluster2 groups to form a group, its step is as follows actually in us. Take Cluster1 as an example.

Step1. Building and installing the packages
Step2. Server configuration
Step3. Starting the servers
Step4. Client configuration
Step5. Testing your Installation

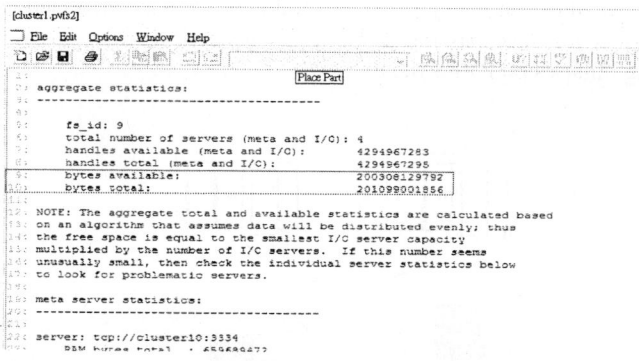

Fig. 2. Results list of Cluster1

We successfully obtain our projected capacity: Cluster1 have 200,308,129,792 bytes available, Cluster2 have 152,531,263,488 bytes available. (Figures 2 and 3), the capacity is small than SAN or NAS, but we assure that the capacity of the said system can be very large due to good hard disk.

Our experiment expressed that it can additionally provide a large storages space in Computing Grid surely. We established a platform of large storages for supplying to

GridFTP, Avaki [8], something like DataGrid middleware or use XML's DataGrid Access Software Application by himself.

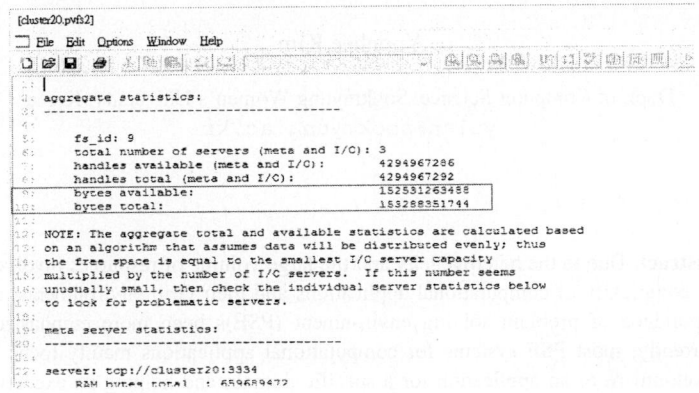

Fig. 3. Results list of Cluster2

4 Conclusion and Future Work

As the internet bandwidth is increasing constantly, the PVFS is used in Local, now, it accesses to the whole world gradually, in opposition, and the security question is the primary guiding principle in the future. There is a quite space to improve in this system, such as: how to combine the capacity of Cluster1 with Cluster2, although it didn't be experimented, we conduct a well design method. We have the confidence that we can create a more big space for DataGrid.

References

[1] R. Buyya, High Performance Cluster Computing: System and Architectures, Vol. 1, Prentice Hall PTR, NJ, 1999.
[2] R. Buyya, High Performance Cluster Computing: Programming and Applications, Vol. 2, Prentice Hall PTR, NJ, 1999.
[3] I. Foster, The Grid: A New Infrastructure for 21st Century Science, available at http://www.gridtoday.com/02/0805/100191.html
[4] I. Foster, Internet Computing and the Emerging Grid, available at http://www.nature.com/nature/webmatters/grid/grid.html
[5] I. Foster, C. Kesselman, and S. Tuecke. "The Anatomy of the Grid: Enabling Scalable Virtual Organizations," International Journal of Supercomputer Applications, 15(3), 2001. Available at http://www.globus.org/research/papers/anatomy.pdf
[6] A Quick Start Guide to PVFS2, Available at http://www.pvfs.org/pvfs2/pvfs2-quickstart.html
[7] Global Grid Forum, Available at http://www.ggf.org/
[8] Avaki, Available at http://www.avaki.com/

A Grid-Enabled Workflow PSE for Computational Applications[1]

Yoonhee Kim

Dept. of Computer Science, Sookmyung Women's University, Korea
yulan@sookmyung.ac.kr

Abstract. Due to the heterogeneity and the large volume of resources involved; the complexity of computational applications and their Grid environments, the importance of problem solving environment (PSE)s been more emphasized. Currently, most PSE systems for computational applications mainly focus on development of an application for a specific domain and helping its execution with static resource configuration but does not consider of general form of PSE toolkit for its deployment to extended domains. This paper proposed a Grid-enabled PSE called as a Computing Environment for Grid Applications (CEGA) and discuss how it is evolving to develop a computational application in a style of workflow model and incorporate Grid computing services to extend its range of services and handle information for development, deployment, execution and maintenance for an application as well as an application requirement itself. In addition, the paper provides the architecture of CEGA and its implementation for development, execution and visualization of an application in detail.

1 Introduction

High performance problem solving computing environments capitalize on the emerging high speed network technology, parallel and distributed programming tools and environments, and the proliferation of high performance computers. Recently, there have been increased interests in building large-scale high performance distributed computing application over Grid environment.

The concept of Grid computing has been investigated and developed to enlarge the concept of distributed computing environment to create infrastructure that enables integrated services for resource scheduling, data delivery, authentication, delegation, information service, management and other related issues [1]. As the Grid provides integrated infrastructure for solving problems, interfacing services such as web portal to access Grid services, PSEs (Problem Solving Environments) have been developed to improve the collaboration among Grid services and reduce significantly the time and effort required to develop, run, and experiment with large scale Grid applications.

---

[1] This Research was supported by the Sookmyung Women's University Research Grants 2004.

However, most PSEs to support parallel and distributed computing focus on providing environments for successful execution of applications and providing reasonable resource scheduling schemes. Due to the lack of adaptability on creating dynamic application configurations due to changes of resource status, the execution of these applications is inefficient. There have been several application-specific tools and PSEs to utilize Grid environment efficiently. ASC Grid Portal [2] is a PSE for large-scale simulation in astrophysics. Hotpage [3] is another PSE targeted toward high performance computing applications. Cactus [4] provides a problem solving environment for developing large-scale distributed scientific applications. GrADS [5] is a toolkit to help users to build applications over heterogeneous resources with ease of use. Similarly, UNICORE [6] provides graphical user interface to access heterogeneous resources uniformly. However, an effort on generalizing a PSE to support development and execution of applications (i.e. applications in workflow management), has been not fully investigated.

A Computing Environment for a Grid Application (CEGA) has been developed to provide a computing environment for a computational application in a workflow model. The CEGA provides an efficient Graphical User Interface (GUI) approach for developing, running, evaluating and visualizing large-scale parallel and distributed applications that utilize computing resources connected by local and/or wide area network. To support Grid services through CEGA, the Server creates application configurations using Resource Specification Language (RSL), which runs over the Globus toolkit [7].

The organization of the remaining sections of the paper is as follows. We present an overview of the CEGA architecture in Section 2. In Section 3 we describe the major functionality in workflow editor for development and visualization in detail. The conclusion is followed in Section 5.

2 The Architecture of CEGA

The CEGA is a workflow based problem solving environment for grid computational applications. It provides transparent computing and communication services for large scale parallel and distributed applications. The architecture of CEGA consists of Workflow Editor, Workflow Engine and Globus (see Fig.1) Globus is the Grid middleware toolkit to launch jobs and collects the results over Grid resources. Workflow Editor helps users to generate a workflow of an application, based on the application logic, specify the input/output and runtime requirements to provide various execution environment without having big efforts for changing their experiment options. To interface between the Editor and Globus, Workflow Engine collects and handles data from the Editor and Globus services, steers the workflow over Globus. In addition, it monitors the status of job execution.

An application is defined as a set of jobs; which are connected to one another based on their job dependency. The execution of jobs can be executed either in parallel or sequence based on the dependency. When the Workflow Engine collects application workflow information from the editor, it controls the order of execution of the jobs based on the dependency over Grid environment as the results of analysis of the workflow information. The Engine generates the as a set of activities in Resource Specification language (RSL), one of which can run over Globus in parallel. Most execution have a set of input and output. The deployment of the data in appropriate locations among the execution of activities is done by the control of the Engine based on the workflow. The Engine checks the job dependency on the graph and divides multiple phases, which means making execution groups(i.e. activities) of jobs in parallel. Each group is mapped to grid resources by means of job scheduling service in Globus. Beside of job steering in the Engine, it provides cooperative administration for dynamic Globus environment such as administrating Grid nodes and coordinating other Grid services, GRAM, MDS, and FTP as examples. The Engine also provides runtime monitoring and collects runtime log data in XML including starting and ending time, and total execution time. Whenever a user wants to monitor the runtime data, the Engine provides them to a visualization tool.

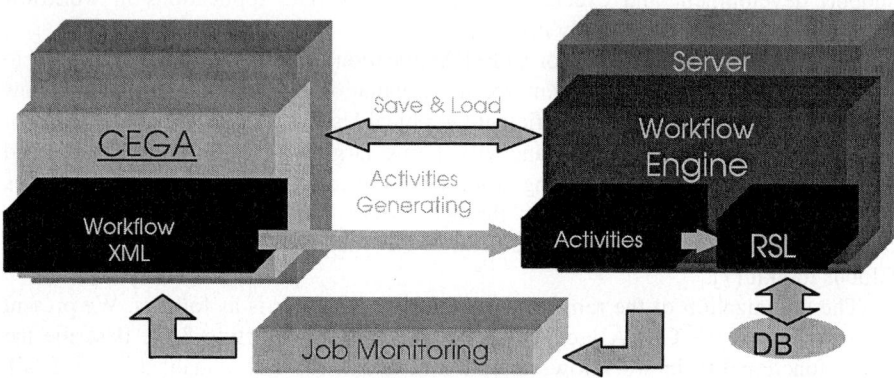

Fig. 1. An Architecture of CEGA

3 CEGA Editing and Monitoring Service

Graphical user interface helps users to develop, modify and execute an application easily over Grid resources. CEGA editor provides workflow patterns which includes various job patterns and linkages. The left side of Fig. 2 shows a simple model of work patterns- basic and join patterns. User can use customized workflow patterns which a user can directly modify on; as well as built-in patterns. As Object List Tree is added in the left side of the window, new object is easily added to the graph with just drag & drop scheme. For editing service, open, save, new, execute and monitor interface is developed on the top menu. Once an application is developed within the editor, the information is passed to the Workflow Engine for workflow management to proceed application execution.

The information of monitoring syntax error and job execution result is displayed on the bottom window in text. At the same time, the color of each job model shows the current status of job execution such as ready, active done, and failure (see Fig. 2).

Currently, CEGA has been developed for a potential energy surface calculation in molecular dynamics simulation, which requires high performance parallel computing. It also provide interface to customize experimental options easily for diverse execution conditions. It reduces deployment cost for experimentation.

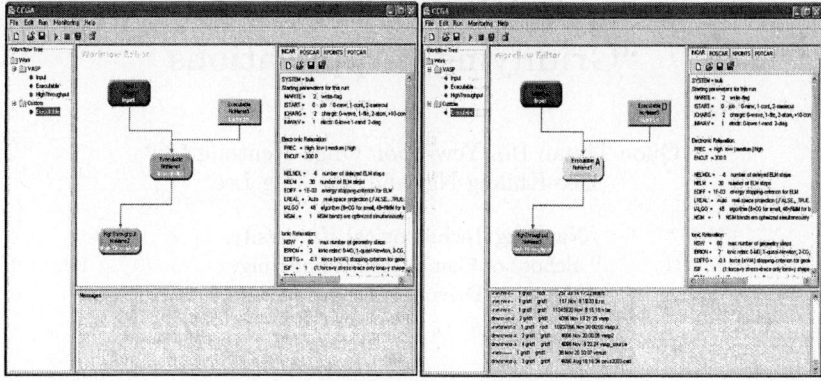

Fig. 2. An example of CEGA editor

4 Conclusion

We describe the architecture of CEGA to provide a parallel and distributed programming environment; it provides an easy-to-use graphical user interface that allows users to develop, run and visualize parallel/distributed applications running on heterogeneous computing resources connected by networks. To support Grid services through CEGA the server creates application configurations using Resource Specification Language (RSL), which runs over the Globus toolkit. This paper shows the functionality of the workflow editor to develop an application and generate application configuration over Grid environment. As it is adapt a workflow model, it can be easily extended to other application domain when diverse workflow patterns are added.

References

1. Foster, C. Kesselman, "The Grid:Blueprint for a New Computing Infrasteructure," Morgan-Kaufmann, 1998.
2. Astrophysics Simulation Collaboratory: ASC Grid Portal, http://www.ascportal.org
3. HotPage, http://hotpage,npaci.edu
4. Cactus Code, http://www.cactuscode.org
5. GrADS Project, http://nhse2.cs.rice.edu/grads/index.html
6. Romberg,M., "The UNICORE Architecture Seamless Access to Distributed Resources," High Performance Distributed Computing, 1999
7. Globus Project, http://www.globus.org
8. J. Novotny, "The Grid Portal Development Kit," Concurrency: Practice and Experience, Vol.00, pp 1–7, 2000

GAD Kit - A Toolkit for "Gridifying" Applications

Quoc-Thuan Ho, Yew-Soon Ong, Wentong Cai[*],
Hee-Khiang Ng, and Bu-Sung Lee

Nanyang Technological University,
School of Computer Engineering,
Nanyang Drive, Singapore 639798

Abstract. In this paper, we present a Grid Application Development toolkit called GAD Kit. It simplifies the "gridifying" process by providing mechanisms to enable existing applications as Grid services and their consumptions. These include features for automatic wrapping of applications as Grid services, service deployment and discovery, metascheduling and seamless access to Grid resources. To facilitate access to Grid resources, GAD Kit was developed based on the standard GridRPC API. Finally, we present the use of GAD Kit for "gridifying" a realistic aerodynamic design application.

Keywords: Grid computing, Grid programming tools, GridRPC.

1 Introduction

Over the recent years, there has been an increasing interests in executing high performance applications over the Grid. A lot of works have been done in the areas of core middleware support for building Grid computing environments, application specific problem solving environments and portal development [1]. However, at present, there has been a lack of user-centric tools and environments that facilitates seamless deployment of existing software components/applications as Grid services. Clearly, the tools to provide a secure yet simple consumptions of these grid resources has been lacking too.

"Gridifying" is defined as the process of transforming an existing application to execute appropriately on a Grid environment. This process involves handling the issues on parallelizing existing applications, deploying applications as Grid services, discovering and consuming of Grid services, last but not least, the scheduling of tasks on the Grid which would involves both at cluster and node levels. Clearly, having general users to perform all these tasks manually in order to be able to use the Grid is time consuming, tedious, and non-trivial.

In this work, we present the GAD Kit to simplify the "gridifying" process by providing mechanisms for seamless enabling of existing applications as Grid

---

[*] Contact Author: email – aswtcai@ntu.edu.sg

services and their consumptions. The rest of the paper is organized as follows. In the second section, we present the basic components of our GAD Kit. In addition, we demonstrate the "gridification" of a realistic application using the GAD Kit in section 3. Finally, the fourth section draws our main conclusions.

2 GAD Kit Architecture and Design

The GAD Kit comprises of a Graphical User Interface (GUI) module, Grid service provider module, Grid service consumer module, and the metascheduler module. Here, to facilitate a common application programming interface that conforms to Grid standards, the GridRPC API [2,3] is used in the GAD Kit. The "gridifying" process in the GAD Kit is accomplished by two main components, namely the Service Provider and Service Consumer modules.

2.1 Service Provider

The service provider module in the GAD Kit provides automatic wrapping and deployment of existing applications as Grid services. To provide a platform-independent development environment for wrapping of existing applications, a standard format for specifying Grid service interfaces based on Grid Function Description (GFD) language is developed in the GAD Kit to accommodate different domain-specific interface. Currently, the problem description interface file format of NetSolve [4] is supported. The GFD language is similar in spirit to CORBA IDL and focusses on the arguments passed to the services. Once applications are wrapped as Grid services, they are deployed automatically onto Grid resources as specified by the users. Rather GAD Kit employs standard Grid technologies such as GridFTP and Globus remote commands to deploy Grid services, i.e, to distribute and install Grid services on resources.

2.2 Service Consumer

The service consumer module provides simple aggregation of Grid resources and offers mechanisms to facilitate consumption of the deployed Grid services. Principally, it produces Grid-enabled client programs that access deployed Grid services. To generate Grid-enabled client programs, templates for consuming Grid services are provided in the GAD Kit. This reduces programming time and eliminate programming errors. Further, a service consumer GUI is provided to user for customization of the templates, for example, selecting which Grid services to call in the client programs. To permit embarrassingly parallelism of Grid services, capabilities of making multiple asynchronous requests are also provided. Resource discovery and metascheduling mechanisms are also included in the GAD Kit. These mechanisms facilitate efficient service of requests across the dynamically changing resources based on the system configuration, speed, and workload information obtained from Globus MDS [5] and Ganglia monitoring toolkit [6].

3 Realistic Airfoil Analysis and Design Using GAD Kit

In this case study, a Genetic Algorithm (GA) for aerodynamic airfoil designs was "gridified" using GAD Kit. The design optimization process was carried through a number of GA generations. In each generation, the Grid-enabled GA produces a population of designs for analysis using the "gridified" airfoil analysis service provided. Subsequently, these analysis results pertaining to the merits of each potential design points are used to generate the new designs for the next generation. The "gridifying" process of this application is outlined in Figure 1(a).

To implement the airfoil analysis Grid service, the users first specify the GFD of the service in the first stage (see Figure 1(b)). The domain-specific interface based on NetSolve is generated automatically. From here, the users can simply transfer their existing codes into the domain-specific interface and customize any output, input arguments necessary for the service. At stage 3, the Grid service code is subsequently deployed on the user specified resources. Note that the GAD Kit registers the service on the Globus MDS automatically and all deployment tasks are completed with the use of standard GridFTP and Globus remote commands.

To consume the deployed Grid services, user first selects the airfoil analysis service from the list of Grid services discovered automatically by the GAD Kit via an in-built GUI. Subsequently, a Grid-enabled client program which takes into account the configurations specified by the users for consuming the airfoil analysis service gets generated automatically. It is worth noting that the generated Grid-enabled client program contains built-in prototypes to perform resource

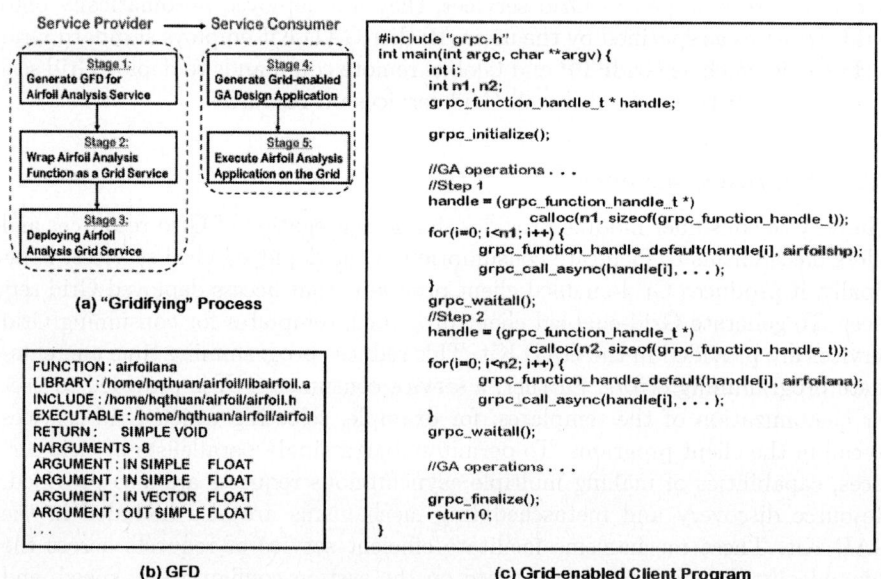

Fig. 1. "Gridifying" of Airfoil Analysis and Genetic Algorithm

discovery (i.e., locate where the airfoil analysis resides in) and metascheduling (i.e., select the cluster that gives maximum throughput). The users may perform further customization to this client program if necessary (see Figure 1(c)).

Traditionally, "gridifying" an application involves dealing with the low-level programming throughout all five stages. Using the GAD Kit, the development time is now spent mainly on specifying the GFD, customizing service and modifying the Grid-enabled program. With the GAD Kit, the "gridifying" process of applications is simplified considerably, contributing significantly to the success of Grid realistic applications.

4 Conclusions

The GAD Kit presented in this paper can simplify the "gridifying" process and offer a seamless and transparent access to Grid resources. It comprises of the GUI module and a set of mechanisms for providing and consuming Grid services. They cover most of mechanisms necessary for Grid application development and free users from tedious low-level programming and the complexity of underlying system. A case study on using the GAD Kit for facilitating embarrassingly parallelism in the aerodynamic design optimization application is also presented briefly.

In our future work, we plan to offer different models for applications. This requires mechanisms for seamless construction of hybrid services from existing services. In addition, extension of the present work to handle multi-level nested services would also be considered.

References

1. C. Lee and D. Talia. Grid Programming Models: Current Tools, Issues, and Directions. In *Grid Computing Making the Global Infrastructure a Reality*, John Wiley & Sons, Ltd., 2003.
2. H. Nakada, S. Matsuoka, K. Seymour, J. Dongarra, C. Lee, and H. Casanova. GridRPC: A Remote Procedure Call API for Grid Computing. Advanced Programming Models Research Group, The Global Grid Forum, July 2002.
3. Q. T. Ho, Y. S. Ong, and W. Cai. "Gridifying" Aerodynamic Design Problem using GridRPC. In *LNCS Vol. 3032, pp. 83-90, Springer-Velag*, 2003.
4. D. Arnold, H. Casanova, and J. Dongara. Innovations of the NetSolve Grid Computing System. In *Concurrency: Practical and Experience 14(13-15): 1457-1479*, 2002.
5. K. Czajkowski, S. Fitzgerald, I. Foster, and C. Kesselman. Grid Information Services for Distributed Resource Sharing. In *Proceedings of the Tenth IEEE International Symposium on High-Performance Distributed Computing (HPDC-10)*, 2001.
6. M. L. Massie, B. N. Chun, and D. E. Culler. The Ganglia Distributed Monitoring System: Design, Implementation, and Experience. February 2003.
7. Nanyang Campus Grid. *http://www.ntu-cg.ntu.edu.sg*

GridCrypt: High Performance Symmetric Key Cryptography Using Enterprise Grids

Agus Setiawan, David Adiutama, Julius Liman,
Akshay Luther, and Rajkumar Buyya

Grid Computing and Distributed Systems Laboratory,
Dept. of Computer Science and Software Engineering,
The University of Melbourne, Australia
{a.setiawan, d.adiutama, j.liman}@pgrad.unimelb.edu.au
{akshayl, raj}@cs.mu.oz.au

Abstract. Today's cryptanalysis on symmetric key cryptography is encouraging the use of larger key sizes and complex algorithms to achieve an unbreakable state. However, this leads an increase in computational complexity. This has promoted many researchers to develop high-performance symmetric key cryptography schemes using approaches such as the use of high-end computing hardware. Peer-to-peer (P2P) or enterprise grids are proven as one of the approaches for developing cost-effective high-end computing systems. By utilizing them, one can improve the performance of symmetric key cryptography through parallel execution. This approach makes it attractive for adoption by businesses to secure their documents. In this paper we propose and develop an application for symmetric key cryptography using enterprise grid middleware called Alchemi. An analysis and comparison of its performance is presented along with pointers to future work.

1 Introduction

Symmetric key cryptography, also called private key or secret key cryptography, is a method that uses the same key for encryption of plain text to generate the cipher text and decryption of the cipher text to get the original plain text. This method is used to secure data for transmission over open networks such as the Internet.

There are two methods that are used in symmetric key cryptography [1]: block and stream. The block method divides a large data set into blocks (based on predefined size or the key size), encrypts each block separately and finally combines blocks to produce encrypted data. The stream method encrypts the data as a stream of bits without separating the data into blocks. The stream of bits from the data is encrypted sequentially using some of the results from the previous bit until all the bits in the data are encrypted as a whole.

Although stream ciphers are designed to encrypt data as a whole, we introduce a new modified hybrid scheme that divides the data into several blocks prior to processing the data with stream cipher. This allows us to divide the stream cipher process into several processes so that we can apply multiprocessing principles to speed up the stream cipher method.

In this paper, we consider three popular encryption algorithms. The first two, DES (Data Encryption Standard) and Blowfish, use the block cipher method and the third one, RC4, uses the stream cipher method. The similarity of these encryption algorithms is that they initialise an S-Box for use in the encryption process derived from the key used for encryption [2]. During decryption, the same key is used to generate an S-Box to decrypt the cipher data.

Developed in 1997, DES implements 16 rounds of symmetric 56-bits key to each 64-bits block of data [7]. Since DES considered not secure enough to be applied in recent computer technology, Triple-DES was developed using three times encryption (encrypt, decrypt, encrypt) on different key which gives cumulative key size of 112-168 bits [5].

Blowfish was developed in 1993 as a replacement for DES using variable-length key (32-488 bits). It is considered faster than DES because it was designed with 32-bit instruction processors [9]. In the first part, Blowfish implements key dependent permutation, which convert variable-length key into several subkey arrays. Then, like DES, it applies 16 rounds of key-dependent permutation and key-data-dependent substitution, using XORs and additions on 32-bit word [8]. As an addition, there are four lookups into indexed array for each round.

Posted on Internet newsgroup without permission from its inventor in 1994 [10], RC4 implements symmetric key up to 2048 bits length, which is considered to be a relatively fast and strong cipher [5]. Using the same algorithm for encryption and decryption, it simply XORes a block of data with the generated random key sequence. In serial operation, each state entry is then exchanged successively based on the key sequence [11].

2 Alchemi

Alchemi [12] is a .NET based grid computing framework developed at the University of Melbourne. It is an open source project which provides middleware for creating an enterprise grid computing environment by harnessing Windows machines. Alchemi supports multithreaded parallel operation in a manner similar to threading in Java or C#, but with their execution on distributed resources. The parallelism is realised at thread level and the programmer has to identify functions to be parallelized and implement them in the form of threads. Currently, inter-thread communication is not supported, so threads must be independent.

Alchemi's main components are manager and executor that support a master-worker parallel model. Alchemi has a number of features that ease the process of setting up of a grid environment in an enterprise. The executors can be setup in dedicated or non-dedicated mode on employees' desktop computers. In non-dedicated mode, Alchemi has no impact on the workstation as far as the user is concerned. The Alchemi manager also requires a Microsoft SQL Server instance, which is available in most companies.

3 Design and Architecture

Alchemi provides a Software Development Kit (SDK) that can be used develop grid applications. The SDK includes a Dynamic Link Library (DLL) that supports object oriented programming model for multithreaded applications. Currently, Alchemi only supports completely parallel threads and does not support inter-thread communication. This affects the design of parallelism in our symmetric key cryptography implementation. While this does not affect the parallelization of block cipher method, we have to use the hybrid scheme discussed above for the stream cipher method.

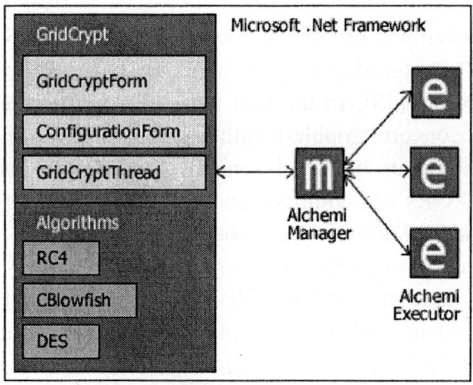

Fig. 1. GridCrypt Architecture

The architecture of GridCrypt is shown in Fig. 1. Our .NET application interacts with Alchemi to enhance the symmetric key cryptography performance. In this application we have developed three main classes. The first class (GridCryptForm) is the interface to control and monitor the progress of the encryption and connection with Alchemi manager. The second class (ConfigurationForm) is the form that can be used to configure the number of threads to be submitted and specify the location of the Alchemi manager. The last class (GridCryptThread) is the thread class that is run under Alchemi and it uses the algorithm classes.

Multithreading Symmetric Key Cryptography

In our design of multithreaded symmetric key cryptography, parallelization is being carried to process the data that need to be encrypted. We use the Task-Farming (master-slave) model for execution and principles of SPMD (Single Program Multiple Data) model for application parallelisation. The effect of this parallelization method is that we have to find a way to divide the files into several blocks so that the process can be done in parallel on each block of data.

We divide the raw file into several blocks based on the configuration form. An analysis of the three algorithms reveals that the size of the block to be able to run each encryption algorithm should be divisible by 8. This is because in the DES and Blowfish algorithm the encryption was done 64 bit (8 byte) at a time, so if the block is not divisible by 8 the encryption algorithm that we implement will simply pad the block so that it will be divisible by 8. The padding is carried our on the last block of the file.

The flow of GridCrypt program is shown in Fig. 2. A Pseudo code for multi-threaded symmetric key cryptography can be found in [13]. It separates the input file into several parts in order to parallelise the encryption process. After the separation of the input file, each part of the file (block) is assigned to thread including the last block whose size is the remainder of the predefined block size. The file separation process is done by reading the file sequentially according to the block size. After the threads return with the encrypted result, GridCrypt writes the encrypted data to a random access file according to the index that is carried within the thread.

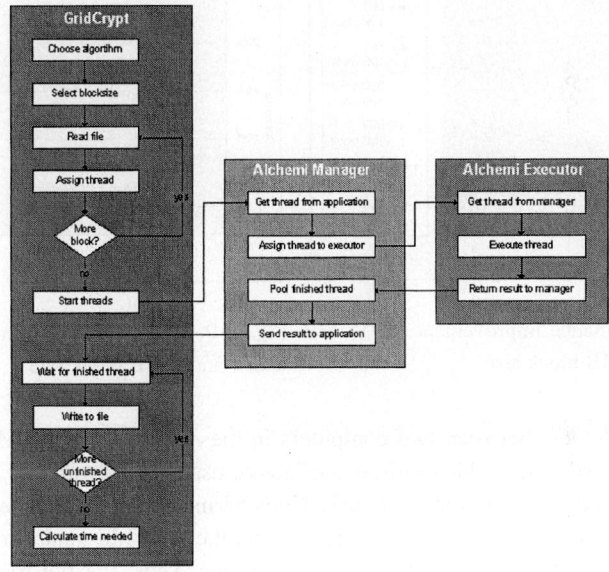

Fig. 2. GridCrypt flow of process

4 Performance Evaluation

We have done a runtime comparison for the GridCrypt application using 8 executor nodes each with the same specification of Pentium IV 2400 MHz processor and 512 MB of memory and running Windows 2000 Professional operating system. All these nodes were interconnected over a shared student laboratory LAN network of 100 Mbps. The Alchemi manager was installed on a separate computer together with SQL Server 2000. A separate user machine was used to initiate the execution of the Grid-Crypt application.

The encryption experiments were conducted on files of size 55 MB and 110 MB with 1 and 2 MB block size. For each file the encryption was carried on 1, 2, 4 and 8 executor nodes. The performance results of these experiments are shown in Fig. 3 and 4.

In all experiments, there was a reasonable performance improvement when 4 and 8 executors were used -- roughly 5% to 20% respectively. This gain is not linear; a similar phenomenon is also observed in [6]. Although there was a reasonable performance improvement when up to 8 executors were used, in some cases, there were drops in speedup gain when number of executors was increased from 4 to 8. This is due to various overhead factors including (a) involvement of large datasets with low computation to communication ratio, (b) existence of serial processing component (file splitting and collating results), (c) the use of slow and shared network, and (d) the overhead of the distributed execution environment (e.g., distribution of executable, initiation of execution on a remote node, and management of threads).

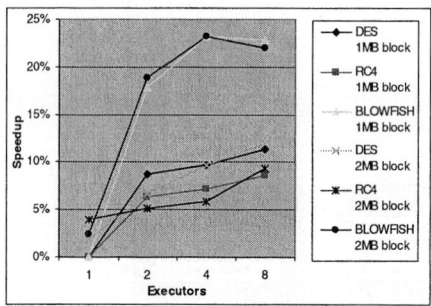
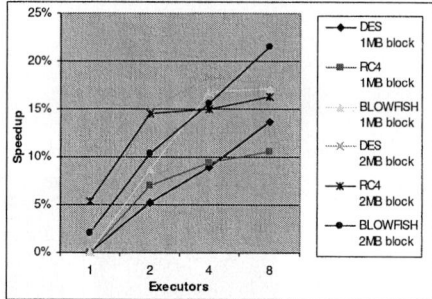

Fig. 3. Performance improvement for 55 MB with 1 and 2 MB block size

Fig. 4. Performance improvement for 110 MB with 1 and 2 MB block size

A file copy test between two computers in the network for 110 MB file took an average of 20 seconds, which indicates effective usable bandwidth of 5.5 MB/sec. in our shared student laboratory network. Considering the data transfer between the GridCrypt application and executor nodes is via the Alchemi manager, data for each work unit has to travel across the network 4 times. Thus, the file transfer overhead alone contributes about 60-70% of the processing time in this experiment. The use of a faster network such as Gigabit Ethernet and faster storage systems will help minimize the overhead. In addition, although this overhead can be approximately halved by bypassing the manager and transferring date files between the user host and executors directly, it violates the current Alchemi security model.

5 Related Works

One of the approaches to increase the performance of symmetric key cryptography was carried by Praveen Dongara and T. N. Vijaykumar [3]. They were implementing Interleaved Cipher Block Chaining method on Symmetric Multiprocessors. This is the case where the effort to improve symmetric key cryptography is focused on the algorithm and hardware. Another related effort carried out by Jerome Burke, John McDonald and Todd Austin [4] adds instruction set support for fast substitutions, general permutations, rotates, and modular arithmetic. Their experiment has shown overall speedup to the symmetric key cryptography. While these two approaches also enhance the performance of symmetric key cryptography, our approach is scalable and cost-effective due to the use of a commodity-based high-performance computing platform.

6 Conclusion

While the performance of enterprise grid symmetric key cryptography that was implemented using Alchemi shows an increase over the single processor version of the symmetric key cryptography, the performance improvement is limited by the I/O and communication overhead. The use of high performance networks can enhance performance. Another way increase performance to transfer the data directly between the user host and executors. However, it violates the current Alchemi security model and requires enhancement of Alchemi security to support rights delegation.

References

1. Wikipedia. Symmetric key algorithm. Updated March 10, 2004. http://en.wikipedia.org/wiki/Symmetric_key_algorithm (June 11, 2004)
2. W. Stallings. Cryptography and Network Security: Principles and Practice, 3rd Edition. Prentice Hall, New Jersey, USA, 2003.
3. Praveen Dongara, T. N. Vijaykumar. Accelerating Private-key cryptography via Multi-threading on Symmetric Multiprocessors. In Proceedings of the IEEE International Symposium on Performance Analysis of Systems and Software (ISPASS), March 2003.
4. Jerome Burke, John McDonald, Todd Austin. Architectural Support for Fast Symmetric-Key Cryptography. Advanced Computer Architecture Laboratory University of Michigan.
5. MyCrypto.net. Encryption Algorithms. http://www.mycrypto.net/encryption/crypto_algorithms.html (June 11, 2004)
6. Daniel M. Pressel. Scalability vs. Performance. U.S. Army Research Laboratory Aberdeen Proving Ground, MD 21005-5066. http://www.hpcmo.hpc.mil/Htdocs/UGC/UGC00/paper/daniel_pressel_scale_paper.pdf
7. searchSecurity.com. Data Encryption Standard. http://searchsecurity.techtarget.com/sDefinition/0,,sid14_gci213893,00.html (June 11, 2004)
8. B. Schneier. The Blowfish Encryption Algorithm -- One Year Later. http://www.schneier.com/paper-blowfish-oneyear.html (June 11, 2004)
9. searchSecurity.com. BlowFish. http://searchsecurity.techtarget.com/sDefinition/0,,sid14_gci213676,00.html (June 11, 2004)
10. R. J. Jenkins Jr. ISAAC and RC4. http://burtleburtle.net/bob/rand/isaac.html (June 11, 2004)
11. VOCALTechnologies, Ltd. RC4 Encryption Algorithm. http://www.vocal.com/RC4.html?glad (June 11, 2004)
12. Akshay Luther, Rajkumar Buyya, Rajiv Ranjan, and Srikumar Venugopal, Alchemi: A .NET-based Desktop Grid Computing Framework, High Performance Computing: Paradigm and Infrastructure, Laurence Yang and Minyi Guo (editors), Wiley Press, New Jersey, USA, Fall 2004. (in print)
13. Agus Setiawan, David Adiutama, Julius Liman, Akshay Luther and Rajkumar Buyya, GridCrypt: High Performance Symmetric Key using Enterprise Grids, Technical Report, GRIDS-TR-2004-6, Grid Computing and Distributed Systems Laboratory, University of Melbourne, Australia, July 7, 2004.

Planning Based Service Composition System

Zhang Jianhong, Zhang Shensheng, and Cao Jian

CIT Lab of Shanghai Jiaotong University, Shanghai, 200030, P.R. China
{zhang-jh, sszhang, cao-jian}@cs.sjtu.edu.cn

Abstract. Automated composition of web services can be realized by using planning techniques in AI. This paper introduces an open and flexible framework for service planning and execution. A hybrid algorithm based on Hierarchical Task Network (HTN) planning and partial order planning (POP) is developed to do service planning. A semantic type-matching algorithm is introduced to matching actions of plan to suitable operations of web services. Compared with other service composition methods, this system has high planning efficiency and good executable ability and can satisfy the need of dynamic business process application.

1 Introduction

The wide availability and standardization of Web services make it possible to compose basic Web services into composite services that provide more sophisticated functionality and create add-on values. However, business process, organization policies and applications change rapidly. And the increase of services caused a vast service space to search, a variety of services to compare and match and different ways to construct composite services. These reasons make it necessary to construct an open, flexible and efficient system for service composition.

There are many service composition standards built such as BPEL4WS[1], DAML-S[2], WSFL, etc. But all the technology assumes that business process is static and predefined and needs vast programming work or human intervention. All these result in poor flexibility and low efficiency. Planning and reasoning about actions in AI has been investigated in service composition. In [3], service composition is addressed by using the Situation Calculus-based programming language CONGOLOG. Both, BPEL4WS specifications and Golog programs are written manually and no assembling of complex flows from atomic message exchanges based on a search process takes place. [5] uses HTN planning system SHOP2 to realize service composition. But the method of solving problem must be predefined and can be used only with OWL-S web service descriptions.

To overcome these problems, we build an open and flexible service composition framework in which service composition problem is viewed as a planning problem.

2 Planning Based Service Composition

Planning can be considered as searching the state space of problem domain to find an action path, which changes the environment from initial states to goal states. In our service composition framework (Fig.1), user's service requirement is mapped as a planning problem firstly. If there is no existing plan that can satisfy user's requirement, the planning engine call the hybrid planning algorithm (see section 3) to generate a plan composed of atomic actions defined in plan library. Then type-matching algorithm is invoked and appropriate services are matched for each atomic action of the plan from the internal/internet UDDI. Then the plan becomes an executable service dependent plan (SDP).

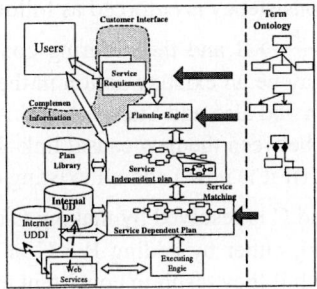

Fig. 1. Planning based Service Composition Framework

Action is the basic unit of the planning model. There are two kinds of action. One kind is atomic action, the basic reuse unit, which will be assigned with some web service for execution. Another kind of action is plan action, which can fulfill more complex service requirement and is composed of atomic actions.

3 Hybrid Planning Algorithm

Compared with other planning algorithm, HTN planning is very efficient. We take a hybrid approach in which action decompositions are used as plan refinements in partial-order planning, in addition to the standard operations of establishing an open condition and resolving conflicts by adding ordering constraints. This algorithm can decide whether a solution exists and can provide interface for user to complement necessary information, has high efficiency and avoid recursive problem.

When executing this planning algorithm, planning engine should obey four rules:

Rule 1: A set of **actions** make up a plan. The "empty" plan contains just the Start and Finish actions.
Rule 2: Each **ordering constraint** is of the form $A \prec B$, which means that action A must be executed before action B.
Rule 3: A **causal link** between two actions A and B in the plan is written as $A \xrightarrow{P} B$, which asserts that p is an effect of the A and a precondition of B. It also asserts that P must remain true from the time of action A to the time of action B. The plan may not be extended by adding a new action C that conflicts with the causal link. An action C conflicts with $A \xrightarrow{P} B$ if C has the effect ¬p and if C could possibly (according to the ordering constraints) come after A and before B.

Rule 4: A set of **open preconditions**. A precondition is open if it is not achieved by some action in the plan.

Algorithm

1. The initial plan contains Start and Finish, the ordering constraint Start $\prec$ Finish, no casual links, and all the preconditions in Finish are open preconditions.

2. The successor function arbitrarily picks one open precondition p on an action B, and generates a successor plan for ever possible consistent way of choosing an action A that achieve p. Consistency is enforced as follows:

- The causal link $A \xrightarrow{P} B$ and the ordering constrain $A \prec B$ are added to the plan. Action A may be an existing action in the plan or a new one. If it is new, add it to the plan and also add Start $\prec A$ and $A \prec$ Finish.
- We resolve conflicts between the new causal link and all existing actions, and between the action A (if it is new) and all existing causal links. A conflict between $A \xrightarrow{P} B$ and C is resolved by making C occur at some time outside the protection interval, either by adding $B \prec C$ or $C \prec A$. We add successor states for either or both if they result in consistent plan.

3. Because only consistent plans are generated, the goal test just needs to check that there are no open preconditions.

4. Select some complicated action a' in Pl(the plan generated above)and for any Decomposition(a, d) method from the plan library such that a and a' unify with substitution θ, we replace a' with d'=SUBST(θ,d).

- First, the action a' is removed from Pl. Then, for each step s in the decomposition d, we need to choose an action to fill the role of s and add it to the plan.
- Hook up the ordering constraints for d in the original plan to the steps in d'.
- Hook up causal links. If $B \xrightarrow{P} a'$ was a causal link in the original plan, replace it by a set of causal links from B to all the steps in d with precondition p that were supplied by the Start step in the decomposition d.

5. Run step4 repeatedly until there is no plan action in the plan.

6. Call type-matching algorithm to find matching service for each action in the plan.

The key to the above planning algorithm is the construction of the plan library. Definitions of actions in the plan library can be abstracted from existing business processes, workflow models or web service description documents. Another important method of constructing the library is to accumulate action definition from problem-solving experience. After the excruciating experience of constructing a plan from scratch, the system can save the plan in the library as a plan action for implementing the high-level action defined by the task.

In this paper, we developed a type-matching approach similar to [6]. The definition of action can map to operation of service. We take a logical interpretation of the problem of type matching and see it as a problem of deciding whether one type structure is a more generic version of another type structure under a certain set of mapping. We use the semantic relations in WordNet[4] as the basis for our algorithm, rather than relying on string matching, synonyms, or "semantic distance values" between words.

When matching service for an action, the labels in each are tokenized using a regular expression, common abbreviations are expanded, compound words are discovered and the words are checked against the hierarchy. For the reason of space, this algorithm is not discussed here.

4 Case study

One example of service composition is as follows: A company in Shanghai wants to participate a trade fair in Shanghai. So, they want to plan the trip, ship the exhibit items and know the weather condition in Shanghai. The task can be achieved by compose a collection of service using the enhanced HTN planning method presented above. The planning process is as Fig. 2.

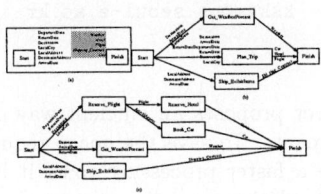

Fig. 2. The planning process of "Participate_Fair" example

Acknowledgements

This research is supported by Natural Funds of China(03DZ19320 and 2003C11009).

References

1. Baldonado, M., Chang, C.-C.K., Gravano, L., Paepcke, A.: The Stanford Digital Library Metadata Architecture. Int. J. Digit. Libr. 1 (1997) 108–121
2. Business Process Execution Language for Web Services, Version 1.1 ftp://www6.software.ibm.com/software/developer/library/ws-bpel11.pdf
3. Ankolenkar A., Burstein M., Hobbs J. R., Lassila O. Adapting golog for composition of semantic web services. In Proc. of KR02, 2002.
4. 4.Jihie Kim and Yolanda Gil, Towards Interactive Composition of Semantic Web Services, 2004 AAAI Spring Symposium. ISWSS'04
5. C. Fellbaum, editor. WordNet: An Electronic Lexical Database. The MIT Press, 1998.
6. Mark Klein and Abraham Bernstein. Searching for services on the semantic web using process ontologies. In Proceedings of SWWS, July 2001.
7. Carman, M.; Serafini, L.; and Traverso, P. 2003. Web service composition as planning. In Workshop on Planning for Web Services, ICAPS 2003.

A Sparse Timestamp Model for Managing Changes in XML Documents*

Geunduk Park[1], Woochang Shin[2], Kapsoo Kim[3], and Chisu Wu[1]

[1] School of Computer Science and Engineering, Seoul National University,
56-1, Shillim-Dong, Kwanak-Gu, Seoul, 151-741, Korea
{dean, wuchisu}@selab.snu.ac.kr
[2] Department of Internet Information, Seokyeong University,
16-1, Jungneung-Dong, Sungbuk-Gu, Seoul, 136-704, Korea
wcshin@imail.skuniv.ac.kr
[3] Department of Computer Education, Seoul National University of Education,
161, Umyeonno, Seocho-Gu, Seoul, 137-070, Korea
kskim@ns.seoul-e.ac.kr

Abstract. This paper proposes an efficient way of managing changes made in XML documents. To save the space required to store various versions and provide a faster processing time, it is essential to reduce the number of parent relations and timestamps that are maintained. To meet these requirements, this paper proposes an augmented tree and the sparse timestamp model (STM).

1 Introduction

The domains of XML are being extended to fields that it was not originally intended to serve. Software engineering is one such field, because XML can provide a common format for all types of software documents and a mechanism for bridging data heterogeneity. Several studies have been conducted and are in progress to apply XML to software documentation [3–6]. The various advantages of XML have led to a rapid increase in the number of documents that make use of it, and this growth has in turn necessitated new methods to manage changes made to XML documents[7].

2 Sparse Timestamp Model

In the Document Object Model (DOM), XML documents are modeled as m-ary trees that are composed of various types of nodes. Accordingly, version control for XML documents can be conceptually converted into version control for m-ary trees.

---

* This work was supported by grant number R01-2003-000-10449-0 from the basic research program of the Korea Science & Engineering Foundation.

A general tree T is a tuple $< N, E, r >$, where N is a set of nodes, E is a set of edges, and r is a root node. A full timestamp model Θ is a tuple $< T, \Psi, \Omega >$, where Ψ is a fully timestamping relation, and Ω is a set of basic operations. In Θ, every node has creation and deletion times, by which the valid nodes in a given version are identified.

[Definition 1]. An augmented tree AT is a tuple $< N, AE, r >$ and $AE = E \cup R$ where R is a set of edges representing revision relations.

A revision sequence starting with n is defined as $n^* = \{n, n_1, n_2, \ldots, n_l\}$. The first and last version of n are designated by n_f and n_l, respectively. A revision sequence can be treated as a single object by replacing it with n^*. The converted tree with this replacement is denoted T^*, and is defined as $T^* =< N^*, E^* >$. In addition, timestamps for n^* are defined as follows:

- $\Psi_c(n^*) = \Psi_c(n_f)$ and $\Psi_d(n^*) = \Psi_d(n_l)$.

The relation Ψ_c on N^* can be divided into the two partitions, Ψ_{ce} and Ψ_{ci}, where $\Psi_{ce} = \{< c, \Psi_c(c) >| \Psi_c(c) \neq \Psi_c(p) \wedge < p, c >\in E\}$ and $\Psi_{ci} = \{< c, \Psi_c(c) >| \Psi_c(c) = \Psi_c(p) \wedge < p, c >\in E\}$. Similarly, the relation Ψ_d on N^* can be divided into Ψ_{de} and Ψ_{di}.

[Definition 2]. A sparsely node-timestamping relation Ψ' is a partial relation from N^* to V and $\Psi' = \Psi'_c \cup \Psi'_d$, where $\Psi'_c = \Psi_{ce}$ and $\Psi'_d = \Psi_{de}$. With this definition, Ψ' from N to V is defined as follows:

- If $< n^*, \Psi'_c(n^*) >\notin \Psi'_c$, then $\Psi'_c = \Psi_c - \{< n_f, \Psi_c(n_f) >\}$.
- If $< n^*, \Psi'_d(n^*) >\notin \Psi'_d$, then $\Psi'_d = \Psi_d - \{< n_l, \Psi_d(n_l) >\}$.

[Definition 3]. A sparsely edge-timestamping relation ψ is a partial relation from AE to V and satisfies the followings:

- $\psi(e_{pc}) = t$ iff $\Psi'(c) = t$, if $e_{pc} \in E$.
- $\psi_c(e_{nn'}) = t$ iff $\Psi'_c(n') = t \wedge \Psi'_d(n) = t$, if $e_{nn'} \in R$.

Let Ω' be a set of basic operations, where $\Omega' = \{insert', delete', update'\}$. If each operation in Ω' is performed in version v, its semantics are defined as follows:

- If $T' =< N', E', r >$ is inserted into $AT =< N, AE, root >$ as a child of n, where $E(n) = \phi$, $S(insert') \Rightarrow (N = N \cup N') \wedge (E = E \cup E') \wedge (E = E \cup \{< n, r >\}) \wedge (\psi_c = \psi_c \cup \{< e_{nr}, v >\})$.
- If $AT' =< N', AE', r' >$ is deleted from $AT =< N, AE, r >$ and $< n, r >\in E$, $S(delete') \Rightarrow (e_{nr}.deleted = true) \wedge (\psi_d = \psi_d \cup \{< e_{nr}, v >\})$.
- If n is updated to n' in $AT =< N, AE, r >$ and $< m, n >\in E$, $S(update') \Rightarrow (N = N \cup n') \wedge (R = R \cup < n, n' >) \wedge shiftRight(e_{nn'}) \wedge (\psi_c = \psi_c \cup \{< e_{nn'}, v >\})$.

Instead of actually deleting AT', $delete'$ set the delete flag of e_{nr} true. And the predicate, $shiftRight$ is defined in Table 1.

Table 1. The *retrieve* procedure

Input AT : The augmented tree controlled by STM.
x : The version number to retrieve.
Output T : The xth version of AT.

---
do $< v, e_{nr}, type >$ in TStack where v is from cno to $x + 1$
    if $e_{nr} \in E \wedge < e_{nr}, v > \in \psi_c$, $e_{nr}.deleted = true$
    if $e_{nr} \in E \wedge < e_{nr}, v > \in \psi_d$, $e_{nr}.deleted = false$
    if $e_{nr} \in R$, shiftLeft(e_{nr})
end do
$T =$ copyTreeFollowingPR(AT)
do $< v, e_{nr}, type >$ in TStack where v is from $x + 1$ to cno
    if $e_{nr} \in E \wedge < e_{nr}, v > \in \psi_c$, $e_{nr}.deleted = false$
    if $e_{nr} \in E \wedge < e_{nr}, v > \in \psi_d$, $e_{nr}.deleted = true$
    if $e_{nr} \in R$, shiftRight(e_{nr})
end do
return T

$shiftRight(e_{nn'}) \Rightarrow (E = E \cup \{< m, n' >\} - \{< m, n >\}) \wedge$
$(E = E \cup \{< n', k > | k \in E(n)\}) \wedge (E = E - E(n)\})$.
$shiftLeft(e_{nn'}) \Rightarrow (E = E \cup \{< m, n >\} - \{< m, n' >\}) \wedge$
$(E = E \cup \{< n, k > | k \in E(n')\}) \wedge (E = E - E(n')\})$.

[Definition 4]. A sparse timestamp model Θ' is a tuple $< AT, \psi, \Omega' >$.

To efficiently access the edges to which timestamps are assigned, they are stored in a stack structure, rather than in the edges themselves. This stack is called a stack for timestamps, or a TStack. If $< e_{nn'}, v > \in \psi$, an element, $< v, e_{nn'}, type >$ is stored in the TStack, where

$$type = \begin{cases} C, \text{ if } < e_{nn'}, v > \in \psi_c \\ D, \text{ if } < e_{nn'}, v > \in \psi_d \end{cases}$$

In STM, retrieval of versions can be made by sequentially reading records stored in the TStack from the top element, and by performing a rollback operation that adjusts invalid edges. The semantics of *rollback* are defined depending on the condition of an invalid edge, and are shown in Table 1. In Table 1, cno denotes the current version number, and the procedure copyTreeFollowingPR() copies the augmented tree along with edges representing parent relations, disregarding edges representing revision relations.

3 Experimental Results

In attempts to efficiently manage changes made in trees and XML documents, various techniques have been developed, such as HiP[1], and SPaR[2]. Because HiP has better performance among proposed approaches so far[1], this paper presents experimental results of STM and HiP.

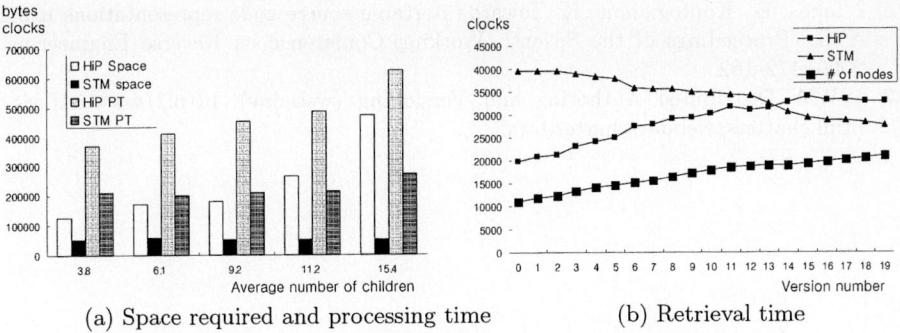

(a) Space required and processing time   (b) Retrieval time

Fig. 1. Performance comparison of HiP and STM

In HiP, the time and storage required to process an operation is proportional to the number of children. In contrast, STM only requires a timestamp for an operation regardless of the number of children. Accordingly, STM has better performance in terms of space and processing time(PT) required to construct version trees as shown in Figure 1(a). Figure 1(b) shows retrieval time to get a specific version using each method. When retrieving versions close to the latest version, STM has better performance because HiP has the overhead to visit additional h-nodes. In contrast, When retrieving versions close to the first version, HiP is superior to STM because retrieval time of STM is proportional to the number of elements in TStack.

STM is efficient in terms of space and processing time and has reasonable performance to get versions close to the latest version. To speed up retrieval of older versions in STM, techniques to reduce the number of timestamps in TStack are necessary.

References

1. E. J. Choi, Y. Kwon, An Efficient Method for Version Control of a Tree Data Structure, Software : Practice and Experience, vol.27, no 7, pp.797-811, July 1997.
2. S.-Y. Chien, V.J. Tsotras, C.Zaniolo, D. Zhang, Storing and Querying Multiversion XML Documents using Durable Node Numbers, In Proc. of the 2nd International Conference on Web Information Systems Engineering, 2001.
3. Object Management Group. OMG-XML Metadata Interchange (XMI)Specification v1.2. January 2002.
4. Nentwich, C., Capra, L., Emmerich, W., Finkelstein, A. xlinkit: A consistency checking and smart link generation service. ACM Transactions on Internet Technology 2002; 2(2):151–185.
5. Badros, G. J. JavaML: a markup language for java source code. Computer networks. 2000; 33(1):159–177.

6. Mamas, E., Kontogiannis, K. Towards portable source code representations using XML. Proceedings of the Seventh Working Conference on Reverse Engineering. 2000; 172–182.
7. WWW Distributed Authoring and Versioning (web-dav). http://www.ietf.org/html.charters/webdav-charter.html.

Author Index

Abdul Latif, Aishah 168
Abdul Rashid, Nur'Aini 13, 248
Abdul Salam, Rosalina 13, 168, 248
Abdullah, Rosni 13, 168, 248
Adiutama, David 872
Apduhan, Bernady 68
Azhari, Afreen 160

Bae, Hae-Young 62
Bae, Misook 25
Bai, Yingcai 72, 829
Baik, Sung Wook 42
Bala, Jerzy 42
Beadle, Patch 127, 192, 791, 795
Bhardwaj, Dheeraj 94
Bin, Ni 188
Birn, First 257
Bo, Song 689
Buyya, Rajkumar 872

Cai, Wentong 868
Calaiselvy 314
Cao, Lei 318
Cao, Zhenfu 662
Cha, Eui-Young 799
Cha, Hojung 401
Cha, Hwangho 301
Chang, Wen-Kui 860
Changqing, Yuan 689
Chen, Bo 772
Chen, Gang 367
Chen, Hanhua 345
Chen, Hansheng 72
Chen, Kefei 591
Chen, Shudong 155
Chen, Xiong 376
Cheng, Kai 218
Ching Lian, Chua 740
Cho, Dong-Sub 729
Cho, HyunJoon 322
Cho, J.W. 586
Cho, Jae-Hyun 172, 176
Cho, Ju Sang 42
Cho, Tae Ho 782

Cho, Youngjoo 293
Choi, Bong-Sik 446
Choi, Dae-Sik 650, 654
Choi, Jin-Hwan 624
Choi, Jong-Soo 106
Chu, Wanming 196
Chua, Ching-Lian 1
Chuan, Zhan 180
Chuanshan, Gao 702
Chun, Junchul 116
Chung, Ilyong 293
Chung, MinYoung 519
Chung, Sang-Hwa 406, 446, 451
Chung, Yongwha 833
Cohen, Jeremy 94

Davy, John R. 230
Deepa L. 86
Dilin, Mao 702
Ding, Jianguo 72
Doh, Kyu B. 111
Dou, Jun 429
Dou, Wenhua 681
Du, Qing-feng 46, 213
Du, Yujun 310

Fan, Pingzhi 619, 666
Fan-Yuan, Ma 50, 54
Fang, Bin-Xing 613
Fang, Bingxing 839
Fang, Binxing 81, 410
Fei, Liu 50, 54
Flahive, Andrew 68
Fujita, Satoshi 337
Fung, Yu-Fai 441

Gang, Peng 202
Gao, Ming 341
Gegang, Peng 702
George, Bindya 86
Goryachev, Andrew 5
Guan, Yong Liang 164
Guan, Zhihong 326

Haron, Fazilah 58, 230
Hasegawa, Yukihiro 149

He, Mingxing 619
Hiraki, Kei 305
Hirasawa, Shoichi 305
Ho, Liang-Yoong 1
Ho, Quoc-Thuan 868
Hong, Chul-Eui 238
Hong, Chuleui 234, 787
Hong, Feng 310, 341
Hong, Jeongwoo 301
Hong, Sangcheol 719
Hong, Seongsoo 803
Hong, Soon Jwa 642
Hong, Taeyoung 301
Horng, Shi-Jinn 243
Hou, Meng-Shu 763
Hu, Mingzeng 81, 410, 839
Huah Yong, Chan 58
Huang, I-Hsuan 600
Huang, Jinxia 127
Huang, Joshua 318
Huang, Kedi 363
Huang, Linpeng 76
Huang, Z.Y. 505
Huang, Zhiyi 497
Husain, Wahidah 13
Hwang, Buhyun 25
Hwang, ChongSun 17
Hwang, Eenjun 280

Iimura, Ichiro 202
Ismail, Bukhary Ikhwan 58

Jang, Hankook 406
Je, Sung-Kwan 799
Jeong, JongMin 694
Jeong, Ok-Ran 729
Jeong, Sangjin 549
Jeong, Yeonkwon 719
Jermiin, L.S. 274
Jia, Zhaoqing 768
Jia-Di, Yu 50
Jian, Cao 878
Jiang, Jehn-Ruey 267
Jiang, Yu 410
Jianghu, Yang 702
Jianhong, Zhang 878
Jiazhi, Zeng 424
Jidong, Zhao 424
Jin, Hai 345
Jing-Yi, Zhang 332

Jingli, Zhou 226
Jinyuan, You 604
Jo, Eun Hwan 736
Joarder, Md Rajibul Alam 160
Joo, Miri 748
Joo, Young-Hoon 176
Jung, Kwang-Chul 62
Jung, Mi Gyoung 121

Kaderali, Firoz 619
Kaneko, Keiichi 149
Kang, Eung-Kwan 106
Kang, Hyung Woo 642
Kang, Sungho 539
Keat, Martin Chew Wooi 168
Keum, Young Wook 698, 724
Kim, Boon-Hee 493
Kim, Byung Joo 184
Kim, Chang-Suk 799
Kim, Daegeun 685
Kim, Dong-Wook 106
Kim, DongKyu 650
Kim, Doo-Hyun 420, 736
Kim, Heeyoul 586, 608
Kim, HyeSuk 131
Kim, Hyo 527
Kim, Hyung Jun 297
Kim, Il Kon 184
Kim, Jae-Won 706
Kim, Jangha 748
Kim, Jin-Tae 106
Kim, Jinsoo 519
Kim, Jong 638
Kim, Kapsoo 882
Kim, Kwang-Baek 9, 172, 176
Kim, Kyeongwha 111
Kim, LaeYoung 464
Kim, Miyoung 131
Kim, Moon Hae 736
Kim, Pyungsoo 396
Kim, Pyung Soo 670
Kim, R Young-Chul 848
Kim, Sang-Moon 446
Kim, Sangwook 748
Kim, Soo-Hong 420
Kim, Soon-Gohn 752
Kim, Tae-Hyung 803
Kim, Taehae 833
Kim, Wonil 234, 238, 787
Kim, Woon-Yong 848

Kim, Woonyon   549
Kim, Yeong-Joon   238
Kim, Yeongjoon   234, 787
Kim, Yoonhee   864
Kim, Young-Chan   493
Kim, Young-Ho   98
Kim, Young-Kook   98
Kim, Youngkeun   396
Ko, Kwang-Man   752
Koh, Kern   401, 807
Kondoh, Takuya   811
Koyanagi, Mitsumasa   564
Krishnan, Arun   1, 5, 740
Kumar, Resmy S.   86
Kurino, Hiroyuki   564
Kusakabe, Shigeru   811

Law, Choi Look   164
Lee, Bu-Sung   868
Lee, Do-Hoon   549
Lee, Dong Hoon   642
Lee, DongWoo   17, 322
Lee, Eunyoung   748
Lee, GueeSang   131
Lee, Heejo   638
Lee, Hyo Jong   257
Lee, Inkyu   706
Lee, Jaewon   586, 608
Lee, Kanghee   748
Lee, Kyu-Woong   62
Lee, Minho   396
Lee, Sang-Hun   549
Lee, SeongHoon   17, 322
Lee, SuKyoung   459, 464
Lee, Sung-Tae   98
Lee, Sungyoung   144
Lee, Travis   5
Lee, Wankwon   322
Lee, Wonjun   706, 711
Lee, Young Sam   670
Lee, Yun-Bae   98
Lei, Li   332
Lertnattee, Verayuth   38
Li, Bin   613
Li, Dong   76
Li, Ji   383
Li, Juan   140
Li, Keqiu   554
Li, Kuan-Ching   856, 860

Li, Ming   596
Li, Mingliu   76, 155, 829
Li, Minglu   310, 318, 341, 545,
   744, 768
Li, Shiqun   591
Li, Tian-rui   21
Li, Xiangxue   591
Li, Yamin   196
Li, Ying   310, 341, 545
Li, Youping   558
Li, Zhancheng   192, 795
Li, Zhiye   376
Liang Yong, Ho   740
Liang, Yue   337
Liao, Chun-Sheng   856
Lim, Yun-Ping   1
Liman, Julius   872
Liming, Zhang   188
Lin, Chen   604
Liu, Gang   839
Liu, Hui   744
Liu, Jian   136, 140
Liu, Jingao   596
Liu, Yang   136
Liu, Zhe   564
Liwen, Huang   226
Long, Dongyang   596
Lu, Cunwei   218
Lu, Xian-Liang   763
Luther, Akshay   872

Ma, Fanyuan   155, 829
Ma, Jianguo   558
Ma, JoongSoo   694
Ma, Joongsoo   719
Ma, Jun   21
Manivannan, D.   284
Martí Campoy, Antonio   531
McGough, Steve   94
Men, Chaoguang   570
Min, Huang   455, 689
Min, Kyongpil   116
Ming-Lu, Li   50, 54
Ming, Zhang   424
Minghua, Chen   455
Minglu, Li   604
Minh Hai, Nguyen Thi   252
Mizuhito, Ogawa   628
Moon, Byung In   539

Moon, Daesung 833
Moon, Jongsub 654
Myung, Jihoon 706, 711

Na, Jong Whoa 30
Nakayama, Shigeru 202
Nam, Dong Su 549
Nam, Jae-Hyun 9
Nam, Yunyoung 280
Newhouse, Steven 94
Ng, Hee-Khiang 868
Nguyen, Ngoc Chi 144
Nii, Manabu 90
Niwa, Junpei 815
No, Jaechun 527

Oh, Am-Suk 9
Oh, Gun-Tak 98
Oh, Soo-Cheol 406, 451
Ok, MinHwan 685
Ong, Yew-Soon 868
Othman, Fazilah 248

Pan, Chieh-Tung 860
Park, Bok-Nyong 711
Park, Byoung Seob 698, 724
Park, Choonsik 650
Park, Eung Ki 549
Park, Eungki 650
Park, Eung-Ki 654
Park, Geunduk 882
Park, Hansol 736
Park, Hyun-Jung 172
Park, Jaehyung 519
Park, Jeenhong 624
Park, Jin-Won 833
Park, Myong-soon 685
Park, Sejin 446
Park, Soo Hong 670
Park, Soohong 396
Park, Sung Soon 527
Park, Sungyong 778
Park, Taesoon 577
Parveen, Sharmin 160
Peng, Chao 349
Peng, Liang 844
Peng, Shietung 196
Peng, Teh Chee 13
Perles Ivar, Angel 531

Pethick, Mark 497
Poon, Ting-C 111
Prak, Goorack 116
Purvis, M. 505

Qian, Haifeng 662
Qian, Xing 180
Qing, Ming 21
Qu, Wenyu 582

Rafique, Shahida 160
Rahayu, Wenny 68
Rao, Ruonan 768
Rodríguez, Francisco 531
Rong, Henry 318
Rui, Shi 674
Ryu, Dae-Hyun 633

Sakagami, Hitoshi 90
Sakaguchi, Tomoya 90
Sandnes, Frode Eika 354
Sang, Yingpeng 666
Sang-Dong, Jang 715
Sarda, Deepak 5
Sarwar, Hasan 160
See, Simon 367, 372, 844
Seo, Dae-Wha 624
Seo, Hee Suk 782
Seo, Jung-Taek 650, 654
Seo, Jungtaek 748
Setiawan, Agus 872
Shen, Hong 349, 416, 554, 582, 666
Shen, Minfen 127, 192, 791, 795
Shen-Sheng, Zhang 332
Shengsheng, Yu 226
Shensheng, Zhang 878
Sherly, Elizabeth 86
Shi, Jin-Qiao 613
Shim, JeoungChill 564
Shin, Ilhoon 807
Shin, Seung-Jung 633
Shin, Woochang 882
Shin, Y.H. 807
Shon, Tae-Shik 654
Shui, Yu 54
Singh, Shailendra 58
Sinnen, Oliver 354
Song, Bo 469
Song, Jie 367, 372
Song, Jiyoung 778

Song, JooSeok 464
Soong, Boon Hee 164
Sun, Lisha 791, 795
Susumu, Horiguchi 252
Suzuki, Yasuto 149

Tak, Dongkil 293
Takahashi, Yutaka 90
Tang, Francis 1, 5, 740
Tang, Jianqi 81
Taniar, David 68
Tantikul, Tongchit 284
Teh, Ying Wah 34
Theeramunkong, Thanaruk 38
Tian, Hui 416
Tian, Jinwen 136, 140
Till, M. 274
Toh, Da-Jun 5
Tsu Yong, Foo 314
Tsurusawa, Hidenobu 202
Turner, Jessica 257

Ushijiam, Kazuo 218

Wang, Haiying 429
Wang, Hua O. 326
Wang, Liang 326
Wang, Xuehui 681, 363
Wang, Yuh-Rau 243
Wei Ping, Lee 314
Wei, Qing-Song 46, 213
Wen-Ju, Zhang 54
Wendong, Xiao 188, 455
Werstein, P. 505
Werstein, Paul 497
Won, Yonggwan 519
Wu Woan, Kim 715
Wu, Chisu 882
Wu, Jin 136, 140

Xiang, Limin 218
Xianliang, Lu 180
Xiao, Wendong 164, 376
Xiaoqin, Huang 604
Xin, Li 628
Xing, Ling 558
Xingwei, Wang 455, 689
Xiong, Chen 188

Xiaozong, Yang 674
Xu, Dengyuan 383
Xu, Weiling 127, 791, 795
Xu, Yang 21
Xu, Yuedong 326
Xue, Qingshui 662

Yamakami, Toshihiko 756
Yan, Liu 702
Yang, Chao-Tung 856, 860
Yang, Cheng-Zen 600
Yang, Jihoon 778
Yang, Xiaozong 570
Yang, Zhonghua 367, 372
Ye, Tang 332
Yim, Keun Soo 401
Yoon, H. 586
Yoon, Hongil 539
Yoon, HyoSun 131
Yoon, Hyunsoo 608
Yoon, Yong-In 106
You, Jinyuan 768
Youn, Jaehwan 577
Yu, Jiadi 310, 341, 545
Yu, Yong 441
Yuanqiao, Wen 226
Yue, Liquan 469
Yun, Ilgun 539
Yun-Ming, Ye 50
Yunlong, Zhao 674

Zaitun, Abu Bakar 34
Zeng, Huaxin 383, 429, 469
Zhan, Chuan 763
Zhan, Hongli 81, 839
Zhang, Jun 72, 829
Zhang, Lei 363, 681
Zhang, Liang 155
Zhang, Minghu 345
Zhang, Yuzheng 192
Zhao, Jianjun 218
Zheng, Peng 424
Zhou, B.B. 274
Zhou, Mingtian 772
Zhou, Xu 763
Zomaya, A. 274
Zou, Deqing 345
Zou, Hengming 484

Lecture Notes in Computer Science

For information about Vols. 1–3239

please contact your bookseller or Springer

Vol. 3356: G. Das, V.P. Gulati (Eds.), Intelligent Information Technology. XII, 428 pages. 2004.

Vol. 3340: C.S. Calude, E. Calude, M.J. Dinneen (Eds.), Developments in Language Theory. XI, 431 pages. 2004.

Vol. 3339: G.I. Webb, X. Yu (Eds.), AI 2004: Advances in Artificial Intelligence. XXII, 1272 pages. 2004. (Subseries LNAI).

Vol. 3338: S.Z. Li, J. Lai, T. Tan, G. Feng, Y. Wang (Eds.), Advances in Biometric Person Authentication. XVI, 707 pages. 2004.

Vol. 3337: J.M. Barreiro, F. Martin-Sanchez, V. Maojo, F. Sanz (Eds.), Biological and Medical Data Analysis. XI, 508 pages. 2004.

Vol. 3336: D. Karagiannis, U. Reimer (Eds.), Practical Aspects of Knowledge Management. X, 523 pages. 2004. (Subseries LNAI).

Vol. 3334: Z. Chen, H. Chen, Q. Miao, Y. Fu, E. Fox, E.-p. Lim (Eds.), Digital Libraries: International Collaboration and Cross-Fertilization. XX, 690 pages. 2004.

Vol. 3333: K. Aizawa, Y. Nakamura, S. Satoh (Eds.), Advances in Multimedia Information Processing - PCM 2004, Part III. XXXV, 785 pages. 2004.

Vol. 3332: K. Aizawa, Y. Nakamura, S. Satoh (Eds.), Advances in Multimedia Information Processing - PCM 2004, Part II. XXXVI, 1051 pages. 2004.

Vol. 3331: K. Aizawa, Y. Nakamura, S. Satoh (Eds.), Advances in Multimedia Information Processing - PCM 2004, Part I. XXXVI, 667 pages. 2004.

Vol. 3329: P.J. Lee (Ed.), Advances in Cryptology - ASIACRYPT 2004. XVI, 546 pages. 2004.

Vol. 3323: G. Antoniou, H. Boley (Eds.), Rules and Rule Markup Languages for the Semantic Web. X, 215 pages. 2004.

Vol. 3322: R. Klette, J. Žunić (Eds.), Combinatorial Image Analysis. XII, 760 pages. 2004.

Vol. 3321: M.J. Maher (Ed.), Advances in Computer Science - ASIAN 2004. XII, 510 pages. 2004.

Vol. 3321: M.J. Maher (Ed.), Advances in Computer Science - ASIAN 2004. XII, 510 pages. 2004.

Vol. 3320: K.-M. Liew, H. Shen, S. See, W. Cai, P. Fan, S. Horiguchi (Eds.), Parallel and Distributed Computing: Applications and Technologies. XXIV, 891 pages. 2004.

Vol. 3316: N.R. Pal, N.K. Kasabov, R.K. Mudi, S. Pal, S.K. Parui (Eds.), Neural Information Processing. XXX, 1368 pages. 2004.

Vol. 3315: C. Lemaître, C.A. Reyes, J.A. González (Eds.), Advances in Artificial Intelligence – IBERAMIA 2004. XX, 987 pages. 2004. (Subseries LNAI).

Vol. 3312: A.J. Hu, A.K. Martin (Eds.), Formal Methods in Computer-Aided Design. XI, 445 pages. 2004.

Vol. 3311: V. Roca, F. Rousseau (Eds.), Interactive Multimedia and Next Generation Networks. XIII, 287 pages. 2004.

Vol. 3309: C.-H. Chi, K.-Y. Lam (Eds.), Content Computing. XII, 510 pages. 2004.

Vol. 3308: J. Davies, W. Schulte, M. Barnett (Eds.), Formal Methods and Software Engineering. XIII, 500 pages. 2004.

Vol. 3307: C. Bussler, S.-k. Hong, W. Jun, R. Kaschek, D.. Kinshuk, S. Krishnaswamy, S.W. Loke, D. Oberle, D. Richards, A. Sharma, Y. Sure, B. Thalheim (Eds.), Web Information Systems – WISE 2004 Workshops. XV, 277 pages. 2004.

Vol. 3306: X. Zhou, S. Su, M.P. Papazoglou, M.E. Orlowska, K.G. Jeffery (Eds.), Web Information Systems – WISE 2004. XVII, 745 pages. 2004.

Vol. 3305: P.M.A. Sloot, B. Chopard, A.G. Hoekstra (Eds.), Cellular Automata. XV, 883 pages. 2004.

Vol. 3303: J.A. López, E. Benfenati, W. Dubitzky (Eds.), Knowledge Exploration in Life Science Informatics. X, 249 pages. 2004. (Subseries LNAI).

Vol. 3302: W.-N. Chin (Ed.), Programming Languages and Systems. XIII, 453 pages. 2004.

Vol. 3299: F. Wang (Ed.), Automated Technology for Verification and Analysis. XII, 506 pages. 2004.

Vol. 3298: S.A. McIlraith, D. Plexousakis, F. van Harmelen (Eds.), The Semantic Web – ISWC 2004. XXI, 841 pages. 2004.

Vol. 3295: P. Markopoulos, B. Eggen, E. Aarts, J.L. Crowley (Eds.), Ambient Intelligence. XIII, 388 pages. 2004.

Vol. 3294: C.N. Dean, R.T. Boute (Eds.), Teaching Formal Methods. X, 249 pages. 2004.

Vol. 3293: C.-H. Chi, M. van Steen, C. Wills (Eds.), Web Content Caching and Distribution. IX, 283 pages. 2004.

Vol. 3292: R. Meersman, Z. Tari, A. Corsaro (Eds.), On the Move to Meaningful Internet Systems 2004: OTM 2004 Workshops. XXIII, 885 pages. 2004.

Vol. 3291: R. Meersman, Z. Tari (Eds.), On the Move to Meaningful Internet Systems 2004: CoopIS, DOA, and ODBASE, Part II. XXV, 824 pages. 2004.

Vol. 3290: R. Meersman, Z. Tari (Eds.), On the Move to Meaningful Internet Systems 2004: CoopIS, DOA, and ODBASE, Part I. XXV, 823 pages. 2004.

Vol. 3289: S. Wang, K. Tanaka, S. Zhou, T.W. Ling, J. Guan, D. Yang, F. Grandi, E. Mangina, I.-Y. Song, H.C. Mayr (Eds.), Conceptual Modeling for Advanced Application Domains. XXII, 692 pages. 2004.

Vol. 3288: P. Atzeni, W. Chu, H. Lu, S. Zhou, T.W. Ling (Eds.), Conceptual Modeling – ER 2004. XXI, 869 pages. 2004.

Vol. 3287: A. Sanfeliu, J.F. Martínez Trinidad, J.A. Carrasco Ochoa (Eds.), Progress in Pattern Recognition, Image Analysis and Applications. XVII, 703 pages. 2004.

Vol. 3286: G. Karsai, E. Visser (Eds.), Generative Programming and Component Engineering. XIII, 491 pages. 2004.

Vol. 3285: S. Manandhar, J. Austin, U.B. Desai, Y. Oyanagi, A. Talukder (Eds.), Applied Computing. XII, 334 pages. 2004.

Vol. 3284: A. Karmouch, L. Korba, E.R.M. Madeira (Eds.), Mobility Aware Technologies and Applications. XII, 382 pages. 2004.

Vol. 3283: F.A. Aagesen, C. Anutariya, V. Wuwongse (Eds.), Intelligence in Communication Systems. XIII, 327 pages. 2004.

Vol. 3282: V. Guruswami, List Decoding of Error-Correcting Codes. XIX, 350 pages. 2004.

Vol. 3281: T. Dingsøyr (Ed.), Software Process Improvement. X, 207 pages. 2004.

Vol. 3280: C. Aykanat, T. Dayar, İ. Körpeoğlu (Eds.), Computer and Information Sciences - ISCIS 2004. XVIII, 1009 pages. 2004.

Vol. 3278: A. Sahai, F. Wu (Eds.), Utility Computing. XI, 272 pages. 2004.

Vol. 3275: P. Perner (Ed.), Advances in Data Mining. VIII, 173 pages. 2004. (Subseries LNAI).

Vol. 3274: R. Guerraoui (Ed.), Distributed Computing. XIII, 465 pages. 2004.

Vol. 3273: T. Baar, A. Strohmeier, A. Moreira, S.J. Mellor (Eds.), <<UML>> 2004 - The Unified Modelling Language. XIII, 454 pages. 2004.

Vol. 3271: J. Vicente, D. Hutchison (Eds.), Management of Multimedia Networks and Services. XIII, 335 pages. 2004.

Vol. 3270: M. Jeckle, R. Kowalczyk, P. Braun (Eds.), Grid Services Engineering and Management. X, 165 pages. 2004.

Vol. 3269: J. Lopez, S. Qing, E. Okamoto (Eds.), Information and Communications Security. XI, 564 pages. 2004.

Vol. 3268: W. Lindner, M. Mesiti, C. Türker, Y. Tzitzikas, A. Vakali (Eds.), Current Trends in Database Technology - EDBT 2004 Workshops. XVIII, 608 pages. 2004.

Vol. 3267: C. Priami, P. Quaglia (Eds.), Global Computing. VIII, 377 pages. 2004.

Vol. 3266: J. Solé-Pareta, M. Smirnov, P.V. Mieghem, J. Domingo-Pascual, E. Monteiro, P. Reichl, B. Stiller, R.J. Gibbens (Eds.), Quality of Service in the Emerging Networking Panorama. XVI, 390 pages. 2004.

Vol. 3265: R.E. Frederking, K.B. Taylor (Eds.), Machine Translation: From Real Users to Research. XI, 392 pages. 2004. (Subseries LNAI).

Vol. 3264: G. Paliouras, Y. Sakakibara (Eds.), Grammatical Inference: Algorithms and Applications. XI, 291 pages. 2004. (Subseries LNAI).

Vol. 3263: M. Weske, P. Liggesmeyer (Eds.), Object-Oriented and Internet-Based Technologies. XII, 239 pages. 2004.

Vol. 3262: M.M. Freire, P. Chemouil, P. Lorenz, A. Gravey (Eds.), Universal Multiservice Networks. XIII, 556 pages. 2004.

Vol. 3261: T. Yakhno (Ed.), Advances in Information Systems. XIV, 617 pages. 2004.

Vol. 3260: I.G.M.M. Niemegeers, S.H. de Groot (Eds.), Personal Wireless Communications. XIV, 478 pages. 2004.

Vol. 3259: J. Dix, J. Leite (Eds.), Computational Logic in Multi-Agent Systems. XII, 251 pages. 2004. (Subseries LNAI).

Vol. 3258: M. Wallace (Ed.), Principles and Practice of Constraint Programming – CP 2004. XVII, 822 pages. 2004.

Vol. 3257: E. Motta, N.R. Shadbolt, A. Stutt, N. Gibbins (Eds.), Engineering Knowledge in the Age of the Semantic Web. XVII, 517 pages. 2004. (Subseries LNAI).

Vol. 3256: H. Ehrig, G. Engels, F. Parisi-Presicce, G. Rozenberg (Eds.), Graph Transformations. XII, 451 pages. 2004.

Vol. 3255: A. Benczúr, J. Demetrovics, G. Gottlob (Eds.), Advances in Databases and Information Systems. XI, 423 pages. 2004.

Vol. 3254: E. Macii, V. Paliouras, O. Koufopavlou (Eds.), Integrated Circuit and System Design. XVI, 910 pages. 2004.

Vol. 3253: Y. Lakhnech, S. Yovine (Eds.), Formal Techniques, Modelling and Analysis of Timed and Fault-Tolerant Systems. X, 397 pages. 2004.

Vol. 3252: H. Jin, Y. Pan, N. Xiao, J. Sun (Eds.), Grid and Cooperative Computing - GCC 2004 Workshops. XVIII, 785 pages. 2004.

Vol. 3251: H. Jin, Y. Pan, N. Xiao, J. Sun (Eds.), Grid and Cooperative Computing - GCC 2004. XXII, 1025 pages. 2004.

Vol. 3250: L.-J. (LJ) Zhang, M. Jeckle (Eds.), Web Services. X, 301 pages. 2004.

Vol. 3249: B. Buchberger, J.A. Campbell (Eds.), Artificial Intelligence and Symbolic Computation. X, 285 pages. 2004. (Subseries LNAI).

Vol. 3246: A. Apostolico, M. Melucci (Eds.), String Processing and Information Retrieval. XIV, 332 pages. 2004.

Vol. 3245: E. Suzuki, S. Arikawa (Eds.), Discovery Science. XIV, 430 pages. 2004. (Subseries LNAI).

Vol. 3244: S. Ben-David, J. Case, A. Maruoka (Eds.), Algorithmic Learning Theory. XIV, 505 pages. 2004. (Subseries LNAI).

Vol. 3243: S. Leonardi (Ed.), Algorithms and Models for the Web-Graph. VIII, 189 pages. 2004.

Vol. 3242: X. Yao, E. Burke, J.A. Lozano, J. Smith, J.J. Merelo-Guervós, J.A. Bullinaria, J. Rowe, P. Tiňo, A. Kabán, H.-P. Schwefel (Eds.), Parallel Problem Solving from Nature - PPSN VIII. XX, 1185 pages. 2004.

Vol. 3241: D. Kranzlmüller, P. Kacsuk, J.J. Dongarra (Eds.), Recent Advances in Parallel Virtual Machine and Message Passing Interface. XIII, 452 pages. 2004.

Vol. 3240: I. Jonassen, J. Kim (Eds.), Algorithms in Bioinformatics. IX, 476 pages. 2004. (Subseries LNBI).